Gender, Race, and Class in Media

A Critical Reader

Fifth Edition

Gail Dines

Wheelock College

Jean M. Humez

University of Massachusetts, Boston

Bill Yousman

Sacred Heart University

Lori Bindig Yousman

Sacred Heart University

Editors

Los Angeles | London | New Delhi
Singapore | Washington DC | Melbourne

FOR INFORMATION:

SAGE Publications, Inc.
2455 Teller Road
Thousand Oaks, California 91320
E-mail: order@sagepub.com

SAGE Publications Ltd.
1 Oliver's Yard
55 City Road
London, EC1Y 1SP
United Kingdom

SAGE Publications India Pvt. Ltd.
B 1/I 1 Mohan Cooperative Industrial Area
Mathura Road, New Delhi 110 044
India

SAGE Publications Asia-Pacific Pte. Ltd.
3 Church Street
#10–04 Samsung Hub
Singapore 049483

Acquisitions Editor: Terri Accomazzo
Content Development Editor: Anna Villarruel
Editorial Assistant: Erik Helton
Marketing Manager: Amy Lammers
Typesetter: Hurix Systems Pvt. Ltd.
Proofreader: Lawrence Baker
Indexer: Molly Hall
Cover Designer: Anthony Paular

Printed in the UK

Names: Dines, Gail, editor.

Title: Gender, race, and class in media : a critical reader / [edited by] Gail Dines, Wheelock College.

Description: Fifth edition. | Thousand Oaks, California : SAGE, [2018] | Includes bibliographical references and index.

Identifiers: LCCN 2017034116 | ISBN 9781506390796 (pbk. : alk. paper)

Subjects: LCSH: Mass media and culture—United States. | Mass media and sex—United States. | Mass media and race relations—United States. | Social classes in mass media. | Mass media—Social aspects—United States. | Popular culture—United States. | United States—Social conditions—1980-

Classification: LCC P94.65.U6 G46 2018 | DDC 302.23/0973—dc23 LC record available at https://lccn.loc.gov/2017034116

This book is printed on acid-free paper.

FSC
www.fsc.org
MIX
Paper from responsible sources
FSC® C011748

18 19 20 21 10 9 8 7 6 5 4 3

CONTENTS

PREFACE

Despite the introduction of two new members to the editorial team, the overall goal of the fifth edition of *Gender, Race, and Class in Media* remains the same as in previous editions: to introduce undergraduate and graduate students to some of the richness, sophistication, and diversity that characterizes contemporary media scholarship, in a way that is accessible and builds on students' own media experiences and interests. We intend to help demystify the nature of **popular culture** and **emergent media** by examining their production, analyzing the **texts** of some of the most pervasive forms or **genres**, and exploring the processes by which audiences make meaning out of media images and stories—meaning that helps shape our economic, cultural, political, and personal worlds. We start from the position that, as social beings, we construct our realities out of the cultural norms and values that are dominant in our society. Media and popular culture are among the most important producers and reproducers of such norms and values.

We have designed this as a volume to help teachers (1) introduce the most powerful theoretical concepts in contemporary media studies; (2) explore some of the most influential and interesting forms of contemporary popular culture; and (3) focus on issues of **gender** and **sexuality, race,** and **class** from a **critical** perspective. Most of the readings in this book take an explicitly critical perspective that is also informed by a diversity of approaches, such as **political economy, feminism, cultural studies, critical race theory,** and **queer theory.** We have chosen readings that make the following assumptions, as we do: (1) that industrialized societies are stratified along lines of gender and sexuality, race, and class; (2) that everyone living in such societies "has" gender and sexuality, race, and class, and other aspects of social identity that help structure our experience; and (3) that economic and other resources, advantages, and privileges are distributed inequitably, in part because of power dynamics involving these categories of experience (as well as others, such as age, ethnicity, religion, national origin, ability, or disability). Our selection of material has been guided by our belief that an important goal of a critical education is to enable people to conceptualize social justice clearly and work toward it more effectively. For us, greater social justice would require a fairer distribution of our society's economic and cultural resources. In the current political era, we see these commitments as more urgent than ever.

Our book is situated within both media studies and cultural studies. When Gail Dines and Jean M. Humez started working on the first edition of *Gender, Race, and Class in Media* in the early 1990s, cultural studies was a relatively new academic field in the United States, although it had been popular for some time in England (where it originated at The Center for Contemporary Cultural Studies at the University of Birmingham). The cultural studies approach has now been dominant in U.S. media studies for more than a generation. Cultural studies has heavily influenced several other interdisciplinary fields concerned with social issues and representation, such as American studies and gender and women's studies.

The field of cultural studies is actually **multidisciplinary,** drawing on insights and approaches from history, critical race studies, literary studies, philosophy, sociology, and psychology. Because of its **progressive** politics and because it offers a much broader and apparently more democratic definition of culture than was used in humanistic studies such as literary criticism in the past, many scholars and students particularly interested in race, gender, sexuality, and class have been attracted to its theories and potential for **activism.** (For a more extended discussion of the development of multiculturalism and cultural studies in the last decades of the 20th century, see Douglas Kellner's reading in Part I.)

In this fifth edition, we continue to emphasize three separable but interconnected areas of analysis: political economy, **textual analysis,** and **audience reception.** It is crucial to integrate all three to provide a holistic understanding of the entire media culture communication process, from production through consumption. Indeed, one of the initial goals of cultural studies was to contextualize the media text within the wider society that informs its production, construction, consumption, and, more recently, distribution along a range of **media platforms.**

Traditionally, political economy has looked at the ways the profit motive affects how texts are produced within a society marked by class, gender, and racial inequality. Who owns and controls the media? Who makes the decisions about content? How does financing affect and shape the range of texts produced? In what other ways does the profit motive drive production? These are central questions political economists ask. Examining this economic component is still essential to an understanding of what eventually gets produced and circulated in the mainstream commercial media industries. However, with the advent of **new media** technologies that enable consumers to produce and widely distribute their own content, we must broaden our view of production, as many of the readings in this book do.

Media representations are never just mirrors or "reflections of reality" but, rather, always artfully constructed creations designed to appeal to our emotions and influence our ideas, and especially our consumer behavior. Therefore, to educate ourselves as consumers, we need tools to help us closely examine the ways all cultural texts—from TV sitcoms, dramas, or reality shows to video games, YouTube videos, and social media sites—are structured, using complex combinations of words, sounds, and visual languages. Critical textual analysis provides a special focus on how to analyze the **ideological** significance of media texts—that is, to look at how, through the use of certain codes and conventions, they create or transmit meanings that may challenge or reinforce the economic, social, cultural, and political status quo.

Media studies has long acknowledged that audiences also have a role in creating the meanings of media texts, and for at least a generation, ethnographic audience reception research has focused on this dimension. By observing and talking with actual consumers of media texts—as opposed to critics—much has been learned about how we are active as we interpret, make sense of, understand, and use such texts within our everyday social and private lives. These studies have played an important role in complicating the older view of media audiences as passive, or even brainwashed, recipients of prepackaged meanings. Clearly, gender, race, ethnicity, class, sexuality, political beliefs, age, religion, and more are important factors that can help explain the different meanings that various audiences appear to take away from an advertisement, movie, video game, blog, or sitcom. Studies of **fans**—those dedicated consumers of media texts who build community around their experiences of consumption—go even further in exploring how consumers of media texts can produce meanings quite different from those intended by the original text producers. With the advent of new media aided by the Internet, the debate over audience exploitation versus empowerment has only intensified.

However we conceptualize the media audience in the age of the Internet, it is still vital to study all three components of media representations—production, text, and consumption—to understand how such texts can and do strengthen—or perhaps in some ways undermine—our dominant systems and ideologies of gender and sexuality, race, and class inequality.

In this fifth edition, we have maintained our thematic focus on gender and sexuality, race, and class, because we believe that media studies needs to address the issues of social inequality that continue to plague our society and undermine its democratic potential, perhaps even more now than when the first edition of this anthology appeared. Some of the readings in this book employ an **intersectional** analysis—that is, one that complicates each of these social categories by examining how they interact with one another. Whenever possible, we have selected articles that give voice to the multiple levels of analysis needed to make media studies a truly **multicultural** endeavor. We acknowledge the ever-intensifying interrelationships among media cultures globally while continuing to focus primarily on the North American examples of media texts that we see as most likely to be familiar to instructors and students working with this book.

For the fifth edition, we again located, read, and discussed many new journal articles and book chapters. We reached out to colleagues who do media research and teach media courses, and we listened to students to learn what they found compelling in former editions. Twenty-seven chapters in this edition are either new or substantially updated. This reflects both the rapid evolution of the field and our desire to provide analysis of relatively recent and current media texts likely to be familiar to students. Several "classic" readings (like Janice Radway's **ethnography** of women who are voracious readers of romance novels), which first appeared in earlier editions, still offer important and clearly articulated historical and theoretical insights into media analysis.

We've grouped our selections into thematic sections that highlight some of the important changes that have taken place in the worlds of popular culture and emerging media over the past several years and that also reflect our experience of student interests. As in the fourth edition, we include an index of individual reading topics, which will allow instructors to create alternative groupings of readings to suit their own course designs. We hope that instructors and students will find the themes and genres represented in this collection provocative, stimulating, and an invitation to engage in further thinking, research, and perhaps even media activism.

In condensing previously published journal articles and book chapters, we have often had to omit quite a lot of detail from the originals, while preserving central arguments and challenging ideas. The omissions are carefully noted with the use of ellipses (. . .). By judiciously cutting the overall length, we have aimed to make cutting-edge scholarship as accessible as possible for undergraduate and graduate students alike. Our brief introductory essays to each section highlight key concepts and identify some interesting connections among the readings in that section. We continue to welcome comments from users of this book about our selections, about what worked well in the classroom and what did not. We especially invite suggested articles for future editions.

At the end of the book, we provide some supplementary resources for the teacher. In addition, we have included a selective list of the many media activist organizations easily located on the Internet. We hope this will be useful for those who, inspired by the progressive ideals espoused by many of the writers in this collection, would like to explore this kind of grassroots consumer and citizens' activism on behalf of a more democratic media culture in the future.

DIGITAL RESOURCES

Visit **http://study.sagepub.com/dines5e** to access online resources including articles from previous editions, video links, web resources, eFlashcards, recommended readings, SAGE journal articles, and more.

Password-protected **Instructor Resources** include the following:

- A **Microsoft® Word test bank** is available containing multiple choice, true/false, short answer, and essay questions for each part. The test bank provides a diverse range of prewritten options as well as the opportunity for editing any question or inserting personalized questions to assess students' progress and understanding.

- **Sample course syllabi** for semester and quarter courses provide suggested models for use when creating the syllabi for courses.

- Lively and stimulating **class activities and course projects** that can be used in class to reinforce active learning. The activities apply to individual or group projects.

- **Video and multimedia links** that appeal to students with different learning styles.

- **Web exercises** direct both instructors and students to useful and current websites, along with creative activities to extend and reinforce learning or allow for further research on important chapter topics.

- **Articles from prior editions** are also included online.

The open-access Student Study Site includes the following:

- Mobile-friendly **eFlashcards** reinforce understanding of key terms and concepts that have been outlined in the chapters.

- **Video and multimedia links** appeal to students with different learning styles.

- **Web exercises** direct readers to useful and current web resources, along with creative activities to extend and reinforce learning or allow for further research on important chapter topics.

- Interesting and relevant **articles from prior editions** of the book provide a jumping-off point for course assignments, papers, research, group work, and class discussion.

Throughout our book, key concepts important for students to discuss and digest appear in boldface. These are defined in more detail in the Glossary at the end of the volume. Some instructors have found it useful to assign the Glossary itself as a reading early in a course, for the benefit of students new to media theory and critical cultural studies.

ACKNOWLEDGMENTS

We are immensely grateful to the colleagues and students who have contributed over the years to all of our thinking about the issues and questions raised in this book. They are far too many to be mentioned individually, but they include faculty and students at Sacred Heart University, the University of Massachusetts Boston, and Wheelock College, as well as colleagues and associates with whom we have worked in multiple other locations.

Many writers contributed original essays and edited articles that have been included in the five editions thus far. This anthology could obviously not exist without their scholarship and their willingness to allow us to edit and include their work.

We would also like to thank Terri Accomazzo, Anna Villarruel, and Tori Mirsadjadi at SAGE Publications, for their belief in the book, their encouragement in urging a new edition, and their careful work in bringing the fifth edition into print.

We are indebted to the faculty who provided feedback on the content of previous editions and suggestions for the fifth edition: Vanessa T. Ament, Ball State University; Jennifer Dunn, Dominican University; Kristen M. Kalz, University of Missouri Columbia; Tracy Everbach, University of North Texas; Felicia LeDuff Harry, Nicholls State University; Tamara Zellars Buck, Southeast Missouri State University; Karen Schermerhorn, University of Hartford; Laura Hahn, Humboldt State University; Jan Semmelroggen, Nottingham Trent University; Christopher T. Gullen, Westfield State University; Francine Edwards, Delaware State University; Angela Pettitt, Penn State University-Shenango; Christine Scodari, Florida Atlantic University; Antoinette Charfauros McDaniel, Baldwin Wallace University; Jennifer Fogel, SUNY-Oswego; Merrill Morris, University of North Georgia; Anne Osborne, SI Newhouse School, Syracuse University; Ingrid Semaan, University of Connecticut; Colleen Kappeler, Carthage College; Chyng Sun, New York University; Sherry R. Boyd, North Lake College; and Christopher Bell, University of Colorado Colorado Springs.

And again, we salute the members of our families, who provided much-needed moral support and love as we pursued our research and editorial labors. Lori and Bill want to give special thanks to Rachel, Nathan, and Kayla Yousman. We couldn't ask for a better litter.

A CULTURAL STUDIES APPROACH TO MEDIA

Theory

In this book, we offer a selection of critical examinations of popular culture and emergent media to exemplify a powerful method of analysis you will be able to apply on your own to other examples. In this way, we hope to promote and support critical **media literacy.** While there are many ways to think about media literacy, for the purposes of this book, we argue that in a postindustrial society dominated by corporate media and commercial messages media literacy can be one tool to help limit the **discursive** power of media in our lives. While a sophisticated level of media literacy cannot replace other efforts to democratize our society's economic and cultural resources, in our view, it does give audiences the skills necessary to analyze and question the ideologies that often work at a subtextual level within media narratives and images.

We begin with media theory because we think students will find it useful to have a good grasp of several central concepts, illustrated in an introductory way here, before going on to tackle later readings in which an understanding of these concepts is often presumed. In the media theory section, we especially highlight the central concepts and terms of the field of cultural studies as applied to **media culture.** As in all the other sections of this book, the chapters in this section are in dialogue with one another in many ways. In these opening comments, we give only one possible reading of the ways their main themes connect.

We open with "Cultural Studies, Multiculturalism, and Media Culture," by Douglas Kellner (I.1). This essay sets out the three-part approach to cultural studies (political economy/production, textual analysis, and audience reception/consumption) that characterizes this field. Like Kellner, we believe that to understand a media artifact such as a TV show, advertisement, social media site, or online digital game, one must be able to understand the socioeconomic context in which it is created (political economy/ production); analyze its constructed meaning(s) through careful attention to its particular visual/verbal/ auditory languages, or **codes** (textual analysis); and determine its actual impact on individuals and groups and how these audiences contribute to the meaning-making process, and even to the production and distribution of cultural products (audience consumption/production). In addition, Kellner points to the importance of intersectional considerations of gender, sexuality, race, class, and more, as categories of difference and social analysis in cultural studies work.

In "The Meaning of Memory" (I.2), an important historical background piece that sheds light on how and why corporations came to dominate media culture so heavily in the United States, George Lipsitz shows how the needs of the national economy in the post–World War II period facilitated the development of mass television production. He explores how the increase in the sale of televisions and the development of a group of situation comedies were used to transform a traditional, ethnic immigrant ideology that stressed values of community, thrift, and commitment to labor unions into an **American Dream ideology** that stresses **individualism, consumerism,** and suburban domesticity—values consistent with the needs of the expanding postwar **capitalist** economy.

In subsequent decades, media industries have changed dramatically as a result of mergers and buyouts. Commercial entertainment today is a highly profit-oriented business controlled for the most part by a small number of giant corporations. In "The Economics of the Media Industry" (I.3), David P. Croteau and William D. Hoynes focus on the concentration of ownership in these industries, showing why this is an important problem in a purportedly democratic society.

Giant media **conglomerates** are able to "assemble large portfolios of magazines, television stations, book publishers, record labels, and so on to mutually support one another's operations" (a process called "horizontal integration"). They also use "vertical integration"—"the process by which one owner acquires all aspects of production and distribution of a single type of media product"—to gain further control over the market. As the authors point out,

> In this era of integrated media conglomerates, media companies are capable of pursuing elaborate cross-media strategies, in which company-owned media products can be packaged, sold, and promoted across the full range of media platforms. Feature films, their accompanying soundtracks and DVD/Blu-ray Disc releases, spin-off television programs, and books, along with magazine cover stories and plenty of licensed merchandise can all be produced and distributed by different divisions of the same conglomerate. (p. 28)

In these ways, corporate media giants benefit economically from conglomeration and integration and, arguably, make it "more difficult for smaller media firms to compete," but even more worrisome is the potential for such conglomerates to translate media ownership into political power. Offering examples from the United States (Michael Bloomberg), Europe (Italy's Silvio Berlusconi), and the United Kingdom and Australia (Rupert Murdoch), the authors warn that "owners can systematically exclude certain ideas from their media products." Building on political economist Herb Schiller's concept of "the corporate voice," they ask us to consider whether "the corporate voice has been generalized so successfully that most of us do not even think of it as a specifically corporate voice: That is, the corporate view has become 'our' view, the 'American' view, even though the interests of the corporate entities that own mass media are far from universal" (p. 32).

One way of thinking about how the corporate view becomes woven into dominant ways of thinking about the world is the theory of **hegemony** that James Lull explores in his chapter (I.4). While Karl Marx was one of the first major social thinkers to explore how the ideologies of the ruling class become the mainstream ideas of the time, theorists such as Antonio Gramsci, Louis Althusser, and Stuart Hall helped develop the more nuanced concept of hegemony that Lull defines as "the power or dominance that one social group holds over others" (p. 34). As Lull points out,

> Owners and managers of media industries can produce and reproduce the content, inflections, and tones of ideas favorable to them far more easily than other social groups because they manage key socializing institutions, thereby guaranteeing that their points of view are constantly and attractively cast into the public arena. (p. 34)

Though many critical studies of media owned by private companies use the concept of hegemony, at first it seems more difficult to apply this notion to the Internet, which has been seen as a kind of "public sphere" in which many voices are heard, because there are often-obscured, profit-oriented entities in control of production and distribution of online content. Indeed, somewhat grandiose and utopian claims were made in some circles about the new era of free expression and democratic cultural production the Internet would bring with it. But as John Bellamy Foster and Robert W. McChesney remind us in "The Internet's Unholy Marriage to Capitalism" (I.5), there is a need to think more critically about the relationship between the Internet and capitalism. They argue: "There was—and remains—extraordinary democratic and revolutionary promise in this communication revolution. But technologies do not ride roughshod over history, regardless of their immense powers. They are developed in a social, political, and economic context" (p. 37).

The authors provide an account of the Internet's origins and an extensive analysis of the ways its development has been shaped by market forces. They conclude:

> In a world in which private riches grow at the expense of public wealth, it should not surprise us that what seemed at first the enormous potential of the internet—representing a whole new realm of public wealth, analogous to the discovery of a whole new continent, and pointing to the possibility of a vast new democratic sphere of unrestricted communication—has vaporized in a couple of decades. (p. 41)

Like the Internet, television was also considered by some as a medium that could help spread knowledge, debate, and diverse perspectives around the globe. However, as Michael Morgan and James Shanahan's chapter on television and the **cultivation** of **authoritarianism** (I.6) demonstrates, television narratives are no less ideological than other forms of media storytelling in their contributions to our perceptions and attitudes about the world and our place in it. Morgan and Shanahan's contribution to this volume is based in the important theory of cultivation first advanced by the late media scholar George Gerbner. Gerbner posited that in the television age much of our sense of reality came to us through the screens that dominated our living rooms. As Morgan and Shanahan explain,

> Gerbner and his colleagues argued that heavy viewers of television drama tended, over time, to absorb images and lessons from the consistent messages of television's story system. Noting that television messages often tend toward a formulaic demonstration of power that includes the frequent use of violence, Gerbner et al. showed that heavy television exposure cultivates a sense of fear, anxiety, and mistrust, with worrisome implications. (p. 46)

Morgan and Shanahan's chapter focuses on the 2016 election season and the rise of Donald Trump as they ask, "might television viewing . . . contribute to the level of support for the candidacy of Donald Trump?" (p. 47) Operating out of the assumption that stories matter and that television is more than "just entertainment," cultivation researchers argue that television texts, like all media and popular culture texts, contain ideological messages that influence the worldviews of their audiences.

Analysis of the ideological dimensions of popular images and narratives is thus an important component in understanding how media texts work, especially when linked with background knowledge about the producers' political and economic interests; however, as suggested by the Morgan and Shanahan chapter, there is another element that students of media culture need to take into account. Cultivation research is based in comparison of the content of television messages to the knowledge, attitudes, and beliefs of heavy viewers of those messages. Thus, these researchers go beyond analysis of content to examine the impact of that content on audiences. And, irrespective of whether any media text appears to encode dominant or subversive cultural ideas, Kellner's cultural studies approach also reminds us that we cannot simply assume that we know how consumers of media texts actually read or **decode** them (constructing meaning from texts for themselves). For that piece of the equation, we must turn to studies of audience reception—how particular media consumers understand and use media texts.

Scholars widely agree that consumers of the media should not be conceptualized as passive pawns of media imagery, completely controlled by the dominant culture, but there are several different ways of understanding audience activity. First, according to the influential concept of **oppositional readings,** initiated by Stuart Hall (and also discussed by Kellner in I.1), the meaning of media texts cannot be established by only one critic's decoding of the text—no matter how subtle and full—because all texts are to some degree "open" (**polysemic,** or capable of multiple meanings). Therefore, we must also seek to know how audiences, both as individuals and as members of various communities, bring different experiences and complex identities to the processes of reading/viewing by which they actually feel, think about, and come to understand these texts.

According to Hall's paradigm, audience members may do one of three things in relation to the intended or **preferred meanings** encoded in the text: (1) accept them uncritically and read the text as its producers intended, (2) produce a **negotiated reading** (partially **resisting** the encoded meaning), or (3) create an oppositional reading of their own, completely rejecting the preferred meaning of the text.

Janice Radway's classic ethnographic research into audience reception of romance novels was an early and influential study of how specific readers actually engage with a mass media text. In "Women Read the Romance" (I.7), Radway looks closely at how a group of White lower-income women in the 1970s and 1980s negotiated with the genre of the romance novel, in terms of both the books they selected and the ways they actually read the text and appropriated and changed its meanings. Radway acknowledges that "romance reading . . . can function as a kind of training for the all-too-common task of reinterpreting a spouse's unsettling actions as the signs of passion, devotion, and love" (p. 58). Yet she sees, in these women's selection of certain books as favorites and their rejection of others, an active tendency to critique certain patriarchal masculine behaviors, substituting an ideal of the "nurturing" male that might have been missing in their own family lives. Through the act of reading itself, she argues, this group of women romance readers escaped temporarily from familial demands on their time, and Radway interprets this action as potential **resistance** to, or refusal to accept completely, the patriarchal restrictions on their lives. While encouraging respect for women's own experiences as cultural consumers, however, Radway warns that we should not confuse modes of resistance that reside in textual consumption with more practical, real-world modes of resistance (such as organized protest against the patriarchal abuses women meet in real life).

Radway's work helped establish the field of media audience studies, which has since developed into a rich body of research and interpretation. At the same time, over the past two decades or so, a distinct subfield of audience study has emerged, devoted to one particularly active kind of text consumer—the fan. In an early and influential essay, "*Star Trek* Rerun, Reread, Rewritten: Fan Writing as Textual Poaching" (I.8), Henry Jenkins III drew our attention to "a largely unexplored terrain of cultural activity, a subterranean network of readers and writers who remake [media texts] in their own image." For Jenkins and many who have been influenced by his work,

> "fandom" is a vehicle for marginalized subterranean groups (women, the young, gays, etc.) to pry open space for their cultural concerns within dominant representations; it is a way of appropriating media texts and rereading them in a fashion that serves different interests, a way of transforming mass culture into popular culture. (p. 63)

Drawing on the theories of Michel de Certeau and his own studies of fans organized around their mutual appreciation of the long-running science fiction television series about space exploration by a team of diverse characters, Jenkins brought to light a fascinating body of fan fiction, written for the most part by female fans, whom he conceptualized as

> reluctant poachers who steal only those things that they truly love, who seize televisual property only to protect it against abuse by those who created it and who have claimed ownership over it. In embracing popular texts, the fans claim those works as their own, remaking them in their own image. . . . Consumption becomes production; reading becomes writing; spectator culture becomes participatory culture. (p. 68)

Following Jenkins's lead, contemporary fandom studies foreground the **agency** and creativity of culture consumers who go on to produce their own cultural materials, often through such "poaching" of ideas and materials from the original mass-produced texts. Emergent digital technologies have clearly added to the opportunities available to do-it-yourself cultural producers outside of the commercial world of the media industries, including fans. Moreover, some individuals and groups have taken advantage of **social networking** platforms to facilitate not only fandom but also political activism.

Some critical media theorists have warned (as Kellner does) of the dangers of overemphasizing the power of media audiences to resist or effectively challenge the dominant ideologies that normalize social and economic inequities, simply through their activities as consumers—even if they become devoted fans. After all, as Morgan and Shanahan's chapter reminds us, it is the heaviest users of media content that are most likely to accept the ideological tendencies of the content they love, without even being consciously aware that they are being influenced.

Throughout this section of the anthology, the notions of both media power and resistance to that power have already frequently surfaced, as they will throughout the rest of the book. Richard Butsch provides us with a detailed and challenging discussion of these notions in our final chapter of the section, "Reconsidering Resistance *and* Incorporation" (I.9). Some strands of cultural studies work on the media tend to ignore the more structured analysis of political economy, which foregrounds the inequality of access to media resources. Butsch's chapter is both a critique of an overly celebratory use of the idea of audience resistance and a call for a more nuanced understanding of how resistance and "incorporation" (the process by which resistance is co-opted and contained within hegemony) work together. In this way, he works to bridge competing paradigms within media studies.

We have aimed in this book to contribute to the project Butsch calls for. We invite you, the reader, to engage in a critical analysis of your own media consumption, exploring how you may be at times resisting the dominant ideologies while at other times unwittingly internalizing the "corporate voice" and weaving it into your own social construction of reality.

1

CULTURAL STUDIES, MULTICULTURALISM, AND MEDIA CULTURE

Douglas Kellner

Radio, television, film, popular music, the Internet and social networking, and other forms and products of media culture provide materials out of which we forge our very identities, including our sense of selfhood; our notion of what it means to be male or female; our conception of class, ethnicity and race, nationality, sexuality; and division of the world into categories of "us" and "them." Media images help shape our view of the world and our deepest values: what we consider good or bad, positive or negative, moral or evil. Media stories provide the symbols, myths, and resources through which we constitute a common culture and through the appropriation of which we insert ourselves into this culture. Media spectacles demonstrate who has power and who is powerless, who is allowed to exercise force and violence and who is not. They dramatize and legitimate the power of the forces that be and show the powerless that they must stay in their places or be oppressed.

We are immersed from cradle to grave in a media and consumer society, and thus it is important to learn how to understand, interpret, and criticize its meanings and messages. The media are a profound and often misperceived source of cultural pedagogy: They contribute to educating us how to behave and what to think, feel, believe, fear, and desire—and what not to. The media are forms of pedagogy that teach us how to be men and women. They show us how to dress, look, and consume; how to react to members of different social groups; how to be popular and successful and how to avoid failure; and how to conform to the dominant system of norms, values, practices, and institutions. Consequently, the gaining of critical media literacy is an important resource for individuals and citizens in learning how to cope with a seductive cultural environment. Learning how to read, criticize, and resist sociocultural manipulation can help one empower oneself in relation to dominant forms of media and culture. It can enhance individual sovereignty vis-à-vis media culture and give people more power over their cultural environment.

In this chapter, I will discuss the potential contributions of a cultural studies perspective to media critique and literacy. From the 1980s to the present, cultural studies has emerged as a set of approaches to the study of culture, society, and politics. The project was inaugurated by the University of Birmingham Centre for Contemporary Cultural Studies, which developed a variety of critical methods for the analysis, interpretation, and criticism of cultural artifacts. Through a set of internal debates, and responding to social struggles and movements of the 1960s and 1970s, the Birmingham group came to focus on the interplay of representations and ideologies of class, gender, race, ethnicity, and nationality in cultural texts, including media culture. They were among the first to study the effects on audiences of newspapers, radio, television, film, advertising, and other popular cultural forms. They also focused on how various audiences interpreted and used media culture differently, analyzing the factors that made different audiences respond in contrasting ways to various media texts, and how they made use of media in their personal and social lives in a multiplicity of ways.[1]

Through studies of youth subcultures, British cultural studies demonstrated how culture came to constitute distinct forms of identity and group membership for young people. In the view of

---

This piece is an original essay that was commissioned for this volume. It has been updated from an earlier version that appeared in the third edition.

cultural studies, media culture provides the materials for constructing views of the world, behavior, and even identities. Those who uncritically follow the dictates of media culture tend to "mainstream" themselves, conforming to the dominant fashion, values, and behavior. Yet cultural studies is also interested in how subcultural groups and individuals resist dominant forms of culture and identity, creating their own style and identities. Those who obey ruling dress and fashion codes, behavior, and political ideologies thus produce their identities as members of specific social groupings within contemporary U.S. culture, such as White, middle-class, conservative American men, or lesbian African American women, for instance. Persons who identify with subcultures, such as punk culture or Latino subcultures, dress and act differently than those in the mainstream and thus create oppositional identities, defining themselves against standard models.

Cultural studies insists that culture must be studied within the social relations and system through which culture is produced and consumed and that the study of culture is thus intimately bound up with the study of society, politics, and economics. Cultural studies shows how media culture articulates the dominant values, political ideologies, and social developments and novelties of the era. It conceives of U.S. culture and society as a contested terrain, with various groups and ideologies struggling for dominance (Kellner, 1995, 2010). Television, film, music, and other popular cultural forms are thus often liberal or conservative, or occasionally express more radical or oppositional views—and can be contradictory and ambiguous as well in their meanings and messages.

Cultural studies is valuable because it provides some tools that enable individuals to read and interpret culture critically. It also subverts distinctions between "high" and "low" culture by considering a wide continuum of cultural artifacts, from opera and novels to soap operas and TV wrestling, while refusing to erect any specific elite cultural hierarchies or canons. Earlier mainstream academic approaches to culture tended to be primarily literary and elitist, dismissing media culture as banal, trashy, and not worthy of serious attention. The project of cultural studies, in contrast, avoids cutting the field of culture into high and low, or popular versus elite. Such distinctions are difficult to maintain and generally serve as a front for normative aesthetic valuations and, often, a political program (i.e., either dismissing mass culture for high culture/art or celebrating what is deemed "popular" while scorning "elitist" high culture).

Cultural studies allows us to examine and critically scrutinize the whole range of culture without prior prejudices toward one or another sort of cultural text, institution, or practice. It also opens the way toward more differentiated political, rather than aesthetic, valuations of cultural artifacts in which one attempts to distinguish critical and oppositional from conformist and conservative moments in a given cultural artifact. For instance, studies of Hollywood film show how key 1960s films promoted the views of radicals and the counterculture and how film in the 1970s was a battleground between liberal and conservative positions; late 1970s films, however, tended toward conservative positions that helped elect Ronald Reagan as president (see Kellner & Ryan, 1988). During the Bush–Cheney era, there were many oppositional films, such as the work of Michael Moore, and liberal films that featured black heroes and anticipated the election of Barack Obama (Kellner, 2010). For instance, African American actor Will Smith was the top grossing U.S. actor during the Bush–Cheney era, Denzel Washington won two Academy Awards and played a wide range of characters, and Morgan Freeman played a president, corporate executive, crime figure, and even God, attesting that U.S. publics were ready to see African Americans in major positions in all arenas of society. This is not to say that Hollywood "caused" Obama's surprising victory in 2008 but that U.S. media culture anticipated a black president.

There is an intrinsically critical and political dimension to the project of cultural studies that distinguishes it from objectivist and apolitical academic approaches to the study of culture and society. British cultural studies, for example, analyzed culture historically in the context of its societal origins and effects. It situated culture within a theory of social production and reproduction, specifying the ways cultural forms served either to further social domination or to enable people to resist and struggle against domination. It analyzed society as a hierarchical and antagonistic set of social relations characterized by the oppression of subordinate class, gender, race, ethnic, and national strata. Employing the Italian sociologist Antonio Gramsci's (1971) model of hegemony and counterhegemony, it sought to analyze "hegemonic" or ruling, social, and cultural forces of domination and to seek "counterhegemonic" forces of resistance and struggle. The project was aimed at social transformation and attempted to specify forces of domination and resistance to aid the process of political struggle and emancipation from oppression and domination.

For cultural studies, the concept of ideology is of central importance, for dominant ideologies serve to reproduce social relations of domination and subordination.[2] Ideologies of class, for instance, celebrate upper-class life and denigrate the working class. Ideologies of gender promote sexist representations of women, oppressive ideologies of sexuality promote homophobia, and ideologies of race use racist representations of people of color and various minority groups. Ideologies make inequalities and subordination appear natural and just and thus induce consent to relations of domination. Contemporary societies are structured by opposing groups who have different political ideologies (liberal, conservative, radical, etc.), and cultural studies specifies what, if any, ideologies are operative in a given cultural artifact (which could involve, of course, the specification of ambiguities and ideological contradictions). In the course of this study, I will provide some examples of how different ideologies are operative in media cultural texts and will accordingly provide examples of ideological analysis and critique.

Because of its focus on representations of race, gender, sexuality, and class, and its critique of ideologies that promote various forms of oppression, cultural studies lends itself to a multiculturalist program that demonstrates how culture reproduces certain forms of racism, sexism, and biases against members of subordinate classes, social groups, or alternative lifestyles. Multiculturalism affirms the worth of different types of culture and cultural groups, claiming, for instance, that Black; Latino; Asian; Native American; lesbian, gay, bisexual, transgendered, and questioning (LGBTQ); and other oppressed and marginalized voices have their own validity and importance. An insurgent multiculturalism attempts to show how various people's voices and experiences are silenced and omitted from mainstream culture, and struggles to aid in the articulation of diverse views, experiences, and cultural forms from groups excluded from the mainstream. This makes it a target of conservative forces that wish to preserve the existing canons of White male, Eurocentric privilege, and thus attack multiculturalism in cultural wars raging from the 1960s to the present over education, the arts, and the limits of free expression.

Cultural studies thus promotes a critical multiculturalist politics and media pedagogy that aims to make people sensitive to how relations of power and domination are "encoded" in cultural texts, such as those of television and film, or how new technologies and media such as the Internet and social networking can be used for oppositional pedagogical or political purposes (Kahn & Kellner, 2008). A critical cultural studies approach also specifies how people can resist the dominant encoded meanings and produce their own critical and alternative readings and media artifacts, as well as new identities and social relations. Cultural studies can show how media culture manipulates and indoctrinates us and thus can empower individuals to resist the dominant meanings in media cultural products and produce their own meanings. It can also point to moments of resistance and criticism within media culture and thus help promote development of more critical consciousness.

A critical cultural studies approach—embodied in many of the articles collected in this reader—thus develops concepts and analyses that will enable readers to analytically dissect the artifacts of contemporary media culture and gain power over their cultural environment. By exposing the entire field of culture and media technology to knowledgeable scrutiny, cultural studies provides a broad, comprehensive framework to undertake studies of culture, politics, and society for the purposes of individual empowerment and social and political struggle and transformation. In the following pages, I will therefore indicate some of the chief components of the type of cultural studies I find most useful for understanding contemporary U.S. society, culture, and politics.

COMPONENTS OF A CRITICAL CULTURAL STUDIES APPROACH

As a theoretical apparatus, cultural studies contains a threefold project of analyzing the production and political economy of culture, cultural texts, and the audience reception of those texts and their effects in a concrete sociohistorical context.

This comprehensive approach avoids too narrowly focusing on one dimension of the project to the exclusion of others. To avoid such limitations, I propose a multiperspectival approach that (a) discusses production and political economy, (b) engages in textual analysis, and (c) studies the reception and use of cultural texts.[3]

PRODUCTION AND POLITICAL ECONOMY

Since cultural production has been neglected in many modes of recent cultural studies, it is important to stress the importance of analyzing cultural texts within their system of production and distribution, often referred to as the political economy of culture.[4] Inserting texts into the system of culture within which they are produced and distributed can help elucidate features and effects of the texts that textual analysis alone might miss or downplay. Rather than being an antithetical approach to culture, political economy can actually contribute to textual analysis and critique. The system of production often determines, in part, what sorts of artifacts will be produced, what structural limits will determine what can and cannot be said and shown, and what sorts of audience effects the text may generate.

Study of the codes of television, film, or popular music, for instance, is enhanced by studying the formulas and conventions of production, which are shaped by economic and technical, as well as aesthetic and cultural, considerations. Dominant cultural forms are structured by well-defined rules and conventions, and the study of the production of culture can help elucidate the codes actually in play. Because of the demands of the format of radio or music television, for instance, most popular songs are 3 to 5 minutes long, fitting into the format of the distribution system, just as the length of content on YouTube or Twitter has technical constraints. From the early years of the Internet to the present, there have been legal and political conflicts concerning file sharing of music, other forms of media culture, and information, situating media culture in a force field of political conflict. Because of their control by giant corporations oriented primarily toward profit, film and television production in the United States is dominated by specific genres such as talk and game shows, soap operas, situation comedies,

action/adventure series, reality TV series, and so on, which are familiar and popular with audiences. This economic factor explains why there are cycles of certain genres and subgenres, sequelmania in the film industry, crossovers of popular films into television series, and a certain homogeneity in products constituted within systems of production marked by relatively rigid generic codes, formulaic conventions, and well-defined ideological boundaries.

Likewise, study of political economy can help determine the limits and range of political and ideological discourses and effects. My study of television in the United States, for instance, disclosed that the takeover of the television networks by major transnational corporations and communications conglomerates in the 1980s was part of a "right turn" within U.S. society, whereby powerful corporate groups won control of the state and the mainstream media (Kellner, 1990). For example, during the 1980s, all three networks were taken over by major corporate conglomerates: ABC was taken over in 1985 by Capital Cities, NBC was taken over by GE, and CBS was taken over by the Tisch Financial Group. Both ABC and NBC sought corporate mergers, and this motivation, along with other benefits derived from Reaganism, might well have influenced them to downplay criticisms of Reagan and generally support his conservative programs, military adventures, and simulated presidency.

Corporate conglomeratization has intensified further, and today Time Warner, Disney, Rupert Murdoch's News Corporation, Viacom, and other global media conglomerates control ever more domains of the production and distribution of culture (McChesney, 2000, 2007). In this global context, one cannot really analyze the role of the media in the Gulf War, for instance, without also analyzing the production and political economy of news and information, as well as the actual text of the Gulf War and its reception by its audience (see Kellner, 1992). Likewise, the ownership by conservative corporations of dominant media corporations helps explain mainstream media support of the Bush–Cheney administration and its policies, such as the wars in Afghanistan and Iraq (Kellner, 2003, 2005).

Looking toward entertainment, female pop music stars such as Madonna, Britney Spears, Beyoncé, and Lady Gaga deploy the tools of the glamour industry and media spectacle to become icons of fashion, beauty, style, and sexuality, as well as purveyors of music. And in appraising the full social impact of pornography, one needs to be aware of the immense profits generated by the sex industry and the potential for harm endemic to the production process of, say, pornographic films and videos, and not just dwell on the texts themselves and their effects on audiences.

Furthermore, in an era of globalization, one must be aware of the global networks that produce and distribute culture in the interests of profit and corporate hegemony. The Internet and new media link the globe and distribute more culture to more people than at any time in history, yet giant media conglomerates and institutions, such as the state, that can exert censorship continue to be major forces of cultural hegemony (see McChesney 2013). Yet political economy alone does not hold the key to cultural studies, and important as it is, it has limitations as a single approach. Some political economy analyses reduce the meanings and effects of texts to rather circumscribed and reductive ideological functions, arguing that media culture merely reflects the ideology of the ruling economic elite that controls the culture industries and is nothing more than a vehicle for capitalist ideology. It is true that media culture overwhelmingly supports capitalist values, but it is also a site of intense struggle between different races, classes, genders, and social groups. It is also possible in the age of new media and social networking for consumers to become producers of their own media content and form, including oppositional voices and resistance. Thus, to fully grasp the nature and effects of media culture, one needs to develop methods to analyze the full range of its meanings and effects that are sensitive to the always mutating terrain of media culture and technology.

TEXTUAL ANALYSIS

The products of media culture require multidimensional close textual readings to analyze their various forms of discourses, ideological positions, narrative strategies, image construction, and effects. "Reading" an artifact of media culture involves interpreting the forms and meanings of elements in a music video or television ad as one might read and interpret a book. There has been a wide range of types of textual criticism of media culture, from quantitative content analysis that dissects the number of, say, episodes of violence

in a text to qualitative study that examines representations of women, Blacks, or other groups, or applies various critical theories to unpack the meanings of the texts or explicate how texts function to produce meaning. Traditionally, the qualitative analysis of texts attended to the formal artistic properties of imaginative literature—such as style, verbal imagery, characterization, narrative structure, and point of view. From the 1960s on, however, literary-formalist textual analysis has been enhanced by methods derived from semiotics, a system for investigating the creation of meaning not only in written languages but also in other, nonverbal codes, such as the visual and auditory languages of film and TV.

Semiotics analyzes how linguistic and nonlinguistic cultural "signs" form systems of meanings, as when giving someone a rose is interpreted as a sign of love or getting an A on a college paper is a sign of mastery of the rules of the specific assignment. Semiotic analysis can be connected with genre criticism (the study of conventions governing long-established types of cultural forms, such as soap operas) to reveal how the codes and forms of particular genres construct certain meanings. Situation comedies, for instance, classically follow a conflict/resolution model that demonstrates how to solve certain social problems with correct actions and values, and they thus provide morality tales of proper and improper behavior. Soap operas, by contrast, proliferate problems and provide messages concerning the endurance and suffering needed to get through life's endless miseries, while generating positive and negative models of social behavior. And advertising shows how commodity solutions solve problems of popularity, acceptance, success, and the like.

A semiotic and genre analysis of the film *Rambo* (1982), for instance, would show how it follows the conventions of the Hollywood genre of the war film that dramatizes conflicts between the United States and its "enemies" (see Kellner, 1995). Semiotics describes how the images of the villains are constructed according to the codes of World War II movies and how the resolution of the conflict and happy ending follow the tradition of Hollywood classical cinema, which portray the victory of good over evil. Semiotic analysis would also include study of the strictly cinematic and formal elements of a film such as *Rambo,* dissecting the ways camera angles present Rambo as a god or how slow-motion images of him gliding through the jungle code him as a force of nature. Formal analysis of a film also includes how lighting is used to code characters as "good" or "evil," or how any of the technical features of film production can help generate meanings.

Similarly, a semiotic analysis of James Cameron's *Avatar* (2009) would reveal how the images in the film present an anti-militarist and pro-ecological agenda, although the narrative form celebrates a White, male savior, replicating more conservative narratives. *Avatar* also demonstrates how fantasy artifacts can project a wealth of political and ideological meanings, often ambiguous or contradictory. Discussions of *Avatar* have also generated heated debates in the politics of representation, concerning how the film has represented gender, sexuality, race, the military, and the environment, as well as other themes and dimensions of the film (see Kellner, 2010).

The textual analysis of cultural studies thus combines formalist analysis with critique of how cultural meanings convey specific ideologies of gender, race, class, sexuality, nation, and other ideological dimensions. Ideologies refer to ideas or images that construct the superiority of one class or group over others (i.e., men over women, Whites over people of color, ruling elites over working-class people, etc.) and thus reproduce and legitimate different forms of social domination. Ideological textual analysis should deploy a wide range of methods to fully explicate each dimension of ideological domination across representations of class, race, gender, and sexuality, and other forms of domination and subordination and to show how specific narratives serve interests of domination and oppression, contest it, or are ambiguous (as with many examples of media culture). Each critical method focuses on certain features of a text from a specific perspective: The perspective spotlights, or illuminates, some features of a text while ignoring others. Marxist methods tend to focus on class, for instance, while feminist approaches highlight gender, critical race theory emphasizes race and ethnicity, and gay and lesbian theories explicate sexuality. Yet today, the concept of "intersectionality" is often used, and many feminists, Marxists, critical race scholars, and other forms of cultural studies depict how gender, class, race, sexuality, and other components intersect and co-construct each other in complex cultural ways (see Crenshaw, 1991).

Various critical methods have their own strengths and limitations, their optics and blind spots. Traditionally, Marxian ideology critiques have been strong on class and historical contextualization and weak on formal analysis, while some versions are highly "reductionist," reducing textual analysis to denunciation of ruling class ideology. Feminism excels in gender analysis and in some versions is formally sophisticated, drawing on such methods as psychoanalysis and semiotics, although some versions are reductive, and early feminism often limited itself to analysis of images of gender. Psychoanalysis in turn calls for the interpretation of unconscious contents and meaning, which can articulate latent meanings in a text, as when Alfred Hitchcock's dream sequences project cinematic symbols that illuminate his characters' dilemmas or when the image of the female character in *Bonnie and Clyde* (1967), framed against the bar of her bed, suggests her sexual frustration, imprisonment in middle-class family life, and need to revolt.

Of course, each reading of a text is only one possible reading from one critic's subjective position, no matter how multiperspectival, and may or may not be the reading preferred by audiences (which themselves will be significantly different according to class, race, gender, ethnicity, ideology, and so on). Because there is a split between textual encoding and audience decoding, there is always the possibility for a multiplicity of readings of any text of media culture (Hall, 1980b). There are limits to the openness or polysemic nature of any text, of course, and textual analysis can explicate the parameters of possible readings and delineate perspectives that aim at illuminating the text and its cultural and ideological effects. Such analysis also provides the materials for criticizing misreadings, or readings that are one-sided and incomplete. Yet to further carry through a cultural studies analysis, one must also examine how diverse audiences actually read media texts and attempt to determine what impact or influence they have on audience thought and behavior.

AUDIENCE RECEPTION AND USE OF MEDIA CULTURE

All texts are subject to multiple readings depending on the perspectives and subject positions of the reader. Members of distinct genders, classes, races, nations, regions, sexual preferences, and political ideologies are going to read texts differently, and cultural studies can illuminate why diverse audiences interpret texts in various, sometimes conflicting, ways. Media culture provides materials for individuals and communities to create identities and meanings, and cultural studies work on audiences detects a variety of potentially empowering uses of cultural forms. One of the merits of cultural studies is that it has focused on audience reception and fan appropriation, and this focus provides one of its major contributions, although there are also some limitations and problems with the standard cultural studies approaches to the audience.[5]

Ethnographic research studies people and their groups and cultures and is frequently used in an attempt to determine how media texts affect specific audiences and shape their beliefs and behavior. Ethnographic cultural studies have indicated some of the various ways audiences use and appropriate texts, often to empower themselves. For example, teenagers use video games and music television to escape from the demands of a disciplinary society. Males use sports media events as a terrain of fantasy identification, in which they feel empowered as "their" team or star triumphs. Such sports events also generate a form of community currently being lost in the privatized media and consumer culture of our time. Indeed, fandoms of all sorts, from *Star Trek* fans ("Trekkies"/"Trekkers") to devotees of various soap operas, reality shows, or current highly popular TV series, also form communities that enable them to relate to others who share their interests and hobbies. Some fans, in fact, actively re-create their favorite cultural forms (see examples in Jenkins, 1992; Lewis, 1992; and Gray, Sandvoss, & Harrington, 2007). Other studies have shown that audiences can subvert the intentions of the producers or managers of the cultural industries that supply them, as when astute young media users laugh at obvious attempts to hype certain characters, shows, or products (see de Certeau, 1984, for more examples of audiences constructing meaning and engaging in practices in critical and subversive ways).

The emphasis on active audience reception and appropriation, then, has helped cultural studies overcome the previously one-sided textualist orientations to culture and also has directed focus to the actual political effects texts may have. By combining quantitative and qualitative research, audience reception and fandom studies—including some of the chapters in this reader—are providing important contributions to how people interact with cultural texts.

Yet I see several problems with reception studies as they have been constituted within cultural studies, particularly in the United States. Importantly, there is a danger that class will be downplayed as a significant variable that structures audience decoding and use of cultural texts. Cultural studies in England were particularly sensitive to class differences—as well as subcultural differences—in the use and reception of cultural texts, but I have noted many dissertations, books, and articles in cultural studies in the United States in which attention to class has been downplayed or is missing altogether. This is not surprising, as a neglect of class as a constitutive feature of culture and society is endemic in the American academy in most disciplines.

There is also the reverse danger, however, of exaggerating the constitutive force of class and downplaying, or ignoring, such other variables as gender and ethnicity. Staiger (1992) noted that Fiske, building on Hartley, lists seven "subjectivity positions" that are important in cultural reception—"self, gender, age-group, family, class, nation, ethnicity"—and proposes adding sexuality. All these factors, and no doubt more, interact in shaping how audiences receive and use texts and must be taken into account in studying cultural reception, for audiences decode and use texts according to the specific constituents of their class, race or ethnicity, gender, sexual preference, and so on.

Furthermore, I would warn against a tendency to romanticize the "active audience" by claiming that all audiences produce their own meanings and denying that media culture may have powerful manipulative effects. There is a tendency within the cultural studies tradition of reception research to dichotomize between dominant and oppositional readings (Hall, 1980b). "Dominant" readings are those in which audiences appropriate texts in line with the interests of the dominant culture and the ideological intentions of a text, as when audiences feel pleasure in the restoration of male power, law and order, and social stability at the end of a film such as *Die Hard*, after the hero and representatives of authority eliminate the terrorists who had taken over a high-rise corporate headquarters. An "oppositional" reading, in contrast, celebrates the resistance to this reading in audience appropriation of a text. For example, Fiske (1993) observed (and implicitly approved) resistance to dominant readings when homeless individuals in a shelter cheered the violent destruction of police and authority figures during repeated viewings of a videotape of *Die Hard*.

Fiske's study illustrates a tendency in cultural studies to celebrate resistance per se without distinguishing between types and forms of resistance (a similar problem resides with indiscriminate celebration of audience pleasure in certain reception studies). For example, some would argue that the violent resistance to social authority valorized in this reading of *Die Hard* glamorizes brutal, masculinist behavior and the use of physical violence to solve social problems. It is true that theorists of revolution, including Jean-Paul Sartre, Frantz Fanon, and Herbert Marcuse, among others, have argued that violence can be either emancipatory, when directed at forces of oppression, or reactionary, when directed at popular forces struggling against oppression. In contrast, many feminists and those in the Gandhian tradition see all violence against others as a form of brutal, masculinist behavior, and many people see it as a problematic form of conflict resolution. Thus, audience pleasure in violent resistance cannot be valorized per se as a progressive element of the appropriation of cultural texts. Instead, difficult discriminations must be made as to whether the resistance, oppositional reading, or pleasure in a given experience should be understood as progressive or reactionary, emancipatory or destructive.

Thus, while emphasis on the audience and reception was an excellent correction to the one-sidedness of purely textual analysis, I believe that in recent years, cultural studies has overemphasized reception and textual analysis while underemphasizing the production of culture and its political economy. This type of cultural studies fetishizes audience reception studies and neglects both production and textual analysis, thus producing populist celebrations of the text and audience pleasure in its use of cultural artifacts. This approach, taken to an extreme, would lose its critical perspective and put a positive gloss on audience experience of whatever is being studied. Such studies also might lose sight of the manipulative and conservative effects of certain types of media culture and thus serve the interests of the cultural industries as they are presently constituted.

No doubt, media effects are complex and controversial, and it is the merit of cultural studies to make the analysis of such effects an important part of its agenda. Previous studies of the audience and reception of media privileged ethnographic studies that selected slices of the vast media audiences, usually from the sites where researchers themselves lived. Such studies are invariably limited, and broader effects research can indicate how the most popular artifacts of media culture have a wide range of effects.

One new way to research media effects is to use Google, or databases that collect media texts, to trace certain effects of media artifacts through analysis of references to them in the journalistic media. Likewise, a new terrain of Internet audience research studies how fans act in chat rooms or on fansites devoted to their favorite artifacts of media culture. New media such as Facebook, YouTube, Twitter, and other social networking sites produce forums for more active audiences, as well as new sites for audience research. As audiences critically discuss or celebrate their preferred artifacts of media culture and, in some cases, produce their own versions, disseminated to audiences throughout the Internet and via new digital technologies, media culture expands its reach and power while audiences can feel that they are part of their preferred cultural sites and phenomena. Studies are proliferating in this field, examining how Facebook, YouTube, Twitter, and other new media are used by individuals and groups in diverse ways, from sharing pictures and media content to social networking to political expression and organizing and pedagogical purposes (Kellner & Kim, 2010).

TOWARD A CULTURAL STUDIES THAT IS CRITICAL, MULTICULTURAL, AND MULTIPERSPECTIVAL

To avoid the one-sidedness of textual analysis approaches or audience and reception studies, I propose that cultural studies itself be multiperspectival, getting at culture from the perspectives of political economy, text analysis, and audience reception, as outlined above. Textual analysis should use a multiplicity of perspectives and critical methods, and audience reception studies should delineate the wide range of subject positions, or perspectives, through which audiences appropriate culture. This requires a multicultural approach that sees the importance of analyzing the dimensions of class, race and ethnicity, and gender and sexual preference within the texts of media culture, while also studying their impact on how audiences read and interpret media culture.

In addition, a critical cultural studies approach attacks sexism, heterosexism, racism, and bias against specific social groups (i.e., gays, intellectuals, seniors, etc.) and criticizes texts that promote any kind of domination or oppression. As an example of how considerations of production, textual analysis, and audience readings can fruitfully intersect in cultural studies, let us reflect on the Madonna phenomenon. Madonna came on the scene in the moment of Reaganism and embodied the materialistic and consumer-oriented ethos of the 1980s ("Material Girl"). She also appeared in a time of dramatic image proliferation, associated with MTV, fashion fever, and intense marketing of products. Madonna was one of the first MTV music video superstars who consciously crafted images to attract a mass audience. Her early music videos were aimed at teenage girls (the Madonna wannabes), but she soon incorporated Black, Hispanic, and minority audiences with her images of interracial sex and multicultural "family" in her concerts. She also appealed to gay and lesbian audiences, as well as feminist and academic audiences, as her videos became more complex and political (e.g., "Like a Prayer," "Express Yourself," "Vogue," etc.).

Thus, Madonna's popularity was in large part a function of her marketing strategies and her production of music videos and images that appealed to diverse audiences. To conceptualize the meanings and effects in her music, films, concerts, and public relations stunts requires that her artifacts be interpreted within the context of their production and reception, which involves discussion of MTV, the music industry, concerts, marketing, and the production of images (see Kellner, 1995). Understanding Madonna's popularity also requires focus on audiences, not just as individuals but as members of specific groups—such as teenage girls, who were empowered by Madonna in their struggles for individual identity, or gays, who were also empowered by her incorporation of alternative images of sexuality within popular mainstream cultural artifacts. Yet appraising the politics and effects of Madonna also requires analysis of how her work might merely reproduce a consumer culture that defines identity in terms of images and consumption. It would make an interesting project to examine how former Madonna fans view the superstar's evolution and recent incarnations, such as her many relationships and marriages and ongoing world tours, as well as to examine how contemporary fans view Madonna in an age that embraces pop singers such as Beyoncé and Lady Gaga.

Likewise, Michael Jackson's initial popularity derived from carefully managed media spectacles, first in the Jackson Five and then in his own career. Jackson achieved his superstar status, like Madonna, from his MTV-disseminated music videos and spectacular concert performances, in which promotion, image management, and his publicity apparatus made him the King of Pop. While, like Madonna, his frequent tabloid and media presence helped promote his career, media spectacle and tabloids also derailed it, as he was charged with child abuse in well-publicized cases. After his death in 2009, however, Jackson had a remarkable surge in popularity as his works were disseminated through the media, including new media and social networking sites.

CULTURAL STUDIES FOR THE 21ST CENTURY

As discussed above, a cultural studies that is critical and multicultural provides comprehensive approaches to culture that can be applied to a wide variety of media artifacts, from advertising and pornography to Beyoncé and the *Twilight* series, from reality TV and *World of Warcraft* to Barbie and *Avatar*. Its comprehensive perspectives encompass political economy, textual analysis, and audience research and provide critical and political perspectives that enable individuals to dissect the meanings, messages, and effects of dominant cultural forms. Cultural studies is thus part of a critical media pedagogy that enables individuals to resist media manipulation and increase their freedom and individuality. It can empower people to gain sovereignty over their culture and struggle for alternative cultures and political change. Thus, cultural studies is not just another academic fad but, rather, can be part of a struggle for a better society and a better life.

NOTES

1. For more information on British cultural studies, see Agger (1992); Durham and Kellner (2012); During (1992, 1998); Fiske (1986); Grossberg (1989); Grossberg, Nelson, and Treichler (1992); Hall (1980b); Hammer and Kellner (2009); Johnson (1986–1987); O'Connor (1989); and Turner (1990). The Frankfurt school also provided much material for a critical cultural

studies approach in its works on mass culture from the 1930s through the present; on the relation between the Frankfurt school and British cultural studies, see Kellner (1997).

2. On the concept of ideology, see the Centre for Contemporary Cultural Studies (1980), Kellner (1978, 1979), Kellner and Ryan (1988), and Thompson (1990).

3. This model was adumbrated in Hall (1980a) and Johnson (1986–1987), and guided much of the early Birmingham work. Around the mid-1980s, however, the Birmingham group began to increasingly neglect the production and political economy of culture (some believe that this was always a problem with their work), and the majority of their studies became more academic, cut off from political struggle. I am thus trying to recapture the spirit of the early Birmingham project, reconstructed for our contemporary moment. For a fuller development of my conception of cultural studies, see Kellner (1992, 1995, 2001, 2010).

4. The term *political economy* calls attention to the fact that the production and distribution of culture take place within a specific economic system, constituted by relations between the state and economy. For instance, in the United States, a capitalist economy dictates that cultural production is governed by laws of the market, but the democratic imperatives of the system mean that there is some regulation of culture by the state. There are often tensions within a given society concerning how many activities should be governed by the imperatives of the market, or economics, alone and how much state regulation or intervention is desirable to ensure a wider diversity of broadcast programming, for instance, or the prohibition of phenomena agreed to be harmful, such as cigarette advertising or pornography (see Kellner, 1990; McChesney, 2007).

5. Influential cultural studies that have focused on audience reception include Ang (1985, 1996), Brunsdon and Morley (1978), Fiske (1989a, 1989b), Jenkins (1992), Lewis (1992), Morley (1986), and Radway (1983). On "fandom," see Gray, Sandvoss, and Harrington (2007).

REFERENCES

Agger, B. (1992). *Cultural studies.* London: Falmer.

Ang, I. (1985). *Watching* Dallas. New York: Methuen.

Ang, I. (1996). *Living room wars: Rethinking media audiences for a postmodern world.* London: Routledge.

Brunsdon, C., & Morley, D. (1978). *Everyday television: "Nationwide."* London: British Film Institute.

Centre for Contemporary Cultural Studies. (1980). *On ideology.* London: Hutchinson.

Crenshaw, K. W. (1991). Mapping the margins: Intersectionality, identity politics, and violence against women of color. *Stanford Law Review, 43*(6), 1241–1299.

de Certeau, M. (1984). *The practice of everyday life.* Berkeley: University of California Press.

Durham, M. G., & Kellner, D. (Eds.). (2012). *Media and cultural studies: Key works* (Rev. 2nd ed.). Malden, MA: Blackwell.

During, S. (1992, 1998). *Cultural studies.* London: Routledge.

Fiske, J. (1986). British cultural studies and television. In R. C. Allen (Ed.), *Channels of discourse* (pp. 254–289). Chapel Hill: University of North Carolina Press.

Fiske, J. (1989a). *Reading the popular.* Boston: Unwin Hyman.

Fiske, J. (1989b). *Understanding popular culture.* Boston: Unwin Hyman.

Fiske, J. (1993). *Power plays, power works.* London: Verso.

Gramsci, A. (1971). *Selections from the prison notebooks of Antonio Gramsci* (Q. Hoare & G. Nowell Smith, Eds.). New York: International.

Gray, J., Sandvoss, C., & Harrington, C. L. (Eds.). (2007). *Fandom: Identities and communities in a mediated world.* New York: New York University Press.

Grossberg, L. (1989). The formations of cultural studies: An American in Birmingham. *Strategies, 22,* 114–149.

Grossberg, L., Nelson, C., & Treichler, P. (1992). *Cultural studies*. New York: Routledge.

Hall, S. (1980a). Cultural studies and the Centre: Some problematics and problems. In S. Hall, D. Hobson, A. Lowe, & P. Willis (Eds.), *Culture, media, language: Working papers in cultural studies, 1972–79* (pp. 15–47). London: Hutchinson.

Hall, S. (1980b). Encoding/decoding. In S. Hall, D. Hobson, A. Lowe, & P. Willis (Eds.), *Culture, media, language: Working papers in cultural studies, 1972–79* (pp. 128–138). London: Hutchinson.

Hammer, R., & Kellner, D. (2009). *Media/cultural studies: Critical approaches*. New York: Peter Lang.

Jenkins, H. (1992). *Textual poachers*. New York: Routledge.

Johnson, R. (1986–1987). What is cultural studies anyway? *Social Text, 16,* 38–80.

Kahn, R., & Kellner, D. (2008). Technopolitics, blogs, and emergent media ecologies: A critical/reconstructive approach. In B. Hawk, D. M. Rider, & O. Oviedo (Eds.), *Small tech: The culture of digital tools* (pp. 22–37). Minneapolis: University of Minnesota Press.

Kellner, D. (1978, November–December). Ideology, Marxism, and advanced capitalism. *Socialist Review, 42,* 37–65.

Kellner, D. (1979, May–June). TV, ideology, and emancipatory popular culture. *Socialist Review, 45,* 13–53.

Kellner, D. (1990). *Television and the crisis of democracy*. Boulder, CO: Westview.

Kellner, D. (1992). *The Persian Gulf TV war*. Boulder, CO: Westview.

Kellner, D. (1995). *Media culture: Cultural studies, identity, and politics between the modern and the postmodern*. London: Routledge.

Kellner, D. (1997). Critical theory and British cultural studies: The missed articulation. In J. McGuigan (Ed.), *Cultural methodologies* (pp. 12–41). London: Sage.

Kellner, D. (2001). *Grand Theft 2000*. Lanham, MD: Rowman & Littlefield.

Kellner, D. (2003). *From September 11 to terror war: The dangers of the Bush legacy*. Lanham, MD: Rowman & Littlefield.

Kellner, D. (2005). *Media spectacle and the crisis of democracy*. Boulder, CO: Paradigm.

Kellner, D. (2010). *Cinema wars: Hollywood film and politics in the Bush/Cheney era*. Malden, MA: Blackwell.

Kellner, D., & Kim, G. (2010). YouTube, critical pedagogy, and media activism. *Review of Education/Pedagogy/Cultural Studies, 32*(1), 3–36.

Kellner, D., & Ryan, M. (1988). *Camera politica: The politics and ideology of contemporary Hollywood film*. Bloomington: Indiana University Press.

Lewis, L. A. (1992). *Adoring audience: Fan culture and popular media*. New York: Routledge.

McChesney, R. (2000). *Rich media, poor democracy: Communications politics in dubious times*. New York: New Press.

McChesney, R. (2007). *Communication revolution: Critical junctures and the future of media*. New York: New Press.

McChesney, R. (2013). *Digital disconnect: How capitalism is turning the Internet against democracy*. New York: New Press.

Morley, D. (1986). *Family television*. London: Comedia.

O'Connor, A. (1989, December). The problem of American cultural studies. *Critical Studies in Mass Communication, 6,* 404–413.

Radway, J. (1983). *Reading the romance*. Chapel Hill: University of North Carolina Press.

Staiger, J. (1992). Film, reception, and cultural studies. *Centennial Review, 26*(1), 89–104.

Thompson, J. (1990). *Ideology and modern culture*. Cambridge, UK: Polity Press and Stanford University Press.

Turner, G. (1990). *British cultural studies: An introduction*. New York: Unwin Hyman.

THE MEANING OF MEMORY

Family, Class, and Ethnicity in Early Network Television Programs

George Lipsitz

2

THE MEANING OF MEMORY

. . . In the midst of extraordinary social change, television became the most important discursive medium in American culture. As such, it was charged with special responsibilities for making new economic and social relations credible and legitimate to audiences haunted by ghosts from the past. Urban ethnic working-class situation comedies provided one means of addressing the anxieties and contradictions emanating from the clash between the consumer present of the 1950s and collective social memory about the 1930s and 1940s.

The consumer consciousness emerging from economic and social change in postwar America conflicted with the lessons of historical experience for many middle- and working-class American families. The Great Depression of the 1930s had not only damaged the economy, it also undercut the political and cultural legitimacy of American capitalism. Herbert Hoover had been a national hero in the 1920s, with his credo of "rugged individualism" forming the basis for a widely shared cultural ideal. But the depression discredited Hoover's philosophy and made him a symbol of yesterday's blasted hopes to millions of Americans. In the 1930s, cultural ideals based on mutuality and collectivity eclipsed the previous decade's "rugged individualism" and helped propel massive union organizing drives, anti-eviction movements, and general strikes. President Roosevelt's New Deal attempted to harness and co-opt that grass roots mass activity in an attempt to restore social order and recapture credibility and legitimacy for the capitalist system (Romasco 1965). The social welfare legislation of the "Second New

Deal" in 1935 went far beyond any measures previously favored by Roosevelt and most of his advisors, but radical action proved necessary for the Administration to contain the upsurge of activism that characterized the decade. Even in the private sector, industrial corporations made more concessions to workers than naked power realities necessitated because they feared the political consequences of mass disillusionment with the system (Berger 1982).

World War II ended the depression and brought prosperity, but it did so on a basis even more collective than the New Deal of the 1930s. Government intervention in the wartime economy reached unprecedented levels, bringing material reward and shared purpose to a generation raised on the deprivation and sacrifice of the depression. In the postwar years, the largest and most disruptive strike wave in American history won major improvements in the standard of living for the average worker, both through wage increases and through government commitments to insure full employment, decent housing, and expanded educational opportunities. Grass roots militancy and working-class direct action wrested concessions from a reluctant government and business elite— mostly because the public at large viewed workers' demands as more legitimate than the desires of capital (Lipsitz 1981).

Yet the collective nature of working-class mass activity in the postwar era posed severe problems for capital. In sympathy strikes and secondary boycotts, workers placed the interests of their class ahead of their own individual material aspirations. Strikes over safety and job control far outnumbered wage strikes, revealing aspirations to control the process of production that conflicted with capitalist labor-management relations. Mass demonstrations demanding government employment and housing programs indicated a collective political response to problems previously adjudicated on a personal level. Radical challenges to the authority of capital (like the 1946 United Auto Workers' strike demand that wage increases come out of corporate profits rather than from price hikes passed on to consumers), demonstrated a social responsibility and a commitment toward redistributing wealth, rare in the history of American labor (Lipsitz 1981:47–50).

Capital attempted to regain the initiative in the postwar years by making qualified concessions to working-class pressures for redistribution of wealth and power. Rather than paying wage increases out of corporate profits, business leaders instead worked to expand the economy through increases in government spending, foreign trade, and consumer debt. Such expansion could meet the demands of workers and consumers without undermining capital's dominant role in the economy. On the presumption that "a rising tide lifts all boats," business leaders sought to connect working-class aspirations for a better life to policies that insured a commensurate rise in corporate profits, thereby leaving the distribution of wealth unaffected. Federal defense spending, highway construction programs, and home loan policies expanded the economy at home in a manner conducive to the interests of capital, while the Truman Doctrine and Marshall Plan provided models for enhanced access to foreign markets and raw materials for American corporations. The Taft-Hartley Act of 1947 banned the class-conscious collective activities most threatening to capital (mass strikes, sympathy strikes, secondary boycotts); the leaders of labor, government, and business accepted as necessity the practice of paying wage hikes for organized workers out of the pockets of consumers and unorganized workers, in the form of higher prices (Lipsitz 1981).

Commercial network television played an important role in this emerging economy, functioning as a significant object of consumer purchasers as well as an important marketing medium. Sales of sets jumped from three million during the entire decade of the 1940s to over five million a *year* during the 1950s (*TV Facts* 1980:141). But television's most important economic function came from its role as an instrument of legitimation for transformations in values initiated by the new economic imperatives of postwar America.

For Americans to accept the new world of 1950s' consumerism, they had to make a break with the past. The depression years had helped generate fears about installment buying and excessive materialism, while the New Deal and wartime mobilization had provoked suspicions about individual acquisitiveness and upward mobility. Depression era and war time scarcities of consumer goods had led workers to internalize discipline and frugality while nurturing networks of mutual support through family, ethnic, and class associations. Government policies after the war encouraged an atomized acquisitive consumerism at odds with the lessons of the past. At the same time, federal home loan policies stimulated migrations to the suburbs from traditional, urban ethnic working-class neighborhoods. The entry of television into the American home disrupted previous patterns of family life and encouraged fragmentation of the family into separate segments of the consumer market.[1] The priority of consumerism in the economy at large and on television may have seemed organic and unplanned, but conscious policy decisions by officials from both private and public sectors shaped the contours of the consumer economy and television's role within it.

COMMERCIAL TELEVISION AND ECONOMIC CHANGE

Government policies during and after World War II shaped the basic contours of home television as an advertising medium. Government-sponsored research and development during the war perfected the technology of home television while federal tax policies solidified its economic base. The government allowed corporations to deduct the cost of advertising from their taxable incomes during the war, despite the fact that rationing and defense production left business with few products to market. Consequently, manufacturers kept the names of their products before the public while lowering their tax obligations on high wartime profits. Their advertising expenditures supplied radio networks and advertising agencies with the capital reserves and business infrastructure that enabled them to dominate the television industry in the postwar era. After the war, federal antitrust action against the motion picture studios broke up the "network" system in movies, while the FCC sanctioned the network system in television. In addition, FCC decisions to allocate stations on the narrow VHF band, to grant the networks ownership and operation rights over stations in prime markets, and to place a freeze on the licensing of new stations during the important years between 1948 and 1952 all combined to guarantee that advertising-oriented programming based on the model of radio would triumph over theater TV, educational TV, or any other form (Boddy 1985; Allen 1983). Government decisions, not market forces, established the dominance of commercial television, but these decisions reflected a view of the American economy and its needs which had become so well accepted at the top levels of business and government that it had virtually become the official state economic policy.

Fearing both renewed depression and awakened militancy among workers, influential corporate and business leaders considered increases in consumer spending—increases of 30% to 50%—to be necessary to perpetuate prosperity in the postwar era (Lipsitz 1981:46, 120–121). Defense spending for the Cold War and Korean Conflict had complemented an aggressive trade policy to improve the state of the economy, but it appeared that the key to an expanding economy rested in increased consumer spending fueled by an expansion of credit (Moore and Klein 1967; Jezer 1982). Here too, government policies led the way, especially with regard to stimulating credit purchases of homes and automobiles. During World War II, the marginal tax rate for most wage earners jumped from 4% to 25%, making the home ownership deduction more desirable. Federal housing loan policies favored construction of new single family detached suburban housing over renovation or construction of central city multifamily units. Debt-encumbered home ownership in accord with these policies stimulated construction of 30 million new housing units in just twenty years, bringing the percentage of home-owning Americans from below 40% in 1940 to more than 60% by 1960. Mortgage policies encouraging long term debt and low down payments freed capital for other consumer purchases, while government highway building policies undermined mass transit systems and contributed to increased demand for automobiles (Hartman 1982:165–168). Partly as a result of these policies, consumer spending on private cars averaged $7.5 billion per year in the 1930s and 1940s, but grew to $22 billion per year in 1950 and almost $30 billion by 1955 (Mollenkopf 1983:111).

For the first time in U.S. history, middle-class and working-class families could routinely expect to own homes or buy new cars every few years. Between 1946 and 1965 residential mortgage debt rose three times as fast as the gross national product and disposable income. Mortgage debt accounted for just under 18% of disposable income in 1946, but it grew to almost 55% by 1965 (Stone 1983:122). In order to insure eventual payment of current debts, the economy had to generate tremendous expansion and growth, further stimulating the need to increase consumer spending. Manufacturers had to find new ways of motivating consumers to buy ever increasing amounts of commodities, and television provided an important means of accomplishing that end.

Television advertised individual products, but it also provided a relentless flow of information and persuasion that placed acts of consumption at the core of everyday life. The physical fragmentation of suburban growth and declines in motion picture attendance created an audience more likely to stay at home and receive entertainment there than ever before. But television also provided a locus redefining American ethnic, class, and family identities into consumer identities. In order to accomplish this task effectively, television programs had to address some of the psychic, moral, and political obstacles to consumption among the public at large.

The television and advertising industries knew that they had to overcome these obstacles. Marketing expert and motivational specialist Ernest Dichter stated that "one of the basic problems of this prosperity is to give people that sanction and justification to enjoy it and to demonstrate that the hedonistic approach to life is a moral one, not an immoral one" (Jezer 1982:127). Dichter went on to note the many barriers that inhibited consumer acceptance of unrestrained hedonism, and he called on advertisers "to train the average citizen to accept growth of his country and its economy as *his* growth rather than as a strange and frightening event" (Dichter 1960:210). One method of encouraging that acceptance, according to Dichter, consisted of identifying new products and styles of consumption with traditional, historically sanctioned practices and behavior. He noted that such an approach held particular relevance in addressing consumers who had only recently acquired the means to spend freely and who might harbor a lingering conservatism based on their previous experiences (Dichter 1960:209). . . .

FAMILY FORMATION AND THE ECONOMY—THE TELEVISION VIEW

Advertisers incorporated their messages into urban ethnic working-class comedies through indirect and direct means. Tensions developed in the programs often found indirect resolution in commercials. Thus Jeannie MacClennan's search for an American sweetheart in one episode of *Hey Jeannie* set up commercials proclaiming the abilities of Drene shampoo to keep one prepared to accept last minute dates and of Crest toothpaste to produce an attractive smile (*Hey Jeannie:* "The Rock and Roll Kid"). Conversations about shopping for new furniture in an episode of *The Goldbergs* directed viewers' attention to furnishings in the Goldberg home provided for the show by Macy's department store in exchange for a commercial acknowledgment (*The Goldbergs:* "The In-laws").

But the content of the shows themselves offered even more direct emphasis on consumer spending. In one episode of *The Goldbergs,* Molly expresses disapproval of her future daughter-in-law's plan to buy a washing machine on the installment plan. "I know Papa and me never bought anything unless we had the money to pay for it," she intones with logic familiar to a generation with memories of the Great Depression. Her son, Sammy, confronts this "deviance" by saying, "Listen, Ma, almost everybody in this country lives above their means—and everybody enjoys it." Doubtful at first, Molly eventually learns from her children and announces her conversion to the legitimacy of installment buying by proposing that the family buy two cars so as to "live above our means—the American way" (*The Goldbergs:* "The In-laws"). In a subsequent episode, Molly's daughter, Rosalie, assumes the role of ideological tutor to her mother. When planning a move out of their Bronx apartment to a new house in the suburbs, Molly ruminates about where to place her furniture in the new home. "You don't mean we're going to take all this junk with us into a brand new house?" asks an exasperated Rosalie. With traditionalist sentiment Molly answers, "Junk? My furniture's junk? My furniture that I lived with and loved for twenty years is junk?" But in the end she accepts Rosalie's argument—even selling off all her old furniture to help meet the down payment on the new house, and deciding to buy new furniture on the installment plan (*The Goldbergs:* "Moving Day").

Chester A. Riley confronts similar choices about family and commodities in *The Life of Riley.* His wife complains that he only takes her out to the neighborhood bowling alley and restaurant, not to "interesting places." Riley searches for ways to impress her and discovers from a friend that a waiter at the fancy Club Morambo will let them eat first and pay later, at a dollar a week plus ten percent interest. "Ain't that dishonest?" asks Riley. "No, it's usury," his friend replies. Riley does not borrow the money, but he impresses his wife anyway by taking the family out to dinner on the proceeds of a prize that he received for being the one-thousandth customer in a local flower shop. Though we eventually learn that Peg Riley only wanted attention, not an expensive meal, the happy ending of the episode hinges totally on Riley's prestige, restored when he demonstrates his ability to provide a luxury outing for the family (*Life of Riley:* R228).

The same episode of *The Life of Riley* reveals another consumerist element common to this subgenre. When Riley protests that he lacks the money needed to fulfill Peg's desires, she answers that he would have plenty if he didn't spend so much on "needless gadgets." His shortage of cash becomes a personal failing caused by incompetent behavior as a consumer. Nowhere do we hear about the size of his paycheck, relations between his union and his employer, or, for that matter, the relationship between the value of his labor and the wages paid to him by the Stevenson Aircraft Company. Like Uncle David in *The Goldbergs*—who buys a statue of Hamlet shaking hands with Shakespeare and an elk's tooth with the Gettysburg address carved on it—Riley's comic character stems in part from a flaw which in theory could be attributed to the entire consumer economy: a preoccupation with "needless gadgets." By contrast, Peg Riley's desire for an evening out is portrayed as reasonable and modest—as reparation due her for the inevitable tedium of housework. The solution to her unhappiness, of course, comes from an evening out rather than from a change in her own work circumstances. Even within the home, television elevates consumption over production; production is assumed to be a constant—only consumption can be varied. But more than enjoyment is at stake: unless Riley can provide her with the desired night on the town, he will fail in his obligations as a husband (*Life of Riley:* R228; *The Goldbergs:* "Bad Companions"). . . .

"Mama's Birthday," broadcast in 1954, delineated the tensions between family loyalty and consumer desire endemic to modern capitalist society. The show begins with Mama teaching Katrin to make Norwegian potato balls, the kind she used long ago to "catch" Papa. Unimpressed by this accomplishment, Katrin changes the subject and asks Mama what she wants for her upcoming birthday. In an answer that locates Mama within the gender roles of the 1950s, she replies, "Well, I think a fine new job for your Papa. You and Dagmar to marry nice young men and have a lot of wonderful children—just like I have. And Nels, well, Nels to become president of the United States" (Meehan and Ropes 1954). In one sentence Mama has summed up the dominant culture's version of legitimate female expectations: success at work for her husband, marriage and childrearing for her daughters, the presidency for her son—and nothing for herself.

But we learn that Mama does have some needs, although we do not hear it from her lips. Her sister, Jenny, asks Mama to attend a fashion show, but Mama cannot leave the house because she has to cook a roast for a guest whom Papa has invited to dinner. Jenny comments that Mama never seems to get out of the kitchen, adding that "it's a disgrace when a woman can't call her soul her own," and "it's a shame that a married woman can't have some time to herself." The complaint is a valid one, and we can imagine how it might have resonated for women in the 1950s. The increased availability of household appliances and the use of synthetic fibers and commercially processed food should have decreased the amount of time women spent in housework, but surveys showed that home-makers spent the same number of hours per week (51 to 56) doing housework as they had done in the 1920s. Advertising and marketing strategies undermined the potential of technological changes by upgrading standards for cleanliness in the home and expanding desires for more varied wardrobes and menus for the average family (Hartmann 1982:168). In that context, Aunt Jenny would have been justified in launching into a tirade about the division of labor within the Hansen household or about the possibilities for cooperative housework, but network television specializes in a less social and more commodified dialogue about problems like housework: Aunt Jenny suggests that her sister's family buy her a "fireless cooker"—a cast iron stove—for her birthday. "They're wonderful," she tells them in language borrowed from the rhetoric of advertising. "You just put your dinner inside them, close 'em up, and go where you please. When you come back your dinner is all cooked" (Meehan and Ropes 1954). Papa protests that Mama likes to cook on her woodburning stove, but Jenny dismisses that objection with an insinuation about his motive, when she replies, "Well, I suppose it *would* cost a little more than you could afford, Hansen" (Meehan and Ropes 1954). By identifying a commodity as the solution to Mama's problem, Aunt Jenny unites the inner voice of Mama with the outer voice of the sponsors of television programs. . . .

Prodded by their aunt, the Hansen children go shopping and purchase the fireless cooker from a storekeeper who calls the product "the new Emancipation Proclamation—setting housewives free from their old kitchen range" (Meehan and Ropes 1954). Our exposure to advertising hyperbole should not lead us to miss the analogy here: housework is compared to slavery, and the commercial product takes on the aura of Abraham Lincoln. The shopkeeper's appeal convinces the children to pool their resources and buy the stove for Mama. But we soon learn that Papa plans to make a fireless cooker for Mama with his tools. When Mama discovers Papa's intentions she persuades the children to buy her another gift. Even Papa admits that his stove will not be as efficient as the one made in a factory, but Mama nobly affirms that she will like his better because he made it himself. The children use their money to buy dishes for Mama, and Katrin remembers the episode as Mama's happiest birthday ever (Meehan and Ropes 1954).

The stated resolution of "Mama's Birthday" favors traditional values. Mama prefers to protect Papa's feelings rather than having a better stove, and the product built by a family member has more value than one sold as a commodity. Yet the entire development of the plot leads in the opposite direction. The "fireless cooker" is the star of the episode, setting in motion all the other characters, and it has unquestioned value even in the face of Jenny's meddlesome brashness, Papa's insensitivity, and Mama's old-fashioned ideals. Buying a product is unchallenged as the true means of changing the unpleasant realities or low status of women's work in the home.

This resolution of the conflict between consumer desires and family roles reflected television's social role as mediator between the family and the economy. Surveys of set ownership showed no pronounced stratification by class, but a clear correlation between family size and television purchases: households with three to five people were most likely to own television sets, while those with only one person were least likely to own them (Swanson and Jones 1951). The television industry recognized and promoted its privileged place within families in advertisements like the one in the *New York Times* in 1950 that proclaimed,

"Youngsters today need television for their morale as much as they need fresh air and sunshine for their health" (Wolfenstein 1951). Like previous communications media, television sets occupied honored places in family living rooms, and helped structure family time; unlike other previous communications media, they displayed available commodities in a way that transformed all their entertainment into a glorified shopping catalogue. . . .

NOTE

1. Nielsen ratings demonstrate television's view of the family as separate market segments to be addressed independently. For an analysis of the industry's view of children as a special market, see Patricia J. Bence (1985), "Analysis and History of Typology and Forms of Children's Network Programming From 1950 to 1980."

REFERENCES

Allen, Jeanne. 1983. The Social Matrix of Television: Invention in the United States. In *Regarding Televison*. E. Ann Kaplan, ed. Pp. 109–119. Los Angeles: University Publications of America.

Berger, Henry. 1982. Social Protest in St. Louis. Paper presented at a Committee for the Humanities Forum. St. Louis, Missouri. March 12.

Boddy, William. 1985. The Studios Move Into Prime Time: Hollywood and the Television Industry in the 1950s. *Cinema Journal* 12(4):23–37.

Dichter, Ernest. 1960. *The Strategy of Desire*. Garden City: Doubleday.

Goldbergs, The. 1955. Moving Day. Academy of Television Arts Collection. 35F34I. University of California, Los Angeles.

———. 1955. The In-laws. Academy of Television Arts Collection. F32I8. University of California, Los Angeles.

———. 1955. Bad Companions. Academy of Television Arts Collection. F32I9. University of California, Los Angeles.

Hartmann, Susan. 1982. *The Home Front and Beyond*. Boston: Twayne.

Hey Jeannie. 1956. The Rock and Roll Kid. Academy of Television Arts Collection. University of California, Los Angeles.

Jezer, Marty. 1982. *The Dark Ages*. Boston: South End.

Life of Riley. 1953. Academy of Television Arts Collection. R228. University of California, Los Angeles.

Lipsitz, George. 1981. *Class and Culture in Cold War America: A Rainbow at Midnight*. New York: Praeger.

Meehan, Elizabeth, and Bradford Ropes. 1954. *Mama's Birthday*. Theater Arts Collection. University Research Library. University of California, Los Angeles.

Mollenkopf, John. 1983. *The Contested City*. Princeton: Princeton University Press.

Moore, Geoffrey, and Phillip Klein. 1967. *The Quality of Consumer Installment Credit*. Washington, D.C.: National Bureau of Economic Research.

Romasco, Albert U. 1965. *The Poverty of Abundance*. New York: Oxford University Press.

Stone, Michael. 1983. Housing and the Economic Crisis. In *America's Housing Crisis: What Is to Be Done?* Chester Hartman, ed. Pp. 99–150. London and New York: Routledge and Kegan Paul.

Swanson, Charles E., and Robert L. Jones (1951). Television Ownership and Its Correlates. *Journal of Applied Psychology* 35:352–357.

TV Facts. 1980. New York: Facts on File.

Wolfenstein, Martha. 1951. The Emergence of Fun Morality. *Journal of Social Issues* 7(4):15–25.

THE ECONOMICS OF THE MEDIA INDUSTRY

David P. Croteau and William D. Hoynes

Agreat deal of the media content we consume is produced by media companies and most of the media in the United States and other Western democracies are for-profit businesses. Like all businesses, they are influenced by issues such as profitability, cost containment, and evolving ownership patterns. To understand the media, then, we must have some sense of the economic dimension of the media industry. (For a more in-depth treatment of the economic dynamics that shape the media industry, see Croteau and Hoynes 2006; for a focus on the global dimension of media, see Flew 2007.)

CONCENTRATION OF OWNERSHIP

One of the clearest trends in media ownership is its increasing concentration in fewer hands. In his classic book, *The New Media Monopoly,* Ben Bagdikian (2004) argued that ownership of media had become so concentrated that by the mid-2000s only five global firms dominated the media industry in the United States, operating like a cartel. Bagdikian identified the five dominant companies as Time Warner, The Walt Disney Company, Viacom, News Corporation, and Bertelsmann, all multimedia entertainment conglomerates that produce and distribute newspapers, magazines, radio, television, books, and movies. According to Bagdikian, "This gives each of the five corporations and their leaders more communication power than was exercised by any despot or dictatorship in history" (Bagdikian 2004: 3).

In the years since the publication of *The New Media Monopoly,* the media landscape has changed considerably. For example, in 2006 Viacom split into the CBS Corporation and Viacom, Inc. But even in the face of such change, media ownership remains highly concentrated in the 2010s. Within each sector of the media industry, a few large companies tower above their smaller competitors. For example,

Movies. The global motion picture industry is dominated by six companies—Comcast's Universal Pictures, Viacom's Paramount Pictures, Time Warner's Warner Bros., Walt Disney Studios, the News Corporation's 20th Century Fox, and Sony Pictures Entertainment. In 2012, Sony led the way with worldwide box office revenues of $4.4 billion, with less than half of its ticket sale revenue ($1.77 billion) in North America. Its top film, the James Bond movie *Skyfall,* made more than $1 billion at the global box office. Time Warner was a close second at the global box office, with $4.25 billion in 2012 ticket sales. The remaining four major motion picture companies each brought in more than $2 billion in global ticket sales in 2012: Fox ($3.7 billion), Disney ($3.6 billion), Universal ($3.13 billion), and Paramount ($2.4 billion) (McClintock 2013). In addition, some of the leading "independent" film companies are owned by the industry giants—Focus Features (Comcast), Fox Searchlight (News Corporation), Sony Pictures Classics (Sony/Columbia), Paramount Vantage (Paramount), and New Line (Time Warner).

Television. Unlike other media sectors, broadcast television has become somewhat less concentrated since the 1990s when FOX joined ABC, CBS, and NBC to expand the number of major broadcast networks to four. In 2006, Warner Bros. and CBS partnered to launch a 5th broadcast network, the CW Network, after the two partners shut down

Croteau, D. P., & Hoynes, W. D. (2014). "The economics of the media industry." In *Media/society: Industries, images, and audiences* (5th Ed.). Thousand Oaks, CA: SAGE.

their separate fledgling networks WB and UPN. While cable television has offered the most new programming, the major cable television channels are often owned by the same companies that own the broadcast networks. For example, Time Warner (co-owner of the CW Network) owns CNN, HBO, TBS, TNT, Cartoon Network, truTV, Turner Classic Movies, and Cinemax. The News Corporation (owner of Fox) also owns FOX News, FOX Business, FX, SPEED, FUEL TV, Fox Movie Channel, Fox Soccer Channel, and National Geographic. Disney (owner of ABC) owns ESPN, Disney Channels Worldwide, ABC Family, and SOAPnet Networks; and Disney is also part-owner of several other major cable channels, including A&E, Lifetime Television, the History Channel, and the Biography Channel.

The major players in the television industry are leaders in other media sectors as well. Comcast, owner of NBCUniversal, is the nation's largest cable television company and the nation's largest Internet service provider, as well as one of the major players in television production and distribution. In addition, the broadcast television networks and the major movie studios typically share owners. Four of the five broadcast networks are owned by media conglomerates with major film studios: ABC (Disney), NBC (Universal), Fox (Twentieth Century Fox), and CW (Warner Brothers). And these major movie studios are the leading producers of prime-time programming for network television, accounting for about 90 percent of the series on the major networks (Kunz 2009). This kind of ownership structure makes it very difficult for independent producers to consistently get their programs on broadcast television.

Book Publishing. The global English-language book market is dominated by the "Big Five" publishers—Penguin Random House, HarperCollins (owned by News Corporation), Simon & Schuster (owned by CBS Corporation), Hachette Book Group, and Macmillan. Some analysts believe that additional consolidation of the book industry is on the horizon (Pfanner and Chozick 2012).

U.S. Magazines. Time Inc. (property of Time Warner, which operates, among others, the premium cable television network HBO, Warner Brothers, and CNN) towers above its competitors. Its 21 U.S. publications in print, online, and via mobile devices reach more than 138 million

people (nearly half the U.S. adult population) and control a 21.5 percent share of domestic magazine advertising spending (Time Inc. 2013).

Recorded Music. Only three companies are responsible for the vast majority of U.S. music sales. Universal Music Group, Sony Music Entertainment, and Warner Music Group accounted for more than 87 percent of total U.S. music sales in 2012 (Christman 2013). (Universal purchased the number four music company, EMI, in late 2012, but European antitrust regulations required Universal to sell some of EMI's labels. In early 2013, Universal sold Parlophone—the label with rights to albums by a variety of popular artists, such as Coldplay, Radiohead, and Pink Floyd—to Warner Music Group.) Each of the big three controls a number of smaller labels and local subsidiaries.

Radio. Clear Channel, with more than 850 radio stations in 2012, is the dominant player in the U.S. radio industry. Clear Channel's radio stations and online and mobile applications reach 237 million listeners in the United States each month (Clear Channel 2013). . . .

The major media companies own vast portfolios of products, spanning the range of media formats and delivery systems. Indeed, the media giants own such a dizzying array of entertainment and news media that the scale of their operations may surprise many readers. Because most products carry a distinct name, rather than the label of the corporate owner, most media users are unaware that a large number of media outlets are actually owned by a single corporation. In the world of newspapers, for example, chains such as Gannett and MediaNews own newspapers all over the country. . . . In 2013, Gannett owned more than 80 daily newspapers, including *USA Today,* the best-selling newspaper in the United States, alongside hundreds of websites and 23 television stations in the United States (Gannett 2013). MediaNews Group, the second largest newspaper publisher in the country, owns more than 60 newspapers, including the *Denver Post,* the *Detroit News,* and the *San Jose Mercury News* along with 450 websites and more than 200 specialty magazines (MediaNews Group 2013). At the newspaper chains, each paper has a different name, and it is not always apparent to readers that a paper is part of a national chain. Similarly, in book publishing, the major companies have so many different imprints that even a conscientious reader is unlikely to know the common owners of the different imprints. For example, Bertelsmann's Penguin Random House, far and away the largest English language book publisher in the world, owns more than 75 publishing imprints. . . .

CONGLOMERATION AND INTEGRATION

Concentration of media ownership means that fewer corporations own the media. At the same time that concentration of ownership has been occurring, conglomeration has been taking place. That is, media companies have become part of much larger corporations, which own a collection of other companies that may operate in highly diverse business areas.

Much as in other industries, the largest media companies are growing in size and reach as they purchase or merge with their competitors. In the United States, media outlets are among the most attractive properties to both potential investors and buyers. While some high-profile mergers ultimately fail—including AOL-Time Warner (which split into two companies in 2009) and Viacom-CBS (split in 2006)—the process of conglomeration in the media industry is continuous. For example,

- Google purchased over 125 companies between 2001 and 2013, including YouTube (2006), online advertising company Doubleclick (2007), the Zagat restaurant guide (2011), and GPS navigation firm Waze (2013).

- Yahoo bought about 80 companies, including Internet radio site Broadcast.com (1999), job search engine HotJobs.com (2002), and the blogging site Tumblr (2013).

- In addition to dozens of newspapers, the News Corporation bought 20th Century Fox (1984), the Metromedia group of television stations (1986), MySpace (2005) (later sold), and Dow Jones, owner of *The Wall Street Journal* (2007).

- AOL bought early online service provider Compuserv (1997), the web browser Netscape (1998), the Moviefone data base (1999), Mapquest (1999), the online music store MusicNow (2005), and the news/entertainment site *The Huffington Post* (2011).

- The cable giant Comcast purchased a number of smaller cable companies over the years, including AT&T Broadband (2001). It partnered with Sony to buy MGM and its production studio, United Artists (2005), and NBC Universal—acquiring a controlling stake in 2011 and the remainder in 2013 (see Figure 3.1).

- Walt Disney Company acquired (and later sold) Miramax Films (1983), CapCities/ABC (1995), Marvel Entertainment (2005), Pixar animation studios (2006), and Lucasfilm (2012)—owner of the *Star Wars* franchise.

Media—in both news and entertainment forms—are a key segment of the American economy and are attractive to growing conglomerates. The media industry produces high visibility, substantial profits, and a major item for export to other countries.

Concentration has affected the relationships among various media organizations within a single conglomerate. Economic analysts have long used the terms *horizontal integration* and *vertical integration* to describe two types of ownership concentration in any industry. In the media industry, vertical integration refers to the process by which one owner acquires all aspects of production and distribution of a single type of media product. For example, a movie company might integrate vertically by acquiring talent agencies to acquire scripts and sign actors, production studios to create films, manufacturing plants to produce DVDs, and various venues to show the movies, such as theater chains, premium cable channels, broadcast television networks, and Internet-based streaming services. The company could then better control the entire process of creating, producing, marketing, and distributing movies. Similarly, a book publisher might integrate vertically by acquiring paper mills, printing facilities, book binderies, trucking firms, and Internet booksellers. . . .

Horizontal integration refers to the process by which one company buys different kinds of

FIGURE 3.1 ■ Anatomy of a Media Conglomerate: Comcast Corporate Holdings	
Cable Television	● Largest video provider in the United States, through Comcast Cable—more than 22 million subscribers
Internet Service	● Largest residential Internet service provider in the United States—19.4 million customers
Phone Service	● 4th largest phone company in the United States—10 million customers
Broadcast Television	● NBC television network ● Telemundo, Spanish language network ● 10 NBC-owned local television stations ● 15 Telemundo-owned local television stations
Cable Television Networks	● USA Network ● Syfy ● E! ● CNBC ● MSNBC ● Bravo ● Golf Channel ● Oxygen ● NBC Sports Network ● Style ● MLB Network (joint venture with Major League Baseball) ● NHL Network (joint venture with National Hockey League) ● 10 regional sports networks ● 3 regional news networks
Film	● Universal Pictures ● Focus Features
Internet Sites	● Hulu (online video) ● Fandango (movie ticket sales) ● Daily Candy (fashion and restaurant news) ● Television Without Pity (TV fan site)
Theme Parks	● Universal Studios Florida ● Universal Studios Hollywood
Sports and Entertainment	● Philadelphia Flyers, NHL hockey team ● New Era Tickets ticketing company ● Wells Fargo Center sports arena

Source: Comcast Corporate website.

FIGURE 3.2 ■ Vertical and Horizontal Integration in the Media Industry

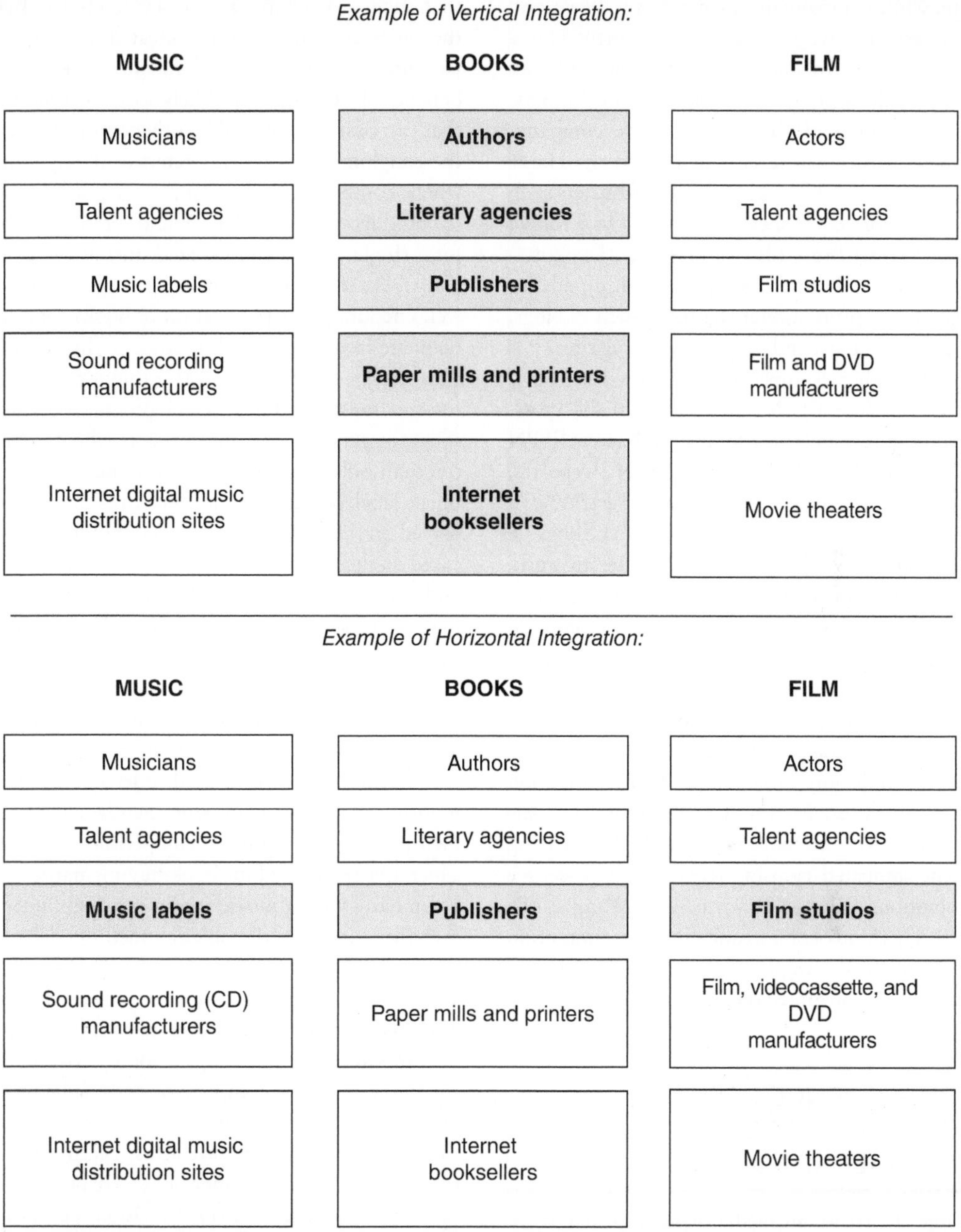

Example of Vertical Integration:

MUSIC	BOOKS	FILM
Musicians	**Authors**	Actors
Talent agencies	**Literary agencies**	Talent agencies
Music labels	**Publishers**	Film studios
Sound recording manufacturers	**Paper mills and printers**	Film and DVD manufacturers
Internet digital music distribution sites	**Internet booksellers**	Movie theaters

Example of Horizontal Integration:

MUSIC	BOOKS	FILM
Musicians	Authors	Actors
Talent agencies	Literary agencies	Talent agencies
Music labels	**Publishers**	**Film studios**
Sound recording (CD) manufacturers	Paper mills and printers	Film, videocassette, and DVD manufacturers
Internet digital music distribution sites	Internet booksellers	Movie theaters

Note: Shaded, bold-faced companies are owned by the same corporation.

media, concentrating ownership across differing types of media rather than up and down through one industry. In horizontal integration, media conglomerates assemble large portfolios of magazines, television stations, book publishers, record labels, and so on to mutually support one another's operations. In a classic example, when

Warner Bros. released the 2001 film *Harry Potter and the Sorcerer's Stone,* its then-parent company AOL Time Warner pursued an elaborate multimedia strategy to cash in on the Harry Potter franchise. AOL's online services provided links to various Harry Potter web pages, including sites for purchasing the Harry Potter merchandise that

AOL sold. The company's movie information site, Moviefone, promoted and sold tickets to the film, while company magazines *Time, People,* and *Entertainment Weekly* featured prominent Harry Potter stories. In addition, AOL Time Warner used its cable systems and cable networks for massive promotion of the film, and the company-owned Warner Music Group released the Harry Potter soundtrack. More recent blockbusters such as *The Avengers* (Disney 2012), *The Dark Knight Rises* (Warner Bros. 2012), and *Avatar* (Fox 2009) have employed similar strategies, taking advantage of new promotional channels, such as blogs, smartphone apps, and social networking sites.

In another example, Disney turned its sports cable franchise ESPN into a multimedia cross-promotional vehicle, developing ESPN.com, ESPN Classic, ESPN2, ESPNEWS, ESPN Deportes, ESPNU, the ESPN Radio Network, *ESPN: The Magazine,* an ESPN news service, ESPN3 (a broadband service), and ESPN Mobile, all working together to promote Disney's growing list of ESPN products. Such cross-media promotion can be a very powerful strategy. One experimental study found that a coordinated television and print ad campaign for a television program was far more effective than single-media campaigns; cross-media campaigns "resulted in higher attention from audiences, improved memory, greater perceived message credibility . . . and higher viewing intent compared to using repetitive single-source promotions" (Tang, Newton, and Wang 2007: 132). This kind of opportunity for cross-promotion is one of the driving forces behind the growth of horizontally integrated media companies.

CONSEQUENCES OF CONGLOMERATION AND INTEGRATION

While the trends in media ownership may be of interest in themselves, our prime concern is with the relationship between ownership and the media product. What are the consequences of integration, conglomeration, and concentration of ownership?

Integration and Self-Promotion

The economic factors propelling both vertical and horizontal integration are clear: Owners perceive such arrangements as both efficient and profitable.

The cultural consequences are more ambiguous. However, an institutional approach suggests that such ownership patterns are likely to affect the types of media products created. In particular, integrated media conglomerates seeking the benefits of "synergy" are likely to favor products that can best be exploited by other components of the conglomerate. (Synergy refers to the dynamic where components of a company work together to produce benefits that would be impossible for a single, separately operated unit of the company.) For example, horizontal integration may well encourage the publication of books that can be made into movies and discourage the publication of those that cannot. Or it might encourage the creation of TV talent search programs because they can generate new musical acts who are contractually obligated to record for the company's music label, featured in the company's magazines, played on the company's radio stations, and showcased on their websites. More generally, promotion and marketing are likely to dominate the decision-making process within a horizontally integrated media industry.

Vertical integration becomes especially significant when the company that makes the product also controls its distribution. For example, a corporation that owns a mail-order book-of-the-month club is likely to prominently feature its own publications, limiting competitors' access to a lucrative segment of the book-buying market. Or a company with a movie studio can highlight its own films on its movie cable channel.

The possibilities for fully using horizontal and vertical integration are startling. In this era of integrated media conglomerates, media companies are capable of pursuing elaborate cross-media strategies, in which company-owned media products can be packaged, sold, and promoted across the full range of media platforms. Feature films, their accompanying soundtracks and DVD/Blu-ray Disc releases, spin-off television programs, and books, along with magazine cover stories and plenty of licensed merchandise, can all be produced and distributed by different divisions of the same conglomerate—with each piece serving to promote the broader franchise. One consequence of integration, then, is an increase in media cross-promotion and, perhaps, a decrease in media products that are not suitable for cross-promotion. It also makes it more difficult for smaller media firms to compete with the major corporations who can use their vast and diverse holdings to saturate consumers during their promotional campaigns.

The Impact of Conglomeration

What has the growth of large multimedia firms over the past few decades meant for the news, television, radio, films, music, and books we receive? In other words, to what extent does conglomeration affect the media product? The loudest warnings about the impact of conglomeration have come from within the news industry, in part because some news media had traditionally been sheltered from the full pressure of profit making. For example, for much of television history, respectable television news divisions were understood to represent a necessary public service commitment that lent prestige to the major broadcast networks. They were not expected to turn a substantial profit. However, that changed with the takeover of news operations by major corporate conglomerates during the 1980s.

Ken Auletta's *Three Blind Mice* (1991) paints a vivid picture of the clash that ensued during that time, when new corporate owners took over the major television networks and their news divisions. For those who worked at NBC News, for example, the purchase of the network by General Electric led to conflicts about the meaning and role of television news. In most of these conflicts, the new corporate owners ultimately prevailed. As Auletta tells it, when General Electric took over as the new owners of NBC, they

> emphasized a "boundaryless" company, one without walls between News, Entertainment, Sales, and other divisions. . . . At NBC's annual management retreat in 1990, many of the 160 executives questioned why Sales or Entertainment couldn't have more input into news specials, or why News tended to keep its distance from the rest of the company, as if it were somehow special. (p. 564)

General Electric chair Jack Welch even specified that *Today Show* weather reporter Willard Scott should mention GE lightbulbs on the program. According to former NBC news president Lawrence Grossman, "It was one of the perks of owning a network. . . . You get your lightbulbs mentioned on the air. . . . People want to please the owners" (Husseini 1994: 13).

Since that time, the network news programs have faced stiff competition from the 24-hour cable news channels, yet they are expected to turn a profit by attracting audiences that owners expect and advertisers demand. One result has been an increased emphasis on entertainment and celebrities on the network news—what former CBS news anchor Dan Rather called "the Hollywood-ization of the news" due to the growth of "stupid celebrity stories" (*Brill's Content* 1998: 117). The changes that were seen as a threat to serious broadcast news in the 1980s and '90s are now the norm in the industry, with the broadcast networks now routinely incorporating entertainment, celebrities, human interest, and other light fare into their broadcasts. . . .

Conglomeration has affected print journalism as well. Some critics have long argued that corporate takeovers of print media put the emphasis on attracting and entertaining consumers rather than on informing citizens (Squires 1993). In this context, newspapers become increasingly colorful, focus attention on the lives of celebrities, and print sensationalistic stories about dramatic and bizarre happenings. One example is NewsCorp's head Rupert Murdoch—now best-known as the owner of FOX—who launched his career by buying up newspapers in Australia and England and converting them into down-market tabloids that specialized in sex, scandal, and celebrities. This was epitomized by his purchase of Britain's *The Sun,* which became notorious—and popular—for its scandalous coverage, even adopting a "Page Three" feature—a daily photo of a topless or nude model (Braid 2004). The 2011 phone-hacking scandal in England, which led to the shutdown of Murdoch's British tabloid *News of the World,* showed how far profit-focused news organizations can go in search of a story. Hundreds, and perhaps thousands, of phones were hacked by reporters at the newspaper, who sought titillating information about crime victims, their families, and celebrities. In the report on the scandal commissioned by the British government, Lord Justice Leveson concluded that "there has been a recklessness in prioritising sensational stories, almost irrespective of the harm that the stories may cause and the rights of those who would be affected (perhaps in a way that can never be remedied), all the while heedless of the public interest" (The Leveson Inquiry 2012: 10). . . .

Media Control and Political Power

Can concentrated media ownership be translated into undue political influence? Most people recognize the importance of such a question in examining the government's control of media in totalitarian nations. It is clear in such situations that state ownership and exclusive access are likely to affect media products. In the United States, most discussion about the First Amendment and free speech also focuses on the possibility of government censorship. This discussion is generally blind, however, to the impact of corporate ownership.

In addressing this concern, Bagdikian (2004) has argued that the United States has a "private ministry of information," metaphorically referring to the type of government-led propaganda system that exists in totalitarian societies. In the case of the contemporary United States, however, private interests, not the government, largely control this information system. Bagdikian suggests that when a small number of firms with similar interests dominate the media industry, it begins to function in a way similar to a state information system. It is hard to question the underlying argument that those who own large media conglomerates have at least the potential to wield a great deal of political power.

How might ownership of media translate into political power? It is possible that those building media empires could use their media outlets to promote a very specific political agenda. Furthermore, when media barons become candidates for major office, their media holdings can be invaluable political resources. Perhaps the starkest example of this in a Western democracy is the case of Silvio Berlusconi in Italy, who managed to use ownership of private media to gain public office—which then enabled him to influence public media.

Silvio Berlusconi, a media magnate and the dominant force in Italian broadcasting and publishing, was elected prime minister three times (1994, 2001, and 2008). For Berlusconi, ownership of television and radio clearly had great political value; he owned strategic assets that were unavailable to other political actors. In the 2001 electoral campaign, he was given four times the exposure of his rival candidate on the television networks that he owns. After winning that election, he went on to effectively control 90 percent of Italian television programming (*The Economist* 2001). That's because Italian prime ministers have the right to replace the boards of directors of the three public television channels, known as RAI, and thus can influence RAI's editorial choices. In subsequent election campaigns, Berlusconi not only had his own private television networks as a political resource, but he also influenced the public channels.

Berlusconi's domination of television was so great that, after the 2001 election and again in 2004, the European Federation of Journalists called for new regulations limiting media ownership. In 2004, both the European Parliament and the Council of Europe condemned the open conflict of interest between Berlusconi's role as prime minister and that of media magnate. The corrosive effect of this arrangement on Italian democracy was so serious that Freedom House, an independent watchdog group that produces annual rankings of freedom and democracy around the world, downgraded Italian freedom of the press from "free" to "partially free" (Freedom House 2004). After Berlusconi launched a series of attacks and lawsuits against the press, Reporters Without Borders (2009) declared that Berlusconi "is on the verge of being added to our list of Predators of Press Freedom," which would be a first for a European country (Ginsborg 2005; Hine 2001). Berlusconi resigned as prime minister in 2011 in the midst of a sex scandal. In 2013, however, he was once again a prominent figure in national politics, and he lost a close election for a fourth term as prime minister.

Though the media environment is quite different largely because of the vast size of the U.S. media industry, private media ownership can be a huge political asset in the United States too. Media entrepreneur Michael Bloomberg amassed a fortune selling technology and media products to businesses. He drew on the widespread recognition of his brand-name line of Bloomberg business media products—and the enormous profits they have generated for him—in his successful campaign to become New York City mayor in 2001. In the process, he spent $69 million of his own money—more than $92 per vote. Bloomberg won reelection in 2005 then successfully had the term-limit law changed so he could run again (and win again) in 2009. There has long been speculation that Bloomberg, one of the 10 wealthiest people in the United States as of 2012 (Forbes 2012), will one day launch a presidential bid.

In some cases, owners of media companies have direct control over media products and thus are able to exert political influence by promoting ideas that enhance their interests. Conservative media magnate Rupert Murdoch, for example, has used a variety of his News Corporation's media holdings to advance his political and economic goals. In 1975, he had his Australian newspapers slant the news so blatantly in favor of his conservative choice for prime minister that Murdoch's own journalists went on strike in protest. His British papers played a crucial role in the 1979 election of British conservative Margaret Thatcher. In 1995, Murdoch financed the multimillion-dollar start-up of the high-profile conservative U.S. magazine *The Weekly Standard*. In 1996, Murdoch's News Corporation initiated a 24-hour news channel, Fox News Channel (headed by Rush Limbaugh's former executive producer and long-time Republican Party political consultant, Roger Ailes), that many have argued promotes a consistent conservative agenda (Ackerman 2001; Aday 2010; McDermott 2010). When Murdoch's News Corporation bought Dow Jones in 2007, it took over as owner of *The Wall Street Journal*, one of the most influential—and editorially conservative—papers in the country.

More recently, Charles and David Koch, the billionaire brothers who helped support the Tea Party movement and who provide major funding to the conservative movement more broadly, sought to purchase the Tribune Company, the owner of several prominent newspapers, including the *Los Angeles Times* and the *Chicago Tribune*. News of the Koch brothers' interest in the newspapers sparked concern among journalists worried that the Kochs were primarily interested in the potential political value of the newspapers. The Koch brothers later dropped their efforts to buy the company.

However, some media outlets, especially news outlets, rely on a perception of objectivity or evenhandedness to maintain their legitimacy. Journalists often see themselves as members of a sort of fourth estate, complementing the executive, legislative, and administrative branches of government. Their job is to act as watchdogs over politicians (Louw 2010; Schultz 1998). As a result, with perhaps the exception of Fox News, most major news media outlets will not consistently and blatantly promote a single political agenda. Instead, viewers are more likely to find such an approach on cable programs that focus on analysis and commentary or on the growing number of ideologically driven websites and blogs.

The process of using media to promote a political agenda is more complex than simply feeding people ideas and images that they passively accept. Owners can use media sites to disseminate a specific position on a controversial issue or to help legitimize particular institutions or behaviors. Just as important, owners can systematically exclude certain ideas from their media products. While control of information or images can never be total, owners can tilt the scales in particular directions quite dramatically.

Ownership by major corporations of vast portfolios of media gives us reason to believe that a whole range of ideas and images—those that question fundamental social arrangements, under which the media owners are doing quite well—will be visible primarily in low-profile media. This does not mean that all media images and information are uniform. It means that some ideas will be widely available, while others will be largely absent. For example, stories critical of gridlock in the federal government are frequent; in contrast, stories critical of capitalism as an economic system that can facilitate inequality are very rare. There is no way of proving the connection, but the media's focus on the shortcomings of the government, rather than of the private sector, seems consistent with the interests of the corporate media owners.

This process is most obvious in products that directly address contemporary social and political events, but it also happens in entertainment products. Consider, for example, the depiction of gays and lesbians on prime-time television. For most of U.S. television history, there were virtually no gay or lesbian characters. As gay rights advocates made advances in the 1980s and 1990s, gay and lesbian characters began appearing, though infrequently and in often superficial depictions. Also, gay characters faced constraints that heterosexual characters did not; for example, they typically did not kiss, even as popular television continued to become more explicit in depictions of heterosexual sex. It was not until 2004 that the first television drama series to revolve around a group of lesbian, gay, bisexual, and transgendered characters appeared; *The L Word* ran from 2004 to 2009 on the premium cable channel Showtime. There is no conspiracy here. More likely, a small number of profit-making firms that rely on mass audiences and major advertisers simply avoided potential controversies that might threaten their bottom line. As network executives and major advertisers began to define such images as more acceptable to mainstream audiences, lesbian and gay characters have become more commonplace and more diverse in recent years (GLAAD 2012). . . .

The political impact of concentrated corporate ownership, however, is both broader and subtler than the exclusion of certain ideas in favor of others. Herbert Schiller (1989) argues that "the corporate voice" has been generalized so successfully that most of us do not even think of it as a specifically corporate voice. That is, the corporate view has become "our" view, the "American" view, even though the interests of the corporate entities that own mass media are far from universal. One example of this is the entire media-generated discourse—in newspapers, television, radio, and magazines—about the American economy, in which corporate success provides the framework for virtually all evaluations of national economic well-being. Quarterly profits, mergers and acquisitions, productivity, and fluctuations in the financial markets are so widely discussed that their relationship to the corporate voice is difficult to discern. The relationship between corporate financial health and citizen well-being, however, is rarely discussed explicitly—even in times of serious financial crisis. During the economic crises of 2008–2009, the U.S. news media were remarkably unquestioning of the message from both government and the private sector that a massive and immediate bailout of banks, Wall Street firms, and other corporate interests was absolutely essential.

A concentrated media sphere can also undermine citizens' capacity to monitor their government's war-making powers. McChesney (2008: 98) argues that "those in power, those who benefit from war and empire, see the press as arguably the most important front of war, because it is there that consent is manufactured, and dissent is marginalized. For a press system, a war is its moment of truth." The 2003 U.S.-led invasion of Iraq was justified by the alleged presence of weapons of mass destruction (WMD) in Iraq. The news media reported these WMD charges uncritically, relying on official sources and without in-depth investigation, effectively affirming the Bush administration's rationale for war. According to one study of U.S. news media coverage in the first three weeks of the Iraq war, pro-war U.S. sources outnumbered antiwar sources by 25 to 1, thus making it very difficult for citizens to access critical perspectives on the war (Rendall and Broughel 2003).

One possible political consequence of the concentration of media ownership is that, in some ways, it becomes more difficult for alternative media voices to emerge. Because mass media outlets in all sectors of the media industry are large mass-production and mass-distribution firms, ownership is restricted to those who can acquire substantial financial resources. In the age of multimillion-dollar media enterprises, freedom of the press may be left to those few who can afford to own what has become a very expensive press.

The Internet offers the possibility for small producers to create professional-looking alternative media—from websites and blogs to mobile apps and streaming video. However, without a means to effectively promote such sites, and without the budget to pay for staff to continuously produce substantive new content that continues to draw users, most online alternative media are limited to relatively small niche audiences. Television and the major daily newspapers—along with the online content associated with these major media—are still the main sources of news for most of the population.

In the end, ownership of the means of information becomes part of larger patterns of inequality in contemporary societies, and large media conglomerates can use their capacity to shape media discourse and their substantial financial resources to influence public policy. In this sense, mass media institutions are no different from other social institutions; they are linked to the patterned inequality that exists throughout our society. . . .

REFERENCES

Ackerman, Seth. 2001. "The Most Biased Name in News: Fox News Channel's Extraordinary Right-Wing Tilt." *Extra!*. July/August. Retrieved from http://www.fair.org/index.php?page =1067

Aday, Sean. 2010. "Chasing the Bad News: An Analysis of 2005 Iraq and Afghanistan War Coverage on NBC and Fox News Channel." *Journal of Communication* 60 (1): 144–164.

Auletta, Ken. 1991. *Three Blind Mice: How the TV Networks Lost Their Way.* New York: Random House.

Bagdikian, Ben. 2004. *The New Media Monopoly.* Boston: Beacon Press.

Braid, Mary. 2004. "Page Three Girls—The Naked Truth." *BBC News Online.* September 14. Retrieved from http://news.bbc.co.uk/2/hi/uk_news/magazine/3651850.stm

Christman, Ed. 2013. "Universal Music Still Market Top Dog in 2013." *Billboard.biz.* January 3. Retrieved from http://www.billboard.biz/bbbiz/industry/record-labels/universal-music-still-market-top-dog-in-1008068352.story

Clear Channel. 2013. About Us. Retrieved from www.clearchannel.com/Corporate/

Croteau, David and William Hoynes. 2006. *The Business of Media: Corporate Media and the Public Interest.* 2nd ed. Thousand Oaks, CA: Pine Forge/Sage.

The Economist. 2001. "Fit to Run Italy?" Retrieved from http://www.economist.com/node/593654?story_id=593654

Flew, Terry. 2007. *Understanding Global Media.* New York: Palgrave.

Freedom House. 2004. *Freedom of the Press 2004: A Global Survey of Media Independence.* Lanham, MD: Rowman & Littlefield Publishers, Inc.

Forbes. 2012. "The Forbes 400: The Richest People in America." Retrieved from http://www.forbes.com/forbes-400/

Gannett. 2013. Our Brands. Retrieved from http://www.gannett.com/section/BRANDS&template=cover

Ginsborg, Paul. 2005. *Silvio Berlusconi: Television, Power and Patrimony.* London, UK: Verso.

GLAAD. 2012. *Where We Are On TV: 2012–2013 Season.* Retrieved from http://www.glaad.org/publications/whereweareontv12

Hine, David. 2001. "Silvio Berlusconi, the Media and the Conflict of Interest Issue." *Italian Politics: A Review* 17: 261–276.

Husseini, Sam. 1994. "NBC Brings Good Things to GE." *Extra!* November/December, p. 13.

The Leveson Inquiry. 2012. *An Inquiry into the Culture, Practices, and Ethics of the Press: Executive Summary.* November. London: The Stationary Office.

Louw, Eric P. 2010. *The Media and the Political Process.* 2nd ed. Thousand Oaks, CA: Sage.

McChesney, Robert W. 2008. *The Political Economy of Media.* New York: Monthly Review Press.

McClintock, Pamela. 2013. "Sony Pictures No. 1 in 2012 Worldwide Box Office Market Share." *The Hollywood Reporter.* January 2. Retrieved from http://www.hollywoodreporter.com/news/sony-pictures-no-1-2012-407575

McDermott, Terry. 2010. "Dumb Like a Fox." *Columbia Journalism Review.* 48 (6): 26–32.

MediaNews Group. 2013. Audience Reach: Market Leadership. Retrieved from http://www.medianewsgroup.com/CONSUMERS/Pages/AudienceReach.aspx

Pfanner, Eric and Amy Chozick. 2012. "Random House and Penguin Merger Creates Global Giant." *The New York Times.* October 30. Page B1.

Rendall, Steve and Tara Broughel. 2003. "Amplifying Officials, Squelching Dissent." *Extra!* May/June. Retrieved from http://www.fair.org/index.php?page=1145

Reporters Without Borders. 2009. "Reporters Without Borders in Rome to Defend Press Freedom." October 5. Retrieved from http://en.rsf.org/italy-reporters-without-borders-in-rome-05–10–2009,34647.html

Robischon, Noah. 1998. "Browser Beware." *Brill's Content,* August, pp. 40–44.

Schiller, Herbert. 1989. *Culture, Inc.* New York: Oxford University Press.

Schultz, Julianne. 1998. *Reviving the Fourth Estate.* New York: Cambridge University Press.

Squires, James. 1993. *Read All About It! The Corporate Takeover of America's Newspapers.* New York: Times Books.

Tang, Tang, Gregory D. Newton, and Xiaopeng Wang. 2007. "Does Synergy Work? An Examination of Cross-Promotion Effects." *The International Journal on Media Management* 9 (4): 127–134.

Time Inc. 2013. Company Profile. Retrieved from http://www.timeinc.com/aboutus/companyprofile.php

4 HEGEMONY

James Lull

Hegemony is the power or dominance that one social group holds over others. This can refer to the "asymmetrical interdependence" of political-economic-cultural relations between and among nation-states (Straubhaar, 1991) or differences between and among social classes within a nation. Hegemony is "dominance and subordination in the field of relations structured by power" (Hall, 1985). But hegemony is more than social power itself; it is a method for gaining and maintaining power.

Classical Marxist theory, of course, stresses economic position as the strongest predictor of social differences. Today, more than a century after Karl Marx and Friedrich Engels wrote their treatises about capitalist exploitation of the working class, economic disparities still underlie and help reproduce social inequalities in industrialized societies. . . . Technological developments in the twentieth century, however, have made the manner of social domination much more complex than before. Social class differences in today's world are not determined solely or directly by economic factors. Ideological influence is crucial now in the exercise of social power.

The Italian intellectual Antonio Gramsci—to whom the term *hegemony* is attributed—broadened materialist Marxist theory into the realm of ideology. Persecuted by his country's then fascist government (and writing from prison), Gramsci emphasized society's "super structure," its ideology-producing institutions, in struggles over meaning and power (1971; 1973; 1978; see also Boggs, 1976; Sassoon, 1980; and Simon, 1982). A shift in critical theory thus was made away from a preoccupation with capitalist society's "base" (its economic foundation) and towards its dominant dispensaries of ideas.

Attention was given to the structuring of authority and dependence in symbolic environments that correspond to, but are not the same as, economically determined class-based structures and processes of industrial production. Such a theoretical turn seems a natural and necessary development in an era when communications technology is such a pervasive and potent ideological medium. According to Gramsci's theory of ideological hegemony, mass media are tools that ruling elites use to "perpetuate their power, wealth, and status [by popularizing] their own philosophy, culture and morality" (Boggs, 1976: 39). The mass media uniquely "introduce elements into individual consciousness that would not otherwise appear there, but will not be rejected by consciousness because they are so commonly shared in the cultural community" (Nordenstreng, 1977: 276). Owners and managers of media industries can produce and reproduce the content, inflections, and tones of ideas favorable to them far more easily than other social groups because they manage key socializing institutions, thereby guaranteeing that their points of view are constantly and attractively cast into the public arena.

Mass-mediated ideologies are corroborated and strengthened by an interlocking system of efficacious information-distributing agencies and taken-for-granted social practices that permeate every aspect of social and cultural reality. Messages supportive of the status quo emanating from schools, businesses, political organizations, trade unions, religious groups, the military and the mass media all dovetail together ideologically. This inter-articulating, mutually reinforcing process of ideological influence is the essence of hegemony. Society's most entrenched and powerful institutions—which all depend in one way or another on the same sources for economic support—fundamentally agree with each other ideologically.

Hegemony is not a *direct* stimulation of thought or action, but, according to Stuart Hall, is a "framing [of] all competing definitions of reality within [the dominant class's] range bringing all alternatives within their horizons of thought. [The dominant class] sets the limits—mental and structural—within which subordinate classes 'live' and make sense of their subordination in such a way as to sustain the dominance of those ruling over them" (1977: 333). British social theorist Philip Elliott suggested similarly that the most potent effect of mass media is how they subtly influence their audiences to perceive social roles and routine personal activities. The controlling economic forces in society use the mass media to provide a "rhetoric [through] which these [concepts] are labeled, evaluated, and explained" (1974: 262). Television commercials, for example, encourage audiences to think of themselves as "markets rather than as a public, as consumers rather than citizens" (Gitlin, 1979: 255).

But hegemony does not mature strictly from ideological articulation. Dominant ideological streams must be subsequently reproduced in the activities of our most basic social units—families, workplace networks, and friendship groups in the many sites and undertakings of everyday life. Gramsci's theory of hegemony, therefore, connects ideological representation to culture. Hegemony requires that ideological assertions become self-evident cultural assumptions. Its effectiveness depends on subordinated peoples accepting the dominant ideology as "normal reality or common sense . . . in active forms of experience and consciousness" (Williams, 1976: 145). Because information and entertainment technology is so thoroughly integrated into the everyday realities of modern societies, mass media's social influence is not always recognized, discussed, or criticized, particularly in societies where the overall standard of living is relatively high. Hegemony, therefore, can easily go undetected (Bausinger, 1984).

Hegemony implies a willing agreement by people to be governed by principles, rules, and laws they believe operate in their best interests, even though in actual practice they may not. Social consent can be a more effective means of control than coercion or force. Again, Raymond Williams: "The idea of hegemony, in its wide sense, is . . . especially important in societies [where] electoral politics and public opinion are significant factors, and in which social practice is seen to depend on consent to certain dominant ideas which in fact express the needs of a dominant class" (1976: 145). Thus, in the words of Colombian communication theorist Jesús Martín-Barbero, "one class exercises hegemony to the extent that the dominating class has interests which the subaltern classes recognize as being in some degree their interests too" (1993: 74).

Relationships between and among the major information-diffusing, socializing agencies of a society and the interacting, cumulative, socially accepted ideological orientations they create and sustain is the essence of hegemony. The American television industry, for instance, connects with other large industries, especially advertising companies but also national and multinational corporations that produce, distribute, and market a wide range of commodities. So, for example, commercial TV networks no longer buy original children's television shows. Network executives only want new program ideas associated with successful retail products already marketed to children. By late 1990 more than 20 toy-based TV shows appeared on American commercial TV weekly. Television also has the ability to absorb other major social institutions—organized religion, for instance—and turn them into popular culture. The TV industry also connects with government institutions, including especially the federal agencies that are supposed to regulate telecommunications. The development of American commercial broadcasting is a vivid example of how capitalist economic forces assert their power. Evacuation of the legislatively mandated public service ideal could only have taken place because the Federal Communications Commission stepped aside while commercial interests amassed power and expanded their influence. Symptomatic of the problem is the fact that government regulators typically are recruited from, and return to, the very industries they are supposed to monitor. . . .

HEGEMONY AS AN INCOMPLETE PROCESS

Two of our leading critical theorists, Raymond Williams and Stuart Hall, remind us that hegemony in any political context is indeed fragile.

It requires renewal and modification through the assertion and reassertion of power. Hall suggests that "it is crucial to the concept that hegemony is not a 'given' and permanent state of affairs, but it has to be actively won and secured; it can also be lost" (1977: 333). Ideological work is the winning and securing of hegemony over time. . . . Ideology is composed of "texts that are not closed" according to Hall, who also notes that ideological "counter-tendencies" regularly appear in the seams and cracks of dominant forms (Hall, 1985). Mediated communications ranging from popular television shows to rap and rock music, even graffiti scrawled over surfaces of public spaces, all inscribe messages that challenge central political positions and cultural assumptions.

Counter-hegemonic tendencies do not inhere solely in texts. They are formulated in processes of communication—in the interpretations, social circulation, and uses of media content. As with the American soldiers' use of military gas masks as inhaling devices to heighten the effect of marijuana smoke, or the homeless's transformation of supermarket shopping carts into personal storage vehicles, ideological resistance and appropriation frequently involve reinventing institutional messages for purposes that differ greatly from their creators' intentions. Expressions of the dominant ideology are sometimes reformulated to assert alternative, often completely resistant or contradictory messages. . . .

Furthermore, resistance to hegemony is not initiated solely by media consumers. Texts themselves are implicated. Ideology can never be stated purely and simply. Ways of thinking are always reflexive and embedded in a complex, sometimes contradictory, ideological regress. . . .

Audience interpretations and uses of media imagery also eat away at hegemony. Hegemony fails when dominant ideology is weaker than social resistance. Gay subcultures, feminist organizations, environmental groups, radical political parties, music-based formations such as punks, B-boys, Rastafarians, and metal heads all use media and their social networks to endorse counter-hegemonic values and lifestyles. Indeed, we have only just begun to examine the complex relationship between ideological representation and social action.

REFERENCES

Bausinger, H. (1984). Media, technology, and everyday life. *Media, Culture & Society*, 6, 340–52.

Boggs, C. (1976). *Gramsci's Marxism*. London: Pluto.

Elliott, P. (1974). Uses and gratifications research: A critique and a sociological alternative. In J. G. Blumler and E. Katz (eds.), *The Uses of Mass Communications: Current Perspectives on Gratifications Research*. Beverly Hills, CA: Sage.

Gitlin, T. (1979). Prime-time ideology: The hegemonic process in television entertainment. *Social Problems*, 26, 251–66.

Gramsci, A. (1971). *Selections from the Prison Notebooks*. New York: International.

Gramsci, A. (1973). *Letters from Prison*. New York: Harper and Row.

Gramsci, A. (1978). *Selections from Cultural Writings*. Cambridge, MA: Harvard University Press.

Hall, S. (1977). Culture, media, and the "ideological effect." In J. Curran, M. Gurevitch, and J. Woollacott (eds.), *Mass Communication and Society*. London: Edward Arnold.

Hall, S. (1985). Master's session. International Communication Association. Honolulu, Hawaii.

Martín-Barbero, J. (1993). *Communication, Culture and Hegemony*. Newbury Park, CA: Sage.

Nordenstreng, K. (1977). From mass media to mass consciousness. In G. Gerbner (ed.), *Mass Media Policies in Changing Cultures*. New York: Wiley.

Sassoon, A. S. (1980). *Gramsci's Politics*. New York: St. Martin's.

Simon, R. (1982). *Gramsci's Political Thought*. London: Lawrence and Wishart.

Straubhaar, J. (1991). Beyond media imperialism: Asymmetrical interdependence and cultural proximity. *Critical Studies in Mass Communication*, 8, 39–59.

Williams, R. (1976). *Key Words: A Vocabulary of Culture and Society*. New York: Oxford University Press.

THE INTERNET'S UNHOLY MARRIAGE TO CAPITALISM

John Bellamy Foster and Robert W. McChesney

The United States and the world are now a good two decades into the Internet revolution, or what was once called the information age. The past generation has seen a blizzard of mind-boggling developments in communication, ranging from the World Wide Web and broadband, to ubiquitous cell phones that are quickly becoming high-powered wireless computers in their own right. Firms such as Google, Amazon, Craigslist, and Facebook have become iconic. Immersion in the digital world is now or soon to be a requirement for successful participation in society. The subject for debate is no longer whether the Internet can be regarded as a technological development in the same class as television or the telephone. Increasingly, the debate is turning to whether this is a communication revolution closer to the advent of the printing press.[1]

The full impact of the Internet revolution will only become apparent in the future, as more technological change is on the horizon that can barely be imagined and hardly anticipated.[2] But enough time has transpired, and institutions and practices have been developed, that an assessment of the digital era is possible, as well as a sense of its likely trajectory into the future.

Our analysis in this article will focus on the United States—not only because it is the society that we know best, and the Internet's point of origin, but also because it is there, we believe, that one most clearly finds the integration of monopoly-finance capital and the Internet, representing the dominant tendency of the global capitalist system. This is not meant to suggest that the current U.S. dominance of the Internet is not open to change, or that other countries may not choose to take other paths—but only that all alternatives in this realm will have to struggle against the trajectory now being set by U.S. capitalism, with its immense global influence and power. . . .

The Internet, or more broadly, the digital revolution is truly changing the world at multiple levels. But it has also failed to deliver on much of the promise that was once seen as implicit in its technology. If the Internet was expected to provide more competitive markets and accountable businesses, open government, an end to corruption, and decreasing inequality—or, to put it baldly, increased human happiness—it has been a disappointment. . . .

We do not argue that the initial sense of the Internet's promise was pure fantasy, although some of it can be attributed to the utopian enthusiasm that major new technologies can engender when they first emerge. (One is reminded of the early-twentieth-century view of the Nobel Prize-winning chemist and philosopher of energetics, Wilhelm Ostwald, who contended that the advent of the "flying machine" was a key part of a universal process that could erase international boundaries associated with nations, languages, and money, "bringing about the brotherhood of man."[3]) Instead, we argue that there was—and remains—extraordinary democratic and revolutionary promise in this communication revolution. But technologies do not ride roughshod over history, regardless of their immense powers. They are developed in a social, political, and economic context. And this has strongly conditioned the course and shape of the communication revolution.

This economic context points to the *paradox of the Internet* as it has developed in a capitalist society. The Internet has been subjected, to a

From John Bellamy Foster and Robert W. McChesney, "The Internet's Unholy Marriage to Capitalism," *Monthly Review* online (2011). Volume 62, Issue 10. Reprinted with permission of *Monthly Review*.

significant extent, to the capital accumulation process, which has a clear logic of its own, inimical to much of the democratic potential of digital communication, and that will be ever more so, going forward. What seemed to be an increasingly open public sphere, removed from the world of commodity exchange, seems to be morphing into a private sphere of increasingly closed, proprietary, even monopolistic markets.

. . . We hope to provide a necessary alternative way to imagine how best to develop the Internet in contrast to the commodified, privatized world of capital accumulation. This does not mean that there can be no commerce, even extensive commerce, in the digital realm, but merely that the system's overriding logic—and the starting point for all policy discussions—must be as an institution operated on public interest values, at bare minimum as a public utility.

It is true that in any capitalist society there is going to be strong, even at times overwhelming, pressure to open up areas that can be profitably exploited by capital, regardless of the social costs, or "negative externalities," as economists put it. After all, capitalists—by definition, given their economic power—exercise inordinate political power. But it is not a given that all areas will be subjected to the market. Indeed, many areas in nature and human existence cannot be so subjected without destroying the fabric of life itself— and large portions of capitalist societies have historically been and remain largely outside of the capital accumulation process. One could think of community, family, religion, education, romance, elections, research, and national defense as partial examples, although capital is pressing to colonize those where it can. Many important political debates in a capitalist society are concerned with determining the areas where the pursuit of profit will be allowed to rule, and where it will not. At their most rational, and most humane, capitalist societies tend to preserve large noncommercial sectors, including areas such as health care and old-age pensions, that might be highly profitable if turned over to commercial interests. At the very least, the more democratic a capitalist society is, the more likely it is for there to be credible public debates on these matters.

However—and this is a point dripping in irony—such a fundamental debate never took place in relation to the Internet.

. . . The lack of debate about how the Internet should be developed was due, to a certain extent, to the digital revolution exploding at precisely the moment that neoliberalism was in ascendance, its flowery rhetoric concerning "free markets" most redolent. The core spirit was that businesses should always be permitted to develop any area where profits could be found, and that this was the most efficient use of resources for an economy. Anything interfering with capitalist exploitation was bad economics and ideologically loaded, and was usually advanced by a deadbeat "special interest" group that could not cut the mustard in the world of free market competition and so sought protection from the corrupt netherworld of government regulation and bureaucracy.[4] This credo led the drive for "deregulation" across the economy, and for the privatization of once public sector activities.

The rhetoric of free markets was adopted by all sides in the communications debate in the early 1990s, as the World Wide Web turned the Internet seemingly overnight into a mass medium. For the business community and politicians, the Internet was all about unleashing entrepreneurs, slaying monopolies, promoting innovation, and generating "friction-free capitalism," as Bill Gates famously put it.[5] There was great money to be made. Even those skeptical toward corporations and commercialism tended to be unconcerned, if not sanguine, about the capitalist invasion, as the power of this apparently magical technology could override the efforts of dinosaur corporations to tame it. There was plenty of room for everybody. The Internet bubble of the late 1990s certainly encouraged capitalism's embrace of the Internet, and U.S. news media could barely contain themselves with their enthusiasm for the happy couple. Capitalism and the Internet seemed a marriage made in heaven.

INTERNET SERVICE PROVIDERS

A more sober analysis, however, can locate certain inconsistencies, if not contradictions, in ascribing so called "free markets" to the Internet, beyond the fact that the Internet's very existence was a testament to public sector investment. . . .

First, the dominant wires that would come to deliver Internet service provider (ISP) broadband access for Americans were and are controlled by the handful of firms that dominated telephone and cable television. These firms were all local monopolies that existed because of government monopoly licenses. In effect, they have been the recipients of enormous indirect government subsidies through their government monopoly franchises. . . . The telephone companies had lent their wires to Internet transmission and, over the course of the 1990s, they—soon followed by the cable companies—realized it was their future, and a very lucrative one, at that. All the more so, considering that ISP's are the only entry point to the Internet and digital networks.

These telephone and cable giants came to support the long process of what was called the "deregulation" of their industries that came to a head in the 1990s, not because they eagerly anticipated ferocious new competition, but because they suspected deregulation would allow them to grow ever larger and have more monopolistic power. . . .

Deregulation has led to the worst of both worlds: fewer enormous firms with far less regulation.[6] To top it off, the political power of these firms in Washington, D.C. and state capitals has reached Olympian heights. . . . Unlike firms in many other nations, U.S. telephone and cable firms are not required to allow competitor broadband ISPs access to their wires, so there is virtually no meaningful competition in the now crucial broadband ISP industry. Fully 18 percent of U.S. households have access to no more than a single broadband provider—a monopoly. . . . Meanwhile, four companies control the mushrooming U.S. wireless market, and the two leaders—AT&T and Verizon—are in the process of amassing one hundred million subscribers each. With dreams of converting the Internet into an expanded version of cable television, all of these firms have spectacular incentive to "privatize" the Internet as much as possible, and to use their control over broadband access as a bottleneck where they can exact additional tolls on users. Moreover, with little meaningful competition, as the FCC acknowledges, these firms have no particular incentive to upgrade their networks.[7]

Remarkably, the United States, which created and first developed the Internet, and which ranked, throughout the 1990s, close to first in world Internet connectivity, now ranks between fifteen and twenty in most global measures of broadband access, quality of service, and cost per megabit.[8] There is no incentive to terminate the "digital divide," whereby poor and rural Americans remain unconnected to broadband far beyond the rates in other advanced nations; a digital underclass encourages people to pay what it takes to avoid being unconnected. There is a striking comparison here to health care, where Americans pay far more than any other nation per capita, but get worse service, due to the parasitic existence of the health insurance industry. President Barack Obama said that if the United States were starting from scratch, it would obviously make more sense (from a public welfare standpoint) to have a publicly run health care system, and no private health insurance industry.[9] The same overall logic applies to broadband Internet access, in spades. . . .

MARKET CONCENTRATION IN MULTIPLE AREAS

. . . Capitalist development of Internet-related industries has quickly, inexorably, generated considerable market concentration at almost every level, often beyond that found in non-digital markets. What this means is that there are multiple areas where private interests can get a chokehold on the Internet and seize monopoly profits, and they are all being pursued. Google, for example, holds 70 percent of the search engine market, and its share is increasing. It is on pace to challenge the market share that John D. Rockefeller's Standard Oil had at its peak. Microsoft, Intel, Amazon, eBay, Facebook, Cisco, and a handful of other giants enjoy considerable monopolistic power as well. The crucial Wi-Fi chipset market, for example, is a duopoly where two firms have 80 percent of the market between them.[10] Apple, via iTunes, controls an estimated 87 percent market share in digital music downloads and 70 percent of the MP3 player market.[11]

This, too, runs directly counter to the notion of the Internet as a generator of competition and consumer empowerment, and as a place for an alternative to the top-down corporate system to prosper. Writers like Clay Shirky and Yochai Benkler wax eloquent about the revolutionary potential for collaborative and cooperative work online. Some of this has carved out an important niche on the Internet, which stands as a tangible reminder of how different the Internet could look. They point to peer-to-peer activities, the Open Source movement, Mozilla Firefox, WikiLeaks, and the Wikipedia experience. We find this work illuminating and encouraging, and it points to the great potential of the Internet that we have only begun to tap.[12]

But this collaborative potential, arguably the democratic genius of the Internet, runs up against the pressure of capital to consolidate monopoly power, create artificial scarcity, and erect fences wherever possible. At nearly every turn, industries connected to the Internet have transitioned from competitive to oligopolistic in short order. To a large extent, this is a familiar story: any sane capitalist wants to have as much market power and as little competition as possible. By conventional economic theory, concentration in markets in general is bad for the efficient allocation of resources in an economy. Monopoly is the enemy of competition, and competition is what keeps the system honest.

. . . Most important, the Internet adds to the mix what economists term "network effects," meaning that just about everyone gains by sharing use of a particular service or resource. Information networks, in particular, generate "demand-side economies of scale," related to the capture of customers as opposed to supply-side economies of scale (prevalent in traditional oligopolistic industry) related to cost advantages as scale goes up.[13] The largest firm in an industry increases its attractiveness to consumers by an order of magnitude as its gets a greater market share—similar to how a hurricane picks up speed as it crosses the ocean on a hot summer day—and makes it almost impossible for competitors with declining shares to remain attractive or competitive. . . .

Google is a classic example of economies of scale and monopoly power; as it grows larger, its search engine becomes ever more superior to erstwhile competitors, not to mention it gains the capacity to build up traditional barriers-to-entry and scare away anyone trying to mess with it.[14] Its network effects are so large that it has drowned out all other search engines, allowing it to prosper by selling data derived from its network to others (as well as prominently positioning paid-for "sponsored links"), marketing the vast mine of data at its disposal. In the old days, such "winner take all" markets were termed "natural monopolies."[15]

Likewise, consider Microsoft, which has been able to exploit the dependence of a wide range of software applications on its underlying operating system in order to lock in its operating system seemingly permanently, allowing it to enjoy long-term monopoly-pricing power. Any competitor, seeking to introduce a new, rival operating system, is faced with an enormous "applications barrier to entry."[16] "Apps" have thus become key to the construction of barriers of entry and monopoly power, not only in relation to information technology in general, but also, more crucially today, in relation to the Internet.

Along these lines, new devices, such as the iPhone and the iPad, carry with them applications specific to a given device that are designed to lock customers in a whole commercial domain that mediates between them and the Internet—quite differently than the Web—and that generates "network effects" and rising sales for the producer. The more that a particular device becomes the interface for whole networks of applications, the more customers are drawn in, and the exponential demand-side economies of scale take over. This directly translates into enormous economic power, and the ability to determine much of the technological landscape. Once such economic power is fully consolidated and people become increasingly dependent on a new device, network prices can be leveraged up. . . .

Such monopolistic firms accrue huge amounts of cash with which they can gobble up any potential competitor or promising upstart attempting to create a new commercial sector on the Internet. These corporate giants use their monopoly base camps to make expeditions to conquer new areas in the Internet, especially those in proximity to their monopoly undertaking. Google, for example, has a purported $33 billion in cash to play with. It has spent many billions making several dozen key Internet acquisitions, averaging around one acquisition per month, over the past several years. In just the first three quarters of 2010, Google reported that it made forty distinct acquisitions.[17] Microsoft, with $43 billion in cash on hand, has a similar record. Apple is sitting on $51 billion in cash to play with.

The idea that new technological breakthroughs will create competition online is increasingly absurd, and if it does somehow happen, it will only be a temporary stop on the way to more monopoly. The exceptional case is not actual competition—that is not even in the range of outcomes—but, instead when a new application avoids being conquered by an existing giant and creates another new monopolistic powerhouse (a new Facebook, for example) because the upstart is able to escape the clutches or enticements of an existing giant laden with cash, and create its own "walled garden" of economic value. The name of the game in such "walled gardens" of value is to exploit what economists now sometimes call "an enhanced surplus extraction effect," that is, the increased ability to fleece those walled within.[18]

Even more dire by the standards of conventional economics is the manner in which this monopoly power permits giant Internet firms effectively to control the policy-making process and rigidify their power with minimal public "interference." To the extent there are genuine policy debates, it is because powerful firms and sectors—much like King Kong and Godzilla—square off against one another. The most striking manner in which this political power manifests itself is with regard to electromagnetic spectrum, which can be defined as "the resource on which all forms of electronic wireless communication rely—the range of frequencies usable for the transmission of information." There is an enormous amount of unused spectrum that could be put to use—greater than the amount actually in use—but the incumbent spectrum users prefer the artificial scarcity that rewards them, and the government obliges. In 2011 AT&T alone has license to $10 billion worth of spectrum that is laying fallow, while it lobbies to have more spectrum diverted to it.[19] . . .

In the realm of the Internet, a state-corporate alliance has developed that is matched perhaps only in finance and militarism. It makes a mockery of traditional economics, with its emphasis on an independent private sector responding to a competitive market. It also makes a mockery of the traditional liberal notion that capitalist democracy works because economic power and political power are in two distinct sets of hands, and that these interests have strong conflicts that protect the public from tyranny. Examples of how large communication corporations and the national security state work hand-in-hand are beginning to proliferate. The one that was exposed—and is singularly terrifying—concerned how, for much of the past decade, AT&T illegally and secretly monitored the communications of its customers on behalf of the National Security Agency.[20] . . .

This integration of corporations and the state leads us to reappraise one of the greatest claims for the Internet: the notion that the Internet was impervious to control or censorship, and is the tool of the democratic activist. The same Internet, for both commercial and political reasons, can provide an unparalleled instrument for surveillance.[21] This does not mean that activists cannot use the Internet to do extraordinary organizing, merely that this has to be balanced with the notion that the Internet can make individual privacy from state and corporate interests difficult, if not impossible. The monopoly-capitalist development of the Internet has given more weight to the antidemocratic tendency. . . .

The Paradox of the Internet

In a world in which private riches grow at the expense of public wealth, it should not surprise us that what seemed at first as the enormous potential of the Internet—representing a whole new realm of public wealth, analogous to the discovery of a whole new continent, and pointing to the possibility of a vast new democratic sphere of unrestricted communication—has vaporized in a couple of decades. Competitive strategy in this sphere revolves around the concept of the lock-in of customers and the leveraging of demand-side economies of scale, which allow for the creation of massive concentrations of capital in individual firms.

Like the elimination of free land in the United States, the Internet is being transformed into a few dominant spaces that are thereby able to exploit their scarcity value. The effective "closure" (or displacement) of much of the free public space on the Internet, which now seems to be occurring, means that what was once clearly a form of public wealth in new communicative possibilities, as measured by use values—that is, in the new, universal human capacities it seemed to promise—is giving way to a very different type of system. Here exchange value dominates, and the disappearance of those use values associated with relatively free communication comes to be registered as a gain in wealth, since it produces massive private riches overnight.

. . . An innovation is commercially developed, and a market created, only by finding a way to "wall" off a sector of public wealth and effectively privatize and monopolize it, leading to huge returns. Information, which is a public good—by nature available to all and, if consumed by one person, still available to others—is, in this way, turned into a scarce private commodity through the exercise of sheer market power.

All of this is possible, however, only with the cooperation of the public sector. The privatization and monopolization of the Internet requires a state, which, in partnership with capital, neither provides the population with the alternatives necessary to develop access to this public domain, nor protects it against Internet robber barons. The state, in effect, looks the other way when it sees new realms of economic wealth being made out of "nothing" (the value attributed to, say, the electromagnetic spectrum outside market exchange) and fails to move against rapid concentration of capital, even facilitating the latter.

The FCC's approval of the 2011 merger of Comcast and NBC Universal is a case in point. As FCC Commissioner Michael Copps stated, in his lone dissenting vote: the merger "opens the door to cable-ization of the Internet." According to Copps, this creates "the potential for walled gardens, toll booths, content prioritization, access fees to reach end users, and a stake in the heart of independent content production."[22] Public wealth, free access, net neutrality, and a democratic communicative sphere are all losers. In this way, the real wealth of the Internet, like a newly discovered land that has not yet been explored, is given away to private interests—before the population has been able to realize or even to imagine the full material use value of such a realm, if managed in the public interest.

Communication is more than an ordinary market. Indeed, it is properly not a market at all. It is more like air or water—a form of public wealth, a commons. When Aristotle said that human beings were *social animals*, he might just as well have said that we are *communicative animals*. We know that the human brain coevolved with language (a social characteristic).[23] The development of social relations and democratic forms, as well as science, culture, etc., are all communicative. The rise of the Internet as a form of free communication, seemingly without limits, thus raises the prospect of vast new realms of human sociability and enhanced democratic possibilities. Yet, rather than a means of expanding human sociability, the Internet is being turned into the opposite: a new means of alienation. There is nothing natural in this process; at bottom it remains a social choice.

The moral of the story is clear. People in the United States and worldwide must redouble their efforts to address the paradox of the Internet at all levels of the analysis presented herein. The outcome is far from certain, and the issues are still very much in play. A global network of resistance is both necessary and feasible. Indeed, in view of the nature of the Internet and the stakes involved, it seems fair to say that these issues will only become more encompassing in coming years. How this battle plays out will go a long way toward determining our future as social animals.

NOTES

1. For a discussion of this point, see Robert W. McChesney, *Communication Revolution* (New York: The New Press, 2007), ch. 3.

2. For important recent discussions of the negative implications of the digital revolution, see Nicholas Carr, *The Shallows: What the Internet Is Doing to Our Brains* (New York: W.W. Norton, 2010); Sherry Turkle, *Alone Together: Why We Expect More from Technology and Less from Each Other* (New York: Basic Books, 2011).

3. Wilhelm Ostwald, "Breaking the Boundaries," *The Masses* (February 1911), 15–16.

4. See Ha-Joon Chang, *23 Things They Don't Tell You About Capitalism* (New York: Bloomsbury Press, 2010) for a superb discussion of this point and debunking of the other ideological ballast underpinning neoliberal economics.

5. Bill Gates, *The Road Ahead* (New York: Viking, 1995), 180.

6. For a revealing discussion of the 1990s lobbying by the telephone companies, see Tim Wu, *The Master Switch: The Rise and Fall of Information Empires* (New York: Alfred A. Knopf, 2010).

7. The information in this paragraph comes from *Connecting America: The National Broadcasting Plan* (Washington, D.C.: Federal Communications Commission, 2010), 37–38.

8. For OECD data see OECD, Directorate for Science, Technology and Industry, OECD Broadband Portal, http://oecd. org. See also: James Losey and Chiehyu Li, *Price of the Pipe: Comparing the Price of Broadband Service Around the Globe* (Washington, DC: New America Foundation, 2010).

9. Lynn Sweet, "Obama on why he is not for single payer health insurance. New Mexico town hall transcript," *Chicago Sun Times,* May 14, 2009, http://blogs.suntimes.com. Of course, Obama's statement was partly meant to justify acceding to the demands of the insurance companies, since a truly rational course, he implied, was no longer possible. He was wrong. It would still make more sense today from a health care standpoint to move to a publicly run health care system, but vested interests, which benefit from the present system, stand in the way.

10. Sascha D. Meinrath, James W. Losey, and Victor W. Pickard, "Digital Feudalism: Enclosures and Erasures from Digital Rights Management to the Digital Divide," *CommLaw Conspectus,* vol. 19, no. 2 (2011).

11. Adam L. Penenberg, "The Evolution of Amazon," *Fast Company* (July 2009), 66–74.

12. Yochai Benkler, *The Wealth of Networks* (New Haven: Yale University Press, 2006); Clay Shirky, *Cognitive Surplus: Creativity and Generosity in a Connected Age* (New York: The Penguin Press, 2010).

13. Carl Shapiro and Hal R. Varian, *Information Rules* (Boston: Harvard Business School Press, 1999), 173.

14. Matthew Hindman, *The Myth of Digital Democracy* (Princeton: Princeton University Press, 2009), 84–86. Hindman does a superb job of demonstrating the immense capital expenses Google incurs to assure its dominance, and that all but guarantee no other firm can or will challenge it in the search engine market.

15. Jia Lynn Yang, "Google: A 'Natural Monopoly'?" *Fortune,* May 10, 2009, http:// money.cnn.com.

16. Hal R. Varian, Joseph Farrell, and Carl Shapiro, *The Economics of Information Technology* (Cambridge: Cambridge University Press, 2004), 37, 49, 71–72; Richard Gilbert and Michael L. Katz, "An Economist's Guide to *US v. Microsoft,*" *Journal of Economic Perspectives* 15, no. 2 (2001): 30.

17. Google, Inc., "Quarterly Report Form 10-Q," September 30, 2010. http://investor.google.com/ documents/20100930_google_10Q. html.

18. Anderson, "The Web Is Dead," 127; Varian, Farrell, and Shapiro, *The Economics of Information Technology,* 14.

19. Karl Bode, "AT&T Wants FCC to Free More Spectrum—For Them to Squat On," *Broadband DSL Reports,* January 14, 2011, http://dslreports.com.

20. See Wu, 249–52.

21. Evgeny Morozov, *The Net Delusion: The Dark Side of Internet Freedom* (New York: Public Affairs, 2011).

22. "FCC's Copps Fears 'Cable-ization of the Internet," January 20, 2011, http://broad castengineering.com.

23. Terence W. Deacon, The Symbolic Species: The Co-evolution of Language and the Brain (New York: W.W. Norton, 1997).

TELEVISION AND THE CULTIVATION OF AUTHORITARIANISM

A Return Visit from an Unexpected Friend

Michael Morgan and James Shanahan

The emergence and victory of Donald Trump in the tumultuous 2016 Presidential election raises many critical and challenging questions for communication scholars. At the outset of the Republican political primary season, no political expert or pundit predicted that Trump would last long. He was widely seen as an amusing distraction in an otherwise crowded field, one who was sure to fizzle out quickly. Trump dumped all forms and rules of traditional campaigning and immediately began an assault on immigration, targeting Mexicans as "criminals, drug dealers, rapists, etc." and proposing to build a wall (to be paid for by Mexico) to keep out future undocumented immigrants. He went on to offer a barrage of "politically incorrect" proposals, insults, offenses, and inconsistencies that normally would have derailed a campaign. He quickly evolved a strategy based on a "strongman" personality that many saw as raising the specter of a dangerous authoritarianism moving to the forefront of American politics. In the end, to the surprise of most, this strategy worked.

Trump's success in the 2016 election reintroduced a factor that we have not thought much about recently: the role of media in creating fervent support for one perceived as a strong leader. Historically, leaders identified as "authoritarian" (such as Hitler, Perón, or Berlusconi) may represent sharply distinct political philosophies and regimes, ranging from traditional fascism to nationalism to right-wing populism. But what such leaders share in common are their efforts to control and manipulate the media. Those efforts in turn raise questions about the power of media to generate allegiance to those leaders and consent for

their actions. With populism and nationalism on the rise around the world, these questions take on additional urgency.

Indeed, Trump's use of media and the role of media in his election have been the focus of extensive attention. Many . . . observers have pointed to his use of social media to bolster his personal charisma and build his movement. Tweeting in particular allowed him to circumvent the gatekeeping role of traditional news media, even while he exploited their near fixation with him, giving him an enormous amount of free (and for the media, ratings-rich) coverage.

The specific media tactics used by Trump, along with the practices of media institutions during the campaign, deserve . . . serious scholarly study. Our concern here, however, is with a broader and more subtle issue: what are the dynamics within the media cultural environment that may have contributed to Trump's popularity? Could television—which continues to occupy more of Americans' leisure time than any other activity or medium (U.S. Bureau of Labor Statistics, 2016)—play a role in cultivating a cultural climate that made Trump's triumph possible? We are not talking about news and campaign coverage, but about the role of general, everyday programming, about television content, largely entertainment, that carries no *explicit* political messages and few if any direct references whatsoever to Trump. Following the theoretical assumptions, methodological procedures, and previous findings of cultivation analysis (Gerbner, Gross, Morgan, & Signorielli, 1982; Gerbner, Gross, Morgan, Signorielli, & Shanahan, 2002; Shanahan & Morgan, 1999), this study asks if heavy television viewing contributes to the kind

From Morgan, M. and Shanahan, J. (2017). Television and the cultivation of authoritarianism: A return visit from an unexpected friend. *The Journal of Communication.* Reprinted with permission of John Wiley & Sons.

of authoritarian mindset that may have helped elect Donald Trump.

THEORIES OF AUTHORITARIANISM

Authoritarianism has been a much-studied (and much contested) construct since the 1950s. Gaining impetus and momentum from the events of World War II and the rise of worldwide Fascist movements, it has been adduced as a "root cause" of attitudes such as ethnocentrism, nationalism, and anti-Semitism. The idea is that the authoritarian "personality" is one who is subservient to power above him or her, and abusive of power to those below. Authoritarians favor conformity; liberal attitudes that support and celebrate freedom of speech or social diversity are abhorrent to authoritarians' sense of things. They also prize law and order, and believe force and power are often necessary to create it. Strong leaders are seen as more desirable than those who work toward consensus or compromise through democratic means (see Adorno, Frenkel-Brunswik, Levinson, & Sanford, 1950; Altemeyer, 1998; Hetherington & Weiler, 2009).

The basics of authoritarianism were most famously laid out by Adorno et al. in *The Authoritarian Personality* (1950). They developed a scale (the "F" scale, for Fascism) that was intended to measure persons' tendencies toward authoritarian values. The scale assessed responses to statements such as "Obedience and respect for authority are the most important virtues children should learn," "What this country needs most, more than laws and political programs, is a few courageous, tireless, devoted leaders in whom the people can put their faith," and "The true American way of life is disappearing so fast that force may be necessary to preserve it." . . . This work became one of the most well-traveled lanes of the social-psychological research highway.

Many different versions and re-workings of the idea have appeared in the literature (Robinson, Shaver, & Wrightsman, 2013). Adorno et al.'s version, as indicated by the use of the word "personality" in their title, sought to describe a psychological trait acquired very early in life. There were Freudian tinges to their analysis:

A basically hierarchical, authoritarian, exploitive parent-child relationship is apt to carry over into a power-oriented, exploitively dependent attitude towards one's sex partner and one's God and may well culminate in a political philosophy and social outlook which has no room for anything but a desperate clinging to what appears to be strong and a disdainful rejection of whatever is relegated to the bottom . . . [and] the formation of stereotypes and of ingroup-outgroup cleavages. (Adorno et al., 1950, p. 971)

Not surprisingly, there have been many critiques of this work. Martin (2001) has called it "the most deeply flawed work of prominence in political psychology" (p. 1). . . . [W]ith the benefit of hindsight, we can see that Adorno et al. were greatly affected by a "confirmation bias" (Martin, 2001, p. 5) in their approach, using data selectively . . . to confirm something that they already knew existed.

Improvements were made by Altemeyer, both conceptually and in terms of measurement, as he focused on something he called "right-wing authoritarianism" (Altemeyer, 1988). Apart from the narrowed focus, Altemeyer proposed a different psychological mechanism from Adorno et al.: social learning. He adopted Bandura's theories to argue that authoritarianism was something that could be learned (or unlearned). . . .

A third stance comes from the work of Stenner and others who argue that authoritarianism is a predisposition that can be catalyzed by events. . . . When external threats disturb authoritarians' perception of equilibrium, latent tendencies are activated and they respond with attitudes and behavior that we typically associate with authoritarianism.

In total then, we have views that authoritarianism is a personality trait (Adorno et al.), a socially learned construct (Altemeyer), or a predisposition that only emerges under certain conditions (Stenner). While authoritarianism is no longer thought to reflect a personality "type" (Roiser & Willig, 2002), the consistency across these views is that authoritarians are seen as "rigid thinkers who perceive the world in black-and-white terms. . . . Authoritarians obey. They seek order. They follow authoritarian leaders. They eschew diversity, fear 'the other, . . . act aggressively toward others. . . ." (MacWilliams, 2016b, p. 717).

CULTURE AND AUTHORITARIANISM: THE ROLE OF TELEVISION

Given that Bandura and others have noted that social learning can involve vicarious agents of socialization (Bandura & Walters, 1977), the role of media in fostering authoritarianism has received some attention. Amongst well-known theories of media effects, cultivation analysis (Gerbner & Gross, 1976; Gerbner, et al., 2002) offers a close complement to the social learning perspective that Altemeyer favored. Moreover, media images can contribute to our conceptions of social reality, in ways that structure our perceptions and give us frames of meaning; this may fit with Stenner's concept of authoritarianism as a "predisposition." Thus, authoritarianism may be "acquired" through social learning processes, but still remain latent unless and until the "right" conditions emerge; television may be one source of that social learning and one basis for that predisposition.

Gerbner and his colleagues argued that heavy viewers of television drama tended, over time, to absorb images and lessons from the consistent messages of television's story system. Noting that television messages often tend toward a formulaic demonstration of power that includes the frequent use of violence, Gerbner et al. showed that heavy television exposure cultivates a sense of fear, anxiety, and mistrust, with worrisome implications. Although most public debate about television violence had focused on sensational cases of possible imitation, they argued that "We should look at the majority of people who become more afraid, anxious, and reliant on authority; they may grow up asking for more protection or worse to gain security" (Gerbner, Gross, Morgan, Signorielli, & Jackson-Beeck, 1979, p. 196). These words have a certain prescience to them in the midst of the Trump phenomenon.

From an initial focus on violence and victimization, cultivation research expanded in the 1980s to examine a far broader range of topics and issues. Thus it is not surprising that cultivation theorists eventually tended to focus more explicitly on the issue of authoritarianism and political outlooks in general. Gerbner, et al. first outlined a view of television's relation to ideology in a piece called "Charting the mainstream: Television's contributions to political orientations" (1982). They found that heavier viewers of television were more likely to blend and converge toward a conservative view of the world on such issues as freedom of speech, minority rights, race, and sexuality, although they tended to define themselves as "moderates." This process, called "mainstreaming," means that "otherwise" disparate social groups are more similar to each other when they are heavy viewers. For instance, liberals and conservatives are more likely to hold similar views about social issues such as abortion when they are heavy viewers. The implication is that television cultivates a shared cultural mainstream. These mainstreaming patterns have been consistently observed in replications of the original work (Shanahan & Morgan, 1999).

The first cultivation study to explicitly examine whether heavy exposure to the culture of television could be tied specifically to authoritarian values was conducted in Argentina (Morgan & Shanahan, 1991). . . . When the survey data were collected in the mid-1980s, Argentina was just emerging from a brutal authoritarian military regime, so it was decided to include questions that tapped support for nascent "democratic" values, such as freedom of speech, attitudes toward conformity, and so on. The study found that heavy viewing adolescents in Argentina were indeed more likely to support authoritarian over democratic values.

This work was replicated with American adolescents (Shanahan, 1995, 1998), and linked back to Gerbner's mainstreaming ideas regarding the homogenizing role of television (Gerbner, Gross, Morgan, & Signorielli, 1980). Shanahan noted that "Television apparently holds back political development for heavy viewers" (1998, p. 494). In this view, adolescents—as they mature—progress from a fairly normal state of "adolescent authoritarianism" (Duriez, Soenens, & Vansteenkiste, 2007) toward a more nuanced understanding of the world that involves solving problems by other-than-authoritarian means. Heavy adolescent viewers show less of this progression; Shanahan (1998) termed this a "retardation" of political attitude development, with the attitudes of older heavy viewing adolescents generally in line with those of their younger counterparts.

What is the relevance of the rise of Donald Trump to this earlier research on television and the cultivation of authoritarian perspectives? Many in the popular press and the public eye have criticized Trump for having authoritarian tendencies, or have decried the authoritarianism of his supporters. When it became clear that he would be the candidate, Senator Elizabeth Warren tweeted that Trump "incites supporters to violence, praises Putin, and is 'Cool with being called an authoritarian'" (Warren, 2016). Similarly, Shapiro (2016) condemned him as "the embodiment of the authoritarian temptation that has imperiled liberty since the days of the Roman Republic" (para. 5). Stanley (2016) writes that Trump employs a narrative of "wild disorder . . . as a display of strength, showing he is able to define reality and lead others to accept his authoritarian value system" (para. 13). Hundreds, if not thousands, of statements denouncing Trump for his authoritarian qualities can easily be found.

MacWilliams (2016a) goes further, arguing that authoritarianism was really the *only* predictor of support for Donald Trump during the primary campaign. . . . MacWilliams found that no other variable—including education, income, gender, age, ideology, and religiosity—significantly predicted support for Trump. Moreover, in a book that some see as uncannily forecasting the rise of Trump, Hetherington and Weiler (2009) found authoritarianism to be a primary driver of polarization in American politics, based on an obsession with law and order, immigration, fear of change, and the need for a strongman leader to meet an array of threats. MacWilliams (2016b) argues that this authoritarian-driven partisan polarization, along with "increasing fear of real and imagined threats, and terrorist incidents abroad and at home," (p. 716) is exactly what has propelled Trump (see also Choma & Hanoch, 2016). Although racial and gender attitudes played an important role (Blair, 2016), along with education and many other factors (Rothwell & Diego-Rosell, 2016), authoritarianism is especially deeply implicated in the emergence of support for Trump.

Accordingly, the question arises: if (1) television viewing cultivates values and perspectives conducive to authoritarianism, and if (2) authoritarianism is a driving force behind support for Trump, then might television viewing—directly, or indirectly through authoritarianism—contribute to the level of support for the candidacy of Donald Trump? That is what the current study investigates.

METHODS

The data analyzed here come from an online survey conducted by the research firm Qualtrics from May 16-18, 2016 (N = 1053), about two months before the party conventions were held and six months before the general election. . . . Our sample was drawn to represent gender equally and insure variance across age. . . . The sample is nearly evenly split between males (49.9%) and females (50.1%). The average age of the sample is 43.93. . . . The racial breakdown of the sample is as follows: 82.5% white, 6.6% African American, 5.9% Hispanic, 2.4% Asian-American, and 1.2% Native American. . . . [A]bout a fifth (22.2%) have no more than a high school education, while 28.0% have at least some college and 37.8% a two- or four-year college degree.

Participants were asked questions designed to tap into a range of political beliefs and values. To measure authoritarianism, we used the same four-item measure as MacWilliams (2016b). This scale . . . has been used as a measure of authoritarianism by dozens of political science scholars (e.g., Federico & Tagar, 2014; Feldman & Stenner, 1997; Henry, 2011; Sears, Van Laar, Carrillo, & Kosterman, 1997). We asked respondents:

> Although there are a number of qualities that people feel that children should have, every person thinks that some are more important than others. Here are some pairs of desirable qualities. For each pair, which one do you think is more important for a child to have:
>
> - independence (25.5%) or respect for their elders (74.5%)?
>
> - curiosity (32.5%) or good manners (67.5%)?
>
> - self-reliance (68.9%) or obedience (31.1%)?
>
> - being considerate (74.6%) or being well-behaved (25.4)?

The percent of respondents selecting each option is given in parentheses. In each case, the first answer indicates an emphasis on autonomy in child-rearing, while the second is considered to reflect more authoritarian child-rearing values. . . .

The index predicts intolerance toward outgroups, racism, moral absolutism, less trust, support for limits on freedom of speech, punitive policies toward crime, an emphasis on law and order, and more. It has also been found to be stable over time (Gerber, Huber, Doherty, & Dowling, 2013).

At the time our data were collected (May 2016), among major party candidates only Hillary Clinton, Bernie Sanders, and Donald Trump were still in the race. The few remaining Republicans, including Ted Cruz, had just recently dropped out; Trump was the presumptive nominee although he had not yet been formally named. We asked respondents which of those remaining three they would most likely vote for if the Presidential election were to be held "today." Response options also included "Don't Know," "Other" (with a write-in) and "Don't know but leaning toward" (with a write-in). About five percent of the sample said they didn't know, but were leaning toward one of the three candidates; including those "leaning towards," 32.3% said they would vote for Trump, 24.8% for Sanders, and 24.1% for Clinton. Most of the rest either said they didn't know for whom they would vote (12.6%) or wrote in some other candidate (2.6%).

To measure television viewing, we asked respondents: "Think about all the ways that you may watch television these days—including on a TV set live or on a DVR or On Demand, or streaming on a laptop, and so on. Altogether—taking all these into account—on an average day, how many hours would you say you spend watching TV?" . . .

Although news viewing is not centrally relevant to cultivation research in general, it clearly may play an important role in the case of electoral politics. Accordingly, we asked respondents how often they watch the news on each of the broadcast networks (ABC, CBS, and NBC, combined here into a single measure) and cable news channels (Fox, MSNBC, and CNN, analyzed individually). These were 5-point scale responses that ranged from "never" to "very often." . . .

In this study, news viewing is analyzed for comparative purposes and is used as an important control, but since this is a cultivation analysis, our major focus is on overall television exposure.

RESULTS

Confirming earlier cultivation research, heavy overall television viewers score significantly higher on the scale of authoritarianism. . . . Heavier viewers of broadcast network news are also significantly more authoritarian, as are viewers of Fox News; exposure to neither CNN nor MSNBC is related to authoritarianism. . . . [We also found] a significant link between authoritarianism and intention to vote for Trump. . . .

[T]here is no [direct] association between television viewing and supporting Trump (with the exception of watching Fox News). . . . Nonetheless, the indirect effect of television viewing on supporting Trump through authoritarianism *is* significant, [even with controls for] sex, age, education, political ideology, and race. . . . [T]he indirect effect model positing that television viewing contributes to favoring Trump *through authoritarianism* is supported for overall viewing, for watching news on the broadcast networks, and for watching Fox News. . . .

We tested the potential moderating role of age, sex, education, political ideology, race, and the individual news outlets. (That is, the indirect effect of Overall TV → Authoritarianism → Trump may vary for people of different education levels, or who are watching different news channels, and so on.) The indirect effect is fairly stable . . . it does not vary by age, education, race, or watching network news (or MSNBC). But four cases of significant moderated mediation were found: for political ideology, sex, watching Fox News, and watching CNN. . . .

The subgroup breakdown shows that the indirect effect remains significant in all cases. . . . However . . . there are differences in the strength of the indirect effect. For example, the size of the indirect effect decreases from the liberal to the conservative side of the political spectrum. This decrease is reminiscent of a classic and common mainstreaming pattern, in which cultivation on political issues (toward conservative views) is much more pronounced among liberals (Gerbner, et al., 1982).

The indirect effect is also larger for females than for males. Finally, the indirect effect of television viewing on backing Trump by way of authoritarianism is moderated by watching either Fox News or CNN, but in opposite ways. The indirect effect is greater for those who rarely watch Fox News and for those who more frequently watch CNN.

In these four cases, the stronger indirect effect is found within the group that is "otherwise" least likely to say they will vote for Trump: liberals, females, light viewers of Fox News, and heavy viewers of CNN. This finding suggests a complex kind of mainstreaming, given that support for Trump is "already" high for males, conservatives, and Fox News viewers. . . .

DISCUSSION

There have been thousands of studies on authoritarianism, including many in the U.S. political context, not to mention studies of the innumerable cases of authoritarian political structures around the world. But, at least in the United States, there has been a strong and longstanding assumption that, despite occasional ripples, the rise of an authoritarian political regime simply "can't happen here." That is, we have believed that while a *caudillo*-type ruler espousing nationalistic and racist sentiments might appeal to a few (or more) on the marginal fringes, such a figure could never gain serious traction as a possible leader of the US. The 2016 election has challenged that assumption and brings a need for understanding.

We explored the relationships among amount of overall television viewing, authoritarianism, and support for Donald Trump in the 2016 election. Authoritarianism was measured with a scale of attitudes toward childrearing that has no explicit political or religious dimensions, a scale that is very commonly used for this purpose by political scientists. There was no association between amount of viewing and the intention to vote for Trump, but we found a significant and consistent indirect effect of television viewing, through authoritarianism, on supporting him. This indirect effect holds under a variety of important controls, and appears to be even stronger among liberals, females, light Fox News viewers, and heavy CNN viewers. . . .

From a cultivation theory standpoint, our results are consistent with the idea that television viewing in the U.S. context provides a supportive environment for authoritarian values. Viewing broadcast news or Fox News, but not CNN or MSNBC, also tends to be positively related to authoritarianism. Of course, we are not arguing that television viewing is the dominant or determining factor driving authoritarianism. Obviously, we have had the same type of television

system in place for many years without authoritarians coming to power. . . .

Cultivation suggests that message systems contribute to background tendencies and factors that can emerge when conditions are ripe. Authoritarianism behaves in much the same way, remaining latent and then emerging in times of crisis. In the current situation, many complex factors and processes explain both authoritarianism and the rise of Trump. Although television is not likely to be the most powerful or decisive among these, the indirect effect we have uncovered is persistent, significant, and theoretically coherent.

Others are beginning to explore the importance of culture in conditioning support (or lack thereof) for someone like Trump. For example, Mutz (2016) found that *Harry Potter* readership apparently acts as something of an antidote against him, based on the series' "messages of tolerance for difference and opposition to violence and punitive policies" (p. 728). Writing in the online magazine *Slate,* Canfield (2016) argued that prime-time television is in many ways dominated by "Trump's America," that is, filled with programming that is "xenophobic," "fearmongering," "billionaire-boosting," and "science-rejecting"—especially on ratings leader CBS, with its older and whiter audience. Although television appears to offer "broad and depoliticized entertainment," and "harmless prime-time escapism," he argues that it actually "reinforces the exclusionary agenda put forth by the Trump campaign."

Our data suggest that television in the U.S. commercial model continues to play an important role in the cultivation of authoritarianism. Over twenty years ago, in reference to Argentina, we wrote: "Television asks people to be receptive to strong government" (Morgan & Shanahan, 1995, p. 198). We can say the same about the US today. Again, authoritarianism tends to be more latent than manifest for many; it is only under conditions of threat or fear of threat that the "resort" to authoritarianism comes. As MacWilliams (2016b) claims, Trump's support came both from those who were already disposed to authoritarianism and from those who were activated to it by fear. The long-standing claim of cultivation research that heavy viewing contributes to fear and mistrust comes to mind.

In the US, the fear that marked the post-9/11 environment meant support for Bush administration policies that were certainly more militaristic than average, and in which conventional regard for civil liberties was sometimes disregarded. In other words, threat brought about tendencies toward a slightly more manifest authoritarianism. The move to the Obama administration seemed to be a softening, but at the same time political polarization was heating up and seemed to create even more of a safe communication space for authoritarianism, at least within some base political subgroups. It now seems clear that there is a substantial segment of the American population that will quite readily support these views under the right conditions. . . .

Following the theory and methods of cultivation analysis, our primary independent variable is overall amount of television viewing—a measure that has long been contentious in critiques of cultivation research (Shanahan & Morgan, 1999; Morgan, Shanahan, & Signorielli, 2015). . . . While cultivation does not assume that all programming imparts identical messages or that differences among types of programs are trivial or irrelevant, the argument is simply that most regular, heavy viewers, over time, will tend to be more exposed to entertainment programs that present certain common, consistent, and stable messages about life and society that cut across many different channels and types of programs. These programs routinely present formulaic violence, along with gender and ethnic/racial stereotypes that persist despite substantial changes. They also have historically created in- and out-groups; all of these are features that would tend to nourish latent manifest authoritarianism among heavy viewers.

Even in an era when television is increasingly less "mass" than it used to be, the cultivation perspective suggests that message commonalities still exist that are more or less resistant to change and that contribute to the cultivation of insecurity, fear, and mistrust. Where the minorities who are tagged as outgroups may change (women, gays, blacks), new ones (Hispanics, Muslims) emerge that provide the grist for the fear factory that television can still embody. Interestingly, Trump has chosen the two outgroups that allow him to cover

two bases: Muslims provide the security threat and Mexicans the economic and crime threat (see Hellwig & Sinno, 2016, for an interesting parallel in Britain); these two groups are also linked with crime, violence, and terror in television entertainment. This may also feed into the common dramatic theme of the strong leader-hero who single-handedly will protect us from danger and restore the rightful order of things. . . .

We hope this study helps counter the common notion that cultivation implies a one-way causal influence from television to attitude or behavior. From the start, Gerbner envisioned cultivation as a systemic process, both reflecting and reproducing cultural patterns. Again, our findings are quite consistent with Gerbner's arguments about television violence and support for strong law-and-order policies. Moreover, they also open the door to the idea that cultivation can operate in an indirect, mediated manner, beyond any direct evidence of associations between amount of exposure and attitudes. In the same way, the study suggests that these "indirect cultivation" patterns may themselves reveal mainstreaming, as shown by our analysis of moderated mediation. We think these findings point cultivation research in some new and intriguing directions.

The largely unexpected ascendance of Donald Trump is a complex phenomenon, a product of many factors, forces, and currents coming together in a unique way. This study suggests that plain-old, regular, everyday television viewing should be considered a piece of the larger puzzle. There were many other media factors in the election—endless months of campaign coverage, intense scrutiny of the role of new and traditional media, "real" and "fake" news and much more. In terms of media cultivating support for authoritarian values, our data point to a very real effect of media and "entertainment" in American culture and politics. It remains to be seen whether the cultivation of support for Trump through authoritarianism is part of a one-time historical anomaly or signals a deeper and more long-lasting trend that will translate into authoritarian leaders and policies in the future.

REFERENCES

Adorno, T. W., Frenkel-Brunswik, E., Levinson, D. J., & Sanford, R. N. (1950). *The authoritarian personality.* New York: Harper & Row.

Altemeyer, B. (1998). The other "authoritarian personality." *Advances in experimental social psychology, 30,* 47–92.

Altemeyer, B. (2006). *The authoritarians*. Retrieved from http://members.shaw.ca/jeanaltemeyer/drbob/TheAuthoritarians.pdf

Bandura, A., & Walters, R. H. (1977). *Social learning theory*. Englewood Cliffs, NJ: Prentice Hall.

Blair, K. L. (2016). A 'basket of deplorables'? A new study finds that Trump supporters are more likely to be Islamophobic, racist, transphobic and homophobic. *USApp–American Politics and Policy Blog*. Retrieved from http://blogs.lse.ac.uk/usappblog/2016/10/10/a-basket-of-deplorables-a-new-study-finds-that-trump-supporters-are-more-likely-to-be-islamophobic-racist-transphobic-and-homophobic/

Choma, B. L., & Hanoch, Y. (2016). Cognitive ability and authoritarianism: Understanding support for Trump and Clinton. *Personality and Individual Differences, 106*, 287–291.

Duriez, B., Soenens, B., & Vansteenkiste, M. (2007). In search of the antecedents of adolescent authoritarianism: The relative contribution of parental goal promotion and parenting style dimensions. *European Journal of Personality, 21*(4), 507–527.

Federico, C. M., & Tagar, M. R. (2014). Zeroing in on the right: Education and the partisan expression of authoritarianism in the United States. *Political Behavior, 36*(3), 581–603.

Feldman, S., & Stenner, K. (1997). Perceived threat and authoritarianism. *Political Psychology, 18,* 741–70.

Gerbner, G., & Gross, L. (1976). Living with television: The violence profile. *Journal of Communication, 26*(2), 173–199.

Gerbner, G., Gross, L., Morgan, M., & Signorielli, N. (1980). The "Mainstreaming" of America: Violence profile No. 11. *Journal of Communication, 30*(3), 10–29.

Gerbner, G., Gross, L., Morgan, M., & Signorielli, N. (1982). Charting the mainstream: Television's contributions to political orientations. *Journal of Communication, 32*(2), 100–127.

Gerbner, G., Gross, L., Morgan, M., Signorielli, N., & Jackson-Beeck, M. (1979). The demonstration of power: Violence Profile No. 10. *Journal of Communication, 29*(3), 177–196.

Gerbner, G., Gross, L., Morgan, M., Signorielli, N., & Shanahan, J. (2002). Growing up with television: Cultivation processes. In J. Bryant & D. Zillman (Eds.), *Media effects: Advances in theory and research* (2nd ed., pp. 43–67). Hillsdale, NJ: Erlbaum.

Hellwig, T., & Sinno, A. (2016). Different groups, different threats: public attitudes towards immigrants. *Journal of Ethnic and Migration Studies,* 1–20. https://doi.org/10.1080/1369183x.2016.1202749

Henry, P. J. (2011). The role of stigma in understanding ethnicity differences in authoritarianism. *Political Psychology, 32*(3), 419–438.

Hetherington, M. J., & Suhay, E. (2011). Authoritarianism, threat, and Americans' support for the war on terror. *American Journal of Political Science, 55*(3), 546–560.

Hetherington, M. J., & Weiler, J. D. (2009). *Authoritarianism and polarization in American politics*. New York: Cambridge University Press.

MacWilliams, M. (2016a, Jan 17). The one weird trait that predicts whether you're a Trump supporter. *Politico Magazine*. Retrieved from http://www.politico.com/magazine/story/2016/01/donald-trump-2016-authoritarian-213533

MacWilliams, M. C. (2016b). Who decides when the party doesn't? Authoritarian voters and the rise of Donald Trump. *PS: Political Science & Politics, 49*(4), 716–721.

Martin, J. L. (2001). The authoritarian personality, 50 years later: What questions are there for political psychology? *Political Psychology, 22*(1), 1–26.

Morgan, M. & Shanahan, J. (1991). Television and the cultivation of political attitudes in Argentina. *Journal of Communication, 41*(1), 88–103.

Morgan, M., & Shanahan, J. (1995). Democracy tango: Television, adolescents, and authoritarian tensions in Argentina. Cresskill, NJ: Hampton Press.

Morgan, M., Shanahan, J., & Signorielli, N. (2015). Yesterday's new cultivation, tomorrow. *Mass Communication and Society, 18*(5), 674–699.

Mutz, D. (2016). Harry Potter and the Deathly Donald. *PS: Political Science and Politics, 49*(4), 722–729.

Robinson, J. P., Shaver, P. R., & Wrightsman, L. S. (Eds.). (2013). *Measures of Personality and Social Psychological Attitudes: Measures of Social Psychological Attitudes* (Vol. 1). San Diego, CA: Academic Press.

Roiser, M., & Willig, C. (2002). The strange death of the authoritarian personality: 50 years of psychological and political debate. *History of the Human Sciences, 15*(4), 71–96.

Rothwell, J. T., & Diego-Rosell, P. (2016). Explaining nationalist political views: The case of Donald Trump. Retrieved from https://papers .ssrn.com/s013/papers.cfm?abstract_id=2822059

Sears, D. O., Van Laar, C., Carrillo, M., & Kosterman, R. (1997). Is it really racism?: The origins of white Americans' opposition to race-targeted policies. *The Public Opinion Quarterly, 61*(1), 16–53.

Shanahan, J. (1995). Television viewing and adolescent authoritarianism. *Journal of Adolescence, 18*(3), 271–288.

Shanahan, J. (1998). Television and authoritarianism: Exploring the concept of mainstreaming. *Political Communication, 15,* 483–496.

Shanahan, J., & Morgan, M. (1999). *Television and its viewers: Cultivation theory and research.* London: Cambridge University Press.

Shapiro, W. (2016, Sept. 5). "Dear Republican Sirs: It's up to you to save the republic." *Roll Call.* Retrieved from http://www.rollcall.com/opinion-analysis/319/?dcz=

Stanley, J. (2016, Nov. 4). "Beyond lying: Donald Trump's authoritarian reality." *New York Times.* Retrieved from http://nyti.ms/2eacuoC

Stenner, K. (2005). *The authoritarian dynamic.* Cambridge: Cambridge University Press.

Stenner, K. (2009). Three kinds of conservatism. *Psychological Inquiry, 20*(2–3), 142–159.

U.S. Bureau of Labor Statistics. (2016). "American time use survey summary." Retrieved from https://www.bls.gov/news.release/atus.nr0.htm

Warren, E. (2016, May 04). @realDonaldTrump incites supporters to violence, praises Putin, and is "cool with being called an authoritarian." [Tweet]. Retrieved from https://twitter.com/elizabethforma/status/727691296727519233?ref_src=twsrc%5Etfw

7

WOMEN READ THE ROMANCE

The Interaction of Text and Context

Janice Radway

The interpretation of the romance's cultural significance offered here has been developed from a series of extensive ethnographic-like interviews with a group of compulsive romance readers in a predominantly urban, central midwestern state among the nation's top twenty in total population.[1] I discovered my principal informant and her customers with the aid of a senior editor at Doubleday whom I had been interviewing about the publication of romances. Sally Arteseros told me of a bookstore employee who had developed a regular clientele of fifty to seventy-five regular romance readers who relied on her for advice about the best romances to buy and those to avoid. When I wrote to Dot Evans, as I will now call her, to ask whether I might question her about how she interpreted, categorized, and evaluated romantic fiction, I had no idea that she had also begun to write a newsletter designed to enable bookstores to advise their customers about the quality of the romances published monthly. She has since copyrighted this newsletter and incorporated it as a business. Dot is so successful at serving the women who patronize her chain outlet that the central office of this major chain occasionally relies on her sales predictions to gauge romance distribution throughout the system. Her success has also brought her to the attention of both editors and writers for whom she now reads manuscripts and galleys.

My knowledge of Dot and her readers is based on roughly sixty hours of interviews conducted in June 1980 and February 1981. I have talked extensively with Dot about romances, reading, and her advising activities as well as observed her interactions with her customers at the bookstore. I have also conducted both group and individual interviews with sixteen of her regular customers and administered a lengthy questionnaire to forty-two

of these women. Although not representative of all women who read romances, the group appears to be demographically similar to a sizable segment of that audience as it has been mapped by several rather secretive publishing houses.

Dorothy Evans lives and works in the community of Smithton, as do most of her regular customers. A city of about 112,000 inhabitants, Smithton is located five miles due east of the state's second largest city, in a metropolitan area with a total population of over 1 million. Dot was forty-eight years old at the time of the survey, the wife of a journeyman plumber, and the mother of three children in their twenties. She is extremely bright and articulate and, while not a proclaimed feminist, holds some beliefs about women that might be labeled as such. Although she did not work outside the home when her children were young and does not now believe that a woman needs a career to be fulfilled, she feels women should have the opportunity to work and be paid equally with men. Dot also believes that women should have the right to abortion, though she admits that her deep religious convictions would prevent her from seeking one herself. She is not disturbed by the Equal Rights Amendment and can and does converse eloquently about the oppression women have endured for years at the hands of men. Despite her opinions, however, she believes implicitly in the value of true romance and thoroughly enjoys discovering again and again that women can find men who will love them as they wish to be loved. Although most of her regular customers are more conservative than Dot in the sense that they do not advocate political measures to redress past grievances, they are quite aware that men commonly think themselves superior to women and often mistreat them as a result.

Janice Radway, "Women Read the Romance: The Interaction of Text and Context," was originally published in *Feminist Studies*, Volume 9, Number 1 (Spring 1983): 56–68, by permission of the publisher, Feminist Studies Inc.

In general, Dot's customers are married, middle-class mothers with at least a high school education.[2] More than 60 percent of the women were between the ages of twenty-five and forty-four at the time of the study, a fact that duplicates fairly closely Harlequin's finding that the majority of its readers is between twenty-five and forty-nine.[3] Silhouette Books has also recently reported that 65 percent of the romance market is below the age of 40.[4] Exactly 50 percent of the Smithton women have high school diplomas, while 32 percent report completing at least some college work. Again, this seems to suggest that the interview group is fairly representative, for Silhouette also indicates that 45 percent of the romance market has attended at least some college. The employment status and family income of Dot's customers also seem to duplicate those of the audience mapped by the publishing houses. Forty-two percent of the Smithton women, for instance, work part-time outside the home. Harlequin claims that 49 percent of its audience is similarly employed. The Smithton women report slightly higher incomes than those of the average Harlequin reader (43 percent of the Smithton women have incomes of $15,000 to $24,999, 33 percent have incomes of $25,000 to $49,999—the average income of the Harlequin reader is $15,000 to $20,000), but the difference is not enough to change the general sociological status of the group. . . .

When asked why they read romances, the Smithton women overwhelmingly cite escape or relaxation as their goal. They use the word "escape," however, both literally and figuratively. On the one hand, they value their romances highly because the act of reading them literally draws the women away from their present surroundings. Because they must produce the meaning of the story by attending closely to the words on the page, they find that their attention is withdrawn from concerns that plague them in reality. One woman remarked with a note of triumph in her voice: "My body may be in that room, but I'm not!" She and her sister readers see their romance reading as a legitimate way of denying a present reality that occasionally becomes too onerous to bear. This particular means of escape is better than television viewing for these women, because the cultural value attached to books permits them to overcome the guilt they feel about avoiding their responsibilities. They believe that reading of any kind is,

by nature, educational.[5] They insist accordingly that they also read to learn.[6]

On the other hand, the Smithton readers are quite willing to acknowledge that the romances which so preoccupy them are little more than fantasies or fairy tales that always end happily. They readily admit in fact that the characters and events discovered in the pages of the typical romance do not resemble the people and occurrences they must deal with in their daily lives. On the basis of the following comments, made in response to a question about what romances "do" better than other novels available today, one can conclude that it is precisely the unreal, fantastic shape of the story that makes their literal escape even more complete and gratifying. Although these are only a few of the remarks given in response to the undirected question, they are representative of the group's general sentiment.

Romances hold my interest and do not leave me depressed or up in the air at the end like many modern day books tend to do. Romances also just make me feel good reading them as I identify with the heroines.

The kind of books I mainly read are very different from everyday living. That's why I read them. Newspapers, etc., I find boring because all you read is sad news. I can get enough of that on TV news. I like stories that take your mind off everyday matters.

Different than everyday life.

Everyone is always under so much pressure. They like books that let them escape.

Because it is an escape, and we can dream. And pretend that it is our life. I'm able to escape the harsh world a few hours a day.

It is a way of escaping from everyday living.

They always seem an escape and they usually turn out the way you wish life really was.

I enjoy reading because it offers me a small vacation from everyday life and an interesting and amusing way to pass the time.

These few comments all hint at a certain sadness that many of the Smithton women seem to share because life has not given them all that it once promised. A deep-seated sense of betrayal also lurks behind their deceptively simple expressions of a need to believe in a fairy tale. Although they have not elaborated in these comments, many of the women explained in the interviews that despite their disappointments, they feel refreshed and strengthened by their vicarious participation in a fantasy relationship where the heroine is frequently treated as they themselves would most like to be loved.

This conception of romance reading as an escape that is both literal and figurative implies flight from some situation in the real world which is either stifling or overwhelming, as well as a metaphoric transfer to another, more desirable universe where events are happily resolved. Unashamed to admit that they like to indulge in temporary escape, the Smithton women are also surprisingly candid about the circumstances that necessitate their desire. When asked to specify what they are fleeing from, they invariably mention the "pressures" and "tensions" they experience as wives and mothers. Although none of the women can cite the voluminous feminist literature about the psychological toll exacted by the constant demand to physically and emotionally nurture others, they are nonetheless eloquent about how draining and unrewarding their duties can be.[7] When first asked why women find it necessary to escape, Dot gave the following answer without once pausing to rest:

> As a mother, I have run 'em to the orthodontist. I have run 'em to the swimming pool. I have run 'em to baton twirling lessons. I have run up to school because they forgot their lunch. You know, I mean really. And you do it. And it isn't that you begrudge it. That isn't it. Then my husband would walk in the door and he'd say, "Well, what did you do today?" You know, it was like, "Well, tell me how you spent the last eight hours, because I've been out working." And I finally got to the point where I would say, "Well, I read four books, and I did the wash and got the meal on the table and the beds are all made and the house is tidy." And I would get defensive like, "So what do you call all this? Why should I have to tell you because I certainly don't ask you what you did for eight hours, step by step."

> But their husbands do that. We've compared notes. They hit the house and it's like

"Well, all right. I've been out earning a living. Now what have you been doin' with your time?" And you begin to be feeling, "Now, really, why is he questioning me?"

Romance reading, as Dot herself puts it, constitutes a temporary "declaration of independence" from the social roles of wife and mother. By placing the barrier of the book between themselves and their families, these women reserve a special space and time for themselves alone. As a consequence, they momentarily allow themselves to abandon the attitude of total self-abnegation in the interest of family welfare which they have so dutifully learned is the proper stance for a good wife and mother. Romance reading is both an assertion of deeply felt psychological needs and a means for satisfying those needs. Simply put, these needs arise because no other member of the family, as it is presently constituted in this still-patriarchal society, is yet charged with the affective and emotional reconstitution of a wife and mother. If she is depleted by her efforts to care for others, she is nonetheless expected to restore and sustain herself as well. As one of Dot's customers put it, "You always have to be a Mary Poppins. You can't be sad, you can't be mad, you have to keep everything bottled up inside."

Nancy Chodorow has recently discussed this structural peculiarity of the modern family and its impact on the emotional lives of women in her influential book, *The Reproduction of Mothering,*[8] a complex reformulation of the Freudian theory of female personality development. Chodorow maintains that women often continue to experience a desire for intense affective nurturance and relationality well into adulthood as a result of an unresolved separation from their primary caretaker. It is highly significant, she argues, that in patriarchal society this caretaker is almost inevitably a woman. The felt similarity between mother and daughter creates an unusually intimate connection between them which later makes it exceedingly difficult for the daughter to establish autonomy and independence. Chodorow maintains, on the other hand, that because male children are also reared by women, they tend to separate more completely from their mothers by suppressing their own emotionality and capacities for tenderness which they associate with mothers and femininity. The resulting asymmetry in human personality, she concludes, leads to a situation where men typically cannot fulfill all of a woman's emotional needs. As a consequence, women turn to the act of mothering as a way of vicariously recovering that lost relationality and intensity.

My findings about Dot Evans and her customers suggest that the vicarious pleasure a woman receives through the nurturance of others may not be completely satisfying, because the act of caring for them also makes tremendous demands on a woman and can deplete her sense of self. In that case, she may well turn to romance reading in an effort to construct a fantasy-world where she is attended, as the heroine is, by a man who reassures her of her special status and unique identity.

The value of the romance may have something to do, then, with the fact that women find it especially difficult to indulge in the restorative experience of visceral regression to an infantile state where the self is cared for perfectly by another. This regression is so difficult precisely because women have been taught to believe that men must be their sole source of pleasure. Although there is nothing biologically lacking in men to make this ideal pleasure unattainable, as Chodorow's theories tell us, their engendering and socialization by the patriarchal family traditionally masks the very traits that would permit them to nurture women in this way. Because they are encouraged to be aggressive, competitive, self-sufficient, and unemotional, men often find sustained attention to the emotional needs of others both unfamiliar and difficult. While the Smithton women only minimally discussed their husbands' abilities to take care of them as they would like, when they commented on their favorite romantic heroes they made it clear that they enjoy imagining themselves being tenderly cared for and solicitously protected by a fictive character who inevitably proves to be spectacularly masculine and unusually nurturant as well.[9]

Indeed, this theme of pleasure recurred constantly in the discussions with the Smithton women. They insisted repeatedly that when they are reading a romance, they feel happy and content. Several commented that they particularly relish moments when they are home alone and can relax in a hot tub or in a favorite chair with a good book. Others admitted that they most like to read in a warm bed late at night. Their association of romances with contentment, pleasure, and good feelings is apparently not unique, for in conducting a market research study, Fawcett discovered that when asked to draw a woman reading a romance, romance readers inevitably depict someone who is exaggeratedly happy.[10]

The Smithton group's insistence that they turn to romances because the experience of reading the novels gives them hope, provides pleasure, and causes contentment raises the unavoidable question of what aspects of the romantic narrative itself could possibly give rise to feelings such as these. How are we to explain, furthermore, the obvious contradiction between this reader emphasis on pleasure and hope, achieved through vicarious appreciation of the ministrations of a tender hero, and the observations of the earlier critics of romances that such books are dominated by men who at least temporarily abuse and hurt the women they purportedly love? In large part, the contradiction arises because the two groups are not reading according to the same interpretive strategies, neither are they reading nor commenting on the same books. Textual analyses like those offered by Douglas, Modleski, and Snitow are based on the common assumption that because romances are formulaic and therefore essentially identical, analysis of a randomly chosen sample will reveal the meaning unfailingly communicated by every example of the genre. This methodological procedure is based on the further assumption that category readers do not themselves perceive variations within the genre, nor do they select their books in a manner significantly different from the random choice of the analyst.

In fact, the Smithton readers do not believe the books are identical, nor do they approve of all the romances they read. They have elaborated a complex distinction between "good" and "bad" romances and they have accordingly experimented with various techniques that they hoped would enable them to identify bad romances before they paid for a book that would only offend them. Some tried to decode titles and cover blurbs by looking for key words serving as clues to the book's tone; others refused to buy romances by authors they didn't recognize; still others read several pages *including the ending* before they bought the book. Now, however, most of the people in the Smithton group have been freed from the need to rely on these inexact predictions because Dot Evans shares their perceptions and evaluations of the category and can alert them to unusually successful romantic fantasies while steering them away from those they call "disgusting perversions."

When the Smithton readers' comments about good and bad romances are combined with the conclusions drawn from an analysis of twenty of their favorite books and an equal number of those they classify as particularly inadequate, an illuminating picture of the fantasy fueling the romance-reading experience develops.[11] To begin with, Dot and her readers will not tolerate any story in which the heroine is seriously abused by men. They find multiple rapes especially distressing and dislike books in which a woman is brutally hurt by a man only to fall desperately in love with him in the last four pages. The Smithton women are also offended by explicit sexual description and scrupulously avoid the work of authors like Rosemary Rogers and Judith Krantz who deal in what they call "perversions" and "promiscuity." They also do not like romances that overtly perpetuate the double standard by excusing the hero's simultaneous involvement with several women. They insist, one reader commented, on "one woman—one man." They also seem to dislike any kind of detailed description of male genitalia, although the women enjoy suggestive descriptions of how the hero is emotionally aroused to an overpowering desire for the heroine. . . .

According to Dot and her customers, the quality of the ideal romantic fantasy is directly dependent on the character of the heroine and the manner in which the hero treats her. The plot, of course, must always focus on a series of obstacles to the final declaration of love between the two principals. However, a good romance involves an unusually bright and determined woman and a man who is spectacularly masculine, but at the same time capable of remarkable empathy and tenderness. Although they enjoy the usual chronicle of misunderstandings and mistakes which inevitably leads to the heroine's belief that the hero intends to harm her, the Smithton readers prefer stories that combine a much-understated version of this continuing antagonism with a picture of a gradually developing love. They most

wish to participate in the slow process by which two people become acquainted, explore each other's foibles, wonder about the other's feelings, and eventually "discover" that they are loved by the other.

In conducting an analysis of the plots of the twenty romances listed as "ideal" by the Smithton readers, I was struck by their remarkable similarities in narrative structure. In fact, all twenty of these romances are very tightly organized around the evolving relationship between a single couple composed of a beautiful, defiant, and sexually immature woman and a brooding, handsome man who is also curiously capable of soft, gentle gestures. Although minor foil figures are used in these romances, none of the ideal stories seriously involves either hero or heroine with one of the rival characters.[12] They are employed mainly as contrasts to the more likable and proper central pair or as purely temporary obstacles to the pair's delayed union because one or the other mistakenly suspects the partner of having an affair with the rival. However, because the reader is never permitted to share this mistaken assumption in the ideal romance, she knows all along that the relationship is not as precarious as its participants think it to be. The rest of the narrative in the twenty romances chronicles the gradual crumbling of barriers between these two individuals who are fearful of being used by the other. As their defenses against emotional response fall away and their sexual passion rises inexorably, the typical narrative plunges on until the climactic point at which the hero treats the heroine to some supreme act of tenderness, and she realizes that his apparent emotional indifference was only the mark of his hesitancy about revealing the extent of his love for and dependence upon her.

The Smithton women especially like romances that commence with the early marriage of the hero and heroine for reasons of convenience. Apparently, they do so because they delight in the subsequent, necessary chronicle of the pair's growing awareness that what each took to be indifference or hate is, in reality, unexpressed love and suppressed passion. In such favorite romances as *The Flame and the Flower, The Black Lyon, Shanna,* and *Made for Each Other,* the heroine begins marriage thinking that she detests and is detested by her spouse. She is thrown into a quandary, however, because her partner's behavior vacillates from indifference, occasional brusqueness, and even cruelty to tenderness and passion. Consequently, the heroine spends most of her time in these romances, as well as in the others comprising this sample, trying to read the hero's behavior as a set of signs expressing his true feelings toward her. The final outcome of the story turns upon a fundamental process of reinterpretation, whereby she suddenly and clearly sees that the behavior she feared was actually the product of deeply felt passion and a previous hurt. Once she learns to reread his past behavior and thus to excuse him for the suffering he has caused her, she is free to respond warmly to his occasional acts of tenderness. Her response inevitably encourages him to believe in her and finally to treat her as she wishes to be treated. When this reinterpretation process is completed in the twenty ideal romances, the heroine is always tenderly enfolded in the hero's embrace and the reader is permitted to identify with her as she is gently caressed, carefully protected, and verbally praised [with] words of love.[13] At the climactic moment (pp. 201–2) of *The Sea Treasure,* for example, when the hero tells the heroine to put her arms around him, the reader is informed of his gentleness in the following way:

> She put her cold face against his in an attitude of surrender that moved him to unutterable tenderness. He swung her clear of the encroaching water and eased his way up to the next level, with painful slowness. . . . When at last he had finished, he pulled her into his arms and held her against his heart for a moment. . . . Tenderly he lifted her. Carefully he negotiated the last of the treacherous slippery rungs to the mine entrance. Once there, he swung her up into his arms and walked out into the starlit night.
>
> The cold air revived her, and she stirred in his arms.
>
> "Dominic?" she whispered.
>
> He bent his head and kissed her.
>
> "Sea Treasure," he whispered.

Passivity, it seems, is at the heart of the romance-reading experience in the sense that the final goal of the most valued romances is the creation of perfect union in which the ideal male, who is masculine and strong, yet nurturant, finally admits his recognition of the intrinsic worth of the heroine. Thereafter, she is required to do nothing more than exist as the center of this paragon's attention. Romantic escape is a temporary but literal denial of the demands these women recognize as an integral part of their roles as nurturing wives and mothers. But it is also a figurative journey to a utopian state of total receptiveness in which the reader, as a consequence of her identification with the heroine, feels herself the passive *object* of someone else's attention and solicitude. The romance reader in effect is permitted the experience of feeling cared for, the sense of having been affectively reconstituted, even if both are lived only vicariously.

Although the ideal romance may thus enable a woman to satisfy vicariously those psychological needs created in her by a patriarchal culture unable to fulfill them, the very centrality of the rhetoric of reinterpretation to the romance suggests also that the reading experience may indeed have some of the unfortunate consequences pointed to by earlier romance critics.[14] Not only is the dynamic of reinterpretation an essential component of the plot of the ideal romance, but it also characterizes the very process of constructing its meaning because the reader is inevitably given more information about the hero's motives than is the heroine herself. Hence, when Ranulf temporarily abuses his young bride in *The Black Lyon,* the reader understands that what appears as inexplicable cruelty to Lyonene, the heroine, is an irrational desire to hurt her because of what his first wife did to him.[15] It is possible that in reinterpreting the hero's behavior before Lyonene does, the Smithton women may be practicing a procedure which is valuable to them precisely because it enables them to reinterpret their own spouse's similar emotional coldness and likely preoccupation with work or sports. In rereading this category of behavior, they reassure themselves that it does not necessarily mean that a woman is not loved. Romance reading, it would seem, can function as a kind of training for the all-too-common task of reinterpreting a spouse's unsettling actions as the signs of passion, devotion, and love.

If the Smithton women are indeed learning reading behaviors that help them to dismiss or justify their husbands' affective distance, this procedure is probably carried out on an unconscious level. In any form of cultural or anthropological analysis in which the subjects of the study cannot reveal all the complexity or covert significance of their behavior, a certain amount of speculation is necessary. The analyst, however, can and should take account of any other observable evidence that might reveal the motives and meanings she is seeking. In this case, the Smithton readers' comments about bad romances are particularly helpful.

In general, bad romances are characterized by one of two things: an unusually cruel hero who subjects the heroine to various kinds of verbal and physical abuse, or a diffuse plot that permits the hero to become involved with other women before he settles upon the heroine. Since the Smithton readers will tolerate complicated subplots in some romances if the hero and heroine continue to function as a pair, clearly it is the involvement with others rather than the plot complexity that distresses them. When asked why they disliked these books despite the fact that they all ended happily with the hero converted into the heroine's attentive lover, Dot and her customers replied again and again that they rejected the books precisely because they found them unbelievable. In elaborating, they insisted indignantly that they could never forgive the hero's early transgressions and they see no reason why they should be asked to believe that the heroine can. What they are suggesting, then, is that certain kinds of male behavior associated with the stereotype of male machismo can never be forgiven or reread as the signs of love. They are thus not interested only in the romance's happy ending. They want to involve themselves in a story that will permit them to enjoy the hero's tenderness *and* reinterpret his momentary blindness and cool indifference as the marks of a love so intense that he is wary of admitting it. Their delight in both these aspects of the process of romance reading and their deliberate attempt to select books that will include "a gentle hero" and "a slight misunderstanding" suggest that deeply felt needs are the source of their interest in both components of the genre. On the one hand, they long for emotional attention and tender care; on the other, they wish to rehearse the discovery that a man's distance can be explained and excused as his way of expressing love.

It is easy to condemn this latter aspect of romance reading as a reactionary force that reconciles women to a social situation which denies them full development, even as it refuses to accord them the emotional sustenance they require. Yet to identify romances with this conservative moment alone is to miss those other benefits associated with the act of reading as a restorative pastime whose impact on a beleaguered woman is not so simply dismissed. If we are serious about feminist politics and committed to reformulating not only our own lives but those of others, we would do well not to condescend to romance readers as hopeless traditionalists who are recalcitrant in their refusal to acknowledge the emotional costs of patriarchy. We must begin to recognize that romance reading is fueled by dissatisfaction and disaffection, not by perfect contentment with woman's lot. Moreover, we must also understand that some romance readers' experiences are not strictly congruent with the set of ideological propositions that typically legitimate patriarchal marriage. They are characterized, rather, by a sense of longing caused by patriarchal marriage's failure to address all their needs.

In recognizing both the yearning and the fact that its resolution is only a vicarious one not so easily achieved in a real situation, we may find it possible to identify more precisely the very limits of patriarchal ideology's success. Endowed thus with a better understanding of what women want, but often fail to get from the traditional arrangements they consciously support, we may provide ourselves with that very issue whose discussion would reach many more women and potentially raise their consciousnesses about the particular dangers and failures of patriarchal institutions. By helping romance readers to see why they long for relationality and tenderness and are unlikely to get either in the form they desire if current gender arrangements are continued, we may help to convert their amorphous longing into a focused desire for specific change. . . .

TABLE 7.1 ■ Select Demographic Data: Customers of Dorothy Evans			
Category	*Responses*	*Number*	*%*
Age	(42) Less than 25	2	5
	25–44	26	62
	45–54	12	28
	55 and older	2	5
Marital Status	(40) Single	3	8
	Married	33	82
	Widowed/Separated	4	10
Parental Status	(40) Children	35	88
	No children	4	12
Age at Marriage	Mean 19.9		
	Median 19.2		
Educational Level	(40) High school diploma	21	53
	1–3 years of college	10	25
	College degree	8	20
Work Status	(40) Full or part time	18	45
	Child or home care	17	43
Family Income	(38) $14,999 or below	2	5
	15,000–24,999	18	47
	25,000–49,999	14	37
	50,000+	4	11
Church Attendance	(40) Once or more a week	15	38
	1–3 times per month	8	20
	A few times per year	9	22
	Not in two (2) years	8	20

Note: (40) indicates the number of responses per questionnaire category. A total of 42 responses per category is the maximum possible. Percent calculations are all rounded to the nearest whole number.

NOTES

1. All information about the community has been taken from the 1970 U.S. Census of the Population *Characteristics of the Population,* U.S. Department of Commerce, Social and Economic Statistics Administration, Bureau of the Census, May 1972. I have rounded off some of the statistics to disguise the identity of the town.

2. See Table 7.1.

3. Quoted by Barbara Brotman, "Ah, Romance! Harlequin Has an Affair for Its Readers." *Chicago Tribune,* 2 June 1980. All other details about the Harlequin audience have been taken from this article. . . .

4. See Brotman (1980), cited above. All other details about the Silhouette audience have been drawn from Brotman's article. . . .

5. The Smithton readers are not avid television watchers. . . .

6. The Smithton readers' constant emphasis on the educational value of romances was one of the most interesting aspects of our conversations, and chapter 3 of *Reading the Romance* discusses it in depth. Although their citation of the instructional value of romances to a college professor interviewer may well be a form of self-justification, the women also provided ample evidence that they do in fact learn and remember facts about geography, historical customs, and dress from the books they read. Their emphasis on this aspect of their reading, I might add, seems to betoken a profound curiosity and longing to know more about the exciting world beyond their suburban homes.

7. For material on housewives' attitudes toward domestic work and their duties as family counselors, see Ann Oakley, *The Sociology of Housework* (New York: Pantheon, 1975) and *Woman's Work: The Housewife, Past and Present* (New York: Pantheon. 1975); see also Mirra Komorovsky, *Blue Collar Marriage* (New York: Vintage, 1967) and Helena Znaniecki Lopata, *Occupation: Housewife* (New York: Oxford University Press, 1971).

8. Nancy Chodorow, *The Reproduction of Mothering: Psychoanalysis and the Sociology of Gender* (Berkeley: University of California Press, 1978). I would like to express my thanks to Sharon O'Brien for first bringing Chodorow's work to my attention and for all those innumerable discussions in which we debated the merits of her theory and its applicability to women's lives, including our own.

9. After developing my argument that the Smithton women are seeking ideal romances which depict the generally tender treatment of the heroine, I discovered Beatrice Faust's *Women, Sex, and Pornography: A Controversial Study* (New York: Macmillan, 1981) in which Faust points out that certain kinds of historical romances tend to portray their heroes as masculine, but emotionally expressive. . . .

10. Daisy Maryles, "Fawcett Launches Romance Imprint with Brand Marketing Techniques," *Publishers Weekly* 216 (3 Sept. 1979), 69.

11. Ten of the twenty books in the sample for the ideal romance were drawn from the Smithton group's answers to requests that they list their three favorite romances and authors. . . . I also added *Summer of the Dragon* (1979) by Elizabeth Peters because she was heavily cited as a favorite author although none of her titles were specifically singled out. Three more titles were added because they were each voluntarily cited in the oral interviews more than five times. . . . Seven were added because Dot gave them very high ratings in her newsletter. Because I did not include a formal query in the questionnaire about particularly bad romances, I drew the twenty titles from oral interviews and from Dot's newsletter reviews.

12. There are two exceptions to this assertion. Both *The Proud Breed* by Celeste DeBlasis and *The Fulfillment* by LaVyrle Spencer detail the involvement of the principal characters with other individuals. Their treatment of the subject, however, is decidedly different from that typically found in the bad romances. Both of these books are highly unusual in that they begin by detailing the extraordinary depth of the love shared by hero and heroine, who marry early in the story. The rest of each book chronicles the misunderstandings that arise between heroine and hero. In both books the third person narrative always indicates very clearly to the reader that the two are still deeply in love with each other and are acting out of anger, distrust, and insecurity.

13. In the romances considered awful by the Smithton readers, this reinterpretation takes place much later in the story than in the ideal

romances. In addition, the behavior that is explained away is more violent, aggressively cruel, and obviously vicious. Although the hero is suddenly transformed by the heroine's reinterpretation of his motives, his tenderness, gentleness, and care are not emphasized in the "failed romances" as they are in their ideal counterparts.

14. Modleski has also argued that "the mystery of male motives" is a crucial concern in all romantic fiction (p. 439). Although she suggests, as I will here, that the process through which male misbehavior is reinterpreted in a more favorable light is a justification or legitimation of such action, she does not specifically connect its centrality in the plot to a reader's need to use such a strategy in her own marriage. While there are similarities between Modleski's analysis and that presented here, she emphasizes the negative, disturbing effects of romance reading on readers. In fact, she claims the novels "end up actually intensifying conflicts for the reader" (p. 445) and cause women to "reemerge feeling . . . more guilty than ever" (p. 447). While I would admit that romance reading might create unconscious guilt, I think it absolutely essential that any explanation of such behavior take into account the substantial amount of evidence indicating that women not only enjoy romance reading, but feel replenished and reconstituted by it as well. See Tania Modleski, "The Disappearing Act: A Study of Harlequin Romances," *Signs* 5 (Spring 1980), 435–48.

15. Jude Deveraux, *The Black Lyon* (New York: Avon, 1980), 66.

STAR TREK RERUN, REREAD, REWRITTEN

Fan Writing as Textual Poaching

Henry Jenkins III

In late December 1986, *Newsweek* (Leerhsen, 1986, p. 66) marked the 20th anniversary of *Star Trek* with a cover story on the program's fans, "the Trekkies, who love nothing more than to watch the same 79 episodes over and over." The *Newsweek* article, with its relentless focus on conspicuous consumption and "infantile" behavior and its patronizing language and smug superiority to all fan activity, is a textbook example of the stereotyped representation of fans found in both popular writing and academic criticism, "Hang on: You are being beamed to one of those *Star Trek* conventions, where grown-ups greet each other with the Vulcan salute and offer in reverent tones to pay $100 for the autobiography of Leonard Nimoy" (p. 66). Fans are characterized as "kooks" obsessed with trivia, celebrities, and collectibles; as misfits and crazies; as "a lot of overweight women, a lot of divorced and single women" (p. 68). . . .

Fans appear to be frighteningly out of control, undisciplined and unrepentant, rogue readers. Rejecting aesthetic distance, fans passionately embrace favored texts and attempt to integrate media representations within their own social experience. Like cultural scavengers, fans reclaim works that others regard as worthless and trash, finding them a rewarding source of popular capital. Like rebellious children, fans refuse to read by the rules imposed upon them by the schoolmasters. For fans, reading becomes a type of play, responsive only to its own loosely structured rules and generating its own types of pleasure.

Michel de Certeau (1984) has characterized this type of reading as "poaching," an impertinent raid on the literary preserve that takes away only those things that seem useful or pleasurable to the reader. "Far from being writers . . . readers are travelers; they move across lands belonging to someone else, like nomads poaching their way across fields they did not write, despoiling the wealth of Egypt to enjoy it themselves" (p. 174). De Certeau perceives popular reading as a series of "advances and retreats, tactics and games played with the text" (p. 175), as a type of cultural bricolage through which readers fragment texts and reassemble the broken shards according to their own blueprint, salvaging bits and pieces of found material in making sense of their own social experience. Far from viewing consumption as imposing meanings upon the public, de Certeau suggests, consumption involves reclaiming textual material, "making it one's own, appropriating or reappropriating it" (p. 166). . . .

In this chapter, I propose an alternative approach to fan experience, one that perceives "Trekkers" (as they prefer to be called) not as cultural dupes, social misfits, or mindless consumers but rather as, in de Certeau's term, "poachers" of textual meanings. Behind the exotic stereotypes fostered by the media lies a largely unexplored terrain of cultural activity, a subterranean network of readers and writers who remake programs in their own image. "Fandom" is a vehicle for marginalized subterranean groups (women, the young, gays, etc.) to pry open space for their cultural concerns within dominant representations; it is a way of appropriating media texts and rereading them in a fashion that serves different interests, a way of transforming mass culture into a popular culture.

I do not believe this essay represents the last word on *Star Trek* fans, a cultural community that is far too multivocal to be open to easy description.

From Jenkins, H., III. (1988). *Star Trek* rerun, reread, rewritten: Fan writing as textual poaching. *Critical Studies in Mass Communications, 5*(2), 85–107. Copyright © National Communication Association, reprinted by permission of Taylor & Francis Ltd. (http://www .tandfonline.com) on behalf of The National Communication Association.

Rather, I explore some aspects of current fan activity that seem particularly relevant to cultural studies. My primary concern is with what happens when these fans produce their own texts, texts that inflect program content with their own social experience and displace commercially produced commodities for a kind of popular economy. For these fans, *Star Trek* is not simply something that can be reread; it is something that can and must be rewritten in order to make it more responsive to their needs, in order to make it a better producer of personal meanings and pleasures.

No legalistic notion of literary property can adequately constrain the rapid proliferation of meanings surrounding a popular text. Yet, there are other constraints, ethical constraints and self-imposed rules, that are enacted by the fans, either individually or as part of a larger community, in response to their felt need to legitimate their unorthodox appropriation of mass media texts. E. P. Thompson (1971) suggests that eighteenth and nineteenth century peasant leaders, the historical poachers behind de Certeau's apt metaphor, responded to a kind of "moral economy," an informal set of consensual norms that justified their uprisings against the landowners and tax collectors in order to restore a preexisting order being corrupted by its avowed protectors. Similarly, the fans often cast themselves not as poachers but as loyalists, rescuing essential elements of the primary text misused by those who maintain copyright control over the program materials. Respecting literary property even as they seek to appropriate it for their own uses, these fans become reluctant poachers, hesitant about their relationship to the program text, uneasy about the degree of manipulation they can legitimately perform on its materials, and policing each other for abuses of their interpretive license. . . .

FANS: FROM READING TO WRITING

The popularity of *Star Trek* has motivated a wide range of cultural productions and creative reworkings of program materials: from children's backyard play to adult interaction games, from needlework to elaborate costumes, from private fantasies to computer programming. This ability to transform personal reaction into social interaction, spectator culture into participatory culture, is one of the central characteristics of fandom. One becomes a fan not by being a regular viewer of a particular program but by translating that viewing into some type of cultural activity, by sharing feelings and thoughts about the program content with friends, by joining a community of other fans who share common interests. For fans, consumption sparks production, reading generates writing, until the terms seem logically inseparable. In fan writer Jean Lorrah's words (1984, p. 1):

> Trekfandom . . . is friends and letters and crafts and fanzines and trivia and costumes and artwork and filksongs [fan parodies] and buttons and film clips and conventions—something for everybody who has in common the inspiration of a television show which grew far beyond its TV and film incarnations to become a living part of world culture.

Lorrah's description blurs all boundaries between producers and consumers, spectators and participants, the commercial and the home crafted, to construct an image of fandom as a cultural and social network that spans the globe.

Many fans characterize their entry into fandom in terms of a movement from social and cultural isolation, doubly imposed upon them as women within a patriarchal society and as seekers after alternative pleasures within dominant media representations, toward more and more active participation in a community receptive to their cultural productions, a community where they may feel a sense of belonging. . . .

For some women, trapped within low paying jobs or within the socially isolated sphere of the homemaker, participation within a national, or international, network of fans grants a degree of dignity and respect otherwise lacking. For others, fandom offers a training ground for the development of professional skills and an outlet for creative impulses constrained by their workday lives. Fan slang draws a sharp contrast between the mundane, the realm of everyday experience and those who dwell exclusively within that space, and fandom, an alternative sphere of cultural experience that restores the excitement and freedom that must be repressed to function in ordinary life. One fan writes, "Not only does 'mundane' mean 'everyday life,' it is also a term used to describe narrow-minded, pettiness, judgmental, conformity, and a shallow and silly nature. It is used by people who feel very alienated from society" (Osborne, 1987, p. 4). To enter fandom is to escape from the mundane into the marvelous.

The need to maintain contact with these new friends, often scattered over a broad geographic area, can require that speculations and fantasies about the program content take written form, first as personal letters and later as more public newsletters, "letterzines" or fan fiction magazines. Fan viewers become fan writers. . . .

Although fanzines may take a variety of forms, fans generally divide them into two major categories: "letterzines" that publish short articles and letters from fans on issues surrounding their favorite shows and "fictionzines" that publish short stories, poems, and novels concerning the program characters and concepts.[1] Some fan-produced novels, notably the works of Jean Lorrah (1976, 1978) and Jacqueline Lichtenberg (1976), have achieved a canonized status in the fan community, remaining more or less in constant demand for more than a decade.[2]

It is important to be careful in distinguishing between these fan-generated materials and commercially produced works, such as the series of *Star Trek* novels released by Pocket Books under the official supervision of Paramount, the studio that owns the rights to the *Star Trek* characters. Fanzines are totally unauthorized by the program producers and face the constant threat of legal action for their open violation of the producer's copyright authority over the show's characters and concepts. Paramount has tended to treat fan magazines with benign neglect as long as they are handled on an exclusively nonprofit basis. Producer Gene Roddenberry and many of the cast members have contributed to such magazines. Bantam Books even released several anthologies showcasing the work of *Star Trek* fan writers (Marshak & Culbreath, 1978).

Other producers have not been as kind. Lucasfilm initially sought to control *Star Wars* fan publications, seeing them as a rival to its officially sponsored fan organization, and later threatened to prosecute editors who published works that violated the "family values" associated with the original films. Such a scheme has met considerable resistance from the fan community that generally regards Lucas' actions as unwarranted interference in its own creative activity. Several fanzine editors

have continued to distribute adult-oriented *Star Wars* stories through an underground network of special friends, even though such works are no longer publicly advertised through *Datazine* or sold openly at conventions. A heated editorial in *Slaysu,* a fanzine that routinely published feminist-inflected erotica set in various media universes, reflects these writers' opinions:

> Lucasfilm is saying, "you must enjoy the characters of the *Star Wars* universe for male reasons. Your sexuality must be correct and proper by my (male) definition." I am not male. I do not want to be. I refuse to be a poor imitation, or worse, someone's idiotic ideal of femininity. Lucasfilm has said, in essence, "this is what we see in the *Star Wars* films and we are telling you that this is what you will see." (Siebert, 1982, p. 44)

C. A. Siebert's editorial asserts the rights of fanzine writers to consciously revise the character of the original texts, to draw elements from dominant culture in order to produce underground art that explicitly challenges patriarchal assumptions. Siebert and the other editors deny the traditional property rights of textual producers in favor of a right of free play with the program materials, a right of readers to use media texts in their own ways and of writers to reconstruct characters in their own terms. Once characters are inserted into popular discourse, regardless of their source of origin, they become the property of the fans who fantasize about them, not the copyright holders who merchandise them. Yet the relationship between fan texts and primary texts is often more complex than Siebert's defiant stance might suggest, and some fans do feel bound by a degree of fidelity to the original series' conceptions of those characters and their interactions.

GENDER AND WRITING

Fan writing is an almost exclusively feminine response to mass media texts. Men actively participate in a wide range of fan-related activities, notably interactive games and conference planning committees, roles consistent with patriarchal norms that typically relegate combat—even combat fantasies—and organizational authority to the masculine sphere. Fan writers and fanzine readers, however, are almost always female. Camille Bacon-Smith (1986) has estimated that more than 90% of all fan writers are female. The greatest percentage of male participation is found in the "letter-lines," like *Comlink* and *Treklink,* and in "nonfiction" magazines, like *Trek* that publish speculative essays on aspects of the program universe. Men may feel comfortable joining discussions of future technologies or military lifestyle but not in pondering Vulcan sexuality, McCoy's childhood, or Kirk's love life.

Why this predominance of women within the fan writing community? . . .

A particular fascination of *Star Trek* for these women appears to be rooted in the way that the program seems to hold out a suggestion of nontraditional feminine pleasures, of greater and more active involvement for women within the adventure of professional space travel, while finally reneging on those promises. Sexual equality was an essential component of producer Roddenberry's optimistic vision of the future; a woman, Number One (Majel Barrett), was originally slated to be the Enterprise's second in command. Network executives, however, consistently fought efforts to break with traditional feminine stereotypes, fearing the alienation of more conservative audience members (Whitfield & Roddenberry, 1968). Number One was scratched after the program pilot, but throughout the run of the series women were often cast in nontraditional jobs, everything from Romulan commanders to weapon specialists. The networks, however reluctantly, were offering women a future, a "final frontier" that included them.

Fan writers, though, frequently express dissatisfaction with these women's characterizations within the episodes. In the words of fan writer Pamela Rose (1977, p. 48), "When a woman is a guest star on *Star Trek,* nine out of ten times there is something wrong with her." Rose notes that these female characters have been granted positions of power within the program, only to demonstrate through their erratic emotion-driven conduct that women are unfit to fill such roles. Another fan writer, Toni Lay (1986, p. 15), expresses mixed feelings about *Star Trek*'s social vision:

> It was ahead of its time in some ways, like showing that a Caucasian, all-American, all-male crew was not the only possibility for

space travel. Still, the show was sadly deficient in other ways, in particular, its treatment of women. Most of the time, women were referred to as "girls." And women were never shown in a position of authority unless they were aliens, i.e., Deela, T'Pau, Natira, Sylvia, etc. It was like the show was saying "equal opportunity is OK for their women but not for our girls."

. . . Indeed, many fan writers characterize themselves as "repairing the damage" caused by the program's inconsistent and often demeaning treatment of its female characters. Jane Land (1986, p. 1), for instance, characterizes her fan novel, *Kista,* as "an attempt to rescue one of *Star Trek*'s female characters [Christine Chapel] from an artificially imposed case of foolishness." Promising to show "the way the future never was," *The Woman's List,* a recently established fanzine with an explicitly feminist orientation, has called for "material dealing with all range of possibilities for women, including: women of color, lesbians, women of alien cultures, and women of all ages and backgrounds." Its editors acknowledge that their publication's project necessarily involves telling the types of stories that network policy blocked from airing when the series was originally produced. A recent flier for that publication explains:

> We hope to raise and explore those questions which the network censors, the television genre, and the prevailing norms of the time made it difficult to address. We believe that both the nature of human interaction and sexual mores and the structure of both families and relationships will have changed by the 23rd century and we are interested in exploring those changes.

Telling such stories requires the stripping away of stereotypically feminine traits. The series characters must be reconceptualized in ways that suggest hidden motivations and interests heretofore unsuspected. They must be reshaped into full-blooded feminist role models. While, in the series, Chapel is defined almost exclusively in terms of her unrequited passion for Spock and her professional subservience to Dr. McCoy, Land represents her as a fiercely independent woman, capable of accepting love only on her own terms, ready to pursue her own ambitions wherever they take her, and outspoken in response to the patronizing attitudes of the command crew. Siebert (1980, p. 33) has performed a similar operation on the character of Lieutenant Uhura, as this passage from one of her stories suggests:

> There were too few men like Spock who saw her as a person. Even Captain Kirk, she smiled, especially Captain Kirk, saw her as a woman first. He let her do certain things but only because military discipline required it. Whenever there was any danger, he tried to protect her. . . . Uhura smiled sadly, she would go on as she had been, outwardly a feminine toy, inwardly a woman who was capable and human.

Here, Siebert attempts to resolve the apparent contradiction created within the series text by Uhura's official status as a command officer and her constant displays of "feminine frailty." Uhura's situation, Siebert suggests, is characteristic of the way that women must mask their actual competency behind traditionally feminine mannerisms within a world dominated by patriarchal assumptions and masculine authority. By rehabilitating Uhura's character in this fashion, Siebert has constructed a vehicle through which she can document the overt and subtle forms of sexual discrimination that an ambitious and determined woman faces as she struggles for a command post in Star Fleet (or for that matter, within a twentieth century corporate board room).

Fan writers like Siebert, Land, and Karen Bates (1982; 1983; 1984), whose novels explore the progression of a Chapel-Spock marriage through many of the problems encountered by contemporary couples trying to juggle the conflicting demands of career and family, speak directly to the concerns of professional women in a way that more traditionally feminine works fail to do. These writers create situations where Chapel and Uhura must heroically overcome the same types of obstacles that challenge their male counterparts within the primary texts and often discuss directly the types of personal and professional problems particular to working women. . . .

The fan community continually debates what constitutes a legitimate reworking of program materials and what represents a violation of the special reader-text relationship that the fans hope to foster. The earliest *Star Trek* fan writers were careful to work within the framework of the information explicitly included within the broadcast episodes and to minimize their breaks with series conventions. In fan writer Jean Lorrah's words (1976, p. 1), "Anyone creating a *Star Trek* universe is bound by what was seen in the aired episodes; however, he is free to extrapolate from those episodes to explain what was seen in them." Leslie Thompson (1974, p. 208) explains, "If the reasoning [of fan speculations] doesn't fit into the framework of the events as given [on the program], then it cannot apply no matter how logical or detailed it may be." As *Star Trek* fan writing has come to assume an institutional status in its own right and therefore to require less legitimization through appeals to textual fidelity, a new conception of fan fiction has emerged, one that perceives the stories not as a necessary expansion of the original series text but rather as chronicles of alternate universes, similar to the program world in some ways and different in others:

> The "alternate universe" is a handy concept wherein you take the basic *Star Trek* concept and spin it off into all kinds of ideas that could never be aired. One reason Paramount may be so liberal about fanzines is that by their very nature most fanzine stories could never be sold professionally. (L. Slusher, personal communication, August 1987)

Such an approach frees the writers to engage in much broader play with the program concepts and characterizations, to produce stories that reflect more diverse visions of human interrelationships and future worlds, to rewrite elements within the primary texts that hinder fan interests. Yet, even alternate universe stories struggle to maintain some consistency with the original broadcast material and to establish some point of contact with existing fan interests, just as more faithful fan writers feel compelled to rewrite and revise the program material in order to keep it alive in a new cultural context.

BORROWED TERMS: KIRK/ SPOCK STORIES

The debate in fan circles surrounding Kirk/Spock (K/S) fiction, stories that posit a homo-erotic relationship between the show's two primary characters and frequently offer detailed accounts of their sexual couplings, illustrates these differing conceptions of the relationship between fan fiction and the primary series text.[3] Over the past decade, K/S stories have emerged from the margins of fandom toward numerical dominance over *Star Trek* fan fiction, a movement that has been met with considerable opposition from more traditional fans. For many, such stories constitute the worst form of character rape, a total violation of the established characterizations. Kendra Hunter (1977, p. 81) argues that "it is out of character for both men, and as such comes across in the stories as bad writing. . . . A relationship as complex and deep as Kirk/Spock does not climax with a sexual relationship." Other fans agree but for other reasons. "I do not accept the K/S homosexual precept as plausible," writes one fan. "The notion that two men that are as close as Kirk and Spock are cannot be 'just friends' is indefensible to me" (Landers, 1986, p. 10). Others struggle to reconcile the information provided on the show with their own assumptions about the nature of human sexuality: "It is just as possible for their friendship to progress into a love-affair, for that is what it is, than to remain status quo. . . . Most of us see Kirk and Spock simply as two people who love each other and just happen to be of the same gender" (Snaider, 1987, p. 10). . . .

What K/S does openly, all fans do covertly. In constructing the feminine countertext that lurks in the margins of the primary text, these readers necessarily redefine the text in the process of rereading and rewriting it. As one fan acknowledges, "If K/S has 'created new characters and called them by old names,' then all of fandom is guilty of the same" (Moore, 1986, p. 7). Jane Land (1987, p. ii) agrees: "All writers alter and transform the basic *Trek* universe to some extent, choosing some things to emphasize and others to play down, filtering the characters and the concepts through their own perceptions."

If these fans have rewritten *Star Trek* in their own terms, however, many of them are reluctant to break all ties to the primary text that sparked their creative activity and, hence, feel the necessity to legitimate their activity through appeals to textual fidelity. The fans are uncertain how far they can push against the limitations of the original material without violating and finally destroying

a relationship that has given them great pleasure. Some feel stifled by those constraints; others find comfort within them. Some claim the program as their personal property, "treating the series episodes like silly putty," as one fan put it (Blaes, 1987, p. 6). Others seek compromises with the textual producers, treating the original program as something shared between them.

What should be remembered is that whether they cast themselves as rebels or loyalists, it is the fans themselves who are determining what aspects of the original series concept are binding on their play with the program material and to what degree. The fans have embraced *Star Trek* because they found its vision somehow compatible with their own, and they have assimilated only those textual materials that feel comfortable to them. Whenever a choice must be made between fidelity to their program and fidelity to their own social norms, it is almost inevitably made in favor of lived experience. The women's conception of the *Star Trek* realm as inhabited by psychologically rounded and realistic characters insures that no characterization that violated their own social perceptions could be satisfactory. The reason some fans reject K/S fiction has, in the end, less to do with the stated reason that it violates established characterization than with unstated beliefs about the nature of human sexuality that determine what types of character conduct can be viewed as plausible. When push comes to shove, as Hodge and Tripp (1986, p. 144) recently suggested, "Non-televisual meanings can swamp televisual meanings" and usually do.

CONCLUSION

The fans are reluctant poachers who steal only those things that they truly love, who seize televisual property only to protect it against abuse by those who created it and who have claimed ownership over it. In embracing popular texts, the fans claim those works as their own, remaking them in their own image, forcing them to respond to their needs and to gratify their desires. Female fans transform *Star Trek* into women's culture, shifting it from space opera into feminist romance, bringing to the surface the unwritten feminine countertext that hides in the margins of the written masculine text. Kirk's story becomes Uhura's story and Chapel's and Amanda's as well as the story of the women who weave their own personal experiences into the lives of the characters.

Consumption becomes production; reading becomes writing; spectator culture becomes participatory culture. . . .

NOTES

1. Both Lorrah and Lichtenberg have achieved some success as professional science fiction writers. For an interesting discussion of the relationship between fan writing and professional science fiction writing, see Randall (1985).

2. Although a wide range of fanzines were considered in researching this essay, I have decided, for the purposes of clarity, to draw my examples largely from the work of a limited number of fan writers. While no selection could accurately reflect the full range of fan writing, I felt that Bates, Land, Lorrah, and Siebert had all achieved some success within the fan community, suggesting that they exemplified, at least to some fans, the types of writing that were

desirable and reflected basic tendencies within the form. . . .

3. The area of Kirk/Spock fiction falls beyond the project of this particular paper. My reason for discussing it here is because of the light its controversial reception sheds on the norms of fan fiction and the various ways fan writers situate themselves toward the primary text. For a more detailed discussion of this particular type of fan writing, see Lamb and Veith (1986), who argue that K/S stories, far from representing a cultural expression of the gay community, constitute another way of feminizing the concerns of the original series text and of addressing feminist concern within the domain of a popular culture that offers little space for heroic action by women.

REFERENCES

Bacon-Smith, C. (1986, November 16). Spock among the women. *The New York Times Book Review,* pp. 1, 26, 28.

Bates, K. A. (1982). *Starweaver two.* Missouri Valley, IA: Ankar Press.

Bates, K. A. (1983). *Nuages one.* Tucson, AZ: Checkmate Press.

Bates, K. A. (1984). *Nuages two.* Tucson, AZ: Checkmate Press.

Blaes, T. (1987). Letter. *Treklink, 9,* 6–7.

de Certeau, M. (1984). *The practice of everyday life.* Berkeley: University of California Press.

Hodge, R., & Tripp, D. (1986). *Children and television: A semiotic approach.* Cambridge: Polity Press.

Hunter, K. (1977). Characterization rape. In W. Irwin & G. B. Love (Eds.), *The best of Trek 2* (pp. 74–85). New York: New American Library.

Lamb, P. F., & Veith, D. L. (1986). Romantic myth, transcendence, and *Star Trek* zines. In

D. Palumbo (Ed.), *Erotic universe: Sexuality and fantastic literature* (pp. 235–256). New York: Greenwood Press.

Land, J. (1986). *Kista.* Larchmont, NY: Author.

Land, J. (1987). *Demeter.* Larchmont, NY: Author.

Landers, R. (1986). Letter. *Treklink, 7,* 10.

Lay, T. (1986). Letter. *Comlink, 28,* 14–16.

Leerhsen, C. (1986, December 22). *Star Trek's* nine lives. *Newsweek,* pp. 66–73.

Lichtenberg, J. (1976). *Kraith collected.* Grosse Pointe Park, MI: Ceiling Press.

Lorrah, J. (1976). *The night of twin moons.* Murray, KY: Author.

Lorrah, J. (1978). The Vulcan character in the NTM universe. In J. Lorrah (Ed.), *NTM collected* (Vol. 1, pp. 1–3). Murray, KY: Author.

Lorrah, J. (1984). *The Vulcan academy murders.* New York: Pocket.

Marshak, S., & Culbreath, M. (1978). *Star Trek: The new voyages*. New York: Bantam Books.

Moore, R. (1986). Letter. *Treklink, 4*, 7–8.

Osborne, E. (1987). Letter. *Treklink, 9*, 3–4.

Randall, M. (1985). Conquering the galaxy for fun and profit. In C. West (Ed.), *Words in our pockets* (pp. 233–241). Paradise, CA: Dustbooks.

Rose, P. (1977). Women in the federation. In W. Irwin *&* G. B. Love (Eds.), *The best of Trek 2* (pp. 46–52). New York: New American Library.

Siebert, C. A. (1980). Journey's end at lover's meeting. *Slaysu, 1*, 28–34.

Siebert, C. A. (1982). By any other name. *Slaysu, 4*, 44–45.

Snaider, T. (1987). Letter. *Treklink, 8*, 10.

Thompson, E. P. (1971). The moral economy of the English crowd in the 18th century. *Past and Present, 50*, 76–136.

Thompson, L. (1974). *Star Trek* mysteries—Solved! In W. Irwin & G. B. Love (Eds.), *The best of Trek* (pp. 207–214). New York: New American Library.

Whitfield, S. E., & Roddenberry, G. (1968). *The making of Star Trek*. New York: Ballantine Books.

RECONSIDERING RESISTANCE *AND* INCORPORATION

Richard Butsch

For a century, American cultural elites and intellectuals have criticized commercial leisure for giving people the wrong ideas. Much of this has been criticism of commercial entertainment and media, that is, mass culture. The more widely used term "commercialization," as well as the more technical "commodification" have been used with negative connotations by social commentators, reformers, and researchers warning of mass culture's corrupting influences on aesthetics, community, and class consciousness.

Art and literary figures have long blamed commercialism, that is, commercial entertainment, amusements and media, for undermining artistic taste and support of the arts. Nathaniel Hawthorne's famous misogynous statement about "scribbling women" was directed at popular novels and magazines. Actors, playwrights, and drama critics bemoaned what they called the commercialization of theater in late nineteenth and early twentieth century America, blaming the Theater Syndicate, and its commercial success in particular, for low aesthetic standards in drama. Modernists and mass culture critics through the twentieth century abhorred commercialization for aesthetic degradation (Huyssen, 1986; Li, 1993), moral debasement (Boyer, 1978) and social disintegration (Giner, 1976; Kornhauser, 1959).

Political economists use the more technical term "commodification" to indicate an ongoing expansion of commercial exchange into all areas of human activity, gradually turning all of human intercourse into a "universal market" (Braverman, 1974). In recent years, journal articles have described commercial inroads into areas that most people consider inappropriate. These include such personal areas as renting wombs and purchasing pregnancies (Resnik, 1998; Rothman, 1987), the patenting of genes and animals (Berlan, 1989), advertising in schools (Molnar, 1996), the packaging of ethnic identity (Castile, 1996; Lee, 1992; Richer, 1988) and privatization of public services such as policing (Loader, 1999; McMullan, 1996). Commodification has also been dreaded in the choice between development and conservation of parks and wilderness (Swinnerton, 1999).

Trading in identity, bodies, and personal or public services crosses a moral threshold and transforms social relations traditionally regulated by values that transcend money into exchange relations regulated by money. As part of this change, leisure, instead of being a haven from alienated wage work, now becomes like work, an environment of commodity consumption in which treasured aspects of social relations (based on attachment and commitment rather than self-interest) and personal identity (based on character rather than clothes) are lost.

During the twentieth century, criticism of commercialization and commodification has usually presumed that such processes and their agents control those who consume these products and services, shaping and corrupting people's thoughts, behavior and relationships as they participate in monetary exchanges and inhabit the cultural environments built for these purposes. Critics, in other words, tend to emphasize domination of the masses, and cast people as victims of commercial culture.

In the mid-1970s, the new field of cultural studies broke ranks with those who shared this premise. Cultural studies introduced the idea that, while commodity culture is powerful, the victory is never total, and people regularly resist

From Butsch, R. (2001). Considering resistance and incorporation. *Leisure Sciences, (23)*2, 71–79. Reprinted by permission of Taylor & Francis Ltd. (http://www.tandf.co.uk/journals).

the domination that is so feared. In particular, they saw this resistance in the leisure activities of working class youth—clubbing, dancing, dress, motorbiking, drug use, "hanging out" (Hall & Jefferson, 1976).

Cultural studies arose as a reaction to traditional Marxist criticism of popular culture. Orthodox Marxists as well as humanistic Marxists, such as the Frankfurt School, shared a base and superstructure model that presumed the unquestioned dominance of ideas legitimating the existing social structure (Williams, 1973). According to this deterministic model, the economic structure would inevitably generate a culture that justified it and its beneficiaries, and the mass of the population would be "duped" into false consciousness by these justifications (Jay, 1973; Swingewood, 1977). Popular culture and leisure were particularly problematic in this respect, the new "opiate of the masses." Working class resistance, which was presumed to occur in political and economic realms (political parties and labor unions), was prevented by cultural production of false consciousness in the realm of leisure. Workers did not "throw off their chains" because they were persuaded from watching television and enjoying their new car that capitalism was good for them. This was a rather pessimistic model since it left little room for popular resistance to evolve.

Cultural studies rejected this model and instead offered a more optimistic model in which people were not suffering from false consciousness, but rather contended against cultural institutions and elites, often reinterpreting commodities to produce their own subculture serving their own interests. Other scholars disputed the significance of such cultural resistance and continued to emphasize the overwhelming power of capitalist institutions to control culture and create false consciousness.

Since that time the concept of cultural resistance has been under regular attack from many quarters, including from within cultural studies, and there has been endless debate over commodification versus resistance, what Richard Johnson two decades ago called "intellectual ping-pong," in which sides have taken absolutist partisan positions, each oversimplifying the argument of the other side and dismissing it (Johnson, 1981, p. 386). In response to the rancorous debate there also arose recurring calls for an end to the debate and a search for a synthesis (Clarke, 1990; Grossberg, 1995; Johnson, 1981).

My purpose here is to repeat this call for a truce and suggest an avenue for synthesis of the foci of both sides of the debate. The path I propose first is to acknowledge the validity of both the strength of hegemony and of the significance of resistance. Second, I propose to seek a differentiated vocabulary for different levels of resistance. Third, I seek to reintegrate into the analysis a side of the dialectic of hegemony proposed by Raymond Williams, but generally neglected in cultural studies. That side is "incorporation," a process that in many ways reflects the concerns of those critical of resistance studies and that overlaps the process of commodification. To describe this path I will retrace some of the theoretical roots of cultural studies to retrieve this concept of incorporation and reinstate it in the framework as originally conceived.

RETRACING FORGOTTEN PATHS

Studies of the ideological power of monopoly capital and studies of resistance both have contributed greatly to our understanding of modern society. At the same time, domination studies have focused too narrowly on the (admittedly great) power of corporations and media monopoly; and resistance studies have been too singularly focused on resistance or alternate readings. Now, we need to take the next step, to analyze the *relationship between* resistance and incorporation, to look at their interaction. We need to understand not simply domination or resistance, but domination and resistance.

Both concepts are central to Raymond Williams' essay, "Base and Superstructure in Marxist Cultural Theory," first published in *New Left Review* (1973) and later elaborated into his book, *Marxism and Literature* (1977). In this essay, Williams first introduces an idea of cultural opposition, though he does not use the term resistance. Williams' purpose in this essay is to critique the traditional Marxist concepts of base, superstructure and ideology as too deterministic. The base referred to the economic structure, the mode of production. The superstructure included the other institutions presumed to be derivative of the base (e.g., law, education, arts, and leisure), institutions whose purpose was the production, dissemination, and application of ideas. Both their organization and the ideas they propagated were determined by the base. The base was material, the superstructure ideational. In the traditional model, the form of the superstructure and, thus, the dominant ideas of a society, are determined by the base. In other words, the predominant ideas are controlled by and justify the existing order and, thus, the existing power structures. Such ideas are so dominant that most people most of the time are duped into a false consciousness that prevents opposition. In more concrete terms, commercialized leisure dupes most people into acceptance and cooperation with the enterprise of monopoly capital.

Williams argued that this concept of ideological control was too rigid and too extensive. He did not dispute the power of monopoly capital to shape the prevailing ideas of an era. But he rejected the assumption of inevitability and totality. Instead he suggested a more flexible concept of cultural hegemony that acknowledged concentrated power, but also allowed for "space" in which people might create and sustain their own ideas different from or opposed to and, on occasion, prevailing over those promoted by concentrated power. He conceived of alternative and oppositional cultures resisting domination; he considered these cultures never to be a given, but always a contingency. In his own words,

> We have to emphasize that hegemony is not singular; indeed that its own internal structures are highly complex, and have to be continually renewed, recreated and defended; and by the same token, that they can be continually challenged and in certain respects modified. (1973, p. 8)

He argued that hegemony is always contingent and in a continual struggle that is never certain or final, that resistance (without using that word in his essay) is perennial, although the degree of it varies historically. The incompleteness, contingency, and struggle are necessary concepts to account for historical change.

Unlike later resistance studies, Williams continued to acknowledge the power of hegemonic forces. He began his explanation of his model with a description of hegemony as a central system of practices, meanings and values which we can properly call dominant and effective . . . which are organized and lived . . . a sense of reality for most people . . . beyond which it is very difficult for most people of the society to move, in most areas of their lives (1973, p. 9).

He cautioned that hegemony is not static and therefore is capable of countering resistance. He said, "We can only understand an effective and dominant culture if we understand the real social *process* on which it depends: I mean the process of *incorporation*" (p. 9), the process whereby resistances are corralled and rearticulated within the framework of hegemony. He argued that hegemony is "active and *adjusting*" (p. 9) and flexible. Incorporation is the dominant cultural response to challenges and the means to overcome them. Williams never lost sight of the power of hegemony, its dominance. Yet at the same time, he also insisted that there is also space, sometimes more, sometimes less, for "other senses of reality" (p. 9), alternative or oppositional.

Williams seems to have been thinking in terms of more self-consciously organized and overtly political movements when he conceived of alternative and oppositional cultures. In a subsequent book, *Culture* (1981), he described anti-establishment arts movements of the nineteenth and twentieth centuries, such as the Pre-Raphaelites and the Bloomsbury Group, as oppositional cultural movements. The new field of cultural studies was likewise concerned with opposition to hegemony, but they were focused on popular, commercial culture, on what youth in particular did with commodities, on leisure.

Early classics of cultural studies recognized the importance of incorporation, even when not pursuing it. Dick Hebdige's *Subculture: The Meaning of Style* (1979, pp. 92–99) is probably the most widely cited study of resistant subcultures, including mods, skinheads, punk, teddy boys, and reggae. It became the prototype of studies that celebrated subcultural style as resistance. Yet Hebdige also discussed their incorporation in commodity form back into the dominant culture. Quoting Henri Lefebvre (1971), Hebdige said that oppositional ideas, such as these subcultures, are often subverted by being commodified and resold as fashionable styles, stripped of their more dangerous content. At the same time, an ideological form of incorporation in other sectors, especially media, translates the messages of such subcultures into trivia or meaningless spectacle, again stripping away dangerous elements. News stories depict them as innocuous adolescent rebellion, blunting the class and political content of their message. (Other news stories characterize them as dangerous and to be repressed. Another study, *Policing the Crisis* [Hall, Critcher, Jefferson, Clarke, & Roberts, 1978], examined this aspect of dominant culture response.).

Unfortunately, Hebdige's treatment of incorporation was secondary and overshadowed by his more elaborate and persuasive presentation of resistance. Hebdige's emphasis and its reception is understandable in terms of the debate at the time, since resistance was the side of the equation that had been ignored and needed elaboration. Domination, the power of hegemony, was already a well-developed topic of study and needed little elaboration. The idea of resistance was new, exciting and eye-opening. Students and faculty at the University of Birmingham's Centre for Contemporary Cultural Studies (CCCS), birthplace of cultural studies, immersed themselves in projects on resistance.

The center's work on resistance was introduced in *Resistance Through Rituals* (1976), a collective effort led by Stuart Hall along with several CCCS students who would later gain renown, among them Ian Chamber, John Clarke, Paul Corrigan, Chas Critcher, Simon Firth, Tony Jefferson, Angela McRobbie, Graham Murdoch, Paul Willis and Hebdige. Some of this work preceded Williams' original essay—though Williams had been talking about these ideas for some time before. *Resistance* was inspired more by sociologist Howard Becker's formulation of labeling theory and Phil Cohen's studies of East London subcultures than by Williams. It focused on deviance and proposed a then new interpretation of deviant subculture as an expression of subordinate class and generational resistance to labeling that denied the dominant culture as valid and themselves as deviant. Problematic for the authors was not the power of hegemony but the category of deviant. Hegemony was a given. They showed how deviance, understood as resistance, was a response to hegemony.

Like Williams, however, the authors of *Resistance* never forgot the significance of hegemonic power. Indeed the book presumed its dominance as something from which these subcultures were trying to "win space," to avoid suffocation so to speak. They used the term "resistance," instead of Williams' concept of alternative and oppositional culture, because they wanted to avoid Williams' suggestion of a fully formed culture and more developed class consciousness. Williams wrote of opposition in terms of the grand historical sweep

of classes and modes of production supplanting each other, for example, the bourgeoisie of capitalism replacing the aristocracy of feudalism. At CCCS, they focused on the sources of change at the microsocial level—hence the interest in the American sociology of deviance—as people live their everyday lives surrounded by the dominant culture, but subverting it by adapting this culture to their own purposes. They had in mind something less grand in scope and less fully formed than Williams did. Their idea was simply a "refusal" to be taken in, to succumb, to conform to the dominant. Unfortunately, usage of the term has gravitated toward a suggestion of something more forceful, self-conscious, politically motivated, fully formed, and *effective* than was originally intended.

Far from submissive, deviant subcultures such as the skinheads studied by John Clarke (1990, pp. 99–102) rebelled against the efforts to control and define them. These working class youth exhibited a fierce sense of "us," embattled against a society that described them with contempt and attempted to control their behavior and appearance. Instead of behaving as they were told in school, in reaction to government control of their daily lives through social workers' visits and to the unfavorable comparisons to middle class hippies, lower working class youth of the 1960s created their own identity and community in the form of violent rituals of football hooliganism. One skinhead quoted by Clarke summed it up.

> All these dummoes at school who always do what they're told . . . end up being Coppers . . . social workers [are] really authority pretending to be your friend. They try to get you to do things and if you don't do them, they've got the law on their side. . . . With all this lot against us, we've still got the yids, Pakis, 'ippies on our backs. (1990, p. 100)

The consciousness of belonging to a despised and dominated class and the refusal to submit is at the core of a third cultural studies work that first appeared as an essay in *Resistance,* Paul Willis' *Learning to Labor* (1977), centered on English working class adolescent boys' refusal to cooperate with school authorities from teachers on up, rejecting the values and promises the school made as false and as requiring a rejection of their own background. Willis deftly described the delicate and intimate interweaving of resistance and incorporation in the delinquent acts of the boys at school, leisure pursuits and work. He showed how the lads in and around Birmingham England incorporated themselves into the hierarchy of work and class through their very acts of resistance. In resisting they were "learning to labor." Their very rebelliousness helped to consign them to their place in the class structure. It did provide them some space to sustain their own self-constructed identities, something that can be very important to subordinate groups attempting to save their self-respect. Willis' book continues to be one of the best examples of attending to the relationship between resistance and incorporation. Unfortunately it did not inspire emulation or extension to other areas besides education and work.

The director of CCCS at the time, Stuart Hall, also consistently acknowledged the power of the dominant culture while arguing that this power was resisted. In "Encoding/Decoding" (1980, 1994), originally given as a talk in the 1970s, Hall included a category of "preferred reading," the intended meaning of media messages. Alternative or oppositional readings had to work against its grain. In "Deconstructing the Popular," presented in the late 1970s, Hall echoed Williams' words that popular culture is "partly where hegemony arises, and where it is secured . . . [but also] where struggle for and against a culture of the powerful is engaged" (1981, p. 239). His formulation begins and ends with recognizing the power of the dominant culture, as well as resistance to domination. He sees popular culture as an especially important arena where this struggle takes place in today's world.

LOSING OUR PATH

Cultural studies began to go off the track when new converts neglected incorporation and failed to bring it back into the equation once we had established the existence of resistance and the need to take it into account. This was made worse by the universal application of resistance as a single, undifferentiated concept of divergence from the dominant culture. Even Williams' original distinction between "alternative" and "oppositional" cultures faded into the background, as those two concepts were supplanted in the scholarly discourse by the undifferentiated "resistance." By the 1980s,

lacking a nuanced vocabulary for different kinds of resistance (such as suggested by Butsch, 2000, pp. 292–294), some, even within cultural studies, began to criticize the use of a label that had been used to describe significant cultural actions for relatively trivial and self-indulgent behavior.

Some cultural studies scholars adopted Michel de Certeau's (1984) idea of "making do" to describe oppositional stances not significant enough to warrant being called resistance, but still constituting a refusal to complete subordination. According to de Certeau, people carve out space of their own in a cultural sense and make do with what cultural autonomy they can hold onto. They may live in a world of advertising and mass produced products, but they construct a world with these products in ways not predetermined by the products or producers. Nor are they duped by ads and media imagery. They do not overthrow this world of corporate power. But they do make a place of their own within it. A range of terms for different levels of refusal would help greatly to clarify analysis and reduce criticism.

Hall's *Resistance Through Rituals* (1976, pp. 42–45) talks about resistance in similar terms of "winning space" from the dominant culture, not in terms of explicit political opposition. Stuart Hall, in "Deconstructing the Popular" (1981), wrote about popular culture and leisure not so much as explicit opposition, but as a ground to prepare opposition. Resistance in these early formulations, then, was not proposed as some grand assault on the status quo, but as the ground from which might arise some political force. In Hall's words, popular culture is "not a sphere where socialism, socialist culture—already fully formed—might be simply expressed, but it is one of the places where socialism might be constituted" (1981, p. 239).

The failure of our vocabulary to differentiate levels of refusal made it easier to lump all resistance studies as exaggerated extremes, and left us to choose either political economy or cultural studies as mutually exclusive and hostile camps. This in turn closed off explorations of approaches incorporating both views.

There followed a genre of essays calling for a more balanced approach. I will mention only three. John Clarke (1990) characterized the two extreme positions as "populism versus pessimism." He presented a simple but clear map of the basic differences, noting positive and negative aspects of both positions, and then called for a synthesis that puts an end to our "oscillation" between the two. The same sensitivity to both forces was espoused by Justin Lewis and Sut Jhally (1994) and by Herman Gray (1994) in his response to them. All three claimed cultural studies as their ground, all agreed that one extreme or the other is inadequate and that we need take account of determination as well as semiotic space for resistance and evasion.

Yet years after several such calls for synthesis, we still lack an approach that integrates the two forces. We need to focus on this nexus instead of looking exclusively at the resistance or the domination side of the equation. We need to return Williams' concept of incorporation to its place in the equation without displacing some concept of resistance. We need a more nuanced concept of resistance, perhaps several distinct terms for different levels of refusal or opposition. Most important, we need to focus on the connection between resistance and incorporation, to transcend a focus on either one individually and look at how they operate together, how the balances and tensions between the two processes work, how the contradictions of their relationship operate. Incorporation is akin to processes that are at the heart of analyses of commodification, but is also integral to the formulation of opposition by Raymond Williams and of resistance in early formulations of cultural studies. Hopefully such integrated studies will interest both sides to this debate and build common ground.

TRACING A NEW PATH

What would such a combined approach look like? Consider, for example, the incorporation of resistive subcultures into fashionable new commodities. Incorporation often takes place through commodification, that is, incorporating an alternative or oppositional idea in a commodity, often using the idea to sell or advertise the product by presenting it as avant garde or different from the mass. The universal market is ever searching for new commodities and new packaging. Alternative and oppositional cultures are treated by corporations as simply sources of new products or styles.

The dialectic of resistance and incorporation, particularly in the form of commodification, has been explored in terms of the path of avant-garde art movements. Critiques of modernists have argued that the antibourgeois stance of

modernism was incorporated quickly into commodity capitalism (Huyssen, 1986; Li, 1993; Williams, 1982). These studies have emphasized the victories of commodification over resistance.

Another example is the incorporation of two explicitly oppositional subcultures, classic examples of resistance, American hippie subculture in the 1970s and hip-hop subculture in the 1990s (Frank, 1997; Watkins, 1998). They were quickly commodified by corporations. The clothing industry adopted hippie and hip-hop dress styles, stripping or taming their original symbolism and substituting values compatible with consumption. Advertisements of large corporations co-opted their subcultural slogans. Music of both movements that advocated revolt was distributed by major record companies.

Most studies however continue to focus on either incorporation or resistance, but not the relation between the two. For example, Thomas Frank's *The Conquest of Cool* (1997) and S. Craig Watkins' *Representing* (1998) are outstanding new pieces of scholarship on incorporation, but they focus on one half of the relationship. As Hebdige's *Subculture* (1979) acknowledged, both books recognize resistance, but that is overshadowed by concentrating on incorporation. Neither takes as the central purpose understanding the relationship between resistance and incorporation. What is missing in most research is the next step of analysis after incorporation. We should not presume that incorporation is the end of the story of resistance, but should rather pose it as an empirical question. Is there a resistance to incorporation itself, a new stage of resistance, so to speak? Does one resistance die with its incorporation, with new resistances emerging elsewhere? Are they in turn incorporated, and so on? Wherever we leave off telling the story, we should not make it appear that this is the end, but leave open the possibility of continuation. As Williams said, hegemony is never complete, nor is resistance. Such research is daunting, but necessary to progress in understanding consumption, culture and power.

Another approach is to examine cases in which domination went awry, to discover the relation between domination and resistance, just as I have suggested for incorporation and resistance. One approach looks at the process beginning with domination and moving toward resistance; the other begins with resistance and moves toward domination (through incorporation).

In the 1980s, huge electronics corporations tried to introduce a new consumer product, the video disc. They failed because consumers simply refused to buy them (Butsch, 2000). People exercised economic power. Can cultural power be exercised against economic power? Isn't the decision to buy or not a cultural decision? How about resisting a heavily hyped cultural product like a movie, book, or music CD? Movie studios spend tens of millions on movie ads and yet success seems mostly determined by word of mouth. How does this work? Who's in control? Are there resistive and incorporative forces at work?

Here is where the future of leisure studies and cultural studies lies, weaving together the threads of domination, resistance, and incorporation in order to understand leisure and popular culture in an era of hyper commodification and consumption. We have examined the individual threads enough. They are conceptually and empirically sound. Now we can weave our tapestry of power and struggle.

AFTERWORD: CHANGES IN MEDIA AND AUDIENCE STUDIES OVER THE PAST DECADE

In 2001, I framed the issue as subcultural resistance of active audiences facing the framing power of centralized mass media, including its power to incorporate and co-opt audiences. Since then much has changed. The media landscape has changed remarkably. Digital convergence, the Internet, and mobile media have created an everywhere, ever-on environment and changed audiences into users, or what some have called "prosumers," both producing and consuming media content. Industrial convergences and concentration have created multimedia giants with global reach much greater than once envisioned by sociologist Herbert Schiller (1969). Politics have changed, too. Across the globe, neoliberal politics has privatized public media and supplanted the public service model with a market model to justify deregulation and enable media monopoly. In some cases, an older power-elite conspiracy theory seems more appropriate than Williams' (1977) concept of hegemony, which he conceived to explain a subtler form of domination in post-war Western democracies.

Our understanding of media industry and especially of audiences has grown as well, in ways that enable a synthesis of hegemony and resistance in the production and reception of media texts. The concept of active audiences that accompanied the idea of resistance has led us also to discover a good deal more. Resistance and its companion communication model of encoding/decoding (Hall, 1980) were largely conceived within the framework of "short-term" media effects, focusing on the impact of a single media message. More recent research into audience history, studies of entire genres (e.g., sitcom, telenovela, reality shows), and the impact of media per se has provided a picture of "long-term," cumulative effects of repetition across time and media that are presumed in the concept of hegemony and in critiques of media monopoly.

In hindsight, resistance can be seen as a conceptual passage that led from the study of effects to a broad theoretical and empirical plain with a far richer understanding of audiences and audiencing than either effects or resistance enabled. This new framework more readily allows structural and macro considerations that typify concerns about media monopoly and thus connect our understandings of audiences with those of media industry and production. Resistance was conceived in a culturalist framework and as a result lent itself to broader cultural explorations such as ideas of "embeddedness," "net locality," and collective concepts of audiences.

The first idea, that of embeddedness (Silverstone, 1994) grew from addressing family (Lull, 1990; Morley, 1986) and group structure at the micro level of television viewing. It places media experience within the living context of audiences, understanding media as part of the whole immediate social environment, and has notably contributed to this broadened horizon in understanding audiences. What people do with media and their messages is influenced by the situation within which they do it, whether in the home or elsewhere, alone or with others, and often while focused or multitasking.

Second, the idea of "net locality" characterizes some new research on media companies that links the virtual and physical locations of audiences (Gordon & de Sousa e Silva, 2011) and has begun to interweave analysis of Internet users' (audience) behavior with studies of the organization and actions of media companies. This research potentially bridges the macro approach of corporate policies and the micro analysis of audiences' responses. It places the interface between audiences and media industries at the very center of its focus, and shows promise for further integration of ideas about hegemony and resistance.

A third new idea focuses on audiences on a macro level, as collectivities such as publics in a democratic polity, or as crowds that potentially contest government or corporate authority, or as communities (Butsch & Livingstone, 2013; Carpentier, 2011; Harindranath, 2009; Livingstone, 2005). This macro level is the same turf as political economy, thus presenting a possible convergence. It situates audiences in a larger framework where they are positioned vis-à-vis the centralized power of hegemony and domination.

Additionally, three new areas of research have begun to explore links between production, text, and consumption, connecting our knowledge of media industries, texts, and audiences: (1) cultural production studies, (2) global media studies, and (3) discourse studies. These show promise for further convergence of our understanding of active audiences with that of media monopoly's influence over audiences.

Critiques of cultural imperialism and media monopoly (Bagdikian, 2000; Baker, 2007; Schiller, 1976) have presumed that concentration of cultural production truncates the range of ideas to those that are consistent with the interests of power elites. However, research demonstrating how this actually happens, whether by conspiracy or by structural constraints, has been sparse. Yet we need such research to demonstrate not "short-term" effects of a single text, as might happen in the wake of a conspiracy, but "long-term" effects of organizational structures producing a steady stream of similarly themed texts that may shape the culture and widespread values and beliefs.

Earlier American sociological research linked production organization and process to specific cultural content (Tuchman, 1988). Studies of the production of news demonstrated how objectivism, dependence on sources, and time constraints resulted in much news composed of prearranged "routine events" (Molotch & Lester, 1974). Peterson and Berger (1975) explained how record industry oligopoly constrained the range of commercial recorded music. A new generation of cultural production studies (Hesmondhalgh, 2006; Holt & Perren, 2009; Mayer, Banks, & Caldwell, 2009) has wedded this older American research to cultural studies to reveal organizational processes by which outcomes grow as resolutions of strains and resistances within

organizations. For example, Laura Grindstaff (2002) demonstrated how the reality show format produced an emphasis on manipulating participants into the emotional labor of the "money shot," and constructed a differential characterization of social class in the process. However, production studies linking the production process to the resulting texts remain sparse. Hesmondhalgh (2006) explains the importance of this link. Butsch (1989; Chapter VII.52 in this volume) has welded together insights of multiple studies of production processes for American domestic situation comedies to explain how these resulted in specific content about social class.

Global media studies has forged a connection between industry studies and audience studies, partly through the experience of actual global companies (Volkmer, 2012). The concept of "glocal" has been used to describe the failure of global media to reach cross-culturally to disparate audiences and the strategies by global corporations such as STAR TV to resolve this by revising production and distribution to tailor content to local cultures and audiences (Chadha & Kavoori, 2000).

Another new approach has examined hegemonic discourses about audiences that reveal institutional goals in relation to the social control of populations. One such example is Livingstone and Lunt (2011), on the "implied audience" in regulation. Looking at British regulation, they find a remarkably consistent framing of audiences as consumers, to the neglect of audiences as citizens. This seems a good example of corporate efforts to incorporate audiences into a hegemonic structure of consumption (bread and circuses) and to distract them away from their role as citizens. U.S. regulation took a similar path in abandoning the trustee model (also the basis of the BBC) to make good citizens in favor of a market model based on audiences as consumers buying the media they prefer. Butsch (2008) finds that American elite discourses over two centuries judged audiences against standards of good citizenship. Butsch and Livingstone (2013) compare such discourses about audience across diverse cultures and governing structures around the world.

In sum, we now have ways to understand audiences and industries that interweave audience and production studies; so we are moving toward a more holistic picture of production, texts, and reception.

REFERENCES

Bagdikian, B. (2000). *Media monopoly* (6th ed.). Boston: Beacon Press.

Baker, C. E. (2007). *Media concentration and democracy: Why ownership matters*. Cambridge, UK: Cambridge University Press.

Berlan, J. P. (1989). The commodification of life. *Monthly Review, 41*, 24–30.

Boyer, P. (1978). *Urban masses and moral order in America, 1820–1920*. Cambridge, MA: Harvard University Press.

Braverman, H. (1974). *Labor and monopoly capital*. New York: Monthly Review Press.

Butsch, R. (1989). How does it happen: The television industry, the production process, and images of class. In L. Chorbajian (Ed.), *Introduction to critical sociology* (pp. 25–34). Boston: Ginn.

Butsch, R. (2000). *The making of American audiences*. Cambridge, UK: Cambridge University Press.

Butsch, R. (2008). *The citizen audience: Crowds, publics, and individuals*. London: Routledge.

Butsch, R., & Livingstone, S. (2013). *Meanings of audiences*. London: Routledge.

Carpentier, N. (2011). New configurations of the audience? In V. Nightingale (Ed.), *Handbook of media audiences* (pp. 190–212). Malden, MA: Wiley Blackwell.

Castile, G. P. (1996). The commodification of Indian identity. *American Anthropology, 98*(4), 743–749.

Chadha, K., & Kavoori, A. (2000). Media imperialism revisited: Some findings from the Asian case. *Media Culture Society, 22*(4), 415–432.

Clarke, J. (1990). Pessimism versus populism: The problematic politics of popular culture. In R. Butsch (Ed.), *For fun and profit: The transformation of leisure into consumption* (pp. 28–44). Philadelphia: Temple University Press.

de Certeau, M. (1984). *The practice of everyday life* (S. Rendall, Trans.). Berkeley: University of California Press.

Frank, T. (1997). *The conquest of cool: Business culture, counterculture and the rise of hip consumerism*. Chicago: University of Chicago Press.

Giner, S. (1976). *Mass society*. New York: Academic Press.

Gordon, E., & de Sousa e Silva, A. (2011). *Net locality: Why location matters in a networked World*. Malden, MA: Wiley Blackwell.

Grindstaff, L. (2002). *The money shot: Trash, class, and the making of TV talk shows*. Chicago: University of Chicago Press.

Grossberg, L. (1995). Cultural studies vs. political economy. *Critical Studies in Mass Communication, 12*(1), 72–81.

Hall, S. (1980). Encoding/decoding. In S. Hall, D. Hobson, A. Lowe, & P. Willis (Eds.), *Culture, media, language: Working papers in cultural studies, 1972–79* (pp. 128–138). London: Hutchinson.

Hall, S. (1981). Notes on deconstructing "the popular." In R. Samuels (Ed.), *People's history and socialist theory* (pp. 227–240). London: Routledge & Kegan Paul.

Hall, S. (1994). Reflections upon the encoding/decoding model: An interview with Stuart Hall. In J. Cruz & J. Lewis (Eds.), *Viewing, reading, listening: Audiences and cultural reception* (pp. 253–274). Boulder, CO: Westview Press.

Hall, S., Critcher, C., Jefferson, T., Clarke, J., & Roberts, B. (1978). *Policing the crisis: Mugging, the state, and law and order*. London: Macmillan.

Hall, S., & Jefferson, T. (1976). *Resistance through rituals: Youth subcultures in post-war Britain*. London: Hutchinson.

Harindranath, R. (2009). *Audience-citizens: The media, public knowledge, and interpretive practice*. New Delhi: Sage.

Hebdige, D. (1979). *Subculture: The meaning of style*. London: Methuen.

Hesmondhalgh, D. (2006). Media organizations and media texts. In D. Hesmondhalgh (Ed.), *Media production*. Berkshire, UK: Open University Press.

Holt, J., & Perren, A. (Eds.). (2009). *Media industries: History, theory and method*. Malden, MA: Wiley Blackwell.

Huyssen, A. (1986). *After the great divide: Modernism, mass culture, postmodernism.* Bloomington: Indiana University Press.

Jay, M. (1973). *The dialectical imagination: A history of the Frankfurt School.* Boston: Little, Brown.

Johnson, R. (1981). Against absolutism. In R. Samuels (Ed.), *People's history and socialist theory* (pp. 386–396). London: Routledge & Kegan Paul.

Kornhauser, W. (1959). *The politics of mass society.* New York: Free Press.

Lee, D. O. (1992). Commodification of ethnicity. *Urban Affairs Quarterly, 28,* 258–275.

Lefebvre, H. (1971). *Everyday life in the modern world.* New York: Harper.

Lewis, J., & Jhally, S. (1994). The politics of cultural studies; and Gray, H. Response. *American Quarterly, 46*(1), 114–121.

Li, V. (1993). Selling modernism: Resisting commodification, commodifying resistance. *English Studies in Canada, 19*(1), 35–44.

Livingstone, S. (Ed.). (2005). *Audiences and publics.* Bristol: Intellect Press.

Livingstone, S., & Lunt, P. (2011). The implied audience of communication policy making. In V. Nightingale (Ed.), *Handbook of media audiences* (pp. 169–189). Malden, MA: Wiley Blackwell.

Loader, I. (1999). Consumer culture and the commodification of policing and security. *Sociology, 33*(2), 373–392.

Lull, J. (1990). *Inside family viewing: Ethnographic research on television's audiences.* London: Routledge.

Mayer, V., Banks, M., & Caldwell, J. (Eds.). (2009). *Production studies: Cultural studies of media industries.* Abingdon, UK: Routledge.

McMullan, J. L. (1996). The new improved monied police. *British Journal of Criminology, 36,* 85–108.

Molnar, A. (1996). *Giving kids the business: The commercialization of America's schools.* Boulder, CO: Westview Press.

Molotch, H., & Lester, M. (1974). News as purposive behavior: On the strategic use of routine events, accidents, and scandals. *American Sociological Review, 39*(1), 101–112.

Morley, D. (1986). *Family television: Cultural power and domestic leisure.* London: Comedia.

Peterson, R. A., & Berger, D. (1975). Cycles in symbol production: The case of popular music. *American Sociological Review, 40*(2), 158–173.

Resnik, D. (1998). The commodification of human reproductive materials. *Journal of Medical Ethics, 24*(6), 388–393.

Richer, S. (1988). Fieldwork and the commodification of culture. *Canadian Review of Sociology and Anthropology, 25,* 406–420.

Rothman, B. K. (1987). Reproductive technology and the commodification of life. *Women and Health, 13* (1–2), 95–100.

Schiller, H. (1969). *Mass communications and American Empire.* New York: A. Kelley.

Schiller, H. (1976). *Communication and cultural domination.* White Plains, NY: International Arts and Science Press.

Silverstone, R. (1994). *Television and everyday life.* London: Routledge.

Swingewood, A. (1977). *The myth of mass culture.* Atlantic Highlands, NJ: Humanities Press.

Swinnerton, G. (1999). Recreation and conservation. In E. Jackson & T. Burton (Eds.), *Leisure studies: Prospects for the twenty-first century* (pp. 199–231). State College, PA: Venture.

Tuchman, G. (1988). Mass media institutions. In N. Smelser (Ed.), *Handbook of sociology* (pp. 601–626). Newbury Park, CA: Sage.

Volkmer, I. (2012). *The handbook of global media research.* Malden, MA: Wiley Blackwell.

Watkins, S. C. (1998). *Representing: Hip-hop culture and the production of Black cinema.* Chicago: University of Chicago Press.

Williams, R. (1973). Base and superstructure in Marxist cultural theory. *New Left Review, 82,* 3–16.

Williams, R. (1977). *Marxism and literature.* New York: Oxford University Press.

Williams, R. (1981). *Culture.* London: Fontana.

Williams, R. (1982). *Sociology of culture.* New York: Schocken Books.

Willis, P. (1977). *Learning to labor: How working class kids get working class jobs.* New York: Columbia University Press.

REPRESENTATIONS OF GENDER, RACE, AND CLASS

The chapters in this section apply many of the theoretical concepts discussed in Part I to the analysis of **gender** and sexuality, race, and class in media production, texts, and audience reception. This book contextualizes theory with an understanding of how media texts may either contribute to or undermine the social, cultural, economic, and political inequalities that persist in the twenty-first century. The linkage of media theory and politics is particularly important within cultural studies, which, as indicated in Part I, is concerned with the lived experience of economically and socially subordinate individuals and groups and with making visible the ways in which media may challenge or reinforce inequalities. Media are one of the primary institutions that socially construct our notions of gender, sexuality, race, and class.

What do we mean when we say that we view gender (and sexuality), race, and class as "social constructs"? To take this approach means to question the explanatory role of biology or "nature" in social arrangements and power imbalances. Instead, we shift our attention to the social, cultural, economic, and political forces that shape and reshape these conceptual categories over time and place. Many examples can be offered of the "instability" (changeable or shifting nature) of these concepts, which are dependent on both historical and cultural contexts that condition how we conceptualize difference. Take race, gender, and sexuality for example. Racial categories have mutated over the decades, as have norms of gender and sexuality, which also differ from culture to culture. The mutability of these concepts offers proof that biology and nature cannot fully explain differences among groups and individuals. Furthermore, we operate from the assumption that none of these socially constructed categories can be considered in isolation from one another. Thus, we advocate for an intersectional approach that recognizes that gender and sexuality, race, class, and other markers of difference all play equally powerful roles in shaping both power relations and our own senses of identity.

We begin this section with Wesley Morris's (II.10) reflections on recent cultural events that have challenged how we think about our own racial, gendered, and sexual identities. Morris writes: "Gender roles are merging. Races are being shed. In the last six years or so . . . we've been made to see how trans and bi and poly-ambi-omni we are" (p. 85). Looking at a wide range of recent news events and cultural texts, Morris challenges us to consider what identity means in the modern media age:

> For more than a decade, we've lived with personal technologies—video games and social-media platforms—that have helped us create alternate or auxiliary personae. We've also spent a dozen years in the daily grip of makeover shows, in which a team of experts transforms your personal style, your home, your body, your spouse. (p. 86)

Theory can provide us with ways to try and better understand changing cultural times. For example, critical race theory challenges many of our unexamined myths about race and power, and asks us to consider White supremacy not as an aberration but as a routine force of domination in modern society. Looking back, in the 1960s, 70s, and 80s, the civil rights movement, the Black power movement, and subsequent antiracist organizing and activism mobilized many vigorous campaigns focusing public attention on denigrating racial representations that buttressed an inequitable economic and political status quo. Academic fields such as Black studies, Africana studies, Latina/o studies, Asian American studies, and Native American studies developed important critiques of taken-for-granted but demeaning imagery originating from the "White imaginary" (the culturally dominant ideas, attitudes, and feelings about "race"). Building on this base, the 1990s saw the development of sophisticated studies in critical race theory and **postcolonial theory** that critiqued Western European and U.S. historical narratives of "progress," "civilization," and assimilation. In such narratives, the politically and culturally dominant (White, Eurocentric) group defined the terms and projected criminality, poor morals, lack of intelligence and sophistication, and a host of other demeaning characteristics upon the racial "Other"—whether African, Arab, Latina/o, East or South Asian, Pacific Islander, or indigenous (Native American). Such historical perspectives help us understand the role of "race" both within U.S. culture and globally.

Thanks to the political work undertaken by antiracist movements, as a society we have developed some awareness of the more overt racist images of the past. But as the late Stuart Hall, one of the key founders of British cultural studies, points out in the classic piece "The Whites of Their Eyes" (II.11), we still need to educate ourselves about "inferential racism," which he defines as

> those apparently naturalized representations of events and situations referring to race, whether "factual" or "fictional," which have racist premises and propositions inscribed in them as a set of unquestioned assumptions. (p. 91)

Hall's chapter provides an exemplary explanation of how ideology works to shape our perceptions of the world and other people. He also reminds us that while many overt racist representations may have faded, their traces still remain in movies, television shows, advertisements, and other forms of popular culture. Sometimes it may even seem that overt racist images also still persist in forms such as Native American sports mascots. In the introduction to his book *Redskins: Insult and Brand* (excerpted here), C. Richard King (II.12) discusses the continuing use of a racist slur and cartoon image by the National Football League (NFL) franchise based in America's capitol. King demonstrates the important social impact of representation when he says:

> The word has deep connections to the history of anti-Indian violence, marked by ethnic cleansing, dispossession, and displacement. It is a term of contempt and derision that targets indigenous people. As much a weapon as a word, then, it injures and excludes, denying history and humanity. Its lingering presence undermines the pursuit of equality, inclusion, and empowerment by American Indians. (p. 93)

The intransigence of both fans and ownership of the Washington professional football team, and their defensive deflection of criticism, exemplifies the slow and uneven nature of social change. Staying with professional sports, one of the most powerful forms of popular culture around the globe, we find another underlying assumption about race that has historical resonance in media representations—the myth of African American hypersexuality. This imputed hypersexuality has played a part in the creation of "otherness" and has historically legitimized acts of violence, such as the rape of Black women and the lynching of Black men.

Drawing on sports media coverage of tennis athletic stars Serena and Venus Williams, James McKay and Helen Johnson (II.13) contextualize what they call the "sexual grotesquerie" in these recent media texts, by placing them within a larger context of historic denigration of Black bodies by Europeans and

Euro-Americans. Acknowledging that "the exceptional performances of the Williams sisters have provoked complex and ambivalent narratives of qualified praise and grudging approval, as well as subtle and overt racism and sexism" (p. 101]), these scholars argue that contemporary socially constructed images of Black women need to be understood as linked to historically deep ideologies of Blacks as embodying a deviant sexuality.

Like McKay and Johnson, Rosemary Pennington's chapter (II.14) also utilizes an intersectional approach to cultural analysis that takes into account race, gender, and sexuality. Pennington draws on the late Edward Said's conceptualization of the theory of **Orientalism** in her examination of the popular music star Katy Perry, and, in particular, a music video that "reproduce[s] a centuries old discourse which frames the culture, people, and objects coming out of the East as things to be possessed, consumed, and tamed by those in the West (p. 107)." Orientalist representations grew out of Western imperialist policies toward Asia and the Middle East, first manifesting themselves in narrative accounts by European travelers and paintings by European artists. However, media critics like Pennington argue that Orientalist thinking persists in modern forms of media like movies and music videos that continue to frame the Middle East as an exotic and dangerous place peopled by savage, untrustworthy men and hypersexual women.

Raka Shome (II.15) next offers a compelling chapter that provides another example of underlying racist assumptions beneath "apparently naturalized representations" of gender, sexuality, and race. In her study of White femininity in the context of transnational "motherhood" narratives in popular culture, Shome points to a phenomenon that is "simultaneously gendered, racialized, and heterosexualized": the visual or narrative representation of the White woman "saving, rescuing, or adopting international children from underprivileged parts of the world" (p. 117). Analyzing many examples of this phenomenon (featuring celebrities like Princess Diana, Angelina Jolie, and Madonna), she shows that the media construction of heroic maternal **Whiteness** is dependent upon, and further reproduces, the denigration of women of color as mothers. As Shome writes,

> The white mother can only occupy the position of a "global mother" by erasing the non-white maternal body from visions of global domesticity. The white mother's **subject position** is thus ironically dependent on the necessary failure of the non-white native mother. (p. 121)

Femininity in its **hegemonic** form (White, domesticated, heterosexual) is a powerful ideological formation that, like race, seems "natural" until we begin to explore its historical evolution. As we discuss further in the introduction to Part V, challenges from feminist theory and queer theory and activism have changed the very meaning of the terms *gender* and *sexuality*. Where those categories were once thought of in fixed biological terms, many (if not most) scholars now understand that gender roles and sexual practices are social constructions whose meaning is always contextual and varies widely through time and across cultures and individuals.

While popular culture has, on some level, acknowledged that gender and sexual identities are more fluid than was once thought, and film and TV representations have become somewhat more diverse, Kay Siebler (II.16) shows that there is still a strong tendency to caricature and **stereotype,** and in general to "reinforce gender rigidity" (p. 127). This is especially the case with **transgender** people who, according to Siebler, "are reduced to very un-queer definitions of masculinity and femininity, maleness and femaleness" (p. 127). As she points out, in the context of commercial media products, "the presence of a traditionally marginalized group does not necessarily equate to advancement" (p. 127).

Siebler also looks at how members of the transgender community construct their own identities, often influenced by the resources commercial media and the Internet provide. She acknowledges "the digital world has opened up communities for transgender people where none have existed before. There is less isolation and perhaps less struggle because of the resources, social networks, and virtual communities provided on the Internet" (p. 131). At the same time, Siebler offers an important critique of the ways in which some of these virtual communities and forums "also serve to create a codified version of limited ways of being transgender. A transgender norm becomes established so that even transgender people are no longer queering gender . . . " (p. 131).

Our final category of analysis, social class, is unfortunately less well represented in media scholarship than gender, sexuality, and race. The comparative absence of class analysis in the scholarship reflects the fact that as a society we seem to be more attuned to unequal treatment based on race and gender than to economic inequality, and this in turn reflects the history of social movement activity in the twentieth and twenty-first centuries. A robust labor movement arose during the decades of the most intensive industrialization in the United States to challenge the absolute right of **capitalism** to exploit working people's labor, but corporate backlash, regressive politics, and a subsequent sharp decline in both union membership and labor movement visibility have been accompanied by a corresponding decline in the national conversation about the disruptive social effects of a highly unequal distribution of wealth. In 2010, the Occupy Wall Street movement briefly highlighted the alarmingly severe gap in wealth between the top 1% of Americans and everyone else, but as of this writing very little has changed in the national and international policies that advance increasing inequality. If anything, the election of Donald Trump in 2016, and his installation of corporate CEOs at the highest levels of government, represents a further retreat from the fight for equality.

Michael J. Lee and Leigh Moscowitz's chapter, "The 'Rich Bitch'" (II.17), offers an unusually strong discussion of the class dimensions of the reality TV series *Real Housewives of New York City (RHW-NYC)*, and one that also demonstrates the importance of considering the intersectional aspects of social identity too often discussed in isolation from one another. This chapter is also notable for its focus on the wealthy, rather than the poor, and for its insight into the use of affluent women as the target for a class-based hostility toward the rich that lies just below the surface of envy and admiration. As the authors write, "According to the logic of *RHW-NYC,* rich women, not rich men, spend frivolously, project false appearances, backstab, gossip, and leave their children's care to paid staff" (p. 134).

While Lee and Moscowitz point out that there is a "populist promise" underlying the sardonic portrait of the rich as unenviable "figures of scorn and pity," they see the promise as limited in part by the desired target audience of the show, labeled "affluencers" by the Bravo network itself. (This audience can enjoy judging the badly behaved super-wealthy, without having to reflect uneasily on their own material privilege.) Similarly problematic for Lee and Moscowitz is the fact that viewers of *RHW-NYC* are "invited to conclude that the rich are undeserving because these women violate traditional gender roles so flagrantly" (p. 142).

The above-mentioned 2016 presidential election also highlighted issues of race, gender, and class norms under threat. This is the concern of the last chapter in this section of the book, Jackson Katz's analysis of gendered political **discourse** on conservative talk radio, as best known through *The Rush Limbaugh Show,* and how this discourse helped paved the way for the Trump victory. In this newly updated essay, Katz looks closely at how during a period when "white men's unquestioned dominance in the family and workplace are in the process of a long-term decline," a media genre denying these changes provides listeners "with an alternate media universe where the old order of male dominance and white supremacy is still intact" (p. 146). Katz suggests that Limbaugh's critics have tended to miss the "gendered nature of Limbaugh and company's contempt for liberals," and he draws attention to right-wing media discourse giving Republicans credit for superior "manhood." In Katz's view,

> Embedded firmly within the talk radio hosts' scathing critique of liberalism is a barely suppressed well of anger at the progressive changes in the gender and sexual order over the past forty years and the concomitant displacement of traditional patriarchal power. (p. 149)

The issues related to gender, sexuality, race, and class ideology in media culture that have been highlighted here will be important to bear in mind throughout subsequent chapters, where a wide array of media cultural forms are examined in more depth, through our organization into thematic sections that we hope will be of interest.

10

THE YEAR WE OBSESSED OVER IDENTITY

Wesley Morris

2015's headlines and cultural events have confronted us with the malleability of racial, gender, sexual and reputational lines. Who do we think we are?

A few weeks ago, I sat in a movie theater and grinned. Anne Hathaway was in "The Intern," perched on a hotel bed in a hotel robe, eating from a can of overpriced nuts, having tea and freaking out. What would happen if she divorced her sweet, selfless stay-at-home dad of a husband? Would she ever meet anybody else? And if she didn't, she would have no one to be buried next to—she'd be single for all eternity. And weren't the problems in her marriage a direct result of her being a successful businesswoman—she was there but never quite present? "The Intern" is a Nancy Meyers movie, and these sorts of cute career-woman meltdowns are the Eddie Van Halen guitar solos of her romantic comedies.

But what's funny about that scene—what had me grinning—is the response of the person across the bed from Hathaway. After listening to her tearful rant, this person has had enough: Don't you dare blame yourself or your career! Actually, the interruption begins, "I hate to be the feminist, of the two of us. . . ." *Hate to be* because the person on the other side of the bed isn't Judy Greer or Brie Larson. It's not Meryl Streep or Susan Sarandon. It's someone not far from the last person who comes to mind when you think "soul-baring bestie." It's Robert freaking De Niro, portrayer of psychos, savages and grouches no more.

On that bed with Hathaway, as her 70-year-old intern, he's not Travis Bickle or the human wall of intolerance from those Focker movies. He's Lena Dunham. The attentiveness and stern feminism coming out of his mouth are where the comedy is. And while it's perfectly obvious what Meyers is doing to De Niro—girlfriending him—that doesn't make the overhaul any less effective. The whole movie is about the subtle and obvious

ways in which men have been overly sensitized and women made self-estranged through breadwinning. It's both a plaint against the present and a pining for the past, but also an acceptance that we are where we are.

And where are we? On one hand: in another of Nancy Meyers's bourgeois pornographies. On the other: in the midst of a great cultural identity migration. Gender roles are merging. Races are being shed. In the last six years or so, but especially in 2015, we've been made to see how trans and bi and poly-ambi-omni- we are. If Meyers is clued into this confusion, then you know it really has gone far, wide and middlebrow. We can see it in the instantly beloved hit "Transparent," about a family whose patriarch becomes a trans woman whose kids call her Moppa, or in the time we've spent this year in televised proximity to Caitlyn Jenner, or in the browning of America's white founding fathers in the Broadway musical "Hamilton," or in the proliferating clones that Tatiana Maslany plays on "Orphan Black," which mock the idea of a true or even original self, or in Amy Schumer's comedic feminism, which reconsiders gender confusion: Do uncouthness, detachment and promiscuity make her a slut, or a man?

We can see it in the recently departed half-hour sketch comedy "Key & Peele," which took race as a construct that could be reshuffled and remixed until it seemed to lose its meaning. The sitcom "Black-ish" likewise makes weekly farcical discourse out of how much black identity has warped—and how much it hasn't—over 50 years and across three generations. "Unbreakable Kimmy Schmidt" turns selfhood into a circus, introducing us to a lower-middle-class Native American teenager who eventually succeeds at becoming a rich white lady, and to other characters who try out new selves every 10 minutes, as if they're auditioning for "Snapchat: The Musical." Last month, Ryan Adams released a remake of Taylor Swift's album "1989," song for song, as a rock record that combines a male voice with a perspective that still sounds like a woman's, like Lindsey Buckingham trying on Stevie Nicks's clothes. Dancing on the fringes of mainstream pop are androgynous black men like Le1f, Stromae and Shamir.

What started this flux? For more than a decade, we've lived with personal technologies—video games and social-media platforms—that have helped us create alternate or auxiliary personae. We've also spent a dozen years in the daily grip of makeover shows, in which a team of experts transforms your personal style, your home, your body, your spouse. There are TV competitions for the best fashion design, body painting, drag queen. Some forms of cosmetic alteration have become perfectly normal, and there are shows for that, too. Our reinventions feel gleeful and liberating—and tied to an essentially American optimism. After centuries of women living alongside men, and of the races living adjacent to one another, even if only notionally, our rigidly enforced gender and racial lines are finally breaking down.

There's a sense of fluidity and permissiveness and a smashing of binaries. We're all becoming one another. Well, we are. And we're not.

In June, the story of a woman named Rachel Dolezal began its viral spread through the news. She had recently been appointed president of the local chapter of the N.A.A.C.P. in Spokane, Wash. She had been married to a black man, had two black sons and was, by most accounts, a black woman. Her white biological parents begged to differ. The ensuing scandal resurrected questions about the nature of identity—what compelled Dolezal to darken her skin, perm her hair and pass in reverse? She might not have been biologically black, but she seemed well past feeling spiritually white.

Some people called her "transracial." Others found insult in her masquerade, particularly when the country's attention was being drawn, day after day, to how dangerous it can be to have black skin. The identities of the black men and women killed by white police officers and civilians, under an assortment of violent circumstances, remain fixed.

But there was something oddly compelling about Dolezal, too. She represented—dementedly but also earnestly—a longing to transcend our historical past and racialized present. This is a country founded on independence and yet comfortable with racial domination, a country that has forever been trying to legislate the lines between whiteness and nonwhiteness, between borrowing and genocidal theft.

We've wanted to think we're better than a history we can't seem to stop repeating. Dolezal's unwavering certainty that she was black was a measure of how seriously she believed in integration: It was as if she had arrived in a future that hadn't yet caught up to her.

It wasn't so long ago that many Americans felt they were living in that future. Barack Obama's election was the dynamite that broke open the country. It was a moment. It was *the* moment. Obama was biological proof of some kind of progress—the product of an interracial relationship, the kind that was outlawed in some states as recently as 1967 but was normalized. He seemed to absolve us of original sin and take us past this stupid, dangerous race stuff. What if suddenly anything was possible? What if we could be and do whatever and whoever we wanted? In that moment, the country was changing. *We* were changing.

Before Obama ran for president, when we tended to talk about racial identity, we did so as the defense of a settlement. Black was understood to be black, nontransferably. Negro intellectuals—Ralph Ellison and Albert Murray and James Baldwin, for starters—debated strategies for equality and tolerance. Some of them asserted that to be black was also to be American, even if America begged to differ. For most of those many decades, blackness stood in opposition to whiteness, which folded its arms and said that was black people's problem. But Obama became everybody's problem. He was black. He was white. He was hope. He was apocalypse. And he brought a lot of anxiety into weird relief. We had never really had a white president until we had a black one.

This radical hope, triggered by Obama, ushered in a period of bi- and transracial art—art that probed the possibility that we really had transcended race, but also ridiculed this hope with an acid humor. During Obama's past year in office, those works of art have taken on an even darker, more troubled tone as we keep looking around and seeing how little has really changed.

When the Dolezal story broke, I was partway through Nell Zink's "Mislaid," one of the four new satirical novels of race I read this year—Jess Row's "Your Face in Mine," Paul Beatty's "The Sellout" and Mat Johnson's "Loving Day" were the others. (I also read Fran Ross's long-lost, recently reissued "Oreo.") But Zink's was the only one that felt like an energy reading of Dolezal. Zink's white heroine, Peggy, has run off with her daughter, Mireille, and decided to take the birth certificate of a dead black girl named Karen Brown and use it for Mireille, while changing her own name to Meg.

The next year, Karen was 4 years old going on 5 and still blond. Nonetheless registering her for first grade as a black 6-year-old was easy as pie.

Maybe you have to be from the South to get your head around blond black people. Virginia was settled before slavery began, and it was diverse. There were tawny black people with hazel eyes. Black people with auburn hair, skin like butter and eyes of deep blue-green. Blond, blue-eyed black people resembling a recent chairman of the N.A.A.C.P.

Zink's marveling description of what blackness looks like implies that it could welcome anyone. She draws a phenotypic loophole through which a sympathetic impostor or a straight-up cynic can pass.

Each of these books wrestles with the fact of race while trying to present it as mutable, constructed, obscuring. In Beatty's novel, a young black farmer in modern Los Angeles reluctantly takes on a vulgar former TV minstrel star as his slave.

Blackness, according to this book, is as much a scam as it is a cultural identity; the undercurrents of tragedy keep lapping at the harbor of farce. Row's novel is also a satire, but an eerily calm one in which a white man has "racial reassignment" surgery and becomes black. Row, who like Zink is white, takes guilt to an astounding allegorical extreme: The surest cure for white oppression is to eliminate whiteness.

Whatever else is going on with Dolezal psychologically, you can read into her proud reassignment a sense of shame.

But racial transgression works the other way too. "Hamilton" is a musical biography about the very white, very dead Alexander Hamilton, in which

most of the cast is "other," including Lin-Manuel Miranda, the show's Nuyorican creator and star. Some of its audacity stems from the baldness of its political project: In changing the races of the founding fathers from white to brown, it pushes back against the currents of racial appropriation. It also infuses the traditional melodies of the American musical with so many genres of hip-hop and R & B, sometimes in a single number, that the songs themselves become something new. Political debates are staged as rap battles. Daveed Diggs's Thomas Jefferson becomes the best good thing that never happened at the Source Awards. Artistically, Miranda has created a great night out. Racially, the show tags the entertainment industry status quo with color. It's obviously musical theater. But damn if it's not graffiti too.

Naturally, this new era has also agitated a segment of the populace that is determined to scrub the walls. That, presumably, is where Donald Trump comes in: as the presidential candidate for anyone freaked out by the idea of a show like "Hamilton." Trump is the pathogenic version of Obama, filling his supporters with hope based on a promise to rid the country of change. This incarnation of Trump appeared not long after Obama's election, determined to disprove the new president's American citizenship. On Trump's behalf, an entire wing of conservatism—the so-called birthers—devoted itself to the removal of a mask that Obama was never wearing. Part of Trump's appeal is his illusion of authenticity. His blustering candor has currency in a landscape of android candidates. Yet his magnetism resides in paranoia, the fear that since Obama's election ushered in this shifting, unstable climate of identity, the country has been falling apart.

It's a paranoia that pop culture captured first: In the last six years, Hollywood has provided a glut of disaster spectacles, armageddon scenarios and White House sackings. But the USA Network's "Mr. Robot," which ended its first season last month, might have gotten at that sense of social collapse best. Created by Sam Esmail, an Egyptian-American, the show pits technology against the economy and its unstable protagonist against himself. The plot concerns a group of anarchist hackers conspiring to topple a corporation; with it go the stability of world markets and everybody's financial debt. But it's also a mystery about the identity of its protagonist, a mentally ill, morphine-addicted hacker named Elliot. We think he's obeying the commands of the show's title character, the head of a hacktivist outfit, but it turns out that he has been commanding himself all along. Significant parts of this world are figments of his delusion. Elliot is at least two people. Some of the dark excitement of this show is that he might be even more.

"Mr. Robot" is worst-of-times TV, reflecting a mood of menacing instability. Over the course of its 10 episodes, almost no one was who they appeared to be. A straight married man seemed to think nothing of his sleeping with a gay work underling (and neither did his wife). A character who seemed, to my eyes at least, to be a transgender woman at some point appeared as a conventional man. Was that a coming out? A going in? Both? This isn't a show I watched for what was going to happen but for who people were going to turn into, or who they wanted to turn out to be. It's a show about the way your online profile can diverge from your real-life identity, yes, but also the way you can choose a self or a self can choose you.

There's also the choice to ignore the matter of identity—until, of course, it starts to aggravate your complacency. Not far into the flap over Dolezal, another alarming story took over the news, a story that challenged the myths white America tells itself about progress. This story was about Atticus Finch, the protagonist of Harper Lee's 1960 classic, "To Kill a Mockingbird." Atticus single-handedly fought racism in the fictitious Alabama town of Maycomb, and he became a window through which we could see a version of tolerance, someone holy enough to put on stained glass or money. But in "Go Set a Watchman," the sequel to "To Kill a Mockingbird," published in July, Atticus was given a scandalous status update: He had been aged into a racist.

I can't recall the last time the attitudes of a single fictional character led the national news. But there was bigoted old Atticus, on the front pages, being discussed on cable. One of the most iconic white antiracists had grown fond of white supremacy. It raised an uncomfortable question: If you had identified with the original Atticus Finch, did his Archie Bunkerization make a racist out of you too?

The public hand-wringing was a perverse refreshment because, even if only for a few days, it left white people dwelling on race as intensely as nonwhite people. This new Atticus was a betrayal of white liberal idealism, feeding a suspicion that that idealism was less than absolute—that it could suddenly, randomly turn against the people it purported to help.

It was almost as if Lee knew, in 1957, about the mood of the country in 2015—about the way a series of dead black men and women would further cleave apart the country; about the massacre of nine black churchgoers by a young white supremacist in a South Carolina church, and the ensuing debate over the Confederate flag; about the fear of inevitable, inexorable racial, gender and sexual evolution; about the perceived threats to straight-white-male primacy by Latino immigrants, proliferating Spanish, same-sex marriage, female bosses and a black president.

The yearning to transcend race keeps coming up against the bedrock cultural matter of separateness. But the tectonic plates of the culture keep pushing against one another with greater, earthquaking force. The best show in our era about that quake—about the instability of identity and the choosing of a self—has been "Key & Peele." For five seasons, in scores of sketches, two biracial men, Keegan-Michael Key and Jordan Peele, became different women and different men of different ethnicities, personalities and body types. They were two of the best actors on television, hailing from somewhere between the lawlessness of improv comedy and the high-impact emotionalism of Anna Deavere Smith's one-woman, zillion-character plays. "Key & Peele" granted nearly every caricature a soul.

The show started as a commentary on the hilarious absurdity of race, but it never fully escaped the pernicious reality of racism. The longer it ran, the more melancholy it became, the more it seethed. In the final episode, its anger caught up with its fancifulness and cheek, exploding in an old-timey musical number called "Negrotown," which opens with a black man (Key) being arrested by a white cop one night while walking down a dark alleyway. He says he's innocent of any wrongdoing and asks why he's being arrested, intensifying the cop's anger. Entering the police cruiser, he hits his head on the car door. Suddenly, a homeless man (Peele) arrives on the scene and offers to take the black guy off the cop's hands. The cop gratefully acquiesces.

Taking the disoriented man by the hand, the homeless guy leads him through an alley door. They find themselves on the threshold of a sunny neighborhood. The homeless guy is now dressed in a three-piece suit the color of pink grapefruit meat, and he begins to sing in a camped-up, zero-calorie Paul Robeson baritone about this new place, "where there ain't no pain, ain't no sorrow." Black people in bright clothes are dancing in the streets, singing in giddy verse about the special virtues of their town: You can get a cab to pick you up, have a loan application approved, even wear a hoodie without getting shot. Plus: "There's no stupid-ass white folks touching your hair or stealing your culture, claiming it's theirs."

But it's clear from the start that the "neighborhood" is a studio backlot, and the dancers are costumed in the colors of Skittles, and their dancing involves a lot of grinning and spinning and stretching out their arms—shuffling. Black freedom looks like a white 1940s Hollywood director's idea of it. At the end of the number, the dancers stand frozen with their arms raised in a black-power salute, as if waiting for someone to yell "cut." No one does.

The dream melts away, and we're back with the guy being arrested, passed out on the ground. The cop starts shoving him into the cruiser. "I thought I was going to Negrotown," he says.

"Oh, you are," the cop replies, as the piano riff from the song starts to play and the car drives off.

The show left us with a dream of Edenic self-containment as the key to black contentment—a stunning contradiction of all its previous sketches. It was a rebuke to both racial integration and ghettoization. It split me open. I cried with laughter at the joke of this obviously fake place as a kind of heaven. I cried with sadness, because if you're in Negrotown, you're also in a special ring of hell.

The bitterness of the sketch made me wonder if being black in America is the one identity that won't ever mutate. I'm someone who believes himself to have complete individual autonomy, someone who feels free. But I also know some of that autonomy is limited, illusory, conditional. I live knowing that whatever my blackness means to me can be at odds with what it means to certain white observers, at any moment. So I live with two identities: mine and others' perceptions of it. So much of blackness evolving has been limited to whiteness allowing it to evolve, without white people accepting that they are in the position of granting permission. *Allowing.* If that symbiotic dynamic is going to change, white people will need to become more conscious that they, too, can be perceived.

It could be that living with recycled conflict is part of the national DNA. Yet it's also in our natures to keep trying to change, to discover ourselves. In "Far From the Tree," Andrew Solomon's landmark 2012 book about parenting and how children differentiate themselves, he makes a distinction between vertical and horizontal identity. The former is defined by traits you share with your parents, through genes and norms; the latter is defined by traits and values you don't share with them, sometimes because of genetic mutation, sometimes through the choice of a different social world. The emotional tension in the book's scores of stories arises from the absence of love for or empathy toward someone with a pronounced or extreme horizontal identity—homosexuality or autism or severe disability. Solomon is writing about the struggle to overcome intolerance and estrangement, and to better understand disgust; about our comfort with fixed, established identity and our distress over its unfixed or unstable counterpart.

His insights about families apply to us as a country. We're a vertical nation moving horizontally. We're daring to erase the segregating boundaries, to obliterate oppressive institutions, to get over ourselves. Nancy Meyers knows it. Sam Esmail knows it. So, in his way, does Donald Trump. The transition should make us stronger—if it doesn't kill us first.

11

THE WHITES OF THEIR EYES

Racist Ideologies and the Media

Stuart Hall

We begin by defining some of the terms of the argument. 'Racism and the media' touches directly the problem of *ideology,* since the media's main sphere of operations is the production and transformation of ideologies. . . .

I am using the term ideology to refer to those images, concepts and premises which provide the frameworks through which we represent, interpret, understand and 'make sense' of some aspect of social existence. Language and ideology are not the same—since the same linguistic term ('democracy' for example, or 'freedom') can be deployed within different ideological discourses. But language, broadly conceived, is by definition the principal medium in which we find different ideological discourses elaborated.

Three important things need to be said about ideology in order to make what follows intelligible. First, ideologies do not consist of isolated and separate concepts, but in the articulation of different elements into a distinctive set or chain of meanings. In liberal ideology, 'freedom' is connected (articulated) with individualism and the free market; in socialist ideology, 'freedom' is a collective condition, dependent on, not counterposed to, 'equality of condition,' as it is in liberal ideology. The same concept is differently positioned within the logic of different ideological discourses. One of the ways in which ideological struggle takes place and ideologies are transformed is by articulating the elements differently, thereby producing a different meaning: breaking the chain in which they are currently fixed (e.g. 'democratic' = the 'Free' West) and establishing a new articulation (e.g. 'democratic' = deepening the democratic content of political life). This 'breaking of the chain' is not, of course, confined to the head: it takes place through social practice and political struggle.

Second, ideological statements are made by individuals: but ideologies are not the product of individual consciousness or intention. Rather we formulate our intentions *within ideology.* They pre-date individuals, and form part of the determinate social formations and conditions into which individuals are born. We have to 'speak through' the ideologies which are active in our society and which provide us with the means of 'making sense' of social relations and our place in them. The transformation of ideologies is thus a collective process and practice, not an individual one. Largely, the processes work *unconsciously,* rather than by conscious intention. Ideologies produce different forms of social consciousness, rather than being produced by them. They work most effectively when we are not aware that how we formulate and construct a statement about the world is underpinned by ideological premises; when our formations seem to be simply descriptive statements about how things are (i.e. must be), or of what we can 'take-for-granted.' 'Little boys like playing rough games; little girls, however, are full of sugar and spice' is predicated on a whole set of ideological premises, though it seems to be an aphorism which is grounded, not in how masculinity and femininity have been historically and culturally constructed in society, but in Nature itself. Ideologies tend to disappear from view into the taken-for-granted 'naturalized' world of common sense. Since (like gender) race appears to be 'given' by Nature, racism is one of the most profoundly 'naturalized' of existing ideologies.

Third, ideologies 'work' by constructing for their subjects (individual and collective) positions

Extract from *Silver Linings: Some Strategies for the Eighties* (George Bridges and Ros Brunt, eds.), Lawrence & Wishart, 1981, "The Whites of Their Eyes: Racist Ideologies and the Media," by Stuart Hall, pp. 28–52.

of identification and knowledge which allow them to 'utter' ideological truths as if they were their authentic authors. This is not because they emanate from our innermost, authentic and unified experience, but because we find ourselves mirrored in the positions at the centre of the discourses from which the statements we formulate 'make sense.' Thus the same 'subjects' (e.g. economic classes or ethnic groups) can be differently constructed in different ideologies. . . .

Let us look, then, a little more closely at the apparatuses which generate and circulate ideologies. In modern societies, the different media are especially important sites for the production, reproduction and transformation of ideologies. Ideologies are of course, worked on in many places in society, and not only in the head. The fact of unemployment is, among other things, an extremely effective ideological instrument for converting or constraining workers to moderate their wage claims. But institutions like the media are peculiarly central to the matter since they are, by definition, part of the dominant means of *ideological* production. What they 'produce' is, precisely, representations of the social world, images, descriptions, explanations and frames for understanding how the world is and why it works as it is said and shown to work. And, amongst other kinds of ideological labour, the media construct for us a definition of what *race* is, what meaning the imagery of race carries, and what the 'problem of race' is understood to be. They help to classify out the world in terms of the categories of race.

The media are not only a powerful source of ideas about race. They are also one place where these ideas are articulated, worked on, transformed and elaborated. We have said 'ideas' and 'ideologies' in the plural. For it would be wrong and misleading to see the media as uniformly and conspiratorially harnessed to a single, racist conception of the world. Liberal and humane ideas about 'good relations' between the races, based on open-mindedness and tolerance, operate inside the world of the media. . . .

It would be simple and convenient if all the media were simply the ventriloquists of a unified and racist 'ruling class' conception of the world. But neither a unifiedly conspiratorial media nor indeed a unified racist 'ruling class' exists in anything like that simple way. I don't insist on complexity for its own sake. But if critics of the media

subscribe to too simple or reductive a view of their operations, this inevitably lacks credibility and weakens the case they are making because the theories and critiques don't square with reality. . . .

Another important distinction is between what we might call 'overt' racism and 'inferential' racism. By *overt* racism, I mean those many occasions when open and favourable coverage is given to arguments, positions and spokespersons who are in the business of elaborating an openly racist argument or advancing a racist policy or view.

By *inferential* racism I mean those apparently naturalized representations of events and situations relating to race, whether 'factual' or 'fictional,' which have racist premises and propositions inscribed in them as a set of *unquestioned assumptions*. These enable racist statements to be formulated without ever bringing into awareness the racist predicates on which the statements are grounded. . . .

An example of *inferential* racist ideology is the sort of television programme which deals with some 'problem' in race relations. It is probably made by a good and honest liberal broadcaster, who hopes to do some good in the world for 'race relations' and who maintains a scrupulous balance and neutrality when questioning people interviewed for the programme. The programme will end with a homily on how, if only the 'extremists' on *either side* would go away, 'normal blacks and whites' would be better able to get on with learning to live in harmony together. Yet every word and image of such programmes are impregnated with unconscious racism because they are all predicated on the unstated and unrecognized assumption that the *blacks* are the *source of the problem*. Yet virtually the whole of 'social problem' television about race and immigration—often made, no doubt, by well intentioned and liberal minded broadcasters—is precisely predicated on racist premises of this kind. . . .

Recent critics of imperialism have argued that, if we simply extend our definition of nineteenth century fiction from one branch of 'serious fiction' to embrace popular literature, we will find a second, powerful strand of the English literary imagination to set beside the *domestic* novel: the male-dominated world of imperial adventure which takes *empire,* rather than *Middlemarch* as its microcosm. I remember a graduate student, working on the construction of race in popular literature and culture at the end of the Nineteenth Century, coming to me in despair—racism was so *ubiquitous,* and at the same time, so *unconscious*—simply assumed to be the case—that it was impossible to get any critical purchase on it. In this period, the very idea of *adventure* became synonymous with the demonstration of the moral, social and physical mastery of the colonizers over the colonized.

Later, this concept of 'adventure'—one of the principal categories of modern *entertainment*—moved straight off the printed page into the literature of crime and espionage, children's books, the great Hollywood extravaganzas and comics. There, with recurring persistence, they still remain. Many of these older versions have had their edge somewhat blunted by time. They have been distanced from us, apparently, by our superior wisdom and liberalism. But they still reappear on the television screen, especially in the form of 'old movies' (some 'old movies,' of course, continue to be made). But we can grasp their recurring resonance better if we identify some of the base image of the 'grammar of race.'

There is, for example, the familiar *slave-figure:* dependable, loving in a simple, childlike way—the devoted 'Mammy' with the rolling eyes, or the faithful field-hand or retainer, attached and devoted to 'his' Master. The best known extravaganza of all—*Gone With the Wind*—contains rich variants of both. The 'slave-figure' is by no means limited to films and programmes *about* slavery. Some 'Injuns' and many Asians have come on to the screen in this disguise. A deep and unconscious ambivalence pervades this stereotype. Devoted and childlike, the 'slave' is also unreliable, unpredictable and undependable—capable of 'turning nasty,' or of plotting in a treacherous way, secretive, cunning, cut-throat once his or her Master's or Mistress's back is turned: and inexplicably given to running away into the bush at the slightest opportunity. The whites can never be sure that this childish simpleton—'Sambo'—is not mocking his master's white manners behind his hand, even when giving an exaggerated caricature of white refinement.

Another base-image is that of the 'native.' The good side of this figure is portrayed in a certain primitive nobility and simple dignity. The bad side is portrayed in terms of cheating and cunning, and, further out, savagery and barbarism. Popular culture is still full today of countless savage and restless 'natives,' and soundtracks constantly repeat the threatening sound of drumming in the night, the hint of primitive rites and cults. Cannibals, whirling dervishes, Indian tribesmen, garishly got up, are constantly threatening to overrun the screen. They are likely to appear at any moment out of the darkness to decapitate the beautiful heroine, kidnap the children, burn the encampment or threaten to boil, cook and eat the innocent explorer or colonial administrator and his lady-wife. These 'natives' always move as an anonymous collective mass—in tribes or hordes. And against them is always counterposed the isolated white figure, alone 'out there,' confronting his Destiny or shouldering his Burden in the 'heart of darkness,' displaying coolness under fire and an unshakeable authority—exerting mastery over the rebellious natives or quelling the threatened uprising with a single glance of his steel-blue eyes.

A third variant is that of the 'clown' or 'entertainer.' This captures the 'innate' humour, as well as the physical grace of the licensed entertainer—putting on a show for The Others. It is never quite clear whether we are laughing with or at this figure: admiring the physical and rhythmic grace, the open expressivity and emotionality of the 'entertainer,' or put off by the 'clown's' stupidity.

One noticeable fact about all these images is their deep *ambivalence*—the double vision of the white eye through which they are seen. The primitive nobility of the ageing tribesman or chief, and the native's rhythmic grace always contain both a nostalgia for an innocence lost forever to the civilized, and the threat of civilization being over-run or undermined by the recurrence of savagery, which is always lurking just below the surface; or by an untutored sexuality, threatening to 'break out.' Both are aspects—the good and the bad sides—of *primitivism.* In these images, 'primitivism' is defined by the fixed proximity of such people to Nature.

Is all this so far away as we sometimes suppose from the representations of race which fill the screens today? These *particular* versions may have faded. But their *traces* are still to be observed, reworked in many of the modern and up-dated images. And though they may appear to carry a different meaning, they are often still constructed on a very ancient grammar.

12 REDSKINS
Insult and Brand
C. Richard King

*R*edskin is a problem. It is an outdated reference to an American Indian. It is best regarded as a racial slur on par with other denigrating terms. In fact, while similar terms have been crossed out of our collective vocabulary as inappropriate and offensive . . . it still finds use. Most visibly, it remains the moniker of the Washington professional football team, long anchoring its brand and traditions. This should unsettle us. The word has deep connections to the history of anti-Indian violence, marked by ethnic cleansing, dispossession, and displacement. It is a term of contempt and derision that targets indigenous people. As much a weapon as a word, then, it injures and excludes, denying history and humanity. Its lingering presence undermines the pursuit of equality, inclusion, and empowerment by American Indians. Indeed, this continued use of a racial slur as the name of a professional sports team, the ongoing defense of it, and the willingness of the franchise, the National Football League (NFL), and their media partners to profit from it pose an even more troubling set of problems.

Sportscaster Bob Costas seemed to recognize as much when in October 2013, during halftime of the Sunday Night Football game between Dallas and Washington, he offered a sharply worded critique of the latter's team name, describing it as a "slur" and an "insult."[1] In denouncing the continued use of the moniker, he followed a growing number of high-profile journalists, from Peter King and Bill Simmons to Christine Brennan and Dave Zirin. At the same time, he joined media figures, including Howard Stern, Matthew Berry, and John Oliver, and athletes, like Billy Mills, Mike Tyson, and Martina Navratilova, who have all publicly spoken out against the name.[2] And in the subsequent NFL season, use of the team name declined by 27 percent, as sportscasters "deferred to 'Washington' more often."[3] Costas's comments, moreover, echoed the long-standing position of the National Congress of American Indians (NCAI) and nearly a dozen tribes. And they found support in positions taken by a number of professional organizations, including the American Studies Association, the American Sociological Association, and the Organization of American Historians; religious groups; and news outlets, like *Mother Jones,* the *Seattle Times,* and the *Washington City Paper.*[4] Even Larry Dolan, owner of the Cleveland Indians, infamous for its continued use of the caricature Chief Wahoo, has remarked, "If we were the Redskins, the day after I owned the team, the name would have been changed."[5]

These changing attitudes coincide with a recent ruling in *Blackhorse et al. v. Pro Football, Inc.,* which stripped the team of several of its trademarks (and was upheld by a federal court in the first round of appeals). They unfold alongside, if not in direct response to, Change the Mascot, a well-orchestrated campaign spearheaded by the National Congress of American Indians and the Oneida Nation, and a growing grassroots movement, armed with social media. The shifts in public opinion, moreover, find resonance in recent calls for action from members of the U.S. Congress, including fifty U.S. senators who demanded change in a letter to the organization, in President Obama's statement that he would think about changing the team name, and in efforts by the Obama administration to block the building of new stadium in the District of Columbia so long as the franchise has its current moniker. Some seventy years after its inception, the name makes many people uncomfortable. Some, in fact, are so uneasy, they have resolved not to use it. These individual epiphanies, actions, and condemnations together direct attention to a shift around popular understandings of racial images, ideas, and identities. While all of these actions were undoubtedly fomented by a broader movement within Indian Country intent on reclaiming dignity, sovereignty, and humanity, in part by bringing stereotypes like mascots to an end, Costas did not highlight these unsettling politics. Instead, he anchored his critique in the seemingly settled truths found in dictionaries, where the word is defined as an offensive, antiquated, and insulting reference to an American Indian.

As a scholar who has written about the history and significance of Native American mascots for more than two decades, I have long known the franchise to exemplify the practices associated with playing Indian in athletics, offering some of the most vivid and troubling examples of popular uses and understandings of American Indians.[6] Among the most prominent and profitable in sport, the organization since its inception has offered insights into the privileges and pleasures associated with taking and remaking Indianness. This alone would merit study and reflection, but in recent years, something even more significant has begun to unfold. Recent events suggest to me that we have reached something of a critical juncture, which makes this an especially opportune moment to reflect on the past, present, and possible futures of the Washington professional football team.

Perhaps most obviously, a dynamic, multifaceted opposition has converged around the moniker and logo. While far from united, this critical mass has its roots in Indian Country and has important connections to broader struggles for self-determination and decolonization. Unprecedented in size, scope, and diversity, it has made the once-unremarkable, and often-celebrated, team and its traditions the subject of debate, rendering them increasingly indefensible. In doing so, it has actively challenged anti-Indian racism, while pushing to restore dignity and humanity to indigenous people.

The ongoing debate, moreover, has fostered a shifting defense of the organization and its use of American Indians, which has appealed to and exposed the complex contours of racial politics and cultural identity today. Much of the defense casts the franchise and fans in a positive light, stressing that they have good intentions and mean to convey honor with the moniker, logo, and associated practices. And more, it has stressed indigenous support, highlighting the importance of public opinion polls as well as endorsements of the team by prominent individuals and reservation communities. Importantly, the defense is about more than Indianness. In particular, it turns in spoken and unspoken ways on whiteness. On the one hand, it invokes the attachments and sentimentality of white fans to legitimate the team and its traditions. On the other hand, it derives from and defends a series of entitlements or prerogatives anchoring a long history of owning Indians and Indianness in U.S. settler society.

Current events also focus our understanding of the past. They provide much-needed critical distance to assess the creation of the brand and its broader significance. That the team would have settled on its name unselfconsciously underscores how deep the entitlement and attachment to things "Indian" were at the time and how deeply embedded anti-Indian racism was in American public culture. It was, not to overstate things, a paradoxical love of imagined Indians and a loathing of actual, embodied Indians that continues to this day. Not surprisingly, the franchise, in common with other sports teams, Hollywood films, and commercial culture generally, traded in stereotypical renderings of Native Americans that, like the moniker, distorted and dehumanized them. To fans, journalists, and owners alike, the logo, fight song, and marching band all were in good fun. And while they meant no harm, a point many make today, these traditions create hostile environments that do in fact harm. Then, as now, such images and attitudes encouraged a kind of thoughtlessness. Such thoughtlessness allowed people to take the team and its traditions for granted without the burdens of history or introspection.

Finally, the critical juncture produced by recent events may be the beginning of the end. It is certainly a moment of change, a moment when countless people call for the team to change, when individuals create new team names and logos, and when many others imagine a time after the current moniker and mascot have been changed. Of course, this moment of change and what it has brought into being are about much more than the brand, its use of a slur, or even the intransigence of the current owner. The issue is about dignity and respect, combating anti-Indian racism while furthering self-determination and decolonization. As such, when the name changes, for that action to be of lasting and meaningful importance, it must be paired with deeper transformations, including education, coming to terms with the past, and expressing honor for indigenous people by honoring treaties made with native nations.

The critical juncture . . . has been marked by public condemnations of the team and calls for change, which have heightened public awareness of the word and its origins. Recent events likely played a key role in the increase in online searches. In 2014 Dictionary.com dubbed the team name, along with *caliphate, Ebola,* and *sociopath,* one of its eleven trending words.[7] Growing interest and increased attention, moreover, may explain why Americans generally remain supportive of the franchise but have growing unease about the word. A recent survey, for instance, found that 83 percent of Americans indicated they would not use the word in a conversation with a Native American.[8] One pizza restaurant in Washington DC learned how profoundly attitudes have shifted around the term. In fall 2014, when it ran a promotion, "Redskins score, You score," the reaction from its customers was so negative that it felt compelled to issue an apology less than six hours later. It read in part, "We are listening to all of your feedback. . . . We agree that the use of the name is wrong, offensive, and hurtful to all. In our future promotions and emails, we will make sure not to make the same mistake."[9]

Whatever the precise cause, the conservative columnist Charles Krauthammer rightly concludes that words and public usage of and attitudes toward them change:

> Fifty years ago the preferred, most respectful term for African Americans was Negro. The word appears 15 times in Martin Luther King's "I have a dream" speech. . . . The preferred term is now black or African American. With a rare few legacy exceptions, Negro carries an unmistakably patronizing and demeaning tone.

> If you were detailing the racial composition of Congress, you wouldn't say: "Well, to start with, there are 44 Negroes." . . . Similarly, regarding the further racial breakdown of Congress, you wouldn't say: "And by my count, there are two redskins." It's inconceivable, because no matter how the word was used 80 years ago, it carries invidious connotations today.[10]

For Krauthammer, like Costas and growing numbers of people, these changing sensibilities do not simply argue against use of the slur to describe an American Indian, they also argue against its continued use as a name for a professional football team.

Even as the past few years have witnessed an unparalleled push toward and increasing momentum for change, it would be wrong to conclude that concern with the team and its traditions is of recent origin or driven by forces outside of Indian Country. For more than four decades, American Indians and their allies have voiced their opposition. They have appealed to the ownership, held rallies and demonstrations at NFL games, and filed lawsuits to strip the team of its trademarks. They have created art, produced public service announcements, and formed organizations devoted to change. They have funded studies, launched protests on social media, and lodged complaints with governmental bodies, like the Federal Communications Commission. Through it all, they have worked to developed a diverse coalition within and beyond Indian Country and across cultural and racial lines in the nation's capital. These efforts have had noticeable impacts on public opinion. They have also prompted the franchise and the league to repeatedly respond to questions and criticism, secure support among indigenous people—often through questionable, if not fraudulent, means—and wage a series of public relations campaigns.

Even as Costas, Congress, and myriad others have called the team and its name into question, it has remained one of the most valuable franchises in professional sports. It has an easily recognizable and familiar brand, which is at once hugely popular and highly profitable. It is, according to *Forbes,* the third most valuable NFL franchise.[11] By way of comparison, in 2014 the Bureau of Indian Affairs had a total operating budget of $2.6 billion, while the team had a total value of $2.4 billion and total revenues of $395 million.[12] The franchise's ownership has bristled at the ongoing critique, suggesting that the team name is in fact quite positive, enjoying support from the majority of Americans and American Indians. Far from being an ethnic slur, the team has long asserted, its moniker conveys respect and honor. The franchise, moreover, has sought to reframe the controversy through a sophisticated promotional campaign rooted in focus groups, polls, and philanthropic initiatives. The National Football League, for its part, has actively defended the team, endorsed its interpretation of the name and its origins, and supported it in court. And even as more journalists and news outlets have spoken out against the team name, according to the *Washington Business Journal,* in an editorial ending its use of the moniker, "The vast majority of media outlets continue to use it. Our sister paper, the *Sports Business Journal,* reported last week that 44 of 48 major newspapers—those in cities with NFL teams along with the *Wall Street Journal, L.A. Times* and *USA Today*—still use the name."[13] Finally, fans largely have continued to support the team. Disappointing play has not diminished pride or attendance appreciably. And many are quite vocal in defense of the team and its traditions of social media. Nevertheless, merchandise sales, in a possible sign of things to come, were down 35 percent in 2014.[14] Despite this and in keeping with the general support of the organization, according to *Forbes,* the valuation and revenues for the team rose during the same period.[15]

The ongoing struggle lends itself to binary thinking, moral declarations, and public denunciations. To many, either the moniker is respectful or it is racist. It is a stereotype or not. Such arguments, whatever their merits, simplify the conflict and its cultural import. They discourage full understanding of the significance of the debate, competing claims, and key words. Indeed, the struggle over the team name, what it means, and why it matters raises important questions about popular perceptions of American Indians, the cultural life of brands, and existing obstacles to inclusion and equality. It also encourages deeper reflection on race and racism, the shifting contours of American attitudes and identities, and the possibilities and limitations of change in consumer society.

Some of these complexities find expression in the city that has long celebrated the franchise. Washington DC exemplifies racial politics in the United States. Built in part by slave labor, on land taken from native nations, the seat of American democracy was long marked by pronounced segregation and black-white racial tensions. For much of its first three decades in DC, the team played off these tensions, endeavoring to cast itself as the team of the South. Even as the city has changed, the centrality of race has not, and a rising Latino population has introduced a new dynamic that has complicated established assumptions. Economic and demographic shifts, moreover, have fostered a whitening of the urban core, increasingly pushing the poor and people of color to the margins. For all of this, on any given Sunday, residents of the metropolitan area form an imagined community united in shared identification with a team and becoming cultural citizens by exalting imaginary Indians. Even as they dress in feathers and sing the praises of their braves on the warpath, fans erase indigenous people. They make claims on and through images of them but disclaim their histories or continued relevance. In the process, they forget the past and its legacies. They forget about dispossession, displacement, and death. Few will remember that the team currently plays on the ancestral territory of the Piscataway Tribe or that the capital is built on the homelands of the Patawomeck Tribe. And even as they don its colors or sing its fight song, fewer still will acknowledge the ways in which a professional football team continues to profit from anti-Indian stereotypes and stories.

The creation, consumption, and contestation of the brand, then, have emerged and evolved in a context marked by the interplay of racisms. What the team means and how individuals and institutions make sense of it can be understood only in light of overlapping identities, ideologies, and exclusions. Perhaps most obviously, the moniker and logo reflect the force of anti-Indian racism to dehumanize and deny. As such, they underscore the importance and invisibility of U.S. settler society, particularly the ingrained prerogatives of taking and remaking land, culture, and identity, which actively contribute to the erasure and exclusion of indigenous people. At the same time, arguments around the team and its traditions also reveal the centrality of a model of black-white race relations for assessing the shape and significance of racism generally.

Of course, one cannot speak of settler colonialism, prevailing understandings of race and racism, or the team and its traditions without talking about the construction of whiteness. The assumptions, aspirations, and anxieties of Euro-Americans not only introduce Indianness into athletics in the form of mascots and monikers but anchor the ongoing defense of them as well. At root, this cultural complex, as embodied by the Washington professional football team, turns on owning Indians. The franchise has long regarded Indianness as a resource or raw material to exploit for pleasure and profit. The establishment of its brand depended on embellishments of pseudo-Indian motifs. In fact, over its first three decades, the organization elaborated on popular stereotypes and romantic images of American Indians to create a logo, rituals, marching band, cheer squad, and identity. Fans and the franchise alike have felt entitled to use Indians and Indianness as they have seen fit. Even as the franchise ownership has become uneasy with outside criticism of its name, the organization has fought to prop up the brand through philanthropy that some interpret as little more than bribery and fake instances of indigenous support for its racist image. Anxiety, along with entitlement, has shaped the origin, elaboration, and defense of the brand. Jennifer Guiliano has identified the historic anxieties that prompted the emergence of American Indian mascots. She has argued in particular that the changing shape and significance of white masculinities in the wake of modernity, urbanization, and industrialization gave rise to American Indian mascots and monikers like those associated with the Washington professional football team.[16]

Today a new set of anxieties paces the defense of the team and its traditions; specifically, it reflects the shape and significance of white masculinities in the wake of multiculturalism, feminism, and postindustrialization. Arguments for the team and its traditions, then, often hinge on other issues, circle around whites and whiteness, and display deep-seated resentments about a changing world as much as they purport to pay homage and convey respect. Thus, while it may be easy to see the team name as a slur, it is difficult, even for many critics, to recognize and respond to the ways that attachment, entitlement, identity, and anxiety shape the debate and stymie change. Ultimately, the name, the team, and the brand matter not just because they reference an offensive racial slur or profit on hurtful stereotypes. They have pressing significance because of how they encourage anti-Indian racism, reinforce white privilege, and perpetuate distorted understandings of people and the past. As Amanda Blackhorse, lead plaintiff in a current legal challenge, notes, "Native American people have been targeted for their race, their land, and their resources. So when the dominant culture believes they are superior to the indigenous population they will dehumanize and dominate us for their own good. This includes the dehumanization of our entire being, especially our identity."[17] Clearly part of a deeper history and larger struggle, the prerogative to imagine and exploit popular ideas about American Indians for pleasure and profit, as the franchise has long done, negatively affects indigenous people, belittling, disempowering, and marginalizing them on any given Sunday. For Blackhorse, this pattern raises two questions seldom asked: "Why have we not achieved true self-determination as indigenous people?" and "Why is it that in this day and age are we still fighting for common decency to be respected by our non-native counterparts?"[18]

Tracing the history of the team and studying the defense of its use of racial slur may be a first and necessarily partial step toward addressing these big questions. Such efforts offer an important opportunity to better comprehend the problem posed by *R*dskin* today, creating an important means of combating the ongoing dehumanization of indigenous people in the United States. Echoing Blackhorse, for the franchise and its fans, for the league and its media partners, for politicians and the public, the key challenge posed by the critique of the team and its traditions might be phrased as two overlapping questions: How do we stop the dehumanization of indigenous peoples? And how do we create new stories and spaces, reimagine self and society, and otherwise transform traditions to rehumanize them?

NOTES

1. Kogod, Sarah. "Bob Costas on Redskins Name: 'It's an Insult, a Slur.'" *Washington Post*, October 13, 2013. http://www.washingtonpost.com/blogs/dc-sports-bog/wp/2013/10/13/bob-costas-on-redskins-name-its-an-insult-a-slur/.

2. Anderson, Monica. "How Media Organizations Are Handling the Redskins Name." Pew Research Center, October 30, 2013. http://www.pewresearch.org/2013/10/30/how-media-organizations-are-handling-the-redskins-name/; Beaujon, Andrew. "Here's a List of Outlets and Journalists That Won't Use the Name 'Redskins.'" Poynter Mediawire, June 19, 2014. http://www.poynter.org/news/mediawire/256258/heres-a-list-of-outlets-and-journalists-who-wont-use-the-name-redskins/.

3. Burke, Timothy. "'Redskins' Mentions Down 27% on NFL Game Broadcasts in 2014." *Deadspin*, December 30, 2014. http://regressing.deadspin.com/redskins-mentions-down-27-on-nfl-game-broadcasts-in-1676147358.

4. Anderson, Monica. "How Media Organizations Are Handling the Redskins Name." Pew Research Center, October 30, 2013. http://www.pewresearch.org/2013/10/30/how-media-organizations-are-handling-the-redskins-name/; Beaujon, Andrew. "Here's a List of Outlets and Journalists That Won't Use the Name 'Redskins.'" Poynter Mediawire, June 19, 2014. http://www.poynter.org/news/mediawire/256258/heres-a-list-of-outlets-and-journalists-who-wont-use-the-name-redskins/; Keene, "Who Has Spoken Out?" On the ethics of using the name in news coverage, see Jensen, Robert. "Banning 'Redskins' from the Sports Page: The Ethics and Politics of Native American Nicknames." *Journal of Mass Media Ethics 9* (1994): 16–25; Lindsay, Peter. "Representing Redskins: The Ethics of Native American Team Names." *Journal of the Philosophy of Sport 35* (2008): 208–24.

5. Wulf, Steve. "Why Use of Native American Nicknames Is an Obvious Affront." ESPN, September 3, 2014. http://espn.go.com/espn/otl/story/_/id/11426021/why-native-american-nicknames-stir-controversy-sports.

6. On the team, see Coombe, Rosemary J. "Sports Trademarks and Somatic Politics: Locating the Law in Critical Cultural Studies." In *SportCult*, edited by R. Martin and T. Miller, 262–88. Minneapolis: University of Minnesota Press, 1999; Goddard, Yves. "'I Am a Red-Skin': The Adoption of a Native-American Expression (1769–1826)." *European Review of Native American Studies 19*, no. 2 (2005). http://anthropology.si.edu/goddard/redskin.pdf; Sigelman, Lee. "Hail to the Redskins? Public Reactions to a Racially Insensitive Team Name." *Sociology of Sport Journal 15* (1998): 317–25; Strong, Pauline Turner. "The Mascot Slot: Cultural Citizenship, Political Correctness, and Pseudo-Indian Sports Symbols." *Journal of Sport & Social Issues 28* (2004): 79–87; Waggoner, Linda M. "On Trial—The Washington R*dskins' Wily Mascot: Coach William Lone Star Dietz." Montana: *The Magazine of Western History 63*, no. 1 (Spring 2013): 24–47. http://nmai.si.edu/sites/1/files/pdf/seminars-symposia/WaggonerWEBSpr2013.pdf. Good introductions to the subject of American Indian mascots include Davis, Laurel R. "Protest against the Use of Native American Mascots: A Challenge to Traditional, American Identity." *Journal of Sport and Social Issues 17* (1993): 9–22; Guiliano, Jennifer. Indian Spectacle: College Mascots and the Anxiety of Modern America. New Brunswick NJ: Rutgers University Press, 2015; King, C. Richard. "Re/Claiming Indianness: Critical Perspectives on Native American Mascots." Special Issue, *Journal of Sport and Social Issues 28*, no. 1 (2004); King, C. Richard. *The Native American Mascot Controversy: A Handbook*. Lanham md: Scarecrow Press, 2011; King, C. Richard. *Unsettling America: Indianness in the Contemporary World*. Lanham MD: Rowman and Littlefield, 2013;

..... *Frontier, Masculinity, and Whiteness in Native American Mascot Representations.* Lanham MD: Rowman and Littlefield, 2014. Importantly, only Staurowsky deals exclusively with professional athletics, in her studies of the Cleveland Indians.

7. "11 Trending Words of 2014." Dictionary .com, December 18, 2014. http://blog .dictionary.com/trending-words-2014/.

8. Brady, Erik. "Poll: 83% Would Not Call Native American a 'Redskin.'" USA Today, November 20, 2014. http://www.usatoday .com/story/sports/nfl/redskins/2014/11/20/ washington-redskins-poll-name-controversy- daniel-snyder/19297429/.

9. Steinberg, Dan. "Pizza Chain Apologizes for Using 'Wrong, Offensive, and Hurtful' Redskins Name." Washington Post, September 19, 2014. http://www.washingtonpost.com/ blogs/dc-sports-bog/wp/2014/09/19/pizza- chain-apologizes-for-using-wrong-offensive- and-hurtful-redskins-name/.

10. Krauthammer, Charles. "Redskins and Reason." Washington Post, October 17, 2013. http://www.washingtonpost.com/ opinions/charles-krauthammer-redskins- and-reason/2013/10/17/cbb11eee-374f-11e3- ae46-e4248e75c8ea_story.html.

11. "Washington Redskins Valuation." Forbes, August 2014. http://www.forbes.com/teams/ washington-redskins/.

12. Odle, Mairin. "What's in a Name? On Sports Teams and Scalp Bounties." *Junto* (blog), December 22, 2014. http://earlyamericanists .com/2014/12/22/guest-post-whats-in- a-name-on-sports-teams-and-scalp- bounties/.

13. Fruehling, Douglas. "We Won't Use Redskins Anymore." *Washington Business Journal*, August 1, 2014. http://www .bizjournals.com/washington/print- edition/2014/08/01/we-won-t-use-redskins- anymore.html.

14. Ley, Tom. "Washington Merchandise Sales Are Down 35 Percent," *Deadspin*, September 5, 2014. http://deadspin.com/ washingtons-merchandise-sales-are-down- 35-percent-1631023843.

15. "Washington Redskins Valuation." Forbes, August 2014. http://www.forbes.com/teams/ washington-redskins/.

16. Guiliano, Jennifer. *Indian Spectacle: College Mascots and the Anxiety of Modern America.* New Brunswick NJ: Rutgers University Press, 2015.

17. Blackhorse, Amanda. "This Is What Dehumanization Looks Like." *Indian Country Today*, March 20, 2015. http:// indiancountrytodaymedianetwork .com/2015/03/20/blackhorse-what- dehumanization-looks-159694.

18. Ibid.

13

PORNOGRAPHIC EROTICISM AND SEXUAL GROTESQUERIE IN REPRESENTATIONS OF AFRICAN AMERICAN SPORTSWOMEN

James McKay and Helen Johnson

Go Back To The Cotten [sic] Plantation Nigger. (Banner in the stands when Althea Gibson walked on court to defend her US Open title in 1958)

That's the way to do it! Hit the net like any Negro would! (Racist male heckling Serena Williams before she served at the 2007 Sony Ericsson Championships in Miami)

In this paper we use sport to encourage 'white' people to deconstruct the privileged lens through which they construct and view 'black' people. More specifically, we analyse how sections of the media have framed tennis champions Serena and Venus Williams as threats to sport's racist and sexist regime. Like other sportswomen of colour, the Williams sisters have challenged racist and sexist stereotypes and inspired millions of females around the world (Hargreaves, 2000, 2007). However, given that Althea Gibson and Serena Williams were subjected to blatant racism at tennis tournaments nearly 50 years apart, we should not be sanguine about the social constraints that African American sportswomen still encounter. . . .

AFRICAN AMERICAN SPORTSWOMEN AS THREATS TO GENDER AND RACIAL HIERARCHIES

Rowe (1990, p. 409) argues that gender hierarchies are threatened whenever women's bodies are deemed to be excessive: 'too fat, too mouthy, too old, too dirty, too pregnant, too sexual (or not sexual enough) for the norms of conventional gender representation.' Following Schulze (1990, p. 198), we can add muscularity to this list of corporeal transgressions: '[t]he deliberately muscular woman

disturbs dominant notions of sex, gender, and sexuality, and any discursive field that includes her risks opening up a site of contest and conflict, anxiety and ambiguity.' While muscularity in women and men is becoming an increasingly desirable body type, it is, in the twenty-first century, hyper-muscularity in women that threatens heteronormative gender relations (Heywood & Dworkin, 2003). . . .

Hyper-muscularity as both a new social phenomenon and a denigrating stereotype is especially evident in sport, which has embodied in the past the 'natural' superiority of men in contrast to the 'otherness' of female athletes as objects of ridicule, weakness, inferiority, decoration, passivity and as erotically desirable yet transgressive, but which is now searching for new ways to disparage the powerful and therefore 'uppity' African American sportswomen. . . .

A common strategy of reasserting masculine hegemony in sport is via 'pornographic eroticism,' in which sexuality is constructed as the 'primary characteristic of the person represented' (Heywood, 1998). Heywood distinguishes 'pornographic eroticism' from 'athletic eroticism,' in which sexuality is 'one dimension of human experience, as a quality that emerges from the self-possession, autonomy, and strength so evident in the body of a female athlete.' Although Heywood refers to bodybuilding, examples of 'pornographic

From McKay, J., & Johnson, H. (2008). Pornographic eroticism and sexual grotesquerie in representations of African-American Sportswomen. *Social Identities, 14*(4), 491–504. Reprinted by permission of Taylor & Francis Ltd., www.tandf.co.uk/journals

eroticism' are prevalent in most sports (Glenny, 2006; Messner, Dunbar & Hunt, 2002; Messner, Duncan & Cooky, 2003).

While Heywood's concept of 'pornographic eroticism' is useful for explaining how female athletes in general are recuperated by the media, the negative coverage of the Williams sisters that we analyse below demonstrates that African American sportswomen also threaten racial hierarchies. Hence, we propose that the racialized anxieties that drive censorious responses to African American sportswomen are most effectively understood when situated within the historical context of black women's enslavement, colonial conquest, and exhibition as ethnographic 'grotesquerie.' The categorization of black women's bodies as hyper-muscular and their targeting for lascivious comment mirrors the public and pseudo-scientific response to nineteenth century exhibits of Saartjie Baartman, the South African woman labeled the 'Hottentot Venus' (Hobson, 2003, p. 87). Thus, we also use Hobson's concept of 'sexual grotesquerie,' which, in turn, was suggested by Morgan's (1997) analysis of European explorers' writings about Africa that depicted African women's bodies as mythic and monstrous. . . .

THE 'GHETTO CINDERELLAS'

On Tuesday the story was Maria Sharapova's Swan Lake dress. On Wednesday it was Tatiana Golovin's red knickers. Yesterday it was Venus Williams' hot pants. . . . [C]overage of men's tennis tends to focus on tennis. Not so the women's game, especially in the first week of a Grand Slam event when the lack of depth in the field means the opening rounds serve as a glorified warm-up for the 'big beasts.' (Moore 2007)

'Pornographic eroticism' is particularly prominent in media coverage of women's tennis, where many players' physiques and performances are the objects of a constant gaze and are monitored for 'excess' (Harris & Clayton, 2002; Kennedy, 2001; Miller, McKay & Martin, 1999; Stevenson, 2002). Anna Kournikova has been criticized for trading on her looks and displaying more style than substance; Amelie Mauresmo was reproached for being openly lesbian and having a strong body and powerful topspin backhand; former world number 1 Justine Henin is belittled for having a drab image, while Maria Sharapova

has been nicknamed 'The Glamazon,' to describe her combination of conventional good looks, statuesque physique, and powerful forehand (she also has been dubbed 'Shriekapova' and 'Belle of the Decibel' and censured for having a 'banshee-like grunt'); Daniela Hantuchova has been accused of being an anorexic, while Casey Dellacqua and Marion Bartoli have been condemned for allegedly being overweight. For instance, journalist Sue Mott (2007) described 2007 Wimbledon singles finalist Bartoli as 'more Friar Tuck than Maid Marion.'

Matthew Syed (2008) contends that

there has always been a soft-porn dimension to women's tennis, but with the progression of Maria Sharapova, Ana Ivanovic, Jelena Jankovic and Daniela Hantuchova to the semi-finals of the Australian Open, this has been into the realms of adolescent (and non-adolescent) male fantasy.

He complains that Western society has not 'reached a place where heterosexual men can acknowledge the occasionally erotic dimension of watching women's sport without being dismissed as deviant' thus articulating the unreflective, heterosexual, white male-centred viewpoint that is normative in mainstream media.

The Williams sisters also have been subjected to the carping critical gaze that both structures and is a key discursive theme of 'pornographic eroticism.' Of great significance, however, is that they also have been constructed by derogatory racial, sexual and class stereotypes associated with African Americans. . . .

Since 1999 the Williams sisters have dominated international women's tennis by winning 14 Grand Slam singles titles (Serena eight, Venus six), five women's doubles and four mixed doubles Grand Slam titles, and gold medals in singles (Venus) and women's doubles at the Olympics. The Williams sisters began playing sport early while living in Compton, an economically impoverished area of Los Angeles, before moving to Florida while young. Whereas many tennis prodigies attend private tennis academies, the Williams sisters trained under the unorthodox regime of their father, Richard, a sharecropper's son from Louisiana. Serena and Venus have become wealthy international sporting superstars and celebrities, with incomes estimated at over $US100 million from endorsement contracts with firms such as McDonald's, Nike, Wilson, Estée Lauder, and

Reebok. Thus, they have been constructed within a 'ghetto-to-glory' narrative: a journalist referred to their ascent as a 'fairy tale, that astonishing narrative of the "ghetto Cinderella"' (Adams, 2005); one described Venus as a former 'teenage curio from a Los Angeles ghetto' (Muscat, 2007); and another stated that, 'Only in America would Venus have risen from her cradle of crack dealers and grunge courts to contest the women's singles final at Wimbledon' (Mott, 2000). Patton (2001, p. 122) refers to these sorts of narratives as 'an Africanized version of the Horatio Alger story in which athletics provides a route out of the ghetto.'

The exceptional performances of the Williams sisters have provoked complex and ambivalent narratives of qualified praise and grudging approval, as well as subtle and overt racism and sexism (Douglas, 2002, 2005; Schultz, 2002; Spencer, 2001, 2004). Media coverage of the Williams sisters is not always negative, because their performances are too extraordinary to be completely denigrated. For instance, in the lead-up to the 2003 French Open, Serena appeared in an action shot on the cover of *Sports Illustrated* with the caption 'Awesome.' Journalist Will Buckley (2007, p. 15) compared the Williams sisters to male legends like Pele, Muhammad Ali, Roger Federer, Tiger Woods, and Jack Nicklaus, rating them as the 'greatest duo' in sporting history. However, such praise co-exists with both subtle and overt racism and sexism. The Williams sisters have been criticized for lacking 'commitment' by refusing to conform to the Spartan training regime of professional tennis, restricting their playing schedules, having too many 'off-court interests' in acting, music, product endorsements, fashion and interior design, and their Jehovah's Witness religion. They have been accused of fixing matches against one another, cheating, and engaging in unsporting behaviour. They have been called arrogant, aloof, and self-absorbed; indicted for putatively ostentatious lifestyles and wearing expensive jewelry while not assisting African Americans affected by Hurricane Katrina; and disparaged for competing while wearing beaded cornrows and/or tinted hairstyles and 'tacky' outfits. At the 2002 US Open Serena was condemned for wearing a black 'catsuit,' and in 2003 her appearance at a public function was disparaged as a 'hooker look' by *The Washington Post*'s fashion writer:

She wore an orange crochet hussy dress modeled after something that Wilma Flintstone might choose. The low-cut dress, with its embroidered bodice, had a hemline that looked like it had been gnawed by Dino. . . . Her admirers paint a picture of poise and exuberance, talent and physical grace. One only wishes that Williams would use her wealth and notoriety to paint herself in equally flattering terms. (PostWatch, 2002)

In an article about the 2007 Wimbledon tournament, entitled 'Street style gives Venus her deadly cutting edge,' Venus was compared poorly to her vanquished opponent Akiko Morigami:

Williams the elder is urban hip-hop, a swirling, whirling, street babe who believes tennis is a sport best played at full volume. . . . With Williams wearing an ill-fitting vest and hot-pants outfit that might have been plucked off the *Primark* bargain rail, Morigami, the ultimate in femininity, won the consolation fashion stakes in her broderie anglaise skirt and scalloped sleeved top. (Philip, 2007)

The title of another article about Wimbledon condensed many of the above points. Although Venus was portrayed in an 'action shot,' the title was, 'Williams has designs on title despite host of outside distractions.' Much of the material was devoted to suggesting that Venus had played in her underwear, to her preoccupation with her interior design company, to the gold handbag she brings courtside, and to her guitar-playing skill (Smith, 2007). While Serena and Venus have been described as the 'Sisters Sledgehammer' (Bierley, 2004) and as having an 'Amazonian physique and piranha mentality' (Mott, 2000), Daniela Hantuchova, in contrast, was portrayed as playing tennis 'with grace and artistry, words that appeared to have been all but crushed by the blitzkrieg that was Venus and Serena Williams' (Viner, 2007).

Such commentary has often been anchored by the stereotypes to which we have alluded of black people being constructed as animalistic and closer to nature. Following Venus' victory at Wimbledon in 2000, a journalist hailed her as a 'role model for blacks' and lamented that black people had not been given more opportunities to participate in sport, because 'there is a natural physical superiority about those of African origin . . . only centuries of repression has prevented them becoming masters of so many sports' (Miller, 2000). Serena was described as a 'cat woman' at the 2002 US Open (Schultz, 2002), and Venus' quarterfinal victory over Sharapova at Wimbledon in 2007 was headlined 'Dying swan devoured as giant bird of prey returns to SW19,' with Barnes (2007) writing that, 'The dying swan [Maria Sharapova] slunk out in her tutu, savaged to death by a giant bird of prey—a Californian condor, if you like.' Marion Bartoli's loss to Venus in the final was attributed to the 'immense hard luck that Venus can chase from side to side like a cheetah on the run' (Mott, 2007), and Venus was also depicted as 'a panther, sensing a wounded animal' (White, 2007).

The Williams sisters arrived at the 2006 Australian Open in the unusual situation of being ranked lowly due to injuries and long lay-offs. Their commitment, fitness, and weight were targeted even before competition began. In 'Aussie defeat is the bottom line for overweight Serena,' British journalist Alix Ramsay (2006) claimed that

Both Venus and Serena were unfit, unprepared and under-done as the Open began. . . . Swanning into Melbourne as only they can, the sisters were seen shopping and posing around town. They certainly acted the part of superstar athletes but they certainly did not look it. Serena, in particular, was patently overweight and pictures of her larger-than-life figure were splashed across every newspaper in the land. . . . Clearly the sisters, 'cross-over celebrities' both, are too busy to devote their time exclusively to tennis.

Journalists' fixation with Serena's diet, weight, fitness, and appearance then shifted into categories of 'pornographic eroticism' and 'sexual grotesquerie.' Her breasts and bottom were fetishized via headlines such as, 'Size up Serena Williams at your own risk' (Stevens, 2006), 'Serena out to kick butt' (Epstein, 2006), and 'Easybeat? Fat chance' (Crawford, 2006a), and photographs of her allegedly abnormal gluteal muscles and weight. When asked about her physical status, Serena commented that: 'Honestly, I've never read any comments about my fitness. I don't read the papers. I saw (a picture) of me running. And I was like, "Wow, my hamstring muscle is that big?" I had no idea my muscle was like that. But that's about it' (Epstein, 2006). One newspaper used the headline 'Serena Shocked by Pictures,' but selectively printed Serena's comment about her hamstring being large, thereby suggesting she was alarmed (Crawford, 2006b). In one of Australia's 'quality' newspapers, journalist Stephen Gibbs (2006) compared Serena with Maria Sharapova in his article 'Big bum rap for Serena.'

Serena Williams has this great big arse. Some tennis commentators seem able to ignore the urge to record that for posterity and instead have concentrated on her career. . . .

Righto. This is the spot for a sentence that starts: 'Before the letters of complaint come flooding in from the hairy-armpit brigade . . . ' This may or may not be interesting but, in fact, they never do. Those sentences are written for female colleagues and partners rather than letter-writing lesbians.

[But] Sharapova is a Russian glamour girl and can apparently play a bit, too. She is tanned, teenaged, firm of bottom and pert of breast. She has for some time been ranked No. 1 by the tennis world as the female player heterosexual males most want to up-end.

But that is not how they put it in the media, just as we don't say Serena Williams has a big arse.

. . . The authoritative discourse of 'science' was . . . used by a journalist, who consulted a sports medicine specialist about Serena's physique, and was advised that, 'It is the African-American race. They just have this huge gluteal strength. With Serena, that's her physique and genetics' (Stevens, 2006). The media attributed early upset losses by both Serena and Venus to excess weight, lack of commitment, and interest in 'frivolous' pursuits outside tennis, while an Australian journalist 'joked' that the quick exit of local hero Lleyton Hewitt was due to his dislike for the Rebound Ace courts, which were 'more dangerous than trying to steal Serena Williams's lunch box' (Hinds, 2006).

While Serena publicly stated during the 2007 Australian Open that her critics were haters who simply served to motivate her, such defiance intensified media attention. For instance, Hinds (2007a) wrote that Serena's game has always been about as subtle as a 'kick in the groin,' she had 'bludgeoned her way to seven grand slam titles with the swing of her executioner's blade,' and she had a 'chip on her shoulder.' He also alluded to her displeasure over losing a challenge to the electronic officiating system, Hawk-Eye, by posing the rhetorical question: 'Is she a Hawk-Eye hater, too?' (Hinds, 2007a). Despite struggling in the preliminary rounds, Serena reached the final, only to receive ongoing criticism that her progress highlighted the inferior status of women's tennis:

That she has reached the final speaks volumes for her competitive spirit and determination, while once again underlining the general lack of intelligence and creative ability of the other leading players. . . . Williams has played so few tournaments in the last 13 months that her success here rather makes a mockery of the circuit. Why play at all if you can get to a grand slam final with virtually no previous match-play? . . . Williams should not have been able to get to the final with such ease. The fact that she has must be deeply embarrassing. (Bierley, 2007)

Serena easily defeated top-seeded Maria Sharapova in the final, an outcome that could have been embedded in several stock heroic sporting narratives: 'Champion rises to the occasion,' 'Comeback Queen,' or 'Serena battles through adversity.' Instead, her triumph was narrativized in recurrent deprecating and sexualized scripts: 'Champ focused on retail therapy after responding to critics' (Scott, 2007); 'Serena ignores the knockers' (Pearce, 2007); 'Cyclone Serena slams Maria and her knockers' (in which Serena was described as 'the game's Alpha female'—Niall, 2007a); and 'Sharapova and the critics dealt a blow by Williams' sledgehammer' (in which Serena was said to resemble a 'wrecking ball' and to have an 'Exocet return'—Niall, 2007b). Hinds (2007b) reported her success via a mock attack on the behaviour of the highly respectable and respected men's champion, Roger Federer, with the sarcastic conclusion: 'See, Serena, you were right. We can hate anyone. It's just that you make it so much easier.' Serena's post-match response to the barrage of criticism was as powerful and as eloquent as her tennis:

I have a large arse and it always just looks like I'm bigger than the rest of the girls, but I have been the same weight for I don't know how long. If I lost 20 pounds, I'm still going to have these knockers, forgive me, and I'm still going to have this arse.

While the narratives of 'pornographic eroticism' were used to portray Griffith-Joyner nearly 20 years earlier, a journalist described a match by Serena at Wimbledon in 2007 in terms that had hardened into those of 'sexual grotesquerie':

Cartoonists would have been hard pressed to create Serena. First there was the body—all bosom, bottom and muscle. In her skintight faux leather bodysuit she gave Lara Croft a run for her money. (The great kinkster cartoonist Robert Crumb told me that she was his ideal woman; his idea of heaven was to be given a piggyback by Serena.) (Hattenstone, 2007)

At the 2008 Australian Open, the fixation turned to Venus with one newspaper article using the title, 'Venus Williams with a superior posterior' (Johnson, 2008). Jessica Halloran (2000), in a story entitled 'Venus win helps keep focus on bottom line,' reported that television commentator Roger Rasheed practically started salivating when admiring Venus's rear end during her first-round win. Venus then fielded questions about Rasheed's comment with grace and humor in the post-game interview.

CONCLUSION

Our study shows that despite their outstanding sporting achievements, the Williams sisters have been subjected to the 'gender-specific images that deem black bodies as less desirable if not downright ugly' (Collins, 2004, p. 284); that is, their bodies have been positioned by the 'sexually grotesque.' The complex and ambivalent ways in which the Williams sisters have been constructed—exotic/erotic yet deviant and repulsive, athletic yet animalistic and primitive, unfeminine yet hyperfeminine, muscular yet threateningly hyper-muscular—is a reinscription of the 'Hottentot Venus' genealogy. . . .

However, the very contradictions of their lived experiences as sportswomen provide some African-American sportswomen with the discursive tools to re-imagine and re-work their experiences in new ways, as the Williams sisters' responses to the media demonstrate. Paying attention to the multifaceted discourses and symbolic expressions through which African American people construct new forms of social identities has contributed to sociological understandings of marginalized people's responses to racism. Listening to the positive responses of African American women to negative readings of their corporeality could enable the sports industry to cultivate what Hobson (2003, p. 98) calls a black feminist aesthetic that recognizes the black female body as 'beautiful and desirable' in its distinction from stereotypes of white beauty.[1]

Of greater significance, however, is the need for 'white' people to deconstruct their privileged perspectives and the powerful lenses through which they construct and view 'black' people, to develop a new critical race consciousness that can inform sporting commentary and media narratives. Since sport both reinforces and reproduces the 'persistent,' 'resurgent,' and 'veiled' forms of white power that permeate society (King, Leonard & Kusz, 2007, p. 4), a systematic targeting and 'outing' of racist and sexist narratives in sport has the potential to enable African American women and men to envision and achieve equality within a broader framework of social justice.[2]

NOTES

1. Creef (1993) and Fabos (2001) have shown how Asian and Asian-American women figure skaters have also been inscribed by racist and sexist narratives.

2. For alternatives to the prevailing able-bodied, racist, sexist, and commodified representations of sportswomen, see the book, exhibition, and educational outreach programs based on Jane Gottesman's collection of photographs, which emphasize diversity and inclusion (Gottesman, 2003; *Game Face: What Does a Female Athlete Look Like?*).

REFERENCES

Adams, T. (2005, January 9). Selling the sisters. *The Observer.* Retrieved July 1, 2005 from http://observer .guardian.co.uk/osm/story/0,,1 383632.00.html

Barnes, S. (2007, July 5). Dying swan devoured as giant bird of prey returns to SW19. *Timesonline.* Retrieved July 5, 2007 from http://www.timesonline .co.uk/tol/sport/columnists/simon_barnes/article 2028764.ece

Bennett, M., & Dickerson, V. (2001). Introduction. In M. Bennett & V. Dickerson (Eds.), *Recovering the black female body: Self-representations by African American women* (pp. 1–12). New Brunswick, NJ: Rutgers University Press.

Bierley, S. (2004, January 14). Sisters sledgehammer lured towards siren song of celebrity. *The Guardian.* Retrieved June 1, 2007 from http://sport.guardian .co.uk/columnists/story/0,,1122498,00.html

Bierley, S. (2007, January 26). Fighting Williams sets up Sharapova showdown. *The Guardian.* Retrieved January 28. 2007 from http://sport.guardian.co.Uk/ australianopen2007/story/0,,1998879,00.html

Buckley, W. (2007, September 16). Ali? Laver? Best? No, the Williams sisters. *The Observer,* p. 15.

Collins, P. H. (2004). *Black sexual politics: African Americans, gender, and the new racism.* New York: Routledge.

Crawford, C. (2006a, January 15). Easybeat? Fat chance. *The Sun-Herald,* p. 34.

Crawford, C. (2006b, January 15). Serena shocked by pictures. *The Sunday Mail,* p. 23.

Creef, E. T. (1993). Model minorities and monstrous selves: The winter Olympic showdown of Kristi Yamaguchi and Midori Ito; or: 'How to tell your friends apart from the Japs.' *Visual Anthropology Review, 9*(1), 141–146.

Douglas, D. D. (2002). To be young, gifted, black and female: A meditation on the cultural politics at play in representations of Venus and Serena Williams. *Sociology of Sport Online, 5*(2). Retrieved July I, 2006 from http://physed.otago .ac.nz/sosol/v5i2/v5i2_3.html

Douglas, D. D. (2005). Venus, Serena, and the Women's Tennis Association (WTA): When and where 'race' enters. *Sociology of Sport Journal, 22*(3), 256–282.

Epstein, J. (2006, January 15). Serena out to kick butt. *MensTennisForums.com.* Retrieved January 16, 2006 from http://www.menstennisforums.com/ archive/index.php/t-63698.html

Fabos, B. (2001). Forcing the fairy tale: Narrative strategies in figure skating competition coverage. *Sport in Society, 4* (2), 185–212.

Game Face: What does a female athlete look like? Retrieved January 28, 2007 from http://www .gamefaceonline.org/4_5_press.html

Gibbs, S. (2006, January 21). Big bum rap for Serena. *The Age,* p. 63.

Gilman, S. (1985). *Difference and pathology.* Ithaca, NY: Cornell University Press.

Glenny, G. H. (2006). Visual culture and the world of sport. *The Scholar & Feminist Online.* Retrieved January 30, 2007 from http://www .barnard.edu/sfonline/sport/glenny_ 01.htm

Gottesman, J. (2003). *Game face: What does a female athlete look like?* New York, NY: Random House.

Hadfield, W. (1988, September 30). Fast as a cheetah but Flo-Jo no cheater. *The Australian,* p. 33.

Hadley Freydberg, E. (1995). Sapphires, spitfires, sluts, and superbitches: Aframericans and Latinas in contemporary American film. In K. M. Vaz (Ed.), *Black women in America* (pp. 222–243). Thousand Oaks, CA: Sage.

Halloran, J. (2008, January 18). Venus win helps keep focus on bottom line. *The Sydney Morning Herald.* Retrieved January 18, 2008 from http://www.smh.com.au/news/tennis/venus-win-helps-keep-focus-on-bottom-line/2008/01/17/1200419971695.html

Hargreaves, J. (2000). *Heroines of sport: The politics of difference and identity.* London: Routledge.

Hargreaves, J. (2007). Sport, exercise, and the female Muslim body: Negotiating Islam, politics, and male power. In J. Hargreaves & P. Vertinsky (Eds.), *Physical culture, power and the body* (pp. 74–100). London: Routledge.

Harris, J., & Clayton, B. (2002). Femininity, masculinity, physicality and the English tabloid press: The case of Anna Kournikova. *International Review for the Sociology of Sport, 37*(3/4), 397–413.

Hattenstone, S. (2007, January 31). Serena's triumph over tragedy a weepy classic. *The Guardian.* Retrieved January 31, 2007 from http://sport.guardian.co.uk/columnists/story/0,,2002277,00.html

Heywood, L. (1998). Athletic vs pornographic eroticism: How muscle magazines compromise female athletes and delegitimize the sport of bodybuilding in the public eye. *Mesomorphosis Interactive, 1*(1). Retrieved July 1, 2007 from http://www.mesomorphosis.com/exclusive/heywood/eroticism01.htm

Heywood, L., & Dworkin, S. L. (2003). *Built to win: The female athlete as cultural icon.* Minneapolis, MN: University of Minnesota Press.

Hinds, R. (2006, January 30). Crocks, shocks and 'nots' did the Open proud. *The Sydney Morning Herald,* p. 54.

Hinds, R. (2007a, January 26). Surrounded by 'haters,' rampaging American plays angry. *The Age,* p. 62.

Hinds, R. (2007b, January 28). I hate to admit it, Serena, but we can even dislike Federer. *The Sun-Herald,* p. 59.

Hobson, J. (2003). The 'batty' politic: Toward an aesthetic of the black female body. *Hypatia, 18*(4), 87–105.

Johnson, M. (2008, January 18). Venus Williams with a superior posterior. *The Telegraph.* Retrieved January 18, 2008, from http://www.telegraph.co.uk/sport/main.jhtml?xml=/sport/2008/01/18/stjohn118.xml

Kennedy, E. (2001). She wants to be a sledgehammer: Tennis femininities in British television. *Journal of Sport & Social Issues, 25*(1), 56–72.

King, C. R., Leonard, D. J., & Kusz, K. W. (2007). White power and sport: An introduction. *Journal of Sport & Social Issues, 31,* 3–10.

Messner, M. A., Dunbar, M., & Hunt, D. (2002). The televised sports manhood formula. *Journal of Sport & Social Issues, 24,* 380–394.

Messner, M. A., Duncan, C. M., & Cooky, C. (2003). Silence, sports bras, and wrestling porn: Women in televised sports news and highlights shows. *Journal of Sport & Social Issues, 27,* 38–51.

Miller, D. (2000, July 10). Victor deserves role model status. *The Sunday Telegraph.* Retrieved June 15, 2005 from www.telegraph.co.uk:80/et?ac=003087666203340&rtmo=aq4CWX4J&atmo=99999999&pg-/et/00/7/9/strole09.html

Miller, T., McKay, J., & Martin, R. (1999). Courting lesbianism. *Women and Performance: A Journal of Feminist Theory, 11*(1), 211–234.

Moore, G. (2007, June 29). Williams' fashion statement the hot topic. *The Independent.* Retrieved June 29, 2007 from http://sport.independent.co.uk/tennis/article2720027.ecc

Moore, K. (1988, July 25). Get up and go. *Sports Illustrated.* Retrieved June 12, 2005 from sportsillustrated.cnn.com/olympics/features/joyner/flashback2.html

Morgan, J. L. (1997). 'Some could suckle over their shoulder': Male travelers, female bodies, and the gendering of racial ideology, 1500–1770. *William and Mary Quarterly, 54,* 167–92.

Morton, P. (1991). Introduction. *Disfigured images: The historical assault on Afro-American women.* Westport, CT: Greenwood Press.

Mott, S. (2000, December 14). Wimbledon: Triumph of American values. *The Daily Telegraph*. Retrieved June 30, 2006 from http://www.telegraph.co.uk/sport/main.jhtml;jsessionid=TP5GNFRXV0LFLQFIQMFSFFWAVCB00IV()?xml=/sport/tennis/stmott08.xml

Mott, S. (2007, July 9). Star quality is no match for Venus. *The Daily Telegraph*. Retrieved July 9, 2007 from http://www.telegraph.co.uk/sport/main.jhtml?xml=/sport/2007/07/09/stmott109.xml

Muscat, J. (2007, June 28). Molik stirs the lighting character in Williams. *Timesonline*. Retrieved June 29, 2007 from http://www.timesonline.co.uk/tol/sport/tennis/article1996666.ece

Niall, J. (2007a, January 28). Cyclone Serena slams Maria and her knockers. *The Sydney Morning Herald*, p. 54.

Niall, J. (2007b, January 28). Sharapova and the critics dealt a blow by Williams' sledgehammer. *The Age*, p. 54.

Patton, C. (2001). 'Rock hard': Judging the female physique. *Journal of Sport & Social Issues, 25*(2), 118–140.

Pearce, L. (2007, January 24). Serena ignores the knockers. *The Sydney Morning Herald*. Retrieved January 25, 2007 from http://www.smh.com.au/ncws/tennis/serena-ignores-the-knockers/2007/01/23/1169518709298.html

Peterson, C. (2001). Foreword: Eccentric bodies. In M. Bennett & V. Dickerson (Eds.), *Recovering the black female body: Self- representations by African American women* (pp. ix–xvi). New Brunswick, NJ: Rutgers University Press.

Philip, R. (2007, July 3). Street style gives Venus her deadly cutting edge. *The Daily Telegraph*. Retrieved July 3, 2007 from http://www.telegraph.co.uk/sport/main.jhtml?xml=/sport/2007/07/03/Stphil103.xml

PostWatch. (2002). *Defending the trashy*. Retrieved July 1, 2006 from http://postwatch.blogspot.com/2002_08_25_post watch_archive.html

Ramsay, A. (2006, January 22). Aussie defeat is the bottom line for overweight Serena. *News.scotsman.com*. Retrieved August 14, 2006 from http://sport.scotsman.com/tennis.cfm?id=105902006

Rowe, K. (1990). Roseanne: Unruly woman as domestic goddess. *Screen, 31*(4), 408–419.

Schultz, L. (2002). Reading the catsuit: Serena Williams and the production of blackness at the 2002 US Open. *Journal of Sport & Social Issues, 29*(3), 338–357.

Schulze, L. (1990). On the muscle. In J. Gaines & C. Herzog (Eds.), *Fabrications: Costume and the female body* (pp. 59–78). London: Routledge.

Scott, B. (2007, January 28). Champ focused on retail therapy after responding to critics. *The Sun-Herald*, p. 57.

Sharpley-Whiting, T. D. (1999). *Black Venus: Sexualized savages, primal fears, and primitive narratives in French*. Durham, NC: Duke University Press.

Smith, G. (2007, June 29). Williams has designs on title despite host of outside distractions. *The Times*, p. 104.

Spencer, N. E. (2001). From 'child's play' to 'party crasher': Venus Williams, racism and professional Women's tennis. In D. L. Andrews & S. J. Jackson (Eds.), *Sport stars: The cultural politics of sporting celebrity* (pp. 87–101). London: Routledge.

Spencer, N. E. (2004). Sister Act VI: Venus and Serena Williams at Indian Wells: 'Sincere fictions' and white racism. *Journal of Sport & Social Issues, 28*(2), 115–135.

Stevens, M. (2006, January 12). Size up Serena Williams at your own risk. *The Sun-Herald*, p. 57.

Stevenson, D. (2002). Women, sport and globalization: Competing discourses of sexuality and nation. *Journal of Sport & Social Issues, 26*, 209–225.

Syed, M. (2008, January 24). They play great. They look great. So what, exactly, is the problem? *The Times*. Retrieved January 24, 2008 from http://www.timesonline.co.uk/tol/sport/tennis/article3241414.ece

Vertinsky, P., & Captain, G. (1998). More myth than history: American culture and representations of the black female's athletic ability. *Journal of Sport History, 25*, 532–561.

Viner, B. (2007, June 15). There is way too much emphasis on how we look. Focus on my game. *The Independent*. Retrieved June 15, 2007 from http://sport.independent.co.uk/tennis/article2659628.ece

White, C. (2007, January 28). Williams silences critics. *The Telegraph*. Retrieved January 28, 2007 from http://www.telegraph.co.uk/sport/main.jhtml?xml=/sport/2007/OI/28/stlina28.xml

DISSOLVING THE OTHER

14

Orientalism, Consumption, and Katy Perry's Insatiable Dark Horse

Rosemary Pennington

INTRODUCTION

". . . the core of white privilege is the ability to consume anything, anyone, anywhere" (Alcoff, 1998, p. 19).

Pop star Katy Perry courts controversy with the performance choices she makes. In November 2013, Perry came under fire for a performance that was labeled an instance of yellowface after she chose to sing her song *Unconditionally* at the American Music Awards dressed as a Japanese geisha (Lang, 2013). Perry and her backup dancers were dressed in kimonos, Perry's cut to show off her cleavage, and sported white powdered faces as they danced on stage with rice paper umbrellas under falling cherry blossoms (Feeney, 2013). Whether the performance was racist or not was hotly debated in social media, with Dr Ravi Chandra (2013) writing on *Psychology Today's* The Pacific Heart blog "If you don't think Katy Perry was racist—let me ask you, what if she had performed in blackface? Perhaps a costume isn't the same as changing skin color to you, but it is agonizingly close for me." In July 2014, Perry was again accused of treating a racial identity like a costume when she wore a hair style frequently seen in the African American community and used a "blaccent" in her video for the song *This Is How We Do* (Callahan, 2014). This research is focused on a controversy that sits between these two. Earlier in 2014, Perry was fending off accusations of being anti-Muslim after she destroyed a piece of jewelry with the word *Allah* written in Arabic on it in the music video for her single *Dark Horse* (Lee, 2014). Drawing less anger was the

fact that the brown-skinned man attached to that piece of jewelry was also destroyed in the process; audiences were also seemingly unbothered by White Perry's portrayal of a Cleopatra-like character nor the video's setting in a DayGlo version of ancient Egypt.

Dark Horse comes off Perry's fourth studio album, *Prism*. . . . *Prism* was marketed as a showcase for a grownup Perry, featuring a darker mood than the bubble gum pop *Teenage Dream*. In the video for *Dark Horse*, it would seem as though Perry's artistic maturity came at a very destructive price. Guided by research coming out of postcolonial studies as well as scholarship on the function of music videos, this qualitative textual analysis shows that the maturity of Perry's character in *Dark Horse* is created through the destruction of Orientalized men of color, reproducing a centuries old discourse which frames the culture, people, and objects coming out of the East as things to be possessed, consumed, and tamed by those in the West.[1]

ORIENTALIST IMAGINARIES

Ancient Egypt has long held a special place in the Western imagination. The early 1800s saw a renewed interest in Egyptian history and culture in the United States and Europe (DeLapp, 2011; McAlister, 2005; Trafton, 2004), fueling the consumption of all things Egyptian (Trafton, 2004) including art objects and mummies themselves (Meskell, 1998). In her discussion of European consumption of Oriental objects in the 19th century, Parameswaran (2002) argues this consumption was quite political in that it was designed to

From Pennington, R. (2016). Dissolving the Other: Orientalism, consumption, and Katy Perry's insatiable Dark Horse. *Journal of Communication Inquiry, 40*(2), 111–127.

"contain the threat posed by the colonized and reinvent the Western Self through consumption of the non-Western Other" (p. 298).

Orientalism, Edward Said (1978) wrote, is a conceptualization of the *Orient,* or East, which places it in opposition to the *Occident,* or West. It is a discourse which serves to codify difference (Said, 1978) while also portraying "non-Western peoples as the Other of a Western Self" (Coronil, 1996, p. 52). Said, and Orientalism, have their critics—Prakash (1995) notes Orientalism has been criticized for painting both East and West with a too broad brush, essentializing both East and West. However, Said (1985) insists that "underlying much of the discussion of Orientalism is a disquieting realization that the relationship between cultures is both uneven and irremediably secular" (p. 100). It is that unevenness that is often reflected in media representations. One way it manifests is through rhetorical strategies deployed by Orientalists depicting *The East* as soft, feminine, and irrational, in need of the saving grace of rational Western masculinity (Said, 1978). The Orient has been feminized through visual depictions of harems full of veiled women and via language that links the very landscape to soft, curving, female bodies. The bodies of Western women also contoured the shape of Orientalism and empire but in a very different way.

Writing of the way bodies were surveilled during the height of European imperialism McCombe (2008) suggests that "as part of the process of maintaining power through discourse, the colonizer must insist that the colonial body be a known and predictable quantity" (p. 26). Colonial power was predicated upon the creation of racialized and gendered understandings of identity in which non-Whites were forever cast as the other who needed taming and from whom things could be taken (Lugones, 2007). Within colonial discourses of identity, men were framed as the actors in sexual relationships, the ones who controlled reproduction, while women were to be acted upon, used for reproductive purposes. Colonized women were seen as sexual objects (Hoganson, 2001; Lugones, 2007; Stoler, 1989) while White, colonizing women were seen as harbingers of gentility and civilization (Rafael, 1995; Stoler, 1989).

Woollacott (1997) reminds us that "critics of Orientalism tend to 'write out gender'" when White women were often just as invested in the maintenance of colonies, and colonial categories, as White men. One way to help maintain those boundaries was through the policing of sexual behavior (Hoganson, 2001). This, in turn, helped produce narratives in which colonized men were often reduced to little more than sexual beasts (Lugones, 2010; Mutekwa, 2009; Spanakos, 1998; Stoler, 1989). The focus on the sexual behavior of colonized men, on their supposed hypersexuality, was used to sharpen the conceptual contrast between colonizer and colonized—the colonizer was in control of his impulses; the colonized was not. It served to sharpen contrasts between *Us* and *Them* in policy but also in media narratives of colonial life.

Orgad (2012) reminds us that media "representations call on viewers momentarily to become intimate with others . . . to develop an imaginary bond with, and then, usually, forget about and move on" (p. 190). Such representations give us access to images and narratives we can then use to craft moments of engagement with those we imagine as the other. This relates to Said's (1978) concept of *imaginary geography* in that imaginaries, such as imaginary geography, are constructions designed to orient us to our world. For Said (1978), the imaginary geography of Orientalism produced a physical understanding of the Orient that Orientalist artists, scholars, and painters helped fashion; an understanding designed to highlight differences and to mask similarities or, even, on the ground realities all in the pursuit of the commodification of the Orient and its consumption.

MUSIC VIDEOS, COMMODIFICATION, AND LIBERATION

Music videos "have an avowedly commercial agenda" (Railton & Watson, 2005, p. 52), often serving "as advertisement for albums and tours" (Roberts 1990, p. 4). Aufderheide (1986) suggests that they represent a "merging of artistic and commercial production" (p. 58), as they are designed to showcase the musical artist while also inducing the audience to consume the artist's merchandise. This commercial aspect of music videos has meant they often dwell in the familiar (Railton & Watson, 2005). Or, music videos can make the unfamiliar seem less strange by allowing "one to move past a number of strange or disturbing images while neither worrying about them nor forgetting them completely" (Vernallis, 2001, p. 22).

This tension between accessibility and novelty, or strangeness, can serve as both a site of resistance for female artists to wage "sex as a weapon" in the fight against gender stereotyping (James, 2015; Roberts, 1990) as well as a space where stale ideas about gender roles and what is appropriate female sexual behavior are reified (Andsanger & Roe, 2003; Bradby 1993; Railton & Watson, 2005). Female artists are more frequently sexualized than their male counterparts (Andsanger & Roe, 2003), with male artists often being framed as the authors of their music and female artists as an object through which a performance flows (Bradby, 1993). . . .

Artists can at times leverage sexual objectification to produce what James (2015) calls a "look, I Overcame" discourse—in that the artists seemingly break free of sexual expectations— or, in the case of Orientalist discourses, to create a kind of exotic multiculturalism in which race and ethnicity are deployed strategically to create a sense of sexual empowerment as women are portrayed as liberal subjects, free to be whomever they long to be (McGee, 2012). All of this shaped by a female artist's need to sell not only her music to her audience but herself as well (Andsanger & Roe, 2003; Bradby, 1993; James, 2015; McGee, 2012; Railton & Watson, 2005).

This research . . . examines Perry's *Dark Horse* music video through the lens of postcolonial studies in order to understand how the video perpetuates Orientalist framings of East and West. Shome and Hegde (2002) suggest postcolonial studies can be useful in the study of communication because it "provides a historical and international depth to the understanding of cultural power" (p. 252) while Fernandez (1999) points out both postcolonial studies and media studies (particularly the study of electronic media) provide entry points for the exploration of a multiplicity of cultural understandings. Orientalism and postcolonial studies were also judged pertinent to this study of a music video because of its location in Egypt—a country whose long experience of colonization dates to ancient times and which is still recovering from its encounter with Europe's more recent imperial expansions.

AN ORIENTALIST'S EGYPTIAN DREAM

The *Dark Horse* video opens as the camera zooms in on a boat silhouetted against the setting sun. One imagines the vessel floating down the Nile River as a pyramid and palm trees appear in the background. In case this was not enough to alert the audience to the fact we are now in Egypt, black text appears just above the boat which proclaims this to be "Memphis, Egypt a crazy long time ago. . . ." There are five figures on what seems to be an Egyptian barge—two muscly men, painted green and blue, manning prow and stern while two females wearing all gold and sporting the heads of cats flank the reclining Witch of Memphis, Katy Perry.[2] Perry, the center of this tableau, wears a short white shift resembling those found on figures carved on buildings throughout Egypt as well as a white wig covered, in part, by what appear to be blue hieroglyphs. A series of four electronically produced musical notes is repeated several times as the camera zooms in on the barge, giving the scene an overall trippy feeling. As Perry, now framed in a close-up, turns to the camera and sings, "I knew you were, you were going to come to me," the audience gets the feeling they have come to her in an Egypt that is meant to reflect more a dream than reality. If so, it is the reflection of an Orientalist dream.

Dark Horse is a visual feast. Peeters (2004) suggests music videos are often more concerned with spectacle than narrative, and Perry's video is nothing if not spectacular. She embeds nods to ancient Egypt throughout *Dark Horse,* frequently through her use of hieroglyphics as accessories. They appear on wigs, on Juicy J's (her *Dark Horse* collaborator) sunglasses, and floating in the air around a centrally framed Perry as she sings "So, you want to play with magic?" Perry's deployment of hieroglyphics, among the most recognized products of ancient Egypt, works to make the Egypt she's created seem less strange—most viewers will have seen hieroglyphics at some point in their lives—while the way she deploys them, as accessories, positions herself front and center. They, and the Egypt they represent, are meant to be consumed by Perry as well as by her audience. The nonlinear way the video is edited together, moving from barge to throne room, to a Perry surrounded by gold, floating hieroglyphs helps the audience navigate this strange landscape, latching onto what is familiar (Railton & Watson, 2005) while allowing the unfamiliar to fly by (Vernallis, 2001). It works to create both an idea of Egypt, and an idea of an Egyptian Perry, as consumable; easily swallowed by viewers.

This echoes the ways in which Egypt was produced as a consumable product during the colonial era. Although not a British colony at the time, Saglia (2002) points out that Egyptian art and culture were mimicked and replicated in early 17th century British luxury goods. Meskell (1998) reminds us that it was not simply culture and art that was consumed—actual Egyptian bodies were consumed, both figuratively in the unwrapping of ancient mummies as well as literally via their ingestion as ground powders meant to spark lax libidos. Egypt has long been made accessible through consumption; in this sense, Perry's video fits neatly beside expensive British China and snake oil salesman's wares.

In her work on *Sex and the City,* Arthurs (2003) notes that media narratives have fashioned a story of the modern woman that situates her liberation within the context of consumption. Globalized western feminism, as it moved from first to second wave, was woven into the tapestry of capitalism so that to be a fully modern and empowered woman one had to consume (Eisenstein, 2010). This commodity feminism (Goldman, Heath, & Smith, 1991) helps shape an understanding of the modern woman that does more to reinforce patriarchy and hegemonic understandings of gender roles than it does to challenge them (as the consumption is often focused on making women prettier or more attractive; McRobbie, 2008). Although the actions in her *Dark Horse* video take place "a crazy long time ago," Perry clearly situates herself within the context of the liberated woman being a consuming woman. If Marilyn Monroe taught us that "diamonds are a girl's best friend" and Carrie Bradshaw showed us that the modern woman is defined by what she buys, then Katy Perry in *Dark Horse* is the very epitome of modern femininity. This becomes all too clear as we begin to meet her *Dark Horse* suitors.

EATING HEARTS AND MARGINALIZING MEN

After we are introduced to Perry via Nile River barge, the camera moves us into what seems to

be an ancient Egyptian throne room. The space reminds viewers of pillars or ruins they may have seen in documentary programs about ancient Egypt; the structure is painted in bright colors that may, or may not, resemble those that once adorned the palaces and temples of various Egyptian kingdoms. The camera zooms in on Perry sitting atop a throne. The shot is framed at a low angle, establishing Perry's authority over the scene (Vernallis, 2001) as more of the cat-headed women and brightly painted male servants attend her. Looming just behind is the giant silver head of a sphinx. The staging of the space, and of Perry, is reminiscent of Elizabeth Taylor's entrance into Rome on the sphinx in the 1963 film *Cleopatra.* Shin (2012) suggests Taylor's depiction of the pharaoh was wrapped up in capitalist discourses of colonial whiteness which were driven by excess and by consumption; a White Cleopatra was a Cleopatra that was easy for Americans to see and consume. Cleopatra has often served as an accessible stand-in for Egypt in Western media as her racial ambiguity (scholars debate whether she was White like her Greek forebears may have been or a Black African) has made any possible strangeness seem less potent (McCombe, 2008; Riad, 2011; Shin, 2012), and has made her sexuality less dangerous.

Danger lurks in Perry's throne room as what appears to be the first of five suitors walks a red carpet (a reminder of Perry's life as a superstar outside the video) toward her. The camera follows the man into the room so that the eye is focused on his glimmering golden cape and headdress, as well as the muscular blue backs of Perry's male servants. Typically, it is women who appear fragmented in music videos (Schoppmeier, 2015; Vernallis, 1998; Vernallis, 2008), with this fragmentation indicating their existence as sexual objects. In *Dark Horse,* this is reversed, as it is the men in the video who are sometimes reduced to close-ups of body parts, it is the men who will be on display, not the pop star. When we finally get a look of this first suitor's face, we see he wears a golden eye patch over his right eye, and he is covered in golden necklaces—originally one of those necklaces had the Arabic word for god, *Allah,* inscribed on it, but this was scrubbed from the video after it was heavily criticized by Muslim groups for being blasphemous. He rubs his hand along his chest as Perry sings "Make me your Aphrodite," and it is clear that she has found his appearance pleasing. The juxtaposition of the suitor's attractive body and the reference to the Greek goddess of love (and sex) conjures up the phantom of the hypersexual colonized man with his uncontrollable lusts (Lugones, 2010; Spanakos, 1998).

The camera cuts to Perry on the barge singing "Don't make me your enemy," and when we return to the throne room, we see the man pulling from his belt an enormous diamond. Perry inspects the diamond, runs her tongue over her teeth when suddenly we see blue lightning shoot from the sphinx above her throne and the man crumbles to dust as the sphinx tells him, too late to be a warning, "There's no going back."

We do not know why Perry has destroyed her suitor. The look of glee that washes over her face as she runs her eyes over his body and as she examines the jewel he has brought her seems to indicate she is pleased with the suitor and with his gift, and yet he is turned to dust. Both Mutekwa (2009) and Stoler (1989) have discussed the ways indigenous, colonized masculinities would be punished for the merest whiff of sexual impropriety with White women. The focus on sexual behavior reduced colonized men to little more than threatening beasts with threatening lusts that had to be controlled, avoided, and ultimately punished (Lugones, 2010). Perry, in her destruction of this first suitor, seems to be punishing him for the lust the glimpse of his body may have provoked in her. But she does not simply punish him, she utterly destroys him with his jewelry transformed into a glittering grill to adorn her blazing white teeth. Much as Coronil (1996) suggests happens in Occidentalist media representations of East and West, Perry has dissolved the other into herself, in this instance by turning the other into an accessory to be worn and, later one imagines, discarded.

The next suitor to dare tempt Perry is a corpusculent man of vaguely Asian extraction. His body seems to be oiled, and he is clothed in robes that suggest a passing resemblance to rosewood Buddhas sold in tiny, cramped markets found in Chinatowns and hippy college communities all over the United States. As with the prior suitor, the camera lingers over his bare chest and the large golden ropes which adorn it, emphasizing both his wealth and his girth. Unlike his predecessor, this man does not offer jewels, instead the carts rolling down the carpeted walkway are laden with Twinkies, Cheetos, and other types of junk

food that both emphasize his obesity as well as the wanton consumption on display in Perry's throne room. As she sings "It's a yes or a no, no maybe . . . ," the Buddha gestures to the large piles of food he's brought with him as Perry's eyes grow big and she licks her lips in anticipation. It is a cartoonish moment that heightens the absurdity of the spectacle taking place on screen. "Just be sure," Perry sings, "before you give it all to me" as she eats what seems to be a Cheeto—a Cheeto, it turns out, that is flaming hot. As Perry desperately gestures for something to drink, the suitor upends his enormous drinking vessel to find it empty. Suddenly, there's a flash of blue lightning, the man turns to dust and in his place stands a large metal goblet full of liquid that Perry then drinks. She literally consumes this second of her suitors, dissolving him utterly into herself. Often music videos shirk narrative in the pursuit of spectacle (Peeters, 2004; Vernallis, 2008), but there seems to be a clear narrative developing in Katy Perry's throne room. One which positions her as all powerful and all consuming. The production company which helped shape Perry's vision for the *Dark Horse* video says it was imagined as an epic film, one focused on Perry's toying with her would be suitors (Mirada, n.d.). After the destruction of the first two men in the video, Perry's warnings "to be sure before giving it all" to her take on a particular urgency as other suitors arrive. After the dissolving of Perry's Buddha, two other men are quickly dispatched. One, a bare chested Black man, presents Perry a bouncing lowrider-esque golden chariot; the other, whose brown skin we can see only on his bare arms, walks in carrying two bowls laden with gold and jewels and wearing a golden chainmail veil. For no discernable reason, the charioteer is transformed into yellow fuzzy dice to adorn the new chariot; the second suitor is turned into a reptile skin purse when he pulls back his veil to reveal a crocodile's head. The case of this suitor is especially interesting, though he is given less screen time than any of the other men.

Many gods of ancient Egypt had human bodies with animal heads—among them Sobek, the Egyptian god of crocodiles (Oakes & Gahlin, 2002), whom the veiled suitor appears to be referencing. Sobek was a god associated with both fertility and death (Sebek, n.d.). He was a violent god and one, as Allen (2005) suggests, who was prone to hypersexual behavior. In her discussion of the way gender was produced in European colonies and the way that race and gender intersected to create a hierarchy of civilized behavior, Lugones (2010) points out that colonized men were imagined as being hypersexual creatures, barely in control of their most animalistic urges. Perry's version of Sobek, wearing a broad grin that seems almost lecherous, conjures up this framing of men of color as hypersexed animals; this conjuring in turn serves as a kind of justification for the destruction of her suitors. By this point in the video, all the suitors have been men of color whose dress suggests they come from the historic Orient—their skin color and the imaginary geography they seem to inhabit makes them suspect and a threat that must be dealt with.

By the end of the video, the only suitor to have survived this dealing with is the man who most resembles *the familiar*—a man whose light skin seems to suggest he could be of the same Western background as Perry herself; or that he might, at the very least, be able to pass. Although his gift of a floating, neon pink pyramid seems pleasing, he is also the victim of Perry's brand of magic. However, unlike the other men, he is not annihilated; instead, he's turned into a small dog with a human head. His gift has pleased Perry enough that he now gets to exist as a lapdog while she climbs his pyramid and sprouts wings, suggesting a transformation from the pharaoh Cleopatra into the goddess Isis. Isis, it is worth noting, was among the most important deities in ancient Egypt (Oakes & Gahlin, 2002; Shaw, 2004), worshipped as a mother goddess as well as "the giver of death" through her association with her husband Osiris, considered the judge of the dead (Murray, 1994). Andsanger and Roe (2003) suggest that metamorphosis in music videos can "create the illusion that an artist has evolved into a different being, generally a more mature and edgier version of his or her former self" (p. 88). In the *Dark Horse* music video, it is Perry's giving of death to the men of color who would woo her that leads to her transformation into a goddess; it is the dealing of destruction that suggests her transformation from bubble gum pop star into mature musical artist.

The destruction, transformation, and consumption of the Orientalist imaginings of men in *Dark Horse* exemplifies Bhabha's (1994) assertion that constructions of colonial otherness create objects of "desire and derision." We, the viewers, are meant to find Perry's annihilation of the suitors, her sporting of a glittery grill, and her wanton consumption amusing. The suitors are attractive, their presents are desired, but they themselves are nothing more than playthings at which we all laugh and then forget as the next victim, with his gifts, comes into view. A "brand of 'empowered' modern femininity" within capitalism is based on consumption that serves to reinforce patriarchy more than it serves to upend it (Parameswaran, 2002). At the same time, Orientalism has informed a strain of Orientalist feminism that has helped construct "a binary opposition between a civilised West and an uncivilised East" (Ho, 2010, p. 433). It's a strand of feminism in which liberated White, modern, Western women know best and, much like their colonial predecessors (Hoganson, 2001; Woollacott, 1997), reinscribe Orientalist and racist understandings of difference instead of challenging them.

Perry, through her performance of an empowered woman who symbolically consumes Orientalized men one after another, is reinforcing a hegemonic understanding of the place of men and women in, specifically, capitalist society even though her consumption takes place in ancient Egypt. She is a golden winged, liberated, powerful woman who owes her position to her ability to consume all she can. Given the song's lyrics and the video's visuals, we are left with the expectation that Perry's hunger for things and for power is insatiable and that she will ride her dark horse into the ground to get what she wants, but she will do so by reinforcing heterosexist and Orientalist understandings of male and female bodies.

REPACKAGING ORIENTALISM AS EMPOWERMENT

As with any media text, there are any number of meanings that could be drawn from this music video. One feminist reading of this text might suggest that the juxtaposition of lyrics about a strong, determined woman with the visual destruction of male suitors implies a kind of liberation but a liberation at the price of whom? In an interview, Perry claimed *Dark Horse* was the story of a man-eating woman; the kind of woman a man should love only if he was comfortable loving the machine of his destruction (Garibaldi, 2013). That Perry, a

White American woman, and *Dark Horse* director Mathew Cullen, a White American man, chose to visually represent this story through the destruction of men of color—men who seem to represent several Orientalist stereotypes—in the video suggests an understanding of East and West fueled by colonial prejudices. . . . It also reinforces Alcoff's (1998) assertion, quoted at the beginning of this essay, that " . . . the core of white privilege is the ability to consume anything, anyone, anywhere" (p. 19). That privilege is made clear not only by Perry's consumption of men of color but also through the adoption of Egypt as a backdrop and pharaoh then goddess as persona.

The core of White feminist privilege has, in part, been fleshed out by a capitalist framing of freedom where, to be free, is to consume (Eisenstein, 2010). Within this framework, the *Dark Horse* video becomes a reflection of a capitalist notion of liberation founded upon the consumption of "the other." It is difficult to overlook the way it reproduces a centuries old rhetoric of power and race in which " . . . whiteness can be read as the assertion of privilege, power, and historically specific, gender and class-related cultural identity in a racially hierarchical social system" (Woollacott, 1997, p. 1027). Katy Perry's position as a White woman in the video is not a problem because she destroys an amulet with the word *Allah* inscribed on it, though some might find it blasphemous, and it was the action that caused the most criticism—it is a problem because her White privilege allows her to continue the domination of the symbolic West over the symbolic East and perpetuates the idea that the Orient is a fecund place ripe for consumption. Her wanton destruction of her suitors is evidence of their inferiority and recalls the ways in which colonized peoples were categorized as, at times, non-human within colonial structures of power (Lugones, 2010).

Stoler (1989) notes that, in European colonies, White women seldom enjoyed sexual freedom, and so Perry's performance could be read as transgressive in that she clearly has the freedom to do as she wishes with her suitors in her dreamscape Egypt; however, her seeming contempt for, her consumption of, and her destruction of men of color in her *Dark Horse* video perpetuates a discourse of White dominance over people categorized as other. Perry punishes each suitor for the possible threat they present to her position of power much the way

colonized men of color were punished for the possible sexual threat they posed to White colonial women (Stoler, 1989). Orgad (2012) notes that "we need the other in order to establish and maintain a sense of who we are" (p. 81). Throughout *Dark Horse,* Katy Perry uses Orientalized men of color to define who she is—a liberated Western woman; a pop icon who can devour what she wants when she wants; a beautiful female who can allow herself to be momentarily objectified because, in the end, she holds all the power in her interactions with the men she encounters.

Repackaging a centuries old Orientalist discourse about East and West, Perry is free to consume, appropriate, and destroy while the men who visit her throne room are not. As Powell (2011) suggests, it is especially important to dig through this construction of race and power in popular media "because of the overload of information in society, it is almost impossible for the public to critique messages on race and culture in any useful way" (p. 93). Perry's AMA performance was quickly labeled yellowface because she chose to represent herself as a geisha; somehow, though, her dressing as a pharaoh and her destruction of men of color in *Dark Horse* did not create the same kind of outrage. Yes, there was the furor over the *Allah* necklace, but there were few, if any, bloggers declaring Perry's vision of Egypt a display of racism. The question to ask ourselves is why? Is it simply because the onslaught of media messages people receive every day wearies them? Or is it because the destruction of men of color in a former colony fits into larger Orientalist narratives of the inferiority of the East and, so, their destruction seems familiar and fails to provoke?

CONCLUSION

When Katy Perry first came onto the music scene, she was seen as just another iteration of the pop music ingénue. While bright blue wigs, whipped cream spurting breasts, and latex outfits might have signaled a one and done career for Perry, she's been rather savvy in not getting boxed into one particular type of music or performance. She has proven to be a chameleon of sorts which has translated into huge international tours and immense wealth. In 2014 alone, Perry earned 40 million dollars (Forbes, 2015). Perry is not only one of the bestselling female artists of all time; she's one of the bestselling artists ever. *Prism* is her third album to sell at least one million copies (Caulfield, 2014).

Even with her success, it would be easy to write someone like Katy Perry off, to pretend that her music, her videos, and her costumes don't matter in the long run because they are little more than pop fluff. But that would be shortsighted. As of this writing, the official *Dark Horse* video has more than 1.2 billion views on YouTube. Unofficial uploads have received tens of thousands of views. Entertainment media are often treated as trivial and, yet, music videos like those produced by Katy Perry reach a wide audience. To overlook the power of popular media because it is fluff is to decide what that media tells a huge portion of the public is unimportant. Katy Perry, the framing of

men of color in her video, and her cultural appropriation matter because they reach a broad audience and serve to reinforce a racist and prejudicial understanding of the world that only sharpens dichotomies.

In reflecting on *Orientalism* Said wrote, "The challenge to Orientalism and the colonial era of which it is so organically a part was a challenge to the muteness imposed on the Orient as object" (1985, p. 93). Although it is a music video, muteness abounds in Katy Perry's *Dark Horse* as the servants who seem to be stand-ins for ancient Egyptians, as well as her seemingly Oriental suitors, all say nothing. Egypt says nothing, it is simply an imaginary geography on which Perry places herself and which reflects a dream, her Orientalist dream, more than anything else.

NOTES

1. Official *Dark Horse* video: http://www.youtube.com/watch?v¼0KSOMA3QBU0

2. For the video Perry adopted the name Katy Pätra—a play on the name of Egypt's famous

female pharaoh Cleopatra. However, for the sake of clarity, I will continue referring to her as Katy Perry during my analysis and discussion.

REFERENCES

Alcoff, L. M. (1998). What should white people do? *Hypatia, 13*(3), 6–26.

Allen, J. P. (2005). *The ancient Egyptian pyramid texts.* Atlanta, GA: Society of Biblical Literature.

Andsanger, J., & Roe, K. (2003). What's your definition of dirty, baby? Sex in music video. *Sexuality & Culture, 7,* 79–97.

Arthurs, J. (2003). Sex and the city and consumer culture: Remediating postfeminist drama. *Feminist Media Studies, 3*(1), 83–98.

Aufderheide, P. (1986). Music videos: The look of sound. *Journal of Communication, 36,* 57–78.

Bernard, H. R. (2011). *Research methods in anthropology: Qualitative and quantitative approaches* (5th ed.). New York, NY: Rowman & Littlefield Publishers, INC.

Bhabha, H. K. (1994). *The location of culture.* London, England: Routledge.

Bradby, B. (1993). Sampling sexuality: Gender, technology and the body in dance music. *Popular Music, 12*(2), 155–176.

Callahan, Y. (2014, July 31). Katy 'the Queen of Cultural Appropriation' is at it again. *The Root.* Retrieved from http://www.theroot.com/blogs/the_grapevine/2014/07/katy_the_queen_of_cultural_appropriation_perry_is_at_it_again.html

Caulfield, K. (2014, January 10). Chart moves: Katy Perry's 'PRISM' hits 1 million in sales, One Republic returns to Top 10. *Billboard.com.* Retrieved from http://www.billboard.com/biz/articles/news/5869527/chart-moves-katy-perrys-prism-hits-1-million-in-sales-onerepublic-returns

Chandra, R. (2013, November 24). Yes, Katy Perry's performance was racist, here's why. *Psychology Today.* Retrieved from http://www.psychologytoday.com/blog/the-pacificheart/201311/yes-katy-perry-s-performance-was-racist-here-s-why

Coronil, F. (1996). Beyond occidentalism: Toward nonimperial geohistorical categories. *Cultural Anthropology, 11*(1), 51–87.

DeLapp, K. M. (2011). Ancient Egypt as Europe's intimate stranger.' In H. V. Bonavita (Ed.), *Negotiating identities: Constructed selves and others* (pp. 171–192). Amsterdam, the Netherlands: Rodopi.

Eisenstein, H. (2010). Feminism seduced: Globalisation and the uses of gender. *Australian Feminist Studies, 25*(66), 413–431.

Feeney, N. (2013, November 25). Katy Perry's 'geisha-style' performance needs to be called out. *The Atlantic.* Retrieved from http://www.theatlantic.com/entertainment/archive/2013/11/katy-perrys-geisha-style-performance-needs-to-be-called-out/281805/

Fernandez, M. (1999). Postcolonial media theory. *Art Journal, 58*(3), 58–73.

Forbes. (2015, May 30). *The world's most powerful celebrities.* Retrieved from http://www.forbes.com/celebrities/list/#tab: overall

Fursich, E. (2009). In defense of textual analysis—Restoring a challenged method for journalism and media studies. *Journalism Studies, 10*(2), 238–252.

Garibaldi, C. (2013, August 29). Katy Perry's "Dark Horse" is a "warning." *MTV News.* Retrieved from http://www.mtv.com/news/articles/1713269/katy-perry-dark-horse-prism.jhtml

Goldman, R., Heath, D., & Smith, S. L. (1991). Commodity feminism. *Critical Studies in Mass Communication, 8,* 333–351.

Hoganson, K. L. (2001). As badly off as the Filipinos: U.S. women's suffragists and the imperial issue at the turn of the twentieth century. *Journal of Women's History, 13*(2), 9–33.

Ho, C. (2010). Responding to Orientalist feminism: Women's rights and the war on terror. *Australian Feminist Studies, 25*(66), 434–439.

Isis. (n.d.). In *Encyclopædia Britannica online.* Retrieved from http://www.britannica.com/EBchecked/topic/295449/Isis

James, R. (2015). *Resilience & melancholy: Pop music, feminism, Neoliberalism.* Alresford, UK: Zero Books.

Lang, N. (2013, November 29). Settling the Katy Perry controversy: 'Yellowface' is not beautiful. *The Los Angeles Times.* Retrieved from http://articles.latimes.com/2013/nov/29/news/la-ol-katy-perry-american-music-awards-yellowface-20131127

Lee, A. (2014, February 28). Katy Perry edits 'Dark Horse' video after petition objects to Arabic religious symbol. *The Hollywood Reporter.* Retrieved from http://www.hollywoodreporter.com/earshot/video-katy-perry-edited-dark-684345

Lugones, M. (2007). Heterosexualism and the colonial/modern gender system. *Hypatia, 22*(1), 186–209.

Lugones, M. (2010). Toward a decolonial feminism. *Hypatia, 25*(4), 742–759.

McAlister, M. (2005). *Epic encounters: Culture, media & U.S. interest in the Middle East since 1945* (2nd ed.). Berkeley, CA: University of California Press.

McCombe, J. P. (2008). Cleopatra and her problems: T.S. Eliot and the fetishization of Shakespeare's Queen of the Nile. *Journal of Modern Literature, 31*(2), 23–38.

McGee, P. (2012). Orientalism and erotic multiculturalism in popular culture: From princess Rajah to pussycat dolls. *MSMI, 6*(2), 209–238.

McKee, A. (2003). *Textual analysis: A beginner's guide.* London, England: Sage Publications.

McRobbie, A. (2008). Young women and consumer culture. *Cultural Studies, 22*(5), 531–550.

Meskell, L. (1998). Consuming bodies: Cultural fantasies of ancient Egypt. *Body & Society, 4*(1), 63–76.

Mirada. (n.d.). *Katy Perry 'dark horse': How to build a neo-ancient Egyptian hip-hop epic.* Retrieved from http://mirada.com/stories/katy-perry-dark-horse

Murray, A. S. (1994). *Who's who in mythology: Classic guide to the ancient world.* London, England: Bracken Books.

Mutekwa, A. (2009). Gendered beings, gendered discourses: The gendering of race, colonialism and anti-colonial nationalism in three Zimbabwean novels. *Social Identities: Journal* for the Study of Race, Nation and Culture, 15(5), 725–740.

Oakes, L., & Gahlin, L. (2002). Ancient Egypt: An illustrated reference to the myths, religions, pyramids and temples of the land of the pharaohs. London, England: Hermes House.

Orgad, S. (2012). Media representation and the global imagination. Malden, MA: Polity Press.

Parameswaran, R. (2002). Local culture in global media: Excavating colonial and mater-ial discourses in national geographic. Communication Theory, 12(3), 287–315.

Peeters, H. (2004). The semiotics of music videos: It must be written in the stars. Image & Narrative: Online Magazine of the Visual Narrative. Retrieved from http://www.ima-geandnarrative .be/inarchive/issue08/heidipeeters.htm

Powell, K. A. (2011). Framing Islam: An analysis of U.S. media coverage of terrorism since 9/11. Communication Studies, 62(1), 90–112.

Prakash, G. (1995). Orientalism now. History and Theory, 34(3), 199–212.

Rafael, V. L. (1995). Colonial domesticity: White women and the United States rule in the Philippines. American Literature, 6(4), 639–666.

Railton, D., & Watson, P. (2005). Naughty girls and red blooded women: Representations of female heterosexuality in music video. Feminist Media Studies, 5(1), 51–63.

Riad, S. (2011). Invoking Cleopatra to examine the shifting ground of leadership. The Leadership Quarterly, 22, 831–850.

Roberts, R. (1990). "Sex as a weapon": Feminist rock music videos. NWSA Journal, 2(1), 1–15.

Rothman, L. (2014, February 21). There's a very good reason why Katy Perry's 'Dark Horse' video is set in ancient Egypt. Time. Retrieved from http://time.com/9233/katy-perry-dark-horse-egypt/

Saglia, D. (2002). Consuming Egypt: Appropriation and the cultural modalities of romantic luxury. Nineteenth-Century Contexts: An Interdisciplinary Journal, 24(3), 317–332.

Said, E. (1978). Orientalism. New York, NY: Vintage.

Said, E. (1985). Orientalism reconsidered. Cultural Critique, 1, 89–107.

Schoppmeier, S. (2015). "Hottentot Barbie" as a multicultural star: The commodification of race in Nicki Minaj's music videos. Aspeers: Emerging Voices in American Studies, 8, 49–70.

Sebek. (n.d.). In Encyclopædia Britannica online. Retrieved from http://www.britannica.com/EBchecked/topic/531238/Sebek

Shaw, I. (2004). Ancient Egypt: A very short introduction. Oxford, England: Oxford University Press.

Shin, G. (2012). If it be love indeed, tell me how much: Elizabeth Taylor, Richard Burton, and White pleasure after empire. Reconstruction: Studies in Contemporary Culture, 12(1), 4.

Shome, R., & Hegde, R. S. (2002). Postcolonial approaches to communication: Charting the terrain, engaging the intersections. Communication Theory, 12(3), 249–270.

Spanakos, A. P. (1998). The canvas of the other: Fanon and recognition. DisClosure: A Journal of Social Theory, 7(1), 147–161.

Stoler, A. L. (1989). Making empire respectable: The politics of race and sexual morality in 20th century colonial cultures. American Ethnologist, 16(4), 634–660.

Trafton, S. (2004). Egypt land: Race and nineteenth-century American Egyptomania. Durham, NC: Duke University Press.

Vernallis, C. (1998). The aesthetics of music video: An analysis of Madonna's 'Cherish.' Popular Music, 17(2), 153–185.

Vernallis, C. (2001). The kindest cut: Functions and meanings of music video editing. Screen, 42(1), 21–48.

Vernallis, C. (2008). Music video, song, sound: Experience, technique and emotion in Eternal Sunshine of the Spotless Mind. Screen, 49(3), 277–297.

Woollacott, A. (1997). All this is the empire, I told myself: Australian women's voyages "home" and the articulation of colonial whiteness. The American Historical Review, 102(4), 1003–1029.

"GLOBAL MOTHERHOOD"

The Transnational Intimacies of White Femininity

Raka Shome

In October 2005, ABC news published an online story about a Midwestern woman in Ohio who, inspired by images of Angelina Jolie's adoption of an Ethiopian child, expressed a desire to do the same.[1] The woman, Ann Charles Watt, recalled that: "I remember being at the store and seeing Angelina on the cover of, I think it was *People* magazine," and I said "Oh my gosh! We can do this" [i.e. adopt from Ethiopia]. Watt, along with her husband Jason Hillard, enthusiastically noted that "in the grand scheme of things, she changed our lives . . . Angelina . . . probably brought us an African child." Ann Watt's husband reinforced this enthusiasm by adding that *"we're inviting a whole new genealogy to our family line. We invite culture and diversity into our family* and those are things that inspired me to adopt" (emphasis added). Ann and Jason's enthusiasm here has to do not only with their decision of international adoption but also that they would be able to bring a "new genealogy" of "culture and diversity" into their "family."

This story is important because it is representative of a growing transnational phenomenon (that is simultaneously gendered, racialized, and heterosexualized) that is marking the late twentieth and early twenty-first century's media and cultural landscape. This is a phenomenon in which it is now becoming commonplace and even fashionable to see white Western women saving, rescuing, or adopting international children from underprivileged parts of the world, and rearticulating them through *familial* frameworks that recenter white Western (and especially North Atlantic) heterosexual kinship logics. From the exhaustive images of Princess Diana with children of the world in the 1990s, to more recent images of celebrity adoption

(such as by Angelina Jolie, Madonna, Mia Farrow, and Meg Ryan), to representations of white women as U.N. "good will" ambassadors (such as Nicole Kidman, Susan Sarandon, Audrey Hepburn, and Angelina Jolie), to numerous websites of international adoption in nations such as the U.S. and U.K. that specifically target middle-and upper-class white women, a discourse of what I term *global motherhood* has surfaced as a logic through which white womens' bodies are spilling into the global community and offering visions and hopes of a multicultural global family. . . .

This essay examines the representational logics through which white women are represented as "global mothers" in popular culture, and how such representations manifest new transnational formations of whiteness (and race more broadly). It is particularly concerned with the visualities, myths, and desires that are spun as well as concealed through images of white women representing transnational maternity in popular culture. . . .

REPRESENTATIONS OF "GLOBAL MOTHERHOOD"

In order to examine the representational logics of global motherhood, I focus on a range of celebrity white women such as Princess Diana, Angelina Jolie, Madonna, and white female movie stars serving as United Nations' good will ambassadors. Although I address representations of many white women, much of my focus remains on Princess Diana, given that she was the first woman in the current neoliberal regime of the late twentieth century who was so extensively visualized as a global mother and imbricated in a logic of humanitarian borderlessness through which she was styled as a global caretaker. Indeed, no other white woman in history has been visualized as a site of global intimacies—of love, care, desire—to the extent that Diana has been; just to think of Diana is to think of her with children of the world. And it is these images that today make it commonplace for us to engage with other celebrity white women such as Angelina Jolie endlessly adopting and caring for children of the world. Indeed, as Jolie herself recently stated (as reported by one of her friends) she wants to be the Diana of the twenty-first century. . . .

RAYS OF LIGHT

In representations of white women as transnational mothers, we often find them moralized through visual logics that represent them as angelic figures emanating compassion, love, and healing. Dyer (1997) has written about the relationship between the aesthetics of photographic technology and whiteness. He has noted how in media culture white women are often bathed through soft white light that represents them as pure, divine, and angelic. "Idealised white women are bathed in and permeated by light. It streams through them and falls on to them. . . . In short they glow" (p. 127). He further argues that the "angelically glowing white woman is an extreme representation precisely because it is an idealisation" in which white women become the symbol of "white virtuousness and the last word in the claim that what made whites special as a race was their non-physical, spiritual, and indeed ethereal qualities" (p. 127).

White women who come to signify transnational motherhood are not only bathed in a halo of virtuousness but they are also always beautiful. Beauty is frequently associated with the production of life; it serves as an "exemplary image for the furtherance of life" (Colebrook, 2006, p. 138).

> We regard as beautiful anything that will serve to realize life's potential—anything that is fertile, productive, and conducive to self recognition and self maintenance (p. 138).

Women visually coded as ordinary looking generally do not grace our screens as carrying the potential for producing and sustaining life. Although this is not surprising—given that women who

signify global motherhood tend to be celebrities and hence beautiful—such representations, however, highlight an underlying intersectional logic in which heterosexuality, race, class, gender, and internationality come together in constructing the "global mother" and highlighting her life giving abilities. Women whose bodies are "out of place"— the "white trash" woman, the lesbian woman, the non-white woman, the non-Western woman—are usually not celebrated as global mothers in popular culture. Lacking in desirability and civility, they do not glow and hence cannot "further life" and further it in a way that conforms to the purities and moralities associated with an idealized reproductive body.

Diana's images, for instance, are often saturated in visual codes that moralize her beautiful body. This is seen especially in lighting techniques. For instance, a famous image that circulated in many magazines was of Diana with children in Africa. Diana is sitting on a bamboo bench with hungry children who have probably just been handed food by Diana. The visual organization of the image is situated in a play of light and darkness. The sunlight falls on Diana; the photograph has been deliberately composed to emphasize Diana through that light. We notice that the light *flows up* to Diana's body, centralizing her and she literally glows. When reprinted in a popular commemorative book, *Diana: An extraordinary life* (1998, pp. 384–385) this image is narratively positioned by the copy headline— "Lighting up the third world." This copy text positions Diana as the carrier of light; it invites us to view Diana's body through the trope of light (and life) and the "third world" around her through darkness and death. Many of the other visual components in the image are also in darkness—the background, for instance, is in darkness where we only see hazy ill-defined silhouettes of children. Some of the children sharing the bench with her, with eating bowls in their hands, are in shadows that by contrast again visually emphasize the light on Diana. . . .

Verbal narratives often shore up the meanings imbedded in such visual techniques; for instance, Diana is frequently represented through the language of a healer. Reports describe her in terms such as:

> Diana used her power just like a magic wand, waving it in all kinds of places where there was hurt. . . . And everywhere she used it, there

were changes, almost like a fairy tale. (*People,* February 2, 1998, p. 84)

Or

These children were victims of cancer, mines, Aids, leprosy or hunger [. . . .] She would cuddle and stroke them. She would kiss them— whatever their condition. . . . *When she left, they would describe her as an angel.* (*Daily Mail,* 1997, September 6, p. xix) (emphasis added)

This theme, where Diana is seen as having some innate power to heal, is also dominant in other representations of white women. When controversies around Madonna's adoption of baby David in Malawi were exploding, Madonna justified her adoption saying that when she saw baby David in the clinic, she was "transfixed" by him. The sense one gets is that an inner spiritual pull drew her to this adoption. Meg Ryan also recently described her adoption of a baby from China as a "metaphysical kind of labor." [2] In such representations white femininity, associated with the spiritual/metaphysical, seems to transcend time and space as its transnational love becomes coded as something authentic, almost something that exists a priori in relation to the body. Constructing an inward "essence" for white femininity, such representations reproduce a universalism which equates whiteness with spirit and not corporeality. And as Dyer (1997) has noted, historically this has been a classic mode through which whiteness has reproduced its universality and godliness.

Other visual assemblages also play a role in attributing goodness and spirituality to the white maternal body. Especially important is the *Madonna-Child trope* which functions as a significant representational framework. The Madonna-Child image, evoking associations of Mary with Jesus, has had significant visual power in Western religious discourses. Reproduced in the art of Raphael, DaVinci, Michelangelo, and Salvador Dali, it is saturated with connotations of salvation and love, and has historically functioned to represent white women through compassion and morality. Briggs (2003), for instance, has illustrated the prevalence of the Madonna/Child image in post– cold war U.S. narratives and has demonstrated how this trope informed foreign policy, international aid, and family values discourses.

Representations of global motherhood frequently draw on this Madonna/Child trope.

Consider an image of Diana cradling a cancer-ridden baby in Pakistan (Owen, 1997). Diana's eyes are closed in compassion (notice again how the light falls on Diana). The child looks up at Diana with devotion. Diana's hand is touching the hand of the child as though giving it life. Similarly, in a recent image of Jolie in the British magazine *Hello* (May 2, 2006, p. 77) Jolie is carrying baby Zahara and looking out into the endless desert, a peaceful smile gracing her face. The starkness of the landscape confers an other-worldly quality to the mother/child image. Additionally, many international adoption agencies take on names such as *Adopt an Angel, Angels Haven Outreach, Adoption Blessings Worldwide,* and *Cradle of Hope* that rhetorically invoke religiosity imbedded in the Madonna/Child trope that then gets associated with white women's adoptive desires.

Discursive operations of the Madonna/Child image through which white women are positioned in relation to deprived children of the global south also manifest what Bashford (2006) calls "global biopolitics" (p. 67). For example, the children that Diana visits in "other worlds" are usually unhealthy—they are sick children, often abandoned by their families (read: the nation). Given the normalized assumption that a modern body is a healthy body, for it has the apparatus to attend to its care and development, the unhealthy body of the child signifies the non-modern future of its nation. And the rescue/healing of that unhealthy body from its nation, by white female cosmopolitan subjects such as Diana or Jolie, moralizes a movement from the darkness of non-modernity to the light of modernity. Such global biopolitics where health, race, and nation collide, manifest a larger phenomenon of late twentieth century in which the very battle over modern belonging is being fought out on the terrain of health. From AIDS to SARS, the social representations of diseases have played an important role in imperial cultural projects, in securing borders, prohibiting cross-national flows of populations, and framing nations through the language of disease whereby health becomes spatialized (Briggs, 2003; Bashford, 2006; Cartwright, 2003; Patton, 1992; Treichler, 1999). For instance, Madonna justified to Oprah her controversial adoption, stating that:

"I beg all of those people to go to Africa" she said, "and see what I saw and walk through those villages. . . . *To see mothers dying, with Kaposi sarcoma lesions all over their bodies.*

To see open sewers everywhere. To see what I saw." (*USA Today*, 2006, emphasis added)

Singer Bono supported Madonna's actions to Britain's *Sun* newspaper, stating that "Madonna should be applauded for helping to take a child out of the worst poverty imaginable." He also despaired that "the situation is so desperate in the third world continent that parents are willing to give up their children if there is a chance for them to have a better life" (Exposay, 2006). Place and nation here begin to symbolize a crisis in hygiene that ultimately suggests a crisis in the modernity of such nations—a crisis which, however, conceals larger geopolitical struggles related to toxic dumping, environmental pollution, the need for cheap mobility of pharmaceutical products to the global south, the neoliberal destruction of local economies, the need for greater international aid, and the history of Western colonialisms.

The visual contrast between bodies reinforces this struggle that is fought out on the terrain of health. For instance, when the robust, toned, tall body of Diana (i.e. healthy) that has been built up with gym equipment, modern yoga, swimming, and other body-care technologies (technologies of the modern) is visually juxtaposed with the starving and undernourished bodies of children in the global south, the white female body's (read the nations) "built up" superiority in relation to the damaged bodies of the children becomes highlighted. Camera angles and lighting are often organized to inspire awe towards Diana's body: we often look *up* at Diana's body (or at least her body is at eye level with our gaze) while we look *down* at the native children around her body. . . .

TRANSNATIONAL MATERNITIES AND "ETHICS OF CARE"[3]

Imperialism has always been about a struggle over maternities. Sometimes this struggle has been explicit, as during slavery in the U.S. when the black mother's body was regularly raped by white plantation owners and the child of the rape recirculated as plantation labor. At other times the struggle has silently informed grand narratives of imperial enlightenment, as with cases of white women in British imperialism supporting the empire's cultural mission as teachers, governesses, and missionaries by enculturating upper-class children of the colonized in manners of "civilization."

If narratives of imperialism are also grand narratives about modernity, then underlying visions of the modern have always lurked in the politics of domesticity, home, and family (Stoler, 1997, 2002). To produce modern subjects is to ensure that the home as the basic unit of the nation is civilized, for home is the site for the production of the nation's future. In Western imperial discourses, where white heterosexual femininity functions as a signifier of "homeliness," the non-white non-Western mother by contrast often functions as a failure of civil "homeliness." In contemporary Anglo-centric discourses, for example, the non-white mother is often a failed mother. Within the U.S. black mothers are "crack mothers," Latina mothers are seen as overly breeding children while unable to look after them, and Native American mothers are seen as suffering from Fetal Alcohol Syndrome.

Imaginations about a "global family" that circulate in adoption discourses are often underpinned by such a logic of failed non-white, non-Western motherhood. For example, a U.S. adoption agency, International Adoption Help, invokes the trope of maternal abandonment to encourage U.S. families to adopt from Guatemala. It emphasizes that "the easiest way to understand the type of child/children that become available for adoption in Guatemala is to realize" the processes of "abandonment" and "relinquishment" at work. Abandonment, explains the text, is "when a child has been abandoned by his/her biological family, or when parental rights have been terminated by the Guatemalan government due to neglect" and "relinquishment" is when a Guatemalan mother relinquishes the child's care to a lawyer because of her inability to give maternal care. The invocation of a crisis in Guatemalan motherhood enables the invitation to white U.S. mothers to step in and rescue those children.

Such a logic of maternal abandonment also informs representations of Diana as a "global mother." [4] In a popular book *Diana: An extraordinary life* (1998) a particular chapter (from which an image was discussed earlier) is entitled "Lighting up the third world." The chapter offers a detailed description of the conditions of children in Brazil:

> As Diana quickly learned, Brazil, a spectacular country full of beautiful tourist sights had a *horrifying secret*—a mass of starving homeless children, many *abandoned by their mothers and their societies*. . . . When Diana arrived, she saw only the tiniest remnants of these human

cast-offs: ten children aged from five months to five years *left in the streets by their mothers who were drug addicts or prostitutes. . . .* (1998, p. 392, emphasis added)

Brazilian mothers here are failed mothers; metaphors of prostitution and drug addiction frame their bodies. Their bodies thus cannot nurture their children—the future of the nation and the world.[4]

A BBC program, *The Diary of a Princess* (1997), that chronicles Diana's humanitarian work with British Red Cross in Angola, also invokes the logic of failed non-Western motherhood. The program is replete with images of sick and dying babies, and children with broken limbs from landmine explosions. A particular moment in the film captures Diana's arrival at a health clinic where local mothers are waiting with their babies. On Diana's arrival, a young mother hands over her highly overweight baby to Diana. Diana cuddles the baby, laughs, and then asks: "he weighs a ton. What has she been feeding him?" At this moment we see the baby's mother, partly eclipsed in the frame by Diana, standing in the background with a shy smile, not understanding the conversation.

While a humorous and affectionate moment, the image of a white mother examining a black baby while that baby's mother stands in the background, rendered into silence, is poignant and revealing. The poignancy emerges from the erasure of the African mother by the global motherhood of Diana. The passage of the highly overweight baby from the native mother to Diana is a performative moment through which competing visions of global domesticity are staged in which one (white maternal domesticity) negates the other (non-white maternal domesticity). The question "what has she been feeding him?" is addressed to the local male officials around Diana and not to the native mother as she cannot speak English. The male native officials become a point of mediation between the white woman and the native mother. A complex positionality of the third-world mother in relation to the white mother becomes visible here. As Diana addresses her query to the local official, this address situates the native men in a position that invites them to "speak for" the native mother. . . .

The white mother can only occupy the position of a "global mother" by erasing the non-white maternal body from visions of global domesticity. The white mother's subject position is thus ironically dependent on the necessary failure of the non-white native mother. . . .

UNITED COLORS OF CHILDREN

Today, a continental collecting of impoverished children is becoming a way through which to represent a seamless global family in popular culture. In a 2006 interview, Angelina Jolie noted that she and Brad wanted to travel the world to find babies from different countries to adopt:

I want to create a rainbow family. That's children of different religions and cultures from different countries. I believe I am meant to find my children in the world and not necessarily have them genetically. (MailOnline, 2006)

Reports of how they were first planning to adopt in Russia but then adopted from Ethiopia, or how they were planning to adopt from India and name the child India "to honour its homeland" illustrate the pervasiveness of a "worldliness" in which collecting children becomes a way of engaging with different national cultures, and the children become a commodity through which race/culture can simply be bought, and engaged with, at will. As Jolie once stated: "do you balance the race, so there's another African person in the house for Zahara, after another Asian person in the house for Mad? . . . We think so" (Fox News, 2006). (Similarly, Madonna in an interview with Oprah reinforced such a history-blind and individualized cosmopolitan logic when she claimed that her natural children simply did not notice the "difference" of the adopted baby from Malawi: "they've [her natural children] never once mentioned the difference in his skin colour or questioned his presence in our life" (Pilkington, 2006).

. . . Colorful visual regimes of "global motherhood" ultimately constitute a symbolic exchange between nations; how the child figures in this exchange becomes crucial to analyze, for the representation of the child makes a larger statement about the ways in which the relationality between nations and their domesticities are conceptualized in Western media discourses (Castaneda, 2002). . . . It is important to note that the figure of the child does not represent a threat to our sense of self in the (white) West. A child lacks agency. As Castaneda (2002) notes, a "child is not only in the making but is also malleable—and so can be made" (p. 3). This is unlike the adult—a fully formed human being—whose adultness cannot be so easily be stripped of its national history. In contrast, the child enables an easy dehistoricization and a *re-historicization* that is non-threatening to the white national self.

There is also the issue of what Ahmed (2004) calls "affective economies" (p. 117). Feelings and emotions, argues Ahmed, are not merely psychological matters; rather they "mediate the relationship" between "the psychic and the social, and between the individual and the collective" (p. 119). They function as sites of bonding through which national and, in this case, transnational attachments are fostered. The child, as opposed to the adult, easily functions as a love object and thus inspires bonding in ways that the adult cannot. We can love the child of another nation *out of its history* in ways we cannot for the adult, for to be a child is to be (seemingly) without much of a history and memory. Consequently, feelings of affection that the figure of the child invites in the white mother are also feelings that can be mobilized in the larger imagination of a loving (and dehistoricized) global family. . . .

One reason why we in the West can feel pity and compassion for these starving, abandoned children is because we are simultaneously invited to hate the underlying conditions of their nations. We are meant to feel gratitude that we are not them. This underlying gratitude mobilizes our pity and speaks to our sense of superiority that then invites care from us. The irony is this: our hatred of the conditions that have produced the native child always interrupts our capacity to seriously love the child on *an equal cultural level,* for to love the child with dignity and equality is to love its nation and culture with dignity. Thus, romantic internationalism (Malkki, 1994) mobilizes our love in the West as conditions of attachment to underprivileged nations but it simultaneously reifies our underlying disgust for these nations.

. . . The Sponsor-a-child section of the adoption agency Children's International states:

> We unite sponsors with children around the world—bringing different nations and cultures together. So take a peek by clicking below and learn about the children and their countries, their traditions and their lives.

When a potential sponsor clicks on the image of a child from a country, s/he is directed to a section that provides cultural descriptions of traditions of that particular country—from food and cultural festivals, to language and social norms. One could almost be shopping for a tourist place to visit. In choosing to adopt a child, one chooses to affiliate with a particular nation that takes one's fantasy. Jolie expresses this touristic logic when she notes

to *People:* "there is something . . . about waking up and travelling somewhere and finding your family. . . . Sooner or later, I'll end up everywhere" (*People,* January 11, 2006). In such language, the child becomes a route for the white woman to enter a particular nation/culture even while the child, in such representations, becomes rooted in that culture as it is often made to embody the markers of its exotic national difference. . . .

Such representations of internationally adopted children frequently contrast with representations of domestic trans-racial adoption (in the U.S. for instance). International adoption receives far greater attention in the media, especially made popular by celebrities; it is seen as more exciting than domestic adoption. U.S. adoption agencies note that "there is an idea that because these kids [domestic kids] come from unfortunate circumstances, that they are juvenile delinquents," a view confirmed by Rita Soronen, executive director of *Dave Thomas Foundation,* to Fox News.[5] Ortiz and Briggs (2003) explain that in discourses of transnational adoption there is greater sentimentalization attached to a child from an "other" nation than from within the nation. One reason for this, they argue, is that underclass children (usually children of color) within the U.S. are already racialized in ways that make their body threatening: they are already coded as products of violent, drug cracking, antisocial families that have transgressed the bounds of proper citizenly belonging. Hence these children are often perceived as psychologically damaged or flawed in character. In contrast, international children while perceived as unhealthy and non-modern, do not represent delinquency or violence, and hence are less threatening. They are simply seen as needing rescuing by the modernizing Western family.[6] Although recent films such as *The Blind Side* (2009) have represented trans-racial domestic adoption, the film reinforces many of the stereotypes of black pathology that strengthen the perception that domestic kids are products of dangerous, toxic environments. To be sure, the film is based on a factual story, but the very selection of this content for representational purposes tends to reinforce anxieties around black pathology.

CONCLUSION

Contemporary representations of global motherhood make visible new logics of whiteness that are imbricated in a politics of the transnational. . . .

The discussion offered in this essay for instance, invites us to ask how whiteness—in particular the white family form—today is being bolstered by, and remaking itself through, particular kinds of transnational flows—in this case of children who occupy positions of extreme global otherness. . . .

This essay has also underscored the importance of a transnational contextual analysis of whiteness. Given that whiteness is a contextual formation, and that national contexts today are shaped by, as well as shaping, transnational relations of power, ignoring transnational linkages in the production of whiteness is limiting, for it can potentially perpetuate a view that power relations of whiteness within the nation are somehow disconnected from larger transnational struggles and flows (see also Shome, 2010). Examining whiteness through the methodological lens of the transnational also enables us to avoid conceiving whiteness as though its logics are the same wherever and whenever. A transnational *contextual* analysis of whiteness recognizes that the power of whiteness lies precisely in its ability to constantly shift its strategies of reproduction in response to the changing contours of the nation, and that those contours are always imbricated in larger international and geopolitical relations.

NOTES

2. http://www.femalefirst.co.uk/celebrity/ MegRyan-22693.htm

3. I borrow the term from Michel Foucault.

4. See Dorow (2006) for a different discussion about maternal abandonment.

5. http://www.Foxnews.com/entertainment /2009/04/03/domestic-vs-international- adoption celebrities-overlooking-american-children.

6. http://www.Foxnews.com/entertainment /2009/04/03/domestic-vs-international-adoption celebrities-overlooking-american-children.

REFERENCES

Ahmed, S. (2004). Affective economies. *Social Text*, 22, 117–139.

Anagnost, A. (2000). Scenes of misrecognition: Maternal citizenship in the age of transnational adoption. *Positions*, 8, 299–421.

Bashford, A. (2006). Global biopolitics and the history of world health. *History of the human sciences*, 19, 67–88.

Berlant, L. (1991). *Anatomy of a national fantasy*. Chicago, IL: University of Chicago Press.

Berlant, L. (1997). *The queen of American goes to Washington city*. Durham, NH: Duke University Press.

Berlant, L. (2000). Intimacy: A special issue. In L. Berlant (Ed.), *Intimacy* (pp. 18). Chicago, IL: University of Chicago Press.

Blunt, A. (1999). The flight from Lucknow: British women travelling and writing home. In J. Duncan & D. Gregory (Eds.), *Writes of passage* (pp. 92–113). New York, NY: Routledge.

Briggs, L. (2003). Mother, child, race, nation: The visual iconography of rescue and politics of transnational and transracial adoption. *Gender and History*, 15, 179–200.

Briggs, L. (2006). Making "American" families: Transnational adoption and U.S. Latin America foreign policy. In A. Stoler (Ed.), *Haunted by empire: Geographies of intimacy in North American history* (pp. 344–364). Durham, NH: Duke University Press.

Cartwright, L. (2003). Photographs of waiting children. *Social Text*, 21, 83–109.

Castaneda, C. (2002). *Figurations: Child, bodies, worlds*. Durham, NH: Duke University Press.

Colebrook, C. (2006). Introduction. *Feminist Theory* (special issue on Beauty), 7, 131–142.

Diana: An extraordinary life. (1998). London, UK: Orbis Publishing Limited.

Dorow, S. (2006). *Transnational adoption*. New York, NY: New York University Press.

Dyer, R. (1997). *White*. New York, NY: Routledge.

Eng, D.L. (2003). Transnational adoption and queer diasporas. *Social Text, 76*, 21, 137.

Exposay (2006, November 13). Bono praises Madonna for African adoption. Retrieved from http://www.exposay.com/bono-praises-madonna-for-adoption/v/6011

Fox News. (2006, December 14). Angelina Jolie: I'm on the pill. Retrieved from http://www.foxnews.com/story/0,2933,236522,00.html

Gilroy, P. (2005). *Postcolonial melancholia.* New York, NY: Columbia University Press.

Grewal, I. (1996). *Home and harem.* Durham, NH: Duke University Press.

Kaplan, C. (1995). A world without boundaries: The Body Shop's trans/national geographics. *Social Text, 43,*45–66.

Kaplan, C. (2001). Hillary Rodham Clinton's Orient: Cosmopolitan travel and global feminist subjects. *Meridians: Feminism, Race, Transnationalism, 2,* 219–240.

MailOnline (2006, October 26). Angelina set to adopt another baby. Retrieved from http://www.dailymail.co.uk/tvshowbiz/article-412751/Angelina-set-adopt-baby.html

Malkki, L. (1994). "Citizens of humanity": Internationalism and the imagined community of nations. *Diaspora, 3,*41–68.

Marre, D., & Briggs, L. (Eds.). (2009). *International adoption: Global inequalities and the circulation of children.* New York, NY: New York University Press.

Nakayama, T.K. & Krizek, R. (1995). Whiteness as strategic rhetoric. *Quarterly Journal of Speech, 81,* 291–309.

Nakayama, T.K., & Martin, J. (Eds.). (1999). *Whiteness: The communication of social identity.* Oakland, CA: Sage Publication.

Ortiz, A., & Briggs, L. (2003). The culture of poverty, crack babies, and welfare cheats: The making of the "healthy white baby crisis." *Social Text, 76,* 21,39–57.

Owen, Nicholas (1997). *Diana: The People's Princess.* Carlton Books.

Patton, C. (1992). From nation to family: Containing African AIDS. In H. Abelove, D. Halperan, & M. Barale (Eds.), *Lesbian and gay studies reader* (pp. 127–138). New York, NY: Routledge.

People, January 11, 2006. Angelina Jolie Pregnant. Retrieved from: http://www.people.com/people/archive/article/0.20145123.000.html

Pilkington, E. (2006, October 26). Confessions on a TV show: Oprah hears Madonna's side of the story. *The Guardian.* Retrieved from http://www.guardian.co.uk/world/2006/oct/26/arts.usa

Ram, K., & Jolly, M. (1998). *Maternities and modernities.* Berkeley: University of California Press.

Shohat, E. & Stam, R. (1994). *Unthink-ing Eurocentrism: Multiculturalism and the media.* UK: Routledge.

Shome, R. (2006). Transnational feminism and communication studies. *Communication Review, 9*(4), 255–267.

Shome, R. (2010). Internationalizing critical race communication studies: Transnationality, space, and affect. In T. Nakayama & R. Halualani (Eds.), *Handbook of Critical Intercultural Communication* (pp. 149–170). Malden, MA: Blackwell Publishing.

Spivak, G. (1988). Can the subaltern speak? In L. Grossberg & C. Nelson (Eds.), *Marxism and the interpretation of culture* (pp. 271–313). Urbana: University of Illinois Press.

Stoler, A. (1997). *Race and the education of desire.* Durham, NH: Duke University Press.

Stoler, A. (2002). *Carnal knowledge and imperial power.* Berkeley: University of California Press.

Stoler, A. (2006). Tense and tender ties. In A. Stoler (Ed.), *Haunted by empire: Geographies of intimacy in North American history* (pp. 2367). Durham, NH: Duke University Press.

Treichler, P. (1999). How to have theory in an epidemic: Cultural chronicle of AIDS. Durham, NH: Duke University Press.

USA Today (2006). Retrieved from http://www.foxnews.com/story/0,2933,236522,00.html

Volkman, T. (2003). Transnational adoption. *Social Text, 74,* 21,1–5.

Wells, K. (2009). *Childhood in a global perspective.* Cambridge, MA: Polity.

Wiegma, R. (1999). Whiteness studies and the paradox of particularity. *Boundary, 2, 26,* 115–150.

16

TRANSGENDER TRANSITIONS

Sex/Gender Binaries in the Digital Age

Kay Siebler

Tim Curry, in a black corset, big-girl-cha-cha shoes, elbow-length black gloves, and sexy garters, will forever be the quintessential queer for a generation of Americans. But that generation, of which I proudly count myself a member, is now just a bunch of geezers. What Curry's character of Dr. Frank-n-Furter in the cult classic *Rocky Horror Picture Show* did for us was show us queerness that could be celebrated, queerness that could be embraced, queerness that was hip, and cool. If we did not want to be just like Curry *and* his character, we wanted to be his friend. In fact, many of us spent a better part of our teens and twenties learning to perform his specific brand of queer in our rooms, at parties, and in the front of movie theaters all over the country.

The Rocky Horror Picture Show (1975) provides a celebratory portrayal of a "Transvestite from Transylvania," although we never see Dr. Frank-n-Furter out of drag. The language of the time did not accommodate anything but transsexuals or transvestites. There was no such term as "transgender" or the umbrella term of "queer" other than as an epithet. Judith Butler's theories on gender as performance were yet to be written. Yet for the fans of this film and musical (the London musical *The Rocky Horror Show* debuted in 1973), Dr. Frank-n-Furter was not a drag queen—although the character self-identified as a transvestite. He was not trying to perform femaleness. He had a sexy bulge in his black briefs; there were no breasts in his laced-up bustier. He was the first media representation of a delightful transgender person before we had the language to describe him as thus. He was dancing on the grave of the oppressive systems that rigidly link sex with gender and sexuality; he remains a glorious model for people

who play with gender. He thrilled us, even if—in the mid 1970s—we did not know exactly why. We knew he was bolder, different, and seemingly more fun and joyful than any other transvestite we had ever seen on the silver screen.

At that time Dr. Frank-n-Furter's ambiguity was part of the appeal. Today we are far less comfortable with the sort of ambiguity embodied by transgender people. We want them to be either/or: pre-op or post-op, transvestite or transsexual. There are few representations in mainstream media of a transgender person who defies these categories. Characters or people may define themselves as transgender, but they are modifying their bodies into the accepted codes for masculine male or feminine female. Unfortunately, the Internet serves to reinforce these binaries. Locating a transqueer identity online, that is, a person who is not "transitioning" with hormones and surgery to a specific gender identity, is difficult. What the digital realm tells users and viewers is that "trans" means "transitioning," not moving outside of systems defining sex and gender. . . . For all the strides we have made as a culture of embracing and complicating queerness in the Digital Age—for all the communities and groups that the Internet offers to queer folks finding their way in the world—we have taken a step backwards in relation to breaking out of the gender/sex binaries. . . .

THE DANGEROUS MOVES OF DEFINITIONS

Before we go any further, we need to first enter the prickly business of defining terms. . . . Queer is the umbrella term for people who resist the

From Siebler, K. (2012). Transgender transitions: Sex/gender binaries in the digital age. *Journal of Gay & Lesbian Mental Health,* 16(1), 74–99. Reprinted by permission of Taylor & Francis Ltd., www.tandfonline.com.

binaries. There are various identities within the context of identifying as queer. People who were, 20 years ago, described as "hermaphrodite" (people having biological characteristics of both sexes) now name themselves "intersex." Language shifted because the intersex community wanted to name themselves rather than being named by the medical profession. One will occasionally still encounter the term "hermaphrodite" in reference to a person who is intersex, but the preferred term of those claiming the identity is intersex.

Only in the past 20 years has the intersex community come out and talked about their experiences. Previously, when an intersex child was born, pediatric surgeons were called upon to "fix" the baby, that is, create a distinct penis or vagina. As the child grew and went through puberty, hormones were given to ensure the surgical assignment had been "correct." Most intersex babies grew up not knowing what had happened to them. Today, medical professionals are more attuned to the sensitivity of the intersex individual and counsel parents on letting their child decide who he or she will become. Yet in a world where gender is a primary way we interact with the world, raising a child to be gender-neutral is no small feat.

A transsexual may or may not come into the world intersex. A transsexual is an individual who undergoes hormones and surgery in an effort to feel at home in hir[1] body. Transsexuals are identified as Female-to-Male (FTM) or Male-to-Female (MTF). A transsexual may identify as intersex, but once zhe begins the transition to create a distinctly male or female body, zhe moves into the category of transsexual. Once a transsexual has transitioned for any period of time, he or she may no longer identify as trans as he or she feels zhe is now accepted as a masculine male or feminine female.

A transgender person is someone who occupies the borderlands between communities and identities. A transgender person may be intersex, but may not be. With the feminist and gay/lesbian rights movements of the 1970s, the term "transgender" was coined. At that time, most transgender people eschewed the idea that they needed surgery or hormones to modify their body. Today transgender people see hormones and surgery as a way to "pass" in a heteronormative world that mandates a rigid gender/sex binary. . . .

Genderqueer or transgender people reject the terms "transvestite" or "cross dresser" as ways of describing themselves because these terms imply a superficial or playful performance of gender. . . . The transgender/genderqueer person rejects and resists categorization: "The Genderqueer has an identity that is unrecognizable in the gender binary" (Saltzburg, 2010, p. 18). As Leslie Feinberg, a self-defined transgender warrior, describes the identity in the film, *Outlaw,* that profiles hir life (Lebow, 1994): "Not everybody who is differently gendered is gay."

Feinberg, as a gender warrior, defies the either/or categories and instead identifies as both/all. Saltzburg's research found this to be indicative of the transmasculine people she interviewed. "Many participants conceptualized genderqueer as a **'both/neither' identity**. . . . This means there is a sense of being more than one gender at a time, or being in between genders" (*bold in original text*) (2010, p. 43). Feinberg describes this identity as a transgender warrior; Saltzburg defines it as genderqueer. Both are articulating the identity of those who actively resist and defy the gender binary. Therefore, this population is less likely to feel the need for hormones and surgery. These are the people whose perspectives and identities are disappearing or lost to us in the Digital Age. . . .

PASSING ON THE QUEER

. . . Where many media theorists have argued that the Internet offers a disembodiment—a way of transforming the physical body into a digital identity—that is liberating, the Internet more often serves to reinforce a rigid trans body type. For example, in his research regarding online ads by and for transgender people (2010), Daniel Farr discovered that there was very little play within the categories of trans people. Descriptors of identity were reduced to "FTM" and "MTF," using easy shorthand that simplifies, as opposed to complicates, the gender system. Farr writes, "The use of MTF and FTM are problematic when engaging with transgender persons given the mélange of embodiment and social enactments, but were exceptionally common terms among the personal ads" (p. 91). Farr found that the majority of people posting ads included descriptors about their bodies, with the focus on convincing their audience they were "real" men or women (p. 93). . . .

There has been limited research on transgender people and online communities (Gauthier & Chaudoir, 2004). Despite the dearth of research, it makes sense that transgender people would seek out online communities more than other queer populations as they are a minority within a minority. Transgender people face disproportionate violence (Lombardi et al., 2001). People of minority communities find that the Internet provides a feeling of safety and anonymity (Farr, 2010, pp. 89–90). But as transgender people may seek out on-line communities to escape violence and find acceptance, these communities may only accept them if they have certain gender characteristics. The dominant narrative found in online queer spaces is one of reductive definitions of trans bodies and trans identity. . . .

THE FTM BODY: OUR RIGHT TO STARE

Transgender bodies are discussed, displayed, and regulated much more rigidly on the Internet than the physical bodies of others within the queer community. . . . Popular television shows and films reinforce gender rigidity, and online fan sites debate and celebrate these representations. Max, the trans character on *The L Word,* is a fascinating example of how online fans expressed mixed responses to fictionalized trans people. In season four (2006), the character Moira was introduced, a slight, butch lesbian. By mid-season Moira was transitioning to Max with the help of hormones, cross-dressing, and crotch stuffing. Top surgery was discussed. Max has transitioned across three seasons. He is referred to as a "trans-man" instead of a "butch lesbian" because of his choice to use hormones. Max is no longer considered a lesbian because he uses hormones, but without surgery, Max still has the vagina and breasts that code him as female (Edwards, 2010, p. 167). Among the lesbian and trans communities there was much Internet discussion about the Max character. One online viewer expressed typical frustration with Max's gender ambiguity on the "After Ellen Forum" electronic bulletin board, writing: "Also, L word STILL has no butch characters. Moira/Max does not count because he's a transgender man which isn't the same thing! L word is making it look as if the natural progression for butch women is to eventually become transgender" (Edwards, 2010, p. 168). Many online lesbians expressed frustration that finally there was a butch

lesbian on *The L Word* and she turned out to be trans, echoing what Judith Halberstam refers to at the "butch/FTM border wars" (Coogan, 2006, p. 18). It seems no one was willing to see Max as a transgender person, where binaries of sex and gender are queered. News media tells us there is either/or, we cannot see anything else, we cannot *be* anything else. Queer, in relation to transgender people, is not really queer in the Digital Age. Instead trans-gender people are reduced to very un-queer definitions of masculinity and femininity, maleness, and femaleness. . . .

TRANNIES ARE THE NEW BLACK/"CHICKS WITH DICKS"

The cultural curiosity of trans identity permeates popular media. From Ru Paul's or Tyra Banks' talk shows to *Queer Eye for the Straight Guy* or *Law and Order,* the laptop screen and the television screen bring us images of MTF transgender people as an intriguing oddity or amusement. Transgender people, typically in various stages of surgical and hormonal transitioning, are appearing on the "hip" television programs with predictable regularity: *Nip and Tuck* (Famke Janssen plays Ava Moore), *America's Next Top Model* (Isis King plays herself), VH1's *I Want to Work for Diddy* (Laverne Cox plays herself). ABC's *Dirty Sexy Money* (Candis Cayne plays Carmelita), *Ugly Betty* (Rebecca Romijn plays Alexis Meade), and *All My Children* (Jeffery Carlson plays Zoe) are popular television shows that have clamored onto the "Trannies are the New Cool" bandwagon. The Internet discussions (blog posts and comments on fan websites) regarding these characters connect these television shows to the digital world.

Some may argue that the mainstream presence of trans people is revolutionary, but as many media theorists have pointed out (Clark, 1969; Leifer, Gordon, & Graves, 1974; Berry, 1998; Hartley, 1999; Padva, 2007), the presence of a traditionally marginalized group does not necessarily equate to advancement. MTF people are typically portrayed as high drag. They have big hair, lots of make-up, push-up bras, and large implants that they are happy to display through low-cut bodices. They often carry the stereotypically gay catty (snap, snap, swish) attitudes that straight audiences love. The MTF transqueers can easily be read as gay men dressing in drag and playing to the stereotypes both of hyper-feminine females and comedic drag performers. A thread on a Facebook discussion board ("Nigel, is this your daughter/son?") focused on transgender people, making a direct connection between trans representations on television and "real world" trans people. The posts (presumably written by non-trans people) contained references to stereotypical trans identity. A person using the screen name of Jessica posted, "I've seen transgender people on television, and there's always something different about their voices and their body shape. I think MTV Real World had a chick with a d*** recently" ("Nigel," 2010). The vernacular of "chick with a dick" reflects how the complexity of trans identity is reduced to male/female—the genitalia; the physical manifestation of the body is what counts. To further codify the sex/gender connection, body aesthetics of MTF trans people *must* ascribe to hyper feminine ideals. Femininity costs money and means body modification.

In *Girl Inside* (Gallus, 2007), the filmmaker follows Madison, a college-aged transgender person, as she goes through the gradual steps of transitioning to female: first her Adam's apple is shaved, then she takes hormones, finally the genital surgery. The most interesting parts of this film are the relationships that are portrayed. Madison has a close and loving relationship with her 80-year-old grandmother who accepts her transition and attempts to teach her about the standards of femininity, and tutors Madison in the power that resides in being feminine. This hyper-feminine fixation can be attributed to a postfeminist cultural moment where people have been duped into believing that feminine sexual power is a form of real and sustained power within the culture. Rosalind Gill, in writing of cisfemales (women who were born female) and the effects of media on their bodies, states:

> One of the most striking aspects of post feminist media culture is its obsessive preoccupation with the body. . . . [F]emininity is defined as bodily property rather than (say) a social structural or psychological one. Instead of caring or nurturing or motherhood being regarded as central to femininity (all, of course, highly problematic and exclusionary) in today's media it is possession of a "sexy body" that is presented

as women's key (if not sole) source of identity. (Gill, p. 255)

Transgender characters such as Laverne Cox on *I Want to Work for Diddy*, Carmelita on *Dirty Sexy Money*, and Isis King on *America's Top Model* all fit the "chick with a dick, gay Barbie" stereotype of MTF transqueers. Cox has an interview clip on the VH1 website where she talks about trans politics, the lack of portrayals of transqueers on television, and connects the struggles of transgender people with the Civil Rights movement ("Transgendered People on Television," 2008). She is articulate, smart, and politically astute. But these dynamics of her politics and intellect never make it to the *I Want to Work for Diddy* show where she plays a stereotypical "gay Barbie" with big hair, Valley Girl language, and glamorous fashion. This image is reiterated in Cox's casting in the reality show *TRANSform*. In *TRANSform*, Cox plays one of three *Charlie's Angels*-type trannies who do makeovers of cisgender women (VH1, 2010). The promotional materials for this show, entitled *TRANSform Me*, pose Cox and her two co-stars (Jamie Clayton and Nina Poon) with hair dryers and hair products instead of guns but striking a pose that calls back to the *Charlie's Angels* television show logo of the 1970s. The postfeminist illusion is that these transgender women are taking up the *Charlie's Angels* torch by doing makeovers instead of fighting crime because they are, after all, Barbie beautiful. One could argue that *all* women in pop culture media outlets, trans or not, manifest the Barbie Aesthetic. If they did not, they would not be on the screen. The interesting twist with *TRANSform Me* is that the trans women are so Stepford Wife feminine that they can give advice to cisfemales on how to be/become/buy-their-way to the ideal femininity.

The only MTF transqueers who are allowed to escape this hyper-feminine, make-up and product-dependent aesthetic that permeates the MTF representation in the Digital Age, are trans *children*. Tyra Banks on her talk show *The Tyra Show* aired an episode on transgender children in January 2010. Because the market has been saturated with MTF transgender adults, media puts a new edge on the topic by talking about children who identify as trans. On one episode of *The Tyra Show*, Banks brags that "*The Tyra Show* has the daytime exclusive" of airing interviews with transgender children. She follows that statement by interviewing two children, a six-year-old (Josie) and her transgender sister, Jade. The parents sit by the two tykes, smiling nervously. Jade describes being transgender as having a birth defect. Banks reduces that analogy to hinting that the birth defect is the child's penis that is "just not supposed to be there"—again distilling the trans identity to genitalia (2010). Although all the people (from the children to the parents) interviewed on this episode of *The Tyra Show* are articulate and on-the-mark in talking about the complexities of being transgender or having a trans-gender child, the format and Bank's own approach gives the program a sensational quality, as if the concept of a transgender child is bizarre. The focus is, if not an unveiling and displaying of the body, a discussion of body parts that define biological sex.

The above genres of reality shows or talk shows show trans people talking about their "real" lives for the consumption of the audience. Candis Cayne, a MTF transqueer, has made the cross-over from reality show to serialized drama. According to Ryan Baber at Reuters.com, ABC's *Dirty Sexy Money* was the first television show that cast a transgender person to play a transgender character in prime time. The character Carmelita (played by Cayne) is a transgender person who is involved with a married man. The actor Candis Cayne (a.k.a. Candi Cayne) blurs the line between drag queen and transgender person. She is often described as a "female impersonator" (ETonline, 2007) or "transsexual" (Roberts, 2007). Other web postings or online articles describe Cayne as transgender. Some interviews avoid the politics of naming altogether by simply referring to her as a spokesperson for an unnamed cause or describing her as having "transitioned" ("Access Extended," 2010). Cayne's identity as a trans person cast to play a trans character is seen as a victory by many in the queer rights community. The issue of casting nontrans people to play trans people is an abiding critique, similar to the critique leveled against directors who cast straight actors to play gay and lesbian characters.

We see this in transfeminine representations where legs, cleavage, youth and the Barbie aesthetic are primarily portrayed. There are no other sorts of representations to counter this hyper-sexualized, hyper-feminine ideal that pivots on capitalist models of gender facilitated by product consumption.

"The body is presented simultaneously as women's source of power *and* as always unruly and requiring constant monitoring, surveillance, discipline and remodeling (and consumer spending) in order to conform to ever narrower judgments of female attractiveness. . . . Women's bodies are evaluated, scrutinized and dissected . . . and are always at risk of 'failing'" (Gill, p. 255). In order *not* to "fail" at being female or feminine, both cisfemales and trans-feminine people must resort to surgery and consumption of more and more products that define femininity. The body, be it female or trans, is not acceptable in its natural state.

DIGITAL TRANS BODIES OF MATTER

Digital space, films and television shows serve to teach transqueers what the current standards are for being trans in this world. These texts codify just one version of trans identity that transqueers must manifest to be accepted. Angela McRobbie and Janice Winship analyzed the discourses in women's magazines and how a highly restrictive femininity is constructed, centering on romance, domesticity, and caring (2004). As a result, females of all ages in the culture internalize that restrictive femininity and aspire to it by dieting, buying beauty products, and dressing to accommodate. To an even larger degree, this is true of trans people who feel they have to be über-feminine or hyper-masculine to prove their identity as "real" or true females/males. The standards of beauty and the standards of body are hooked into the capitalistic culture of consumption: consuming undergarments made specifically for trans "passing," consuming clothing, makeup, and beauty products, consuming various types of surgeries. Without this consumption mandate, would there be these rigid gender standards of how to be trans? Most media theorists argue that the capitalist culture creates the *need* for body modification or body insecurity. If there were no body insecurity, there would be no need for the products. Therefore, it is the goal of the marketers to make the viewing public feel insecure enough to buy.

We trust our screens to inform us how we should be, perceiving it as "real." Zizek writes, "The postmodern universe is the universe of naive trust in the screen which makes the very quest for what lies behind it irrelevant" (*Plague,* p. 134). The technology of this postmodern moment creates both disillusionment and the idea that technology is reality; objective reality and technology become blurred. What technology delivers to us, we believe to be real; the virtual reality of the computer screen is confused with the physical world in which we live. Therefore, the information, language, and representations encountered in that virtual world are seen as truth. The ramifications of new media reinforcing the rigidity of the sex/gender systems results in the demand for more hormones and more surgeries. Zizek believes the virtual world inside the screen "jeopardizes our most elementary perceptions of our own bodies. It cripples our own phenomenological attitudes toward the bodies of others. We suspend our knowledge of what actually exists and conceive of that surface (the computer interface) as directly expressing the soul" (1997, p. 137). Yet we believe we are not affected by the cyber-texts we consume.

In research conducted by Bryson et al., regarding queerness and digital texts, they found people were in denial about how much they folded the digital world into their own. Bryson et al. write, "It was relatively common for participants to describe daily practices of living as highly mediated by a range of Internet technologies and spaces, and their lives as relatively insulated from any cybercultural 'effects' or 'affects'" (Bryson et al., 2006, p. 798).

Websites, films, and television are making gender more rigid. New media may support alternative genders, but only those alternative genders that require the assistance of hormones and surgery. Carroll and Gilroy (2002) wrote about treatment approaches for transgender people. Rather than counseling patients to assume either a male or female role, counselors are more likely to encourage patients to explore other identities and options even as the screen-mediated world sends the opposite message. Carroll and Gilroy challenge counseling educators and counselors to embrace a "trans positive" approach, affirming various gender identities. These counselors will have little chance of success against the digital onslaught of gender/sex binaries.

The Internet feeds trans people the notion that gender means capitalist consumption with images, banner ads on web pages, and websites that exist only to sell products to transqueers. The website *Susan's Place Transgender Resources* is an example

of a hybrid site that initially purports to provide "resources," but getting products to help one pass is the dominant function of the site. The name suggests that there may be some support groups listed or organizations that advocate for trans people. And there are, but there are also various links to surgeons, places to buy clothing, where to shop, what kind of surgery is available, and where to buy prostheses. The "academic" link is empty. The *Transgender Care* website is one that focuses on surgery, hormones, and hair removal; the "care" advertised has a cost, both literally and figuratively.

. . . Buck Angel, a muscular, tattooed, bald man who harkens back to Mr. Clean, has a well-known body that matters in the digital space. Angel is not afraid to queer his image by letting us know that he does not have a penis. The line Angel is most known for is, "It isn't what is between your legs that makes your gender" (*Buck Angel Entertainment,* 2010). Angel resists the mandate of being fully female or male, although Angel has had top surgery and presumably is taking hormones. Angel has a web site devoted to his own brand of queer politics and his "Public Cervix Announcement" is popular on YouTube (2010). Angel's web-site *Buck Angel Entertainment's* (http://buckangelentertainment .com/) tag line promises "Agency, Advocacy, Lectures, Workshops and Media Projects." His public service announcement (PSA) about cervical cancer screenings advises transmen to continue to get annual pap and pelvic exams. Responses posted by viewers are overwhelmingly hostile, calling Angel a "monster" and a "synthetic male" (among other things). He also has a YouTube PSA on transgendered women getting prostate exams.

Buck Angel's website, as well as websites such as *Transgender Law and Policy Center, Transgender Forum Community Center,* and *National Association of Gay, Lesbian, Bisexual, and Transgender Centers,* offer essential information on where a transgender person can go to find community, information, and support. There are more websites peddling products, surgery, and testimonials of the one "true" trans way. The Internet offers a singular and unified pedagogy of transgender identity: be who you are, but you need to spend money to align your body with who you really are; your natural state is one that is unnatural and needs remediation. . . .

The digital world has opened up communities for transgender people where none have existed before. There is less isolation and perhaps less struggle because of the resources, social networks, and virtual communities provided on the Internet. However, these virtual communities and forums also serve to create a codified version of limited ways of being transgender. A transgender norm becomes established so that even transgender people are no longer queering gender in the way that Dr. Frank-n-Furter did in the 1970s. The Transgender Warrior that Leslie Feinberg describes is being co-opted by the capitalist culture so that a buck—and a Buck Angel—can be made. This commodification of queerness is not exclusive to transgender people, but this group seems the most vulnerable because the "products" they are persuaded to purchase are not new wardrobes or cars. Instead, the capitalist culture has successfully convinced transgender people that they must purchase surgeries and hormones, body parts or the removal of them, to embody their "true" identity. In a culture where consumption is a way of life, a way to validate one's existence, a way to display one's status and worth, queerness has been co-opted. The Digital Age has obliterated the transqueers who embrace the borderlands of gender fluidity and replaced it with "gender as consumption."

NOTE

1. A note on pronouns: when the person I am referring to has designated a specific pronoun for himself or herself, I use that pronoun. If the person I am referring to has not designated a pronoun, or if I am generally speaking about trans people, I will use the gender-neutral pronouns of "hir" and "zhe." These terms are embraced by many activists in the trans community as a way of shaping language to reflect their reality. Standard Written English does not allow for a gender-neutral third person singular or gender-neutral pronoun referring to a person.

REFERENCES

Access Extended: Candis Cayne Talks Chastity (Chaz) Bono's Transgender Transformation. (2010). *Access Hollywood*. Retrieved from www.accesshollywood.com

Anderson, J. (Writer/Director). (2003). *Normal* [Television movie]. United States: Avenue Picture Productions.

Angel, B. (2010, February 23). Buck Angel's public cervix announcement. *You Tube*. Retrieved from http://www.youtube.com/watch?v=XuNFmZHv00& feature=related

Applegate, K., Chermol, C., Medina, B., Miskowiec, B., Moriarity, J., & Redmann, R. (Executive Producers). (2010, January 27). *The Tyra Banks Show* [Television broadcast]. New York, NY: Warner Brothers Broadcasting Company.

Babenco, H. (Director). (1985). *Kiss of the Spider Woman* [Motion picture]. United States: HB Films.

Baber, R. (2008, April 25). TV has never seen more transgender characters. *Reuters*. Retrieved from http://www.reuters.com/article/idUSN2534139520080425

Bastian, R., Cooper, L., Dungan, S., Macy, W., & Moran, L. (Producers), & Tucker, D. (Writer/Director). (2005). *Transamerica* [Motion picture]. United States: Belladonna Productions.

Becker, A. E. (1995). *Body, self, and society: The view from Fiji*. Philadelphia, PA: University of Pennsylvania.

Berlanti, G. (Producer). (2007, October 31). *Dirtysexymoney* [Television broadcast]. Los Angeles, CA: ABC.

Berry, G. (1998). Black family life on television and the socialization of the African American child: Images of marginality. *Journal of Comparative Family Studies, 29*(2), 233–242.

Bryson, M., MacIntosh, L., Jordan, S., & Lin, H.-L. (2006). Virtually queer? Homing devices, mobility and un/belongings. *Canadian Journal of Communication, 31*, 791–814.

Buck Angel Entertainment. (2010). Available from http://buckangelentertainment.com/

Butler, J. (1999). *Gender trouble* (First ed.). London, England: Routledge.

Carroll, L., & Gilroy, P. J. (2002). Transgender issues in counselor preparation. *Counselor Education and Supervision, 41,* 233–242.

Carstarphen, M., & Zavoina, S. (Eds.). (1999). *Sexual rhetoric: Media perspectives on sexuality, gender, and identity.* Westport, CT: Greenwood Press.

Clark, C. (1969, Spring). Television and social controls: Some observations on the portrayals of ethnic minorities. *Television Quarterly, 18*–22.

Collins, D., Eric, R., Metzler, D., Panzanaro, J., & Williams, M. (Producers). (2006, August 1). *Queer eye for the straight guy* [Television broadcast]. New York, NY: Bravo.

Coogan, K. (2006). Fleshy specificity: (Re)considering transsexual subjects in lesbian communities. *Journal of Lesbian Studies, 10*(1/2), 17–41.

De Lauretis, T. (1989). *Technologies of gender: Essays on theory, film, and fiction.* Basingstoke and London, England: Macmillan.

Edwards, M. (2010). Transconversations: New media and community. In C. Pullen & M. Cooper (Eds.), *LGBT identity and online new media* (pp. 159–172). London, England: Routledge Press.

Eonline. ETonline. (2007, September 26). Retrieved from http://www.etonline.com/news/2007/09/54395/

Farr, D. (2010). A very personal world: Advertisement and the identity of trans-persons on craigslist. In C. Pullen & M. Cooper (Eds.), *LGBT identity and online new media* (pp. 87–99). London, England: Routledge Press.

Feder, S., & Hollar, J. (2006). *BoyI am* [Film].

Feinberg, L. (1993). *Stone butch blues.* Ithaca, NY: Firebrand Books.

Feinberg, L. (2004, January 12). Reading my author afterward. *WBAI.org.* Retrieved from http://wbai.org/index.php?option=comcontent&task=view&id=741&Itemid=127

Gallus, M. (Director). (2007). *Girl inside* [Motion picture]. United States: Women Make Movies.

Gauthier, D. K., & Chaudoir, N. K. (2004). Tranny boyz: Cyber community supports in negotiating sex and gender mobility among female to male transsexuals. *Deviant Behavior, 25,* 375–398.

Gill, R. (2007). *Gender and the media.* Cambridge, England: Polity.

Gray, M. L. (2010). From websites to Wal-Mart: Youth, identity work, and the queering of boundary publics in small town USA. In C. Pullen & M. Cooper (Eds.), *LGBT identity and online new media* (pp. 288–298). London, England: Routledge Press.

Hansbury, G. (2005). The middle men: An introduction to the transmasculine identities. *Studies in Gender and Sexuality, 6,* 241–264.

Harrison, D. (2010). No body there: Notes on queer migration to cyberspace. *The Journal of Popular Culture, 43*(2), 286–310.

Hartley, J. (1999). *Uses of television.* New York, NY: Routledge.

Hichon, J., & Reaves, S. (1999). Media mirage: The thin ideal as digital manipulation. In M. Carsarphen & S. Zavoina (Eds.), *Sexual rhetoric* (pp. 65–76). Westport, CT: Greenwood Press.

Hill, R. J. (2004, Summer). Activism as practice. *New Direction for Adult and Continuing Education, 102,* 85–96.

Hudson's FTM Resource Guide. (2004). Retrieved from http://www.ftmguide.org/

Jordan, N. (Writer/Director). (1992). *The Crying Game* [Motion picture]. United States: Miramax Films.

Kimball, M. M. (1986). Television and sex-role attitudes. In T. M. Williams (Ed.), *The impact of television: A natural experiment in three communities* (pp. 265–301). New York, NY: Academic Press.

Lebow, Alisa. (Writer/Director). (1994). *Outlaw* [Documentary]. United States: Women Make Movies.

Leifer, A. D., Gordon, N. J., & Graves, S. B. (1974). Children's television: More than mere entertainment. *Harvard Educational Review, 44*(2), 213–245.

Lombardi, M., Wilchins, R., Priesing, D., & Malouf, D. (2001). Gender violence: Transgender experiences with violence and discrimination. *Journal of Homosexuality, 42*(1), 89–101.

McCarthy, M. (1992). The thin ideal, depression and eating disorders in women. *Behavioral Research Therapy, 28,* 205–215.

MacDonald, K. (Writer/Director) (2006). *Black and white* [Documentary]. United Kingdom: Women Make Movies.

McGee, M. (2005). *Self-help Inc.: Makeover culture in American life.* Oxford, England: Oxford University Press.

Nevins, S. (Executive Producer), & Davis, K. (Director). (2001). *Southern Comfort* [Motion picture]. United States: Home Box Office (HBO).

Nigel, is that your daughter/son? (2010). *Facebook.* Retrieved November 17, 2010, from www.facebook.com

Padva, G. (2007). Media and popular culture representations of LGBT bullying. *Journal of Gay & Lesbian Social Services, 19*(3–4), 105–118.

Roberts, G. (2007, September 25). Transsexual actress joins mainstream American drama. *Pink News.* Retrieved from http://www.pinknews.co.uk/news/articles/2005-5553.html/

Roen, K. (2002). Either/or and both/neither: Discursive tensions in transgender politics. *Signs, 27,* 501–522.

Ross, K. (2010). *Gendered media: Women, men and identity politics.* Lanham, MD: Rowman and Littlefield.

Rosskam, J. (Writer/Director). (2005). *Transparent* [Documentary]. San Francisco, CA: Frameline.

Saltzburg, N. (2010). Developing a model of transmasculine identity. (Unpublished doctoral dissertation). University of Miami, Coral Gables, FL.

Sawyer, T. (2003). Hail the Prada-worshipping queer. *Alternet.* Retrieved from www.alternet.org

Shernoff, M. (2000). Cyber counseling for queer clients and clinicians. *Journal of Gay & Lesbian Social Services, 11*(4), 105–113.

Stasi, L. (2003, August 26). Flame out! Linda isn't happy with how gay TV turned out. *New York Post.* Retrieved August 13, 2010, from nypost.com

Stice, E. M., & Shaw, He. E. (1994). Adverse effects of the media portrayed thin-ideal on women and linkages to bulimic symptomatology. *Journal of Social and Clinical Psychology, 13*(3), 288–308.

Tan, A. S. (1977). TV beauty ads and role expectations of adolescent female viewers. *Journalism Quarterly, 56,* 283–288.

TransBucket. (2010). Retrieved from http://www.transbucket.com

Transgendered People on Television. (2008, September 11). *VHI.* Retrieved from http://www.vh1.com/video/misc/275123/transgendered-people-on-tv.jhtml

Veneruso, T. (2001). Interview with Max from Southern Comfort. *New Wave Films.* Retrieved from http://www.nextwavefilms.com/ulbp/max.html

Ward, L. M. & Harrison, K. (2005). The impact of media use on girls' beliefs about gender roles, their bodies, and sexual relationships: A research synthesis. In E. Cole & J. Henderson Daniel (Eds.), *Featuring females: Feminist analysis of media* (pp. 3–23). Washington, DC: American Psychological Association.

Zizek, S. (1989). *The sublime object of ideology.* London, England: Verso.

Zizek, S. (1997). *The plague of fantasies.* London, England: Verso Press.

THE "RICH BITCH"

17

Class and Gender on the Real Housewives of New York City

Michael J. Lee and Leigh Moscowitz

As the US economy collapsed in 2008 and 2009, a record number of viewers tuned in to Bravo each week to gawk at the consumptive, ostentatious lives of six Manhattan socialites. Bravo perfected its formula for "recession-proof television" in its reality docudrama series, the *Real Housewives of New York City* (*RHW-NYC*), which puts the lives of Alex, Jill, Bethenny, Ramona, LuAnn, and Kelly on display as objects of fascination, envy, and scorn (Guthrie 2009, p. 3). Between the characters' summer homes in the Hamptons, banter about the size of strangers' "p.p.'s" (private planes), $30,000-per-year pre-schools with full-time nutritionists on staff, and week-long jaunts to St. Bart's, *RHW-NYC* is not focused on how the "fortunate few make their fortunes but on how they spend them" (Stanley 2008, p. E1). As *Broadcasting & Cable* magazine reported, "The poster girls for conspicuous consumption are scoring record ratings while Americans are losing their jobs in record numbers" (Guthrie 2009, p. 4).

The *Real Housewives* franchise, which includes five additional shows set in Orange County, Atlanta, New Jersey, Washington DC, and Beverly Hills, is one of the most popular of a bevy of reality television programs about conspicuous consumption. *RHW-NYC* is, at its core, a show about rich women and, as such, resembles television forerunners about lives lived in luxury's lap such as MTV's *Cribs* or *Lifestyles of the Rich and Famous*. However, as we argue in this essay, *RHW-NYC* complicates the scholarly conversation about the role of class on television (Gans 1995; Grindstaff 2002; Kendall 2005). Rather than valorizing the rich and demonizing the poor like its predecessors, *RHW-NYC* takes aim at the consumptive lives of its arriviste heroines.

Nevertheless, the populist scorn the show provokes is not gender-neutral; its sights are set on the rich, to be sure, but only rich women, especially those who transgress the traditional gender roles of supportive friend, nurturing mother, doting wife, and ceaseless caretaker. According to the logic of *RHW-NYC*, rich women, not rich men, spend frivolously, project false appearances, backstab, gossip, and leave their children's care to paid staff. Indeed, the failure of a different reality series about status-obsessed men reveals that when it comes to casting wealthy, out-of-touch villains, female socialites are hard to beat. Fox Reality channel's short-lived *Househusbands of Hollywood* could not leave its viewers aghast like the housewives could. Describing the "chasm in watchability" between the househusbands and housewives series, one entertainment writer quipped, "I found myself wondering what their wives were doing" (Alston 2009, p. 75).

In this essay, we employ the concept of irony to analyze how *RHW-NYC* creates rich women as objects of cultural derision, well-heeled jesters in a populist court. *RHW-NYC* primes its savvy, upscale audience to judge the extravagance of female scapegoats harshly in tough economic times. In failed quests to perform the public role of esteemed aristocrats, these women are shown as neglecting their private duties as mothers. In ironic scenes dubbed "winks" by the show's producers, *RHW-NYC* primes cultural expectations about class and gender behaviors only to show a "housewife" failing to measure up to the standard on both accounts. Their class and gender flops are inter-related; the lure of class status produces inconsiderate mothers. In the world of *RHW-NYC*, money destroys, rather than enables, self-awareness, friendships, and, most importantly,

From Michael J. Lee and Leigh Moscowitz (2012), "The 'Rich Bitch,'" *Feminist Media Studies*. Vol. 12, No. 4, 1–19. Reprinted by permission of the publisher (Taylor & Francis Ltd., www.tandf.co.uk/journals).

competent mothering. Ultimately, *RHW-NYC* uses ironic "winks" to produce a provocative, recession-era, post-feminist drama about rich women too crass to be classy, too superficial to be nurturing, and too self-obsessed to be caring. These are self-professed "working mothers" who work little and mother even less.

Building on feminist media scholarship about portrayals of class and gender, this project offers the opportunity to examine the ways in which normative conceptions of class and gender cohere to produce an archetypal, trans-historical villain typified by the mythology around historical figures like Marie Antoinette, fictional television characters like *Dynasty*'s Alexis Carrington, and cinematic villains like Cruella Deville, a performance we term the "rich bitch." Sacrificing motherhood, empathy, and altruism, the rich bitch, a bourgeois feminine character done up as a cartoonish trope, pursues selfish material gains single-mindedly. Always gendered (female), always classed (leisure), and almost always racialized (white), she functions at a cultural crossroads where class antagonisms can be articulated and traditional gender roles can be reasserted. The figure of the rich bitch fuels class-based contempt by reinforcing anti-feminist tropes. . . .

IRONIC PORTRAYAL AND "THE BRAVO WINK"

RHW-NYC depicts the lives of five New York City "real housewives" whose day-to-day lives are comprised of gala events, high-profile charity auctions, see-and-be-seen functions, and, to a far lesser extent, motherhood and familial bonds. Each program is divided into vignettes that accentuate the cultural type each housewife occupies. Ramona Singer, to provide one example, the entrepreneur and self-described "MILF," frequently organizes "girls-only" events such as group Botox trips. Jill Zarin, the established "Jewess" socialite whose husband oversees a family-owned fabric company, obsesses about the remodeling of her posh Manhattan apartment. Bethenny Frankel, the youngest of the housewives and now subject of her own spin-off reality series, is tagged the "runaway bride" whose celebrity chef career complicates her personal relationships with men. LuAnn de Lesseps, a former model and countess by marriage, is cast as the stereotypical, if unconvincing, "classy" socialite: wealthy, snooty, and judgmental. Alex

McCord, a graphic designer whose marriage to an eccentric hotelier is a topic of ridicule among the housewives, is marked as a social climber on the outside of the elite circle of the fabulously wealthy. Kelly Bensimon, the author, model, equestrian, and, in her words, Manhattan "tastemaker," was a second-season addition to *RHW-NYC*.

These wealthy characters violate, both consistently and flagrantly, the performative conventions of wealth and femininity. Disrupting long-held linkages between wealth and manners, economic class and behavioral class, these wealthy characters are rough and rude even though their cultural type suggests formality and urbanity. We use the concept of irony both to make sense of how *RHW-NYC* is a vivid post-feminist narrative in which wealthy stars contravene class and gender norms out of indifference or ignorance.

. . . What generally signifies an ironic move is the violation of an audience assumption that is deeply engrained or has been recently primed (Booth 1974; Burke 1969). . . . Irony is a code that invites participation in the completion of a communicative act. Sarcastic irony is an illustrative example. When a friend declares *Desperate Housewives* to be "the greatest show in television history," auditors are prodded to discern whether the speaker's hyperbolic formulation, peculiar over-emphasis of "greatest show," or sly smirk are evidence that the intended meaning was the exact opposite of the statement's literal meaning. . . . Given its utility in shaming, ridiculing, inducing laughter, and exposing hypocrisy, some cultural critics have even heralded irony's potential in "creating the conditions of possibility for a genuine democratic environment to develop" (Tabako 2007, p. 27; Rorty 1989).

Irony is central to the production, composition, and narrative of *RHW-NYC*. Even the show's basic premise, showing audiences the lives of "real housewives," is itself a layered irony. These so-called "real housewives" live lives most would find surreal, and none are actual housewives. Two of the six women, moreover, are not even married. Beyond these fundamental ironies, the show depicts several other, but no less galling, ironies: a group of friends who are not actually friends, rich people with no class, and wealthy who profess, but do not conduct, hard work.

Ironic framing is, in fact, the Bravo producers' chief métier. Andy Cohen, Bravo executive and host of the *Real Housewives* reunion specials, explains that the show is intentionally coded to highlight hypocrisy: "We do something with the editing that is called the Bravo wink. We wink at the audience when someone says 'I'm the healthiest person in the world' and then you see them ashing their cigarette. We're kind of letting the audience in on the fun" (Cohen 2009). This ironic viewing is only possible because the show is framed for Bravo viewers, television's most educated and upscale audience that considers itself "'hip to television'" (Dominus 2008).

Such ironic scenes are, nevertheless, not unique to Bravo. Some reality television shows, as Dubrofsky notes, gain dramatic purchase in climactic scenes in which female contestants, previously portrayed as well-mannered contenders, are overcome by uncontrollable emotions and display them "in a way that is unexpected and breaks social norms" (2009, p. 356). Such scenes are structured as acts of unmasking in which a hidden truth about a person is revealed in a surprising, even shocking, way. Even without the emotional spasm, "wink" scenes are of a similar species in the sense that they are designed to expose and reduce female characters and engage the viewing audience in the process. As a housewife brags about being a doting mother or a hard worker, *RHW-NYC* cuts to images of ignored children and a luxuriating mother. These are scoff-inducing scenes in which a housewife says something so patently false, so comically contradicted by several shows' worth of evidence, that the housewife becomes ridiculous and other-worldly, someone who must have descended from another planet ill-equipped to manage life on this one.

CLASS TRANSGRESSIONS

Economic class, of course, is definable in strictly economic terms: as personal income, as familial wealth, as net worth, or, in Marxist terms, as the relationship of an individual to the mode of production (Kendall 2005, pp. 12–13). Class, nevertheless, is also definable as a cultural construct tethered to a range of behavioral expectations. As Laura Grindstaff clarifies, "Class, especially in the context of television, is also a performance, a social script involving, among other things, language use, mannerisms, and dress" (2002, p. 31). Although the recent scholarly focus on class as a performance is often indebted to contemporary theorists, foundational thinkers about class were also sensitive to issues of culture and identity.

Writing in 1899, Thorstein Veblen notes how the "consumption" of "excellent goods" signified wealth whereas a lack, in either quantity or quality, of such goods was viewed as a "mark of inferiority or demerit" (1967, p. 74). The enactment of personal taste, nevertheless, would collapse minus the delicate, polished manners useful in projecting an "apparently natural" image of effortless class (Lane 2000, p. 52). What Veblen calls "manners and breeding," decorousness and etiquette befitting social hierarchies, were vital when exhibiting a "reputable degree of leisure" (1967, p. 46).

Extending Veblen's focus on the repertoire of upper-class signifiers, Pierre Bourdieu explores how the performance of upper class-ness is more a symphony than a solo; it requires the integration of seemingly disparate elements into a fluent whole. Typical conversational "banalities" about art or literature, for example, are "inseparable from the steady tone, the slow, casual diction, the distant or self-assured smile, the measured gesture, the well-tailored suit and the bourgeois salon of the person who pronounces them" (Bourdieu 1984, p. 174). These status markers are, in Bourdieu's terms, cultural capital, the means of reifying class hierarchy. As he explains, the "manner" in which "symbolic goods" are employed is an "ideal weapon in strategies of distinction, that is, as Proust put it, 'the infinitely varied art of marking distances'" (Bourdieu 1984, p. 66).

Veblen was an early chronicler of the process by which the cultural meaning of wealth was disciplined in the late nineteenth century. Gentility and refinement, two markers of behavioral class, became strongly correlated with the upwardly mobile economic classes during the period (Veblen 1967, pp. 48–49). The expectation that the wealthy would be well-mannered and personally reserved was popularized in etiquette manuals, finishing schools, and broader social and educational trends in the nineteenth century (Grindstaff 2002, p. 268). Such socialization was not uniform across social stratas, however; the expectation of etiquette "was especially true for upper-class white women, whose participation in public life was precarious, and for whom the stakes of transgression were high" (Grindstaff 2002, p. 268).

Whereas the management and suppression of public emotion has been construed as a middle and upper-class phenomenon, the embodiment of emotion has been construed as a working and lower-class phenomenon; this perception has been persistently reinforced by myriad talk shows and reality television programs (Grindstaff 2002, p. 246). It is un-ironic to see the impoverished inhabitants of a trailer park come to blows on a nationally televised daytime talk show because public displays of physicality and emotionality are associated with poverty. The link between "class and emotional expressiveness" rests on the faulty assumption that the working poor are innately predisposed toward public paroxysms and that the rich are naturally geared toward private, mannered dispute resolutions (Grindstaff 2002, p. 143). By this cultural logic, it would be highly ironic for hedge fund managers to throw chairs at one another on the same daytime program. Rich people, quite simply, do not publicize their hysterics because they do not profit from social scorn; they do not televise their outbursts because they do not need the money. It is one thing for even the newly moneyed to commit a social indelicacy that would attract the judging eyes of an elite strata within the upper class and quite another to participate in a shouting match at a charity dinner (Season Two, Episode Four). The latter behavior might be judged as boorish across classes. . . .

WEALTH AND SOCIAL CLASS

Nearly every aspect of the characters' economic lives is framed ironically in ways that lampoon a character as bumbling, mindless, or disgraceful. Typically, an *RHW-NYC* episode is edited to couple audio of a character's platitudinous pontifications about "class" or "grace" with video of the character's tactlessness. The characters defy nearly every image of the poised, high-society sophisticate committed to social graces and well-mannered to a fault. . . .

LuAnn is coded as the prototypically pretentious socialite. When this code is coupled with the show's ironic frame, LuAnn is exposed before viewers as a judgmental hypocrite. *RHW-NYC* becomes a prosecutorial vehicle. Much like the cigarette-ashing health nut described by the show's producer, audiences are presented video evidence of LuAnn's professed values followed by images of her contradictory behavior. The producers pursue this ironic line through much of the second season as LuAnn parlays her new, Bravo-driven celebrity

status into a book deal, *Class With the Countess*. The dramatic irony, demonstrated unsubtly in "wink" scenes, is that the joke is on LuAnn. With Bravo's assemblage of audacious quotations about class and footage of her behavioral record, viewers can see her missteps, point out her hypocrisies, and evaluate her class performance. As Bethenny quips about LuAnn's repeated gaffes, "Not very countess-like. It's dis-countess" (Season Two, Episode Nine). Ultimately, LuAnn has performed her class incorrectly.

Like LuAnn, the show paints the other housewives as obsessed by questions of personal authenticity. Each housewife frets over whether she projects a "real," "genuine," "ladylike," "down-to-earth," and, of course, "classy" image. Of equal importance, *RHW-NYC* depicts these women as militant enforcers and harsh critics of the ways in which their acquaintances live up to these standards of authenticity as well. The women become the class police who misunderstand the concept they attempt to enforce. Ramona, for example, polices other characters' class performances while violating her own standards. After Jill refuses her second-row seat at a fashion event—"This is bullshit," Jill exclaims—Ramona stares intently into the camera and snidely isolates a point of difference between them: "I'm not into that kind of status. I could care less who sits where. It was not a normal reaction, or ladylike, or classy, or elegant, more importantly" (Season One, Episode Four). Ramona states that she and Bethenny are united as friends because each is "anti-hypocrisy" (Season Two, Episode Five). Ramona dismisses Alex and Simon for similar reasons: "They aren't real, and I don't have time for people who aren't real" (Season Two, Episode Three). Bravo frames these class ironies as perpetrated by women with no shame, women whose money obstructs self-examination. The characters are highly conscious of the high-ideal of the poised socialite yet framed as doubly incapable of attaining the ideal or of realizing the disparity.

WEALTH AND SOCIAL LIFE

A second irony of class performances on *RHW-NYC* is that money precludes a rewarding social life. *RHW-NYC* dramatizes the housewives' relational difficulties by implying that wealth and anomie among women are linked. To be sure, several principal characters on the show espouse basic feminist bromides. All of the housewives profess to be strong, independent women. All of the housewives have successful careers. "In New York, women work. Women have to work," Jill instructs (Season Two, Episode Nine). All of the women profess a desire to bond with other women and maintain an active social life. The original cast members later berate the newcomer, Kelly, for fixating on men. "You are not a girl's girl," Bethenny yells. "I am a girl's girl," Kelly protests (Season Two, Reunion One). In the same vein, all are suspicious, in some senses more than others, of traditional gender roles with regards to household duties like cooking, cleaning, and child-rearing. Viewers even witness Ramona, in several scenes, use painful examples from her childhood to teach her daughter feminist lessons. Ramona urges her daughter to avoid relying on men, exhorting her "to make her own money" to achieve "the greatest self-worth" and "independence as a woman" (Season One, Episode Six).

The cast members speak a language of women's empowerment; nevertheless, in their relationships with other women, their consumerist lifestyles, and their obsession with personal appearance, the characters become post-feminist cautionary tales rather than feminists. Put differently, the characters dress consumerist desires in a feminist idiom. . . . The housewives figure plastic surgery, losing weight, looking youthful, going out, and dressing provocatively as the liberation of their essential womanhood. Ramona, for instance, sees plastic surgery as sisterly bonding. She says to her friends in a plastic surgeon's office, "I believe women should share . . . and I have this friend who is a doctor who has some new machines to make us look beautiful." "To good girlfriends and a great doctor," she toasts in a scene typifying the Bravo "wink." Same-sex closeness between women is achieved by indulging their common desire to look "eighteen forever" (Season One, Episode Eight).

Conflict is not a prelude to greater inter-personal connectedness; it is the basis of their relationships. In many cases, the housewives' competitive tensions bubble over into televised catfights, produced and edited for the delight of audiences. When Ramona and LuAnn offer Bethenny competing dating advice at a cancer benefit, Ramona dismisses LuAnn's comments as nonsense: "What

do you know? You got married very young. You married a man twice your age" (Season Two, Episode Four). Similarly, a spat between Kelly and Bethenny at an arthritis event reveals their animosity to be mutual and visceral. Kelly establishes social hierarchy: "We're not the same." "This is you," she says holding her left hand low, and "this is me," she concludes raising her other hand above her head (Season Two, Episode Four). When asked about the incident at the reunion show, Bethenny is direct; Kelly is a "piece of shit" (Season Two, Reunion Two).

On the surface, *RHW-NYC* shares much with *Sex and the City,* another show that addressed issues of class, sex, and inter-personal relationships by conjuring consumerist and post-feminist narratives about a group of affluent white women in Manhattan (Arthurs 2003; Brasfield 2006; Gerhard 2005). Several of the New York housewives make sense of their social lives in terms of iconic *Sex and the City* images (Season Two, Episodes 11 and 12). Nevertheless, *RHW-NYC* can be productively read as the anti–*Sex and the City*. The *Sex and the City* characters live fabulously in Manhattan; they maintain strong inter-personal bonds and buy Jimmy Choo shoes. They can "have it all," and even though they may fight, they can have each other too. In *RHW-NYC*'s ironic portrayal of class, the housewives' drive for material possessions and social status destroys the sisterhood; the cattiness overwhelms the camaraderie. In *Sex and the City,* class facilitates social fulfillment. In *RHW-NYC,* women become so consumed by class that their inter-personal connections suffer. . . .

BAD MOMMIES IN MANHATTAN

These real housewives may not be housewives, but four of the five are mothers, and the fifth regrets not having children. (The fifth housewife, Bethenny, became a mother after these shows aired.) One central dynamic in the *Real Housewives* is the collision of the temptations of the housewives' glamorous lives with their motherly obligations. The housewives are shown consistently choosing socializing over mothering and self-maintenance over nurturing, inviting a harsh criticism of mothering which only serves to justify misogynistic gender divisions that presume that "women remain the best primary caretakers of children" (Douglas & Michaels 2004, p. 4). *RHW-NYC* uses gender stereotypes to re-signify the upper class and uses catty and conspicuously consumptive behaviors to reinscribe the notion that mommy should be at home with the kids.

Producers direct much of the audience's attention toward instances of failed mothering, as opposed to failed parenting, participating in a larger overall trend of what Ruth Feldstein (2000) refers to as "mother-blaming." Susan Douglas and Meredith Michaels (2004) have written extensively about the ways in which media culture construct our common-sense notions of how mothers ought to behave, celebrating the "best" mothers and punishing the "worst" mothers. Recent mediated "mommy wars" between falsely polarized "working moms" and "stay at home moms" have turned motherhood into the latest "competitive sport" (Douglas & Michaels 2004, p. 11). As images of intensive mothering drown out notions of egalitarian parenting, "ridiculous, honey-hued ideals of perfect motherhood" dominate popular culture (Douglas & Michaels 2004, p. 2).

In direct violation of these standards of "new momism," viewers of *RHW-NYC* are invited to critique these women as mothers who have chosen their superficial lives over the development of their children (Vavrus 2007). Consistent with the show's cultivation of irony, the mothers' behavior, in some cases, becomes so egregious that the mother-daughter relationship is upended; the mother is childish and the child is authoritative. In a role reversal exemplifying the show's ironic frame, Ramona's twelve-year-old daughter, Avery, adopts the motherly role and scolds her mother about her revealing outfits, her lewd language, and her "embarrassing" behavior. Avery, who is asked in interview segments to critique her mother's behavior, repeatedly refers to her mother's hypersexualized dress and conduct as "ewww," "disgusting," "gross," and "unlady like." After witnessing her mother start a poolside bikini-wrestling match, Avery screams at Ramona: "Oh my god mom, don't! You're such an evil woman," before storming off. Ramona laughs away her daughter's concerns in sexual terms: "We're just a bunch of MILFs" (Season One, Episode Two).

When mothering is prominently featured, producers employ the "Bravo wink" to construct these real mothers as ineffective, neglectful, selfish, superficial, and juvenile. The housewives' relationships with their children are depicted as empty, built on consumptive behaviors and unsolicited, shocking, and even dangerous advice. Excess means are blamed tacitly for the shortage of mothering; a life brimming with extravagance and temptation provides the "pull" that draws mothers outside the home, away from their rightful duties of child-rearing. . . .

NEGLECTING HOME LIFE FOR SOCIAL LIFE

The housewives' home lives and social lives are framed as forced choices, rearticulating post-feminist tensions in leisure-class terms. In a standard scene, a housewife dresses for a night out at a charity event or drinks with friends, and the children are left behind, sullen and abandoned. The scene depicts the glitzy housewife leaving the house and, as a melodramatic score plays, a close-up shot of a sad child fills the screen. The forced choice these women face is not between parenting and work (production), but between mothering and consumptive socializing (consumption): "me-time." What makes their choices even more transgressive of social expectations of mothers is that the "work" they perform at the perceived expense of competent mothering is not really work, but pretend. The housewives are cast as worse than working moms because they choose social obligations and maintaining their external beauty over motherhood, all under the guise of "hard work."

This trope is exemplified by LuAnn, who is often shown siding with sociality over her two children. Noel, her ten-year-old son, at one point begs to come out with his mother and she lies and explains that "children don't go to this restaurant" (Season One, Episode Seven). In the following scene, viewers witness what LuAnn "deserted" her children for: a "girls night out" of drinking, clubbing, and "window shopping" for dildos at a sex shop with her twenty-three-year-old niece, violating not only her responsibilities as mother and nurturer, but normative boundaries assigned by her age and social status. LuAnn arrives at the "bohemian" bar clearly exasperated, greets her niece who is half her age, and directs the bartender who is pouring her cocktail to "make it on the stronger side." To her niece, Nicole, she exclaims, "Yippee! You don't know how happy I am to get out of the house because it has been so grueling" (Season One, Episode Seven). Employing the "wink," producers juxtapose these scenes that mount evidence of absentee mothering with

LuAnn's admission to viewers that it "feels great to get out" of the house when her husband is out of town and "forget about being a mom." Rather than identify with and celebrate LuAnn's "escape" from her motherly duties, viewers are primed to jeer at her pathetic attempt to reclaim her youth as she buys gaudy trinkets, giggles girlishly at dildos in a sex shop window, and pretends to enjoy the band playing at the "bohemian" dive bar. . . . Her desperation to drink from the fountain of youth is not only rendered a failure but an unworthy diversion from her legitimate role of familial caretaker.

OUTSOURCING MOTHERHOOD

Highlighting another irony of "working motherhood" on the *Real Housewives* series, the housewives' children are not nurtured by their mothers but by an expensive array of *au pairs,* live-in nannies, wellness centers, and high-end pre-schools. Motherhood is outsourced. LuAnn's children are "raised" by their second mother, a Pilipino housekeeper named Rosie. In one telling scene, LuAnn is busily preening for an evening out with a girlfriend and ordering Rosie what to make for the kids' dinner. Noel, clearly upset, accuses his mother of neglect: "All my friends, their parents are home every single night. Are you going to be back early?" In a separate interview, LuAnn justifies to viewers: "They [the children] always try to pull the guilt trip on me. I, of course, feel for him, but I don't let it override me and what I have to do in my own social life." It is up to Rosie to counsel Noel: "When he asks 'When are my parents going to be back?' I just say 'They love you very much,' and he says, 'I love you, Rosie'" (Season One, Episode Five). Rosie directly addresses LuAnn's absenteeism and the consequences of outsourcing motherhood in a personal interview. Rosie says to viewers, "I want them [LuAnn and the Count] to spend more quality time with the kids. I don't want the children growing up saying, 'You weren't there.'"

In this family, viewers are repeatedly reassured that Rosie plays the role of the substitute mother. Rosie, LuAnn explains, "is like mom when I'm gone." While LuAnn socializes, she employs quality paid labor to provide the nurturing, care, and love the children are otherwise missing from their relationship with their parents. Rosie explains, "I raise them how I raise my kids. They treat me like a second mother. I am always there for them whenever to give whatever they need." In contrast

to negative working class depictions on television, viewers are invited to empathize with Rosie's plight, to "side" with her and see her as the true mother-figure in the household. Rosie does the heavy-lifting in the household, not only in terms of the care and upkeep of the home, but also in the rearing and nurturing of the children.

As LuAnn farms out the domestic work of parenting and housework to Rosie, Jill attempts to solve problems facing her thirteen-year-old daughter Ally by sending her to a posh "detox" center in Martha's Vineyard. Through careful editing, it becomes evident that "detox" is code for "weight loss," despite Jill's failed attempts to mask the trip as being primarily about curing Ally's "arthritis." The center is run by the author of *How to Lose 21 Pounds in 21 Days,* and video footage of her time there makes it clear the program focuses on purge dieting made up entirely of liquid meals. Jill is thrilled when Ally returns a week later eleven pounds thinner, drastic weight loss for a young teen. In a scene intended to make audiences squirm uncomfortably, Jill pokes at her daughter's mid-section while she screams in delight at the prospect of weight loss, "Oh my god! Where'd my daughter go?" (Season One, Episode Three).

CLASSING CHILDREN

The housewives' failures as mothers are not limited to absenteeism or substituting shoe shopping for emotional intimacy. Alex's failures, in particular, stem from her attempts to manufacture worldly, learned adults out of young children. Her class anxieties have infiltrated her parenting style, and frequent scenes of Johan and Francois running, screaming, and defiant attest to her limitations as a mother.

. . . As involved, hyper-attentive parents, one narrative arch involves Alex and Simon's often barely concealed attempts to break into the right social circle, and the importance of their children in that quest. They named them pretentiously (Johan and Francois); they employ a French *au pair;* they try to cajole the children to order food in French at fancy restaurants; they tour fifteen Manhattan preschools.

Alex, of all the characters, hews most closely to popular media representations of "new momism," a logic that naturalizes "intensive mothering" (Douglas & Michaels 2004). But in this social climate, this kind of doting only serves to destroy effective parenting practices. These children are spoiled, and even the best, most well-intentioned attempts to set boundaries, instill work ethic, and inspire a fulfilled life inevitably fail. Johan and Francois are shown violating the standards of good behavior expected from children of such a wealthy family. At the formal dinner party that concludes Season One, Alex and Simon sit idly as the children scream incessantly and poke guests' food, ruining a thirty-dollar hamburger in one instance. The camera focuses intently on the other housewives as they exchange judgmental glances, eye rolls, and catty commentary. Ramona scolds: "My daughter would never be able to do that . . . I've never seen that before in my life." This dinner party footage is replayed repeatedly, slowed down for dramatic effect, and colored in sepia tone to place it in the past. It serves as ammunition for another powerful "Bravo wink" whenever the Van Kempens espouse their views on effective parenting, especially in Season Two when they reveal they are writing a book of their "collection of experiences" they gleaned from raising their children. The Van Kempens are subjected to the ridicule of their show-mates, as producers juxtapose the footage of the dinner party as LuAnn makes a mockery of their book: "The way the Van Kempen children behave, I wouldn't say they would be the authority on writing a book about childhood behavior." Just as the housewives police one another's class performances, they also criticize each other's mothering skills; they fail to adhere to the standards they preach in both instances. Not only are viewers invited to level harsh criticisms against the characters' failed attempts at mothering. Often these criticisms are channeled through the characters themselves, who act out their own version of the "mommy wars" for the delight of TV audiences.

CONCLUSION: THE DOWNSIDE OF THE POPULIST PROMISE

The ironies of the housewives' performances of class and gender alienate viewers from identifying with the six women of *RHW-NYC* on two levels. First, the characters, through some outlandish display of wealth or an ill-considered comment about another character's looks, spouse, or parenting, mark themselves as poorly behaved. In these instances, any judgment viewers make about the characters' excessive purchases or materialistic

values draws upon the audience's latent senses of class consciousness and social decorum. Such judgments are primed by displays of the characters' deviant behaviors. Second, these primed judgments are reinforced by standards the characters set for themselves. That is, the show uses outlandish behavior to mark these characters' difference, and deviance, from an audience's most basic aspirations of tactful consumption and social grace, but it also highlights through "winks" their failure to live up to their own criteria. By juxtaposing the characters' stated behavioral ideals with their numerous televised transgressions, *RHW-NYC* compounds many viewers' latent judgments with an explicit invitation to label these women as hypocrites. In the end, these women are a far cry from hegemonic conceptions of motherhood perpetuated by popular media forms. The show is entertaining precisely because they fail to meet these standards. As one reality producer said, "*Housewives* isn't as much about them being rich as it is about them being spoiled, senseless and self-obsessed. No matter what the economy is, people are always going to tune in that" (Guthrie 2009, p. 4).

The show, of course, is not a cultural phenomenon solely because it broadcasts rich bitch villains; that is only part of its force. Fans of *RHW-NYC* are empowered as judges and invited to conclude that those with the most deserve the least. Many viewers delight in witnessing "the women on the show program bicker nakedly, flaunting diamonds—and talons—with equal hauteur" (La Ferla 2009, p. 2). On *RHW-NYC,* as with other reality TV formats, viewer-judges are supplied evidence of repeated violations of class performances: vulgar behavior, conspicuous consumption, poor relationships, and bad mothering. The host of the season-ending reunion episodes showcases this audience empowerment by reading viewers' condemnatory emails and blog posts on air. For instance, regarding Jill's consumptive lifestyle, the host says, "We got thousands of viewer emails, many of them very pointed," before asking, "Do you feel any responsibility for the [economic] crash?" (Season Two, Reunion One). Another email read during the reunion show illustrates how the producers feature emails that are pointed and personal. One viewer tells Kelly, "You need to seek professional help." Many of these emails feature an accusation of hypocrisy by an angered viewer. One viewer, for example, emailed Kelly: "If you're so private, why would you do a reality show?" (Season Two, Reunion Two).

On these season-finales-as-trials, the characters have to explain themselves and atone for bad behavior. Such scenes, when coupled with hours of footage of the rich defiling themselves in numerous ways, reflect deep class anguish within the US political culture and express a potentially powerful populist sentiment. The upper-class is not evidence of an economic system that rewards hard labor or elite education. They are neither models for imitation or spectacles for amazement. Reading critical emails that identify the hypocrisy of these rich women is the mass mediation of a leveling of social hierarchy. The rich not only become accessible and accountable for their behavior, they become less than the audience. They are scapegoats for economic crises, figures of scorn and pity, morality tales of lives led wastefully. Their Manhattan social lives, their profligate purchases, the location of their summer homes, and the baroque renovations of their high-rises are motivated by status anxiety. They appear as simple rats unaware of their unnecessary race, rich automatons enslaved by extravagance. . . .

RHW-NYC, to be sure, is not overt, class-based vitriol, but it has an antagonistic undertone. Historically, images of villainous or buffoonish elites have fueled progressive class politics in which the downtrodden, priced-out farmers, and even the forgotten middle class has exposed a fat cat banker or a corrupt robber-baron to highlight gross inequalities in the social conditions produced by industrial capitalism. Whether motivated by Marx, the Christian social gospel, or simple egalitarianism, whether decried as the "super-rich," in Huey Long's words, or the "economic royalists," in Franklin Roosevelt's language, a critique of the rich as too rich has accompanied calls for income redistribution, social safety nets, progressive taxation, workers' rights, and, ultimately, social democracy (Kazin 1995, p. 110).

Considering Bravo's upscale branding to some of the most desirable audience demographics on television, however, the populist promise of *RHW-NYC* may be limited. It is not the downtrodden, laid-off worker who is empowered but a relatively affluent and well-educated audience that is encouraged to see themselves as superior to the extremely wealthy. The show's themes may nourish class antagonisms, but Bravo's audience is not exactly the working-class heroes of Left fables. Bravo dubs its audience "affluencers," a catchy name for its young, chic, stylish, and upward-aspiring demographic, a quarter of whom make over $100,000 a year (Dominus 2008). The show's mockery and prosecution of tremendously wealthy women may also let the merely affluent Bravo audience off the hook. In their role as viewer-judge, they may conclude that some rich people do their class comically wrong and nothing more politically potent than that. As one television programmer explained, "Viewers can enjoy all the vapid consumerism . . . without imagining that they're falling sway to the very forces that make that show catnip for advertisers" (Dominus 2008).

Potentially empowering though this critique may be, its seductiveness also exists at the intersection of populist class ideals and anti-feminist gender tropes. Viewers of *RHW-NYC* are invited to conclude that the rich are undeserving because these women violate traditional gender roles so flagrantly. The housewives are convicted for failing to live up to the June Cleaver image of mom as an omnipotent nurturer. Moreover, parental mistakes on the show are consistently framed as maternal mistakes. When the children act up, the ostensible judgment is that the mother should become a better disciplinarian. In the world of *RHW-NYC,* strong fatherly figures are noticeably absent, but only mothers, not fathers, are persecuted for their absence. This economic morality tale mirrors other vaguely Faust-ish tales in which individuals sell their souls for social status. Money, so the bromide goes, is the root of all evil. In the case of *RHW-NYC,* however, the evil that money engenders is specific to women, specific to the stereotype of the pampered rich wife, and specific to six women transgressing their roles as mothers and caregivers. Although *RHW-NYC* offers the viewing public a wealthy villain to judge, scapegoating women during an unfolding economic crisis smacks of retrograde gender politics.

REFERENCES

Alston, Joshua. (2009) 'The limp factor,' *Newsweek*, 23 & 31 Aug., p. 75.

Arthurs, Jane. (2003) '*Sex and the City* and consumer culture: remediating postfeminist drama,' *Feminist Media Studies*, vol. 3, no. 1, pp. 83–99.

Baym, Geoffrey. (2010) *From Cronkite to Colbert: The Evolution of Broadcast News*, Paradigm Publishers, Boulder, CO.

Booth, Wayne A. (1974) *A Rhetoric of Irony*, University of Chicago Press, Chicago.

Bourdieu, Pierre. (1984) *Distinction: A Social Critique of the Judgment of Taste*, trans. Richard Nice, Harvard University Press, Cambridge, MA.

Brasfield, Rebecca. (2006) 'Rereading *Sex and the City*: exposing the hegemonic feminist narrative,' *Journal of Popular Film & Television*, vol. 34, no. 3, pp. 130–139.

Brown, Laura S. (2005) 'Outwit, outlast, out-flirt? the women of reality TV,' in *Featuring Females: Feminist Analyses of Media*, eds Ellen Cole & Jessica H. Daniel, American Psychological Association, Washington, DC.

Burke, Kenneth. (1961) *The Rhetoric of Religion*, University of California Press, Berkeley, CA.

Burke, Kenneth. (1969) *Grammar of Motives*, University of California Press, Berkeley.

Butsch, Richard. (2003) 'Ralph, Fred, Archie, and Homer: why television keeps re-creating the white male working-class buffoon,' in *Gender, Race and Class in Media: a Text-Reader*, eds Gail Dines & Jean M. Humez, 2nd edn, Sage Publications, Thousand Oaks, CA, pp. 575–585.

Class Dismissed: How TV Frames the Working Class. (Videorecording) (2005) Media Education Foundation, Northampton, MA.

Cohen, Andy. (2009) 'Bravo exec on the art of creating "reality"', *National Public Radio*, 19 Aug.

Dominus, Susan. (2008) 'The affluencer,' *The New York Times Magazine*, 2 Nov., pp. MM38–48, [Online] Available at: http://www.nytimes.com/2008/11/02/magazine/02zalaznick-t.html?pagewanted=all.

Douglas, Susan & Michaels, Meredith. (2004) *The Mommy Myth: The Idealization of Motherhood and How It Has Undermined All Women*, Free Press, New York.

Dubrofsky, Rachel E. (2009) 'Fallen women on reality TV: a pornography of emotion,' *Feminist Media Studies*, vol. 9, no. 3, pp. 353–368.

Dubrofsky, Rachel E. & Hardy, Antoine. (2008) 'Performing race in *Flavor of Love* and The *Bachelor*,' *Critical Studies in Media Communication*, vol. 25, no. 4, pp. 373—392.

Fairclough, Kirsty. (2004) 'Women's work? *Wife Swap* and the reality problem,' *Feminist Media Studies*, vol. 4, no. 2, pp. 344–360.

Feldstein, Ruth. (2000) *Motherhood in Black and White: Race and Sex in American Liberalism, 1930–1965*, Cornell University Press, Ithaca, NY.

Fernandez, James W. & Huber, Mary T. (2001) 'The anthropology of irony,' in *Irony in Action: Anthropology, Practice, and the Moral Imagination*, eds James W. Fernandez & Mary T. Huber, University of Chicago Press, Chicago, pp. 1–40.

Galewski, Elizabeth. (2007) 'The strange case for women's capacity to reason: Judith Sargent Murray's use of irony in "on the Equality of the Sexes" (1790),' *Quarterly Journal of Speech*, vol. 93, no. 1, pp. 84–108.

Gans, Herbert. (1995) *The War Against the Poor: The Underclass and Antipoverty Policy*, BasicBooks, New York.

Gerhard, Jane. (2005) '*Sex and the City*,' *Feminist Media Studies*, vol. 5, no. 1, pp. 37–49.

Gies, Lieve. (2008) 'Reality TV and the jurisprudence of *Wife Swap*,' in *Law and the Media: the Future of an Uneasy Relationship*, ed. Lieve Gies, Routledge-Cavendish, New York.

Gill, Rosalind. (2007) 'Postfeminist media culture: elements of a sensibility,' *European Journal of Cultural Studies*, vol. 10, no. 2, pp. 147–166.

Gill, Rosalind & Arthurs, Jane. (2006) 'Editors' introduction: new femininities?,' *Feminist Media Studies*, vol. 6, no. 4, pp. 433–451.

Grindstaff, Laura. (2002) *The Money Shot: Trash, Class, and the Making of TV Talk Shows*, University of Chicago Press, Chicago.

Guthrie, Marisa. (2009) 'VH1 working on reality concept about upscale Aspen ski bunnies,'

Broadcasting & Cable, 23 Feb., pp. 3–4, [Online] Available at: http://www.broadcastingcable.com/article/174568-VH1_Working_on_Reality_Concept_About_Upscale_Aspen_Ski_Bunnies.php (6 January 2011).

Heider, Don. (ed.) (2004) *Class and News,* Rowman & Littlefield, Lanham, MD.

Hendershot, Heather. (2009) 'Belabored reality: making it work on *the Simple Life* and *Project Runway,*' in *Reality TV: Remaking Television Culture,* eds Susan Murray & Laurie Ouellette, New York University Press, New York, pp. 243–259.

Hofstadter, Richard. (1996) *The Paranoid Style in American Politics: and Other Essays,* Harvard University Press, Boston.

Kazin, Michael. (1995) *The Populist Persuasion: an American History,* Cornell University Press, Ithaca, NY.

Kendall, Diana. (2005) *Framing Class: Media Representations of Wealth and Poverty in America,* Rowman & Littlefield, New York.

La Ferla, Ruth. (2009) 'TV royalty, but no longer a housewife,' *the New York Times,* 15 Apr., p. E1.

Lane, Jeremy F. (2000) *Pierre Bourdieu: a Critical Introduction,* Pluto Press, London.

Lauzen, Martha M., Dozier, David M. & Cleveland, Elizabeth. (2006) 'Genre matters: an examination of women working behind the scenes and on-screen portrayals in reality and scripted prime-time programming,' *Sex Roles: a Journal of Research,* vol. 55, no. 7–8, pp. 445–456.

Martin, Christopher. (2004) *Framed: Labor and the Corporate Media,* Cornell University Press, Ithaca, NY.

McRobbie, Angela. (2004) 'Post-feminism and popular culture,' *Feminist Media Studies,* vol. 4, no. 3, pp. 255–264.

Mills, C. Wright. (1956) *The Power Elite,* Oxford University Press, New York.

Olson, Kathryn M. & Olson, Clark D. (2004) 'Beyond strategy: a reader-centered analysis of irony's dual persuasive uses,' *Quarterly Journal of Speech,* vol. 90, no. 1, pp. 24–52.

Ouellette, Laurie. (2003) 'Inventing the cosmo girl,' in *Gender, Race and Class in Media: a Text-Reader,* eds Gail Dines & Jean M. Humez,, 2nd edn, Sage Publications, Thousand Oaks, CA, pp. 116–128.

Ouellette, Laurie & Hay, James. (2008) *Better Living through Reality TV,* Blackwell Publishing, Malden, MA.

The Real Housewives of New York City. (television series) (2008–2010) Bravo, USA.

Ringrose, Jessica & Walkerdine, Valerie. (2008) 'Regulating the abject: the TV make-over as site of neo-liberal reinvention toward bourgeois femininity,' *Feminist Media Studies,* vol. 8, no. 3, pp. 227–246.

Rorty, Richard. (1989) *Contingency, Irony, and Solidarity,* Cambridge University Press, New York.

Sgroi, Renee M. (2006) '*Joe Millionaire* and women's positions: a question of class,' *Feminist Media Studies,* vol. 6, no. 3, pp. 281–294.

Skeggs, Beverly. (1997) *Formations of Class and Gender,* Sage, London.

Skeggs, Beverly. (2005) 'The making of class and gender through visualizing moral subject formation,' *Sociology,* vol. 39, no. 5, pp. 965–982.

Stanley, Alessandra. (2008) 'New Yorkers sure love to spend. Who knew?,' *the New York Times,* 15 Mar., p. E1.

Tabako, Tomasz. (2007) 'Irony as a pro-democracy trope: Europe's last comic revolution,' *Controversia,* vol. 5, no. 2, pp. 23–53.

Vavrus, Mary D. (2007) 'Opting out moms in the news,' *Feminist Media Studies,* vol. 7, no. 1, pp. 47–63.

Veblen, Thorstein. (1967) *The Theory of the Leisure Class,* the Viking Press, New York.

Waggoner, Catherine Egley. (2004) 'Disciplining female sexuality in *Survivor,*' *Feminist Media Studies,* vol. 4, no. 2, pp. 217–220.

Wray, Matt. (2006) *Not Quite White: White Trash and the Boundaries of Whiteness,* Duke University Press, Durham, NC.

18

FROM RUSH LIMBAUGH TO DONALD TRUMP

Conservative Talk Radio and the Defiant Reassertion of White Male Authority

Jackson Katz

Donald Trump's 2016 campaign slogan "Make America Great Again" (MAGA) is one of those catchy phrases that carries much greater weight than the sum of its words. While an object of derision and caricature on the cultural and political left—mostly for the putatively racist implications of its timing after two terms of the first African American president, Barack Obama, for millions of (mostly White) Americans MAGA captured an essential truth. The America they remembered and romanticized was fading from view amidst the dizzying pace of social change over the past half-century, especially the changes associated with the country's intensifying racial, ethnic, gender and sexual diversity.

A popular progressive restatement of the right-wing catchphrase alleged that Trump wanted to "Make America White Again." But a careful examination of the Trump campaign's rhetoric and stage-managed rallies, bolstered by exit poll results, reveals that race *and* gender anxieties and resentments animated the bombastic real estate developer's political rise. A more finely tuned rewrite of the famous phrase might read: "Put White Men Back on Center Stage Again," which aptly captures Trumpism as an aspirational political movement.

But White men were already on center stage in a critically important theater in U.S. media culture: conservative talk radio. In fact, the same reactionary sociocultural forces that fueled the phenomenal success of Rush Limbaugh and other conservative talkers over the past generation arguably paved the way for Trump's election as president of the United States. This article outlines some of those forces, with particular attention

to the ways in which conservative talk radio, like Trumpism, champions the reassertion of an idealized, throwback White masculinity as the solution to America's myriad problems at home and abroad.

THE RISE OF CONSERVATIVE TALK RADIO

The recent historical context for the rise of Trumpism was set at least as far back as the 1990s, long before the real estate developer and reality TV star who energized the movement emerged as a serious candidate for the 2016 Republican presidential nomination. In particular, that decade saw the rise of a militantly antigovernment conservatism, which was catalyzed in part by White men's continuing loss of economic power and an accompanying loss of familial and cultural authority, especially in the working and middle classes. Not coincidentally, the 1990s was also the decade in which the influence of conservative talk radio increased dramatically. Over the past three decades, Rush Limbaugh, Sean Hannity, and a number of charismatic White male talk radio and cable TV hosts have risen to cultural prominence and have done so—like Donald Trump—by selling a brand of authoritarian, bellicose, and at times verbally abusive White masculinity, which for reasons of identity politics and history has touched a nerve with millions of listeners—especially (but not exclusively) White men.

In the real world of the 21st century, White men's unquestioned dominance in the family and workplace are in the process of a long-term decline. But not when you turn on right-wing AM

This piece is an original essay that was commissioned for this volume. It is updated from the version that appeared in the fourth edition.

talk radio or *Fox News Channel*, which together reach an audience of as many as 50 million people (Draper, 2016). People don't generally travel to those precincts to seek out new ideas about the possibilities of democratic governance and citizenship in an increasingly diverse and interconnected world—and they don't get it there. Instead, right-wing hosts typically speak with an old-school masculine authority that recalls an idealized past, when (White) men were in control in the public and private spheres, and no one was in a position to actively challenge their power. They provide their listeners with an alternate media universe where the old order of male dominance and White supremacy is still intact, even if they've (sometimes) cleaned up the cruder rhetorical expressions of sexism and racism. It is both fitting and revealing that one of the signature on-air promotions for Rush Limbaugh's top-rated radio program features an announcer boldly proclaiming that Rush is "America's anchorman," slyly invoking association with the memory (if not the liberal politics) of the late Walter Cronkite, a paternal and authoritative television presence as the chief anchor of the CBS Evening News in the 1960s and 1970s who was known as the "most trusted man in America."

Of course not all conservative talk hosts are White men. There are women, such as Laura Ingraham, a former law clerk for Supreme Court Justice Clarence Thomas, and a handful of men of color, such as the African American conservative libertarian Larry Elder. The Los Angeles-based Elder's signature characteristic, and perhaps the key feature of his popularity with a largely White male audience, is his performance of an angry Black man persona. But unlike the angry Black man who elicits fear and resentment in the White racist imagination, Elder's anger typically is directed at the usual objects of conservative scorn: antiracist White liberals, feminists and progressives of all stripes. Elder is the Black man who literally gives voice to sentiments—especially about race—that White conservatives are reluctant to say out loud, for fear of being labeled as racists.

But women and Black men are the exceptions on conservative talk radio, which remains a bastion of White men's power and center stage for the airing of a myriad of cultural and political grievances on the part of conservative White men. On the air and in their public personae, the (White) men who personify the genre—such as

Limbaugh, Hannity, Mark Levin and Michael Savage—typically shun nuance, rarely concede points in arguments, or even acknowledge the validity of opposing viewpoints. This is, arguably, less a result of their personal stubbornness than it is an occupational imperative: the simplicity of their ideology and arguments and their exaggerated self-confidence are the very source of their popularity. In the midst of a society in transition, in which the old *Father Knows Best* certainties are a figment of the idealized past, these men provide a comforting patriarchal presence, just as the reactionary ideology they champion seeks to roll back the democratizing social changes that have disrupted White men's cultural centrality.

In recent years, bloggers, journalists, and scholars have begun to move beyond dismissive caricatures of talk radio as merely entertainment or simplistic populist chatter and pay closer attention to its cultural and political influence. This is long overdue. There is ample data that demonstrate the powerful role talk radio plays in elections; one study showed that in the 2010 midterm elections 78% of talk radio listeners voted, compared to 41% of eligible voters (Harrison, 2011). There has been some discussion of the racial politics of talk radio. In a book-length study of "outrage media," the authors suggest that many conservatives fear being perceived as racist, and thus find comfort in the "safe political environs" provided by "outrage" programs in which conservative racial resentment is normalized and defended (Berry & Sobieraj, 2014). But with the exception of ongoing feminist criticism of the crude sexism that persists among too many male political commentators in media, there has been very little gendered analysis of talk radio's role in establishing and enforcing a certain kind of old school White manhood.

TALK RADIO AND THE PROMOTION OF TRADITIONAL GENDER IDEOLOGY

Conservative talk radio programs are typically hosted by strong, charismatic White men whose personal style ranges from verbal bomb throwers like Michael Savage to more cerebral and less-caffeinated types like Michael Medved. But almost all of them share a belief not only in conservative orthodoxies like "smaller government" and the virtues of a "free market," but also in traditional gender and sexual ideologies. One way this tra-ditionalist belief plays out conversationally is in the near-constant refrain from right-wing talkers that the problems of the country are linked to the supposed "softness" of liberal men. For example, it is common to hear qualities like compassion and empathy—especially in men—equated with weakness and femininity; a major theme of Rush Limbaugh's social commentary is that the "chicki-fication" of American society is linked to our cul-tural decline (Limbaugh, 2011). In fact, one of the most popular rhetorical techniques conservative talk hosts use is a variation of the rational-public sphere/emotional-private sphere binary. Men in patriarchal cultures have employed this binary for centuries to justify the perpetuation of their familial, religious, economic, and political control over women. The idea is that men are more ratio-nal, and hence better equipped to handle public matters of the economy and foreign policy than women, who are said to be more "emotional," and thus more suited to the private sphere of caregiv-ing and maintaining relationships. Feminist the-orists and popular writers have critiqued—and discredited—this falsely gendered dichotomy for decades, but it continues to animate conservative talk radio—one of the chief sources of news and political commentary for millions of White men.

On his nationally syndicated radio program, the Los Angeles-based conservative talk host Den-nis Prager regularly declares that liberal thought is based on the heart, not on the mind. In his book *Still the Best Hope: Why the World Needs American Values to Triumph,* Prager (2012) outlines what he calls the "feelings-based nature" of liberalism. Of course the "feelings" of empathy or compassion that Prager and other conservatives deride as inca-pable of competing with conservative "logic" has long been devalued in public discourse as femi-nine. In fact, conservative propagandists have so thoroughly feminized the word "liberal" that in recent years few Democratic candidates of either sex wanted to claim the label. Male candidates feared being unmanned, while female politicians didn't want to be seen in narrow, stereotypical terms as merely a "women's candidate."

Critiquing these linguistic practices is not merely a rhetorical exercise, because all of this talk has significant material consequences. For exam-ple, talk radio plays an important role in national debates about military spending and foreign policy,

because daily discussion and on-air dialogue and disputation about these matters helps to define what course of action "manly" men should support. This, in turn, helps to define the political space in which politicians, especially presidents, have to operate. As many observers have noted, for decades Democrats have often supported or acquiesced in the advancement of militaristic policies in part out of fear of being accused of being "soft" on defense. Even before he was elected president, Barack Obama had been the target of relentless mockery and ridicule on conservative talk radio. The line of attack varied from issue to issue, but its essence was usually the same: Obama was Jimmy Carter II: a weak and vacillating leader who (in Obama's case) gave good speeches but was in way over his head. The growing troubles in the world were the result not of complex historical and economic forces, but instead were caused by weak leadership in the White House. This right-wing narrative—replayed endlessly on talk radio for nearly a decade—played a crucial role in setting the stage for the emergence of a leader—Donald Trump—who would "get tough" and (finally) get things done.

RUSH KNOWS BEST

Any serious discussion about the cultural and political significance of talk radio has to begin with Rush Limbaugh. Since the early 1990s Lim-baugh's astounding political influence on the right—and in the Republican Party—has been an open secret. He has been the top-rated radio talk show host in America since *Talkers* magazine started the rankings in 1991. His weekly audience is estimated at approximately 15 million listeners. Over the past two decades Limbaugh's influence has grown to the point that David Frum described him as the "unofficial spokesman for the Republi-can Party." Limbaugh's audience is made up not only of casual listeners and die-hard "dittoheads," but includes a significant percentage of the politi-cal class in and outside of the Washington Beltway, especially conservatives. In 1994, dubbed "The Year of the Angry White Male," when Republi-cans gained control of Congress for the first time in 40 years, Limbaugh was asked to address the new GOP legislators and was named an honor-ary member of the freshman class (Chafets, 2010). As Karl Rove said of Limbaugh, "He's a leader.

If Rush engages on an issue, it gives others courage to engage" (Wilson, 2011, p. 252).

It is notable—although hardly surprising—that Rush Limbaugh's listeners are 72% male, over 90% White and skew 50+ years old. Presumably, a key part of the appeal of conservative talk radio to its predominantly older White male audience resides in its reinforcement of traditional masculinity in the face of a culture where epochal economic transformations and progressive social movements have shaken old certainties about what constitutes a "real man." In this context it is important to note that Limbaugh not only articulates a set of conservative moral precepts and reactionary politics. He also performs a kind of cartoonish masculinity from an era gone by. For example, he loves to talk about football, and he is frequently photographed smoking expensive cigars. He regularly celebrates the military and in the mid-2000s was a prominent defender of the conduct of U.S. service members in the disgraceful episode of the Abu Ghraib prison in Iraq, which he dismissed as a "fraternity prank."

Limbaugh's retrograde attitudes toward women are well-known. According to his biographer, the thrice-divorced Limbaugh has "a fair amount" of Hugh Hefner in him (Chafets, 2010, p. 204). Limbaugh has a long history of making explicitly sexist and dismissive statements about women—especially feminists. Early in his career, he published his "Undeniable Truths of Life," which included this: "Feminism was established so as to allow unattractive women easier access to the mainstream of society" (Limbaugh, 2008). He is also the media personality most responsible for popularizing the term *feminazi,* which links feminists, who are among those at the forefront of democratic advocacy and nonviolence, with Nazis, the embodiment of masculine cruelty and violence. In Limbaugh-land, Democratic women who demand to be treated as men's equals are castrating "feminazis," and Democratic men are either neutered wimps or gay. This antiwoman and antifeminist anger finds expression in the commercial world of talk radio in a way that is inconceivable in other forms of mainstream political discourse.

In fact, the source of Limbaugh's immense popularity on AM radio has some interesting parallels to Howard Stern's popularity on FM, and later on satellite radio. Under the guise of self-consciously constructed personae—Limbaugh as the fun-loving conservative truth-teller, Stern as naughty rock-and-roll bad boy—both men function as the id of their respective audiences. They say things that men in more responsible or respectable contexts may believe but would never say out loud. For example, few men in public life—particularly Republican candidates and officeholders—would dare criticize sexual harassment laws when women comprise 53% of the electorate. But Rush Limbaugh, who repeatedly refers to accomplished women, including women in politics, as "babes," female journalists as "infobabes" and "anchorettes," and lesbians as "lesbos," boasts that a sign on his door reads "Sexual harassment at this work station will not be reported. However . . . it will be graded" (Edsall, 2006). Outside of a handful of short-lived boycotts by feminist activists that resulted in some of his advertisers pulling their support for his program, Limbaugh has largely sidestepped significant financial repercussions for his repeated expressions of open misogyny. Nonetheless it is notable that in 2016–17, two of the most powerful figures in conservative media, Fox News Channel founding president and CEO Roger Ailes, and that network's biggest star, Bill O'Reilly, lost their jobs at Fox due to multiple allegations of sexual harassment against them.

To be sure, Limbaugh is not without his many critics and detractors. For many years he has been the subject of mainstream media interest—and concern. One *Time* magazine cover story that appeared as far back as 1995 was headlined "Is Rush Limbaugh Good for America? Talk Radio is only the beginning. Electronic populism threatens to short-circuit representative democracy" (*Time,* 1995). A 2008 cover story in the *New York Times Magazine* profiled Limbaugh's political influence, as well as offered readers a glimpse at the lavish lifestyle afforded him due to his financial success (Chafets, 2008). But not everyone recognizes the extent of his political clout. When the controversy over Limbaugh's misogynous tirade against Georgetown law student Sandra Fluke erupted in 2012, Al Neuharth, founder of *USA Today,* wrote that "the real problem with Rush Limbaugh is that people take him seriously. He's a clown. If you listen to his radio program regularly, it should be to get your daily laugh" (Neuharth, 2012).

Critics of Limbaugh and other right-wing talk radio hosts often point to the coarsening of political discourse to which the talkers have contributed. Former vice-president Al Gore describes what he terms the "Limbaugh-Hannity-Drudge axis" as a kind of "fifth column in the fourth estate" that is made up of "propagandists pretending to be journalists" (Gore, 2007, p. 66). Gore claims that what most troubles him about these right-wing polemicists is their promotion of hatred as entertainment—particularly their mean-spirited hostility toward liberals and progressives. But what most of right-wing radio's progressive critics overlook or downplay is the gendered nature of Limbaugh and company's contempt for liberals. Embedded firmly within the talk radio hosts' scathing critique of liberalism is a barely suppressed well of anger at the progressive changes in the gender and sexual order over the past 40 years and the concomitant displacement of traditional patriarchal power. Limbaugh is perhaps the most overt in his open hostility not only toward feminist women, but also the men who support them. He calls these men the "new castrati," and ridicules them for having "lost all manhood, gonads, guts and courage throughout our culture and our political system" (Media Matters, 2011).

In the media character he self-created, Limbaugh's unrestrained narcissism drives him to broadcast to his audience an inflated sense of himself as a "man's man," while his political agenda seeks to reinforce the link between manly strength and political conservatism. He accomplishes this rhetorically, in part, by relentlessly attacking the femininity of feminist women, and the masculinity of men who support gender equality. Limbaugh's brash and boorish persona, and his belief that White men's cultural centrality is, in the title of his first book, "The Way Things Ought to Be," help set the stage for the political rise of another bombastic media performer: Donald J. Trump.

LIMBAUGH AND OTHER CONSERVATIVE TALKERS PROVIDE THE TEMPLATE FOR TRUMP

During the 2016 presidential campaign, Sean Hannity—who is the second most highly-rated talk radio host (after Limbaugh) and a Fox News Channel mainstay—became a vociferous supporter of Donald Trump, providing the eventual Republican nominee and president with many millions of dollars of free (and largely fawning) media coverage. But while Hannity eagerly insinuated himself into the Trump story, Rush Limbaugh's entire career can be seen as an extended prelude to

Trump's climb to the pinnacle of power. In fact, when Rush Limbaugh praised a Donald Trump speech on June 22, 2016 that the *New York Times* said contained a "torrent of criticism" aimed at Hillary Clinton, he was really congratulating himself. Trump "basically said things about Hillary Clinton that you just do not hear Republicans saying," the right-wing talk radio icon said. "You just do not hear Mitt Romney say this, for example. You would not hear the Bush family talk this way about Hillary. You . . . would not hear it" (Schwartz, 2016, para. 2). Limbaugh's point—variations of which he has made for years—is that "establishment types" can't or won't be this blunt in their criticism. "But Trump can say this as an outsider, he can say this stuff as a nonmember of the elite or the establishment" (Schwartz, 2016, para. 3).

Limbaugh might outwardly have been lauding the brashness of the billionaire real estate developer, but any critical Limbaugh-listener could hear the gushing self-congratulation just beneath the surface of those remarks. For perhaps the best way to describe the Big Talker is the "outsider who can say stuff that is normally out of bounds in polite company"—a cleverly constructed persona that the college drop-out from Cape Girardeau, Missouri has parlayed into a long and amazingly lucrative career in conservative talk radio. Limbaugh's unparalleled popularity owes a great deal to his willingness to say things—especially sexist, racist, and homophobic things—that more respectable Republicans would never utter in public: especially those who have to face the voters. And for close to 30 years his legions of fans have loved him for it. In this sense, Limbaugh's affection for Donald Trump is about more than his recognition of a kindred spirit; it is actually yet another manifestation of his narcissism.

Consider the many similarities between the two men. They're both aging heterosexual White men of German American ethnicity who were born 5 years apart and grew up as the sons of authoritarian, deeply patriarchal and professionally highly successful fathers. They both have reaped rich rewards in life despite—or is it because of?—displaying levels of narcissistic toxicity that are notable even in the puffed-up precincts of New York City real estate and conservative media. They are both frequent supporters of aggressive military action, including torture, but each deftly avoided military service during the Vietnam War era.

Trump avoided serving through a series of deferments common to members of his social class, Limbaugh by claiming an anal boil rendered him unfit for service. They are both members of the 1% who inhabit worlds of almost unimaginable wealth and privilege, living in luxury dwellings in New York City and mansions in south Florida, flying around the world on private jets. They both love to golf. They both repeatedly make misogynous comments and refuse to apologize for them. They both have had at least three wives. And they are both fake populists who have used aggressive language and verbal bullying tactics against their adversaries to wrangle their way to the heights of cultural and political influence in the United States of America.

Consider how Rush Limbaugh's career in talk radio might have paved the way for Donald Trump's political ascension. For almost three decades, Limbaugh fashioned himself a tribune of the people, a man with the guts to defend average (White) folks from an ongoing assault waged by liberal politicians and cultural elites against traditional American values. Many liberals and progressives see Limbaugh as a pompous and bigoted blowhard, and they are perplexed and dismayed by his continuing popularity. At the same time, Limbaugh is revered on the right as a champion of the little White guy (and gal) who have been trampled for a generation by multiculturalism, feminism, the gay rights movement, and the myriad of unsettling cultural transformations they have catalyzed. While progressives look at Limbaugh and see a bloated bully who routinely targets individuals and groups with less power, his fans see him as a man armed only with a very large microphone and the confidence and courage to shovel sand against the rising tides of social change.

Perhaps the most concise way to explain these radically different perceptions is that while the left sees many of Limbaugh's pronouncements as offensive, the right sees them as defensive. And because he's defending them, they're willing to overlook or excuse his more than occasional intemperate outbursts. It's quite similar to how millions of Trump supporters see the reality TV star who was elected to be the 45th president of the United States. Like Limbaugh, Trump is a man of privilege whose class sympathies lie with the rich, but who nonetheless has been able to market himself as someone who is on the side of average (White) Americans. A crucial part of Trump's appeal to downwardly mobile

White men is his image as the "blue-collar billionaire" who will do what it takes to bring back good jobs for working-class people. He has managed to maintain this illusion despite the reality that, as Matt Taibbi wrote, "Trump had spent his entire career lending his name to luxury properties that promised exclusivity and separation from exactly the sort of struggling Joes who turned out for his speeches" (Taibbi, 2015) and despite his enthusiasm for the failed idea of trickle-down economics—i.e. cutting taxes on the wealthy as a way to create jobs for the working class (Taibbi, 2015).

But in Trumpworld, you're a "populist" not because you advocate economic policies that actually benefit working people, but because you're dismissive of "politically correct" elites who refuse to talk honestly and say what every red-blooded White American man supposedly knows to be true—especially about matters of race, gender, and sexuality. Trump learned during his campaign for the presidency what Rush Limbaugh has known for decades. On the right, the way to build an audience—or a voter base—is to convince people you're on their side and are willing to fight back—and hit hard—against the forces that are holding them down. For Limbaugh, those forces are, generally speaking, the enemy within: snobby "libs," the "drive-by media," "feminazis," "environmentalist wackos," Black Lives Matter activists. The objects of Trump's rhetorical aggression are more likely to be "outsiders," either far-away actors like China and ISIS, or closer to home, Mexican and Muslim immigrants (and Muslim Americans).

What these men's rhetorical appeals have in common is they identify and target specific enemies for people to get angry with—especially those who reside on the lower rungs of economic and social power. It's much easier to direct people's anger downward (or sideways) than it is to level with them that their very real problems—including the loss of millions of well-paying jobs and a chance for social mobility for the next generation—are rooted in the impersonal forces of global capitalism. It's much easier to bash Democrats or dark-skinned others than it is to critique decades of conservative economic and social policy—promulgated by class-peers and ideological fellow-travelers of the real estate mogul and radio star—that have gutted the middle class and dramatically exacerbated income inequality.

CONCLUSION

This chapter outlined some of the ways that conservative talk radio is not simply "entertainment." Rather, it has a profound influence not only on elections, but on the very nature of public discourse, and thus ultimately on public policy, on issues ranging from women's health to climate change. Until now, little attention has been paid in cultural studies scholarship to the important cultural and political role of conservative talk radio, and even less to how this cultural phenomenon functions in the gender order. Considering the important "public pedagogical" role that charismatic hosts play in their embodiment and modeling of an influential version of conservative White masculinity, and the influence this has on contemporary American political dialogue and debate, much more empirical research and analysis of conservative talk radio's social and political impact is necessary. This need has taken on even greater urgency since the stunning political success of Donald Trump, a former reality TV star who performs a kind of crude, loud-mouthed, throwback White masculinity that has been a regular presence on the airwaves for the past generation, but which is now ensconced at the pinnacle of cultural and political power.

REFERENCES

Berry, J., & Sobieraj, S. (2014). *The outrage industry: political opinion media and the new incivility."* New York: Oxford University Press.

Chafets, Z. (2008). Late period Limbaugh. *The New York Times Magazine.* July 6. Retrieved from http://www.nytimes.com/2008/07/06/magazine/06Limbaugh-t.html?pagewanted=all&_r=0 p. 3.

Chafets, Z. (2010). *Rush Limbaugh: an army of one.* New York: Sentinel.

Draper, R. (2016, October 2). How Donald Trump's candidacy set off a civil war within the right-wing media. *The New York Times Magazine,* 38.

Edsall, T. (2006). *Building red America: The New Conservative Coalition and the drive for permanent power.* New York: Basic Books.

Gore, A. (2007). *The assault on reason.* New York: Penguin.

Harrison, M. (2011, October). Qualitative aspects of the talk radio audience. *Talkers Magazine,* 8.

Limbaugh, R. (2011). Chickification of America: NFL cancels game because of snow. RushLimbaugh.com. Retrieved from http://www.rushlimbaugh.com/daily/2011/01/04/chickification_of_america_nfl_cancels_game_because_of_snow

MacNicol, G. (2011, May 2). Rush Limbaugh MOCKS the idea that Obama is responsible for capture of Bin Laden: "Thank God for President Obama!" *Business Insider.* Retrieved from http:///www.businessinsider.com/rush-limbaugh-thank-god-for-president-obama-2011-5

Media Matters. (2011, March 8). Limbaugh describes the new castrati.

Neuharth, A. (2012, March 19.) Limbaugh is a clown so let's laugh at him. *USA Today.*

Politico. (2011, May 2). Limbaugh mocks Obama for bin Laden hit. Retrieved from http://www.politico.com/blogs/onmedia/0511/Limbaugh_mocks_Obama_for_bin_Laden_hit.html

Prager, D. (2012). *Still the best hope: Why the world needs American values to triumph.* New York: Broadside Books.

Schwartz, I. (2016, June 23). Limbaugh on Trump: Finally, a Republican (other than me) tells the truth about Hillary Clinton. *Real Clear Politics.* Retrieved from http://www.realclearpolitics.com/video/2016/06/23/limbaugh_on_trump_finally_a_republican_other_than_me_tells_the_truth_about_hillary_clinton.html.

Taibbi, M. (2015, December 29). "In the year of Trump, the joke was on us." *Rolling Stone.*

Time magazine. (1995, January 23.) Cover.

Wilson, J. (2011) *The most dangerous man in America: Rush Limbaugh's assault on reason.* New York: St. Martin's.

READING
MEDIA TEXTS
CRITICALLY

M edia scholars recognize that media **texts** are never simple, however transparent they may seem to be on the surface. Because media texts are relatively open to interpretation, or polysemic (discussed in the introduction to Part I), there is frequently room to make readings that go at least partially against dominant ideologies (**counterhegemonic** readings). However, in our everyday media engagement, we don't always attend closely to the mechanisms and techniques that influence the way we make meanings out of texts. This inattention makes us more likely to internalize the messages encoded in the stories and images and to become passive rather than active (and potentially resistant) readers, listeners, and viewers.

In this section, we have assembled a group of chapters that provide a variety of models for how to **deconstruct** or get underneath the surface of media texts, in order to understand how they **encode ideologies** of gender, sexuality, race, and class. We acknowledge that some readers may find that close analysis interferes with the pleasure of consuming media texts. But if you are one of those readers, we would invite you to join media scholars in finding the special pleasure (and power) available to those who become critical readers of texts. As audiences build critical media literacy skills, a dual consciousness can develop, enabling us both to enjoy the text and simultaneously take pleasure in decoding and critiquing its more subtle and nuanced meanings.

We begin with a particularly good example of how one might do a close reading of polysemic media texts—those with multiple possible meanings. *Cosmopolitan* has been a wildly popular magazine for decades, one that ostensibly offers empowering messages to women and girls, yet functions within a consumerist and **patriarchal** ideology that equates female power and success with expensive beauty products and a sex life built around pleasing men. Laurie Ouellette (III.19) analyzes both *Cosmopolitan* and the best-selling book *Sex and the Single Girl* (1962) by Helen Gurley Brown, the editor who made the magazine such a major success in the 1960s and 1970s. Ouellette's intersectional approach reveals how the book and the magazine took on the cultural mission of teaching working-class White women about the supposed path to upward mobility. According to Ouellette,

> Brown's advice offered a gendered success myth to women who found themselves taking on new roles as breadwinners, but who lacked the wages, education, professional skills, and social opportunities to recognize themselves in more conventional, male-oriented upward-mobility narratives. (p. 164)

For these White working-class women in the prefeminist 1960s, learning to fake a middle-class version of femininity was supposedly the key to real class mobility, through ensnaring a well-off man. How to snare that man? The answer the texts provided was through possessions, beauty, and sex. Yet simultaneously, as suggested by its name, *Cosmopolitan* seemed to offer women an entry into the **public sphere**—the world outside of the home that had long been denied to them.

Ouellette's chapter thus reminds us that there is no one completely dominant perspective encoded throughout mass media. She writes: "The cultural discourse Brown articulated legitimated sexism and the capitalist exploitation of women's labor, while simultaneously expressing hardships and desires in a voice that spoke with credibility to an expanding class of pink-collar women" (p. 157). As cultural studies scholars often emphasize, drawing upon the complex concept of power articulated by Michel Foucault, competing voices and alternative perspectives always arise to contest hegemonic formulations, in an ongoing and decentralized struggle for superiority. Thus, even in a socially conservative time and place like the early 1960s, there is always some space for power to play out in subtle ways.

In the early 21st century, one place within mass media production where arguably counterhegemonic views can be found is in the more narrowly targeted commercial entertainment media such as cable TV networks. For example, Comedy Central's *The Daily Show* slyly conveys dissident political views by parodying the conventions of the mainstream television news format. Jamie Warner (III.20) compares the show's tactics to those practiced by activist "culture jammers," who are "rebelling against the hegemony of the messages promoting global capitalism." In this case, the target was frequently the "branding techniques" politicians and political parties use "to drown out dissident messages," and the method for subverting those "brand" messages is "dissident humor":

> Like other culture jammers, *The Daily Show* subversively employs emotional and aesthetic modalities similar to those employed by political branding itself, thus interrupting it from within. Unlike many culture jammers, however, *The Daily Show*'s reliance on a humorous version of parody means that they can add their voices to the conversation in a seemingly innocuous way. (After all, it is *just* a joke.) (p. 169)

Another example of a potentially subversive humorous TV show is *The Simpsons,* the long-running edgy satirical animation series on the Fox Network that has been very popular with young people. Gilad Padva (III.21) situates *The Simpsons* within "the popular subgenre of animated TV sitcoms in the late 1990s and 2000s," which "integrates semi-anarchistic humor and spectacular imagery that often challenge conventional ethnic, social, gender and sexual patterns of representation." Using an episode from *The Simpsons* called "Homer Phobia," which lampoons the leading character Homer Simpson for knee-jerk antigay attitudes, Padva deconstructs the text, showing how it **encodes** a celebration of "queer counterculture" and is open to different readings for those "in the know": "Although straight audiences too enjoy this episode, its hyperbolic scenes particularly empower gay viewers, who likely identify the linguistic maneuvers and decode the queer meanings" (p. 179).

Candace Moore (III.22) presents another example of a media text in which forbidden truths rupture the smooth surface of social harmony. Ellen DeGeneres, the stand-up comic who famously "came out" as a lesbian on her sitcom in 1997, has since adopted what is called "an everywoman approach" on her talk show, launched in 2003 and still popular with viewers. According to Moore, DeGeneres has been critiqued for failing to embrace her lesbian identity in her post-sitcom media work. However, by closely analyzing the persona and self-presentation of DeGeneres on this show, Moore is able to see a strategy more subtle than simply denying her lesbianism or returning to the closet, as some of her critics would have it. Moore argues that "she performs queerness through what implicitly 'exceeds' her stand-up jokes and sit-down talk, and, physically, through the ritual action of her daily dance sequence" (p. 182). Through these methods, perhaps DeGeneres escapes being such a "convenient screen" for hate-mongers or bearing the responsibility of being a spokesperson for all of gay America, while she still maintains a *televisibility* of queer identity.

Despite the preceding examples, we should remember that the popular culture environment is far from a utopian safe space for nontraditional gender roles and queerness. Without doubt, sports radio is a major producer of hegemonic masculinity, yet even here, according to David Nylund's chapter (III.23), there may be some contesting of **homophobia.** Interestingly, Nylund found that well-known sports radio talk show host Jim Rome unexpectedly critiqued the use of homophobic slurs by callers, thus opening up space through his show for the questioning of dominant gender notions. Nylund is careful to point out, however, that "Rome's location of the problem of homophobia in a few bigoted, intolerant individuals leaves unchallenged the larger societal structures that perpetuate heterosexism" (p. 195).

Another place where lessons of gender, race, and class are taught is on television, including enormously successful, so-called reality television shows like *Duck Dynasty*. In her intersectional critical reading, Shannon E. M. O'Sullivan (III.24) shows how the performance of the role of "redneck" on this program is based in particular hegemonic notions of race, class, and gender. Despite their actions and appearance on the show itself, Sullivan's attention to auxiliary media about the Robertson family at the center of the *Duck Dynasty* brand demonstrates the performative nature of identity:

> In the collection of photographs that reemerged . . . the Robertsons can be seen on the beach and on the golf course, embodying stereotypical yuppie appearances, before their careers on A&E. The Robertson men look clean-shaven with short haircuts, as they pose wearing khakis and button-down shirts. These images sharply contrast with their trademark long beards, hair, and camouflage. (p. 202).

Thus, a wealthy, media-savvy father and sons are reimagined in their "reality" show as "authentic" representatives of the White male working-class despite the economic truths of the family's more than comfortable class position. O'Sullivan sums up the hegemonic power of this representation of race, class, and gender:

> In short, the most popular reality television program on US cable television to date promotes the dominant myth that the United States is a classless society, in which there are no structural barriers to upward social mobility. It also reinforces the prevailing perception that white, rural, heteronormative men are "real men." Thus, it promotes white, heteronormative male supremacy. (p. 207)

While the world of rap and hip-hop might seem as far away from *Duck Dynasty* as can be imagined, in the next chapter Guillermo Rebollo-Gil and Amanda Moras (III.25) analyze how in this form of popular culture ideologies of race and gender also play out in complex ways. While critiquing the violence and **misogyny** of some rap music Rebollo-Gil and Moras argue that the lyrics and images of hip-hop should be examined within the context of the White supremacist nature of both the music industry and the larger U.S. culture. For example, they note: "the sexualized images of black women in Hip Hop must also be understood as a reflection of white patriarchal commodification of black sexuality" (p. 210). And, in discussing gangsta rap, the authors remind us:

> [W]hile it is true that this Hip Hop sub-genre is problematic and troubling as it pertains to its exponents' treatment of women, for example, the music and its artists are put under fire more for what they are perceived to be because of their race than on account of what they actually say or do. The censorship of the music then can be understood to be more a product of white racism than of hurtful or offensive rap speech given the various other places in mainstream US popular culture where misogyny is both tolerated and promoted. (p. 211)

In the last chapter in this section, Bill Yousman (III.26) offers a critical reading of a variety of 21st century media texts that construct and reinforce racist ideologies by equating Blackness with criminality. He argues that there are real social costs that accrue from the proliferation of racist cultural texts:

> Media images and narratives play a crucial role in shaping our perceptions of key social issues, including race, crime, policing, and incarceration. These beliefs inflect public opinion about the proper state responses to crime, often leading to a fearful and punitive mindset that is easily exploited for political purposes. (p. 217)

However, Yousman also notes the counter-hegemonic possibilities afforded by the emergence of new technologies and social media platforms that aid social justice movements like #blacklivesmatter in creating their own texts that challenge White supremacy, both in media and popular culture and in the wider social formation.

As demonstrated by this and other chapters in this section, decoding media texts is never simple, because they work on multiple levels of meaning and have polysemic potential. Once you learn to read them critically, however, it makes them even more interesting. Students usually find courses that develop critical media literacy "eye-opening" and intellectually transforming—but as you share your new insights into the depths of the texts with friends who just want to be entertained, be prepared to be told "you're reading too much into it." Deconstructing media texts, however, should not be thought of as a process of "over analyzing." Instead it should be recognized as part of what the linguist and political scholar Noam Chomsky often referred to as "intellectual self-defense."

19

INVENTING THE COSMO GIRL
Class Identity and Girl-Style American Dreams
Laurie Ouellette

I am a materialist, and it is a materialistic world.

—*Helen Gurley Brown[1]*

In February 1997, a former secretary named Helen Gurley Brown stepped down from her position as the editor-in-chief of *Cosmopolitan,* the hugely successful consumer magazine she developed for the "single girl" market in the mid-1960s. Still an American cultural icon, Brown was suddenly back in the media spotlight, espousing her credo on topics ranging from sex and the workplace to the Cosmo Girl, the fictionalized woman she invented to characterize the magazine's imagined 18- to 34-year-old female reader. Just as feminist historians have recognized Brown's role in partly subverting patriarchal sexual ideologies (Douglas, 1994; Ehrenreich et al., 1986), media commentators framed the departure by casting Brown as the feminine piper of the sexual revolution.[2] What cannot be explained by a singular focus on sexual politics, however, are the class-specific dimensions of Brown's message and popular appeal.

This chapter analyzes Helen Gurley Brown's early advice to women as a cultural discourse that managed some of the social and economic tensions of the 1960s and early 1970s, while also offering certain women the symbolic material to enable them to think about themselves as historical subjects in new ways. John Fiske's understanding of discourse is especially helpful for making sense of Brown's position as a capitalist media maven and an immensely popular spokeswoman for everygirl. As Fiske argues, discourse is a "system of representation that has developed socially in order to make and circulate a coherent set of meanings about an important topic area" (1987: 14). Discourses are ideological insofar as their "meanings serve the interests of that section of society within which the discourse originates and which works ideologically to naturalize those meanings into common sense," but they are not conspiratorial or "produced" by individual authors or speakers (1987: 14). Rather, discourses are socially produced and often institutionalized ways of making sense of a certain topic that "preexist their use in any one discursive practice," and that construct "a sense, or social identity, of us" as we speak them (Fiske, 1987: 14–15).

. . . I wish to show how Brown's advice spoke to major changes in women's economic and sexual roles, while also constructing a suggested social identity for her "working girl" readers. . . . The cultural discourse Brown articulated legitimated sexism and the capitalist exploitation of women's labor, while simultaneously expressing hardships and desires in a voice that spoke with credibility to an expanding class of pink-collar women.

Based on my examination of *Cosmopolitan* magazine (1965–75) as well as Brown's books, recordings and interviews during this period, I am suggesting that she articulated a girl-style American Dream that promised transcendence from class roles as well as sexual ones. Brown was one of the first mainstream figures to free women from the guilt of premarital sex by advising them to disregard the patriarchal double standard. But she was also concerned with shaping and transforming the class position of the Cosmo Girl through

From Laurie Ouellette, "Inventing the Cosmo Girl." *Media, Culture and Society* (1999), 21, 359–383. Reprinted with permission of SAGE Publications.

a combination of self-management strategies, performative tactics, sexuality, and upwardly mobile romance.[3] At a time when the term often seems in danger of slipping from the critical vocabulary, Brown's advice to women offers a case study in the cultural construction of class—not as an economic category or even a relationship in the Marxist sense, but as a fragmented and sexualized identity. As Brown explained,

> There are girls who . . . don't want to be that driven, to have that many affairs; they don't want more than one man or one dress at a time. They don't care about jewelry and they don't want a sable coat or Paris for the weekend. . . . But "my girl" wants it. She is on the make. Her nose is pressed to the glass and she does get my message. These girls are like my children all over the country. Oh, I have so much advice for them. . . . (Quoted in *Guardian Weekly*, 1968)

INVENTING THE COSMO GIRL

In 1962, at the age of 42, Brown wrote the best-seller *Sex and the Single Girl* (1962) and became an overnight celebrity. According to Brown, the book was an unabashed self-help credo for "the girl who doesn't have anything going for her . . . who's not pretty, who maybe didn't go to college and who may not even have a decent family background" (quoted in Didion, 1965: 35). Drawing partly from Brown's experience as a woman who held 18 secretarial jobs before she was promoted to an advertising copywriter and then married at the age of 37, the book offered step-by-step advice on personal appearance, budget apartment dwelling, working, and, above all, flirting. Brown guided women through encounters with men who were not their husbands, instructing them how to attract the best ones, date them, cajole dinners and presents out of them, have affairs, and eventually marry the most eligible man available. In a year when "married people on television slept in twin beds" (Douglas, 1994: 68) and the sexual revolution remained the prerogative of men and student counterculture types, *Sex and the Single Girl* suggested that ordinary women could lead fully sexual lives outside marriage (Brown, 1962: 11). Brown critiqued mandatory motherhood, advised birth control, condoned divorce, encouraged women to work outside the home, and

recommended sexual and financial independence within boundaries. However, the book was by no means anti-marriage: As Brown explained, it was a response to the "man shortage," a guide to attracting desirable men while remaining "single in superlative style" ("A Proposal for *Cosmopolitan*," n.d.).

Sex and the Single Girl was mocked by intellectuals, reviewed, as one journalist observed, "only to provide a fixed target for reviewers eager to point up (amid considerable merriment) the superiority of their own perceptions over those of Mrs. Brown" (Didion, 1965: 36). But the book appealed to hundreds of thousands of women who were living out a growing gap between "girlhood and marriage" made possible by shifting urban migration patterns and the expanding pink-collar labor force (Ehrenreich et al., 1986: 54). *Single Girl* sold more than two million copies in three weeks, due to extensive publicity and Brown's rigorous efforts to get in touch with the kind of women critics derided as "subliterate and culturally deprived" (Didion, 1965: 36). Following the book's initial success, Brown was interviewed extensively in the press, appeared as a frequent guest on radio and television talk shows, and sold the motion-picture rights to *Single Girl* to Hollywood. She wrote a series of follow-up books, including *Sex and the Office* (1964) and *Sex and the New Single Girl* (1970a), recorded best-selling lectures with names like *Lessons in Love* (1963), and wrote a syndicated newspaper column called "Woman Alone." While early feminist leaders like Betty Friedan found Brown's message "obscene and horrible," few could deny that she had developed an "astonishing rapport with America's single-girldom" (quoted in Welles, 1965: 65).

In 1965, Brown took her credo and her phenomenal sales figures to Hearst Publications, owners of *Cosmopolitan* magazine, and became the magazine's new editor-in-chief. With close monitoring by Hearst, she transformed *Cosmopolitan* from a fledgling intellectual publication into a "compendium of everything I know about how to get through the emotional, social and business shoals that confront a girl, and have a better life" (Brown, 1970a: 7). Brown maintained such strict control over the magazine that critics began to ridicule the singular, gushy voice that permeated article after article, but the editorial formula she devised drew new readers (Brown, 1965). Circulation rose by more than 100,000 the first year alone, advertising sales grew 43 percent (*Newsweek*, 1966: 60), and a series of self-help books distributed through the *Cosmopolitan* Book-of-the-Month Club were equally successful. By the mid-1970s, *Cosmopolitan* was reaching more than two million readers, advertising sales were still soaring, 12 foreign-language editions had been launched, and Brown was a celebrity who claimed to embody much of the advice she distributed through her media enterprise.[4] Due to Brown's characterizations and the "I'm that Cosmopolitan Girl" advertising campaign, which she helped write, the fictionalized Cosmo Girl had entered the cultural lexicon as a sexualized symbol of pink-collar femininity. Before elaborating on her construction, it is useful to sketch out the historical context during which she arose.

As the economist Julie Matthaei has shown, the growth of the service sector has been "central in the absorption of female labor" (1982: 282). In the 1960s, as the U.S.A. moved rapidly toward a post-Fordist economy, women entered the paid workforce in greater numbers, and began to stay there for longer periods of time, earning approximately 59 cents on the male dollar (Howe, 1977: 3). According to the U.S. Department of Labor, between 1962 and 1974, the number of employed women rose by 10 million, or 45 percent. Some women entered the male-dominated professions, but the majority entered "feminine" pink-collar jobs, and the largest gain occurred in secretarial and clerical occupations that often required no college education (Howe, 1977: 10–11). Women were already the mainstay of these occupational fields, but the capitalist expansion of the service sector was a new development, as was the growing number of women working for prolonged periods of time to support themselves (and families) in these positions.[5] *Sex and the Single Girl* spoke directly to unmarried working women, and *Cosmopolitan* was the first consumer magazine to target single "girls with jobs" with feature articles, advice columns, budget fashions and advertisements for mainly "feminine" consumer items, such as cosmetics, personal care products, lingerie, and clothing.[6] The magazine also featured advertisements for temporary employment agencies, training centers and correspondence schools where women could learn stenography, typing, and dictation and similar clerical skills. Hearst's interest in hiring Brown to address self-sufficient working women was thus linked to their emergence as a consumer market capable of purchasing certain goods and services with their own wages.[7]

Cosmopolitan's pink-collar orientation and economic base is especially clear when compared to that of its nearest competitor, *Ms.* magazine. Critics have observed that when *Ms.* debuted in 1972 as a voice of the women's movement, it tended to emphasize the goals and aspirations of liberal feminism and college-educated women. Editorial material aimed at pink-collar women was less typical, and the female consumer hailed by "dress-for-success" fashions and durable consumer goods differed from the one hailed by *Cosmopolitan* (McCracken, 1993: 278–80; Valverde, 1986: 81). Both magazines claimed to serve independent working women, but market research found *Ms.* readers had higher incomes and were more than twice as likely to have attended college. More than a third of *Ms.* readers (as opposed to virtually no *Cosmopolitan* readers) also held advanced degrees (Harrington, 1974). Critics, however, downplayed the social and economic basis of the skew and blamed Brown for the "Two Faces of the Same Eve," explaining that intelligent women with graduate degrees were not apt to be called "little Cosmo Girl" or buy a magazine whose editor insists that ideas be made "baby simple" (Harrington, 1974: 12). With considerable scorn, Brown was characterized as the "working girl's Simone de Beauvoir" of her era (*Newsweek,* 1966: 60).

In the U.S.A., women's mass entry into the workforce is often attributed to the second wave of the women's movement. However, when we consider the stratification within the female labor force, Barbara Ehrenreich's thesis that "male revolt" from the traditional breadwinning role was an earlier and more significant catalyst seems highly plausible. Breadwinning, according to Ehrenreich, was an informal economic contract rooted in the family wage system, and as such it was dependent upon the voluntary cooperation of men:

> Men are favored in the labor market, both by the kinds of occupations open to them and by informal discrimination within occupations, so that they earn, on the average, 40 percent more than women do. Yet nothing compels them to spread the wealth to those—women and children—who are excluded from work or less generously rewarded for it. Men cannot be forced to marry; once married, they cannot be forced to bring home their paychecks, to be reliable job holders, or, of course, to remain married. In fact, considering the absence of legal coercion, the surprising thing is that men have for so long, and, on

the whole, so reliably, adhered to what might be called the "breadwinner" ethic. (1983: 11)

Once held together by popular culture, expert opinion and religious expectations, the breadwinning ethic began to unravel around the time the Beats, with their flagrant celebration of male freedom, appeared on the scene, says Ehrenreich (1983: 12; 52). When *Playboy* magazine debuted in 1953, she argues, "male revolt" was expressed in a broader context. While *Playboy* is often associated with the mainstreaming of soft-core pornography, it also promoted a "Dale Carnegie–style credo of male success" rooted in free enterprise, a strong work ethic and materialistic consumption. The only difference between conventional success mythology and Hugh Hefner's message was that men were not encouraged to share their money, says Ehrenreich. Wives and single women were depicted as shrews and "gold-diggers," while bachelors were advised to pursue sex on a casual basis to avoid getting snared in a "long term contract" (1983: 46). By the 1970s, alimony reductions and no-fault divorce laws—however progressive in the feminist sense—had legitimated male revolt at the official level of the state. For the first time in U.S. history, observed sociologist Jane Mansbridge, "society was beginning to condone a man leaving his family on the sole grounds that living with them and providing for them made him unhappy" (1986: 108).

Brown's advice spoke to the social and economic flux generated by these shifts by offering a modified sexual contract, and by presenting certain women, who may no longer have recognized their place in male-oriented American Dream mythology, with the discursive material to envision themselves as upwardly mobile sexual agents. Brown was clear in her wish for women to see themselves in the fictionalized persona of the Cosmo Girl. "A guy reading *Playboy* can say, 'Hey, That's me.' I want my girl to be able to say the same thing," she explained (quoted in *Providence Journal*, 1965). While her advice was often antagonistic, the social structure that was the cause of the dilemma was never challenged. . . .

THE BEAUTIFUL PHONY

. . . Brown's credo required an understanding of identity as something that could always be reworked, improved upon, and even dramatically

changed. *Sex and the Single Girl* promised every girl the chance to acquire a stylish and attractive aura by copying fashion models and wealthy women (Brown, 1962: 189–94). Expenditures on clothing, cosmetics, and accessories were presented as necessary investments in the construction of a desirable (and thus saleable) self. *Cosmopolitan* columns with names like "So You're Bored to Death with the Same Old You" (1972) extended these possibilities by offering women the ability to construct a "whole new identity," defined in terms of fashion and style. According to the column, "A new lipstick will really not work a sudden transformation, but have you considered going further? Perhaps even to the point of changing everything (hair, makeup, clothes, manner), in short, changing your type?" (*Cosmopolitan,* 1972: 172). Other articles with names like "Yes, You Can Change Your Image" (De Santis, 1969) stressed the fluidity of female subjectivity, encouraging readers to make themselves over and even construct multiple selves, often to meet the demands and opportunities of prolonged courtship.

To "get into the position to sink a man" it was not necessary that a woman be beautiful, but she had to know how to create "an illusion of beauty" (Brown, 1962: 204). Phoniness was often celebrated as a form of trickery—a way to create a prettier, sexier, and more desirable self beyond one's allotted means. Even the *Cosmopolitan* cover girl was exposed as a "fake," her breasts made to appear more alluring with masking tape and Vaseline (Kent, 1972; Reisig, 1973). According to another column called the "The Beautiful Phony" (*Cosmopolitan,* 1966a), "naturalness" was an imposed value that destroyed the possibility of such illusions. Taking sides with the imagined reader, it opened with the advice:

They're always telling you to be the most natural girl in the world and you want to cooperate but, well, they just ought to see you in your natural state. Pale, lashless, lusterless, bustless and occasionally, after a grinding day at the typewriter, almost fingernail-less! Darling, not another apology! (1966a: 104)

Instead, "new looks" created with wigs, and false eyelashes, tinted contact lenses, fake beauty spots, false toenails, false fingernails, nose surgery, padded bras, false derrieres, and fake jewelry were recommended. Another article explaining "Why I

Wear My False Eyelashes to Bed" (Cunningham, 1968) presented the problem of a shower with a lover, a situation where the investments of a highly produced femininity (and hence its material rewards) might be erased. Recommending hurling soap suds in his eyes so "he won't be able to see how you look" (Cunningham, 1968: 18), it got to the core of Brown's advice by linking femininity to the modified sexual contract she espoused.

The aspirations of the Cosmo Girl were white, heterosexual, and upper-middle class. "Other" women were sometimes acknowledged in *Cosmopolitan* articles like "What It Means to Be a Negro Girl" (Guy, 1966), but they were not presented as models for emulation, primarily because Brown's mobility credo forbade it. White working-class culture appeared more often, but as a reference point for makeover and improvement. Similar to femininity, class was presented as a malleable identity that could be easily changed through performative tactics, covert strategies, and cultural consumption.

Unlike her feminist contemporaries who believed in the possibilities of a female sex class (Firestone, 1970; Millett, 1970), Brown was especially concerned with improving the lot of women stuck lower on the economic ladder. While her most radical suggestion may have been to carry Karl Marx's *Das Kapital* as a way to meet potential eligibles (1962: 63), the Cosmo Girl was often addressed as a have-not, and was offered instructions to remedy the situation. Instead of critiquing the capitalist distribution of resources or the politics of wage labor, reworking one's identity was presented as an individual route to mobility. The extent to which these narratives constructed a feminine version of American Dream mythology is revealed by Brown's own version of the Horatio Alger story:

> We have two Mercedes-Benzes, one hundred acres of virgin forest near San Francisco, a Mediterranean house overlooking the Pacific, a full-time maid and a good life. I am not beautiful, or even pretty . . . I didn't go to college. My family was, and is, desperately poor and I have always helped support them. . . . But I don't think it's a miracle that I married my husband. I think I deserved him! For seventeen years I worked hard to become the kind of woman who might interest him. (Brown, 1962: 4–5)

Drawing from John Berger (1972), Ellen McCracken has shown how commercial women's magazines trade on female insecurities by offering a temporary "window to a future self" rooted in male visions of idealized femininity and consumer solutions (1993: 13). Jackie Stacey discusses something similar in her analysis of women and film stars, but proposes that the perpetual gap between "self and ideal" is the subjective space where female identities are negotiated (1993: 206). In *Sex and the Single Girl,* Brown extended these processes by constructing an idealized, but never fully realized, class subjectivity for her readers, which then manifested in the fragmented identity of the fictionalized Cosmo Girl. Although rooted in upper-class reverence and materialistic desires, her advice is difficult to dismiss as entirely co-optive or advertising-driven, because it was presented as a guide to overcoming the gendered class barriers Brown encountered. Her path to success stressed the conventional motto of hard work and conspicuous consumption, but it also required covert strategies and performative behaviors on the part of the Cosmo Girl. As I see it, the tenuous sense of agency Brown's advice offered is central to the tension between class fluidity and class consciousness in the politicized sense.

Women were essentially advised to "pass" as members of the bourgeoisie, by studying and copying its presumably superior tastes, knowledges, and cultural competencies. This performative strategy was rooted in the unauthorized acquisition of what Pierre Bourdieu (1984) calls "cultural capital," or the symbolic resources that signify and legitimate class dominance in capitalist democracies. In the U.S.A., the myth of equality of opportunity proposes that anyone can gain access to economic capital (what wealth buys) through individual effort and talent, while the cultural capital that breeds success is inherited via "proper" family socialization or acquired through extended years of schooling (Jhally and Lewis, 1992: 69). Brown subverted these intersecting mythologies in a roundabout way by revealing pink-collar barriers to the American Dream, and by partly subverting the uneven distribution of cultural capital. According to Brown's girl-style American Dream, anyone—even the Cosmo Girl—could appropriate the surface markers of cultural capital. Once acquired, these surface markers of class position could be traded for economic capital (or access to it) on the dating and marriage market.

The credibility of this advice was rooted in the fact that women who may have married directly into the lower classes were spending longer periods of time working as office workers. Under the ambiguous label "pink collar," they encountered men with more education, money, and resources. Brown's advice encouraged women to exploit these opportunities, and prepared them to do so by offering a basic introduction to upper-class customs and cultural traditions. "Some girls have it . . . some don't. But that elusive little quality separating the haves from the [have-]nots is within everyone's grasp," claimed one *Cosmopolitan* article (Geng, 1970: 92).

Since the advice was always tempered to the experience of the Cosmo Girl, the reader was allowed to participate in two class cultures simultaneously, which encouraged a fragmented class subjectivity. However, the point of the lessons was to conceal one's working-class lineage. Thus, *The Cosmo Girl's Guide to the New Etiquette* warned women about common phrases that were "instant lower-class betrayals" (Brown, 1970b: 55). Similarly, *Cosmopolitan* articles with names like "Poor Girl Paintings" (*Cosmopolitan,* 1966c), "If You Don't Know Your Crepes From Your Coquilles" (Matlin, 1969), "Go Ahead, Pretend You're Rich" (Barnes and Downey, 1968), "Good Taste" (Johnson, 1974), and "Live Beyond Your Means" (de Dubovay, 1975) presented lessons on the ways of the educated, wealthy, and culturally sophisticated.

This advice often involved appropriating cultural signifiers of class, particularly European cuisine, art, foreign languages, and good books. One especially vivid example here was "A Handbook of Elegant Starvation," a *Cosmopolitan* guide to maintaining a "desirable image" while pursuing the arts and getting by on unemployment insurance (Dowling, 1966). According to the article, which offered detailed instructions for serving "Bogus Beef Bourguignon" to a male dinner guest, "The clue to faking it on $12.50 a week is a front. You've got to keep up a front—an aura of prosperity—at all times" (1966: 30). Another article proposed that an ordinary secretary, who "would probably expire from malnutrition if she didn't have a dinner date at least two nights a week," could easily pass as a member of the New York "jet set" or a corporation president's daughter (Tornabene, 1966: 43). By extending the aura of cultural capital to the female masses, this discourse subverted the myth that class is inevitable or natural. However, it also upheld the class pyramid and reproduced social and cultural hierarchies. . . .

PINK-COLLAR SEXUALITY

Feminist historians have suggested that what was potentially transforming about *Cosmopolitan* magazine was the emphasis placed on female sexuality (Douglas, 1994; Ehrenreich et al., 1986).[8] Features on female orgasm, birth control, masturbation, casual sex, and sexual experimentation appeared under Brown's editorship, while quizzes with names like "How Sexy Are You?" (*Cosmopolitan,* 1969) invited ordinary women into the sexual revolution, and *Cosmopolitan's Love Book* (Brown, 1972) offered them instructions on the new sexual protocol. At the close of the 1970s, Brown hired a sociologist to survey the sexual practices of *Cosmopolitan* readers, and they were found to be the most experienced group in western history (Wolfe, 1981). However, what a focus on sexual politics cannot fully explain are the class dimensions of Brown's discourse on female sexuality, as epitomized by her credo "Poor girls are not sexy!" (1962: 108).

. . . Sexual fantasies presented in *Cosmopolitan* fiction excerpts and in *Cosmopolitan's Love Book* encouraged women to identify with female heroines whose male sexual partners (or desired partners) were above them socially and economically. . . . Female desire was linked to what the male object represented socially and economically. As Brown explained in *Sex and the Single Girl,* a woman is "more favorably disposed toward a man who is solvent and successful than someone without status. She prefers a tycoon to a truck driver no matter how sexy the latter looks peering down at her from the cab of his chrome chariot" (1962: 227).

Cosmopolitan's "Bachelor of the Month" column was similarly constructed. This sought-after eligible was always solvent and socially established, as were the men presented as desirable in articles like "It's Just as Easy to Love a Rich Man" (Lilly, 1965), "How Much Will He Earn?" (Sloane, 1966), "The Big Catch" (Blyth, 1972), and "Used Men: A Definitive Guide for the Selective Shopper" (Price, 1972). When acknowledged, working-class men were almost always presented as undesirable, as epitomized by the juxtaposition in February 1966 of two *Cosmopolitan* profiles, one featuring "Six Current (But Perennial) Fascinators" (1966d), the other featuring "10 Most Wanted Men (by the FBI)" (Reed, 1966). While the first roster was comprised of men characterized as rich, famous, successful, charming, and attractive, the second opened with the warning "You've seen the most fascinating men, now read about the most feared" (Reed, 1966: 72). Police mug shots were accompanied by one-liners detailing the physical characteristics of the men as well as their occupations, which included clerk, dishwasher, hospital orderly, tractor driver, and mason's helper.

While female sexual desire was linked to upward mobility through men, the construction of female sexual desirability in *Cosmopolitan* was linked to the cultural codes of the working-class prostitute. Indeed, sexually explicit representations of women were the only places readers were encouraged to forge positive identifications with working-class traditions. Bourgeois tastes were transgressed by these images, especially on the cover, where the desirability of the model was constructed through class-coded signifiers such as exposed cleavage, teased hair, heavy make-up, and flamboyant and suggestive costumes.[9] The sexualized Cosmo Girl was not the wholesome middle-class sex object of the era, and she appeared to contradict Brown's discreet schemes for mobility. However, the sexualized imagery also offered an entry point into the modified sexual contract Brown espoused.

In the 1960s, when college-educated women were beginning to demand and sometimes secure equality in the professional workplace, most pink-collar office workers were not so fortunate. Brown articulated an alternative way to get men to part with their disproportionate share of power and resources. She subverted the moral shame surrounding sex and reframed the sexual code as an individual ethic and a commodity exchange. In this sense, her advice was rooted in the history of working-class women's sexual practices.

Kathy Peiss, for example, has shown how a turn-of-the-century system of "treating" allowed young, unmarried workers to trade "sexual favors" ranging from flirting and kissing to sexual intercourse for small presents, meals, and admissions to amusement parks, which they could not otherwise afford (1983: 78). Some "charity girls" appropriated the look of a prostitute, using "high-heeled shoes, fancy dresses, costume jewelry, elaborate pompadours and cosmetics" to attract male attention (1983: 78). The system of treating was also present in the workplace, says Peiss, where sexual harassment was rampant (1983: 78–9). Brown's advice articulated an updated sexual barter system, by encouraging the Cosmo Girl to never go dutch, but to instead coax gifts, dinners, vacations, groceries, and cash presents from male dates, bosses, colleagues, and

partners. Her revised sexual contract promoted women's sexual freedom and financial independence, while also encouraging the exchange of sexual "favors" for material comforts and luxuries. Perhaps the most significant difference between the system Peiss describes and what Brown articulated is that the Cosmo Girl was encouraged to pursue men who may have been off limits in earlier eras. . . .

While the mainstream women's movement strove for equality in the workplace, Brown often framed sexual activity in terms of work and achievement. "Sex is a powerful weapon for a single woman in getting what she wants from life," she explained to an interviewer (quoted in *San Francisco,* 1962). A similar message was conveyed in her memoir, where Brown described the ability to bring a man to orgasm as a "specialty" every upwardly mobile girl should acquire (1982: 212). Occasionally, *Cosmopolitan* explained the advantages of being "kept" and "slightly kept" girls (Baumgold, 1970; Condos, 1974), and articles glamorizing upscale prostitution were not uncommon. However, these explicit cases of sexual trading were not nearly as prevalent as the sexualization of the office, especially the relationship between male superiors and female secretaries. Again, this pattern drew from and reworked historical assumptions about the role of women in offices. . . .

By the 1960s, office work was a rapidly growing occupational field, and women were an expanding part of the labor force. By the time *Sex and the Single Girl* appeared, almost one of every three employed women worked in clerical and secretarial jobs (Matthaei, 1982: 282), and by 1974 women held four out of five jobs in this category (Howe, 1977: 10). The capitalist expansion of the service sector opened the field to women outside the middle class, while women with college degrees were struggling to move into male-dominated professions. What remained was the middle-class respectability of office work compared to factory work and other working-class wage labor (Matthaei, 1982: 282). Despite the low pay and dead-end nature of most pink-collar jobs, this made it easier for women to see themselves as upwardly mobile. . . .

Cosmopolitan elevated the sexual worth of the secretary by suggesting that "a secretary is not necessarily rich, beautiful or brilliant, but she is the most sought-after female since King Kong chased Fay Wray" (Lewis, 1969: 133). Likewise, the rewards for working for women were defined through the types of men one encountered. In *Sex and the Single*

Girl, Brown promoted secretarial jobs because they were "all-time great spots" for meeting men (1962: 37). *Cosmopolitan* articles with titles like "Secretaries Who've Made Very, Very Good" (James, 1969), "Be a 9-to-5 Show Off" (Fisher, 1970), and "Hollywood Secretaries" (*Cosmopolitan,* 1975a) also glamorized secretarial jobs as excellent places to meet well-connected bosses, dreamy executives, and traveling salesmen with expense accounts. One article even recommended "A Different Job Every Day" (Fahey, 1966), contracted through temporary employment agencies, as a chance to meet dozens of eligible men in a single week. The low pay, insecurity, and lack of benefits offered by the growing temporary workforce were obscured. . . .

Brown clearly understood women's subordination in the office, but she did not directly challenge it because "in an ideal world, we might move onward and upward by using only our brains and talent, but since this is an imperfect world, a certain amount of listening, giggling, wriggling, smiling, winking, flirting and fainting is required in our rise from the mailroom" (1964: 3). . . .

There were exceptions to these patterns, especially after 1970, when Brown proclaimed herself a friend of women's lib and *Cosmopolitan* began to negotiate feminist discourse, however haltingly. Several feminist articles were published, including an excerpt in November 1970 from Kate Millett's book *Sexual Politics* (1970) critiquing the gendered aspects of economic inequality and the ideology of heterosexual romance. As was typical, however, it was shockingly out of place, juxtaposed with a fashion spread proclaiming "Be His Fortune Cookie in Our Gala Gypsy Dress" (*Cosmopolitan,* 1970). Liberal feminist demands for professional equality had a more lasting impact on Brown's thinking, and on the partial incorporation of conventional success mythology in *Cosmopolitan.* While she continued to value street smarts over a college degree and to promote the sensational opportunities offered by secretarial work, Brown modified her credo to suggest that the Cosmo Girl might be both a sex object and a "high powered" executive (Brown, 1982: 19–20).

GIRL-STYLE AMERICAN DREAMS

Many pink-collar women may have found the Cosmo Girl's fragmented identity as an upwardly mobile sexual agent more attractive and even more feasible than what the mainstream women's movement offered. Brown's advice offered a gendered success myth to women who found themselves taking on new roles as breadwinners, but who lacked the wages, education, professional skills, and social opportunities to recognize themselves in more conventional, male-oriented upward-mobility narratives. She articulated, in feminine terms, the materialistic desires that so often underpin popular structures of feeling in a consumer-oriented nation where the class structure is officially denied. Brown's reworking of American Dream mythology involved the construction and reconstruction of a desirable self, the presentation of identity as self-made, the valorization of femininity as a creative production, the partial subversion of natural class distinctions, the refusal of Victorian sexual norms, and the expression of multiple hardships and frustrations—all within a framework that legitimated capitalism, consumerism, and patriarchal privilege. However, to dismiss the fragmented, sexualized class identity she promoted as wholly co-optive or less than "real" would be to lose touch with the way social beings construct a sense of self.

As Stuart Hall suggests with his theory of articulation, there is no necessary link between economics and class. Class awareness is a social construct, produced in a political sense only when individual experiences are articulated as a "political force," enabling subjects to enter the stage as historical agents (Hall, 1986: 55). Brown's advice encouraged women to rework their identities on the basis of upper-class ideals, and to assess their current situations and future possibilities on the basis of those constructions. One of the consequences of the discourse may have been the way it positioned women as individual competitors in the quest for mobility, rather than part of a growing female labor force with many differences, to be sure, but with collective interests and bargaining power. Characterizing her own self-transformation, for example, Brown explained that "early on you have to separate yourself in the head from those people (friends, family, colleagues) you don't want to be like . . . be one of the girls, but also don't be one of the girls" (1982: 38).

Helen Gurley Brown's historical resonance as the "working girl's Simone de Beavoir" suggests the need to take the cultural construction of class seriously. . . .

NOTES

1. Quoted in *Time* (1965: 60).

2. See, for example, Brown's appearance, 25 January 1997, on CNN's *Larry King Live*.

3. Mariana Valverde (1986) also observed the promotion of mobility in *Cosmopolitan,* arguing that what both the Cosmo Girl and the Ms. woman of the 1980s wanted, despite their different paths to achievement (e.g., getting a man vs. merit), was to be white, upper-middle class, and heterosexual. While she sees both magazines imposing unified capitalist and patriarchal ideologies on women (a view similar to early feminist Marxist criticism), I see Brown's advice in poststructuralist terms, as a contradictory, historically specific and productive discourse that constructed a social identity for pink-collar women.

4. Harrington, 1974. In 1997, *Cosmopolitan* had a U.S. circulation of 2.5 million, resulting in $156 million in estimated annual advertising revenue (Pogrebin, 1997).

5. In 1940, about one-third of employed Americans were in white-collar occupations, while in 1959 nearly half were due to the expanding service economy and the growing number of women who joined the "white-collar ranks." However, many of these jobs were "essentially manual" in that they were routine, repetitive, and sometimes minimally skilled. They paid less than the professions and often less than skilled blue-collar work, but were "rated" above traditional working-class wage labor because they were perceived as "cleaner" and more "dignified" (Packard, 1959: 25–6). Advertisers played on the social ambiguity, promising status through consumer goods. In this [chapter] I refer to non-professional white-collar jobs taken up predominantly by women as pink-collar. For more on the post-Fordist economy see Harvey (1990: 121–97).

6. Brown envisioned the "untapped" market for *Cosmopolitan* as single women, divorcees, and widows, separated, and "otherwise neglected wives" who worked outside the home. Working married women who were (because of their independent attitude) "women on their own" were considered a secondary market ("A Proposal for *Cosmopolitan,*" n.d.; "Statement for Advertisers," n.d.). Early marketing discourse inflated the spending power of the magazine's readers, describing them as well educated, high income, and "working in top occupations," despite statistic[s] that contradicted these generalizations. Thus, there was overlap between the class performativity Brown encouraged and the strategies used to court advertisers. While the Cosmo Girl was constructed as single and sexually free, a high percentage of readers were married. This would suggest that they too were drawn to the magazine's guide to changing sexual and economic roles.

7. Products and services said to be bought by *Cosmopolitan* readers included cosmetics, perfumes, fashion and personal products, wines and liquors, travel, miscellaneous, and mail order (*Cosmopolitan* Advertising Kit, 1965). The first three categories comprised most of the advertising according to my research.

8. Ehrenreich et al. note that Brown championed independence and guiltless sex at a time when few women "could imagine options other than marriage and full-time motherhood" (1986: 56). Susan Douglas (1994) also cites Brown as a key figure in the transformation of female sexuality.

9. As McCracken argues, "If the *Cosmopolitan* cover photo presents women with an ideal image of their future selves, it is an image at the other end of the social spectrum from that of the affluent *Vogue* or *Bazaar* cover" (1993: 158). While she sees this image as an invitation to male fantasy and sexual voyeurism, I see it rooted in the class dimensions of Brown's revised sexual code.

REFERENCES

Barnes, J. and M. Downey (1968) "Go Ahead—Pretend You're Rich," *Cosmopolitan* (July): 54–5.

Baumgold, J. (1970) "The Slightly Kept Girl," *Cosmopolitan* (Sept.): 154.

Berger, J. (1972) *Ways of Seeing.* London: Penguin Books.

Blyth, M. (1972) "The Big Catch," *Cosmopolitan* (Jan.): 128–36.

Bourdieu, P. (1984) *Distinction: A Social Critique of the Judgment of Taste.* Cambridge, MA: Harvard University Press.

Brown, H. G. (1962) *Sex and the Single Girl.* New York: Bernard Geis Associates.

Brown, H. G. (1963) *Lessons in Love.* New York: Crescendo Records.

Brown, H. G. (1964) *Sex and the Office.* New York: Bernard Geis Associates.

Brown, H. G. (1965) "New Directions for *Cosmopolitan,*" *The Writer* (July): 20.

Brown, H. G. (1970a) *Sex and the New Single Girl.* New York: Bernard Geis Associates.

Brown, H. G. (ed.). (1970b) *The Cosmo Girl's Guide to the New Etiquette.* New York: Cosmopolitan Books.

Brown, H. G. (ed.). (1972) *Cosmopolitan's Love Book: A Guide to Ecstasy in Bed.* New York: Cosmopolitan Books.

CNN Television. (1997) Interview with Helen Gurley Brown, *Larry King Live* (25 Jan.).

Condos, B. (1974) "I Was Kept," *Cosmopolitan* (May): 60, 66–74.

Cosmopolitan Advertising Kit, July 1965, HGB papers, Box 8, Folder 12.

Cosmopolitan (1966a) "The Beautiful Phony" (March): 104–7.

Cosmopolitan (1966b) "*Cosmopolitan* Interviews Hugh M. Hefner" (May): 76–81.

Cosmopolitan (1966c) "Poor Girl Paintings" (Aug.): 88.

Cosmopolitan (1966d) "Six Current (But Perennial) Fascinators" (Feb.): 66–71.

Cosmopolitan (1969) "How Sexy Are You?" (April): 54–6.

Cosmopolitan (1970) "Be His Fortune Cookie in Our Gala Gypsy Dress" (Nov.): 104.

Cosmopolitan (1975a) "Hollywood Secretaries" (Aug.): 36.

Cosmopolitan (1975b) "How to Sink into a Man" (Nov.): 48–9.

Cunningham, L. (1968) "Why I Wear My False Eyelashes to Bed," *Cosmopolitan* (Oct.): 46–51.

de Dubovay, D. (1975) "Live Beyond Your Means," *Cosmopolitan* (Aug.): 132–4.

De Santis, M. (1969) "Yes, You Can Change Your Image," *Cosmopolitan* (April): 91–3.

Didion, J. (1965) "Bosses Make Lousy Lovers," *Saturday Evening Post* (30 Jan.): 34–8.

Douglas, S. (1994) *Where the Girls Are: Growing Up Female with the Mass Media.* New York: Time Books.

Dowling, C. (1966) "A Handbook of Elegant Starvation," *Cosmopolitan* (Oct.): 30–2.

Ehrenreich, B. (1983) *The Hearts of Men.* New York: Anchor Books.

Ehrenreich, B. et al. (1986) *Re-Making Love: The Feminization of Sex.* New York: Anchor Books.

Fahey, P. (1966) "A Different Job Every Day," *Cosmopolitan* (Oct.): 128–31.

Ferguson, M. (1983) *Forever Feminine: Women's Magazines and the Cult of Femininity.* London: Heinemann.

Firestone, S. (1970) *The Dialectic of Sex.* New York: Quill Press (repr. 1993).

Fisher, K. (1970) "Be a 9-to-5 Showoff," *Cosmopolitan* (Nov.): 150–1.

Fiske, J. (1987) *Television Culture.* New York: Routledge.

Geng, V. (1970) "A Little Bit of Class," *Cosmopolitan* (Oct.): 92–7.

Greller, J. (1966) "Night School Isn't All Education," *Cosmopolitan* (July): 87–8.

Guardian Weekly (1968) newspaper clipping (12 Nov.) HGB papers, Box 7, Folder 3.

Guy, R. (1966) "What It Means to Be a Negro Girl," *Cosmopolitan* (July): 76–81.

Hall, S. (1986) "On Postmodernism and Articulation: An Interview," *Journal of Communication Inquiry* 10(2): 45–60.

Harrington, S. (1974) "Two Faces of the Same Eve: *Ms.* Versus *Cosmo*," *New York Times Magazine* (11 Aug.): 10–11, 36, 74–6.

Harvey, D. (1990) *The Condition of Postmodernity*. London: Blackwell.

Hennessy, R. (1993) *Materialist Feminism and the Politics of Discourse*. New York: Routledge.

Howe, L. (1977) *Pink Collar Workers*. New York: G. P. Putnam's Sons.

James, T. (1969) "4 Secretaries Who've Made Very, Very Good," *Cosmopolitan* (June): 134–5.

Jhally, S. and J. Lewis (1992) *Enlightened Racism: The Cosby Show, Audiences and the Myth of the American Dream*. Boulder, CO: Westview.

Johnson, N. (1974) "Good Taste!" *Cosmopolitan* (Feb.): 122–31.

Joyce, P. (ed.) (1995) *Class*. New York: Oxford University Press.

Kent, R. (1972) "Cover Girl: Behind the Scenes," *Cosmopolitan* (Aug.): 94–117.

Lewis, B. (1969) "Today's Secretary—Wow!" *Cosmopolitan* (June): 133.

Lilly, D. (1965) "It's Just as Easy to Love a Rich Man," *Cosmopolitan* (July): 66–9.

Mansbridge, J. (1986) *Why We Lost the ERA*. Chicago: University of Chicago Press.

Matlin, P. (1969) "If You Don't Know Your Crepes From Your Coquilles, Or How to Order From a French Restaurant," *Cosmopolitan* (April): 96–9.

Matthaei, J. (1982) *An Economic History of Women in America*. New York: Schocken.

McCracken, E. (1993) *Decoding Women's Magazines*. New York: St Martin's.

Millett, K. (1970) *Sexual Politics*. Garden City, NY: Doubleday.

Newsweek (1966) "Down with "Pippypoo" (18 July): 60.

Packard, V. (1959) *The Status Seekers: An Exploration of Class Behavior in America*. New York: David McKay.

Peiss, K. (1983) "'Charity Girls' and City Pleasures: Historical Notes on Working-Class Sexuality, 1880–1920," pp. 74–87 in Ann Snitow et al. *Powers of Desire*. New York: Monthly Review Press.

Pogrebin, R. (1997) "Changing of Guard at Cosmo," *New York Times* (13 Jan.): D1.

Price, R. (1972) "Used Men: A Definitive Guide for the Selective Shopper," *Cosmopolitan* (Aug.): 68–73.

"A Proposal for Cosmopolitan from Helen Gurley Brown" (n.d.) Helen Gurley Brown papers, Sophia Smith Collection, Smith College, Northampton, MA (hereafter HGB papers), Box 14, Folder 4.

Providence Journal (1965) newspaper clipping (1 July) HGB papers, Box 8, Folder 1.

Reed, R. (1966) "10 Most Wanted Men (by the FBI)," *Cosmopolitan* (Feb.): 72–81.

Reisig, R. (1973) "The Feminine Plastique," *Ramparts* (March): 25–9, 53–5.

San Francisco News Call Bulletin (1962) "Single Gal's Quandary" (6 July) HGB papers, Box 8, Folder 3.

Sloane, L. (1966) "How Much Will He Earn?" *Cosmopolitan* (Feb.): 30–7.

Stacey, J. (1993) *Star Gazing: Hollywood Cinema and Female Spectatorship*. London: Routledge.

"Statement from Helen Gurley Brown for Advertisers" (n.d.) HGB papers, Box 14, Folder 3.

Time (1965) "Big Sister" (9 Feb.): 60.

Tornabene, L. (1966) "How to Live Beautifully on $100 a Week," *Cosmopolitan* (Aug.): 42–7.

Valverde, M. (1986) "The Class Struggles of the Cosmo Girl and the Ms. Woman," *Heresies* 18: 78–82.

Welles, C. (1965) "Soaring Success of the Iron Butterfly," *Life* (19 Nov.): 65–6.

Wolfe, L. (1981) *The Cosmo Report*. New York: Arbor House.

POLITICAL CULTURE JAMMING

20

The Dissident Humor of The Daily Show with Jon Stewart

Jamie Warner

Armed with branding techniques honed and perfected in the commercial marketplace, politicians and political parties have attempted to drown out dissident messages to better "sell" their own political policies, a dagger in the heart of deliberative democrats who argue that democracy cannot survive without open, ongoing, and rational political conversation. In fact, much of contemporary democratic theory rests on two propositions: (a) the public sphere is populated with multiple and disparate voices who can and will engage each other, and (b) these conversations will be rational. Jürgen Habermas's (1962/1989) *The Structural Transformation of the Public Sphere* is perhaps the most important of the recent statements of this position (Habermas, 1973/1975, 1998; see also Bennett & Entman, 2001; Carey, 1989; White, 1995). Indeed, many scholars posit some version of accessible, public, substantive, rational conversations among numerous and diverse participants as *the* prerequisite for a healthy democracy. . . .

Political elites and their consultants have no such concerns. Rather than fretting over possible barriers confronting marginal voices, politicians instead want their voices, agenda, and framing of issues to crowd out divergent voices because such dominant status helps contribute to the success of their specific political agendas (Lakoff, 2002, 2004). In the past two decades, politicians have increasingly utilized what are known as "branding" techniques of commercial marketers to just such an end, in the hopes of persuading the citizen/consumer to trust their "product"—their platform and policy positions—to the exclusion of all others. These branding techniques, relying on emotional rather than rational appeals, are used in the attempt to achieve automatic, unreflective

trust in the branded product, whether that product is a Popsicle, a Palm Pilot, or a political party. Although such brand hegemony is obviously profitable in terms of money and/or power for the hegemon, it works to the detriment of the tenets of democratic theory, both by talking over viable voices and conversations in the public sphere, and by operating through calculated emotional appeals. How, in the name of the healthy democracy described previously, can one *disrupt* the transmission of the dominant political brand messages so that competing conversations can occur?

One intriguing model comes from the same realm as the original branding techniques, the media saturated world of consumer capitalism, where an insurgent movement known as "culture jamming" is at the forefront of this type of disruption. Culture jammers are a loose collection of media activists who are rebelling against the hegemony of the messages promoting global capitalism. Spearheaded by media activist Kalle Lasn of the Media Foundation and his *Adbusters* magazine, culture jammers utilize a wide variety of tactics to destabilize and challenge the dominant messages of multinational corporations and consumer capitalism. Rather than simply using factual information, rational argumentation, legal language, and traditional political tactics to oppose capitalist institutions directly, culture jamming turns the commercial techniques of image and emotion back on themselves through acts of what Christine Harold (2004) calls "rhetorical sabotage" (p. 190).

As politicians and political parties increasingly utilize the branding techniques of commercial marketers to "sell" their political agendas, it follows that similar jamming techniques could be employed to call those branding techniques into

From Warner, J. (2007). Political culture jamming: The dissident humor of *The Daily Show With Jon Stewart. Popular Communications,* 5(1), 17–36. Reprinted by permission of Taylor & Francis Ltd. http://www.tandfonline.com.

question. In this chapter, I argue that the comedian Jon Stewart and his fake news program, *The Daily Show With Jon Stewart,* act as *political* culture jammers. Through their own humorous version of news parody, *The Daily Show* writers and comedians disseminate dissident interpretations of current political events, potentially jamming the transmission of the dominant political brand message. Like other culture jammers, *The Daily Show* subversively employs emotional and aesthetic modalities similar to those employed by political branding itself, thus interrupting it from within. Unlike many culture jammers, however, *The Daily Show*'s reliance on a humorous version of parody means that they can add their voices to the conversation in a seemingly innocuous way. (After all, it is *just* a joke.) . . .

THE FETISH OF POLITICAL BRANDING

See, in my line of work you got to keep repeating things over and over and over again for the truth to sink in, to kind of catapult the propaganda. (George W. Bush, quoted in Froomkin, 2005)

. . . The basic assumption behind branding is simple: Consumers are not "rational" shoppers. Instead, they are busy people, possessing neither the time nor the inclination to do detailed comparisons of sneakers, sunglasses, or fabric softeners. This time crunch creates an opening for marketers. Knowing that many consumers cannot or will not do research based on quality and/or price, marketers instead strive to cultivate a *relationship* with consumers that inspires loyalty for that particular brand. Trust in a particular brand allows the consumer to take a time-saving shortcut at the supermarket or mall, as well as get the supposed value, and, hopefully, the status that marketers strive to attach to the brand. Thus, the key to establishing this lucrative connection with consumers is through the play of emotion, rather than the dissemination of information: "Marketing is no longer about selling. It's about creating relationships with customers that cultivate an emotional preference for your brand" (Travis, 2000, cited in Hiebert, 2001; see also Gobe, 2001,

2002). The particular relationship to be cultivated with consumers depends on the type of image that marketers believe will best sell their product to its target demographic: dependable, practical, good value for the price, safe, or the much coveted yet ever elusive "cool."

Politicians and their political consultants have fully embraced the logic and tactics of branding in the political arena. Although the normative value of the migration of these marketing tactics into the political sphere, via the media, has been widely disputed, its efficacy has not, at least from the point of view of the politicians themselves (Newman, 1999). It is obvious why parties and politicians would see brand loyalty as a desirable outcome. Citizens, like consumers, are busy people, and cultivating trust in the "Republican" or "Democratic" brand works to save the citizen/consumer time, in the form of information costs, while providing the politician or party a solid base of support. Many of the same branding techniques used to sell soap and MP3 players are exploited for political gain, including market research techniques, the proliferation of emotional messages across various media through the use of sound bites and talking points, and repetition/saturation strategies within each medium. In addition to creating a sense of familiarity, an important part of building trust, repetition of carefully researched emotional messages (e.g., talking points) helps locate a party or politician as one of the "top of mind" or "dominant" brands—the first or, hopefully, the only brand that comes to mind in response to a particular stimulus (Carter, 1999, cited in Karlberg, 2002, p. 7). The ultimate goal in political branding is the same as in commercial branding: the creation of such unquestioning trust in the brand that the citizen/consumer allows the brand [to] do the "thinking" for him or her.

CULTURE JAMMING

How does one call these very effective branding techniques into question, so that alternative voices can get into the conversation? The success of global consumer capitalism and the marketing techniques that go with it, specifically the branding techniques mentioned previously, have spurred many internal and external critiques and rebellions, often lumped together under the term culture jamming (e.g., Klein, 2000, 2002; Roddick, 1994; Talen, 2003). Current culture jammers, such as media activist Kalle Lasn, place themselves on a "revolutionary continuum" with anarchists, Dadaists, surrealists, the Situationists, the Sixties hippie movement, and early punk rockers, among others (Lasn, 1999, p. 99; see also Dery, 1993). According to Lasn, the primary goal of culture jammers is *détournement,* a French term borrowed from the Situationists of the 1950s and 1960s. Translated literally as a "turning around," Lasn (1999) defines the concept of *détournement* as "a perspective-jarring turnabout in your everyday life" (p. xvii), which is instigated by "rerouting spectacular images, environments, ambiences and events to reverse or subvert their meaning, thus reclaiming them" (p. 103).

Specifically, Lasn and his fellow culture jammers want to reverse, subvert, and reclaim our identity as brand-trusting pawns of consumer capitalism. For example, Lasn's Web site (www .adbusters.org) constantly runs multiple ongoing antibrand campaigns, and these do utilize traditional, rational techniques such as boycotts and petition drives against heavily branded corporations such as Nike and Tommy Hilfiger. However, *Adbusters* is perhaps best known for its attempts to jam the dominant brand images with alternative images, what Lasn calls subvertisements. These images use the same branding technologies and design layouts that advertisers do, with a problematizing twist: "A well produced print 'subvertisement' mimics the look and feel of the target ad, prompting the classic double-take as viewers realize what they're seeing is the very opposite of what they expected" (Lasn, 1999, p. 131). Successful *Adbuster* subvertisments include those parodying alcohol, cigarettes, and the fast food industry, as well as the fashion establishment.

One of *Adbusters'* best-known subvertisements revolved around the Calvin Klein *Obsession* ads of the 1990s. The original and very successful print ads for the perfume featured close-ups of young, beautiful, tan, taut bodies with the words "Obsession for Men" or "Obsession for Women" across the top of the ad. Exploiting what Lasn calls "leverage points" or logical contradictions in the underlying logic of consumer capitalism, *Adbusters* attacks Calvin Klein, not with facts and figures demonstrating how the empty quest to buy beauty and status is dangerous, but instead with perverted mirror images (1999, p. 130). . . .

In what follows, I argue that *The Daily Show With Jon Stewart* functions as what I call "political culture jamming" by working in much the same way: disseminating dissident images with messages designed to provoke the same type of *détournement* or subversion of the dominant meaning that Lasn and his fellow culture jammers seek. . . .

POLITICAL CULTURE JAMMING: *THE DAILY SHOW WITH JON STEWART*

In January 2004, the Pew Research Center for the People and the Press released the results of a survey designed to discover where Americans get their political news. One of the most interesting findings involved a relatively new phenomenon: 21% of those 18–29 regularly learned about the presidential campaign and its candidates on comedy programs (compared with 23% who said they regularly learned this information from network news). Overall, 50% of the 18–29 demographic said that they at least "sometimes" learn about the campaign from these shows, compared with 27% of the 30–49 demographic and 12% of people 50 and older. . . .

One of the most popular of these comedy shows—with an estimated 1.3 million viewers per night—is *The Daily Show With Jon Stewart,* a 30-min "newscast" that airs Monday through Thursday at 11:00 p.m. EST on the cable network *Comedy Central* (Hall, 2005). . . .

The Daily Show is a funny and often sharply critical parody of a television news broadcast; the entire cast is made up of comedians. In fact, in his videotaped acceptance of the Television Critics Association Award, Stewart recommended that one of the other, legitimate nominees, *60 Minutes* perhaps, should investigate how a *fake* news program won the award for "Outstanding Achievement in News and Information" (Kurtz, 2003). It is this seeming lack of seriousness within the serious format of a cable/network news broadcast, however, that makes *The Daily Show* both a popular and a cogent critic. Like the *Adbuster* subvertisements, *The Daily Show* inserts its voice into the political conversation by plagiarizing the aesthetics of the media, in this particular case, the news media. It is a copy, but a copy that has been strategically altered to highlight political "leverage points": factual errors, logical contradictions, and incongruities in the dominant political brand messages and the media that disseminates them.

Matter Out of Place: Parodic Format

The first political culture jamming technique employed by *The Daily Show* is a metatechnique, one that most explicitly resembles the aesthetics of the *Adbusters'* subvertisements discussed previously: news parody format. This twisted mimicking of the newscast format is the first and most important jamming technique and the entire show makes sense only within this format. Just as the subversive parody of the *Obsession* ad must closely approximate the actual ad to be effective, the news parody must closely resemble an actual news television broadcast, and *The Daily Show* does. The anchor, Jon Stewart, presents the top stories of the day, complete with the video over his right shoulder, and conducts interviews. Correspondents, many of whom are now becoming celebrities in their own right, do segments and interviews on current events. Watching the show with the volume turned down might not alert you to the fact that this is anything other than one of the myriad news options now available. Turning the volume up should let you in on the secret. Here Stewart is interviewing "senior media analyst" Stephen Colbert about the media coverage of the U.S. invasion of Iraq in March 2003:[1]

Stewart: What should the media's role be in covering the war?

Colbert: Very simply, the media's role should be the accurate and objective description of the hellacious ass-whomping we're handing the Iraqis.

Stewart: Hellacious ass-whomping? Now to me, that sounds pretty subjective.

Colbert: Are you saying it's not an ass-whomping, Jon? I suppose you could call it an "ass-kicking" or an "ass-handing-to." Unless, of course, you love Hitler.

Stewart: [stammering] I don't love Hitler.

Colbert: Spoken like a true Hitler-lover.

Stewart: I'm perplexed. Is your position that there's no place for negative words or even thoughts in the media?

Colbert: Not at all, Jon. Doubts can happen to everyone, including me. But as a responsible journalist, I've taken my doubts, fears, moral compass, conscience, and all-pervading skepticism about the very nature of this war and simply placed them in this empty Altoids box. [Produces box] That's where they'll stay, safe and sound, until Iraq is liberated. (Miller, 2003)

This is obviously not a typical network or cable news interview. . . .

What are the consequences of choosing to intentionally misuse the newscast format? Parodying the sober and seemingly impartial language and layout of a newscast gives the content an air of legitimacy and respectability. This seemingly weighty format then allows an automatic contrast with the humorous content—out of which incongruity, a prerequisite for most humor, can flow.[2] . . .

Matter Out of Time: Strategic Use of Video

The mimicking of the news format at a metalevel, however, is a necessary but not sufficient condition for the specific political culture jamming of *The Daily Show*. There is nothing inherently subversive about parody, which can just as easily be employed in the service of the dominant political message as in the critique of that message. Within the larger parodic format of the show, however, *The Daily Show* also presents the political content in a way that calls into question the *substantive* claims of the dominant brand message, as well as the media that unproblematically disseminates it.

The second technique employed by *The Daily Show*—the strategic use of video clips—thus works inside the meta-technique of the news parody. Similar to the parodic format of the show, the use of video is designed to disrupt the dominant political message by presenting various types of "matter out of time" using video clips. As previously stated, there is usually one video screen above Stewart's right shoulder just as there is on network and cable news shows. Often Stewart will turn his head and talk to the video clips, stopping the video to pose questions and make comments. . . . Stewart's own comments provide the matter that is out of time; news anchors do not usually interject such comments during "serious" news programs. . . . However, the most effective way *The Daily Show* uses video is to strategically juxtapose video clips to highlight leverage points. . . . The branding techniques are exposed as orchestrated techniques and so can be examined explicitly and critically, rather than operating in the background where they are most successful. . . .

Technically, the audience is left to draw their own conclusions, although those conclusions are channeled in a certain direction by the specific sequence of video, as the following 2003 segment demonstrates:

Stewart: . . . When you combine the new mandate that criticizing the Commander in Chief is off limits in wartime with last year's official disbanding of the Democratic Party, we're left at the all time low in the good old fashion debate category. Now I know you're thinking: But Jon, every time I want to have a calm, honest discussion about these kinds of issues, I'm shouted down and harassed by the Dixie Chicks and their ilk. Well, tonight it all changes. . . . So first, joining us tonight is George W. Bush, the 43rd President of the United States. . . . Taking the other side, from the year 2000, Texas Governor and presidential candidate, George W. Bush. *(Split screen of Governor Bush on the left and President Bush on the right. "Bush vs. Bush" logo between them.)*

Stewart: Mr. President, you won the coin toss. The first question will go to you. Why is the United States of America using its power to change governments in foreign countries?

President Bush: We must stand up for our security and for the permanent rights and the hopes of mankind.

Stewart: Well, certainly that represents a bold new doctrine in foreign policy, Mr. President. Governor Bush, do you agree with that?

Governor Bush: Yeah, I'm not so sure that the role of the United States is to go around the world and say, "This is the way it's gotta be."

Stewart: Well, that's interesting. That's a difference of opinion, and certainly that's what this country is about, differences of opinion. Mr. President, let me just get specific: Why are we in Iraq?

President Bush: We will be changing the regime of Iraq for the good of the Iraqi people.

Stewart: Governor, then I'd like to hear your response on that.

Governor Bush: If we're an arrogant nation, they'll resent us. I think one way for us to end up being viewed as the ugly American is to go around the world saying, "We do it this way, so should you." . . . ("Bush vs. Bush," n.d.)

Again, Stewart makes no direct comment, simply presenting the matter out of time and allowing the audience to decide how to interpret this information. Is this an example of the notorious flip-flopping [of George W. Bush]? Or does this simply represent a wise policy change due to 9/11? Stewart does not say. He simply presides over the clips. Although Stewart will often alternate looking pained or amused, as the videos are playing, rarely does he directly offer his own opinion on the video clips. By customarily adhering to this tactic, *The Daily Show* manages to stay suggestive rather than didactic, provocative rather than sermonizing or moralizing.

Dialectics That Matter: Stewart's Socratic Interview Style

. . . Although the interview is a common technique used on television news broadcasts, Stewart often employs what is called "Socratic irony" as a rhetorical tactic to point out incongruities, inconsistencies, and internal contradictions in the interviewee's argument, without directly offering his own opinion, as well as without appearing confrontational. In the Platonic dialogues, Socrates routinely adopted an ignorant or tentative tone, asking simple and direct questions to his often dense interlocutors, with the seemingly innocent goal of getting to the "truth." However, his questions were neither simple nor innocent, and Socrates would use his interlocutors' answers to suggest that they should not be quite so confident in their assertions, as well as to make his own substantive points (Colebrook, 2002, p. 87; see also Seery, 1990; Vlastos, 1991). In addition, Socrates' self-effacing demeanor and rather halting comments add to the perception of his sincerity, a mode of personal presentation that Stewart also utilizes.

Discussing the public's perception of the war in Iraq in the summer of 2005 with "senior military analyst" Stephen Colbert, Stewart, like

Socrates, plays the straight man, strategically setting up the interviewee to make the substantive point for him:

Stewart: . . . When the Vice President says that the insurgency is in its last throes and Donald Rumsfeld says that that could mean 12 years, isn't that contradictory?

Colbert: Well, Jon, as a member of the cynical, knee-jerk reaction media, liberal, Ivy League, Taxachusetts elite, I can see how you would find a discrepancy between the words "last throes" and "12-year insurgency." But your mistake is looking at what's happening in Iraq on a human scale. The Administration is looking at it from a *geological* perspective. After all, it took a billion years for the earth to cool . . . ("Administrative Discrepancies," n.d.)

Here Stewart plays the calm, polite voice of reason to Colbert's vastly overstated and thus comical position. Like Socrates in the Platonic dialogues, he is *just* asking questions. . . .

By feigning ignorance and constantly insisting that *The Daily Show* is only for laughs, Stewart can operate stealthily. Unlike his culture jamming counterparts who are openly hostile to consumer capitalism and use the violent language of revolution in their fight to be heard, Stewart's self-effacing humor fosters both a sense of trust with those interviewed on the show and a sense of camaraderie with the audience. Further, any attempts by those who were the butt of the joke to attack *The Daily Show*'s credibility could easily falter, as Stewart would be the first one to agree that he is stupid and that the show means nothing. After all, it is *just* a joke.[3] Criticizing *The Daily Show* could come close to admitting that one had no sense of humor, something nobody, especially a politician, would be eager to admit. Employing this Socratic stance—one of Socrates' most famous quotations is "All I know is that I know nothing"—Stewart can create a dissident message that raises questions about both the dominant political and media brands (Colebrook, 2002, p. 87).

NOTES

1. Colbert [who now has his own spinoff show: Ed.] is also senior war correspondent, senior religious correspondent, senior UN analyst, senior White House correspondent, senior psychology correspondent, senior "death" correspondent (for stories that report on the death penalty), and senior child molestation expert (for stories on the Catholic Church).

2. George Test (1991) calls this technique the "irony of misused form" (p. 169). For a detailed discussion of the role of incongruity in humor, see Morreall (1987).

3. In his book chronicling the "new political television" of comedians Bill Maher, Dennis Miller, and Jon Stewart, Jeffrey Jones (2005) argues that Stewart's persona is like that of the court jester or fool, speaking truth to power without fear of retaliation because he has the ability to make everyone laugh.

REFERENCES

Administrative discrepancies. (n.d.). *The Daily Show with Jon Stewart.* Retrieved October 2, 2005, from http://www.comedycentral.com/shows/the_daily_show/videos/stephen_colbert_index.jhtml

Bauder, D. (2004, February 29). Stewart delivers news to younger viewers. *The Associated Press.* Retrieved October 19, 2005, from http://www.washingtonpost.com/wp-dyn/articles/AI6704–2004Feb29.html

Baym, G. (2005). *The Daily Show:* Discursive integration and the reinvention of political journalism. *Political Communication, 22,* 259–276.

Bennett, W. L., & Entman, R. (Eds.). (2001). *Mediated politics: Communication in the future of democracy.* New York: Cambridge University Press.

Bush vs. Bush. (n.d.). *The Daily Show with Jon Stewart.* Retrieved August 8, 2004, from http://www.comedycentral.com/tv_shows/

thedailyshowwithjonstewart/videos_corr.jhtml?
startIndex=25 &p=stewart

Carey, J. (1989). *Communication as culture: Essays on media and society.* Boston: Unwin Hyman.

Colebrook, C. (2002). *Irony in the works of philosophy.* Lincoln: University of Nebraska Press.

Dery, M. (1993). *Culture jamming: Hacking, slashing and sniping in the empire of the signs.* Westfield, NJ: Open Pamphlet Series.

Froomkin, D. (2005, May 25). The ostrich approach. *Washington Post.* Retrieved August 10, 2005, from http://www.washingtonpost .com/wp-dyn/content/blog/2005/05/25/ BL2005052501250.html

Gobe, M. (2001). *Emotional branding: The new paradigm for connecting brands to people.* New York: Allworth.

Gobe, M. (2002). *Citizen brand: 10 commandments for transforming brands in a consumer democracy.* New York: Allworth.

Habermas, J. (1975). *Legitimation crisis* (T. McCarthy, Trans.). Boston: Beacon. (Original work published 1973)

Habermas, J. (1989). *The structural transformation of the public sphere: An inquiry into a category of bourgeois society* (T. Burger, Trans.). Cambridge, MA: MIT University Press. (Original work published 1962)

Habermas, J. (1998). *Between facts and norms: Contributions to a discourse theory of law and democracy* (W. Rehg, Trans.). Cambridge, MA: MIT Press.

Hall, S. (2005). Colbert's "Daily Show" Spinoff. *Eonline.* Retrieved April 15, 2006, from http:// www.eonline.com/News/Items/0,1,16481,00.html

Harold, C. (2004). Pranking rhetoric: "Culture jamming" as media activism. *Critical Studies in Media Communication, 21,* 189–211.

Hiebert, R. (2001). Review of *Emotional branding: How successful brands gain the irrational edge* and *Adbusters: Journal of the mental environment. Public Relations Review, 27,* 244–245.

Jones, J. (2005). *Entertaining politics: New political television and civic culture.* New York: Rowman & Littlefield.

Karlberg, M. (2002). Partisan branding and media spectacle: Implications for democratic communication. *Democratic Communique, 18,* 1–21.

Klein, N. (2000). *No logo.* New York: Picador.

Klein, N. (2002). *Fences and windows: Dispatches from the front lines of the globalization debate.* New York: Picador.

Kurtz, H. (2003, July 27). No holds barred: Alternative news outlets smack down convention coverage. *The Washington Post,* p. C1. Retrieved October 15, 2005, from LexisNexis database.

Lakoff, G. (2002). *Moral politics: How liberals and conservatives think* (2nd ed.). Chicago: University of Chicago Press.

Lakoff, G. (2004). *Don't think of an elephant!* White River Junction, VT: Chelsea Green.

Lasn, K. (1999). *Culture jam: How to reverse America's suicidal consumer binge—and why we must.* New York: Quill.

Miller, L. (2003, April 8). TV's boldest new show. Retrieved August 8, 2004, from http:// archive.salon.com/ent/tv/feature/2003/04/08 stewart/index_np.html

Morreall, J. (1987). *The philosophy of laughter and humor.* Albany: State University of New York.

Newman, B. (1999). *Handbook of political marketing.* Thousand Oaks, CA: Sage.

Roddick, A. (1994). *Body and soul: Profits with principles—The amazing success story of Anita Roddick & The Body Shop.* Pittsburgh, PA: Three Rivers Press.

Seery, J. (1990). *Political returns: Irony in politics and theory, from Plato to the antinuclear movement.* Boulder, CO: Westview.

Talen, B. (2003). *What should I do if Reverend Billy is in my store?* New York: New Press.

Test, G. (1991). *Satire: Spirit and art.* Tampa: University of South Florida Press.

Vlastos, G. (1991). *Socrates: Ironist and moral philosopher.* Cambridge, UK: Cambridge University Press.

White, S. (Ed.). (1995). *The Cambridge companion to Habermas.* Cambridge, UK: Cambridge University Press.

EDUCATING *THE SIMPSONS*

21

Teaching Queer Representations in Contemporary Visual Media

Gilad Padva

The visual media, mainly popular films and TV programs, offer an excellent tool for high school and university educators to encourage sexual tolerance, and in particular to promote a supportive attitude towards queer students. . . . I have selected "Homer's Phobia" as a case study here because of the significant popularity of this Emmy Award–winning 15th episode of the *Simpsons'* 8th season, aired on February 16, 1997. . . . I offer a scholarly counter-cultural analysis of this episode in regard to its politics of sexuality and gay-straight alliance, and to its visualized sociolinguistic strategies of subverting homophobia and sissy-phobia. . . .

QUEERING THE SIMPSONS

. . . The popular subgenre of *animated* TV sitcoms in the late 1990s and 2000s . . . integrates semi-anarchistic humor and spectacular imagery that often challenge conventional ethnic, social, gender *and* sexual patterns of representation. This subgenre includes, for example, *Beavis & Butthead, King of the Hill, Daria, Family Guy, The Kid,* and *The Simpsons. The Simpsons,* in particular, is one of the world's most successful American television exports, syndicated in over 60 countries since 1991 (Chocano, 2001). In its imaginative, disruptive, and even surrealistic way, this subgenre often criticizes conservatism, bigotry, and prejudice with humor. . . .

Jonathan Gray (2003) suggests that *The Simpsons* has turned on its family sitcom brethren, situating its action within an anti-suburb that is depicted as xenophobic, provincial, and narrowminded. Brilliantly parodying the traditional family sitcom neighborhood, *The Simpsons'* town of Springfield satirizes and challenges rather than extols the American Dream. This series criticizes the hypocrisy within the American educational system, religious, political, and even economic systems (Tingleff, 1998). Notably, through Bart, Homer, and Grandpa, *The Simpsons* even challenges categories of male sexuality. Sam Tingleff notes that the relationship between the vicious, albeit decrepit Mr. Burns, who owns the local nuclear plant, and his younger assistant Smithers, is a consistent attack on male sexual norms. Smithers' loyalty comes not from monetary desires, but his quasi-sexual attraction towards Mr. Burns.

Furthermore, the males of *The Simpsons* challenge categories of male sexuality and demonstrate its flexibility. For instance, Homer shaves his "bikini zone" for a presumed swimsuit competition; he kisses his secretary Carl (voice of the gay icon Harvey Fierstein) on the lips, and later mistakenly calls his wife "Carl" in bed; his favorite song is "It's Raining Men"; and he says Oliver North was "just poured into that uniform." And in one episode, when Grandpa Simpson can't take his pills, the elder turns into a woman, later accepting flowers and a date from a male suitor (Tingleff, 1998). Moreover, when Lenny, Homer's co-worker, is dying, he sees a heaven full of Carls. On the other hand, Homer suggests that Lisa could win a class election over Nelson by starting a rumor that he's gay. And when a Gay Pride parade passes the Simpson's house, Homer disapproves of his dog's attempt to hook up with an effeminate, leather-clad dog.

In the gay classic episode "Homer Phobia" (written by Ron Hauge and directed by Mike B. Anderson, 1997), the Simpsons befriend "John," a

From Padva, G. (2008). Educating *The Simpsons:* Teaching queer representations in contemporary visual media. *Journal of LGBT Youth,* 5(3), 57–73. Reprinted by permission of Taylor & Francis Ltd., www.tandf.co.uk/journals.

mustachioed kitsch trader (resembling and voiced by the cult filmmaker and gay icon John Waters). The fact that he is gay makes Homer fear his potential effect on Bart. After a series of ridiculous attempts to turn Bart into a "real man" (and consequent arguments with his wife Marge), Homer assures his son that his love for him is unconditional, whether he is straight or gay.

The anti-homophobic contribution of this episode to the empowerment of GLBT young viewers is based on its three political premises: celebrating queer counter-culture, embracing straight-gay alliance, and promoting diversity and multiculturalism.

CELEBRATING QUEER COUNTER-CULTURE

The Simpsons' friendship with John starts during their visit to the latter's "Cockamamie's" antique store. Marge tries to sell Grandma's Civil War doll to John in order to pay an exorbitant Springfield Gas Company bill. John tells her that the doll is nothing but a Johnny Reb bottle from the early 1970s. Homer counters that it's still better than the junk that John is selling, and he wonders how a grown man can love a nostalgic box or a toy. John replies: "It's camp! The tragically ludicrous? The ludicrously tragic?" Eventually, Homer invites John over to see their home, which is "full of valuable worthless crap." John is delighted.

Camp is defined in the *Oxford Dictionary* (1996) as "Affected, theatrically exaggerated; effeminate; homosexual." Susan Sontag (1999 [1964]) categorically defined camp as a vision of the world in terms of a particular kind of style.

> It is the love of the exaggerated, the "off," of things-being-what-they-are-not. . . . The androgyne is certainly one of the great images of Camp sensibility. . . . What is most beautiful in virile men is something feminine; what is most beautiful in feminine women is something masculine. (p. 56)

Jack Babuscio identified camp with queer subculture based on *gay* sensibility "as a creative energy reflecting a consciousness that is different from the mainstream; a heightened awareness of certain human complications of feeling that spring from the fact of social oppression" (1999 [1978], pp. 117–18). . . .

The *Simpsons* episode's visual vocabulary is dominated by camp. For instance, John wears flamboyant, striped shirts from the 1970s and his store contains many telling artifacts: Godzilla toy, piggy bank, pink flamingo (echoing John Water[s]'s eponymous cult film), a statue of an Easter Island native head, cola bottle, floral wall decoration, etc. All these items are highly camp, as they are related to kitsch, extravagance, "good" bad taste, artificiality, style, and retrostyle, and also to feminine or "girly" behavior, demonstrated in John's clothing choices and his coy intonation and gestures.

Ironically, John finds the Simpsons extremely camp. He is thrilled by the corn-printed curtain in their kitchen, the color scheme, the rabbit ears antenna, the Hi-C soft drink and Lisa's necklace ("Pearls on a little girl! It's a fairy tale!"). Homer asks him if his records have camp value, and John flatters him: "You yourself are worth a bundle, Homer! Why I could wrap a bow around you and slap on a price tag." Homer laughs and starts dancing with John to an Alicia Bridges disco record ("I Love the Nightlife"). Marge comments that Homer has "certainly taken a shine to him."

The next morning, Homer decides to invite John and his wife over for drinks. But Marge does not think John is married. In fact, she tells Homer that "John is a ho-mo-sexual" (adopting the apparently scientific/medical definition). In response, Homer shouts hysterically.

Soon afterwards, Homer sees Bart wearing a Hawaiian shirt, choosing a pink cake over a brown one and dancing to Cher's "Shoop Shoop Song (It's In His Kiss)," wearing a large black wig with a pink bow. Bart's drag show is traumatic for his father. No confusion is allowed over his child's sexual identity and orientation (two concepts Homer repeatedly mixes up). Homer suspects that his son is gay, not because Bart is attracted to boys, but because he does not behave manly enough. Homer sees Bart's dance, not as innocent child's play, but as a *camp* performance, identified (even in Homer's presumably straight mind) with "transvestite" gay identity, and therefore, as extremely, "problematic." He consequently resolves to "normalize" his son. . . .

While Homer is threatened by John's (homo) sexuality and its "effeminizing" influence on

Bart, the female protagonists—wife Marge, their individualistic pre-adolescent daughter Lisa, and baby Maggie—sympathize with their new friend. Marge, in particular, likes gossiping with John, who demonstrates his impressive knowledge of celebrities' secret lives, and she adores him for his sense of humor, creativity, friendship, stylishness and delicacy. These qualities are contrasted to her husband's stupidity, egocentricity, misbehavior, clumsiness and machismo. It is no wonder that Marge immediately becomes John's best (female) friend, his devoted "fag hag."

EMBRACING STRAIGHT-GAY ALLIANCE

The term "fag hag" dates back to the United States in the late 1960s, dismissively directed at women who were considered not attractive enough to socialize with "real men." But like so many derogatory terms, it was reclaimed in the 1990s as a stereotypic term to be worn with pride. In the ideal, gay men introduced their female friends into a world free from sexual harassment, where the emphasis was on fun and where, more often than not, they would find themselves the center of flattering and unthreatening attention. Hence, "[F]ag haggery was in fashion" (Button, 2000, p. 46). . . .

Marge's "sistership" with John is a bonding between a straight woman and a gay man who enjoys his own stylishness, neatness and effeminacy. In contrast to many straight men *and* some sissy-phobic gay men, John celebrates rather than mocks male femininity, sissiness and stylishness. He and Marge share "feminine" insights and feelings in a friendship that signifies an alternative, equal and respectful relationship between a man and a woman in conservative small Springfield.

After Bart points a giant, phallic and colorful plastic pistol at him, Homer's worry becomes stronger. He suspects that his wife is ignoring John's malicious homosexualization of Bart, and he makes foolish attempts to save his son from gayness. For instance, he forces his Bart to look at a huge sexist advertising billboard, showing two female models in bathing suits smoking cigarettes; after a long look at the models, Bart only (homo) erotically wishes for "anything slim."

Homer decides that if he is to turn the boy into a man, Bart will need manhood and virility in his environment. During their visit to the local steel mill, Roscoe, the muscular and mustachioed manager, asks the ultravirile, muscular workers to say hello to the Simpsons. In response, they wave effeminately, "Hello-o." Homer wonders if the whole world has gone insane, watching a slender worker running-in-place while his mate theatrically slaps his back: "Stand still, there's a spark in your hair!" and the worker replies: "Get it! Get it!" Then a tanned bodybuilder in hot pants walks past Homer holding a vat of hot steel and announcing "Hot stuff, comin' through!"—a phrase that echoes gay pornography. Roscoe states, "We work hard. We play hard" and pulls a chain. Surprisingly, a high-tech disco ball descends and the entire mill turns into a nightclub called "The Anvil," with flickering spotlights, smoke effects, dance floors, mustachioed body builders, and muscular young men at work, proudly exposing their torsos. All the workers dance to "Everybody Dance Now," except Homer, who is in shock and leaves this male-only enclave, shading Bart's eyes.

Edmund White (2000 [1980]), in his discussion of the political vocabulary of homosexuality, notes that in the past, feminization, at least to a small and symbolic degree, seemed a necessary initiation into gay life. Today, almost the opposite seems to be true. Many gay men sport beards, army fatigues, work boots, etc. They build up their bodies or are "busy arraying themselves in these castoffs and becoming cowboys, truckers, telephone line-men, football players (in appearance and sometimes also in reality)" (p. 192). In this way, the ultra-virile spectacle at the gay steel mill can be perceived as a high-camp drag show. . . .

Earl Jackson (1995) suggests that a truly subversive gay representational practice must contest not only the gay subject's experience of heterosexist persecution, but also his experience of patriarchal privilege. He notes that certain gay male cultural practices that transvalue deviance as a positive mode of self-identification contain at least an implicit critique of the normative male ideal (and the dominant heterosexual sex/gender system) from which the gay male deviates. Sam Fussell (1999 [1994]) contends that even apparently straight male bodybuilding signs a *reversal* of sex roles, with the bodybuilder taking a traditionally female role: body as object. Further, Fussell observes, "whether it be beefcake or cheesecake, it's still cake . . ." (p. 46).

David Halperin (1995) contends that gay muscles, in particular, deliberately flaunt the visual norms of straight masculinity, which impose discretion on masculine self-display and require that straight male beauty exhibit itself only casually or inadvertently. Brian Pronger (2000) also contends that gay muscles, commercialized as they are, have at least one significant character of drag performances: they are ironic. "Musculature," he notes, "within a gay ironic sensibility signifies the *subversion* of patriarchal power by acting as homoerotic *enticements* to other men" (pp. 689–690).

Homer is not only surprised by the muscular men's queerness. He is also astonished by their proud cultural identity: their dress (and undress), language ("Hot stuff, comin' through!"), behavior (dancing and having fun), and mood (happy), which contradict his image of gays as low-life, dubious and miserable people. This lively discotheque is a demonstration of power, as it presents an alternative culture, part of an alternative camp lifestyle. Homer feels threatened by the spectacular: "This is a nightmare! You're all sick!" He pathologizes gayness as deviation from the "natural" order. Camp, as a queer counter-cultural political praxis, uses its innovative and inspirational deviancy to contest the oppressive social order. This deviation is also political because camp reflects an aesthetic and ethical refusal to be visually hetero-normalized or silenced by dominance (Meyer, 1994; Padva, 2000).

PROMOTING DIVERSITY AND MULTICULTURALISM

Homer's phobia primarily derived from ignorance. His negative reaction towards the gay workers/clubbers is caused by guilt for what he considers his son's deviancy. Pointedly, Homer is not demonized. From this perspective, not only gays but also straight Homer are victims of the same oppressive "natural" sexual order that stigmatizes and discriminates against sexual minorities and imposes restricting hetero-masculine codes of visibility, behavior and sexual expression on men. Although he does not recognize it, Homer too transgresses the (hetero)sexual representational regime, by wearing Hawaiian shirts, dancing with another man, etc.

Homer wonders how it could be possible that a gay son has developed in a straight family. As Eve Kosofsky Sedgwick pointed out (1990), the double-edged potential for injury in the scene of gay coming out results partly from the fact that the erotic identity of the person who receives the disclosure is also apt to be implicated in, and hence perturbed by, it.

In an earlier scene, Homer blames Marge for being "too feminine around the boy" and she replies that if there is actually a problem with Bart worth worrying over, it must be that he's not spending time with his dad. But Homer's own transgressive masculinity might be implicated in his son's suspected homosexuality.

Michael Kimmel (2001) contends that homophobia is a central organizing principle of our cultural definition of manhood. He suggests that homophobia is more than the irrational fear of gay men, more than the fear that straights might be perceived as gay men. David Leverentz (1986) points out that the word "faggot" has nothing to do with homosexual experience or even with fear of homosexuals. Rather, it arises from the depths of manhood: a label of ultimate contempt for anyone who seems sissy, untough, uncool.

Homer, horrified by the gay steel mill/dance club, decides to socialize his son into the hetero-masculine world through a male brotherhood that putatively includes himself, the paranoid local bar-owner Moe, and the town's notorious drunk Bernie—three unappealing male role models. When Bart hears about his dad's plan to go hunting with him and his friends, he whispers: "Something about a bunch of guys alone together in the woods . . . seems kinda gay." The three (straight and narrow) losers get drunk and fall asleep near the bonfire. Homer is shown gently and compassionately holding his sleeping son. Desperate to provide Bart with an animal to kill, the hunting group breaks into a reindeer pen. Homer orders him to shoot a reindeer after Bernie has assured him (ironically) that shooting a reindeer is like killing a beautiful man. Suddenly, the deer attack the unwelcome guests, who are rescued at the last moment by John's Japanese Santa Claus robot.

John has earned Homer's gratitude: "Hey, we owe this guy, and I don't want you calling him a sissy. This guy's a fruit, and a . . . no, wait, wait, wait: queer, queer, queer! That's what you like to be called, right?" and John wittily replies, "Well, that or John." Lisa remarks that this is about as tolerant as her dad gets, so John should be flattered. Here, language demonstrates the change that has occurred in Homer's thinking, when he agrees to use the other's terminology as a sign of respect.

The word "queer," as Cherry Smith (1996) points out, defines a strategy, an attitude, a reference to other identities, and a new self-understanding. "Both in culture and politics," Smith notes, "queer articulates a radical questioning of social and cultural norms, notions of gender, reproductive sexuality and the family" (p. 280).

Embracing the idea of unconditional love, Homer tells Bart in the final scene that he loves him because he is his son, gay or not. Bart looks quite surprised to be identified by his parent as gay, before he has recognized *himself* to be gay. This presents the whole identification process as questionable and contradicts Homer's (and some of the viewers') fixation over gender roles and sexual identities.

The hit song "Everybody Dance Now" (associated with the disco in the steel mill) forms the sound track for the final scene, as John's car drives off and Bart's face is shown in increasing close-ups, matching the rhythm and lyrics, "I've got the power." The makers of the "Homer Phobia" episode dedicated it to the steelworkers of America and, winking, exhorted them to "Keep reaching for that rainbow," metaphorically liberating their hyper-masculine territory from its monologic perception.

This episode's multicultural perspective, embracing diversity and open-mindedness, is based on universal ideas of freedom, liberty, equality, justice, tolerance, solidarity and compassion. The outwardly naive medium of animation here mediates sexual pluralism through (unexpected) comic situations that parody homophobia rather than homosexuals. The creators have knowingly encoded many gay expressions (e.g., "Dad, you are the living end!"), erotic innuendos (e.g., the gay steel workers' dance club is called "The Anvil"), intertextual hints (e.g., Homer recalls the hit song "It's Raining Men"; and John's car beeper plays Judy Garland's "Somewhere Over the Rainbow"). Although straight audiences too enjoy this episode, its hyperbolic scenes particularly empower gay viewers, who likely identify the linguistic maneuvers and decode the queer meanings. In "Homer's Phobia"'s Utopian vision, homophobia is just a phase; the hysterical drama queens are primarily Homer and his bigoted straight friends; and an amplified machismo is as theatrical as a flamboyant drag show.

REFERENCES

Babuscio, J. (1978). The cinema of camp (aka Camp and the gay sensibility). *Gay Sunshine Journal, 35*; reprinted in Cleto, F. (Ed.). (1999). *Camp: Queer aesthetics and the performing subject* (pp. 117–135). Edinburgh: Edinburgh University Press.

Button, S. (2000). Best friends. *Attitude* 75 (July 2000), 46–48.

Chocano, C. (2001). Matt Groening. *Salon*. Retrieved April 2, 2005, from hitp://www.salon.com/people/bc/2001/01/30/groening/print.html

Fussell, S. (1994). Bodybuilder americanus. In Goldstein, L. (Ed.), (1999). *The male body: Features, destinies, exposures* (pp. 43–60). Ann Arbor: The University of Michigan Press.

Gray, J. (2003). *Imagining America: The Simpsons and the anti-suburb go global*. Paper presented at Communication in Borderlands: The 53rd Annual Conference of the International Communication Association, San Diego, California, USA. May 23–27.

Halperin, D. (1995). *Saint Foucault: Towards a gay hagiography*. New York: Oxford University Press.

Jackson, E., Jr. (1995). *Strategies of deviance: Studies in gay male representation*. Bloomington: Indiana University Press.

Kimmel, M. (2001). Masculinity as homophobia: Fear, shame, and silence in the construction of gender identity. In Whitehead, S. M. & Barrett, F. J. (Eds.), *The masculinities reader* (pp. 266–287). Cambridge: Oxford and Malden, MA: Polity.

Leverentz, D. (1986). Manhood, humiliation and public life: Some stories. *Southwest Review, 71*.

Meyer, M. (1994). Introduction: Reclaiming the discourse of camp. In *The politics and poetics of camp* (pp. 1–23). London and New York: Routledge.

The Oxford Dictionary. (1996). Oxford and New York: Oxford University Press.

Padva, G. (2000). *Priscilla* fights back: The politicization of camp subculture. *Journal of Communication Inquiry,* 24(2), 216–243.

Pronger, B. (2000). Physical culture. In Haggerty, G. (Ed.), *Gay histories and cultures: An encyclopedia* (pp. 688–690). New York: Garland Publishing.

Sedgwick, E. K. (1990). *Epistemology of the closet.* Berkeley and Los Angeles: University of California Press.

The Simpsons (1997). Homer Phobia. Created by M. Groening; episode written by R. Hauge; directed by M. Anderson. Distributed by Gracie Films in association with 20th Century Fox Television: retrieved on June 22, 2008, from http://www.snpp.com/epidoses/4F11.html

Smith, C. (1996). What is this thing called queer? In Morton, D. (Ed.), *The material queer: A lesbigay cultural studies reader* (pp. 227–285). Boulder, Colorado and Oxford: Westview Press.

Sontag, S. (1964). Notes on camp. *Partisan Review,* 31(4), 515–530; reprinted in Cleto, F. (Ed.), *Camp: Queer aesthetics and the performing subject* (pp. 53–65). Edinburgh: Edinburgh University Press.

Szalacha, L. (2004). Educating teachers on LGBTQ issues: A review of research and program evaluations. *Journal of Gay & Lesbian Issues in Education* 1(4), 67–79.

Tingleff, S. (1998). "I will not expose the ignorance of the faculty": *The Simpsons* as a critique of consumer culture. *The Simpsons Archive.* Retrieved on April 2, 2005, from http://www.snpp.com/olher/papers/st.paper.html

White, E. (1980). The political vocabulary of homosexuality. In Michaels, L. & Ricks, C. (Eds.), *The state of the language* (pp. 235–246). Berkeley and Los Angeles: University of California Press; reprinted in Burke, L., Crowley, T. & Girvin, A. (Eds.), *The Routledge language and cultural theory reader* (pp. 189–196). London and New York: Routledge.

22

RESISTING, REITERATING, AND DANCING THROUGH

The Swinging Closet Doors of Ellen DeGeneres's Televised Personalities

Candace Moore

Gushing to *The Advocate* about her new girl-friend, comedian Ellen DeGeneres, *Arrested Development* star Portia De Rossi says: "She was so courageous and loud in '97, and now she is doing something that is more subliminal. She's changing the world, she really is" (Kort, "Portia," 40). De Rossi subtly articulates a difference between Ellen's 1997 "coming out" and Ellen's current daily dance into America's living rooms as a beloved daytime talk show host who "happens to be" gay. LGBT activists and media critics slightly disagree, asserting that Ellen may be "softpedaling her lesbianism" on *Ellen: The Ellen DeGeneres Show* to find widespread acceptance (Lo, "The Incredible Story"; Heffernan, "The Perils" E5). As *New York Times* critic Virginia Heffernan puts it: "Ms. DeGeneres no longer wants to talk about being gay, so she discusses pleasant [topics]: décor, holidays and the fridge" (E5). Host of a mainstream variety show that has wowed NBC network executives by pulling in impressive numbers of its targeted demographic—women ages 25–54 (Deeken 30; Schnuer S1)—and hyped as an "everywoman approach" ("The Ellen DeGeneres Show"), DeGeneres avoids the topic of her own homosexuality and actively closes down conversation in which the very word or concept comes up.

. . . Not verbally addressing queer identity on her talk show is understandable from DeGeneres's personal perspective. Her career all but collapsed not long after the glow of her public coming-out party died down.

"To come out," according to [queer theorist David M.] Halperin,

is precisely to expose oneself to a different set of dangers and constraints, to make oneself into a convenient screen onto which straight people can project all the fantasies they routinely entertain about gay people, and to suffer one's every gesture, statement, expression, and opinion to be totally and irrevocably marked by the overwhelming social significance of one's openly acknowledged homosexual identity. (30)

Following Ellen DeGeneres's self-outing, her private life (with ex-girlfriend Anne Heche) became unbearably public—their love affair's ups and downs became unending fodder for gossip columnists and paparazzi, who stalked the new couple. Ellen's groundbreaking sitcom was also summarily canceled the next year, due to advertiser pullouts, public attacks from the religious right, and, arguably, sabotage by the ABC network itself in imposing parental advisories because of the show's portrayals of same-sex romance. (Such advisories were not, of course, placed on programs that tackled more explicitly sexual subjects with heterosexual leads) (Gross 162). Throughout these trials, DeGeneres became an important icon of political courage for the LGBT community, even though she candidly expressed that she had neither intended her coming out as a political statement nor wished to become a poster-woman for the queer cause. . . .

Since its launch in 2003, Ellen has crafted herself a talk-show persona on *Ellen: The Ellen DeGeneres Show,* who linguistically sidesteps the word or concept of homosexuality. However, she performs queerness through what implicitly

---

"exceeds" her stand-up jokes and sit-down talk, and, physically, through the ritual action of her daily dance sequence. Through these methods, perhaps DeGeneres escapes being such a "convenient screen" for hate-mongers or bearing the responsibility of being a spokesperson for all of gay America, while she still maintains a *televisibility*[1] of queer identity. Demonstrating how Ellen's coming out and her return to the closet become enacted again and again, ad infinitum, on television, my textual analysis involves queer ruptures on the primarily heterosexual text of Ellen's current Emmy-winning daytime talk show. Seeing "being in the closet" and "being out" as performances that are constantly negotiated socially—either actively resisted or reinscribed—rather than one-time denials or declarations of sexuality that hold, this chapter highlights ambiguous moments in DeGeneres's daily show. In specific instances that I explore, DeGeneres gestures rhetorically or symbolically to her sexual preference, absurdly omits or redirects possible discussions of homosexuality, or is subtly or not-so-subtly "called out" as gay by her celebrity guests. . . .

Repetition and reiteration is a central theme in Ellen's show, with her daily dances, recurring verbal noises and catch phrases. I ultimately argue that Ellen's many repetitious behaviors also serve as multiple self-outings. Anna McCarthy suggests that perhaps queer visibility on television is only permissible as spectacle; such televisibility becomes dangerous to heteronormativity when it presents queer lives and loves as "quotidian" ("Ellen: Making Queer Television History" 597). By repeatedly dancing to the same songs and expressing the same verbal ticks over and over again, Ellen seeks in the opening sequences of her talk show to present the out-of-the-ordinary repeatedly, until its very performance, occurring daily, becomes un-alarming and even infectiously celebratory.

During her ritual opening dance, Ellen looks into the camera, directly addressing the audience, and then follows by breaking the proscenium arch, dancing out into the pulsating, cheering, similarly dancing live studio audience. Her daily dances, set to a handful of uplifting disco, hip hop, and R&B songs, with their awkward, non-choreographed moves, together with her wide, toothy grin, seem to proclaim a message of self-acceptance: *This is me! I'm great just the way I am, and you can be great just the way you are too!* Her dance moves

themselves evoke nostalgia for the gay-steeped, 1970s-era culture of disco. While Ellen does not remind her audience of her queerness over and over again verbally, Ellen does repeat acts that are both absurd and permissible, causing the most bizarre squawks and awkward dance moves to become a commonplace sight, and a site for pleasure.

SUBLIMINAL RITUALS

While De Rossi's claim that Ellen is "changing the world" might represent the overstated rhetorical flourish of the lovestruck, De Rossi's use of the word "subliminal," meaning "below the threshold of conscious perception" (*Webster's II New Riverside University Dictionary* 1994: 1154), to describe what Ellen is "doing," does astutely point out the very *liminality* of Ellen's ritualistic daily performances.[2] To put it in other terms, De Rossi is here distinguishing between a media *event* and a repeated media *ritual*. A media *event* is a one-time, idiosyncratic phenomenon that acts as an exception to the usual rules of both television flow and content, and, if planned, is often surrounded by quite a bit of promotional hype (Hubert 31; McCarthy, "Ellen: Making Queer Television History" 593). A repeated media *ritual* also temporarily upends or stretches convention (only to reinstate it); however, it is less outwardly eventful; in fact, it gradually becomes perceived as a part of the normal flow, and signifies through repetition, over time, or through multiple broadcasts (Couldry 24). One punctuates the Nielsen's ratings, the other has the potential to slowly, rather than rapidly, shift consciousnesses through a process of slow audience acclimation to, and reinforcement of, difference.

ENCODING/DECODING THE DANCE

When asked why Ellen DeGeneres does not address her homosexuality on her talk show, lesbian actress and screenwriter Guinevere Turner (*Go Fish, The L Word*) declared emphatically "How could you dance like that and not be gay? That's a way of saying with every opening representation, I'm gay!" ("Personal Interview" 2005). Marusya Bociurkiw, in a recent critical essay published in *Canadian Woman Studies,* concurred with Turner's view that Ellen's lesbianism is palpable in her dancing: "As the music, usually hip hop, is played, Ellen's body is on display in a manner that is decidedly not heteronormative. Here DeGeneres displays the grace and confidence that her accessible, self-deprecating, 'kook' act disavows. DeGeneres looks like a butch lesbian dancing alone, in a club" (176).

However, these interpretations are just that, individualized readings of a polysemic text, and sometimes we see what we want to see. Furthermore, "what a dyke dancing looks like" is a nearly impossible thing to put one's finger on. Just as lesbians are a diverse, rather than homogeneous group, comprising women of varying ethnicities, cultural backgrounds, styles, classes, gender presentations, and so on, their dance moves likely vary enormously. So while a general consensus remains among these readings, that "something's queer" here, I try to show, through examining prior precedents of Ellen expressing herself physically—whether through physical humor or through dance—that not only does her opening "dance with herself" (and thus the viewer) represent a daily declaration of queer identity, but that she has previously coded it to mean exactly that.

Rather than revisit the coming-out media event of Ellen's "Puppy Episode" (4.22 and 4.23, April 30, 1997), which has been explored in depth by Anna McCarthy, Susan J. Hubert, and Steven Capsuto, among others, I concentrate instead on two pre-coming-out episodes from the second season of *Ellen*—texts, which, like her talk show, operate "doubly." In "The Fix Up" (2.5, October 19, 1994), Ellen's dance moves are first foregrounded, and in "Thirty Kilo Man" part 1 and 2 (2.23, May 10, 1995; 2.24, May 17, 1995), her character has a heterosexual love affair that reads as unmistakably queer.

ELEVATOR MUSIC ON EARLY *ELLEN*

Early *Ellen* is best described as ABC's version of *Seinfeld*'s sitcom about nothing, since both half-hour shows center around known stand-up comedians and their witty banter about insignificant, repetitious, or everyday matters with friends. During the three seasons prior to Ellen DeGeneres's/ Ellen Morgan's doubly momentous 1997 coming out, Ellen's character on the middling-rated

sitcom was consistently stuck in a weekly cycle of dates-gone-wrong with guys, that, for an array of incidental and sometimes extravagantly bizarre reasons, just do not fit. In "The Gladiators" (2.19, March 1, 1995) for instance, Ellen's new beau, Nitro, a gladiator from the then-popular television show, *American Gladiators*,[3] is snapped away from her by an ultra-buff woman (Ice), leading the bookstore owner to jealously beat the pumped-up woman to a pulp with a padded lance.

The sitcom's season with the most overtly heterosexual storylines, the second, is also the season with the most queer subtext. Disney would not okay the idea of Ellen Morgan's coming out until more than a year later, when blatant hints began to be worked into the weekly scripts (Gross 157). Ellen's obsessive man-shopping in season two is painted by the writers and producers as downright absurd, but what will serve as the alternative (asexuality, in most of season three, before facing her queer identity), is not quite clear yet. Journalist for *The San Francisco Examiner,* Joyce Millman, caught on early. In the spring of 1995, in a column entitled "The Sitcom that Dare Not Speak Its Name," the television critic prematurely outed Ellen Morgan: "As a gal sitcom, *Ellen* doesn't make any sense at all, until you view it through the looking glass, where the unspoken subtext becomes the main point. Then is Ellen is transformed into one of TV's savviest, funniest, slyest shows. Ellen Morgan is a closet lesbian" (B1).

In "The Fix Up" (2.5, October 19, 1994) of season two, the episode opens with Ellen inside an elevator—the enclosed space that arguably acts as the show's metaphorical stand-in for a closet. Ellen's adventures in (or waiting for) an elevator are a reoccurring trope on the show. Given the sitcom's frequent meta-references to sitcom history (see McCarthy, "Ellen: Making Queer Television History" 607–614), perhaps this trope, seen throughout the second season, is also a tip of the hat to the historically common "meat locker" sitcom scenario, wherein people with differences get stuck in a small space, often a meat locker or an elevator, and overcome differences (Sconce 104–105). In this case, the elevator's only other passenger exits, and finding herself alone, Ellen openly acknowledges the song playing over the loud speakers, Aretha Franklin's "Respect," by first tapping her feet, then swinging from side to side and lip-synching. As the song builds to crescendo, Ellen is observed flailing, rocking her head along to the words, and jumping into the air, landing with thumps. As audience members, we are in anticipation for the elevator doors to suddenly open and or Ellen to be "found out." Instead, Franklin's rousing tune halts abruptly and a male authoritarian voice comes over the loud speakers: "Excuse me, ma'am, this is security" the voice interrupts. "Please refrain from jumping in the elevator." The camera offers a shot from above, looking down at Ellen, as she immediately looks up to the speaker, with a petrified deer-in-the-headlights acknowledgment that she is being surveyed. She then cradles her head down in her hand, in embarrassment, before the camera cuts away.

This scene might be read divorced from any queer subtext, as mere silliness in an elevator, with Ellen as the 1990s Lucy Ricardo, always getting herself into a new kind of trouble. However, the larger text of the sitcom suggests the elevator as a contained closet, within which Ellen Morgan can finally release herself, be happy with who she is, until she is again reminded, reprimanded by a voice from outside, that others do not approve of her lifestyle. This is particularly suggested by the content of the dialogue between Ellen and her mother that immediately follows, and furthermore by the theme (failed heterosexual daring, what else?) of "The Fix Up."

In the scene that follows, Ellen's mother asks her a question over coffee that reoccurs, rephrased, throughout the series: "So, are you seeing anyone these days?" When Ellen's answer implies no, her mom continues in full fuss mode: "I just worry about you. You're not immortal . . . I just want you to be happy." Ellen retorts, "You know it's possible to be happy without a man." "Must you joke about everything?" her mom returns, and then promptly tries to fix Ellen up with someone she grew up with. Described by Ellen as the "weird" kid in the neighborhood who ate bugs, he has matured into an adult man who is not peculiar at all; in fact, Ellen seems to find him quite charming. In a plot reversal, he ends up finding Ellen entirely "weird," through the usual comedy of errors. "The Fix Up" is a stereotypical example of the pre-coming-out plotline, wherein events beyond Ellen's control, but generally propelled at least partially by her neurotic behavior, spiral, causing Ellen ultimately to be rejected by her possible heterosexual love interest, rather than force the thirty-something to

own up to the fact that she is not truly interested in the first place. There are also instances where Ellen rejects men; these generally involve Ellen's discovery that the man she thought was a dreamboat has an impossible-to-stand trait.

The "date that always goes wrong" plot is finally frustrated and complicated in the two-part season two finale, "Thirty Kilo Man" (2.23 and 2.24, May 10, 1995, and May 17, 1995). The first part of the finale opens in Ellen's apartment, with Ellen's mother asking her about her plans for the weekend. When Ellen makes a joke about getting a "Chia Date," so that she can sprinkle it and "watch it grow," Ellen's mom pulls out the claws: "You know what the problem with you is, Ellen? You're too picky. You always look for a man's faults. Greg was too nice, Roger watched too much TV, Carl was a drag." "Drag king, mother," Ellen corrects, "I know I nitpick . . ." As the episode continues, Dan, a man she was interested in during an earlier episode but rejected after discovering that he delivered pizza for a living, returns from Italy with a new, more prestigious job. The first ever return "beard" is also the one that actually ends up in bed with Ellen. A "next day" scenario finds Ellen strutting out from her bedroom in a robe, hair mussed, puffing on an imaginary cigarette. Dan emerges fully dressed and primped, and she kisses him, mumbling, "No fair, you brushed your teeth." "Sorry," he practically sings. They touch their way into the living-room, and in full soap-opera pitch, Dan gushes: "I never want this feeling to end. Ellen Morgan, I think I'm falling in love with you." In this scene, Ellen is scripted and choreographed into the position of the stereotypical man in a classic romance, who swaggers out of the bedroom, while Dan is the stereotypical woman, who rushes to say effusive things, to say "I love you" right away.

Later, when Dan comes back from work, Ellen backs him into the couch and gets on top, kissing him. His beeper starts to vibrate in his pants, she pauses to say, "What's that?" and then keeps kissing him, pressing into him, moaning "You are such a considerate man!" She grabs the cordless phone from the coffee table. "Okay, it stopped. What's your number?" This joke on his beeper as vibrator, a device implied as more pleasurable than perhaps his penis, again with the classic roles switched (her as the "horny" one), plays on the notion that, although he is a man, they are in a "lesbian" affair.

This joke is toyed with even further in part two of the finale, when he figuratively "brings a U-Haul," moving in with her right away, and they spend all waking moments together. In their every dialogue and physical interaction, Ellen plays butch to Dan's femme, and the season uses the potential of their hetero-homo romance continuing as a cliff-hanger to the next season. Here the sitcom *Ellen* playfully *queers* heterosexual scenarios, since it cannot yet show a queer one. Ellen's otherness is continually the underlying gag.

In "Three strikes" (2.21, March 29, 1995), Ellen, forced under court order to live with her parents, is made, by her mother, to wear a dress. As she walks through work, the laugh track goes wild; Ellen in a flowery dress in which she looks awkward is a joke in and of itself. Ellen Morgan's (and, really, Ellen DeGeneres's) queerness is what always exceeds the text, both with her dates that do not work, and with the one, Dan, that does.

HETEROSEXUAL TALK

Ellen's closeted verbal discourse around the topic of her sexuality on *Ellen: The Ellen DeGeneres Show* functions similarly to the coded scripting of her pre-out counterpart, Ellen Morgan, on *Ellen.* . . .

Generally, when the topic of her own sexuality is broached, live, Ellen DeGeneres defers the question within a heterosexual paradigm, in which straight desire is always the point-of-reference, the norm. Like a pre–"Puppy Episode" Ellen Morgan, who cannot seem to find the right man, Ellen DeGeneres never enunciates the nature of her desire on air, but always enunciates, rather, *what her desire is not.*

Two live tapings of *Ellen: The Ellen DeGeneres Show* demonstrate this point. In a November 10, 2005, interview with Jake Gyllenhaal, the young actor comes out on stage with 400 white roses for Ellen, to congratulate her on her 400th live talk show (3.49, November 10, 2005). When they sit down together, Ellen immediately declares Jake "cute" and gives him a publicity suggestion: "More shots with your shirt off," showing a clip of him naked from the waist up in *Jarhead.* Her studio audience, mostly women, cheer at the top of their lungs. "You should take it off right now," Ellen urges. "You don't have to . . . It's only going to help

you." Gyllenhaal unbuttons his top button then closes it again. "It's my 400th show," begs Ellen. "Roses are sweet and everything . . . I'll give 'em back if you'll take your shirt off." Gyllenhaal becomes bright red and laughs, clearly bashful.

Ellen here mimics Rosie O'Donnell's "passing" as straight. Rosie O'Donnell, who came out as a lesbian after her popular television talk show wrapped, perfected "passing" by regularly harping on her ambiguously sexualized obsession with *Top Gun* star Tom Cruise. Gyllenhaal is verbally worshiped like Cruise; however, Ellen camps the faked crush even further, demonstrating her "passing" clearly as shtick. Acting similarly as a facilitator for straight women in their fantasies, DeGeneres's play act has a distinct difference from O'Donnell's: DeGeneres's homosexuality is a known secret—a secret the audience knows in an iconic way—and she trades on this knowledge to make her interaction funny.

"It's not for me," Ellen asserts, looking Gyllenhaal in the eye, smiling. He can barely talk; he refuses to budge, but good naturedly. "It's not for me!" she insists again, making it clear, as if he did not get it the first time, that she is not trying to sexually harass him; besides, she's gay. They share an understanding glance. "Are you single right now? I should ask that. Not for me, again, I don't care, but the women in the audience want to know." After the commercial break, Gyllenhaal loosens the collar of his shirt and exposes the top of his chest.

The sustained tease of Gyllenhaal's potential strip that never happens acts as a promotional para-text for the film *Jarhead.* Ellen even spells this out: "If you want to see what the rest of that looks like, you have to go see the movie *Jarhead.*" Ellen focuses entirely on *Jarhead* and on her flirtation with Gyllenhaal about taking off his shirt. She gives his other about-to-release-film, *Brokeback Mountain,* an ever-so-quick mention at the end, but does not ask Gyllenhaal one question about this "film with Heath Ledger" (as she summarizes it), nor does she mention that the film deals with a homosexual romance between Gyllenhaal's and Ledger's characters. While implying that her own homosexuality gives her the social mobility to be so openly cheeky with him, without it constituting any kind of gender upheaval or sexual come-on, Ellen has, in this exchange, played butch to Gyllenhaal's femme, much like Ellen Morgan did with Dan, placing him in the position of the looked at, the desirable. . . . She insists, however, on her non-desire, and does not name why it is that she is not attracted to him—that is supposedly "understood," it goes without saying. Gyllenhaal gets visibly uncomfortable with his position as object, but becomes visibly more comfortable when Ellen finally asks whether he is single, since "the women in the audience want to know," because she is offering him the space of normal heterosexual identity by default. Therefore, she intelligently also skirts the question of his sexuality. Ellen comes out through negation, although a denial of a heterosexual desire for one person does not necessarily imply homosexuality. The way she addresses the subject matter is very crafty— to those that do not want to be reminded of the nature of her desires, she does not dare speak its name; to those that do, she is, at least, honest.

In a special event edition of *Ellen: The Ellen DeGeneres Show* that aired on November 30, 2005, celebrating Ellen's twenty-fifth anniversary as a stand-up comedian, a similar incident takes place (3.63). Ellen's "anniversary" special revolves around clips shown from Ellen's career as a stand-up comedian, allowing her to poke fun at her many bad haircuts. Guest celebrities visit to reminisce about Ellen's start in "show biz." Jay Leno, for instance, discusses getting Ellen her first gig on the Johnny Carson Show, a show that obviously inspired her own. Her first Carson appearance was featured most prominently during the hour, and the fact that she was the first female comedian ever invited to be interviewed by Carson after her act was underscored. . . . Strangely, however, her sitcom was conspicuously missing from this retrospective. (Consider, for example, a retrospective on Jerry Seinfeld that fails to mention *Seinfeld* . . . .) By focusing only on Ellen's stand-up career, not only was her sitcom and her "coming out" conveniently occluded from the history of Ellen that the talk show offers, but no clips with any gay content were shown. Ellen rehistoricizes herself as a stand-up comedian first and foremost, and an asexual one at that.

David Spade joins Ellen on this episode, and we learn through their conversation that they met twenty years ago when the two traveled comedy circuits together, Spade opening for Ellen's headlining act. Spade admits a secret: "We used to do some of these gigs together . . . I had a big crush on her . . . then I got the news." Ellen becomes visibly embarrassed and just laughs for a long while, while Spade turns it into a joke: "What it was, was the fact that you had a Walkman . . . and a sweet mullet." "I thought you were adorable," Ellen finally responds, "No interest, other than the fact that you were adorable. Although I did . . . I had a crush on you and you know it." She goes right from this statement into a clip of David Spade's vintage comedy. Those of us that are "in" on the joke, read David's crush on Ellen as real, and Ellen's crush on David as purely platonic. Again here Ellen discursively frames her queerness through expressing what she does not desire, and even that in a very mixed-up way, as is evident in the statement, "No interest, other than the fact that you were adorable." What does that mean? Ellen does not outright deny her homosexuality; when it comes up, she deflects mention of "gayness" with the double-speak and coded strategies of her pre-coming-out sitcom character. DeGeneres is comfortable expressing her nonheterosexuality (in a specific instance—so that it could be read as follows: she just does not like him) on air, but not her homosexuality directly.

John Limon points out that DeGeneres's strategy of "skirting" is not only admitted, but defined, in her book *My Point . . . and I Do Have One:*

> Someone recently wrote a letter . . . asking "Why does Ellen DeGeneres always wear pants and never skirts?" I'm guessing that the person who wrote that letter meant skirt, a noun signifying an article of clothing, and not skirt, a verb defined as, "to evade or elude (as a topic of conversation) by circumlocution." Because, if they mean the verb skirt, well, they're dead wrong. I'm always skirting. (DeGeneres 93; quoted in Limon 115)

Limon identifies DeGeneres's "skirting" as a form of "escapist art" that refuses "to put all kidding aside," and where "what is made visible . . . is evasion" (116–117). Her verbal skirts act as denials of reality that constantly rely on reality as their vanishing point. Rather than expressing information that can be pinned down or literally understood, she replaces objective "truths" with tangential flights of fancy, distractions, wordplay, while presenting the journey of the skirt itself as having *subjective* and transient values—of imagination, pleasure, possibility.

Limon lyrically asks of DeGeneres's skirting: "Is knowledge of the body repressed or unlearned? Is the body itself decoded or disclaimed?" (121). He dubs DeGeneres "an inverse Lenny Bruce, whose shame existed to be displayed as pride" (121). The notion that DeGeneres's *pride* (with all of the meanings attached to that word) exists to be *displayed* as shame, as the case may be, is a savvy way to view beneath her linguistic skirts. If skirting is DeGeneres's verbal strategy for, at least on the surface, distancing her comedy from the bodily, from *her body* and the material consequences of the world, while leaking other meanings, DeGeneres's physical displays, especially her dances, convey and rely on utter embodiment: the body engaged in ritual.

INTERPRETIVE DANCE

. . . . Ellen's choice to deflect or redirect the question of her homosexuality in potentially heterosexual discursive terms on her talk show is one strategy to remove herself from the confessional paradigm, wherein an implied authority outside of herself (like the voice in Ellen Morgan's elevator), "the one who listens" (in the case of her show, the audience), is the implied judge or cheerleader of her private life. Instead, Ellen *performs* her daily dances—illustrating both her control over what is expressed and her pleasure in expressing it. Here Ellen presents her queerness, individuality, difference, otherness, in an expressive act that broadcasts her self-love, and as part of a daily ritual that is ultimately not all about her. Her daily dance also becomes a boundary-crossing ritual shared with all, where she encourages others (her studio audience and viewers at home) to join her—to get up and dance *themselves*. For Ellen, dancing

with oneself becomes dancing with the watching world, fulfilling the wish of the final refrain of the 1980s Billy Idol tune, "Dancing With Myself": "If I had a chance, I'd ask the world to dance." Dancing with oneself on television *presents* a dance *of oneself* to be received, shared, and potentially reciprocated.

Opening the stand-up special *Ellen DeGeneres: The Beginning,* which first aired on cable channel HBO on July 23, 2000, Ellen briefly addresses her coming-out saga before performing a dance about the very subject (set to disco music that devolves into chants of "nah nah, nah nah, nah"). A comedy special such as this one, on a pay cable network such as HBO, offers DeGeneres a markedly less censored venue in which to express herself than on network television, daytime or prime time. In her introduction, Ellen offers an extremely telling speech that I end this chapter with, because I believe it not only introduces Ellen's specific dance performance that night, but frames both her discursive closet and her soon-to-be-daily dance as "out." Speaking her mind about what should now be said, or not said, about her sexuality, Ellen successfully encodes the media ritual of dancing, later to appear on *Ellen: The Ellen DeGeneres Show,* as a performance of queerness that expresses meaning where words have been found to fail:

> Since I made the decision to come out three years ago, my life has been very interesting . . . I knew that people would want me to talk about it. Some people may not want me to talk about it. So I went back and forth, trying to decide should I talk about it, should I not talk about it, and ultimately I decided: No, I don't want to talk about it. It's been talked about enough, what can I say? I feel it would be best expressed through interpretive dance.

NOTES

1. I use the word *televisibility* to refer to instances of visibility on television by queer subjects.

2. [Liminality refers to an in-between, or transitional, phase or state of consciousness. Ed.] . . .

3. *American Gladiators* (1989–1997, CBS) featured body builders competing against

contestants on an obstacle course. Nitro was a regular gladiator and sometime co-host on the sensationalistic game show. Featuring *American Gladiators* on *Ellen* obviously served as an ABC-CBS cross-promotion.

REFERENCES

Bociurkiw, Marusya. "It's Not About the Sex: Racialization and Queerness in *Ellen* and *The Ellen DeGeneres Show*." *Canadian Woman Studies* 24:2–3 (2005): 176–182.

Couldry, Nick. *Media Rituals: A Critical Approach*. London: Routledge, 2003.

Deeken, Aimee. "Syndies Score in February." *Mediaweek* March 14, 2005: 30.

DeGeneres, Ellen. *My Point . . . And I Do Have One*. New York: Bantam, 1996.

"*The Ellen DeGeneres Show*: About the Show." Warner Bros.com. December 31, 2006. http://ellen.warnerbros.com/showinfo/about.html.

Gross, Larry. *Up from Invisibility: Lesbians, Gay Men and the Media in America*. New York: Columbia University Press, 2001.

Halperin, David M. *Saint Foucault: Towards a Gay Hagiography*. New York: Oxford University Press, 1995.

Heffernan, Virginia. "The Perils of Pleasant, or Spacey, on Talk Shows." *New York Times,* September 16, 2003. E5

Hubert, Susan J. "What's Wrong with This Picture? The Politics of Ellen's Coming Out Party." *Journal of Popular Culture* 33:2 (1999): 31–37.

Kort, Michele. "Welcome Back to the L World." *The Advocate* February 1, 2005: 40–45.

———. "Portia Heart & Soul." *The Advocate,* September 13, 2005: 40–46.

Limon, John. *Stand-up Comedy in Theory, or, Abjection in America*. Durham and London: Duke University Press, 2000.

Lo, Malinda. "Does the L Word Represent? Viewer Reactions Vary on the Premiere Episode." *AfterEllen.com: Lesbian and Bisexual Women in Entertainment and the Media.* January 2004. May 3, 2006. http://www.afterellen.com/tv/thelword/reaction.html.

McCarthy, Anna. "Ellen: Making Queer Television History." *GLQ* 7:4 (2001): 593–620.

———. "Must-see Queer TV: History and Serial Form in Ellen." *Quality Popular Television: Cult TV, the Industry and Fans.* Ed. Mark Jancovich and James Lyons. London: BFI, 2003. 88–102.

Millman, Joyce. "The Sitcom that Dare Not Speak Its Name." *San Francisco Examiner* March 19, 1995: B1.

Schnuer, Jenna. "*The Ellen DeGeneres Show*: Upbeat Host Gains Fans, Feel-Good Marketers." *Advertising Age* May 16, 2005: S1.

Sconce, Jeffrey. "What If? Charting Television's New Textual Boundaries." *Television After TV: Essays on a Medium in Transition.* Eds. Lynn Spiegel and Jan Olsson. Durham: Duke University Press, 2004. 93–112.

Turner, Guinevere. "Lipstick Los Angeles." *OUT Traveler Magazine.* December 2004. http://www.thelwordonline.com/lipstick_LA.shtml

———. *Personal Interview with Candace Moore.* March 28, 2005.

Turner, Victor. *From Ritual to Theatre: The Human Seriousness of Play.* New York: PAJ Publications, 1982.

23

WHEN IN ROME
Heterosexism, Homophobia, and Sports Talk Radio
David Nylund

The Jim Rome Show reflects a growing cultural trend in the United States—sports talk radio. According to sportswriter Ashley Jude Collie (2001), Jim Rome is the "hippest, most controversial, and brutally honest voice" (p. 53) in mediated sports. In addition to his nationally syndicated radio program that airs on more than 200 stations, the 40-year-old hosts ESPN's *Rome Is Burning,* a weekly 1-hr television sports talk show (and his second show on ESPN). Rome began his radio career broadcasting University of California, Santa Barbara (UCSB), basketball games. After graduating from UCSB in 1986 and serving seven non-playing radio internships, Rome earned a local weekend job at XTRA in San Diego, a powerful 77,000-watt station. The "clever fashioning of a streetwise persona" (Mariscal, 1999), his raspy voice, staccato delivery, and fiercely independent opinions separated him from the talk radio crowd, and he soon moved into hosting a primetime radio show. Eventually, his popularity earned him a television spot on ESPN2, *Talk2,* a cable show that Rome hosted in the early 90s. The Noble Sports Network syndicated Rome's radio show in 1995, and Premiere Radio Networks acquired the rights to the show 1 year later. Rome also hosted Fox Sports Net's *The Last Word,* a sports talk television program that ran from 1997 to 2002.

However, despite the variety of venues in which he plays, it is the radio show's format that contributes to Rome's controversiality and popularity. Loyal callers, whom he calls "clones," phone in with their opinion (referred to as a "take") on what's happening in the world of sports. Rome listens intently and either "runs" the caller with a buzzer (meaning he disconnects the call) or he

allows them to finish their take and says, "rack 'em" (meaning he saves the call as an entry into the huge call-of-the-day contest). As opposed to other talk radio programs where there is some dialogical interaction between the caller and hosts, Rome and his callers do not engage in a back-and-forth interchange. The caller's comments are highly performative, full of insider language, and monological. Rome silently listens to the call and only comments when the caller is finished with his or her monologue or Rome disconnects the call. Rarely, if ever, does a caller disagree with Rome.[1] "Huge" calls are those that Rome considers good "smack" speech—his term for sports talk that is gloatful, uninhibited, and unbridled. According to Rome, only the strong survive in this 3-hr dose of smack and irreverence. Rome's in-group language and his unique interaction (or lack thereof) make his radio show distinctive. His "survival of the fittest" format is responsible for the show's reputation as sports version of hate-speech radio (Hodgson, 1999).

The Jim Rome Show epitomizes the growing trend of talk radio. Presented as a medium in which citizens/callers can freely "air their point of view," talk radio has become a very popular forum for large numbers of people to engage in debate about politics, religion, and sports. The media culture, with talk radio as a prominent discourse, plays a very powerful role in the constitution of everyday life, shaping our political values, gender ideologies, and supplying the material out of which people fashion their identities (Kellner, 1995). Hence, it is crucial for scholars to furnish critical commentary on talk radio; specifically, we should critique those radio texts that work to reinforce inequality.

From David Nylund, "When in Rome: Heterosexism, Homophobia, and Sports Talk Radio." *Journal of Sport and Social Issues* (2004), 28(2), 136–168. Reprinted with permission of SAGE Publications.

Talk radio formats, particularly political talk radio, exploded in the 1980s as a result of deregulation, corporatization of radio, and niche marketing (Cook, 2001).[2] Deregulation, which loosened mass-media ownership and content restrictions, renewed interest in radio as a capitalist investment and galvanized the eventual emergence of its two 1990s prominent showcase formats: hate radio talk shows and all-sports programming (Cook, 2001). By the late 1990s, there were more than 4,000 talk shows on 1,200 stations (Goldberg, 1998).[3] Sports talk radio formats have, according to cultural studies scholar Jorge Mariscal (1999), "spread like an unchecked virus" (p. 111). Currently, there are more than 250 all-sports stations in the United States (Ghosh, 1999).

As a result of deregulation and global capitalism, new media conglomerates emerged as the only qualified buyers of radio programming.[4] Infinity Broadcasting, the largest U.S. company devoted exclusively to owning and operating radio stations, owns WFAN[5] and Sacramento's local all-sports station, 1140 AM. Its competing company, Premiere Radio Network, owns the popular nationally syndicated programs hosted by Howard Stern, Rush Limbaugh, Dr. Laura, and Jim Rome. . . . Talk radio is aimed at a very desirable demographic: White middle-class men between the ages of 24 and 55 years. Research shows that talk-radio listeners are overwhelmingly men who tend to vote Republican (Armstrong & Rubin, 1989; Hutchby, 1996; Page & Tannenbaum, 1996). The most popular program, the *Rush Limbaugh Show,* has 20 million daily listeners who laugh along with the host as he rants and vents, opening a channel for the performance of the angry White male. . . . Douglas (2002) argued that although most of the research on talk radio is on the threat it poses to democracy, what is obvious, but far less discussed, is talk radio's central role in restoring masculine hegemony:

> Talk radio is as much—maybe even more— about gender politics at the end of the century than it is about party politics. There were different masculinities enacted on the radio, from Howard Stern to Rush Limbaugh, but they were all about challenging and overthrowing, if possible, the most revolutionary of social movements, feminism. The men's movement of the 1980s found its outlet—and that was talk radio. (Douglas, 2002, p. 485)

Similarly, sports talk radio, according to Goldberg (1998), enacts its White hegemony via hypermasculine posing, forceful opinions, and loudmouth shouting. Sports talk radio "pontificates, moralizes, politicizes, commercializes, and commodifies—as it entertains" (p. 213). Although Rome's masculine style is different from Limbaugh's and Stern's, all three controversial hosts have built reputations through their rambunctious, masculinist, and combative styles (Farred, 2000). With White male masculinity being challenged and decentered by feminism, affirmative action, gay and lesbian movements, and other groups' quest for social equality, sports talk shows, similar to talk radio in general, have become an attractive venue for embattled White men seeking recreational repose and a nostalgic return to a prefeminist ideal (Farred, 2000).

This chapter offers a critical analysis of the most prominent sports talk-radio program, *The Jim Rome Show.* My study does not critique and dissect *The Jim Rome Show* in isolation from other media texts or discourses about sports; rather, I aim to provide a historicized and contextualized study based in cultural studies methodology. I show how *The Jim Rome Show* is situated within a broader set of social, gender, racial, political, economic, and cultural forces. In particular, I examine the ways in which the show reinforces and (less obviously) calls into question heterosexism as well as what gender scholars call hegemonic masculinity. . . .

As a casual listener to *The Jim Rome Show* over the past 3 years, I have noticed themes of misogyny, violence, and heterosexual dominance appear to recur with considerable frequency. Rome's persona embodies an aggressive masculinity with unassailable expertise and authority. This aggressive persona climaxed in 1994 on the set of Rome's ESPN show *Talk 2* while interviewing NFL quarterback Jim Everett. During the interview, Everett knocked Rome off his chair after Rome taunted Everett by calling him "Chris" (i.e., female tennis star, Chris Evert), a veiled reference to the quarterback's reputed lack of toughness.

Rome's reference to Everett as "Chris" on the show was not the first time he had done so. In fact, Rome has used this term on Everett throughout the 1993 NFL season on his local radio show on XTRA 690 AM. This hypermasculine event increased Rome's fame and reputation among some of his audience as a host who "tells it like it is" even if it means insulting someone. However, many in the media criticized Rome's lack of professionalism and predicted the end of his career (Sports Illustrated Editors, 1994). Although Rome left ESPN2 soon after the Everett incident, his radio career slowly continued to grow to the prominence it now holds. Rome's reputation as intolerant and abusive continues to this day because his rapid-fire, masculinist-laden opinion on sports provoked OutSports.com—a Web site that caters to gay and lesbian sports fans—to refer to him as "the commentator who makes a name for himself by saying stupid things with an obnoxious style, that for some reason, attracts many straight sports fans" (Buzinski, 2000, p. 5).[6]

As a cultural studies scholar and committed sports fan, I am compelled to study *The Jim Rome Show* to examine the sexism and homophobia present in the show. When in Rome, do the clones do as the Romans do? This question led me to conduct a textual analysis that identifies those features that appear to reinforce or promote homophobia and sexism. I also researched audiences in various sports bars in the United States to achieve a better understanding of what *The Jim Rome Show* means to listeners. I was particularly curious whether certain audience members resist the dominant, hegemonic, textual themes. . . .

HEGEMONIC THEMES

My analysis of the text confirms that much of the discourse on the show contains themes of misogyny, violence, and heterosexual dominance including themes that reinforced sexism and lesbian baiting. The following examples highlight these instances.

The first is from an infamous program dated July 23. On this date, Rome was commenting on the breaking story that several professional male athletes (Patrick Ewing, Terrell Davis, and Dekembe Motumbo) had testified in an Atlanta court that they regularly attended a strip club (The Gold Club) and engaged in sex acts with some of the club's dancers.[7] This tabloidlike story was a great opportunity for Rome to engage in his sardonic "smack" talk. Here are Rome's acerbic comments on Patrick Ewing's admission that he received free oral sex at the Gold Club:

Want some free oral sex Patrick [Ewing]? Nah, I'm good. Maybe next time! Come on! He said he'd been there 10 times. He said he had free oral sex 2 times. And by the way, who's going to say "no" to free oral sex? I mean, clones, would you like some free oral sex? Who's going to say no to that [laughing]? Most athletes go to a club or restaurant and get comped some free drinks, chicken wings. . . . not Patrick, he gets comped free oral sex.

[later in his monologue] Meanwhile, a former stripper testified. And it's a good thing. We finally have some good testimony. She testified that she performed sex acts or witnessed other dancers perform sex acts on celebrities including Terrell Davis and Dekembe Motumbo. So in response to the proverbial question, "who wants to sex Motumbo?" The answer obviously is whichever skank's turn it is at the Gold Club.

In this section of the transcript, Rome employs a very common, taken-for-granted discourse—"the heterosexual male sexual drive discourse" (Hare-Mustin, 1994). This dominant ideology is predicated on the notion that women are objects (Rome misogynistically refers to the dancers as "skanks") who arouse men's heterosexual urges, which are assumed to be "natural and compelling" (Hare-Mustin, 1994, p. 24). Accordingly, men cannot control their primitive sexual yearnings, and women are blamed for inflaming them. This assumption, reproduced by Rome's rhetorical question, "who is going to turn down 'free' oral sex," reinforces women's subjugation as they become defined as existing solely for men's pleasure.

Rome's language takes on homophobic tones later in the same program. In this excerpt, Rome ridicules a former dancer's testimony:

Finally we are getting somewhere. I thought Ewing's testifying of getting "hummers" was going to be the best that the trial had to offer. Thankfully, it's not in fact, not even close! After Patrick was done humiliating himself, one of the hookers got on the stand. That's when it really got good. A former dancer at the club starting naming names! This is just the beginning. This "tramp" also testified that she went back to the hotel room of a former wrestling executive, to perform sex acts, not on him, but on his wife! Now, we are getting somewhere. Sex with athletes; lesbian sex acts with the wives of executives. That's what I was hoping for from the beginning! And this tramp also added that she and another dancer performed a lesbian sex show for Ewing and some friends before he was given free oral sex by other dancers. And perhaps the most amazing thing, this tramp that ratted everybody out, is now working at a day care center in Georgia. Wonderful. Who wouldn't want to leave their kids with a woman who used to be a hooker? There's no one I would trust my kids with more than a woman who used to perform lesbian sex shows for NBA centers and had sex with wrestling executives' wives. What a perfect person to have around children! Man, I can't wait to see what happens today in the trial. I wonder who else's life will be ruined today?

Many of the callers on the September 9 program also reproduced male hegemony during their takes. Here is the call of the day:

Dan: [Contemptuously] I feel sorry for those skanks. I mean Ewing, Motumbo![8] Hopefully, the dancers got time and a half! I guess America has finally found a job worse than Assistant Crack Whore. About the only thing good to come out of this sordid mess is that Motumbo finally found a bar where his pickup line works.

Rome: [Laughing] Good job Dan!

Rome and his production staff chose this take as the call of the day, and in doing so, they support offensive, masculinist humor.[9] Dan's behavior reflects a common social practice for many men—the desire to earn the homosocial approval of other, more powerful men such as Jim Rome. Rome has power over the discourse and decides that Dan's wit gives him the right to enter the homosocial space of male privilege. Yes, Dan attempts to hold the players accountable for their behavior. However, the underlying tone of Dan's comments—"crack whore" and "skanks"—are racialized and sexist.

Rome's comments on athletes receiving oral sex at a strip club references the Clinton/Lewinsky affair and the increasing media focus on sex scandals in the lives of public figures. Although the "tabloidization" of the media has many negative consequences, Lumby (2001) posited that it is not completely destructive. In fact, the increased media attention on private sexuality is because

of, in part, the "feminist project of politicizing the private sphere and its attendant issues, such as sexual harassment, domestic violence, and child care" (p. 234). "Bad" tabloid style press may actually stem from some "good" political motives that have focused on issues that were once seen as merely personal. Yet the media focus on Clinton and Rome's focus on athletes at the Gold Club elides a feminist analysis of structures of power (Clinton with an intern or famous athletes with female sex workers). Hence, the entertainment value of sex scandals undermines the feminist goal of politicizing the private and reinforces "patriarchal sexuality morality: a proscription of sexual behavior outside the bounds of heterosexual monogamous marriage and the violation of that proscription by powerful and privileged males" (Jakobsen, 2001, p. 307).

ENTERTAINMENT AND MALE HEGEMONY

How do fans themselves make sense of and respond to Rome's problematic masculinist commentary? Not surprisingly, many of the fans I spoke to found it humorous; "It's entertaining" was the most common response. In fact, 2 days after Rome's acerbic comments about the incidents at the Gold Club, the topic came up with George (all the names of my research participants have been changed to preserve anonymity), a 27-year-old White male, in a sports bar in Sacramento. While inquiring about what he finds appealing about Rome, he replied,

> I listen every day. He tells like it is. He lets it rip. He doesn't hold back. I like that! And he's entertaining! He pokes fun at people like the other day when Rome went off about the Ewing (Gold Club incident). It's funny! It reminds me of locker room humor. Yes, I get a kick out of his smack talk. It's pure entertainment. Like when he trashes NASCAR and the WNBA.

His friend, John (a 26-year-old White male), echoed similar sentiments:

> Yeah, Rome is hilarious. I thought it was hilarious when he called Jim Everett, "Chris." That's what sticks in my head when someone says something about Rome. He's kind of like the Rush Limbaugh or Howard Stern of sports

talk radio. Like he thinks he's God. But I don't mind it because he's entertaining. And it's a way for him to get the ratings and the market share. I admire that because I am a stockbroker. You need to market yourself to stand out. You need to be aggressive and controversial to be successful in today's society. The show makes men cocky—like the clones. I listen to it for the entertainment. And he does know his sports.

Such comments are fairly representative of the participants that I interviewed. Many men valorize Rome's "transnational business masculinity," a term coined by Council (2000) to describe egocentrism, conditional loyalties, and a commitment to capital accumulation. In addition, as stated above, many participants found the program pleasurable because Rome is knowledgeable, authoritative, and comedic. Implied here is the notion that listening to Rome is a natural as well as an innocent pleasure. One person, when asked about the so-called harmlessness of the program, said, "If you don't like it, turn the radio dial. No one is forcing you to listen. It's just entertainment!" This is a common response to critiques of the negative effects of media culture and audience pleasure. Yet amusement is neither innate nor harmless. Pleasure is learned and closely connected to power and knowledge (Foucault, 1980). As media scholar Douglas Kellner (1995) observed,

> We learn what to enjoy and what we should avoid. We learn when to laugh and when to cheer. A system of power and privilege thus conditions our pleasures so that we seek certain socially sanctioned pleasures and avoid others. Some people learn to laugh at racist jokes and others learn to feel pleasure at the brutal use of violence. (p. 39)

The media industry, therefore, often mobilizes pleasure around conservative ideologies that have oppressive effects on women, homosexuals, and people of color. The ideologies of hegemonic masculinity, assembled in the form of pleasure and humor, are what many of my participants found most enjoyable about *The Jim Rome Show,* including Rome's aggressive, masculinist, "expert" speech that ridicules others. Thus, many of the pleasurable aspects of the program may encourage certain male listeners to identify with the features of traditional masculinity.

CALLING *THE ROME SHOW*: HOMOSOCIALITY AND APPROVAL

I was also interested in what listeners of the program thought of callers' comments and if they had ever called the program themselves. Many enjoyed listening to callers such as Dan and found their commentary to constitute comical moments of the show. I was particularly interested in what calling in to the show might mean for men who subscribe to traditional masculinity. One of the main aspects of traditional masculine homosociality involves men's striving and competing for prestige and approval within their peer groups (Wenner, 1998). This striving provides the basis for an affiliation. Many people I interviewed stated that the ultimate compliment would be for Jim Rome to approve of their take if they called. To have your call "racked" by the leading sports media personality would be a revered honor. What's more, from within the terms of hegemonic masculinity, having one's call rejected may signify a "failure" of masculinity. The following dialogue occurred between me and Fred (a 44-year-old Black male):

David: Have you called the program before?

Fred: No, I never have called. I thought about calling but I would hate to get run [Rome disconnecting the call]. Man that would hurt! I sometimes think, "Man, I could give a good take . . . but if I call and "suck" . . . you know . . . get run, start stuttering . . . man that would be embarrassing.

David: What would be embarrassing about getting run?

Fred: It's embarrassing 'cause it's Jim Rome. He's the man [laughing]! He's the pimp in the box![10] Man, if you get racked and are the caller of the day, you're the man!

. . . When asked why *The Jim Rome Show* and other sports talk radio programs are so popular among heterosexual men, about one half of the men told me that they feel anxious and uncertain because of the changes in men's work and women's increasing presence in the public sphere. Moreover, several participants believed that sports talk provides a safe haven for men to bond and reaffirm their essential masculinity. Here's what a 27-year-old White male said in a bar in Tampa:

> It's [*The Jim Rome Show*] a male bonding thing, a locker room for guys in the radio. You can't do it at work, everything's PC (politically correct) now! So the Rome Show is a last refuge for men to bond and be men. It's just in your car, Rome, and it's the audience that you can't see. I listen in the car and can let that maleness come out. I know it's offensive sometimes to gays and women . . . you know . . . when men bond . . . but men need that! Romey's show gives me the opportunity to talk to other guy friends about something we share in common. And my dad listens to Romey also. So my dad and I bond also.

This comment is telling about the mixed effects of sports talk. On one hand, sports talk radio allows men to express a "covert intimacy"[11] (Messner, 1992) and shared meaning about a common subject matter. This bonding can bring forth genuine moments of closeness and should not necessarily be pathologized or seen as completely negative. However, much of the bonding is, as the interviewee stated, "offensive sometimes to gays and women." Many of the men I interviewed were speaking in a group context in the presence of other male peers. The gender displays (sexist and homophobic jokes, for example) by the men I interviewed in the homosocial space of a sports bar were interesting to observe as they confirmed Messner's (2002) point that men in groups define and solidify their boundaries through aggressive misogynistic and homophobic speech and actions. Underneath this bonding experience are homoerotic feelings that must be warded off and neutralized through joking, yelling, cursing, and demonizing anybody who does not conform to normative masculinity. Pronger (1990) argued the arena of sports is paradoxical: on one hand, sports is a primary site for the expression of heterosexual masculinity, and on the other hand, there is a powerful homoerotic undercurrent subliminally present in sports. Sports radio operates similarly as an extension of this paradoxically homosocial and homoerotic space. Shields (1999), in his analysis of sports radio, stated, "It would be impossible to overstate the degree to which sports talk radio is shadowed by the homosexual panic implicit in

the fact that it consists almost entirely of a bunch of out-of-shape White men sitting around talking about Black men's buff bodies" (p. 50). . . .

COUNTERHEGEMONIC THEMES

As the above analysis illuminates, *The Jim Rome Show* reinforces male hegemony. However, a close reading of the show reveals some contradiction and fissures to hegemony. The following transcripts of the program exemplify times when the text and its voices (Jim Rome, audience members) partially subvert hegemonic masculinity and homophobia. The first example is from the show dated April 30 when the topic of bigotry was raised by Rome. Here, Rome, in his belligerent vocal style, is taking issue with the homophobic comments made by Chicago Cubs pitcher, Julian Tavarez, about San Francisco Giants fans:

> Julian Tavarez, a pitcher for the Cubs said this about San Francisco Giants fans— his words not mine—"they are a bunch of a-holes and faggots". . . . You know, it would be nice to go a week without some racist or bigot comment . . . but no, Julian. Nice job Julian. . . . And here's a thought, Julian Rocker [reference to John Rocker, a pitcher who became famous for making racist and homophobic comments during an interview in *Sports Illustrated*], just because San Francisco has a significant gay population, I would be willing to bet that not everybody at a Giants game is a homosexual. Maybe. Can't document that. Just a thought . . . I feel pretty secure in saying that? How do you come up with this garbage? I mean how do you get to the point where the proper response to heckling fans is to drop racist, anti-Semitic, or homophobic bombs on people? And even if you had those bigoted views, you would have the sense to keep it [to] yourselves. They might realize that not everybody hates everybody else. I think there is only one solution to this problem of overcrowding in the racist frat house. We are going to have to have honorary members.

In this instance, the host clearly positions himself as antiracist and antihomophobic. This stance is noteworthy and a possible contradiction to dominant sports talk discourse. Rome uses his masculine authority to stand against the intolerance often engendered by homophobia.

Rome's comments on the subject appear to be progressive and reasonable.[12] On closer examination, however, Rome's location of the problem of homophobia in a few bigoted, intolerant individuals leaves unchallenged the larger societal structures that perpetuate heterosexism. The stance taken up by the host is rooted within liberal discourse, which reduces analysis to an individual, private endeavor (Kane & Lenskyj, 2000; Kitzinger, 1987) and forecloses any serious discussion of homophobia as structural and political issues related to power, gender, and sexuality. When Rome denounces a few athletes as "bigots," it prevents a wider analysis of the link between the institution of organized sports and its heterosexual, masculinist, and homophobic agenda. Addressing the thorny questions of sexuality, politics, power, and privilege would be a risky and bold move for *The Jim Rome Show,* as it would offer a more radical challenge to the institution of heterosexual privilege and sports.

The next seemingly subversive segment relates to an editorial letter in the May 2001 issue of *Out* magazine. In that issue, the editor in chief, Brendan Lemon, stated that his boyfriend was a Major League baseball player. Lemon did not give names, but hinted that the player was from an East Coast franchise. Rome and other mainstream media programs reacted quickly to the editorial. A media firestorm resulted in a rumor mill: Players, fans, owners, and sports talk radio hosts swapped guesses and anxieties over the athlete's identity.

On May 18, Rome's monologue pondered the questions. What would happen if that person's identity became public? What would it mean for baseball, gays, and lesbians in sports in general, and for the man himself? Given that Lemon's boyfriend would be the first athlete in one of the "big four" major league team sports (baseball, football, basketball, and hockey) to come out "during" his career, what effect would this have on the institution of sport? Rome decided to pose this question to one of his interview participants that day, well-respected baseball veteran Eric Davis.

Rome: What would happen if a teammate of yours, or any baseball player, would come out of the closet and say, "I am gay"? What would the reaction be like? How badly would that go?

Eric: I think it would go real bad. I think people would jump to form an opinion because everybody has an opinion about gays already. But I think it would be a very difficult situation because with us showering with each other . . . being around each other as men. Now, you're in the shower with a guy who's gay . . . looking at you . . . maybe making a pass. That's an uncomfortable situation. In society, they have never really accepted it. They want to come out. And if that's the case, fine, but in sports, it would definitely raise some eyebrows. . . . I don't think it should be thrown at 25 guys saying, "yeah I am gay."

[Rome changes the subject . . . no follow-up]

Rome asks a pointed question to Davis whose predictable homophobic response warrants more follow-up questions. Yet Rome shifts the subject to something less problematic, letting Davis off the hook. After Rome ends the interview, he addresses Davis's comments in another monologue:

That's [Eric Davis] a 17-year respected major league ballplayer. And I think that's a representative comment of a lot of these guys. . . . He is [a] very highly regarded guy. This is why I asked him the question. And he answered it very honestly. He would be concerned about having gay teammate. . . . For instance, when he's showering. Personally, I don't agree with the take. It's my personal opinion. However, I posed the question to see what the reaction would be. And this is what I have been saying since this story broke. This is why it would not be a good thing. This is why the editor of that magazine clearly was wrong and has never been in a locker-room or clubhouse. That's why it hasn't happened. Eric Davis' reaction is what you would expect. Not everybody would feel that way, but a large majority would. It would make it nearly impossible for a gay player to come out.

Here, Rome is aware of the difficulties that would occur for an openly gay ballplayer. However, he shares his opinion in the safety of his "expert" monologue, not in the presence of Eric Davis. He does not risk compromising his masculinity or his relationship with Davis by endorsing this unusually progressive stance in the presence of a famous ballplayer such as Davis. However, when a listener calls immediately after the Davis interview, Rome responds differently:

Joe: I never imagined my first take would be on gays but I had to call. Being gay, it matters to no one but gays themselves. Why don't you guys, girls or gays . . . whatever you guys are. Just do us a favor, do yourselves a favor and keep it to yourselves. I mean . . . [Rome runs the caller with the buzzer and disconnects the call]

Rome: I think that's a very convenient response— "It's an issue only because you make it an issue." I don't agree with that, frankly. It's an issue because they are often persecuted against, harassed, assaulted, or killed in some cases. That's why it is an issue. They are fired from jobs, ostracized. It's not only an issue because they are making it an issue. What you are saying is keep your mouth shut, keep it in the closet; you are not accepting them for who they are and what they are. It's not an issue because they are making it an issue. It's an issue because of people saying things like, "keep your mouth shut. . . . We don't want you around. . . . We don't want to know you people exist." That's why it's an issue because of that treatment.

Again, Rome takes a strong stance against homophobia and demonstrates a fairly nuanced appreciation of the injustices of homophobia and heterosexism. This position is worth mentioning, particularly in the context of a program referred to as "The Jungle," with an audience of mostly men steeped in traditional masculinity and for whom heterosexuality is the unquestioned norm. Rome's antihomophobic stance represents a fissure in hegemonic masculinity. It can potentially foster a new awareness in Rome's listeners and invite new voices into this important conversation about masculinity and sexuality, potentially spurring a rethinking of masculinity and sports. Cutting off the first-time caller because of his homophobic comment could be viewed as a productive accountable maneuver, which is notable because straight men do not have a rich history of holding

other straight men responsible for homophobic slurs.[13]

The historic May 18 radio show generated further substantive discussion on the issue of sports and heterosexual dominance in various media sites. This included a two-part show on Jim Rome's Fox TV show, *The Last Word,* titled "The Gay Athlete." The show's guests included two out athletes: Diana Nyad and Billy Bean. The show's discussion was very rich, with the host asking fairly nuanced and enlightened questions. Since this show, Rome has interviewed other athletes who have come out since they left professional sports, including football players, Esera Tuaolo and David Kopay. In these interviews, Rome asked perceptive questions about the prevalence of homophobia in male sports and applauded their courage in coming out. ESPN also addressed the same topic and conducted a poll that showed that a substantial number of sports fans would have no problem with a gay athlete (*Outside the Lines,* 2001). What's more, the *Advocate* magazine published an article by cultural critic Toby Miller (2001) where he argued that the media firestorm generated by Brendan Lemon's article could potentially create a moment "for unions and owners of the big four to issue a joint statement in support, to show that queers are a legitimate part of the big leagues" (p. 3). . . .

It is important to note that Rome's interviewing of out athletes such as Billy Bean and David Kopay is a unique outcome in the world of heteronormative sports. To allow visibility of the gay athletes cannot be taken lightly in terms of its potential ramifications. Yet it is equally important to ask which athletes are allowed to become visible? What is their social location? How is their sexuality represented? Virtually all the gay athletes who have been on *The Jim Rome Show* are White males (an exception is Esera Tuaolo who is Samoan) who define homosexuality as an essentialist identity. Foucault (1980) contended that although visibility opens up some new political possibilities, it is also "a trap" because it creates new forms of surveillance, discipline, and limits. Sure, Bean and Kopay are given space to discuss their experience as a gay athlete, however it must be contained within a very limited, private discourse. Scholar Lisa Duggan (2001) claimed that much of the recent visibility of gays and lesbians is framed within a post-Stonewall, identitarian, private discourse. She referred to this discourse as homonormativity—"a politics that does not contest dominant heteronormative assumptions and institutions, but upholds and sustains them, while promising the possibility of a demobilized gay constituency and a privatized, depoliticized gay culture anchored in domesticity and consumption" (p. 179). According to Duggan, homonormativity is privatizing, much as heteronormativity is, and each lends support to the other. As much as

Rome's recognition of gays in the sporting world is noteworthy, it is very much contained with a homonormative frame that reproduces the sex and gender binary. Hence, Rome's show, although it may be influenced by traditional gay and lesbian identity polities, is not a queer space. Athletes, including women who perform a more transgressive, non-normative sexuality, are invisible in sports radio. . . .

NOTES

1. Rome's relationship with his caller, similar to most talk-show power relations between caller and host, is quite asymmetrical. Hutchby (1996) in his study of the discourse in talk radio stated that although the host has an array of discursive and institutional strategies available to him or her to keep the upper hand, occasionally callers have some resources available to resist the host's powerful strategies. Hence, Hutchby argued that power is not a monolithic feature of talk radio. Hutchby's argument does not appear to work with *The Jim Rome Show* as callers hardly ever confront Rome's authority. Rather, Rome's callers want his approval.

2. Deregulation was championed by then FCC chairman Mark Fowler who sold it as a form of media populism and civic participation. However, this public marketing campaign masked increased economic consolidation and increased barriers to entry into this market for all but very powerful media conglomerates such as Infinity Broadcasting and Premiere Radio. Commenting about the success of conservative White male talk radio due to deregulation of the 1980s, Douglas (2002) claimed that Reaganism was successful by "selling the increased concentration of wealth as move back toward democracy" (p. 491).

3. In 1960, there were just two radio stations in the United States that were dedicated to talk radio formats (Goldberg, 1998).

4. The other significant deregulatory move in the 1980s was the abandonment of the Fairness Doctrine, which the FCC announced it would no longer enforce. The doctrine required stations to offer access to air alternative opinions when controversial issues were discussed. The goal of the doctrine was to promote a balance of views. Opponents of the doctrine, including Fowler and Reagan, felt it inhibited freedom of speech. Stations, they argued, avoided giving airtime to opinionated individuals because of the requirement to broadcast competing points of view. Unrestricted by the Fairness Doctrine's mandate for balance, Limbaugh and a legion of ultraconservative imitators took off the gloves and revived the financial state of AM radio.

5. The largest sports station in the United States, based in New York, WFAN is also the largest ad-billing radio station in the United States.

6. In a recent interview in *Sports Illustrated,* Rome stated he regrets the Everett interview and has matured into a well-reasoned interviewer. In the article, Rome stated that he was "wiser" because of being married and having a child (Deitsch, 2003).

7. The court in Atlanta was prosecuting the owner of the Gold Club for mob connections and other illegalities. This event received a great deal of media attention.

8. Ewing and Motumbo are Black men. The caller of the day, Dan, is implying that they are unattractive men. Dan's disdainful "smack talk" could be understood to reproduce racist representations of Black athletes.

9. As a sidebar, Cook (2001) challenged the common notion that radio talk shows are a natural two-way dialogue between the caller and host that allow the caller to "freely air their point of view" (p. 62). The production

process reveals that it is a complex, mediated process that constrains the dialogue through a range of in-studio control techniques. These hidden maneuvers include off-air talk decisions on what gets included on the program, what gets omitted, and time control cues. Cook argued that examining the complex relational politics in radio talk is important to examine to contest its negative power and influence.

10. The term *pimp in the box* refers to Rome's "pimping" of NHL hockey in Los Angeles during 1992–1993 when the Los Angeles Kings made it to the Stanley Cup Finals. Rome's show was the first in Los Angeles to actively talk about hockey on sports talk stations and book hockey players as guests. This made national news as Wayne Gretzky was to appear on the show following every playoff game the Kings played that season to the point where Gretzky thanked Rome during a televised interview after the Kings won Game 7 of the Western Conference Finals to advance to the finals. After thanking Kings management and players he said, "To my friend Jim Rome, we've got the karma going."

11. Messner (1992) defined "covert intimacy" as doing things together rather than mutual talk about inner lives.

12. When I refer to Rome in this section, I am referring not to Rome, the individual person. Rather, I am referring to Rome's discourse.

13. However, it is important to note that Rome asserts his authority over a person with less power—a first-time caller. Rome doesn't take this strong a stance with Eric Davis, a high-status person who likely has more influence within the sports world. This textual example reveals the power relations of talk radio; hosts and famous athletes have more authority than callers.

REFERENCES

Armstrong, C. B., & Rubin, A. M. (1989). Talk radio as interpersonal communication. *Journal of Communication, 39*(2), 84–93.

Buzinski, J. (2000, July 13). *Week in review*. Available at www.outsports.com

Buzinski, J. (2001, May 20). *Give the media good marks: Coverage of closeted gay baseball player was positive and non-judgmental*. Available at www.outsports.com

Collie, A. J. (2001, August 8). Rome rants. *American Way*, pp. 50–54, 56–57.

Connell, R. W. (2000). *The men and the boys*. Berkeley: University of California Press.

Cook, J. (2001). Dangerously radioactive: The plural vocalities of radio talk. In C. Lee & C. Poynton (Eds.), *Culture and text: Discourse and methodology in social research and cultural studies* (pp. 59–80). New York: Rowman & Littlefield.

Deitsch, R. (2003, May 12). Under review: Rome returning. *Sports Illustrated, 98,* 28.

Douglas, S. J. (2002). Letting the boys be boys: Talk radio, male hysteria, and political discourse in the 1980s. In M. Hilmes & J. Loviglio (Eds.), *Radio reader: Essays in the cultural history of radio* (pp. 485–504). New York: Routledge.

Duggan, L. (2001). The new homonormativity: The sexual politics of neoliberalism. In R. Castronovo & D. D. Nelson (Eds.), *Materalizing democracy: Toward a revitalized cultural politics* (pp. 175–194). Durham, NC: Duke University Press.

Farred, G. (2000). Cool as the other side of the pillow: How ESPN's *Sportscenter* has changed television sports talk. *Journal of Sport & Social Issues, 24*(2), 96–117.

Foucault, M. (1980). *Power/knowledge: Selected interviews and other writings, 1972–1977* (Colin Gordon, Ed. & Trans.). New York: Pantheon.

Ghosh, C. (1999, February 22). A guy thing: Radio sports talk shows. *Forbes,* p. 55.

Goldberg, D. T. (1998). Call and response: Sports, talk radio, and the death of democracy. *Journal of Sport & Social Issues, 22*(2), 212–223.

Hare-Mustin, R. T. (1994). Discourses in the mirrored room: A postmodern analysis of therapy. *Family Process, 33,* 19–35.

Hodgson, E. (1999, August 18). King of smack. *Fastbreak—The Magazine of the Phoenix Suns,* pp. 1–5.

Hutchby, I. (1996). *Confrontation talk: Arguments, asymmetries, and power on talk radio.* Mahwah, NJ: Lawrence Erlbaum.

Jakobsen, J. K. (2001). He has wronged America and women: Clinton's sexual conservatism. In L. Berlant & L. Duggan (Eds.), *Our Monica, ourselves: The Clinton affair and the national interest* (pp. 291–314). New York: New York University Press.

Kane, M. J., & Lenskyj, H. J. (2000). Media treatment of female athletes: Issues of gender and sexualities. In L. W. Wenner (Ed.), *Mediasport* (pp. 186–201). New York: Routledge.

Kellner, D. (1995). *Media culture: Cultural studies, identity, and politics between the modern and postmodern.* New York: Routledge.

Kimmel, M. (1994). Masculinity as homophobia. In H. Brod & M. Kaufman (Eds.), *Theorizing masculinities* (pp. 119–141). Thousand Oaks, CA: Sage.

Kitzinger, C. (1987). *The social construction of lesbianism.* Newbury Park, CA: Sage.

Lumby, C. (2001). The President's penis: Entertaining sex and power. In L. Berlant & L. Duggan (Eds.), *Our Monica, ourselves: The Clinton affair and the national interest* (pp. 225–236). New York: New York University Press.

Mariscal, J. (1999). Chicanos and Latinos in the jungle of sports talk radio. *Journal of Sport & Social Issues, 23*(1), 111–117.

Messner, M. A. (1992). *Power at play: Sports and the problem of masculinity.* Boston: Beacon.

Messner, M. A. (2002). *Taking the field: Women, men, and sports.* Minneapolis: University of Minnesota Press.

Miller, T. (2001, June). Out at the ballgame. *Advocate,* pp. 1–3.

Outside the lines: Homophobia and sports. (2001, May 31). ESPN.com. Available at http://espn.go.com/otl

Page, B. I., & Tannenbaum, J. (1996). Populistic deliberation and talk radio. *Journal of Communication, 46*(2), 33–53.

Pronger, B. (1990). *The arena of masculinity: Sports, homosexuality, and the meaning of sex.* New York: St. Martin's.

Shields, D. (1999). *Black planet: Facing race during an NBA season.* New York: Crown.

Sports Illustrated Editors. (1994, April). The fall of Rome. *Sports Illustrated, 80,* 14.

Wenner, L. W. (1998). The sports bar: Masculinity, alcohol, sports, and the mediation of public space. In G. Rail & J. Harvey (Eds.), *Sports and postmodern times: Gender, sexuality, the body, and sport* (pp. 301–322). Albany: State University of New York Press.

PLAYING "REDNECK"

24

White Masculinity and Working-Class Performance on Duck Dynasty

Shannon E. M. O'Sullivan

INTRODUCTION

Playing redneck has become a popular trope in A&E's reality television program, *Duck Dynasty,* the highest-rated nonfiction series in cable television history; peaking with a record audience of 11.8 million viewers for its season four premiere in August 2013 (Cohen). . . . The series centers on the wealthy Robertson family of West Monroe, Louisiana. Despite their economic largesse, the male members of the clan in particular, loudly proclaim their "redneck" credentials. They are devoted to hunting and fishing, wearing camouflage, and sport long, unkempt beards with lengthy, unruly hair to match. Headed by their patriarch Phil, who originally made his millions by establishing Duck Commander—a family business that manufactures duck calls for hunters—the program documents their lifestyle (Magary).

Each episode across the show's nine seasons replicates a highly formulaic trajectory. The Robertson men are often depicted outdoors either hunting or fishing, and the Robertson women typically appear in the home performing domestic duties, particularly cooking. At times, traditional gender roles are hyperbolically enforced. Phil frequently makes remarks regarding who in the family is appropriately behaving in accordance with redneck standards and who is deviating in a "yuppie" fashion. Each episode ends with Phil leading a Christian prayer as the whole family enjoys dinner together, while Willie, Phil's son and CEO of Duck Commander, recaps the lesson of the episode in narrative form.

One of the core themes of the show is that not only do the family members—especially Phil—habitually invoke their redneck identities but they also frequently assert their superiority in relation to so-called "yuppies." Although the term "yuppies" commonly refers to young (white) urban professionals, Phil applies the term generously to anyone who does not embrace his lifestyle of hunting and fishing. The show discursively configures rednecks as authentically masculine and yuppies as feminine, which therefore implies the superiority of the former over the latter in this patriarchal context.

After controversy arose following a revelation of Phil's homophobic and racist comments in late 2013, the family's starkly contrasting appearances before the reality show also resurfaced in the popular media (Walton). Through a series of widely publicized photographs, it emerged that the Robertson men had fully embraced so-called "yuppie" appearances before their careers on A&E (Luzer). The popularity of *Duck Dynasty* raises critical questions about social class in the United States, particularly in terms of how social class is embodied and performed. Judith Butler's work on gender performativity can illuminate the Robertsons' performance of a redneck lifestyle, which they display despite their comparatively large economic capital. Pierre Bourdieu's theorizing of class and its relationship with various forms of capital (economic, social, cultural, and symbolic) also aids in understanding the complexity of class as a social category. The theoretical framework of intersectionality, which views social categories as intersecting and mutually constitutive, further elucidates the complex relationship among social class, whiteness, and hegemonic masculinity as illustrated on *Duck Dynasty.*

David McKillop, general manager and executive vice president of A&E, sums up the appeal of

From O'Sullivan, S.E.M. (2016). Playing "Redneck": White masculinity and working-class performance on *Duck Dynasty. The Journal of Popular Culture, (49)*2. Reprinted with permission of John Wiley & Sons.

the Robertson family: "The Robertsons represent a lot of things we as Americans cherish: self-made wealth, independence, three generations living together" (Cohen). Given the show's record ratings, A&E has tapped into salient aspects of US culture, which, despite the controversy over Phil's remarks, remain remarkably high for cable television (Kissell). The Robertson family has also generated $400 million in sales from *Duck Dynasty* merchandise—establishing the Louisiana clan as a highly marketable brand (Boorstin). Narratives of rugged individualism and upward social mobility remain hegemonic, especially in the current neoliberal discourse and in reality television by extension (Skeggs and Wood 2–3). It is not surprising then that the family's rags-to-riches story has broad-based appeal in the United States.

Typical A&E viewers are comparatively affluent, with nearly two-thirds falling within the coveted 18–54 age demographic ("Network Demographics: A&E"). To solicit advertisers, networks desire such audiences with higher disposable income. According to National Media, a Republican ad-buying firm, the typical *Duck Dynasty* viewer resides in Southern and/or rural areas that characteristically lean Republican (Geraghty). The Robertsons' performance of a "redneck" lifestyle, including each episode ending with a family dinner where Phil leads a Christian prayer, provides the perfect imagery for the politically conservative side of the so-called "culture wars" in the United States (Douthat). Not unexpectedly, then, the show's core viewership seems primarily confined to the Republican red states.

PLAYING "REDNECK"

Duck Dynasty perfectly captures the inherent tension of social class operating simultaneously as both a socioeconomic category and as a lifestyle orientation in mainstream US discourse. These dual conceptions are not necessarily mutually exclusive, but in the case of the Robertsons, their comparative wealth indicates that their identity as rednecks resides in their self-conscious performance of a particular lifestyle.

As Michael Zweig notes in *The Working-Class Majority,* social class is not solely about income, but about power and autonomy in the workplace and society at large (4). For example, adjunct professors may have more freedom and flexibility over their work than construction workers, even though adjunct professors likely make considerably less money. In this instance, construction workers would typically be coded as working class, and adjunct professors as middle class—albeit there remains room for debate here . . . .

Bourdieu's conception of capital is highly pertinent for analyzing social class on *Duck Dynasty.* He characterizes the various forms of capital an individual can acquire as the following: "economic capital (money and property), cultural capital (cultural goods and services including educational credentials), social capital (acquaintances and networks), and symbolic capital (legitimation)" (Swartz 74). Phil Robertson not only has a comparatively large amount of economic capital but he also has the cultural capital of a master's degree in education (Strauss). Furthermore, Phil's prominence as a successful business owner and reality television star affords him a significant degree of social capital. One could deduce that Phil and the other male Robertsons adopted their current appearances in order to attain the symbolic capital that the "redneck" image confers in the United States . . . the appearances and consumption practices associated with white, rural, working-class men hold tremendous symbolic power as markers of masculine authenticity. Based on Bourdieu's understanding of social class, the Robertson family possesses far too many forms of capital to be truly considered "rednecks"—at least in the socioeconomic sense.

With Bourdieu's configuration of social class in mind, one can then analytically juxtapose the perceptions of the redneck identity as both a working-class designation and as a particular lifestyle orientation—both marked by white, rural masculinity. The latter conceptualization of redneck is of particular interest in a neoliberal discourse that deemphasizes class consciousness. Charles Reagan Wilson describes the contemporary, neoliberal characterization of a redneck in the mainstream discourse: "The Southern working-class version of redneck is becoming the national version, and it's good-natured, it has humor, and in some ways, it's a *performance* [emphasis added]" (qtd. in Watts 5).

Playing "redneck" can be further understood through Judith Butler's work on gender performance, in which Butler treats gender as an embodied social construction that one always already "does" or "performs." Helen Wood and Beverly Skeggs also theoretically ground their understanding of class performativity using Butler's framework: "Perform*atives* are unconscious repeated gendered and classed enactments, while performances are full-blown conscious actions. What we often see on reality television is the performative made explicit" (17). In the case of *Duck Dynasty,* however, the Robertsons seem to be performing as redneck in a way that is entirely self-conscious and calculated.

To further illustrate the relevance of class performativity to the analysis of reality television more broadly, Vicki Mayer explains how her experience in the industry illuminates the importance of understanding social categories in relation to how they are performed: "My experience with the reality casting process revealed its emphasis on embodied performances. Casters search not only for people within certain demographics but also for those who act appropriately to the demographic" (189). Reality television programs typically seek out those who embody certain class-based characteristics that reflect their actual socioeconomic status; thus, the Robertsons presenting as rednecks despite their economic largesse becomes all the more incongruous. Another central irony of class performativity on reality television is that these performances are separated from the wider reality of structural inequality. . . . Hence, the Robertsons are presented as ordinary *individuals* who embody a particular set of characteristics coded as redneck, in accordance with the dominant neoliberal paradigm.

In the collection of photographs that reemerged following Phil's controversial remarks, the Robertsons can be seen on the beach and on the golf course, embodying stereotypical yuppie appearances, before their careers on A&E (Luzer). The Robertson men look clean-shaven with short haircuts, as they pose wearing khakis and button-down shirts. These images sharply contrast with their trademark long beards, hair, and camouflage. These photos of course prompted several mainstream media commentators to decry the Robertsons as "fake" (Lowry). Critics drew parallels between the drag show, as a site of gender performance, and the Robertsons' redneck performance, as is evidenced in a headline from the Daily Kos: "Duck Dynasty is a Fake Yuppies-in-Red-Neck-Drag Con Job" (Walton).

As Drew Magary notes in the now infamous *GQ* profile on Phil, *Duck Dynasty*'s $400-million merchandising empire includes an iPhone game, which according to the press release, describes the goal of the game as follows: "'As players successfully complete the challenges, their beards grow to epic proportions and they start to transform from a yuppie into a full-blown redneck!'" (qtd. in Magary). The irony of the game's description in relation to the Robertson men's real-life transformation from yuppies to rednecks is comical. As Daniel Luzer effectively summarizes regarding the photographs in *Washington Monthly,*

> Indeed, Jep and Phil (who has a master's degree in education from Louisiana Tech University) might think of themselves as rednecks. And they surely enjoy hunting and fishing. But if ol' frosted tipped, barefoot on the beach Willie is a redneck, I don't know what a real southern gentleman even is. A&E appears to have taken a large clan of affluent, college-educated, mildly conservative, country club Republicans, common across the nicer suburbs of the old south, and repackaged them as the Beverly Hillbillies.

It is apparent that A&E recognized the potential profitability of marketing the family as a redneck brand. Therefore, the Robertson men perform in redneck drag for the cameras. They embrace this performance as a chance to be perceived as authentically masculine on a national stage. As per the rhetoric surrounding the recent popular explosion of blue-collar and redneck reality television series more broadly (Lloyd), *Duck Dynasty* is not intended to be about social class, but about rugged individualism, white rural masculinity, and perceived authenticity.

REALITY TELEVISION'S LOVE AFFAIR WITH "REAL MEN"

Duck Dynasty is part of a recent proliferation of reality television programs that document blue-collar and redneck lifestyles, including *Deadliest Catch, Ice Road Truckers, Ax Men, Gold Rush, Swamp Loggers, Hillbilly Handfishin',* and *Mountain Men.* Robert Lloyd points out the central irony that despite these programs centering on working-class subjects, that social class is not intended to be essential to the narrative: "Blue collars and rednecks aside, these series are not really about class. A little financial struggle is good for the narrative. . . . but by and large these are not people operating on the margins." Lloyd's review reflects a hegemonic reading of programs featuring working-class subjects in the United States: Signifiers of social class and structural inequalities are reduced to secondary plot devices, in which the myth of the classless society, rugged individualism, and the potential for upward social mobility is preserved.

Duck Dynasty is a peculiar standout among these programs given the family's considerable wealth. Although they are occasionally filmed on the job in the Duck Commander warehouse, unlike the protagonists in other blue-collar reality series, the Robertsons are a family that has already "arrived." Either way, social class's lack of centrality in this subgenre of reality television is not only ironic, but also remarkably consistent with mainstream US discourse, in which individualism is continually emphasized at the expense of class consciousness (Skeggs and Wood 1–3). The predominance of narratives that ignore economic barriers to upward social mobility are particularly damaging as the effects of the global economic recession endure, and US workers face continued economic and political marginalization in the neoliberal era. Wood and Skeggs contextualize the role reality television plays in reifying the naturalization of class inequality: " . . . we think it is important to discuss television's intervention in class formations, particularly at a time when political rhetoric is diverting the blame for structural inequality onto personal, individualised failure" (2). Therefore, if the Robertsons were able to make it, then there is no excuse for all those who fail to achieve upward economic mobility.

Despite *Duck Dynasty* deviating from the formula of the other blue-collar reality programs in terms of the absence of both economic struggle and the threat of bodily injury from a dangerous occupation, the show still shares certain characteristics with its counterparts that are highly illustrative of US culture. In the public consciousness, the term "working class" itself is often associated with white, blue-collar males, despite both deindustrialization and the demographic diversity of working-class experience. As Zweig explains in *The Working Class Majority,* "Identifying the

working class with factories may foster the notion that the 'working class' means men, or even just white men. Think again: less than half of the working class labor forces, about 46 percent, are white men" (31).

Although the factory itself is not a site featured on the blue-collar reality shows, the association between white masculinity and working-class life remains. It is also crucial to historicize the diversity of the US working class, in that women and people of color were excluded from the "labor aristocracy" as a result of the intersecting systems of oppression of sexism and racism (Arnold 6–7). The location of the union-organized factory whose workers were largely white and male became the dominant signifier of the term "working class," whereas women and people of color engaged in migrant and domestic work were not identified in the mainstream discourse as such (Glenn). The multiracial and gendered realities of working-class life need greater illumination both historically and into the present.

These programs situate their "stars" as hardworking *individuals* who embody white male, working-class aesthetics. In "Masculinity and Authenticity: Reality TV's Real Men," Christopher Lockett notes the perceived connection between rugged individualism, masculinity, and authenticity:

> That this idealization of working-class masculinity takes place by way of reality television speaks to its preoccupation with an authentic masculinity, one best accessed unalloyed and unmediated. We should not however be surprised that the men portrayed in these series are familiar, as they possess the same attraction as a Clint Eastwood or John Wayne character, and indeed trade on the same frontier mythos that informs the Western as a popular genre.

The Robertson men and all other white men who embody blue-collar or redneck aesthetics are then considered the "real men" of the United States. Thus, redneck performativity confers a perceived legitimacy and symbolic power. Lockett noticeably omits the centrality of these subjects' whiteness, which is a vital component of what constitutes the show's imagery of "real men." This oversight reflects how whiteness is rarely specified as a noteworthy racial identity in mainstream US discourse, since it is hegemonically configured as the norm.

As Daniel Luzer's article in *Washington Monthly* indicates, A&E is self-consciously promoting the men of *Duck Dynasty* as the archetype of "real" or "authentic" men: "But the ZZ top bearded, camo-wearing mountain men, this fusion of 'Cajun redneck culture and Ozark redneck culture' is [*sic*] entertainment industry idea of what real America looks like." Lockett echoes a similar sentiment and ties the emergence and popularity of this brand of reality television to Sarah Palin's discourse about "real America" during her 2008 vice presidential campaign. Palin was one of the few prominent politicians who publicly came to Phil Robertson's defense on her Twitter account when A&E temporarily suspended him from production for his homophobic and racist comments (Stampler).

This imagined notion of "real America" does not typically include the white urban working class, but specifically pertains to those white men who reside in rural areas and live a life on the former frontier. Although the frontier is a social construction of the US cultural imaginary, as per Frederick Jackson Turner's "frontier thesis," it remains an integral backdrop to hegemonic constructions of white masculinity and perceived authenticity, particularly on the blue-collar reality shows (Lockett). Campbell, Bell, and Finney succinctly capture the interconnectivity concerning white, rural masculinity, and cultural legitimacy both politically and economically:

> But there will be no blush on President George Bush's face as he faces the cameras at the next photo opportunity at his Crawford, Texas ranch. Wearing his boots and Stetson, posing with his horses, leaning on the rail of his cattle yards, clearing brush, and striding out across his land, Bush uses the imagery of rural life to portray not just a persona of authority and control but a *masculine* persona of authority and control. . . . Real men don't drink lattes. They drink beer, smoke Marlboros, and ride their SUVs through mud and up mountains. . . . *Real men are rural men* [emphasis added]: this cultural idea wields not only enormous political power but enormous economic power. (102)

The authors illustrate the relationship among hegemonic perceptions of authentic masculinity,

lifestyle/consumption practices, and geographic location—all of which collectively interact and result in the suppression of the identification of these characteristics as overt signifiers of social class. Furthermore, they explicate the ways in which whiteness and maleness have become normalized to the extent that there is a remarkable lack of awareness of these social categories as racial and gendered constructions, respectively (8). Hence, the implicit promotion of the Robertsons as representing "real America." The term "real America" is highly revealing in terms of the discourse that underpins white male supremacy.

One of the most ironic tropes within the blue-collar reality genre is that despite these programs centering on working-class subjects, their experiences are narrowly framed as examples of "rugged individualism" and "tests of manhood," as opposed to emphasizing the common struggles of the working class in the neoliberal era. In the case of *Duck Dynasty,* their occupation of running the family business is not explicitly articulated as such, but their recreational/lifestyle activities, primarily hunting and fishing, are situated as assertions of masculinity and individuality. . . .

Interestingly, the Robertson men primarily emphasize their masculinity through their rural dress and outdoor leisure activities rather than their wealth. This suggests that the Robertsons downplay their economic capital in favor of portraying an authentically masculine redneck image. In addition, they also want to distance themselves from the feminized yuppie identity, which implies an accumulation of wealth and upward social mobility. Their objection resides not in the accumulation of wealth unto itself, but in adopting the lifestyle orientation commonly associated with it. Considering the salience of narratives of upward mobility in the United States, it seems *Duck Dynasty* promotes the possibility of upward economic mobility only to the extent that one's "authentic" masculinity remains intact. Thus, the Robertson men shed the yuppie appearances they had embraced, and ironically attempt to distance themselves from it by denouncing it, especially Phil, through their on-camera performances. *Duck Dynasty* encapsulates the fraught conceptions of social class as both a socioeconomic category and cultural sensibility—both with significant racial and gendered dimensions.

Multiple masculinities exist in society, which are specific to hierarchies of race, class, sexual orientation, and place (Campbell, Bell, and Finney 8). The boundaries that constitute hegemonic masculinity in the United States are clearly demarcated along lines of race (whiteness), region (rural/South), and a relatively subordinate, vaguely working-class identity that masquerades as rugged individualism. Hegemonic masculinity—a concept originally conceived by R. W. Connell in 1987—is described in *Country Boys* as "the version of masculinity that is considered legitimate, 'natural,' or unquestionable in a particular set of gender relations" (10). Rural or "redneck" masculinity is then considered the most authentic in current mainstream US discourse because it is commonly associated with "real men." Prominent political figures, such as former President George W. Bush, publicly embracing an image of rural masculinity reveals the extent of its perceived legitimacy: "Rural occupational and general 'country boy' representations are often appropriated by individuals for self-serving political and commercial purposes. Like the banners of God and flag, rural 'salt-of-the-earth' occupations confer widespread legitimacy" (Campbell, Bell, and Finney 269). Because of the Robertson men's transformation, they sought to perform redneck identities for popular appeal and commercial benefit. Therefore, *Duck Dynasty* is a critical site of analysis for exploring how white, rural masculinity has become hegemonic.

"PHIL'S WAY OF LIFE" AND "REDNECK LOGIC"

The word redneck is widely documented as having its roots as a derogatory term uttered by aristocratic whites in reference to white male rural laborers in the American South, particularly Mississippi, in the late nineteenth century (Huber and Drowne 434–35). Despite its negative connotation, the term seems to have gone mainstream in recent years (Watts 4–5). Edward W. Morris succinctly encapsulates the parameters of the term in his ethnographic study of a rural school: "The term 'redneck' is a well-known popular culture identity that implies being blue-collar, rebellious, and southern. On a more tacit level, 'redneck' also strongly represents masculinity and whiteness. . . . This identity is unabashedly white, but opposed to middle- and upper-class whiteness" (741). Morris explicates the interconnectivity of race and gender within social class in terms of white masculinity

being essential to the redneck identity, as is demonstrated in *Duck Dynasty*. He further explains the resurgence of the term in the rural location of his study, as a result of the subjects there investing more in their whiteness and masculinity because of their comparative economic marginalization:

> Uses of the term 'redneck' captured a sense of pride embedded in living in this 'rough,' white working-class, rural location. Through the implication of toughness and opposition to elitist sophistication, this regional category offered a classed and raced template consistent with local hegemonic masculinity. (742)

Phil Robertson's continual usage of the word redneck is almost always in relation to his criticism of yuppies (young urban professionals or young upwardly mobile professionals). Phil uses the terms redneck and yuppie in a context that does not overtly signify class; he uses them as expressions that represent two divergent and gendered lifestyle orientations. It seems the redneck versus yuppie dichotomy in many ways mirrors the gender binary. The redneck lifestyle is constructed as authentically masculine, while the yuppie lifestyle is situated as feminine and inauthentic, and therefore, subordinate. According to Phil throughout the series, yuppies are not "real men" because they live in urban/suburban areas, have professional occupations, wear formal attire, and do not hunt or fish.

This central theme in *Duck Dynasty* is encapsulated in the compilation clip entitled "Yuppies" from the first season (2012). The clip summarizes Phil's characterizations of whom he identifies as a yuppie. It not only includes Phil's comments but also his son Jep and Jep's spouse Jessica's opinions about what being a yuppie means:

Phil [to his grandson]: Don't marry some yuppie girl . . . find you a kind-spirited country girl . . . if she knows how to cook. . . . now there's a woman.

Jep: A dude that's clean-shaved, that's wearing like a shirt and tie, oh he's a yuppie . . . pretty much anybody that doesn't spend time in the woods, that's a yuppie.

Jessica: City people that, you know, don't generally know anything about hunting or live that lifestyle.

Tellingly, Phil's conception of the ideal woman is heavily tied to traditional domestic duties, such as cooking. This suggests by logical extension that so-called yuppie women do not fulfill these roles adequately. Again, the identification of the term yuppie as a category of social class is subsumed by rhetoric that characterizes it solely as a lifestyle orientation tied to geographic location. Although Phil and the others do not state it explicitly here, it is implied that men are typically the ones who fish and hunt, while women remain in the kitchen. Throughout the series, the men and women of *Duck Dynasty* strictly adhere to these ascribed gender roles, including Phil's wife Miss Kay. These roles are only occasionally transgressed, such as when Phil takes his granddaughters fishing in season four's second episode, "So You Think You Can Date?"

In the context of *Duck Dynasty,* rednecks and yuppies are defined in relation to one another. In the compilation clip "Phil's Way of Life" from the first season (2012), it is clear that Phil articulates the differentiation between these two categories in highly gendered terms. For example, he reiterates the importance of women being able to cook, and refers to men that cook as "girlie men." This clip also captures his condemnation of technology as something "real men" do not rely on. He then comically asserts his opinion regarding the connection between masculine sexual prowess and hunting: "If you catch squirrels for your woman, your woman will never cut you off in bed." Although the terms redneck and yuppie are not specifically mentioned in this clip, their signifiers remain present. The yuppies versus rednecks—us versus them—binary is one of the show's most salient aspects.

Season one's fifth episode, "Redneck Logic," centers on the Robertson men trudging through the Louisiana swamp with their rifles, blowing up old duck blinds, and then rebuilding them for their future hunting expeditions. Although Phil is reluctant to be rid of an old duck blind, his son Willie offers the following observation: "Let me tell you a little bit about redneck logic: If you wanna take something away from him, just blow it up, because then he's gonna be so enamored by the fire that he'll forget all about what he's losing." The connectivity between redneck identity and hegemonic masculinity is overt. As per Willie's commentary, rednecks are assumed male,

anti-intellectual, and easily transfixed by activities and displays that are coded in the popular discourse as authentically masculine.

After one of the old duck blinds is spectacularly lit aflame, Phil returns to his home where his wife, Miss Kay, can be seen cooking dinner. Phil informs Miss Kay about having used explosives to demolish the duck blind: "Willie—he's the one that concocted that scheme. A Redneck stunt if I ever seen one." Interestingly, this scene segues to Miss Kay commenting on how the family upholds traditional gender roles: "It's never dull being married to a Robertson. Never. It's just like you know, 'I'm the man, you're the woman.' . . . We're like in the cave, but not really, we're in modern times." Although Miss Kay does not appear to contest the Robertson men's preference for traditional gender roles, she recognizes the dynamic as antiquated. Again, policing traditional gender roles is a common current that runs through the series.

Later in the episode, the Robertson men decide to assemble a new duck blind out of an old recreational vehicle. Phil hurls a possum from the RV at Willie, causing him to amusingly run and fall to the ground. Phil remarks about Willie's reaction: "What would happen if you threw a possum on a man? Married a yuppie girl, living in a subdivision. That's what happens to you—a possum will scare you." Phil feminizes Willie by claiming that he married a "yuppie girl," and therefore, yuppies are presumed feminine and associated with cowardice. The terms redneck and yuppie are deployed in a highly gendered context that naturalizes (white) masculine dominance. The class dimensions of these expressions remain obscured.

Another highly illuminating moment is when the Robertson men hire a whole crew to build the new duck blind. Willie then comments about their economic largesse: "Being a wealthy redneck does have its advantages, 'cause no matter how dumb an idea is, we can always hire an entire redneck army to make sure the job gets done." The idea of a "wealthy redneck" may seem incongruous, but as per its usage in neoliberal discourse, redneck now signifies a white, rural masculine lifestyle. The specific class implications of redneck are becoming sublimated by its association with hegemonic masculinity. Again, the Robertson men embrace redneck performativity because of the legitimacy and symbolic power it confers in the US cultural context.

CONCLUSION

Duck Dynasty propagates the notion that the redneck identity is a self-styled lifestyle orientation exemplified through the embodied performance of white, rural, working-class masculinity. It strengthens the hegemony of the intersecting social categories that comprise the redneck identity, respectively, at the expense of class consciousness, since the show divorces the term redneck from its working-class associations and the reality of structural economic inequality. In short, the most popular reality television program on US cable television to date promotes the dominant myth that the United States is a classless society, in which there are no structural barriers to upward social mobility. It also reinforces the prevailing perception that white, rural, heteronormative men are "real men." Thus, it promotes white, heteronormative male supremacy. The fact that the Robertson men had to play redneck in order to be viewed as authentically masculine speaks to the power and perceived legitimacy of white, rural, working-class masculinity in mainstream US culture.

Duck Dynasty is a particularly rich site of analysis for understanding the complex obfuscation of social class in mainstream US discourse. It reveals how race and gender are inextricably linked to class formations, and further illuminates how these social categories can be deployed to obscure concurrent class identifications. The complexity and diversity of working-class experience in the United States is not reflected in much of the mainstream media landscape, including reality television. Not only are white, male working-class subjects overrepresented, they are not marked in the mainstream discourse as raced and gendered identities. The normalization of maleness and whiteness contributes to these working-class subjects being constructed as neutral individuals, which lends itself to hegemonic narratives of rugged individualism, the suppression of class consciousness, and the maintenance of white male supremacy. In the case of *Duck Dynasty,* these wealthy white males self-consciously perform a redneck identity in order to find legitimacy, broad-based appeal, and commercial success. This popular program speaks volumes about hegemonic understandings of race, gender, and social class in the contemporary US neoliberal context.

REFERENCES

Arnold, Kathleen R. *America's New Working Class: Race, Gender, and Ethnicity in a Biopolitical Age.* University Park: Pennsylvania State UP, 2008. Print.

Boorstin, Julia. "As 'Duck Dynasty' Returns to TV, Merchandisers Cash In." CNBC.com. CNBC, 15 Jan. 2014. Web. 11 Mar. 2015.

Bourdieu, Pierre. "What Makes Social Class: On the Theoretical and Practical Existence of Groups." *Berkeley Journal of Sociology* 32 (1987): 1–17. Web.

Butler, Judith. "Performative Acts and Gender Constitution: An Essay in Phenomenology and Feminist Theory." *Theatre Journal* 40.4 (1988): 519–31. Print.

———. *Gender Trouble: Feminism and the Subversion of Identity.* New York: Routledge, 1990. Print.

Campbell, Hugh, Michael Bell, and Margaret Finney. *Country Boys: Masculinity and Rural Life.* University Park: Pennsylvania State UP, 2006. Print.

Cohen, Noam. "'Duck Dynasty' Season Opens to Record Ratings." NYTimes.com. *The New York Times,* 15 Aug. 2013. Web. 11 Mar. 2015.

Connell, Raewyn. *Gender and Power: Society, the Person, and Sexual Politics.* Stanford, CA: Stanford UP, 1987. Print.

Douthat, Ross. "The Persistence of the Culture War." NYTimes.com. *The New York Times,* 7 Feb. 2012. Web. 11 Mar. 2015.

Geraghty, Jim. "The Huge, GOP-Leaning Audience for 'Duck Dynasty.'" National Review Online. *National Review,* 23 Aug. 2013. Web. 11 Mar. 2015.

Glenn, Evelyn Nakano. *Unequal Freedom: How Race and Gender Shaped American Citizenship and Labor.* Cambridge, MA: Harvard UP, 2002. Print.

Huber, Patrick, and Kathleen Drowne. "Redneck: A New Discovery." *American Speech* 76.4 (2001): 434. Communication & Mass Media Complete. Web. 3 Mar. 2015.

Kissell, Rick. "A&E's 'Duck Dynasty" Opens Season 6 with More Declines." Variety.com. Penske Business Media, 12 June 2014. Web. 11 Mar. 2015.

Lloyd, Robert. "Blue-collar, Redneck Reality Series Surging." E.standard.net. *Standard-Examiner,* 4 Dec. 2011. Web. 11 Mar. 2015.

Lockett, Christopher. "Masculinity and Authenticity: Reality TV's Real Men." *Flow* 13.1 (2010): n. p. 15 Oct. 2010. Web. 11 Mar. 2015.

Lowry, Brian. "Dear 'Duck Dynasty' Fans: You Do Know It's All Fake, Right?" Variety.com. Penske Business Media, 20 Dec. 2013. Web. 11 Mar. 2015.

Luzer, Daniel. "Duck Decoy: How the Entertainment Industry Made the Duck Dynasty Family into Rednecks." Washingtonmonthly.com. *Washington Monthly,* 9 Jan. 2014. Web. 11 Mar. 2015.

Magary, Drew. "What the Duck?" GQ. *Conde Nast,* Jan. 2014. Web. 11 Mar. 2015.

Mayer, Vicki. (2011). "Reality Television's 'Classrooms': Knowing, Showing and Telling about Social Class in Reality Casting and the College Classroom." *Reality Television and Class.* Ed. Helen Wood and Beverly Skeggs. London: Palgrave Macmillan, 2011. 185–96. Print.

Morris, Edward W. "'Rednecks,' 'Rutters,' and 'Rithmetic: Social Class, Masculinity, and Schooling in a Rural Context." *Gender & Society* 22.6 (2008): 728–51. Web.

National TV Spots. "Network Demographics: A&E." Web. 10 Mar. 2015.

"Phil's Way of Life." Online video clip. A&Etv.com. A&E. Web. 11 Mar. 2015.

"Season 1, Episode 5: Redneck Logic." *Duck Dynasty.* A&E. 4 Apr.

"Season 4: Episode 2: So You Think You Can Date?" *Duck Dynasty.* A&E. 21 Aug. 2013. Television.

Skeggs, Beverly, and Helen Wood. "Introduction: Real Class." *Reality Television and Class.* Ed. Helen Wood and Beverly Skeggs. London: Palgrave Macmillan, 2011. 1–29. Print.

Stampler, Laura. "Sarah Palin Defends *Duck Dynasty* Star Suspended for Anti-Gay Remarks." Time.com. Time Inc., 19 Dec. 2013. Web. 11 Mar. 2015.

Strauss, Valerie. "'Duck Dynasty's' Phil Robertson Is a Former Teacher with a Master's Degree." WashingtonPost.com. Nash Holdings, 20 Dec. 2013. Web. 11 Mar. 2015.

Swartz, David. *Culture & Power: The Sociology of Pierre Bourdieu.* Chicago: U of Chicago P, 1997. Print.

Walton, Vyan F. "Duck Dynasty Is a Fake Yuppies-in-Red-Neck-Drag Con Job." *Daily Kos.* Kos Media, 20 Dec. 2013. Web. 11 Mar. 2015.

Watts, Trent. "Introduction: Telling White Men's Stories." *White Masculinity in the Recent South.* Ed. Trent Watts. Baton Rouge: Louisiana State UP, 2008. 1–29. Print.

"Yuppies." Online video clip. A&Etv.com. A&E. Web. 11 Mar. 2015.

Zweig, Michael. *The Working-Class Majority: America's Best Kept Secret.* Ithaca: Cornell UP, 2000. Print.

BLACK WOMEN AND BLACK MEN IN HIP HOP MUSIC

25

Misogyny, Violence, and the Negotiation of (White-Owned) Space

Guillermo Rebollo-Gil and Amanda Moras

INTRODUCTION

For some, the problem is the vulgarity of the language or the crudeness of speech. For others, it is the violence in the lyrical content; the seemingly unavoidable nihilism that envelops many of the genre's stars. Many of us abhor the misogyny in the music and videos; the unabashed glorification of crime and the unrelenting objectification of black women. Yet a good number of us cannot help but purchase the albums and focus instead on the lyrical dexterity of the artists or on the potential for social and political critique present in the music. All in all, most every outsider to rap or Hip Hop music has an opinion about the seemingly troublesome character of the genre and rightly so. The complex history of the art form and its present international popularity and commercial success demands it of us. Hip Hop as a cultural and economic powerhouse invites a critical eye. It deserves our scrutiny.

Of particular importance are those aspects of the music that frequently appear in the midst of political debates and media hype. Often, these aspects are scrutinized not with the intent of acquiring greater and more nuanced understandings of the art form, but rather to further one political agenda or produce a nice sound bite. The misogyny in rap music is one such case. Often, the treatment of black women in Hip Hop is brought up only to highlight the alleged moral depravity of the artists or the wantonness of so-called Black ghetto culture rather than as a critical and necessary discussion of patriarchy and violence. It is used as yet another tool by which white American

critics and politicians further stigmatize the black male as violent and/or criminal. Consequently, these types of analyses offer no real critique of the misogyny in rap or possible mechanisms to combat it. Furthermore, the issue is often broached as if Hip Hop music existed in some type of social vacuum where the larger US racial and social structure had no bearing on the production and distribution of the musical product (hooks). Therefore, what are needed are analyses that look at the misogyny in rap within the greater social context the music is embedded in. Specifically, it would be wise to examine the place that black women and black men occupy in relation to one another within the genre as well as the place that the genre occupies in relation to white American culture. This article then explores the space afforded to both black women and men in Hip Hop music in an effort to unravel and examine the role that white centered structures play in the making and marketing of the music to the mass public.

RAP MUSIC: THE BASICS

The history of rap music embodies the complex character of a particular musical genre rooted in some of the most downtrodden urban communities in the East Coast of the United States. Rap originated in the late 1970s in the South Bronx during a time marked by extreme political conservatism and economic downfall (Rose, "Fear"). According to Rose, it began as an apolitical party music played in gatherings in public parks or in individual homes. Because it arose and developed,

From Rebollo-Gil, G. & Moras, A. (2012). Black women and black men in hip hop music: Mysogyny, violence, and the negotiation of (white-owned) space. *The Journal of Popular Culture, (45)*1. Reprinted with permission of John Wiley & Sons.

however, during such a time, the music garnered a high level of social significance within the communities that birthed it. Rap quickly became one of the premier forms of expression for the youngest members of the inner city black and Latino communities in New York, which were the hardest hit by the conservative politics and the economic decline during said epoch. Rap then, irrespective of its particular subject matter and stated purpose during its initial stages, must be viewed as an important socio-political innovation. It became one of the few social spaces where disenfranchised "minority" youth could assume and secure a public voice, and it served as vehicle through which members of these communities could express their angst and speak freely (Rose, "Fear"). The music has its roots here.

Rap's popularity and audience, however, grew considerably throughout the nineties (Ogbar), and the genre itself has expanded over time to make room for many technological, lyrical and thematic innovations. Even more telling of the genre's ever expansive reach has been its ability to cross national borders and mix and mesh with other musical styles and genres, reinventing itself in each setting to reflect the needs and desires of each community that practices it. Taking this into consideration, it would be ludicrous to reduce the music's lyrical content to sex and violence, and this would end up negating the potential for social critique and social action the music ultimately harbors. It is important, however, to note that a considerable portion of the rap music produced for radio and video airplay does contain obscene amounts of sexist talk and images. By the same token, not all rappers' references to violence serve to draw attention to the more tragic aspects of inner city life and many of these references are not actually critiques of said violence. On many occasions, sex and violence are present in rap songs solely because they sell.

The popularity of rap music has been both the cause and product of the music's increased commercialization. It seems like everything from candy and soda, to sneakers and vitamin water, to adult video and liquor advertisements feature the music, voice and/or presence of some of rap's most popular stars. This "Boom," however, is not all positive. According to Kitwana, when it comes to the mainstream and commercial portrayal of rap music and its stars, "often highlighted are those aspects of rap which . . . reinforce negative stereotypes about blacks" (24). These stereotypes include images of black males as angry, violent, and/or otherwise dangerous creatures that are manipulated simply to increase sales and have the end result of moving the music further away from its inner city origins.

Furthermore, although at first glance the high number of black-owned record labels would lead one to believe that the genre is mostly at the hands of African Americans, larger, white-owned corporations continue to control the music's distribution channels. This, according to Kitwana, "forces rap artists to come to terms with what is seen by corporate owned recording studios as currently marketable in order to secure any serious form of mass distribution" (23).

Considering that what has been and continues to be marketable is the image of the young, poor, foul-mouthed black male with a criminal or otherwise violent past offering consumers a sneak peek into "his life," we must question as to what degree is Hip Hop a reflection of gender relations and patriarchy within urban poor black communities? We push the reader to frame this question, however, within the same white dominated social structure Hip Hop is produced and marketed under. Recognizing how white racism informs and conceptualizes these relationships is necessary for critical analysis. The history of black sexualities, for example, includes larger systems of institutionalized rape, sexual exploitation, commodification, stereotypes, and the selling of fear and promiscuity as ideologies justifying racial apartheid. White fear and commodification of black sexuality has long been a major component of recreating a system of institutionalized racism (West). This treatment of black sexuality plays an integral role in the racist power hierarchy in America. By portraying African Americans as exotic, erotic, or oversexed, one decontextualizes their experience, marginalizes them, and removes the possibility of a self defined sexuality. It also obscures the metaphorical and physical rape of Women of Color: if they are always willing, they cannot be forced (Hill-Collins, *Black Sexual Politics*).

The "urgencies" of black communities must also be placed in this framework. The high incarceration rates of black men and supposed shortage of marriageable black men, leading to the construct of the ENDANGERED BLACKMAN (Hill-Collins, *Black Sexual Politics*), are also the results of high concentrations of poverty, police brutality, racial profiling, and heavy policing of black and/or poor neighborhoods and racist educational, occupational, and criminal justice systems. This crisis of black men has actual and severe effects on black communities. Hip Hop then exacerbates this image of criminality, at times even obscuring a criminal justice system that actively persecutes black men, by purporting a seemingly voluntary and lauded criminal identity. The overrepresentation of black men in the prison industrial system then appears to be the direct product of overly increasing black male criminality as opposed to a systematic and institutionalized system of white supremacy.

Furthermore, images of black women as domineering, freaks, bitches, mammies, and baby's mammas are reflective of this racist imagery. The rates of black female-headed households (in 2002 about 43% of black households were headed by single women) are targeted as the cause for the supposed "decline" of black families (Hill-Collins, *Black Sexual Politics*). Hip Hop music has an especially complex relationship with single mothers. On the one hand, the presentation of baby mamma drama and single mothers as "gold-diggers" is a misogynistic devaluation of black women, and obscures the actual challenges single mothers face in US society. On the other hand, Hip Hop music is not the cause of increased numbers of single mother households or the supposed disintegration of families.

"THE MUSIC'S IN CRISIS"

There is no doubt that Hip Hop sells. The genre, however, is in crisis. The growing acceptance and commercial appeal of this 30-year-old musical style and culture has led to the increased homogenization of the music and lyrics for the purposes of mass consumption. Hip Hop artists are also in crisis. Along with the recent catapulting of black rappers and producers to nationwide celebrity status is the targeting of these same musicians by the police and other law enforcement agencies across the country. The New York Police Department, for example, has even gone so far to establish a Hip Hop task force. This unit, according to Clark, "often works in tandem with FBI agents to monitor the activities of rappers" (130). Moreover,

Hip Hop music in general has been labeled by the media as gangster or criminal, prompting influential political and religious leaders to target and drive campaigns against specific artists through the years (Russell-Brown).

In her book *Underground Codes: Race, Crime and Related Fires,* Russell-Brown dedicates a chapter to examining the relationship between gangsta rap—a subgenre which emphasizes gun play, misogynistic beliefs, and makes constant references to criminal enterprises (Williams Crenshaw)—and crime. Here, Russell-Brown notes social science's inability to find a clear causal link between gangsta rap and crime: "There is a wide gulf between the dismissal of gangsta rap as a deviance-inducing art form and empirical data. The research simply does not support a direct link between listening to gangsta rap music and involvement in crime" (54). What Russell-Brown does find is an extreme abhorrence for this particular form of black cultural and artistic expression that has no parallel with any other form of white "deviant" music such as heavy metal. According to the author, this difference can be attributed to white America's conception of the black male as criminal or deviant, regardless of whether or not he is wearing baggy pants or has a microphone in his hand.

Consequently, contrary to mainstream white America's view of heavy metal, where a bunch of outlaws are trying to contaminate well-mannered and decent white teens, gangsta rap actively attracts and gathers an already young, black, male and therefore assumed to be criminal element (Rose, "Fear"). Thus, while it is true that this Hip Hop sub-genre is problematic and troubling as it pertains to its exponents' treatment of women, for example, the music and its artists are put under fire more for what they are perceived to be because of their race than on account of what they actually say or do. The censorship of the music then can be understood to be more a product of white racism than of hurtful or offensive rap speech given the various other places in mainstream US popular culture where misogyny is both tolerated and promoted.

In spite of this, some still may argue that rappers willingly attract this monitoring and censorship due to their blatant embracing of a criminal lifestyle both on and off the stage. Some of the most popular rap acts go by the names of former Mafia kingpins, actual and fictitious drug dealers, and even corrupt Latin American dictators. In Hip Hop, you find names like Nas Escobar, Scarface, Mussolini, Capone and Noreaga. You see music videos that are modeled after popular gangster films like *Casino* and *The Godfather* (Ogbar). Entire album concepts are based on drug deals gone bad (i.e., Reakwon's "Only Built for Cuban Links") or drug deals done well (i.e., Jay-Z's "Reasonable Doubt"). More telling, however, is the [large] number of rappers, past and present, who have either been arrested for suspected criminal activity, been linked to a criminal enterprise, or have been convicted of a particular offense. . . .

Hip Hop insiders point to a possible large-scale plan to target rap artists. They view Hip Hop culture as being under constant watch. In their minds, major media outlets, music-related businesses, and the criminal justice system are somehow colluding to either end Hip Hop music altogether or take African Americans completely out of it (Clark). Consequently, while the music is in fashion, its creators continue to be the focus of an unruly and unjustified surveillance. The establishment of specialized police units as well as the nationwide scrutiny placed into the culture's codes, language, and business practices by media analysts and politicians among others speak to the tragically unique position in which black American artists find themselves. They are both "larger than life and less than human at the same time" (Tate 4).

RAP AS TRUCULENT MALE SPEECH

Rap or Hip Hop music has always been feminine. Since its creation, black male rappers have expressed their love and devotion for the art form they practice in ways very much akin to the traditional manner in which heterosexual men attempt to woo heterosexual women (Pough). Rap records are filled with seemingly heart-felt and passionate tales of the way in which rap somehow "saved" and "rescued" black male rappers from difficult situations. Many artists boast about how rap has been the only constant in their life (it is people who fail). Consequently, men's ability to rap is always portrayed by them as pure. It is always great, always a God-send. It is what brings them fame, money, success (it is people who want to take it away). Therefore, rap is always to be valued and never to be misused or betrayed. The lives and fate of actual human beings, however, is another matter.

One of the most popular critiques leveled against rap music is that it is too violent. So-called gangsta rap has frequently been on the forefront of national debates concerning the amount of violence in the media and its effects on America's youth (Williams Crenshaw). Political pundits and television analysts have even gone so far as to pinpoint and blame individual rap stars for real life tragic events such as the shootings at Columbine. Artists and fans, on the other hand, defend the product they create and consume stating that "these are simply songs about reality and not reality itself" (Kitwana 53). More critical analysts, however, look past the controversy and acknowledge that while one particular musical form cannot be made responsible for the violence in America, indiscriminate talk about violence does in fact contribute to the creation of a social climate in which violence is viewed as acceptable (Kitwana, hooks, Russell-Brown).

The crisis in rap music right now is that due to gangsta rap's commercial success, elements of that subgenre have come to spread and define rap music as a whole. Thus, on the one hand, nearly all male rappers "trying to make it" market themselves as gangsters and on the other, the media tend to solely cover artists and events related to this one facet of rap (Kitwana). In the end, everything that has to do with rap is seen either as violent or gangster.

According to Kitwana, male rap artists glorify violence in three main contexts: as a symbol of macho power, as a cure-all for disputes between blacks, and as a necessity for individual protection (43). Popular rap songs are replete with black male bodies being riddled by bullets, plopping to the ground and dying. Individual male valor and honor often depend on the ability of the male speaker to quickly do away with his presumed (black) enemies without concern or regret. The fact is that in gangsta rap, African American men "are defined and assume the identity of losers, victims that enthusiastically achieve their role as statistics, killers void of spiritual centers, rapists and fighters only against black life and possibilities" (Kitwana 55). This subgenre has a very troubling and disturbing paradox at its center: the most potent and grandiose displays of black masculinity are only possible through the vicious, graphic and constant portrayal of black males' physical and spiritual demise. Interestingly enough, however, it is black women and black womanhood who are the most persecuted, attacked, and damaged by this music.

THE RAP ON WOMEN: THIS ONE GOES OUT TO ALL THE FREAKS OUT THERE

As noted, rap has always been feminine. What it has not been is pro-woman. Pough writes, "Hip Hop gendered as feminine has no agency. She is something men rappers love, something they do. She does not act; she is acted upon" (94). The fact is that much of black male rappers' energy is spent trying to either keep women quiet or getting them to shut up. The rest is spent trying to get them into bed or in some cases even condoning or bragging about sexual assault/rape which ultimately has the same silencing effect. Kitwana states, "As inanimate objects women have no opinions. In fact, a thinking woman who questions incites the physical violence of her male peers" (53). Journalist Nelson George offers further insight on this matter stating that, "there was and remains a homoerotic quality to hip hop culture . . . that makes women seem aside from sex, nonessential" (127). The problem then in Kitwana's eyes is not that black male artists frequently talk about sex, but rather, the problem lies in the "graphic, often crude, violent, self-hating, women-hating and anti-black, abusive sexual representations" (33) they refer to when exploring sexual themes. What is even more troubling is that there appears to be an enormous audience willingly consuming these images. This audience includes young black women. Pough writes, "both in the beginning and now, female hip hop heads are part of the crowds at shows and support rap by buying the music even when most of it is sexist and degrading to black womanhood" (9). It thus becomes important to consider the character of black women's involvement in the music. A crucial part of this analysis is determining whether or not black women have the space in rap to respond to the dominant male visions of their womanhood.

BLACK FEMALE RAPPER'S (MUTED) SPEECH

According to Rose, black women rappers' songs must be viewed "as part of a dialogic process with male rappers" (*Black Noise* 147). In her view, what's important is to visualize and analyze the way in which black female rappers work both within and against the dominant sexual and racial narratives in the genre. Before one can do that, however, it is necessary to address the sheer lack of black female rappers in the first place.

Common industry knowledge suggests that it takes much more than talent and good songs for an artist to sell records. It also takes money, employee hours, and aggressive marketing and public relation campaigns (Smith). Common industry knowledge also suggests that female rappers do not receive an equal or even comparable amount of financial support to that which male rappers receive (Smith). Consequently, not only are an individual female artist's chances for financial success dim, but one artist's lack of success seriously reduces the chances of other female rappers getting a record deal and having their work widely distributed. Thus, female artists' speech is actively being muted before their voice even makes it on a record.

Once on the record, black women's voices face even more and possibly greater difficulties. Their artistic persona—the way in which they choose to present and market themselves—is fraught with contradictions. Smith writes, "a girl rapper has to be soft but hard; sweet but serious; sexy but respectable; strong but kind of weak; smart but not too loud about it . . . a hip hop girl, like a regular girl, has got to mix her own ingredients carefully" (127). Furthermore, when it comes to the actual content of their songs, "women's lyrics are often still viewed by men and women themselves as not valid . . . women's versions of reality are somehow suspect" (Smith 126). Thus, for the most part, label executives, artists, producers, and listeners alike seem to overwhelmingly favor men's versions of reality. Consequently, they give more credence and validity to men's tales and portrayals of black womanhood than to those that black women generate on their own. The few female artists who do manage to get their voice heard through national and international channels and whose lyrical skills are respected within the industry constantly have to disprove rumors about their sexuality. Smith makes it crystal clear: "a female can't be tough or strong or clear or exceptionally skillful at hip hop unless she sacrifices the thing that makes her a real girl . . . we need to consider why women have to be touched by either dyke- or ho-ism in order to be marketable hip-hoppers" (127).

In rap, women's voices are actively silenced through sex and/or rape. The violence of the sexual act in men's tales of conquest focuses on making the black female body silent, on meticulously reducing women's selfhood to the physical and then fracturing and severing parts of that physicality until what remains is selfless, senseless, fuck-able and mute. Williams Crenshaw (1993) writes:

> We hear about cunts being fucked until backbones are cracked, asses being busted, dicks rammed down throats, and semen splattered across faces. Black women are cunts, bitches, and all purpose hoes. . . . Occasionally, we do hear women's voices and those voices are sometimes oppositional. But the response to opposition typically returns to the central refrain: 'Shut up bitch. Suck my dick.' (122)

Williams Crenshaw's comments bring us back to Rose's proposition of visualizing black women rappers as active participants in a "dialogic process" with their male counterparts. According to Rose, male artists' misogynistic lines find contestation in women's "caustic," "witty," and "aggressive" raps indicting men for their mistreatment of women in heterosexual love relationships. In these raps, women challenge men's depictions of them as "gold-diggers" or "hoes" and in Rose's mind, they address the many fears and concerns that black female consumers may have. However, as it is made abundantly clear in Williams Crenshaw's comments, male rappers' physical force always seems to give them the last word and reduces black women's role in rap music to their unwilling participation in the male-centered sexual act. Women's space in rap is thus limited to that in which the male figure forces them.

"THE MUSIC'S NOT SAFE"

Black women cannot speak freely in rap music. This reality makes rap an unsafe space for black womanhood. According to Hill-Collins, safe spaces are characterized and defined by the free flow of speech in between black women, who, at that moment, are shielded from mainstream society. Safe spaces thus, by definition, imply an exclusion of outside elements, of outside structures. Their power lies in that they are "free of surveillance by more powerful groups" (Hill-Collins, *Black Feminist Thought* 111). Rap music as a black male dominated art form and as a white corporate

controlled enterprise is not at all free of that surveillance. Black women's interests are not only unrepresented in the music but one of the music's principal themes is the continual negation of their existence as active, speaking, social actors. Furthermore, despite the genre's recent profitability and international visibility, rap still has a conflicting relationship with mainstream white American culture. It is still actively attacked, blamed for any number of social ills, and frequently labeled as deviant. Rap still implies difference and that difference is mostly racial. Consequently, black women rappers, in difficult times, must often represent the genre as a whole. Their defense of the music vis-à-vis mainstream white society often implies a defense of the misogyny in rap. Anything other than this blanket defense would be interpreted as treason by their black male counterparts and could possibly harm their career. Therefore, black feminist identities in rap have to be negotiated within this framework.

TALKING BACK: CLAIMING NEW SPACES

Forman argues that rap must be understood as a tool for communicating socio-cultural perspectives, one that may be used to empower women and create critical dialogue. He uses the metaphor of "coming to voice" to refer to the collective representation black women can find in rap. Forman asserts that black women have already begun to "generate their own discourse of empowerment" through Hip Hop. He cites two important indicators of this shift: the carrying of black female experience into the public domain and the creation of role models for female fans.

However, in formulating a critical dialogue about rap music and feminism, we must ask whose black womanhood is being brought to the public sphere, and is this womanhood truly female defined? It is evident that the most prevalent images of black womanhood in rap are not of successful, assertive, female rappers, but instead, of near naked, unrealistic, back-up dancers used to enforce the masculinity and sexual prowess of those male rappers for whom they dance. The image of the respected and successful female rapper is still marginal at best.

This marginalization from mainstream success is amplified for feminist rappers who cater less to a white audience (Roberts). Rap music is situated in a predominately white and patriarchal culture industry, constraining the expression of black women (Shelton). According to Chuck D (as cited in Stephens and Phillips 13), 70% of the consumers of Hip Hop culture and music are white and the majority of corporate backing of the Hip Hop industry is from white-owned corporations. While those most visible in the industry remain black males (Stephens and Phillips), thorough analysis of women's place within rap music must recognize that black female marginalization in Hip Hop goes further beyond the gender relationships between black men and women.

Furthermore, the sexualized images of black women in Hip Hop must also be understood as a reflection of white patriarchal commodification of black sexuality. Historically, whites have perpetuated images of hyper-sexuality among African Americans, often portraying them naked with exaggerated sexual organs (Feagin). As Feagin notes, "The white world drew the black woman's body as excessively and flagrantly sexual, quite different from the emerging ideology of purity and modesty which defined the white women's body" (113). Furthermore, both white supremacist images of black sexuality and hip hop's portrayal of black women and male/female sexual relationships dictate a compulsory heterosexuality that fosters homophobia and racism explicating the interconnections between institutionalized heterosexism and institutionalized racism (Hill-Collins, *Black Sexual Politics*).

Unfortunately, most of our conversations concerning the creation of "safe spaces" for black women in rap begin with the assumption that Hip Hop has been and continues to be a "safe space" for black males. However, as we have attempted to showcase in our analysis of black men and women's situated positions within the genre, neither of the two are privileged voices. Consequently,

negotiating an accurate and un-oppressive image for black women in rap music is not an intra-racial dialogue. In order to critically understand the misogyny in rap music and eventually surpass it, the issue must be addressed as more than simply a reflection of gender relations within black communities. It must be treated as a reflection of institutionalized images of blackness in the white imagination, which influence the production of the music and mediate the relationship between its makers and its consumers.

CONCLUSION

The majority of resistance against misogyny and violence in rap music thus far has been constructed as a "gendered" issue, instead of a civil rights agenda. We are not claiming here that male rappers are not responsible for their treatment of women, only that they are constrained by an industry they do not control. By denying the possibilities of empowerment for both black men and women in rap, we ignore the political nature of the genre. When we hear our white students who vehemently oppose affirmative action in the most racist of terms, singing along with rapper Kanye West about the need for reparations, we cannot help but stand in awe at the artistic ingenuity of the genre. What other trend has had such large-scale abilities to bring the experience of being black in America to such mainstream venues? Looking forward, rap music does not exist in a vacuum. Although the genre may appear to be artist-controlled, it is subject to the same institutionalized racist forces as our board rooms, schools, and public offices. Therefore, any analysis that does not simultaneously discuss the racist, patriarchal, capitalist hierarchy within which rap exists does not move the music toward liberatory practice.

REFERENCES

Clark, Alvin. "Stranger Among Us." *The Source: The Magazine of Hip-Hop Music, Culture and Politics* 162 (March 2003). Print.

Feagin, Joe. *Racist America*. New York: Routledge, 2000. Print.

Forman, Murray. "'Movin' Closer to an Independent Funk': Black Feminist Theory, Standpoint,

and Women in Rap." *Women's Studies* 23 (1994): 35–55. Print.

George, Nelson. *Hip Hop America*. New York: Viking Press, 1998. Print.

Hill-Collins, *Patricia. Black Feminist Thought: Knowledge, Consciousness and the Politics of Empowerment*. New York: Routledge, 2000. Print.

———. *Black Sexual Politics.* New York: Routledge, 2004. Print.

hooks, bell. *We Real Cool: Black Men and Masculinity.* New York: Routledge, 2004. Print.

Kitwana, Barry. *The Rap on Gangsta Rap: Gangsta Rap and Visions of Black Violence.* Chicago: Third World Press, 1994. Print.

Ogbar, Jeffrey. "Slouching toward Bork: The Culture Wars and Self- Criticism in Hip-Hop Music." *Journal of Black Studies* 30 (1999): 164–83. Print.

Pough, Gwendolyn D. *Check It While I Wreck It: Black Womanhood, Hip Hop Culture and the Public Sphere.* Boston: Northeastern UP, 2004. Print.

Roberts, Robin. "Music Videos, Performance and Resistance: Feminist Rappers." *Journal of Popular Culture* 25 (1991): 141–52. Print.

Rose, Tricia. "'Fear of a Black Planet': Rap Music and Black Cultural Politics in the 1990s." *Journal of Negro Education* 60.3 (1991): 276–90. Print.

———. *Black Noise: Rap Music and Black Culture in Contemporary America.* London: Wesleyan UP, 1994. Print.

Russell-Brown, Katheryn. *Underground Codes: Race, Crime and Related Fires.* New York: New York UP, 2004. Print.

Shelton, Marla L. "Can't Touch This! Representations of the African American Female Body in Urban Rap Videos." *Popular Music and Society* 21.3 (1997): 107–16. Print.

Smith, Danyell. "Ain't a Damn Thing Changed: Why Women Rappers Don't Sell." *Rap on Rap: Straight up Talk on Hip Hop Culture.* Ed. A. Sexton. New York: Delta Publishing, 1995. 125–28. Print.

Stephens, Dionne P., and Layli D. Phillips. "Freaks, Gold Diggers, Divas and Dykes: The Socio-Historical Development of Adolescent African American Women's Sexual Scripts." *Sexuality and Culture* Winter 2003, 21(4): 3–49. Print.

Tate, Greg. "Introduction: Nigs R Us, or How Blackfolk Became Fetish Objects," *Everything but the Burden: What White People Are Taking from Black Culture.* Ed. Greg Tate. New York: Broadway Books, 2003: 1–14. Print.

West, Cornell. *Race Matters.* New York: Vintage, 1994. Print.

Williams Crenshaw, Kimberle. "Beyond Racism and Misogyny: Black Feminism and 2 Live Crew." *Words That Wound: Critical Race Theory, Assaultive Speech and the First Amendment.* Eds. M.J. Matsuda, Charles R. Lawrence III, Richard Delgado, and Kimberle Crenshaw. Boulder: Westview Press, 1993: 111–16. Print.

26

"[IN]JUSTICE ROLLS DOWN LIKE WATER..."

Challenging White Supremacy in Media Constructions of Crime and Punishment

Bill Yousman

"No, no, we are not satisfied and will not be satisfied until justice rolls down like water and righteousness like a mighty stream."

Martin Luther King Jr.

Since the earliest days of American mass culture, newspapers, films, then television shows, and now blogs and social media have vilified Blacks, Asians, Latino/as, Arabs, and indigenous people, painting them as violent, criminal, savage threats to the White social order (Stabile, 2006). In this chapter I explore the intertwined nature of the cultural and criminal justice industries, arguing for analysis of the connections among media representations, the public imagination, public opinion, and public policy. Media images and narratives play a crucial role in shaping our perceptions of key social issues, including race, crime, policing, and incarceration. These beliefs inflect public opinion about the proper state responses to crime, often leading to a fearful and punitive mindset that is easily exploited for political purposes.

While a comprehensive historical overview of the relationship between racial representation in media and racial bias in the criminal justice system is beyond the scope of this chapter, I will focus on several key trends in the last decade, a time when the media and cultural environment has paradoxically experienced both tremendous change and a remarkable level of consistency.

Perhaps the most obvious and significant change in media comes from the proliferation of digital technologies that have fragmented the means of content production and distribution once controlled by a handful of multinational corporations. To point to just three key examples, Facebook and Twitter both became public platforms in 2006, and the iPhone was introduced to the consumer market in 2007. As is often discussed in the popular press, diverse individuals and groups now have the ability to become media producers, shooting photographs and videos with smartphones and other devices and immediately uploading them to Facebook, Instagram, Twitter, Snapchat, YouTube, and countless numbers of blogs.

Yet, despite these advances, concentration in media ownership has only intensified, the society of the spectacle, as Guy Debord (1967) dubbed an entertainment and commodity-obsessed culture, has achieved seemingly unchallengeable hegemony, and the most powerful players in the media industries now possess even more wealth and a longer global reach than ever before. Despite technological and industrial changes, corporate media systems continue to frame people of color as a problem while transforming violence and suppression into the stuff of entertainment. New media racism is not the same as old media racism, and contemporary cultural constructions of crime and violence usually rely on inferential rather than overt calls for White control of people of color, yet the traces of historical patterns of White supremacist representation persist (Hall, 2015).[1]

This piece is an original essay that was commissioned for this volume.

By way of example, we might consider the critically lauded Netflix program, *Orange Is the New Black (OITNB).* This well-regarded and popular series exemplifies how popular media may provide insights into aspects of American culture that most members of the audience will not experience firsthand, while simultaneously reifying and commodifying the deep-seated racial anxieties of White viewers. Set inside a women's prison, and based on a best-selling memoir by a White upper-middle class author, *OITNB* offers viewers a more nuanced and complex glimpse of the race, gender, and sexual politics behind prison life than perhaps American television ever has. Yet, like its predecessor, HBO's *Oz,* as an entertainment product *OITNB* cannot help but turn incarceration into a commodity spectacle, a brief distraction that so-called "ordinary Americans" can relax with on the couch while simultaneously surfing the web or playing games on their tablets and smartphones. Also like *Oz, OITNB* depicts an alien, and often scary, prison environment inhabited by threatening people of color but viewed through the lens of a White protagonist (Yousman, 2009).

Many of the shortcomings of *OITNB* are caused primarily by the economic structure of the U.S. corporate television industry: The program's creator has said that she would never have been able to pitch a show that focused on Latina or Black women in prison (McIlveen, 2013). Despite these constraints, *OITNB* does challenge many television norms as it makes visible the generally invisible, including the racial disparities at the heart of mass incarceration, sexual abuse in women's prisons, and the struggles of queer and trans prisoners. In particular, the framing of *OITNB* challenges the notion of a postracial, colorblind society, as Enck and Morrissey (2015) argue,

> OITNB uses narratives of contrast, identification, and disidentification to provide important insights into the wide range of institutional disadvantages that so often ensnare women of color in the clutches of the PIC (e.g., poverty and homelessness, sexual abuse and domestic violence, interventions by Child Protective Services and the foster care system, and the War on Drugs). . . . OITNB helps to accentuate vast differences in opportunity and access where normally we are trained to expect

similarity (e.g., through myths of color blindness and equal opportunity). (p. 312)

The media environment in the second decade of the 21st century is thus one that is marked by deep contradictions. By way of another example, activist groups like Black Lives Matter have seized the moment by employing digital media to convey their powerful message of resistance to the militarized and lethal policing of Black communities, while Fox News has simultaneously become the most watched cable news outlet, at least partially by offering a voice to those who call for the ramping up of an even harsher, more punitive, White supremacist state.

Nowhere do these contradictions play out more clearly than in the world of social media. In many ways the emergence of digital and mobile media technologies has intensified concerns that media critic Neal Postman noted a generation ago in a famous passage from his 1985 book, *Amusing Ourselves to Death.* Here, Postman calls on the dystopian visions of both George Orwell and Aldous Huxley to frame his concern about the distractions wrought by the hyperentertainment values of the television era:

> What Orwell feared were those who would ban books. What Huxley feared was that there would be no reason to ban a book, for there would be no one who wanted to read one. Orwell feared those who would deprive us of information. Huxley feared those who would give us so much that we would be reduced to passivity and egoism. Orwell feared that the truth would be concealed from us. Huxley feared the truth would be drowned in a sea of irrelevance. Orwell feared we would become a captive culture. Huxley feared we would become a trivial culture. . . . In *1984* . . . people are controlled by inflicting pain. In *Brave New World,* they are controlled by inflicting pleasure. In short, Orwell feared that what we hate will ruin us. Huxley feared that what we love will ruin us. (Postman, 1985, p. xix)

In the iPhone, Facebook, Instagram, Twitter, Snapchat era, Huxley and Postman's warnings seem even more prescient, more germane, more disturbing. How can activists hope to arouse attention, outrage, and action against police brutality and the mass incarceration state while the public is too busy posting selfies and pictures of their food to Instagram while playing Candy Crush on their phones? Meanwhile, Orwell's nightmare also seems more real every week as both governments and corporations employ new technologies to watch us day and night, the ultimate vision of the panoptic state that Foucault (1977) dissected in *Discipline and Punish.*

Yet, this is only one way of thinking about the current media environment. In fact, contradictions abound: concurrent with the phenomena described earlier, the past decade has also seen social justice movements embrace digital technologies and the possibilities they present for independent media production and the distribution of dissenting ideas across previously imposing boundaries.

As in the Occupy movement and the Arab Spring, activists who seek to challenge White supremacy in the criminal justice system also utilize tools that they simply did not possess in previous eras. For example, a recent YouTube search for the keywords "Prison-Industrial Complex" returned almost 20,000 results, including long and short documentaries, interviews with and speeches by Angela Davis, Mumia Abu-Jamal, Michelle Alexander and other activists and authors, news reports from international and alternative media outlets like Al Jazeera and Democracy Now!, and critically oriented comics, music videos, and more.

At the same time, the proliferation of mobile technologies and new possibilities for the distribution of digital media content has enabled a new genre of citizen-produced journalism. Thus, numerous videos of police brutality directed at people of color are continually being uploaded to social media and distributed widely, calling the public's attention to abuses that historically occurred mostly in darkness. This sort of homemade media also includes social media sites dedicated to raising the public's consciousness about their own rights when dealing with the police and other authorities.

Beyond the social media engagement of individuals, activist organizations like Critical Resistance, whose mission statement reads in part: "Critical Resistance seeks to build an international

movement to end the prison industrial complex (PIC) by challenging the belief that caging and controlling people makes us safe" (Critical Resistance, n.d., n.p.), now have their own websites. Meanwhile Facebook, Twitter, and other platforms offer new communication possibilities for social movements like #BlackLivesMatter that are confronting longstanding abuses of the criminal justice system.

The activist voice that social media and digital technologies amplify pushes even profit-centered media institutions to pay occasional attention to issues of police brutality, mass incarceration, and the White supremacist criminal justice system. Michelle Alexander's highly acclaimed *The New Jim Crow* was praised in magazines like *Forbes* and *Newsweek* and became a best seller upon publication in 2010. In September 2015, another mass market magazine, *The Atlantic,* published a long cover story by Ta-Nehisi Coates entitled "The Black Family in the Age of Mass Incarceration," and in 2016 Netflix released *13th*, an Academy Award–nominated documentary about the history of racism in the U.S. justice system

But the contradictions continue. Despite progress and new developments such as those noted above, television news programs still largely ignore the issue of mass incarceration while American popular culture is still rife with spectacles of violence that represent people of color and the poor as dangerous savages in dire need of a strong authoritarian state in order to keep "us" safe from "them" (Hall, 2015). Hollywood films have historically framed people of color as murderers, gang members, and terrorists, set in opposition to a wealth of noble White defenders. Recently, the film *American Sniper* (2014) portrayed a real Navy SEAL, who killed over 160 people and referred to Iraqis as "savages," as a hero. After seeing the film, journalist Max Blumenthal tweeted: "I counted 4 Iraqi child characters in *American Sniper.* Two were 'terrorists.' One was son of a 'terrorist.' The fourth was tortured to death."

Hollywood is far from the only media industry that converts the demonization of people of color into the color of money. It is commonplace for music videos to uncritically celebrate "thugs and gangsters" even while close attention to the lyrics of many hip-hop artists reveals a much more complex representation of the intersections of crime and poverty. Television crime dramas like the top-rated *NCIS* and *CSI* focus on an array of mostly White criminal investigators lined up against the evildoers. So-called reality television programs like *Cops* and *America's Most Wanted* regularly feature tales of primarily White police "defending" communities against people of color, immigrants, and the poor, while documentary prison shows like MSNBC's *Lockup* and National Geographic's *Lockdown* may expose some of the actual conditions that prisoners live under, but also tend to focus on gang violence, heinous crimes, riots and near-riots, death threats, and other extreme situations.

Even the peaceful Black Lives Matter movement is framed as a terrorist organization, the responsible party when it comes to violent confrontations between the police and men and women of color. One of the core ideas behind media framing theory is that media narratives emphasize and elaborate on certain ideas while others are marginalized or excluded. As Entman (2002) explains,

> To frame is to select some aspects of a perceived reality and make them more salient in a communicating text, in such a way as to promote a particular problem definition, causal interpretation, moral evaluation, and or treatment recommendation for the item described. (p. 391)

Thus when individuals and activist organizations engage in resistance to authoritarian abuses of power, the very thing that sparked the confrontation may be left out of the frame altogether. Ta-Nehisi Coates (2015) writes about this in relation to responses to the Baltimore protests subsequent to the suspicious death of Freddie Gray while in police custody in 2015. While media pundits and state officials decried the actions of some of the enraged protestors, there were many crucial facts and questions that remained unspoken: facts like the Baltimore police department having paid out settlements to over 100 victims of police brutality over the preceding 4 years, and questions like "What specifically is the crime here? What particular threat did Freddie Gray pose? Why is mere eye contact and then running worthy of detention at the hands of the state? Why is Freddie Gray dead?" (2015, n.p.). In essence, What is the history and context behind these events? What *caused* the protests, why are people protesting, and why isn't this

at least as salient as the violent actions of some of the protestors?

In much the same manner, when Fox News hosts and guests alike claim that Black Lives Matter is a hate group that is responsible for violence against the police, or when a *Washington Times* headline in 2015 reads: "Black Lives Matter is a Terrorist Group," not only is there no evidence for such allegations, but they also serve as a distraction from the actual issues that catalyzed the emergence of Black Lives Matter and other activist groups. This type of framing occurs in both corporate media outlets and on numerous blogs and social media sites. On one influential right-wing website, for example, protestors were referred to as "hoodie-wearing thugs," Black Lives Matter activists were described paradoxically as both "spoiled children" and "an existential threat." They were also framed as "angry and ignorant, with a hair trigger temper and a long list of grievances that have no factual basis." No mention however, of why they might be angry or what those grievances really are. Instead we are told that what they want is a "bloody revolution leading to a socialist/anarchist America" (Stranahan, 2016, n.p.).

This is just one example of proliferating blogs, websites, podcasts, and social media posts that offer firm evidence that there is no necessary correspondence between progressive politics and the use of digital media technologies to promote a social cause. The same tools that offer the potential for social justice mobilization can just as easily be used by reactionary forces committed to backlash and retrenchment.

The connections between media and justice suggest that activists must fight for a transformation of our media system even as they fight for a transformation of the criminal justice system. These twin battles are needed now more than ever as our lives become ever more saturated with any-place anytime mediated culture. As scholars like Robert McChesney (2013) have pointed out, the rise of the Internet has not diminished the problems of concentration of ownership, hypercommercialism, and a narrow public sphere focused on entertainment and celebrity culture at the expense of in-depth coverage of public affairs and well-funded investigative journalism. While it is true that it is easier now to create and distribute essays, podcasts, photos, and videos, independent producers still do not have access to the halls of power where public policy is set, or the hidden spaces of our society, like prisons, where the consequences of those policies play out in horrific ways.

To put it simply, we can record ourselves in our bedrooms ranting about police brutality and encourage all of our "friends" to watch us on You-Tube. More generously, if we happen to be in the right place at the right time we can even record instances of police abuse on the streets and post them online. This has been crucial in bringing wider attention to the state-sponsored violence that people of color and the poor have long experienced but has been hidden or denied for decades. But there are limitations even to this. Aspiring citizen journalists and documentarians can't follow those taken by the police into the vehicles and backrooms where much of the abuse happens out of sight; they can't get inside our local jails and detention centers or federal prisons, or interview prisoners, and investigate the conditions that they live under. Furthermore, without the promotional muscle of the big media organizations, there is no assurance that the alternative narratives produced will make a lasting mark on the public consciousness. The problems of White supremacy, police brutality, repressive surveillance, and mass incarceration are too significant for us to hope for the random luck that allows the occasional message to "go viral."

In addition to sounding a note of caution about the limitations of the new media environment for those on the outside working for change, it is important to acknowledge that the possibilities for the incarcerated are exponentially more constrained. Both governments and corporations have denied prisoners access to social media. In Alabama, for example, a prisoner lost 6 months of a reduced sentence for good behavior because she violated a prison regulation by going on Facebook to look at pictures of her children. In South Carolina, a prisoner who posted on Facebook was given 37 years in solitary confinement (Shourd, 2015). These are just two examples, but across the U.S. prison system there are thousands of prisoners who have been severely punished for using social media. In 2014 Pennsylvania passed a law in response to a recorded commencement speech by Mumia Abu Jamal that was heard by just 20 graduates of a small Vermont college. The so-called Mumia Bill allows any crime victim to file a civil suit when any communication by a prisoner might have caused them "mental anguish."

These examples demonstrate the need for both more First Amendment rights for the incarcerated and for more media access to prisons and prisoners. Prison reformers and prison abolition activists should also pursue initiatives that will force media outlets to investigate the issue of mass incarceration. The initial success of the Black Lives Matter movement in, at the very least, pushing big media to talk about them is a model that prison activists should heed. This type of activism can be a catalyst for change. Facebook, for example, pursued a policy of automatically taking down prisoner pages at the behest of prison authorities without asking for any rationale or justification from the institutions. Now, however, and only due to pressure from the Electronic Frontier Foundation and other groups, Facebook is at least beginning to ask for evidence that a prisoner is using social media to cause harm before they shut down the site (Shourd, 2015).

We also need to support critical media literacy education efforts that can encourage the public to analyze the distorted messages about race and crime that fuel White supremacy in the criminal justice system and to respond with counterhegemonic media of their own. While media literacy is a term that has in many ways been co-opted by big media companies and conservative educators as a public relations strategy to placate critics, activists, and reformers, truly critical media literacy still holds the potential to empower audiences, allowing them to deconstruct media stories and images, challenge corporate media institutions, and create and seek out alternative media. Critical media literacy education does not shy away from dealing with issues of power, who gets to tell the stories, and the relationship between the type of media we have and whether we will live under democratic or totalitarian social arrangements (Yousman, 2016).

Thus social justice activists should create, distribute, and support critical media literacy curricula, campaigns, and initiatives at all grade levels, in K–12 and higher education, and in nonschool settings such as youth programs and community organizations that work with both children and adults. In our media-saturated society, critical media literacy education is not just for children.

There are several important already-existing critical media literacy organizations that should be brought into a much-needed coalition of media and social justice activists, such as the Media Education Foundation, located in western

Massachusetts, who produce and distribute documentaries about key media and cultural issues, including a number of videos that deal with the issues of patriarchy, sexism, racism, classism, and White supremacy that are so germane to the Black Lives Matter movement and other movements for social justice. Similarly, the California-based Project Censored has shed light on underreported public issues such as the tragedy of mass incarceration since the mid-1970s. One of their recent compendiums of the top censored stories each year includes an analysis of how many people U.S. police murder annually and who those victims of police violence are. In collaboration with the Action Coalition for Media Education (ACME), the nation's leading independent, critical media literacy organization, Project Censored, has recently created the Global Critical Media Literacy Project (GCMLP) whose mission is to employ "a service-learning based media literacy education model to teach digital media literacy and critical thinking skills, as well as to raise awareness about corporate and state-engineered news media censorship around the world" (Frechette, Higdon, & Williams, 2015, p. 199).

Meanwhile, groups like Free Press call for reform of the corporate media system and, in their own words, hope to

create a world where people have the information and opportunities they need to tell their own stories, hold leaders accountable, and participate in our democracy. We fight to save the free and open internet, curb runaway media consolidation, protect press freedom, and ensure diverse voices are represented in our media. (Free Press, n.d., n.p.)

This is just a small sample of the possibilities for media education, alternative media production, and media reform and activism that the new era of digital technologies enables. It is crucial to not fall victim to technological determinism, however, and accept the myth of the digital panacea. Although oft-quoted, the words of Frederick Douglass from a pre–Civil War speech could not be more germane to those who wish to avoid this trap: "If there is no struggle there is no progress. Those who profess to favor freedom and yet deprecate agitation are men who want crops without plowing up the ground; they want rain without thunder and lightning. They want the ocean without the awful roar of its many waters. This struggle may be a moral one, or it may be a physical one, and it may be both moral and physical, but it must be a struggle. Power concedes nothing without a demand. It never did and it never will" (Douglass, 1857, n.p.).

NOTES

1. It should also be noted, however, that in the Trump/Brexit/Le Pen era we are experiencing a resurgence of overt, blatant, virulent racist rhetoric in many places around the globe.

REFERENCES

Coates, T. (2015, April 27). Nonviolence as compliance. *The Atlantic.com.* Retrieved from http://www.theatlantic.com/politics/archive/2015/04/nonviolence-as-compliance/391640/

Critical Resistance (n.d.) *Mission.* Retrieved from http://criticalresistance.org/about/

Debord, G. (1967) (2004). *The society of the spectacle* (D. Nicholson-Smith, trans.). New York: Zone.

Douglass, F. (1857, August 3). *West India emancipation,* speech delivered in Canandaigua, New York. Text available at http://www.blackpast.org/1857-frederick-douglass-if-there-no-struggle-there-no-progress

Enck, S. M., & Morrissey, M. E. (2015). If *Orange is the New Black,* I must be color blind: Comic framings of post-racism in the prison-industrial complex. *Critical Studies in Media Communication, 32*(5), 303–317.

Entman, R. M. (2002). Framing: toward clarification of a fractured paradigm. In D. McQuail (Ed.), *McQuail's reader in mass communication theory* (pp. 390–397). London: Sage.

Foucault, M. (1977). *Discipline and punish: The birth of the prison.* London: Penguin.

Frechette, J., Higdon, N., & Williams, R. (2015). A vision for transformative civic engagement:

The Global Critical Media Literacy Project. In M. Huff & A. L. Roth (Eds.), *Censored 2016: Media freedom on the line* (199–215). New York: Seven Stories Press.

Free Press. (n.d.) *What we do.* Retrieved from https://www.freepress.net/about

Hall, S. (2015). The whites of their eyes: Racist ideologies and the media. In G. Dines & J. M. Humez (Eds.), *Gender, race and class in media* (4th ed.; pp. 104–107). Thousand Oaks, CA: Sage.

McChesney, R. W. (2013). *Digital disconnect: How capitalism is turning the Internet against democracy.* New York: New Press.

McIlveen, H. (2013, July 10). New Netflix show "Orange Is the New Black" is a complex look at sex, gender, and prison. *Bitchmedia.* Retrieved from https://bitchmedia.org/post/new-netflix-show-orange-is-the-new-black-is-a-complex-look-at-sex-gender-and-prison

Postman, N. (1985). *Amusing ourselves to death: Public Discourse in the age of show business.* New York: Penguin.

Shourd, S. (2015, June 4). Facebook now a place for prisoners, too. *The Daily Beast.* Retrieved from http://www.thedailybeast.com/articles/2015/06/04/facebook-now-a-place-for-prisoners-too.html

Stabile, C. (2006). *White victims, Black villains: Gender, race, and crime news in US culture.* New York: Routledge.

Stranahan, L. (2016, January 2). Black Lives Matter: We saw it coming, now here's what's coming next. *Breitbart.com.* Retrieved from http://www.breitbart.com/big-government/2016/01/02/black-lives-matter-saw-coming-now-heres-whats-coming-next/

Yousman, B. (2009). *Prime time prisons on U.S. TV: Representation of incarceration.* New York: Peter Lang.

Yousman, B. (2016). Who's afraid of critical media literacy? In M. Huff & A. L. Roth (Eds.), *Censored 2017* (pp. 369–416). New York: Seven Stories Press.

PART IV

ADVERTISING AND CONSUMER CULTURE

Acentral theme of the chapters in this section is the role of media industries in the production and maintenance of an overwhelmingly consumption-oriented cultural environment. Critics of such a culture point to a long list of social and political costs related to unchecked consumption of world resources, including environmental degradation, the dangerously increasing gap between rich and poor nations, erosion of political democracy, and even climate change—but the global corporate drive to increase levels of consumption seems largely unaffected by these warnings.

In the **consumer** culture, we live in a world saturated with advertising **imagery** urging us to buy and consume more and more products as a supposed path to self-transformation and happiness. As Sut Jhally says in "Image-Based Culture" (IV.27), which introduces this section, "In the contemporary world, messages about goods are all pervasive—advertising has increasingly filled up the spaces of our daily existence . . . it is the air that we breathe as we live our daily lives" (p. 230). Any discussion of the role of media within a capitalist economy has to foreground the role of advertising, both as an industry in its own right and, in Jhally's words, as a "discourse through and about objects." Because advertising legitimizes and glamorizes consumption as a way of life, it is critical to our ability to think for ourselves that we learn to analyze not just the meanings of advertising texts but also the place of the advertising industry in our society.

As Jhally points out, "Fundamentally, advertising talks to us as individuals and addresses us about how we can become happy" (p. 230). In the past, advertisements told us that the key to happiness was our ability to keep up with the consumption patterns of our next-door neighbors. But economist Juliet Schor, in "The New Politics of Consumption" (IV.28), points to the "upscaling of lifestyle norms" that characterizes "the new consumerism." Schor argues that a by-product of the consumerist ideology in the United States is that "luxury, rather than mere comfort, is a widespread aspiration." She points to the role of television, in particular, in contributing to this "upscaling of lifestyle norms." Schor continues:

> Because television shows are so heavily skewed to the "lifestyles of the rich and upper middle-class," they inflate the viewer's perceptions of what others have, and by extension what is worth acquiring—what one must have in order to avoid being "out of it." (p. 236)

In addition to ramping up our material desires, a consumerist ideology attempts to turn everything into a product that can be sold, even movements of dissent and social justice, as demonstrated by Ian Bogost (IV.29) in his take on the controversy over a 2017 ad for Pepsi that attempted to utilize imagery reminiscent of Black Lives Matter protests to sell a sugary soft drink. As Bogost points out, "Before it's an ad for shampoo or cat food or cola, every advertisement is first an ad for capitalism." In other words, the underlying message of all advertisements is that constant consumption of mass produced goods and services is a lifestyle to which we should all aspire. Keeping this in mind, Bogost's analysis reveals that, despite the pushback the ad received, it was still a win for the Pepsi corporation:

> All [the] criticisms are dead-on. But they don't matter, because the ad is an undeniable success. Yes, true, it coopts the politics of protest, particularly as they surround race relations in America today. But that's not the ad's goal, so the public's objection is ultimately irrelevant to Pepsi's mission. The ad's point is to put the consumer in a more important role than the citizen anyway. And to position Pepsi as a facilitator in the utopian dream of pure, color-blind consumerism that might someday replace politics entirely. (p. 240)

The controversy over the ad generated free publicity for the Pepsi brand, and when the company announced plans to pull the ad it could then position itself as a concerned global citizen, who listened to the public and responded to their concerns. This was certainly not the first time advertisers attempted to co-opt a social movement. For example, in the late 1960s, tobacco companies notoriously capitalized on the growing women's liberation movement by incorporating images of "feminist empowerment" into campaigns that targeted young women.

Feminist scholars interested in the ways that the consumption of products plays a central role in constructing hegemonic femininity have traced several important changes in media culture over the past half century through the present, using commercial media and advertising messages directed at women as windows into this topic. The women's movement of the 1960s critiqued a number of patriarchal institutions as agencies of women's subordination in a male-dominated social order. Advertising images that confined women either to roles as wives and mothers or treated women's bodies as sex objects were an early and continuing target of feminist organizing and calls for change. Recounting her experience seeking advertisers to support the pioneering *Ms* magazine in its early days, the iconic feminist Gloria Steinem reminds us, in "Sex, Lies, and Advertising" (IV.30), how advertisers targeting women as consumers subscribed to very limited notions of what constitutes femininity (i.e., dependency, constant concern with beauty, fixation on family and nurturance, fear of technology) and consequently "feminine" buying patterns. Feminist efforts to redefine gender ideals for advertisers in the 1970s and 1980s met with disbelief, resistance, and downright hostility. Steinem's essay reveals the extent to which advertisers also assumed the right to control editorial content of the content surrounding the ads—citing, among other practices, efforts to censor perspectives that might conflict with the interests of advertisers.

Thanks in large part to the feminist activist work to raise awareness about **sexism** in advertising representations, as well as to social and occupational changes since the 1970s, it is no longer broadly acceptable for advertisers to depict women in just a narrow range of occupations, nor primarily as wives and mothers. However, there is a proliferation today of advertising that employs **hypersexualized** representations of the female body (for more on hypersexualization in popular culture generally, see Part V of this anthology). Feminist scholars are not all in agreement over what such hypersexualization means for women's lives. Some argue that such **representations** are merely updated versions of traditional exploitation for profit ("sex sells"); others maintain that hypersexualized imagery is empowering for women and girls.

Rosalind Gill takes on this debate in "Supersexualize Me!" (IV.31). She questions the degree to which representations of young women aggressively emulating a media-constructed hypersexuality are truly about female agency. At the same time Gill points to the categories of women who are still denied visibility in the world conjured up by advertising imagery: "older women, disabled women, fat women and any woman who is unable to live up to the increasingly narrow standards of female beauty and sex appeal that are normatively required" (p. 252).

One series of ads that would seem, at first glance, to make visible a much wider range of female body types and ages was the much-discussed "Dove Campaign for Real Beauty." Dove developed a branding strategy that included apparently nonconventional images featuring "real women" rather than models, and a so-called Movement for Self-Esteem, based on a corporate website. As Dara Persis Murray argues (IV.32), this was a strategy that **co-opted** feminist critical perspectives, encouraging consumers of beauty products "to think of themselves as insurgents" without actually having to do the work and pay the price of "true non-conformity and dissent" (p. 257). After analyzing both the ad texts and the branding strategy as a whole, Murray concludes critically that "real beauty" can be seen as yet another "oppressive beauty ideology." By signing the online declaration ("Join the Movement")—and incidentally providing the company with a list of consumers—Murray argues,

> Girls and women work to become neoliberal subjects who accept responsibility to develop and perform Dove-approved "self-esteem" behaviors (requiring self-judgment and self-monitoring of one's emotional state) that are integral to the pursuit of "real beauty." (p. 261)

Such an ideology "reinforces the value of female beauty and its pursuit by garnering women's agreement with its values of ideological and material consumption" (p. 261).

Advertising, however, is not the only media genre that generates and reinforces scrutiny of **gendered,** racialized, and sexualized bodies in order to generate consumerism and thereby profit. In recent years, there has been a massive growth in gossip industry magazines and websites, which spectacularize every aspect of celebrities' lives, including their diets, clothing, sexual antics, "baby bumps," and children. As Kirsty Fairclough shows in her chapter on gossip blogs (IV.33), female celebrities in particular are subjected to "hyperscrutiny" in today's media. In Fairclough's view,

> Female celebrities have become the chief site upon which contemporary tensions and anxieties surrounding femininity, motherhood, body image, cosmetic surgery, marriage and ageing are now played out. (p. 265)

Reminding us that "in popular culture the older female body is particularly vilified" (p. 266), Fairclough is attentive to the spotlight that the gossip industries shine on female aging. Although there has been a trend in recent years for Hollywood to allow older women some visibility in film, she notes that the gossip discourses about these women "are always structured in terms of how well the actress is managing her ageing process." In the context of a so-called **postfeminist** ideology, as well as the hyperscrutiny of the new gossip culture, Fairclough points to "a new beauty norm . . . that suggests youth must be held in limbo through the use of cosmetic procedures throughout adult life and for as long as possible" (p. 270).

Like Hollywood stars, athletes are also often branded **commodity** celebrities, and in the case of Olympians, Momin Rahman and Sean Lockwood (IV.34) show that their job is to present an authentic persona of heroic athleticism, so that the increasingly commercialized spectacle of the Olympic Games can be "enjoyed primarily for its demonstration of human endeavour rather than as another form of consumption" (p. 274). The authors analyze institutional discourses related to the Olympic Games held in London in the summer of 2012, against the backdrop of the ideal of noble athletic amateurism associated with the Games since the 19th century. As they argue,

> . . . Reiterations of amateurism have become a central part of the modern Olympic discourse, and indeed provide a distinctive Olympic dimension to the "authenticity" that is foregrounded to distract audiences from the commercialization of the Games. (p. 277)

We end this section on advertising and consumer culture with Jonathan Hardy's chapter (IV.35) on the recent HBO vampire series *True Blood*. Hardy's "mapping" of all the ways in which online and social media platforms were used to create a buzz around this cable TV program, and to help it "establish both cult status and popular appeal" (p. 283), brings together many of the themes of this section of the book: advertising, marketing, consumerism, celebrity, and emerging digital media trends.

Hardy's chapter is also a particularly good example of new directions in political economic analysis, taking account of the new proliferation of media outlets and the ways in which they now operate synergistically—to create a greater impact through interlinked operations than could be achieved by each outlet working on its own. In Hardy's words,

Commercial **intertextuality** is used to describe the production and interlinking of texts like blockbuster films or TV series with allied paratexts and products, such as spin-offs, reversionings, promos, online media, books, games and merchandise. (p. 279)

Hardy points out the blurring of categories once considered separate in media studies, including "corporate/independent, professional/amateur, and as *True Blood* illustrates, . . . commercial/autonomous textuality" (p. 279). The research in this chapter highlights "the increasing diversity of transmedia intertextual space and its tensions and contradictions" (p. 284). It is these very tensions and contradictions that necessitate the kind of complex, multifaceted, and nuanced analysis Kellner calls for in chapter I.1. Production, textual analysis, and audience reception have become far less discrete, separable categories than ever before. Along the way, postindustrial nations have adopted consumer culture in ways never imagined by early manufacturers and advertisers. Whether the world can sustain this type of hyperconsumption is looking more and more in doubt.

27

IMAGE-BASED CULTURE
Advertising and Popular Culture
Sut Jhally

Because we live inside the consumer culture, and most of us have done so for most of our lives, it is sometimes difficult to locate the origins of our most cherished values and assumptions. They simply appear to be part of our natural world. It is a useful exercise, therefore, to examine how our culture has come to be defined and shaped in specific ways—to excavate the origins of our most celebrated rituals. For example, everyone in this culture knows a "diamond is forever." It is a meaning that is almost as "natural" as the link between roses and romantic love. However, diamonds (just like roses) did not always have this meaning. Before 1938 their value derived primarily from their worth as scarce stones (with the DeBeers cartel carefully controlling the market supply). In 1938 the New York advertising agency of N.W. Ayers was hired to change public attitudes toward diamonds—to transform them from a financial investment into a *symbol* of committed and everlasting love. In 1947 an Ayers advertising copywriter came up with the slogan "a diamond is forever" and the rest, as they say, is history. As an N.W. Ayers memorandum put it in 1959: "Since 1939 an entirely new generation of young people has grown to marriageable age. To the new generation, a diamond ring is considered a necessity for engagement to virtually everyone."[1]

This is a fairly dramatic example of how the institutional structure of the consumer society orients the culture (and its attitudes, values, and rituals) more and more toward the world of commodities. The marketplace (and its major ideological tool, advertising) is the major structuring institution of contemporary consumer society.

This of course was not always the case. In the agrarian-based society preceding industrial society, other institutions such as family, community, ethnicity, and religion were the dominant institutional mediators and creators of the cultural forms. Their influence waned in the transition to industrial society and then consumer society. The emerging institution of the marketplace occupied the cultural terrain left void by the evacuation of these older forms. Information about products seeped into public discourse. More specifically, public discourse soon became dominated by the "discourse through and about objects."[2]

At first, this discourse relied upon transmitting information about products alone, using the available means of textual communication offered by newspapers. As the possibility of more effective color illustration emerged and as magazines developed as competitors for advertising dollars, this "discourse" moved from being purely text-based. The further integration of first radio and then television into the advertising/media complex ensured that commercial communication would be characterized by the domination of *imagistic* modes of representation.

Again, because our world is so familiar, it is difficult to imagine the process through which the present conditions emerged. In this context, it is instructive to focus upon that period in our history that marks the transition point in the development of an image-saturated society—the 1920s. In that decade the advertising industry was faced with a curious problem—the need to sell increasing quantities of "nonessential" goods in a competitive marketplace using the potentialities offered by printing and color photography. Whereas the initial period of national advertising (from approximately the 1880s to the 1920s) had focused largely in a celebratory manner on the products

From Jhally, Sut. (1990, July). Image-based culture: Advertising and popular culture. *The World & I Online,* 506–519. Reprinted by permission of *The World & I.*

themselves and had used text for "reason why" advertising (even if making the most outrageous claims), the 1920s saw the progressive integration of people (via visual representation) into the messages. Interestingly, in this stage we do not see representations of "real" people in advertisements, but rather we see representations of people who "stand for" reigning social values such as family structure, status differentiation, and hierarchical authority.

While this period is instructive from the viewpoint of content, it is equally fascinating from the viewpoint of *form;* for while the possibilities of using visual imagery existed with the development of new technologies, there was no guarantee that the audience was sufficiently literate in visual imagery to properly decode the ever-more complex messages. Thus, the advertising industry had to educate as well as sell, and many of the ads of this period were a fascinating combination where the written (textual) material explained the visual material. The consumer society was literally being taught how to read the commercial messages. By the postwar period the education was complete and the function of written text moved away from explaining the visual and toward a more cryptic form where it appears as a "key" to the visual "puzzle."

In the contemporary world, messages about goods are all pervasive—advertising has increasingly filled up the spaces of our daily existence. Our media are dominated by advertising images, public space has been taken over by "information" about products, and most of our sporting and cultural events are accompanied by the name of a corporate sponsor. There is even an attempt to get television commercials into the nation's high schools under the pretense of "free" news programming. Advertising is ubiquitous—it is the air that we breathe as we live our daily lives.

ADVERTISING AND THE GOOD LIFE: IMAGE AND "REALITY"

I have referred to advertising as being part of "a discourse through and about objects" because it does not merely tell us about things but of how things are connected to important domains of our lives. Fundamentally, advertising talks to us as individuals and addresses us about how we can become happy. The answers it provides are all oriented to the marketplace, through the purchase of goods or services. To understand the system of images that constitutes advertising we need to inquire into the definition of happiness and satisfaction in contemporary social life.

Quality of life surveys that ask people what they are seeking in life—what it is that makes them happy—report quite consistent results. The conditions that people are searching for—what they perceive will make them happy—are things such as having personal autonomy and control of one's life, self-esteem, a happy family life, loving relations, a relaxed, tension-free leisure time, and good friendships. The unifying theme of this list is that these things are not fundamentally connected to goods. It is primarily "social" life and not "material" life that seems to be the locus of perceived happiness. Commodities are only weakly related to these sources of satisfaction.[3]

A market society, however, is guided by the principle that satisfaction should be achieved via the marketplace, and through its institutions and structures it orients behavior in that direction. The data from the quality of life studies are not lost on advertisers. If goods themselves are not the locus of perceived happiness, then they need to be connected in some way with those things that are. Thus advertising promotes images of what the audience conceives of as "the good life": Beer can be connected with anything from eroticism to male fraternity to the purity of the old West; food can be tied up with family relations or health; investment advice offers early retirements in tropical settings. The marketplace cannot directly offer the real thing, but it can offer visions of it connected with the purchase of products.

Advertising thus does not work by creating values and attitudes out of nothing but by drawing upon and rechanneling concerns that the target audience (and the culture) already shares. As one advertising executive put it: "Advertising doesn't always mirror how people are acting but how they're *dreaming*. In a sense what we're doing is wrapping up your emotions and selling them back to you." Advertising absorbs and fuses a variety of symbolic practices and discourses, it appropriates and distills from an unbounded range of cultural references. In so doing, goods are knitted into the fabric of social life and cultural significance. As such, advertising is not simple manipulation, but what ad-maker Tony Schwartz calls "partipulation," with the audience participating in its own manipulation.

What are the consequences of such a system of images and goods? Given that the "real" sources of satisfaction cannot be provided by the purchase of commodities (merely the "image" of that source), it should not be surprising that happiness and contentment appear illusory in contemporary society. Recent social thinkers describe the contemporary scene as a "joyless economy,"[4] or as reflecting the "paradox of affluence."[5] It is not simply a matter of being "tricked" by the false blandishments of advertising. The problem is with the institutional structure of a market society that propels definition of satisfaction through the commodity/image system. The modern context, then, provides a curious satisfaction experience—one that William Leiss describes as "an ensemble of satisfactions and dissatisfactions" in which the consumption of commodities mediated by the image-system of advertising leads to consumer uncertainty and confusion.[6] The image-system of the marketplace reflects our desires and dreams, yet we have only the pleasure of the images to sustain us in our actual experience with goods.

The commodity image-system thus provides a particular vision of the world—a particular mode of self-validation that is integrally connected with what one *has* rather than what one *is*—a distinction often referred to as one between "having" and "being," with the latter now being defined through the former. As such, it constitutes a way of life that is defined and structured in quite specific political ways. Some commentators have even described advertising as part of a new *religious* system in which people construct their identities through the commodity form, and in which commodities are part of a supernatural magical world where anything is possible with the purchase of a product. The commodity as displayed in advertising plays a mixture of psychological, social, and physical roles in its relations with people. The object world interacts with the human world at the most basic and fundamental of levels, performing seemingly magical feats of enchantment and transformation, bringing instant happiness and gratification, capturing the forces of nature, and acting as a passport to hitherto untraveled domains and group relationships.[7]

In short, the advertising image-system constantly propels us toward things as means to satisfaction. In the sense that every ad says it is better to buy than not to buy, we can best regard advertising as a *propaganda* system for commodities. In the image-system as a whole, happiness lies at the end of a purchase. Moreover, this is not a minor propaganda system—it is all pervasive. It should not surprise us then to discover that the problem that it poses—how to get more things for everyone (as that is the root to happiness)—guides our political debates. The goal of *economic growth* (on which the commodity vision is based) is an unquestioned and sacred proposition of the political culture. As the environmental costs of the strategy of unbridled economic growth become more obvious, it is clear we must, as a society, engage in debate concerning the nature of future economic growth. However, as long as the commodity image-system maintains its ubiquitous presence and influence, the possibilities of opening such a debate are remote. At the very moment we most desperately need to pose new questions within the political culture, the commodity image-system propels us with even greater certainty and persuasion along a path that, unless checked, is destined to end in disaster. . . .

The visual image-system has colonized areas of life that were previously largely defined (although not solely) by auditory perception and experience. The 1980s [saw] a change in the way that popular music commodities (records, tapes, compact discs) were marketed, with music videos becoming an indispensable component of an overall strategy. These videos were produced as commercials for musical commodities by the advertising industry, using techniques learned from the marketing of products. Viewing these videos, there often seems to be little link between the song and the visuals. In the sense that they are commercials for records, there of course does not have to be. Video makers are in the same position as ad makers in terms of trying to get attention for their message and making it visually pleasurable. It is little wonder then that representations involving sexuality figure so prominently (as in the case of regular product advertising). The visuals are chosen for their ability to sell.

Many people report that listening to a song after watching the video strongly affects the interpretation they give to it—the visual images are replayed in the imagination. In that sense, the surrounding commodity image-system works to fix—or at least to limit—the scope of imaginative interpretation. The realm of listening becomes subordinated to the realm of seeing, to the influence of commercial images. There is also evidence suggesting that the composition of popular music is affected by the new video context. People write songs or lines with the vital marketing tool in mind.

SPEED AND FRAGMENTATION

In addition to issues connected with the colonization of the commodity image-system of other areas of social life (gender socialization, politics, children's play, popular cultural forms), there are also important broader issues connected with its relation to modes of perception and forms of consciousness within contemporary society. For instance, the commodity information-system has two basic characteristics: reliance on visual modes of representation and the increasing speed and rapidity of the images that constitute it. It is this second point that I wish to focus on here. . . .

The visual images that dominate public space and public discourse are, in the video age, not static. They do not stand still for us to examine and linger over. They are here for a couple of seconds and then they are gone. Television advertising is the epitome of this speed-up. There is nothing mysterious in terms of how it arose. As commercial time slots declined from sixty seconds to thirty seconds (and recently to fifteen seconds and even shorter), advertisers responded by creating a new type of advertising—what is called the "vignette approach"—in which narrative and "reason-why" advertising are subsumed under a rapid succession of lifestyle images, meticulously timed with music, that directly sell feeling and emotion rather than products. As a commercial editor puts it of this new approach: "They're a wonderful way to pack in information: all those scenes and emotions—cut, cut, cut. Also they permit you a very freestyle approach—meaning that as long as you stay true to your basic vignette theme you can usually just drop one and shove in another. They're a dream to work with because the parts are sort of interchangeable."[8]

The speed-up is also a response by advertisers to two other factors: the increasing "clutter" of the commercial environment and the coming of age, in terms of disposable income, of a generation that grew up on television and commercials. The need for a commercial to stand out to a visually sophisticated audience drove the image-system to a greater frenzy of concentrated shorts. Again, sexuality became a key feature of the image-system within this.

The speed-up has two consequences. First, it has the effect of drawing the viewer into the message. One cannot watch these messages casually; they require undivided attention. Intensely pleasurable images, often sexual, are integrated into a flow of images. Watching has to be even more attentive to catch the brief shots of visual pleasure. The space "in between" the good parts can then be filled with other information, so that the commodity being advertised becomes a rich and complex sign.

Second, the speed-up has replaced narrative and rational response with images and emotional response. Speed and fragmentation are not particularly conducive to *thinking*. They induce *feeling*. The speed and fragmentation that characterize the commodity image-system may have a similar effect on the construction of consciousness. In one series of ads for MTV, a teenage boy or girl engages in a continuous monologue of events, characters, feelings, and emotions without any apparent connecting theme. As the video images mirror the fragmentation of thoughts, the ad ends with the plug: "Finally, a channel for the way you think." . . .

NOTES

1. See Edward Epstein, *The Rise and Fall of Diamonds* (New York: Simon & Schuster, 1982).

2. This is discussed more fully in William Leiss, Stephen Kline, and Sut Jhally, *Social Communication in Advertising* (Toronto: Nelson, 1986).

3. See Fred Hirsch, *Social Limits to Growth* (Cambridge: Harvard University Press, 1976).

4. Tibor Scitovsky, *The Joyless Economy* (New York: Oxford University Press, 1976).

5. Hirsch, *Social Limits*.

6. William Leiss, *The Limits to Satisfaction* (Toronto: Toronto University Press, 1976).

7. See Sut Jhally, *The Codes of Advertising* (New York: St. Martin's Press, 1987) and John Kavanaugh, *Following Christ in a Consumer Society* (New York: Orbis, 1981).

8. Quoted in Michael Arlen, *Thirty Seconds* (New York: Penguin, 1981), 182.

28

THE NEW POLITICS OF CONSUMPTION

Why Americans Want So Much More Than They Need

Juliet Schor

In contemporary American culture, consuming is as authentic as it gets. Advertisements, getting a bargain, garage sales, and credit cards are firmly entrenched pillars of our way of life. We shop on our lunch hours, patronize outlet malls on vacation, and satisfy our latest desires with a late-night click of the mouse.[1]

Yet for all its popularity, the shopping mania provokes considerable disease: many Americans worry about our preoccupation with getting and spending. They fear we are losing touch with more worthwhile values and ways of living. But the discomfort rarely goes much further than that; it never coheres into a persuasive, well-articulated critique of consumerism. By contrast, in the 1960s and early 1970s, a far-reaching critique of consumer culture was a part of our political discourse. Elements of the New Left, influenced by the Frankfurt school, as well as by John Kenneth Galbraith and others, put forward a scathing indictment. They argued that Americans had been manipulated into participating in a dumbed-down, artificial consumer culture, which yielded few true human satisfactions.

For reasons that are not hard to imagine, this particular approach was short-lived, even among critics of American society and culture. It seemed too patronizing to talk about manipulation or the "true needs" of average Americans. In its stead, critics adopted a more liberal point of view and deferred to individuals on consumer issues. Social critics again emphasized the distribution of resources, with the more economistic goal of maximizing the incomes of working people. The good life, they suggested, could be achieved by attaining a comfortable, middle-class standard of living. This outlook was particularly prevalent in economics, where even radical economists have long believed that income is the key to well-being. While radical political economy, as it came to be called, retained a powerful critique of alienation in production and the distribution of property, it abandoned the nascent intellectual project of analyzing the consumer sphere. Few economists now think about how we consume, and whether it reproduces class inequality, alienation, or power. "Stuff" is the part of the equation that the system is thought to have gotten nearly right.

Of course, many Americans retained a critical stance toward our consumer culture. They embody that stance in their daily lives—in the ways they live and raise their kids. But the rejection of consumerism, if you will, has taken place principally at an individual level. It is not associated with a widely accepted intellectual analysis, and an associated *critical politics of consumption.*

But such a politics has become an urgent need. The average American now finds it harder to achieve a satisfying standard of living than 25 years ago. Work requires longer hours, jobs are less secure, and pressures to spend more intense. Consumption-induced environmental damage remains pervasive, and we are in the midst of widespread failures of public provision. . . . Many Americans have long-term worries about their ability to meet basic needs, ensure a decent standard of living for their children, and keep up with an ever-escalating consumption norm.

In response to these developments, social critics continue to focus on income. In his impressive analysis of the problems of contemporary American capitalism, *Fat and Mean,* economist

Reprinted by permission of Juliet Schor.

David Gordon emphasized income *adequacy*. The "vast majority of U.S. households," he argues, "can ᵇarely make ends meet.... Meager livelihoods ᵃ *typical* condition, an *average* circumstance." ᵗhile, the Economic Policy Institute focuses ᵉ distribution of income and wealth, arguing ʈhat the gains of the top 20 percent have jeopardized the well-being of the bottom 80 percent. Incomes have stagnated and the robust 3 percent growth rates of the 1950s and 1960s are long gone. If we have a consumption problem, this view implicitly states, we can solve it by getting more income into more people's hands. The goals are redistribution and growth.

It is difficult to take exception to this view. It combines a deep respect for individual choice (the liberal part) with a commitment to justice and equality (the egalitarian part). I held it myself for many years. But I now believe that by failing to look deeper—to examine the very nature of consumption—it has become too limiting. In short, I do not think that the "income solution" addresses some of the most profound failures of the current consumption regime.

Why not? First, consuming is part of the problem. Income (the solution) leads to consumption practices that exacerbate and reproduce class and social inequalities, resulting in—and perhaps even worsening—an unequal distribution of income. Second, the system is structured such that an *adequate* income is an elusive goal. That is because adequacy is relative and defined by reference to the incomes of others. Without an analysis of consumer desire and need, and a different framework for understanding what is adequate, we are likely to find ourselves, twenty years from now, arguing that a median income of $100,000—rather than half that—is adequate. These arguments underscore the social context of consumption: the ways in which our sense of social standing and belonging comes from what we consume. If true, they suggest that attempts to achieve equality, or adequacy of individual incomes, without changing consumption patterns will be self-defeating.

Finally, it is difficult to make an ethical argument that people in the world's richest country need more, when the global income gap is so wide, the disparity in world resource use so enormous, and the possibility that we are already consuming beyond the Earth's ecological carrying capacity so likely. This third critique will get less attention

in this essay—because it is more familiar, not because it is less important—but I will return to it in the conclusion.

I agree that justice requires a vastly more equal society, in terms of income and wealth. The question is whether we should also aim for a society in which our relationship to consuming changes, a society in which we consume *differently*. I argue here for such a perspective: for a critique of consumer culture and practices. Somebody needs to be for quality of life, not just quantity of stuff. And to do so requires an approach that does not trivialize consumption, but accords it the respect and centrality it deserves.

THE NEW CONSUMERISM

A new politics of consumption should begin with daily life, and recent developments in the sphere of consumption. I describe these developments as "the new consumerism," by which I mean an upscaling of lifestyle norms; the pervasiveness of conspicuous, status goods and of competition for acquiring them; and the growing disconnect between consumer desires and incomes.

Social comparison and its dynamic manifestation—the need to "keep up"—have long been part of American culture. My term is "competitive consumption," the idea that spending is in large part driven by a comparative or competitive process in which individuals try to keep up with the norms of the social group with which they identify—a "reference group." Although the term is new, the idea is not.

Thorstein Veblen, James Duesenberry, Fred Hirsch, and Robert Frank have all written about the importance of relative position as a dominant spending motive. What's new is the redefinition of reference groups: today's comparisons are less likely to take place between or among households of similar means. Instead, the lifestyles of the upper middle class and the rich have become a more salient point of reference for people throughout the income distribution. Luxury, rather than mere comfort, is a widespread aspiration.

One reason for this shift to "upscale emulation" is the decline of the neighborhood as a focus of comparison. Economically speaking, neighborhoods are relatively homogeneous groupings. In the 1950s and 1960s, when Americans were keeping up with the Joneses down the street, they typically compared themselves to other households of similar incomes. Because of this focus on neighbors, the gap between aspirations and means tended to be moderate.

But as married women entered the work-force in larger numbers—particularly in white-collar jobs—they were exposed to a more economically diverse group of people, and became more likely to gaze upward. Neighborhood contacts correspondingly declined, and the workplace became a more prominent point of reference. Moreover, as people spent less time with neighbors and friends, and more time on the family-room couch, television became more important as a source of consumer cues and information. Because television shows are so heavily skewed to the "lifestyles of the rich and upper middle class," they inflate the viewer's perceptions of what others have, and by extension what is worth acquiring—what one must have in order to avoid being "out of it."

Trends in inequality also helped to create the new consumerism. Since the 1970s, the distribution of income and wealth has shifted decisively in the direction of the top 20 percent. The share of after-tax family income going to the top 20 percent rose from 41.4 percent in 1979 to 46.8 percent in 1996. The share of wealth controlled by the top 20 percent rose from 81.3 percent in 1983 to 84.3 percent in 1997. This windfall resulted in a surge in conspicuous spending at the top. Remember the 1980s—the decade of greed and excess? Beginning with the super-rich, whose gains have been disproportionately higher, and trickling down to the merely affluent, visible status spending was the order of the day. Slowed down temporarily by the recession during the early 1990s, conspicuous luxury consumption intensified during the recent boom. Trophy homes, diamonds of a carat or more, granite countertops, and sport utility vehicles became the primary consumer symbols of the late 1990s. Television, as well as films, magazines, and newspapers, ensure that the remaining 80 percent of the nation is aware of the status purchasing that has swept the upper echelons.

In the meantime, upscale emulation had become well established. Researchers Susan Fournier and Michael Guiry found that 35 percent of their sample aspired to reach the top 6 percent of the income distribution, and another 49 percent aspired to the next 12 percent. Only 15 percent reported that they would be satisfied with "living a comfortable life"—that is, being middle class. But 85 percent of the population cannot earn the six-figure incomes necessary to support upper-middle-class lifestyles. The result is a growing aspirational gap, and with desires persistently outrunning incomes, many consumers find themselves frustrated. One survey of U.S. households found that the level of income needed to fulfill one's dreams doubled between 1986 and 1994, and by 1999 it was more than twice the median household income.

. . . The new consumerism, with its growing aspirational gap, has begun to jeopardize the quality of American life. Within the middle class—and even the upper middle class—many families experience an almost threatening pressure to keep up, both for themselves and their children. They are deeply concerned about the rigors of the global economy, and the need to have their children attend "good" schools. This means living in a community with relatively high housing costs. For some households this also means providing their children with advantages purchased on the private market (computers, lessons, extracurriculars, private schooling). Keeping two adults in the labor market—as so many families do, to earn the incomes to stay middle class—is expensive, not only because of the second car, child-care costs, and career wardrobe. It also creates the need for time-saving—but costly—commodities and services, such as take-out food and dry cleaning, as well as stress-relieving experiences. Finally, the financial tightrope that so many households walk—high expenses, low savings—is a constant source of stress and worry. While precise estimates are difficult to come by, one can argue that somewhere between a quarter and half of all households live paycheck-to-paycheck.

These problems are magnified for low-income households. Their sources of income have become increasingly erratic and inadequate, on account of employment instability, the proliferation of part-time jobs, and restrictions on welfare payments. Yet most low-income households remain firmly integrated within consumerism. They are targets for credit card companies, who find them an easy mark. They watch more television, and are more exposed to its desire-creating properties. Low-income children are more likely to be exposed to commercials at school, as well as at home.

The growing prominence of the values of the market, materialism, and economic success make financial failure more consequential and painful.

These are the effects at the household level. The new consumerism has also set in motion another dynamic: it siphons off resources that could be used for alternatives to private consumption. We use our income in four basic ways: private consumption, public consumption, private savings, and leisure. When consumption standards can be met easily out of current income, there is greater willingness to support public goods, save privately, and cut back on time spent at work (in other words, to "buy leisure"). Conversely, when lifestyle norms are upscaled more rapidly than income, private consumption "crowds out" alternative uses of income. That is arguably what happened in the 1980s and 1990s: resources shifting into private consumption, and away from free time, the public sector, and saving. Hours of work have risen dramatically; saving rates have plummeted; and public funds for education, recreation, and the arts have fallen in the wake of a grassroots tax revolt. The timing suggests a strong coincidence between these developments and the intensification of competitive consumption. . . . Indeed, this scenario makes good sense of an otherwise surprising finding: that indicators of "social health" or "genuine progress" (i.e., basic quality-of-life measures) began to diverge from Gross Domestic Product in the mid-1970s, after moving in tandem for decades. Can it be that consuming and prospering are no longer compatible states? . . .

Americans did not suddenly become greedy. The aspirational gap has been created by structural changes—such as the decline of community and social connection, the intensification of inequality, the growing role of mass media, and heightened penalties for failing in the labor market. Upscaling is mainly defensive, and has both psychological and practical dimensions.

Similarly, the profoundly social nature of consumption ensures that these issues cannot be resolved by pure acts of will. Our notions of what is adequate, necessary, or luxurious are shaped by the larger social context. Most of us are deeply tied in to our particular class and other group identities, and our spending patterns help reproduce them.

Thus, a collective, not just an individual, response is necessary. Someone needs to address the larger question of the consumer culture itself. But doing so risks complaints about being intrusive, patronizing, or elitist. . . .

CONSUMER KNOWS BEST

The recent consumer boom rested on growth in incomes, wealth, and credit. But it also rested on something more intangible: social attitudes toward consumer decision making and choices. Ours is an ideology of noninterference—the view that one should be able to buy what one likes, where one likes, and as much as one likes, with nary a glance from the government, neighbors, ministers, or political parties. Consumption is perhaps the clearest example of an individual behavior that our society takes to be almost wholly personal, completely outside the purview of social concern and policy. The consumer is king. And queen.

This view has much to recommend it. After all, who would relish the idea of sumptuary legislation, rationing, or government controls on what can be produced or purchased? The liberal approach to consumption combines a deep respect for the consumer's ability to act in her own best interest and an emphasis on the efficiency gains of unregulated consumer markets: a commitment to liberty and the general welfare.

Cogent as it is, however, this view is vulnerable on a number of grounds. Structural biases and market failures in the operation of consumer markets undermine its general validity; consumer markets are neither so free nor so efficient as the conventional story suggests. The basis of a new consumer policy should be an understanding of the presence of structural distortions in consumers' choices, the importance of social inequalities and power in consumption practices, a more sophisticated understanding of consumer motivations, and serious analysis of the processes that form our preferences. . . .

A POLITICS OF CONSUMPTION

. . . But what should a politics of consumption look like? To start the discussion—not to provide final answers—I suggest seven basic elements:

1. *A right to a decent standard of living.* This familiar idea is especially important now because

it points us to a fundamental distinction between what people need and what they want. In the not very distant past, this dichotomy was not only well understood, but the basis of data collection and social policy. Need was a social concept with real force. All that's left now is an economy of desire. This is reflected in polling data. Just over 40 percent of adults earning $50,000 to $100,000 a year, and 27 percent of those earning more than $100,000, agree that "I cannot afford to buy everything I really need." One third and 19 percent, respectively, agree that "I spend nearly all of my money on the basic necessities of life." I believe that our politics would profit from reviving a discourse of need, in which we talk about the material requirements for every person and household to participate fully in society. Of course, there are many ways in which such a right might be enforced: government income transfers or vouchers, direct provision of basic needs, employment guarantees, and the like. For reasons of space, I leave that discussion aside; the main point is to revive the distinction between needs and desires.

2. *Quality of life rather than quantity of stuff.* Twenty-five years ago quality-of-life indicators began moving in an opposite direction from our measures of income, or gross domestic product, a striking divergence from historic trends. Moreover, the accumulating evidence on well-being, at least its subjective measures (and to some extent objective measures, such as health), suggests that above the poverty line, income is relatively unimportant in affecting well-being. This may be because what people care about is relative, not absolute income. Or it may be because increases in output undermine precisely those factors that do yield welfare. Here I have in mind the growing worktime requirements of the market economy, and the concomitant decline in family, leisure, and community time; the adverse impacts of growth on the natural environment; and the potential link between growth and social capital.

This argument that consumption is not the same as well-being has great potential to resonate with millions of Americans. Large majorities hold ambivalent views about consumerism. They struggle with ongoing conflicts between materialism and an alternative set of values stressing family, religion, community, social commitment, equity, and personal meaning. We should be articulating an alternative vision of a quality of life, rather than a quantity of stuff. That is a basis on which to argue for a restructuring of the labor market to allow people to choose for time, or to penalize companies that require excessive hours for employees. It is also a basis for creating alternative indicators to the GNP, positive policies to encourage civic engagement, support for parents, and so forth.

3. *Ecologically sustainable consumption.* Current consumption patterns are wreaking havoc on the planetary ecology. Global warming is perhaps the best known, but many other consumption habits have major environmental impacts. Sport utility vehicles, air conditioning, and foreign travel are all energy-intensive and contribute to global warming. Larger homes use more energy and building resources, destroy open space, and increase the use of toxic chemicals. All those granite countertops being installed in American kitchens were carved out of mountains around the world, leaving in their wake a blighted landscape. Our daily newspaper and coffee are contributing to deforestation and loss of species diversity. Something as simple as a T-shirt plays its part, since cotton cultivation accounts for a significant fraction of world pesticide use. Consumers know far less about the environmental impacts of their daily consumption habits than they should. And while the solution lies in greater part with corporate and governmental practices, people who are concerned about equality should be joining forces with environmentalists who are trying to educate, mobilize, and change practices at the neighborhood and household levels.

4. *Democratize consumption practices.* One of the central arguments I have made is that consumption practices reflect and perpetuate structures of inequality and power. This is particularly true in the "new consumerism," with its emphasis on luxury, expensiveness, exclusivity, rarity, uniqueness, and distinction. These are the values that consumer markets are plying, to the middle and lower middle class. (That is what Martha Stewart did at Kmart.)

But who needs to accept these values? Why not stand for consumption that is democratic, egalitarian, and available to all? How about making "access," rather than exclusivity, cool, by exposing the industries such as fashion, home decor, or tourism, which are pushing the upscaling of desire? This point speaks to the need for both cultural change and policies that might facilitate it. Why not tax high-end "status" versions of products while allowing the low-end models to be sold tax-free?

5. *A politics of retailing and the "cultural environment."* The new consumerism has been associated with the homogenization of retail environments and a pervasive shift toward the commercialization of culture. The same mega-stores can be found everywhere, creating a blandness in the cultural environment. Advertising and marketing are also pervading hitherto relatively protected spaces, such as schools, doctors' offices, media programming (rather than commercial time), and so on. In my local mall, the main restaurant offers a book-like menu comprising advertisements for unrelated products. The daily paper looks more like a consumer's guide to food, wine, computer electronics, and tourism and less like a purveyor of news. We should be talking about these issues, and the ways in which corporations are remaking our public institutions and space. Do we value diversity in retailing? Do we want to preserve small retail outlets? How about ad-free zones? Commercial-free public education? Here too public policy can play a role by outlawing certain advertising in certain places and institutions, by financing publicly controlled media, and enacting zoning regulations that take diversity as a positive value.

6. *Expose commodity "fetishism."* Everything we consume has been produced. So a new politics of consumption must take into account the labor, environmental, and other conditions under which products are made, and argue for high standards. This argument has been of great political importance in recent years, with public exposure of the so-called global sweatshop in the apparel, footwear, and fashion industries. Companies fear their public images, and consumers appear willing to pay a little more for products when they know they have been produced responsibly. There are fruitful and essential linkages between production, consumption, and the environment that we should be making.

7. *A consumer movement and governmental policy.* Much of what I have been arguing for could occur as a result of a consumer's movement. Indeed, the revitalization of the labor movement calls out for an analogous revitalization of long dormant consumers. We need independent organizations of consumers to pressure companies, influence the political agenda, provide objective product information, and articulate a vision of an appealing and humane consumer sphere. We also need a consumer movement to pressure the state to enact the kinds of policies that the foregoing analysis suggests are needed. These include taxes on luxury and status consumption, green taxes and subsidies, new policies toward advertising, more sophisticated regulations on consumer credit, international labor and environmental standards, revamping of zoning regulations to favor retail diversity, and the preservation of open space. There is a vast consumer policy agenda that has been mainly off the table. It's time to put it back on.

NOTE

1. Sources for much of the data cited in this [chapter] can be found in the notes to *The Overspent American: Why We Want What We Don't Need* (Harper Perennial, 1999) or by contacting the author.

29

PEPSI'S NEW AD IS A TOTAL SUCCESS

Ian Bogost

Before it's an ad for shampoo or cat food or cola, every advertisement is first an ad for capitalism.

Without a privately-controlled industry jockeying to compete with one another for consumer dollars, there's no need for advertising. People would wash their hair with Shampoo, and feed their cats with Cat Food, and quench their thirst with Cola. Without competition, there would be no need to advertise in the first place.

Especially when it comes to commodities. There are some differences between colas—the taste and the ingredients, for example. But the main difference is on the can rather than in it. The branding, and the sensibilities that branding conveys.

[Recently], Pepsi released an ad that takes a strong, if bizarre, brand position on contemporary politics. In the spot, dubbed "Jump In," Kendall Jenner abandons a photo shoot to join a passing march. To do so, she sheds a blonde wig and slips in among a diverse throng of variously-toned participants in a seemingly-innocuous protest. Eventually, Jenner meets an equally innocuous policeman keeping order. She hands him a cold Pepsi, and the crowd of protesters rejoices. "Live for Now," the spot concludes, topped by the Pepsi brand mark.

The ad has been almost universally panned online. A tone-deaf take on "protest as brunch." An absurdist parody of the long, unfinished project of civil-rights activism in America. A trivialization of today's street unrest.

All these criticisms are dead-on. But they don't matter, because the ad is an undeniable success. Yes, true, it coopts the politics of protest, particularly as they surround race relations in America

today. But that's not the ad's goal, so the public's objection is ultimately irrelevant to Pepsi's mission. The ad's point is to put the consumer in a more important role than the citizen anyway. And to position Pepsi as a facilitator in the utopian dream of pure, color-blind consumerism that might someday replace politics entirely.

Controversy is no stranger to consumer marketing today. In early 2016, Coca-Cola launched an online ad campaign that let users overlay their own taglines onto GIFs of people enjoying the company's soft drinks. Aware of the dangers of user-generated content, Coke built a many-thousand-entry "profanity API" to prevent objectionable ads. Writing about the campaign last year, I cataloged the various concepts Coke knew it didn't want people to associate with its brand. Those included vulgarity, drugs, and other brand names—but also weirder things, like references to science, music, and even tacos.

But it still couldn't stop people from making Coke GIFs that mocked the company directly. For a time, social media swelled with user-generated sneers at Coke, fashioned by means of the very tool that was meant to prop the brand up. Take that, capitalism! Hoisted on its own petard.

The only problem: Capitalism is an immensely resilient institution. The ironic, contra-Coke GIFs couldn't help but become transformed back into brand-compatible Coca-Cola messaging. Even the neo-Marxist agitators fashioning Coke-facilitated critiques of consumer capitalism might occasionally drink soft drinks. And when they do, their brains will have to contend with the dissonance of feeling affinity for Coca-Cola, thanks to the company having facilitated sneers at its own expense.

IT'S POSSIBLE TO UNDERSTAND THE PEPSI PROTEST AS A MARCH FOR THE POWER OF PEPSI BRANDING INSTEAD OF SOCIAL JUSTICE

The Pepsi "Jump In" ad plays a similar trump card. In a statement, the company claims that the spot "captures the spirit and actions of those people that jump into every moment." In so doing, according to Pepsi anyway, the brand unites people from different backgrounds around the shared delight of refreshment. For those predisposed to an apolitical reading of consumer advertising—and let's face it, that's most people—the result might land near its target, even if it doesn't do so with the memorable aplomb of, say, Coca-Cola's famous 1971 "Hilltop" ad.

But those who object to the ad's brazen appropriation of political malcontent in general and organized protest in particular also have a role to play in Pepsi's proposal for brand unity. The march shown in the ad is so nondescript as to invite offense. The supposed protesters carry generic signs: Peace, many read, or Unity. Another sign reads, "Join the Conversation," a glib quip often used by media companies and brand marketers to spur engagement on social media or website comment sections. Here too, Pepsi wins in advance. For what else are the rightfully-angry critics of "Jump In" doing but "joining the conversation?" That call is clearly being met by everyone yammering against it on social media. To embrace all voices and perspectives isn't a bad bet for a commodity soft-drink manufacturer.

Critics aren't wrong to see the protest as a milquetoast mockery of the real agitation for social justice in the streets in America. In particular, the ad neuters one of the most memorable images of protest in recent memory, that of a woman facing-off with riot police in a mid-2016 Baton Rouge demonstration.

PEOPLE DON'T BUY COLA FOR ITS SOCIAL REALISM. THEY BUY IT TO FEEL GOOD ABOUT THEMSELVES

But the ad's interpretive possibilities don't end with this explanation. It's equally possible to understand the Pepsi protest as a march for the power of Pepsi branding instead of social justice. It may seem preposterous or even revolting to advance this interpretation, but that doesn't make it any less viable. After all, the ad ends with a clear admission of the march's purpose: to deliver ice-cold Pepsi cola to the (prominently unmilitarized) police who quirkily mistook an innocent, branded march for a political protest.

At a time when so much is worthy of protest, it might seem insane to imagine a big company like Pepsi greenlighting such a tone-deaf take. But it's equally likely that Pepsi is banking on this exact social anxiety as an invitation for branded levity. Today's political climate is distressing for many people in America. For some of them, the answer to such distress is protest and agitation. But for others, salve comes in dreaming of a near future in which all that anxiety melts away, like a cool soda quenching a big thirst.

Pepsi steps in here, offering a hypothetical resolution to politics by a more powerful force in America—consumer capitalism. The cooption of specific scenes of protest, like the Baton Rouge moment, offers an alternative reality in which people line the streets to share soda rather than to lament (or defend) racial inequity. If only everyone would first identify as a consumer, reasons Pepsi, then they wouldn't have to see one another as black or white, man or woman, citizen or immigrant. Don't be surprised; after all, people don't buy cola for its social realism. They buy it to feel good about themselves, even if temporarily. And let's be real: that's also why people post on social media, in large part.

In 2008, Pepsi changed its brand mark to the current, off-axis rendition of the longstanding swirly-circle. The next year, a document circulated online, claiming to be a design strategy document from the agency that managed the rebrand. It was a thing of ghastly nonsense, mixing references to art and philosophy with obfuscated drafting guides for the geometries of vessels and brand images. Dubbed a sphere, the Pepsi brand was theorized as a cosmic body, with gravitational pull that might naturally draw shoppers toward it in supermarkets. Pepsi reportedly paid $1 million for this consulting service.

Is it real? That's the first question most sensible people ask about the branding document. But in truth, it doesn't matter. Brand marketing is black magic, conducted largely to eke out incremental changes in consumer commodity purchasing behavior. And within the corporate world, chief marketing officers and brand managers also need to establish and maintain their own future necessity. Part of capitalism's job is to reproduce itself.

But even if the branding document is not real, it might as well be, and it easily could be, which is not much different. After the document's leak in 2009, some media outlets reported that "others believe it is a clever hoax released as part of a 'viral marketing campaign' by the drink's firm to get attention on the internet." Plausible enough.

And so too, the "Jump In" ad succeeds even in its failure. As I write this, *The Wall Street Journal* reporter Jennifer Maloney reports that Pepsi has seen the error of its ways and plans to pull the ad. "Clearly we missed the mark," the company's statement reads. "We did not intend to make light of any serious issue."

The genius of this decision is that it satisfies everyone. The Kardashian fanatics got their Kendall Jenner fix. The agitators get to feel that they have successfully redressed a big brand company; a minor victory in a time of so many defeats. The earnest, probably-white folk who enjoyed Pepsi's alternative to constant politicization got their saccharine status-quo—and now they also get a branded excuse to issue a counter-offensive against the progressives who insisted on bringing politics into innocuous soft drinks (surely it's coming). The media get their scoops, and their thinkpieces (like this one). And these outcomes, incompatible though they are, all return attention to Pepsi—which is all it really wanted in the first place.

30 SEX, LIES, AND ADVERTISING

Gloria Steinem

When *Ms.* began, we didn't consider *not* taking ads. The most important reason was keeping the price of a feminist magazine low enough for most women to afford. But the second and almost equal reason was providing a forum where women and advertisers could talk to each other and improve advertising itself. After all, it was (and still is) as potent a source of information in this country as news or TV and movie dramas.

We decided to proceed in two stages. First, we would convince makers of "people products" used by both men and women but advertised mostly to men—cars, credit cards, insurance, sound equipment, financial services, and the like—that their ads should be placed in a women's magazine. Since they were accustomed to the division between editorial and advertising in news and general interest magazines, this would allow our editorial content to be free and diverse. Second, we would add the best ads for whatever traditional "women's products" (clothes, shampoo, fragrance, food, and so on) that surveys showed *Ms.* readers used. But we would ask them to come in *without* the usual quid pro quo of "complementary copy."

We knew the second step might be harder. Food advertisers have always demanded that women's magazines publish recipes and articles on entertaining (preferably ones that name their products) in return for their ads: clothing advertisers expect to be surrounded by fashion spreads (especially ones that credit their designers); and shampoo, fragrance, and beauty products in general usually insist on positive editorial coverage of beauty subjects, plus photo credits besides. That's why women's magazines look the way they do. But if we could break this link between ads and editorial content, then we wanted good ads for "women's products," too. . . .

I thought then that our main problem would be the imagery in ads themselves. Carmakers were still draping blondes in evening gowns over the hoods like ornaments. Authority figures were almost always male, even in ads for products that only women used. Sadistic, he-man campaigns even won industry praise. (For instance, *Advertising Age* had hailed the infamous Silva Thin cigarette theme, "How to Get a Woman's Attention: Ignore Her," as "brilliant.") Even in medical journals, tranquilizer ads showed depressed housewives standing beside piles of dirty dishes and promised to get them back to work.

Obviously, *Ms.* would have to avoid such ads and seek out the best ones—but this didn't seem impossible. *The New Yorker* had been selecting ads for aesthetic reasons for years, a practice that only seemed to make advertisers more eager to be in its pages. *Ebony* and *Essence* were asking for ads with positive black images, and though their struggle was hard, they weren't being called unreasonable. . . .

The fact that *Ms.* was asking companies to do business in a different way meant our saleswomen had to make many times the usual number of calls—first to convince agencies and then client companies besides—and to present endless amounts of research. I was often asked to do a final ad presentation, or see some higher decision maker, or speak to women employees so executives could see the interest of women they worked with. That's why I spent more time persuading advertisers than editing or writing for *Ms.*, and why I ended up with an unsentimental education in the seamy underside of publishing that few writers see (and even fewer magazines can publish).

From Steinem, Gloria. "Sex, Lies, and Advertising." *Ms. Magazine,* July/August 1990. Reprinted with permission of Gloria Steinem and *Ms. Magazine.*

Let me take you with us through some experiences, just as they happened:

1.   Cheered on by early support from Volkswagen and one or two other car companies, we scrape together time and money to put on a major reception in Detroit. We know U.S. carmakers firmly believe that women choose the upholstery, not the car, but we are armed with statistics and reader mail to prove the contrary: a car is an important purchase for women, one that symbolizes mobility and freedom.

But almost nobody comes. We are left with many pounds of shrimp on the table, and quite a lot of egg on our face. We blame ourselves for not guessing that there would be a baseball pennant play-off on the same day, but executives go out of their way to explain they wouldn't have come anyway. Thus begins ten years of knocking on hostile doors, presenting endless documentation, and hiring a full-time saleswoman in Detroit: all necessary before *Ms.* gets any real results.

This long saga has a semi-happy ending: foreign and, later, domestic carmakers eventually provided *Ms.* with enough advertising to make cars one of our top sources of ad revenue. Slowly, Detroit began to take the women's market seriously enough to put car ads in other women's magazines, too, thus freeing a few pages from the hothouse of fashion-beauty-food ads.

But long after figures showed a third, even a half, of many car models being bought by women, U.S. makers continued to be uncomfortable addressing women. Unlike foreign carmakers, Detroit never quite learned the secret of creating intelligent ads that exclude no one, and then placing them in women's magazines to overcome past exclusion. (*Ms.* readers were so grateful for a routine Honda ad featuring rack and pinion steering, for instance, that they sent fan mail.) Even now, Detroit continues to ask, "Should we make special ads for women?" Perhaps that's why some foreign cars still have a disproportionate share of the U.S. women's market.

2.   In the *Ms.* Gazette, we do a brief report on a congressional hearing into chemicals used in hair dyes that are absorbed through the skin and may be carcinogenic. Newspapers report this too, but Clairol, a Bristol-Myers subsidiary that makes dozens of products—a few of which have just begun to advertise in *Ms.*—is outraged. Not at newspapers or newsmagazines, just at us. It's bad enough that *Ms.* is the only women's magazine refusing to provide the usual "complementary" articles and beauty photos, but to criticize one of their categories—*that* is going too far.

We offer to publish a letter from Clairol telling its side of the story. In an excess of solicitousness, we even put this letter in the Gazette, not in Letters to the Editors where it belongs. Nonetheless—and in spite of surveys that show *Ms.* readers are active women who use more of almost everything Clairol makes than do the readers of any other women's magazine—*Ms.* gets almost none of these ads for the rest of its natural life.

Meanwhile, Clairol changes its hair coloring formula, apparently in response to the hearings we reported.

3.   Our saleswomen set out early to attract ads for consumer electronics: sound equipment, calculators, computers, VCRs, and the like. We know that our readers are determined to be included in the technological revolution. We know from reader surveys that *Ms.* readers are buying this stuff in numbers as high as those of magazines like *Playboy,* or "men 18 to 34," the prime targets of the consumer electronics industry. Moreover, unlike traditional women's products that our readers buy but don't need to read articles about, these are subjects they want covered in our pages. There actually *is* a supportive editorial atmosphere.

"But women don't understand technology," say executives at the end of ad presentations. "Maybe not," we respond, "but neither do men—and we all buy it."

"If women *do* buy it," say the decision makers, "they're asking their husbands and boyfriends what to buy first." We produce letters from *Ms.* readers saying how turned off they are when salesmen say things like "Let me know when your husband can come in."

After several years of this, we get a few ads for compact sound systems. Some of them come from JVC, whose vice president, Harry Elias, is trying to convince his Japanese bosses that there is something called a women's market. At his invitation, I find myself speaking at huge trade shows in Chicago and Las Vegas, trying to persuade JVC dealers that showrooms don't have to be locker rooms where women are made to feel unwelcome.

But as it turns out, the shows themselves are part of the problem. In Las Vegas, the only women around the technology displays are semi-nude models serving champagne. In Chicago, the big attraction is Marilyn Chambers, who followed Linda Lovelace of *Deep Throat* fame as Chuck Traynor's captive and/or employee. VCRs are being demonstrated with her porn videos.

In the end, we get ads for a car stereo now and then, but no VCRs; some IBM personal computers, but no Apple or Japanese ones. We notice that office magazines like *Working Woman* and *Savvy* don't benefit as much as they should from office equipment ads either. In the electronics world, women and technology seem mutually exclusive. It remains a decade behind even Detroit.

4. Because we get letters from little girls who love toy trains, and who ask our help in changing ads and box-top photos that feature little boys only, we try to get toy-train ads from Lionel. It turns out that Lionel executives *have* been concerned about little girls. They made a pink train, and were surprised when it didn't sell.

Lionel bows to consumer pressure with a photograph of a boy *and* a girl—but only on some of their boxes. They fear that, if trains are associated with girls, they will be devalued in the minds of boys. Needless to say, *Ms.* gets no train ads, and little girls remain a mostly unexplored market. By 1986, Lionel is put up for sale.

But for different reasons, we haven't had much luck with other kinds of toys either. In spite of many articles on child-rearing—an annual listing of nonsexist, multiracial toys by Letty Cottin Pogrebin; Stories for Free Children, a regular feature also edited by Letty; and other prizewinning features for or about children—we get virtually no toy ads. Generations of *Ms.* saleswomen explain to toy manufacturers that a larger proportion of *Ms.* readers have preschool children than do the readers of other women's magazines, but this industry can't believe feminists have or care about children.

5. When *Ms.* begins, the staff decides not to accept ads for feminine hygiene sprays or cigarettes: they are damaging and carry no appropriate health warnings. Though we don't think we should tell our readers what to do, we do think we should provide facts so they can decide for themselves. Since the antismoking lobby has been pressing for health warnings on cigarette ads, we decide to take them only as they comply.

Philip Morris is among the first to do so. One of its brands, Virginia Slims, is also sponsoring women's tennis and the first national polls of women's opinions. On the other hand, the Virginia Slims theme, "You've come a long way, baby," has more than a "baby" problem. It makes smoking a symbol of progress for women.

We explain to Philip Morris that this slogan won't do well in our pages, but they are convinced its success with some women means it will work with *all* women. Finally, we agree to publish an ad for a Virginia Slims calendar as a test. The letters from readers are critical—and smart. For instance: Would you show a black man picking cotton, the same man in a Cardin suit, and symbolize the antislavery and civil rights movements by smoking? Of course not. But instead of honoring the test results, the Philip Morris people seem angry to be proven wrong. They take away ads for *all* their many brands.

This costs *Ms.* about $250,000 the first year. After five years, we can no longer keep track. Occasionally, a new set of executives listens to *Ms.* saleswomen, but because we won't take Virginia Slims, not one Philip Morris product returns to our pages for the next 16 years.

Gradually, we also realize our naiveté, in thinking we *could* decide against taking cigarette ads. They became a disproportionate support of magazines the moment they were banned on television, and few magazines could compete and survive without them: certainly not *Ms.*, which lacks so many other categories. By the time statistics in the 1980s showed that women's rate of lung cancer was approaching men's, the necessity of taking cigarette ads had become a kind of prison.

6. General Mills, Pillsbury, Carnation, Del Monte, Dole, Kraft, Stouffer, Hormel, Nabisco: you name the food giant, we try it. But no matter how desirable the *Ms.* readership, our lack of recipes is lethal.

We explain to them that placing food ads *only* next to recipes associates food with work. For many women, it is a negative that works *against* the ads. Why not place food ads in diverse media without recipes (thus reaching more men, who are now a third of the shoppers in super-markets anyway), and leave the recipes to specialty magazines like *Gourmet* (a third of whose readers are also men)?

These arguments elicit interest, but except for an occasional ad for a convenience food, instant coffee, diet drinks, yogurt, or such extras as avocados and almonds, this mainstay of the publishing industry stays closed to us. Period.

7.   Traditionally, wines and liquors didn't advertise to women: men were thought to make the brand decisions, even if women did the buying. But after endless presentations, we begin to make a dent in this category. Thanks to the unconventional Michel Roux of Carillon Importers (distributors of Grand Marnier, Absolut Vodka, and others), who assumes that food and drink have no gender, some ads are leaving their men's club.

Beermakers are still selling masculinity. It takes *Ms.* fully eight years to get its first beer ad (Michelob). In general, however, liquor ads are less stereotyped in their imagery—and far less controlling of the editorial content around them—than are women's products. But given the underrepresentation of other categories, these very facts tend to create a disproportionate number of alcohol ads in the pages of *Ms.* This in turn dismays readers worried about women and alcoholism.

8.   We hear in 1980 that women in the Soviet Union have been producing feminist *samizdat* (underground, self-published books) and circulating them throughout the country. As punishment, four of the leaders have been exiled. Though we are operating on our usual shoestring, we solicit individual contributions to send Robin Morgan to interview these women in Vienna.

The result is an exclusive cover story that includes the first news of a populist peace movement against the Afghanistan occupation, a prediction of *glasnost* to come, and a grass-roots, intimate view of Soviet women's lives. From the popular press to women's studies courses, the response is great. The story wins a Front Page award.

Nonetheless, this journalistic coup undoes years of efforts to get an ad schedule from Revlon. Why? Because the Soviet women on our cover *are not wearing makeup.*

9.   Four years of research and presentations go into convincing airlines that women now make travel choices and business trips. United, the first airline to advertise in *Ms.,* is so impressed with the response from our readers that one of its executives appears in a film for our ad presentations. As usual, good ads get great results.

But we have problems unrelated to such results. For instance: because American Airlines flight attendants include among their labor demands the stipulation that they could choose to have their last names preceded by "Ms." on their name tags—in a long-delayed revolt against the standard, "I am your pilot, Captain Rothgart, and this is your flight attendant, Cindy Sue"— American officials seem to hold the magazine responsible. We get no ads.

There is still a different problem at Eastern. A vice president cancels subscriptions for thousands of copies on Eastern flights. Why? Because he is offended by ads for lesbian poetry journals in the *Ms.* Classified. A "family airline," as he explains to me coldly on the phone, has to "draw the line somewhere."

It's obvious that *Ms.* can't exclude lesbians and serve women. We've been trying to make that point ever since our first issue included an article by and about lesbians, and both Suzanne Levine, our managing editor, and I were lectured by such heavy hitters as Ed Kosner, then editor of *Newsweek* (and later of *New York Magazine*), who insisted that *Ms.* should "position" itself *against* lesbians. But our advertisers have paid to reach a guaranteed number of readers, and soliciting new subscriptions to compensate for Eastern would cost $150,000, plus rebating money in the meantime.

Like almost everything ad-related, this presents an elaborate organizing problem. After days of searching for sympathetic members of the Eastern board, Frank Thomas, president of the Ford Foundation, kindly offers to call Roswell Gilpatrick, a director of Eastern. I talk with Mr. Gilpatrick, who calls Frank Borman, then the president of Eastern. Frank Borman calls me to say that his airline is not in the business of censoring magazines: *Ms.* will be returned to Eastern flights.

10.   Women of color read *Ms.* in disproportionate numbers. This is a source of pride to *Ms.* staffers, who are also more racially representative than the editors of other women's magazines. But this reality is obscured by ads

filled with enough white women to make a reader snowblind.

Pat Carbine remembers mostly "astonishment" when she requested African American, Hispanic, Asian, and other diverse images. Marcia Ann Gillespie, a *Ms.* editor who was previously the editor in chief of *Essence,* witnesses ad bias a second time: having tried for *Essence* to get white advertisers to use black images (Revlon did so eventually, but L'Oréal, Lauder, Chanel, and other companies never did), she sees similar problems getting integrated ads for an integrated magazine. Indeed, the ad world often creates black and Hispanic ads only for black and Hispanic media. In an exact parallel of the fear that marketing a product to women will endanger its appeal to men, the response is usually, "But your [white] readers won't identify."

In fact, those we are able to get—for instance, a Max Factor ad made for *Essence* that Linda Wachner gives us after she becomes president—is praised by white readers, too. But there are pathetically few such images.

11. By the end of 1986, production and mailing costs have risen astronomically, ad income is flat, and competition for ads is stiffer than ever. The 60/40 preponderance of edit over ads that we promised to readers becomes 50/50; children's stories, most poetry, and some fiction are casualties of less space: in order to get variety into limited pages, the length (and sometimes the depth) of articles suffers; and, though we do refuse most of the ads that would look like a parody in our pages, we get so worn down that some slip through. . . . Still, readers perform miracles. Though we haven't been able to afford a subscription mailing in two years, they maintain our guaranteed circulation of 450,000.

Nonetheless, media reports on *Ms.* often insist that our unprofitability must be due to reader disinterest. The myth that advertisers simply follow readers is very strong. Not one reporter notes that other comparable magazines our size (say, *Vanity Fair* or *The Atlantic*) have been losing more money in one year than *Ms.* has lost in 16 years. No matter how much never-to-be-recovered cash is poured into starting a magazine or keeping one going, appearances seem to be all that matter. (Which is why we haven't been able to explain our fragile state in public. Nothing causes ad-flight like the smell of nonsuccess.)

My healthy response is anger. My not-so-healthy response is constant worry. Also an obsession with finding one more rescue. There is hardly a night when I don't wake up with sweaty palms and pounding heart, scared that we won't be able to pay the printer or the post office; scared most of all that closing our doors will hurt the women's movement.

Out of chutzpah and desperation, I arrange a lunch with Leonard Lauder, president of Estée Lauder. With the exception of Clinique (the brainchild of Carol Phillips), none of Lauder's hundreds of products has been advertised in *Ms.* A year's schedule of ads for just three or four of them could save us. Indeed, as the scion of a family-owned company whose ad practices are followed by the beauty industry, he is one of the few men who could liberate many pages in all women's magazines just by changing his mind about "complementary copy."

Over a lunch that costs more than we can pay for some articles, I explain the need for his leadership. I also lay out the record of *Ms.:* more literary and journalistic prizes won, more new issues introduced into the mainstream, new writers discovered, and impact on society than any other magazine: more articles that became books, stories that became movies, ideas that became television series, and newly advertised products that became profitable: and, most important for him, a place for his ads to reach women who aren't reachable through any other women's magazine. Indeed, if there is one constant characteristic of the ever-changing *Ms.* readership, it is their impact as leaders. Whether it's waiting until later to have first babies, or pioneering PABA as sun protection in cosmetics, *whatever* they are doing today, a third to a half of American women will be doing three to five years from now. It's never failed.

But, he says, *Ms.* readers are not *our* women. They're not interested in things like fragrance and blush-on. If they were, *Ms.* would write articles about them.

On the contrary, I explain, surveys show they are more likely to buy such things than the readers of, say, *Cosmopolitan* or *Vogue.* They're good customers because they're out in the world enough to need several sets of everything: home, work, purse, travel, gym, and so on. They just don't need to read articles about these things. Would he ask a men's magazine to publish monthly columns on how to shave before he advertised Aramis products (his line for men)?

He concedes that beauty features are often concocted more for advertisers than readers. But *Ms.* isn't appropriate for his ads anyway, he explains. Why? Because Estée Lauder is selling "a kept-woman mentality."

I can't quite believe this. Sixty percent of the users of his products are salaried, and generally resemble *Ms.* readers. Besides, his company has the appeal of having been started by a creative and hardworking woman, his mother, Estée Lauder.

That doesn't matter, he says. He knows his customers, and they would *like* to be kept women. That's why he will never advertise in *Ms.*

In November 1987, by vote of the Ms. Foundation for Education and Communication (*Ms.*'s owner and publisher, the media subsidiary of the Ms. Foundation for Women), *Ms.* was sold to a company whose officers, Australian feminists Sandra Yates and Anne Summers, raised the investment money in their country that *Ms.* couldn't find in its own. They also started *Sassy* for teenage women.

In their two-year tenure, circulation was raised to 550,000 by investment in circulation mailings, and, to the dismay of some readers, editorial features on clothes and new products made a more traditional bid for ads. Nonetheless, ad pages fell below previous levels. In addition, *Sassy,* whose fresh voice and sexual frankness were an unprecedented success with young readers, was targeted by two mothers from Indiana who began, as one of them put it, "calling every Christian organization I could think of." In response to this controversy, several crucial advertisers pulled out.

Such links between ads and editorial content was a problem in Australia, too, but to a lesser degree. "Our readers pay two times more for their magazines," Anne explained, "so advertisers have less power to threaten a magazine's viability."

"I was shocked," said Sandra Yates with characteristic directness. "In Australia, we think you have freedom of the press—but you don't."

Since Anne and Sandra had not met their budget's projections for ad revenue, their investors forced a sale. In October 1989, *Ms.* and *Sassy* were bought by Dale Lang, owner of *Working Mother, Working Woman,* and one of the few independent publishing companies left among the conglomerates. In response to a request from the original *Ms.* staff—as well as to reader letters urging that *Ms.* continue, plus his own belief that *Ms.* would benefit his other magazines by blazing a trail—he agreed to try the ad-free, reader-supported *Ms.* you hold now, and to give us complete editorial control.

31

SUPERSEXUALIZE ME!¹

Advertising and the "Midriffs"

Rosalind Gill

For the last four decades the notion of objectification has been a key term in the feminist critique of advertising. Its centrality to the feminist critical lexicon lay in its ability to speak to the ways in which media representations help to justify and sustain relations of domination and inequality between men and women. In particular, processes of objectification were held to be the key to understanding male violence against women:

> Adverts don't directly cause violence . . . but the violent images contribute to the state of terror. Turning a human being into a thing, an object, is almost always the first step towards justifying violence against that person. . . . This step is already taken with women. The violence, the abuse, is partly the chilling but logical result of the objectification. (Kilbourne, 1999: 278)

It is difficult to over-estimate the importance of this argument for feminism (and also for understandings of racism and other relations of brutality); it has been central to feminist activism around advertising and media representations more generally. However, I want to suggest that a number of significant changes have taken place in the regime of representation that mean that the notion of objectification no longer has the analytic purchase to understand many contemporary constructions of femininity. Increasingly, young women are presented not as passive sex objects, but as active, desiring sexual subjects, who seem to participate enthusiastically in practices and forms of self-presentation that earlier generations of feminists regarded as connected to subordination. . . .

This shift was emblematic of a wider transformation happening in advertising in the early 1990s. Robert Goldman (1992) has argued that advertisers were forced to respond to three challenges at this time. First, there was the growing experience of 'sign fatigue' on the part of many media audiences fed up with the endless parade of brands, logos and consumer images. Like its millennial sibling, compassion fatigue, sign fatigue showed itself in what we might call a weariness of affect, an ennui and a disinclination to respond. Secondly, advertisers had to address increasing 'viewer scepticism,' particularly from younger, media-savvy consumers who had grown up with fast-paced music television and were the first generation to adopt personal computers and mobile phones as integral features of everyday life. To get through to this generation, who regarded themselves as sceptical and knowing in relation to commercial messages, advertisers had to adapt. They increasingly came to produce commercials that mocked the grammar and vocabulary of advertising and effaced their own status as advertisements. Thirdly, advertisers needed to address feminist critiques of advertising and to fashion new commercial messages that took on board women's anger at constantly being addressed through representations of idealized beauty.

Goldman argued that advertisers' response to this third challenge was to develop what he called 'commodity feminism'²—an attempt to incorporate the cultural power and energy of feminism whilst simultaneously domesticating its critique of advertising and the media. Commodity feminism takes many different forms. It consists of adverts that aim to appease women's anger and to suggest that advertisers share their disgruntlement with

From Rosalind Gill, "Supersexualize Me! Advertising and the 'Midriffs.'" In Feona Attwood (ed.) (2009), *Mainstreaming Sex: The Sexualization of Western Culture*. New York: I. B. Taurus, 93–99.

images of thin women, airbrushed to perfection. It is found in adverts that attempt to articulate a rapprochement between traditional femininity and characteristics which are coded as feminist goals; independence, career success, financial autonomy. It may be identified in gender-reversal adverts or in revenge adverts that mock or turn the tables on men. Elsewhere I have considered a number of shifts in the representation of gender in advertising in some detail (Gill, 2007a).[3] In the remainder of this chapter, however, I will turn my attention to perhaps the major contemporary shift in the sexual representation of women: the construction of a young, heterosexual woman who knowingly and deliberately plays with her sexual power and is forever 'up for it': the midriff.

SEXUALIZATION AND THE MIDRIFFS

The midriff is a part of the body between the top of the pubis bone and the bottom of the rib cage. This part of the female body has been the site of erotic interest in many non-Western cultures for a long time. In the West, the recent upsurge of interest in the midriff can be traced back to the visual presentation of Madonna in the late 1980s in which her pierced belly button and toned abdomen became features for erotic display in dance routines. For almost a decade, between the mid-1990s and the mid-2000s, revealing the midriff was central to young women's fashion in the West, with low-hung hipster jeans and cropped or belly top, exposing a pierced navel at the front and the familiar 'whale back' (visible g-string) from behind. Increasingly, the lower back has also become a site for elaborate tattoos.

This style was so widespread for such a long time that the term 'midriffs' has become a shorthand employed by advertisers and marketing consultants (Quart, 2003). In one sense it signals a generation—primarily women in their 20s and 30s, but sometimes also girls in their teens and women in their early 40s—defined by their fashion tastes. More tellingly, the midriffs can be understood in relation to a particular sensibility: a sensibility characterized by a specific constellation of attitudes towards the body, sexual expression and gender relations.

Advertising aimed at the midriffs is notable for its apparently 'sexualized' style but this is quite different from the sexual objectification to which second-wave feminist activists objected. In today's midriff advertising, women are much less likely to be shown as passive sexual objects than as empowered, heterosexually desiring sexual subjects, operating playfully in a sexual marketplace that is presented as egalitarian or actually favourable to women.

Midriff advertising has four central themes: an emphasis on the body, a shift from objectification to sexual subjectification, a pronounced discourse of choice and autonomy, and an emphasis upon empowerment.

Perhaps the most striking feature of midriff advertising is the centrality of the body. If in the 1950s the home was the ideal focus for women's labour and attention, and the sign used to judge their 'worth,' in the new millennium it is the body. Today, a sleek, controlled figure is essential for portraying success, and each part of the body must be suitably toned, conditioned, waxed, moisturized, scented and attired. In advertising, more and more parts of the body come under intense scrutiny: Dove's summer 2006 campaign alerts us that the newest must-have accessory is beautiful armpits, lest we forget to use all the products necessary to render this part of the body acceptable.

Today, the body is portrayed in advertising and elsewhere as the primary source of women's capital. This may seem obvious and taken-for-granted, but it is, in fact, relatively new. Surveillance of women's bodies constitutes perhaps the largest type of media content across all genres and media forms. Women's bodies are evaluated, scrutinized and dissected by women as well as men and are always at risk of 'failing.' This is most clear in the cultural obsession with celebrity which plays out almost exclusively over women's bodies. . . . In the very recent past, women's cooking, domestic cleanliness or interior design skills were the focus of advertisers' attention to a much greater extent than the surface of the body. But there has been a profound shift in the very definition of femininity so that it is now defined as a bodily property rather than a social or psychological one. Instead of caring or nurturing or motherhood, it is now possession of a 'sexy body' that is presented as women's key source of identity. . . .

There has also been a shift in the way that women's bodies are presented erotically. Where once sexualized representations of women in the media presented them as the passive, mute objects of an assumed male gaze, today women are presented as active, desiring sexual subjects who choose to present themselves in a seemingly objectified manner because it suits their liberated interests to do so. . . . The notion of objectification does not seem to capture this; a better understanding would come from the Foucaultian idea of (sexual) subjectification, which speaks to the way that power operates through the construction of particular subjectivities.

A crucial aspect of both the obsessional preoccupation with the body and the shift from objectification to sexual subjectification is that this is framed in advertising through a discourse of playfulness, freedom, and, above all, *choice.* Women are presented not as seeking men's approval but as *pleasing themselves;* in doing so, they just happen to win men's admiration. . . .

Dee Amy-Chinn (2006) eloquently captures this double-edged postfeminist emphasis on women pleasing themselves, in the title of her article about lingerie advertising: 'This is just for me(n).' Such advertising hails active, heterosexual young women, but does so using a photographic grammar directly lifted from heterosexual pornography aimed at men. The success—and this is what is novel about this—is in connecting 'me' and 'men,' suggesting there is no contradiction—indeed no difference—between what 'I' want and what men might want of 'me.' This is clearly complicated. There is no necessary contradiction or difference between what women and men want, but equally it cannot be assumed that their desires are identical. What is most interesting is the sophisticated 'higher' development of ideology and power relations, such that the ideological is literally made real. This takes the form of constructions of femininity that come straight out of the most predictable templates of male sexual fantasy, yet which must also be understood as authentically owned by the women who produce them. Part of their force lies precisely in the fact that they are not understood as ideological, or indeed are understood as *not* ideological. . . .

Almost as central to midriff advertising as the notions of choice and 'pleasing one's self,' is a discourse of feminine *empowerment.* Contemporary advertising targeted at the midriffs suggest, above all, that buying the product will empower you. . . . What is on offer in all these adverts is a specific kind of power—the sexual power to bring men to their knees. Empowerment is tied to possession of a slim and alluring young body, whose power is the ability to attract male attention and sometimes female envy. . . . A US advert for lingerie dares to make explicit that which is usually just implied. Showing a curvaceous woman's body from the neck down, clad in a black basque and stockings, the advert's text reads, 'while you don't necessarily dress for men, it doesn't hurt, on occasion, to see one drool like the pathetic dog he is.'[4] This is 'power femininity': a 'subject-effect' of 'a global discourse of popular post-feminism which incorporates feminist signifiers of emancipation and empowerment, as well as circulating popular postfeminist assumptions that feminist struggles have ended, that full equality for all women has been achieved, and that women of today can "have it all"' (Lazar, 2006).

SUPERSEXUALIZE ME: MIDRIFF ADVERTISING AND POSTFEMINISM

What, then, are we to make of the shift in the way that women are presented sexually? In offering up representations of women who are active, desiring sexual subjects, who are presented as powerful and playful, rather than passive or victimized, has advertising pointed to more hopeful, open or egalitarian possibilities for gender relations? I do not think so. On the contrary, I want to argue that midriff advertising re-sexualizes women's bodies, with the excuse of a feisty, empowered postfeminist discourse that makes it very difficult to critique.

Let us examine first some of the exclusions of midriff advertising. Most obviously this includes anyone living outside the heterosexual norm. Contemporary midriff advertising operates within a resolutely hetero-normative economy, in which power, pleasure and subjectivity are all presented in relation to heterosexual relationships. Indeed, the parallel growth of a kind of 'queer chic' (Gill, 2008) seems to locate homosexuality in terms of style and aesthetics rather than sexuality. A cynic might suggest that the greater visibility of hyper-feminine/hyper-sexualized lesbians in advertising may be a way for advertisers to evade charges of sexism, whilst continuing to present women in a highly objectified manner.

Others excluded from the empowering, pleasurable address of midriff advertising are older women, disabled women, fat women and any woman who is unable to live up to the increasingly narrow standards of female beauty and sex appeal that are normatively required. These women are never accorded sexual subjecthood. The figure of the 'unattractive' woman who seeks a sexual partner remains one of the most vilified in popular culture. . . .

Sexual subjectification, then, is a highly specific and exclusionary practice, and sexual pleasure is actually irrelevant here; it is the power of sexual attractiveness that is important. Indeed, the two are frequently and deliberately confused in midriff advertising.

The practice is also problematic for what it renders invisible, what Robert Goldman has called the 'diverse forms of terror experienced by women who objectify themselves.' He explains:

> There is the mundane psychic terror associated with not receiving 'looks' of admiration—i.e., not having others validate one's appearance. A similar sense of terror involves the fear of 'losing one's looks'—the quite reasonable fear that ageing will deplete one's value and social power. A related source of anxiety involves fear about 'losing control' over body weight and appearance . . . and there is a very real physical terror which may accompany presentation of self as an object of desire—the fear of rape and violence by misogynist males. (1992: 123)

Midriff advertising is notable not only for its success in selling brands but also—much more significantly—for its effective rebranding or reconstruction of the anxieties and the labour involved in making the body beautiful, through a discourse of fun, pleasure and power. The work associated with disciplining the feminine body to approximate the required standards is made knowable in new ways that systematically erase pain, anxiety, expense and low self-esteem. See, for example, the way that the application of boiling wax to the genital region and then its use to pull out hairs by their roots can be discursively (re)constructed as 'pampering' (Sisters, I don't think so!).

Goldman is correct, too, to point to the erasure of violence in such advertising. It seems literally to have been conjured away. In one advert, an attractive young woman is depicted wearing just a bra, her arm stretched high in the internationally recognized gesture for hailing a taxi. 'I bet I can get a cab on New Year's Eve 1999,' she declares, laughing. Here, again, exposed breasts are a source of male attention-grabbing power, a way to defeat the notorious concerns about taxi queues on the millennium eve. But the representation is entirely shorn of any suggestion of the violence that might threaten a woman so scantily attired, late at night, in the midst of large numbers of men who are drinking heavily. More generally, the depiction of heterosexual relations as playful, and women as having as much—if not more—power as men in negotiating them, is at odds with statistics, which give an extraordinarily sobering picture of the levels of violence by men against women.[5] . . .

Midriff advertising articulates a thoroughgoing individualism in which women are presented as entirely autonomous agents, no longer constrained by any inequalities or power imbalances. The pendulum swing—from a view of power as something obvious and overbearing which acts upon entirely docile subjects, towards a notion of women as completely free agents who just 'please themselves'—does not serve feminist or cultural understandings well. It cannot explain why the look that young women seek to achieve is so similar. If it were the outcome of everyone's individual, idiosyncratic preferences, surely there would be greater diversity, rather than a growing homogeneity organized around a slim, toned, hairless body. Moreover, the emphasis upon choice sidesteps and avoids all the important and difficult questions about how socially constructed ideals of beauty are internalized and made our own.

The notion of choice has become a postfeminist mantra. The idea that women are 'pleasing themselves' is heard everywhere: 'women choose to model for men's magazines,' 'women choose to have cosmetic surgery to enhance the size of their breasts,' 'women choose to leave their children in Eastern Europe or in the Global South and come and make a better life in the rich countries.' Of course, at one level, such claims have some truth: some women do make 'choices' like this. However, they do not do so in conditions of their own making, and to account for such decisions using only a discourse of free choice is to oversimplify, both in terms of analysis and political response. We need urgently to complicate our understandings of choice and agency in this context (Gill, 2007b).

Finally, I would argue that midriff advertising involves a shift in the way that power operates: it entails a move from an external, male-judging gaze, to a self-policing, narcissistic gaze. In this sense it represents a more 'advanced' or pernicious form of exploitation than the earlier generation of objectifying images to which second-wave feminists objected—because the objectifying male gaze is internalized to form a new disciplinary regime. Using the rather crude and clunky language of oppression, we might suggest that midriff advertising adds a further layer of oppression. Not only are women objectified, as they were before, *but through sexual subjectification they must also now understand their own objectification as pleasurable and self-chosen.* If, in earlier regimes of advertising, women were presented as sexual objects, then this was understood as something being done to women. In contemporary midriff advertising, however, some women are endowed with the status of active subjecthood so that they can 'choose' to become sex objects, because this suits their liberated interests. One of the implications of this shift is that it renders critique much more difficult.

. . . Goldman's analysis of commodity feminism discussed earlier in this chapter . . . stresses the ongoing struggle between advertising and feminism, . . . that, so far, . . . has largely been resolved in favour of the advertising industry, with feminist ideas ransacked, cannibalized, incorporated, and 'domesticated.' To contest this, there are three fronts on which feminists must engage: first, to articulate a language and cultural politics of resistance to midriff advertising, preferably one that is funny, feisty, sex-positive and inclusive; second, to rethink agency and choice in more sophisticated terms that reject the existing dualisms; and finally, to push for—or create—more diverse representations of gender and sexuality.

NOTES

1. This title owes a debt to Morgan Spurlock's powerful critique of the fast-food industry, *Super Size Me* (2004).

2. Commodity feminism is, of course, an homage to Marx and Engels's notion of commodity fetishism.

3. See also Gill (2008) for a discussion of sexualization that looks at the rise of 'queer chic' in advertising, the erotic depiction of men's bodies, and the increasing use of the grammars of heterosexual pornography in advertising.

4. Elsewhere (2007a) I have considered the offensive depiction of male sexuality in such adverts.

5. It is estimated that there were 190,000 incidents of serious sexual assault and 47,000 female victims of rape in 2001 in England and Wales. Research by Amnesty International in the UK published in November 2005 found that a blame culture exists against women who have been raped, with up to one-third of people who were questioned seeing a woman as responsible if she was wearing revealing clothing, had been drinking or had had a number of sexual partners.

REFERENCES

Amy-Chinn, D. (2006). "This is just for me(n): Lingerie advertising for the post-feminist woman." *Journal of Consumer Culture* 6(2).

Gill, R. (2007a). "Critical respect: Dilemmas of choice and agency in feminism (A response to Duits and Van Zoonen)." *European Journal of Women's Studies* 14(1).

Gill, R. (2007b). "Postfeminist media culture: Elements of a sensibility." *European Journal of Cultural Studies.*

Gill, R. (2008). "Beyond 'sexualization': Sexual representations in advertising." *Sexualities.*

Goldman, R. (1992). *Reading ads socially.* London; New York, Routledge.

Kilbourne, J. (1999). *Can't buy my love: How advertising changes the way we think and feel.* New York, London, Touchstone.

Lazar, M. (2006). "'Discover the power of femininity!' Analysing global 'power femininity' in local advertising." *Feminist Media Studies* 6(4).

Quart, A. (2003). *Branded: The buying and selling of teenagers.* London, Arrow Books.

Rushkoff, Douglas. (2001). *The Merchants of Cool.* Documentary film aired on *Frontline,* PBS.

Spurlock, Morgan. (2004). *Super Size Me.* Documentary film.

Walby, Sylvia and Jonathan Allen. (2004). *Domestic Violence, Sexual Assualt and Staulking: Findings from the British Crime Survey.* Home Office Study 276. Home Office Research, Development and Statistics Directorate.

32

BRANDING "REAL" SOCIAL CHANGE IN DOVE'S CAMPAIGN FOR REAL BEAUTY

Dara Persis Murray

In June 2010, the Dove Movement for Self-Esteem launched at the G(irls) 20 Summit. Modeled after the G20 Summit, this convention brought together young women from the same countries[1] represented at the G20 Summit to discuss education, health, and economic initiatives that could stimulate girls' activism and advancement in their communities. The ideological intersection of the Movement (a brand extension of Dove's Campaign for Real Beauty, or CFRB) and the G(irls) 20 Summit reflects the complex and often problematic meanings of feminism that circulate in popular culture: the blending of active female citizenship with empowerment via consumption in the marketplace.

This chapter explores CFRB's branding strategy, wherein its "real beauty" messaging merges co-opted feminist discourse and "a postfeminist sensibility" (Gill 2007, p. 254). A feminist semiotic analysis suggests that, under a guise of corporate altruism that democratizes female beauty, CFRB endorses global postfeminist citizenship. The findings suggest that CFRB may reflect a social change in the relationship between corporations and audiences that carries perilous meanings for the future roles of feminists and practices of female citizenship in global consumer culture. CFRB offers a rich site for unpacking the production and consumption of popular meanings of feminism, social change, female citizenship, and female beauty at this cultural moment.

DOVE GETS THE WORD OUT

Dove is a brand of personal care products such as soaps, body washes, and body lotions manufactured by the Unilever Corporation. Since 1957, Dove's mainstay product has been the Beauty Bar. In 2002, Unilever reassessed Dove's marketing strategy with its public relations firm, Edelman, and its advertising/marketing agency, Ogilvy & Mather, to create a unified global image to generate brand loyalty. Discussing her view of the global brand, Ogilvy's Chairman and Chief Executive Officer Shelly Lazarus stated, "It means figuring out what is universal about the brand—those things that transcend where it happens to be manufactured, or where it started" (O'Barr, Lazarus & Moreira 2008). Lazarus's statement indicates that in today's market, a brand needs to reach audiences' emotions by building a platform that drives ideological alliance with the corporate identity before the act of material consumption.

CFRB was largely shaped by women in industry and as research subjects. Female members of Ogilvy & Mather's CFRB team included Lazarus, two creative directors, an art director, a writer, and producer. Lazarus is a graduate of Smith College (an all-women's institution listing numerous feminist icons among its alumni), where she sat on its Board of Trustees. Although Lazarus has not publicly aligned herself with feminism, others have identified her as "a strong feminist. . . . Yet Lazarus's feminist love of economic empowerment prevents her from acknowledging the ways in which capitalism can hurt the powerless" (Dyer 2004, p. 191). Moreover, Dove commissioned women[2] to direct its foundational research and conduct much of the Campaign's research.

The construction of CFRB was based on Dove's 2003 global research study, "The Real Truth About Beauty." This research involved the participation of thirty-two hundred women, ages

From Murray, D. P. (2012). Branding "real" social change in Dove's campaign for real beauty. *Feminist Media Studies, 12*(4), 1–19. Reprinted by permission of Taylor & Francis Ltd., www.tandf.co.uk/journals.

eighteen through sixty-four, in ten countries, in a twenty to twenty-five-minute long telephone interview. The study found that less than 2 percent of women feel beautiful; 75 percent want representations of women to reflect diversity through age, shape, and size; and 76 percent want the media to portray beauty as more than physical (Etcoff, Orbach, Scott & D'Agostino 2004). These responses suggested a market for a new philosophy of beauty that was "a great opportunity to differentiate the brand from every [other] beauty brand" (Fielding, Lewis, White, Manfredi & Scott 2008), according to Alessandro Manfredi, Dove's Global Brand Director. CFRB has been identified as a cause marketing effort (Lachover & Brandes 2009), which associates corporate identities with social problems to benefit the corporate image, "distracting attention from their [the corporation's] connections as to why these social problems continue to exist" (Stole 2008, p. 21). This article advances that CFRB is a *cause branding* strategy that merges messages of corporate "concern and commitment for a cause" (Cone 2000) with the participation of women and girls for the same social goals, further concealing corporate aims.

In line with their findings, Dove announced its challenge to the dominant ideology of beauty: it would feature "real" women and girls of "various ages, shapes and sizes" (Campaign for Real Beauty 2008). The campaign launched in England in 2004, and was soon exported to Canada and the United States; CFRB is currently marketed in thirty-five countries.[3] The branding strategy was executed through television and print advertising, billboards, new media, and national and grassroots outreach. The Dove Self-Esteem Fund is a brand extension that serves as the site for in-person and online workshops that provide "self-esteem toolkits" for girls and "parent kits" for mothers/mentors. In the United States, the Fund has partnered with multiple national nonprofit girls' organizations (Girl Scouts, Girls Inc., and Boys & Girls Clubs of America) to facilitate these workshops. As an example of CFRB's international events that engage female audiences, Dove "call[ed] on women from the Middle East to write about someone they find beautiful and the reasons they see a different kind of 'real beauty.' Participants could be treated to a luxury five-star treatment for two" (Dove Exposes the Beauty Myth 2007) in return.

The Dove Movement for Self-Esteem launched in Canada and the United States in Fall 2010.

A FEMINIST PERSPECTIVE ON BEAUTY

In the twentieth and twenty-first centuries, the beauty and fashion industries have produced powerful media images communicating the dominant ideology of female beauty as ultra-thin, tall, sexual bodies. Consumption of these images has resulted in a cultural norm of women and girls disciplining their bodies (Bordo 2003). The beauty industry's discourse connects ideological and physical nonconformity to the dominant ideology with a woman's inability to fulfill her gender role or experience happiness (Bartky 1990). The struggle of women and girls to physically emulate media images has manifested itself in eating disorders and body image issues, while the lack of a fulfilled identification may result in low self-esteem (Kilbourne 1999).

Dove's stated call to arms echoes feminist and feminist media studies scholarship that addresses how representations in popular culture convey often-problematic meanings of gender and beauty. In its advocacy of women's rights and egalitarian roles, the feminist position argues for social change of oppressive social structures (Dworkin 1974). By contrast, the postfeminist position contends that gender equality and female empowerment have been achieved in the public sphere. Postfeminism has immense power in western culture, as noted by feminist media studies scholar Rosalind Gill, who names our current time a "postfeminist media culture" (2007, p. 249). Significantly, she advances that postfeminism can be interpreted as "a sensibility" (2007, p. 254) whose messaging includes:

> the notion that femininity is a bodily property; the shift from objectification to subjectification; the emphasis upon self-surveillance, monitoring and discipline; a focus upon individualism, choice and empowerment; the dominance of a makeover paradigm; the articulation or entanglement of feminist and antifeminist ideas . . . and an emphasis upon consumerism and the commodification of difference. (Rosalind Gill 2007)

The postfeminist position easily aligns with corporate interests, situating messages of women's freedom in the marketplace as "empowered consumer[s]" (Tasker & Negra 2007, p. 2). This identity lies at the intersection of consumerism and neoliberal governmentality, thereby separating meanings of female citizenship from civic engagement (McRobbie 2008, p. 533). The emergent neoliberal postfeminist citizen links meanings of empowerment and choice to ideological and material consumption.

The postfeminist citizen's pursuit of beauty engages her consumer power and self-governance, aligning her identity with the goals of institutional power. In postfeminist media culture, the body is a site of attention for the postfeminist citizen since it is promoted as integral to female identity (Gill 2007, p. 255). Consumption of the dominant ideology of beauty involves absorbing representations and meanings of hypersexual women and, increasingly, girls. Agreement with these messages may make it difficult for postfeminist citizens to understand their sexuality in "healthy, and progressive ways" (Durham 2008, p. 39). This feminist analysis will consider the political, social, and economic meanings in CFRB's texts and address how female identity may be shaped as postfeminist citizenship through the myth of "real beauty."

SELF-BRANDING BY EMBRACING POPULAR FEMINISM

A strategy for accomplishing audience identification with texts is the co-option of discourse; importantly, such appropriation highlights social issues as a means of generating sales (Danesi 2002). Alignment with co-opted subcultural signs allows consumers to think of themselves as insurgents; yet, since their rebellion occurs through consumerism, they do not "pay the social price of true non-conformity and dissent" (Danesi 2002, p. 197).

Sociologist Robert Goldman terms this tactic "commodity feminism," wherein advertisers attempt "to reincorporate the cultural power of feminism" (Goldman 1992, p. 130) and, in so doing, depoliticize the feminist message. . . .

Branding enlists audiences to support a corporate brand identity that is managed by the corporation to produce its desired

outcome. . . . Importantly for this study, cause branding is a specific type of branding that blends corporate and individual identities through brand communication and audience participation. Cause branding "falls at the intersection of corporate strategy and citizenship and is fast becoming a 'must do' practices [sic] for the 21st century" (Cone 2000), therefore positioning corporations to implement their identities to attract and retain consumers through a depth of involvement that draws on their emotions, actions, and identities to drive brand commitment.

It is important to consider the practice of self-branding when thinking about girls and women who consume cause branding messages. While media studies scholars have examined the meanings of textual signs, a study of current consumer culture entails an exploration of the ways in which individuals are encouraged to become a self-branded "commodity sign" (Hearn 2008, p. 201) using "the narrative and visual codes" (Hearn 2008, p. 198) promoted by institutional power (corporations, advertisers, and so on). . . . This analysis considers how CFRB's meanings of popular feminism and social change convey the message that audiences should self-brand as postfeminist "real" beauties. . . .

Analysis of Dove's "Real Beauty" Print Texts

CFRB's texts integrate feminist politics from the three waves[4] through the pictorial signs of "real" women and the use of feminist discourse to foster audience identification based on physical attributes, age, and generational feminist politics. The pictorial signs of women signify their age, which corresponds with a feminist wave, and all the women are photographed against a white background. These images inaugurate the campaign's mission with representations of five women of distinctly varied ages, signifying a unification of women from the three waves. The first word of CFRB—"Campaign"—acknowledges a political intention. Linguistic signs in the CFRB texts connote the politics of the feminist waves: specifically, the first wave's focus on suffrage; the second wave's focus on collective—"we"—political action by women; and the third waves focus on individual difference—in gender, ethnicity, race, etc.—or micro-politics. The print launch comprised six images: portraits of five women (three close-ups of faces and two body shots at a distance) and one composite picture of them. The five women pose with questions that address the dominant ideology of beauty; each question offers two options as a response. The CFRB manifesto accompanies the composite image, stating:

> For too long, beauty has been defined by narrow, unattainable stereotypes. It's time to change all that. Because Dove believes real beauty comes in many shapes, sizes, colors and ages. It's why we started the campaign for real beauty. And why we hope you'll take part. Together, let's think, talk, debate and learn how to make beauty real again. Cast your vote at campaignforrealbeauty.com. (Dove Manifesto 2004)

The three close-up photos represent women from each wave. Their images are accompanied by ballot boxes next to descriptive labels, posed as questions: "wrinkled? wonderful?" (First Wave), "gray? gorgeous?" (Second Wave) and "flawed? flawless?" (Third Wave). The dark-skinned ninety-ish woman wearing a colorful headscarf smiles, with the text beside her asking, "Will society ever accept old can be beautiful?" This query signifies the difficulties involved in changing societal views regarding the role of women (First Wave). The smiling fifty-ish Caucasian woman wears a black turtleneck and, looking over her shoulder at the audience, the text beside her raises the only question of those in this set that invites discussion, rather than a yes/no response: "Why aren't women glad to be gray?" This question signifies the consciousness-raising ideology of dialogue relevant to her era (Second Wave). The text beside the twenty-ish, red-haired Caucasian woman, wearing a white tank top, poses a question that seemingly derives from her freckled appearance, "Does beauty mean looking like everyone else?" This inquiry signifies the ideology of difference in her wave (Third Wave).

Additionally, two women belonging to the Third Wave are photographed from head to thighs and are presented next to the ballot box signifier. One image ("half empty? half full?") depicts a slim, smiling, short-haired, small-breasted black woman in a white tank top and jeans with her hands in her back pockets; the text beside her

breast questions, "Does sexiness depend on how full your cups are?" This phrasing suggests optimism or pessimism, an intertextual reference to the rhetorical expression, "Is the glass half empty or half full?" The other image ("oversized? outstanding?")[5] depicts a full-figured, smiling, large-breasted Caucasian woman in a strapless black cocktail dress with hands crossed behind her head; the text, positioned at her hips, asks, "Does true beauty only squeeze into a size 6?" Both of their confidently smiling visages connote an optimistic, "real beauty" answer to the ballot box question posed next to them. . . .

The composite representation of all five women is accompanied by the CFRB manifesto. . . . The corporate message is visually constructed as more important than the women: the paragraph of copy occupies more space on the page than all the women together, the text occupies more vertical space than the strip of photos, and the copy concludes with a blue color whose length and vibrancy are more visually compelling than the women. Further, this blue copy relays information about Dove and CFRB: the campaign website, the Dove icon, and a request to "Cast your vote." The copy emphasizes Dove as the organizer, catalyst, and vehicle for change: "it's time to change all that . . . it's why we started the campaign for real beauty." . . .

Self-Esteem Fund: Television and Viral Video Texts

Dove took CFRB's messaging "a step further and [focused on] talk about self-esteem" (Branding Evolution 2007) by launching two texts in 2006 to brand the Dove Self-Esteem Fund, which was established by and is primarily financed by Unilever/Dove. These texts encourage ideological identification for girls and adult female audiences (mentors/mothers). Girl audiences may identify with the "real" girls in CFRB's television advertisement and viral video through sharing their physical attributes, ages, and, significantly, their emotional states. These texts are designed to arouse emotions against the dominant ideology of beauty and garner support for "real beauty." The mentors/mothers identification is mobilized through acceptance of the Fund's leadership and mission: to save girls' psychological and physical health via an emphasis on "self-esteem" (a crucial component of the "real beauty" ideology). Women can also economically bond with Dove by making donations to the Fund.

"True Colors" debuted during the February 2006 Superbowl XL Game, at a cost of $2.4 million dollars for forty-six seconds. The spot ran during this time to make contact with the largest audience possible, in keeping with Dove's goal (which was achieved) of reaching one million young girls by 2008. In "True Colors," Dove represents itself as a facilitator and problem-solver, declaring: "let's change their minds/we've created the Dove self-esteem fund/because every girl deserves to feel good about herself/and see how beautiful . . . she really is/help us . . . get involved at" the CFRB website. . . .

"True Colors" offers a range of emotions in the expressions of "real" girls of various sizes and ethnicities. The emotional song, "True Colors," is performed by The Girl Scouts Chorus. At first, the girls' faces reflect innocence or ambivalence, bolstered by linguistic signs connoting feelings of victimization—"hates her freckles," "thinks she's ugly," "wishes she were blonde," "afraid she's fat"—because they do not meet the dominant ideology of beauty. The lyrics simultaneously elevate the poignant portraits and offer an intimate relationship with the person ("I") in the music and the girls in the text: "Show me a smile then, don't be unhappy, can't remember when, I last saw you laughing, If this world makes you crazy and you've taken all you can bear, You call me up, because you know I'll be there." Halfway through the video, an emotional shift occurs following the encouraging syntagm, "Let's change their minds" against a white background. The lyrics also become positive: "And I'll see your true colors shining through." Accompanying this phrase is a group of smiling girls euphorically pumping their hands in the air, an intertextual reference to the feminist iconic image of "Rosie the Riveter," whose slogan was "We Can Do It!" Another phrase, "We've created the Dove Self-Esteem Fund," appears next, also against a white background. Smiling girls appear throughout the rest of the text, accompanying Dove's announcement of leadership via the Fund and the lyrics: "I see your true colors, And that's why I love you, So don't be afraid, To let them show, You're beautiful like a rainbow." The white background on which the pivotal text for the film's message appears signifies light, symbolizing

Dove as the caring narrator ("I") and the ray of light illuminating the public perception of female beauty and girls' "real beauty."

"Evolution" launched on YouTube at no cost to Dove or Ogilvy & Mather other than its production expenses. Near its commencement, a screen displays the words "a Dove film." . . .

"Evolution" depicts a woman's makeover using the tools (physical, technological) that are employed by the beauty industry to transform a "real" woman into a supermodel. The subject appears to be in her twenties and sits on a stool, staring without affect into the camera. Bright lights suddenly turn on; the footage speeds up in a choppy, fast-forward simulation; and music plays in synchrony with the rapid projection of images. The woman is presented as a site of work for make-up artists and hair stylist. During the transformation, the camera zooms in on her face, removing any indicators of her tank top to imply a state of undress. The image is manipulated through Photoshop, and her final representation as the dominant beauty appears on a billboard that two girls walk past and briefly acknowledge, connoting acceptance of the manufactured image as a cultural norm. . . .

At the conclusion of the film, [the tagline] "no wonder our perception of beauty is distorted," implicitly acknowledges a social problem that relates to the dominant ideology. . . . The logo that appears, "the Dove self-esteem fund," shows the upward flight of three blue doves in ascending size (from small to large). . . . Their upward direction connotes unity and positive direction for the future. However, this optimistic sign diverts from the messaging, which positions the corporation to usurp the feminist role of engendering social change for women and displaces the influential role of the women who share girls' everyday lives onto institutional power. Moreover, through the Fund, Dove asks mothers/mentors and girls to endorse the oppressive female role as an ideological and material consumer.

Dove Movement for Self-Esteem Website

The Dove Movement for Self-Esteem is primarily an online branding strategy through social media and the corporate website. Achieving online popularity (over ten million views) and more popular discourse for the brand than "True Colors" (and for minimal cost), The Movement may be an effort drawing on the success of "Evolution" as a low cost, high impact text. It is a site of interactivity, a critical process for understanding the agency and subjectivity of users.

. . . The Movement brings together the "real beauty" ideology from CFRB's print texts with the Fund's positioning of Dove as the site for women's and girls' activism. The centerpiece of the Movement is acceptance of its mission, which is executed when women and girls acknowledge their participation by signing a "declaration" to "Join the Movement." A declaration denotatively affords power to the audience by offering the opportunity to make a choice and assert oneself. Yet the Movement's language communicates a hegemonic relationship between the corporate leader and its followers, asking users to join "our Movement," "our vision," and "our cause." The declaration itself amounts to providing their email address, first and last name, zip code, and age, as well as an answer to an "optional" question: "What advice would you give to your 13 year old self? We'll collect these messages and deliver them to girls to build self-esteem in the next generation" (Our Vision: Join Us 2010). . . .

That the Movement may be using the declaration to create a list of consumers under the guise of participation for social change is not surprising: CFRB was formulated on the findings from a global research study and Dove has conducted numerous global and national studies[6] throughout the Campaign. The Movement can be seen as a form of market research, and the Movement's participants are its research subjects. The work of media studies theorist Mark Andrejevic is of particular importance here, as he contends that it is critical to question the politics of participation by users, who may be involved in "the labor of detailed information gathering and comprehensive monitoring . . . in the name of their own empowerment . . . and to view such participation as a form of power sharing" (2007, p. 15). Scholarship on Dove's user-generated marketing raises issues of users' labor on behalf of the brand (Duffy 2010) and users' discourse may support the patriarchal view that women's role is to pursue the dominant ideology (Lachover & Brandes 2009). In light of these voices, the Movement's declaration serves as a contractual agreement between audiences and the "real beauty" ideology, whose potential for the liberation of women and girls is questionable. . . .

PRODUCING A POSTFEMINIST CAMPAIGN AND SELF-BRANDED POSTFEMINIST CITIZENSHIP

CFRB and its brand extensions (the Fund and the Movement) created and advanced a myth of "real beauty." This ideology mandates female audiences to practice psychological self-improvement and physical subjectification as a means of liberation from the dominant ideology of beauty. This section explores the production (concentrating on the politics of women's participation in CFRB) and potential consumption (in connection with self-branded identity and postfeminist citizenship) of "real beauty" to consider its promise to facilitate audience liberation.

In addition to the aforementioned participation of women from Ogilvy & Mather, CFRB's partnership with the Woodhull Institute for Ethical Leadership further highlights women's involvement in this branding strategy. Woodhull is a nonprofit women's organization named after feminist Victoria Woodhull. Its website describes its partnership by employing the key words of feminist activism—"social change": "The Woodhull Institute of Ethical Leadership has partnered with the Dove CFRB to share success building tools through online training sessions that promote ethical development and empower women to act as agents of positive social change" (Woodhull 2007). Of note, Woodhull's co-founder and most public figure is Naomi Wolf, who may be known to popular audiences for her bestselling critique of the beauty industry, *The Beauty Myth*. Three years later, Wolf advocated a postfeminist position in her subsequent (and lesser known) book. However, for audiences who remember Wolf from her argument in *The Beauty Myth* and are not versed in postfeminism, this partnership may pose conflicting meanings of feminist involvement with the beauty industry. As one journalist notes, "To go from writing *The Beauty Myth* to touring with Dove and singing its praises is a big jump" (M.K. Johnson 2008). At the same time, the author optimistically queries whether Wolf is actually "spreading her message about the hypocrisy of the beauty industry, all on Dove's dime? Savvy audience members would certainly catch the irony, and Dove can laugh all the way to the bank. Everybody wins" (M.K. Johnson 2008).

Several "self-esteem" partners (nonprofit girls' organizations that draw on feminist ideologies) similarly bolster CFRB/Dove's credibility to audiences. The participation of these female-focused groups extends the brand into community spaces in a grassroots way that may read as "feminist" for popular audiences. These groups thereby function as a kin network that aids in the development of a CFRB community. The strategy surrounding Dove with these partnerships may operate to reduce popular attention to Unilever's other brands; after all, Unilever manufactures Slimfast (a diet plan), Fair & Lovely Fairness Cream (a skin lightening product), and Axe deodorant (whose advertisements, targeted at men, portray objectified women). Unilever's ownership structure suggests it is a site of fractured ideological credibility that circulates knotty popular meanings of feminism and social change.

By asking girls and women to partner with the corporate ideology in a similar manner as the aforementioned organizations, The Movement potentially enlists global postfeminist citizenship through the support of yet *another* oppressive beauty ideology. By signing the declaration, girls and women work to become neoliberal subjects who accept responsibility to develop and perform Dove-approved "self-esteem" behaviors (requiring self-judgment and self-monitoring of one's emotional state) that are integral to the pursuit of "real beauty."

. . . Becoming "a real beauty" necessitates ideological and material labor on the self that originates from acceptance of the "real beauty" myth: support of CFRB's hegemonic views of female beauty, agreement with Dove as the site for social change and female activism about beauty (even if it displaces the roles of feminists, mothers, and mentors in individuals' lives and in cultural ideology), work to achieve Dove's meaning of self-esteem, and embrace of women's traditional role as consumers.

. . . The rationale for women's and feminists' support of CFRB may lie in the postfeminist belief that contemporary women are consumers with agency. Or, feminists might welcome CFRB's representations as a positive change in a mediascape

that is otherwise saturated with the dominant ideology of beauty. It is important to stress, however, that the feminist task is to realize social change that revolutionizes social structures, not to support corporate strategies that seek audiences' brand attachment.

. . . Ultimately, it seems that "who wins" in CFRB's effort is the corporation. At first, CFRB resulted in enormous financial success for Dove and industry acclaim for Ogilvy & Mather and Edelman Public Relations, which spearheaded CFRB's marketing. Sales figures indicate that Dove's revenues increased following its launch: 12.5 percent in 2005 and 10.1 percent in 2006 (Neff 2007). In 2006, CFRB swept the highest awards[7] in the advertising industry and its sister industry, public relations. In 2007, however, sales growth dwindled to 1.2 percent (Neff 2007), and industry pundits questioned whether sales were connected to advertisements for Dove's Pro-Age product line (featuring unclothed women over age fifty) that perhaps "went a step too far in embracing aging in all its naked, wrinkled and sagging glory" (Neff 2007). The same year, controversy over the realness of CFRB's texts may have impacted sales when retoucher Pascal Dangin implied in an interview that he had altered the Pro-Age texts (Collins 2008). While Dove denied any textual modifications and Dangin retracted his statements, the public realization that there had (or could have) been retouching may have generalized to a lack of textual and brand authenticity. In 2008, although the "brand reportedly gained $1.2 billion in value" (Molitor 2008) since CFRB's launch, Dove's unhappiness with its sales led to a re-assessment of CFRB. The Movement may be CFRB's tactic to restore its integrity with audiences to bolster sales. More than previous CFRB strategies, the Movement incites ideological brand commitment through focusing on women's "depth of involvement, the engagement, the participation and the commitment of moving people to take action" (Molitor 2008). The Movement may also be a way for Dove to publicly emphasize the brand bond with consumers, thereby minimizing the role of industry insiders.

"Real beauty" is an oppressive ideology that reinforces the value of female beauty and its pursuit by garnering women's agreement with its values of ideological and material consumption. At its core is a paradox: while apparently decrying it, "real beauty" embraces conformity to hegemonic beauty standards through both corporate instigation for brand attachment and women's striving to be part of what they may feel is a positive beauty ideology. "Real beauty," then, is "diluted by its contradictory imperative to promote self-acceptance and at the same time increase sales by promoting women's consumption of products that encourage conformity to feminine beauty ideology" (Johnson & Taylor 2008, p. 962). CFRB's "real" women, whose beauty deviates from the beauty norm in size and/or color, lend credibility to the campaign and invite female audiences to self-brand as a "real beauty"; yet, this identity aligns with being a consumer of a corporate brand strategy that positions itself in the feminist role as an advocate for social change that promises to empower women. The stakes are high for audiences who agree with CFRB's meanings of "real beauty," and may intensify when such popularized meanings of empowerment are drawn on and reinforced as cultural norms by future brands. . . . Like cause marketing, this cause branding strategy "is merely a cleverly disguised ploy to mask some of the fundamental problems for which the very same marketing forces are directly or indirectly responsible" (Stole 2008, p. 34). Within this consumer context, commercial connotations are attached to popular messages and practices of philanthropy (Stole 2008).

There is much work to be done to arrive at a strong collective feminist voice of what empowering female beauty means for current and future audiences. As feminist media studies scholar Angela McRobbie suggests, this action may "entail the resuscitation and re-conceptualization of feminist anti-capitalism" (2008, p. 548). . . . CFRB's partnership between female cultural producers and a corporation is problematic at best.

NOTES

1. Countries represented at The G(irls) 20 Summit and the G20 Summit are Argentina, Australia, Brazil, Canada, China, France, Germany, India, Indonesia, Italy, Japan, Mexico, Russia, Saudi Arabia, South Africa, South Korea, Turkey, UK, USA and the European Union.

2. Women who participated included Dr. Jennifer Scott and Heidi D'Agostino of research firm StrategyOne; Dr. Nancy Etcoff, Harvard psychologist; and Dr. Susie Orbach, author of *Fat Is a Feminist Issue*.

3. See "Welcome to Dove" for a list of countries.

4. Industry insiders confirmed that there is no single database for global CFRB texts. A search of texts in the major markets where CFRB was created (the UK, the US, and Canada) found minor differences in the images and language that did not substantially alter the messaging. The US texts were selected since they are among the first set of texts, the United States is a major market, and they were accessible. This analysis thus focuses on the US texts.

5. The feminist movement is generally regarded as comprising three "waves" whose dates are as follows: the first wave occurred from the late nineteenth century to the 1930s; the second wave occurred from the 1960s to the 1980s; the third wave began in the 1990s and characterizes the present time.

6. The author was granted permission to reproduce the First-Wave and Third-Wave portraits and Third-Wave body shots, but not the Second-Wave portrait and composite portrait of the women (these images, accordingly, are not included in the article).

7. The UK version says, "fat? fit?" and the Canadian version asks, "fat? fab?" These sentiments are strikingly similar to the US version.

8. "Beyond Stereotypes" (2005) collected information from 3,300 girls and women from ten countries; "Beauty Comes of Age" (2006) surveyed 1,450 women from nine countries; and "Real Girls, Real Pressure" (2008) surveyed 1,029 American girls.

9. Awards include: Cannes Advertising's Grand Effie Award, Cannes' Film Grand Prix and Cyber Grand Prix, Global Campaign of the Year by *Advertising Age*, Consumer Launch Campaign of the Year by *PR Week*, and Best of Silver Anvil Award from the Public Relations Society of America.

REFERENCES

About The Movement (WEB PAGE) (2010) *Dove/Unilever,* [Online] Available at: http://www.dovemovement.com/movement/about (1 November 2010).

Andrejevic, Mark (2007) *iSpy: Surveillance and Power in the Interactive Era,* University Press of Kansas, Lawrence.

Arvidsson, Adam (2006) *Brands: Meaning and Value in Media Culture,* Routledge, New York.

Bartky, Sandra Lee (1990) *Femininity and Domination: Studies in the Phenomenology of Oppression,* New York, Routledge.

Bignell, Jonathan (1997) *Media Semiotics: An Introduction,* St. Martin's Press, New York.

Bordo, Susan (2003) *Unbearable Weight: Feminism, Western Culture, and the Body,* University of California Press, Berkeley.

Branding Evolution: The Dove Story (Web Page) (2007) *The Manufacturer,* [Online] Available at: http://www.themanufacturer.com/us/content/5640/Branding_evolution%3A_the_Dove_story (10 October 2010).

Byerly, Carolyn M. & Ross, Karen (2006) *Women & Media: A Critical Introduction,* Blackwell Publishing, Malden.

Campaign for Real Beauty (Web Page) (2008) *Dove/Unilever,* [Online] Available at: http://www.dove.us/#/CFRB/arti_cfrb.aspx[cp-document id=7049726]/ (1 April 2008).

Collins, Lauren (2008) 'Pixel perfect: Pascal Dangin's virtual reality,' *The New Yorker,* [Online] Available at: http://www.newyorker.com/reporting/2008/05/12/fa_fact_collins?currentPage=all (14 May 2008).

Color Wheel Pro (Web Page) (2010) *QSX Software Group,* [Online] Available at: http://www.color-wheel-pro.com/color-meaning.html (2 June 2008).

Cone, Carol L. (2000) 'Cause branding in the 21st century,' *Public Service Advertising Research Center,* [Online] Available at: http://www.psaresearch.com/causebranding.html (5 October 2010).

Cruikshank, Barbara (1993) 'Revolutions within: self-government and self-esteem,' *Economy and Society,* vol. 22, no. 3, pp. 327–344.

Danesi, Marcel (2002) *Understanding Media Semiotics,* Oxford Publishing Press, New York.

Dove Exposes the Beauty Myth to Reveal 'Real Beauty' to Women in the Middle East (Press Release On Web Page) (2007) Dove/Unilever, [Online] Available at: http://www.campaignforrealbeauty.ae/press.asp?url=press.asp&section=news&id=7221 (3 June 2008).

Dove Manifesto (Print) (2004) [Online] Available at: http://www.coloribus.com/adsarchive/prints/dove-skincare-products-dove-manifesto-6606505/ (5 June 2008).

Duffy, Brooke Erin (2010) 'Empowerment through endorsement? Polysemic meaning in Dove's user-generated advertising,' *Communication, Culture & Critique,* vol. 3, pp. 26–43.

Durham, Meenakshi Gigi (2008) *The Lolita Effect: The Media Sexualization of Young Girls and What We Can Do About It,* The Overlook Press, New York.

Dworkin, Andrea (1974) *Woman Hating,* E.P. Dutton, New York.

Dyer, Stephanie (2004) 'Lifestyles of the media rich and oligopolistic,' in *Censored 2005: The Top 25 Censored Stories,* ed. Peter Phillips, Seven Stories Press, New York.

Etcoff, Nancy, Orbach, Susie, Scott, Jennifer & D'agostino, Heidi (2004) 'The real truth about beauty: a global report: findings of the global study on women, beauty and well-being' [Online] Available at: http://www.campaignforrealbeauty.com/uploadedfiles/dove_white_paper_final.pdf (5 June 2008).

Evolution. (videorecording) (2006) [Online] Available at: http://www.youtube.com/watch?v=iYhCn0jf46U (10 October 2010).

Fielding, Daryl, Lewis, Dennis, White, Mel, Manfredi, Alessandro & Scott, Linda (2008) 'Dove campaign roundtable, *Advertising & Society Review,* vol. 9, no. 4 [Online] Project MUSE,

Available at: http://muse.jhu.edu.proxy.libraries.rutgers.edu/ (22 October 2010).

Fiske, John (2000) 'The codes of television, in *Media Studies: A Reader,* eds Paul Marris & Sue Thornham, New York University Press, New York, pp. 220–230.

Gill, Rosalind (2007) *Gender and the Media,* Polity, Cambridge.

Goldman, Robert (1992) *Reading Ads Socially,* Routledge, New York.

Hearn, Alison (2008) '"Meat, mask, burden:" probing the contours of the branded "self,"' *Journal of Consumer Culture,* vol. 8, no. 2, pp. 197–217.

Jenkins, Henry (2006) *Convergence Culture: Where Old and New Media Collide,* New York University Press, New York.

Jhally, Sut (2003) 'Image-based culture: advertising and popular culture,' in *Gender, Race, and Class in Media: A Text-Reader,* eds Gail Dines & Jean M. Humez, Sage Publications, Thousand Oaks, CA.

Johnson, M. K. (2008) 'Is Naomi Wolf pulling punches for Dove's real beauty campaign?,' *Lucire,* [Online] Available at: http://lucire.com/insider/20080215/is-naomi-wolf-pulling-punches-for-doves-real-beauty-campaign (10 June 2010).

Johnston, Josee & Taylor, Judith (2008) 'Feminist consumerism and fat activists: a comparative study of grassroots activism and the dove real beauty campaign,' *Signs: Journal of Women in Culture and Society,* vol. 33, no. 4, pp. 941–966.

Kilbourne, Jean (1999) *Can't Buy My Love: How Advertising Changes the Way We Think and Feel,* Simon & Schuster, New York.

Lachover, Einat & Brandes, Sigal Barak (2009) 'A beautiful campaign? Analysis of public discourse in Israel surrounding the Dove campaign for real beauty,' *Feminist Media Studies,* vol. 9, no. 3, pp. 301–316.

McRobbie, Angela (2008) 'Young women and consumer culture: an intervention,' *Cultural Studies,* vol. 22, no. 5, pp. 531–550.

Molitor, Dori (2008) 'In Dove we trust,' *The Hub Magazine,* [Online] Available at: http://www.hubmagazine.com/html/2008/may_jun/womanwise.html (1 October 2010).

Neff, Jack (2007) 'Soft soap,' *Advertising Age,* vol. 78, no. 38, p. 1.

O'Barr, William M., Lazarus, Shelly & Moreira, Marcio (2008) 'Global advertising,' *Advertising & Society Review,* vol. 9, no. 4 [Online] Project MUSE, Available at: http://muse.jhu.edu.proxy.libraries.rutgers.edu/ (1 October 2010).

Our Vision: Join Us (Web Page) (2010) Dove/Unilever, [Online] Available at: http://www.dovemovement.com/declaration/sign (5 October 2010).

Seiter, Ellen (1992) 'Semiotics, structuralism, and television,' in Channels of Discourse, *Reassembled: Television and Contemporary Criticism,* ed. Robert C. Allen, The University of North Carolina Press, Chapel Hill.

Stole, Inger L. (2008) 'Philanthropy as public relations: a critical perspective on cause marketing,' *International Journal of Communication,* vol. 2, pp. 20–40.

Tasker, Yvonne & Negra, Diane (2007) 'Introduction: feminist politics and postfeminist culture,' in *Interrogating Postfeminism: Gender and the Politics of Popular Culture,* eds Yvonne Tasker & Diane Negra, Duke University Press, Durham, pp. 1–25.

True Colors (videorecording) (2006) [Online] Available at: http://video.google.com/videoplay?docid=1731400614466797113# (2 June 2008).

Welcome to Dove (web page) (2010) [Online] Available at: http://www.dove.com/?ref=dove (1 October 2010).

Williamson, Judith (1978) *Decoding Advertisements: Ideology and Meaning in Advertising,* Marion Boyars Publishers, New York.

Woodhull (Web Page) (2007) *The Woodhull Institute for Ethical Leadership,* [Online] Available at: http://www.woodhull.org/gallery/index.php (20 June 2008).

33

NOTHING LESS THAN PERFECT

*Female Celebrity, Ageing, and
Hyper-Scrutiny in the Gossip Industry*

Kirsty Fairclough

INTRODUCTION

. . . Female celebrities have become the chief site upon which contemporary tensions and anxieties surrounding femininity, motherhood, body image, cosmetic surgery, marriage and ageing are played out. The corporeal is the principal means by which the famous women are now represented; it is the celebrity's face and body that become the locus for discussion in both printed and online discourse. These bodies are still revered and aspired to, but they are also exposed, examined and scrutinised in order to reveal their corporeal construction. In an increasingly individualistic culture, a woman's outward appearance represents her entire selfhood, and it is both pertinent and timely to examine the flow of discourses about ageing and cosmetic surgery that circulate in and out of celebrity culture.

Popular discourses surrounding female celebrities and cosmetic surgery most often emerge from a post-feminist perspective. Post-feminism is a term made up of multiple and conflicting meanings, and in this context, I refer to Rosalind Gill's conception of post-feminism as a distinctive sensibility consisting of a number of interrelated themes. These include 'Femininity as a bodily property; the shift from objectification to subjectification; an emphasis upon self surveillance, monitoring and self-discipline; a focus on individualism, choice and empowerment; the dominance of a makeover paradigm; and a resurgence of ideas about natural sexual difference' (Gill 2007, p. 148). These themes have provided the basis for analysis by some feminist scholars and are a useful touchstone from which to ground this analysis. In celebrity culture, transgression of post-feminist norms is subject to excoriating attack, particularly in the case of ageing and cosmetic surgery. The

age narrative is a central trope in gossip culture where the perpetual discussion of the age of female celebrities and whether their behaviour, lifestyle and look are 'age appropriate' reflects a deeply entrenched double standard.

GOSSIP TROPES AND AGEING

Celebrity gossip is of course nothing new. Gossip mavens such as Louella Parsons and Hedda Hopper were prolific during the Hollywood Studio System and often operated in conjunction with the studios. Later, the gossip industry began to provide the public with more salacious rumour and scandal about Hollywood stars through magazines such as *Confidential*. In the digital era, the gossip industry is thriving. From well-known gossip mavens such as *Perezhilton* and *Laineygossip* to spin-off sites associated with tabloid and gossip magazines such as *US Weekly* and *Heat,* the celebrity gossip blog is now firmly embedded within celebrity culture and is hinged on the hyper-scrutiny of the famous. . . .

The gender politics of contemporary celebrity is highly visible through the gossip blog, often a more derisive alternative to the printed gossip magazine, which actively deconstructs the female celebrity image in ways that are distinctly post-feminist in that they encourage and privilege hyper-femininity and perpetual transformation, and often espouse conservative views regarding gender roles. Celebrity gossip magazines and blogs lock women in a seemingly endless process of reinventing the neo-liberal self, providing sites to negotiate this self through evaluating celebrities and their lifestyle choices, allowing the facade of choice to be deeply inscribed within it. In this

From Fairclough, K. (2012). Nothing less than perfect: Female celebrity, ageing and hyperscrutiny in the gossip industry. *Celebrity Studies, 3*(1), 90–103. Reprinted by permission of Taylor & Francis Ltd., www.tandf.co.uk/journals.

context, gossip bloggers have the ability to essentially eradicate the carefully crafted image that the entertainment industry works to cultivate and maintain. As Anne-Helen Petersen suggests, 'As new media technology makes New Hollywood's mechanisms visible, gossip bloggers utilise this visibility to influence consumption. Bloggers illuminate the star system, and in so doing, alter our expectations and understanding of stars and their importance in society today' (Petersen 2007).

It is certainly not new to suggest that ageing as represented in the mainstream media is linked to a range of negative connotations. In popular culture the older female body is particularly vilified. Ageing is configured in contemporary society as a kind of narcissistic problem and exists as an embarrassing reminder to a celebrity-obsessed transformation focused society that ultimately there is no successful way to fight it. Audiences are constantly bombarded with ways to overcome the ageing 'problem' through advertising, marketing, the visibility of youthful older people in celebrity culture and through the promotion of a lifestyle trajectory that suggests there is no need to succumb to old age any longer, as the technologies exist to stave it off or at least keep it at bay. . . .

To this end, there has been both an intensification of the visibility and sexual objectification of the older woman in popular culture, particularly on US and UK television with series such as *Desperate Housewives* (Channel 4 2004–present), *Cougar Town* (ABC 2009–present) and *Mistresses* (BBC 2008–2010) . . . , all of which feature the relationships between groups of women post-forty. This may be seen as a positive shift in the representation of 'older' women and is in line with more general societal attitudes, where representations of ageing have undergone seismic shifts in recent years. More active populations, lifestyle industries creating an idealised older age and cosmetic surgery developments and its accessibility have contributed to a perceived 'ageless' society. This idea became entrenched in popular culture as the baby boomer generation aged. . . . Yet as a consequence of these shifts, and especially in a post-feminist context, women are not allowed to grow old naturally and are encouraged to fight the ageing process at every turn, as there is apparently no reason not to engage with technologies to stave off ageing when they are seemingly available to all. This places further responsibility on the individual in a neo-liberal context, where they must be in complete control of their own lives and ageing process. Indeed, in a post-feminist, neo-liberal society, ageing is not something to be feared, but must be both celebrated and fought; women must battle nature in order to look much younger to adhere to and maintain the fantasy of the sexualised middle-aged woman. In this stage of life, women are encouraged to adopt strict regimes in order to be considered still attractive and youthful. . . .

AGEING IN THE SPOTLIGHT

It has long been stated that male-dominated Hollywood is notoriously ageist against women. Men can continue long and successful careers in the film industry as they age, and yet their women peers struggle to continue to secure lead roles and are rendered almost invisible. Actors, such as Harrison Ford, Michael Douglas, Sylvester Stallone and Clint Eastwood, continue to undertake major roles whilst moving beyond middle age. Women are far less visible in major roles as they age, and the normative structure for women in roles post-fifty is that their ageing is part of the narrative, as seen in recent films such as *Mamma Mia* (2008), *The Women* (2008), *Sex and the City 1* (2008), *Sex and the City 2* (2010) and *It's Complicated* (2009). For men, ageing is rarely considered part of the nexus of their characters. Indeed, the male is often portrayed as the ageless 'hero,' where the film disregards their age, imagining that time has stood still for the character, especially in reference to a sequel or franchise. Hollywood has long fed age anxieties and it has become an oft-repeated exhortation that there are few interesting roles for older actresses in Hollywood. However, the recent visibility of older women on screen and the greater coverage of older women in the gossip industry in general has been posited as a progressive move towards inclusivity. Yet, discourses surrounding these women are first and foremost framed in terms of narratives of ageing, which are always structured in terms of how well the actress is managing her ageing process.

This utopian ideal of transcending time through cosmetic surgery is firmly ensconced in celebrity culture and its seductive aura is one that has been routinely criticised by feminists and cultural studies scholars alike. Cosmetic surgery in celebrity culture attempts to judge women by a particular beauty norm. This norm aims to construct women as ageless, the face must be taut and smooth, but must no longer adhere to the often-mocked early advances in face lift technologies, such as the 'wind tunnel' look of the 1980s and 1990s, it must be devoid of wrinkles and the body must be toned and slender, with evidence of the disciplined, yet discreet work that has been undertaken to achieve it. Indeed, it would appear that the older woman may well be visible in gossip culture, but she should never look her age.

GOSSIP, SURGERY AND HYPER-SCRUTINY

. . . The culture of hyper-scrutiny that exists within the gossip industry is explicit and contradictory. Aside from well-known gossip mavens, sites such as awfulplasticsurgery.com and famousplastic.com track alleged celebrity surgery in minute detail and allow readers to view detailed images of celebrity surgery. Such sites present categories such as *Bad Brow Lift, Bad Cheekbone Implants* and *Awful Plastic Surgery Victims* and simultaneously deride and revere the processes of surgical transformation, both mocking the celebrity but offering the reader advice and guidance on surgical procedures, where to gain advice, and so on. . . .

Sites such as these present their versions of 'appropriate' and 'inappropriate' age maintenance with sections featuring 'monstrous' examples of surgery, those that congratulate celebrities for getting their surgery 'right' and those that deride the celebrity for attempting to transcend time or more pertinently, making visible the signs of labour involved in maintaining a youthful look. They highlight the perceived difficulties in attempting to maintain an appropriately feminine public image, career and private life. . . .

Many gossip sites offer the reader paths of negotiation regarding staving off the ageing process where correct and incorrect versions of celebrity ageing are presented and justified. This kind of discourse is not exclusive to individual bloggers: in August 2010 the following discussion of Madonna appeared on *Femail,* the UK's *Daily Mail* newspaper online site and was widely disseminated across a number of gossip sites:

With her fresh complexion and taut skin, she would have been the envy of many women half her age. In fact, Madonna looked so youthful as she arrived at her 52nd birthday party in London

at the weekend that some even drew favourable comparisons with her 13-year-old daughter Lourdes. Sadly for the singer, however, there was one telltale sign that she has not been immune to the ageing process. A look at her hands as she clutched her black bag and a chunky gold crucifix showed that there are some things that even careful make-up and a tough gym regime can't hide. (www.mailonline 2010a)

Here Madonna is both praised for her 'fresh complexion' and 'taut skin,' usually represented as the result of numerous cosmetic interventions, and she is then compared with a teenager. The strict regime that Madonna undergoes to maintain her look is commended, but it is also made clear that not *even* Madonna, the foremost example of extreme health and beauty discipline, is 'immune' to ageing and that this is a 'sad,' but inevitable state. In gossip culture these discourses can be deeply contradictory where not to engage in practices of transformation means certain descent into career oblivion and engaging in too 'obvious' a way suggests desperation. Famous women are not considered 'true stars' if they make the signs of labour too obvious in the gossip industry. Female celebrities have long been hounded by the media for attempting to remain youthful by utilising the technologies available to them. British actress Lesley Ash was one of the first high-profile women to experience such vitriolic responses. In 2003 Ash underwent a collagen lip filler procedure that went wrong, giving her unnaturally large lips, which was deemed the 'Trout Pout' by British tabloid newspapers. She was then vilified in the press and gossip industry as an example of selfish indulgence; a desperate woman trying to stave off ageing.

SURGICAL AND AGEING TYPOLOGIES IN THE GOSSIP INDUSTRY

I want now to consider how typical discourses in the gossip industry and blog in particular, generally place female celebrities into surgical and ageing categories, which I shall identify here as the 'gruesome,' the 'desperate' and the 'sanctioned.' These categories effectively outline the flow of discourse that pervades gossip culture in relation to female celebrity and place women into particular groups, which are then often integrated into their star images and become part of the circulation of discourse in relation to their celebrity status.

The gruesome

Most apparent is the celebrity as gruesome object. . . . These gruesome women are positioned as abject freaks, who lie outside the boundaries of appropriate and acceptable feminine selves. They possess a macabre and morbid look, which operates as a reminder of the perils of both ageing and indulging in excessive cosmetic surgery. Celebrities such as Cher, Lil' Kim, Joan Rivers, Priscilla Presley, Joan Van Ark, LaToya Jackson, Alicia Douvall, Janice Dickinson, Melanie Griffith, Courtney Love, Lara Flynn Boyle and, most notoriously, Jocelyn Van Wildenstein are routinely discussed in these terms. . . .

Cher regularly features in discourses surrounding the gruesome version of the celebrity face. She has been perceived as the poster girl for cosmetic surgery since the 1990s, and formerly her look was praised in terms of how well she appeared to transcend her age. More recently, however, the tone of coverage in gossip culture has become increasingly malicious. At the December 2010 premiere of her film *Burlesque,* Cher was described as looking glamorous and youthful on the red carpet (Daily Mail 2010b). However, close ups later revealed face lift tape hidden just beneath her jaw line. She was predictably vilified across the gossip industry and was seen as desperately attempting to cling on to youth, but this moment was also widely seen as an acceptable improvement on her 'natural' look when she was photographed shortly after in natural daylight. Cher's *faux pas* was perceived as bizarre, gruesome and monstrous, a rather pathetic attempt to hold back, literally, her already heavily surgically enhanced face. Indeed, the celebrity that makes their cosmetic surgery too obvious, as in Cher's case, and becomes cast as gruesome is rejected by culture and becomes a spectacle to be ridiculed rather than revered. . . . Despite her seemingly following all the 'acceptable' paths, the result is that of a face that embodies both horror and fascination. As with all cosmetic surgery narratives in gossip culture, this is deeply problematic and contradictory and these women then become part of the carnivalesque matrix of post-feminist makeover culture, operating as both spectacle and caveat, warning the reader that there is a price to pay for overindulging in technologies of cosmetic surgery.

The desperate

The second category constructed by the gossip industry is the 'desperate.' Celebrities in this group are generally over forty and have often had successful careers. They are configured as desperate to remain youthful in order to suspend time and reclaim their once glittering careers and images, but are often constructed as failing at both. Examples of such women include Nicole Kidman, Meg Ryan, Sharon Stone and Pamela Anderson. They are positioned as rarely, if ever, making any public acknowledgement of cosmetic surgery and are pursued by the gossip industry on precisely these terms. Here the celebrity is both maligned and praised, often treated as anxiously attempting to remain relevant to the extent that the reconfiguring of their celebrity through cosmetic surgery becomes more visible than their actual work. A pertinent example of this is Nicole Kidman who appears regularly in the gossip industry and whose star image has been altered considerably by gossip culture. Generally considered a serious and accomplished actress, her star image is becoming more tenuous and is at times located in the category of 'has-been' in some quarters of the gossip industry. High-profile bloggers such as Perez Hilton and Lainey Liu of *Laineygossip* have been scathing in their discussion of Kidman. Both appear to hinge their dislike on Kidman's lack of authenticity, based on the fact that she appears to have undergone various cosmetic procedures but refuses to acknowledge them. *Laineygossip* has taken particular issue with this invisibility of the 'authentic' self by renaming Kidman 'Granny Freeze.' Subsequently, *Laineygossip* has also named Kidman's body parts and has given them a particular narrative of their own. Kidman's supposedly collagen-enhanced lips are now deemed by the blogger as 'Third Lip.' Hilton regularly states that she has a 'frozen face' and discussion surrounding Kidman suggests that she is no longer relevant to the industry, having become old and inauthentic. Consider the following 2010 post from *Perezhilton. com:*

> Nicole Kidman is a stickler for denying that she has had any work done, even though you could build an ice rink on her forehead. But it's actually another part of her anatomy that got people's attention at Wednesday's CMA Awards—her lips! Sources are claiming that the actress showed up at the event with hubby Keith Urban looking like she had just had her

lips done. One witness said she looked 'freak-ish' and compared her to Meg Ryan! Ouch! It is obvious she has had massive amounts of Botox put in her face, but the lips . . . we're not sure. They sure look like they've been plumped, but we wouldn't go as far to call them freakish. Maybe it's just because we've seen worse. What do you think? *(PerezHilton.com)*

Here Hilton suggests Kidman should be open with the public regarding cosmetic surgery in order to gain approval and popularity. Kidman is compared with Meg Ryan, whose star image has plummeted in recent years, post lip augmentation. No longer perceived as America's favourite romantic comedy sweetheart, she is repeatedly represented as a bitter older woman. These celebrities operate in a difficult space: they are considered fraudulent, yet appealing, ugly yet beautiful, has-beens, yet in demand. These are the women who face the most vitriol, represented as oscillating between nostalgic notions of a better version of themselves and a reinvented youthful version of middle age that is balanced precariously between the beautiful and the grotesque.

The sanctioned

Lastly, the sanctioned refers to those celebrities who are positioned by the gossip industry as age-ing well and who have purportedly employed the technologies of cosmetic surgery in 'acceptable' ways according to the post-feminism and who are held up as beautiful, womanly and appropriately feminine. Examples in this category include Demi Moore, Halle Berry, Charlize Theron, Cindy Crawford, Andie McDowell and Sandra Bullock.

What links these women is their ability to remain 'ageless,' as if they have frozen middle age and left it somehow suspended. This is widely praised in gossip culture, but is of course precarious.

Demi Moore is a particularly good example of a celebrity who is depicted as engaging in such practices, since she is often held up as the epitome of cosmetic surgery 'done right.' Moore starred in a number of successful films during the 1990s including *Ghost* (1990), *A Few Good Men* (1992) and *Indecent Proposal* (1993), resulting in her being one of the highest paid Hollywood actresses of the decade. More recently she has repositioned herself in the industry. She is married to actor Ashton Kutcher, 15 years her junior, and is consistently

featured in the gossip industry as a celebrity who has managed to negotiate the ageing process skil-fully. Rather than entering the category of the abject, freakish or desperate, despite her repeated denial of surgery, she is desirable and 'appropri-ately' feminine . . .

Moore also became an early Twitter user, dem-onstrating her knowledge of the mechanisms of the blogosphere and social networking, regularly posting commentary in response to particular sto-ries about her look, age and surgery rumours in the gossip industry and also cementing her status as youthful. Her ability to suspend time and her visibility and participation in gossip culture have both revived her star image and brought her to the attention of a new generation of fans.

Yet, this group is not immune to derogatory discussion. Perez Hilton routinely comments upon Moore's image and suggests that she is ageing well, whilst behaving in ways that are age inappropriate. In a 2010 post, for example, he commented:

> Isn't she a little old for this?! Demi Moore may have felt the need for everyone to look at her because the 47-year-old actress took to her Twitter to post pics of her bikini body. The pho-tos were given the caption, 'Maybe this is more like summer!' It's not that she doesn't look great, but we're starting to understand where her daughters get the need to let their goods hang out. Grow up, honey! *(PerezHilton.com)*

In gossip culture, discourse surrounding cosmetic surgery is most concerned with the celebrities' visible management of ageing and how well they tap into technologies that will allow youth to be extended through the face. This linking of age and surgery becomes the nexus of post-feminist rhetoric, assuming that the reader can become as beautiful and youthful as Moore if they only use the technologies available to become an empowered and appropriately feminine older woman. It is these markers of femininity that are linked with Moore and her youthful look, the long, glossy hair, the lean body, the wrinkle-free face.

She is often pitted against other actresses of her generation such as Meg Ryan, who is repre-sented as desperate, old and frumpy because she failed to employ cosmetic technologies suc-cessfully, whilst Moore is youthful, fun and hyper-feminine. . . .

BOTOX BABIES

There are other types of discourse reverberating around female celebrity and ageing in gossip culture. Recently, media attention has focused on the issue of much younger women undergoing cosmetic procedures before they reach an age where the visible signs of ageing are even present. It must be recognised that many have never known anything but a culture where cosmetic surgery is performed on women routinely. There has been growing 'concern' in the gossip industry regarding the use of cosmetic surgery on women and young girls who are deemed too young, certainly propelled by the 23-year-old star of MTV's reality series *The Hills* (2006–2010) Heidi Montag and her much publicised cosmetic procedures. The term 'Botox Babies' has been used to describe young women who undergo surgical enhancement, such as singer Charice Pempengco, who recently appeared on television having Botox at 18 years old, as she reportedly wanted to look 'fresh' for her appearance on the hit US television show *Glee*. Heidi Montag represents the results of the era's cultural pressure and appears to have succumbed to the crippling images of beauty that abound in popular culture.

Montag reportedly underwent 10 surgical procedures in a single day including a chin reduction, liposuction and rhinoplasty, resulting in an extreme physical transformation that was unveiled through the gossip industry. The work prompted widespread condemnation from the media who were quick to label her 'Franken-Heidi' and 'Franken-Barbie,' relating her surgeries to mental health problems. . . .

Montag's face is now a composite of what is culturally coded as beautiful, sexual and feminine. Her almond-shaped eyes, petite nose, full lips, large breasts and tightly sculpted body are constructed from a set of norms that are valued culturally, yet they appear at odds with an individual in early womanhood. Indeed, Heidi seems to be gazing out, trapped from underneath her face, her surgeries speaking for her, telling her that she is her 'best self.' Montag may well function as the epitome of a post-feminist culture that places so much emphasis on the image that a woman so young felt she had to conform, to make her, in her words, 'like Barbie' (www.people.com 2010) and assist her in reclaiming some sense of agency, now she has become effectively a living embodiment of a Barbie doll. Montag has been widely condemned because her surgery appears far removed from the current prescribed look, which in order to remain within the boundaries of acceptability should not reveal the work. The trickery lies in the ability to disguise the labour involved in order to maintain the alignment of the inner self and the outer self.

However, the contradictory nature of the ways in which cosmetic surgery is represented in popular culture, as indulgent, excessive and unnecessary, pitted against desirable, necessary and normal, complicates and fragments the ideal self so it becomes hopelessly unstable. The juxtaposition of fear and desire associated with cosmetic surgery and the complexity and intertwined nature of celebrity and makeover cultures makes the boundaries of acceptable and desirable cosmetic surgery even narrower and ever more elusive.

Youthful beauty as evidenced in celebrity culture now appears to be the only type of beauty to aspire to. Weber suggests celebrity functions as a playing field on which a fascinated and perplexed culture negotiates sites of identity (Weber 2009, p. 235). Indeed individuals use celebrity as a nexus of identity negotiation. Through the matrix of post-feminism and gossip culture, a new beauty norm has been created advocating the use of cosmetic procedures on younger women, a norm that suggests youth must be held in limbo through the use of cosmetic procedures throughout adult life and for as long as possible. . . .

REFERENCES

A Few Good Men, 1992. Film. Directed by Rob Reiner. USA: Castle Rock Entertainment.

Blum, V., 2003. *Flesh wounds: the culture of cosmetic surgery.* Berkeley, CA: University of California Press.

Cougar Town, 2009–present. Film. Directed by Michael McDonald. USA: Doozer/Coquette Productions.

Daily Mail, 2010a. Madonna, still a smooth operator at 52 as she celebrates birthday with daughter

Lourdes. *Daily Mail* 16 Aug. [online]. Available from: http://www.dailymail.co.uk/tvshowbiz/article-1303369/Madonna-smooth-operator-52—hands-havent-stood-test-time-face.html [Accessed 20 August 2010].

Daily Mail, 2010b. So that's why you need face tape, Cher . . . 24 hours after red carpet appearance, 64-year-old shows her natural side. *Daily Mail* 15 Dec. [online]. Available from: http://www.dailymail.co.uk/tvshowbiz/article-1338296/Cher-64-shows-needed-facelift-tape-Burlesque-premiere.html [accessed 15 December 2010].

Desperate Housewives, 2004–present. Film. Directed by Larry Shaw. USA: Cherry Alley Productions.

Ghost, 1990. Film. Directed by Gerry Zucker. USA: Paramount Pictures.

Gill, R., 2007. Postfeminist media culture: elements of a sensibility. *European journal of cultural studies*, 10, 147–166.

Gilleard, C., 2005. Cultural approaches to the ageing body. *In:* J. Bengtson, V. Coleman, and P. Kirkwood, eds. *The Cambridge handbook of age and ageing.* Cambridge: Cambridge University Press, 156–163.

Good Morning America, 1975–present. Film. Directors various. USA: ABC News.

Hills, 2006–2010. Film. Directed by Hisham Abed. USA: Reel Security/ MTV.

Indecent Proposal, 1993. Film. Directed by Adrian Lyne. USA: Paramount Pictures.

It's Complicated, 2009. Film. Directed by Nancy Meyers. USA: Universal Pictures.

Jones, M., 2008. *Skintight: an anatomy of cosmetic surgery.* London: Berg.

Mamma Mia!, 2008. Film. Directed by Phylilda Lloyd. USA: Universal Pictures.

Mistresses, 2008–2010. BBC.

Negra, D. and Holmes, S., 2008. Going cheap? Female celebrity in the reality, tabloid and scandal genres. *Genders special issue* [online], 48.

Available from: http://www.genders.org/g48/g48_negraholmes.html [accessed 10 April 2011].

Petersen, A., 2007. Celebrity juice, not from concentrate: Perez Hilton, gossip blogs, and the new star production. *Jump cut: A review of contemporary media*, Spring, 49.

Sex and the City 1, 2008. Film. Directed by Michael Patrick King. USA: New Line.

Sex and the City 2, 2010. Film. Directed by Michael Patrick King. USA: New Line.

Shildrick, M., 2002. *Embodying the monster: encounters with the vulnerable self.* London: Sage.

The Hills, 2006–2010. MTV.

The Women, 2008. Film. Directed by Diane English. USA: Picture house Entertainment.

Wearing, S., 2007. Subjects of rejuvenation: aging in postfeminist culture. *In:* Y. Tasker and D. Negra, eds. *Interrogating postfeminism; gender and the politics of popular culture.* Durham, NC: Duke University Press, 277–311.

Weber, B., 2009. *Makeover TV: selfhood, citizenship and celebrity.* Durham, NC: Duke University Press.

Woodward, K., 2006. Performing age, performing gender. *NWSA journal*, 18 (1), 162–189.

www.abcnews.com, 2010. Heidi Montag interview prompts huge response. *www.abcnews.com* 20 Jan. [online]. Available from: http://abcnews.go.com/GMA/Entertainment/heidi-montag-interview-plastic-surgery-prompts-huge-response/story?id=9610622 [accessed 12 April 2011].

www.people.com, 2010. Heidi Montag; my surgeries aren't an addiction. *www.people.com* 19 Jan. [online]. Available from: http://www.people.com/people/article/0,,20337744,00.html [accessed 12 April 2011].

Available from: www.laineygossip.com

Available from: www.perezhilton.com [accessed 16 December 2010].

HOW TO "USE YOUR OLYMPIAN"

34

The Paradox of Athletic Authenticity and Commercialization in the Contemporary Olympic Games

Momin Rahman and Sean Lockwood

INTRODUCTION

... Drawing on research on sports celebrity and modern celebrity culture, we discuss how the transformation of the Olympics into a media entertainment event affects the authenticity of the athletes who literally embody the positive aspects of 'Olympism'; the ideals that underpin the event and movement or, in more commercial terms, the meaning of the Olympic brand. The following is an example of the commercial use of Olympic athletes:

> The British Olympic Association is delighted that you have visited the britisholympians site and we hope that you take the next step of making a booking and using one of our Olympians to help you achieve your business objectives . . . (From *Guidelines on the Use of Olympians,* British Olympic Association)[1]

To illustrate the role of authenticity within this commercialization, we investigate a range of institutional discourses drawn from the International Olympic Committee (IOC), London 2012, the British Olympic Association (BOA), and Lloyds TSB Bank, a major corporate sponsor of the London 2012 Games. . . . We argue that the tension between authenticity and commercialization is inevitable given that media and corporate finances are necessary to fund the Games, and therefore that this paradox must be managed to emphasize the positive side of this dialectic—the authenticity of motivation and fans' enjoyment of the same. Central to this management is the promotion of Olympic athletes as embodiments of the authentic Olympic ideal, which includes their construction as 'heroic' individuals who participate to excel

rather than make money. However, this discourse is contradictory because the representation of athletes occurs within and draws on a celebrity and commodity culture that primarily serves the accumulation strategies of corporations. Moreover, the tacit assumption within this contemporary discourse of sporting heroism is that the Games of antiquity provide a precedent for authentic motivation based on athletic amateurism. We demonstrate, however, that this appeal was driven first by the requirements of legitimizing the modern Games, and subsequently by the need to manage the paradox of commercialization. The ancient Olympics have therefore become part of the wider discourse of authenticity that is deployed in contemporary times to facilitate the continued commercial and cultural viability of the Games in a mediatized and commodity culture.

THE OLYMPICS AND ENTERTAINMENT CULTURE: PARADOXES IN THE 'BRAND' THROUGH COMMERCIALIZATION

Whilst the modern Games began in 1896 in modest fashion, their international impact was established by Stockholm 1912 (Barney, 2007). However, the only media available to these and other pre-Second World War Games were the contemporary forms of radio, press, and cinema newsreel. The subsequent modern Olympic Games developed concurrently with the growth of television and its relationship with sport in general (Smart, 2005; Wenn and Martyn, 2007; Whannel, 2009). Whannel explains that 'The emergence of television in the 1930s enabled a combination of the immediacy and uncertainty of

From M. Rahman and S. Lockwood (2011), "How to 'use your Olympian': The Paradox of Athletic Authenticity and Commercialization in the Contemporary Olympic Games." *Sociology,* 45, 815–829. Reprinted with permission of SAGE Publications, Ltd.

live sport, the domestic context of radio, and the drama and spectacle of newsreel' (2009: 208). He describes how television was first used to broadcast the 1936 Berlin Olympics in local cinemas, and how public broadcast was expanded during the London Olympics of 1948, albeit to a limited audience of those with sets in the London area. In contrast, the London 2012 Olympics was a global 'mega-event' experienced not only through television but also through other forms of media such as print and websites that commented on the events and, moreover, create a simultaneous, communal global audience that is increasingly rare in the on-demand and subscription formats of most televised sport (Whannel, 2009). Television media technology is therefore a distinct aspect of the context in which the modern Olympic Games has existed since the mid-20th century (Smart, 2005; Whannel, 2002, 2009).

This mediatization is, however, fundamentally about commercialization, primarily the impact that the availability of media finances has had on the organization of sport. According to Whannel:

> Television transformed sport into a set of commodified global spectacles, producing huge audiences and massive new sources of income. Sport in turn provided television with an endless supply of major spectacular events and an enduring form of pleasurable and popular viewing. (2009: 206)

When a sport is popular enough, guaranteeing a significant audience, the governing bodies can demand huge monies for the broadcast rights both at national levels and internationally for 'mega-events.'[2] In the case of the Olympics, this process began in 1960 when the IOC licensed television rights for both summer and winter Games for the first time, in partnership with the local organizing committees. The IOC took direct control of negotiations starting with Barcelona in 1992, allowing considerations of the Olympic Movement and brand to outweigh specific local or national agendas and local attempts to keep the majority of revenues (Wenn and Martyn, 2007: 311).

The mediatization and commercialization are linked because the media provide larger audiences who are also potential consumers, not only of the sporting event as media product, but also of associated advertising and branding. This media/commercial equation has clearly influenced the activities of the Olympic Movement, specifically

transforming it into a more explicitly corporate operation, as characterized by Wenn and Martyn:

> Fuelled by the revenues generated from television rights, the activities commonly associated with corporate enterprise flourished inside the halls of power of the organisation's Lausanne headquarters. Television matters aside, it was in the areas of product advertising and consumer sales, often identified as *marketing,* that the IOC became linked to what is commonly referred to as *commercialism.* (2007: 315)

This commercialization has been inevitable, largely because of the wider development of sport as a commercialized leisure and entertainment industry that is dependent on both corporate media and commodity corporate finances. Since the latter part of the 20th century, sport has increasingly become a central component of the wider media entertainment industry that consists of globalized transnational and multi-corporate organizations which deploy cross-media and cross-national delivery (Law et al., 2002; Maguire, 1999; Smart, 2005). The Olympic Movement has not only become drawn into these economic structures, but it has also been able to promote its unique identity to capitalize on funding sources: there is clearly a positive 'branding' effect of the Olympic discourse, both in hosting the event and for companies associated with it through sponsorship. In the case of the former, Zhang and Zhao detail the specific and concerted efforts of the Chinese authorities to secure the Games for Beijing and to use them to 'rebrand' the city (2009: 251). Although the authors remain sceptical as to whether economic or rebranding efforts were successful in this case, this example does demonstrate the attraction of the Olympic Games as a globally recognized mega-event that has specific, positive brand associations. Moreover, the IOC is aware of this power and commissioned research to define, refine, and promote its brand, resulting in an advertising campaign in 2000 called 'Celebrate Humanity,' which was 'the first fully global marketing campaign to attempt to communicate the values embodied within the Olympic movement' (Maguire et al., 2008a: 70). The researchers comment, however, that:

> . . . the 'message' becomes embedded in a broader process of commerce whereby the media/marketing/advertising/corporate nexus is concerned less with the values underpinning

Olympism *per se* ... and more with how such values can help build markets, construct and enhance brand awareness and thus create 'glocal' consumers/identities. (2008a: 74)

... Within the context of this inevitable commercialization, however, remains the perceived 'authenticity' of the Olympics as an athletic event and a brand, one that can therefore be enjoyed primarily for its demonstration of human endeavour rather than as another form of consumption. Broadly speaking, the Olympics are seen to represent a combination of the following: sport for its own sake; the pursuit of achievement and self-improvement through sport but also through associated cultural and educational programmes; and national pride but in a spirit of peace, mutual understanding, and friendship. This discourse of the Olympics is expressed in various ways by the institutions of the movement, primarily through the IOC's mission statements and in the promotion of specific games such as London 2012.

... Specific iterations are derived from the concept of 'Olympism' that is defined in the Olympic Charter thus:

1. Olympism is a philosophy of life, exalting and combining in a balanced whole the qualities of body, will and mind. Blending sport with culture and education, Olympism seeks to create a way of life based on the joy of effort, the educational value of good example and respect for universal fundamental ethical principles.

2. The goal of Olympism is to place sport at the service of the harmonious development of man, with a view to promoting a peaceful society concerned with the preservation of human dignity. (http://www.olympic. org/Documents/Olympic%20Charter/ Charter_en_2010.pdf)

In the context of the Olympics as part of sports media entertainment culture, a paradox exists wherein the commercialization of the Games is potentially undermining its brand power, the meanings of which are antithetical to consumerism. For example, the key messages of the Celebrate Humanity campaign in 2000 mentioned above focus on issues such as 'hope,' 'dreams' and inspirations,' 'friendship,' 'fair play,' and 'joy in effort' (Maguire et al., 2008a), echoing the ideals of modern Olympism which emphasize peaceful international relationships, education through sport, and a focus on human greatness.[3] Indeed, a critical perspective on contemporary IOC marketing efforts would suggest that they are there simply to veil the commercialism behind the Games, or at the very least to justify it as necessary for the Games to exist by providing the funds required to facilitate the rarefied Olympic atmosphere in which such ideals can still be pursued (Maguire et al., 2008a). ...

THE CONTEMPORARY CONTEXT FOR SPORTS STARS: CELEBRITY AND AUTHENTICITY

... Sport has increasingly become part of the wider media entertainment structure of globalized trans-national and multi-corporate organizations (Law et al., 2002; Maguire, 1999; Smart, 2005). Moreover, the media broadcasts themselves have been joined by commercial sports commodity products, associated with specific individuals, teams and nations, as well wider commodity branding through endorsement and sponsorship deals (Andrews and Jackson, 2001; Smart, 2005). This media-driven commercialization of sport has converged with the emergence of modern celebrity as a historically distinct form of fame, dependent on the development of mass media technologies throughout the 20th century and the significant expansion of mass consumption in late capitalism (Marshall, 1997; Rojek, 2001; Turner, 2004). In his critique of the consumerist and indi-vidualist society of the post-war period, Lasch (1979) bemoans the 'degradation of sport' into entertain-ment show business culture. One consequence of this 'degradation' has been an increasing emphasis on individual 'stars,' and so sporting figures have been transformed into sporting celebrities. The sta-tus of celebrity beyond their own sport is a distinc-tive aspect of contemporary sports stars, derived from the transformation of sport from amateur community-based leisure into a globalized and mediatized 'entertainment' industry. Moreover, this industry uses the technologies and strategies of wider celebrity culture to provoke consumption of its own media products, associated sports commodi-ties, and, crucially, wider commodity brands. Thus:

... commercial corporations have come to rec-ognize that sport and sporting figures offer a rare, if not unique, quality of authenticity from which their brands can derive substantial benefit by association. . . . From the 1980s, sport events and sporting figures have been increasingly valued as the means through which all sorts of products and services, including those not related to sport at all could be marketed to consumers. (Smart, 2005: 144)

However, this branding is potentially a threat to the athletes' cultural resonance because it can make them seem more like corporate functionaries than genuinely motivated enthusiasts for their sport (Smart, 2005). The premise of the threat is that commercialization is a negative aspect of contemporary sports industries because it renders sport as just another indistinct form of consumerism, removing any enthusiasm from its audience. This argument, however, must be understood in terms of historical scale given that some level of economic burden has always been part of organized sport, both for players requiring equipment and wages if they were professionals, and for fans to buy tickets to events. The issue in contemporary times has become the large-scale finances available in many sports through commercialization and mediatization, requiring an associated increase in economic burdens for fans, and rewarding athletes to the extent that 'Making money is now an important part of sport and professional participants have to work hard at their games because it is their job to do so' (Smart, 2005: 5). Furthermore, the commercialization of teams and sport industries has removed the close identification of traditional fan and team, whereby the latter, collectively and individually, 'were the apotheosis of the culture of their cities, symbolizing not only the heart and soul of the spectators who watched them but the spirit of the associated community' (Rojek, 2006: 684). The separation of fans from their teams through mediatization and the consequent positioning of fan as consumer and athletes as highly paid wage labourers are seen as less genuine than either an emotional identification with a team or sports star, or the athlete as motivated by the opportunity to excel. This tension is managed by emphasizing the genuine basis of emotional attachment in fans, focused on the authenticity of their heroes (Smart, 2005: 194–8). The inevitability of commercialization is therefore alleviated by promoting the authenticity of the sporting event, not only at the level of the event

as brand as described in the previous section, but also through its particular sports stars. Authenticity is a key issue here precisely because it serves two symbiotic purposes: its presence is seen to promote brands and products through positive association, and it can also be deployed to manage the potentially disruptive consequences of this commercialization. We suggest that this latter function is more relevant to the Olympics: athletes' 'authenticity' is invoked to emphasize the purity of the event, distracting fans and audiences from their overt interpellation as consumers (Maguire et al., 2008b), and reiterating the actual Games as an arena for human achievement rather than a global media and commercial mega-event (Whannel, 2009).

The construction of the authenticity of sports stars is two fold: first, they are seen to achieve status through their talent and hard work at training that talent, rather than through inherited or class privilege. This resonates with the democratization of fame during the 20th century, whereby media 'stars' have been increasingly drawn from 'ordinary' backgrounds, or at least have celebrity personae that emphasize their ordinary origins (Rojek, 2001; Turner, 2004). This serves to model the idea that 'ordinary' people—from the newly enfranchised masses in democracies—do matter in mass capitalist society, and may even one day become rich, powerful and famous using their talents. As Rojek argues, sporting heroes have become part of the mediatized celebrity elite partly because 'In societies based around the meritocratic ideal, sport is also one of the paradigmatic institutions that articulate and elaborate the meritocratic ideal and reinforce achievement culture' (2006: 680–1). Rojek argues that the 'achievement culture' modelled by sports stars serves social integration by reinforcing the values needed for the discipline of work, but it does so by focusing our attention on heroic or exceptional individuals. Nike's reinvention and global expansion drew precisely on this achievement culture in both its advertising and branding, and in its sponsorship of athletes who embodied the hard-working and heroic ethos, most notably Michael Jordan (Goldman and Papson, 1998). Moreover, Nike's promotion of athletic celebrity illustrates a central point about celebrity culture: the pivotal affinity between consumer culture and the emergence of contemporary celebrity culture. Sports stars make great 'celebrity-commodities' (Turner, 2004: 34) precisely because they fulfil the function of modelling desire for their fans as consumers: sports celebrities embody both the work ethic of achievement culture *and* luxurious and exceptional lifestyle consumerism.

The second dimension of athletes' authenticity is the potential for heroism that is seen to underpin their professional activities. In his study on footballers in Britain and how they became media stars during the 1990s, Whannel argues that the 20th century saw more emphasis on sports as an arena for heroism (2002). He challenges arguments that describe a gradual erosion of 'authentic' heroism during the 20th century in favour of an emphasis on mass media entertainment stars, exemplified by Daniel Boorstin's (2006) characterization of the decline of heroes in favour of celebrities. Boorstin suggests that the interest in 'greatness' of achievement has gradually been replaced by the media-driven interest in the banalities of celebrities' lives, and hence we no longer have true heroes in our culture. Whannel argues, however, that while sports stars have replaced more traditional 'heroes' such as explorers, adventurers, scientists, and military men, athletes retain some of the authenticity of such extraordinary figures because 'the cultures of sport still depend in part on a constant re-enacting of the heroic' (2002: 46). The unpredictability of sporting contests is a key dimension of this authenticity in that it allows for 'heroic' or extraordinary performances in specific, limited, and never to be repeated time frames, resulting in both urgency and demands on participants to excel beyond expectations, to achieve 'greatness' (Smart, 2005). The 2010 World Cup demonstrates this in full measure, with many favoured teams knocked out at the league stage or surviving only through penalty kick deciders. Spain, a team that had perpetually missed the finals, eventually won the competition, but only through a last-minute goal in extra time, providing dramatic tension and finally matching long-held national expectation. Earlier in 2010 at the Winter Olympics, the Canadian men's hockey team beat their eternal American rivals in the gold medal game, but only after their youthful captain Sidney Crosby scored in overtime, provoking an outpouring of Canadian media stories on these national heroes. Goodman et al. (2002) demonstrate that adverts using Olympians also draw predominantly on narratives of heroism, illustrating that the commercial use of these celebrities relies directly on the perceived authenticity of athletic heroism. . . .

THE MODERN CONSTRUCTION OF OLYMPISM AND THE APPEAL TO ANCIENT AUTHENTICITY

As already discussed, heroism is a dominant discourse in the construction of sport (McKay et al., 2000; Whannel, 2002), but this heroism is often based on archetypes, many of which are drawn from eternal cultural myths (Goodman et al., 2002). In the case of the Olympics, an important archetype has been the ancient amateur athlete and his participation purely for the sake of sport—rather than for economic gain—which is certainly echoed in the contemporary discourses described above. . . .

The modern Olympics were established under the leadership of Pierre Frédy, Baron de Coubertin, a wealthy French aristocrat. Coubertin's original aim was to reform the French educational system to include athletic training, based on the model of the British public school system. When, however, he was unable to raise interest in this scheme, he turned his attention to establishing the international Olympics. Support for this was sought through an appeal to his fellow aristocrats and their contemporary notion of amateur sport. At a congress held in 1894 in Paris, delegates voted to re-establish the Olympic Games under the leadership of an already-formed IOC, restricting participation to amateurs, defined as those who received absolutely no monetary gain from athletics (and thereby impeding the participation of the working class, who would be discouraged by the expense involved in training and travelling to the games) (Young, 1984). The first Games held in 1896 in Athens were a moderate success, and Coubertin decided that the second should be staged in Paris. The IOC was reformed at this time, including nine new members of the European titled aristocracy. Also at this time, Coubertin began to promote the idea that ancient Greek Olympians were both aristocratic and amateur, and that their competition was based on the ideal of sport for its own sake (Young, 1984: 73). . . .

The simple truth, however, is that Greek athletes who participated in the Olympic Games and other athletic festivals were not amateurs but professionals, at least in the modern sense of the terms. . . . Victorious athletes were lavishly rewarded on their return home, as best demonstrated by evidence from Athens which shows that an Athenian Olympic victor would receive an immediate cash award and free meals for life at public expense (Kyle, 1987: 127, 146–7).[4] There is evidence that other cities took things a step further, paying Olympians to compete for them rather than their own home towns (Young, 1984: 141–2). The acceptance of monetary awards and particularly payment would have made any of these athletes professional, by modern definition, and disqualified all from competing in the pre-1980s Olympics. . . .

Although professional athletes are now an accepted presence in the modern Olympic Games, the authenticity of amateurism has become so ingrained that it is still, if only tacitly, invoked. If we turn to the example of the Lloyds TSB 'Local Heroes' programme, we can see attempts to emphasize the amateurism central to sporting authenticity that still exists. The programme:

. . . is an initiative to support the future stars of Team GB and Paralympics GB in the lead up to London 2012 and beyond. Follow their journey as they pursue their sporting dreams. For

every Olympic and Paralympic medalist, there are thousands of genuine hopefuls struggling without recognition or funding. (http://www.facebook.com/lloydstsblocalheroes)

These 'local heroes' need the financial support of the bank's donations to achieve their goals, suggesting that they are not yet established enough to have significant commercial sponsorship and that they are, therefore, amateurs who do not receive direct payment for their athletic activities. The ancient Greek Olympics have been used to legitimize and authenticate ideals of amateurism in the modern Games, but this discourse is based on the misinterpretation and occasional falsification of historic evidence. Nonetheless, the reiterations of amateurism have become a central part of the modern Olympic discourse, and indeed provide a distinctive Olympic dimension to the 'authenticity' that is foregrounded to distract audiences from the commercialization of the Games. . . .

NOTES

1. The British Olympic Association's website http://www.britisholympians.com/guidelines.aspx was accessed on 14 January 2011, but the site was folded into the London 2012 preparations and these guidelines deleted.

2. The other major sporting mega-event is, of course, the World Cup. The global television rights in 2002 and 2006 were sold for almost USD$2 billion (Smart, 2005: 90) and, more recently, FIFA completed the worldwide sale of television rights for the 2010 World Cup, 18 months before the tournament began (http://www.fifa.com/aboutfifa/tv/

index.html). No details of the revenue are provided on FIFA's official website, but various media news reports USD$2.7 billion as the price of broadcast rights for South Africa 2010.

3. All institutions of the Olympic movement are governed by the Olympic Charter and contain many references to promoting the fairness, equality, and friendship of sporting contests, see http://multimedia.olympic.org/pdf/en_report_122.pdf

4. The intrinsic monetary value of these awards has been debated (e.g. Instone, 1986).

REFERENCES

Andrews DL and Jackson SJ (2001) *Sports Stars: The Cultural Politics of Sporting Celebrity*. London: Routledge.

Barney RK (2007) The Olympic Games in modern times. In: Schaus GP and Wenn SR (eds) *Onward to the Olympics: Historical Perspectives on the Olympic Games, Part II.* Waterloo, ON: Wilfred Laurier University Press.

Barney RK, Wenn SR and Martyn SG (2002) *Selling the Five Rings: The International Olympic Committee and the Rise of Olympic Commercialism.* Salt Lake City, UT: University of Utah Press.

Boorstin DJ (2006) From hero to celebrity: The human pseudo-event. In: Marshall PD (ed.) *The Celebrity Culture Reader*. New York and London: Routledge.

Chatziefstathiou D (2007) The history of marketing an idea: The example of Baron Pierre de Coubertin as a social marketer. *European Sport Management Quarterly* 7(1): 55–80.

Christensen P (2007) The transformation of athletics in sixth-century Greece. In: Schaus GP and Wenn SR (eds) *Onward to the Olympics: Historical Perspectives on the Olympic Games, Part I.* Waterloo, ON: Wilfred Laurier University Press.

Crowther NB (2007) The Ancient Olympic Games through the centuries. In: Schaus GP and Wenn SR (eds) *Onward to the Olympics: Historical Perspectives on the Olympic Games, Part I.* Waterloo, ON: Wilfred Laurier University Press.

Evjen HD (1987) Review of Young. *The Classical Journal* 82(3): 268–71.

Gardiner EN (1910) *Greek Athletic Sports and Festivals.* London: Macmillan.

Gardner P (1892) *New Chapters in Greek History.* London: Putnam's and Sons.

Goldman R and Papson S (1998) *Nike Culture: The Sign of the Swoosh.* London: Sage.

Goodman JR, Duke LL and Sutherland J (2002) Olympic athletes and heroism in advertising: Gendered concepts of valor? *Journalism and Mass Communication Quarterly* 79(2): 374–93.

Instone S (1986) Review of Young. *The Journal of Hellenic Studies* 106: 238–9.

Kyle DG (1987) *Athletics in Ancient Athens.* Leiden: E.J. Brill.

Lasch C (1979) *The Culture of Narcissism.* New York: Warner Books.

Law A, Harvey J and Kemp S (2002) The global sport mass media oligopoly. *International Review for the Sociology of Sport* 37(3–4): 279–302.

McKay J, Messner MA and Sabo D (2000) *Masculinities, Gender Relations and Sport.* Thousand Oaks, CA: Sage.

Maguire J (1999) *Global Sport: Identities, Societies, Civilisations.* Cambridge: Polity.

Maguire J, Barnard S, Butler K and Golding P (2008a) 'Celebrate humanity' or 'consumers?': A critical evaluation of a brand in motion. *Social Identities* 14(1): 63–76.

Maguire J, Barnard S, Butler K and Golding P (2008b) Olympism and consumption: An analysis of advertising in the British media coverage of the 2004 Athens Olympic Games. *Sociology of Sport Journal* 25(2): 167–86.

Mahaffy JP (1879) *Old Greek athletics.* Macmillan's Magazine 36: 61–9.

Marshall PD (1997) *Celebrity and Power: Fame in Contemporary Culture.* Minneapolis, MN: University of Minnesota Press.

Miller SG (2004) *Ancient Greek Athletics.* New Haven, CT: Yale University Press.

Olympic.org (n.d.) Revenue Sources and Distribution. Available at: http://www.olympic.org/en/content/The-IOC/Financing/Revenues/?Tab=1

Poliakoff MB (1989) Review of Young. *The American Journal of Philology* 110(1): 166–71.

Rojek C (2001) *Celebrity.* London: Reaktion Books.

Rojek C (2006) Sports celebrity and the civilizing process. *Sport in Society* 9(4): 674–90.

Smart B (2005) *The Sport Star: Modern Sport and the Cultural Economy of Sporting Celebrity.* London: Sage.

Turner G (2004) *Understanding Celebrity.* London: Sage.

Wenn SR and Martyn SG (2007) Juan Antonio Samaranch's score sheet: Revenue generation and the Olympic Movement, 1980–2001. In: Schaus GP and Wenn SR (eds) *Onward to the Olympics: Historical Perspectives on the Olympic Games, Part II.* Waterloo, ON: Wilfred Laurier University Press.

Whannel G (2002) *Media Sports Stars: Masculinities and Moralities.* London: Routledge.

Whannel G (2009) Television and the transformation of sport. *The Annals of the American Academy of Political and Social Science* 625: 205–18.

Young DC (1984) *The Olympic Myth of Greek Amateur Athletics.* Chicago: Ares.

Zhang L and Zhao SX (2009) *City branding and the Olympic effect: A case study of Beijing.* Cities 26: 245–54.

35

MAPPING COMMERCIAL INTERTEXTUALITY

HBO's True Blood

Jonathan Hardy

Commercial intertextuality is used to describe the production and interlinking of texts like blockbuster films or TV series with allied para-texts and products, such as spin-offs, reversion-ings, promos, online media, books, games and merchandise. For critical political economists such commercial intertextuality is mainly read in terms of synergistic corporate communications that seek to maximize profits by cultivating and exploiting audiences and fans (Meehan, 1991, 2005). Corporate transmedia storytelling, such as the *Matrix* franchise, serve to create 'narra-tively necessary purchases' (Proffitt et al, 2007: 239). For scholars working in a cultural studies tradition—culturalists—commercial intertex-tuality can be read quite differently, as material that is fashioned in autonomous and creative ways for self-expression and social communica-tion, generating new forms of participation, and collaboration amongst prosumers (Jenkins, 1992, 2002, 2006). While such divergent readings have reflected underlying clashes between 'critical' and culturalist scholarship, this article explores scope for more integrative approaches through a case study of cross-media promotion and intertextual-ity in HBO's vampire drama *True Blood*.[1]

Discussing *Star Wars: the Phantom Menace* (Lucasfilms 1999) Nick Couldry writes (2000:70):

> If we place *The Phantom Menace* in its own wider context (the *Star Wars* series, all the associated fan literatures and practices, the whole his-tory of cross-marketed merchandise-saturated Hollywood blockbuster films), it is clear that we need to understand not one discrete text but a vast space of more or less interconnected texts, and how that space is ordered.

Couldry's notion of the ordering of textual space is usefully synthesizing, encouraging consideration of ordering as shaped by corporations but also other media practices. . . .

. . . Textual 'space' includes various kinds of discourse, from corporate 'speech' to the dis-courses of critics and commentators, intergroup and interpersonal communication. Yet there is blurring and hybridization across each category, corporate/independent, professional/amateur, and, as *True Blood* illustrates, across commercial/ auton-omous textuality.

TRUE BLOOD: MAPPING CORPORATE INTERTEXTUAL SPACE

True Blood is a fantasy horror entertainment series on HBO, the premium cable/multiplatform ser-vice owned by Time Warner. HBO, a quality brand ('It's not television. It's HBO'), was seek-ing a new hit on Sunday evenings, the traditional showcase for original material. The failure of series like *John From Cincinnati* and *Lucky Louie* had left HBO (dubbed 'HB-over') without a replacement for previous hits such as *Sex and the City* and *The Sopranos*. Promoting shows meant encouraging new subscribers to pay premium monthly fees. The first series aired in September 2008 shortly before the USA officially entered recession, when such subscriptions were vulnerable to household cut-backs. This was the context for HBO's investment in an extensive, expensive and innovative cross-media marketing campaign.

True Blood is a television show based on novels, *The Southern Vampire Mysteries,* by Charlaine Har-ris. The stories, the tenth of which was published

From Jonathan Hardy (2011), "Mapping Commercial Intertextuality: HBO's *True Blood.*" *Convergence,* 17: 7–17. Reprinted with permis-sion of SAGE Publications, Ltd.

in 2010, were bestsellers, providing a rich source of (inter-corporate) intertextuality. The *Twilight* franchise and later the CW's *The Vampire Diaries,* added to the resonance and intertextual reworking of vampire myths and iconography, whose rich cultural history continues to provide malleable resources for contemporary storytelling. Harris's nine books featured in *USA Today's* top 100 US book sales in 2009, while 17 per cent of total book sales that year were related to vampires or the paranormal (DeBarros et al., 2010). The stories and *True Blood* envision a world in which vampires 'live' alongside humans, able to feed off a synthetic blood product marketed as Tru Blood (discovered in Japan two years before the events in the drama begin). Set in Louisiana, the story has a powerful resonance of segregation, racism and bigotry, as well as 'Deep South' ingredients of swamps, sex, and religious fervour. There is a Vampire Rights Amendment being debated at the start of the series; with pronounced connotations of civil rights and gay liberation, Tru Blood has enabled Vampires to 'come out of the coffin.' Described by *USA Today* (Bianco, 2010: 9) as a 'blood-spattered, sex-obsessed, fabulously wild camp-vamp funfest,' the show succeeded in building a large, majority female, audience, averaging 6.8 million per week for the first series, with a young, mainly college-educated and upscale profile. The central character, Sookie Stackhouse, is a telepathic woman attracted to a supernatural lover whose mind she cannot read and who is a mix of old-style, 'Southern' gentility (being 173 years old) and sexually charged, predatory animal. The lead writer and executive producer for the show is Alan Ball, who produced HBO's earlier hit *Six Feet Under.* Describing the show's appeal, Ball stated 'women love the storytelling and the romance, and men love the sex and violence' (Carter, 2009). Ball said he had pitched *True Blood* to HBO as 'popcorn television for smart people' (Associated Press, 2008a; *Rolling Stone,* 2008).

True Blood engages a complex mix then of intertextuality from the broadest cultural levels to the more proprietary and 'authorially' inflected, such as contemporary culture wars. The title sequence used 'handheld' and art-house cinema styles to provide an unsettling montage of images including Ku Klux Klansmen and signage ('God Hates Fangs'), identifying vampires with themes of otherness, eroticism, miscegenation,

danger and intolerance. Corporate intertextuality ranged across the various branded and co-branded elements, including that of producer, actors, visual images used across marketing, and sound, notably the music tracks used in promos and show. There was extensive inter-firm cross-promotion: Harris's publishers Orion, and retailers, cross-promoted the HBO series, while Harris herself cross-promoted the show via interviews, her official website and other fan sites.

Promoting *True Blood*

HBO and its enlisted marketers have won awards and industry acclaim for an inventive campaign that has combined traditional and cutting edge marketing techniques for promotions in the USA and HBO's international markets. Most of these techniques, as distinct from treatments, are traceable to earlier innovation and comparable campaigns such as Showtime's *Dexter* (Young, 2010) or Fox's *24* (Scolari, 2009), however the campaign exemplified a highly developed cross-media strategy. HBO has a privileged site for its own self-/cross-promotion, and trailers and promos have been intensively used to promote the series on HBO channels. During the first series, these included explicitly intertextual trailers; one featured enthusiastic notices from professional media critics, another appreciation from fan sites and bloggers. Both highlight core brand features: confirming quality, promoting a cult-fan engagement, while also appealing to a broader audience. Another promotional theme has been to play, in startling and creative ways, with the conceit of vampires 'living' alongside humans, and thus as 'consumers' for marketed services from coffin fittings to dating agencies. Audiovisual promotions included a pre-launch mockumentary (disguised as a news show), together with documentaries on vampire (inter)texts and cultural representation.

All contemporary 'event' television promotion is cross-platform, but HBO, seeking to make sense of a proprietary, non-advertising TV service and a franchise attractive to its other sales divisions, media partners and advertisers, had particular incentives to launch a cross-channel campaign, one which made innovative use of online and social media platforms. Promos and trailers were run across HBO's broadcast channel, its non-linear VOD service HBO On Demand, and online.

For series 3, HBO produced six 'minisodes,' first shown as webisodes on Yahoo! TV, then posted on HBO.com (n.d.) and subsequently shown on HBO following repeats of series 2. Exemplifying transmedia storytelling, and 'overflow' (Brooker, 2001), the minisodes were also posted to the official *True Blood* Facebook page with over 1.4 million fans. At a tertiary promotional level, a promo for the minisodes proclaimed (voice-over):

> You crave new blood. You're hungry for more of the story. Now sink your teeth into six *True Blood* mini episodes. Not from last season— won't been seen in the new season. All New. Written by *True Blood* creator Alan Ball. Beginning May 2, every Sunday night right after a season 2 encore presentation at eight. Get ready for the new season with a drop of *True Blood*.

Against the textual bias of 'intertextuality,' the visual and aural dimensions must be reincorporated. A Depeche Mode track was used for a celebrated series 2 promotion, for series 3 a trailer was re-edited with the track 'Teeth' by Lady Gaga, while Snoop Dog crafted a cross-promotional rap homage, 'Oh Sookie.' Jace Everett's track 'Bad things' from the title sequence, climbed the alt-country sales charts, and the soundtracks were sold alongside the DVDs. Featured music and episode titles also add layers of inter-aural resonance, such as title use of the Cowboy Junkies' song 'To love is to bury.'

Marketing—using print, TV, radio and outdoor advertising, competitions and sweepstakes— was used extensively, but often in innovative ways. In New Zealand, outdoor billboard posters featured marked-out wooden stakes and stencilled instructions reading 'In case of Vampires, snap here.' In the USA, guerrilla marketing tactics included street teams with fake petitions for and against vampires (with heightened resonance in a presidential election year), as well as stunts involving 'Fangbanger' girls (the pejorative term used in *True Blood* for women who sleep with vampires) appearing in bars. However, amongst the most innovative aspects was an extensive cross-platform campaign, with significant investment online. This began with a teaser campaign in May 2008 involving viral outreach to a few influential bloggers amongst fantasy and horror fans and gamers. The strategy was contracted to Campfire NYC,

a small marketing firm specializing in online and guerrilla marketing whose founders had developed the successful strategy for *The Blair Witch Project* (Marshall, 2002). Such viral strategies can overcome resistance to conventional media marketing and benefit from fans' own marketing efforts (Murray, 2004). For *True Blood,* Campfire (2009) pursued a similar strategy of distributing teaser material, alternate reality game (ARG) puzzles, and even posting capsules of '*blood*' in unmarked envelopes. In fact, there was no corporate branding for HBO at all in the first phase of the online campaign, a feature repeated in some later promotions. Bloodcopy.com (n.d.) was launched as the main site for stories and activity.

For the first series a cross-media marketing campaign for Tru Blood was developed using the iconography of an adult drink, with taglines such as 'Real blood is for suckers' 'All flavor. No bite.' Videos spread virally some three months before the series aired explaining how Tru Blood enabled vampires to 'come out,' while faux TV spots appeared on cable and late-night network TV advertising vampire-targeted products (Stanley, 2008). HBO also developed elaborate fake websites to support the concept. A fully functioning website for vampires, the American Vampire League, was modelled on such progressive organizations as the American Civil Liberties Union. In contrast to sites' multiethnic diversity, the other fake site, the Fellowship of the Light, features the iconography of a fundamentalist Christian organization. Opposing 'interspecies' relationships, the site displays a near exclusive array of white Anglo-Saxon models. Common to all these campaigns was a sophisticated, and knowing, intertextuality, from the graphic layout of websites to the images and text.

More overt programme promotions appeared towards launch. Time Warner's deal with YouTube (and subsequently with Yahoo! TV) led to advertisements, trailers and proprietary clips being made available online, hyperlinked and copied by numerous emergent fan sites. HBO's vp advertising and promotions, Zach Enterlin, told *Brandweek*, 'From the start, we knew this was just so much bigger than print ads and 30-second spots. We wanted a campaign that's as rich as the series. . . . The whole campaign has been about popping through in a really crowded environment, and using promotional content to tell a story' (Stanley, 2008). According to Gregg Hale, a partner at Campfire, 'We built this on solid storytelling and the idea of immersing people in this world. . . . We never tried to fool anybody; we wanted to give them an entertaining experience and a way down the rabbit hole' (cited in Stanley, 2008).

By the time the second series was promoted in 2009, HBO was working with six different creative and media-buying agencies. Campfire produced Bloodcopy.com (n.d.), a fake vampire blog and news site, and viral videos for the campaign; Digital Kitchen, crafted 'vampire product' tie-in ads; Ignition produced radio ads; Red Creative did the same for online ads; Omnicom Group's PHD placed media advertising, while Deep Focus organized online media buying for parts of the campaign (Steinberg, 2009). For the second series, Tru Blood was marketed to fans, manufactured by Omni Consumer Products, a company specializing in creating 'real' products from fictional ones (Stanley, 2009a). A striking series of fake ads for vampire products featuring real brands were produced by Digital Kitchen, who had created the acclaimed title sequence for the first series (Alston, 2008). Ecko Unlimited, Geico, Gillette, Harley-Davidson, MINI and Monster.com all signed up to the HBO co-funded campaign, with taglines including 'Dead Sexy' (Gillette), 'Feel the wind in your fangs' (Mini), and 'Outrun the Sun' (Harley-Davidson).

HBO's campaign included faux evening weather reports on radio stations for vampires; a cinema advertisement made to look like local business ads; a weekly news magazine shown on HBO platforms that included a segment called 'The Vampire Report.' PHD won awards for its media campaign that included an 8-page vampire insert in *am New York* newspaper, a first-ever cover wrap-around for *The Los Angeles Times,* and a 12-page intra-firm advert in *Entertainment Weekly* (Moses, 2010). *Vanity Fair* featured party-photos of celebrities with fangs. Inter-firm cross-promotion included Warner Home Video's tie-up with fashion label Saint Augustine Academy for a vampire-inspired show at the Australian Fashion Week to promote the season 2 DVD.

There was extensive intra-firm advertising and editorial cross-promotion across Time Warner's holdings. *Entertainment Weekly* (2009), owned by Time Warner, featured *True Blood*'s star Stephen Moyer on the cover for a special feature on vampires, and numerous celebratory news, reviews and feature articles, such as 'Bring on the Blood' (Spines et al., 2009; Stack, 2009). Amongst extensive coverage for the third series in 2010 were a six-page cover story (18 June), previews (8 January, 9 April), and reviews (25 June). The corporate 'texts' produced and heavily cross-promoted included an original comic book, merchandise and series releases on DVD and Blu-ray. The series 2 release (involving another agency, BBDO) incorporated social media features so that, for the minority with internet linked Blu-ray players, users could post viewing status updates directly to their Facebook and Twitter accounts, share favourite scenes with friends, access the live feeds and receive gifts (Lezzie, 2010). For series 3, HBO launched new teaser posters, the minisodes, cross-promotional inserts in Time Warner's *Entertainment Weekly* and third-party media, including sponsorship (with 3D glasses) of the centrefold model in *Playboy* magazine. IDW Publishing produced a comic-book adaptation of the show, written by Ball. Mobile marketing specialists Medialets worked with PHD to launch an iPhone app that generated bloody fingerprints when users touched the screen.

This was a highly successful promotional strategy. *True Blood* was a domestic hit in the USA, becoming HBO's most successful show since *The Sopranos* and boosting subscriptions (Associated Press, 2008b). Extending the franchise, the first series DVD, released in May 2009, was the best-selling TV programme in June, while the series topped the iTunes chart for purchased TV episodes that month and remained a bestseller. The audience built steadily, increasing to 2.4 million for series 1 (Steinberg, 2009; Stelter, 2008). The second series premiered with a record-setting 3.7 million audience (Hibberd, 2009) peaking at 5.3 million, the largest audience HBO had achieved for five years since *The Sopranos* (Toff, 2009). The second series attracted weekly audiences of 10–12 million (made up of the Sunday show, repeat screenings, VOD and online access), from a subscription base around a third of the size of free-to-air TV. *True Blood* also sold successfully overseas. In Britain it was shown on News Corporation's FX channel on BSkyB, and then on free-to-air when the public service broadcaster Channel Four screened the first series in Autumn 2009.

TRUE BLOOD AND THE ORDERING OF TEXTUAL SPACE

HBO's strategy involved a sophisticated effort to establish both cult status and popular appeal. Through the targeting of fan networks, buzz marketing and invitations for immersion, HBO's corporate strategy sought to cultivate fan engagement and use this as a tool to generate interest and publicity amongst wider audiences. There was a revealing moment of collision and controversy, however. In May 2009 the business and news weblog network site Gawker Media featured Bloodcopy, the fake blog purporting to be written by a vampire. Campfire and HBO staged Gawker Media's 'acquisition' of Bloodcopy as part of a paid sponsorship deal, and promoted it via a public relations strategy to business and technology reporters. Described as an adverblog (Steinberg, 2009), Bloodcopy was syndicated through Gawker sites such as the gadget site Gizmodo and gaming site Kotaku. Under the deal, Gawker was to create six original posts for the blog per day. However, this marketing—masquerading as vampire news—generated a backlash from users whose complaints eventually led to suspension of the blog. Some Gawker users complained that marketing discourse was not being adequately identified. In response, Chris Batty, Gawker's vp of sales and marketing, dismissed critics of the advertorial as 'humorless' (Seward, 2009), while Courteney Monroe, who led HBO's marketing, welcomed the exposure, commenting 'it contributed to the noise' (Stanley, 2009b). However, beyond the issue of disclosure, the incident highlighted broader issues concerning corporate speech masquerading as autonomous speech, and the boundaries between 'interested' and 'independent' speech. If the fake vampire advertisements were playful masquerades, the corporate masquerading of autonomous textual production was more troubling, marking the complex friction between top-down (corporate) and bottom-up autonomous media practices. HBO closed Bloodcopy in September 2009, but resurrected it as a microsite for series 3, enabling fans to participate in live conversations on Twitter.

The online intertextual space for *True Blood* stretches from corporate sites to autonomous fan sites, some organized around the series, stars and characters, some around the novels, and others with greater distance from the megatext, connected to fantasy, gaming, horror and other networks. The off-air relationship between co-stars Anna Paquin and Stephen Moyer generated other intertextual connections. HBO has six official dedicated sites, while there are more than 30 major fan sites, together with Facebook and Twitter sites, forums and message boards. *True Blood* has also generated numerous fan sites around the world, notably in the UK, Italy, Spain, France, Germany, Poland, Serbia and Brazil. One of the leading fan sites True-blood.net (n.d.) has a predominantly US audience (57%) but with significant traffic from the UK (11%) and Canada (7%), followed by Australia, Sweden and Norway. The site's demographic profile (February 2009 to 2010) was 55 per cent women, 39 per cent 18–34, 44 per cent college educated and 11 per cent from graduate school (Quantcast, 2010).

As other studies show (Hills, 2002; Jenkins, 1992), there is evidence of a textual hierarchy in which some fans favour more independent sites over corporate ones, and sites declare their independence with varying intensity. Yet, while only a full study can do justice to the multiplicity of fan/audience texts, there is evidence that the boundaries between corporate/autonomous and commercial/non-commercial blur and merge. Already, in *Textual Poachers* (1992) Jenkins feared that division between fan autonomy and corporate directedness was breaking down, expressing in the final pages fears that the fan autonomy and authenticity which structures his account was being undermined by growing commercialism. Popular fan sites such as True-Blood.tv (n.d.), financed by advertising, contain prominent links to HBO merchandise. The commercial intertextuality of official merchandise is prominent across all the most popular 'independent' sites. Commodified intertextual flows thus extend into more 'autonomous' textual spaces. Yet a counter-flow is also discernible. Enabled by media corporations efforts to encourage online participation is the space created within 'controlled' sites such as HBO's Trueblood. wiki (n.d.) for critical fan discussions, for instance on the show's double standards in regard to male and female nudity.

The spectrum from corporate to autonomous texts is important for normative-critical analysis but also complex, often opaque, at points of intersection. *True Blood* Twitter, for instance, is 'officially endorsed' but not 'affiliated' to HBO. The corporate wiki's textual space is polyvocal, official promotions run alongside 'autonomous,' albeit policed, exchanges. Leading fan sites, part-supported by advertising, incorporate HBO promotions, link to official merchandise, and in various ways 'trade' with HBO to secure privileged access to stars (interviews), news, and materials. Commercial intertexuality ranges from authorized texts/merchandise in official sites to unlicensed products, such as t-shirts. *True Blood* illustrates the increasing diversity of transmedia intertextual space and its tensions and contradictions. Online sites and allied promotions provided opportunities for immersion in story elaboration. For its architects, the strategy sought to engage with perceived audience demand for complexity, sophistication and subtlety, across both brand communications and media texts. This created space for participation, pleasure, creativity and play. However, this agency needs to be examined in the context of the shaping influence on reading and consumption from those managing such narrative brands.

CONCLUSION

This discussion has argued for the importance of examining how corporate activity seeks to order (inter)textual space, while emphasizing that this requires analysis of the multiple sites and contending forces of communicative exchange. HBO invested heavily in shaping textual space and extended commercial intertextuality through cross-media promotion, online and social media engagement. An important focus, as the Bloodcopy incident reveals, concerns the manner in which boundaries are negotiated as commercial speech extends into spaces governed by expectations of independence. Yet, an integrative analysis is required of the plural dynamics of textual production and interaction along a corporate-autonomous axis. Far from diminishing critical accounts, this strengthens attention to the power dynamics structuring textual space, the manner in which economic structures, imperatives of commodification and corporate interests impose constraints on that space, and the manner in which these are negotiated and contested. It requires efforts to reincorporate 'control' and 'pleasure' narratives (Meyrowitz, 2008), overcome the divide between 'contextual' and 'textual' analysis (Caldwell, 2006:104), and remain alert to the articulation of creativity and meaning as well as commerce. How the problems of synergistic corporate speech and commercialism might be evaluated alongside the pleasures of the (inter)texts is beyond the scope of this piece. Yet, both critical political economy and cultural studies are needed to trace the increasing complexity, and implications, of corporate (inter) textual proliferation.

NOTE

1. For more general discussion on political economy and cultural studies integration see Babe (2008), Kellner (1998, 2009), Hesmondhalgh (2007, 2009), Hardy (2010b).

REFERENCES

Alston J (2008) Give HBO Some Credit. *Newsweek* 152(12) 22 September: 14.

Associated Press (2008a) Vampires, well, come to life in 'True Blood' (3 September), URL (accessed 12 February 2010): http://today.msnbc.msn.com/id/26513974

Associated Press (2008b) 'True Blood' a well-timed hit for HBO, MSNBC. (23 November) URL (accessed 12 February 2010): http://today.msnbc.msn.com/id/27821649

Babe RE (2008) *Cultural Studies and Political Economy: Towards a New Integration.* Lanham, MD: Lexington Books.

Bennett T and Woollacott J (1987) *Bond and Beyond: The Political Career of a Popular Hero.* Basingstoke: Macmillan.

Bianco R (2010) Wild, weird *True Blood* packs full-throated fun. *USA Today, Life* section (11 June): 9.

Bloodcopy.com (n.d.) URL (accessed October 2010): http://www.bloodcopy.com/

Brooker W (2001) Living on Dawson's Creek: Teen viewers, cultural convergence, and television overflow. *International Journal of Cultural Studies* 4(4): 456–472.

Caldwell J (2004) Convergence television: Aggregating form and repurposing content in the culture of conglomeration. In: Spigel L and Olsson J (eds) *Television After TV: Essay on a Medium in Transition.* Durham, NC: Duke University Press, 41–74.

Caldwell J (2006) Critical industrial practice: Branding, repurposing, and the migratory patterns of industrial texts. *Television & New Media* 7(2): 99–134.

Campfire (2009) Campfire wins four IAB MIXX awards for HBO's *True Blood.* News release 24 September. New York: Campfire. URL (accessed 27 September 2010): http://campfirenyc.com/press.html

Carter B (2009) With a little 'True Blood,' HBO is reviving its fortunes. *New York Times-Business* (12 July): 1.

Couldry N (2000) *Inside Culture.* London: SAGE.

De Barros A, Donahue D, Memmott C, Minzesheimer B and Wilson C (2010) Trends, triumphs of 2009 book year. *USA Today, Life* section (14 January): 4.

Entertainment Weekly (2009) 20 greatest vampires of all time (31 July): cover, 30–33.

Fiske J (1987) *Television Culture.* London: Routledge.

Grey J (2010) *Show Sold Separately: Promos, Spoilers, and Other Media Paratexts.* New York: New York University Press.

Gripsrud J (1995) *The Dynasty Years.* New York: Routledge.

Hardy J (2010a) *Cross-Media Promotion.* New York: Peter Lang.

Hardy J (2010b) The contribution of critical political economy. In: Curran J (ed.) *Media and Society.* London: Bloomsbury, 186–209.

HBO.com (n.d.) URL (accessed October 2010): http://www.hbo.com/

Heszmondhalgh D (2007) *The Cultural Industries* (2nd edition). London: SAGE.

Hesmondhalgh D (2009) Politics, theory and method in media industries research. In: Holt J and Perren A (eds) *Media Industries: History, Theory, and Method.* Malden, MA: Wiley-Blackwell, 245–255.

Hibberd J (2009) 'True Blood' returns to biggest HBO audience in years. *Hollywood Reporter* (16 June). URL (accessed 15 February 2010): http://livefeed.hollywoodreporter.com/2009/06/true-blood-season-two-premiere-ratings.html

Hills M (2002) *Fan Cultures.* London: Routledge.

Jenkins H (1992) *Textual Poachers: Television Fans and Participatory Culture.* New York: Routledge.

Jenkins H (2002) Interactive audiences? In: Harries D (ed.) *The New Media* Book. London: BFI, 157–170.

Jenkins H (2006) *Convergence Culture.* New York: New York University Press.

Kellner D (1998) Overcoming the divide: Cultural studies and political economy. In: Ferguson M and Golding P (eds) *Cultural Studies in Question.* London: SAGE, 102–120.

Kellner D (2009) Media industries, political economy and media/cultural studies: An articulation. In: Holt J and Perren A (eds) *Media Industries: History, Theory, and Method.* Chichester: Wiley-Blackwell, 95–107.

Levine E (2005) Fractured fairy tales and fragmented markets: Disney's weddings of a lifetime and the cultural politics of media conglomeration. *Television & New Media* 6(1): 71–88.

Lezzie T (2010) The Work. *Advertising Age* 81(22) 31 May: 23.

Marshall PD (2002) The new intertextual commodity. In Harries D (ed.) *The New Media Book.* London: BFI, 69–81.

Marshall PD (2004) *New Media Cultures.* London: Arnold.

Meehan E (1991) 'Holy commodity fetish, Batman!' The political economy of a commercial intertext.

In: Pearson RE and Uricchio W (eds) *The Many Lives of the Batman: Critical Approaches to a Superhero and his Media*. New York: Routledge, 47–65.

Meehan E (2005) *Why TV Is Not Our Fault*. Lanham, MD: Rowman and Littlefield.

Meyrowitz J (2008) Power, pleasure, patterns: Intersecting narratives of media influence. *Journal of Communication* 58(4): 641–663.

Moses L (2010) PHD: HBO's *True Blood*. *Brandweek* 51(24) 14 June: 22.

Murray S (2004) Celebrating the story the way it is: Cultural studies, corporate media and the contested utility of fandom. *Continuum,* 18(1): 7–25.

Ono KA and Buescher DT (2001) Deciphering Pocahontas: Unpacking the commoditization of a Native American woman. *Critical Studies in Media Communication* 18(1): 23–43.

Proffitt JM, Yune Tchoi D and McAllister MP (2007) Plugging back into the matrix: The intertextual flow of corporate media commodities. *Journal of Communication Inquiry* 31(3): 239–254.

Quantcast (2010) true-blood.net audience profile. URL (accessed 2 February 2010): www.quantcast .com/true-blood.net

Rolling Stone (2008) 'True Blood.' *Rolling Stone* 1061 (18 September): 101.

Sandvoss C (2005) *Fans*. Cambridge: Polity.

Scolari CA (2009) Transmedia storytelling: Implicit consumers, narrative worlds, and branding in contemporary media production. *International Journal of Communication* 3: 586–606.

Seward ZM (2009) Gawker VP says sponsored posts will bring in majority of revenue one day. *Nieman Journalism Lab* (27 May). URL (accessed 10 July 2009): http://www.niemanlab .org/2009/05/gawker-vp-says-sponsored-posts-will-bring-in-majority-of-revenue-one-day/

Spines C, Bentley J and Semingran A (2009) Bring on the blood. *Entertainment Weekly* (26 June): 23–24.

Stack T (2009) 'True Blood.' *Entertainment Weekly* 1063 (4 September 2009): 22–23.

Stanley TL (2008) HBO tempts consumers with 'trublood.' *Brandweek* (18 July). URL (accessed 6 December 2009): http://www.brandweek.com/ bw/content_display/news-and-features/promotion/ e3i3a2b5d0d04f5 fd1cba7c2bcb81329ccd#

Stanley TL (2009a) HBO markets bloodsucker beverage. *Brandweek* 50(29) 3 August: 21.

Stanley TL (2009b) Courteney Monroe. *Brandweek* 50(32) 14 September: 18.

Steinberg B (2009) Advertising for HBO's 'True Blood' bends truth a bit. *Advertising Age* (28 May). URL (accessed 6 February 2010): http://adage.com/mediaworks/article?article_id=136942

Stelter B (2008) *'True Blood'* renewed. *New York Times* 19 September: 6.

Toff B (2009) ARTS, BRIEFLY, 'True Blood' is boiling for HBO, *New York Times* 27 August: 2.

True-blood.net (n.d.) URL (accessed October 2010): http://true-blood.net/True-Blood.tv (n.d.) URL (accessed October 2010): http://true-blood.tv/

Trueblood.wiki (n.d.) URL (accessed October 2010): http://truebloodwiki.hbo.com

Waetjen J and Gibson TA (2007) Harry Potter and the commodity fetish: Activating corporate readings in the journey from text to commercial intertext. *Communication and Critical/Cultural Studies* 4(1): 3–26.

Young A (2010) 'Dexter' vs. 'True Blood': The battle of two killer media plans. *Advertising Age* (20 May). URL (accessed 1 July 2010): http://adage .com/mediaworks/article? article_id=144011

PART V

REPRESENTING SEXUALITIES

This section explores how hegemonic representations of gender and sexuality are both reinforced and challenged throughout mainstream media. Looking across genres and media platforms, these chapters question the ideologies surrounding sex, sexuality, and hegemonic masculinity and femininity. Close attention is paid to how social structures and institutions impact media representations of gender and sexuality as well as how particular audiences and communities respond to those images. At the same time, these readings explore the performative nature of gender and sexuality and offer examples of how gender and sexual binaries can be challenged.

As a way of foregrounding the many ways critical media scholars analyze mainstream representations of heterosexuality, we begin this section with a discussion of **pornography.** In recent years, scholars have argued that there has been a "**pornification**" of popular culture. In other words, the codes and conventions of pornography have seeped into the wider culture, often to the point that such representations are so normalized that they are rendered invisible. In the first two chapters of this section, we provide a brief and selective introduction to the contemporary pornography industry—both in terms of how its business practices function, and how its representations shape our understanding of our own humanity within a hypermediated society.

Pornography itself has been held up to feminist scrutiny and divisive debate for many years, and it is not our intent to represent these sometimes heated debates here. However, in the first chapter Robert Jensen (V.36) employs a **radical feminist** framework to analyze the production and consumption of contemporary pornography. Jensen explains that, "Radical feminism opposes patriarchy, the system of institutionalized male dominance, and understands gender as a category that established and reinforces inequality. The goal is the end of—not accommodation with—patriarchy's gender system and other domination/subordination dynamics" (p. 292). Thus, a radical feminist critique highlights four elements of much pornographic content (**objectification,** hierarchy, submission, and violence), which ultimately work to eroticize men's domination over women. While "pornographers and their allies have advanced their underlying libertarian sexual ethic, which focuses on individual choices in the moment and ignores or downplays the constraints and opportunities that structure choices," Jensen argues that pornography relies on sexual exploitation and perpetuates gender inequality (p. 291). Ultimately, Jensen advocates for a sexual ethic that acknowledges the implications of misogynistic mediated storytelling and questions how pornography shapes our understanding of what it means to be human.

In the next chapter, Gail Dines (V.37) employs a complementary political economic approach to examine the actual business practices of the wide-ranging pornography industry. Dines explores "how porn as an industry works within a global economic system that often serves to define the nature of the content produced, and the way the corporatization of porn has resulted in a monopolistic system of distribution" (p. 298). The large scale and reach of the porn industry means that it has become part of hegemonic culture. While many are aware that technological advancements have led to the proliferation of pornography, few acknowledge the integral role the porn industry has played in helping to create these technologies—from VCRs and DVD players to streaming video on mobile devices. Likewise, video sharing, downloading, and web-based subscriptions make the violent gendered representations of pornography more easily accessible. Just as in mainstream media, industrial concentration has led to a handful of companies controlling the distribution of the majority of pornographic texts. These few companies have formed their own lobbying group, the Free Speech Coalition, which works to fend off government regulation. The pornography industry's legal strategies may result in the further mainstreaming of disturbing content such as childlike representations of women, "teen porn," as well as dehumanizing and violent sex acts that compromise performers' health.

In her chapter, "The Pornography of Everyday Life," Jane Caputi (V.38) further explores the theme of eroticized sexual degradation in pornography-inspired pop culture imagery. Closely analyzing advertisements, Caputi argues that when the degrading codes from porn filter into mainstream culture, they are framed as sexy and alluring. Even when "everyday" porn is not representing sexuality as entwined with female degradation, according to Caputi it is still founded "in conventional notions of gender, [where] women and men are opposite and unequal, with specific gendered attributes, such as masculine aggression and feminine passivity" (p. 308).

We can find other examples of "everyday pornography" throughout media and popular culture, such as the immensely popular vampire romance series, *The Twilight Saga,* by Stephenie Meyer. Victoria E. Collins and Dianne C. Carmody (V.39) offer a **content analysis** of instances of abusive behavior directed toward Bella, the heroine of the series. They also argue that the books and films must be seen as examples of contemporary popular culture that continues to represent violence against women as "an acceptable expression of love in adolescent relationships" (p. 320). For Collins and Carmody, although "critics disagree about the presentation of adolescent relationships in the *Twilight* series" their own study "examined the book series with special attention to behaviors that are commonly associated with dating and intimate partner violence" (p. 321). They conclude by calling for the use of these books in "programs to prevent dating violence" and more generally in the education of teens about the mythology of "romantic dominance" in traditional heterosexuality:

> To recognize behaviors that were previously presented as chivalrous and romantic as clear examples of control, stalking, abuse, and intimidation may offer young people new insights into the insidious and often-subtle nature of abuse and control. In this way, the *Twilight* series could continue to influence young lives, but in a new way. (p. 326)

While the first four chapters of this section focus on **heteronormative** masculinity and femininity, the remaining four chapters offer broader representations of gender and sexuality. The term *gender* has acquired a whole new range of associations in light of feminist and queer theory emerging from activist movements and **postmodern** scholarship. Historians of gender and sexuality, like Michel Foucault, have pointed out that the very terms we use to describe the concept of fixed and opposite sexual orientations— "heterosexuality" and "homosexuality"—are only a little more than a century old. These terms were produced within a late 19th-century medical discourse developed by the emerging professional health fields of psychology and sexology. Through the cultural dominance of the new medical discourse in the 20th century, heterosexuality came into being as a norm against which same-sex attraction and love (as well as many other desires and sexual behaviors) could be defined as threateningly deviant or "other." Queer theory questions traditional ideas of "normal" and "deviant" in the realms of both gender and sexuality by arguing against the commonsense notion that there are only two genders (masculine and feminine) and two kinds of desire or attraction (straight and gay). In queer theory, gender, sexuality, and desire are all seen as ambiguous, shifting, unstable, and too complex to fit neatly into **binary** (either/or) systems.

Even the most entrenched forms of heteronormative popular culture can be a site of "queering" or shifting representations of gender and sexuality. Take, for example, hip-hop, a music genre that has long been derided for its homophobic and misogynistic imagery and lyrics. With the emergence of a new subgenre, alternative R&B, hegemonic heterosexual masculinity is being challenged. In order to understand the ways that gender and sexuality are represented in alternative R&B, Frederik Dhaenens and Sander De Ridder (V.40) conducted a textual analysis comparing the work of two different artists: Frank Ocean and The Weeknd. The authors contextualize hip-hop and R&B within a "history of racism and systematic oppression" that degrades and emasculates Black men (p. 330). In the face of these obstacles, the sexism, misogyny, and homophobia embodied by hegemonic masculinity can be understood (but not excused) as an act of self-preservation and as a strategy for autonomy and control. Yet, Dhaenens and De Ridder argue that the music of Frank Ocean and The Weeknd deviates from these conventions (albeit in different ways). For instance, Ocean's songs showcase diverse male characters that engage in nonnormative or nonbinary behaviors in regards to gender and sexuality. The Weeknd features tropes of hegemonic masculinity, but as a type of reflective critique. Therefore, the authors suggest both artists offer **counterhegemonic** alternatives to masculinity by "questioning what it means to be a man in R&B and hip hop culture" (337).

Problematic sexual representations in media culture are also of strong concern within the LGBT (lesbian, gay, bisexual, transgender) communities. Despite some important advances in gay and lesbian visibility in media culture in recent years, representations of sexuality in mainstream pop culture continue to be, for the most part, overwhelmingly heterosexual. Part of the reason for this is the ongoing homophobia that media producers assume continues to characterize the majority of media consumers. Although progress has been made by **activists** in raising awareness of new audiences for complex representations of nonnormative sexuality and gender, producers of mainstream media culture still shy away from representing sexual and gender minorities in richly textured ways.

Jay Clarkson (V.41) studies "the politics of gay representation" through an examination of "the discourse of . . . StraightActing.com, an Internet discussion board for self-identified straight-acting gay men." He argues that in their talk about "the nature of their and other gay men's visibility . . . they demonize an effeminate gay stereotype, which they perceive as dominating media representations of gay men" (p. 340). Viewing "the flamer" and other gender transgressives as limiting the progress of full gay and lesbian integration into the society's mainstream, posters to the discussion board "argue that increased visibility of straight-acting gay men has the potential to undo what they see as the negative consequences of the prevalence of effeminate gay stereotypes" (p. 344). But for Clarkson, such a conservative and defensive visibility strategy is wrongheaded and only contributes to the narrowing of public understanding of the complexities of gender and sexuality while reinforcing hegemonic notions.

Femininity in its hegemonic form (White, domesticated, heterosexual) is similarly a powerful ideological formation that seems "natural" until we begin to explore its historical evolution. The artificiality or "constructedness" of femininity is the focus of Mary F. Rogers's provocative brief chapter, "Hetero Barbie?" (V.42). As Rogers writes, the iconic Barbie doll's femininity "entails a lot of artifice, a lot of clothes, a lot or props such as cuddly poodles and shopping bags, and a lot of effort." Indeed, Rogers playfully raises the possibility that Barbie may not be heterosexual at all and indeed may not even be a woman: Barbie may be a drag queen. Much in the tradition of cross-dressing stars like RuPaul, Barbie's ultrafeminine presence may signal the ironic exaggeration that drag performances enact (p. 347).

As Rogers's chapter suggests, drag performance, cross-dressing, and a myriad of other types of gender-bending activities, behavior, and identities now highly visible in 21st century culture certainly suggest the futility of attempts to maintain that once traditional categories are fixed by nature. The influential feminist philosopher and queer theorist Judith Butler has likened gender to a theatrical performance—a matter of gradually learned role-playing, with no necessary correlation to one's biological sex (Butler, 1999).

In the final chapter in this section, Joanna Mansbridge (V.43) expands on the notion of gender and drag performance by comparing two popular media representations of Muslim femininity—the veiled woman and the belly dancer. Far from universal **signifiers,** belly dancing and veiling take on multiple meanings depending on the cultural context and historical moment. For the Western audience, the "women's bodies are used as sites onto which multiple differences—political, religious, sexual, and cultural—are either imaginatively resolved (belly dancing) or reinforced (the veil)" (p. 349). However, Mansbridge argues that beyond commercial media representations, veiling and belly dancing are a form of "cultural drag" that complicate binary depictions of gender, colonialism, and sexuality. In some contexts, media representations of belly dancing "can promote the idea of a global femininity and sexual democracy" while in other contexts they function "as a performance of cultural assimilation" (p. 354). Likewise, though some public discourse surrounding veiling positions Muslim women as victims of patriarchal oppression, Mansbridge suggests that it can be understood as a symbol of protest against cultural imperialism and the hegemony of sexualized femininity.

Since the first edition of *Gender, Race, and Class in Media* in 1994, there has been a proliferation of images in media culture that make nonhegemonic genders and sexualities visible through a range of representations that are nuanced and complex. In large part this increased nuanced visibility is due to the organization of activists on local and national levels to both educate and agitate for media representations that speak to the diversity of gendered identities and sexualities that are embodied in the contemporary world. Several instances of such grassroots media activism, along with examples of fan engagement, are found in Part VIII of this anthology.

36 PORNOGRAPHIC VALUES
Hierarchy and Hubris
Robert Jensen

Political debates grow out of differing answers to one of our most fundamental questions, "What does it mean to be human?" This is especially true of the pornography debate.

That question reminds us that all political positions are based on underlying moral claims. In this context, "moral" does not mean preachy judgments about conventional rules, especially for sexual behavior, but rather how we might balance a yearning for self-realization with the need for stable, respectful communities that make it possible for individuals to fulfill their potential, as free as possible from the constraining effects of systems of domination. What do we owe ourselves and what obligations do we have to others? Answers not only vary among individuals within a culture and between different cultures but also change over time with new challenges, hence "what does it mean to be human at this particular moment in history?"

Despite the cliché "you can't legislate morality," there are moral claims at the core of all political proposals. Every position in the pornography debate is based on a sexual ethic, and the outcome of the political struggle will advance the underlying ethic.

I have been involved in that debate—within feminism and progressive politics as well as the wider culture—for a quarter century. More than ever, I believe the radical feminist critique of pornography provides the best framework for understanding the production and consumption of graphic sexually explicit material. In that quarter century, the trends—in the pornography industry, the material it produces, and the ways images are used (Dines, 2010; Jensen, 2011)—demonstrate the compelling nature of that analysis, even though in that same period this radical feminist critique has been eclipsed by postmodern and liberal positions (Taormino, Penley, Shimizu, & Miller-Young, 2013) that either celebrate or capitulate to an increasingly pornographic culture.

To state it bluntly, over the past 25 years, the pornographers and their allies have won, and radical feminism has lost. There is more pornography, more easily available, and much of it more openly cruel and degrading to women and more overtly racist than ever. Pornographers and their allies have advanced their underlying libertarian sexual ethic, which focuses on individual choices in the moment and ignores or downplays the constraints and opportunities that structure choices.

How does a pornographic culture answer the question about "being human," in regard to our relationship to each other and to mediated images?

Pornography's answer about human relationships and the nature of power: The domination/subordination dynamic is inevitable, because it is the way humans are designed. So get used to the same old hierarchy.

Pornography's answer about images and the nature of technology: The more mediated our lives, the better, because it gives us a sense of control over our experience. So get used to a new level of hubris.

My response: Both these answers are wrong, with destructive consequences beyond pornography. This article explains the feminist

From Jensen, R. (2016). Pornographic values: Hierarchy and hubris. *Sexualization, Media & Society,* 1–5.

critique of pornography, analyzes the corrosive nature of hierarchical power and technological hubris, and poses questions about a healthy sexual ethic.

PORNOGRAPHY: A RADICAL FEMINIST CRITIQUE

"Radical" is often used to dismiss people or ideas as "crazy" or "extreme," but here it describes an analysis that seeks to understand, address, and eventually eliminate the root causes of inequality. Radical feminism opposes patriarchy, the system of institutionalized male dominance, and understands gender as a category that established and reinforces inequality. The goal is the end of—not accommodation with—patriarchy's gender system and other domination/subordination dynamics.

Radical feminists understand men's efforts to control women's sexuality and reproduction as a key feature of patriarchy. As feminist philosopher Frye (1992) puts it,

> For females to be subordinated and subjugated to males on a global scale . . . billions of female individuals, virtually all who see life on this planet, must be reduced to a more-or-less willing toleration of subordination and servitude to men, and [t]he primary sites of this reduction are the sites of heterosexual relation and encounter. (p. 130)

Beyond the sex/gender system, radical feminism's focus on the way in which patriarchy normalizes hierarchy leads not just to a critique of men's domination of women but also to a deeper understanding of systems of power more generally. While not sufficient by itself, the end of patriarchy is a necessary condition for liberation more generally.

Radical feminism addresses many issues, including men's violence and the sexual exploitation of women and children. Pornography, prostitution, and stripping are the major sexual-exploitation industries in the contemporary United States, presenting objectified female bodies to men for sexual pleasure. Boys and vulnerable men are also used in the exploitation industries that cater to gay men, but the vast majority of people used are girls and women. In heterosexual pornography, the negative psychological and physical consequences for female performers are far more dramatic than for male performers (Whisnant & Stark, 2004).

The critical feminist analysis demonstrates that pornography is not "just sex on film," but sex routinely presented within a domination/subordination dynamic. Pornography eroticizes men's domination of women, along with other forms of inequality, especially racism. This analysis, developed within the larger feminist project of challenging men's violence against women, was first articulated clearly by Andrea Dworkin (1979) who identified what we can call the elements of the pornographic:

1. Objectification: when "a human being, through social means, is made less than human, turned into a thing or commodity, bought, and sold."

2. Hierarchy: "a group on top (men) and a group on the bottom (women)."

3. Submission: when acts of obedience and compliance become necessary for survival, members of oppressed groups learn to anticipate the orders and desires of those who have power over them, and their compliance is then used by the dominant group to justify its dominance.

4. Violence: "systematic, endemic enough to be unremarkable and normative, usually taken as an implicit right of the one committing the violence" (Dworkin, 1988, p. 266–267).

This framework, developed further by Dworkin along with MacKinnon (1987), sparked organizing efforts for a civil rights approach to replace failed obscenity laws (MacKinnon & Dworkin, 1997). Although the law didn't change, this analytic framework continues to be useful in understanding the pornography industry's expansion (Dines, 2010). As pornography depicting relatively conventional sexual acts became commonplace, producers of "gonzo" pornography (industry terminology for movies with no pretense of plot, in which performers acknowledge the camera and speak directly to the audience) dominated the market and pushed the limits of social norms and women's bodies with the routine use of double penetrations (vaginal and anal penetration by two men at the same time), double vag (two men penetrating a woman vaginally), double anal (two men penetrating a woman anally), gagging (forcing the penis down a woman's throat so far that she gags), and ass-to-mouth (a man removing his penis from a woman's anus and placing it directly into her mouth or the mouth of another woman).

Although there is variation in the thousands of pornographic films produced commercially each year, the main themes have remained consistent: (1) all women always want sex from men, (2) women like all the sexual acts that men perform or demand, and (3) any woman who resists can be aroused by force, which is rarely necessary because most of the women in pornography are the "nymphomaniacs" of men's fantasies (Jensen, 2007, p. 56–57). While both men and women are portrayed as hypersexual, men typically are the sexual subjects who control the action and dictate the terms of the sex. Women are the sexual objects that fulfill male desire.

The radical feminist critique highlights not only that much of pornography is pornographic, reflecting, and reinforcing patriarchy's domination/subordination dynamic, but that pop culture is increasingly pornified (Paul, 2005). Pornography is a specific genre, but those elements of the pornographic also are present in other media.

PORNOGRAPHY'S HIERARCHY

It is common to distinguish between sex categories based on biological realities of reproduction (male and female) and gender categories based on culture (men and women). While we have limited understanding of how differences in male and female biology might influence intellectual, emotional, and moral differences between the sexes, there is no evidence those differences are relevant to political status: Men and women have equal claim to citizenship.

The denial of equality to women is a product of patriarchy, typically rationalized with God or evolution. "Gender fundamentalists," whether conservatives rooted in theology or secular folk offering sociobiology/evolutionary psychology arguments for patriarchal practices (Buss, 1994), assert that there are large differences between male and female humans that are largely immutable, despite considerable evidence to the contrary

(Zell, Krizan, & Teeter, 2015). The equality claim, which is accepted in the formal political sphere, is routinely ignored in other realms of contemporary life—people assert the need for, or inevitability of, inequality, most notably in sexual behavior, intimate relationships, and family life. Gender fundamentalists refuse to consider whether patriarchal ideology is consistent with decent answers to "what does it mean to be human?"

In the version of patriarchy dominant in the United States, the sexual-exploitation industries are a routine part of contemporary culture. Some aspects are criminalized and other aspects regulated, but the vast majority of men have some experience with at least one of these industries that buy and sell women's bodies for sex.

Whatever one's view of the role of intimacy and sexuality in human society, it is difficult to imagine achieving gender equality when members of one group (women) can routinely be bought and sold by members of another group (men) for sexual pleasure. Supporters of the sexual-exploitation industries focus on women's right to choose to participate in these activities. While individual choice is a component of any free society, people choose within parameters set by larger cultural and economic forces. To define freedom as choice, abstracted from the reality of a society and its values/norms/practices, is simplistic. To contend that such a thin conception of freedom can produce gender equality is to obscure hierarchy. Under conditions of real equality, it is hard to imagine that such exploitation practices would exist.

PORNOGRAPHY'S HUBRIS

Human beings are storytelling animals, and stories often deal with intimacy and sexual behavior. Humans also are tool making animals, and we have invented increasingly complex tools for telling stories. What we might call "pornographic fundamentalists" believe it is a good thing for people to tell any sexual stories they find arousing, and "media fundamentalists" believe it is a good thing for people to use every media technology to tell all stories.

Fundamentalists refuse to consider whether specific sexual stories told with specific media technologies are consistent with our best answers to "what does it mean to be human?" That pornographic/media fundamentalism does not just critique narrow-minded moralistic judgments but rejects the possibility of any deeper moral evaluation of these cultural practices.

Do the sexual stories of the pornography industry, which so routinely celebrate men's dominance, advance self-realization? Do those stories help build stable, respectful communities? Does the intensity of graphic sexually explicit images delivered through film/video enhance our capacity to achieve these goals? Exploring sexual themes in art can help people struggle with the power and mystery of desire, but what are the long-term effects of reducing sex to pleasure acquisition through a screen? Do those mediated experiences erode our ability to connect to each other sexually in person? Is it possible that sex and intimacy are realms of human experience that do not translate well to explicit representation in mass media?

My experience has led to clear choices for myself, but these are not questions that have single, definitive answers for all. Fearful of the conversation, pornographic/media fundamentalists tend to avoid these questions and try to marginalize anyone who wants to ask them. Better that we check our hubris—the assumption that our ability to do something means we have the wisdom to understand what we are doing and can control its effects—and proceed with caution.

A SEXUAL ETHIC: WHAT IS SEX FOR?

Radical feminism challenges us to ask an often overlooked question: What is sex for? Of the ways people might understand sexuality in their lives, which are most consistent with self-realization and stable, respectful communities? At times, especially within certain religious traditions, rigid answers to the question have been imposed on people in ways that were routinely constraining and sometimes inhumane. But because some people have answered a question badly does not mean we should, or can, avoid the question (Jensen, 2014).

Sex is central to reproduction but clearly plays a role in human life far beyond reproduction. The varied ways that different societies have made sense of these questions indicates that there likely is no single answer for all times and places. Even within an individual's life, sex can play a different role at different times. As young people, sex may be primarily about exploring ourselves and our limits as we mature, while as adults, the most important function of sex may be to foster intimacy within a primary relationship. In general, we can think of sex as a form of communication, a way we learn not only about others but about ourselves. We can collectively try to understand which conceptions of sex are most healthful without claiming definitive knowledge or the right to impose judgments on others.

An analogy to food is helpful. Just as we recognize that sex is more than the acquisition of pleasure, eating is more than just the acquisition of calories. U.S. food companies tend to encourage what Berry (1990, p. 147) calls "industrial eating," just as pornography offers a kind of "industrial sex." Eating processed fast food is a different experience than eating food to which one has a more direct connection in production or preparation. Processed fast food creates distance between us and the living world, and the same is true of processed fast sex. In both cases, people's reflexive response often is, "But I like it." Fast food and fast sex both are efficient at producing a certain type of pleasure, but what is lost in normalizing those forms of pleasure?

CONCLUSION

What does it mean to be human at this particular moment in history? Our answer must be consistent with core progressive principles of dignity (all people have the same claim to being human), solidarity (human flourishing depends on loving connections to others), and equality (dignity and solidarity are impossible without social and economic justice).

A sexual ethic consistent with these widely held moral principles would reject the hierarchy of patriarchy, and hierarchy more generally, recognizing that systems of domination and subordination are inherently abusive. When there is no common understanding of what roles sex plays in our lives, people are more likely to get hurt more often, not just psychologically but physically. In patriarchy, those injuries will be endured mostly by women and children. The conversation about a sexual ethic is not a restriction of anyone's freedom but a part of the quest for a more expansive freedom for all.

A sexual ethic consistent with just, sustainable communities would question the technologizing of all human activity. That does not mean that mediated storytelling with sexual themes is inherently negative, only that we need to consider not only the pleasures of sex through technology but the deeper implications. We need not romanticize a mythical golden age to recognize that what we call progress does not always enhance the quality of our lives.

Radical feminist critics of pornography are often accused of being prudes, or the more academically fashionable pejorative "sex negative," but critiquing the negative aspects of patriarchal sex is not prudish. It is not antisex to critique a pornographic culture that accepts overtly misogynistic and racist images designed to produce sexual stimulation, which are easily accessible not only to adults but to children at the beginning stages of their sexual development.

A friend, who does not share the radical feminist position, once suggested I was "overwrought" about the subject. Would it be better to be underwrought? Or to not be wrought at all? My level of "wroughtness" is based on research and critical thinking, along with my experience and the experiences of hundreds of people I have talked to in the course of this work—men who have told me they feel trapped by their habitual use of pornography, which was undermining their ability to be truly intimate with a partner; women whose partners lost interest in intimacy and sex once the men started using pornography habitually; and other women whose partners started demanding degrading and/or painful sexual acts they had seen in pornography. Are those people overwrought in their struggles?

Our pornified and pornographic culture leaves us with challenging questions: Why do so many people need films of other people having sex to feel sexual, and why do so many people want pictures of sex that eroticize domination/subordination? Why are most of those people men? Are we afraid that we can't transcend patriarchal ideas that are deeply woven into the fabric of contemporary society and that we cannot turn away from the screens that proliferate in our lives? Are we afraid that we have not only become consumers of goods but consumers of the most basic human experiences?

Those questions have nothing to do with a fear of sex but rather identify reasonable fears of who, or what, we have become in hypermediated patriarchal society. If we were to look to pornography for answers to this most basic question—what does it mean to be human at this particular moment in history?—it is difficult to imagine a just, sustainable human future. Our task is to face those fears and imagine the future differently.

REFERENCES

Berry, W. (1990). *What are people for?* San Francisco, CA: North Point Press.

Buss, D. M. (1994). *The evolution of desire: Strategies of human mating.* New York, NY: Basic.

Dines, G. (2010). *Pornland: How porn hijacked our sexuality.* Boston, MA: Beacon.

Dworkin, A. (1979). *Pornography: Men possessing women.* New York, NY: Perigee. (Reprint edition, Dutton, 1989).

Dworkin, A. (1988). *Letters from a war zone.* London, England: Secker & Warburg. (Reprint edition, Dutton, 1989).

Frye, M. (1992). *Willful virgin.* Freedom, CA: Crossing Press.

Jensen, R. (2007). *Getting off: Pornography and the end of masculinity.* Cambridge, MA: South End Press. Retrieved from http://robertwjensen.org/

Jensen, R. (2011). Pornography as propaganda. In G. Sussman (Ed.), *The propaganda society: Promotional culture and politics in global context* (pp. 159–174). New York, NY: Peter Lang.

Jensen, R. (2014). Pornographic and pornified: Feminist and ecological understandings of sexually explicit media. In J. Held & L. Coleman (Eds.), *The philosophy of pornography: Contemporary perspectives* (pp. 53–70). Lanham, MD: Rowman & Littlefield/Scarecrow Press.

MacKinnon, C. A. (1987). *Feminism unmodified: Discourses on life and law.* Cambridge, MA: Harvard University Press.

MacKinnon, C. A., & Dworkin, A. (1997). *In harm's way: The pornography civil rights hearings.* Cambridge, MA: Harvard University Press.

Paul, P. (2005). *Pornified: How pornography is transforming our lives, our relationships, and our families.* New York, NY: Times Books.

Taormino, T., Penley, C., Shimizu, C. P., & Miller-Young, M. (Eds.). (2013). *The feminist porn book: The politics of producing pleasure.* New York, NY: Feminist Press.

Whisnant, R., & Stark, C. (Eds.). (2004). *Not for sale: Feminists resisting prostitution and pornography.* North Melbourne, Australia: Spinifex Press.

Zell, E., Krizan, Z., & Teeter, S. R. (2015). Evaluating gender similarities and differences using metasynthesis. *American Psychologist, 70*(1), 10–20.

"THERE IS NO SUCH THING AS IT"

Toward a Critical Understanding of the Porn Industry

Gail Dines

37

The mid-1990s . . . can be seen as the golden age of critical media studies, with scholars such as Sut Jhally, Eileen Meehan, Stuart Hall, Robert McChesney, and Janet Wasko calling for a paradigm shift away from simple cause and effect (often called the "Magic Bullet Theory" in communication) toward a more nuanced understanding of how media is produced, distributed, and consumed within a society characterized by class, race, and gender inequality. Building on the insights of Marx, Althusser, Gramsci, and the Birmingham School for Contemporary Cultural Studies, much of the scholarship sought to interrogate the ways in which media ownership and control serve to limit, shape, and, in some cases, determine the nature of the media products that circulate in mainstream culture.

By 2014 these debates had been largely marginalized, and the field seemed to have been taken over by articles written by scholars who were openly and uncritically celebrating media forms that in the past would have been subject to rigorous academic analysis. This was especially true in the case of feminist media studies. Rather than looking at how corporate-owned media affect the way in which girls and women construct gender and sexual identities that produce and reproduce hegemonic gender relations, scholars were now arguing that we needed to take a more positive approach to media targeted to women. Starting from the premise that media texts are polysemic (open to multiple meanings), feminist media scholars—often sounding more like fans than researchers—began to argue, often without any research to back up their claims, that women and girls may actually be empowered by hypersexualized images that objectify women because they offer a kind of pleasure that comes with being noticed and desired by men (see, e.g., Johnson, 2002).

This paradigm shift caused one of the most prolific and well-respected feminist media scholars, Angela McRobbie, to write a 2008 article that she termed an "intervention in the field of feminist media and cultural studies" that "to ignore the force field within which . . . cultural forms circulate is to abandon the ethical and the political underpinning of feminist media and cultural studies scholarship" (McRobbie, 2008, p. 544), she called on scholars to bring back a feminist critique of how media images shape and construct a consumer-driven femininity. McRobbie specifically pointed to the way in which *Sex and the City* was hailed by some feminist media scholars as a show that celebrated women's sexual power. Missing from this critique, McRobbie pointed out, is "a prior, or old-fashioned feminist vocabulary which was concerned with the power of these media forms, and their role in producing sexual objectification, differentiation and subordination . . ." (p. 540). This results in what McRobbie called a "complicitous critique" (p. 539) that "appears to suspend critical engagement with the wider political and economic conditions which shape the very existence, as well as the circulation and availability, of these forms" (p. 539).

This article draws upon and develops McRobbie's concept of a "complicitous critique" to explain why so many scholars writing in the field of women's studies ignore the socio-economic dynamic within which porn is produced, distributed, and consumed that shapes the very products that circulate within the mainstream market. . . . Thus, my major concern here is how (to use McRobbie's terms) the "wider political and economic conditions" shape the way in which porn is produced and distributed. This involves taking a critical approach to how porn as an industry works within a global economic system that often serves to define the nature of the content produced, and the way the corporatization of porn has resulted in a monopolistic system of distribution.

Moreover, arguing that pornography operates as an industry means that we need to examine how it uses its corporate dollars to establish legitimacy and lobby for political and legal change. Lobbying is a central part of the porn industry's business plan, because any legal restrictions on content, production, and distribution could reduce profits. Corporations abhor regulation of any sort. As this article will show, the porn industry, despite its efforts to portray itself as progressive and sexually liberating, is especially aggressive in organizing against regulation so that it can continue to grow in market size and mainstream acceptability. The industry seeks to operate in an almost regulation-free zone and has attempted to shred existing and proposed protections for porn performers against injury, the transmission of STDs, and the exploitation of minors.

WHAT IS "IT": MAPPING THE PORN INTERNET INDUSTRY

In 2011, at a plenary session of a conference in London called *Pornified? Complicating Debates about the "Sexualization of Culture,"* pro-porn scholars Feona Attwood, Clarissa Smith, and Martin Barker argued that there is no such thing as "it." The "it" they were referring to was the porn industry, and their reasoning was that because there are so many sub-genres of porn circulating on the Internet, there couldn't possibly be a cohesive industry. While this is a rather strange argument given the way management scholars analyze industries—nobody would argue, for example, that there is no such thing as a car industry because there are lots of different types of cars on the road—it also speaks to the ways in which much of what passes for scholarship today in the world of pro-porn studies is little more than simplistic musings rather than rigorous research. No

attempt was made at this plenary session to explore how pornography is produced and distributed, if indeed there is no industry actually organizing the production and distribution of those products that are accessed when a consumer types the word "porn" into Google. Moreover, as the conference continued, it became clear that these scholars, by sounding more like fans than researchers, were falling into the very trap that McRobbie had warned against.

Ironically, the porn industry would be the first group to disagree with the argument that a porn industry does not exist. In a 2000 interview, Andrew Edmond, president and CEO of Flying Crocodile, a $20-million pornography Internet business, discussed how surprising it is that so few people understand the scale and scope of the industry. Edmond's explanation for this was that "a lot of people [outside adult entertainment] get distracted from the business model by [the sex]. It is just as sophisticated and multilayered as any other market place. We operate just like any Fortune 500 company" (Edmond, 2000).

Indeed, since 2000, the porn industry has become even more sophisticated and multilayered. In 2009, Steven Yagielowicz, a well-known porn industry journalist, stated in an article for *XBIZ News:*

> The corporatization of porn isn't something that will happen or is happening, it is something that has happened—and if you're unaware of that fact then there truly is no longer a seat at the table for you. It's Las Vegas all over again: the independent owners, renegade mobsters and visionary entrepreneurs pushed aside by mega-corporations that saw a better way of doing things and brought the discipline needed to attain a whole new level of success to the remaining players. (Yagielowicz, 2009)

So there is clearly an "it," and this "it" requires detailed and rigorous analysis if we are to understand the ways in which the mainstream porn industry develops and functions within the wider economic systems of global capitalism. One reason for this is that the scale of the pornography business has important cultural implications. The entertainment industries do not just influence us; they constitute our hegemonic culture, our identities, our conceptions of the world, and our norms of acceptable behavior. Moreover, in the absence of thorough and robust sex education programs in schools, porn fills the knowledge gap for children and youth and thus becomes an important player in the development of adolescent sexual templates.

This is especially worrisome given the findings of a comprehensive content analysis of contemporary porn by Bridges and her team (2010). They found that the majority of scenes from 50 of the top-rented porn movies contained both physical and verbal abuse targeted at the female performers. Physical aggression, which included spanking, open-hand slapping, and gagging, occurred in over 88% of scenes, while expressions of verbal aggression—calling the woman names such as "bitch" or "slut"—were found in 48% of the scenes. The researchers concluded that 90% of scenes contained at least one aggressive act if both physical and verbal aggression were combined (Bridges et al., 2010). An industry of this magnitude and reach that so blatantly produces images of violence against women is a worthy area of investigation within feminist media studies because it plays a role in constructing notions of gender and gender relations.

An obvious starting point in developing a map of the porn industry is an analysis of how porn is a key driver of technological innovations and pioneers new business models that subsequently permeate the wider economy (Coopersmith, 2006). In turn, evolving technologies and business techniques have shaped the content and format of pornography. A key factor driving the growth of the porn market has been the development of technologies that allow users to buy and consume porn in private on almost any device with a screen, without embarrassing trips to seedy stores or video rental shops. Porn does not just benefit from these technologies, however; it has helped create the technologies that expand its own market. As Blaise Cronin and Elizabeth Davenport put it, "Certainly, it is universally acknowledged by information technology experts that the adult entertainment industry has been at the leading edge in terms of building high-performance Web sites with state-of-the art features and functionality" (Cronin & Davenport, 2001).

Porn has proven to be a reliable, highly profitable market segment that has accelerated the development of media technologies from VCRs and DVDs to file sharing networks, video on demand for cable, streamed video over the Internet for PCs, and, most recently, video for hand-held devices (Coopersmith, 2006). Video uses vast quantities of data, and the demand for porn has driven the development of core cross-platform technologies for data compression, search, and transmission. A common pattern across these various technologies is for pornography to blaze the trail, then gradually decline as a proportion of total business as the technology matures and develops more general commercial use (Coopersmith, 2006).

The porn industry has also been a pioneer of new business models that help to make commercial video profitable, opening the way for the commercial viability of video-sharing websites such as YouTube and television series downloads to cellphones and iPods. The porn industry has been able to exploit the unregulated, freewheeling nature of business on the web, which has made it very easy for small companies to enter new markets with very little capital. It has also allowed them to pursue international strategies, since the jurisdictional ambiguity of Internet geography facilitates the avoidance of taxation and regulation. Porn has led the way in obtaining free content from users, repackaging and then reselling it. The porn industry has also developed marketing devices that have been adopted by other Internet sectors, such as free "supersites" that build traffic and cross-link to numerous providers, generating advertising and pay-per-click revenues. It has also been a leader in the development of web-based subscription business models, anti-fraud security, and micro-payment systems for pay-per-view customers (Coopersmith, 2006).

Porn as a major industry engages in the normal business activities that other industries pursue. Porn businesses raise capital, hire managers and accountants, undergo mergers and acquisitions, organize trade shows, have their own lobbying group (the Free Speech Coalition), and enter into co-marketing arrangements with other companies. The Private Media Group was the first diversified, adult-entertainment company to gain a listing on the Nasdaq exchange (though it should be noted that porn businesses have struggled to raise capital through public share offerings). There is now an investment firm that deals specifically with the porn industry. Called AdultVest, the company boasts that it brings together accredited investors, hedge funds, venture capital funds, private equity funds, investment banks, and broker dealers with growing adult entertainment companies and gentlemen's clubs who are looking to sell their business, raise capital, or go public. Investors can utilize their AdultVest.com membership to research a wide variety of private placements, reverse mergers, IPO's, public offerings, buyouts, joint ventures, and business opportunities.

While these activities are in themselves unremarkable business operations, they signal that porn is becoming a mainstream, everyday business—a legitimate enterprise being taken more seriously by Wall Street, the media, and the political establishment. The porn business is embedded in a complex value chain that links not just film producers and distributors, but also bankers, software producers, Internet providers, cable companies, and hotel chains. These other businesses become allies and collaborators with a vested interest in the growth and continued viability of the porn business. Banks, for example, make money from the porn industry as the revenue it generates is invested in stocks, bonds, mutual funds, and so forth. Indeed, everyone in the supply chain, from production to consumption, is complicit in building and strengthening the porn industry.

RECENT SHIFTS IN THE PORN INDUSTRY

The conventional wisdom today is that porn is on the decline and hemorrhaging money, thanks to free porn sites and increased piracy. While profits may be down, however, it is a mistake to see this as evidence of a dying industry. Indeed, it is actually a sign of a successful, maturing industry that is moving from a mom-and-pop model of small, backstreet players to a more legitimate, mainstream industry characterized by fierce competition and increasing concentration in the hands of a few large firms.

What has happened to porn is typical of industries that grow and mature. The Internet served to enable rapid market growth and attracted a proliferation of new entrants eager to make what

appeared to be easy money. This led to intense competition, falling prices and profits, and, as documented by Theroux (2012), lower pay for the performers. But the weeding out of some unprofitable firms and a wave of acquisitions have led to the consolidation of the industry and the emergence of a few large, more professionally managed businesses operating in multiple market segments through a variety of distribution channels. These big players have gained a level of economic, political, and cultural clout that is reshaping the industry politically, culturally, and legally.

While many people think of *Playboy, Penthouse,* and *Hustler* as the movers and shakers of the porn industry, it is actually a company that few outside the industry have ever heard of that has played the most significant role in reshaping the entire business strategy of porn. Originally called Manwin, this Luxembourg-based company (renamed MindGeek in 2013 after CEO Fabian Thylmann stepped down following his arrest on charges of tax evasion) advertises itself on its website as driving

the state of technology forward, developing industry-leading solutions enabling faster, more efficient delivery of content every second to millions of customers worldwide. The Company is committed to enhancing its technological capabilities and thrives on a sustainable growth trajectory built on innovation and excellence. (MindGeek, n.d.)

Boasting that it has "over 1000 employees worldwide" and is expanding "with the acquisition and licensing of some of the most iconic brands in entertainment media," it is impossible to know from clicking on the major pages of its website that this company is the biggest distributor of porn in the world. However, according to an article on the website therichest.com, MindGeek

is hands down the number one distributor of porn in the world. If you're surprised that companies such as Reality Kings and Brazzers didn't make the list don't be. MindGeek owns all of those, to better break it down, Reality Kings owns 38 pornographic sites and Brazzers 35. Making MindGeek (MG) hold a strong monopoly on the industry. . . . They are among the top three bandwidth consumption companies on earth, operating more than 73 websites in all-free, paid and webcam. (DiVirgilio, 2013)

This level of industry concentration has angered a lot of smaller players who are being pushed out of the market by MindGeek. One of the main reasons for this is that MindGeek owns the top eight free porn sites (called "tube sites" in the industry) that offer an enormous amount of free porn that is funded by ads for paid sites, live webcam sites, penis enlargers, and so-called escort services. According to an article by David Auerbach on the Slate website, the sites are made up largely of pirated material, and MindGeek is notorious for making it difficult for the original producers—often small-time, mom-and-pop shops with few resources—to get the pirated material removed (Auerbach, 2014). In addition, given their extensive ownership of both paid and free porn sites, most major studios and well-known porn performers have economic ties to MindGeek. The result is that both producers and performers are in the "difficult situation of seeing their work pirated on sites owned by the same company that pays them" (Auerbach, 2014). Auerbach continues by making the important point that this means that few people in the industry feel comfortable about speaking publicly against MindGeek, a situation made worse by the fact that MindGeek also has influence over the major trade publications by virtue of its advertising dollars (Auerbach, 2014).

Thus, in a clever marketing ploy, much of the content on the free porn websites comes from MindGeek's paid sites and acts as a teaser to get viewers interested so that they can then "monetize" the free porn with advertising and by diverting the consumer to paid sites. So, rather than destroying the porn industry, free porn is expanding the consumer base for paid porn. Feras Antoon, CEO of Brazzers, is quoted in *New York Magazine* as claiming that free porn sites have so "vastly enlarged the total universe of porn consumers that the number of those who pay has ballooned along with it" (Wallace, 2011). Given the revenues that MindGeek generates, it is taken very seriously on Wall Street and by politicians and policymakers because it is a major funder of the porn lobby. It is this concentration of economic power that is key to understanding why any rigorous and serious analysis of the porn industry must follow the industry's money trail.

PORN INDUSTRY'S WINS AND LOSSES: USING ECONOMIC POWER TO LOBBY FOR (AND AGAINST) LEGISLATION

One of the key markers of a mature industry is that it has developed the capacity and resources for corporate legal and political activity by financing industry associations and lobbying groups. Chief among these is the Free Speech Coalition (FSC), founded in 1991, which describes itself as "the trade association of the adult entertainment industry based in the United States" and has been active in working to change laws, develop PR campaigns, and to promote itself as a beacon in the protection of free speech for all. Its stated mission is to serve as an organization that "helps limit the legal risks of being an adult business, increases the profitability of its members, promotes the acceptance of the industry in America's business community, and supports greater public tolerance for freedom of sexual speech" (Free Speech Coalition, n.d.).

In reality, mainstream positioning requires that an industry present a more socially responsible face and pursue modes of self-regulation that try to eliminate the more blatant abuses while fending off more unwelcome governmental regulation.

By way of exploring the role that the FSC has played in making the political and legal landscape more hospitable to the porn industry, I will focus on three major battles that the coalition has undertaken in the last decade or so. These have yielded mixed results that include some losses . . . and a major win . . . I will begin with the latter, since this has had the largest, most profound impact on the content and distribution of porn in the last decade.

Ashcroft v. Free Speech Coalition (2002)

In 2002, the FSC brought a case to the U.S. Supreme Court designed to change the 1996 Child Pornography Prevention Act, which prohibited any image that "is, or appears to be, of a minor engaging in sexually explicit conduct."

Arguing that the term "appears to be" limited the free speech of pornographers, the coalition succeeded in removing this "limitation," and the law's scope was narrowed to cover only those images in which an actual person (rather than one who appears to be) under the age of 18 was involved in the making of porn. Thus, the path was cleared for the porn industry to use either computer-generated images of children or real porn performers who, although age 18 or over, are "childified" to look much younger.

Since that 2002 decision, there has been an explosion in the number of sites that childify women, as well as those that use computer-generated imagery. Pseudo Child Pornography (PCP) sites that use adults (those people defined by law as 18 years of age or over) to represent children are never referred to as child pornography by the industry. Instead, almost all of those sites that childify the female porn performer are found in the sub-genre called "teen-porn" or "teen-sex" by the industry. There are any number of ways to access these sites, the most obvious one being through Google. Typing "teen porn" into Google yields over 16 million hits, giving the user his[1] choice of thousands of porn sites. A number of the hits are actually for porn portals where "teen porn" is one sub-category of many, and when the user clicks on that category, a list of sites comes up that runs over 90 pages.

Many of the actual sites in this category have the word "teen" in their names—for example, *Solo Teen, Solo Teen Babe, Sexy Teen Girl, Teen Cuties,* and *Solo Teen Girls.* When the user clicks on any one of these sites, the first and most striking feature is the body shape of the female porn performers. In place of the large-breasted, curvaceous bodies that populate regular porn websites, one sees small-breasted, slightly built women with adolescent-looking faces that are relatively free of makeup. Many of these performers do look younger than 18, but they do not look like children, so the pornographers use a range of techniques to make them appear more childlike than they actually are. Most common among these are the use of children's clothes and props such as stuffed animals, lollipops, pigtails, pastel-colored ribbons, ankle socks, braces on the teeth, and, of course, the school uniform. It is not unusual to see a female porn performer wearing a school uniform, sucking a lollipop, and hugging a teddy bear while she masturbates with a dildo.

Evidence as to just how this victory on the part of the FSC shaped the content of mainstream porn can be found in the fact that "teen porn" has grown rapidly and is now the largest single genre whether measured by search-term frequency or proportion of websites.

. . . a Google Trends analysis indicated that searches for "teen porn" have more than tripled between 2005 and 2013, and that teen porn was the fastest-growing genre in this period. Total searches for teen-related porn reached an estimated 500,000 daily by March 2013, far larger than other genres and representing approximately one-third of total daily searches for pornographic websites. Moreover, the content of the three most popular "porntubes," the portals that serve as gateways to online porn, contained about 18 million teen-related pages—again, the largest single genre and about one-third of the total content.

Holder v. Free Speech Coalition (2013)

The Child Protection and Obscenity Enforcement Act of 1988 (known as 2257) requires primary and secondary producers of pornography to keep records on file demonstrating that all porn performers on a set are at least 18 years of age. The porn industry has been fighting this law for well over a decade on the basis that such record keeping is, in their words, "overly burdensome" for free speech. This battle reached a climax in June 2013 in the James A. Byrne Federal Courthouse in Philadelphia when U.S. District Court Judge Michael Baylson upheld federal regulation 2257.

Why is the overturning of 2257 such a priority for the porn industry? The answer lies in the fact that the age documentation requirements of 2257 represent a key component of the legal struggle to prevent child pornography from becoming widespread on free porn websites. Given that content is loaded onto tube sites from a variety of sources, some of which the owner of the tube site controls, and some of which are not under direct control, it would require an investment in information technology infrastructure to keep track of age verification documents across the value chain, which increasingly extends internationally. Thus the distributors (defined as secondary producers) such as MindGeek could be held responsible for uploading child pornography that would make them run afoul of the law. One way to avoid this is to succeed in getting 2257 struck down. . . .

Moreover, the production side of the pornography industry operates in terms of an internationally fragmented supply chain in which production is dispersed across the globe. This dispersion can be seen in the list of content producers on You-Porn.com, the second-largest porn site on the Internet. As evidenced by the list of custodians of 2257 records for the 180 official content producers (see http://www.youporn.com/information/), pornography production takes place in numerous smaller studios located not only in the United States but also Canada and Europe, including Cyprus, the Czech Republic, the UK, Hungary, and The Netherlands. For example, on YouPorn.com, many of the listed custodian sites are no longer operational. . . .

While the FSC was fighting 2257 in court, it boasted on its site that it was a member of the porn industry-backed non-profit group Adult Sites Against Child Pornography (ASACP). ASACP was founded in 1996 by the porn industry and claims that it "battles child pornography through its Reporting Hotline" and is "dedicated to online child protection." Both ASACP and the FSC have similar membership and funding from porn industry players across the value chain, from producers to online distributors to webmasters. . . . This strategy of pursuing Corporate Social Responsibility (CSR) is typical for industries facing challenges to their legitimacy and embroiled in legal battles to protect their interests.

Measure B (County of Los Angeles Safer Sex in the Adult Film Industry Act)

More pornography is produced in the Greater Los Angeles area than in any other part of the English-speaking world, so it is no surprise that activists have focused their efforts in this location when organizing to improve the health and safety of porn performers. Without doubt the most successful of these has been the passage of Measure B in the County of Los Angeles in November 2012. This law, authored by the AIDS Healthcare Foundation (AHF), mandates the use of condoms in porn scenes that contain anal or vaginal penetration and also requires production companies to both obtain a health permit and to notify performers of the requirement of condom use during filming. Repeated failure to do so can result in civil fines or misdemeanor charges.

Given that the most popular porn websites depict acts that include gagging with a penis; pounding anal sex; spitting into the mouth of a woman; ATM (ass-to-mouth) transitions, in which the penis goes from the anus to the mouth without washing; ejaculation onto the body and sometimes into the eye; and bukkake (wherein any number of men ejaculate onto a woman's body, or into a cup that she then drinks), it is no surprise that there have been a number of STD outbreaks, including HIV, on porn sets in the last decade. In researching my book *Pornland* (Dines, 2010), I watched hundreds of scenes from the most popular porn movies, and I regularly saw a mixture of saliva, semen, feces, and vomit on the set.

The now-shuttered Adult Industry Medical Health Care Association, which was the Los Angeles-based voluntary organization in charge of testing performers, had a list on its website of possible injuries and diseases to which porn performers were prone. These included HIV; rectal and throat gonorrhea; tearing of the throat, vagina, and anus; and chlamydia of the eye. In a study published in the December 2012 issue of *Sexually Transmitted Diseases* that examined 168 sex industry performers (67% were female and 33% were male), 47 (28%) were diagnosed with a total of 96 infections. . . . These findings led the authors to conclude that "Adult film industry performers in California are workers in a legal industry and should be subject to the same workplace safety standards from which workers in other industries benefit" (Rodriguez-Hart et al., 2012).

Even though there was a massive campaign against this measure—orchestrated by the porn industry and supported by business organizations . . . the measure passed with 55.9% of the vote. It is worth noting that some of the "premier partners" of VICA include Chase Bank, Walmart, Southwest Airlines, and Vons (a Safeway company). One of the biggest contributors to the effort to defeat Measure B was Manwin (now MindGeek). . . .

According to records obtained by the AHF, Manwin not only donated over $300,000 to fight Measure B, but also had banner ads reading "Vote No on B" splashed across its porn sites. On its Brazzers site, the banner was directly above an image of a woman being anally penetrated by a condom-free penis. In addition to Manwin, questionable supporters opposing the measure included the Coalition for Senior Citizenry, which gives its address as 2350 Hidalgo Avenue, Los Angeles, but has a disconnected phone number; and the Council of Concerned Women Voters, which has no phone number and no web presence—and also resides at 2350 Hidalgo Avenue, Los Angeles. Along with support from these purported grass-roots—or "astroturf"—organizations, money flowed in from major porn studios such as Vivid and porn companies such as Flynt Management Group and John Stagliano, owner of the hardcore porn company Evil Angel. Predictably, the campaign committee against Measure B was established through the FSC.

Diane Duke, FSC's executive director, is on record as saying that Measure B was not about "performer health and safety" but rather about "government regulating what happens between consenting adults" (*Los Angeles Times,* 2012). In place of employees being paid per scene by porn owners who control their wages and working conditions, the industry reframes workers as "consenting adults" having sex that just so happens to end up on film that is distributed through the porn industry and generates profits for its capitalist owners. As a way to further render invisible the power inequality between the owners of porn companies and their employees, the industry used some performers to make the case that Measure B was an infringement on workers' rights. Porn actress Amber Lynn was quoted as saying that "The idea of allowing a government employee to come and examine our genitalia while we're on set is atrocious" (Castillo, 2012). Nina Hartley, a long-time performer and pornographer, claimed that condoms are actually dangerous to the performers' health because "condom burn . . . can create micro abrasions in the vagina or anal canal," exposing them to potential pathogens (Herriman, 2011).

Why was the porn industry so opposed to Measure B? It projects an image of itself as an industry run by a bunch of cool and hip renegade artists who are at the cutting edge of protecting our freedoms. In reality, they abhor any government regulations that cut into profit. And there is no doubt whatsoever that requiring performers to use condoms will have a major economic impact on the porn industry. Porn consumers do not want condoms. As the veteran porn performer Ron Jeremy so eloquently put it: "Hey, dicks, it's really quite simple. . . . No matter how you slice it, the viewers don't want to see them" (Crocker, 2012).

Why is this? The fantasy of porn is that the female performer is an object who exists to be penetrated, dehumanized, and then disposed of. The narrative of porn is that she is not someone to worry about, care for, or protect from physical harm. On the contrary, porn sex is about pushing her to her bodily limits and then moving on to the next, and the next, and the next. Given this, it would simply make no sense for the men, during a porn shoot, to take the time or trouble to open a condom, put it on, check to make sure that it covers the penis so she won't be infected, and then start pounding away at her. Condoms mean that she matters, and porn is all about her not mattering.

Another big problem for the industry is that a condom would ruin the "money shot"—the term pornographers use to describe the final scene, in which the man ejaculates onto the body, face, or into the eye of the woman. The best explanation for this comes from the veteran porn actor and producer Bill Margold, who is quoted as saying: "The most violent we can get is the cum shot in the face. Men get off behind that, because they get even with the women they can't have. We try to inundate the world with orgasms in the face" (Stoller & Levine, 1993; quoted in Jensen, 2007, p. 69).

CONCLUSION

As evidenced in the discussion above, the argument made by some pro-porn scholars that there is no "it" to study contradicts the wealth of empirical evidence that porn has now grown into a major industry with sophisticated marketing, technologies, and public relations companies. The increasing concentration of the distribution end of the industry enhances the profitability of the leading firms by generating economies of scale and scope and giving them substantial market power over the fragmented upstream producers and suppliers of porn materials. This market power brings with it political power to lobby and wage PR campaigns. Like other mature industries that generate harmful impacts, the porn industry wages legal and lobbying strategies against existing and proposed regulations while simultaneously pursuing CSR policies that discursively link the industry to wider social aspirations such as sexual emancipation and free speech, and attempt to draw a line between acceptable and unacceptable porn (child porn), reflecting pragmatic concessions while protecting key markets, such as teen porn.

As the porn industry increasingly flexes its muscles in the economic, cultural, and political spheres of governance in which it is embedded, it is a matter of urgency that feminist media scholars become less "curiously timid" (Gill, 2011) in their thinking. Following Rosalind Gill's call for a "bigger" and "bolder" analysis that allows us to "get angry again" (Gill, 2011), feminist media scholars need to bring back some of the "old-fashioned feminist

vocabulary" (McRobbie, 2008) that formed the cornerstone of an unapologetic, rigorous, and transformative feminism. Rather than espousing views that synchronize well with the industry perspective, feminists need to develop a research and activist agenda that interrogates (and undermines) the porn industry's role in legitimizing and cementing the economic and social subordination of women. Absent such a project, feminism becomes one more movement to be co-opted by the neoliberal hegemony that rebrands capitulation as resistance.

NOTE

1. I refer to the user in the masculine since the majority of porn consumers are men. While it is impossible to provide an accurate breakdown of male and female consumers, Mark Kernes, senior editor of the pornography trade magazine *Adult Video News,* stated: "Our statistics show that 78% of the people that go into adult stores are men. They may have women with them, but it's men, and 22%, conversely, is women or women with other women or women alone" (Kernes, 2005).

REFERENCES

AdultVest. (n.d.). Retrieved March 23, 2009, from http://www.adultvest.com/index.php

Auerbach, D. (2014, October 23). Vampire porn: MindGeek is a cautionary tale of consolidating production and distribution in a single, monopolistic owner. *Slate.* Retrieved June 21, 2015, from http://www.slate.com/articles/technology/technology/2014/10/mindgeek_porn_monopoly_its_dominance_is_a_cautionary_tale_for_other_industries.html

Bridges, A., Wosnitzer, R., Scharrer, E., Sun, C., & Liberman, R. (2010). Aggression and sexual behavior in best-selling pornography videos: A content analysis update. *Violence Against Women,* 16, 1065–1085.

Castillo, M. (2012, November 7). L.A. County porn shoots must use condoms. *CBS News.* Retrieved June 21, 2015, from http://www.cbsnews.com/news/la-county-porn-shoots-must-use-condoms/

Coopersmith, J. (2006). Does your mother know what you really do? The changing nature and image of computer-based pornography. *History and Technology, 22*(1), 1–25.

Crocker, L. (2012, January 6). Condom initiative by anti-AIDS group threatens porn industry. *The Daily Beast.* Retrieved June 21, 2015, from http://www.thedailybeast.com/articles/2012/01/06/condom-initiative-by-anti-aids-group-threatens-porn-industry.html

Cronin, B., & Davenport, E. (2001). E-rogenous zones: Positioning pornography in the digital economy. *Information Society, 17,* P41.

Dines, G. (2010). *Pornland: How porn has hijacked our sexuality.* Boston: Beacon Press.

DiVirgilio, A. (2013, January 12). *Money in pornography: One of the most misunderstood industries.* Retrieved June 21, 2015, from http://www.therichest.com/expensive-lifestyle/money/money-in-pornography-one-of-the-most-misunderstood-industries/

Edmond, A. (2000, October). Interview. *Brandweek, 41,* p. 1Q48.

Free Speech Coalition. (n.d.). *FSC history.* Retrieved June 21, 2015, from http://freespeechcoalition.com/fsc-history/

Gill, R. (2011). Sexism reloaded, or, it's time to get angry again. *Feminist Media Studies, 11*(1), 61–71.

Herriman, R. (2011, June 27). The porn industry fights back: A few words with Michael Whiteacre, Part 2. *Examiner.com.* Retrieved June 21, 2015, from http://www.examiner.com/article/the-porn-industry-fights-back-a-few-words-with-michael-whiteacre-part-2

Jensen, R. (2007). *Getting off: Pornography and the end of masculinity.* Boston: South End Press.

Johnson, M.L. (Ed.). (2002). *Jane sexes it up: True confessions of feminist desire.* New York: Avalon.

Kernes, M. (2005, January 7). Interview with Robert Jensen, Adult Entertainment Expo, Las Vegas, NV.

Los Angeles Times. (2012, January 17). Retrieved June 21, 2015, from http://latimesblogs.latimes.com/lanow/2012/01/la-approves-condom-rule.html

McRobbie, A. (2008). Young women and consumer culture. *Cultural Studies, 22*(5), 531–550.

MindGeek. (n.d.). *Full steam ahead: Pioneering the future of online traffic.* Retrieved June 21, 2015, from www.mindgeek.com

Rodriguez-Hart, C., Chitale, R.A., Rigg, R., Goldstein, B.Y., Kerndt, P.R., & Tavrow, P. (2012). Sexually transmitted infection testing of adult film performers: Is disease being missed? *Sexually Transmitted Diseases, 39*(12), 989–994. doi:10.1097/OLQ.0b013e3182716e6e

Stoller, R.J., & Levine, I.S. (1993). *Coming attractions: The making of an X-rated video.* New Haven, CT: Yale University Press.

Theroux, L. (2012, June 5). How the Internet killed porn. *The Guardian.* Retrieved June 21, 2015, from http://www.theguardian.com/culture/2012/jun/05/how-internet-killed-porn

Wallace, B. (2011, January 30). The geek-kings of smut. *New York Magazine.* Retrieved June 21, 2015, from http://nymag.com/news/features/70985/

Yagielowicz, S. (2009). The state of the industry. *XBIZ News.* Retrieved March 20, 2009, from http://www.xbiz.com/articles/106157/

38

THE PORNOGRAPHY OF EVERYDAY LIFE [1]

Jane Caputi

The subject of sexual degradation in the service of domination flooded world consciousness after May 2004, when horrific "trophy" photos that American soldiers took of Iraqi prisoners at Abu Ghraib prison in Iraq were released to the public. They showed Iraqi men stripped, bound, and forced into situations both sides believed to be denigrating—simulating homosexual sex, crawling on the floor, posing for sexual display, and wearing women's underwear on their heads. In one photo, naked men are made to pile on top of one another, with their buttocks in the air. (Image 1) Standing nearby, smiling and giving a "thumbs-up" gesture are a pair of White soldiers, male and female. Shocked and appalled, many recognized the behavior in these photos as torture, meant to humiliate and break the spirit of the prisoners.

What was not widely acknowledged, however, was how often we see women being posed and treated in precisely these ways and worse, not only in pornography, but also in fashion magazines, music videos, and advertising around the world, including the United States. And these are not generally recognized as humiliating, torturous and spirit-breaking; rather, they are passed off as normal or even "sexy."

For example, a photo in an issue of *Vibe* magazine (which appeared before the release of the Abu Ghraib photos) is structured around a scene that is eerily similar to one I just described (Image 2). Two Black men are seated at a bar. To their left, a Black woman (we see only the back of her head) in a very short skirt and stiletto heels bends over the bar, exposing her "panties" and with her partially bared buttocks up in the air. One man grins widely and the other gives a "thumbs-up" gesture. This image is overt in its contempt for the nameless and faceless Black woman pictured as a throwaway sex object.

A famous White woman, movie star Michelle Williams, gets similar treatment, although less egregiously, in her pose for a luxury fashion magazine. (Image 3) Williams, outside and alone amid lush greenery, stands awkwardly, tilting her head and body in a childish manner. She wears one designer's sweater and awkwardly holds up another's hat; her bottom half is covered only by a third designer's briefs. Basically, Williams is *de-pantsed,* a colloquial expression meaning to "remove someone's trousers as a joke or as a punishment."[2] Such pictorial modes probably just look normal to most viewers, though they would not if it were a male celebrity posed and dressed in that degrading way.

As these examples indicate, this chapter is not about "x-rated" porn. Rather, it is about a "habit of thinking" (Williams, 1995, p. 123)—an everyday pornographic discourse (words and pictures) normalizing, sexualizing, and gendering humiliation and hierarchy. "The man" is the one on top, and the objectified, exposed, and denigrated one is "the woman" (even when, sometimes a woman plays the masculine role and vice versa).

Catharine MacKinnon and Andrea Dworkin (Dworkin, 1989, pp. 253–275) originally shifted the debate around pornography from the issue of morality to one of power relations. They define pornography as "the graphic, sexually explicit subordination of women" or men, children or transsexuals "used in the place of women." Their extended discussion delineates specific elements, including women, being put into "postures or positions of sexual submission, servility or display," "scenarios of degradation, injury, abasement, torture," "dehumanizing objectification" and women

---

This piece is an original essay that was commissioned for this volume. It is updated from the version that appeared in the fourth edition. Although the images referenced in this article do not appear in this book, a list with all the source information is provided at the end of the article.

being defined as "whores by nature" (incapable of ever saying *no* to sex, being basically made for sex). Pornography, in this view, is not about the "joy of sex" but about the domination and "denigration of women and a fear and hatred of the female body" (Kaplan, 1991, p. 322).

What is believed to be denigrating is culturally specific—contingent upon social, religious, and moralistic systems. For example, sexuality and nakedness is not intrinsically a source of shame, nor is being in a physically lower position, which, really, is just closer to the Earth. It is our beliefs that make these shameful. Intersecting oppressions based in sex, race, class, and other factors depend upon hierarchies. To construct a hierarchy, you start by fragmenting and simplifying something whole and complex (like human), then creating two parts that distort complexity, like man and woman, and then declare one part superior and opposite to the other. Everyone and everything gets split up and put into a top-down hierarchy: high over low, Heaven over Earth, light over dark, mind over body, spirit over sex. Everyone and everything that can be associated with the top half is seen as superior, while those relegated to the bottom are stigmatized.

My plan in this chapter is to criticize select popular representations that transmit and normalize this everyday pornographic paradigm. Some readers might see them the same way I do; others might not. Popular culture is not monolithic and representations are open to interpretation. My intent is to suggest that the pornographic "habit of thinking" underlies and supports oppressions, including not only sexism, but also homophobia, transphobia, racism, colonization, and ecocide (wanton destruction against the Earth and nature). Pornography is everyday, not just in the sense that coded versions of it populate mainstream images, but also because its precepts underlie mainstream ideas and practices.

Gender Pornography

In conventional notions of gender, women and men are opposite and unequal, with specific gendered attributes, such as masculine aggression and feminine passivity. However different and unequal, the story goes, men and women still are (and must be!) attracted to each other, and *only* to each other. These gender norms thereby normalize and make "sexy" inequality, domination, and even violence and are reflected in conventional representations of "ideal," that is heteronormative, couples.

In most mainstream advertising images, the heteronormative couple is the only romantic configuration represented. The man is upright, taller, stronger, richer, older, bolder, and colder. He does not wear makeup or color his hair. He is self-contained, stands firmly on the ground and is dressed, often, in a business suit or some other status-oriented or functional garb. In short, he is in the power position. The woman, however, often has glazed eyes and is unsteady, often due to the shoes she is wearing or because she is tilting to one side, jutting out one hip or turning one foot out and over. With great frequency, she is "put down," (literally placed on the floor) or constrained (up against a wall, or in the man's grip). She is shorter, warmer, weaker, vulnerable, and younger. Sometimes, she is in a state of partial or even total undress, and what she does wear is coded as alluring. She is "sex" and she is accessible. In short, she is represented as socially powerless.

Even when both people in such common representations are undressed, the man is clearly the dominant partner. Gucci makes a fragrance called "Guilty"; one ad (2013) shows an embracing, apparently naked, White man and White woman (from the shoulders up). (Image 4) The man is unsmiling, steady, and looks directly at the viewer, while the woman is turned to the side, has her mouth partly open, and her head tilted back, baring her throat (standard body language indicating submission). His hand comes around her neck, with the thumb pressed up against the side of her neck, suggesting that he could easily apply pressure on her neck, while her arms are loosely draped over his shoulders.

Calvin Klein ads are known for their tendency to glorify sexual objectification and abuse of girls and women, suggesting child sexual abuse, domestic violence, and gang rape. The most insidious are perhaps the more subtle as these often slip under our critical radar. Consider a 2007 ad for CKIN2U fragrance. It shows a young White couple, posed against a gray concrete wall. (Image 5) He is taller and leaning over her, while her back is against that wall. His left hand presses into the wall, while his right tugs on her long hair. His look is determined, hers dazed. Both wear jeans, but hers are low cut and a good deal of skin is showing. His belt is undone and her hand is wrapped limply around its end. The situation is clearly sexual, but with an obvious power differential. He seems determined to get "IN2" her, while she is passive. Moreover, he is backing her up against that unyielding barrier. The phrase "up against the wall" means literally to be trapped, cornered and put into a situation with no escape and no options. Pressure and coercion, not consent, is the sexually charged dynamic here.

This same version of power-over sex is more obvious in another fragrance ad from the same year. This one is for "Sean Jean Unforgiveable Woman," a product line created by the hip-hop star, P. Diddy Combs. (Image 6) An African American couple is featured in what appears to be a sexual situation, once again with a wall as backdrop. This time, the man (Combs) crushes the woman, whose back is to him, up against that wall. Both of his arms are around her, holding her there. In profile, her eyes are closed, her right arm flails back as if in futile resistance. The perfume's name, "Unforgivable Woman," implies that she has done something to deserve this sexualized punishment. When taking in such images, we should know that from 2 to 4 million women are victims of domestic violence every year in the United States, that rape is a core element in that abuse, and that Black women are reported to experience domestic violence at a rate 35% higher than that of White women, and about 2.5 times the rate of women of other races (Rennison & Welchans, 2000). This is a continuing legacy of U.S. racism, which continues to impoverish Black people and also make helping services much less accessible to women of color.[3]

The rightness of male sexual domination of women is assumed, even when there seems to be a challenge. A photo illustrating a 2007 *Cosmopolitan* article (Benjamin, 2007) shows a White woman lying on top and clearly over a White man in bed. The theme of the piece is that some men entertain a fantasy of a girlfriend playing the role of "boss lady" in bed. But nothing is really that different here. The sexuality is still focused on domination and submission, and his "boss lady" fantasy is something "secret," to be enacted only "every once in a while" and only in the bedroom. Proper gender roles remain in place: The onus is placed on the woman to fulfill the man's fantasies. As the "boss lady" reference indicates, our

hierarchical social institutions, including work, the family, schools, churches, and the military, are based in someone "on top" ordering someone else around. But why not shared leadership? Why not consensus as the basis for decision making?

These everyday hierarchies begin with the imbalance of power required by proper gender roles and influence the ways many of us fantasize and express our desires. After the legalization of marriage equality, the social pressure to be heterosexual is lessening, but particularly in some families, areas of the country, and faith traditions, that pressure remains strong. So too is the ideology that the only people who are attractive embody conventional masculine dominance and feminine submission. Gender porn underlies the popularity of E. L. James's *Fifty Shades of Grey* trilogy, as it absurdly promises that a "virginal good girl . . . can lead the dark bad boy to salvation (Gay, 2011, p. 197). Roxane Gay argues compellingly that "the books are, essentially, a detailed primer for how to successfully engage in a controlling abusive relationship" (p. 201). Once again, as in other favorites like *Pretty Woman* and *Twilight,* a troubled man's unfolding and increasing control over a woman is deceptively presented as the ultimate love story.

The trilogy famously features BDSM (bondage and discipline, sadism and masochism) sexuality, which explicitly sexualizes domination and submission. But many who practice BDSM diverge from the traditional power imbalances (and silences) in conventional sexual relationships around the crucial issue of consent (Jolles, 2016). They put forth an ethic of explicit consent for all sexual activities. What feminists call explicit and enthusiastic consent (Friedman & Valenti, 2008) needs to be part of all sexual relationships. Still, our ability to consent freely often remains compromised by social inequalities and hatreds (including self-hatreds) based in gender, sex, race, age, sexuality, ability, and so on. Sometimes, an experience of childhood sexual abuse can result in someone having difficulty maintaining boundaries, or learning to associate sexuality with domination and abuse, either as victim or perpetrator.

Whatever our choice of sexual practices, I hope that we affirm enthusiastic consent and consider the ways that sexualities have been and continue to be formed in an unequal world long based in sexualized hierarchies. Yearning for something better, we might also continue to imagine and generate sexual desires and practices reflective of a culture based in justice, freedom, equality, community, and reverence for life, human and nonhuman.

Sex-and-Violence

The normalization of sexual domination fused into conventional gender roles manifests vividly in the ways that slang words for sexual intercourse equate it with violence: *fucking, nailing, screwing, hitting on, banging, beating the pussy up,* and so on. The first two official definitions of the verb *fuck* are "to engage in heterosexual intercourse" and "to harm irreparably; finish; victimize" (Sheidlower, 1999, pp. 117, 124). In this schema, "the man" (or masculine-identified partner) is the one doing the "fucking" and the one getting "fucked" is "the girl" (even if this partner is male). In this scheme, "manhood" can never just be a given, but must be perpetually proven. A man must regularly demonstrate that he is the one "on top," that he has no trace of what is defined as "feminine." This setup leaves boys and men constantly vulnerable and liable to humiliation and functions as the basis for misogyny as well as homophobia. When boys and men and also women and girls sexually harass boys and men with words, they call them *woman, whore, pussy, bitch,* as well as *sissy, faggot* and *punk,* putting them in the place of the woman. To prove manhood, men, one way or another, have to assert domination, most efficiently and most effectively by being violent (Gilligan, 1996).

A 2009 ad for Dockers takes on the role of the homophobic, misogynist bully, showing a male figure from the top of his head to his knees. (Image 7) From the waist down, we see only pants-clad legs. Above, an outline of the body is filled in by a stream of screaming words scolding that man and proclaiming that a "genderless" society has stripped them of their manhood and left them "stranded on the road between boyhood and androgyny." Dockers demands that all males "answer the call of manhood," take charge, and "WEAR THE PANTS." This is a resounding call for gender conformity in behavior as well as dress. In mainstream American culture since the 1960s, women can mostly get away with wearing pants, but men still cannot wear skirts in most situations. Men who do cross-dress in popular representations can be acceptable only if they present themselves as obvious comic characters, whose maleness and

heterosexuality are still apparent. Some element of cross-dressing for women is allowed as long as it can be presented as titillating for men, and as long as the women are clearly straight, feminine, seductive, and often partly undressed. If not, they too are punished.

The Dockers ad is a call for sexist domination. Dockers' mandate to "wear the pants" intends to make us think of what is inside the pants and fall sway to the pornographic notion that the penis inherently is an instrument of violence. Male heroes in popular culture invariably are pictured not only wearing pants, but also wielding weapons, usually guns, and the bigger the better. In Freudian psychoanalysis, as well as popular understandings, these weapons are phallic symbols.

In 2012 Adam Lanza, a small, weak, mentally disturbed, 20-year-old White man from a wealthy family, first killed his mother and then six adult women and 20 children at a Newtown, Connecticut elementary school. He used two weapons, including a Bushmaster assault rifle belonging to his mother; he then killed himself. Most such crimes are committed by White and relatively privileged young men, though often ones who do not fit a masculine ideal. It is interesting to look at the ways that the Bushmaster rifle had been advertised, not to suggest that it had any direct influence on Adam Lanza, but to see it as evidence of the kind of overall gender pornography that links men with violence and sets them in opposition to women. The Bushmaster rifle in earlier ads was touted as coming replete with a "man card," which would allow men to avert "complete humiliation." (Image 8) This card, the ad proclaimed, also bestowed "rights and privileges," including being able to "belch loudly" and "leave the seat up." Implicit in this kind of language is a suggestion that women constrain, oppress, and humiliate boys and men and that gun violence is a way to get revenge, if not their "right and privilege."

On Valentine's Day 2013, the celebrated Olympic hero, Oscar Pistorius (nicknamed "the Blade Runner" due to his use of two prosthetic legs) shot four bullets through a bathroom door in his bedroom in the middle of the night, killing his girlfriend, Reeva Steenkamp, who had been spending the night with him. In 2016, he was sentenced to 6 years in prison. He had claimed innocence, saying that he believed he was shooting an intruder and hadn't noticed that Steenkamp was no longer in their bed. Many suggest, instead, that this might have been a lethal episode of domestic violence. Horribly, an earlier Nike ad featuring Pistorius had happily equated him to a bullet. It showed him sprinting, with the caption "I am the bullet in the chamber," together with Nike's "Just do it" slogan and logo. (Image 9)

One of the posters for the antihero superhero film *Deadpool* (2016) features Deadpool (played by Ryan Reynolds) lying on the ground, going against conventional gender posing. (Image 10) But this is a joke, spoofing Burt Reynold's 1972 nude pose for *Cosmopolitan* and there is a significant difference. Burt hides his genitals with his arm, but Ryan Reynolds, instead, dangles a gun right over his crotch. Visual metaphors both comic and serious relentlessly equate the penis to a gun. These contribute to a gender pornography that fuses sex to violence and also implies that maleness itself is innately violent. They try to make us forget that neither a male nor a penis is innately like a weapon, permanently hard, mechanical, and lethal. On the contrary, the penis is more often soft, always sensitive, often fertile and, like all of life, fragile (Dyer, 1993; Marcus, 1992). When the penis is represented as a weapon, rape becomes its purpose, intercourse becomes a kind of murder, and the will to hurt becomes definitive of being a man.

Sexual Assault and Harassment

Journalist Mickey Rapkin (2014) wrote a profile of Travis Kalanick, the founder of Uber, the "on-demand car service," for *Vanity Fair*. Rapkin (2014) reports that when he teased Kalanick "about his skyrocketing desirability," Kalanick responded "with a wisecrack about women on demand: 'Yeah, we call that Boob-er.'" This quip—reducing women to a body part, ordered up when desired—evinces an attitude characteristic of a culture of sexual harassment and discrimination. According to widely publicized information from a former female employee, the Uber workplace is just such a culture (Fowler, 2017), something the company is now internally investigating.

During the 2016 presidential campaign, a leaked tape from 2005 featured another famous billionaire, this time Republican candidate Donald Trump, also making statements many found troubling. He boasted about how his fame and money gave him license to kiss women and "do anything," even "grab them by the pussy" without their consent. When outrage ensued, as these actions constitute criminal sexual assault, Trump insisted this was merely "locker room banter" and thus inconsequential. Many of his supporters agreed and Trump went on to be elected president of the United States. At least 13 women have accused Donald Trump of forcibly kissing them or touching them without their consent and several are now suing him (Pagones, 2017).

Even if this is just "talk," that kind of talk does normalize sexual assault, minimizes its harm, and encourages men to do it. This pornographic habit of thinking is matched throughout our visual culture where women (often reduced to body parts) are everywhere on display, where men act and women get acted on.

This setup is at the foundation of what feminist theorist Sharon Marcus (1992) calls the "rape script." Habitually, she says, our culture represents men's bodies as penetrating, aggressive forces and women's bodies as inner and open spaces to be invaded, occupied and owned, a body without will or capacity for violence, including defensive violence.

A 2007 ad for business loans offered by J.P. Morgan Chase is set in a dress store. (Image 11) The ad features a young, demure Asian woman. Asian women are stereotypically represented as hypersexual—either dangerous "Dragon Ladies" or docile and submissive sex slaves. This woman stands with eyes and head downcast and holds a sign at womb level reading "OPEN." Flanking her are frocks, draped on headless mannequins. Visually, the composition suggests that the women, like the store, is "open," completely available, without will (indicated by her lowered, submissive gaze) and without even a voice to protest (the headless mannequins). A 2005 ad for St. Pauli Girl beer draws similarly on the rape script and indicates that alcohol facilitates the assault: "It's hard to get some girls to open up. Others just need a bottle opener." (Image 12) In other words, get her drunk.

One of the most extreme, and notorious, rape-friendly ads is one for Dolce Gabbana that appeared in 2007. (Image 13) It shows a blank-looking and passive White woman in a bathing suit pinned to the ground by one White man, while four others look on. International protests ensued for its too obvious suggestion of gang rape and D&G pulled the ad. A few years later, undeterred, Calvin Klein issued a very similar ad; again protests ensued and the ad was banned in Australia. This enthusiasm for rape persists. In 2015, a Bloomingdales' billboard in New York City glorified this rapist scenario: a White man looks appraisingly at a White woman, unaware of his gaze. The copy urges him to "Spike your best friend's eggnog when they're not looking." Again, thankfully, protests ensued and the ad was withdrawn (Dostis, 2015).

On occasion, imagery suggests male-on-male rape, as in a Dolce Gabana ad from 2008. This showed an all-White male group, with a seemingly passed out young White man on the floor. (Image 14) There was no widespread protest but there should have been. Due to homophobia and gender norms, the subject of male-on-male rape is still so locked up in denial and taboo that any outcry was foreclosed.

The Sexual Double Standard

Male supremacists would have us believe that all cultures have been and are now patriarchal. But patriarchy is relatively new in human culture, dating back 5 to 7 millennia (Lerner, 1986) and is not, even today, universal.

A complex sexual double standard abides at the foundation of patriarchal culture. First of all, there are different rules for men and women. Men are not stigmatized by having multiple sex partners, but women are excoriated as "sluts," as all "used up." The reasons go back to the origins of patriarchy when women and their children were first deemed the property of men. This is why women go from bearing their father's name to their husband's upon marriage; why brides are supposed to be "virgins," and hence undamaged "goods"; and why abortion was first made a crime (the fetus was part of the holdings and future wealth of the father).

In this schema, women are split into "private" or "public" property, *aka* "good girls" or "bad girls," and if "good," their chastity is key to their father's or husband's honor. A 2016 popular Super Bowl ad for Hyundai, "First Date," is premised upon this primal sexist setup.[4] Comedian Kevin Hart plays a father intent on preserving his daughter's virginity (no mother is viewed in the ad). When a date comes calling, Hart hands him the keys to his car (why doesn't the daughter drive?) and then uses the car's high-tech location

features to stalk his daughter and intervene throughout her date to keep them from even kissing. Stalking is a criminal offense, but this commercial makes it seem normal "dad" behavior and all in good fun.

All the actors in this commercial seem middle class and all are the same race, African American. This is significant as the sexual double standard is heavily influenced along lines of race, ethnicity, class, and sexuality. "Good girls" are affiliated with men who have social standing. They must be "pure," faithful, and chaste, or their own men may well turn on them, even kill them to maintain "honor." When prominent men deplore other men's sexually assaultive behavior on the grounds that they "have wives, sisters, and daughters," this does not condemn the sexual assault. It just means that they don't want "their" women to be treated this way. Implicitly, it remains fine for men to treat the women socially beneath them that way—enslaved women, colonized women, racially stigmatized women, poor women, sex workers, lesbians, sexually autonomous women, unveiled women, even women out in public unescorted by a man. These stereotypes animate "rape myths," deeming "bad girls" unrapeable and also helping to exculpate the men who prey on them.

Soap ads have a long history of projecting these ideologies. One from 1995 shows an upright, young blonde White woman in a white blouse, alongside the word *PURE*. It looks, on the one hand, like an endorsement of female chastity and on the other, a neo-Nazi poster evoking White-supremacist notions of "purity" of blood. (Image 15) The other side of that stereotype is rendered in a 1995 ad for Diesel jeans. It shows a dark-skinned woman, who, the copy announces, is a "dangerous animal . . . using the planet as a toilet." (Image 16) She is laid out on Zebra-striped sheets and her jeans are unzipped, signaling her absolute sexual availability to all men. Significantly, even the "pure" woman has some skin showing between her shirt and her jeans, signifying that she too is open and available to the "right" men.

These same themes are more recapitulated in a 2011 ad for Dove Body Wash. (Image 17) This shows three towel-clad women in a "before/after" progression. A larger Black woman occupies the "before" position on the left. She poses sexily, with hand on jutting hip. Succeeding her is a lighter-skinned and thinner Latina, making a more reserved but similar sexual gesture. The "after" position is held by a thin and demurely posed White woman. Dove argu-ably is equating "White" to "clean." This is not as obvious as the 1995 ads, but sometimes innuendo is potent nonetheless, as the meaning bypasses critical awareness, but sinks in subconsciously.

Distorted notions of purity and dirtiness are used not only to promote sexism and racism, but also homophobia and transphobia. In March of 2005, an extraordinary interfaith alliance of male religious leaders formed to try to stop an international gay pride festival in Jerusalem. One leader stated the groups' aim: "We can't permit anybody to come and make the Holy City dirty" (Goodstein & Myre, 2005). A 2004 ad for gum makes a similar point. (Image 18) It shows a young White woman, with short brown hair, minimal makeup, and wearing a button-down shirt and tie. A sewer cover is shoved into her mouth. The copy reads: "Dirty Mouth, Clean it up with Orbit." The implication here is that it is the cross-dresser, transman, or lesbian who is dirty and should be abused, silenced, and "cleaned up."

This justification of violence against or stig-matization of those who are labeled as "animal-istic," "dark," and "dirty" is linked to an overall pattern of body loathing and concomitant disre-spect for nature (including human nature) and the dark Earth, the original source of *dirt* and the source of all life. Aspects of human life, like our animality, sexuality, defecation, emotional-ity, and aging are cast as "nature" and inferior to (masculine- and usually White-identified) rationality, culture, and "civilization." Accord-ingly, (Mother) Earth is treated as mere matter, body without mind, something for "mankind" to exploit and use. It is no wonder that environmen-tal damage is so often spoken about as *rape* of the Earth. Dominating cultures try to forget that rul-ing men too are human beings, made of earth, a kind of animal, and also that other animals also are *beings,* not things. Men's (and women's) hier-archical violence against those stigmatized by sex, gender, sexuality, race, class, religion, or nation as "dirty," "low," "bestial," and "other" is part of an overall pattern of violence against the Earth.

Objectification and Dehumanization

The now common demand to recognize that "women's rights are human rights" was first intro-duced by Brazilian feminists in 1945 during the conference that created the United Nations. Still today, many state, religious, and social systems do not recognize men's abuses against women as human rights' violations because women are not recognized as full human beings (MacKinnon, 2006). In the world of representation, the denial of women's humanity is performed over and over in everyday pornographic images conflating women with fruit, meat (Adams, 2003), drink, cars, tech devices, and other consumables and commodities (Caputi, 2006). Michelob and Budweiser have fea-tured ads that show a beer bottle as a sexy, young, White woman's body. (Image 19) And the video for "Birthday Song" by 2Chainz with Kanye West shows a female celebrant carrying a chocolate cake in the form of a woman's buttocks (Crunklife, 2012).

Racism and classism intervene, influencing these depictions. The novelist Alice Walker (1980) pungently observes: "Where White women are depicted in pornography as 'objects,' Black women are depicted as animals" (p. 103). Women of color, in particular, are shown in ways suggesting that they are "animals" in our culture where animals also are unjustly defined as property, with no legal rights—something animal rights activists are now challenging in the courts.

The U.S. chattel slave system defined Africans as less than human and treated them as a form of livestock. Patricia Hill Collins (2009) argues that the treatment of enslaved women provided a foun-dation for continuing pornographic stereotypes: the White, good chaste girl; the dark/bad sexual girl; the sexualization of bondage and captiv-ity; and dehumanization. One of the most overt examples of this type is a 1999 ad for Moschino apparel that appeared in *Elle* magazine. A very dark-skinned woman, with a big Afro (both sig-nifying her difference from a White supremacist ideal) is garbed in leopard-skin pants. She stands with legs spread wide and arms flung out against what appears to be a wall. Looking closely, you see that she is literally stapled to fabric, like a doll (or a slave) to be sold. (Image 20)

A parallel racist stereotype associates White-ness with the nonanimal, with civilization, science, technology, and progress. So young, slim, and pretty White women, while also shown as animals, commonly are depicted as futurist fembots. A 2007 Heineken television commercial, which retains a following on YouTube, features a platinum blonde, White-skinned robot who dances, sprouts an addi-tional set of mechanical arms, and produces from her torso a keg of Heineken, from which she pours a glass of beer and offers it to viewers. (Image 21) She then splits into three identical models. Here is the ultimate sex object—decorative, entertaining, interchangeable, and with no possibility of a will of her own, existing only to serve. Numerous You-Tube commentators affirm their sexual attraction to this robot, one (Dominatorxxx) deeming her the "perfect woman."[5]

Sexual objectification fits perfectly into a capitalist-consumer and monocultural society. It sexualizes possession itself, and hence creates a desire to buy and own. Sexual objectification in a capitalist culture also defines women as in need of innumerable products and processes to measure up to desirability standards. This includes even bodily mutilation. A 2008 ad for a center for cosmetic surgery shows an Asian woman naked except for fetish-wear underpants. (Image 22) Lines are drawn from key zones of her body, indicating where she has been worked on, for example, "breast augmentation." The headline claims: "WE CAN REBUILD HER." The unmodified female body is a turnoff to a pornographic culture steeped in misogyny, body loathing, and the technological "fix" for the supposed imperfections of flesh. She must be remade into the perfect consumer object.

Regularly, ads call upon girls and women to be "perfect," possessing "flawless" skin, being impossibly slender, light-skinned, straightened hair, and so on. This kind of perfectionism can be read as a kind of fascism, obliterating diversity, as is clear in a 2013 ad for Louis Vuitton. (Image 23) It shows six women in pairs of three, each pair exactly alike and all six made to seem almost interchangeable except that the two identical White women are in the foreground, two identical Asian women at midrange, and two identical Black women at the back. This image not only makes women interchangeable but underscores the same kind of racial hierarchies and dehumanization that characterized the chattel slave and coolie labor systems in the United States.

Dead and Dismembered

Images of dismembered female bodies are the very stuff of slasher films as well as the "snuff" genre of pornography, which document (or purports to document) an actual sexual murder and mutilation. Symbolic dismemberment and sexy female bodies appearing dead have long been the norm in fashion photography (Caputi, 1987). These too

look "normal"; we might notice them if they were being done to male bodies, but they are not in any comparable way.

In the February 2009 issue of *Details,* a photograph illustrating a story about dating during the economic recession showed a White woman turned upside down and dumped in a garbage can. (Image 24) Dismemberment again is the visual motif as all we can see are her high-heeled feet and legs jutting up in the air. This theme of women's severed legs waving in the air is a common one. When Juergen Teller photographed Victoria Beckham in an ad for Marc Jacob's designs, he didn't present her as a glamorous celebrity, but as something less than human, a kind of "living doll" (Horyn, 2008). In one photo, we see only her bare, high-heeled legs flopping spread-eagled over the side of a shopping bag. (Image 25) A 2017 album from Jidenna shows the singer with his head pillowed upon the stocking-clad thigh of a woman. (Image 26) We assume this is an actual woman, but she appears without a head and is pictorially sliced down the middle. She is just a partial torso and thighs, wearing a barely there red bodysuit. The attention is all on her open crotch and spilling-out breasts. Visually, there is no "person" there, just parts.

A "virtual snuff" sensibility has informed countless images in advertising and fashion tableau since the 1970s. Models are showcased in positions suggesting that they are dead: suffocated under plastic bags; heads without bodies, bodies without heads; laid out in gift-boxes; sprawled brokenly on stairs, streets, and boutique floors (Caputi, 2006). A disturbing 2012 ad for a Canon camera shows a young Asian woman on her back, and seemingly washed up at the edge of a lake. (Image 27) She wears a drenched top and short skirt. Her face is blank, water is pooling up in the cavity at the base of her neck, her eyes are closed and her head and arms, resting on the shore's edge, are flung back and out. She could be dead. A few yards away, we see a White man's head and arms as he stands in water that comes up to his neck. He is training a camera on her. The copy reads: "When was the last time something inspired you to be creative?" One possible interpretation of this bizarre scenario is that the man has killed the woman and is now documenting this act in a "snuff" photo. Her destruction becomes his "creativity."

One 2015 ad for the TV series *Murder in the First* shows the stereotypic dead woman.

Written on the closed eyelids of an attractive White woman, implicitly raped and murdered, is the phrase "Dead Girls Don't Talk." (Image 28). Why is this Ok? Why doesn't this look like a hate crime? And can we also see beyond to its rape-murder's relation to other forms of hate crime, including those committed against the Earth?

Monica Sjöö and Barbara Mor (1991) suggest that those silenced, killed, and tortured "images. . . . of female flesh . . . are really our species' maps of the mutilated earth" (p. 411). A 2009 ad for Global Fruits juice shows the Earth strangled and squeezed dry by a pair of male hands. (Image 29) Paralleling the abused and murdered images of women in our popular culture are countless images of the Earth carved up, dismembered, diminished, objectified, targeted, and violated along parallel lines (Caputi, 2016).

Reality Bites Back

In early 2017, an advertising campaign was launched for *Calvin Klein by Appointment*, a "14-look made-to-order collection." Each look is modeled by a girl or woman and shown opposite a pair of white Calvin Klein briefs. One features supermodel Abby Lee Kershaw, spread out on a concrete floor, and wearing only a short, American-flag style skirt. Her eyes are blank and doll-like; her hands are placed to hide her breasts. (Image 30) According to promotional materials, this campaign, was "rolled out simultaneously" with the 2017 Women's March, a worldwide movement protesting the inauguration of Donald Trump. According to creative director Pieter Mulier, this image signifies, like the marches, a "woman feeling empowered" (Yotka, 2017).

This statement is fashionista fakery. The actual marching, protesting and upright women waved signs, including ones declaring "Pussy Grabs Back."[6] They demanded women's human rights, gender, racial, economic, and environmental justice and an end to men's sexual violence against them. None of these aims are even remotely suggested or supported by the Kershaw image. The woman in the picture is once again on the floor, positioned as a helpless and virtually lifeless sex object. The supposedly inevitable and dominating male presence is suggested by the larger-than-life briefs.

Sexual violence is verbal, emotional, psychological, and physical. Psychological sexual violence takes forms aimed at destroying the self-esteem of the victim while enhancing that of the abuser: insults, belittlement, cultivation of anxiety and despair, humiliation, blaming, shaming, accusing, denigration, disrespect, and *reality control*. Reality control is when the abuser denies the actuality of what is going on, creates an atmosphere of threat, and blocks the victim's awareness of alternative ways of living and being.

Repeated, negative mass representation of a group is a public form of psychological abuse. It is a form of spirit-breaking destruction meant to squelch resistance and destroy self-esteem. At the same time, such negative representation feeds the sense of omnipotence of the dominators and says that this world of violence and inequality is the only world possible. Such representation simultaneously blocks awareness of alternative ways of living and being, and stifles the development of any imagination other than the pornographic one.

Numerous theorist/activists counter with alternatives. Sharon Marcus calls for a discourse, verbal and visual, of the female body/mind as no longer "object, property, and . . . inner space," but as powerful, capable of will, capable even of violence. bell hooks (1993) asks heterosexual women to cease sexualizing the dominating "hard man" and to eroticize, instead, equal and respectful relationships. Patricia Hill Collins (2004) puts forth an ethic of "honest bodies that are characterized by sexual autonomy and soul, expressiveness, spirituality, sensuality, sexuality, and an expanded notion of the erotic as a life force" (p. 287).

Collins draws on poet Audre Lorde (1984), who extols what she calls the "erotic," a cosmic force of connectivity and creativity that courses through unfettered sexuality as well as creative work and play. The erotic rejoins body and mind, sex and spirit and is, Lorde claims, our birthright, our bodily access to forces of creativity, ecstasy, and connection and also the energy source that enables us to resist oppression and transform ourselves and our world.

In ancient understandings, the erotic as a cosmic creative force was represented by the figure of a (sex) goddess, sometimes a bisexual divinity, sometimes a mother, sometimes not. She is pictured variously as naked, outside, surrounded by animals or herself part animal, and with spread legs to signify the vulva as sacred and powerful. Patriarchal religions came to power, in part, by defaming and profaning that goddess and trying to eliminate her as a rival by turning her into pornography (Caputi, 2004). Susan L. Taylor (2006), former editorial director of *Essence* magazine, proclaims that now is the time for "Goddess to awaken from patriarchy's trance." She claims that this happens every time "women step into our power." Some will resonate with this symbol; others will generate new ones. This is as it should be, for diversity—as well as fun, pleasure, joy, care, freedom, and reverence for others—is fundamental to the erotic principle.

NOTES

1. My film, *The Pornography of Everyday Life* (Caputi, 2006), distributed by Berkeley Media, www.berkeleymedia.com, incorporates much of this material. This article is an update and revision of my article appearing in a previous edition of this anthology and a related one in Caputi (2004). I thank Melissa Aldana, Shela O'Hea, Lauren Walleser, Ann Scales, Mary Caputi, Peter Cava, Andria Chediak, Rebecca Whisnant, Nicole Calvert, and many students who gave me some of these materials and/or discussed them with me. A list of the sources of the images analyzed in this chapter appears after the references.

2. See http://www.dictionary.com/browse/depants? s=t.

3. For more information see a fact sheet complied by the Institute on Domestic Violence in the African American Community, University of Minnesota (http://www.idvaac.org/media/publications/FactSheet.IDVAAC_AAPCFV-Community%20Insights.pdf).

4. Ad can be viewed at http://www.superbowlcommercials.co/latest-updates/hyundai-super-bowl-commercial-with-kevin-hart/.

5. Ad and comments available at http://www.youtube.com/watch? v=1 -NfrBgYIEQ.

6. This slogan appeared on a T-shirt created in November 2016, at http://www.femalecollective.org/product/pussy-grabs-back.

REFERENCES

Adams, C. (2003). *The Pornography of Meat.* New York: Continuum.

Benjamin, J. (2007, September). The sex he secretly craves. *Cosmopolitan.*

Caputi, J. (2004) *Goddesses and monsters: Women, myth, power and popular culture.* Madison: University of Wisconsin Popular Press.

Caputi, J. (2016). *Feed the green: Feminist voices for the Earth.* DVD. Distributed by Women Make Movies.

Collins, P. H. (2004). *Black sexual politics: African Americans, gender, and the new racism.* New York: Routledge.

Collins, P. H. (2009). *Black feminist thought: Knowledge, consciousness, and the politics of empowerment* (2nd ed.). New York: Routledge.

Crunklife (2012, September 13). Cake! Cake! Cake! Cake!: Let's take 2Chainz to school. *Crunk Feminist Collective.* Retrieved from http://www.crunkfeministcollective.com/2012/09/13/cake-cake-cake-cake-lets-take-2chainz-to-school/

Dostis, M. (2015, November 13). Five other controversial ads in light of Bloomingdale's 'inappropriate' date rape ad. *Daily News.* Retrieved from http://www.nydailynews.com/news/national/bloomingdale-date-rape-ad-joins-5-controversial-ads-article-1.2434214, last visited Feb. 28, 2017.

Dworkin, A. (1989). *Pornography: Men possessing women.* New York: Penguin.

Dyer, R. (1993). Male sexuality in the media. In *The matter of images: Essays on representation* (pp. 111–112). New York: Routledge.

Fowler, S. J. (2017, February 18). Reflecting on one very strange year at Uber [Blog post]. Retrieved from https://www.susanjfowler.com/blog/2017/2/19/reflecting-on-one-very-strange-year-at-uber

Friedman, J., & Valenti, J. (2008). *Yes means yes!: Visions of female sexual power and a world without rape.* Seattle: Seal Press.

Gay, R. (2011). *Bad feminist.* New York: HarperCollins.

Gilligan, J. (1996). *Violence: Reflections on a national epidemic.* New York: Random House.

Goodstein, L., & Myre, G. (2005, March 31). Clerics Fighting a gay festival for Jerusalem. *New York Times.*

hooks, b. (1993). Seduced by violence no more. In E. Buchward, P. Fletcher, & M. Roth (Eds.), *Transforming a rape culture* (pp. 351–356). Minneapolis: Milkweed.

Horyn, C. (2008, April 10). When is a fashion ad not a fashion ad? *New York Times.*

James, E. L. (2012). *Fifty shades of grey trilogy.* New York: Vintage.

Jolles, M. (2016). Pleasure, pain, and the feminist politics of rough sex. In S. Tarrant (Ed.), *Gender, sex, and politics* (pp. 263–274). New York: Routledge.

Kaplan, L. J. (1991). *Female perversions: The temptations of Emma Bovary.* New York: Doubleday.

Kelly, V. (2007). What is it about the walls? In M. Ochoa & B. K. Ige (Eds.), *Shout out: Women of color respond to violence* (pp. 3–25). Emeryville, CA: Seal Press.

Lerner, G. (1986). *The creation of patriarchy.* New York: Oxford.

Lorde, A. (1984). Uses of the erotic: The erotic as power. In *Sister outsider* (pp. 53–59). Trumansburg, NY: The Crossing Press.

MacKinnon, C. A. (2006). *Are women human? And other international dialogues.* Cambridge: Harvard University Press.

Pagones, S. (2017, January 21). "Women accusing Trump of sexual assault refuse to back down. *New York Post.* Retrieved from http://nypost.com/2017/01/21/woman-accusing-trump-of-sexual-assault-refuse-to-back-down/

Rapkin, M. (2014, February 27). Uber cab confessions. *GQ.* Retrieved from http://www.gq.com/story/uber-cab-confessions

Rennison, M. & Welchans, W. (2000). *Intimate partner violence* (NCJ 178247). Washington, DC: U.S. Department of Justice, Office of Justice Programs, Bureau of Justice Statistics. Retrieved from http://www.bjs.gov/content/pub/pdf/ipv.pdf

Sheidlower, J. (Ed.) (1999). *The F-word* (2nd ed.). New York: Random House.

Sjöö, M., & Mor, B. (1991). *The great cosmic Mother: Rediscovering the religion of the Earth* (2nd ed.). San Francisco: HarperSanFrancisco.

Taylor, S. L. (2006, October). The goddess within. *Essence.*

Walker, A. (1980). Coming apart. In Laura Lederer (Ed.), *Take back the night: Women on pornography,* (pp. 95–104). New York: Bantam Books.

Williams, P. J. (1995). *The rooster's egg: On the persistence of prejudice.* Cambridge, MA: Harvard University Press.

Yotka, S. (2017, January 22). Calvin Klein launches made-to-measure service. *Vogue.* Retrieved from http://www.vogue.com/article/calvin-klein-by-appointment-2.

LIST OF IMAGES

8. Bushmaster, "Man Card" ads, 2012. (See two of the relevant ads and read commentary at Hamilton Nolan, "Bushmaster Firearms, Your Man Card Is Revoked," Gawker, Dec. 17, 2012. Retrieved at http://gawker.com/5969150/bushmaster-firearms-your-man-card-is-revoked?post=55340293

9. Busbee, J. (2013, February 14). Oscar Pistorius Nike ad takes on new, chilling resonance after tragedy. *Yahoo! Sports.* Retrieved from http://sports.yahoo.com/blogs/olympics-fourth-place-medal/oscar-pistorius-nike-ad-takes-chilling-resonance-tragedy-182235671–oly.html

10. This poster was designed by Ten30 Studios, available at http://www.impawards.com/2016/deadpool_ver13.htmlm.

11. © JPMorganChase, 2007.

12. Pauli Girl Beer, 2005, © Imported By Barton Beers, Ltd., Chicago.

13. Dolce Gabbana, 2007. Retrieved from http://nextshark.com/people-are-pissed-at-dolce-gabbana-again-for-these-ads-depicting-gang-rape/

14. Dolce Gabbana, 2008. Retrieved from www.bilerico.com/2008/06/dolce_gabbana_sells_gang_rape.php

15. "Pure," © 1994 Neutrogena Corp.

16. Diesel Jeans, source unknown, c. 1995.

17. "Dove Body Wash," 2011. (See the ad and read commentary, including Dove's rebuttal at http://www.huffingtonpost.com/2011/05/23/dove-visiblecare-ad-racist_n_865911.html

18. "Dirty Mouth," © 2004 Wm. Wrigley Jr. Co.

19. Michelob beer ad, 2003, source unknown.

20. Moschino, *Elle,* © 1999.

21. "Heineken: Keg," 2007. Retrieved from http://www.youtube.com/watch?v=1-NfrBgYIEQ

22. New Beauty Center, Ocean Drive, Miami, FL, 2008.

23. Louis Vuitton. Set Design Daniel Buren © ADAGP-Paris & DB 2012, *New York Times Style Magazine,* February 17, 2013.

24. *Details,* February 2009.

25. Photo in *New York Times,* April 10, 2008, accompanying the article by Horyn.

26. "Jidenna," *The Chief,* album cover. Retrieved from http://www.xxlmag.com/rap-music/reviews/2017/02/jidenna-the-chief-album-review/. (The cover is a play on a 1970 Boz Skaggs album cover.)

27. ©2012 Canon U.S.A.

28. *Murder in the First,* © 2014. Turner Entertainment Networks, Inc. This appeared in *People* magazine.

29. Global Fruits, *Backpacker Magazine,* 2009.

30. Calvin Klein by Appointment. Retrieved from http://explore.calvinklein.com/en_GB/page/byappointment

DEADLY LOVE

39

Images of Dating Violence in the "Twilight Saga"

Victoria E. Collins and Dianne C. Carmody

INTIMATE PARTNER AND DATING VIOLENCE

. . . In the past several decades, researchers have documented the prevalence and nature of violence that is perpetrated in the course of heterosexual relationships (Smith-Stover, 2005). Most of this research has focused on intimate partner violence by married or cohabiting partners, with a smaller collection of studies limited to violence among those in dating relationships, especially young people in high school and college (Eckhardt, Jamieson, & Watts, 2002; Gover, Kaukinen, & Fox, 2008). A greater understanding of the behaviors that are common to both intimate partner and dating violence may be gleaned from the following brief review of the literature.

Dating violence is gendered, with females suffering higher rates of victimization and injury than males (Centers for Disease Control and Prevention, 2000). At particular risk are adolescent males and females (Kim-Godwin et al., 2009). This vulnerability has been attributed to adolescents' tendency to exaggerate gender roles, as well as their subscription to fantastical ideals of romance (Prothrow-Stith, 1993). Estimates indicate that 2–9% of male adolescents and 4–20% of female adolescents in the United States have been victims of physical or sexual abuse at the hands their dating partners (Howard, Wang, & Yan, 2007). . . . Female adolescents have also reported greater levels of fear as a direct result of their victimization (O'Keefe, 2005).

Dating has traditionally been defined within the context of heterosexual relationships and is influenced by socially accepted forms of masculinity and femininity. Adelman and Kil (2007) described "conservative dating conflicts," characterized by dominant heterosexual comprehensions of masculinity and femininity, emphasizing the supremacy of intimate, romantic relationships over all other relationships. They noted that these conflicts occur when individuals become isolated from other societal relationships, including those with friends and family members, and can lead to the objectification of dating partners, jealously, and possessiveness. Bernard, Bernard, and Bernard (1985) also noted that strong patriarchal attitudes are linked to an increased risk of violence by men in dating relationships. Dating violence is strongly associated with dominant forms of masculinity and femininity (Black & Weisz, 2003; Feldman & Gowen, 1998).

Researchers have long noted the similarities between dating violence and intimate partner violence, both of which are linked to issues of power and control (Gover et al., 2008). The feminist perspective purports that intimate partner violence results from a social structure that is inherently male dominated and the socialization of males and females into specific gender roles (Pagelow, 1984; Prospero, 2007). These socialization processes reinforce socially appropriate behaviors for both sexes in a patriarchal society that promotes male privilege (Prospero, 2007). Social norms support the use of relationship violence as a means for the male to remain in control of the female (Marin & Russo, 1999).

Tactics that are designed to exert power and control have been identified as strong predictors of dating violence (Kaura & Allen, 2004; Riggs & O'Leary, 1996). In relationships in which power differentials exist and decision making is not shared, dating violence is more likely to occur

From Victoria E. Collins and Dianne C. Carmody (2011). "Deadly Love: Images of Dating Violence in the 'Twilight Saga.'" *Affilia* 26:382. Reprinted with permission of SAGE Publications.

(Felson & Messner, 2000). Instances of violence result from struggles over who is going to make important decisions in the relationship and dissatisfaction over the perceived level of power that each partner possesses (Hendy et al., 2003; Pulerwitz, Gortmaker, & DeJong, 2000; Ronfeldt, Kimerling, & Arias, 1998). Behaviors, such as stalking and threats of homicide and suicide, have been found to be strongly correlated with future violence and homicide (McFarlane et al., 1999; Roehl, O'Sullivan, Webster, & Campbell, 2005). Research has also indicated that 75–90% of femicide victims were stalked prior to their murder (McFarlane et al., 1999), and in a high proportion of femicide cases, the perpetrator committed suicide following the act of homicide (Roehl et al., 2005).

It has been estimated that between 20% and 96% of dating relationships contain psychologically abusive behavior (James, West, Deters, & Armijo, 2000; Jezl, Molidor, & Wright, 1996). The presence of psychological abuse in dating relationships is positively related to the risk of physical violence (Kasian & Painter, 1992). Foshee (1996) identified four types of psychological abuse in adolescent dating relationships: Threatening behavior, which includes threats of physical violence; behavior monitoring, in which the perpetrator forces the victim to communicate where they are physically located; personal insults; and emotional manipulation. In addition, interpersonal violence has been found to be strongly associated with suicide and suicidal ideations for both the perpetrator and the victim of the dating violence (Swahn, Lubell, & Simon, 2004).

Research has also demonstrated that violence and love often become intertwined in adolescent relationships (Black & Weisz, 2003; James et al., 2000; Vezina, Lavoie, & Piche, 1995). In a 1990 study, Carlson found that the majority of adolescents supported the use of violence against a dating partner in some situations. In addition, Bergman's (1992) study of high school students showed that more than 79% of the girls who had experienced dating violence continued to date the perpetrators of that violence.

DATING VIOLENCE AND THE MEDIA

The media have been found to have an impact on a wide range of adolescent issues, such as sexual activity, smoking, substance abuse, body image, obesity, and violence (Brown et al., 2006; Brown &

Witherspoon, 2002; Collins et al., 2004). Although causality has not been established, the media have been found to influence teenagers' attitudes and indirectly to affect behaviors (Brown et al., 2006; Collins et al., 2004). Teenagers are well aware of the way the media shape their attitudes and behaviors (Lavoie, Robitaille, & Hébert, 2000), and they turn to media sources for information on dating and romantic relationships. Borzekowski and Rickert (2001) found that 23% of teenagers used the Internet-accessed information about dating violence.

Violence is not exclusive to television or the Internet and can be found in other forms of media that have a teenage audience. Certainly, movies that are popular among teenagers include considerable violence (Sargent et al., 2002), as do music lyrics and videos (Haynes, 2009; Strasburger, 1995). A large proportion of the media, including music, movies, television, and books, specifically target a teenage audience.

Because violence has been recognized as being an acceptable expression of love in adolescent relationships (Vezina et al., 1995), it is necessary to examine the social messages that teenagers are receiving through the media. Of particular interest is Stephenie Meyer's *Twilight* Saga. This four-book series has a core target audience of teenage girls (Stone, 2009; Young, 2009) and has sold an estimated 40 million copies worldwide since its debut in 2005 (Memmott & Cadden, 2009). The series is centered on the relationship between a 17-year-old girl (Bella) and a 17-year-old vampire (Edward) and has sparked much controversy over the modeling of a healthy relationship for teenagers (McCulloch, 2009; Stone, 2009; Young, 2009). The series also includes a teenager named Jacob, who competes with Edward for Bella's affections.

The series has been said to be attractive to teenage girls because it portrays a "traditional, romantic relationship" and positively frames the issue of abstinence (Stone, 2009). Christian publications have heralded the book series, noting that the characters restrain from engaging in sexual intercourse until they are married (Smith, 2008) and portray themes of immense self-control in the face of temptation. Others, however, have criticized the series for modeling unhealthy, inequitable romantic relationships. In a 2009 article published by MSNBC, the relationship between the two main characters, Bella and Edward, was labeled "controlling" (Young, 2009). Others have argued that the books contain "a dark undercurrent of sexual assault and abuse"

(Editorial, 2009), identifying unhealthy relationship behaviors that are synonymous with stalking, self-harm, and suicide (McCulloch, 2009). Clearly, critics disagree about the presentation of adolescent relationships in the *Twilight* series. The study presented here examined the book series with special attention to behaviors that are commonly associated with dating and intimate partner violence.

THEORETICAL FRAMEWORK

The analysis was guided by feminist theories, which "analyze women's experiences, articulate the nature of social relations between women and men, and provide explanations that support efforts to transform these social relations" (Swigonski & Raheim, 2011, pp. 10–11). Specifically, gender-reform feminism provides the framework (Lorber, 2005). This approach focuses on gender inequality in the social order and its cultural and structural components. To be female in the United States brings a variety of disadvantages, such as lower pay than males for the same work and disproportionate exposure to sexual harassment, sexual assault, and other forms of gender-based violence (Tong, 2009). These disadvantages do not apply equally to all women; wealthy, white, attractive, heterosexual, and able-bodied women tend to have fewer disadvantages. In fact, more recent feminist theorists have argued that we must note the "complexities of multiple, competing, fluid, and intersecting identities" (Gringeri, Wahab, & Anderson-Nathe, 2010, p. 394).

Philaretou and Allen (2001) noted that under societally enforced, strict gender-role guidelines, men are pressured to use aggression and competition in romantic relationships. In this way, masculinity emphasizes sexualized violence and dominance. In an examination of adolescent masculinities, Messerschmidt (2000) also noted that under hegemonic masculinity, which is both youthful and heterosexual, force may be acceptable in romantic relationships. Such gender stereotypes, reinforced by mediated messages, may certainly encourage dating violence and perceptions of romance that reflect traditional gender roles.

METHOD

An ethnographic content analysis (Altheide, 1996) of the four books in the *Twilight* series provided the basis for the study. Table 1 presents brief overviews of the plots of the four books in the series. Prior to the coding, conceptual coding categories were identified, on the basis of previous research on predictors of dating violence (Felson & Messner, 2000; Hendy et al., 2003; Kaura & Allen, 2004). . . . These predictors included physical violence, which was defined as actual or threats of unwanted physical touching, pushing, and hitting; sexual violence, which was defined as unwanted or forced sexual behaviors, including physical harm and violence perpetrated during sexual acts; and controlling behaviors. Controlling behaviors were divided into three subcategories for the purpose of coding. These categories included (a) physical control, which included physically detaining, restraining, or preventing a character from moving in order to obtain compliance; (b) verbal orders, such as demanding that someone do something; and (c) emotional control, which involved one character controlling the dissemination of information to another character, reacting with anger to threaten another character into compliance, or making threats to harm a loved one or himself if the character did not comply with his wishes. In addition, stalking behaviors, such as following and constantly monitoring a partner's location, were coded. Since jealousy is often used to justify such behaviors, it was also included in the analysis. Another category was male aggressiveness, which included the three subcategories of male territorial behavior that emerged during the analysis on the basis of the actor's intent. The first theme involved the display of male aggressiveness to exert territorial dominance over a female. The second theme was the use of aggressiveness or anger to obtain compliance from another character.

The last category involved the male characters' use of aggression as a means of defending a female character, namely, Bella. Finally, on the basis of the findings of Kettrey and Emery (2010), who found that traditional gender roles are a dominant theme presented in magazines for teenagers, particularly the central focus on finding a man, having a romantic relationship, and securing a home, the presentation of traditional gender roles was included in the analysis. During the process of coding the last category, secondary violence emerged, that is, violent acts or threats of violence against Bella that were a direct result of her being involved with Edward or his vampire family. . . .

RESULTS

Situations involving physical violence or threats of immediate physical violence were identified 80 times across the series, and 30% of the physical violence was perpetrated by a male in the course of an intimate relationship. Within this category, 66.7% of the violence was perpetrated by Edward on Bella and 33.3% was perpetrated by Jacob on Bella. Throughout the series, references are made to Edward's desire to drink Bella's blood, either as a mechanism that allows Edward to control both Bella's behavior and the course of their relationship or as a reminder of the power differential between the two characters. Physical violence also occurs when Edward attempts to protect Bella from harming herself or from being harmed by others. Although Edward's intention is not to harm Bella, she suffers physical harm on 16 (20%) occasions. For example, when Bella receives a paper cut while opening a birthday gift, another vampire lunges to attack her, and Edward jumps to her rescue, resulting in injury to Bella, "He threw himself at me, flinging me back across the table. It fell, as did I, scattering the cake and the presents, the flowers and the plates. I landed in the mess of shattered crystal" (Meyer, 2006, p. 28).

Bella is the victim of 96 instances of secondary violence in the book series. The most frequent perpetrators of this secondary violence are other vampires. The story involves a romantic relationship in which Bella's love for Edward repeatedly places her at risk of serious injury or death. In addition, Edward himself poses a threat because of his desire to drink her blood: "They have a name for someone who smells the way Bella does to me. They call her my singer—because her blood sings for me" (Meyer, 2006, p. 490). It is also interesting to note that in *Breaking Dawn,* the fourth book in the series, Bella is expecting Edward's child. Throughout the pregnancy, the nonhuman child causes significant injury to Bella, threatening both her health and her life.

We identified five cases of sexual violence in the four books. All were perpetrated against Bella by either Edward or Jacob. The following excerpt describes sexual violence perpetrated by Edward: "Under the dusting of feathers, large purplish bruises were beginning to blossom across the pale skin of my arm. My eyes followed the trail they made up to my shoulder, and then down across my ribs. I pulled my hand free to poke at a discoloration on my left forearm, watching it fade where I touched and then reappear" (Meyer, 2008, p. 89).

Although Edward and Bella do not engage in sexual intercourse until after they are married, which is in accordance with those who promote the series as advocating abstinence, the sexual relationship they do have is extremely violent.

Another instance of sexual violence involves Jacob and Bella. Jacob physically overpowers Bella and kisses her forcibly against her will. This act occurs twice in the series, and after the first time, Bella retaliates by punching Jacob, inadvertently breaking her hand. Bella's injury and distress are then the cause of amusement for both Jacob and Bella's father, Charlie, which trivializes both Jacob's perpetration of sexual violence and Bella's victimization.

With regard to cases of controlling behavior, 30 cases of the first type of controlling behavior, physical control, were detected, all but two of which involved either Edward or Jacob controlling Bella. The second type of controlling behavior, verbally ordering someone to comply, occurred exclusively between Edward and Bella, with Edward ordering Bella to do something a total of 31 times. For the last type of controlling behavior, emotional control, 58 cases were identified.

Examples of Edward's use of violence for the purposes of controlling Bella's behavior are illustrated by the following quotation, in which Edward intimates Bella, "'Where do you think you're going?' he asked, outraged. He was gripping a fistful of my jacket in one hand" (Meyer, 2005, p. 103), or through asking other characters to restrain her physically, "'Emmett,' Edward said grimly. And Emmett secured my hands in his steely grasp" (Meyer, 2005, p. 382), or by threatening violence to ensure that Bella complies with his wishes, "'No! No! NO!' Edward roared charging back into the room. He was in my face before I had time to blink, bending over me, his expression twisted in rage" (Meyer, 2006, p. 535).

Throughout the series, there are 60 references to self-harm or suicide. The majority of these thoughts and behaviors (60.67%) are Bella's. Within this category, three themes emerged. The first theme is Bella's desire to become a vampire and consequently to go through the process of becoming undead, a process that involves enduring intense pain and death. Bella is willing and eager to endure a painful death to be with Edward forever. The second theme is related to Bella's suicidal ideations when Edward leaves her. Bella's deep depression manifests itself through thoughts of suicide and subsequent reckless behaviors. The last suicidal theme is related to self-harm initiated in an effort to save another character. For example, during a fight with hostile vampires, Bella has the following thoughts, "If I had to bleed to save them, I would do it. I would die to do it" (Meyer, 2007, p. 539). Repeatedly, images of suicide or self-harm are romanticized in this book series.

We identified 14 instances of stalking behavior in the books, 11 (78.6%) of which were perpetrated by Edward against Bella. These behaviors included Edward breaking into Bella's room without her knowledge, listening to her conversations with other people, following her, and monitoring her interactions with others. For example, in *Eclipse* (Meyer 2007, pp. 131–132), Bella visits Jacob against Edward's orders. When she returns, the following ensues, "It came out of nowhere. One minute there was nothing but bright highway in my rearview mirror. The next minute, the sun was glinting off a silver Volvo right on my tail." Edward uses stalking techniques as a means of manipulating and controlling Bella. These behaviors are both minimized and romanticized throughout the series through Bella's response, or lack of response, to them: "'You spied on me?' But somehow I couldn't infuse my voice with the proper outrage. I was flattered" (Meyer, 2005, p. 292).

The content analysis also revealed 31 episodes involving jealousy in the series. Most of these episodes involved Edward's jealousy of Bella's interactions with another male (54.8%), and 41.4% were expressed by Jacob over Bella's interactions with another male. These behaviors manifested themselves in many ways: admitting jealously outright, acting aggressively toward other males, and physically fighting over Bella's attentions.

Edward and Jacob repeatedly express their feelings through anger and aggression. We found 183 instances of male aggressiveness, machismo, or male privilege in the book series. The majority of these behaviors are perpetrated by Edward (44.3%), followed by Jacob (23.5%). Displaying male aggressiveness to exert territorial dominance over a female occurred 43 times (23.5%) and was either presented through expressions of possessiveness by Edward and Jacob toward Bella or establishing dominance when confronted by another male. For example, in *Eclipse,* when Jacob attempts to warm Bella up by getting into her sleeping bag with her, the following occurs:

> Edward snarled, but Jacob didn't even look at him. Instead, he crawled to my side and started unzipping my sleeping bag. Edward's hand was suddenly hard on his shoulder restraining, snow white against the dark skin. Jacob's jaw clenched, his nostrils flaring, his body recoiling from the cold touch. The long muscles in his arms flexed automatically. (Meyer, 2007, p. 490)

In addition, claims of ownership are made concerning Bella. On three occasions, Edward refers to Bella as if she is his property, as in the following example: "'She is mine.' Edward's low voice was suddenly dark, not as composed as before" (Meyer, 2007, p. 341).

We identified the use of aggressiveness or anger to obtain compliance from another character in 23 instances in the series, with 87% of the acts of aggressiveness perpetrated by Edward toward Bella and 13% by Jacob toward Bella. These acts vary from aggressive vocalizations, such as growling, snarling, or shouting, to threatening looks, physical intimidation, and physical restraint. There were also incidents involving the male characters' use of aggression to defend a female character, namely, Bella. These incidents occur 47 times (25.68%) in the series, most frequently by Edward (n = 37) and Jacob (n = 10). It is also interesting to note that the most common descriptive words used to convey expressions of male aggressiveness throughout include "growl, snarl, and hiss." These words are animalistic, normalizing a primitive imagery of male dominance.

Of the 132 representations of traditional gender roles in the four books that we identified, most involved Edward's behavior toward Bella (67.4%) or Jacob's behavior toward Bella (14.4%). Bella is physically saved from harm by male characters seven times (5.3%). Although these events occur relatively infrequently, they are often major events in the story. In one instance, Edward saves Bella from death by stopping a van that is speeding toward her, "Two long, white hands shot out protectively in front of me, and the van shuddered to a stop a foot from my face, the large hands

TABLE 39.1 ■ Plot Overview of the Four Books in the *Twilight* Series

Book Title	Book Number	Number of Pages	Date of Publication	Plot Overview
Twilight	1	498	October 2005	Bella, a 17-year-old, moves to Forks, Washington, to live with her father. She meets and falls in love with Edward, a vampire. Edward is initially attracted to Bella because her blood smells especially good to him, and he desires to kill her and drink her blood. However, with significant restraint, he resists this impulse and pursues a romantic relationship with Bella. Bella finds out that Edward is a vampire, and instead of fearing him, she embraces him as he is. Because of her association with Edward and his family, Bella is exposed to other vampires, one of which tracks and attacks Bella to upset Edward. Edward saves Bella and kills the attacking vampire, James, but not before Bella is bitten by the other vampire. Edward is forced either to let Bella become a vampire herself or suck the venom from the bite, which involves sucking her blood. Edward chooses the latter course of action, preventing Bella from becoming a vampire.
New Moon	2	563	September 2006	On her 18th birthday, Bella receives a paper cut when opening her birthday presents. Edward's brother, Jasper, attacks Bella, but Edward intervenes, saving her. As a result, Edward and his family leave the area. Bella sinks into a depression that lasts months. Bella's depression is made bearable by her relationship with Jacob. Bella also finds that when she acts recklessly, subjecting herself to significant risk of harm, she suffers delusions that allow her to see Edward. Consequently her behavior becomes more reckless. When Jacob distances himself from Bella, she discovers he is a werewolf. Jacob reveals that another vampire is in the vicinity and that he has been protecting the area. It is revealed that the vampire is Victoria, James's disgruntled mate who is there to kill Bella. Following an extremely reckless stunt, in which Bella jumps off a cliff, Edward believes that Bella is dead and plans to kill himself by inciting anger from the vampires' governing body, the Volturi. Alice, Edward's sister, takes Bella to Italy to prevent him from taking such action. They are successful in preventing Edward from ending his life, but the Volturi agree to let them go only if Edward promises to turn Bella into a vampire.
Eclipse	3	629	September 2007	Edward returns to Forks with Bella and promises never to leave again. He does not want Bella to spend time with her friend Jacob because he believes it is too dangerous for her. Victoria is still attempting to kill Bella and begins to create an army of new vampires for the purpose of killing her. Jacob and the wolf pack join forces with Edward and his vampire family to save Bella from Victoria and her newborn vampires. Jacob learns that Bella has agreed to marry Edward. The book ends with a fight in which Edward kills Victoria, and her newborns are defeated. Jacob suffers substantial injuries that require medical attention and significant respite.

Breaking Dawn	4	754	August 2008	Bella and Edward get married, and on their honeymoon they have sexual intercourse. As a result, Bella becomes pregnant. The pregnancy is accelerated because the fetus is not human. Edward wants to terminate the pregnancy because of the harm the baby can and does cause to Bella's body. Bella wants to carry the baby to term. Bella recruits Rosalie to ensure that no one attempts to take her baby from her. The baby causes Bella significant harm, including broken ribs. Jacob learns of the pregnancy and protects Bella from the wolf pack because they want to destroy her child. The pack splits into two, with those who support the protection of Bella siding with Jacob. The baby becomes so strong that it almost kills Bella. Edward has to cut the baby out of her and inject her with his venom to save her. Bella becomes a vampire, but the Volturi hear of Edward and Bella's child and come to Forks to kill the Cullens. The Cullens ask other vampires for help and create a small defensive force. Alice and Jasper disappear. The Volturi come and seek to find an excuse to exterminate the Cullen family. Alice and Jasper return with evidence that Edward and Bella's child is not a threat to vampire discovery and save the day. The Volturi return to Italy.

fitting providentially into a deep dent in the side of the van's body" (Meyer, 2005, p. 56). Traditional gender roles are also emphasized in the chivalrous behaviors exhibited by both Edward and Jacob toward Bella (16.67%). These behaviors include opening doors, lending Bella clothes to ensure her warmth, carrying Bella when she is tired, and giving Bella comfort. Bella is repeatedly depicted as weak and dependent, requiring male protection from harm.

DISCUSSION

Viewed through the lens of dating violence, the *Twilight* series offers many troubling examples of controlling behaviors and violence. Many of these behaviors are minimized, justified, normalized, and sometimes romanticized. The majority of controlling and violent behaviors—physical and sexual violence, stalking, controlling, intimidating, and threatening—are exhibited by male characters. The central characters manifest behaviors that are consistent with traditional gender roles, with Edward and Jacob presenting as aggressive, territorial, and demanding, and Bella presented as subservient and weak. Considering the popularity

of the books and the marketing of their stories to a predominantly teenage audience, these messages are counterintuitive to the promotion of healthy, equitable, nonviolent relationships. This is especially true with regard to sexual violence since the representation of a sexually violent relationship seems to be in direct contradiction to advocating abstinence.

Twilight, published in 2005, was ranked the best-selling book of 2008 by *USA Today,* closely followed by the book's sequels. In 2009, *New Moon,* published in 2006, was ranked number one on the U.S. best-seller list, again followed by the other three books in the series (DeBarros, Cadden, DeRamus, & Schnaars, 2010a). The books have reportedly sold more than 40 million copies worldwide (DeBarros, Cadden, DeRamus, & Schnaars, 2010b), with *Breaking Dawn,* published in 2008, selling 1.3 million copies in the United States the day it was released, debuting at the top of the best-seller lists in Britain, France, Italy, Ireland, and Spain. The books have also been printed in 37 languages, including Vietnamese, Croatian, Chinese, and Latvian (Parsons, 2008).

Given the widespread popularity of the series and the fact that the target audience is predominantly teenage girls (Young, 2009), it is of particular concern that the dominant romantic relationship is presented with behaviors that are characteristic of relationship violence. The presentation of these behaviors in popular fiction clearly does not cause dating violence. However, it is troubling when one of the most popular book series in recent history repeatedly normalizes, minimizes, and romanticizes these behaviors. It reinforces cultural norms that condone men's use of force to obtain a variety of goals.

... Programs to prevent dating violence and educational programs could certainly use examples from these books to illustrate behaviors and attitudes that are related to dating violence. To recognize behaviors that were previously presented as chivalrous and romantic as clear examples of control, stalking, abuse, and intimidation may offer young people new insights into the insidious and often-subtle nature of abuse and control. In this way, the *Twilight* series could continue to influence young lives, but in a new way.

REFERENCES

Ackard, D., Eisenberg, M., & Neumark-Sztainer, D. (2007). Long-term impact of adolescent dating violence on the behavioral and psychological health of male and female youth. *Journal of Pediatrics, 151*, 476–481.

Adelman, M., & Kil, S. H. (2007). Dating conflicts: Rethinking dating violence and youth conflict. *Violence Against Women, 13*, 1296–1318.

Altheide, D. L. (1996). *Qualitative data analysis.* Thousand Oaks, CA: SAGE.

Bergman, L. (1992). Dating violence among high school students. *Social Work, 37*, 21–27.

Bernard, J. L., Bernard, S. L., & Bernard, M. L. (1985). Courtship violence and sex-typing. *Family Relations, 34*, 573–576.

Black, B., & Weisz, A. (2003). Dating violence: Help-seeking behaviors of African American middle schoolers. *Violence Against Women, 9*, 187–206.

Borzekowski, D., & Rickert, V. (2001). Adolescent cybersurfing for health information: A new resource that crosses barriers. *Archives of Pediatric and Adolescent Medicine, 155*, 813–817.

Brown, J. D., L'Engle, K. L., Pardun, C. J., Guo, G., Kenneavy, K., & Jackson, C. (2006). Sexy media matter: Exposure to sexual content in music, movies, television, and magazines predicts black and white adolescents' sexual behavior. *Pediatrics, 117*, 1018–1027.

Brown, J. D., & Witherspoon, E. M. (2002). The mass media and American adolescents' health. *Journal of Adolescent Health, 31*, 153–170.

Carlson, B. E. (1990). Adolescent observers of marital violence. *Journal of Family Violence, 5*, 285–299.

Centers for Disease Control and Prevention. (2000). Youth risk behavior surveillance—U.S. 1999. *Morbidity and Mortality Weekly Report, 49*, 1–96.

Centers for Disease Control and Prevention. (2007). Effectiveness of universal school-based programs for the prevention of violent and aggressive behavior, *Morbidity & Mortality Weekly Report, 56*, 1–11. Retrieved from http://www.cdc.gov/mmwr/preview/mmwrhtml/rr5607a1.htm

Collins, R., Elliott, M., Berry, S., Kanouse, D., Kunkel, D., Hunter, S. B., & Miu, A. (2004). Watching sex on television predicts adolescent initiation of sexual behavior. *Pediatrics, 114*, 280–289.

DeBarros, A., Cadden, M., DeRamus, K., & Schnaars, C. (2010a, January 14). The top 100 books of 2008. *USA Today.* Retrieved from http://www.usatoday.com/life/books/news/2009-01-14-2008-top-100titles_N.htm

DeBarros, A., Cadden, M., DeRamus, K., & Schnaars, C. (2010b, January 15). USA Today's bestselling books: The top 100 for 2009. *USA Today.* Retrieved from http://www.usatoday.com/life/books/news/2010-01-05top-books-2009_N.htm

Eckhardt, C., Jamieson, T. R., & Watts, K. (2002). Anger experience and expression among dating violence perpetrators during anger arousal. *Journal of Interpersonal Violence, 17*, 1102–1114.

Editorial: Frontline: Be critical of stalking, abuse in "Twilight" series. (2009, November 17). *The Western Front.* Retrieved from http://westernfrontonline.net/pdf/fa1109/Nov 17Final.pdf

Feldman, S., & Gowen, L. K. (1998). Conflict negotiation tactics in romantic relationships in high school students. *Journal of Youth and Adolescence,* 27, 691–717.

Felson, R. B., & Messner, S. F. (2000). The control motive in intimate partner violence. *Social Psychology Quarterly,* 63, 86–94.

Foshee, V. A. (1996). Gender differences in adolescent dating abuse prevalence, types, and injuries. *Health Education Research,* 11, 275–286.

Foshee, V. A., Benefield, T., Ennett, S., Bauman, K. E., & Suchindran, C. (2004). Longitudinal predictors of serious physical and sexual dating violence victimization during adolescence. *Preventive Medicine,* 39, 1007–1016.

Gover, A. R., Kaukinen, C., & Fox, K. A. (2008). The relationship between violence in the family of origin and dating violence among college students. *Journal of Interpersonal Violence,* 23, 1667–1693.

Gray, B. (2009, November 21). "New Moon" shatters opening day record. *Box Office Mojo.* Retrieved from http://www.boxofficemojo.com/news/?id=2626&p=.htm

Gringeri, C. E., Wahab, S., & Anderson-Nathe, B. (2010). What makes it feminist? Mapping the landscape of feminist social work research. *Affilia,* 25, 390–405.

Haynes, J. (2009). Exposing domestic violence in country music videos. In L. M. Cuklanz & S. Moorti (Eds.), *Local violence, global media* (pp. 201–217). New York, NY: Peter Lang.

Hendy, H. M., Weiner, K., Bakerofskie, J., Eggen, D., Gustitus, C., & McLeod, K. C. (2003). Comparison of six models for violent romantic relationships in college men and women. *Journal of Interpersonal Violence,* 18, 645–665.

Howard, D., Wang, M., & Yan, F. (2007). Psychosocial factors associated with reports of physical dating violence among U.S. adolescent females. *Adolescence,* 42, 311–327.

James, H. W., West, C., Deters, K. E., & Armijo, E. (2000). Youth dating violence. *Adolescence,* 35, 455–465.

Jezl, D., Molidor, C. E., & Wright, T. L. (1996). Physical, sexual, and psychological abuse in high school dating relationships: Prevalence rates and self-esteem issues. *Child & Adolescent Social Work Journal,* 13, 69–88.

Kasian, M., & Painter, S. L. (1992). Frequency and severity of psychological abuse in a dating population. *Journal of Interpersonal Violence,* 7, 350–364.

Kaura, S. A., & Allen, C. M. (2004). Dissatisfaction with relationship power and dating violence perpetration by men and women. *Journal of Interpersonal Violence,* 19, 576–588.

Kettrey, H. H., & Emery, B. C. (2010). Teen magazines as educational texts on dating violence: The $2.99 approach. *Violence Against Women,* 16, 1270–1294.

Kim-Godwin, Y. S., Clements, C., McCuiston, A. M., & Fox, J. A. (2009). Dating violence among high school students in southeastern North Carolina. *Journal of School Nursing,* 25, 141–151.

Lavoie, F., Robitaille, L., & Hébert, M. (2000). Teen dating relationships and aggression: An exploratory study. *Violence Against Women,* 6, 6–36.

Lorber, J. (2005). *Gender inequality.* Los Angeles, CA: Roxbury Press.

Marin, A. J., & Russo, N. F. (1999). Feminist perspectives on male violence against women: Critiquing O'Neil and Harway's model. In M. Harway & J. M. O'Neil (Eds.), *What causes men's violence against women?* (pp. 18–35). Thousand Oaks, CA: SAGE.

McCulloch, S. (2009, November 11). Star in *Twilight* vampire movies poor role model for girls says Victoria professor. *Times Colonist.* Retrieved from http://www2.canada.com/entertainment/movieguide/starþtwilightþvampireþmovies+poor+role+model+girls+says+victoria+professor/2210174/story.html? id=2210

McFarlane, J., Campbell, J. C., Wilt, S., Sachs, C., Ulrich, Y., & Xu, X. (1999). Stalking and intimate partner femicide. *Homicide Studies,* 3, 300–316.

Memmott, C., & Cadden, M. (2009, August 5). Twilight series eclipses Potter records on bestsellers list. *USA Today.* Retrieved from http://www.usatoday.com/life/books/news/2009-08-03-twilight-series_N.htm

Messerschmidt, J. W. (2000). *Nine lives: Adolescent masculinities, the body, and violence.* Boulder, CO: Westview Press.

Meyer, S. (2005). *Twilight.* New York, NY: Little, Brown.

Meyer, S. (2006). *New moon*. New York, NY: Little, Brown.

Meyer, S. (2007). *Eclipse*. New York, NY: Little, Brown.

Meyer, S. (2008). *Breaking dawn*. New York, NY: Little, Brown.

O'Keefe, M. (2005). Teen dating violence: A review of risk factors and prevention efforts. *VAWnet: National Electronic Network on Violence Against Women Applied Research Forum*. Retrieved from http://new.vawnet.org/Assoc_Files_VAWnet/AR_TeenDatingViolence.pdf

Pagelow, M. D. (1984). *Family violence*. New York, NY: Praeger.

Parsons, C. (2008, November 21). "Twilight" publisher sees film boosting book sales. *Reuter*. Retrieved from http://www.reuters.com/article/idUSTRE4AK03620081121

Pence, E., & Paymar, M. (1993). *Education groups for men who batter: The Duluth model*. New York, NY: Springer.

Philaretou, A. G., & Allen, K. R. (2001). Reconstructing masculinity and sexuality. *Journal of Men's Studies, 9*, 301–321.

Prospero, M. (2007). Young adolescent boys and dating violence: The beginning of patriarchal terrorism? *Affilia, 22*, 271–280.

Prothrow-Stith, D. (1993). *Deadly consequences*. New York, NY: Harper Perennial.

Pulerwitz, J., Gortmaker, S. L., & Dejong, W. (2000). Measuring sexual relationship power in HIV/STD research. *Sex Roles, 42*, 637–660.

Rennison, C. M. (2003, February). *Intimate partner violence 1993–2001: Bureau of justice statistics, crime data brief*. Retrieved from http://bjs.ojp.usdoj.gov/content/pub/pdf/ipv01.pdf

Riggs, D. S., & O'Leary, K. D. (1996). Aggression between heterosexual dating partners: An examination of a causal model of courtship aggression. *Journal of Interpersonal Violence, 11*, 519–540.

Roehl, J., O'Sullivan, C., Webster, D., & Campbell, J. (2005). *Intimate partner violence risk assessment validation study, final report*. Washington, DC: Unpublished manuscript, U.S. Department of Justice.

Ronfeldt, H. M., Kimerling, R., & Arias, I. (1998). Satisfaction with relationship power and the perpetration of dating violence. *Journal of Marriage and the Family, 60*, 70–78.

Sargent, J. D., Heatherton, T. F., Ahrens, M. B., Dalton, M. A., Tickle, J. J., & Beach, M. L. (2002). Adolescent exposure to extremely violent movies. *Journal of Adolescent Health, 31*, 449–454.

Smith, C. (2008, July 9). "Twilight": A positive or negative influence for teens? *Christ and Pop Culture*. Retrieved from http://www.christandpopculture.com/featured/twilight-a-positive-or-negative-influence for-teens/

Smith-Stover, C. (2005). Domestic violence research: What we have learned and where do we go from here? *Journal of Interpersonal Violence, 20*, 448–454.

Strasburger, V. C. (1995). *Adolescents and the media: Medical and psychological impact*. Thousand Oaks, CA: SAGE.

Stone, L. (2009, November 19). Lack of sex attracts teen girls to *Twilight* series: Study. *The Vancouver Sun*. Retrieved from http://www.vancouversun.com/entertainment/Lack+attracts+teenþgirls+Twilightþseries+study/2238456/story.html http://www.crosswalk.com/blogs/liebelt/lack-of-sex-attracts-teen-girls-to-twilight-series-11617033.html

Swahn, M., Lubell, K., & Simon, T. (2004). Suicide attempts and physical fighting among high school students—United States, 2001. *Morbidity and Mortality Weekly Report, 53*, 474–476.

Swigonski, M. E., & Raheim, S. (2011). Feminist contributions to understanding women's lives and the social environment. *Affilia, 26*, 10–11.

Tong, R. (2009). *Feminist thought: A more comprehensive introduction*. Boulder, CO: Westview Press.

Vezina, L., Lavoie, F., & Piche, C. (1995, July). Adolescent boys and girls: Their attitudes on dating violence. Paper presented at the fourth International Family Violence Research Conference, Durham, NH.

Young, S. C. (2009, June 10). Bella no match for Sookie at vampire love: Subservient "Twilight" heroine a terrible model for pre-teen girls. *MSNBC.com*. Retrieved from http://www.msnbc.msn.com/id/31087539

40

RESISTANT MASCULINITIES IN ALTERNATIVE R&B?

Understanding Frank Ocean and The Weeknd's Representations of Gender

Frederik Dhaenens and Sander De Ridder

INTRODUCTION

When rising vocalist Frank Ocean announced his first love was a man via a personal Tumblr post (Ocean, 2012a), hip hop and R&B celebrities (e.g. Beyoncé, Jay-Z, Russell Simmons) spoke out their support for Ocean's coming out. The music press seized the opportunity to speak of a significant change of heart regarding homosexuality within contemporary R&B and hip hop culture (Jonze, 2012). Interestingly, Frank Ocean's sexuality is not the only aspect that distinguishes him from other R&B and hip hop artists. We argue that his public disclosure of same-sex desires links up to an alternative masculinity articulated throughout his work. Even more, he is not alone in performing a masculinity that diverges from a hegemonic masculinity established within contemporary R&B and hip hop culture. Alternative masculinities seem to be at the center of a music culture labeled by the music industry and music press as 'Alt R&B,' 'PBR&B (Pabst Blue Ribbon R&B)' or 'hipster R&B' (DeVille, 2012; Fennessey, 2011; Soderberg, 2012)—genre labels that refer to contemporary artists whose music can be situated on the crossroads between hip hop, soul and contemporary R&B culture. The genre, which we refer to as 'alternative R&B,' is considered both a continuation of contemporary R&B music (e.g. the (neo-)soul singing, stylistic elements or slick production) and a departure from it (e.g. alternative modes of distribution, broaching new and transgressive themes, gaining critical success and being positively received by indie-fan audiences) (Fennessey, 2011; Walters, 2012).

Of interest to this article is the way male artists in alternative R&B negotiate the hegemonic masculine identity of contemporary R&B and hip hop culture. . . . In contemporary Western societies, hegemonic masculinity is conceptualized as practices and embodiment that justify and institutionalize the central position of patriarchal men and the suppression, discrimination or symbolic exclusion of women or of men who embody and/or express alternative masculinities (Connell, 2005; Connell and Messerschmidt, 2005). We start from the argument that in contemporary R&B and hip hop culture, a particular form of hegemonic masculinity is being articulated which, to this day, is hypermasculine, hypersexual and heteronormative (hooks, 2004; Jeffries, 2010; Smalls, 2011; Weitzer and Kubrin, 2009). Bearing in mind that recent studies have shown a decline in explicit homophobia and a renegotiation of masculinities in contemporary Western societies (see Connell and Messerschmidt, 2005; McCormack and Anderson, 2010), we aim to study to what extent these socio-cultural transformations are reflected in a music culture often denoted to reinforce patriarchal gender notions. In other words, do the alternative masculinities represented in alternative R&B *resist* the hegemonic masculine identity in contemporary R&B and hip hop culture? To this end, we conduct a qualitative textual analysis to deconstruct and interpret the gender representations in the work of two alternative R&B artists, namely, Frank Ocean and The Weeknd.

From Dhaenens, F. & De Ridder, S. (2015). Resistant masculinities in alternative R&B?: Understanding Frank Ocean and The Weeknd's representations of gender. *European Journal of Cultural Studies, 18*(3).

MASCULINITIES IN CONTEMPORARY R&B AND HIP HOP CULTURE

To study and understand the negotiation of masculinity by male alternative R&B artists, a discussion is needed on the embodiment and expression of masculinity in contemporary R&B and hip hop culture. Why is it that this particular music culture has been repeatedly argued in public and academic debate to be sexist, misogynistic, homophobic or aggressive (Battan, 2012; hooks, 2004; Jonze, 2012; Smalls, 2011; Weitzer and Kubrin, 2009)? We start by discussing gender norms in relation to Black popular music culture, from which contemporary R&B and hip hop culture emerged.

Hegemonic R&B and hip hop masculinity is grafted onto a history of racism and systematic oppression by White Americans of African-American men (Penney, 2012; Wise, 2001). E. Patrick Johnson (2003) argues that Black masculinity has never been taken for granted. Whether by acts of violence, degradation or emasculation, the manhood of Black men has been constantly scrutinized, questioned and defied. Hence, he argues that strategies of preserving a normal Black male identity have been employed. As a consequence, identities, practices, or norms and values that threaten the 'normality' of Black manhood are being rejected, which enables possibilities to indulge in homophobia, sexism and misogyny. Zooming in on hip hop culture—which came about at the end of the 1970s in Black impoverished inner city communities (Neal, 1997)—the socio-cultural setting has fortified the need for Black young men to embody this masculinity. Different strategies have been applied by men in these neighborhoods. First, men have claimed their masculinity by expressing in public a hypermasculine identity. Derek Iwamoto (2003) considers this a way of showing to their peers and to White mainstream society that despite the racial oppression and socio-economic deprivation, Black men still have control and agency. A second way is by performing homonegative, homophobic or sexist rhymes or songs as a way to ensure a hierarchical superior position. Michael P. Jeffries (2010) considers this practice typical for contemporary R&B and hip hop artists who embody the thug identity. They dissociate themselves from lesbian, gay, bisexual and transgender (LGBT)

and queer identities while representing women in binary inferior roles (the despicable 'gold digging tricks/hoes' vs the worthy 'down-ass chicks') and with little agency. In Ronald Weitzer and Charis E. Kubrin's (2009) analysis of misogynist gangsta rap songs, this translated in objectification, depersonalization and fragmentation of women, in the celebration of sexual activities without responsibility, in measuring sexual success to gain status and respect among its peers, in glorification of gang-banging, the legitimization of violence against women or the celebration of prostitution or pimping. . . . Third, we stress the central role of hypersexuality (Smalls, 2011; Weitzer and Kubrin, 2009). A historical association of the Black body with sexuality is connoted by the practice of expressing and embodying a hypersexual identity. bell hooks (2004) elaborates on the role of sexuality within segregated Black communities. She argues that for many Black men who find themselves in a politically and economic powerless situation sexual prowess and sexual successes are ways to excel. Sexuality becomes a means to gain social status—a practice that is stimulated by, on the one hand, Black peers who reiterate patriarchal and heterosexist discourse and, on the other, White society who expresses a desire for the image of the hypersexual Black stud. For hooks, this rigid and pressured focus on the hypersexual only creates victims: the women who fall victim to the misogynist and heterosexist practices, the Black men who fail to embody the sexual norms and the hypersexual Black men who remain deprived from developing a healthy sexuality.

Yet, the argument that contemporary R&B and hip hop masculinity is predominantly rooted in Black identity politics dismisses the role of heteronormative discourse (Jeffries, 2010; Weitzer and Kubrin, 2009). . . . The essentialized, hierarchical and binary approach to race, gender and sexuality is a pivotal assumption within heteronormative societies. Hegemonic masculinity may thus be considered a means to preserve the supremacy of the heterosexual matrix (Butler, 1999; Halberstam, 2005; Warner, 1999). Weitzer and Kubrin (2009), for instance, argue that the misogynist trope in gangsta rap is not only directed at Black women but at all women. Similarly, Shanté Paradigm Smalls' (2011) illustration of how audiences in the hip hop community were troubled and angered by male soul artists who confuse gender and sexual norms links up to the heteronormative desire for a gender and sexual hierarchy in which identities are clear-cut, stable and easy to control. The example is also illustrative for various heteronormative practices that negotiate alternative masculinities. Even though gender norms in Western societies still demand of men to embody hegemonic masculinity and to disavow other masculinities, the practices have become more complex. Within explicit homophobic environments, excluding gender and sexual others is the norm. However, within liberal environments such as current Western societies, an inclusive and gay-friendly attitude is articulated in relation to a strategy of heterosexual recuperation. Here, heterosexual men will indulge in expressing nonnormative gender behavior or pro-gay attitudes, but they will mostly do so in a way that does not threaten their public image of being a hetero-sexual masculine man (McCormack and Anderson, 2010). . . .

[H]eterosexual recuperation can be found in hip hop culture, where it is used to express homosocial intimacy without running the risk of being labeled as gay. Jeffries (2010) illustrates the practice by discussing rapper Lil' Wayne's use of the phrase 'no homo.' The artist uses the phrase each time he publicly associates himself with or expresses admiration for a fellow male artist to ensure that his public disclosure of same-sex intimacy is not interpreted in sexual terms. Even though used to transgress certain gender norms, Jeffries, nonetheless, reads into the act an expression of heteronormative masculine anxiety, which is equally manifested in other studies on gay panic in hip hop culture (e.g. Penney, 2012). hooks (2004) is the most critical in her analysis of hip hop culture. She argues that there is nothing real about hegemonic Black hip hop masculinity as it only reflects the norms and values of a White supremacist capitalist patriarchal society. She points out the embrace of capitalism, the reiteration of rigid gender roles and patriarchal violence, the neglect of a history of suffering, the disdain of emotional complexity and the refusal to disclose emotions as anything but Black. She compares it to blues music, which she considers a genre that dealt with the pains and joys of everyday life in an honest manner. By contrast, she sees hip hop as emotionally immature and absorbed into the ideology of White Western capitalism. In this perspective, Gilbert B. Rodman's (2006) work

sheds a new light on the gender politics in contemporary R&B and hip hop culture. He argues that an intensified and isolated scrutiny of specific artists within this genre fails to acknowledge the structural and institutional elements in mainstream Western society that instigate and perpetuate racism, misogyny or homophobia. Or, to put it differently, that construct and consolidate the blueprint for hegemonic masculinities. He builds his argument by pointing out a double standard in the treatment of hegemonic masculinity in popular culture. Whereas Black popular music is systematically questioned for its sexist discourse, White popular music genres and artists are exempt from scrutiny. Rodman stresses the irony of this situation by pointing out that hegemonic masculinity is articulated by both White and Black artists and by deconstructing the idea that popular music genres are racially pure forms. . . . Thus, in order to avoid reinforcing the idea that only Black popular music culture articulates hegemonic masculinity, these articulations need to be understood as complex negotiations of genre and culturally specific characteristics (e.g. Black identity politics) and broader ideological strategies of mainstream Western society (e.g. heteronormativity and White Western capitalism).

However, with this article, we also want to acknowledge the progressive potential of contemporary R&B and hip hop culture. In contrast to hooks' (2004) analysis, these genres are potentially able to engage in progressive gender politics. Furthermore, scholars have always nuanced the popular assumption that the genres' gender politics are only invested in reiterating a hegemonic masculine identity. Even though hegemonic masculinity assumes a key position in many contemporary R&B and hip hop tropes—whether by upholding specific heteronormative values or by embodying hypermasculinity—it is challenged in multiple ways (Jeffries, 2010; Weitzer and Kubrin, 2009). First, we want to emphasize the critique that within popular debate, the politics of representation employed by media are being ignored. The exaggeration, reduction and stereotyping in media coverage on R&B and hip hop have fostered the assertion that hip hop artists are 'violent, sexist, homophobic, anti-gay, heteronormative, and male-centered' (Wilson, 2007: 117). In addition to fortifying the violent and patriarchal norms and values, the media represent the

African-American male artist as a unique spectacle of hypermasculinity, ignoring both the artist's agency, his personal complexities and his creative work (McLeod, 2009). Furthermore, instead of engaging in representing the diversity in everyday-life Black masculinities, mainstream media glorify a stereotypical patriarchal male as one of the few mediated role models for other Black youngsters (Iwamoto, 2003). Also, not only mainstream media have reiterated this image, the music industry as well participates in promoting the thug artist and thug life. Considering the hypermasculine identity as profitable, the music industry has encouraged artists to perform this image (Weitzer and Kubrin, 2009). As James B. Stewart (2005) and Watkins (2006) underscore, this packaging of ghetto pop to mainstream audiences is done by both Black and White moguls within the music industry who responded to the success of the genre with suburban White male teens. For some artists, this has resulted in the contradictory situation of becoming affluent by rhyming about their inner city lives (Neal, 1997; Watkins, 2006). Other artists within the genres resolve this issue by refraining from tackling social and political issues and solely singing and rapping about the material benefits and sexual successes of a contemporary R&B and hip hop artist (hooks, 2004; Stewart, 2005; Weitzer and Kubrin, 2009).

Moreover, the discourses on masculinity that circulate in contemporary R&B and hip hop culture are far from monolithic. Even though a hegemonic masculinity is present, a diversity of cultural practices exists within the genres that diverge from or resist the hegemony of the hypermasculine, homophobic and/or heteronormative man. A first form of practices that challenge the superiority of men and the dominance of heteronormativity is offered by female artists within the genres. It concerns female artists who question male dominance and seek to empower women (Weitzer and Kubrin, 2009) or who appropriate the language and behavior of fellow male rappers to expose and deconstruct the heteronormativity that governs the male rappers' masculine pose (Smalls, 2011). Second, there are those male artists within the genres who hold up a mirror and question hegemonic masculinity. This may range from explicit rejections of hypermasculinity to more subtle and complex negotiations. For

instance, Iwamoto's (2003) reading of thug artist Tupac Shakur revealed how, despite performing a hypermasculine identity, he tackles the difficult socio-economic situation of Black women in inner city communities as well as the violence inflicted onto women. A third group of practices concerns male artists who embrace and/or negotiate aspects of queer popular culture—cultural practices that are generally associated with LGBT individuals and/or transgressive gender identities. Joel Penney (2012) speaks of a queer-inflected style in hip hop culture that defies the hegemonic hypermasculine identity in several ways. For instance, heterosexual Black artists sample electronic dance music (EDM) known as queer-friendly, associate with openly gay fashion designers and explicitly critique homophobia. Last, there are the artists who explicitly represent themselves as gender-nonnormative, LGBT and/or queer. These artists embrace the political potential that has typified Black popular music and use the aesthetics and rhetoric of the genres to, first, break a lance for other queer artists within the genres and, second, to deconstruct hegemonic masculinity and heteronormativity in general (Wilson, 2007).[1] For instance, Michael Quattlebaum's artist persona Mykki Blanco—a female rapper—articulates hypermasculinity (using braggadocio as rap style) together with ultrafemininity (style of dress and make-up) in his/her rap performance and thereby unsettles rigid and oppositional gender norms (Battan, 2012).

METHOD

. . . we conducted a textual analysis of the gender representations of two artists within the genre of alternative R&B . . . to, first, investigate how the masculinities performed within the genre are alternatives to the hegemonic norm within R&B and hip hop culture and, second, whether the alternatives qualify as cultural resistances to the norms and values linked to the hegemonic masculine man.

We chose to work with two young Black artists, namely Frank Ocean and The Weeknd, who are considered popular within alternative R&B and representative for the genre. Frank Ocean, the artist persona of Christopher Breaux, is a Black American artist who wrote songs for, among others, Justin Bieber and Beyoncé and who sung as a member of the hip hop collective Odd Future (Odd Future Wolf Gang Kill Them All (OFWGKTA)). Under the name of Frank Ocean, he released his mixtape *Nostalgia, Ultra* (2011) for free, which gathered the attention and praise from the music press. In 2012, he released his first official commercial album *Channel Orange* (Def Jam Recordings, 2012). Since the release of the album coincided with his public disclosure of same-sex feelings (cf. supra), both the critically acclaimed album and the artist became the focal point of Western media attention (Jonze, 2012). Next to Frank Ocean, this article considers the work of The Weeknd, the artist persona of Black Canadian artist Abel Tesfaye. In contrast to Frank Ocean, The Weeknd/Abel Tesfaye remains a mystery. He debuted the work of The Weeknd with the free mixtape *House of Balloons* in 2011, whose work was lauded for its musical and thematic risks. That same year, he released two other mixtapes, namely *Thursday* and *Echoes of Silence*. Again, the music had to speak for itself as The Weeknd was not giving any interviews . . .

FRANK OCEAN: MEN SEARCHING FOR A REAL LOVE

Over the course of two albums, Frank Ocean has engaged in portraying a musical universe that is both aesthetically and thematically diverse. Pinpointing him to solely alternative R&B is already something that can be considered restrictive, as his music blends genre conventions that characterize EDM, alternative rock, (neo-)soul, funk, hip hop and contemporary R&B. He further varies in choice of instrumentations, sound and ways of vocalizing. Similarly, the choice of artists he samples and/or invites to sing or play along reveals Frank Ocean as an artist who refuses to remain in the confines of Black popular music culture. Thematically, Frank Ocean does not take the safe road that is paved with picture-perfect, heteronormative and neoliberal fantasies. Rather than reiterating these commercial tropes, he explores socio-cultural and political issues that typify contemporary Western society. As tackled in early hip hop and soul music (Maultsby, 1983; Stewart, 2005; Watkins, 2006), racial segregation, class distinctions, and community building return as

themes in his music. For some music journalists (e.g. Soderberg, 2012), this is what makes alternative R&B *alternative*. It defies classical, marketable and racialized categorizations, which are traditional marketing strategies regarding Black popular music. By offering his first mixtape for free online, he further undermined the music industry's neoliberal model of making profit. Even though these strategies can be interpreted as niche marketing, they have nonetheless unsettled the aesthetic, thematic and commercial conventions of the genre.

Of interest to this article, however, is the way he represents masculinity. . . . Even though some male artists advocated gender equality (see Iwamoto, 2003), hypermasculinity remains the dominant trope, while the genres' progressive political potential remains tied to class and race issues. Frank Ocean, however, does not follow suit. The 'authentic' male identity often promoted in many hip hop songs is challenged by Frank Ocean's portrayal of diverse male characters. His songs consist of men that vary from traditional, patriarchal figures over men who reevaluate their (masculine) identities to men who are comfortable with engaging in nonnormative gender behavior. By giving these diverse masculinities a stage, Frank Ocean explores the performativity of gender and questions what it means to be a real man. On the first record *Nostalgia, Ultra,* for instance, the male characters include, among others, a workaholic estranged from his female partner in 'Songs 4 Women,' a heartbroken and suicidal man in 'Swim Good,' and a man dealing with the death of his grandfather and the absence of a father in 'There Will Be Tears.' What is interesting about all characters is that, despite their differences, they struggle with how to deal with their emotions. 'There Will Be Tears' is exemplary. Even though he sings about having to hide his tears for his friends, the song itself operates as a public expression of a man crying. This is further emphasized by sampling verses of the eponymous song 'There Will Be Tears' by Mr Hudson. What is being challenged is the idea of having to live up to an ideal of masculinity that, besides being a patriarchal socio-construction, conflicts with the everyday-life emotions of men. Yet, due to societal pressure, they often put on a hypermasculine performance to hide their vulnerability, love or jealousy. For instance, on *Channel Orange*'s 'Thinking Bout

You,' he portrays a male character who is in love for the first time. However, afraid of assuming the vulnerable position in the relation, he conceals his emotions by singing to the other character:

> No, I don't like you, I just thought you were cool enough to kick it
> Got a beach house I could sell you in Idaho, since you think
> I don't love you I just thought you were cute, that's why I kissed you.

He masks his desires and instead articulates traditional masculine behavior. Taking into account that the other character is presumably male,[2] the verses are remarkable in terms of defeminization: he addresses the other man in a hypermasculine lingo, he broaches about property and wealth and he emphasizes that the kiss has nothing to do with love. Yet, at the same time, he uses the hook—sung in a higher and more vulnerable manner—that he is actually thinking about being together forever. In the end, 'Thinking Bout You' portrays a hypermasculine man whose performed masculinity keeps him from happiness . . .

By representing masculinities and critiquing the masculine identity considered hegemonic in R&B and hip hop culture, he is deconstructing the idea of an unchangeable masculinity that is generally taken for granted. A few songs highlight this by undermining fixed ideas regarding men and women. For instance, the insertion of a monologue spoken by Nicole Kidman's character in the film *Eyes Wide Shut* (Kubrick, 1999) in 'LoveCrimes' (*Nostalgia, Ultra*) is significant. As such, he metaphorically gives women agency in his music and allows them to counter ingrained stereotypes regarding women. The character is making a stand for the sexuality of women. She reproaches the evolutionary psychological perspective that justifies men's sexual behavior to 'stick it in every place they can,' while ridiculing men for thinking that women are only interested in security and commitment. By making only these phrases audible, Frank Ocean inserts a plea for female sexual agency while questioning hypersexual and hypermasculine behavior. At other times, he makes explicit his views on gender equality. In 'We All Try' on *Nostalgia, Ultra,* he expresses the following statements:

> I believe a woman's temple
> Gives her the right to choose [. . .]
> I believe that marriage isn't
> Between a man and woman but between love and love.

The verse explicates his support for abortion rights and same-sex marriage, expressed in a song that predates his public coming out. Notwithstanding his sexual identity, the song is significant as it acknowledges the role of politics to bring about emancipation of women and sexual minorities.

Yet, advocating same-sex marriage does not imply he is not critical of the institution of marriage. 'American Wedding' (*Nostalgia, Ultra*)—a song that uses the master track of The Eagles 'Hotel California'—tells the story of a young man and woman who decided to get married, a marriage that did not last long. He refers to the marriage as an American wedding, an institution he describes as having little meaning, unable to last long and due to result in an 'American divorce.' Even though the song can be interpreted as making a case for taking the institution of marriage more seriously, it also allows to be read as critical of the institution itself. In particular, the song consists of a verse that describes the married woman turning in her term papers:

> M-R-S dot Kennedy, she signed her name in pen
> In a fancy fancy cursive, then turned her term papers in
> A thesis on Islamic virgin brides and arranged marriage
> Hijabs and polygamist husbands, those poor un-American girls.

At first sight, the verse reports the woman's socio-cultural critique of Islamic marriage. Yet, the verse implies that the aspects she deplores (e.g. virginity, arranged marriage, polygyny and hijabs) are taken out of its historical and spatial context and are only used to reinforce her American-centric perspective on marriage. Yet, at the same time, the verse evokes the notion that her marriage is not that different from the 'un-American girls.' Emphasizing the practice of taking the husband's last name, she partakes in yet another patriarchally constructed marriage. If anything, Frank Ocean uses his work to stress the value of an emotional commitment rather than to have it institutionalized and rendered empty, hollow or disposable. It is not surprising that many of his songs deal with heartbreak, estranged lovers and unstable relationships. Yet, this does not imply that he promotes heteronormative bliss. As songs such as 'Nature Feels' (*Nostalgia, Ultra*), 'Pink Matter' and 'Monks' (*Channel Orange*) illustrate, sex can be perfectly experienced in a pleasurable way outside of wedlock and without the necessity of love. What he does criticize are the discourses—whether materialized in political institutions or in socio-cultural norms and values—that hamper intimate commitments . . .

Last, the burden of being governed by hegemonic discourses and hegemonic masculinity also affects Frank Ocean as a man with same-sex desires—a theme that became more readable in his music after publicly disclosing that his first love was a man. Take for instance 'Bad Religion' (*Channel Orange*). The song features Frank Ocean confessing his unrequited love for a man to a cab driver. He tells the driver that he has 'three lives balanced on his head like steak knives,' which might be interpreted in terms of feeling forced to embody a fixed sexual identity category even though the identity might not correspond to his desires. Challenging the notion that sexual orientation is a fixed construction, his songs (and his tumblr note) avoid the labels 'gay' or 'homosexual.' Even though he might experience his sexual desires as confusing, he refuses to be confined to a rigid sexual identity category. He challenges the rational categorization in 'Pink Matter.' The song is not only intended as a deconstruction of masculine behavior, it also explores the relation between sexual pleasure and gender identities. Whereas the first verse of the song explores the relation of the male character with women—metaphorically referenced as pink matter—the second verse questions whether 'matter' is so important when it comes to sexual pleasure, as the verse ends with Frank Ocean making a stand for 'pleasure over matter.' Nonetheless, the song also brings to mind the power of hegemonic discourses such as heteronormativity—metaphorically represented as the purple matter—which is able to enforce the idea that sexual identity is fixed, natural and stable. Consequently, when Frank Ocean sings near the end of the song that he has no choice but to stick to blue matter since blue is his favorite color, he adopts a homosexual identity . . .

THE WEEKND: HEGEMONIC MASCULINITY IN CRISIS

With The Weeknd, alternative R&B was given yet another face that unsettled the conventions of contemporary R&B music. Like Frank Ocean, he defied the music industry by releasing his three mixtapes for free on the Internet, all in the same year. The Weeknd's music sounds less varied than Frank Ocean's and remains more close to the contemporary R&B signature in aesthetics and vocalizing. Nonetheless, by sampling, among others, 1960s French pop artist France Gall and a diversity of contemporary alternative rock artists such as Beach House and Cults, he broadens the musical perspective in which he positions himself. Furthermore, he introduces new themes into contemporary R&B by exploring a hedonist life of sex and drugs. Yet, what distinguishes him from the other artists in alternative R&B is his choice to remain a mystery. He conceals his private persona—Abel Tesfaye—as much as possible and refrains from providing background and interpretations to the musical world he creates. Taking into account the subjects he broaches and the questionable roles he assumes, however, both audiences and the music press are left wondering what to make of the songs and of the norms and values the artist holds.

Looking at the subjects in his work, it is remarkable that racial and class issues are largely ignored or left unspoken. Whereas Frank Ocean and other R&B and hip hop acts do engage in explicit and implicit social criticism of racial and class inequalities, The Weeknd portrays himself as a character whose main worries are related to women. Gender relations are at the heart of his music. Almost every song is built around the relation of The Weeknd with a girl/woman he is addressing in the lyrics. Throughout *Trilogy,* these relations are predominantly shaped as unequal. We are presented with a male character who is superior to almost all female characters in the songs, whereas the female characters are muted, objectified and, with the exception of a few songs, nameless and rid of any agency. On top of that, the female characters come across as passive and submissive, who are willingly subjected to his opinions, confessions and seductions. Whereas Frank Ocean represented diverse and contrasting masculinities, The Weeknd represents variations of the hegemonic masculine man. 'High For This' introduces audiences to this man and his attitudes toward women:

Close your eyes, lay yourself beside me
Hold tight for this ride
We don't need no protection
Come alone, we don't need attention.

Sung in an authoritative and seductive voice, he tries to persuade a woman into doing drugs and having sex. As the latter two phrases reveal, The Weeknd knows best. Yet, reading between the lines, the fact that a man convinces a woman of engaging in unsafe sex and doing drugs without priers implies that there is something suspicious with what is going to happen if she follows him. Other songs further fortify this image of a patriarchal deceiver. In 'Lonely Star' and 'Thursday'—two songs that make up one story—he convinces a woman to give up her life and devote herself to him. In return, he promises her 'the clothes, the jewels, the sex, the house' ('Lonely Star'). Yet, he then reveals the condition on which the relation will be based; he will only see her on Thursday. First, the songs reveal him as a patriarch who is not per se interested in loving a woman but rather owning a woman. He is prepared to provide her material wealth in return for sex. She, however, cannot expect an emotional commitment. Second, he is a hypersexual man who wants his (sexual) freedom—whether symbolically or literally—preserved. Even though he assumes often the role of patriarch, he does refer to other types of male characters in his songs. On the one hand, the songs feature men who are ridiculed, despised or threatened with violence if they are current or former boyfriends of the girls he is trying to seduce (e.g. 'What You Need,' 'House of Balloons/Glass Table Girls'). On the other, he references his gang, his 'boys,' who have his back and who come first before the girls (e.g. 'Loft Music,' 'Life of the Party'). In sum, The Weeknd qualifies as a hypermasculine, hypersexual and misogynist R&B and hip hop man.

However, that is just one way of looking at it. Reading The Weeknd's music, three other aspects need to be taken more explicitly into account to fully understand the gender politics of his songs. First, and quite central in his work, is a question of sincerity. Lacking context, each song has the potential to provoke the thought whether the artist supports the hypermasculinity and misogyny expressed by the I-character in his songs. To under-stand his position, we point out the song 'Valerie' as key in unraveling his position toward the hegemonic male identity. The song discusses how 'performance' is a crucial strategy employed by men to ensure their superior position:

There comes a time in a man's life
Where he must take responsibility
For the choices he has made
There are certain things that he must do Things that he must say
Like I love you
And I need you
I only want you
And nobody's going to know if it's true.

The cynical last phrase reveals how he and, according to him, men in general are able to fake a loving and dependable position in a relationship. A woman will never know whether her partner is merely putting on a show or not. Yet, more remarkable about this phrase is the exposure of that performance. Additionally, the last phrase also fortifies our argument that his music is not per se intended as true narratives and experiences. As audiences, we will never be able to know whether what he portrays is true. Yet, by provoking this thought, it does evoke a reading of his music as rather critical of the superiority of hegemonic masculinity.

Furthermore, The Weeknd's musical choices help to read his music culture as rather criticizing men's behavior than supporting it. First, by sampling songs by female artists in which men are critiqued, he allows the samples to operate as challenges to the discourse he expresses in his songs. For example, in 'House of Balloons/Glass Table Girls,' which samples the distinctive guitar riff and hook from Siouxsie and the Banshees' 'Happy House,' the hook of 'Happy House' is used as an ironic and cynic commentary to The Weeknd's attempt to convince his girl that their imbalanced and abusive relationship is perfectly normal:

This is a happy house
We're happy here
In a happy house
Oh this is fun.

As in the original song, the hook mocks the patriarchal exploitation of the male character. Another way of using music to convey a critique of hegemonic masculinity is articulated in specific conjunctions of sound and text. 'Life Of The Party' and 'Initiation' are exemplary for this practice. In the former, the spectrum of sound consists of raging electric guitars, an acoustic guitar that is strummed in an ironic way, and threatening metallic percussion sounds. Meanwhile, The Weeknd moans, sighs and giggles in a lunatic manner while his voice sounds slightly distorted. As The Weeknd is trying to, once again, lure a girl into a room full of men and drugs, the connotation of abuse becomes enhanced in the oppressive and upsetting sound of the song. In 'Initiation,' which features a similar narrative, the technique is pushed to an extreme. Drenched in a charged sound of brooding basses and sketchy break beats, The Weeknd tries to convince a girl into 'meeting his boys.' In return, he promises her his heart. Whether his boys operate as a metaphor for actual boys or for drugs, the threat of falling victim to a gang bang or to a risky drug party is near. Not only the sound operates as a warning, also his manipulated voice—which is rid of any humanity by being electronically lowered and sharpened throughout the song—announces the girl may end up in peril. The hegemonic male has been unmasked as a ghastly debased character.

Third, a few songs explicitly emasculate the hegemonic masculine man. To do so, The Weeknd connects the emasculation to a drug-infused lifestyle. In his music, drugs function as literal and metaphorical obstructions to having a healthy private and public life. Even though many of the male characters express a desire to be together with a woman, they are generally more interested in getting her as high as they are and, eventually, end up alone and/or emotionally detached from these women. In 'Gone,' he boasts to a girl about his skills to satisfy her sexually but ends up apologizing to the girl as he sinks more into his drug trip and eventually fails to perform. 'Gone,' like other songs on *Trilogy*, undermines the powerful and superior position of the hegemonic masculine man. In 'Coming Down,' the main male character acknowledges this. The song is an apology of a guy to a girlfriend after coming down from his drug trip. He expresses remorse and guilt while admitting that he is addicted to his 'friends'— used as a metaphor to the drugs he is on. This song features a rare moment of a male character exposing himself as vulnerable. Yet, other songs, such as 'Wicked Games,' 'The Knowing,' 'The Zone' or 'Rolling Stone' all feature male characters who are confronted with their own emotions and forced to deal with unrequited love, insecurity and jealousy. Yet, rather than negotiating the fact that the hegemonic masculine ideal is unrealistic and accepting their own emotionality, vulnerability and humanity, they indulge in more debauchery, machismo behavior and self-loathing.

In fact, if anything, The Weeknd presents a repertoire that explores a hegemonic masculinity in crisis. As Frank Ocean did in a few songs, The Weeknd holds out a mirror to men and shows them what is wrong with *men* in contemporary Western society. Even though he situates the characters of his songs in an underground community outside civil society, he populates the community with familiar men who consider their patriarchal rights natural and essential and who engage in verbal or physical abuses on their female partners.

CONCLUSION

This article started from the assumption that alternative R&B brought about a new array of masculinities, alternatives to the traditional and dominant characters of masculinity in contemporary R&B and hip hop. Even though Frank Ocean and The Weeknd differ significantly in approach, they both are engaged in questioning what it means to be a man in R&B and hip hop culture. Their representations of masculinity both express a craving for something real—a realness that stretches back to what hooks (2004) described as real in blues music and what she finds lacking in men of contemporary hip hop culture. Looking back at the gender representations in the work of both artists, it seems that only the masculinities in Ocean's world seem to qualify as 'real.' The male characters represented by Ocean are at least attempting to challenge the hegemonic interpretation of masculinity offered by both contemporary R&B and hip hop culture and heteronormative society at large. In the case of The Weeknd, we are predominantly confronted with men having a crisis over what is real. Furthermore, the postmodern approach employed by The Weeknd remains debatable. If anything, the ambiguous approach of exaggerating the gender hierarchies and gender violence rather than 'explicitly' critiquing it, while avoiding to represent a strong nonnormative masculine character and independent, confident female characters, holds the risk of being misinterpreted. For some, the songs may be read by some as a justification of gender and sexual violence, and for others, the thematic connotations may evaporate while listening to the music rather than the lyrics. As such, one may enjoy his crooning and angelic vocalizing while ignoring the ambiguous and unsettling content. In a way, the duplicity that typifies The Weeknd's approach is comparable to the work of other artists within R&B and hip hop culture, particularly White rapper Eminem. Rodman (2006) emphasizes that Eminem's hegemonic masculinity has often been considered autobiographical. As a result, his private and public persona has been held responsible for the use of violent, misogynist and homophobic lyrics. Ironically, Eminem's performance of multiple identities (e.g. Slim Shady and Marshall Mathers) has

seldom been taken into account when interpreting his music. Like The Weeknd, his work allows to be reinterpreted in terms of a hegemonic masculinity in crisis.

To conclude, both Frank Ocean and The Weeknd can be understood as being part of a music culture that reflects the social complexities of masculinities in current Western public spheres. The liberal environments in which contemporary R&B and hip hop operate are less dominated by homophobia, sexism and misogyny and provide spaces for nonnormative gender representations and pro-gay attitudes. However, as the crisis within The Weeknd's work illustrates, the changing of cultural understandings of masculinities is often accompanied by same-old hegemonic recuperations. Moreover, these continuous oscillations between representations of alternative masculinities and hegemonic reinforcements debouch in multiple everyday interpretations and appropriations at the individual, societal and cultural level.

NOTES

1. It should be noted that lesbian, gay, bisexual and transgenders (LGBTs) do not automatically challenge hegemonic masculinity. Like heterosexual and cisgender men, men who experience same-sex desires and transgender men can assume/perform a hegemonic masculine identity and/or express

homophobia and misogyny (Connell and Messerschmidt, 2005).

2. We assume the other character is male, based on the following verse: 'My eyes don't shed tears, but boy they pour when I'm thinking "bout you".'

REFERENCES

Battan C (2012) We invented swag: NYC's Queer Rap. *Pitchfork,* 21 March. Available at: http://pitchfork.com/features/articles/8793-we-invented-swag/ (accessed 5 May 2013).

Butler J (1999) *Gender Trouble: Feminism and the Subversion of Identity* (2nd edn). London: Routledge.

Connell RW (2005) *Masculinities* (2nd edn). Berkeley, CA/Los Angeles, CA: University of California Press.

Connell RW and Messerschmidt JW (2005) Hegemonic masculinity: Rethinking the concept. *Gender & Society* 19(6): 829–859.

DeVille C (2012) The new wave of R&B comes into full bloom. *Stereogum,* 24 December. Available at: http://stereogum.com/1225571/2012-in-review-the-new-wave-of-rb-comes-into-full-bloom/ (accessed 5 May 2013).

Fennessey S (2011) Love vs. money: The Weeknd, Frank Ocean, and R&B's Future Shock. *The Village Voice,* 23 March. Available at: http://blogs.villagevoice.com/music/2011/03/the_weeknd_frank_ocean.php (accessed 5 May 2013).

Halberstam J (2005) *In a Queer Time and Place: Transgender Bodies, Subcultural Lives.* New York and London: New York University Press.

hooks b (2004) *We Real Cool: Black Men and Masculinity*. New York and London: Routledge.

Iwamoto D (2003) Tupac Shakur: Understanding the identity formation of hyper-masculinity of a popular hip hop artist. *The Black Scholar* 33(2): 44–49.

Jeffries MP (2010) Can a Thug (get some) love? Sex, romance, and the definition of a hip hop 'Thug.' *Women and Language* 32(2): 35–41.

Johnson EP (2003) *Appropriating Blackness: Performance and the Politics of Authenticity*. Durham, NC: Duke University Press.

Jonze T (2012) Frank Ocean and the courage to come out. *The Guardian*, 4 July. Available at: http://www.guardian.co.uk/music/2012/jul/04/frank-ocean-courage-come-out (accessed 5 May 2013).

Kubrick S (1999) *Eyes Wide Shut*. [DVD] United Kingdom: Warner Bros. Entertainment Inc. Lawrence J (2012) Sex, drugs and the underground: The Weeknd. *Creative Loafing Charlotte*, 19 October. Available at: http://clclt.com/charlotte/sex-drugs-and-the-underground-the-weeknd/Content?oid=2892484 (accessed 5 May 2013).

McCormack M and Anderson E (2010) 'It's Just not Acceptable Anymore': The erosion of homophobia and the softening of masculinity at an English sixth form. *Sociology* 44(5): 843–859.

McLeod K (2009) The construction of masculinity in African American music and sports. *American Music* 27(2): 204–226.

Maultsby PK (1983) Soul music: Its sociological and political significance in American popular culture. *Journal of Popular Culture* 17(2): 51–60.

Neal A (1997) Sold out on soul: The corporate annexation of Black popular music. *Popular Music and Society* 21(3): 117–135.

Ocean F (2011) *Nostalgia, Ultra*. [online] available at http://www.oddfuture.com/products/frank-ocean-nostalgia-ultra (accessed 5 May 2013).

Ocean F (2012a) Untitled (Blog post). Available at: http://frankocean.tumblr.com/post/33700009336 (accessed 5 May 2013).

Ocean F (2012b) *Channel, Orange*. [CD] United States: Def Jam Recordings.

Penney J (2012) 'We Don't Wear Tight Clothes': Gay panic and queer style in contemporary hip hop. *Popular Music and Society* 35(3): 321–332.

Rodman GB (2006) Race . . . and other four letter words: Eminem and the cultural politics of authenticity. *Popular Communication* 42(2): 95–121.

Smalls SP (2011) 'The Rain Comes Down': Jean Gray and hip hop heteronormativity. *American Behavioral Scientist* 55(1): 86–95.

Soderberg B (2012) Trend of the year: Alt R&B. *Spin*, 6 December. Available at: http://www.spin.com/articles/trend-of-the-year-alt-rb-2012-frank-ocean-weeknd-miguel (accessed 5 May 2013).

Stewart JB (2005) Message in the music: Political commentary in Black popular music from rhythm and blues to early hip hop. *Journal of African American History* 90(3): 196–225.

Walters B (2012) Frank Ocean, Miguel and Holy Other in PBR&B 2.0. *Spin*, 22 August. Available at: http://www.spin.com/articles/frank-ocean-miguel-and-holy-other-usher-in-pbrb-20 (accessed 5 May 2013).

Ward B (1998) *Just My Soul Responding: Rhythm and Blues, Black Consciousness, and Race Relations*. London; Berkeley, CA and Los Angeles, CA: University of California Press.

Warner M (1999) *The Trouble with Normal*. Cambridge, MA: Harvard University Press.

Watkins SC (2006) *Hip Hop Matters: Politics, Pop Culture, and the Struggle for the Soul of the Movement*. Boston, MA: Beacon Press.

The Weeknd (2012) *Trilogy*. [CD] United States: republic records.

Weitzer R and Kubrin CE (2009) Misogyny in rap music: A content analysis of prevalence and meanings. *Men and Masculinities* 12(1): 3–29.

Wilson DM (2007) Post-pomo hip-hop homos: Hip-hop art, gay rappers and social change. *Social Justice* 34(1): 117–140.

Wise SJ (2001) Redefining black masculinity and manhood: Successful Black gay men speak out. *Journal of African American Men* 5(4): 3–22.

Zemeckis R (1994) *Forrest Gump*. [DVD] United States: Paramount Pictures.

THE LIMITATIONS OF THE DISCOURSE OF NORMS

Gay Visibility and Degrees of Transgression

Jay Clarkson

41

Painful.

Both my partner and I are totally straight-acting, very masculine, and when we're in mixed company with someone who's . . . um . . . well, let's just say they open their mouth & their purse falls out, well, we get rather uncomfortable.

Case in point: a big get-together of a bunch of friends last year at the local Macaroni Grille (chain Italian restaurant). Thing is, this is suburban Detroit, not the Castro, and a table full of fourteen guys in a busy restaurant full of middle-class families might get noticed of its own accord!

Add in one of our friends, let's call him "Bill." Not his real name. Bill's 23, lives at home, has no responsibilities, and is finishing up interior design school. He's emaciated thin; we think he lives on ice chips, Dolce & Gabbana anything, and Swarovski crystal trinkets. Both he and another member of our crew decided that this would be the perfect place to turn up their flames from "dull glow" to "viewable-from-space." It was all I could do not to either 1. smack him or 2. flee the building.

Because my one pet peeve, more than anything else with regards to gay men (besides the idiots who believe that HIV is a curable disease and therefore don't use protection) are fags who don't recognize the conditions of their environment. There's a time to flame out (greeting friends in the gay bar) and a time to tone it down (the sideline at an NFL game). Boys who don't change their temperament in accordance with their conditions endanger themselves and those they're with, in my opinion. (roadster_guy)

At the heart of the politics of gay representation are two intersecting considerations: the meanings and functions of visibility, and the role of gender performance in our understanding of sexuality. This chapter continues the discussion of gay visibility and gender transgression that has emerged as a key concept in recent scholarship of GLBTQ (gay, lesbian, bisexual, transgender, and queer) representation in the media. I explore the discourse of the discussion board of StraightActing.com, an Internet discussion board for self-identified straight-acting gay men, to demonstrate how current popular understandings of representational power create divisiveness among groups of gay men who seek to normalize a particular set of gender performances as acceptably gay, at the expense of other performances perceived as more transgressive. . . .

The discourse of visibility on StraightActing. com is useful because the online space functions for self-proclaimed straight-acting gay men to make themselves visible to other gay men. Their discussions include significant debate about the nature of their and other gay men's visibility, of which I have chosen a representative sample. Their discourse mirrors critical understandings of the power of visibility and gender transgression. They demonize an effeminate gay stereotype, which they perceive as dominating media representations of gay men, because they fear that it functions to construct a normative gay identity that is promoted by other gay men and can only be undone with increased visibility of straight-acting gay men. . . . Their argument assumes that transgressive gender performance, not just same-sex desire, is the root of antigay attitudes.

From Jay Clarkson, "The Limitations of the Discourse of Norms: Gay Visibility and Degrees of Transgression." *Journal of Communication Inquiry* (2008), 32 (4), 368–382. Reprinted with permission of SAGE Publications.

Homophobia in this formulation is reduced to a fear of particular gender performances, and not a deeper cultural fear of same-sex attraction. The visibility of straight-acting gay men, or men who cannot be read as gay, may challenge the notion of a hegemonic and monolithic gay identity, but they reflect the historic need for the marginalized to remain obedient, silent, and invisible in order to be recuperated into dominant ideologies (Owen, Vande Berg, & Stein, 2007). I argue that for gay visibility to challenge the hegemonic gender regime, the acceptance of outspoken, disobedient, visible gay men and lesbians is necessary to raise acceptance of all gay people, including those who identify as straight acting, and to recognize the diversity of gay identities.

CONCEPTUALIZING VISIBILITY

It is important to remember that visibility is not in itself an unproblematic concept. Peggy Phelan criticizes identity politics for its reliance on the assumption that a lack of media visibility of a minority group reflects and reproduces inequality, and accordingly, these groups should seek great power through increased visibility. Phelan has quipped, "If representational visibility equals power, then almost-naked young white women should be running Western Culture" (Phelan, 1993, p. 10). She recognizes that equating visibility with power is problematic, for in its supposed promise of liberation it invites increased surveillance. . . . The notion that the power visibility promises may be reduced to quantity is nonsensical, since visibility is often used to signify deviance and not to promote tolerance (see, e.g., Sloop, 2004). . . .

Gay and lesbian media critics have long recognized that media visibility of gay men and lesbians often functions only to make a certain type of homosexual natural and normal (Battles & Hilton-Murrow, 2002; Dyer, 1977; Shugart, 2003). It is important therefore for critics to analyze gay and lesbian visibility to see how it is being used by heterosexual society to define homosexuality. . . . Despite the widely accepted notion that GLBTQ people turn to the media to understand homosexuality, there remains a relative void in research detailing the ways that actual gay people conceptualize visibility in the media or in actual social practice. It is important to look beyond merely examining media texts to

determine how transgressive performances may be constructed, and to actually observe how these transgressive performances are read by those who oppose them. . . .

Degrees of Transgression and the Limits of Normalization

The passage from roadster_guy that begins this chapter reveals the tension over gay visibility that exists even within gay communities.[1] In answering the question "How have your experiences with nelly men been," roadster_guy blames those who are read as gay for their own oppression and advocates invisibility for gay men. He demonstrates a homophobic, but widely accepted and repeated, view: those who do not alter their behaviors to avoid the risk of offending potentially homophobic bystanders are responsible for any disciplinary action that those homophobes may choose to inflict. Furthermore, the fact that he would consider smacking his friend for displaying any sort of gender transgression reveals his reliance on blending into a presumably heterosexual environment at any cost, and his assumption that gender performance is an overtly agentic set of choices to be made.

Given roadster_guy's obvious discomfort with Bill, even before he broadcast his flaming performance to space, it is unclear why Bill is his friend at all. His reaction does reveal how gender transgressors are disciplined differently than those who conform. Most importantly, it reveals that selective homophobia is alive and well within gay communities. It suggests that some gay men fear the gender performances they see as flaming, not only because they do not like them, but also because they fear what those performances may mean to straight people. However, it is these flaming gender performances which represent a heightened degree of transgression that, as the visibility of gay men grows, remains a barometer for gay rights and highlights how the gender and sex regime continues to operate even within gay communities. Potentially, as Halberstam (1998) argues, these transgressors are not simply saying no to the dominant gender regime, but are in fact saying "I don't care" to the system of power, and thus it is more difficult for disciplinary forces to cope with this transgression.

I submit "degrees of transgression" as a metaphor for discussing the political potential of rethinking "normalization" of gay visibility as "conventionalization." This phrasing should remind critics that "flaming gays" remain among the most marginalized members of society, even in some gay communities. Even when these flamers are represented in the media, audiences, including gay men, often are positioned to laugh at gender transgression, not to identify with those who perform it. Furthermore, many assume that the presence of a flamer positions the reader to laugh at the transgression, even if the audience is positioned to identify with the transgressor. The flamer needs to be validated in media texts, and by media audiences, as a critical first step toward the acceptance of these gender performances as legitimate conventions of the larger and more diverse gay community. . . .

NEGATING TRANSGRESSION IN REPRESENTATIONS OF GAY PRIDE

The limits of normalization and the fear of heightened degrees of transgression can be observed in the discourse of StraightActing.com. Several of its members suggest that gay visibility would improve in quality if gay pride parades were abolished and gay men implemented a strategy of being "quietly gay":

> I'm not sure gay pride is working. A gay author, Dan Savage, I think, suggested that once the disease is cured, the cure becomes toxic. Once the cancer is gone, the chemo will kill you. I think the Stonewall/Gay Pride movement was a necessary cure, and brought the gay world to people's attention. But I think that what was once the cure is now toxic. I see more and more of our rights taken away, and more hate crimes, because the flamboyant elements of the gay movement have remained in power after they have ceased to be effective, IMHO.[2]
>
> I suggest a movement called "quietly gay." I think it's important for me to be out to the people closest to me, but as for the rest of the world, they can "do the math." I don't need to be vocal or up front with the world at large. And I think the world would be more accepting if we just lived our lives in our own little world. I think that we are losing because people continue to shove their orientation in people's faces. I think a new vanguard of "normal" men living normal lives would help the movement more at

this moment in time. Thought I'd toss that out for discussion. (James)

James is interpreting Dan Savage, a controversial gay columnist, correctly. Savage does argue that pride has outlived its usefulness and may be more of a hindrance than a help. The article that James is citing argues that gay pride functions to suggest that there is a unified gay community, and warns of the danger of assuming that all gay people look out for each other.

Of course, Savage is correct in asserting that not all gay people are allies, as the discourse of this Web site reveals; however, he is wrong to assume that we are at the point where a cure for societal homophobia is no longer needed. I am not arguing that pride is the solution to homophobia, but Savage's perspective that gay rights have been won is tragically optimistic and ignores the growing amount of antigay physical and political violence, as well as the overwhelming body of legislation that has passed to prevent GLBTQ people from enjoying equal access to citizenship.[3]

James, in his post above, reveals that antigay sentiment is still quite strong among large sections of the American population. However, James attributes this sentiment, and an increase in hate crimes, to the visibility of "flamboyant" gay people, and argues that we should move toward a gay identity that conforms to normative standards of gender identity while retaining nonnormative sexual identities. His comments suggest that invisibility is his preferred strategy and that normalization of his particular gender identity is more important than the acceptance of other conventions of gay identity. James's insistence on reduced visibility for particular types of gay people does recognize that diversity exists, but his strategy of reduced visibility attempts to rhetorically douse those who perform higher degrees of transgression. . . .

James's perspective represents only one side of the debate about visibility on StraightActing.com. Xaphan is the first to challenge James's understanding of the power of gay visibility:

> Ahh, but the chemo doesn't get all the cancer during the first treatment. You need to have repeated treatments and follow up to make sure it's gone. Pride is that treatment. And each year, society as a whole gets a little dose of Queer Chemo.

Pride in Boston started 35 years ago. Since that time we've become more visible, less discriminated against, have more rights, less fears, and now we can marry. We're getting to be cured of the homophobic cancer. Will it all go away? Nope. There are still people that think blacks should go back to Africa and women shouldn't be independent. But, can we improve conditions for a more equal world, yes.

So while Pride is seen by people with clouded vision (nice way of saying ignorant fools) as a show of flamboyance, it is in fact exposure, a dose of the variation of life. If Pride is a foolish display of homosexuality, then what of Mardi Gras, Carnival, and Spring Break. What do these things say of heterosexual people? What do they say of young people? And these are groups who don't require any visibility or more acceptance.

So Pride is the continuation of the homophobia chemotherapy. (Xaphan)

Xaphan recognizes that gay rights have increased since the inception of gay pride events, although whether this is as a consequence is impossible to determine. His comment reveals the assumptions of identity politics: that increased visibility results in increased power, which here is framed as acceptance and civil rights. More importantly, he reveals the power of exposing the invisible in order to challenge interpretations of the visible. His comparison of the heterosexual displays of Spring Break and Mardi Gras to the homosexual "flamboyance" of gay pride reveals the ways in which homosexuality is seen and heterosexuality remains unmarked, because these expressions of heterosexuality are contextualized, and thus seen as only one convention of heterosexuality. Few complain about the display of heterosexuality during Spring Break, although some complain about its graphic nature. Furthermore, this distinction recognizes the diversity in heterosexual sexuality—not just their straightness, but the ways that they may employ their sexuality in public or in private. However, the assumption that Xaphan is revealing is that gay sexuality is defined for the public by the gay pride events: that the norm is public displays of sex and sexuality, not that these are indicative of a particular group within the gay community.

What the discourse about gay pride reveals is not that some of these men believe that visibility does not lead to social change, but instead that they see only specific types of representation leading to social change. The flaming performances that are traditionally associated with gay pride are rejected when James advocates that gay people should quietly emulate heterosexual relationships. In the following comment James elaborates on what "quietly gay" means to him. In doing so he assumes that one can be publicly gay without revealing the private desires that homosexuality entails:

> For me, the couples standing in line to get licenses in San Francisco was a powerful, quiet witness. It said something strong and true about the gay experience, and didn't require any costumes. I'm not asking anyone to sit down and shut up—I'm thinking of becoming visible in a different set of roles. I don't think the public at large benefits from knowing about my private desires, but they can see me working for a candidate, cleaning up a park, being a churchgoer, etc., and do the math from the way I live my life. I think the last election has shown that rather than gaining us rights, the gay pride movement is galvanizing people against us. Showing that we are the same as everybody else, and living our lives with our orientation blended in with the rest of the flavors of our lives, would do more to help the cause now, IMHO. (James) . . .

CONCLUSION

The important difference between norm and convention lies in the insistence on a plurality. However, the intragroup struggle over a dominant convention, revealed in the discourse of StraightActing.com, reveals the danger of the current conceptualization of visibility among gay men. The reliance on this discourse of normalization suggests that what media representations contribute to is a single norm for gay men, and all else are abnormal or less than acceptable. Formulating representational power as normalizing, and not conventionalizing, promotes divisiveness among members of the gay community, struggling over which of their identities may become normalized. Just as heterosexuality is not reduced to a single norm, with its recurring representation in MTV's variety of Spring Break specials and coverage of overt sexual display at Mardi Gras celebrations, homosexuality at gay pride parades may be thought of as contextualized within that moment. The displays of homosexuality are conventions that occur within a particular moment and do not represent homosexuality as a whole, and may not even represent the lives of those who engage in these displays at pride events. A discursive shift to conventionalization may reduce the intergroup struggle over who is represented, by assuming a wider range of degrees of transgression.

The discourse of media stereotypes of gay men reveals both pro- and anti-visibility perspectives. In their calls for inclusion, these men focus on inclusion for those men who adhere to the traditional and perhaps conventional expectations of male behavior. In this discussion group, these particular men want to see a change in the ways gay men are represented. They are angered by the seeming focus on feminine gay representations and want to shift the focus to gay men who act just like "normal" heterosexual men, thus returning feminine gay men to a closet of symbolic annihilation.

Indeed, they want to return to the privileged position of seeming to be just like heterosexual men, so that they can assume some of the power that this position entails. . . .

Some of these men, as well as some media critics, argue that increased visibility of straight-acting gay men has the potential to undo what they see as the negative consequence of the prevalence of effeminate gay stereotypes and those who uphold them. They fail to recognize the liberatory potential of representing higher degrees of transgression. While their argument seems to be that their increased visibility will lead to greater acceptance of homosexuals, they fail to acknowledge that the root of homophobia remains homosexuality. They seek to normalize gay men as "real men," but their strategy for confronting homophobia is limited to challenging the conflation of gender and sexuality, and does not seek acceptance for those whose degrees of transgression are higher. It does not challenge the fear or hatred of gayness. . . .

NOTES

1. StraightActing.com is a privately funded Web site for self-proclaimed straight-acting gay men that can be read by all, but users must register (at no cost) to post. The site is based around the discussion area called the Butch Boards, but also includes a series of straight-acting quizzes and, before a massive server crash in the summer of 2004, personal ads, home pages, and other services. The Butch Boards and the quiz have been restored, but unfortunately the previous content has been irreparably lost, and the discussion boards started anew early in October 2004. In June 2005, the Butch Board included 18 forums ranging from 41 to 310 topics in each. Overall, there were slightly less than 55,000 total posts, ranging widely in length and content. While the forum descriptions suggest that the discussion topics are well organized, there is considerable overlap in topic area from forum to forum. As part of a larger study, I engaged all areas of the discussion board in order to avoid overlooking certain perspectives or favoring one forum's most active posters. This chapter focuses exclusively on the discourse of visibility in these forums.

2. IMHO is a common acronym for "In my humble opinion."

3. Five more states voted to ban same-sex marriage in the 2006 election, bringing the total number to 24.

REFERENCES

Battles, K., & Hilton-Morrow, W. (2002). Gay characters in conventional spaces: *Will & Grace* and the situation comedy genre. *Critical Studies in Media Communication, 19*(1), 87–106.

Dyer, R. (1977). *Gays and film*. London: British Film Institute.

Halberstam, J. (1998). *Female masculinity*. Durham, NC: Duke University Press.

Hequembourg, A., & Arditi, J. (1999). Fractured resistances: The debate over assimilationism among gays and lesbians in the United States. *Sociological Quarterly, 40,* 663–680.

Owen, A. S., Vande Berg, L. R., & Stein, S. R. (2007). *Bad girls: Cultural politics and media representations of transgressive women.* New York: P. Lang.

Phelan, P. (1993). *Unmarked: The politics of performance.* London: Routledge.

Shugart, H. A. (2003). Reinventing privilege: The new (gay) man in contemporary popular media. *Critical Studies in Media Communication, 20*(1), 67–92.

Sloop, J. M. (2004). *Disciplining gender: Rhetorics of sex identity in contemporary U.S. culture.* Amherst: University of Massachusetts Press.

Squires, C. R., & Brouwer, D. C. (2002). In/discernible bodies: The politics of passing in dominant and marginal media. *Critical Studies in Media Communication, 19*(3), 283–311.

42 HETERO BARBIE?

Mary F. Rogers

As they enter their teenage years, if not before, most heterosexual females begin putting a boy or young man at the center of their lives. Moving through puberty toward adulthood, girls and young women find that their popularity at school, their feminine credibility, and much else hinge on their attractiveness to boys and their relationship with one particular boy.[1] As they get heterosexualized, then, girls and young women face pressures to give boys and dating a lot of priority. In turn, they pay increasing attention to the size and shape of their bodies, the range and contents of their wardrobes, the styling of their hair, and the making up of their faces. Barbie epitomizes, even exaggerates, these families mandates. She gives girls endless opportunities to costume her, brush and style her hair, and position her in settings like aerobics class, a school dance, or the shopping mall.

Yet Barbie escapes the typical outcomes of such activities. In the end she seems not to have her heart in her relationship with Ken, who in no way monopolizes her attention. Barbie exudes an independence that deviates from the codes of mainstream femininity. That she is insistently single and perpetually childless means that hers is no "normal" femininity. Again, one comes up short by looking for an explanation in Barbie's teenage status, for she is no teenager when it comes to occupations, travel, and other aspects of her lifestyle. The facts of Barbie's having neither a husband nor a child do not speak for themselves, then. Instead, these circumstances leave Barbie open to multiple, conflicting interpretations. They enlarge this icon's field of meanings and thus the range of consumers she can attract.

Within that field of cultural meanings stands the possibility that Barbie may not be heterosexual.

Indeed, she may not even be a woman. Barbie may be a drag queen. Much in the tradition made widely visible by stars like RuPaul, Barbie may be the ultrafeminine presence that drag queens personify. Her long, long legs and flat hips suggest this possibility. So does her wardrobe, especially her shimmering evening gowns, high heels, heavy-handed makeup, and brilliant tiaras and other headpieces. Barbie's is a bright, glittery femininity never visibly defiled by a Lady Schick or Kotex. This exceptionally, emphatically feminine icon has some appeal among gay men.

That appeal shows up in diverse ways. I have no interest in whether or not this designer or that, this collector or that, this event or that is gay, however. My concern is with the *gay-themed* character of what one comes across in some corners of Barbie's far-reaching world. In many cultural worlds heterocentrism and heterosexism prevail in no uncertain terms. In the world of "Father Knows Best" or the feminine mystique, attention to gender and family center on heterosexuality strongly enough to snuff out alternative readings whereby "transgressive" sexualities such as lesbianism or bisexuality can enter the picture. Commonly intertwined with such heterocentrism are values celebrating heterosexuality as normal and natural while condemning or at least rejecting lesbigay sexualities. The world of Barbie is *relatively* free of such heterocentrism and heterosexism and thus holds *relative* appeal for nonheterosexual people, especially gay men. Lesbians, particularly those inclined toward feminism, are more likely to reject some of the central features of Barbie's world, as are bisexuals who might find her apparent monosexuality unappealing. In any case, Barbie's world allows for nonstraight readings, just

From Rogers, M. F. (1999), *Barbie Culture*. London: SAGE Publications Ltd. Reprinted by permission of SAGE Publications Ltd.

as many other "straight" cultural products do.[2] I tap such possibilities here by treating Barbie's sexual identity as less than certain while arguing that her sweeping appeal revolves around such ambiguities.

As an icon of drag, Barbie illustrates what feminists and culture critics have been saying for some years. In no uncertain terms Barbie demonstrates that femininity is a manufactured reality. It entails a lot of artifice, a lot of clothes, a lot of props such as cuddly poodles and shopping bags, and a lot of effort, however satisfying at times.[3] If Barbie can join drag queens as an exemplar of the constructed character of femininity, she can also be an icon of nonheterosexual femininity. In the extreme Barbie might be a lipstick lesbian, a lesbian fem, or a lesbian closeted more tightly than most who choose not to "come out." She might be a bisexual woman who once cared about and pursued a relationship with Ken but now prefers her "best friend" Midge. Most radically of all, Barbie might be asexual. She might be sexy without being sexual, attractive without being attracted. . . .

Not surprisingly, RuPaul sometimes shows up in Barbie's world. Scott Arend (1995) reports that Ivan Burton, who designs artist dolls, has done a "one-of-a-kind RuPaul." Jim Washburn (1994) says that Michael Osborne, a Barbie doll collector, wants to be buried with what he calls his "RuPaul Barbie, or Ru-Barbie for short." Osborne's favorite doll is made from a My Size Barbie, the 18-inch version of the doll, and has "brown skin, blue eyes and platinum hair."

The feature story on Osborne, which appeared in the *Los Angeles Times,* illustrates how a gay-themed text fits into a mainstream publication, that is, how a gay reading of a supposedly straight text involves little stretch of the nonheterosexual imagination. Twenty-four-year-old Osborne, who has been collecting Barbie dolls since he was thirteen, has nearly 300 of them and makes no attempt to hide his "love" for them. Osborne says he has friends employed by Mattel who help him acquire some of his more unusual dolls, such as a hairless Skipper, Barbie's little sister. Like other collectors, Osborne keeps a lot of his dolls in their original packaging. (NRFB, or Never Removed From Box, enhances the market value of a doll.) Osborne, however, has "play-with dolls, whose outfits he changes monthly." He also shampoos his dolls' hair and gives them permanents. Also,

Osborne once dressed as Barbie at Halloween and claims to have "looked pretty darn snappy." Asked about the possibility that his sizable Barbie collection could be an obstacle to "finding a mate," Osborne responds in terms of "friends who have had rocky relationships with *people* because they did not really like Barbie." Washburn poses the more difficult question: What "if it came down to a choice between giving up the Barbies or the *person?*" Osborne answers, "It depends on the *person,* but probably the *person.*"

Where a heterocentrist text would talk about finding a wife or a woman, this one refers only to mates and people and persons. In view of its subject matter this text readily passes as gay-themed. Along those lines Osborne reports, "I had always liked fashion, always liked doing hair. When people asked what I wanted to be when I grew up, I said I wanted to be a hairdresser and president of Mattel." Osborne's interest in being a hairdresser expresses an interest in what queer theorists, who theorize about nonheterosexual or "transgressive" sexualities, call *non-normative occupations.* Such lines of work are those that attract disproportionate numbers of lesbigay people and are widely considered inappropriate for people of a given gender. The ballet and hairdressing for men and the military and auto mechanics for women are examples. In any event Osborne's interest in a non-normative occupation bespeaks a gay-themed text, as does his claim that "the best times of his life have been Barbie times.." . .

More generally, *Barbie Bazaar* often offers gay-themed fare for those attuned to it. Like most such material, it does not leap out to most readers as lesbigay even while leaving room for "queer" interpretations. . . Often, too, gay-themed material shows up in comments about or articles on doll artists, most of whom appear to be men often working in conjunction with male "partners" to refashion Barbie in designs of their own. In one *Barbie Bazaar* article Pattie Jones (1995), for instance, mentions Jim Faraone, who once designed jewelry for Anne Klein but now "designs hand-beaded Barbie doll outfits." Faraone began collecting in 1986 and now has a thousand Barbie dolls. Two of his artist dolls are pictured in Janine Fennick's *The Collectible Barbie Doll* (1996). One is AIDS Awareness Barbie where the AIDS-awareness red ribbon runs around the back of Barbie's neck, across her breasts, and then crosses at her waist. Also showing up in *Barbie Bazaar* are references to Mattel's participation with collectors and other Barbie fans in AIDS fundraisers, often targeting children with AIDS as beneficiaries. . . .

Barbie thus points to what Jesse Berrett (1996) sees as "mass culture's power to define, commodify, and mutate sexual identity." Put more queerly in terms used in *Out* magazine:

RuPaul's larger-than-life, gayer-than-gay presence on runways, VH1, and New York radio and everywhere else . . . suggests that the mall of America has embraced him not as a novelty but as a genuine homo star. But it doesn't take a drag queen to have an impact. (1997: 96)

Mattel can unintentionally sponsor the same impact, it seems. . . .

NOTES

1. For insights into this state of affairs, see Eder with Evans and Parker (1995), Fine (1992), and Walkerdine (1990).

2. See, for example, Valerie Traub, "The Ambiguities of 'Lesbian' Viewing Pleasure: The (Dis)Articulation of *Black Widow*," in Julia Epstein and Kristina Straub (eds.), *Body Guards: The Cultural Politics of Gender Ambiguity* (New York, Routledge, 1991), pp. 304–9; Bonnie Zimmerman, "Seeing, Reading, Knowing: The Lesbian Appropriation of Literature," in Joan E. Hartman and Ellen Messer-Davidow (eds.),

(En)Gendering Knowledge: Feminists in Academe (Knoxville, University of Tennessee Press, 1991), pp. 92–7.

3. Dorothy E. Smith is one of the best commentators on how pleasurable some of the projects of femininity can be. She talks, for example, about the pleasures of female community built up around such feminine pastimes as clothes shopping. See *Texts, Facts, and Femininity: Exploring the Relations of Ruling* (London and New York: Routledge, 1990), p. 199.

REFERENCES

Arend, S. (1994). Review of mondo Barbie. *Barbie Bazaar, 6*, 51.

Berrett, J. (1996). The sex revolts: Reading gender and identity in mass culture. *Radical History Review, 66*, 210–219.

Eder, D., with Evans, C., & Parker, P. (1995). *School talk: Gender and adolescent culture.* New Brunswick, NJ: Rutgers University Press.

Fennick, J. (1996). *The collectible Barbie doll: An illustrated guide to her dreamy world.* Philadelphia: Courage Books.

Fine, M. (1992). *Disruptive voices: The possibilities of feminist research.* Ann Arbor: University of Michigan Press.

Jones, P. (1995). Viva la Barbie. *Barbie Bazaar, 7*, 63–67.

Walkerdine, V. (1990). *Schoolgirl fictions.* London and New York: Verso.

Washburn, J. (1994). The man who would be Ken. *Los Angeles Times*, 2 August: 1: Life & Style Section.

FANTASIES OF EXPOSURE

43

Belly Dancing, the Veil, and the Drag of History

Joanna Mansbridge

INTRODUCTION

Is it paternalistic of us in the West to try to liberate women who insist that they're happy as they are? No, I think we're on firm ground. If most Saudi women want to wear a tent, if they don't want to drive, then that's fine. But why not give them the choice? . . . If Saudi Arabians choose to kill their economic development and sacrifice international respect by clinging to the 15th century, if the women prefer to remain second-class citizens, then I suppose that's their choice. But if anyone chooses to behave so foolishly, is it any surprise that outsiders point and jeer? (Nicholas Kristof)

In 2011, New Zealand cartoonist Malcolm Evans articulated a pithy truth. His cartoon, "Cruel Culture," shows two women looking at each other, one blond and donning a bikini and sunglasses, the other in a *burqa* with only her eyes showing. The blonde's thought bubble reads, "Everything covered but her eyes. What a cruel male-dominated culture," while the *burqa*-clad woman's thought bubble reads, "Nothing covered but her eyes. What a cruel male-dominated culture." A whole history is embedded in this encounter. The simple dichotomy between oppressed and empowered women structuring most media representations of Western and Muslim femininities upholds broader political divisions, in which individual choice, sexual freedom, and visibility are aligned with Western modernity and democracy, while conformity, modesty, and veiling are aligned with antiquated religious oppression. In both cases, women's bodies are used as sites onto which multiple differences—political, religious, sexual,

and cultural—are either imaginatively resolved (belly dancing) or reinforced (the veil).[1] Saudi women's social agency and public visibility are not merely a matter of choice, but part of complex political, religious, economic, and colonial histories. Kristof's derisive dismissal of them exemplifies the media's failure to think historically and its simplistic deployment of neoliberalized notions of choice. While the stock media image of the veiled Muslim woman threatens neoliberal individualism and its collapsed notions of sexual and political freedom, the image of the belly dancer, as circulated in contemporary Western popular culture, fosters a fantasy of a global (read: universal[2]) femininity that is exposed and free. However, as practiced outside of these commodified media contexts, both veiling and belly dancing take on very different, often contradictory meanings that may reveal the histories (of gender, colonialism, modernity, and multiculturalism) that they "drag" with it.

"Drag"—specifically "cultural drag" and "temporal drag"—offers a way of understanding belly dancing as a theatrical practice that is fraught with ambivalences, fantasies, and unfinished histories. The veil, as a socioreligious practice, is not more authentic within this framework; rather, it is the politicized counterpart to the eroticized fantasy that belly dancing performs. One of the contradictions is that many Arab/Muslim women continue to belly dance for employment and pleasure, while Western women have been drawn to belly dancing as a way to feel more sexually empowered. Moreover, the tradition of male belly dancers remains curiously absent in most historical accounts and contemporary practices,

From Mansbridge, J. (2016). Fantasies of exposure: Belly dancing, the veil, and the drag of history. *Journal of Popular Culture, 49*(1): 29–56. © 2016.

while the tradition of belly dancing as a spiritual, feminist practice is often dismissed as trivial or appropriative. The erasure of belly dancing's queer and feminist histories enables the dance to sustain a fantasy of timeless femininity, a fantasy that upholds broader narratives of modernity that depend, in part, on the circulation of the publicly visible, sexualized female body as a sign of freedom and choice within a free market economy. Popular culture representations of belly dancing and media representations of the veil can work together to project polarized images of Western and Muslim femininities, which are understood through such binaries as exposed/concealed, timeless/time-bound, universal/restricted, accessible/controlled, free/oppressed. This dualistic image system obscures belly dancing's queer and feminist histories and the veil's use as a symbol of protest and practice of subjectification. In a moment when hostilities surrounding the veil are gaining force and belly dancing is permeating popular culture, it seems especially urgent to historicize these practices, along with the public fantasies that cluster around them, and to mark moments when fantasies of exposure become acts of violence, real and imagined. . . .

In her trenchant study *Imagining Arab Womanhood*, Amira Jarmakani traces the ways in which Orientalist images have circulated in twentieth- and twenty-first century US media and popular culture. . . . She calls the discourse and imagery around veils, belly dancing, and harems "cultural mythologies," since they are naturalized, divorced from their historical and cultural context and invested with the meanings of the appropriating culture. And yet the remaining historical traces make them appear "accurate and authentic representations of Arab womanhood" (4–5). Jarmakani historicizes representations of belly dancing, veils, and harems in relation to growing tensions between the United States and the Middle East. For example, as she points out, "contemporary representations of veiled women cast them as categorically oppressed, metaphorically implying the brutal patriarchal system under which they supposedly live," whereas "[i]mages of transparently veiled women in early-twentieth-century advertisements . . . eroticize the scene as they suggest the figure to be a coquettish, easily available harem girl" (8). These shifting attitudes toward the veiled Muslim woman tell us that the

fantasy of exposing the Muslim woman—making her known to a US gaze—are an extension of broader political relations between the United States and the Middle East.

Adding to our understanding of the kinds of fantasies belly dancing promotes in the aftermath of the September 11, 2001 terrorist attacks, Sunaina Maira argues . . . belly dancing performances are entangled with the imperial engagements that link the United States and the Middle East and reveal a deeper politics of imperialism, racialization, and feminism in this moment of US empire. The massive appeal of belly dancing and its growing resonance with white American women since 2001 needs to be situated in relation to contemporary gender and nationalist politics (318). . . .

Despite its global circulation, belly dancing replays a remarkably stable fantasy of heteronormative femininity, affirming Said's claim that the (masculine) gaze of Orientalism sees the Middle East as "static, frozen, fixed eternally," incapable of "development, transformation, human movement" (208). . . .

It is as if this stable fantasy of Middle Eastern women allows imaginative control over Islamic cultures that have become increasingly misunderstood and threatening to Western hegemony. However, belly dancing performs an idea of timeless gender and sexuality to which many Western women are deeply attached . . . belly dancing offers women imaginative control over their bodies and sexualities, giving them access to an experience of gender they find both fascinating and reassuring.

Seeing belly dancing as a form of drag reframes it as a performance of identification, imitation, and longing, wherein fantasy assumes material form and political implications. As a critical lens, cultural drag loosens connotations of authenticity and timelessness associated with belly dancing, emphasizing instead its theatricality, ambivalence, and affective investment in a cross-cultural fantasy of gender identity. Although belly dancers do not perform with the ironic, knowing wink often deployed by gay male drag—the wink that gestures toward the artificiality and duplicity of the performance—*reading* belly dancing as drag complicates claims to cultural authenticity and foregrounds gender and culture as mimetic performances that play out the remainders of intersecting histories—of modernization and colonialism—which are also histories of heterosexualization.

Butler defines drag: "At its best," she writes, "drag is a site of a certain ambivalence, one that reflects the more general situation of being implicated in regimes of power by which one is constituted and, hence, of being implicated in the very regimes of power that one opposes" (*Bodies that Matter* 384). Precisely this ambivalence can be read into Western belly dancing performances, which oscillate between complicity and resistance, fascination and longing, essentialism and performativity. Maira rightly explains, "the performance of belly dance by American women represents not so much their ambivalence about Middle Eastern culture, but their ambivalence about their *own* culture—its individualism, materialism, or restrictive body image ideals" (334). Western women are drawn to belly dancing because it gives them access to a relationship with their bodies and their communities that they have lost or been denied.

Thus, belly dancing also implies an identification with and a desire to learn something from Middle Eastern femininity, which is so persistently and reductively cast as the Western femininity's Other. More precisely, belly dancing suggests a desire to know what Western and Arab/Muslim femininities mean *in relation* to each other. . . . Belly dancing idealizes a mythic Middle Eastern femininity, which is understood as sensual without being degraded and objectified, and this idealization reveals a desire for coherent subjectivity among Western women living in a cultural context saturated with hypersexualized images of female bodies. Butler states: "In imitating gender, drag implicitly reveals the imitative structure of gender itself—as well as its contingency" (*Gender Trouble* 187). Likewise, in imitating a culture—a culture imaginatively projected as a counterimage of Western modernity—belly dancing reveals the imitative, contingent, and historical structure of cultural identity. Western belly dancers long to inhabit a body that is valued, and yet also a body coded as distant, timeless, universal—free from the constraints of culture and history. . . .

BELLY DANCING AND THE DRAG OF HISTORY

"How does Orientalism transmit or reproduce itself from one epoch to another?" Said asks (15). One way is through the bodies, affects, fantasies that keep history alive. As an embodied performance steeped in Orientalist ideas about the Middle East, belly dancing offers a rich example of the way affects and fantasies get translated into history. "Belly dancing" is itself a Western term, coined by American musician and entrepreneur Sol Bloom after seeing Fahreda Mazar Spyropoulos and Fatima Djemille (both of whom were known by the stage name "Little Egypt") perform . . . at the 1893 Chicago World's Fair. Since Fatima Djemille was captured in an early silent film, *Fatima* (dir. James H. White, 1896), the image of the exotic belly dancer has circulated in Western popular culture as a seductive spectacle of cultural and sexual difference. Early twentieth century female burlesque performers took up the dance, which dovetailed with the Salome craze that swept New York in 1907 and became a stock striptease routine. This marks the beginning of the West's enduring fascination with these dances, or so the story goes, and since then belly dancing has been practiced continually in Western countries, with ebbs and flows in popularity. . . .

In the 1960s, as the Women's Liberation Movement was getting off the ground and the gender norms and sexual mores of the 1950s were beginning to loosen, belly dancing was taken up in the United States as leisure activity among middle-class women. Belly dance continued to circulate in this period through old Hollywood films, instructional albums . . . , and through classes taught by former performers. The dance provided women with a fantasy femininity that transcended time and place, encapsulating many Western middle-class women's dream of a sensual body liberated from patriarchy and domesticity, careers and car pools, sexualized images and sexual competition. Barbara Sellers-Young explains that during this period belly dancing was also approached as a vehicle for feminists to reclaim their bodies from a history of patriarchal oppression (141). Since the 1960s, belly dancing has grown in popularity among middle-class women around the world. . . .

As a primarily female-centered practice, belly dancing today is a worldwide industry, with classes, competitions, conventions, university clubs, and associations in cities around the world. Three claims are articulated again and again by contemporary belly dancers: That belly dancing is an *art;* that it is *authentic;* and that it is *empowering.* Designating the dance as art distances it from more explicitly sexual performances, such as stripping. Authenticity—often located in the historically and culturally distant, the ancient or the foreign—is itself a highly manufactured concept that designates, somewhat paradoxically, what has not yet been sullied by the processes of commercialization. . . . Finally, belly dancing is considered an empowering practice. Rosalind Gill crucially problematizes this overused term, empowerment, pointing out that, in our postfeminist neoliberal media environment, notions like *choice, agency,* and *empowerment* have "become commodified—used to sell everything from washing powder to cosmetic surgery." Emptied of its meaning and specificity, "sexual empowerment," she argues, has "become one of the tropes of sexualized culture: everywhere we are confronted by images of empowered female sexuality" (743). "Empowerment" has "itself become a normatively demanded feature of young women's sexual subjectivity, such that they are called on routinely to perform confident, knowing heterosexiness" (737). Belly dancing fosters the feelings of empowerment and sexual confidence necessary to a normative heterosexiness—the "new normal" for young women living in a sexualized culture. Having successfully internalized the processes of objectification, women have learned not only to self-objectify, but also to see this self-objectification as a form of empowerment *because done by choice.*

The development of belly dancing has not been one-directional, however, nor has the dance been entirely divorced from meaningful traditions and values. R.F. Al-Rawi points out that after belly dancing became popular in North America and Europe in the late nineteenth and early twentieth centuries, "Arab dancers began to incorporate Western dancing in their performances." She explains, "The dancing that used to be performed in a highly concentrated, nearly meditative and inward state now took a more extravagant and extroverted turn." Broader movements, frenetic twirls, and seductive costumes "combined with the Western image of the Oriental" to produce the enduring images we associate with belly dancing. . . . For Al-Rawi, belly dancing becomes a libratory, healing, and spiritual practice when it is situated in the dancer's specific cultural and historical context, whatever that may be. Only in its connection to the conditions of a particular time,

place, and performer does the dance become "more than just a dance," but a practice that "refines energy and consciousness"; lends "meaning and depth," "peace," "sensuality and inner freedom" to women's life experience; and provides an "opportunity to express many different selves" (Al-Rawi). In contrast to the stable, timeless femininity that many Western belly dancing performances foster, the dance, if practiced with a historical and cultural consciousness, provides access to multiple identities. . . .

Belly dancing does not signify timelessness and universality in the Middle East, but rather bears the historical traces of colonialism that have imbued the dance with connotations of Western imperialism and sexual immorality (Shay and Sellers-Young 16–17). In conservative parts of the Middle East today, belly dancing is held in strong disrepute. Professional belly dancers are thought to be committing *haram* (a forbidden or sinful act) and routinely face prejudice, except while on stage where they are a source of pleasure for heterosexual male spectators. And as extremism spreads throughout the Middle East, the dance has been increasingly censored; it is outlawed in Iran and Afghanistan, for example, and in Egypt, floor work and exposed midriffs have been banned. In September 2014, a belly dancing reality show was pulled off the air by the government after just one episode ("Egypt's First Reality Show Pulled Off Air"). And yet belly dancers continue to perform in tourist locations in Egypt, such as in hotels, on Nile boat cruises, and in restaurants, catering to a traveling Western gaze that sees the belly dancer as an authentic expression of a Middle Eastern cultural tradition . . .

BELLY DANCING IN CONTEMPORARY POPULAR CULTURE: PERFORMING SEXUAL DEMOCRACY

Belly dancing takes on different meanings in different contexts, and it can both reinforce and resist the sexualization of culture and the sexualization of concepts like democracy and freedom. In twenty-first-century Western popular culture, belly dancing plays out a collective fantasy of cross-cultural relations, in which religious and ethnic differences are displaced by a myth of timeless, global femininity that the dance promotes. In this context, the sensual Middle Eastern woman signifies a kind of universal feminine, while the veiled Muslim woman of the Western imagination operates as the sexual and political Other of this fantasy. Jonathon Brandeis's documentary *American Bellydancer: The Pursuit of Life, Liberty, and Dance* encapsulates the ways in which this dance has been mobilized in twenty-first-century popular culture as a form of cultural knowledge. The film tracks Miles Copeland, founder of IRS Records and former manager of The Police and Sting, as he tries to put together a touring belly dancing show featuring prominent American belly dancers. His stated goal is to bring belly dancing deeper into American culture, thus fostering greater understanding between the United States and the Middle East. However, as the subtitle suggests, the pursuit of the film is inextricably tied to an American ideology of freedom and democracy, as mapped onto and enacted by the bodies of American belly dancers. Sadie and Kaya, semifinalists on season ten of "America's Got Talent," and their popular veil dance offer an explicit example of Western individualism masquerading as a mythologized Middle East. Sadie and Kaya perform a heteronormative, body-focused femininity that is aligned with both patriotism and the American Dream. Here, the exposed Western female body signifies (and sexualizes) the Western concepts of freedom and democracy. Sadie and Kaya relish their real bodies and real dreams before the affectively charged backdrop of a waving American flag, as the applauding audience and appreciative judges affirm their performance. It is the dream of opportunity and stardom reimagined in the most evident avenue available to women—through their sexualized bodies. Sadie's belly dancing performances have even gone viral, garnering upward of twenty-seven million views on YouTube. Born in Sheboygan, Wisconsin, Sadie Marquardt travels to São Paulo, Mexico City, London, and New York City to perform and teach belly dancing, styling herself as a fusion of orientalist fantasy and global pop culture sensation. The biography page of Sadie's Web site features her almond-shaped green eyes peering through a veil that covers the rest of her face and hair. On either side of this visage are smaller images of her, unveiled and posing seductively in a gold belly dancing costume ("Sadie's

Biography"). This particular fantasy of exposure can be read as the unconscious counterpart of the ubiquitous images of veiled Muslim women in the Western media. Sadie's drag symbolically exposes the veiled Muslim woman, while promoting a global femininity paradoxically coded as both timeless and American.

On the British reality television show franchise "Got Talent," belly dancers are common, illustrating the ways in which the imperialist traces of the dance have been translated via the global circulation of Western popular culture. Produced by Simon Cowell, "Got Talent" is cited in the 2014 *Guinness World Records* as the "Most Successful Reality TV Format" of all time ("Simon Cowell's 'Got Talent'"). With over fifty-eight versions, the reality show's worldwide reach is expansive and its brand recognition extremely high. Several belly dancers have appeared on Britain's "Got Talent," including a seventy-one-year-old belly dancer named Jan Price; belly dancer Farah Cicekdag made it to the semi-finals of the 2010 season of "Australia's Got Talent"; and belly dancer Alla Kushnir was the winner of the 2011 season of "Ukraine's Got Talent." Indeed, belly dancers have appeared on the British, American, Australian, Korean, Indian, the Ukrainian, Vietnam, China, *and* the Arab world versions of "Got Talent." The culturally diverse examples of belly dancing's appeal to both performers and audiences, and the commodified image system it circulates within, mobilizes fantasies of femininity and female sexuality to displace and resolve deep cultural differences. . . .

Perhaps the most conspicuous example of belly dancing's global popularity can be seen in Columbian-born singer, songwriter, and choreographer Shakira's trademark belly dancing routine. Shakira's self-exoticization resonates with a younger audience that envisions themselves as cosmopolitan consumers, her blond-haired Latina image operating as an ideal canvas on which to project fantasies of a global femininity. With her Columbian nationality and her status as an American pop culture icon, Shakira embodies a kind of globalized femininity. During her 2007 concert in Dubai, for example, she prefaced her signature concert performance of *"Ojos Asi"*/"Eyes Like Those" with a veil dance that plays with the porous boundaries between visibility and invisibility, as well as between the borders of the cultures she references. . . . Shakira sings part of the song in Arabic and has recorded Spanish and English versions. Significantly, the lyrics of "Eyes Like Those" reinforce sight—visibility and the gaze—as legitimizing force of the song's female persona, who searches the globe from "Bahrain . . . to Beirut" for a gaze that will affirm her as the desired object. The abstracted, desiring gaze for which the woman fruitlessly seeks to find a comparable replacement in her global travels can be read as the hegemonic Western gaze, which affirms and defines a globalized femininity that is visible, heteronormative, sexually available, and "free."

The veil registers symbolically in Shakira's performance as a mobile and permeable boundary that enacts an eroticized movement between exposure and concealment and, more politically, between the hypervisibility of the Western female body and the veiled Muslim female body. As Dox succinctly puts it, "If the idea of women's veiling in daily public life is perceived as oppressive, then shedding a costume veil becomes an act of liberation automatically . . . associated with an industrial, secular, progressive West" (62). Sadie, Kaya and Shakira all use the guise of a mythic Middle Eastern femininity to promote images of (sexual and political) freedom within a Western-defined global democracy. Belly dancing thus performs in these contexts a desire *to know*—to expose and make public—what Muslim women's bodies and sexuality mean. Performing in the mythic guise of the temporally and culturally distant belly dancer, rather than through the more familiar image of the stripper, Western belly dancers rehearse an act of cultural supremacy that says something like, "Look at me, looking like you. And yet I'm free and you are imprisoned."

While belly dancing can promote the idea of a global femininity and sexual democracy, it can also work as a performance of cultural assimilation. In September 2011 on her popular daytime talk show, Ellen Degeneres received a belly dancing lesson from Rosalba. Perhaps the most obvious example of belly dancing as cultural drag, this segment is most striking for the way Degeneres's homonormativity displaces and absorbs cultural difference. Her unthreatening sexual difference works to make the cultural difference signified by the dance unthreatening, and her child-like comic persona transforms the dance's sexual undertones into playful overtones. . . . Rosalba's appearance on

Ellen is a study in contrasts, as the hyperfeminine, exoticized Rosalba teaches the lesbian comedian how to isolate and twist her hips. With a bejeweled bra and gauzy skirt held together by a nude body stocking stretched overtop her typically boyish-butch outfit, Degeneres accentuates her subtly queer sexuality, at the same time as her incongruous appearance mocks the claims to authenticity and timelessness made by so many belly dancers. Ultimately, however, Degeneres's parodic performance does not queer belly dancing, but rather further normalizes her own sexuality and illustrates the way the dance "shores up a multiculturalist or liberal notion of US culture that can consume elements of other cultures" (Maira 334). Ellen's belly dancing performance is a form of cultural drag that mobilizes her homonormativity, whiteness, and unthreatening child-like quality to promote an image of harmonious American multiculturalism.

THE VEIL IN HISTORY, MEDIA, AND POPULAR CULTURE

"It's like they don't want [women] to have a voice" (King), says Samantha to her friends as they watch two Muslim women eating lunch on the patio of a 5-star hotel in Abu Dhabi in Michael Patrick King's *Sex and the City 2*. Leaving New York to escape the depressed and depressing economic environment, Carrie, Samantha, Miranda, and Charlotte travel to the wealthy, exoticized Middle East. What follows thereafter is textbook Orientalism. This scene cited above ends with a glimmer of recognition from Carrie, who somehow sees beyond the veil of the younger Muslim woman and knows that, despite her covering, the two women are, at heart, the same. This message is reinforced later in the film when the four sexually savvy Manhattanites come face to face with five women wearing burqas. As the Muslim women strip off their coverings to reveal haute couture clothing and flashy jewelry, Carrie exclaims, "Louis Vuitton!" in a tone that can only be described as gleeful relief. (They *are* just like us!) And her voiceover reduces what is actually a rarely depicted cross-cultural encounter to an exhibition of hyperconsumerism: "There . . . halfway across the world, under a hundred of years of tradition, was this year's Spring collection" (King). The Middle Eastern women's burqas mask their likeness to the Western women, and it is only after they expose themselves that they can be seen as properly modern, like Carrie and her friends, who operate as the norm against which properly modern femininity is judged. The Muslim women in this scene, and the movie as a whole, simply reflect and reinforce Carrie, Samantha, Miranda, and Charlotte's universal femininity, as defined by the three key characteristics: consumerism, sexual freedom, and heteronormativity. In short, the veil, here, threatens the hegemony of white, heterosexual, US femininity.

As a socio-religious practice and symbolic object, the veil is a complex, contradictory sign at the center of heated debates surrounding the limits of religious freedoms within multicultural societies. As Homa Hoodfar explains, veiling is pre-Islamic. When practiced in connection with seclusion in Greco-Roman and pre-Islamic Iranian and Byzantine empires, veiling was a sign of socioeconomic status. In an Islamic context, veiling practices are culturally specific, and, like belly dancing, intersect with a history of colonial expansion.[3] As a cultural practice and state of Islamic dress (*muhegabba*), the veil symbolizes modesty and religious devotion. And although "veiling is nowhere specifically recommended or even discussed in the Qur'an" (Hoodfar 6), as Susie Hawkins notes, "With a few exceptions, most women in Muslim countries are required to wear some form of Islamic dress." . . . Within an orthodox Islamic context, the veiled Muslim woman metonymically protects the sacredness of Islam, and "Islamists tend to see the role of women as divinely prescribed in Islamic family law" (*Islamic Family Law* 90).

In practice, the veil protects a Muslim woman's body from the male gaze and allows freedom of movement in public, giving women access to education and employment.

As far back as the late-nineteenth and early-twentieth-centuries, the veil has been used by the West to construct an image of the uncivilized Islamic world, which worked to legitimize colonial occupations by the self-proclaimed civilized European nations. As Hoodfar points out, by the late-nineteenth-century, "images of Muslim women were used as a major building block to construct the orient's new imagery, an imagery that is intrinsically linked to the hegemony of western imperialism, particularly that of Britain and France" (8).

Leila Ahmed adds, "Veiling—to *Western* eyes, the most visible marker of the differentness and inferiority of Islamic societies—became the symbol . . . of both the oppression of women. . and the backwardness of Islam" (*Women and Gender in Islam,* 152). Since the nineteenth century and especially since the Arab–Israeli conflicts began in the 1960s, veiled Muslim women have been reduced in the Western imagination to monolithically oppressed victims of a backward culture, either in need of saving by the liberated West, or subordinated, by ultraconservative Islamic regimes, to a reactionary struggle against Western imperialism.

Since the Gulf War and, even more so, since the September 11 attacks, the veil continues to be manipulated by the media as a monolithic sign of antidemocracy and oppression of Muslim women, an image that justifies the West's neocolonial interventions. Ahmed identifies a "startling" new feature of the post–September 11 public discourse: "The subject of women in Islam, and in particular women's oppression and the emblems of that oppression, such as the veil and the burka, became recurring themes in the broad public conversation in America and elsewhere in the West" (*Quiet Revolution,* 194). In *Women as Weapons of War: Iraq, Sex, and the Media,* Kelly Oliver explains, "Reminiscent of the French occupation of Algeria in the 1950s, the US invasion of Afghanistan focused on the plight of Afghan women, whose oppression was seen as epitomized by the veil and the burka" (51). Indeed it was Laura Bush who addressed the nation, making a plea to liberate the women of Afghanistan by using gendered and feminist logic, while the Bush administration and the media made much of the West's success in liberating Afghani "women of cover" (Jarmakani 12). Oliver adds, "Efforts to re-veil women in Iraq seem to be a reaction against U.S. occupation wherein westernization becomes associated with women's sexual freedom as evidenced by their dress and the amount of body covered or revealed" (51). What was construed as a humanitarian effort in the 1990s was, after the September 11 attacks, depicted as an unequivocal "war on terror," with the veiled Muslim woman embodying, at once, the enemy threat and the object in need of saving.

The veiled Muslim woman has become a fixation of a Western gaze that sees concealment (of the female body) as a threat to democracy and exposure as a sign of (sexual) freedom. In light of the rising extremism in the Middle East, veiled Muslim women living in Western countries have become an overburdened sign of all that threatens Western democracy and security. They face increasing judgment in the media and increasing infringements on their public freedoms, such as the 2011 law in France forbidding Muslim women to veil their face, Quebec's Charter of Rights, and the establishment of "burqa bans" across the UK and Europe. And the spate of "veil attacks" reported in the United States, France, UK, and Quebec confirms Muslim women's bodies as a conspicuous and volatile site of political, religious, and ideological conflicts. Islamophobia monitoring group Tell MAMA (Measuring Anti-Muslim Attacks) reports that over half of attacks against Muslims happen against women wearing the veil. Over 700 such attacks were reported to Tell MAMA between May 2013 and February 2014 in France, England, the United States, and Quebec (Aziz). . . . In June 2014, thirty-one-year-old student, Nahid Almanea was stabbed to death on a footpath in Essex, United Kingdom, a murder allegedly instigated by her Islamic dress, which consisted of an abaya and patterned head-scarf (Elgot). There is an urgent need for more dialog relating to these violent responses to veiled Muslim women living in Western countries, which might balance the current monocular focus on the oppression of Muslim women under extremist Islamic regimes.

In a curious replay of the 1980s pornography debates, during which there was an alignment of right-wing conservatives and anti-porn feminists in their shared antipornography stance, calls for banning the *niqab* and the *burqa* are shared by the right and many feminists, who see the veiled Muslim woman as a threat to a free (and Christian) Western society. In France, the ban on full-face veiling has been held in place and supported by a public pronouncement of "a certain idea of living together" (Willsher). As Joan Wallach Scott argues in *Politics of the Veil,* France's laws regulating religious clothing signal the country's failure to integrate its former colonial subjects as full citizens. At the center of the debate, Scott explains, are opposing views of sexuality: In France, as in much of the West, sexual openness stands in for normalcy, emancipation, and individuality, while the sexual modesty implicit in the headscarf and, even more

in the *niqab,* undermines these claims to sexual democracy. Scott rightly points out that France's ban exacerbates religious and ethnic difference by enforcing a cultural homogeneity that is no longer feasible in France. "By refusing to accept and respect the difference of these others," Scott writes, "we turn them into enemies, producing that which we most feared most about them in the first place" (19). The ban in France effectively enforces a historically white Christian hegemony, and in doing so does not allow the veil, or by extension the cultural and religious practices it metonymically invokes, to change French culture. With Britain, Belgium, and Switzerland all now banning face veils, Europe is sending a message of censorship and separatism cloaked as a message of community and secularism. These bans prevent Muslim women from freely moving in public, thus restricting (rather than liberating) them and impeding chances at a diversely integrated community. Furthermore, attempts to ban the *burqa* and *niqab* in Austria—even though these are worn by an extremely small proportion of the Muslim women in that country—are a thinly veiled right-wing campaign that resonates with the very sexism that it purports to oppose: "Too beautiful for a veil," is the phrase printed under a photo of a blonde woman in a Facebook post by Austria Freedom Party leader and Member of Parliament Heinz-Christian Strache, who claims to be challenging the "Islamization of Europe" ("Campaign Against Muslim Veils").

The public discourse around the veil has worked to exacerbate tensions and reduce Muslim women to victims of patriarchy and religious extremism. . . . Chaudhry succinctly summarizes how these debates divest Muslim women of their agency as subject and citizens:

> Neither forced veiling nor de-veiling actually serves the interests of women, although secularists argue that de-veiling "saves" women from patriarchal oppression, and Islamists argue that veiling "saves" women from an objectifying male gaze that turns them into sex objects. In both arguments, a woman's emancipation or subjugation is measured by the amount her body is covered or uncovered. Both arguments infantilize women, expressing a profound mistrust in their ability to make decisions in their own self-interest. Caught in the middle, Muslim women simply cannot win. (Chaudhry)

As seen from a Western gaze, the veiled Muslim woman's seeming lack of individuality, her explicit demonstration of her commitment to Islam (as both religion and community), and her refusal to offer her body as object and spectacle undermines the foundational principles of Western subjectivity and norms surrounding women's public visibility. Hidden from view, she disrupts the free-flowing circuits of heteronormative desire that are rehearsed in everyday encounters and circulated in global popular culture products. As a social and religious practice, as a symbol of protest, and as a seductive belly dancing prop, the veil plays precisely at the boundary between such discursive constructions as exposure and concealment, public and private, empowered and oppressed, which are used to define Muslim and Western women's bodies—along with the cultures they represent—as diametrical opposites. Both enforced veiling and sexualized hypervisibility reduce women to their bodies—to an object to be looked at or concealed—and in doing so undermine their viability as political subjects and citizens.

Contemporary veiling practices of Muslim women around the world exist in complex negotiation with their societies, their religion, their communities, and their individual choices. Some women wear the veil because of cultural enforcement, others by choice, and yet others as protest. Muslim women have historically mobilized the veil as a sign of protest against patriarchal domination, against European colonialism, and more recently, against US cultural imperialism. For example, the veil became a recognizable symbol during the 1979 Iranian revolution, when many young Iranian women willingly adopted the veil as a sign of protest against the corrupt regime of the Shah. However, under the Islamic Republic, the new freedoms promised to women were reneged, and instead "new rules and regulations concerning all aspects of women's lives were announced," including mandatory adoption of the veil (*chador*) (Shirazi 116). In ever growing numbers, Muslim feminists have been wearing the veil as a sign of resistance to a global system defined according to neoliberal Western values of individualism and the free market. Shaista Gohir, chairman of the Muslim Women's Network UK, states that more women have adopted headscarves after the September 11 and July 7, 2005 attacks on the United States and London respectively, in part as a way

to make visible their religious and cultural difference from the West and to show pride in their faith and the community ("British Women Fight Racism with the Veil"). Groups like Muslim Women Against FEMEN wear the veil as a sign of protest against Western imperialism and against feminist groups that see veiling as an unequivocal sign of patriarchal domination. Seen in this light, the veil becomes a sign not of oppression, but of agency—not the sexual agency of neoliberal postfeminism, but the agency of mobilized resistance against unjust systems of domination.

The activist group, Muslim Women against FEMEN (MWAF), for example, wear diverse types of veils, while holding written statements that pointedly respond to misunderstandings surrounding the oppressed Muslim woman of the Western imagination and, specifically to the radical feminist group, FEMEN. The photographs posted on the group's Facebook page show Muslim women from around the world, each claiming the veil as a sign of their freedom and dignity. MWAF define themselves as "Muslim women who want to expose FEMEN for the Islamophobes/Imperialists that they are. We are making our voices heard and reclaiming our agency" ("Muslim Women Against FEMEN"). Interestingly, the word "expose" implies an ideological outing of FEMEN, and not a physical unveiling of the female body. Although not self-defined as a feminist group, MWAF can be read as feminist in their praxis in that they advocate recognition of difference and freedom of choice. With written statements such as, "Silence is complicity" and "Nudity DOES NOT liberate me and I DO NOT need saving," MWAF articulate strong counterclaims to FEMEN's condemnation of the veiled Muslim woman as the emblem of patriarchal oppression and veneration of the naked white woman as a symbol of freedom from that oppression ("Muslim Women Against FEMEN").

FEMEN is a radical feminist group that formed in 2008 in the Ukraine. FEMEN members use their exposed bodies to communicate their political messages, protesting topless around the world, from the Vatican to Moscow, with militant slogans promoting sexual freedom written on their naked torsos. FEMEN activists use their nakedness to demonstrate against sexual exploitation and political corruption, a startlingly literal tactic in the way it equates public exposure with social equality. The group states their aims clearly on the Web site: "Our Mission is Protest. Our Weapon are [*sic*] bare breasts!. . FEMEN's Goal: complete victory over patriarchy" (femen.org/about). Driving the movement is the belief that the naked female body in protest spells the demise of a patriarchal world system because it demonstrates a woman's "right to her body." Echoing claims made by many belly dancers, who seek through the dance to reclaim a more authentic, liberated form of embodiment, FEMEN's mandate begins with an ahistorical appeal origin: "In the beginning, there was the body, feeling of the woman's body, feeling of joy because it is so light and free. Then there was injustice, so sharp that you could feel it with your body" (femen.org/about). Staging a fantasy of exposure in which naked, white female flesh inscribed with words of protest signifies freedom from patriarchy, FEMEN paradoxically reinforces women's bodies as the site of political conflict, reducing a complex cultural, political, and economic history to a matter of public exposure and individual choice. In contrast to FEMEN's essentialism, MWAF continually assert an awareness of history and emphasize the necessity of recognizing cultural difference. As one young woman's Facebook post succinctly puts it, "My freedom looks different than yours" ("Muslim Women Against FEMEN"). Muslim women who wear the veil as a sign of agency, religious commitment, and indivisibility from their community are performing their identities as changeable, relational, and culturally specific—neither the oppressed Muslim woman of the Western media nor the timeless femininity of the Western belly dancer.

As antagonisms between the Middle East and the West intensify and the tensions surrounding multiculturalism become more pronounced; as Muslim women in the diaspora face hostile scrutiny and women activists in the Middle East are violently suppressed; and as Western feminists align themselves with a neoliberal paternalism and Muslim women rail against the imposition of Western norms of gender and sexuality, it seems as though, ideologically, the world is divided to the extreme, even as, geographically, we are living in unprecedented proximity to religious, racial, and ethnic differences. Within this scene, belly dancing offers a fantasy of wholeness and universality. Eroticizing and resolving political tensions with the image of a postfeminist, postracial, universal femininity, belly dancing can uphold an idea of global democracy disguised as an exposed, heterosexual female body. In contrast, the Muslim woman's covered body is used by the Western media as a potent symbol of the oppressive patriarchal Islamic regimes, which Western democracy must continue to expose and fight against. As opposing symbols of competing ideologies, women in the West and the Muslim world learn to see each other as antagonists in a global conflict. In an almost perfect replay of Malcolm Evans's cartoon, MWAF and FEMEN confront one another as moral enemies rather than compatriots of the same political system,[4] in which their bodies are used as an ideological battleground and projected back onto the world as a fantasy of exposure, rather than the drag of history.

NOTES

1. Veil is used broadly here. As both a piece of clothing and as a religious practice in Islam, veiling practices vary across Islamic cultures and countries, as do the terms. The hijab refers to the headscarf and comes from the Arabic word hajaba, or "to hide from view." The niqab is the face veil; abaya is a long cloak worn by Saudi Arabian women; chador is the head and shoulder covering worn by Iranian women; burqa is the full body cloak that covers Muslim women from head to toe. Of these, the niqab and burqa are the most controversial in the West.

2. Following Inderpal Grewal, "global," especially as it is used in twenty-first-century

public discourse, is understood as a cognate for "universal" (Grewal 23).

3. Nations using Islamic law as their national judicial system enforce religious veiling of women, whereas in countries that use combined or secular legal systems, veiling is not a legally enforced practice. For example, whereas countries like Saudi Arabia and Iraq use Islamic law as the nation's judicial system, which extends to the legislated veiling of Muslim women, countries like Malaysia have a parallel legal system, using both common law and Islamic law. A secular Muslim nation like Turkey, moreover, uses only common law; here, the face veil

is illegal, while the headscarf signifies traditionalism within a secular Muslim nation.

4. Bell hooks usefully calls this interlocking system "white supremacist-capitalist-patriarchy."

REFERENCES

Ahmed, Leila. *A Quiet Revolution: The Veil's Resurgence, from the Middle East to America*. New Haven, CT: Yale UP, 2011. Print.

——. *Women and Gender in Islam*. New Haven, CT: Yale UP, 1992. Print.

Al-Rawi, R.F. *Grandmother's Secrets: The Ancient Rituals and Healing Power of Belly Dancing*. Northampton, MA: Interlink, 2012. E-book. 11 Aug. 2015.

American Bellydancer. Dir. Jonathan Brandeis. Mondo Melodia Films, 2005. Film.

Aziz, Shaista. "Why Are People So Obsessed with Muslim Women's Wardrobes?" *The Guardian*. Guardian News and Media Limited, 26 July 2014. Web. 4 Aug. 2014.

"British Women Fight Racism with Veil." *OnIslam*. OnIslam.net, 23 Aug. 2014. Web. 1 Sept. 2014.

Butler, Judith. *Bodies that Matter: On the Discursive Limits of Sex*. New York: Routledge, 2011. Print.

——. *Gender Trouble: Feminism and the Subversion of Identity*. New York: Routledge, 2007. Print.

"Campaign against Full-face Muslim Veils Launched in Austria." *RT*. TV-Novosti, 5 July 2014. Web. 31 Aug. 2014.

Chaudhry, Ayesha. "Don't Politicize Women's Bodies." *The Globe and Mail*. The Globe and Mail, Inc., 5 Aug. 2014. Web. 19 Sept. 2014.

Dox, Donnalee. "Dancing Around Orientalism." *The Drama Review* 50.4 (2006): 52–71. Web. 4 Apr. 2013.

"Egypt's First Belly Dancing Reality Show Pulled Off the Air." *Al-Tahir News Network*. 4 Sept. 2014. Web. 10 Sept. 2014.

Elgot, Jessica. "Student Stabbed To Death On Essex Footpath 'Targeted For Muslim Dress.'" *Huffington Post UK*. AOL (UK) Limited, 19 June 2014. Web. 1 July 2014.

Evans, Malcolm. "Cruel Culture." *Evans Cartoons*. Malcolm Evans, 6 Jan. 2011. Web. 20 Oct. 2014.

"Eyes Like Yours." Shakira. *Metro Lyrics*. Web. 30 May 2014.

Fatima's Coochee Coochie Dance. Dir. James White. H. Edison Manufacturing Company, 1896. Film.

FEMEN. femen.org Web. 22 Aug. 2015.

Gill, Rosalind. "Media, Empowerment and the 'Sexualization of Culture' Debate." *Sex Roles* 66 (2012): 736–45. Web. 10 Oct. 2015.

Grewal, Inderpal. *Transnational America: Feminisms, Diasporas, Neoliberalisms*. Durham, NC: Duke UP, 2005. Print.

Hawkins, Susie. "The Essence of the Veil: The Veil as Metaphor for Islamic Women." *Voices Behind the Veil: The World of Islam Through the Eyes of Women*. Ed. Ergun Mehmet Caner. Grand Rapids, MI: Kregel Publishers, 2013. 93–106. Print.

Hoodfar, Homa. "The Veil in Their Minds and On Our Heads: The Persistence of Colonial Images of Muslim Women." *Resources for Feminist Research / Documentation sur la recherche feminist* 22.3/4 (1995): 5–18. Print.

Jarmakani, Amira. *Imagining Arab Womanhood: The Cultural Mythology of Veils, Harems, and Belly Dancers*. London: Palgrave Macmillan, 2008. Print.

Kristof, Nicholas D. "Saudis in Bikinis." *New York Times*. The New York Times Company, 25 Oct. 2002. Web. 3 Oct. 2014.

Maira, Sunaina. "Belly Dancing: Arab-Face, Orientalist Feminism, and US Empire." *American Quarterly* 602 (2008): 317–45. Print.

"Muslim Women Against FEMEN." *Facebook*. Web. 22 August 2015.

Oliver, Kelly. *Women as Weapons of War: Iraq, Sex, and the Media.* New York: Columbia UP, 2007. Print.

"Sadie's Biography." *Sadie Bellydance: International Performing Artist, Instructor & Choreographer.* Web. 15 May 2014.

Said, Edward. *Orientalism.* New York: Vintage Books, 1978. Print. Sellers-Young, Barbara. "Raks El Sharqi: Transculturation of a Folk Form." *Journal of Popular Culture* 26.2 (1992): 141–52. Print.

Sex and the City 2. Dir. Michael Patrick King. New Line Cinema, 2010. DVD.

Shay, Anthony, and Barbara Sellers-Young. "Belly Dance: Orientalism—Exoticism—Self-Exoticism."

Dance Research Journal 35 (2003): 13–37. Web. 21 May 2013.

Shirazi, Fagheh. "Islamic Religion and Women's Dress Code." *Undressing Religion: Commitment and Conversion from a Cross-Cultural Perspective.* Ed. Linda Arthur. Oxford: *Berg,* 2000. 113–30. Print.

"Simon Cowell's 'Got Talent' Confirmed as World's Most Successful Reality TV Format." 7 Apr. 2014. Web. 16 Oct. 2014.

Wallach, Joan Scott. *Politics of the Veil.* Princeton, NJ: Princeton UP, 2009. Print.

Willsher, Kim. "France's Burqa Ban Upheld by Human Rights Courts." *The Guardian.* Guardian News and Media Limited, 1 July 2014. Web. 2 July 2014.

GROWING UP WITH CONTEMPORARY MEDIA

The potential effects of popular culture on children and young people have always generated much anxiety and controversy, at times even resulting in **media activism** as a countermeasure to media influence. Educators and health professionals have argued that young children are a particularly vulnerable population, given their limited experience of the world and the likelihood that their sense of the boundaries between media **representations** and the real world is less well established than (ideally) that of adults. According to Dafna Lemish (VI.44),

> Most pronounced are concerns over the effects of television violence on children, as well as the potential harm of exposure to sexual portrayals, the effects of advertising on consumer culture, and the more general concern over children's passivity and social disengagement. (p. 364)

In the age of **global media,** concerns about children's television are now being studied on an international level. Lemish explores the current state of the research and argues,

> In summary, empirical evidence suggests that children's television around the world consists primarily of fictional animation programs not produced domestically but purchased from abroad, mainly from the United States and Canada. These programs feature mostly light-skinned characters, with an overwhelming presence of males. Therefore, the White male hegemony seems to be numerically dominant in children's television around the world, just as it is in other aspects of popular culture. (p. 366)

No discussion of commercialized children's media would be complete without an analysis of the vast global reach of the Walt Disney company. As Lee Artz (VI.45) writes, "Disney leads the world in the production and distribution of popular culture" (p. 373). In an attempt to understand why Disney animation has achieved such global dominance, Artz looks at the **political economy** of Disney, exploring it both as industry and producer of ideology. Through **textual analysis** of the **ideologies** encoded in animated feature films of the past decade, Artz argues that "Disney consistently and programmatically produces 'commodities-as-animated-feature films' that promote an ideology preferred by Disney and transnational capitalism—an ideology recently replete with cultural diversity and positive gender roles but still at odds with democracy and creative, participatory social life" (p. 373).

Also addressing issues of **ideology** and **hegemony** in children's popular culture, Karen Goldman (VI.46) looks back at the evolution of the Mattel Corporation's iconic Barbie dolls, which continue to reflect and construct a racialized gender ideology while simultaneously attracting critical analysis from media scholars and activists. The original Barbie **encoded** an idealized White American teenage girl, whose ethnic neutrality was useful for a marketing strategy that stressed a mythical "Americanness." However, over the 40 years since her first release on the toy market, in part because of an evolving marketing strategy—one that targets "ethnic" U.S. consumers and a global market—Mattel has sold "more than one billion dolls" in 150 countries, making Barbie "one of the world's most ubiquitous plastic objects" (p. 380). In her essay, Goldman traces the evolution of "official" Mattel representations of Latina femininity, such as Hispanic Barbie and various "Dolls of the World" Barbies. According to Goldman,

> Behind Mattel's portrayal of Latino/a identity lies a system of representation that sells itself as authentic but that ultimately either depicts Latino/a culture as homogeneous and exotic, or repackages the doll's Latinidad in an assimilated form, whether to make her more attractive to more assimilated Latinos or to market her more effectively in places where ethnic diversity is not particularly marketable. (p. 382)

In another chapter focused on the young female media consumer, Gail Dines (VI.47) argues that popular culture provides today's adolescent girls a narrow and reductive version of femininity—one centering on the **hypersexuality** that is a product of the mainstreaming of pornographic imagery and representations. Reminding us that "in today's image-based culture, there is no escaping the image and no respite from its power" (p. 386), Dines describes in particular the environment produced by the hypersexualization of female celebrities. She offers a strong critique of the impact of this immersion in a "closed system of messages" on preteens and teenaged girls, who are in the critical years for developing sexual and **gender** identities. While she acknowledges that "some girls and young women conform and others resist," she points out that "alternative ideologies such as **feminism** that critique dominant conceptions of femininity are either caricatured or ignored in mainstream media," (p. 389) leaving those who are inclined to resist with far fewer cultural resources than even their mothers may have had.

So far, our chapters in this section have featured primarily political economic or textual analysis, but we now turn to two global audience response studies that focus on how young people make sense of the media in their lives. In the first of these chapters, Sue Jackson and Tiina Vares (VI.48) analyze video diaries of preteen girls in New Zealand to explore how they negotiate their fandom of hypersexualized female pop stars. Aware of cultural and parental concerns over sexualized media, the White middle class girls in this study carefully maintained their engagement with pop music by distinguishing between "good" and "bad" female celebrity role models. Establishing boundaries around age appropriate behavior and "slutty" versus "non-slutty" appearances allowed tweens to enjoy the music of hypersexualized female pop stars while simultaneously dismissing or condemning their hypersexual performances. Through their acceptance and/or rejection of the hypersexual celebrity performance, the young women in this study are able to position their use of media somewhere between asexual childhood innocence and adult hypersexualization. As Jackson and Vares are quick to point out, "media representations of celebrities are not static but plural and in flux, as are girls' responses to them" (p. 396). In other words, while girls may embrace a female celebrity as a role model at one moment, they may reject her behavior or performance at another point in time. However, by adopting this binary way of thinking about female celebrities ("good/bad" or "slutty/non-slutty"), the young women are reinforcing a sexist double bind. Therefore, Jackson and Vares suggest that it is important "to not only encourage their political, gender-focused critiques of hypersexualized media but also to engage with them in conversations about alternative, non-commodified meanings of sexuality" (p. 400).

In the digital age, social media are another site where young people must navigate a complicated terrain of **gender and sexuality**. Michael Salter's (VI.49) chapter on "sexting" examines how young men and women respond to digital images of sexualized bodies circulated by peers. Based on focus group research of Australian young adults ages 18 to 20, Salter reveals a disturbing double standard. Though "social media is the first mass media platform in history where girls and women participate at equal or greater levels than boys and men as content producers, distributers and consumers," young women are being harassed and victimized by young men—often peers who they consider "friends"—who request nude pictures, which they then share (p. 402). For young women, this request requires choosing between two negative outcomes: being labelled a "slut" if they comply with the request or being branded as "stuck up" or a "prude" if they do not. Salter also found that when nudes are circulated without a young woman's consent, not only is she humiliated by the violation of privacy, she is also judged harshly by her female peers, who believe the "sexualised display marks her as the 'bad' or 'slutty' girl deserving retribution" (regardless of the intent and context of the nude) while the male perpetrator goes unscathed (p. 405). In contrast, the focus group noted that young men who choose to make and circulate their own "dick pics" encountered no significant negative consequences for their behavior. Ultimately, Salter's study suggests that new technologies are not inherently panaceas for a more just and equitable society. Rather, social media simply provides a new avenue for promoting unequal gender relations where young women's bodies and sexuality are policed and sexual harassment and abuse by young men is excused.

In addition to social media, children and young people in our digital era devote a large portion of their leisure time to electronic and online games. As John Sanbonmatsu (VI.50) points out, "In the US alone, over 150 million people—more than half the population—play video games" (p. 413). In his provocative essay, he calls our attention to the potential dangers of the alluring, highly realistic simulations that draw so many players into these virtual worlds.

Sanbonmatsu argues that many of the most popular video games reproduce sexist and racist depictions, while also legitimizing a **consumerist** militaristic society that undermines the well-being of individuals, cultures, and the ecosystem. Placing gaming within the socioeconomic context of our contemporary life, he questions why video games are so popular, not only for men and boys but increasingly for women and girls. For Sanbonmatsu, the answer lies in our society's many alienating challenges—the increasing financial problems that working people face, a delegitimization of the state, and the destruction of the environment—all issues that people feel are out of their control. He suggests that, confronted with these problems, "We hunger for escapist forms of entertainment because they offer the illusion of restoring to us something that has been lost—a sense of our own personal agency and efficacy in a world that seems increasingly chaotic, dangerous, and out of control" (p. 421).

A conventional **masculinist** gender bias is not only displayed in the texts of most interactive digital games, as already seen, but also emerges in the actual playing of games by fans. Elena Bertozzi (VI.51), who teaches digital game design, looks at observed gender differences in digital play, finding that despite increased female participation,

> researchers have documented the ways in which gender politics are reconstructed in digital worlds. . . . Given that digital play offers a considerable amount of gender plasticity through avatars, it might seem illogical for gender stereotypes and concerns to persist in digital gaming, but they do. (p. 429)

Bertozzi hypothesizes that such differences "are strongly influenced by the unwillingness of both genders to cross traditional, culturally gendered play lines" (p. 429). She is especially interested in female **resistance** to competing fiercely with men in games, because of the real-world implications of continuing to associate competitive success with masculinity. On the positive side, she reminds us many women are now using game/play activities as a way of practicing competition "at the same level as males" (p. 429). As she writes, "If we recognize the significance and level of difficulty of challenging existing norms, we can better support their initiatives and create structures to help others join them" (p. 429).

As the chapters in this section point out, the social impact of growing up with media is a complicated part of contemporary life, one that grows ever more challenging as digital and mobile forms of media creep increasingly into all of our living spaces and all hours of our days.

44

THE FUTURE OF CHILDHOOD IN THE GLOBAL TELEVISION MARKET

Dafna Lemish

TELEVISION AND CHILDREN: A GLOBAL ISSUE[1]

The nature of relations between children and television is a global issue for a variety of compelling reasons. First, children of both genders and all ages, races, religions, classes, and geographic regions of the world watch television on a regular basis, enjoy it tremendously, and may well learn more about the world from it than from any other socializing agent. Few other social phenomena can be claimed with such confidence as an experience shared by most children in today's world. Whether they view TV in their bedrooms, download it on their computers or mobile phones, share the family set in the living room, or watch it in the classroom or the community center, TV is part of the taken-for-granted, everyday experiences of most children. No other cultural phenomenon has achieved such a magnitude of penetration or global status.

The global status of television can be claimed because similar debates over television's role in the lives of children have emerged globally. On one hand, high hopes and great expectations have been expressed worldwide that television would enrich children's lives, stimulate their imagination and creativity, broaden their education and knowledge, encourage multicultural tolerance, narrow social gaps, and stimulate development and democratization processes. On the other hand, there has been and continues to be great anxiety about the ability of television to numb the senses, develop indifference to the pain of others, encourage destructive behaviors, lead to a deterioration of moral values, suppress local cultures, and contribute to social estrangement.

These oppositional stances in regard to the medium of television—as a "messiah" on one hand and a "demon" on the other—have been discussed widely in public debates in every society that has absorbed the medium. Most pronounced are concerns over the effects on children of television violence, as well as the potential harm of exposure to sexual portrayals, the effects of advertising on consumer culture, and the more general concern over children's passivity and social disengagement. Media debates, public forums, parent and community newsletters, legislative body hearings, educational leaders, broadcasting policymakers—all have contributed to these popular debates framed as "moral panics," exerting public pressure on governing institutions.

The relations of television and children have interested scholars worldwide, mainly in the fields of psychology, media studies, sociology, education, and health professions (see, e.g., Lemish, 2007; Pecora, Murray, & Wartella, 2007). With the advent of new media, these studies have also stimulated a more complex discussion of television as part of a process of convergence of media and multiple screens (e.g., computers, mobile phones, handheld games; Calvert & Wilson, 2008; Lemish, 2013). Their varied disciplinary homes have made a great deal of difference to the kind of theoretical underpinnings brought to their research, the questions posed, the methods applied, and, accordingly, the kinds of findings reported and their interpretation. Furthermore, in this respect, the academic field concerned with the reciprocal relationships between children and television reflects in large degree the changes that have taken place in the various disciplines nourishing this

---

This piece is an original essay that was commissioned for this volume. It has been updated from an earlier version that appeared in the 3rd edition.

scholarly field, in general, and the study of mass media, in particular.

Psychology, the most prominent of the disciplines applied to this area, has focused on the individual child and a host of related issues, such as social learning from television, the effects of television on behavior, development of comprehension of television content, and the uses children make of television and the gratifications they acquire from their viewing behaviors. As the body of literature grew, mainly from Western academic institutions, it became clear that the "strong effects" conclusion that assumes a unidirectional television effect on children is oversimplistic. Other research demonstrated something that common sense and anecdotal data posited for a long time: Children are not passive entities, a la the proverbial "tabula rasa," upon which television messages leave their marks. On the contrary, children are active consumers of television. They react to, think, feel, and create meanings. They bring to television encounters a host of predispositions, abilities, desires, and experiences. They watch television in diverse personal, social, and cultural circumstances that also influence and are part of their discourse and interactions with television. Thus, it has become clear that asking, "What do children do with television?" is just as important a question as, "How does television influence them?"

This paradigm shift led to highlighting the need for cross-cultural research. Clearly, comparative research of this global phenomenon can illuminate many of the questions on the research agenda: Does televised violence affect children differently if they are living in a violent urban center in comparison with a tranquil, isolated village? Are children more frightened by news coverage of war when they are growing up amid armed conflict, in comparison with children for whom war is a fictitious concept? Do children react differently to actors and actresses of European descent who appear in their favorite soap operas and situation comedies if they are living in a dominantly Euro-American society, in comparison with African, Latino, or Asian societies? And what about consumerism—would children raised in rich consumer cultures amid an abundance of products from which to choose interpret advertising differently than those with no financial resources or limited personal property? Pursuing such questions

related to children and television has become a global endeavor for researchers to study, as no single body of knowledge based on contextualized studies in one culture, be it as rich and diverse as possible, can provide us with the in-depth, multifaceted picture necessary to understand this phenomenon in its full global manifestation.

The topic of children and television is of global interest for an additional, crucial reason. Today, children are part of a global audience that transcends local or even regional physical and cultural boundaries in consumption of television programs. As a global phenomenon, television promotes mainly what has been termed "late-modernity" values, typified primarily by commercialism, globalization, privatization, and individualization. This is "achieved" as a result of the fact that children all over the world watch, for example, American-produced cartoons, situation comedies, soap operas, action-adventure serials, and Disney and Hollywood movies. However, they also watch programs that come from other parts of the world, such as Latin-American telenovelas, localized versions of Japanese animations, or the local coproductions of the American *Sesame Street* and the United Kingdom's *Teletubbies*. Worldwide, children complete their homework or chores to the sounds of popular music on MTV and fantasize about love and adventure while watching blockbuster movies broadcast at a later time on their local channels or downloaded to their computers. They cheer for their favorite sports team across continents and seas, follow the news of armed conflicts worlds apart, and admire many of the same celebrities—collecting their memorabilia, hanging their posters, wearing their T-shirts, and following their private lives in the magazines and websites.

Therefore, the study of media and children can no longer remain bound within national borders, as media, children, and young people's well-being are international as well as transnational phenomena involving important issues such as the political economy of media corporations; implications of the centrality of new, border-free technologies; massive migration movements; and rapidly changing understandings and theorizing of multiculturalism, cultural hybridity, and diasporic identities. The monies invested in children and child-targeted entertainment media advance a global market of enormous proportions and varying value. For huge entertainment corporations, children are not future citizens; rather, they are first and foremost consumers (Linn, 2004).

Childhood is not a distinct period in the life cycle from the commercial point of view, one that should be attended to with compassion and responsibility. Rather, on the contrary, it is a distinct market opportunity requiring strong socialization to the consumer-centered lifestyle. Thus, any attempts to advance or lobby for change in the contents of television programs and movies directed at children, to legislate Internet safety, or to develop less violent and more creative computer games for children can no longer be redressed in national isolation. Indeed, cross-cultural studies have demonstrated their potential to reveal the deep ethnocentrism and cultural biases inherent in so many of these texts, understand the complex intertwining of culture and media, and at the same time highlight those aspects of children's lives—their needs, aspirations, pleasures, and anxieties—that seem to be shared universally.

CONTENT CHARACTERISTICS OF CHILDREN'S TELEVISION CIRCULATING GLOBALLY

Given this broad overview, we can discuss one of the pressing questions at the center of studies of children's television: What kind of television programs are traveling around the world? A recent analysis of children's television programs in 24 countries (Götz & Lemish, 2012) presented compelling evidence of the global flow of children's programs. The analysis of 9,000 individual programs (out of about 20,000 recorded in the sample that aired during 2,400 hours of explicit children's television) found that only 23% of the programs were produced or coproduced domestically around the world, while 77% of all fictional programs were "imported." The United States and the United Kingdom, with 83% and 67% shares of the market, respectively, were the countries with the highest percentages of local production, followed by China (53%) and Canada (45%). At the other end of the spectrum, only 1% of the programs broadcast in Hong Kong, Kenya, and New Zealand were produced domestically. The biggest export region of children's television programs was

North America, where 60% of the world children's television production originated, followed by Europe with 28% and Asia with 9%.

Among the sample of programs studied, 69% were fictional shows, 17% were nonfiction, and 7% were mixed genres. Animated programs composed the main share of the fictional programs (84%). There was a much smaller share of children's programs that featured real human beings (9%), mixed formats (5%), or puppet shows (2%).

Another central finding was that there were more than twice as many male characters (68%) than female characters (32%) in children's programs. The percentage of females was much lower in programs without human characters, where creators have the most freedom to construct images (25% as animals, 21% as monsters, 16% as robots, and 13% as other fictional beings). Differences between the various countries were not significant, highlighting that this is a universally biased characteristic. In addition, on the average, 72% of all main characters were coded as Caucasian, including in countries where the dominant skin color is Black (e.g., 69% of characters in children's programming in Kenya and 81% in South Africa were White).

In summary, empirical evidence suggests that children's television around the world consists primarily of fictional animation programs not produced domestically but purchased from abroad, mainly from the United States and Canada. These programs feature mostly light-skinned characters, with an overwhelming presence of males. Therefore, the White male hegemony seems to be numerically dominant in children's television around the world, just as it is in other aspects of popular culture.

IMPLICATIONS FOR FUTURE CHILDHOODS AROUND THE GLOBE[2]

Analysis of the characteristics of the global children's television market can be grounded in the more general discourse of critical approaches to media globalization and its influences on local cultures, indigenous traditions, heritages, and values. Globalization, in this sense, rarely means universal but, rather, refers to the spread of Western-mediated products and images around the globe.

The claim that we live in a world increasingly characterized by Americanization has been put forth repeatedly in intellectual and political thought (e.g., Bloch & Lemish, 2003; Held & McGrew, 2003; Ritzer, 1993). Most notably, in the children's television domain, there are three main American corporations (following recent purchasing and realignments) controlling the market in the United States as well as the rest of the world—the Disney Channel, Nickelodeon, and Cartoon Network ("Ratings Watch," 2009). The competition between television networks for their share of the children's market drives them to differentiate themselves from one another and to create brand identity and loyalty (White & Hall Preston, 2005), characterized, among other markers, by a specific gender and age appeal. Their global success suggests that they have succeeded in maximizing their appeal worldwide. Given these structures of market forces, what, then, are the possible implications of the dominance of North American television programs in constructing childhoods around the world? Let us consider some of the most central influences that emerged in a grounded theory of mediated childhood, via analysis of 135 interviews with producers of children's television from 65 countries around the world (discussed in detail in Lemish, 2010).

Loss of the Local

While this is not a new argument in the discourse of cultural imperialism (Morley, 2006), American programming for children has been strongly criticized around the world on many levels: for being stereotypical of gender and race, for being irrelevant to indigenous cultures, for being too limited in scope of content and issues for children as they mature, for unnecessarily accelerating adulthood, and for encouraging wasteful consumerism. In this study, the longing for more visibility of one's own culture is a strong theme. Exported American television for children has been blamed for its role in perpetuating inappropriate values, including flooding the children's television market with stereotypical representations of an imagined, idealized portrayal of the American way of life, with associated culturally dominant representations of gender and race roles. A partial list of the critique of values identified in the forms of American television broadcast to children around the world includes heavy consumerism, preoccupation

with sex and romance, lack of respect for adults and local cultural traditions, individualism and estrangement from the collective, dominance of the English language and slang, dominance of popular culture, and celebrity adoration. Critiques also cite what is absent in these programs, including the lives, values, and concerns of lower-class children, as well as children growing up in poor-resource societies, in conflict and crisis situations, in nontraditional family arrangements, or on the streets. The lack of buying power of such populations means that they are insignificant to the industry, according to the rules by which this system operates. Accordingly, their needs, aspirations, pleasures, fantasies, and realities are not catered to or reflected on the screens to which children and youth are exposed.

Major social issues shared throughout the world that are of central concern for young people are nonexistent in the lives of the middle-class children portrayed on screens around the world—for example, schooling, life as HIV/AIDS orphans, domestic and sexual violence, safety, health, and economic survival. Rarely represented, too, are the historical values and tales, music, customs and mores, sights and sounds, foods, habits, languages, and ways of lives different from those of the "imaginary center" of the Western world (Appadurai, 1990). As a result, most young viewers see neither themselves nor their lives reflected or presented in authentic ways. Rather, among the results of the heavy dominance of the *imagined* Western world is exposure and informal socialization to a social world where they, and those like them, are marginal, unimportant, even nonexistent. Here, according to the cultivation hypothesis advanced in media studies (Signorielle & Morgan, 1990), we can argue that accumulated exposure to a particular worldview fosters an internalization of that world as an accurate and normative perspective on life. Accordingly, many scholars and media educators argue that media literacy programs should enable participants to challenge images that entrench a perspective on oneself as an "other."

The Dominance of the Western Beauty Myth

In a related argument, children's television is a partner with other industries in perpetuating an unattainable beauty model, particularly for girls. This model exemplifies the intertwining of Western gendered and racialized ideologies, and has been called "the beauty myth" by Naomi Wolf (1991): a homogenization of the desired female "look" as mostly young, thin, attractive, heterosexual, wealthy, and predominantly White. Evidence from the global study presented above (Götz & Lemish, 2012), as well as additional studies (e.g., Bramlett-Solomon & Roeder, 2008; Lemish, forthcoming; Northup & Liebler, 2010), demonstrates the priority given to selected images of Whiteness on television viewed by children, all of which convey the message that Western beauty is superior to any other racial form. Scholars claim that such media representations are disempowering for children worldwide, with impacts on self-identity, national pride, and behavior (including the purchase of products in the pursuit of the unattainable look and plastic surgery that imitates Caucasian features). Concern for young people's desire to forsake their identities and even abandon their distinct racial physical characteristics was among the sources of producer grievance around the world (Lemish, 2010).

Thus, the beauty myth has been perceived to be a well-disciplined effort to control girls, as well as a racialized form of inequity and discrimination. Indeed, Hall (1997) claimed this to be an example of "internal colonization" that occurs when adoption of a dominant representation "succeeds" so that people see and experience themselves as an Other. Black, Filipina, or Latina girls, for example, learn to see themselves through the White masculine perspective that represents and speaks for them. In doing so, they internalize an oppressive point of view of themselves and participate in a "process of whitening that attempts to modernize these identities while bleaching ethnicities" (Nayak & Kehily, 2007, p. 24). Others have referred to this as a form of discrimination based on skin color that is a process of internalized "colorism" (Banks, 2000). Thus, even skin tone may determine different "shades" of racism and create status hierarchies and inequalities within the colored community itself (Celious & Oyserman, 2001).

The struggle to attain the "Western look" also imposes an economic strain on children and their families, as it encourages heavy consumption of leisure goods that in turn fuels production of a variety of products, including clothing, fashion accessories, costly surgeries, and multiple exemplars of Western popular culture. A related concern is that the popular beauty ideals distributed by television for children promote negative self-images and glorification of thinness, as well as encouraging destructive eating disorders (Harrison & Hefner, 2006). On the other hand, the unhealthy eating habits promoted by the American "fast-food" industry paired with a passive physical life encouraged by heavy consumption of television have been found to be correlated with growing obesity among young people in Western societies (Vandewater & Cummings, 2008) and are raising anxiety over possible similar influences worldwide.

Gender Segregation

The dynamics of the television industry in the United States and the insatiable economic needs that drive them contribute in numerous ways to television's gender segregation worldwide. For example, they continue to promote a worldview through which boys and girls are encouraged to inhabit different electronic and cultural spaces. They do so through the contents offered, as well as by serving as a model for younger, resource-poor television industries. The Disney Channel, for example, with its big global hits (e.g., *High School Musical, Hannah Montana*), is clearly perceived as "girls oriented," while the Cartoon Network has been traditionally associated with action-adventure cartoons and an audience of boys. Originally, Nickelodeon was involved in extensive gender experimentation and was a somewhat gender-neutral channel. While its programming decisions have shifted, the channel retains a more balanced approach in its programming than any of the other major networks. Yet it is still perceived by industry professionals to be skewed toward girls (Lemish, 2010). This general division among the networks is strongly reinforced by the industry's working axiom: Although girls will watch boys' shows, boys will not watch girls' shows. Scholars have found that this central belief is shared throughout the industry (Alexander & Owers, 2007; Banet-Weiser, 2004; Lemish, 2010; Seiter & Mayer, 2004).

These trends are gradually shifting due to economic pressures and growing gender equity awareness of both audiences and programmers. Networks are now making an effort to address the issue of gender segregation of channels, employing strategies such as selecting lead characters from both genders, diversifying program genres and narrative styles, and modifying packaging and names. However, it is interesting to note that this increase in network efforts to expand the audience to include both boys and girls is clearly understood as primarily a marketing strategy. Take, for example, Disney's efforts to attract 6- to 14-year-old male viewers to the new Disney XD cable channel and website (Barnes, 2009). This plan does not seem to be aimed at diminishing gender segregation or erasing stereotypes; rather, on the contrary, it is geared toward offering a clearly defined "boys' world"—an X Disney—in addition to the existing girls' one.

Television professionals' construction of their young audiences as largely inhabiting two very different gendered cultural worlds draws heavily on developmental theories as well as market and academic research findings. Studies suggest that the tendency for children to segregate themselves by gender and to play more compatibly with same-sex partners is already evident in early childhood and progressively gains strength by mid-childhood. The causes and consequences of this segregation are a major topic of investigation in child psychology and education (Maccoby, 1998; Mehta & Strough, 2009). Suffice to say, for our purposes, that gender-segregated childhoods provide different contexts for children's social development. This does not necessarily prepare them for mutual understanding and collaboration. This segregation runs parallel to the current popularity of the "Mars and Venus" metaphor (Gray, 1991), according to which men and women are perceived to be essentially different beings with opposing communication styles and emotional needs. This perspective has recruited to its service key elements of the postfeminist sensibility, best represented by the slogan "different but equal" (Shifman & Lemish, 2011). Television and toy industries seem to be capitalizing quite successfully on this popular trend, pushing it to its extremes in their pursuit of ever-expanding markets and profits worldwide.

Earlier research on the gendered nature of media consumption by children and youth found that while, overall, girls do develop an interest

in traditional masculine genres, on the whole, boys continue to show no interest in female genres (Lemish, Liebes, & Seidmann, 2001). The largely descriptive evidence gathered does provide empirical support for the popular axiom applied by children's entertainment industry and media professionals cited above, but we need to provide critical analyses of the data that can unpack and identify the mechanisms creating this phenomenon. For example, according to the feminist analysis of social change, this process could be explained, at least in part, through the observation that, more generally, girls as well as women learn to gradually incorporate typical male perspectives and values into their lives while not abandoning their traditional female responsibilities and interests. This echoes other situations in which socially subordinated groups learn to adjust "up," in an effort to improve status and opportunities. Perhaps the trend of girls' interests in boys' genres (and boys' refusal after a certain age to participate in girls' genres) represents all children's growing sensitivity to the advantageous position that boys hold in societies around the world and the higher value associated with their tastes and interests.

SERVING THE NEEDS OF CHILDREN: PROACTIVE CONCLUSIONS[3]

Television programs for children that travel around the world are big business. Generating profit is the main imperative for the corporation executives who manage these programs; therefore, it is up to consumers and citizens to insist that other concerns must also shape the future of children's television globally. I submit that critical analyses of the content offerings of this major socializer raise serious questions about the industry's ethical conduct and social responsibility.

As delineated in the United Nations Convention on the Rights of the Child (1989), the rights of children include a variety of communication rights: the right to be heard and to be taken seriously, to free speech and to information, to maintain privacy, to develop cultural identity, and to be proud of one's heritage and beliefs. Yet, whether girls and boys live in deprived and resource-poor societies or in overwhelmingly commercialized and profit-driven ones, their voices are for the most part neither heard nor taken seriously. They have limited opportunities to express their needs and opinions or to access much-needed information for their healthy development. Many mass communication efforts do not respect children's privacy and dignity or foster their self-esteem and confidence. Even in the cases in which, seemingly, they are allowed to "voice" their concerns, the opportunity is often only "token" in nature, reflects adults' perspectives, and does not necessarily contribute to their holistic development or problem-solving skills (Kolucki & Lemish, 2011).

Despite cultural differences, children around the world face similar issues of personal safety, as well as anxiety over the future of the globe and their place in it. Television has a responsibility to help all children become courageous adults and active citizens of this world. It could be argued that children's television should contribute to an effort to provide children with a "safe space" that also offers advancing programs that enable them to understand what it is like to live in a society of inclusion. A diverse screen provides more realistic, humane portrayals of current societies around the world and is also central to the well-being of the children growing within those societies. It celebrates girls and boys as children who all face the same challenges and share aspirations, morality, dreams, and hopes; children who need love and friendships, have adventures and overcome difficulties; children who are curious and eager to explore their surroundings and who struggle with their multiple identities; children who try to carve out their place in the world. According to this progressive vision, children's television needs to present young persons who are self-willed, who are positive, and who share their problems and accomplishments. Breaking stereotypes and opening up the screen to blurring gender and racial differences, and offering children real choices that cut across divides can foster a safer and healthier environment for growth and development. Young viewers can be exposed to a range of possibilities relevant to their own lives that also challenge the ways they are brought up to think about their identities.

While these suggestions may seem naive given the competitive nature of the now well-established global television market, and given the critiques of how television can promote the domination of Western modernity's values in other parts of the world, it is crucial to remember that we can build on and expand many of the efforts being made worldwide by dedicated professionals who see television as a social resource that needs to be taken seriously and used responsibly. Indeed, there are professionals working, too, within the commercial world to introduce change from within the system. Others operate in organizations driven by social goals that are not solely profit motivated, as well as not-for-profit alternative and citizen media, which, collectively, offer a spectrum from the conservative to the radical, along with subversive contents (Downing, 2001). These efforts can be framed as part of media reform and democratization movements that seek not only to rebut but also to offer alternatives to the hegemonic control of media corporations (McChesney & Nichols, 2002).

Indeed, many such efforts are integrated within public broadcasting systems funded by the state, particularly in Europe. Many of these efforts in the realm of television for children are dedicated to contextualizing their productions within local cultures and children's needs (Lemish, 2010). Some of the best efforts of such work are presented in international events that bring together professionals involved in creating quality television for children around the globe, such as the Prix Jeunesse in Munich and the Japan Prize in Tokyo, among others (see Cole, 2007). Therefore, the debate over the future of public broadcasting, free journalism, and democracy (e.g., McChesney & Nichols, 2010) also has serious implications for broadcasting to children—a unique population devoid of political and economic power or opportunities to lobby, protest, or bargain for their rights.

Through incorporating concerns for children's well-being and healthy development, television can be enriching and inspiring. It can offer a diverse range of possibilities for complex characters not bound by stereotypes, and it can give voice to their multiple perspectives and experiences. It can constitute a safe environment in which to explore the full range of roles children might wish for themselves, a vision for a different reality, and aspirations for a better world.

NOTES

1. This section is reprinted with some changes, with permission, from my earlier work, Lemish (2007, pp. 1–4).

2. This section draws, with permission, on my earlier work, published in Lemish (2010, Chaps. 3 and 4).

3. This section draws, with permission, on my earlier work, published in Lemish (2010, Chaps. 7 and 8).

REFERENCES

Alexander, A., & Owers, J. (2007). The economics of children's television. In J. A. Bryant (Ed.), *The children's television community* (pp. 57–74). Mahwah, NJ: Lawrence Erlbaum.

Appadurai, A. (1990). Disjuncture and difference in the global economy. *Theory, Culture and Society, 7,* 295–310.

Banet-Weiser, S. (2004). Girls rule! Gender, feminism, and Nickelodeon. *Critical Studies in Media Communication, 21*(2), 119–139.

Banks, T. L. (2000). Colorism: A darker shade of pale. *UCLA Law Review, 47*(6), 1705–1746.

Barnes, B. (2009, April 14). Disney expert uses science to draw boy viewers. *New York Times.*

Bloch, L. R., & Lemish, D. (2003). The megaphone effect: International culture via the US of A. *Communication Yearbook, 27,* 159–190.

Bramlett-Solomon, S., & Roeder, Y. (2008). Looking at race in children's television: Analysis of Nickelodeon commercials. *Journal of Children and Media, 2,* 56–66.

Calvert, S. L., & Wilson, B. J. (Eds.). (2008). *The handbook of children, media, and development.* Chichester, UK: Blackwell.

Celious, A., & Oyserman, D. (2001). Race from the inside: An emerging heterogeneous race model. *Journal of Social Issues, 57*(1), 149–165.

Cole, C. F. (2007). A guide to international events in children's media. *Journal of Children and Media, 1*(1), 93–100.

Downing, J. (2001). *Radical media: Rebellious communication and social movements.* Thousand Oaks, CA: Sage.

Götz, M., & Lemish, D. (Eds.). (2012). *Sexy girls, heroes and funny losers: Gender representations in children's TV around the world.* New York: Peter Lang.

Gray, J. (1991). *Men are from Mars, women are from Venus: A practical guide for improving communication and getting what you want in your relationships.* New York: HarperCollins.

Hall, S. (1997). *Representation: Cultural representations and signifying practices.* Milton Keynes, UK: Open University Press.

Harrison, K., & Hefner, V. (2006). Media exposure, current and future body ideals, and disordered eating among preadolescent girls: A longitudinal panel study. *Journal of Youth and Adolescence, 35,* 153–163.

Held, D., & McGrew, A. (Eds.). (2003). *The global transformations reader: An introduction to the globalization debate* (2nd ed.). Cambridge, UK: Polity.

Kolucki, B., & Lemish, D. (2011). *Communication for children and youth: Good practices that nurture, inspire, excite, educate, and heal.* New York: UNICEF.

Lemish, D. (2007). *Children and television: A global perspective.* Oxford, UK: Blackwell.

Lemish, D. (2010). *Screening gender in children's TV: The views of producers around the world.* New York: Routledge.

Lemish, D. (Ed.). (2013). *The Routledge international handbook of children, adolescents, and media.* New York: Routledge.

Lemish, D. (forthcoming). Boys are . . . Girls are . . . : How children's media and merchandizing construct gender. In C. Carter, L. Steiner, & L. McLaughlin (Eds.), *Routledge companion to media and gender*.

Lemish, D., Liebes, T., & Seidmann, V. (2001). Gendered media meaning and use. In S. Livingstone & M. Bovill (Eds.), *Children and their changing media environment* (pp. 263–282). Hillsdale, NJ: Lawrence Erlbaum.

Linn, S. (2004). *Consuming kids: The hostile take-over of childhood*. New York: New Press.

Maccoby, E. E. (1998). *The two sexes: Growing up apart—coming together*. Cambridge, MA: Belknap Press of Harvard University Press.

McChesney, R., & Nichols, J. (2002). *Our media, not theirs: The democratic struggle against corporate media*. New York: Seven Stories Press.

McChesney, R., & Nichols, J. (2010). *The death and life of American journalism: The media revolution that will begin the world again*. Philadelphia: First Nation Books.

Mehta, C. M., & Strough, J. (2009). Sex segregation in friendships and normative contexts across the life span. *Developmental Review, 29,* 201–220.

Morley, D. (2006). Globalisation and cultural imperialism reconsidered: Old questions in new guises. In J. Curran & D. Morley (Eds.), *Media and cultural theory* (pp. 30–43). New York: Routledge.

Nayak, A., & Kehily, M. J. (2007). *Gender, youth and culture: Young masculinities and femininities*. Hampshire, UK: Palgrave.

Northup, T., & Liebler, C. (2010). The good, the bad, and the beautiful: Beauty ideals on the Disney and Nickelodeon channels. *Journal of Children and Media, 4*(3), 265–282.

Pecora, N., Murray, J. P., & Wartella, E. A. (Eds.). (2007). *Children and television: Fifty years of research*. Mahwah, NJ: Lawrence Erlbaum.

Ratings watch: Disney Channel, Nickelodeon. (2009, December 23). *Kidscreen*. Retrieved from http://www.kidscreen.com/articles/news/20091223/ratingswatch.html

Ritzer, G. (1993). *The McDonaldization of society*. New York: Pine Forge Press.

Seiter, E., & Mayer, V. (2004). Diversifying representation in children's TV: Nickelodeon's model. In H. Hendershot (Ed.), *Nickelodeon nation: The history, politics, and economics of America's only TV channel for kids* (pp. 120–133). New York: New York University Press.

Shifman, L., & Lemish, D. (2011). "Mars and Venus" in virtual space: Post-feminist humor and the Internet. *Critical Studies in Media Communication, 28*(3), 253–273.

Signorielle, N., & Morgan, M. (Eds.). (1990). *Cultivation analysis: New directions in media effects research*. Newbury Park, CA: Sage.

Vandewater, E. A., & Cummings, H. M. (2008). Media use and childhood obesity. In S. L. Calvert & B. J. Wilson (Eds.), *The handbook of children, media, and development* (pp. 355–380). Oxford, UK: Blackwell.

White, C. L., & Hall Preston, E. (2005). The spaces of children's programming. *Critical Studies in Media Communication, 22*(3), 239–255.

Wolf, N. (1991). *The beauty myth: How images of beauty are used against women*. New York: Doubleday.

45

DISNEY: 21ST CENTURY LEADER IN ANIMATING GLOBAL INEQUALITY
Lee Artz

Disney leads the world in the production and distribution of popular culture. Although Google and Facebook may be media giants in assets, neither challenges Disney in entertainment content. Warner, 21st Century Fox, and DreamWorks have had box-office success in feature films, but none come close to Disney in animation: five of the top six gross profits in animation films are Disney. *Frozen* (2013) revenues topped $1.3 billion; Disney/Pixar's *Toy Story 3* (2010) reached $1 billion, as did both *Finding Dory* (2016) and *Zootopia* (2016); while the sci-fi/superhero animated feature, *Big Hero 6* (2014) broke $600 million in ticket sales. Indeed, although the addition of Marvel characters and the Star Wars franchise brings hundreds of millions in revenue, animation remains central to Disney's economic vitality and cultural influence. In the last few years alone, Disney has sold over $100 billion in toys based on characters from its animated features. Disney theme parks, featuring popular film characters and settings, now have more visitors each year than all of the fifty-four national parks in the United States.

Seeking to benefit from the global popularity and profits from its animated features, Disney not only has expanded its US media dominance with ownership of the ABC television network, mass-market radio stations, and cable channels such as ESPN and A&E, it has entered joint ventures, partnerships, and distribution agreements with major media in other nations. In addition to owning UTV Television (India), Patgonik Films (Argentina), and Disney Europe, Disney has agreements with RTL Bertlesmann in Germany, SBS in Sweden, Studio Ghibli in Japan, and Yash Raj studios in India, among many others.

The centrality of animation to Disney's corporate success and the corresponding centrality of Disney animation to global popular culture forms and themes is clear in the attempts by other media majors to emulate the Disney animation formula. A full account requires a political, economic and a cultural studies approach to understand the manifest parallels between Disney's corporate practices (from investment and workplace practices to technological production and mass distribution) and the ideological themes of Disney's animated narratives (including race and gender equality). Indeed, the construction, content, and persuasive appeal of Disney animations suggests that Disney consistently and programmatically produces "commodities-as-animated-feature films" that promote an ideology preferred by Disney and transnational capitalism—an ideology recently replete with cultural diversity and positive gender roles but still at odds with democracy and creative, participatory social life.

In the last decade, Disney has made some significant changes in their representations and storylines, but remains at odds with democracy and social responsibility by globally distributing entertainment narratives that simultaneously soften and normalize messages of social-class hierarchy and antisocial hyper-individualism. Disney's family-friendly entertainment carries appealing coming-of-age tales of common sense that sustain belief in existing social relations of power and hierarchy.

Updated from Lee Artz, "Monarchs, Monsters, and Multiculturalism: Disney's Menu for Global Hierarchy," pages 75–76, 83–84, 87–89, 91–92, 94 from *Rethinking Disney: Private Control, Public Dimensions,* edited by Mike Budd and Max H. Kirsch. © 2005 by Wesleyan University Press and reprinted with permission by Wesleyan University Press.

NATURALIZING HIERARCHY

Hierarchy in a social order indicates a ranking according to worth, ability, authority, or perceived natural attributes. In Disney, hierarchy is normalized by the physical appearance of characters supplemented with complementary rewards such that—in each animation—heroes and heroines are invariably attractive, skillful, worthy, often lucky, but always virtuous, and ultimately powerful—either in active service to the narrative's social order as in *Zootopia* or in deference to the natural hierarchy as in *The Princess and the Frog* (2009), *Frozen,* and *Big Hero 6,* among others.

Early scenes in *Big Hero 6* and *Zootopia* portray the magic of post-modern technology that aesthetically enables "naturally" segregated neighborhoods. Years ago in *The Lion King* (1994) we could not mistake that "natural" social order and its validity. All species bowed before the rightful king, which assured happiness and maintenance of the established hierarchy. The visual metaphors of good and evil were simple and transparent: a regal king and his heir; an evil uncle who covets the kingdom; and lesser, passive animal-citizens overrun by social undesirables in need of leadership. Twenty years later we have an ice princess, a plethora of species-cops, and an industrial corporate order as the backdrop to Disney's coming of age stories. The meanings are animationally inescapable—the heroines and heroes are brightly drawn, muscular, and smoothly curved; the villains are dark, angular, large, and usually imposing. *Tangled's* (2010) Mother Gothel is old, vain, overly voluptuous, darkly clothed, with dark curled hair; Yokai is large, masked, and wears a dark suit in *Big Hero 6;* Dory is threatened by a menacing dark blue and black giant squid with angular tentacles.

In recent films, Disney has modified its template for villains, presenting the good-looking Hans as a royal antagonist in *Frozen* and the diminutive sheep Bellweather as a surprisingly evil antagonist in *Zootopia.* In neither case is the more fundamental hierarchy of power disrupted; Disney has just modernized the narrative, perhaps in deference to public dismay as citizens have witnessed gross malfeasance by politicians, executives, coaches, priests, and others previously assumed to be ethical. In a culture of fear, no one is necessarily what they appear: Disney adjusts accordingly while insisting on the legitimacy of power and authority sustained in its animated hierarchies.

Dialogue and action, especially resolution, resolve any moral ambiguity in a character's appearance. Since *The Lion King* (1994) when Mustafa spoke in the King's English, while Scar, the villain, lurked lazy and foppish in style and speech, Disney has used dialogue to direct viewers to the intended meaning. Not unexpectedly given Disney's pulse taking of popular culture, in recent years, Disney has championed cultural diversity as its secondary mantra to hierarchy, presenting positive images of black people in *The Princess and the Frog* (2009), Asian characters in *Big Hero 6,* and even Polynesian cultures in *Moana* (2017). This is not by accident. As John Lassetter, creative director of Pixar, told *Cinema Blend* in 2016, diversity is "very important to us . . . to have female and ethnic characters. It's grown in importance over time. As you'll see in future films, we're really paying attention to that" (quoted in Reyes, 2016, n.p.). Motivated in part to avoid criticism in the US and in part to expand its international audiences, Disney has discovered that cultural diversity can build hegemonic support for authority and inequality, while also bringing increased profits from large, diverse audiences. Disney exudes diversity without democracy in theme songs, graphic representations, and story lines, as relations of power are cordially maintained throughout. As the Wolf told Little Red Riding Hood's grandmother, "All the better to eat you with my dear!"

Even the ostensibly progressive diversity themes in *Zootopia* reinforce existing social relations under the guise of tolerance for others. Almost all the animals experience prejudice, indicating that everyone is a little bit racist to the exclusion of actual privilege and power. Only the elite-constructed order—the invisible, assumed power of the *Zootopia*—can maintain control over the natural tendencies of dangerous species. The film is about diversity and tolerance, but not about racism and equality. In this animal utopia, no one benefits from bigotry, all suffer a bit: a condition that reinforces and allows discrimination as an individual choice or deficiency unrelated to actual historically-structured race inequality.

The narratives of *Pocahontas, Mulan, Tarzan,* and other Disney animations formed from established templates of elite hierarchy reappear in recent films such as *Toy Story 3* (2010), *Arjun:*

Warrior Prince (2012 in India), and even the feminist-friendly *Frozen* (2013)—albeit with considerable hegemonic variation. In *Pocahontas,* the standard Disney coming-of-age romance offered a feisty, independent heroine in a narrative advocating cultural tolerance. Disney's social relations remain hierarchical: lower-class Anglos worked for Ratcliffe or Smith; native soldiers and villagers followed Powhatan's directives. In the end, the "good" colonialist John Smith intervened to save Powhatan and order the arrest of Ratcliffe; Pocahontas presumably found her true path as a peacemaker and daughter; and the rest of the natives and English adventurers assumed their prescribed subordinate positions, awaiting further orders from their superiors. In *Pocahontas,* two hierarchical orders are defended and left intact, although the extended visual metaphor of John Smith saving Powhatan and wanting to civilize Pocahontas indicates that the colonial is dominant over the indigenous.

At first look *Frozen* appears as a corrective feminist milestone advocating "girl power" and "sisterhood" as the two lead female characters attend to their sibling relationship without heterosexual romantic diversions. No people of color appear in the snow white kingdom of Arendelle, which is by all measures outside any actual societal order and an obvious decision by Disney. Meanwhile, female characters appear decisive, independent, and powerful: Anna is the rescuer; Elsa has the power to freeze the kingdom. And therein is the expressed message: even women can hold and use power—if they are royal elites. Disney secured consent among millions for the modern gloss of female independence, successfully advancing the larger condition of hierarchical power and individual self-interest—not exactly characteristics of a democratic society (or a solid basis for gender equality for that matter).

While the hero and heroine are always attractive by birth, villains are privileged and titled only because of the misplaced magnanimity or whim of a legitimate superior. Villains are unattractive, semi-elite social misfits. Mid-level managers may be objects of derision; the social hierarchy is legitimate. Jafar is a grand vizier, adviser to Sultan; Scar is King Mustafa's disgruntled brother, ineligible for legitimate succession; and Ratcliffe's governorship is a reluctant sop from more worthy elites. Randall of *Monsters, Inc.* remains

on the monsters' payroll only through his deceit, which ultimately is discovered by the hero, Sully. In each of these narratives and many others (e.g., *The Little Mermaid, Beauty and the Beast, The Fox and Hound*), the dominant social class has no villainy, producing only good souls who never abuse their authority. We understand this viscerally by the soft, cuddly caricatures that Disney creates. Abuse comes solely from those elevated beyond their goodness, villains who would reach beyond their status and disrupt the social order. The structure of overworked employees is never questioned: only crustacean Henry J. Waterhouse III must be removed for violating the social responsibility that generations of monster CEOs had felt for the business. But villainy is always undone, because as Disney's Comic Book Art Specifications dictate, only elites can triumph; there is "no upward mobility" in Disney lands. In the fairy-tale world of the dominant, class rules apply: a frog becomes prince only if he was a prince before. Rulers may change among the elite (from Mufasa to Simba, from Sultan to Aladdin, Flik in *A Bug's Life* gets royal privilege, Elsa returns to lead the kingdom, Judy Hopps becomes a cop defending the established order), but the rules and ruled remain. And, in Disney's world, the only just rule is class rule.

Evil henchmen, such as Clayton's sailors or the Huns, are consistently shabbily dressed or disheveled, dark, often bearded, usually armed, speak harshly in short sentences, and mete out their brutality only as long as the villain commands. In Disney, lower-class characters do not act on their own. Large groups are often cast as mob-like in action and graphic: jeering primates terrorize Jane in *Tarzan;* wildebeest stampede without regard for others in *The Lion King;* native warriors huddle around the fire waiting for orders to attack; the Huns shout and howl above the thunder of their horses' hooves; grasshoppers and sharks indiscriminately attack. Whether African, Arabian, North American, Chinese, or nonhuman, few from the good citizenry or evil troops are individualized; even fewer have articulate voices, appearing but as replicates from two or three stencils, graphically reflective of their necessarily subordinate position in Disney's hierarchy. *Zootopia*'s futuristic city did not overcome segregation, but established well-designed separate neighborhoods: Tundratown, Bunny World, Rodentia, and Sahara Square are cute and colorful, species-defined communities that establish the "natural" division of animals and their rightful habitats. In sum, Disney films all play a similar refrain: a stylized, naturalized, and Westernized elite hero combats a privileged antisocial oversized villain, while cute animal sidekicks and thuggish rebels knock about as a shapeless, faceless humanity relegated to the background for elite action. Animating hierarchy centers Disney's vision, whatever the era, geography, or species.

ORDERING COERCION AND POWER

To underscore this essential Disney law, narrative resolution in each film defends and reinforces the status quo. Each film's climax occurs with the preferred social order in place. No one lives happily ever after until the chosen one rules. All is chaos and disorder until Simba returns as monarch, Elsa accepts the throne, San Fransokyo's futuristic order is restored, and Moana becomes the new chief. Even nature withholds its bounty, or freezes over, pending the proper social hierarchy. Nemo's mistake is curiosity about another world: when he leaves the security, safety, and proper place of the coral reef, disaster strikes. Saving China is only a youthful adventure: Mulan's "place in life" is in the family garden. Even the wisest of apes knows Tarzan is superior. The Motunui islanders remain mostly passive, but come alive when Moana rises to chief.

In Disney worlds, true rulers are wise, benevolent, and powerful, and essential to the safety and security of all. Any other social arrangement is unworkable. Villains may attain power, but as nonelite, false leaders, they are ill equipped to rule. Their reign is disastrous and temporary. Soon the hero will save the day and the hierarchy. "As evil is expelled, the world is left nice and clean," and well ordered (Dorfman and Mattelart, 1975, p. 89). Thus, zebras bow, faceless Chinese cheer, and, in general, the working masses rejoice (and happily resume their subservience) upon the triumphant defense of the hierarchy. The pleasant narrative outcome verifies the virtue of hierarchy and models Disney's actual institutional hierarchy in everything from animation production to cruise ships, theme parks, and town life in Celebration, Florida. In its digital production, Disney replaces piecework animation artists with piecework technicians

in a hierarchical structure dedicated to marketing entertainment commodities for shareholder profit—no cooperative here, no creative exchange between artists, technicians, and citizen-parents. The story scripts in narrative and in production and distribution conform to market dictates and capitalist production norms, including corporate elite control.

Preference and justification for elite control can be observed in the attributes of each narrative's leading authority: this character is morally good and invariably benevolent. The sultan may be disoriented, but he is a gentle soul, impervious to evil. A compassionate John Smith—"the perfect masculine companion" (Buescher and Ono, 1996, p. 140)—is willing to sacrifice his own life to avoid further bloodshed. In contrast to the malevolent Huns, Mulan's emperor exudes warmth for his docile subjects. Tarzan demonstrates his human compassion and species superiority in saving his ape family (and Jane). Baymax has a caring healthcare chip and only becomes belligerent and dangerous when Hiro installs a battle chip. Lava monster TeKá becomes friendly goddess Te Fiti when Moana restores her heart. For Disney, all elite authority figures are good, caring, and protective of their wards. In a telling statistical analysis of eleven Disney animations, Hoerner (1996) found that heroic protagonists exhibit 98 percent of all pro-social behavior in the films.

A consistent hierarchal aura organizes moral conflicts and elite responses to challenge in all Disney features. In general, elite heroes and heroines use coercion with impunity, continuing a Disney tradition that dates back to Snow White. Elite coercion varies from the Beast's abuse of Belle to the colonialist's murder of Kocoum. Mulan slaughters dozens of Huns; Tarzan wrestles with Clayton, who accidentally falls to his own death. Hiro intends for Baymax to kill, when he installs the karate battle chip into the robot. Villains Randall, Waterhouse, Hopper, and various aliens are similarly dispatched by elite violence. In addition to coercion, elites frequently employ deceit. Everywhere and always Disney's heroic elites are stronger, smarter, and victorious in the final conflict (even when performing antisocial acts). In each case, the protagonist earns riches, power, and happiness.

In contrast, villains—who almost exclusively exhibit antisocial behavior and violence—suffer calamity or death: Jafar is imprisoned for thousands of years; Scar dies; Kocoum dies; Ratcliffe is arrested; the Hun dies; Clayton dies; Randall and Hopper are ultimately dispatched; Callaghan is imprisoned in San Fransokyo and the predator squid is crushed so Dory can escape. One need not consult a literary critic to understand the moral of these stories. In all fairy tales, good triumphs over evil, but for Disney good is the exclusive genetic and social right of the elite. Elites are attractive, benevolent, good, and successful; villains are often misshapen, always treacherous and evil and never win. The rest of Disney's world is undifferentiated, passive, dependent on elite gratuity, and largely irrelevant except as narrative fodder.

COMMUNITY AND DEMOCRACY

In focusing exclusively on individual elites, Disney dismisses group solidarity and the public interest as unimportant to the story. Although each narrative includes dozens of nonelite characters, they appear primarily as background or as proxies for the protagonists—as exhibited by Nemo's "tank guy" buddies. In fact, "every Disney character stands on either one side or the other of the power demarcation line. All below are bound to obedience, submission, discipline, humility. Those above are free to employ constant coercion, threats, moral and physical repression and economic domination" (Dorfman and Mattelart, 1975, p. 35).

Individualism and competition—the tenets and buzzwords for neoliberal capitalism—are definitional characteristics of Disney's fantasy elites, who have no moral or social peer. Elite ideas and actions are right, good, and ultimately successful. Villains may have ideas and take action, but they are wrong, bad, and doomed to fail. In such a fantasy world, no other ideas or actions are needed; hence Disney's animated public seldom speaks, exhibits limited thought, and undertakes little independent action—and never, ever, does a nonelite character successfully broach the question of equality, democracy, or social justice.

At most, Disney's animated populations appear as "average" characters, either acting irresponsibly as inferiors, squabbling over trifles or passively waiting for mobilization orders from a superior. Most secondary castings are not particularly bright in dialogue or graphic portrayal except

for aides, who are often mischievous but harmless, comic animals: *Zootopia*'s segregated species are a delightfully colorful exception. Less enlightened nonelites tend toward antisocial behavior as thieving hyenas, tormenting monkeys, or devious monsters. Having baser instincts, "bad" nonelites (unshaven, partially dressed, usually large) are also prone to violence and easily misled by nefarious Disney antagonists: Arab bandits work for Jafar; sailors join Clayton in kidnapping; hordes follow the Hun; Randall directs his monster minions; grasshoppers pillage for Hopper; Callaghan/Frei commandeers destructive microbots.

Predictably, according to Disney, most nonelites tacitly or enthusiastically understand that hierarchy is good and support the social order no matter who rules. The citizens of Agrabah bow to the sultan, Jafar, then Aladdin on each successive command; no animals rise up against Scar; the colonists obey Ratcliffe, then Smith; all apes obey Kerchak, then Tarzan; the Queen rules over all bugs; villagers celebrate Elsa's return, and islanders respond happily to Moana as their new chief: long live the monarchy!

According to Disney, workers, sailors, farmers, and other producers are wretched, irrational, chaotic, and passive, unable to act in their own interests—at best they may be motivated to protect the hierarchical social order. Some may be roused to mob action under the wrong leader, but all will be happier if the proper order is fulfilled—the hierarchical natural order of the animal kingdom or the hierarchical social order of an Arab sultanate, Chinese empire, British or ant colony, toy room, scare factory, ocean, ice kingdom, or futuristic metropolis. Group action, in other words, occurs only at the whim of the powerful.

Moreover, in Disney animations, action by leading characters thoroughly shred any semblance of collective interest. Aladdin deserts the orphans and his neighborhood; Pocahontas betrays her nation; Tarzan betrays his family; Mulan deceives her family and compatriots; Simba returns to the pride lands only out of royal duty; Flik imperils the colony; Marlin has no concern beyond Nemo. Dory risks her friends' lives in her self-interested quest. Elsa freezes the entire world. Even socially-responsible Judy Hopps at best protects the status quo of separate but equal tolerance. Disney never animates democracy or social responsibility. Disney heroes in all their wit and wisdom never seek happiness or fulfillment through commitment or improving the human condition. Instead, all Disney animated stars indicate that acting against the public interest in one's search for individual gratification is natural, legitimate, and preferred. Community or family interests or democratic concerns do not appear in Disney, while the box-office success of Fox's *Ice Age* indicates that narratives that include group efforts are creatively and financially possible.

THE REALITIES OF FANTASY

Disney is a world leader in mass entertainment implicated in the globalization of capitalism and a concerted effort to deregulate and privatize world culture. A highly proficient producer and international distributor of capitalist cultural products, Disney advances an ideological content that parallels the social and political requirements of capitalist economic activity: hierarchy, elite coercion, hyper-individualism and social atomism. In particular, Disney's animated features communicate a clear message to the world: The individual elite quest for self-gratification, adventure, and acquisition is good and just—the best of all possible worlds.

Disney themes, characters, and animation style have been thoroughly institutionalized in practice and procedure—from the scriptwriters, animators, and technical producers who create the actual films to the market researchers and integrated marketing directors who conduct product research and focus groups to spot trends and advise editors on socially sensitive issues—all are geared to maximizing corporate profits. Pixar's innovations digitally improve Disney content and productively improve Disney's market dominance. Furthermore, dominance in the production of commodified animation and its spin-offs indicates that Disney's narratives resonate with appreciative mass audiences, suggesting that Disney's hierarchical themes are also culturally acceptable, at least tacitly. Disney has adjusted to a changing world with visibly improved cultural diversity. No longer do shapely white princesses star. From Mulan, Tiana, and Elsa to Moana and Go-Go, female leads are more independent, more self-sufficient and more representative of the diversity of humanity. Disney reaps the benefits of its manifest reforms in box office returns and critical acclaim.

Individual pleasures or meanings derived from Disney commodities reinforce, but should not be confused with, the overreaching, consistent themes of self-fulfillment through consumption. Disney's ability to market popular films and the public's delight in consuming their little pleasures can best be understood as a negotiated hegemonic activity. Like modern advertising, Disney worlds are fanciful, optimistic, and tidy. And like advertising, Disney has become part of everyday life, commercially and culturally institutionalized by design. But in Disney's case, the medium is also the advertisement. Disney products are themselves advertisements for Disney and for its ideological and cultural themes.

While one might hope for a more open system that allows for some nuanced messages, the evidence indicates that Disney's dominance is secured through its conscious and selective application of technology, technique, and globally palatable content, especially apparent in more culturally diverse settings and characters.

Understanding Disney clarifies the global intent of transnational capitalism. With well-considered creative deviation (based on market research) Disney animates and narrates myths with pro-social subtexts (e.g. Judy Hopps, Elsa, Dory, Moana and Riley in *Inside Out* [2015]) that are pleasing to multiple and diverse audiences. None of these animations seriously challenge any particular political perspective and thus remain hegemonically amenable to corporate market and ideological interests. The consent won from appreciative audiences spills over in values and behaviors essential to class relations that require subordinate, accommodating students, employees, and citizens believing inequality is part of the natural condition of life. Disney offers diversity without democracy. The emerging world capitalist culture revels in the ideology distributed by Disney, an ideology that aligns the morals of every animated film to class hierarchy, thereby denigrating and dismissing solidarity, democracy, and concern for community needs and interests.

Those interested in improving world social conditions and human solidarity should take note of the cultural power of animation, narration, and entertainment. Disney's application is one variant extremely useful to global capitalism. The practice of individual consumption of entertainment commodities (which further promote consumerism) subverts collective reflections and discussions that could lead to democratic impulses and relations. Rather than searching for the occasional instance of tweaking by resistive animators or hoping that individual subversive readings may prompt a social movement, those who oppose Disney's autocratic production model and generic diversity should replace them with cooperative creations and narratives.

REFERENCES

Buescher, D. T. and Ono, K. (1996). Civilized colonialism: Pocahontas as neocolonial rhetoric. *Women's Studies in Communication* 19: 127–153.

Dorfman, A. and Mattelart, A. (1975). *How to read Donald Duck: Imperialist ideology in the Disney comic*. New York: Internacional General.

Hoerner, K.L. (1996) Gender roles in Disney films: Analyzing behaviors from Snow White to Simba. *Women's Studies in Communication* 19: 213–22.

Reyes, M. (2016, February). Pixar and Disney are working really hard to be diverse. *Cinema Blend*. Accessed February 20, 2017 http://www.cinemablend.com/new/Pixar-Disney-Animation-Working-Really-Hard-Diverse-71549.html.

LA PRINCESA PLASTICA

46

Hegemonic and Oppositional Representations of Latinidad in Hispanic Barbie

Karen Goldman

In the forty-some years since she emerged from her original mold, Mattel's Barbie doll has become, both as cultural icon and children's plaything, one of the world's most ubiquitous plastic objects. The doll's embodiment of a diversity of feminine images reflects Mattel's efforts to market to continuously changing and increasingly diverse groups of U.S. and international consumers. But is it true, as some observers have contended, that, given the preeminence and persistence of the image of "rich, blonde Barbie" worldwide, resistance, cultural or otherwise, to hegemonic Barbie culture is futile? Barbie scholar Erica Rand (1995) points out that there is often a wide gap between the contexts and narratives that are produced for Barbie by Mattel, which are far from monolithic themselves, and the meanings that are generated by her consumers, whether children at play, collectors, or those who find in Barbie's carefully constructed persona an irresistible target for parody and subversion (26–28). . . .

The often quoted statistics on Barbie's global presence are staggering: more than one billion dolls sold in 150 countries, representing forty-five different nationalities (Barbie Collectibles, 2002). Although there is today a multitude of manifestations of Barbie culture, both hegemonic and oppositional, the point from which they all depart is the original, blue-eyed, blonde Barbie. Barbies are marked as "ethnic" or foreign only to the extent to which they differ from the original doll. In her "unauthorized biography," *Forever Barbie* (1994), M. G. Lord begins a chapter on ethnic Barbie by drawing an analogy between the development of Ruth Handler's original doll and the creation of Caucasian, all-American Hollywood star icons by largely Jewish-run movie studios. Lord asserts that original Barbie's ethnic neutrality differs from and surpasses that of the flesh-and-blood female stars that she resembles because, unlike "real" actresses, Barbie had no biological heredity and was, in fact, better suited than a human actress to exemplify an impossible ideal: "There was no tribal taint in her plastic flesh, no baggage to betray an immigrant past. She had no navel; no parents; no heritage" (160). Barbie's plasticity afforded her creators the luxury of designing her from scratch and literally molding every aspect of her appearance.

Like Hollywood promoters, who need to "design" stars that will engage the identification of the largest number of viewers, Mattel strove to develop a Barbie that would appeal to the greatest number of the doll's target audience: white, middle-class American parents and their daughters. Thus, the company's marketing strategy involved stressing, above all else, the doll's "Americanness." She had to be, in the words of Barbie's admiring biographer, BillyBoy (1987), "the personification of the all-round American girl" (28). In the social environment of the United States of the late 1950s, this meant she had to be Caucasian, blonde, light-skinned, and free of any obvious ethnic markers.

The original Barbie's ethnic neutrality not only served to emphasize the association of middle-class Caucasian femininity with "Americanness," it also served to bolster what Erica Rand refers to as Mattel's "language of infinite possibility" (28). Citing the need to allow children to project their own imagination onto the doll, Ruth Handler went to great lengths to expunge what she perceived as distinguishing characteristics that would give Barbie a distinct look or persona. In a

1990 interview she remarked, "the face was deliberately designed to be blank, without a personality, so that the projection of the child's dream could be on Barbie's face" (quoted in Rand, 40). But, like any cultural product, and despite the claims of her inventor, Barbie has indeed "always already" been inscribed in a manufactured narrative that is strictly circumscribed and defined by her producers. Clearly, within the rigid parameters of the doll's image as projected by Mattel, the possibilities for imagining a nonhegemonic Barbie were limited.

By 1961, Mattel had made the decision to allow Barbie to acquire a specific biography beyond her first name and the qualifier "teenage fashion model." During the early sixties, Barbie was appearing in books, records, and other texts as a blonde pony-tailed teenage fashion model with a personality, an address, a last name, and a boyfriend. While Barbie's and Ken's first names were taken from the real names of Ruth and Elliot Handler's two children, the other names are a veritable tribute to hyperbolic anglocentrism: Barbie's full name is Barbara Millicent Roberts. Ken's surname is Carson, and the two names together are, appropriately, an homage to Mattel's advertising firm: Carson/Roberts. Barbie's parents' names are identified as George and Margaret (only a minor variation of George and Martha, those archetypical grandparents of the nation). Barbie lives a glamorous but otherwise typical teenage life in a small American town called Willows.

Mattel has periodically adjusted Barbie's body, face, and hair in the interest of keeping up with styles and social realities of the day. But during the early years of her existence it was above all clothing and accessories that allowed her to (at least superficially) diversify her look. At first, the outfits marketed for Barbie fell into categories that emphasized her elegance ("Evening Splendor," "Silken Flame"), career aspirations ("Ballerina," "Registered Nurse"), leisure activities ("Ski Queen," "Movie Date"), or special occasions ("Easter Parade," "Bride's Dream"). None of these outfits departed in any substantial way from the standard of Barbie's (and later Ken's) middle-class Caucasian Americanness. By 1964, Barbie and Ken had already acquired many of the accoutrements of the American dream, for example, those appropriately named "dream" accessories: the "dream kitchen" (1964), the "dream house"

(1964), and the sports car (1962). For members of the postwar American middle class who had already attained these assets, travel, particularly to an exotic location, became a status-bearing consumer item, akin to owning a nice house or car (Urry, 2002). In 1964, in a miniature reenactment of the U.S. middle-class's increasing tendency to dedicate capital and leisure time to long-distance travel, Mattel launched the Travel Costume series, and Barbie and Ken become tourists, visiting Japan, Switzerland, Holland, Hawaii, and Mexico. Each travel costume outfit included "charming traditional costumes" for Barbie and Ken, as well as a miniature storybook that narrated the pair's travel adventures.

Central to Barbie's Mexican travel experience is the fact that the dolls (with or without the storybook provided with the outfit) come with a readymade Mattel-produced narrative that highlights the pair's status as Caucasian Americans enjoying leisure adventures, oblivious to the larger narrative that is the largely mestizo Mexican nation and its people. No images of other compete as meaning producer with the Mattel master narrative, for there are no traces of actual people (or doll personalities) in the narrative other than the costumed Caucasian Barbie and Ken. . . .

Mexico is a backdrop for Barbie's and Ken's travel adventure, not unlike the stories of the Little Theatre Costume sets that were sold concurrently, featuring Barbie as a princess of the Arabian Knights, Little Red Riding Hood, Guinevere, and Cinderella. Like the memorable figure of Donald Duck wearing a sombrero and traveling through Mexico on a flying serape in the 1989 Disney cartoon film, *The Three Caballeros,* Ken and Barbie perform their jovial masquerade against a background in which the totality of Mexico is represented as a storybook land. The story and the outfits depict folkloric or traditional elements of Mexican culture that, through caricature, are rendered no more unfamiliar or threatening to American cultural hegemony than the storybook characters. Thus, Ken's and Barbie's masquerading in the Mexico set functions more as an affirmation of the doll's implacable whiteness than any attempt to represent a multicultural opening. . . .

Following a traditional pattern of imperialist penetration, Barbie's (and Mattel's) entry into an international, intercultural environment begins from the position of tourist, that of postcolonial traveler to exotic locations. However, and in spite of the Travel Collection's clear affirmation of the dolls as Anglo and American, even this limited acknowledgment of worlds beyond the United States points, however tenuously, to Barbie's (and Mattel's) imminent initial foray into global expansion. It marks the beginning of what would eventually become the breakup of the monolithic Barbie narrative, in which nonwhite others are not only invisible, but their existence is never even an issue, for it simply does not come into play.

By the late sixties, Barbie's privileging of Caucasian femininity as the standard of American beauty, anachronistically silhouetted against a background of the civil rights movement and increasing ethnic and racial diversity in the United States, was becoming an encumbrance to Ruth Handler's notion that all girls must be able to identify with Barbie. Mattel decided to alter its master narrative in a reversal that reined in Barbie's biography and reintroduced the "language of infinite possibility." In 1967, Mattel launched a rather unconvincing Black Francie doll, followed, in 1968, by Barbie's Black friend Christie. In 1980, Mattel introduced Black and Hispanic Barbie, as well as a "Dolls of the World" Collection. In 1988, Teresa, an Hispanic doll, was introduced, followed by a line of African American "friends of Barbie." In a 1990 interview for *Newsweek,* Mattel product manager Deborah Mitchell proudly announced, "now, ethnic Barbie lovers will be able to dream in their own image" (duCille, 1995, 554).

While it is clear that Mattel was intent on capturing the growing ethnic markets in the United States by developing dolls meant to allow identification by ethnic "others," there is much debate regarding how authentically the dolls actually represent diversity. The representation of Latinidad in the marketing of Hispanic Barbie dolls has followed the recent pattern of many products aimed at Latino consumers. Media scholar Clara Rodriguez (1997) argues that in the popular media in the United States today, Latinos are typically either absent or misrepresented. When they are represented, it is often as negative stereotypes or as exotic foreigners (13–30). Behind Mattel's portrayal of Latino/a identity lies a system of representation that sells itself as authentic but that ultimately either depicts Latino/a culture as homogeneous and exotic, or repackages the doll's Latinidad in an assimilated form, whether to make her

more attractive to more assimilated Latinos or to market her more effectively in places where ethnic diversity is not particularly marketable. . . .

The first Hispanic Barbie doll's bilingual box introduced her as Barbie Hispanica (not the grammatically correct Hispaña). Like the earlier Mexico Travel Barbie, she is stereotypically dressed in a white peasant blouse and a full red skirt, a lace mantilla over her shoulders and a red rose tied around her neck. If the standard for Caucasian Barbie is light-skinned, blonde, and blue-eyed, the U.S. Hispanic version presents those contrasting physical attributes stereotypically associated with Latinas: dark hair, dark eyes, and darker skin. However, in few of the dolls designed to represent Hispanic (or Latina) women is skin tone ever darker than the suntanned Malibu Barbie dolls. Facial features never hint at indigenous or African heritage. What most prominently distinguishes the original Hispanic Barbie from any of the brunette Caucasian Barbies is the doll's paratextual items: clothing and accessories, or, more accurately, her costume. The original Hispanic Barbie, as well as subsequent special editions that celebrate occasions culturally specific to Latinos, such as the Quinceañera Barbie, all sport traditional folkloric clothing that is intended to mark them very clearly as Latinas, and therefore as foreign, exotic other.

In her physical characteristics, posture, and dress, the original Hispanic Barbie very closely resembles the international Hispanic (read: foreign) Dolls of the World, which are designed to reflect "typical" national attributes and dress in folkloric clothing. To Caucasian Barbie's quintessential Americanness, the Dolls of the World represent a quintessentially foreign counterpoint. But, as Wendy Varney argues in her convincing analysis of Australian Barbie, they are essentially American products and bear the Stamp of U.S. cultural imperialism, no matter what the guise. With respect to Latina identity, the Dolls of the World tend to negotiate difference by representing those Latinas as either hyperbolically folkloric (Mexico, Peru) or splashy and exotic (Brazil). Mattel's stated goal in offering the Dolls of the World Collection is to foster international understanding and appreciation of cultural differences. Significantly, the Andalusian Barbie and Mexican Barbie, both of whom are included in the Dolls of the World Collection, differ only superficially from U.S. Hispanic Barbie. They all have fair complexions and long dark hair, each with a large red rose tucked behind one ear. They wear full skirts and blouses, and all three dolls' clothes feature bright red as the predominant color, a characteristic that persists in Mattel's representations of Hispanics. Cultural differences among diverse groups and nationalities are elided, as Latinidad is reduced to one easily consumable, stereotypical identity-in-a-box.

The Peruvian doll, issued in 1999, provides a good example of how notions of Latin American class, race, and ethnicity play out in the real or implied narrative that frames the doll's paratextual positioning. For one thing, the doll is clearly meant to portray the identity of an indigenous Peruvian woman, with her long braids, round face, traditional woven shawl, and matching skirt. However, her facial features are wholly Caucasian, as is her rosy skin tone. In a clear and rather surprising break with standard Barbie design and Mattel's custom of representing racial differences only through what Ann duCille calls the "tint of the plastic," Peruvian Barbie carries a baby, who presumably is meant to be her own. One thing that has consistently defined the essence of Barbie has been her status as a single woman. While she is often depicted as a big sister or caring for children, and she has long been available as a bride, there has never been such a thing as a "Married Barbie," much less a maternal Barbie. Until the recent release of the "Happy Family" dolls, including a "Pregnant Midge" (not Barbie), that comes with a belly containing a removable baby, maternity has been wholly absent in the world of Barbie dolls. In the case of Midge, the issue of paternity is never in question, since, in a throwback to the early years of Mattel's use of heavy-handed biography, the doll wears a wedding ring, and her box provides a narrative identifying the father as Midge's husband, Alan.

The Peruvian doll comes with no such disclaimer. The baby is one more accessory, like Hispanic Barbie's lace mantilla, that identifies her as ethnically other. The representation of the Peruvian Barbie as mother is possible precisely because she is a Doll of the World, that is, she is foreign, and not subject to the rigid conventions of the "American" dolls. In addition, Peruvian Barbie's representation responds to principles of marketing and stereotypes that view Latinos as extremely family-oriented and conservative on the issue of nontraditional roles for women (Deanne et al.,

2000). The presence of the baby, with or without an implied father, is a much more important signifier of Mattel's notion of Latina femininity than any national costume or textual commentary might be.

Following the introduction of the first Hispanic Barbie in 1980, which differed little from the "foreign" Dolls of the World, Mattel favored more culturally assimilated Hispanic dolls that differed little from nonethnic Barbies, beyond adjustments to physical characteristics such as hair color and skin tone. Hispanic Barbie and African American Barbies were simply marketed as differently tinted versions of Caucasian Barbies. Such not-*too*-ethnic dolls were attractive to both ethnic minorities and majority Caucasian buyers, and thus served the dual purpose of appearing to foster diversity while increasing profits. In 1988, Mattel introduced Teresa, a bona fide Latina friend of Barbie. Like Barbie, Teresa has been produced with a multitude of physical characteristics over the years, morphing from a doll with consistently darker skin and hair to one that is often indistinguishable from nonethnic Barbie.

Today, all ethnic Barbie dolls vary in skin tone and hair color, but they typically wear the same clothes and accessories as Caucasian Barbie. It is tempting to consider that Teresa's changing looks signal Mattel's acknowledgment of the tremendous diversity among Latino populations worldwide. But beyond the dye that is used to tint her plastic body, it is hard to appreciate any substantial difference between Teresa and brunette Caucasian Barbies. What renders them similar is far more compelling than what sets them apart. Since recent issues of the Teresa doll don't even include Spanish text on the box, the only remaining link to Teresa's Latina identity is her name, Teresa (whose echo of the distant Spanish mystic Santa Teresa does not go unnoticed by many). . . . Even when Teresa is sold in a way that culturally marks her as Hispanic—for example, as Quinceañera Teresa— she more closely resembles Caucasian Barbie than the Latin American or Spanish Dolls of the World. The ultimate confirmation of her degree of assimilation is her marketing success in regions of the United States that do not have high concentrations of Latinos.

While Mattel has been congratulating itself for promoting diversity in the United States by including Hispanic Barbie and Teresa along with other dolls of color among its products, in Latin American countries where licensed Barbies are produced by regional subsidiaries, the dolls are nearly always modeled on the traditional Hollywood-inspired brands of American beauty: Caucasian and blonde. And although Caucasian blonde Barbie is certainly popular among Latina girls in the United States (Budge, 2003), it is unusual for a Hispanic doll to be marketed in the United States that does not possess those physical characteristics typically attributed to Latinas: darker skin, hair, and eyes. That Hispanic Barbies in the United States are not generally sold as blondes, whereas they very often are in Latin America, points to some of the complexities of racial and ethnic identification and marketing in both countries. As is evident in the success of female celebrities from Eva Peron to XuXa, in Latin American popular culture it is, ironically, the Hollywood-inspired ideal of blonde feminine beauty that prevails. And, given Barbie's relatively hefty price tag in Latin America (about $20), it is precisely the mostly white elite to whom Barbie dolls are marketed. The highest proportion of Barbie ownership in Latin America (outside of Puerto Rico, where a whopping 72 percent of girls own Barbies, is in Argentina (44 percent) and Chile (49 percent), nations that also have the lowest proportion of indigenous peoples, blacks, and mestizos, and the highest proportion of European-descended Caucasians ("Barbie Dolls in Latin America," 2002). Not surprisingly, the most popular Argentine Barbies tend to be those with the most Caucasian features. . . .

Barbie's hegemonic identity and her very ubiquity have always made her an attractive target for parodical representations of subversive intent. These counterhegemonic efforts include guerrilla tactics, such as the Barbie Liberation Organization, which sabotaged toys on store shelves. Other examples include works of criticism and literature that revisit and reinterpret the Barbie image, such as *Mondo Barbie* and *The Barbie Chronicles,* works of visual art, a multitude of Internet sites such as visiblebarbie.com and distortedbarbie.com, as well as the notable 1987 film *Superstar* by Todd Haynes. This film narrates the life of pop music star Karen Carpenter, who died of anorexia in 1983, using Barbie dolls to stand in for the human figures. Like Haynes's film, the majority of these counterhegemonic and often feminist-inspired criticisms target Barbie's absurd body proportions,

her flawless physiognomy, her anachronistic femininity, and the culture of consumption she promotes. Few of them problematize the issues of race, ethnicity, class, and the privileging of U.S. perceptions of foreign others in their analyses. . . .

The Internet has been a prodigious global source of Barbie resistance, parody, and criticism. Pocho.com is a Web site based on *Pocho Magazine,* which has been around since the late eighties. The site, subtitled "Aztlán's número uno source for satire y chingazos," features irreverent and biting satire, a longstanding tradition in Mexican journalism. Though *pocho* literally means faded, it is a disparaging term often used by Mexicans to describe U.S.-assimilated Mexican Americans. The magazine's and Website's appropriation of the term reflects a sentiment that has grown consistently as people of Mexican heritage in the United States proudly embrace their identity as one of fluidity and hybridity. On the site, as in the lives and cultures of Chicanos and other Latinos in the United States, English and Spanish are mixed freely, and articles on Mexican president Vicente Fox are juxtaposed with ones on Ron Unz and Monica Lewinsky. The April 28, 2000, edition featured a satirical story titled "New Latina Barbies Unveiled," announcing that Mattel had launched a line of Barbies in the likeness of Latina celebrities Cameron Diaz, Christina Aguilera, and Jennifer Lopez, as well as a new "Hispanic Family."

The text says, in part, "These dolls accurately capture the cultural pride felt by all of these strong Latina women. . . . We hope little Latina girls feel validated each time they look at their realistic and culturally accurate Latina Barbie dolls" (Sanchez-McNulty, 2000). Of course, the joke, one that Mattel (and Hollywood) never gets, is that all of the dolls look the same; they are blonde, blue-eyed, and have perfectly symmetrical Caucasian features. Of course, this begs the question, posed by duCille with regard to black African American dolls: "What would it take to produce a line of dolls that more fully reflects the wide variety of sizes, shapes, colors, hair styles, occupations, abilities, and disabilities that African Americans—like all people—come in?" (duCille, "Dyes and Dolls," 1995, 559). Clearly, the answer to that question does not lie with Mattel, which proudly asserts that "Today, in her 43rd year, Barbie reflects the dreams, hopes and future realities of an entire generation of little girls who still see her as representing the same American dream and aspirations as when she was first introduced in 1959!" (Barbie.com, 2002).

Perhaps, as she straddles cultures, Hispanic Barbie must strive to (and be animated to) embody what Latina writer and critic Gloria Anzaldua (1999) describes as "a tolerance for ambiguity" that characterizes the new mestiza: "She learns to juggle cultures. . . . Not only does she sustain contradictions, she turns ambivalence into something else" (101). Or perhaps, as Wendy Varney suggests, the Barbie phenomenon is itself inextricably, irrevocably bound up in a white, middle-class American context (3). As such, it is hard to resist the temptation to glimpse, behind each Barbie, regardless of her skin and hair color, facial characteristics and dress, or even the language that she speaks, a little blonde blue-eyed Barbie named Barbie Millicent Robert from Willows.

REFERENCES

Ananova. "Lesbian Barbie Film Banned in Mexico." http://www.ananova.com/news/story/sm_540282.html? menu=news.quirkies (accessed November 11, 2002).

Anzaldua, Gloria. *Borderlands/La Frontera: The New Mestiza* (2nd ed.). San Francisco: Aunt Lute Books, 1999.

Barbie Collectibles, http://www.barbiecollectibles.com/inciex-home.asp (accessed November 12, 2002).

Barbie.com. Mattel Corporation, http://www.barbie.com/ (accessed October 10, 2002).

"The Barbie Doll Story." Mattel Corporation, http://www.shareholder.com/mattel/news/20020428–79139.cf (accessed October 22, 2002).

"Barbie Dolls in Latin America." Zona Latina. http://www.zonalatina.com/Zldata37.html (accessed December 22, 2002).

BillyBoy. *Barbie, Her Life and Times.* New York: Crown Trade Paperbacks, 1987.

Budge, David. "Barbie Is No Living Doll as a Role Model." *Times Education Supplement,* January 7, 2003.

Deanne, Claudia, et al. "Leaving Tradition Behind: Latinos in the Great American Melting Pot." *Public Perspectives* 11, no. 3 (May/June 2000): 5–7.

duCille, Ann. "Barbie in Black and White." In *The Barbie Chronicles: A Living Doll Turns Forty.* New York: Touchstone, 1999.

———. "Dyes and Dolls: Multicultural Barbie and the Merchandising of Difference." In *A Cultural Studies Reader,* ed. Jessica Rajan and Gita Rajan. London: 1995.

"Life in Plastic." *Economist,* December 21, 20–23, 2002.

Lipsitz, George. *Dangerous Crossroads: Popular Music, Postmodernism and the Poetics of Place.* Verso: London, 1994.

Lord, M. G. *'Forever Barbie' The Unauthorized Biography of a Real Doll.* New York: William Morrow, 1994.

Pratt, Mary Louise. *Imperial Eyes: Travel Writing and Transculturation.* London: Routledge, 1992.

Rand, Erica. *Barbie's Queer Accessories.* Durham, NC: Duke University Press, 1995.

Rodriguez, Clara, ed. *Latin Looks: Images of Latinas and Latinos in the U.S. Media.* Boulder, CO: Westview Press, 1997.

Sanchez-McNulty, Maria. "New Latina Barbies Unveiled." *Pocho.* http://www.pocho.com/new/2001/barbies21200barbies31700.htm.

Urry, John. *The Tourist Gaze* (2nd edition). London: Sage, 2002.

Varney, Wendy. "Barbie Australis: The Commercial Reinvention of National Culture." *Social Identities* 4 (June 1998): I6I. http://search.epnet.com/direct.asp?an=873697&db=abh (accessed October 2, 2002).

47 GROWING UP FEMALE IN A CELEBRITY-BASED POP CULTURE

Gail Dines

In today's image-based culture, there is no escaping the image and no respite from its power when it is relentless in its visibility. If you think that I am exaggerating, then flip through a magazine at the supermarket checkout, channel surf, take a drive to look at billboards, or watch TV ads. Many of these images are of celebrities—women who have fast become the role models of today. With their wealth, designer clothes, expensive homes, and flashy lifestyles, these women do seem enviable to girls and young women since they appear to embody a type of power that demands attention and visibility.

For us noncelebrities who can't afford a personal stylist, the magazines dissect the "look," giving us tips on how to craft the image at a fraction of the price. They instruct us on what clothes to buy, what shoes to wear, how to do our hair and makeup, and what behavior to adopt to look as hot as our favorite celebrity. The low-slung jeans, the short skirt that rides up our legs as we sit down, the thong, the tattoo on the lower back, the pierced belly button, the low-cut top that shows cleavage, the high heels that contort our calves, and the pouting glossed lips all conspire to make us look like a bargain-basement version of the real thing. To get anywhere close to achieving the "look," we, of course, need to spend money—lots of it—as today femininity comes in the form of consumer products that reshape the body and face. The magazines that instruct us in the latest "must-have" fashions have no shortage of ads that depict, in excruciating detail, what it means to be feminine in today's porn culture.

While the fashion industry has always pushed clothes that sexualize women's bodies, the difference today is that the "look" is, in part, inspired by the sex industry. We are now expected to wear this attire everywhere: in school, on the street, and at work. Teachers, including elementary school teachers, often complain that their female students look more like they are going to a party than coming to school. It is as if we females now have to carry the marker of sex on us all the time, less we forget (or men forget) what our real role is in this society.

Among hypersexualized celebrities, Paris Hilton ranks high. The story of how she was catapulted to the A-list is one all about porn culture. Once a minor-league celebrity known mainly for her vast bank account, in 2004, her then-boyfriend, Rick Salomon—thirteen years her senior—released a videotape of them having sex, called *1 Night in Paris,* and she instantly became a household name. Thanks to that tape, Hilton is now talked about all over the porn discussion boards as "a filthy slut" who got what she deserved. The fact that Salomon was the one who orchestrated the whole thing (she sued him over the release) does not prevent her from being mocked and derided by porn users and pop culture commentators alike. Over the years, Hilton has been labeled a kind of super "slut"—a term used to demarcate the supposed good girls from the bad. Her antics have garnered a devoted following among girls and young women, as well as massive visibility as one of the most photographed women in the world. Hilton gets away with being anointed as a "slut" because she is fabulously rich; the wealth acts as a kind of upmarket cleansing cream that instantly rubs off the dirt. For most girls and women, however, especially those from the working class, the dirt sticks like mud.

Take, for example, Britney Spears. At seventeen Spears released her debut single, called " . . . Baby One More Time," which became an instant international success. In the accompanying video, Spears is dressed in a school uniform with a knotted shirt that reveals a bare midriff, socks, and braided hair as she writhes around asking her ex-boyfriend to "hit me, baby, one more time." Spears later went on to employ Gregory Dark to direct her videos; Dark is a longtime porn director whose films include *The Devil in Miss Jones, New Wave Hookers,* and *Let Me Tell Ya 'Bout Black Chicks.* Her meltdowns in public, together with the famous image of her sans underwear, have contributed to a kind of public humiliation: we collectively flog her for her trashy ways, yet we put her on a pedestal for embodying a kind of uncouth hot sexiness. Unlike Hilton, Spears was not born into great wealth, so the attacks on her mothering, appearance, and partying tend to carry a subtext of classism in which Spears is described as a trailer-trash slut who, despite her millions, can't escape her roots. . . .

People not immersed in pop culture tend to assume that what we see today is just more of the same stuff that previous generations grew up on. After all, every generation has had its hot and sultry stars who led expensive and wild lives compared to the rest of us. But what is different about today is not only the hypersexualization of mass-produced images but also the degree to which such images have overwhelmed and crowded out any alternative images of being female. Today's tidal wave of soft-core porn images has normalized the porn star look in everyday culture to such a degree that anything less looks dowdy, prim, and downright boring. Today, a girl or young woman looking for an alternative to the Britney, Beyonce, Kim look will soon come to the grim realization that the only alternative to looking fuckable is to be invisible.

One show that popularized porn culture was *Sex and the City,* a show that supposedly celebrated female independence from men. At first glance this series was a bit different from others in its representation of female friendships and the power of women to form bonds that sustain them in their everyday lives. It also seemed to provide a space for women to talk about their own sexual desires, desires that were depicted as edgy, rebellious, and fun. However, these women claimed a sexuality that was ultimately traditional rather than resistant. Getting a man and keeping him were central to the narrative, and week after week we heard about the trials and tribulations of four white, privileged heterosexual women who seemed

to find men who take their sexual cues from porn. . . .

Nowhere is this pseudo-independence more celebrated than in *Cosmopolitan,* a magazine that claims to have "served as an agent for social change, encouraging women everywhere to go after what they want (whether it be in the boardroom or the bedroom)." It is hard to see how *Cosmopolitan* helped women advance in corporate America, given that most of the Cosmo girl's time is taken up with perfecting her body and her sexual technique. But this doesn't stop the magazine from boasting that "we here at *Cosmo* are happy to have played such a significant role in women's history. And we look forward to many more years of empowering chicks everywhere.[1] In porn culture empowering women translates into "chicks" having lots of sex, and no magazine does more than *Cosmopolitan* to teach women how to perform porn sex in a way that is all about male pleasure. . . .

With headlines every month promising "Hot New Sex Tricks," "21 Naughty Sex Tips," "Little Mouth Moves That Make Sex Hotter," "67 New Blow-His-Mind Moves," "8 Sex Positions You Haven't Thought Of," and so on, women seem to experience no authentic sexual pleasure; rather, what she wants and enjoys is what he wants and enjoys. While there might be an odd article here and there on what to wear to climb the corporate ladder, the magazine as a whole is all about "him" and "his" needs, wants, desires, tastes, and, most importantly, orgasm. In *Cosmopolitan,* as in much of pop culture, her pleasure is derived not from being a desiring subject but from being a desired object.

Women's magazines that focus on "him" are not new, as earlier generations were also inundated with stories about "him," but then the idea was to stimulate his taste buds rather than his penis. *Cosmopolitan* is the contemporary equivalent of *Ladies' Home Journal* in that it pretends to be about women, but it is in fact all about getting him, pleasing him, and (hopefully) keeping him. For previous generations of women, the secret to a happy relationship lay in being a good cook, cleaner, and mother—for the young women of today, the secret is, well, just being a good lay. If the reader is going to *Cosmopolitan* for tips on how to build a relationship or ways of developing intimacy, she will be disappointed, as conversation only matters in the world of *Cosmo* if it is about talking dirty.

With its manipulative "We are all girls together" tone coupled with the wise older mentor approach that promises to teach young women all they need to know to keep "him coming back for more," *Cosmopolitan,* like most women's magazines, masquerades as a friend and teacher to young women trying to navigate the tricky terrain of developing a sexual identity in a porn culture. *Cosmopolitan's* power is its promise to be a guide and friend, and it promotes itself as one of the few magazines that really understand what the reader is going through. A promotional ad for *Cosmopolitan* geared toward advertisers boasts that it is "its readers' best friend, cheerleader and shrink."[2]

In *Cosmopolitan,* hypersexualization is normalized by virtue of both the quantity of articles on sex and the degree to which they are explicit. For example, one article instructs the reader, in a somewhat clinical manner, on how to bring a man to orgasm: "While gripping the base of the penis steadily in one hand, place the head between your lips, circling your tongue around the crown. When you sense your guy is incredibly revved up, give his frenulum a few fast tongue licks." For the uninitiated, the magazine explains that the frenulum is "the tiny ridge of flesh on the underside of his manhood, where the head meets the shaft."[3]

Cosmopolitan is quick to suggest using porn as a way to spice up sex. In one article, entitled "7 Bad Girl Bedroom Moves You Must Master," the reader is told to take "the plunge into porn" as it "will add fiery fervor into your real-life bump and grinds." The article quotes a reader who, after watching porn with her boyfriend, evidently ended up "having sex so hot that the porn looked tame in comparison." The article suggests that if the reader feels embarrassed, she should "drive to a store in another neighborhood, shop online, or go to a place that stocks X-rated."

In the world that *Cosmopolitan* constructs for the reader, a world of blow jobs, multiple sexual positions, anonymous porn sex, and screaming orgasms (usually his), saying no to his erection is unthinkable. The options on offer in *Cosmopolitan* always concern the type of sex to have and how often. What is not on offer is the option to refuse his demands since he has (an unspoken and unarticulated) right of access to the female body. Indeed, readers are warned that not having sex on demand might end the "relationship." Psychologist Gail Thoen, for example, informs *Cosmopolitan's* readers that "constant cuddling with

no follow-through (i.e., sex) can be frustrating to guys" and what's more, "he is not going to like it if you leave him high and dry all the time."[5] The reader is pulled into a highly sexual world where technique is the key, and intimacy, love, and connection appear only rarely as issues worthy of discussion. The message transmitted loud and clear is that if you want a man, then not only must you have sex with him, you must learn ways to do it better and hotter than his previous girlfriends.

That the magazine teaches women how to have porn sex is clear in an article that ostensibly helps women deal with the etiquette of how to behave in the morning after the first sexual encounter. Women are told: "Don't Stay Too Long." The article warns women that "just because he had sex with you doesn't mean he's ready to be attached at the hip for the day." Actually, the entire day seems like a long shot—"Bo" informs readers that "I was dating this girl who wanted to hang out the next morning, but after only a couple of hours with her, I realized I wasn't ready to be that close." What advice does *Cosmopolitan* have for women in this situation? "Skip out after coffee but before breakfast."[6]

Media targeted to women create a social reality that is so overwhelmingly consistent it is almost a closed system of messages. In this way, it is the sheer ubiquity of the hypersexualized images that gives them power since they normalize and publicize a coherent story about women, femininity, and sexuality. Because these messages are everywhere, they take on an aura of such familiarity that we believe them to be our very own personal and individual ways of thinking. They have the power to seep into the core part of our identities to such a degree that we think that we are freely choosing to look and act a certain way because it makes us feel confident, desirable, and happy. But as scholar Rosalind Gill points out, if the look was "the outcome of everyone's individual, idiosyncratic preferences, surely there would be greater diversity, rather than a growing homogeneity organized round a slim, toned, hairless body."[7]

This highly disciplined body has now become the key site where gender is enacted and displayed on a daily basis. To be feminine requires not only the accoutrements of hypersexuality—high heels, tight clothes, and so on—but also a body that adheres to an extremely strict set of standards. We need to look like we spend hours in the gym exhausting ourselves as we work out, but whatever the shape of the body, it is never good enough. Women have so internalized the male gaze that they have now become their own worst critics. When they go shopping for clothes or look in a mirror, they dissect themselves piece by piece. Whatever the problem, and there is always a problem—the breasts are too small, the thighs not toned enough, the butt too flat or too round, the stomach too large—the result is a deep sense of self-disgust and loathing. The body becomes our enemy, threatening to erupt into fatness at any time, so we need to be hypervigilant. What we end up with is what Gill calls a "self-policing narcissistic gaze," a gaze that is so internalized that we no longer need external forces to control the way we think or act.[8]

. . . Understanding culture as a socializing agent requires exploring how and why some girls and young women conform and others resist. For all the visual onslaught, not every young woman looks or acts like she take her cues from *Cosmopolitan* or *Maxim*. One reason for this is that conforming to a dominant image is not an all-or-nothing act but rather a series of acts that place women and girls at different points on the continuum of conformity to nonconformity. Where any individual sits at any given time on this continuum depends on her past and present experiences as well as family relationships, media consumption, peer group affiliations and sexual, racial, and class identity. We are not, after all, blank slates onto which images are projected.

Given the complex ways that we form our sexual and gender identities, it is almost impossible to predict, with precision, how any one individual will act at any one time. This does not mean, though, that we can't make predictions on a macro level. What we can say is that the more one way of being female is elevated above and beyond others, the more a substantial proportion of the population will gravitate toward that which is most socially accepted, condoned, and rewarded. The more the hypersexualized image crowds out other images of women and girls, the fewer options females have of resisting what cultural critic Neil Postman called "the seduction of the eloquence of the image."[9]

Conforming to the image is seductive as it not only offers women an identity that is in keeping with the majority but also confers a whole host of pleasures, since looking hot does garner the kind of male attention that can sometimes feel empowering. Indeed, getting people to consent to any

system, even if it's inherently oppressive, is made easier if conformity brings with it psychological, social, and/or material gains. Many women know what it's like to be sexually wanted by a man: the way he holds you in his gaze, the way he finds everything you say worthy of attention, the way you suddenly become the most compelling person in the world. This is the kind of attention we don't normally get from men when we are giving a presentation, having a political conversation, or telling them to do the dishes. No, this is an attention men shower on women they want sexually, and it feels like real power, but it is ephemeral because it is being given to women by men who increasingly, thanks to the porn culture, see women as interchangeable hookup partners. To feel that sense of power, women need to keep sexing themselves up so they can become visible to the next man who is going to, for a short time, hold her in his lustful gaze. . . .

. . . Alternative ideologies such as feminism that critique dominant conceptions of femininity are either caricatured or ignored in mainstream media. Absent such a worldview and a community of like-minded people, many young women speak about feeling isolated and alone in their refusal to conform to the porn culture. The stories are the same: they have a lot of difficulty in negotiating the outsider status that they have been forced to take on. They not only refuse to sex themselves up, they also refuse to have hookup sex, which means that they have a difficult time finding men who are interested in them.

HOOKUP SEX AS PORN SEX

One of the most noticeable shifts in girls' and young women's behavior over the last decade or so is their increasing participation in what is called hookup sex—those encounters that can be anything from a grope to full sexual intercourse but have the common feature that there is no expectation of a relationship, intimacy, or connection.[10] Sex is what you expect, and sex is what you get. In a large-scale survey of 7,000 students, sociologist Michael Kimmel found that by their senior year, "students had averaged nearly seven hookups during their collegiate careers. About one-fourth (24 percent) say that they have never hooked up, while slightly more than that (28 percent) have hooked up ten times or more."[11]

Given its lack of commitment and intimate connection, hookup sex is a lot like porn sex, and it is being played out in the real world. If porn and women's media are to be believed, then these women are having as good a time as the men. But studies are finding that women do hope for more than just sex from a hookup encounter, as many express a desire for the hookup to evolve into a relationship. Sociologist Kathleen Bogle, for example, found in her study of college-age students that many of the women "were interested in turning hookup partners into boyfriends," while the men interviewed "preferred to hookup with no strings attached."[12]

... Studies have found that women who participate in hookups have lower self-esteem and higher levels of depression, and they experience regret over the hookups.[13] Grello and her colleagues, for example, found that the more depressed females had more sex partners, and the more partners they had, the more they regretted the hookup. The authors suggest that one possible explanation for this is that "depressed females may be seeking external validation from sex. They may be maintaining a vicious depressive cycle by unconsciously engaging in sex in doomed relationships. Possibly, these females' negative feelings of self-worth or isolation may increase their desire to be wanted by or intimate with another. Thus, if they sensed a potential romance would result from the encounter, they may have engaged in sexual behavior with a casual sex partner in an attempt to feel better, at least temporarily."[14]

Probably one of the most interesting findings of this study is that males who engaged in hookup sex reported the least depressive symptoms of any group. They also reported feeling more pleasure and less guilt than the females who participated in hookups. One reason for this could be the way that masculinity is socially constructed, since the more sex partners a man has, the more he is conforming to the idealized image of manhood.

With hookup sex comes, for women and girls, an increased possibility of being labeled a slut—a term that is used to control and stigmatize female sexual desire and behavior. There is, after all, no male equivalent of a slut since men who are thought to be highly sexually active are called a stud or a player—labels most men would happily take on. What it means to be a "slut" shifts over time, as previous generations of women carried the label just for having sex before marriage. But for all

of women's so-called sexual empowerment today, the effects of being labeled a slut are as devastating now as they were in the past. A study by academics Wendy Walter-Bailey and Jesse Goodman shows that these girls and young women "often resort to self-destructive behaviors such as drug and alcohol abuse, eating disorders, self-mutilation, academic withdrawal, or risky sexual conduct."[15]

Walter-Bailey and Goodman found that the girls most likely to be labeled as sluts are those who "act too casual and/or flaunt their sexuality" as well as those who "flirt too heavily, blossom too early, or dress too scantily."[16] . . .

Other studies have found that women experience "unwanted sex" (in other words, rape) more frequently in hookups than in dating or long-term relationships. One study in which 178 college students were interviewed found that of the experiences students called "unwanted intercourse," 78 percent occurred during a hookup, as opposed to 8.3 percent on a date and 13.9 percent in an ongoing relationship.[17] This makes perfect sense when we think about the lack of clear borders set up during a hookup. In an ongoing relationship, couples can discuss and negotiate sexual boundaries as the relationship develops, but in a hookup, there will typically be little discussion regarding who is thinking of doing what and how far each one wants to go sexually. Talking or drawing boundaries is not what a hookup is about. . . .

The American Psychological Association's study on the sexualization of girls found that there was ample evidence to conclude that sexualizing girls "has negative effects in a variety of domains, including cognitive functioning, physical and mental health, sexuality, and attitudes and beliefs."[18] Some of these effects include more risky sexual behavior, higher rates of eating disorders, depression, and low self-esteem as well as reduced academic performance. These are the same symptoms found in girls and women who have been sexually assaulted; in terms of effect, then, we appear to be turning out a generation of girls who have been "assaulted" by the very culture they live in. And there is no avoiding the culture. The very act of socialization involves internalizing the cultural norms and attitudes. If the culture is now one big collective perpetrator, then we can assume that an ever-increasing number of girls and women are going to develop emotional, cognitive, and sexual problems as they are socialized into seeing themselves as mere sex objects, and not much else.

Where is female sexual agency in all of this? When feminists in the 1960s and '70s fought for sexual liberation, they fought for the right to want, desire, and enjoy sex—but on their own terms. They argued that their sexuality had been defined by men, and they wanted it back. What they got was not what they expected: a hypersexuality that is generic, formulaic, and plasticized. It is a sexuality that has its roots in porn and is now so mainstream that it is fast becoming normalized. One of the men interviewed by Bogle said he saw hookup culture as a "guy's paradise."[19] Yes, Porn-land is indeed paradise for these men, as it is sex with no strings attached. And for women it is business as usual: men defining our sexuality in ways that serve them, not us. Only now this sexuality is sold to us as empowering. A new twist on an old theme.

NOTES

1. Jennifer Benjamin (2005). "How *Cosmo* Changed the World." *Cosmopolitan,* September 2005, http://www.cosmopolitan .com/about/about-us_how-cosmo-changed-the-world (accessed July 7, 2008).

2. http://www.assocmags.co.za/images/pdfs/ Cosmopolitan%20Rate%20Card.pdf (accessed June 6, 2008).

3. Ronnie Koenig. "Thrill Every Inch of Him," *Cosmopolitan,* June 2006. p. 150.

4. http://www.cosmopolitan.com/sex-love/ sex/420935 (accessed July 7, 2008).

5. "Cuddle Overkill." *Cosmopolitan,* June 2007, p. 137.

6. "You Had Sex—Now What?" *Cosmopolitan,* June 2007, p. 76.

7. Rosalind Gill (2009). "Supersexualize Me!: Advertising and the Midriff," in Feona Attwood, *Mainstreaming Sex: The Sexualization of Western Culture.* London: I.B. Tauris. p. 106.

8. Ibid, p. 107.

9. Neil Postman, *Consuming Images* (PBS Video, 1990).

10. I would like to thank Meg Lovejoy for generously sharing her work and insights on hookup sex and for providing me with a list of resources.

11. Michael Kimmel (2008), *Guyland: The Perilous World Where Boys Become Men* (NY: Harper Books), p. 195.

12. Kathleen Bogle (2008), *Hooking Up: Sex, Dating and Relationships on Campus* (New York: New York University Press), p. 173.

13. Catherine M. Grello, Deborah P. Welsh, and Melinda S. Harper (2006), "No Strings Attached: The Nature of Casual Sex in College Students," *Journal of Sex Research* 43, no. 3): 255; Elaine Eshbaugh and Gary Gute (2008), "Hookups and Sexual Regret Among College Women," *Journal of Social Psychology* 148, no. 1: 77–90.

14. Grello, Walsh and Harper, "No Strings Attached."

15. Walter-Bailey, W. and Goodman, J. (2006). "Exploring the culture of sluthood among adolescents," in *Contemporary Youth Culture: An International Encyclopedia.* (Vol. 2). Westport, CT: Greenwood Press, 280–284.

16. Ibid, p. 282.

17. William Flack Jr., Kimberly A. Daubman, Marcia L. Caron, Nenica A. Asadorian, Nicole R. D'Aureli, Shannon N. Gigliotti, Anna T. Hall, Sarah Kiser, and Erin R. Stine (2007). "Risk Factors and Consequences of Unwanted Sex Among University Students: Hooking Up, Alcohol, and Stress Response." *Journal of Interpersonal Violence,* 22: pp. 139–157.

18. Report of the APA Task Force on the Sexualization of Girls, Executive Summary, http://www.apa.org/pi/wpo/ sexualization_report_summary.pdf. p. 2 (accessed February 5, 2009). The full study can be found at http://www.apa.org/pi/wpo/ sexualization.html (accessed February 5, 2009).

19. Bogle, *Hooking Up,* p. 183.

48

"TOO MANY BAD ROLE MODELS FOR US GIRLS"

Girls, Female Pop Celebrities and "Sexualization"

Sue Jackson and Tiina Vares

The 'sexualization' of pre-teen and younger girls has been a dominating presence in the media and popular press since the mid-years of the millennium's first decade. Books with evocative titles such as *So Sexy So Soon* (Levin and Kilbourne, 2008), *The Lolita Effect* (Durham, 2008), *What's Happening to our Girls?* (Hamilton, 2007) and *Girls Gone Skank* (Oppliger, 2008) alerted parents to the troubling phenomenon of their daughters becoming sexualized as a consequence of their encounters with 'sexualized' media. So too did a succession of policy papers and government and institutional reports published in the UK, USA and Australia secure the 'sexualization' of girls as a pressing social problem (Egan, 2013). Amongst these, the Australia Institute Report, provocatively titled Corporate Paedophilia (Rush and La Nauze, 2006), and the American Psychological Society Task Force Report on the Sexualization of Girls (APA, 2007) exerted a particularly strong influence in highlighting the 'sexualization' of girls as a 'crisis' requiring swift educational and political intervention (Duschinsky, 2013; Lumby and Albury, 2010). Collectively, this body of literature has both underlined the problematic of 'sexualized' representations of women and girls in the media and, perhaps unwittingly, cast girls as the naive and damaged victims of 'sexualization.' In part, the literature's concerns about the negative impact of 'sexualized' media on girls have emanated within feminist critiques of the limited, body-focused and sexist versions of femininity available to girls in 'sexualized' media (e.g. the APA report, 2007) but these concerns have largely been swamped in the public arena by a right-wing conservative rhetoric about the loss of child innocence, morality and decency effected by 'sexualization' (Duschinsky, 2013; Egan, 2013).

Claims about the 'sexualization' of girls have been widely debated, however, and a body of critical interrogation on the topic now exists (e.g. Egan and Hawkes, 2008; Lerum and Dworkin, 2009). . . . A critique particularly relevant to this [chapter] . . . is the absence of girls' perspectives to inform claims made about their assumed 'sexualization' in relation to 'sexualized' media (Renold and Ringrose, 2011). More broadly, commentators have similarly noted the sparseness of research with girls and young women in relation to their negotiation of a sexually saturated popular/celebrity culture (e.g. Evans and Riley, 2013; Renold and Ringrose, 2011). In recent years, a small number of feminist girlhood scholars have sought to address this substantive gap, exploring ways in which girls understand 'sexualized' media and themselves in relation to it (e.g. Charles, 2010; Jackson et al., 2013; Renold and Ringrose, 2011; Ringrose, 2011; Vares et al., 2011). Contributing to and expanding upon this body of work, the intention of this [chapter] is to examine . . . how pre-teen girls negotiate their engagement with 'sexualized' female celebrity representations in popular culture. We argue that an explicitly gendered 'sexualization' discourse re-energizes an 'at-risk' discourse for pre-teen girls, compelling them to warily monitor their participation in sexually saturated pop music culture lest they tarnish their reputation as asexual 'good girls' in the eyes of parents, adults and other girls.

'SEXUALIZED' CELEBRITY CULTURE AND 'SEXUALIZED' GIRLS

Gill explains the 'sexualization of culture' as a 'phrase to capture the growing sense of Western societies as

From Jackson, S. & Vares, T. (2015). "Too many bad role models for us girls": Girls, female pop celebrities and "sexualization." *Sexualities, 18*(4): 480–498.

saturated by sexual representations and discourses, and in which pornography has become increasingly influential and porous, permeating 'mainstream' contemporary culture' (2012: 483). Boundaries in the public sphere have loosened such that sexual practices previously closeted in the private spaces of pornography have entered the mainstream and porno-chic styling has become 'commonplace' (Attwood, 2009). But, as Gill and Attwood point out, it is women who are primarily the objects and subjects of 'sexualization'; in other words, 'sexualization' is expressly gendered. One expression of this gendered 'sexualization' is a porn-styled aesthetic that fashions hyper-femininity (e.g. stiletto heels, heavy make-up) and hypersexuality (e.g. body-exposing and/or clothing emphasizing breast and hips; being perpetually sexually desiring i.e. 'up for it') into a 'classy' hetero-sexiness (Attwood, 2009; Dobson, 2011; McRobbie, 2009). Perhaps more prolifically than any other media platform, the pop music video is a conduit for these expressions of gendered, 'sexualized' porno-chic that have been pulled into the mainstream. Although pop music videos have long been replete with sexual content, performances are said to have become increasingly sexually explicit (Andsager and Roe, 2003) and porn inspired as in, for example, incorporations of pole-dancing and twerking (e.g. Rihanna in *Pour it Up* twerking on a throne; Miley Cyrus in *Can't be Tamed* pole dancing in S and M styled gear[1]).

Yet under a critical public and media eye, female artists walk a fine line in terms of their engagement in 'sexualized' performances, perpetually risking harsh condemnation and concomitant falls in popularity. In the neoliberal gender regime described by McRobbie (2009), young women are subjected to constant surveillance and regulation, granted sexual freedoms on the one hand but attached to regulatory moral conditions of white middle-class respectable femininity on the other (Griffin et al., 2013). These regulatory conditions are clearly seen in celebrity culture. . . . Fairclough (2008) . . . highlights the way in which young female celebrities are encouraged into hypersexual representations of themselves only to then be scorned as a 'famewhore' or 'slut' in a ritual of slut-shaming. As teen stars, Britney Spears and Miley Cyrus both reinvented themselves, moving from sexual innocents to hypersexual performers (Lowe, 2003), in transformations that provoked widespread condemnation. Cyrus

presents a particularly graphic illustration of the teen-adult shift, transforming from 'child innocent' to 'sexy' star overnight with her 'sexually provocative' cover shoot for *Vanity Fair* (Lamb et al., 2013). Since then Cyrus has engaged in increasingly pornified hypersexual performances (as in her *Can't be Tamed* music video) drawing intense public and media reaction. Perhaps in Cyrus's case, continuing negative public and press reaction to her hypersexualization connects with the difficulty of shaking off her 'nice girl' persona in her eponymous role Hannah Montana, which persists through every re-run of the popular TV show.

. . . The morally abject celebrity in celebrity discourse permeates a 'sexualization' of girls' discourse where the 'bad' hypersexualized celebrity occupies a space of both feared and assumed adverse influence on young female consumers (e.g. Durham, 2008; Oppliger, 2008). Notions of the influential celebrity are consistent with common sense understandings about the powerful function of role models in childhood as examples of what and who children may aspire to be. Rather than viewing celebrity as all-powerful and girls as uncritical and susceptible to such power, in this [chapter] we understand girls' relationship to celebrity (and popular culture more broadly) as more complicated. . . . Like celebrities, girls are subject to regulation of their sexuality through a moral discourse of respectable femininity (the 'good girl'; Walkerdine, 1990) but they are also regulated through an age discourse of sexual appropriateness. . . . The taboo of pre-teen and younger girls' sexuality, then, complicates participation in a 'sexualized' media culture since it risks girls being seen as crossing a boundary of age appropriateness, of 'knowing' more sexually than is desirable for their age (Duits and van Zoonen, 2011). Operation of the taboo is evident in girls limiting their participation to spaces safe from adult surveillance. . . .

. . . Renold and Ringrose (2011) capture girls' entanglement in contradictory, competing discourses of girlhood sexuality in the notion of 'schizoid' conditions. Girls' positioning as Lolitas in 'sexualization' discourse can be read through this schizoid lens, Lolita embodying both naive childhood innocence and seductive, agentic sexuality. As Griffin (2004; Griffin et al., 2013) has argued, in late capitalist societies femininity has become an even more 'impossible space' for girls and young women to occupy under contradictory postfeminist conditions where apparent sexual freedoms, amongst others, are clawed back by abiding middle-class respectable femininity and the regulatory discourse of the slut. How pre-teen girls negotiate this 'impossible space' with its competing norms of asexuality and sexual savvy is a crucially important inquiry that is taken up as a key objective of this [chapter].

RESEARCHING GIRLS NEGOTIATING 'SEXUALIZED' CELEBRITY CULTURE

. . . A particularly challenging task for researchers in any area of sexuality research with girls is devising ways to open up opportunities and spaces for girls to speak from positions outside of regulatory, constraining discourses while recognizing the silences those discourses may impose (McClelland and Fine, 2008). With this challenge in mind, the study incorporated video diaries, identified in girlhood research as productive ways for girls to express their perspectives and experiences, especially, on the topic of sexuality (e.g. Driver, 2007). . . .

. . . In the following analyses . . . we present three case studies to illuminate girls' negotiation of 'sexualized' celebrity as a complex, discursively mediated process.

'TOO MANY "BAD" ROLE MODELS FOR US GIRLS': THE GOOD/ BAD CELEBRITY BINARY

Originating in the social sciences, the concept of a role model has a much wider popularized circulation, often used, for example, by adults (e.g. parents, teachers, coaches) to highlight exemplary behaviour and achievements of others to children with encouragement to emulate them. This popular notion of the influential role model in childhood is one that carries a great deal of force and so it is perhaps not surprising that a role model discourse featured so regularly in girls' on-camera talk about female pop celebrities. Celebrities are often assigned tags of 'good' or 'bad' role models in public discourse. . . . Thus girls in our study appropriated common sense understandings of the term role model to delineate the 'good' and the 'bad' celebrities. Although sometimes applied to behaviours such as drug use (e.g. Britney Spears, Lindsey Lohan), girls more frequently used the good/bad

binary in relation to celebrity performances or dress that connoted hypersexuality (e.g. bikini tops and very short mini-skirts, movements or poses that suggested sex). Pop celebrities such as Katy Perry, the Pussycat Dolls and Britney Spears were eminent amongst the 'bad' sexual girls of pop who exposed too much flesh. But the celebrity most frequently mentioned in girls' media diaries was Miley Cyrus. That she did so may reflect that at the time of the study Cyrus made media headlines for her *Vanity Fair* cover shoot in which she appeared in a 'sexually provocative' pose (Lamb et al., 2013), partially clad in a bed-sheet. Questions of age-appropriateness (Miley's age and consideration of the age of her fans) prevailed in girls' talk and their responses ranged from disgust to disappointment and from rejection to acceptance. Condemnation of Cyrus, however, dominated. Cory's narrative was exceptional for the loyalty she displayed toward the star, although this was not without critique. Cory, a NZ European middle-class girl, declared herself to be a 'huge, huge fan of Miley' describing her as 'awesome' despite others 'go[ing] off' her because of the 'scandal' (reference to the *Vanity Fair* cover). Yet, unlike those who condemned and alienated themselves from Cyrus, Cory told us, face to camera:

> but you know I think it's fine because she's like the best role model there is like she's hardly done anything, she just posed for *Vanity Fair* and everything but like it wasn't like she was naked or anything so I am still a huge fan of her and everything but I haven't got any posters of her but I would.

For Cory, the exposure of Cyrus's body on the *Vanity Fair* cover seems not to have crossed a boundary casting the star as a 'bad role model' or, as in other girls' accounts, 'slutty'; here the boundary hinges on full nakedness and in the absence of that, Cory is able to read the performance as scarcely significant. This allows Cory to maintain her position as a 'huge fan' and Cyrus's position as 'the best role model there is.' Nonetheless contradictions permeated Cory's narratives in other video diary entries. In one entry she engaged in talk about celebrities as 'good' and 'bad' role models and in this instance her positioning of Cyrus shows a more complex negotiation around the binary:

> Ok well I'm just talking about like the celebrities I *like* and the celebrities that I think are bad

role models and that I don't really *like*. Um the ones that I do like are people who *don't* do anything bad just because they are a celebrity, people like Ashley Tisdale—I don't (wrinkles nose) really like her that much but like she is a *really* good role model she doesn't do anything bad (laughs) she's a *good* actress she has a *good* life and like she doesn't get us to like her and then just go do something *bad* and like, I like Miley Cyrus, I really, really like Miley Cyrus but it's just like, *tweens* really, really like her, and like *young* tweens as well, like seven, eight year olds so like it's really hard for the younger ones more than the older ones to accept it when she did the *Vanity Fair* thing. So like—there're too many bad [laughs] role models for us girls because we listen to celebrities . . . [omitted text about Cyrus on billboards and posters, in magazines 'everywhere'], people still like her and I still like her I just so wish she hadn't done it cos like it annoyed me because she was *perfect,* she was such a great role model and she's only fifteen so it's like we could kinda relate to her cos in a couple of years we would be her age.

The contradictions running through Cory's talk here are a striking feature of her narrative. Although she 'likes' celebrities who 'don't do anything bad,' which constructs them as 'good role models,' she tells us she is not particularly fond of Ashley Tisdale ('a really good role model, she doesn't do anything bad she's a good actress and has a good life'). In this account of Tisdale, Cory recognizes the 'ideal' celebrity, the one who provides girls like herself with a 'good' example of the way they *should* be in the world—the proverbial 'good girl' discourse of femininity (Walkerdine, 1990). On the other hand, Tisdale's goodness doesn't endear her to Cory, diluting the power of the 'good girl' norm. Cory positions celebrities like Tisdale as a source of powerful influence on girls but is more focused on the 'bad' possibilities of this power than the good. Such arguments about the powerful, negative influences of girls' celebrity 'idols' and their media appearances are widely made in the 'sexualization' of girls discourse and possibly inform Cory's understandings. Cory falls short of positioning Cyrus as having such power yet it is perhaps noteworthy that she mentions Cyrus in the same sentence that, arguably, implicates the star as belonging to the category of a bad role model. However, it is her liking of

Cyrus that is reiterated, which effects a rupturing of a straightforward relationship between 'liking' and celebrity behaviour ('bad' or 'good'). As Lowe (2003) found in her research, girls' rejections of celebrity hypersexy performances still leave spaces for appreciation of other aspects of the subjectivities they perform. Cory's expressed girl culture knowledge that 'tween girls' and 'young tween girls' also like Cyrus supports her own position as a Cyrus fan in that 'liking Miley' is being constructed as normative amongst girls her own age and younger. We suggest that normalizing support for Miley enables Cory to avoid being read (by us) as out of step with what might be considered appropriate for her age.

At the same time, however, the *Vanity Fair* cover violates a norm around what is acceptable to young and 'tween' age girls and Cory uses an age appropriateness discourse in underscoring particular effects of Cyrus's actions. She does so in relation to the seven and eight year old 'young tweens' whom she argues are 'more affected'—which works to position Cory and girls her age as better equipped via maturity to deal with the '*Vanity Fair* thing.' Age is also made salient to the disappointment and annoyance Cory feels in relation to Cyrus; as a star relatively close to the girls in age, with whom they might readily identify, Cyrus represented a possible 'ideal' good-girl self for Cory and other girls and this was no longer available to them. Although Cyrus's violation of acceptability norms does not unsettle 'liking' Miley in Cory's narrative, Cyrus's position as 'best role model' of earlier has slipped into the past tense and she is no longer 'perfect' or a 'great role model.'

'LOOK AT ME, I'M SLUTTY': ROLE MODELS AND THE SLUT/NON SLUT BINARY

A particularly striking pattern in girls' (re)production of the 'good'/'bad' girl binary in their narratives about pop celebrities was their deployment of a 'slut' discourse to navigate such representations. In the following extract this construction of the binary organized around female sexuality structures the talk between Jessica and Joely who are both white middle-class girls aged 13 and in their first year of high school (second year of the project). The girls have chosen, at their own initiation, to meet our request that they 'update' us on popular culture they now engage with by interviewing each other on camera. This segment, with Joely as the interviewer, features their current views on different celebrities. The girls are adept in adopting the 'seriousness' of a TV interview genre but simultaneously convey the humour of the set-up. Underlining denotes words given emphasis.

Joely: Yeah—ummm, what do you normally do—what do you normally watch or listen to on youtube?

Jessica: Um, I <u>usually</u> listen to Lady Gaga or Taylor Swift.

Joely: Yeah, it's probably the same with me. . . .

Joely: And what about Britney Spears, what do you think of her?

Jessica: I quite <u>like</u> her music, and I feel kind of <u>sorry</u> for her because like, she like, had a <u>rough</u> patch and then everyone was like, 'oh, blah blah blah,' but, yeah. I think she <u>has</u> made some mistakes.

Joely: Do you reckon she's a good role model? To young people?

Jessica: *(Scrunches up her face)* Ugh, not really.

Joely: Yeah.

Jessica: But, yeah *(pause)* and some of her, like, I like her <u>music</u>, but her <u>video clips</u> are like, real like.

Joely: Yeah—slutty and stuff? Yeah.

Jessica: She's like, wearing like, <u>nothing</u>, and it's like, <u>ew</u>, sort of thing, so yeah.

Joely: Yeah. Do you think, <u>Lady Gaga's</u> a r . . .—good model, or not really?

Jessica: *(laughs)* I like her songs, but again her video clips are quite—*(sucks air between her teeth)* yeah.

Joely: What about Pink?

Jessica: She's <u>okay</u>, but . . .

Joely: Same again?

Jessica: Yeah.

Joely: Yeah *(laughs)*.

Jessica: <u>All</u> of—but, um, Taylor Swift, I like her songs, and I think she's a good role model. Cos her, her <u>clips</u> aren't like, all like, 'look at me, I'm slutty.'

As the girls work through a list of female artists there is a sense of the normativity and homogeneity of celebrity hypersexual performances as first Britney then Lady Gaga and Pink fail to meet the requirements of a 'good role model'. . . . In negotiating the artists' hypersexual performances, Jessica expressly marks out the distinction between music and video image. She likes the music of Britney, Lady Gaga and Pink but draws a line of separation at their 'slutty' music videos. This appears to be an important boundary-marking from the perspective that liking the music whilst also criticizing the hypersexual video performance of it may work to allow and legitimate (perhaps for adults such as us viewing the girls' video) Jessica's viewing of hypersexual videos. This kind of negotiation is consistent with the argument that girls' engagement with hypersexualized pop culture is not as straightforward as a discourse of influence and imitation suggests (Renold and Ringrose, 2011). A non-linear relationship that interrupts a view-then-do model of girls' 'sexualized' media consumption is further suggested by Jessica's account of Britney. She speaks of Britney's 'rough patch' (widely publicized 'mental breakdown' in 2008) with sympathy and an understanding of making 'some mistakes' whereas Britney the barely clad performer evokes her disgust (expressed as 'ew'). This is a reminder that media representations of celebrities are not static but plural and in flux, as are girls' responses to them. Nonetheless the sexual trumps the psychological as Jessica, with a scrunched up face, registers her rejection of the idea that Britney might be a 'good role model' for 'young people.'

Consistent with Duschinsky's (2013) observation of the good/bad role model as constructed through sexual performance, Britney's 'slutty' video performances—'wearing like *nothing*—construct her as 'other' to a 'good role model' and a figure from whom Jessica affectively distances herself. Together Jessica's visual and verbal expressions of disgust with Britney resonate with meanings of the slut as a figure of abject contempt, a woman who has violated middle-class moral codes of proper femininity and sexuality (Attwood, 2007). At the same time, her distancing from a 'slutty' Britney positions her within a 'sexualization' of girls discourse which constructs girls like Jessica as 'naturally' sexual innocent, imitative and readily tainted by 'sexualization' (Egan, 2013). Against this discourse, Jessica's rejection of Britney as a 'good role model' shores up a position as resistant and critical rather than vulnerable and impressionable, but read through a 'sexualization' of girls discourse rejection also protects a positioning as sexually appropriate for her age. In contrast to Britney, Pink and Lady Gaga Taylor Swift stands as the antithesis to a hyper-sexualized pop culture, her absence of 'slutty' performances marking her out as a 'good role model.' Here, the reciprocity of the good/bad girl binary is implicit: the good role model's existence requires the 'bad slutty other' as her point of moral difference.

Jessica had initially named Lady Gaga as a music celebrity she would 'usually' listen to or watch on YouTube but the 'slutty' tarnish of her video clips is signalled by the sucking in of her breath and an absence of words to describe them. Elsewhere in Jessica's video diary, however, the boundaries of 'slutty' appeared to be a little more slippery than her interview with Joely would suggest. In a later video diary entry the camera is trained on Lady Gaga *Paparazzi* video clip which Jessica and her friend are watching in Jessica's bedroom. Jessica is then heard to exclaim 'Dad!' in a soft but surprised voice, signalling to us that her father has entered the room. The video scene playing at this moment switches between Gaga dressed in a gold metallic Madonna-like body suit raising herself on crutches from a wheelchair to Gaga clad in a BDSM styled black outfit performing sexually evocative movements on a sofa. Jessica's father's voice cannot be heard but we do hear her response: 'It's *not* slutty, this one's not slutty. (*Dad leaves*) Did you see his face?'

Again the slutty/not slutty binary is invoked but this time it organizes around performances of the same celebrity. That Jessica uses the term 'slutty' with her father suggests it may take up earlier conversations about this kind of content with him because to not be 'slutty' suggests a discussion around what 'slutty' might be. Lady Gaga costuming in *Paparazzi* clearly appropriates porno styled features through bared flesh, 'underwear' and corseted body (not to mention acts of 'lesbian

kissing' and an orgasmic sex scene). How then might Jessica's reading of 'not slutty' be understood alongside her earlier categorization of Gaga videos as 'slutty'? . . . Context is closely connected with meanings and we would venture that this is important to Jessica's contradictory accounts of Lady Gaga hypersexual performances. Disavowing the slut in the presence of her father may work to counter the potential risk of disapproval and contamination through association in viewing 'slutty' videos. Separation from the slut assumes particular importance for girls in the context of their awareness of adult/parental concerns that they will emulate the 'sexualized' dress of pop celebrities or want to be like them (Duits and van Zoonen, 2011). The scenario involving Jessica's father underlines the important function of situational context to the ways in which subjectivity is negotiated and managed. Ultimately, though, both sides of the slut/not slut binary exercise similar effects of strategically separating Jessica's own subjectivity from the slut; disgust manages the separation from a 'slutty' Lady Gaga in the interview with Joely whereas disavowal of the slut in her father's presence allows Jessica to protect her position within regulatory age-based requirements related to girls' sexuality (i.e. the inappropriateness of sexual interest and content for young teen girls) as well as to defend against the disparagement of 'her' music (and her generation).

'IT'S ALL ABOUT THE MUSIC': (EN)COUNTERING THE 'SEXY,' 'DODGY' VIDEO

Both Cory and Jessica, in their respective sense-making of Cyrus and Lady Gaga show the complicated pathways around accepting/liking a pop celebrity while also juggling a moral position about the undesirability of 'slutty' or 'bad girl' celebrity subjectivities. For 13-year-old Lily, Avril Lavigne offered an alternative to stars like Lady Gaga and Cyrus who perform 'sexy' subjectivities, which encouraged her to be an ardent Lavigne fan. A white middle-class girl, and a talented musician in her own right, Lily's admiration for Lavigne focused on 'the anger' and 'the swearing' she expressed through her music, the 'fact' she was a skateboarder and, particularly, the relative absence of 'stupid clothes' and acting like 'stupid Barbies' (girls used the term 'Barbies' to denote a porno-chic style) in her music videos. In the following extract

Lily's talk into the camera centres more specifically on 'dodgy, sexy' music videos against which she uses Lavigne's videos as a point of comparison:

> I'll look up like, um, Avril Lavigne ones mostly, but the good thing about her music videos, it's all about the music, not about the kind of dodgy, sexy kind of, um, kind of video, like, where they have to wear like all, next to nothing and, you know, act all, touch themselves and (*shudders*) uggh, it's really <u>weird</u> and everybody's like, everybody <u>likes</u> them because they can sort of look at them and like 'woah!' <u>laugh</u> at them and stuff, but um, but with Avril Lavigne it's all about the <u>music</u> and, and stuff like that, and half of songs don't even <u>have</u> videos, so, yeah. I, kind of, I'll <u>look</u> at the music videos and I'll listen to them for about thirty seconds or ten seconds, and then I'll probably turn most of them off because I'll just be like, ugh, the video is gross, and the music is pointless, but if, if the video is—I don't really care about the video as long as the music's good, but you know, I don't watch it for the video like most people seem to.

The sexual displays Lily views in the music videos violate a middle-class respectability that deems such acts as shameful and deserving of disgust (Tyler and Bennett, 2010). For Lily, Lavigne's appeal is that her videos focus on the music and are devoid of 'dodgy, sexy' features marked out by bodies exposed by wearing 'next to nothing,' but also the performance of 'sexy' as in artists 'touch[ing] them- selves'. . . . A combination of 'sexy'-ness displayed through undress and performance evoke Lily's distaste, signified by her embodied shudder and her expressions of disgust ('gross,' 'ugh'). Lily's affective response might be seen as distancing her from hypersexual display, a negotiation consistent with avoiding the contaminating association of pre-teen girls with sexuality that is constructed within a girls' 'sexualization' discourse.

. . . Lily's narrative positions her, somewhat as she positions Lavigne, as different to an 'everybody' Other and to 'most people.' One point of difference is that Lily finds no amusement in 'sexy' music videos and another is the distaste she experiences in viewing them. In contrast, others are depicted as obtaining a gratuitous experience ('woah!') and having a 'laugh,' reactions that Mulholland (2013) similarly found for high

school students' responses to pornography in her research. Pornification has brought elements of 'illegitimate' private pornography into the mainstream (Attwood, 2009) and music videos provide young people of Lily's age with a 'legitimate' form of pornography inspired representations. Lily does watch these 'legitimate' porn-styled music videos but, maintaining her position as different to 'most people,' she negotiates this viewing through time and reason (watching for music not video). However there is a contradictory thread in tracing Lily's shifting locations from a girl who rejects 'dodgy videos' to a girl who doesn't care about the video if the music is 'good.' In a diary entry made some time later, Lily finds this music/video distinction useful in accounting for an unexpected image of Avril Lavigne on a YouTube clip. The next extract is related to this incident; Lily is with her cousin in the bedroom where they are watching music videos on YouTube; the camera is trained on the computer images throughout.

Lily: This one's Avril Lavigne, it doesn't actually have a music video . . . but I like the song. Oh, I've got that album. (*Laughs. This is in response to an image of an album cover.*)

Rosa: (*laughs*) Whoo—look at her butt!

Lily: Rosa! Well, as I said, we don't watch it for the music video! (*Sings along*): *I know, how far you go.*

In this particular YouTube clip, Lavigne's music plays while a series of still images of her flick across the screen. Lily's cousin responds to an image of Lavigne wearing small tight shorts and a sleeveless fitted top but it is predominantly her pose that connotes sexual titillation. Lavigne is bent over from the waist in side profile with her hips tipped to the side exaggerating her 'butt' and the exposure of her legs in her small shorts. This 'sexualized' pose is what arrests Lily's cousin's attention as she points to Lavigne's 'butt' with the exclamation of 'Whoo—look at her butt.' That the image concurs in some way with those Lily has previously described with recoil, is suggested by both her gentle reprimand of her cousin ('Rosa!') as having said something somewhat inappropriate and her good-humoured reminder that she distances herself from 'dodgy' music videos. Lily has caught herself in a moment of contradiction, aware that all she has previously told us about Lavigne is somewhat undone by her cousin's exposure but she manages this through humour and the useful music/video divide she had constructed earlier. As a declared Lavigne fan, Lily may also be more likely to allow for tolerances of an aberrant act or performance in contrast to the less sympathetic evaluations of non-fans (Zaslow, 2009).

In a competitive music market where sex sells and the 'hot, sexy body' is a marker of postfeminist femininity (Gill, 2009), Lavigne's image is readily understood. For girls like Lily and her cousin, transformations of their favourite stars from 'good role models' or non 'slutty' performers into porno-chic styled subjects presents a challenge: do they abandon their pleasure in the music and the celebrity, do they accept it as a normative part of pop music culture or do they perhaps negotiate a position of both criticism and pleasure? As seen with Jessica, Cory and Lily, negotiations of 'sexy' representations and music videos . . . were a complicated intermingling of affect, pleasure and/or distaste, and age.

CONCLUDING DISCUSSION

As the girls' material suggests, contemporary pop music culture is a stage for female celebrity performances of hypersexuality. In the detailed analysis of the three girls' narratives we have presented here, encounters with these performances can be seen to complicate girls' participation and pleasure as a viewing audience. We argue that discourses of age, sexuality and femininity intersect with girls' social locations as white middle-class 'tweenagers,' constructing the fabric through which complications for girls are interwoven. As young teen girls, cultural discourses of 'childhood innocence' and 'good girl' femininity construct their sexuality as an improper, inappropriate domain for their interests or activities. When girls like Jess, Cory and Lily view the 'raunchy' music videos of the female popstars whose music they like, they enter a taboo domain, crossing the boundary from 'innocence' to an adult, sexual world. This being so, there needs to be careful accounting and explanation that enables participation while avoiding being positioned as transgressors, in violation of their age-drawn cultural code of conduct. . . . In the girls' narratives, expressions of disgust, categorization as bad role models and 'sluts' all worked to avoid misrecognition, strategically distancing the three girls from the 'sexy' performances and scanty dress

styles adopted in music videos and celebrity images. From a different perspective, creating a boundary between the music and a 'dodgy' or 'slutty' video also allowed Jessica and Lily to account for and legitimate watching the videos they condemned.

Consistent with an evaluative process of mis/recognition, a striking feature of the girls' process of negotiation around the sexual displays of female pop celebrities is their appropriation of binaries: 'good' and 'bad' 'role models'; 'slutty' and 'not slutty' celebrities. These binary categories were excavated through appearance, specifically the popstars' scanty, body-baring clothing and subsequently accorded a moral status as undesirable or 'bad.' . . . Girls' orientation toward moral readings of the popstars through their appearance (specifically (un)dress) is contextualized in a society where female dress is not only monitored and regulated for its 'appropriate' expression of sexuality but actively used to reprimand, castigate and blame as, for example, in sexual assaults and rape cases. Nonetheless the good/bad binary occasionally ruptured in moments of contradiction, as for example in celebrities' shifting and contradictory productions of 'self': Lavigne 'did' anger but also 'sexy'; Gaga 'did' 'sexy' but also multiple fantasy identities; Cyrus 'did' sexually provocative but also 'did' nice girl-next-door Hannah Montana. We suggest that these contradictory performances allowed girls some space to manoeuvre, enabling them to remain a fan (Lily, Cory) or to engage in pleasurable viewing and listening (all three girls). In other moments, fractures of the binary came by way of self-contradictions as with Lily's recognition that Lavigne participated in 'sexy' productions of self in common with other popstars in 'dodgy' music videos. Here the binary no longer held up for construction of a 'good,' alternative Lavigne and a 'dodgy,' 'othered' popstar. Similarly, Cory's self-contradictions in both liking 'good role models' and not liking them, fractures the normative pull of the 'good girl' if only in terms of popstar preferences and not practices. . . . However, we would suggest that such contradictions can also be viewed as destabilizing, momentarily, categories of the 'slut,' the 'bad girl,' and the 'good girl' and that 'slipperiness' can produce productive as well as troublesome effects, opening up an alternative space to occupy, temporary though it may be.

Although moments of slippage complicated binaries and provided permissive spaces for engaging with 'sexy' popstars, the powerfulness of regulatory, moralizing discourses of femininity and sexuality is all too evident in girls' appropriation of the 'slut' and the 'bad girl.' We argue that the proliferation of 'sexualization' discourses, emphatically holding media accountable for 'sexualizing' girls in damaging, harmful ways, adds yet another layer of discursive constraint that fetters girls' (a)sexuality to morality, appearance and age. In re-energizing a taboo construction of sexuality for pre-teen girls, a discourse of girls' 'sexualization' compels them to warily monitor their participation in sexually saturated pop music culture in order to avoid its sexually corrupting potential. Although girls' distancing from the hypersexual performances of pop celebrities may also be read positively as rejecting what some would hold to be sexist representations of women (see Gill, 2012), they do so with a regulatory tool that resides in the sexism of the sexual double standard. It is an important project for feminists involved in girls' lives to not only encourage their political, gender-focused critiques of hypersexualized media but also to engage with them in conversations about alternative, non-commodified meanings of sexuality. Without such conversations there is a risk that the dangerous and undesirable constructions of 'sexiness' within girls' 'sexualization' discourse will obscure possibilities of pleasurable, embodied possibilities for feeling 'sexy' as part of a positive sexual sense of self.

ACKNOWLEDGEMENTS

We wish to express our immense gratitude to the girls who so enthusiastically gave their time and energy to participate in this study.

FUNDING

We wish to acknowledge the Royal Society of New Zealand Marsden Fund for the financial support of the research project *Girls, 'tween' Popular Culture and Everyday Life*.

NOTE

1. Rihanna and Miley Cyrus are celebrity popstars with wide appeal to a young 'tween' audience. In the music videos referred to, concerns have circulated in media about the exposure of a young girl audience to the porn-styled clothing and performances that involve 'twerking.' 'Twerking' describes sexually provocative dance moves such as hip-thrusting, gyrations and low squats.

REFERENCES

Andsager J and Roe K (2003) What's your definition of dirty baby? Sex in music video. *Sexuality and Culture* 7(3): 79–97.

APA (2007) American Psychological Association Task Force on the Sexualization of Girls. *Report of the APA Task Force on the Sexualization of Girls*. Washington, DC: American Psychological Association. Available at: www.apa.org/pi/wpo/Sexualisation.html (accessed 30 July 2013).

Attwood F (2007) Sluts and Riot Grrrls: Female identity and sexual agency. *Journal of Gender Studies* 16(3): 233–247.

Attwood F (2009) Introduction: The sexualization of culture. In: Attwood F (ed) *Mainstreaming Sex*. London: I.B.Tauris, pp. xiiii–xx.

Charles C (2010) Raunch culture goes to school? Young women, normative femininities and elite education. *Media International Australia* 135: 61–70.

Dobson A (2011) Heterosexy representations by young women on MySpace: The politics of performing an 'objectified' self. *Outskirts Online Journal* 25 November. Available at: http://www.outskirts.arts.uwa.edu.au/volumes/volume-25 (accessed 30 November 2011).

Driver S (2007) *Queer Girls and Popular Culture*. New York: Peter Lang.

Duits L and van Zoonen L (2011) Coming to terms with sexualization. *European Journal of Cultural Studies* 14(5): 491–506.

Durham MG (2008) *The Lolita Effect*. Woodstock, NY: The Overlook Press.

Duschinsky R (2013) What does sexualization mean? *Feminist Theory* 14(3): 255–264.

Egan D (2013) *Becoming Sexual.* Cambridge: Polity.

Egan RD and Hawkes G (2008) Girls, sexuality and the strange carnalities of advertisements: Deconstructing the discourse of corporate paedophilia. *Australian Feminist Studies* 23(57): 307–322.

Evans A and Riley S (2013) Immaculate consumption: Negotiating the sex symbol in postfeminist celebrity culture. *Journal of Gender Studies* 22(3): 268–281.

Fairclough K (2008) Fame is a losing game. *Genders Online* 48. Available at: http://www.genders.org/g48/g48_fairclough.html (accessed 12 December 2008).

Gill R (2009) Beyond the 'sexualization of culture' thesis: An intersectional analysis of 'six-packs', 'midriffs' and 'hot lesbians' in advertising. *Sexualities* 12(2): 137–160.

Gill R (2012) The sexualization of culture? *Social and Personality Compass* 6(7): 483–498.

Griffin C (2004) Good girls, bad girls: Anglocentricism and diversity in the constitution of contemporary girlhood. In: Harris A (ed) *All About the Girl. Culture, Power and Identity.* London: Routledge, pp. 29–43.

Griffin C, Szmigin I, Bengry-Howell A, et al. (2013) Inhabiting the contradictions: Hypersexual femininity and the culture of intoxication among young women in the UK. *Feminism and Psychology* 23(2): 184–226.

Hamilton M (2007) *What's Happening to Our Girls.* Camberwell, VIC: Penguin.

Jackson S, Vares T and Gill R (2013) The whole playboy mansion image: Girls fashioning and fashioned selves within a postfeminist culture. *Feminism and Psychology* 23(2): 143–162.

Lamb S, Graling K and Wheeler E (2013) Polearized discourse: An analysis of responses to Miley Cyrus's teen choice awards pole dance. *Feminism and Psychology* 23(2): 163–183. Epub ahead of print DOI: 10.1177/0959353512472472482.

Lerum K and Dworkin S (2009) Bad girls rule? An interdisciplinary feminist commentary on the report of the APA Task Force on the Sexualisation of girls. *Journal of Sex Research* 46(4): 250–263.

Levin D and Kilbourne J (2008) *So Sexy So Soon. The New Sexualized Childhood and What Parents Can Do to Protect their Kids.* Random House: New York.

Lowe M (2003) Colliding feminisms: Britney Spears, 'tweens' and the politics of reception. *Popular Music and Society* 26(2): 123–140.

Lumby C and Albury K (2010) Too much? Too young? The sexualization of children debate in Australia. *Media International Australia* 135: 141–152.

McClelland S and Fine M (2008) Writing on cellophane. In: Gallagher K (ed) *Creative, Critical and Collaborative Approaches to Qualitative Research.* New York: Routledge, pp. 232–261.

McRobbie A (2009) *The Aftermath of Feminism.* London: SAGE.

Mullholland M (2013) *Young People and Pornography.* New York: Palgrave Macmillan.

Oppliger P (2008) *Girls Gone Skank: The Sexualization of Girls in American Culture.* Jefferson, NC: McFarland and Company.

Renold E and Ringrose J (2011) Schizoid subjectivities? Re-theorizing teen-girls' sexual cultures in an era of 'sexualization.' *Journal of Sociology* 47(4): 389–409.

Ringrose J (2011) Are you sexy or flirty or a slut? Exploring 'sexualization' and how teen girls perform/negotiate digital sexual identity on social networking sites. In: Gill R and Scharff C (eds) *New Femininities: Postfeminism, Neoliberalism and Identity.* London: Palgrave, pp. 99–116.

Rush E and La Nauze A (2006) *Corporate Paedophilia. Sexualisation of Children in Australia.* Discussion Paper No. 90. Available at: www.tai.org.au/documents/downloads/DP90.pdf (accessed 30 July 2013).

Tyler I and Bennet B (2010) Celebrity chav: Fame, femininity and social class. *European Journal of Cultural Studies* 13(3): 375–393.

Vares T, Jackson S and Gill R (2011) Pre-teen girls read popular culture: Diversity, complexity and contradiction. *International Journal for Media and Cultural Politics* 7(2): 139–154.

Walkerdine V (1990) *Schoolgirl Fictions.* London: Verso.

Zaslow E (2009) Wanna get dirty? Determining authentic sexual subjectivity. In: Zaslow E (ed) *Feminism Inc. Coming of Age in Girl Power Media Culture.* New York: Palgrave Macmillan, pp. 57–82.

49

PRIVATES IN THE ONLINE PUBLIC

Sex(ting) and Reputation on Social Media

Michael Salter

INTRODUCTION

Social media is the first mass media platform in history where girls and women participate at equal or greater levels than boys and men as content producers, distributers and consumers (Ahn, 2011). This has enabled girls and women to access alternative forms of social support, develop new modes and forms of communication and become critically engaged with issues that concern them (Hasinoff, 2013). However, the widespread presence of girls and women on social media has sparked concern over their vulnerability to harm and abuse online. Threats and warnings of sexual violence have historically demarcated the public sphere as unsuitable for girls and women, effectively privatising femininity by constructing the private and domestic sphere as the safest and most appropriate place for girls and women (Gordon and Riger, 1989). This pattern continues in the age of social media with frequent warnings to female users not to be too public or immodest online in order to reduce the risk of sexual harm or reputational damage (Albury and Crawford, 2012). Questions of gender, privacy and publicity are therefore deeply implicated in debates over girls' and women's online safety and their participation in the unfolding publics generated by new media technologies.

Drawing on focus groups with young people aged 18–20 years [old], this [chapter] examines the impact of norms of publicity and privacy on young people as they negotiate technologically mediated intimate and peer relations. The [chapter] describes how digital images of bodies circulate online in a manner that reinforces gender inequalities, as the public feminine body is narrowly conflated with pornography in contrast to the range of meanings that can append to the public masculine body. The exposed feminine body online thus becomes the focal point for pejorative ascriptions of sexual promiscuity and aberration, while the exposed masculine body serves a range of purposes, including its deployment in sexual harassment and intimidation. While these gender differentials were frequently identified by focus group participants, young people struggled to account for them through their preferred vocabulary of gender neutrality and individual choice and tended to hold girls and women responsible for managing the risks of online abuse. . . .

PUBLICITY, PRIVACY AND GENDER ON SOCIAL MEDIA

An 'overriding element in modern masculinity at every social level has been the expected and legitimate connection' with the public sphere (Davidoff, 2003: 17), but women and children have historically been characterised as the natural denizens of the private sphere and unsuited to the rigours of public life (Pateman, 1988). Hence, respectable femininity has been associated with privacy, while masculinity has been attributed to both public and private aspects, granting boys and men an ease of movement from private into public spaces and dialogue that is not shared by girls and women (Davidoff, 2003: 19).

Feminine sexuality has been a point of focus within the gendered ideology of the public/private divide. . . . The mass media is now host to highly sexualised depictions of public femininities as evidence of female advancement that, nonetheless,

From Salter, M. (2016). Privates in the online public: Sex(ting) and reputation on social media. *New Media and Society, 18*(11), 2723–2739.

retain older and more pejorative associations with promiscuity and sexual availability (Gill, 2012). This reflects the incompatible demand that girls and young women should not be 'sluts' (i.e. too public about their sexuality and desires) but should also not be 'prudes' (or too private about their sexuality and desires) (Tolman, 2002: 119–120).

These contradictions are evident on social media, where cultural constructions of (hetero) sexualised femininities provide particularly salient modes of self-display for girls and young women online (Renold and Ringrose, 2011), against the persistent view that girls or women who seek online publicity are 'sluts' deserving humiliation (Poole, 2013). The latter view may be disreputable, but it is championed by vocal groups of young men who consider female participation on social media to be immodest and unfeminine (Jane, 2014). . . . The result of these colliding norms is a tendency to view female participation in online publics as contingent on narrow codes of behaviour and appearance that justify apportioning blame to the girl or woman if she experiences online abuse and harassment (Salter et al., 2013). In comparison, the online self-representations and conduct of boys and men rarely attract such levels of scrutiny and judgement (Karaian, 2014).

Social media is not fully public, in the sense that users have a range of options to restrict access to their accounts and profiles and frequently engage in other strategic practices designed to inhibit unwanted attention (Marwick and boyd, 2014). However, social media business models and software architecture are oriented towards the maximisation of content sharing and user interaction, encouraging the publication of private details within a medium with instantaneous and international reach (Papacharissi and Gibson, 2011). . . . [W]hat is discussed and disseminated on social media can reinforce and perpetuate the status quo as well as challenge it (Fuchs, 2008). In their focus groups with young people, for example, Lippman and Campbell (2014) described how girls who 'sext' (i.e. who make and circulate nude images) were judged negatively by their peers as 'sluts' but girls who do not were labelled 'stuck up' and 'prudes.' It appears that norms of privacy and publicity persist on social media in a manner that can reproduce invidious constructions of femininity and female sexuality. . . .

This [chapter] draws on a focus group study of young Australians aged 18–20 years to examine how they negotiate privacy and publicity in their use of online and digital technology. Eight focus groups were conducted at two universities and one adult education centre, in inner city, outer suburban and rural locations. Focus group participants came from diverse class, ethnic and religious backgrounds, including students from Anglo Australian, Asian, Indian, Middle Eastern, North American and European backgrounds. Focus groups contained between 3 and 10 participants with an average of 7 and were 90 minutes in length each. In the focus groups, participants were asked about their views of media coverage of sexting and related phenomena, their experiences of the social and personal impacts of online and digital technology and their views on the appropriate response to aggravated, coercive or unethical uses of this technology. The majority of volunteers for the study were young women, and hence, much of the focus group discussion was focused on the specific concerns and challenges of female social media users. . . .

GENDER ASYMMETRY IN THE ONLINE PUBLIC

The Internet and social media specifically were ubiquitous in the organisation and arrangement of the social, familial and intimate relations of young people in focus groups. Social media facilitated contact with intimates such as family and friends in ways that other communication technology could not, and it provided an interactive platform for the construction and display of a public persona. Nonetheless, participants were acutely aware that there were multiple and not necessarily complimentary audiences for the information that they placed online about themselves. A suspect photo or status update could have potentially ruinous implications for familial or romantic relationships, friendships or even future employment. Since many participants were students contemplating a professional career, there was considerable disquiet about the reputational impacts of social media on their employability. Katie said,

> You have the right to that [a personal life], and if you want to go out on the Saturday

night and party and get drunk, you should be allowed to do that and it should not affect your business life.

What Katie expresses here is the expectation that public manifestations of personal life on social media will be granted an appropriate degree of protection from intrusive or harmful publicity. While once primarily the concern of famous and influential people, the saturation of social life with cameras and networked computer technology has led to a generalised exposure to the dangers of unwanted publicity and its potential impacts on reputation (Solove, 2007). Participants indicated that both online images and text circulated and travelled on social media and mobile phones in a similar way to gossip and rumour and performed a similar function, providing a salacious topic of conversation in which social capital accrues to the individual who obtains and passes on privileged information.

This introduced a key tension into young people's online practices. A lacklustre response to online self-display can signal, Lyon and Bauman (2013) suggest, a kind of 'social death.' Hence, young people have a strong inducement to provide the kinds of provocative or 'edgy' content that has currency on social media, including images of their own and other's bodies.

Attwood (2011) noted that 'the exposure of the body—male and female—seems to be increasingly central to forms of popular representation and to individual self-expression' (p. 204). However, male and female bodies were not equivalent in online publics. Boys could, for example, deliberately shame themselves in public by engaging in grotesque behaviour, photographing it and circulating it online. A naked photo of a 'guy smashed [drunk] doing a strip [running naked] all the way down the road' might be shared by the boy's friends with the dual intention of humiliating him as well as demonstrating his daring and signalling more generally the solidarity of his friendship circle and the kinds of antics they engage in. In this instance, his nudity is entertaining rather than sexual. Such photos circulated between friends and within peer groups that were not sexualised but rather functioned as a form of 'gross out' humour. Ellen recalled,

One of my friends was peeing and took a picture of himself 'cause he thought it was funny

and sent it to his friend, and then his friend—all his guy friends have this picture of him. I've seen it, but they think it's funny—I don't know that's kind of the case. He doesn't care, he was like I took it I don't care. Maybe that's just the difference between boys and girls.

Hope describes a similar incident in high school in which a male student circulated a photo of his genitals to the entire school bus. She noted the very different consequences such behaviour would have had for a girl:

Once when I was in year 11, I was sitting on the school bus going home and I had my Bluetooth turned on and so did a bunch of other girls and boys around me. This message came and a guy was like, 'Oh receive it, it's really funny,' and I opened it and it was a picture of the genitals of the guy sitting next to me.

They were just both smiling and laughing and all these kids on the bus had a picture of his penis. It wasn't embarrassing for them. He thought it was hilarious but if a girl's vagina, a picture of that was sent around that would not be seen in the same way. She probably wouldn't do it to begin with as a generalisation and it wouldn't be funny. It would be harmful for her. It would be seen as like really brazen and negative.

The intent with which boys crafted images of their bodies tended to influence how those images were interpreted once in online circulation, and a range of meanings could affix to images of male bodies. Such nuances were lacking in relation to images of exposed female bodies, often called 'sexts' in the research literature, although participants in this study generally called them 'nudes.' Girls and women may pose and ape for the camera in a range of ways designed to invoke parody and grotesquerie (Dobson, 2014), but public female nudity could not be deployed to 'gross out' effect. It retained an inherently sexual and pornographic quality with deleterious effects on the social standing of the girl or woman depicted. Andrew stated that publicised male nudity can be 'whatever,' but publicised female nudity means 'slut':

I think that's why it's so embarrassing [for girls] because the guys are 'whatever' [about their own nudity], if a guy sends a picture of a girl around it's like 'oh, look at her, she's a slut, she sent a naked picture,' and then it becomes even more embarrassing because you don't just hear 'naked,' now you think 'she's a slut.'

Focus group participants were very aware of the differential impacts of publicised nudity for girls and women and expressed concern about 'naïve' younger sisters and cousins who placed images of themselves in provocative or revealing clothing on social media. Anxiety over the reputational impacts of female nudity extended into private relations, where girls and women could find a male partner soliciting 'nudes' from them. Peta said,

> I know girls that have been shamed and blamed by their boyfriends for failing to deliver on this image. I know girls that, you know, if the guys didn't have it, they would sulk and would say 'Don't you see I'm doing this out of love for you, I just appreciate you, I love your body I want to have a keepsake of it,' and these girls would really feel upset at themselves for not doing it.

While the self-production of bodily images is framed here by the male partner as harmless and safe, girls and women were conscious of the serious ramifications for the female partner if the 'nude' is made public during or after the relationship. Sontag (1977) observed that photos have an indelibly public quality even when manufactured for private viewing, and the potentially public quality of the erotic image was cited by a number of female participants as the reason they refused to make such images available to intimate partners. For others, their resistance went further and incorporated their objections to the similarities between the 'nude' and the pornography already being consumed by the male partner. Leah recalled,

> I've had a couple of friends who've done it [sent naked images to boyfriends] and what they say is—one of them was like 'I know my boyfriend looks at porn, I know he needs porn to masturbate, and he's saying to me, 'What am I meant to do? I need to masturbate and I want to masturbate over you, so please we have sex I see you all the time, I just want that so I can keep that in my personal home. . . . '

In this account, the self-manufacture of erotic images constitutes, in effect, a form of unpaid sex work that conflates female bodily display with prostitution even in the context of an intimate relationship. The potential publicness of the 'nude' thus threatened the point of delineation between private intimacy and public shame literally—such as when the male partner non-consensually circulated the image—and symbolically—when the 'nude' was viewed as a substitute for or compliment to pornography. This loss of boundaries was reflected in focus group discussions where the term 'whore' or 'slut,' the signifier for 'bad' public feminine sexuality, was frequently used to describe girls or women who take 'nudes' or 'sexy' pictures of themselves, regardless of their intent and context of production. For example, Lana characterised the girls who send 'nudes' as 'attention whores,' particular 'types' of girls who 'can't get boys' and are desperate for male attention:

> It's also usually girls that can't get boys, not because of their looks, but they just don't get boys. They do it for attention, because that's what attracts boys I suppose, they love all that dirty stuff.

In this quote from Lana, an 'attention whore' is both a girl who makes 'nudes' (or, as another female participant put it, someone who 'pornographises' herself) and a girl who is immodest simply because she seeks attention. The role of the boy or man in circulating the photo is sublimated to the girl's or woman's decisions to take and send the image, at which point the girls' sexualised display marks her as the 'bad' or 'slutty' girl deserving retribution (Tolman, 2002). . . .

THE GENDERED ABUSE OF ONLINE PUBLICITY

The different signification of male and female public nudity placed boys and girls in unbalanced positions within the digital visual economy. Boys did not face equivalent risks to girls, and this generated mechanisms through which boys and men can gain socially through the online humiliation and derogation of girls and women. This section describes two such practices that emerged in this study. The first involved the solicitation of a 'nude' from a girl which is then non-consensually circulated to others. The second is the 'dick pic,' in which boys and men send girls and women unwanted and shocking images of their genitals.

The Non-Consensual Circulation of 'Nudes'

In the accounts gathered in this study, the exchange of 'nudes' in the context of a consensual relationship was an intimate practice that could be desired by both parties. However, participants also described incidents in which it was not sexual desire but rather the pursuit of cultural capital among male peers that motivated boys to ask girls for 'nudes.' This occurred at times in a predatory manner as boys and men flattered girls and women in an attempt to gain images from them with the intention of showing them to others later. When asked why boys might show a private 'nude' of a girl to other boys, participants in one focus group suggested,

Natalie:	Look how hot my girlfriend is.
Alan:	Popularity, attention.
Leila:	Yeah, I think it's popularity that a girl actually sent him a photo of herself.

This dynamic has been noted in other research on sexting between young people. In their fieldwork with young people in high school, Ringrose et al. (2013) found that nude images of girls can be used by boys as evidence of their sexual proficiency. This in turn substantiated their claims to popularity and power among male peers. As such, circulating a 'nude' represents a claim to masculine status that confirmed not only the power differentials between boys and girls but also the relative status of the male sender over other male peers. In the following excerpt, a woman in the focus group asks a man follow-up questions about a sexting incident:

Ayla:	Remember that story you were telling us about the popular girl who got photos sent around and how she got teased for a couple of months. I was wondering if anything happened to the guy who sent them, did anyone tease him about it?
Adam:	No, he was [seen as] a champion and that sort of thing.
Ayla:	So guys get praised for like. . . .
Adam:	No, it depends on who you are. If it was me that sent it in high school I'd probably have the shit kicked out of me by someone. But because this guy was also up there, nothing happened to him, it was just like 'oh yeah, sick, man.'
Ayla:	It's like everything else at high school, the hierarchy.

Adam had previously explained that the girl victimised in this incident was a 'popular' girl. It was therefore pertinent that the boy who circulated the image was also 'up there' or popular. Adam indicates that if he had been the one circulating the same image, the outcome would have been very different since he would have been victimising a girl associated with a higher-status group. Such an action would have challenged the stratification of the peer hierarchy as a whole and hence might have invited physical retaliation by the 'popular' boys. However, since a 'popular' boy victimised a girl of equivalent or lesser status, then the social response was 'oh, yeah, sick man.'

There were multiple reports of female classmates and friends who had found themselves the subjects of sustained bullying and harassment, online and offline, once a bodily image was maliciously circulated. Hope's report was typical:

It was a girl in my school, when we were in Year 9 she had a photo of herself in a very gratuitous position and she sent it to the boyfriend and the boyfriend and they broke up and he sent it to everyone in our year. It went viral, and she ended up leaving the school.

Anna noted, 'The experiences that I know about of people [sending nudes], it's been the girl to the guy. It's never been the other way.' The consistently gendered nature of these reports could make participants uncomfortable since participants were at pains to characterise their peer groups as gender equal. This insistence that peer groups are gender equal, McRobbie (2004) suggests, preserves neoliberal narratives of choice, agency and self-determination for young women by disavowing experiences of gendered oppression. In this study, these narratives were in tension with both women's and men's observations of the male predominance in online abuse. Participants sought to resolve this tension by raising the hypothetical possibility of female perpetration, but this was generally countered by the recognition that males are less vulnerable to processes of online shaming and humiliation. In this exchange, Anastasia suggested that girls were simply less motivated to engage in online abuse, but Darren emphasised that, regardless of the intent of the female perpetrator, circulating a 'nude' would not have the same effect on the male target:

> Anastasia: It doesn't happen to guys as much because a girl wouldn't be like 'Oh, I'm going to send his naked picture everywhere.' Unless she was really, really pissed off or something.
>
> Darren: The thing is like, comeuppance, having naked pictures of you being around as a man is like, 'whatever,' you know.

Darren's point here is that even if a girl wanted to circulate explicit images of a boy, perhaps in retaliation against her own victimisation, public male nakedness can be more easily shrugged off. In contrast, the circulation of female 'nudes' was considered 'a big deal' in terms of the humiliation of the girl or woman, potentially triggering the intervention and concern of parents, teachers and sometimes police. Female public nakedness cannot be disentangled from its association with pornography and prostitution, and hence, 'private' female nakedness, once revealed to the public, positions the individual as a 'slut.' The same process of signification cannot be set in train for boys or men although, as will be discussed, online exposure can have reputational impacts for boys and men.

The Dick Pic

Multiple female participants in this study described receiving unsolicited photos of male genitals (known colloquially as 'dick pics') from male acquaintances and friends. This put them in an uncomfortable and difficult position. On the whole, they did not know how to respond or the motivations behind the image. In the following excerpt, Isabella describes being sent a video and

photo of a man's erection after meeting him only briefly:

> Like I was friends with the kid that was like his best friend and then like, one time, I met him, so it was like all right, whatever. And then we spoke for that one time and that was it. And then he sent me snapchats[1] before but it was just, like, normal, but then I saw the video and the photo [of his erection] and I was like nah, that's weird . . . What was he expecting? I have never replied to any snapchats ever, and what are you meant to say back? 'Oh you really look good there.' What am I meant to do?

Male motivations for sending unwanted 'dick pics' were the focus of extended debate among women in focus groups, who were uncertain about the significance of male genital display. Some thought that boys and men were simply trying to initiate a similar exchange of pictures from the girl. Sarah's response was typical:

> Maybe it's reciprocal, because the guys they want to see the girls' genitals, so then they think, 'oh so if I'm a girl I want to see the opposite sexes' genitals.' But that's a really simple way of thinking.

The ubiquity of the dick pic prompted speculation in focus groups about the mysterious nature of male sexuality. They recognised that girls and women might be sexually interested in the male form, but the specific focus on the genitals in the 'dick pic' remained troubling:

> **Lauren:** I don't think girls are that interested in getting images from guys, as guys are from girls.
>
> **Nancy:** Guys are more visual.
>
> **Lauren:** Yeah.
>
> **Nadine:** But like yeah girls would generally never ask for—oh well maybe, but it would be less.
>
> **Stephen:** There are girls out there who will.
>
> **Nadine:** Yeah for sure, but in comparison to the guys. I was going to say if it's like a guy topless, that would be something they would more likely

receive than everything and want to see everything. Well certainly I don't want to see everything.

Discussions on the 'dick pic' frequently turned to essentialist differences between men and women, including notions of masculine sexuality as 'more visual' and genitally focused. One woman suggested, 'They're [males] very visual people, to porn. Girls usually read. They read things.' Such speculation was couched almost exclusively in hegemonic terms that associated male sexuality with uncontrollable drives, visual erotic stimulation and a specifically genital fixation. In contrast, female desire was constructed as a morally superior but more diffuse eroticism that incorporated the face, personality and body rather than just the genitals. While this construct endowed women with sexual choice and moral agency that was not attributed to masculinity, it had a number of pernicious effects. It obscured the harassing and coercive dimensions of sending an unwanted 'dick pic' to a girl who was positioned instead as just 'unlucky' rather than victimised. Nadine said,

Sometimes I think you've just got to be really unlucky. Like one of my really good friends, she was being sent images from a guy who had a girlfriend, but I don't know what his motivation was. He kept sending her stuff that was pretty explicit. She wouldn't give anything in return, but he was and like, she didn't do anything about it, she didn't tell his girlfriend. She told me but I haven't told anyone, like you sort of need to be unlucky.

While girls who received unwanted images from boys were 'unlucky,' Nadine also argued that girls who find their own private images shared by boys 'sort of bring it upon themselves, like in sending it in the first place.' In her account, the locus of control and responsibility in online abuse is fixed within the girl or woman regardless of whether she is being sent unwanted images or having images of her circulated without her consent. Nadine appeared to be articulating an implicit position adopted by many other participants. Female participants discussed the unpleasant and harassing dimensions of being sent unwanted pictures, but they did not hold the male sender accountable for his actions. Instead, there

was some suggestion that perhaps the boys were just proud of their bodies and sent these images to 'celebrate.' Heather said,

Guys who like to work on getting really fit and muscly at the gym, a lot of them to celebrate such a thing take pictures of themselves in a mirror, they're mostly young guys.

The unlikely proposition that repeatedly bombarding a girl or woman with unwanted explicit photos was a symptom of youthful masculine exuberance was symptomatic of the systemic avoidance within focus groups of assigning responsibility to boys and men for online abuse. Interestingly, this was particularly pervasive among female participants. It was typically male participants who identified that online male wrongdoing was often deliberate. Ray said, 'I've got a bunch of female friends who've got pictures of guys' cocks, just randomly [sent to them]. So I mean that—I can compare that to the flasher with the raincoat really.' This was one of the few times in the focus group study in which the male perpetration of online harms such as 'dick pics' were linked to sexual harassment and gendered abuse.

POINTS OF CONFLICT AND CHANGE

In discussions about the non-consensual circulation of 'nudes' and 'dick pics,' a number of common themes emerged. The first was the different moral position assigned to boys and girls depicted in nude or bodily images, which are more likely to be seen as a breach of appropriate feminine but not masculine sexuality. This hints at the taken-for-granted public dimensions of masculinity, including a qualified acceptance of public male sexual self-display and expressions of desire, compared to the more closely policed construction of feminine sexuality as private and discrete. The second was the hyper-visibility of girls and women in the online exchange and circulation of these images. Whether girls and women were depicted in bodily images circulated without their consent, or they received unwanted images of male bodies, they became objects of attention and scrutiny in a manner that boys did not. Hope suggests that the impulse to attribute culpability to the victimised girl, while overlooking wrongdoing by the boy, was a deeply entrenched one:

> What I should be thinking is 'Oh my gosh, so this guy got broken up with, and he decided to ruin this girl's life by sending these around.' But inevitably, I don't know maybe we're culturally conditioned to do this, but we think in that moment 'She was taking a picture of herself, she was in this vain pose, what a stupid idea.'

Nonetheless, the preponderance of incidents of male perpetration of online abuse surfaced in a manner that challenged the ethos of presumptive gender equality that prevailed in focus groups. Social media, as an intensely visible medium, had the effect of rendering the advantages of masculinity as an explicit rather than implicit feature of online exchange. In this sense, it is the very publicness of social media that rendered the gendered inequities of online publics visible and therefore contestable. This section discusses two potential points of conflict and change: (1) the exposure of exploitative online practices and (2) challenging the invisibility of masculinity.

The Exposure of Exploitative Online Practices

While focus group discussions often adhered to an ideology of presumptive gender equality, preferring instead a highly individualised language of choice and agency, the circulation of 'nudes' and 'dick pics' challenged their collective disavowal of gendered explanations of wrongdoing. In focus groups, women described their disappointment and outrage in high school when male friends bonded by sharing 'nudes' with one another. They particularly objected when this activity occurred in front of them, which they saw it as disrespectful towards them and other girls present, if not towards the girl depicted in the image. Donna recalls confronting male friends crowding around another boy's phone: 'They're like "look at this, look at this," and I was like "Are you guys seriously just looking at this right now?"' Another woman recounted an incident in which a female friend found that her male 'best friend' had a 'nude' of her on his phone:

> I was sitting with this group of guys and I look over and there was a photo of a girl, and I was

sitting next to my friend and she was like 'grab that phone,' and she grabbed it and she realised it was her. So that's when it gets awkward, and then she full had a go at it because she's like 'You're my best mate, what are you doing?,' and he's like 'I didn't even know it was you.' So it's so weird.

Some women spoke with sadness about the loss of friendships with boys and men who they felt could no longer be trusted because they had sent them 'dick pics' or had circulated 'nudes' of other girls and women. It was clear that both male and female participants valued their platonic opposite-sex friendships, and these could be put at risk by male perpetration of online abuse. The sharing of pornography within male peer groups is an established homosocial bonding practice (Flood, 2008), and the open display of nude images of girls and women has often been used as a way of marking out male-segregated public spaces. The public nature of social media made such practices visible to girls and women, provoking confrontations as they demanded male adherence to norms of gender equality in deed as well as word.

Challenging the Invisibility of Masculinity

The relative impunity to humiliation enjoyed by boys and men in online publics rests on the taken-for-granted public qualities of masculinity. However, the scrutiny of appearance and behaviour that has attended the entry of girls and women into the public sphere has not left boys and men unscathed. There has been a dramatic increase in the visibility of the male body in the media and popular culture over the last two decades, resulting in significant shifts in masculine self-identity and practices (Gill et al., 2005). The male body has become, for many men and boys, a self-project to be modified and displayed in the achievement of an idealised masculinity (Gill et al., 2005). In this study, focus groups commented in particular on the rise of 'gym culture' and the idealisation of muscular physicality by boys in their teens. This was encapsulated in the 'gym selfie' in which boys and men post photos of their torsos to social media to 'show off' to potential partners and compare themselves with others. These performances represent masculine adjustments to the omnipresent gaze of social media and an increased awareness of both female and male scrutiny of the male form.

The increasing visible dimensions of masculinity could in some cases be used against boys and men who engaged in online abuse. In the following excerpt, Reece describes a situation at high school in which a girl who received an unwanted 'dick pic' retaliated by sending it to others. As previously discussed, it was often assumed by focus group participants that boys are effectively inoculated from such forms of public humiliation since, unlike girls, they can disavow the sexual or erotic implications of the image. However, the consensus position that this boy had a 'peanut,' or a small penis, gave the image a humiliating quality that it might otherwise not have had. Renee said,

> So there was a guy, one of my friends, yeah he sent a picture and it got around, and he wasn't very well . . . ah endowed, very well equipped down there. . . . He sent it to a few girls I think. . . . Everyone was pretty cruel to him about it, they called him 'peanut' for ages, and sometimes we still do call him peanut. It's kind of just become like a thing now. But yeah, we were pretty cruel to him about it.

In this incident, the boy's act of self-objectification in taking and sending an image triggers a comparable process of scrutiny and judgement to those that more commonly attend the circulation of the female 'nude.' The enhanced significance of the displayed body in performances of masculinity, the visual culture of social media and perhaps even the ubiquity of online pornography may all contribute to the positioning of male as well as female bodies as objects of sexualised scrutiny and assessment. This suggests that the relative invisibility of masculinity in online publics is not a fixed advantage, but rather it is in a state of flux, rendering some men and boys vulnerable to online humiliation where they are deemed to have fallen short of masculine ideals. . . .

CONCLUSION

While social media provides girls and women with new pathways to public representation, they must negotiate with norms of publicity and privacy that naturalise male public participation while

marking out girls and women in online publics as highly visible and legitimate objects of public scrutiny and judgement. Pejorative references to sex work and pornography clustered around young people's discussions of 'nudes' in a highly gendered fashion that attributed moral failure to the exposed public female, but not male, body. . . . This tendency was sustained in focus groups by a degendered vocabulary of individual agency and choice that characterised online abuse as the fault of particular 'types' of girls and women. However, as gendered patterns of online abuse became apparent in focus group discussions, they could not be entirely resolved within the normative frameworks of gender neutrality through which young people attempted to make sense out of their experiences. Social media had the effect of opening up homosocial bonding practices centred on female humiliation to public challenge by girls and women. Social media could also decentre masculinity as a privileged subject position and instead constitute it as an object of scrutiny and judgement, which has the potential to ameliorate or rebalance the gender inequities evident in the visual online economy.

As boyd (2014: 56) points out, some Internet commentators have argued that social norms will inevitably adapt to social media in a manner that reduces the threat of privacy invasion or even eliminates the need for privacy altogether. However, the young women and men in this focus group study did not seek to abandon privacy but rather they aspired to its more nuanced degrees. They articulate a desire for reasonable levels of 'privacy in public' (Solove, 2007); in effect, the right to engage in public life including social media on their own terms. This was a right granted, albeit in qualified ways, to young men in ways that it was not to young women, who could instead find publicity being used against them in a manner designed to reinforce traditional norms of private femininity. The focus group study also revealed the extent to which some young women continue to internalise responsibility for gendered victimisation and avoid attributing responsibility to those who perpetrate it, instead endorsing essentialist accounts of male sexuality that naturalised and excused sexual harassment and abuse. Ringrose (2011) has argued for a 'critical pedagogy' in high schools that acknowledges the sexualised and gendered dimensions of online publics and provides young people with the resources to interrogate and negotiate these. This study suggests a need to supplement legal reform and public awareness

campaigns about 'cyber-safety' with clear messages about the responsibility of perpetrators, and not victims, for online abuse.

NOTE

1. Snapchat is a social media network and mobile phone application that enables users to record and send digital images and video that are automatically erased after a brief period.

REFERENCES

Ahn J (2011) Digital divides and social network sites: which students participate in social media? *Journal of Educational Computing Research* 45(2): 147–163.

Albury K and Crawford K (2012) Sexting, consent and young people's ethics: beyond Megan's story. *Continuum* 26(3): 463–473.

Attwood F (2011) Through the looking glass? Sexual agency and subjectification online. In: Gill R and Scharff C (eds) *New Femininities: Postfeminism, Neoliberalism and Subjectivity.* Basingstoke: Palgrave Macmillan, pp. 203–214.

boyd d (2014) *It's Complicated: The Social lives of Networked Teens.* New Haven, CT; London: Yale University Press.

Davidoff L (2003) Gender and the 'great divide': public and private in British gender history. *Journal of Women's History* 15(1): 11–27.

Dobson AS (2014) Laddishness online: the possible significations and significance of 'performative shamelessness' for young women in the post-feminist context. *Cultural Studies* 28(1): 142–164.

Flood M (2008) Men, sex and homosociality: how bonds between men shape their sexual relations with women. *Men and Masculinities* 10(3): 339–359.

Fuchs C (2008) *Internet and Society: Social Theory in the Information Age.* New York; Abingdon: Routledge.

Gill R (2012) Media, empowerment and the 'sexualization of culture' debates. *Sex Roles* 66(11–12): 736–745.

Gill R, Henwood K and McLean C (2005) Body projects and the regulation of normative masculinity. *Body & Society* 11(1): 37–62.

Gordon MT and Riger S (1989) *The Female Fear: The Social Cost of Rape.* New York: Free Press.

Hasinoff AA (2013) Sexting as media production: rethinking social media and sexuality. *New Media & Society* 15(4): 449–465.

Jane EA (2014) 'Back to the kitchen, cunt': speaking the unspeakable about online misogyny. *Continuum* 28(4): 558–570.

Karaian L (2014). Policing 'sexting': Responsibilization, respectability and sexual subjectivity in child protection/crime prevention responses to teenagers' digital sexual expression. *Theoretical Criminology* 18(3): 282–299.

Lyon D and Bauman Z (2013) *Liquid Surveillance: A Conversation.* Cambridge; Malden, MA: Polity Press.

McRobbie A (2004) Notes on postfeminism and popular culture: Bridget Jones and the new gender regime. In: Harris A (ed.) *All about the Girl: Culture, Power and Identity.* New York; Oxon: Routledge, pp. 3–14.

Marwick AE and boyd d (2014) Networked privacy: how teenagers negotiate context in social media. *New Media & Society* 16(7): 1051–1067.

Papacharissi Z and Gibson P (2011) Fifteen minutes of privacy: privacy, sociality, and publicity on social network sites. In: Trepte S and Reinecke L (eds) *Privacy Online: Perspectives on Privacy and Self-Disclosure in the Social Web.* London; New York: Springer, pp. 75–89.

Pateman C (1988) *The Sexual Contract.* Oxford: Polity Press.

Poole E (2013) Hey girls, did you know: slut-Shaming on the internet needs to stop. *USFL Review* 48: 221–260.

Renold E and Ringrose J (2011) Schizoid subjectivities? Re-theorizing teen girls' sexual cultures in an era of 'sexualization.' *Journal of Sociology* 47(4): 389–409.

Ringrose J (2011). Are you sexy, flirty, or a slut? Exploring 'sexualization' and how teen girls perform/negotiate digital sexual identity on social networking sites. In: Gill R and Scharff C (eds) *New Femininities: Postfeminism, Neoliberalism and Subjectivity.* Basingstocke, New York: Palgrave Macmillan, pp. 99–116.

Ringrose J, Harvey L, Gill R, et al. (2013) Teen girls, sexual double standards and 'sexting': gendered value in digital image exchange. *Feminist Theory* 14(3): 305–323.

Salter M, Crofts T and Lee M (2013) Beyond criminalisation and responsibilisation: sexting, gender and young people. *Current Issues in Criminal Justice* 24(3): 301–316.

Solove DJ (2007) *The Future of Reputation: Gossip, Rumor, and Privacy on the Internet.* New Haven, CT: Yale University Press.

Sontag S (1977) *On Photography.* London: Penguin Books.

Tolman DL (2002) *Dilemmas of Desire: Teenage Girls Talk about Sexuality.* Cambridge, MA; London: Harvard University Press.

50

VIDEO GAMES
Machine Dreams of Domination
John Sanbonmatsu

In the space of just a few short decades, the computer video game has emerged from the shadows of geek subcultural obscurity to become the most pervasive entertainment medium in the world. In the US alone, over 150 million people—more than half the population—play video games, with 42% playing games for three hours or more each week (Entertainment Software Association, 2015). By comparison, about 75 million Americans attend professional baseball games each year and 40 million play chess ("National Chess," 2003). In 1980, the video game industry barely existed; today, it dwarfs every other media business but the music industry. In 2015, sales of video game software, hardware, and accessories totaled about $23 billion, twice what Hollywood made at the domestic box office that year.

The very ubiquity and popularity of video games suggests the need for us to pay critical attention to its cultural influence as a powerful new medium.[1] Though video games are often dismissed as trivial or unimportant, the reality is quite otherwise. As I will show, mainstream video game culture interpellates or "hails" us into aggressive and socially destructive forms of subjectivity and play, inviting the player to conceive of the world as little more than an arena for demonstrating mastery and control. Video games reinforce unjust social relations, encourage masculine fantasies of domination, and facilitate the ever more fateful intrusion of capitalism and technological fetishism into the fabric of daily life.

While some critics have depicted video games as benign and even emancipatory, portraying them as opportunities for players to experiment with new virtual identities, hone their hand-eye motor skills, engage in harmless pleasures, or even

challenge capitalism (Gee, 2007; Hourigan, 2003), other critics have been notably less sanguine, with mental health professionals, for example, warning of the highly addictive qualities of video games.[2] Most of the public debate about the societal impact of video games has focused on the question of whether games (and other forms of media violence) either cause or contribute to aggression or violence in society: periodic mass murders by young men who were avid players of first-person shooter (FPS) games have only added fuel to the debate.[3] Apologists for video games argue that studies of media violence have so far produced at best conflicting or ambiguous experimental results in the literature on media violence (Peckham, 2008). However, a number of robust meta-studies have in fact confirmed a link between playing violent games and aggressive behavior. In 2015, the American Psychological Association issued a press release stating that "existing quantitative reviews of the violent video game literature have found a direct association between violent video game use" and aggression, and that "higher amounts of exposure" to such games have been empirically "associated with higher levels of aggression and other adverse outcomes" (American Psychological Association, 2015). In 2016, similarly, a committee of the American Academy of Pediatrics concluded, after studying data from more than 400 studies involving media violence, that there is "a significant association" between exposure to media violence and "aggressive behavior . . . aggressive thoughts . . . angry feelings . . . and physiologic arousal," with video game violence correlated with even higher rates of adverse outcomes than other media. While the correlations between violent media exposure and aggression were only "in the small to moderate

---

This piece is an original essay that was commissioned for this volume. It has been updated from the version published in the third edition.

range," such correlations were nonetheless "stronger than the associations between passive smoking and lung cancer, and many municipalities have banned smoking because of that risk" (American Academy of Pediatrics, 2016).

Notwithstanding the addictive qualities of games and the preponderance of evidence suggesting a relationship between violent media and aggression, the main societal impact of video games is to be found elsewhere, particularly in their role in propagating regressive ideologies and reinforcing existing and unjust relations of power and authority in society. Feminists in particular have noted how much of the content of video games tends to mirror the perspective and values of the White, heterosexual men who create and overwhelmingly play them[4], observing that exaggerated sex stereotypy, misogyny, and simulated violence against women are the norm. Not only are the majority of game protagonists and heroes male, but the latter conform closely to hegemonic norms of masculinity—the stereotype of the aggressive, dominating man idealized by the wider patriarchal culture (Alloway and Gilbert, cited in Kline et al., 2003; Hill, n.d.). By the same token, the "femininity" of female characters is grossly exaggerated in games, with few games modeling a range of female body types for players to inhabit as avatars. Female characters are invariably thin and young, have unrealistic body proportions, and are typically depicted semi-nude or clad in clinging body suits, as in *Lara Croft: Tomb Raider* (Core Design, et al., 1996). In the game *Dead or Alive: Xtreme Beach Volleyball* (Tecmo), the erstwhile game objective is secondary to the player's ability to ogle virtual women's breasts and backsides. Other games have adopted the conventions of mainstream pornography—as in the first-person shooter game *Far Cry 3* (Ubisoft, 2012), in which the player's avatar has "point of view" sex with Citra, the mostly nude warrior-leader of a tribe of island "natives." Meanwhile, dozens if not hundreds of games invite the player to sexually exploit or even kill women within the game space. In the controversial Japanese video game *Rape-lay* the player stalks and rapes a woman and her two daughters (Illusion), while in Rockstar's *Grand Theft Auto* (*GTA*) series, one of the most popular games in industry history, the player can have virtual sex with a prostitute, then torture and murder her.

Online video game culture, like much of Internet culture as a whole, is itself intensely misogynistic, with male players of MMORPS (Massively Multi-Player Online Games) routinely directing derogatory comments towards female players, hounding them out of games, and showering male and female players alike with sexist and homophobic slurs. Male players have furthermore enthusiastically embraced the misogynistic "scripts" handed to them by the game companies. In the case of *GTA IV,* for example, dozens of men have posted videos on YouTube sharing their favorite methods of murdering prostitutes in the game—bludgeoning them with tire irons, knifing or shooting them, burning them alive, and blowing them up with hand grenades after driving their virtual victims to remote corners of the game's vast urban landscape (presumably to escape detection by the game's virtual police). The bodies of the women writhe and fall apart in a fair simulation of actual physical trauma and death, indicating the great attention which male software engineers using "frag physics" lavish on simulated violations of the human body. By essentially inviting male players to participate in simulated atrocities against women, such games trivialize and valorize gender violence. They may also dull players' empathetic responses to real-world victims of violence, especially individuals from vulnerable or subordinate social groups, though the experimental data remains inconclusive.

Hostility toward women and girls in the video game industry broke out into the open in 2014 with the "Gamergate" controversy, when three women involved in the video game industry became targets of a violently misogynistic campaign of "trolling" and threats from male gamers.[5] Gamer and media critic Anita Sarkeesian, in particular, was singled out for torrents of personal abuse for producing *Tropes vs. Women in Video Games,* a series of well-researched online videos deconstructing sexism and racism in video games. In revenge, incensed male gamers circulated a digitally altered photograph of Sarkeesian's face, beaten black and blue and with a broken nose. (Credible death threats against Sarkeesian forced her to cancel a scheduled appearance at the University of Utah in 2014.)

In noting the prevalence of racist representations in games, critics have elicited similar hate-filled responses from the predominantly White, male gamer community.[6] Racial and ethnic stereotypy is in fact the norm, rather than the exception, in mainstream video games, with African Americans and Latinos depicted in numerous games as drug kingpins or prostitutes (never as union organizers, hairdressers, or professors of literature), Asians as martial arts experts or sinister villains (never accountants or farmers), Arabs and Persians as blood-thirsty savages and terrorists (never as nurses, parents with elderly relatives to care for, or civilian casualties of US drone strikes) (Dean, 2005; Leonard 2003).[7] Racist and "Orientalist"[8] representations and narratives meanwhile often go hand in hand with regressive gender roles: as Sarkeesian notes of *Far Cry 3,* for example, while the game's White male protagonist, James Brody, is celebrated as the "white savior" of the indigenous islanders, the natives' leader, Citra, is the embodiment of every stereotype of the "exotic, primitive, mystical, savage, sexualized woman" (Sarkeesian, 2017).[9]

To be sure, not all games promote sexism and racism. Puzzle games like *Tetris* (Pajitnov and Pokhilko, 1987), eschew avatars altogether, and some role-playing games have included positive portrayals of gay or transgender characters (*Gone Home,* The Fullbright Company, 2013; *Mass Effect,* BioWare, 2007). Other games (like the music video game *Dance Dance Revolution* by Konami, 1998) engage in only mildly sexist stereotypy. Even more proactively, a handful of intrepid game designers have consciously encoded positive social values, such as gender equality, nonviolence, or empathy, into the mechanics of their games, producing games that are simultaneously ethical, innovative, and fun to play. Jonathan Blow's *Braid* (Number None, 2009), for example, an Xbox platform game, utilized a surprise ending to challenge the viewer's expectations about gender roles within game narratives, while the strategy game *A Force More Powerful* (International Center on Nonviolent Conflict and York Zimmerman Inc., 1999) invited players to organize a nonviolent student revolt against an authoritarian government in Serbia. Some recent role-playing games, such as *Life Is Strange* (Dontnod Entertainment, 2015) and *Depression Quest* (Quinn, 2013), have meanwhile created realistic female characters and sought to address important social themes, such as mental illness.

However, such games remain outliers, typically underselling the major game studio releases by several orders of magnitude. In the main, video games remain remarkable for the consistency with which they have continued to serve as potent conduits of the ideas and discourses most conducive to maintaining the status quo. Like other branches of what Adorno and Horkheimer termed the "culture industry," the video game industry both mirrors and strengthens existing power relations in society, conforming reality to prevailing ideologies, social expectations, and collective fantasies (Adorno and Horkheimer, 2007). At the same time, however, owing to their immersive and participatory qualities, video games are notably more persuasive as mechanisms of social indoctrination and control than other media.

A generation ago, media theorist Marshall McLuhan observed of the technologically mediated communications of his day that the "medium is the message." What McLuhan meant is that radio, television, and so on, are not neutral carriers of meaning, but themselves intensify, magnify, or otherwise alter the "scale" of our relations with one another (McLuhan, 1994). Today's interactive media, however, take this "message" to a whole other level. If as Ian Bogost observes "the logics that drive our [video] games make claims about who we are, how our world functions, and what we want it to become" (Bogost, 2007), it must be emphasized how much those logics are amplified by the interactive nature of the medium, and in ways that arguably correspond to a qualitative, not merely quantitative, transformation of the human personality. Anyone who has careened down the virtual streets of Chicago in *Project Gotham Racing* (Bizarre Creations, 2001) or joined a platoon of Marines patrolling the dusty streets of a Middle Eastern city in *Call of Duty 4* (Infinity Ward, 2007), can attest to the visceral power of the medium and to the degree to which intense player involvement heightens the psychological cathexis between human, machine, and onscreen narrative. While the video games industry disavows any connection between kids shooting virtual humans in the head and real-life mass shootings by children in our schools, the same industry in other market sectors routinely boasts that video games are without peer among media in shaping human behavior and psychology. As Simon Penny observes, "psychotherapists employ simulation technologies precisely because they have effect in people's lives" (Penny, 2004) and computer simulations are now widely used throughout the economy—by the aviation industry to train pilots, by hospitals to teach surgical techniques, by the finance industry to simulate trading transactions, by companies to train sales personnel in the arts of persuasion, by the nuclear power industry to train plant operators, etc. Mass shooters have found the technology effective, too: Anders Breivik, right-wing anti-Islamic fanatic who massacred 69 people (most of them teenagers) on the island of Utoya in Norway in 2011, has boasted that he trained for the killings on *Call of Duty: Modern Warfare 2* (Infinity Ward, 2005), playing the game for as much as 16 hours a day as part of what he termed his "training-simulation."[10] It is therefore implausible to maintain, as apologists for the video games industry often do, that the simulations we enact as consumers of video games do not in some manner educate and even train us into particular beliefs and behaviors, structuring our perception and thought in ways that we may not even be consciously aware of.[11] And with the shift to virtual reality headsets like Oculus Rift and HTC Vive computer games are poised to exert an even more powerful gravitational pull on our consciousness in the future.

WAR SIMULATION AND THE MILITARIZATION OF EVERYDAY LIFE

Without question, the institution that has capitalized most directly on the power of video games to model and modify human behavior is the Pentagon, which has invested billions of dollars in war simulations to train soldiers to kill and to help commanders engage in more effective battlefield tactics and strategy. Cold War nuclear war planning and the emergence of a permanent war economy in the US after the World War II produced both computerization and with it a new digital culture of war simulation. The video game, it must be recalled, developed organically out of what President Dwight D. Eisenhower termed "the military industrial complex," the institutional nexus between the national security state, private military contractors, and academia. A watershed came in 1961, when academic researchers working for the Department of Defense at MIT developed a digital game called *Spacewar*. Other researchers soon grasped the military potential of combining traditional war game simulations with

computerization. By the late-1970s, the Office of Naval Research established the "Theater-Level Gaming and Analysis Workshop for Force Planning"; by the early-1980s, the US was spending tens of millions of dollars on computer simulations like SIMNET, allowing dispersed participants to engage in real-time "war" over a virtual battlefield (Lenoir and Lowood, 2005); and by the 1990s, the Pentagon had built an elaborate national network bringing commercial video game design companies, university researchers, contractors, and the U.S. military together to form a new "military-industrial-*entertainment*" complex.

Today, video gaming and interactive computer simulations are central to U.S. war-making, from recruitment (*America's Army*, a MMORPG released by the U.S. Army in 2002, played by millions of youth) (Nichols, 2010), to conditioning soldiers (the U.S. Marine Corps adaptation of the FPS video game, *Doom*), to running large-scale battlefield simulations. DARWARS, a DARPA-funded program for the U.S. Joint Chiefs of Staff and Marine Corps, thus uses "webcentric, simulation-based trainers [to] take advantage of widespread PC-based technology, including multi-player games, virtual worlds, intelligent agents, and online communities" (U.S. Department of Defense, 2010),[12] while troops at the U.S. Army's PEO STRI war center (Program Executive Office for Simulation, Training, and Instrumentation) use "computerized simulators known as Reconfigurable Vehicle Tactical Trainers to run anti-bomb missions at Grafenwohr Training Area before they head downrange" (U.S. Army, 2009).

Simulations and combat differ now only in their effects, not in their "game" experience. In Afghanistan and Iraq, thus, NATO pilots who may have received training at PEO STRI use computer-guided weapons systems to drop "smart" munitions on real people, viewing their attacks onscreen, while U.S. Air Force and CIA personnel in Arizona and Nevada remotely pilot Predator and Reaper drones from many thousands of miles away, using flight sim joysticks identical to those used in consumer games to launch attacks that obliterate real human beings in Yemen, Pakistan, and other countries. Meanwhile, when Activision released *Call of Duty: Modern Warfare 2* (Infinity Ward, 2015), the game was widely praised by critics for its supposed attention to "realism." (In 2011, *Modern Warfare 3* raked in over $400 million in sales on its first day—an industry record.) Placed side by side, it was in fact virtually impossible to distinguish between actual video footage of C-130 gunships strafing human targets during night raids in Afghanistan at the time, and *Modern Warfare's* simulation of the same action, so highly detailed were the game's command protocols, infrared images, tactical, ballistics, and flight characteristics.[13] Needless to say, however, what gets described as "realism" in military FPS games, however, is only technological fetishism, not historical, psychological, or human truth. Elided in every war simulation are the actual human consequences of war, the terrible loss, trauma, and suffering, the deaths of children, the cries of wounded soldiers and animals, the grieving of relatives, and so on.

The extraordinary technical verisimilitude of today's military FPS games stems both from improvements in processing power and from the seamless integration of broad swaths of the video game industry with the Pentagon. Game designers cycle back and forth between the U.S. military and private companies, and commercial companies scrupulously model games on the latest in U.S. military doctrine, equipment, and weaponry. Some game companies even manufacture hardware and software for real-world weapon systems. SEGA, at the same time it had a lucrative contract with the Boeing corporation in the 2000s to produce computer boards for a real tactical fighter plane, was also producing *After Burner Climax,* a game which enabled players to select "aircraft from the F-14D Super Tomcat by Northrop Grumman to the F-15E Strike Eagle and F/A-18E Super Hornet by Boeing" ("Take to the Skies," 2017). The military-industrial-entertainment complex in this manner integrates entertainment and killing.

The deeply gendered nature of this project has been observed by a variety of critics, including Kline, Dyer-Witheford, and de Peuter, who observe that the video "game industry, conjured into being by technologically adept and culturally militarized men, made games reflecting the interests of its creators, germinating a young male subculture of digital competence and violent preoccupations" (Kline, et al., 2003, p. 257). Gaming culture has in fact become the main mechanism today for socializing the nation's male youth into militarism and an unthinking, pro-U.S. military worldview, with men and boys

now routinely playing at war using forms of software and hardware that resemble components used at DARWARS or in the Afghan "theater." Children sitting at their computer screens "play" using highly realistic virtual versions of such weapons as the Remington 700, AK-47, M16A4, M1 Garand, Walther PPK, etc., weapons whose onscreen behavior and technical specifications, even simulated recoil and sound, are almost identical to their real counterparts.[14] Meanwhile, aware that virtually every male child growing up today attains technical prowess in destroying virtual objects and enemies using commercial game controllers, the Pentagon has responded by integrating Xbox and Wii controllers into a growing number of its weapons systems and robotics controls (Derene, 2008).[15]

As the philosopher Herbert Marcuse suggested, the form and content of technological artifacts and mass culture in a repressive or destructive order tend to serve the ideological and practical needs of that order (Marcuse, 1968). In this regard, commercial video games do critical ideological work in mobilizing the population for permanent war and foreign aggression, by normalizing and dehistoricizing state violence and demonizing "authorized" enemies of the U.S. state. While many Americans believe that they live in a nation that uses violence as a last resort and then only in self-defense, the sad facts of U.S. foreign policy over the last century tell a quite different story, one of military aggression, counterrevolution, support for brutal dictatorships, violent overthrow of democratic governments, and mass violence (Johnson, 2004, 2005; Chomsky, 2004). Despite these facts, virtually all military FPS games (including historical war games) celebrate U.S. military and technological prowess and supremacy, while depicting America's enemies as worthy only of extermination. The narrative content of FPS games since the September 11 attacks in particular have reiterated the values and policy assumptions of the so-called war on terror, cognitively mapping the world for American soldiers and citizenry alike to prepare them "for colonial exercises of spatial domination"—as in the game *Kuma\War,* which includes mission titles like "Freedom's Heroes: The Road to Baghdad," and which claims to faithfully reenact actual historical battles, including the US invasion of Iraq in 2003 (King and Leonard in Huntemann, 2010; Dyer-Witheford and de Peuter, 2009, p. 101). As Höglund observes, such games serve the interests of the U.S. state by constructing the entire Middle East "as a frontier zone where a perpetual war between US interests and Islamic terrorism" can be enacted. The result is a new Orientalism in which "the gamer involved in a military shooter set in the Middle East is forever performing . . . strategic containment of the Other"—the dark-skinned barbarian perpetually threatening the innocent redoubt of Western civilization (Höglund, 2008; Sisler, 2008).[16]

The racialization and militarization of space has meanwhile also been mapped by games onto domestic urban landscapes. Since the September 11 attacks, as a creeping militarism has taken over our society—the breakdown of cultural, psychological, and even operational barriers between military and civilian life (Bacevich, 2013)—video games have abetted this disturbing trend. Civil society itself is frequently depicted in games as a militarized war zone, a space for players to symbolically enact aggression and thus play out the destructive social "scripts" authorized by the wider culture—particularly against people of color. The *GTA* series, for example, notoriously introduced a range of destructive weaponry into the game's virtual neighborhoods. Players have even modified *GTA V* (Rockstar, 2013) under the rubric of "Urban Warfare"—an all too accurate depiction both of the game's militarism and of the growing, real-world firepower and militarization of police forces in the US (Polasek, 2014). Naturally, however, the game's representation of the colonized is from the perspective of the colonizer: urban poverty, police brutality, crime syndicates, and gang violence are not depicted as serious social problems crying out for concerted citizen action, or governmental reform, but as opportunities for vicarious thrill-seeking by the game's overwhelmingly White, middle class, and male target audience.

CAPITALISM AND INSTRUMENTAL REASON

Even when the content of video games is not overtly violent, the medium conveys an educative "message" that instrumental manipulation of the world, self, and other is both natural and desirable. The cognitive and behavioral modality built into the overwhelming majority of video games is *control* of the representational world, rather than an attitude of *receptivity* towards it. The video game in this regard perfectly distills what Marcuse and other critical theorists termed *instrumental reason:* that is, a form of subjectivity, consciousness, and action in which the entirety of the living world and cosmos gets treated as a "thing" to be manipulated—or even destroyed—at will.

Perhaps the most characteristic feature of instrumental reason is a process under capitalism which the German sociologist Max Weber termed "rationalization," corresponding to the reduction of our "qualitative" experiences and relations with others to purely *quantitative* measures. As the philosopher Hannah Arendt observed of *homo faber* or "Man the maker" (a term sometimes used to designate the human essence),

> his instrumentalization of the world, his confidence in his tools and in the productivity of the maker of artificial objects; his trust in the all-comprehensive range of the means-ends category, his conviction that every issue can be solved and every human motivation reduced to the principle of utility; his sovereignty, which regards everything given as material and thinks of the whole of nature as [a mere thing to be made into whatever we wish]. (Arendt, cited in Scharff and Dusek, 2003).

In the popular video game *Minecraft,* thus, players manipulate blocks to construct (or blow up) cities, farms, buildings, and so on. Notwithstanding the often ingenious and creative ways players have made use of the program, *Minecraft* consistently reinforces a "Cartesian" conception of the natural world, reducing even other sentient animals to the status of homogeneous units of inert matter to be manipulated and disposed of at the player's whim.[17] The roots of this "instrumentalization of the world" are deep: they go back at least far as ancient Greek culture and myth, which celebrated the "cunning" of human reason in its capacity to master and dominate the world. However, it was not until the emergence of capitalist social relations in modern Europe that nature and other animals came to be viewed exclusively as "thing-like," as dead matter to be manipulated at will. It was at this time that the logic of the commodity under capitalist relations—the logic of abstraction and numeracy (what the philosopher Husserl [1970] termed the "mathematization of nature")—emerged as the dominant perceptual template through which Western culture viewed the world.

Computerization represents the ultimate triumph of this process, a victory of the quantitative over the qualitative in our encounters with the real. As critic Michael Heim warns, however, what we "gain in power" through the system of technological abstraction comes at the expense "of our direct involvement with things" (Heim, 1993, p. 18). We learn to think and perceive in fragments, to "outsource" our skills and consciousness to machinic entities, and to treat one another with brutal, offhand indifference. Reality collapses into solipsism: the world seems to organize itself around *my* needs and desires. The human and animal body—the true ground of all our experiences and ways of knowing—is diminished, or becomes a target for expressions of rage and violence. Virtual reality leads to the subject's *disembodiment,* her estrangement from the real, sensuous world.[18] Other sentient animals meanwhile exist in the virtual world solely as objects to be manipulated or exterminated.[19]

The instrumentalist conception of the world achieves its fullest representational expression in first-person shooter games, where the subject's interaction with others is typically represented by a disembodied weapon floating in mid-air. But a similar dynamic pervades strategy games, like Sid Meier's critically acclaimed *Civilization III* (Firaxis, 2001), as well. These games treat history from a social Darwinist perspective, with the God-like player invited to preside over a narrative in which groups of humans or other beings dominate or subdue one another (typically on the basis of their technologies—itself a crude reduction of actual historical processes, which are driven by social rather than technological development) (Friedman, 1999; Galloway, 2006). Instrumentalism also stalks ostensibly innocent games like the lucrative *Sims* franchise, where living processes—whether life in the suburbs or life evolving on another planet (as in *Spore*)—are reduced to the player's cost-benefit decisions. In the original *Sims,* the player lives in a middle class, White suburban neighborhood; she shops, raises a family, pursues a career, forms friendships, dates, etc., all the while keeping an eye on quantitative status bars that allow her to monitor her Sim's biological functions, social status, and so on. Life is reduced to a sequence of strategic moves to maximize one's egoistic interests, with the Sim player assuming the role of a technocratic manager over his or her own virtual life, "controlling and predicting and directing the behavior of a very finely tuned market niche, a 'segment of one'" (Kline et al., 2003, p. 278). As J. C. Herz writes, "everything is an object that yields a measurable benefit when some action is performed on it . . ." (cited in Kline et al., 2003). Other human beings are viewed as a mere means for maximizing one's own self-interest. "Even having children is a means to an end," Kline et al. (2003), observe, "since it is through the interaction of your Sims' kids with the neighbors that adult Sims get to know each other" and that one builds the connections one needs to advance one's career and increase one's income. Embedded in such conceptions of life is what can only be described as a neoliberal ideological framework.[20]

Egoism is by no means an incidental feature of the *Sims* world but is "formally engineered into the game-play" in order to achieve the overriding strategic objective of all commercial gaming culture: to integrate the player into the circuits of real-world capitalist production and consumption (Herz, cited in Kline et al., p. 276). The computer video game is in many ways the "ideal" commodity of post-Fordist capitalism, the exemplary form of a system that now requires "a ceaseless stream of new commodities with ever-shortening product cycles and life-spans" if it is to avoid systemic crisis and breakdown. The information revolution made it possible for capital to circumvent the objective limits of an older "regime" of capital accumulation (Kline et al., 2003, pp. 66). Just as the post-1980s era of speculative finance capital led banking institutions and consumers to invest in "virtual" or fictive financial commodities—credit default swaps and other esoteric derivatives—the need of capital to colonize new markets extended commodity fetishism into the *virtual* realm. Where once computer games had to be tethered to bulky media like cathode-ray TVs, or hulking, stationary consoles at an arcade, today games leap nimbly from cell phone and laptop to iPad and Xbox, heedless of spatial or temporal limits. Whereas chess can be played for free and has remained much the same, with few modifications, for centuries, today's virtual games are highly expensive to produce and are designed to be obsolete within months, thus requiring the consumer to spend money almost continuously. Meanwhile, the game worlds themselves have become commodified. In *Second Life,* for example, players spend real money to buy virtual clothes from the Gap and other real-world, mainstream retail chains, while in *World of Warcraft,* some players use their credit cards to hire sweatshop laborers in China to mine virtual gold for them (Dyer-Witheford and de Peuter, 2009, pp. 137–151; Castronova, 2005).

When commercial video games tap into the thwarted libidinal energies of players, they do so in order to spin virtual flax into the real gold of the capitalist economy. Multinational corporate behemoths like Sony, Entertainment Arts, and Activision spend tens of millions of dollars on marketing campaigns to manipulate the consciousness and behavior of the millions of children, teenagers, and young adults in the industrialized North who together make up the lucrative youth market—in 2000, worth up to $164 billion (Kline et al., 2003, p. 221). As Kline et al., point out,

> . . . [When] one looks at the . . . economic, technological, and cultural forces shaping *The Sims* gamer—not merely as the participant in a . . . scripted and designed play scenario but also as a member of a population among which certain levels of technological familiarity are increasingly normalized, required, and rewarded, and as the target of a high-intensity marketing regime designed to elicit certain levels of consumption activity—much of [his] apparent autonomy and empowerment evaporates. The player reappears as object, not subject, the product of a system . . . partially programmed . . . as much played upon as player. (p. 279)

To some extent, the player actively colludes in these processes himself, cynically, knowing full well that the real game in town is the game of consumerism and profit realization. Yet in truth, the player only dimly comprehends the degree to which his own thoughts, values, and desires have been commandeered and integrated into a regime of power whose destructive features more and more serve to render his own consciousness, his own sovereignty as a thinking subject, effectively obsolete.

CONCLUSION

Drawing upon the psychological theories of Sigmund Freud, Herbert Marcuse offered an account of how the repression of human "libidinal" or instinctual needs by the dominant order of wealth and power has yielded ever more destructive forms of culture. As capitalism becomes more advanced, he suggested, a gap develops between the creative and productive forces of society—our potential to make the world a livable and just one—and pathological forms of social life. Eventually, the result comes to be "a suicidal tendency on a truly social scale" (Marcuse, 1968, p. 268)—perpetual mobilization for war, terrorism, mass destruction of nature and animals, heightened aggressiveness in all arenas of life and culture. In this process of decay, technology plays an especially pivotal role. As the distillation of an "instrumentalist" mentality, technology strengthens the life-denying system and effectively shields it from effective revolt by those whom it has stripped of dignity and power. Rather than being used to enlighten and educate the public, for example, the technologies of mass media are used to blur together existential opposites—death and life, killing and culture, sadism and joy. These new false "unities" then get sold back to us as commodities. As Marcuse wrote:

> The brutalization of language and image, the presentation of killing, burning, and poisoning and torture inflicted upon the victims of neocolonial slaughter is made in a common-sensible, factual, sometimes humorous style which integrates these horrors with the pranks of juvenile delinquents, football contests, accidents, stock market reports, and the weatherman (Marcuse, 1968, p. 259).

Such "brutalization of language and image" is rampant across the media spectrum today, from AM talk shows and television to cinema, social media, and video games. In 2016, the three most popular new games across all platforms were *Call of Duty: Infinite Warfare* (Infinity Ward), *Battlefield I* (Electronic Arts), and *Tom Clancy's The Division* (Ubisoft)—all first-person military shooter games. Those games were followed in popularity by two male-oriented sports games (*NBA 2K17* and *Madden NFL 17*), with the three next most popular games also featuring extremely violent and explicit game play (*Grand Theft Auto V, Overwatch,* and *Call of Duty: Black Ops III*). Notwithstanding the superficial diversity of today's video games, which range from platform and role-playing games to sports, fashion, and dancing games, etc., themes of violence, sadism, and war still predominate, confirming Marcuse's thesis concerning the interpenetration of the entertainment complex and the most violently repressive institutions of society and state (Reisinger, 2017).

Such a system requires a corresponding form of human subjectivity or consciousness in order to maintain itself. People must want—or be made to want—to hurt others in their fantasy life. In 2013, in this regard, one of the most popular paid games downloaded on the iPhone was "Plague Inc." by NDemic, in which the player must try to kill every human being on earth "by evolving a deadly, global Plague," infecting nonhuman animals, water supplies, and particular nations, all the while strategizing to defeat the player's enemy—the human race ("Wipe Out Humanity," the game's trailer urges[21]). That millions of people should now be choosing to pass their idle moments fantasizing about ways to commit mass genocide (indeed, to exterminate the species) tells us everything we might want to know about the truly degraded state of contemporary culture. Of an individual who takes pleasure in designing such a game—or in playing it—we must conclude, following Marcuse, that such a person bears "the marks of a mutilated human being" (Marcuse, 1968). In Freud's theory, the healthy individual in a healthy society channels or "sublimates" his or her instinctual needs into socially productive activities—art, work, family relations, and so on. However, Marcuse believed that our pathological social order requires what he termed "surplus" repression. That is, the system takes the individual's creative powers and now channels them into socially *destructive* forms. Forced to adapt his life-instincts to the external needs of an unjust social order, the individual now effectively "collaborates in his own repression, in the containment of potential individual and social freedom, [and hence] in the release of aggression" (Marcuse, 1968, p. 254).

But "society's ingression into the psyche," as Marcuse terms it, could not gain traction without our own collusion and consent (Marcuse, 1968, p. 254). We hunger for escapist forms of entertainment because they offer the illusion of restoring to us something that has been lost—a sense of our own personal agency and efficacy in a world that seems increasingly chaotic, dangerous, and out of control. Tellingly, the prevalence of omnipotence fantasies in video games has increased in inverse proportion to the citizen-subject's actual power in society—her ability to hold public officials, corporations, and states accountable in an era of globalization. "[H]ere everyone is a god who, if they are not omniscient all at once, can at least entertain whatever information they will to have at any time they wish to have it'" (Kroker and Weinstein, as cited in Balbus, 2005, p. 124.) As the earth's atmosphere goes haywire from global warming, species are hounded to extinction by capitalist development, and our nation's democracy slips into authoritarianism or worse, the digital world becomes a more and more welcoming refuge. Paradoxically, though, the more enmeshed we become in our digital devices, the more we participate in simulations of life, the more estranged we become from real life and from those around us (Turkle, 2011). Shrinking from genuine social connection and political engagement, we may mistake the limitless expanse of a "sandbox" game for a realm of true freedom, forsaking forms of speech and action that might actually make a difference in the real world. In a vain attempt to "escape" from our freedom, and from responsibility to others, we may even embrace the very death fetishism and "desublimated" aggression that is dooming the earth and us along with it.

In 1990, Peter Schumann, the founder and director of the Bread and Puppet Theater (a group that has long strived to defend the redemptive, socially transformative possibilities of the arts), noted the power of commercial media culture to coarsen and cheapen human life:

> The . . . aping of kitchen and bedroom intimacy, and [of] the intimacy of pain—that is what is so demeaning. Real pain in life is a serious relative of death, a terrorizer, usually a visitor of great consequence. The detailed, imitated pain in movies makes a mockery of the vital resources which enable our nature to fight pain or even submit to pain gracefully (Schumann, 1990).

Schumann's remarks seem especially apropos today, as media culture beckons to us not merely to watch spectacles of cruelty and degradation, passively, but to actively enact cruelty and degradation ourselves through our avatars. "Playing violent antisocial games, we come to believe that we are heroically defeating evil enemies. In reality, with every virtual bullet to the head, every virtual knife to the stomach, each virtual punch in the face, we are only laying siege to our own endangered humanity. By mocking suffering and pain, we ally ourselves symbolically and psychologically with the instruments of death, against the vital forces of life" (Sanbonmatsu, 2013). The worst thing about video game culture, in this regard, is the way it burrows down into the marrow of human consciousness to poison the moral imagination as such, limiting our ability even to picture a different kind of world. What we need, though, and need urgently, is an effective simulation of a caring and just society.

NOTES

1. It is no exaggeration to claim, as some authors have, that we are witnessing today "the total engulfing of society in gamelike simulations." Kline, Dyer-Witheford, de Peuter (2003, p. 70).

2. Video game addiction is such a widespread phenomenon in China that thousands of Chinese parents have sent their children to special camps to free them of their addiction (West, 2016). Although mental health professionals remain divided about whether or not to classify compulsive video game use an addiction, the American Psychiatry Association now formally recognizes what it calls "Internet gaming disorder," or "distress or problems functioning" due to excessive online game playing (American Psychiatry Association, 2016).

3. See, for example, media coverage of the video game activity of Dylan Klebold and Eric Harris, who massacred fellow students at Columbine High School in 1999, and of Adam Lanza, who murdered 20 school children and six adults at Sandy Hook Elementary School in 2012 (Madhani, 2013; Simpson & Blevins, 2000).

4. About 76% of game developers are White, and 78% are male—but both figures in fact understate the homogeneity of the industry, because the vast majority of senior-level game developers, managers, and owners are White men (Ong, 2016; "Percentage of Female Developers," 2014).

5. Quinn's sin had been to produce a well-received game called *Depression Quest,* and to have been in a relationship with a game designer who later savaged their relationship online (Parkin, 2014).

6. In 2012, for example, the creators of a website called "Gamers Against Bigotry" were forced to take the site down after its home page was vandalized with racist virtual graffiti (Shreier, 2012).

7. Though less often remarked, classism in video games is also a norm, with poor and working class people, particularly those in urban neighborhoods, depicted as crude, stupid, and violent.

8. "Orientalism," a term originally developed by the literary critic Edward Said, describes any form of representation or discourse that reduces a particular racial group or people to an inferior and typically exoticized "other," precisely as a way of establishing the cultural superiority of the more dominant racial group.

9. In one of the two alternate endings of the game, Citra stabs Brody to death after having sex with him (having now become impregnated with the tribe's future leader), thus uniting two popular themes in many video games—sexually objectified women and explicit violence—through the racist trope of the "voodoo" priestess.

10. Breivik was so taken with one gunsight in the game that he had the real version installed on the rifle, using it in committing his crime. Another killer, Aaron Alexis, who used a U.S. Naval installation as his own first person shooter "game," killing 12, had reportedly played the same game obsessively in the days and weeks leading up to his attack. "He played all the time. That was his passion," a friend of Alexis later told ABC News. "It got so bad—was in his room all the time . . . he'd be late for work" (Castellano, 2013).

11. I myself have found that after playing a highly realistic car racing game set in urban areas around the United States, I began driving more aggressively in the hours after playing the game. I had a similar experience playing *Splinter Cell,* in which the player has to stealthily sneak past enemies (and sometimes kill them) and continually has to find ways of crawling in, through, over, or around built structures. Entering my kitchen after playing the game, I noticed for the first time a vertical water pipe running from the floor to the ceiling—and felt the distinct urge to climb it. Some years ago, a student of mine (who was at that time playing first-person shooter games 40 hours per week) told me that when he spoke to other students around campus, he would suddenly find himself imagining what it would be like "for their heads to explode."

12. I am greatly indebted to Nina Huntemann for her research on military uses of video game technologies.

13. Both the real C-130 footage and the simulacral footage were available on YouTube in April 2010. I want to thank Darius Kazemi for bringing this footage to my attention.

14. In today's FPS games, "bullet penetration now takes into account incredibly fine details, like whether the target is wearing leather or cloth." As a game designer at Ubisoft explains, when "someone shoots through a plant, then a car door, then it hits Level 3 body armor, all of that effects the force of the round," requiring an "excessively complex" programming formula to simulate real-world ballistics (Sofge, 2008).

15. Even ostensibly benign children's games have become inflected with technological aggression and fantasies of domination. In Pokémon, thus, the player's avatar roams the world trying to enslave "as many of several hundred elusive creatures" as possible. "Once you leash one and it becomes part of your menagerie, you then train it and make it more powerful by carrying it around and deploying it in battles against other trainers" (Schiesel, 2010). Similarly, on the website of one educational software company, elementary school children can learn mathematics by blasting away at a phalanx of advancing tanks, in the game *Demolition Division* (Arcademics, 2017).

16. As David Nieborg points out, the U.S. Army's *America's Army MMORPG* "has become a powerful vessel for disseminating U.S. Army ideology and foreign policy to a global game culture" (as cited in Höglund, 2008, p. 9).

17. "Cartesianism" refers to the metaphysics of the 17th century French philosopher, René Descartes, who maintained the universe consisted of only two types of entities, mind and matter or "stuff." Among other things, Descartes concluded that nonhuman animals were nothing but complicated machines. Many critics have rejected Cartesianism dualism, as it is called, on grounds that it obscures the complex and varied nature of consciousness, particularly as it exists in and through the body.

18. South Korea, a nation so obsessed with video games that some citizens have literally played themselves to death, became a tragic proving ground for this estrangement when authorities arrested a couple in 2010 for child abuse and neglect when the parents left "their 3-month-old daughter to starve to death while they raised a virtual daughter online during 12-hour bouts at a cyber cafe." The couple had become addicted to Prius Online (CJ Internet, 2008), a game akin to Second Life (Linden Lab, 2003), where players engage in virtual work and virtual relationships, and "[earn] an extra avatar to nurture once they reach a certain level." One police officer observed: "'The couple seemed to have lost their will to live a normal life because they didn't have jobs and gave birth to a premature baby.... They indulged themselves in the online game of raising a virtual character so as to escape from reality, which led to the death of their real baby.'" The virtual child, ironically named Anima (the Latin word for "breath" or "soul," which in ancient usage meant a living being) flourished; meanwhile, the real baby perished from "severe dehydration and malnutrition" (Frayer, 2010). While one

must of course be careful not to make too much of a single case, the incident serves as a frightening reminder of what can happen when flesh and blood human beings become subordinated to, and indeed absorbed into, the realm of virtual commodities.

19. The most popular game in the world in 2009 was *Farmville* (Zynga, 2009), a Facebook-based application that had been played by more than 60 million people, in which players controlled a simulated farm, planting and harvesting crops and raising animals for slaughter (Quenqua, 2009). In *Deer Drive* (SCS Software, 2010) and hundreds of other hunting games, the object is literally to massacre as many animals, of different species, as quickly as possible. Rather more subtly, in *Endless Ocean Blue World* (Arika, 2010), an otherwise beautifully rendered ocean exploration game for Wii, the player is periodically invited to fire a "pulsar gun" at passing fish. In a twist, however, the player shoots the fish not to kill them, but to "heal" them from some sickness. This apparent concession by the design company

to the ubiquitous first-person shooter genre, however, only seemed to confuse the gamers who played it. Players' comments about the game (seen by the author online), included: "Heal fish? I don't get the theme of this game" and "You have to be kidding me." What indeed is the point of having a gun—that heals?

20. As Chicago School economist Milton Friedman wrote in *Capitalism and Freedom,* his celebration of neoliberal capitalism, "children are at one and the same time consumer goods and potentially responsible members of society" (Friedman, 2002, p. 33). In their separate ways, both Friedman and the *Sims* confirm the hidden logic of capital, which is to reduce all labor, all living beings, to the status of things.

21. An alternative to committing mass genocide as the game objective is to create a virus that would merely enslave humanity. The game is especially chilling given the relative ease with which deadly pathogens can now be genetically engineered in the laboratory (NDemic, 2017).

REFERENCES

Adorno, Theodor, and Max Horkheimer. (2007). *Dialectic of Enlightenment.* Stanford: Stanford University Press.

Alloway, Nola, and Pam Gilbert. (1988). Video Game Culture: Playing with Masculinity, Violence, and Pleasure," in Sue Howard, ed., *Wired-Up: Young People and the Electronic Media.* London: University of London College Press.

American Academy of Pediatrics. (2016). "Virtual Violence" (Policy Statement, Council on Communications and Media), *Pediatrics.* July 2016. Retrieved at http://pediatrics.aappublications.org/content/early/2016/07/14/peds.2016-1298.

American Psychiatry Association. (2016). "Can You Be Addicted to the Internet?" July 20, 2016. Retrieved at https://www.psychiatry.org/news-room/apa-blogs/apa-blog/2016/07/can-you-be-addicted-to-the-internet.

American Psychological Association. (2015). "APA Review Confirms Link Between playing violent video games and aggression" (press release), August

13, 2015. Retrieved at http://www.apa.org/news/press/releases/2015/08/violent-video-games.aspx.

Arcademics. (2017). "Demolition Division." Retrieved at http://www.arcademics.com/games/demolition/demolition.html.

Arika. (2010). *Endless Ocean Blue World* [video game]. Kyoto: Nintendo.

Bacevich, Andrew J. (2013). *The New American Militarism: How Americans Are Seduced By War.* New York: Oxford University Press.

Balbus, Isaac. (2005). *Mourning and Modernity.* New York: The Other Press.

BioWare. (2007). *Mass Effect* [video game]. Redwood City, CA: Electronic Arts.

Bizarre Creations. (2001). *Project Gotham Racing* [video game]. Redwood City, CA: Microsoft.

Blizzard Entertainment. (2016). *Overwatch* [video game]. Irvine, CA: Blizzard Entertainment.

Blizzard Entertainment. (2004). *World of Warcraft* [video game]. Irvine, CA: Blizzard Entertainment.

Bogost, Ian. (2007). *Persuasive Games: The expressive power of video games.* Cambridge: MIT Press.

Castellano, Anthony (2013). "Navy Yard Shooter Aaron Alexis Angry, Frustrated, and Vengeful," *ABC News,* Sept. 17, 2013. Retrieved at http://abcnews.go.com/US/navy-yard-shooter-aaron-alexis-angry-frustrated-vengeful/story?id=20276128

Castronova, Edward. (2005). *Synthetic Worlds: The Business and Culture of Online Games.* Chicago: University of Chicago Press.

Chan, Dean. (2005). "Playing with Race: The Ethics of Racialized Representations in e-Games," *International Review of Information Ethics, 4* (12), pp. 24–30.

Chomsky, Noam. (2004). *Hegemony or Survival.* New York: Henry Holt.

CJ Internet. (2008). *Prius Online* [video game]. Tokyo: Gpotato.

Core Design. (2001). *Lara Croft: Tomb Raider* [video game]. Eidos Interactive.

Derene, Glenn. (2008). "Wii all you can be? Why the military needs the gaming industry," *Popular Mechanics,* May 29, 2008. Retrieved at http://www.popularmechanics.com/technology/military_law/4266106.html.

Dontnod Entertainment. (2015). *Life Is Strange.* [video game]. Tokyo and London: Square Enix and Feral Interactive.

Dyer-Witheford, Nick, and Grieg de Peuter. (2009). *Games of Empire: Global Capitalism and Video Games.* Minneapolis: Univ. of Minnesota Press.

EA Digital Illusions CE AB. (2002). *Battlefield I* [video game]. Redwood City, CA: Electronic Arts.

EA Tiburon. (2016). *Madden NFL 17* [video game]. Redwood City, CA: Electronic Arts.

Entertainment Software Association. (2015). *Essential Facts About the Computer and Video Games Industry.* Entertainment Software Association.

Firaxis Games. (2001). *Civilization III* [video game]. Lyon: Infogrames

Fullbright Company (2013). *Gone Home* [video game]. Portland, OR: Fullbright Company.

Frayer, Lauren. (2010). "Baby starved as couple nurtured virtual kid," *AOL News,* March 10, 2010. Retrieved at http://www.aolnews.com/crime/article/south-korean-couple-nurtured-virtual-child-as-their-baby-starved-police-say/19384636).

Friedman, Milton. (2002). *Capitalism and Freedom.* Chicago: University of Chicago.

Friedman, Ted. (1999). "Civilization and Its Discontents: Simulation, Subjectivity, and Space," in G. Smith, ed., *Discovering Discs: Transforming Space and Place on CD-ROM.* New York: New York University Press, pp. 132–50.

Fromm, Erich. (1994). *Escape from Freedom.* New York: Henry Holt.

Galloway, Alexander. (2006). *Gaming: Essays on Algorithmic Culture.* Minneapolis: University of Minnesota Press.

Game Freak and Creatures, Inc. (1996). *Pokémon* [video game]. Kyoto: Nintendo.

Gee, James Paul. (2007). *What video games have to teach us about literacy and learning,* Second edition. New York: St. Martin's Press.

Heim, Michael. (1993). *The Metaphysics of Virtual Reality.* New York: Oxford University Press.

Hill, Nathalie. (n.d.) "Playing with Patriarchy," *Cerise Magazine.* Retrieved at http://cerise.theirisnetwork.org/archives/9.

Höglund, Johan. (2008). "Electronic Empire: Orientalism Revisited in the Military Shooter," *Game Studies,* vol. 8, no. 1, Sept. 2008.

Hourigan, Ben. (2003). "The utopia of open space in role-playing videogames," paper delivered to the Digital Arts and Culture Conference. Melbourne.

Husserl, Edmund. (1970). *The Crisis of European Sciences and Transcendental Phenomenology.* Evanston, IL: Northwestern University Press.

Infinity Ward. (2016) *Call of Duty: Infinite Warfare* [video game]. Santa Monica: Activision.

Infinity Ward. (2007). *Call of Duty 4* [video game]. Santa Monica, CA: Activision.

Infinity Ward. (2005). *Call of Duty: Modern Warfare 2* [video game]. Santa Monica: Activision.

International Center on Nonviolent Conflict and York Zimmerman Inc. (1999). *A Force More Powerful* [video game]. Hunt Valley, MD: Breakaway Games.

Johnson, Chalmers. (2005). *The Sorrows of Empire*. New York: Metropolitan Books.

Johnson, Chalmers. (2004). *Blowback: The Costs and Consequences of American Empire*. New York: Henry Holt.

King, C. R., and David J. Leonard. (2010). "Wargames as a New Frontier: Securing American Empire in Virtual Space," in Nina B. Huntemann and Matthew T. Payne, eds., *Joystick Soldiers: The Politics of Play in Military Video Games*. New York: Routledge.

Kline, Stephen, and Nick Dyer-Witheford, and Grieg de Peuter. (2003). *Digital Play: Inside the Interaction of Technology, Culture, and Marketing*. Montreal: McGill-Queens University Press.

Konami. (1998). *Dance Dance Revolution* [video game]. Minato: Konami.

Kuma Reality Games. (2004). *Kuma\War* [video game]. New York: Kuma Reality Games.

Lenoir, Tim, and Henry Lowood. (2005). "Theaters of War: The Military-Entertainment Complex," in *Collection—Laboratory—Theater: Scenes of Knowledge in the 17th Century,* ed. by Helmar Schramm, Ludger Schwarte, and Jan Lazardzig (Berlin & New York: Walter de Gruyter, 2005), pp. 427–56.

Leonard, David. (2003). "'Live in Your World, Play in Ours': Race, Video Games, and Consuming the Other," *Studies in Media & Information Literacy Education,* Vol. 3, Issue 4. Nov. 2003, pp. 1–9.

Linden Lab. (2003). *Second Life* [video game]. San Francisco: Linden Lab.

Madhani, Aamer. (2013). "In Newtown Book, 'What-Ifs?' Remain Unanswered," *USA Today,* Dec. 8, 2013. Retrieved at https://www.usatoday .com/story/life/books/2013/12/08/newtown-an-american-tragedy-review/3862821/.

Marcuse, Herbert. (1968). *Negations: Essays in Critical Theory*. Trans. by Jeremy J. Shapiro. Boston: Beacon Press, 1968.

Massive Entertainment. (2016). *Tom Clancy's The Division* [video game]. Rennes, France: Ubisoft.

Maxis. (2008). *Spore* [video game]. Redwood City, CA: Electronic Arts.

Maxis (2000). *The Sims*. Redwood City, CA: Electronic Arts.

McLuhan, Marshall. (1994). *Understanding Media: The Extensions of Man*. Cambridge, MA: MIT Press.

Mojang. (2009). Minecraft [video game]. Sweden: Mojang.

Morris, Chris. (2016). "Level Up! Video Game Industry Revenue Soars in 2015," *Fortune,* Feb. 16, 2016. Retrieved at http://fortune.com/2016/02/16/video-game-industry-revenues-2015/.

"National chess survey reveals the truth about chess: why people play and what scares them away." (2003). *Business Wire,* Dec. 2, 2003.

NDemic. Bristol, UK: Ndemic Creations.

Ndemic Creations. (2012). *Plague Inc.* [video game]. Retrieved at www.ndemiccreations.com/en/25-plague-inc-evolved, May 5, 2017.

Nichols, Randy. (2010). "Target Acquired: *America's Army* and the Video Games Industry," Nina B. Huntemann and Matthew T. Payne, eds., *Joystick Soldiers: The Politics of Play in Military Video Games*. New York: Routledge.

Number None. (2008). *Braid.* [video game]. 2008. Number None/Microsoft Game Studios.

Ong, Sandy. (2016). "The video game industry's problem with racial diversity," *Newsweek,* October 13, 2016. Retrieved at http://www.newsweek .com/2016/10/21/video-games-race-black-protagonists-509328.html.

Pajitnov A., and Pokhilko, V. (1987). *Tetris* [video game]. Spectrum HoloBite.

Parkin, Simon. (2014). "Zoe Quinn's Depression Quest." *New Yorker,* Sept. 9, 2014.

Peckham, Matt. (2008). "Violence in Video Games: A Conversation with Christopher Ferguson, Part One," *PC World,* November 4, 2008. Retrieved at http://www.pcworld.com/article/153278/ferguson_part_one.html.

Penny, Simon. (2004). "Representation, Enaction, and the Ethics of Simulation," in N. Wardrip-Fruin and P. Harrigan, *First Person: New Media as Story, Performance, and Game*. Cambridge: MIT Press.

"Percentage of female developers has more than doubled since 2009." (2014). *Gamespot,* June

24, 2014 (https://www.gamespot.com/articles/percentage-of-female-developers-has-more-than-doubled-since-2009/1100-6420680/)

Polasek, Patrick M. (2014). "A Critical Race Review of GTA V," *Humanity and Society,* Vol. 38 (2), pp. 216-218.

Quenqua, Douglas. (2009). "To Harvest Squash, Click Here," *New York Times,* Oct. 28, 2009. Retrieved at http://www.nytimes.com/2009/10/29/fashion/29farmville.html.

Quinn, Zoe. (2013). *Depression Quest* [video game]. Zoë Quinn.

Reisinger, Dan. (2017). "Here Were the Most Popular Video Games in 2016," *Fortune,* Jan 20, 2017. Retrieved at http://fortune.com/2017/01/20/most-popular-video-games/.

Rockstar North. (2013). *Grand Theft Auto V.* New York: Rockstar Games.

Rockstar North. (2008). *Grand Theft Auto IV* [video game]. New York: Rockstar Games.

Sanbonmatsu, John. (2013). "Virtual Murder," *WPI Journal,* Fall 2013.

Sarkeesian, Anita. (2017). "Not Your Exotic Fantasy," *Feminist Frequency,* January 2017. Retrieved at https://feministfrequency.com/video/not-your-exotic-fantasy/.

Scharff, Robert C., and Val Dusek, eds. (2003). *Philosophy of Technology: The Technological Condition.* New York: Basil Blackwell.

Schiesel, Seth. (2010). "Look Kids: A Way to Slip Pokémon Past Mom." *New York Times,* March 19, 2010, p. C3.

Schumann, Peter. (1990). *The Radicality of the Puppet Theater.* Glover, VT: Bread and Puppet Theater.

SCS Software. (2010). *Deer Drive* [video game]. Kyoto: Nintendo.

Sega. (2006). *After Burner Climax* [video game]. Tokyo: Sega.

Shreier, Jason. (2012). "Anti-Bigotry Gaming Site Defaces with Racial Slurs," *Kotaku,* July 24, 2012. Retrieved at http://kotaku.com/5928723/anti-bigotry-gaming-site-defaced-with-racial-slurs.

Simpson, Kevin, and David Blevins. (2000). "Did Harris Preview Massacre on 'Doom'?" *Denver*

Post, May 4, 2000. Retrieved at http://extras.denverpost.com/news/shot0504f.htm.

Sisler, Vit. (2008). "Digital Arabs: Representation in Video Games," *European Journal of Cultural Studies,* Vol. 11, No. 2, SAGE, 2008, pp. 203–220.

Sofge, Eric. (2008). "Shooting for Realism: How Accurate Are Video Game Weapons?," *Popular Mechanics,* March 25, 2008. Retrieved at http://www.popularmechanics.com/technology/military_law/4255750.html.

"Take to the skies and experience blazing speeds in the world's fastest fighter jets!" (2017). *After Burner Climax* [video game advertisement]. Sega. Retrieved at http://www.sega.com/games/after-burner-climax%E2%84%A2.

Team Ninja. (2003). *Dead or Alive: Xtreme Beach Volleyball.* Tokyo: Tecmo.

Treyarch. (2015). *Call of Duty: Black Ops III* [video game]. Santa Monica, CA: Activision.

Turkle, Sherry. (2011). *Alone Together: Why we expect more from technology and less from each other.* New York: Basic Books.

Ubisoft. (2012). *Far Cry 3* [video game]. Rennes, France: Ubisoft.

Ubisoft. (2002). *Splinter Cell* [video game]. Rennes, France: Ubisoft.

US Army. (2009). PEO STRI press release, Feb. 7, 2009. Retrieved at http://www.peostri.army.mil/ on March 9, 2010

US Army. (2002). *America's Army* [video game]. US Army.

US Department of Defense. (2010.) DARWARS. retrieved at http://www.darwars.org/about/index.html) on March 10, 2010.

Visual Concepts. (2016). *NBA 2K17* [video game]. New York: Take-Two Interactive.

West, James. (2015). "Inside the Chinese Boot Camps Designed to Break Video Game Addiction," *Mother Jones,* March/April 2015. Retrieved at http://www.motherjones.com/media/2015/06/chinese-internet-addiction-center-photos.

Zynga. (2009). *Farmville* [video game]. San Francisco: Zynga.

"YOU PLAY LIKE A GIRL!"

Cross-Gender Competition and the Uneven Playing Field

Elena Bertozzi

51

Much has been written about why females do not play the same games or as many digital games as males do. It is now estimated that females play digital games at least as often as males do, but the levels of complexity of games varies widely (Dillon, 2006). Lucas and Sherry (2004) define casual/traditional games (those preferred by females) as 'non-mental rotation games' and console or complex PC games (preferred by males) as 'mental rotation games.' These terms suggest that playing 'mental rotation' games requires an additional level of training and immersion not required by traditional games. The lack of female engagement in this sphere matters because participating in complex digital play[1] is a predictor of confidence in and competence with digital technology (AAUW, 2000; Bertozzi and Lee, 2007; Oxford, 2005). Some have suggested that the representation of women as passive sex objects prevents women from fully engaging in the medium, while others have posited that the emphasis on violent/shooting-based conflict keeps females from being interested in this type of play (Cassell and Jenkins, 1998; Heintz-Knowles, 2001; Oxford, 2005; Schleiner, 1998). For years, it has been argued that females value social behavior and positive values, and that as soon as games of this type emerge, females will play them. Over the last couple of years, several games have been published that meet these criteria (*Final Fantasy, Animal Crossing, World of Warcraft* [*WOW*], *SIMS*) and there have been significant increases in female players of these games.[2] If anything though, the popularity of these games among males demonstrates that males do not require stereotypical representations of females or violence to enjoy digital gameplay, and that they value social interaction as much as females do.

The lack of female engagement in digital play is related to deeply rooted understandings of gender differences in the culture at large. Playgrounds such as poker tables, Monopoly boards or levels of Halo are affected by gender politics in the larger culture. Players can certainly make a conscious decision to avoid or ignore them, but they exist and affect the play process in both conscious and unconscious ways. It is possible that males seek to play with males and females with females in part because single gender playgrounds are arenas in which players feel somewhat freed from having to deal with the complexities of cross-gender interactions which affect every other area of their lives.

Researchers have documented the ways in which gender politics are reconstructed in digital worlds (Schleiner, 1998; Taylor, 2006; Yee, 2004, 2006). In *Everquest,* for example, players can choose to play as either male or female avatars. The gender of the avatar makes absolutely no difference to the actual abilities or capacities of the avatar. The world is constructed to be gender neutral. Players, however, are affected by the sex of the avatar, in that they treat avatars differently based on their appearance. A delicate-looking female avatar will receive more offers of help and collaboration than a male ogre avatar will. Players are very sensitive to gender politics and are often very savvy about playing as a certain type of avatar when they wish to solicit different types of reactions from other players. Many players will play as both male and female avatars under different circumstances, either for strategic advantage, or because it allows them to replay a game and experience a different set of circumstances.

Given that digital play offers a considerable amount of gender plasticity through avatars, it might seem illogical for gender stereotypes and

---

From Elena Bertozzi, "'You Play Like a Girl:' Cross-Gender Competition and the Uneven Playing Field." *Convergence* (2008), 14, 473–487. Reprinted with permission of SAGE Publications.

concerns to persist in digital gaming, but they do.[3] Players of digital games are sexed and the sex of the player matters. The preponderance of male players in complex digital games makes it virtually certain that females who play these digital games will be playing against males.

This chapter considers the possibility that gender differences in digital play are strongly influenced by the unwillingness of both genders to cross traditional, culturally gendered play lines. The fact that females are routinely punished for challenging males on what is perceived to be their turf may be an important factor in deterring women from digital play. When males play against players whom they believe to be female, they are affected by a range of cultural norms including: standards of civility, their own self definition as male, and culturally sanctioned expressions of sexual desire. When females play against players whom they believe to be male, they are affected by similar issues, but from a different perspective. Analysis of gender differences in digital play behavior should consider these factors. In a huge range of game/play activities, including digital gameplay, some females are competing or attempting to compete at the same level as males. They are forging new paths in difficult territory. If we recognize the significance and level of difficulty of challenging existing norms, we can better support their initiatives and create structures to help others join them.

CIVILITY AND CHIVALRY

When males and females play against one another, problems arise. Although there has recently been much lamenting about the death of civility, and concern that young people are growing up without manners, we still have very strongly felt beliefs about how males and females should interact with one another. One of the most relevant, in terms of play, is that it is wrong for males to be aggressive towards females. Our cultural history includes the understanding that males should be protective of women and seek to help them. This understanding was, of course, based on the idea that females are the 'weaker sex,' and required protection and dominance from a strong male. Although we are moving past this perception to some degree, there is no question that public demonstration of violence or aggression from a male towards a female remains

culturally unacceptable. Such behavior brings to mind issues of wife beating, rape and other serious crimes. Many males are thus understandably reluctant to engage in any behavior that might even suggest aggression towards a female, for fear that this might be misinterpreted (Hargreaves, 1990).

> A boy on a co-ed football squad—or playing against a co-ed squad—faces an irreconcilable conflict between his duty as a man and his duty as a player. As a man, he must never strike a woman. As a player he must strike teammates during scrimmages, and opposing players during games, fairly and within the rules, but with all the force he can muster. (Jeffrey, 2004)

It is therefore complicated to have males and females on certain types of playgrounds, participating as equals. If a male were playing against another male, he might use a number of aggressive tactics including: physical proximity, verbal taunting, feints, and actual aggression, among other things. It can be very difficult for a male to understand how much and to what degree he can use these kinds of behaviors when playing against a female opponent. In order to truly treat each other as equals, males and females have to willfully attempt to ignore years of cultural conditioning, which codifies inequality.

These difficulties can, however, be overcome if the concept of 'play' is correctly understood and applied. The philosophical premise of play is that whosoever steps onto the 'sacred space' (Huizinga, 1955) of the playing field sheds any discrimination/bias/advantage accrued to him or her outside of the playing field. Within that physical space and within the constraints of the rules of that game, contestants are measured purely by their ability to perform that particular action, in that particular place, at that particular time. The success of females at high school wrestling, where females often compete on teams with and against males, for example, demonstrates that this can be accomplished even for contact sports.[4]

CONSEQUENCES OF CHALLENGING MALES

Despite the many changes in male–female relations over the past 50 years and the goals attained by women's rights movements in a variety of areas, play of almost all kinds remains rigidly gendered. From birth, children are given toys and encouraged to play in ways that reinforce cultural stereotypes of gender appropriateness (Martin and Ruble, 2004; Serbin et al., 2001). Toys "R" Us, Mattel, and other toy production and sales companies have separate product and sales teams for products aimed at separate gender markets. Studies on sex-role stereotypes demonstrate that in fact little has changed in the public's perception of what constitutes masculine and feminine traits (Broverman et al., 1972; Conway and Vartanian, 2000). Video game environments tend to emphasize the differences between gendered avatars rather than diminish them (Ray, 2004). Females often have enormous breasts, male avatars are muscular and heroic. Although this is often presented as a reason why females do not play video games, Waem et al. found that hyper-sexualized avatars are actually preferred by both male and female players (2005).

One result of Title IX legislation has been to encourage females to play more and to provide them with better equipment and better training (Dowling, 2000; Roberts, 2005). Enormous gains have been made in female sporting achievement as a result of this legislation. If anything though, these gains have further demarcated the 'separate but equal' approach to sports education in the USA. Play is fundamentally about power: who has the right to exercise it and how it is exercised (Bertozzi, 2003). Many kinds of play behavior reward aggression, competition and violence, within a system of checks and balances that control how these behaviors are expressed. Traditional male play behaviors often reward players for engaging in these behaviors appropriately. Males are taught that seeking power through socially sanctioned means is appropriate, and will result in deserved rewards. Interviews with CEOs and other successful businessmen often mention past or current participation in sporting events that helped them create a 'winning' work ethic. . . .

The tenacity of gender stereotypes becomes apparent when women attempt to cross the boundary lines and compete on the same terms as males (Roth, 2004). The fact that the female placekicker for the University of Colorado football team was subjected to constant hazing and then raped (CNN, 2004) is an example of how females can be overtly punished for putting themselves on a par

with men. The response to events like these often suggests that the harm inflicted on the female in question was somehow deserved, because she put herself in a place where she did not belong:

> Only a few female kickers have played college football, but female high school players are more common. The National Federation of State High School Associations (NFHS), which represents state governing bodies for high school sports, says 1,477 girls participated on the tackle football teams last year at 306 U.S. high schools.
>
> That's a national disgrace. There is a connection between the increasing disrespect shown to women in our society and an ultra-feminist ideology that pushes teenage girls to play a brutal contact sport with teenage boys. (Jeffrey, 2004)

According to this columnist, girls are not freely choosing to participate in football. They are the unwitting pawns of feminist ideology, which places them in an arena in which they are certain to be hurt. This ignores the obvious point that the placekicker in question was not hurt on the field, but in the locker rooms and other social settings, and that she was hurt by her own teammates, not by contact with the opposing team. When Annika Sorenstam dared to challenge the men of the PGA, the media hubbub went on for weeks. Some of Sorenstam's male colleagues made extremely unsportsmanlike comments regarding her ability despite her clear demonstration of competence.

> WOODRUFF: . . . fans of Annika Sorenstam would like to believe that golfer Vijay Singh is eating a big plate of crow for dinner tonight. He's the man who said Sorenstam—quote—'doesn't belong here with the men of the PGA Tour.' And today, Sorenstam became the first woman since World War II to play at a PGA event, the Colonial in Fort Worth, Texas. And judging by her game and her game alone, she belonged there. (CNN, 2003)

Ambivalence towards players who represent themselves as females in digital games has been reported by many players. A player using a female avatar is very frequently subject to sexual innuendo and communication from other players that focuses on aspects of the female body, clothes she is wearing and so on. In her discussion of how she was treated differently while playing as male- and female-identified avatars in online poker environments, Slimmer points out that some males become extremely aggressive when beaten by a player using a female-identified avatar, and that her decision to play as a male-identified avatar resulted in part from real fear of retaliation from enraged male players (2007). This hostility towards women who dare to challenge gender norms in play is due to the fact that their presence on the playing field calls into question the very definition of masculinity.

MASCULINE CULTURAL PLAY NORMS

Cultural norms are often reflected in banter, jokes, idiom and insults. Despite the media presence of many strong and athletically talented women, 'You play/throw/kick like a girl' remains a potent insult. When males play in groups, gendered terms such as 'sissy,' 'pussy' and 'fag,' are used as normal and acceptable putdowns. Some males have to differentiate themselves from females in order to prove their masculinity. In a culture where male traits are valued more highly than female, this process often involves devaluing and 'dissing' females and female traits (Messner, 2002). In fact, publicly devaluing females and feminine traits is considered by some researchers to be an integral part of the development of a culturally accepted 'male' gender persona (Butler, 1990; Connell, 1987; Nelson, 1994; Tolman et al., 2003). In digital gameplay, male conversational exchanges often emphasize the establishment of maleness through choice of language and the explicit enunciation of heterosexist norms (Herring, 2001). Other researchers have argued that in digital gameplay it is even more important for males to establish aggressive masculinity through language precisely because the male body is not present and can only be elicited through speech (Alix, 2007).

When a female steps onto the playing field as an equal, it is disruptive to deeply engrained cultural norms that males are different from females, males are better/stronger/more competent than females, and that males are more aggressive/competitive than females. In cultures where

heterosexist cultural norms are especially powerful, in those very few sporting/play activities where males compete on the same level as females, the sport is branded as somehow 'gay' or appropriate only for homosexual men. In the USA these activities include competitive horseback riding events, such as dressage and hunter/jumper competitions, and dance of any kind.[5] The fact that calling someone or some activity 'gay' remains an insult, further underscores the tenacity of traditional binary gender roles in both analog and digital play activities.

The devaluation of the female in the culture at large creates a dilemma when males and females do compete. The stakes are particularly high for a male in this situation, especially if there are spectators. When a male is competing against a female, he is in a lose/lose situation. If he defeats his female opponent, it is not much of a victory, because the cultural expectation is that she is weak anyway. Beating an opponent that is known to be weaker can actually be seen as a kind of humiliation for the winner in this context. If he loses to the female, however, his defeat is compounded by the humiliation of having been defeated by 'a girl.' If this occurs in front of male spectators he is likely to hear about it for a long time afterward.

FEMALE UNWILLINGNESS TO EXCEL AT CROSS-GENDER PLAY

Can we then assume that cross-gender competition is a win/win situation for females? If the female loses against the male, she is still admired for having dared to challenge someone 'superior' to her. If she wins, however, her victory has a different sort of taint to it. There are several terms in western culture for women who dominate men: 'shrew,' 'bitch' and 'ballbreaker' are examples. A man who is dominated by a woman can be called 'pussy-whipped' among other such terms.

Although a woman who defeats a man publicly at play does enjoy the extra status of beating a 'tough' opponent, she also risks being branded with one of these extremely negatively-valenced terms. If for a male, being beaten by a female is a form of emasculation, then the female who beats him is the agent. She, by winning, risks emasculating him. This is its own sort of catch-22. The female athlete, like any other athlete, simply wants to defeat anyone else in her class. She wants to compete against, and hopefully defeat the strongest contestants in her sport. In competing against a male, however, she has other stakes to consider. If she wins, she demonstrates her own superiority and at the same time is potentially responsible for inflicting a sort of societal harm upon her opponent.

Given the cultural norms that correlate femininity with passivity, females who dare to compete and win at the same level as males often find it necessary to emphasize the fact that they remain sexually 'female.' Florence Joyner, a world record holder in track and field, was notorious for her bright pink running suits and impossibly long nails. Female tennis, a sport long associated with powerful women and lesbianism (Nelson, 1994), now has female players who emphasize their femininity with the type of clothing they wear and their off-court behavior. A recent article in the *New York Times* on top-level female chess players pointed out that the top women players are ranked not only on how well they play the game, but also on their looks (Mclain, 2005). Such behavior suggests that women are not just focusing on success in the game, but are at the same time concerned with protecting their status as sexually viable females, because they feel that this status may be threatened by their successes in play. This may in part explain why hyper-sexualized avatars are often chosen as self-representations.

Another reason for choosing not to defeat males is that the act of doing so may make it more difficult for the female athlete to have sexual relationships with males. Given that male/female sexual relationships continue to reflect cultural stereotypes, a female who is known as someone capable of defeating males (thus potentially emasculating them) may encounter difficulties finding male sexual partners off the playing field. In my game design classes, I routinely ask the males in the class if they would date someone who is able to beat them at the games they consider themselves best at. They always say 'No,' except for the few that say 'It depends how hot she is.' Given the societal cost of defeating men, it is not a surprise that many women prefer to maintain their status as sexually attractive rather than choosing to be winners.

The 'it depends' comment just mentioned, however, does seem to indicate a change in attitudes. There has been a definite increase in the portrayal of strong, competitive athletic females

as sexually attractive. Some female singers, such as Madonna, for example, include physically challenging routines in their performances that show off their sleekly muscled bodies. Advertisements for sportswear aimed at females are now often images of powerful-looking women making statements that suggest that they revel in their athletic abilities. 'Working out' is now a common activity among females both old and young, and many popular women's magazines promote a more physically powerful female self-image (*Fitness, Self,* and *Women's Health,* for example).

Some have argued, however, that the importance of fitness can be seen as just another way of pressuring women to obsess about and objectify their bodies, rather than in fact empowering women (Markula, 2001; Tiggemann and Williamson, 2000). Researchers and doctors who deal with anorexic patients have noted that there are pro-anorexia websites, where girls compete to see who can get by on the least amount of food per day and/or work out for the longest amount of time (Williams, 2006). Ryan's (1995) work on sports such as ice-skating and gymnastics found that these sports promote an ideal of fitness which is in fact damaging to a healthy adult female body, and which idealizes traditional norms of femininity:

> The anachronistic lack of ambivalence about femininity in both sports is part of their attraction, hearkening back to a simpler time when girls were girls, when women were girls for that matter: coquettish, malleable, eager to please. In figure skating especially, we want our athletes thin, graceful, deferential and cover-girl pretty. (Ryan, 1995: 25)

These analyses suggest that play activities may provide women with physical, mental and emotional strength, and help them become more competent and capable in many areas of life, but that for some, the recent emphasis on fitness for women perpetuates an ethos in which females manipulate their bodies, sometimes in explicitly damaging ways, in order to be more attractive to males.

WOMEN ON TOP

. . . Males tend to use play as a way of determining their rank and status within a group. Ranking in the group is achieved by ability/success at the game in question. Rank is mobile. A male can raise or lower his ranking by his play performance at any given time. One of the appealing things about play is that, unlike 'real life,' there is always the chance to play the game again. There is always the opportunity to make the attempt to prove yourself as better than you were the last time. DeBoer points out that although males are playing for the team, they are also always playing for themselves. Better individual performance (within limits) is better for the team overall. Males tend to want each other to excel, and respect each other for the levels of excellence achieved (DeBoer, 2004; Vincent, 2006). Competitiveness between males is overt, socially acceptable and rewarded by status.

Competitiveness between females is much more problematic. Generally it is not overt, and often it does not lead to positive outcomes. Recent books such as *Odd Girl Out* and the film *Mean Girls* (Mark Waters, UK, 2004) have documented the 'culture of hidden female aggression' (Simmons, 2002). Overt female aggression and competitiveness have long been discouraged, but this does not signify that females are any less interested in achieving higher status and pursuing their own personal best interests. Evolutionary theory demonstrates that there is always competition for scarce resources and status within groups. Discouraged, and often punished by cultural norms, female aggression is often more subtle, nuanced and emotionally wounding. Unlike males who can publicly challenge one another to a contest, females tend to express aggression through social shunning and verbal harassment. It is much more difficult to confront this kind of aggression. It is also very complicated for an individual female to figure out how to improve her status.

Social status among young females continues to be determined by different criteria than it is among males. Rather than achieving status through physical strength, athletic skill, or intellectual achievement as is common among males, female rank is often determined by beauty, thinness, blondness, and attractiveness to males. Unfortunately, this does not appear to have changed significantly over the last 20 years. In 1984, Weisfeld et al., in a study on social dominance in adolescence, found that: 'Boys seem to strive for social success mainly through competence in athletics, and girls through cultivating an attractive appearance' (1984: 115). When Simmons asked young girls the traits of the 'ideal girl,' the top five characteristics were: 'Very thin, Pretty, Blond, Fake, Stupid' (Simmons, 2002: 124). She summarizes her results: 'The ideal girl is stupid, yet manipulative. She is dependent and helpless, yet she uses sex and romantic attachments to get power. She is popular, yet superficial. She is fit, but not athletic or strong' (Simmons, 2002: 126). In a 2003 study on the importance of facial attractiveness to social ranking, the authors found that attractiveness was a significant factor in social dominance, and particularly so among females (Gary et al., 2003).

Female status appears to be determined by factors that are difficult to change (prettiness, thinness). It is thus much more difficult for a female to raise her status in the group. If she overtly competes against other females the way males can, there are societal costs. This affects how females engage in gameplay. Not only is overt competition discouraged, but it can also be punished by social ostracism and shunning. Girls learn to be cautious about whether or not to seek improved status within a group and how to go about achieving it. They may also be reluctant to engage in any kind of activity that further diminishes their status in the female hierarchy (becoming very physically fit and/or more dominant, for example). In digital gameplay, however, these considerations disappear. Any player can choose to represent himself/herself as thin, blond, pretty and stupid, and all avatars are fake by definition. Digital play offers female players the opportunity to represent themselves in a way that makes them look like a high ranking analog female, but it also makes the ranking moot given that anyone can achieve it and many players do. . . .

In her book, *Female Chauvinist Pigs,* Ariel Levy (2005) describes . . . women who have succeeded in male dominated fields as 'loophole women' who enjoy and exploit the fact that there are few women around them, because this increases their uniqueness and cachet. They are, in fact, invested in ensuring that other women do NOT succeed in order to maintain this status.

An interview with a senior *World of Warcraft* (*WOW*) player (Lehtonen, 2007), however, suggests that the situation, at least in *WOW,* is more complicated. She points out that women who have invested a great deal of time and energy in raising their ranking in Massively-Multiplayer Online Roleplaying Games have done so generally through diligence, practice and careful construction of social relationships with other players. Hostility towards new female players does exist, but only if those females come into the game and attempt to circumvent the laborious process of earning status in the group through 'serious' gameplay. Some females come into the game and use heteronormative feminine wiles, such as flirting and sexual innuendo, to attempt to make progress in the game by bonding with higher ranked males. This kind of behavior is extremely irritating to experienced female players because it undercuts the idea that females can and should gain status by earning it, the same way males do (Lehtonen, 2007) . . . .

CHANGING THE PARADIGM

Claude Steele developed the term 'stereotype threat' to describe the experience of members of a minority group within the context of a majority group. His studies have demonstrated that dominant stereotypes about minorities will affect performance in certain group situations (Spencer et al., 1999). Elite female gamers playing a complex digital shooting game such as *Counter-Strike* against almost exclusively male opponents are clearly operating in a situation of stereotype threat. They are not just playing the game (as all the other participants are), but they are concurrently disproving a number of stereotypes about females and aggressivity, technology, and willingness to challenge males. Steele has suggested strategies of 'wise schooling' to counteract the effects of stereotype threat in academic environments (Steele, 1997). These strategies include changing attitudes and increasing numbers.

The ability of minority populations to succeed in an environment from which they were previously excluded appears to be related to percentages. Once a certain numeric threshold has been crossed, members of the minority population are less likely to feel the effects of stereotype threat. A study that sought to determine why there remain so few women at high levels of *Fortune 500* companies found that once a critical mass of three women on the board of a company has been reached, other participants stop viewing gender as

the reason underlying female recommendations (Kramer et al., 2006).

POLICY IMPLICATIONS

. . . If game designers are aware of issues related to cross-gender play, these can be relatively easily addressed. Additionally, schools and other institutions hoping to attract women to technology might consider the following suggestions.

(1) *Normalize cross-gender play and competition by making it frequent, routine and pleasurable.* In game worlds, this can be accomplished by having many more female characters present in game narratives, and by having them engage with player avatars across a wide range of activities. Stereotype threat can be countered by increasing the number of the members of a minority population present in the majority population and by providing numerous examples of characters that counter stereotypes.

(2) *Create a broad range of non-playable female characters and female avatars who have attributes not stereotypically considered 'female.'* Certainly popular media will always include traditional, stereotypical representations of women. But by broadening the range of females depicted, female and male players alike can choose to represent themselves as a variety of types of female (muscled and timid, thin, blond and bloodthirsty, maternal and insanely competitive, and so on).

(3) *Reinforce emerging perceptions of physically strong, competitive, aggressive females as sexually desirable.* Cultural norms that penalize women for challenging men are a potent deterrent. Females (like males) want very much to be attractive to others and are unlikely to engage in behavior that they perceive as minimizing their attractiveness. By consciously creating representations of females who successfully defy existing gender norms, new norms will be developed. Given that both male and female players will play as female avatars, perceptions can be changed across genders.

(4) *Increase the number of female players and female avatars in digital games.* Games that have large numbers of female avatars and players, *Second Life* and *Sims* games, for example, are potential models for change. . . .

NOTES

1. This is to differentiate digital games such as *Solitaire, Tetris,* or other games which do not require specialized equipment, software, or training, from games including *World of Warcraft, Counter-Strike, Civilization IV* and others, which are much more complicated to learn and play.

2. It is currently estimated that 16 percent of *WOW* players are female (Yee, 2006) while a surprising 46 percent of *SIMS* players are male (Microsoft, 2004).

3. See E. Castronova's article on gendered avatar pricing for an example of how these stereotypes are concretized economically (Castronova, 2003).

4. 'In 2004–5, there were 4334 girls competing in wrestling on the high school level. This total has increased every year since 1990. This actual number is much higher, as some states that have women competitors do not report them' (Abbott, 2006).

5. The film *Billy Elliot* (Stephen Daldry, UK, 2000) explored the gender issues of ballet.

REFERENCES

AAUW (2000) *Tech Savvy.* Washington, DC: American Association of University Women Educational Foundation.

Abbott, G. (2006) 'Women's High School Wrestling Continues Growth with CIF Regional Tournaments,' *TheMat.com* (USA Wrestling), URL (accessed June 2008): http://www.themat.com/index.php? page=showarticle&ArticleID=13874

Alix, A. (2007) 'Online Game Talk and the Articulation of Maleness,' in *Flow TV* 5 (special issue on video games). University of Texas at Austin. URL (accessed June 2008): http://flowtv.org/?p=53

Bertozzi, E. (2003) 'At Stake: Play, Pleasure and Power in Cyberspace,' PhD dissertation, European Graduate School, URL (accessed June 2008): http://www.egs.edu/resources/elena-bertozzi.html

Bertozzi, E. and Lee, S. (2007) 'Not Just Fun and Games: Digital Play, Gender and Attitudes Towards Technology,' *Women's Studies in Communication* 30(2): 179–204.

Broverman, I. K., Vogel, S. R., Broverman, D. M., Clarkson, F. E. and Rosenkrantz, P. S. (1972) 'Sex Role Stereotypes: A Current Appraisal,' *Journal of Social Issues* 28(2): 59–78.

Butler, J. (1990) *Gender Trouble: Feminism and the Subversion of Identity.* New York: Routledge.

Cassell, J. and Jenkins, H. (1998) *From Barbie to Mortal Kombat: Gender and Computer Games.* Cambridge, MA: MIT Press.

Castronova, E. (2003) *The Price of 'Man' and 'Woman': A Hedonic Pricing Model of Avatar Attributes in a Synthetic World* (CESifo Working Paper Series No. 957). Munich: CESifo.

CNN (2003) CNN News night with Aaron Brown, 22 May, URL (accessed May 2003): http://transcripts.cnn.com/TRANSCRIPTS/0305/22/asb.00.html

CNN (2004) 'University Asks Police to Look Into Alleged Rape,' URL (accessed 5 December 2005): http://www.cnn.com/2004/US/Central/02/18/colorado.football/

Connell, R. W. (1987) *Gender and Power: Society, the Person and Sexual Politics.* Stanford, CA: Stanford University Press.

Conway, M. and Vartanian, L. R. (2000) 'A Status Account of Gender Stereotypes: Beyond Communality and Agency,' *Sex Roles* 43(3–4): 499–528.

DeBoer, K. J. (2004). *Gender and Competition: How Men and Women Approach Work and Play Differently.* Monterey, CA: Coaches Choice.

Dillon, B. (2006) E3 Panel: 'Analyzing World Markets,' *Gamasutra Industry News,* URL (accessed June 2008): http://www.gamasutra.com/php-bin/news_index.php? story=9298

Dowling, C. (2000) *The Frailty Myth.* New York: Random House.

Gary, L. A., Hinmon, S. and Ward, C. A. (2003) 'The Face as a Determining Factor for Social

Manipulation: Relational Aggression, Sociometric Status, and Facial Appearance,' *Colgate University Journal of the Sciences,* pp. 93–114, URL (accessed June 2008): http://groups.colgate.edu/cjs/student_papers/ 2003/Garyetal.pdf

Hack, D. (2006) 'Dealing with the Wind is a Challenge in Hawaii,' *New York Times* Sports Section, Sunday 15 January: 2.

Hargreaves, J. A. (1990) 'Gender on the Sports Agenda,' *International Review for the Sociology of Sport* 25(4): 287–307.

Heintz-Knowles, D. K. (2001) *Fair Play? Violence, Gender and Race in Video Games.* Oakland, CA: Children Now.

Herring, S. (2001) 'Gender and Power in Online Communication,' CSI Working Paper no. WP-01–05, URL (accessed June 2008): http://rkcsi.indiana.edu/archive/CSI/WP/WP01–05B.html

Huizenga, J. (1955). *Homo Ludens: A Study of the Play-Element in Culture.* Boston, MA: Beacon Press.

Jeffrey, T. (2004) 'Ban Girls from Football,' *Townhall.com,* URL (accessed June 2008): http://www.townhall.com/columnists/Terence Jeffrey/2004/02/26/ban_girls_from_football

Kramer, V., Konrad, A. and Erkut, S. (2006) 'Critical Mass on Corporate Boards: Why Three or More Women Enhance Governance,' available from Wellesely Centers for Women's Publications, URL (accessed June 2008): http://www.wcwonline.org/

Lehtonen, E. (2007) In-person interview and email communication with author. (Lehtonen is a World of Warcraft Guild member; character: Jaspre, title: Ascent Position: 2nd Officer.)

Levy, A. (2005) *Female Chauvinist Pigs: Women and the Rise of Raunch Culture.* New York: Free Press.

Lucas, K. and Sherry, J. L. (2004) 'Sex Differences in Video Game Play: A Communication-Based Explanation,' *Communication Research* 31(5): 499–523.

Markula, P. (2001) 'Beyond the Perfect Body: Women's Body Image Distortion in Fitness Magazine Discourse,' *Journal of Sport and Social Issues* 25(2): 158–79.

Martin, C. L. and Ruble, D. (2004) 'Children's Search for Gender Cues: Cognitive Perspectives on Gender Development,' *Current Directions in Psychological Science* 13(2): 67–70.

Mclain, D. L. (2005) 'Sex and Chess. Is She a Queen or a Pawn?,' *New York Times* 27 November: 1.

Messner, M. (2002) *Taking the Field: Women, Men, and Sports.* Minneapolis: University of Minnesota Press.

Microsoft (2004) 'Women Get in the Game,' Microsoft, URL (accessed June 2008): http://www.microsoft.com/presspass/features/2004/jan04/01–08womengamers.mspx

Nelson, M. B. (1994) *The Stronger Women Get, the More Men Love Football: Sexism and the American Culture of Sports.* New York: Harcourt Brace.

Oxford, N. (2005) 'Venus or Mars: The Uneasy Relationship Between Gaming and Gender,' *1up,* URL (accessed June 2008): http://www.1up.com/do/feature? cId=3141723

Ray, S. G. (2004) *Gender Inclusive Game Design: Expanding the Market.* Boston, MA: Charles River Media.

Roberts, S. (2005) *A Necessary Spectacle: Billie Jean King, Bobby Riggs, and the Tennis Match that Leveled the Game.* New York: Crown Publishers.

Roth, A. (2004) 'Femininity, Sports, and Feminism,' *Journal of Sport and Social Issues* 28(3): 245–65.

Ryan, J. (1995) *Little Girls in Pretty Boxes: The Making and Breaking of Elite Gymnasts and Figure Skaters.* New York: Doubleday.

Schleiner, A.-M. (1998) 'Does Lara Croft Wear Fake Polygons?,' *Switch,* URL (accessed June 2008): http://switch.sjsu.edu/web/v4n1/annmarie.html

Serbin, L. A., Poulin-Dubois, D., Colburne, K. A., Sen, M. G. and Eichstedt, J. A. (2001) 'Gender Stereotyping in Infancy: Visual Preferences for and Knowledge of Gender-Stereotypical Toys in the Second Year,' *International Journal of Behavioral Development* 25(1): 7–15.

Simmons, R. (2002) *Odd Girl Out: the hidden culture of aggression in girls.* New York: Harcourt Inc.

Slimmer, J. (2007) 'Kings, Queens, and Jackasses: Playing with Gender in Online Poker,' *Flow TV* 5 (special issue on video games). University of Texas at Austin, URL (accessed June 2008): http://flowtv.org/? p=52

Spencer, S. J., Steele, C. M. and Quinn, D. M. (1999) 'Stereotype Threat and Women's Math Performance,' *Journal of Experimental Social Psychology* 35(1): 4–28.

Steele, C. M. (1997) 'A Threat in the Air: How Stereotypes Shape Intellectual Identity and Performance,' *American Psychologist* 52(6): 613–29.

Taylor, T. L. (2006) *Play Between Worlds: Exploring Online Game Culture.* Cambridge, MA: MIT Press.

Tiggemann, M. and Williamson, S. (2000) 'The Effect of Exercise on Body Satisfaction and Self-Esteem as a Function of Gender and Age,' *Sex Roles* 43(1–2): 119–27.

Tolman, D. L., Spencer, R., Rosen-Reynoso, M. and Porche, M. V. (2003) 'Sowing the Seeds of Violence in Heterosexual Relationships: Early Adolescents Narrate Compulsory Heterosexuality,' *Journal of Social Issues* 59(1): 159–78.

Vincent, N. (2006) *Self-Made Man: One Woman's Journey into Manhood and Back Again.* New York: Viking.

Waem, A., Larsson, A. and Neren, C. (2005) 'Gender Aspects on Computer Game Avatars,' paper presented at the ACM SIGCHI International Conference on *Advances in Computer Entertainment Technology* at the Swedish Institute of Computer Science, Valencia Spain, URL (accessed June 2008): ftp://ftp.sics.se/pub/SICS-reports/Reports/SICS-T—2005–06—SE.pdf

Weisfeld, G. E., Bloch, S. A. and Ives, J. W. (1984) 'Possible Determinants of Social Dominance Among Adolescent Girls,' *Journal of Genetic Psychology* 144(1): 115–29.

Williams, A. (2006) 'Before Spring Break, the Anorexic Challenge,' *New York Times* Sunday Styles 2. April: 1.

Yalom, M. (2004) *Birth of the Chess Queen: A History.* New York: HarperCollins Publishers.

Yee, N. (2004) 'Avatar: Use/Conceptualization and Looking Glass Self': Terranova Blog, URL (accessed 17 May 2006): http://terranova.blogs.com/terra_nova/2004/01/the_avatar_and_.html

Yee, N. (2006) 'WoW Gender-Bending' Daedalus Project, URL (accessed 2 April 2006): http://www.nickyee.com/daedalus/archives/001369.php

STILL WATCHING TELEVISION IN THE DIGITAL AGE

In recent years, debates over the continued relevance of television have emerged due to changes in the media landscape. However, rather than showing a decline in viewership, surveys conducted by Nielsen (2016) and the United States Bureau of Labor Statistics (2015) show that we are actually watching more television in the digital age—with Americans spending almost as much time watching television as they do working. Thus, technological advancements such as DVRs, VOD, and streaming services are not replacing television but rather enable us to break free from rigid network schedules. Furthermore, mobile devices like laptop computers, tablets, and smartphones allow us to bypass the television set altogether. With the ability to access vast amounts of content, it is increasingly important to critically examine how television is produced and consumed, along with its underlying values.

Locating television texts within the context of the politics and economics of media production helps ensure that we understand how most of the media we consume are rooted within a capitalist system that shapes, to varying degrees, the content, narratives, and ideologies of the texts. Richard Butsch (VII.52) provides a good example of this approach in his analysis of how corporate control of the U.S. television industry has resulted in working-class men being portrayed as "buffoons"—"dumb, immature, irresponsible, and lacking in common sense"—on 400 television sitcoms produced over the past 60 years (p. 442). Given the high cost of producing a television series such as a situation comedy, he argues that "television networks' first concern affecting program decisions is risk avoidance" (p. 444). Thus, once a formula has proved successful, network executives favor programs that "repeat the same images of class decade after decade" (p. 444).

While Butsch's chapter focuses on scripted television content, Chris Jordan (VII.53) introduces us to the political economy of global reality TV. Using the example of the wildly popular *Survivor* series, this chapter explores "why reality television is a global staple of domestic and international prime time television," and concludes that such shows fit the economic imperatives of producers, networks, and advertisers in an age of global television. The formulas of a reality TV series lend themselves particularly well to international franchising. Jordan's study shows that

> *Survivor*'s relatively low cost and high ratings potential made the show imminently marketable worldwide. . . . Overseas broadcasters that have licensed the American format of *Survivor* and created their own versions include China's CCTV, the Middle East satellite platform Gulf DTH, South Africa's SABC, Mexico's Televisa, and stations in Scandinavia, Eastern Europe, and throughout Asia. (p. 453)

For the most part, audiences all over the world understand that the content of so-called reality television is far from completely spontaneous, but the appeal lies to a large extent in the voyeuristic expectation that we are going to catch dramatic glimpses of "real life." This makes it all the more important to look closely at such texts and learn how to see through and beyond their surface appearances to analyze how they construct notions of "reality." By way of example, our next two chapters offer readings of the construction of race in television texts, the first warning that mainstream reality-show producers continue to look for stereotypical "ethnic" behavior in competition-style reality shows, and the second pointing to the way contemporary primetime soaps erase racial differences, despite featuring multicultural casts.

In the context of the competition reality show subgenre, Grace Wang (VII.54) shows how the familiar trope of the Asian American "model minority" must be negotiated, and indeed performed, if an Asian American contestant is to succeed. Examining the Bravo network's *Top Chef*, Wang argues "while reality TV programs open up a space for greater representation of racialized minorities, these shows also adhere to, and authenticate, racialized narratives and stereotypes by embodying them in the characters of 'real' people" (p. 457). Drawing on interviews with a contestant outside the context of the show, she demonstrates how the "savvy" Vietnamese American chef picked up on early comments and criticisms by the show's panel of judges, to the effect that "his food communicated neither passion nor a sense of his identity as an individual born in Vietnam," and responded by completely transforming his onscreen persona. According to Wang,

> On *Top Chef*, the nuance of Hung's life story and his multilayered relationship to cuisine were compressed into an easily digestible story of immigrant success achieved through hard work, humility, gratitude, and maintaining one's ethnic heritage and "roots." (p. 461)

In contrast, Kristen Warner (VII.55) explores how Shonda Rhimes adopts a postracial approach to her highly successful scripted medical drama, *Grey's Anatomy*. Warner points out that although Rhimes is one of the only Black, female executive producers of primetime network television, she presents herself as "colorless," reinforcing a **postracial** ideology that works to "divest race from its cultural contexts for herself and her cast" (p. 466). Not only does this distance Rhimes from "the disadvantages women of color in the television industry regularly face," but it also complicates racial representations in her work. Through the process of blindcasting, which does not explicitly specify the race or ethnicity of a character, thus allowing a wide range of actors to audition for the same part, Rhimes was able to build a multicultural cast. Although *Grey's Anatomy* was celebrated by popular media and watchdog groups for its diversity, Rhimes also eschews dialogue, plot points, or characterizations that focus on race or racial difference. As Warner explains, "being 'free' from racial group identification is the crux of post-race ideology because separating an individual from his or her group status also disconnects the person from a historical trajectory of disenfranchisement. The individual alone becomes responsible for her lot in life and cannot claim racism as an injustice or an issue" (p. 468).

Like postracial ideologies, **neoliberal** values shape representations of class in contemporary television. In the next chapter in this section, Daniela Mastrocola (VII. 56) examines how the popular *Gilmore Girls* series contributes to neoliberal dreams of autonomous individuals interacting in a "classless" American society. Neoliberalism masks class differences by promoting "a citizen-as-consumer subjectivity that encourages individuals to purchase displays of wealth as evidence of individual success and social membership, while denying structural sources of poverty and inequality" (p. 474). In this chapter, Mastrocola focuses on the ambiguous class performance of the plucky and likeable Lorelai Gilmore. Throughout the series Lorelai exhibits multiple class identities—she is simultaneously depicted as an upwardly mobile entrepreneur who overcame poverty, a former reluctant debutante with wealthy roots, and a lover of "low class" junk food and popular culture. Mastrocola argues that through "Lorelai's performance as a classless protagonist who simultaneously typifies an economic middle-class fantasy and advantageously performs a working class cultural identity," *Gilmore Girls* employs "a 'best of both worlds' strategy" that undercuts the harsh realities of class inequality and overlooks the need for class solidarity (p. 480).

Considering another popular female-centered television text, *Orange Is the New Black*, Hannah Mueller (VII. 57) investigates gender distinctions in acclaimed prison narratives. Since the 1990s mainstream critics have celebrated prison dramas for their "realistic" and "believable" imagery that is often shocking and extreme. However, television programs like *Oz, Prison Break*, and *Orange Is the New Black*, transform viewers into "penal spectators" that find voyeuristic pleasure in the "fictional fantasies" that are far removed from the realities of the prison-industrial complex (p. 484). As Mueller points out, these representations are grounded in gender and sexual stereotypes where incarcerated males are repeatedly shown as uncontrollable, brutally violent perpetrators of physical and sexual assault while female prisoners are often portrayed as immature, silly, and easily dismissed. The underlying ideologies of "the heavily gendered tropes and stereotypes employed in the representation of male and female prisoners on scripted television significantly influence popular narratives about the cycle of crime, punishment, and recidivism in the United States" (p. 484). Not surprisingly, these gendered caricatures obfuscate social forces that contribute to mass incarceration and instead work to naturalize the idea that prisoners are "born criminals" who are resistant to rehabilitation.

Like television's prison narratives, what we think of as nonfiction television (ranging from reality competitions to cable news) relies on **spectacle** to capture the attention of media-saturated audiences. Media spectacles are outrageous or sensational stories and images that circulate across media platforms and take hold of public consciousness. Douglas Kellner (VII.58) explains that media spectacle played a vital role in the 2016 election of Donald Trump. Through his popular reality television shows, *The Apprentice* and *The Celebrity Apprentice*, Trump emerged as a national celebrity promoting cutthroat capitalism, aggressive masculinity, and authoritarian ideologies. According to Kellner, *The Apprentice* "illustrates what aggressive, highly competitive and sometimes amoral tactics are needed to win and gain success and provided for a generation the message that winning was everything and that losing was devastating" (p. 494). Trump then took this same persona and message to the campaign trail and social media, using Twitter to attack critics, promote his hypercapitalist agenda, and mobilize his supporters. Through inflammatory tweets and speeches, Trump orchestrated media spectacle across both traditional and new media platforms, which placed him continuously in the center of the public eye, which "was a crucial factor in thrusting Trump ever further into the front runner status" (p. 495).

As previously noted, the ways traditional and new media work together are transforming our television experience in the digital age. The final chapter in this section explores how television content and distribution are shifting in response to rapid technological changes in our age of **media convergence**, when the boundaries between commercial and noncommercial media formats and platforms have become less clear and what was formerly broadcast, and then cablecast, television content continues to migrate onto laptops and other mobile electronic devices through the Internet. In this chapter, Mareike Jenner (VII.59) uses the streaming service Netflix as a case study to explore the way technology is changing our understanding of television. Unlike in previous eras of television, "Netflix seems to signal a move away from the medium, its branding strategies, associated viewing patterns, technologies, industry structures or programming" (p. 499). Rather Netflix is representative of "matrix media," meaning that it brings together platforms (film, television, DVD, and online video) that were once thought of as distinct. By employing a subscription model, Netflix has creative and budgetary freedom to partner with respected actors, writers, directors, and producers, which help to solidify the platform's reputation as a purveyor of "quality" television content. Bolstered by critical acclaim and social media buzz, along with its standard practice of releasing an entire season of a program all at once, Netflix series have contributed to the growing phenomenon of binge-watching or watching multiple episodes of a television show back-to-back in one sitting. Jenner posits that while some audiences may no longer use a television set to access content, television narratives are being consumed more voraciously than ever in the digital age. The new television era "does not eliminate existing and familiar concepts of what 'television' is, but it extends them significantly and introduces a range of other media forms and discourses to this matrix" (p. 505). In other words, rather than this being a post-television era, television has a wider reach and is more powerful than ever. The need to analyze and understand television is thus also more important than ever.

52

WHY TELEVISION SITCOMS KEPT RE-CREATING MALE WORKING-CLASS BUFFOONS FOR DECADES

Richard Butsch

Strewn across our mass media are portrayals justifying class relations of modern capitalism. Studies of comic strips, radio serials, television series, movies, and popular fiction reveal a persistent pattern underrepresenting working-class occupations and overrepresenting professional and managerial occupations, minimizing the visibility of the working class. Similar patterns are evident for other subordinate statuses of race, gender, and region.

My own studies of class in prime-time network television family series (Butsch, 1992, 2005, 2014, 2017; Butsch & Glennon, 1983; Glennon & Butsch, 1982) indicate that this pattern persisted over six decades and roughly 400 domestic situation comedies, including such icons as *I Love Lucy, The Brady Bunch, All in the Family,* and *The Simpsons.* In only about 10% of the series were heads of house portrayed as working class (i.e., holding occupations as blue-collar, clerical, or unskilled or semiskilled service workers). Widespread affluence was exaggerated as well. More lucrative, glamorous, or prestigious professions predominated over more mundane ones. Working wives were almost exclusively middle class and pursuing a career. Working-class wives, such as the title character in *Roseanne,* who have to work to help support the family, were rare.

Throughout these decades, the few working-class men were portrayed as buffoons. They are dumb, immature, irresponsible, and lacking in common sense. This is the character of the husbands in almost every sitcom depicting a blue-collar head of house—*The Honeymooners, The*

Flintstones, All in the Family, The Simpsons, and *The King of Queens* being the most famous examples. The man is typically well intentioned, even lovable, but no one to respect or emulate. These men are played against more sensible wives, such as Alice in *The Honeymooners* or Carrie in *King of Queens.*

For most of this history, there were few buffoons in middle-class series. More typically, both parents were wise and worked cooperatively to raise their children in practically perfect families, as in *Father Knows Best, The Brady Bunch,* and *The Cosby Show.* The humor came from the innocent foibles and fumbles of the children. The few middle-class buffoons were usually in the form of the ditzy wife, such as Lucy, while the professional/ managerial husband was the sensible, mature partner. Inverting gender status in working-class but not middle-class sitcoms makes this a statement about class more than gender.

The 1990s brought a temporary increase in the number and percentage of working-class families represented in domestic sitcoms: Of 42 new domestic sitcoms from 1991 to 1999, 16 featured working-class families and 9 of those were Black families. Reverting back to form, in the 2000s, only three new working-class and four African American sitcoms were added. By 2008, working-class sitcoms again disappeared ("TV's Class Struggle," 2008). The depictions of middle-class males became more diverse in these two decades, with shows such as *Home Improvement* and *Two and a Half Men* featuring men who succeeded at work but at home exhibited an

This piece is an original essay that was commissioned for this volume. It is an update of an earlier version, titled "Six Decades of Social Class in American Television Sitcoms" that appeared in the 4th edition.

insistent, adolescent, macho maleness—not buffoons but not super-parents either. Still, the portrayals of working-class men remained relatively unchanged. The successful *King of the Hill* (1997), *The King of Queens* (1998), and *Family Guy* (1999), as well as several shorter-lived series throughout the decade, reproduced the traditional, stereotyped working-class man, cast opposite a capable woman.

In the late 2000s the working-class man as buffoon recurred again in *The Cleveland Show, Raising Hope,* and *Working Class.* In the same period, middle-class sitcoms presented more diverse families and male characters. The capable and successful professional man recurred in *Hank, American Dad,* and *Modern Family. Modern Family* and *The New Normal* also featured competent, professional gay couples, albeit as clichéd stereotypes. Three other shows focused on single mothers, absent a father: *Cougar Town, I Hate My Teen Daughter,* and *Malibu Country.*

Why has television kept reproducing the working-class male caricature across six decades, despite major changes in the television industry? How has it happened? Seldom have studies of the television industry pinpointed how specific content arises. Studies of production have not been linked to studies of content any more than audience studies have been. What follows is an effort to explain the link between sitcom production and the persistent images produced. In the words of Connell (1977), "No evil-minded capitalistic plotters need be assumed because the production of ideology is seen as the more or less automatic outcome of the normal, regular processes by which commercial mass communications work in a capitalist system" (p. 195). Rather it is the outcome of complex structural and cultural factors that shaped a uniform representation of working-class men, even as the television industry has undergone remarkable changes from the 1980s on. I will describe the factors as they worked from the beginnings of TV sitcoms in the late 1940s into the 1980s and then examine what effects on representation were wrought by the growth of cable TV and the VCR in the 1980s, computers and the Internet in the 1990s, and the concomitant restructuring of the industry into a new oligopoly of global multimedia corporations. Finally, I will examine the 2000s and 2010s, which have seen substantial increase of cable networks commissioning new

television series and the start of Internet streaming of shows to digital televisions, computers, and smartphones by companies such as Netflix and Hulu. I will look at three levels of organization: (1) network domination of the industry, (2) the organization of decisions within the networks and on the production line, and (3) the work community and culture of the "creative personnel." I will trace how these levels may explain the consistency and persistence of the portrayals of the working class, underrepresentation of the working class, and specific negative stereotypes of working-class men in prime-time domestic sitcoms.

NETWORK DOMINATION AND PERSISTENT IMAGES

From the mid-1940s to mid-1980s, ABC, CBS, and NBC dominated the television industry. Their average share of households watching television at any given time was 90%. They accounted for more than half of all television advertising revenue in the 1960s and 1970s (Owen & Wildman, 1992). They therefore had the money and the audience to dominate the market as the only buyers of series programming from Hollywood producers and studios. The television series market was thus an oligopsony—a market with only three powerful buyers of sitcoms and many sellers (Federal Communications Commission [FCC] Network Inquiry Special Staff, 1980; Owen & Wildman, 1992).

In the 1980s, cable networks and companies that owned several local broadcast stations independent of the three networks began to challenge the dominance of the "big three." The networks' combined rating shrank from 56.5% of all television households in 1980 to 39.7% in 1990, even including the new Fox Broadcasting network that debuted in 1986 (Butsch, 2000, p. 269; Hindman & Wiegand, 2008). By 1999, the four-network rating had slipped to 28.6% ("Upscale Auds Ease B'casters," 1999), while advertising-supported cable had grown to 23.9% ("Young Auds Seek Web, Not Webs," 1999). Still, only five cable networks had sufficient funds in the 1990s to order original scripted series (Blumler & Spicer, 1990). In 2000, cable networks were beginning to become a factor in the market for new drama and comedy series ("B'cast, Cable: Trading Places,"

2000); yet ABC, CBS, and NBC still accounted for the development of the overwhelming majority of new series. However, by 2008, cable networks had become major buyers of new scripted series ("TV Role Reversal," 2009).

Although the dominance of the broadcast networks had slipped, many of the same factors that shaped their programming decisions shaped the decisions of their cable competitors as well. The more competitive market of more buyers did not result in the innovation and diversity in program development long expected by the FCC (FCC Network Inquiry Special Staff, 1980). Jay Blumler and Carolyn Spicer (1990) and Robert Kubey (2004) interviewed writers, directors, and producers, and found that the promise of more openness to innovation and creativity was short-lived. The high cost of scripted series dictated to any buyers that programs had to attract a large audience and avoid risk.

Using their continued market power relative to independent producers, networks maintained sweeping control over the production decisions of even highly successful producers, from initial idea for a new program to final filming or taping (Bryant, 1969, pp. 624–626; Gitlin, 1983; Pekurny, 1977, 1982; Winick, 1961). In addition, in the 1990s, the FCC freed the broadcast networks from rules established in 1970 to reduce their power. This allowed them to increase ownership of programs and in-house production and re-create the vertical integration of television production of the 1950s and 1960s ("TV's Little Guys Stayin' Alive," 2001). It also enabled the movement of film studios into television ownership and created even larger multimedia corporations.

By the late 2000s, programs streaming via Internet to TVs, computers, tablets, and smartphones threatened TV networks. By 2012, more than 100,000 movies and TV shows were available via Internet (Graser, 2011) and more than 20% of U.S. households had Internet-ready video devices (Lisanti, 2012). These alternative delivery systems began to seriously challenge the broadcast and even cable networks delivering to the standard television set (Carr, 2013). Netflix and other Internet outlets were preparing to order their own first-run series.

All this has significantly disrupted the former oligopsony of broadcast networks. So uniformity and persistence of representations of class are likely

to be less the consequence of a concentrated market of buyers of sitcoms. But television dependence on advertising revenue and its influence on sitcom content remains. It means that more efforts will be made to prevent audiences from skipping advertising—for example, by using product placement within shows and stopping DVRs from fast-forwarding through commercials.

NETWORK DECISION MAKING: PROGRAM DEVELOPMENT

Television networks' first concern affecting program decisions is risk avoidance. Popular culture success is notoriously unpredictable. The music recording industry spreads risk over many records so that any single decision is less significant (Peterson & Berger, 1971; Rossman, 2005). Spreading risk is not a strategy available to networks (neither broadcast nor cable), because only a few programming decisions fill the prime-time hours that account for most income. Networks are constrained from expanding the number of their decisions by their use of the series as the basic unit of programming. The series format stabilizes ratings week to week, but reduces the number of prime-time programming decisions to fewer than 50 for the whole season. So each decision represents a considerable financial risk, not simply in production costs, but mostly in advertising income. Success may produce a windfall. For example, ABC multiplied its profits fivefold from 1975 to 1978 by raising its average prime-time ratings from 16.6 to 20.7 (W. Behanna, personal communication, 1980). But mistakes can cause severe losses. Recently networks have shortened seasons and introduced limited-run series, thereby increasing the number of decisions on filling time slots *per year,* but this reduces the risk of each decision only slightly.

Programming decisions are risky and costly, and network executives' careers rest on their ability to make the right decisions, so they are therefore constrained to avoid innovation and novelty. They stick to tried-and-true formulas, a common complaint even among successful television writers and producers (Brown, 1971; Kubey, 2004; Wakshlag & Adams, 1985). One consequence is the repetition of the same images of class decade after decade.

Networks also prefer personnel who have a track record of success. The result is a small, closed community of proven creative personnel (roughly 500 producers, writers, and directors) closely tied to and dependent on the networks (Gitlin, 1983, pp. 115, 135; Kubey, 2004; Pekurny, 1982; Tunstall & Walker, 1981, pp. 77–79). These proven talents then self-censor their work on the basis of a product image their previous experience tells them the networks will tolerate (Cantor, 1971; Pekurny, 1982; Ravage, 1978), creating an "imaginary feedback loop" (Dimaggio & Hirsh, 1976) between producers and network executives. These same conditions continued to characterize program development in the 1980s, 1990s, and 2000s, because the new buyers of programming—cable networks—operated under the same constraints as broadcast networks—until Internet streaming upset business as usual.

More diverse programming appeared only in the early days of the industry, when there were no past successes to copy—broadcast television in the early 1950s and cable in the early 1980s—or when declining ratings made it clear that past successes no longer worked (Blumler & Spicer, 1992; Turow, 1982b, p. 124). Dominick (1976) found that the lower the profits of the networks, the more variation in program types could be discerned from season to season and the less network schedules resembled one another. For example, in the late 1950s, ABC introduced hour-long Western series to prime time to compete with NBC and CBS (FCC Office of Network Study, 1965). Again, in 1970, CBS purchased Norman Lear's then controversial *All in the Family*—other networks turned it down—to counteract a drift to an audience with demographics (rural and over 50) not desired by advertisers. Increased numbers of working-class and African American sitcoms appeared in the 1990s when television executives feared that the White middle class was turning to other entertainments ("Genre-ation Gap Hits Sitcoms," 1999).

Network acceptance of innovative programs takes much longer than for conventional programs and requires backing by the most successful producers (Turow, 1982b, p. 126). Carsey-Werner, producers of the top-rated *Cosby Show,* produced *Roseanne* when ABC was trying to counter ratings losses (Reeves, 1990, pp. 153–154). Hugh Wilson, the creator of *WKRP in Cincinnati* and *Frank's Place,* described CBS in 1987 as desperate about

slipping ratings: "Consequently they were the best people to work for from a creative standpoint" (Campbell & Reeves, 1990, p. 8). Even as declining ratings spurred networks to try innovative programs in the 1990s, they still tended to hire proven talent within the existing production community. The new ideas that were accepted came from (or through) established figures in the industry. As cable networks began to buy series, they contributed to this pattern by supporting programming that satisfied their niche audience but would offend some portion of the broadcast networks' mass market.

Cable changed television markets from mass to niche so that cable networks that served niches with inexpensive programming and subscription networks not supported by advertising could be more risky and risqué. Yet sitcoms, due in part to production costs, were still targeting a broader mass market. By the 2000s, however, more networks and outlets, and thus more shows, were beginning to push the envelope of what was successful. Internet streaming seems to have further increased diversity of programming and characterization.

Another factor affecting network decisions on content is the need to produce programming suited to advertising, not only in decisions on new series, but also in day-to-day decisions producing each episode. What the audience wants is secondary to ad revenue. Confirming this point, pay-cable networks, not bound by this constraint, have been freer to explore sexual and violent content—as in the *Sopranos*—that may have scared off advertisers but attracts an audience. In matters of content, advertising-supported networks avoid content that will offend or dissatisfy advertisers (Bryant, 1969). For example, ABC contracts with producers in 1977 stipulated the following:

> No program or pilot shall contain . . . anything . . . which does not conform with the then current business or advertising policies of any such sponsor; or which is detrimental to the good will or the products or services of . . . any such sponsor. (FCC Network Inquiry Special Staff, 1980, Appendix C, p. A-2)

Garry Marshall, producer of several highly successful series in the 1970s, stated that ABC rejected a story line for *Mork & Mindy,* the top-rated show for 1978, in which Mork takes TV ads literally, buys everything, and creates havoc. Despite the series' and Marshall's proven success, the network feared advertisers' reactions to such a story line.

An advertiser's preferred program is one that allows full use of the products being advertised. The program should be a complementary context for the ad. In the 1950s, an ad agency rejecting a play about working-class life stated, "It is the general policy of advertisers to glamorize their products, the people who buy them, and the whole American social and economic scene" (Barnouw, 1970, p. 32). Advertisers in 1961 considered it "of key importance" to avoid "irritating, controversial, depressive, or 'downbeat' material" (FCC Office of Network Study, 1965, p. 373). This requires dramas built around affluent characters for whom consuming is not problematic. Thus, affluent characters predominate, and occupational groups with higher levels of consumer expenditure are overrepresented. Even in a working-class domestic sitcom, it is unusual for financial strain to be a regular theme of the show—two exceptions being *The Honeymooners* and *Roseanne.*

A third factor in program decisions is whether the program will attract the *right* audience. Network executives construct a product image of what they *imagine* the audience wants—which, surprisingly, often is not based on actual market research on audiences (Blumler & Spicer, 1992; Pekurny, 1982). Michael Dann, a CBS executive, was "concerned the public might not accept a program about a blue-collar worker" when offered the pilot script for *Arnie* in 1969 (before *All in the Family* proved that wrong and after a decade in which the only working-class family appearing in prime time was *The Flintstones*). Similarly, in 1979, an NBC executive expressed the concern that a couple in a pilot was too wealthy to appeal to most viewers (Turow, 1982b, p. 123). Sitcom producer Lee Rich said, "A television series, to be truly successful, has got to have people you can identify with or dream about being" (Kubey, 2004, p. 102). For the sought-after middle-class audience, then, advertisers prefer affluent, middle-class characters.

Aside from anecdotes such as I have mentioned, almost no research has examined program development or production decisions about class content of programs. My own research found no significant class differences between characters in sitcom pilots compared to those in series from 1973 to 1982, indicating that class biases in content began very early in the decision-making process, when the first pilot episode was being developed (Butsch, 1984). I therefore conducted a mail survey of the producers, writers, or directors of the pilots from 1973 to 1982. I specifically asked how the decisions were made about the occupation of the characters in their pilot. I was able to contact 40 persons concerning 50 pilots. I received responses from 6 persons concerning 12 pilots. Although the responses represent only a small portion of the original sample, they are strikingly similar.

Decisions on occupations of main characters were made by the creators and made early in program development as part of the program idea pitched to networks. In no case did the occupation become a matter of debate or disagreement with the networks. Moreover, the choice of occupation was incidental to the situation or other aspect of the program idea; rather, it was embedded in the creators' conception of the situation. For example, according to one writer, a character was conceived of as an architect "to take advantage of the Century City" location for shooting the series; the father in another pilot was cast as owner of a bakery after the decision to do a series about an extended Italian family; and in another pilot, the creator thought the actor "looked like your average businessman." The particular occupations and even the classes are not necessitated by the situations creators offered as explanations. But they did not seem to be hiding the truth; their responses were open and unguarded. It appears they did not consciously consider whether they wished to portray this *particular* class or occupation; rather, to them, the occupation was derivative of the situation or location or actors they chose. They didn't think of characters explicitly in terms of class but, rather, as a personality type that may conjure up a particular occupation. This absence of any awareness of decisions about class is confirmed by Gitlin's (1983) and Kubey's (2004) interviews with industry personnel.

Thus, the process of class construction seems difficult to document given the unspoken guidelines, the indirect manner in which they suggest class, and the absence of overt decisions about class. Class or occupation is not typically an issue for discussion, as obscenity or race is. The choice of class is thus diffuse and indirect, drawn from a culture that provides no vocabulary to think explicitly and speak directly about class. To examine this further, we need to look at the organization of the production process and the culture of creative personnel.

THE IMPACTS OF TIME CONSTRAINTS, WORK COMMUNITY, AND CULTURE IN TELEVISION SERIES PRODUCTION

Within the production process in Hollywood studios and associated organizations, and in the work culture of creative personnel, we find factors that contribute to the use of simple and repetitious stereotypes of working-class men.

An important factor in television production is the severe time constraint (Kubey, 2004; Lynch, 1973; Ravage, 1978; Reeves, 1990). The production schedule for series requires that a finished program be delivered to the networks each week. Even if the production company had the entire year to complete the traditional season's 22 to 24 episodes, an episode would have to be produced on the average every 2 weeks, including script writing, casting, staging, filming, and editing. This is achieved through an assembly-line process where several episodes are in various stages of production and being worked on by the same team of producer, writers, director, and actors, simultaneously.

Such a schedule puts great pressures on the production team to simplify as much as possible the amount of work and the decisions to be made. The series format is advantageous for this reason: When the general story line and main characters are set, the script can be written following a simple formula. For situation comedy, even the sets and cast do not change from episode to episode.

The time pressures contribute in several ways to dependence on stereotypes for characterization. First, sitcoms are based on central characters rather than plot and development. These characters are coming into the living rooms of people and so, have to likeable and believable (Kubey, 2004). This means that, to sell a new series, writers should offer stock characters (i.e., stereotypes). Writing for the same stock character, week after week, also greatly simplifies the task of producing a script.

Time pressure encourages typecasting as well for the minor characters who are new in each episode. The script is sent to a "breakdown" agency, which reads the script and extracts the description of characters for that episode. The casting agency used these brief character descriptions, not the script, to recommend actors (Turow, 1978). Occupation—and by inference, class—are an important part of these descriptions, identified for 84% of male characters. Not surprisingly, the descriptions are highly stereotyped (Turow, 1980).

Notably, most of the production pressures and processes remain the same in the 2010s, regardless of the vast changes in the television industry landscape, including the new delivery systems of Internet streaming. The three- or four-camera method of filming in front of a live audience favored by Norman Lear in the 1970s is still widely used—notably, by the recent most successful showrunner, Chuck Lorre—even while some sitcoms on cable seeking an edgier or more "discerning" niche market have turned to single-camera filming without a live audience, closer resembling feature-film production (Bissell, 2010). Also, while time pressures may be somewhat reduced due to the dissolution of the traditional season and fewer episodes commissioned at one time, still time remains insistent, forcing production teams to rush from task to task and seek ways to make the process more efficient and less time-consuming. Lorre refers to his own production schedule as "Chuck's Inferno" for its intense pace and pressure, just as Norman Lear had advised him: "You run around like a madman" (Bissell, 2010, p. 33).

Producers, casting directors, and casting agencies freely admit to stereotyping but argue its necessity on the basis of time and dramatic constraints. Typecasting is easier and much quicker. They also argue that to diverge from widely held stereotypes would draw attention away from the action, the story line, or other characters and destroy dramatic effect. In addition, stereotyped stock characters are familiar to audiences, requiring less dramatic explanation. Thus, unless the contradiction of the stereotype is the basic story idea—as in *Arnie,* whose title character was a blue-collar worker suddenly appointed as a corporate executive—there is strong pressure to reproduce existing stereotypes.

The time pressures also make it more likely that the creators will stick to what is familiar to them as well. Two of the most frequent occupations of main characters in family series up to 1980 were in entertainment and writing—that is, modeled on the creators' or lead actors' own lives (Butsch & Glennon, 1983)—and that trend continues today, as many sitcom stars are well-known comics and actors. The vast majority of writers and producers come from upper-middle-class families, with little direct experience with working-class life (Cantor, 1971; Gitlin, 1983; Kubey, 2004; Stein, 1979; Thompson & Burns, 1990). Moreover, the tight schedules and deadlines of series production leave no time for becoming familiar enough with the working-class lifestyle to capture it realistically. Those who have done so (e.g., Jackie Gleason, Norman Lear) had childhood memories of working-class neighborhoods to draw on.

Thus, the time pressure encourages creative personnel to rely heavily on a shared and consistent product image—including diffuse and undifferentiated images of class—embedded in what Elliott (1972) called the media culture. The small, closed community of those engaged in television production, including Hollywood creators and network executives (Blumler & Spicer, 1990; Gitlin, 1983; Stein, 1979; Tunstall & Walker, 1981; Turow, 1982a), shares a culture that includes certain conceptions of what life is like and what the audience finds interesting. According to Norman Lear, the production community draws its ideas from what filters into it from the mass media, which is then interpreted through the lens of members' own class experiences and culture, to guess what "the public" would like and formulate images of class they think are compatible (Gitlin, 1983, pp. 204, 225–226).

The closedness of this community is both reflected in and reinforced by the hiring preference for proven talent already in the community, lack of any apprenticeship system to train new talent, and the importance of social networking or, as one director phrased it, "nepotism" in obtaining work (Kubey, 2004). The production community in the 2000s continues to be small and insular, much like Hollywood as described by Leo Rosten in 1941. Stories of successes repeatedly begin with an intermediary, who was close to a member of that community, through whom the newcomer's work was first brought to the attention of decision makers. For example, sitcom showrunner Chuck Lorre got his first break by virtue of knowing a neighbor of perennial sitcom actress Betty White (Bissell, 2010, p. 36).

Thus, while the consistency of image, underrepresentation, and stereotyping of the working class can be explained by structural constraints, the particular stereotypes grow from a rather diffuse set of cultural images, constrained and framed by the structure of the industry.

It is due to the combination of these structural constraints and work culture, rather than any malignant intent, that the stereotyped working-class males in network sitcoms had continued for seven decades. Only the major restructuring of television in the last decade has moderated the pervasiveness of this representation.

Reaching the vast majority of the population for well over half a century and seeping into everyday conversation, sitcoms have made a significant contribution to our culture's attitude toward the man who makes his living with his hands. It is an attitude based on the presumption, repeated again and again by these sitcoms, that this man is dumb, immature, irresponsible, lacking common sense, often frustrated, and sometimes angry. It is an attitude of public disrespect toward him everywhere else in the public realm. That disrespect is the ultimate "hidden injury" that working-class interviewees expressed to Richard Sennett and Jonathan Cobb (1972) in the early 1970s, just about the time Archie Bunker first appeared on network television.

REFERENCES

Barnouw, E. (1970). *The image empire: A history of broadcasting in the U.S. from 1953.* New York: Oxford University Press.

B'cast, cable: Trading places. (2000, April 24). *Variety,* p. 61.

Bissell, T. (2010, December 6). A simple medium. *New Yorker,* 33–41.

Blumler, J., & Spicer, C. (1990). Prospects for creativity in the new television marketplace. *Journal of Communication, 40*(4), 78–101.

Brown, L. (1971). *Television: The business behind the box.* New York: Harcourt, Brace.

Bryant, A. (1969). Historical and social aspects of concentration of program control in television. *Law and Contemporary Problems, 34,* 610–635.

Butsch, R. (1984). *Minorities from pilot to series: Network selection of character statuses and traits.* Paper presented at the Society for the Study of Social Problems annual meeting, Washington, D.C.

Butsch, R. (1992). Class and gender in four decades of television situation comedy. *Critical Studies in Mass Communication, 9,* 387–399.

Butsch, R. (2000). *The making of American audiences.* Cambridge, UK: Cambridge University Press.

Butsch, R. (2005). Five decades and three hundred sitcoms about class and gender. In G. Edgerton & B. Rose (Eds.), *Thinking outside the box: A contemporary television genre reader* (pp. 111–135). Lexington: University Press of Kentucky.

Butsch, R., & Glennon, L. M. (1983). Social class: Frequency trends in domestic situation comedy, 1946–1978. *Journal of Broadcasting, 27,* 77–81.

Campbell, R., & Reeves, J. (1990). Television authors: The case of Hugh Wilson. In R. Thompson & G. Burns (Eds.), *Making television* (pp. 3–18). New York: Praeger.

Cantor, M. (1971). *The Hollywood TV producer.* New York: Basic Books.

Carr, D. (2013, March 18). Spreading disruption. *New York Times,* pp. B1, B5.

Connell, B. (1977). *Ruling class, ruling culture.* London: Cambridge University Press.

Consoli, J., & Crupi, A. (2007, April 30). DVRs make their presence felt. *MediaWeek, 17*(18), 8–10.

DiMaggio, P., & Hirsch, P. (1976). Production organization in the arts. *American Behavioral Scientist, 19,* 735–752.

Dominick, J. (1976, Winter). Trends in network prime time, 1953–74. *Journal of Broadcasting, 26,* 70–80.

Elliott, P. (1972). *The making of a television series: A case study in the sociology of culture.* New York: Hastings.

Federal Communications Commission Network Inquiry Special Staff. (1980). *Preliminary reports.* Washington, DC: U.S. Government Printing Office.

Federal Communications Commission Office of Network Study. (1965). *Second interim report: Television network program procurement, Part II.* Washington, DC: U.S. Government Printing Office.

Genre-ation gap hits sitcoms. (1999, April 26). *Variety,* p. 25.

Gitlin, T. (1983). *Inside prime time.* New York: Pantheon.

Glennon, L. M., & Butsch, R. (1982). The family as portrayed on television, 1946–78. In National Institute of Mental Health (Ed.), *Television and social behavior: Ten years of scientific progress and implications for the eighties* (Vol. 2, Technical Review, pp. 264–271). Washington, DC: U.S. Government Printing Office.

Graser, M. (2011, December 5). Cyber-bidding war. *Variety,* pp. 1, 35.

Hindman, D., & Wiegand, K. (2008). The big three's prime-time decline. *Journal of Broadcasting and Electronic Media, 52*(1), 119–135.

Kubey, R. (2004). *Creating television: Conversations with the people behind 50 years of American TV.* Mahwah, NJ: Lawrence Erlbaum.

Lisanti, J. (2012, May 21). Games grow home nets. *Variety,* p. 2.

Lynch, J. (1973). Seven days with *All in the Family:* A case study of the taped TV drama. *Journal of Broadcasting, 17*(3), 259–274.

Owen, B., & Wildman, S. (1992). *Video economics.* Cambridge, MA: Harvard University Press.

Pekurny, R. (1977). *Broadcast self-regulation: A participant observation study of NBC's broadcast standards department.* Unpublished doctoral dissertation, University of Minnesota.

Pekurny, R. (1982). Coping with television production. In J. S. Ettema & D. C. Whitney (Eds.),

Individuals in mass media organizations (pp. 131–143). Beverly Hills, CA: Sage.

Peterson, R. A., & Berger, D. (1971). Entrepreneurship in organizations: Evidence from the popular music industry. *Administrative Science Quarterly, 16,* 97–107.

Ravage, J. (1978). *Television: The director's viewpoint.* New York: Praeger.

Reeves, J. (1990). Rewriting culture: A dialogic view of television authorship. In R. Thompson & G. Burns (Eds.), *Making television* (pp. 147–160). New York: Praeger.

Rossman, G. (2005). *The effects of ownership concentration on media content.* Unpublished doctoral dissertation, Princeton University.

Rosten, L. (1941). *Hollywood: The movie colony, the movie makers.* New York: Harcourt Brace.

Sennett, R., & Cobb, J. (1972). *The hidden injuries of class.* New York: W. W. Norton.

Stein, B. (1979). *The view from Sunset Boulevard.* New York: Basic Books.

Thompson, R., & Burns, G. (Eds.). (1990). *Making television: Authorship and the production process.* New York: Praeger.

Tunstall, J., & Walker, D. (1981). *Media made in California.* New York: Oxford University Press.

Turow, J. (1978). Casting for TV parts: The anatomy of social typing. *Journal of Communication, 28*(4), 18–24.

Turow, J. (1980). Occupation and personality in television dramas. *Communication Research, 7*(3), 295–318.

Turow, J. (1982a). Producing TV's world: How important is community? *Journal of Communication, 32*(2), 186–193.

Turow, J. (1982b). Unconventional programs on commercial television. In J. S. Ettema & D. C. Whitney (Eds.), *Individuals in mass media organizations* (pp. 107–139). Beverly Hills, CA: Sage.

TV role reversal. (2009, January 12). *Variety,* p. 1.

TV's class struggle. (2008, September 22). *Variety,* p. 1.

TV's little guys stayin' alive. (2001, February 19). *Variety,* p. 1. Upscale auds ease b'casters. (1999, August 23). *Variety,* p. 34.

Wakshlag, J., & Adams, W. J. (1985). Trends in program variety and prime time access rules. *Journal of Broadcasting and Electronic Media, 29,* 23–34.

Winick, C. (1961). Censor and sensibility: A content analysis of the television censor's comments. *Journal of Broadcasting, 5,* 117–135.

Young auds seek Web, not webs. (1999, January 4). *Variety,* p. 65.

53

MARKETING "REALITY" TO THE WORLD

Survivor, *Post-Fordism, and Reality Television*

Chris Jordan

This chapter analyzes the production, distribution, and consumption of *Survivor* in order to explain why reality television is a global staple of domestic and international prime time television.[1] It argues that intensifying concentration of ownership in the television industry, the worldwide proliferation of commercial television, the fragmentation of the global television audience, and the design of *Survivor,* as a thinly veiled advertisement, account for its success.

The centrifugal trends of media industry ownership concentration and global television audience fragmentation exemplify post-Fordism. . . . The Fordist system of manufacturing and marketing strove to maximize profits by making one commodity appeal to as many consumers as possible for as long as possible (Harvey 145). Under post-Fordism, capitalism responds to the global flow of labor and consumption markets within and between nation-states by transforming local and regional cultures into market segments and mobilizing citizens as consumers. By implementing a post-Fordist strategy of diversifying its products and their marketing in order to incorporate diverse locales, capitalism transforms a problem into an opportunity, as it markets products for both global markets and niche segments to take advantage of the countervailing flows of localism and globalism (Fiske, "Global" 58).

Stuart Hall contends that post-Fordism promotes democracy by globally circulating media products and other consumer goods (62). Reality television programs thus flow both ways between the United States and other nations. As John Fiske argues, globalization thus provokes localization, multiplying histories through migration and diaspora and eroding a sense of nationalism built around the interests of dominant groups ("Global"). . . .

PRODUCTION OF REALITY TELEVISION: THE MEDIUM IS THE ADVERTISER'S MESSAGE

. . . . Charlie Parsons and former rock band singer Bob Geldof developed the concept that became *Survivor* at their British TV production company, Planet 24. When Parsons and Geldof sold Planet 24 in 1999, they retained the rights to *Survive!,* which was being produced in Sweden by the duo's Castaway Productions, under the name *Expedition: Robinson.* The next year, Parsons and Geldof licensed the *Survive!* concept to Mark Burnett, for a U.S. version that ended up launching the reality TV craze in America.

As an independent producer, Burnett faced an uphill battle in gaining access to prime time, because the relaxation of government regulations in the 1990s made it possible for networks to produce many of their own shows. In 2000, all six broadcast networks either owned or co-owned more than half of their new shows, and three of them (ABC, CBS, and WB) owned or co-owned more than 75 percent of their new programs (Schneider and Adalian 70).

Survivor appealed to CBS because the co-production deal it struck with Burnett required no deficit financing, yet offered the network a program with the high quality production values that audiences expect of prime time television. Instead of paying Burnett a fee to license the show, CBS agreed to share the show's advertising revenue with him if he pre-sold sponsorship of the program.

By pre-selling the show, Burnett raised the capital necessary to produce *Survivor,* provided CBS with essentially free prime time programming, and enjoyed a hefty share of the show's advertising revenue.

Advertisers readily sponsored *Survivor* because of its design as a virtual commercial for their products. Burnett acquired eight sponsors before the commencement of principal photography during the first season, selling not only 30-second spots, but also sponsorship space in the show itself. Anheuser-Busch, General Motors, Visa, Frito-Lay, Reebok, and Target paid approximately $4 million each for advertising time, product placement in the show, and a website link (McCarthy, "Sponsors" B1). Even though *Survivor* is one of the most expensive reality shows to date, with production costs escalating from $1 million an episode for the first season to $1.5 million an episode for subsequent editions, it is profitable. With pre-sold sponsorships covering production costs, and 30-second spots commanding $445,000 during the 2001–2002 season, *Survivor* proved that lavishly produced reality television shows could be low-risk and lucrative (Raphael 122).

Burnett's success in pitching *Survivor* to advertisers enabled the producer to circumvent the role of the advertising agency as a liaison between program creator and sponsor, making it even more cost efficient for sponsors. Producers started working directly with products' brand managers, moving away from shows such as *Temptation Island,* with overt sexual innuendo, and towards shows such as *Survivor* (see Littleton). Praised by CBS President Les Moonves as a "great pitchman," Burnett steered away from sexual sensationalism and towards themes of competitive merit, by explaining to advertisers "how much sense it would make for someone on an island a million miles from home to crave a soft drink or something to eat from home" ("Burnett Likes Mad Ave" 3).

At one time, advertisers balked at the insertion of a bag of chips or a soda into a situation comedy or drama, because it might break the audience's suspension of disbelief. However, *Survivor* host Jeff Probst's act of rewarding winners of the show's challenges with Doritos and Mountain Dew integrated the products into a circumstance that abstracted the line between programming and advertising by associating them with adventure and heroism. During *Survivor: Africa,* for example, the word "avalanche" was the answer to a reward challenge. Viewers then saw the winner driving a Chevrolet Avalanche across the African plain to deliver medical supplies to hospitals treating AIDS patients (McCarthy "Sponsors" B1). In 2001, Burnett received $14 million from marketers such as Mountain Dew and General Motors for the production of *Survivor: Africa* (McCarthy, "Also Starring" B1).

The design of *Survivor* as a virtual advertisement raises the issue of how television's goal of selling audiences to advertisers shapes the program. According to Sut Jhally, a television program must be able to attract large numbers of people. Second, it has to attract the "right" kinds of people. Not all parts of the audience are of equal value to advertisers. Television programs will also have to reflect this targeting, excluding demographic groups that lack the spending power to satisfy advertisers. Third, television must not only be able to deliver a large number of the correct people to advertisers, but must also deliver them in the right frame of mind. Programs should be designed to enhance the effectiveness of the ads in them (Jhally 76).

Survivor accomplishes all of these goals. Broadcast during prime time, it attracts a teen demographic sought by advertisers as well as a huge national audience composed of other age groups. According to *Variety, Survivor* delivered during its initial season more teens than *WWF Smackdown,* more young adults than *Friends,* more children than *Wonderful World of Disney,* and more 50-plus viewers than *60 Minutes* (Kissell 19). Rejecting the jittery hand-held camera style of public television documentaries of the 1970s, *Survivor* also boasts high quality production values that associate products woven into its text with adventure, heroism, and escape.

Survivor thus appeals to networks and advertisers because it combines high ratings with relatively low cost in comparison to comedies and dramas. The escalating cost of must-have sport and movie properties, and the success of special effects-driven docudramas such as BBC-Discovery's *Walking with Dinosaurs* during the 2000 television season, put drama budgets under scrutiny and encouraged U.S. producers to co-produce much more drama on the terms of European networks. Compounding the shift away from half-hour comedy shows and towards low-cost reality-entertainment hybrids was the lack of obvious successors to prime time smash hits such as *Seinfeld* [1989–1998] and *Friends*

[1994–2004] (Fry M4). High quality production values and exotic locations became means through which *Survivor* targeted the prime time audience sought by advertisers, distinguished itself from cheaper crime-based reality shows, and blurred the line between prime time drama and reality shows ("TV's Peeper Producers Are Powerhouses" 1).

Reality television shows have thus proliferated on prime time television in recent years because they pose little financial risk for networks, yet offer prime-time-friendly production values and generate huge ratings. The use of Internet and cable television networks also attracts a young audience prized by advertisers. On this basis, *Survivor* became a valuable addition to Viacom's cradle-to-the-grave programming spectrum by enabling CBS, known for its primarily elderly audience, to capture a huge mass audience, as well as a slice of the highly coveted youth audience.

DISTRIBUTION OF *SURVIVOR:* CREATING A GLOBAL FRANCHISE

. . . . While network television enables advertisers to target a huge audience, cable and the Internet can target specific viewer demographics and deliver them to advertisers at a lower cost. Viacom's cross-promotion of *Survivor* on CBS, its cable networks MTV and VH1, and its Internet websites CBS.com and MTV Networks Online enabled CBS to capture a young audience during the show's first episode and deliver it to advertisers along with a mass audience of 15.5 million. During its second week, the show attracted 18.1 million viewers, a 17 percent gain (Schneider and Adalian 70). According to *Variety, Survivor* "gave CBS and Viacom tangible proof that corporate synergy works," by being the first CBS program to get the full marketing treatment from Viacom's youthful properties, MTV and VH1 (Kissell and Schneider 19).

CBS's use of the Internet also promoted interactivity between viewers and *Survivor,* allowing the network to extend the program beyond the confines of the television set, by encouraging audiences to participate in its dramatic trajectory by using other media to stay in touch with the show. Viewers stayed in touch with the program through the official *Survivor* website. Prolific coverage from established news outlets also generated several unsanctioned online homages, as the websites

Survivor Junkie and Megadice offered winner predictions, plot spoilers, conspiracy theories, and other information of varying quality (Bing and Oppelaar 5). Mobile media, such as cellular telephones, offer additional means of promoting this interactivity and provide valuable information about the audience that is impossible to gather from any other source. Text-based advertising campaigns have been conducted in various countries by major brands, including Coca-Cola, Nike, and McDonald's (McCartney C1).

The ability of Viacom to endlessly promote *Survivor* across multiple media improved CBS's ability to quickly capture a large audience, during an era in which the network practice of ordering shows in small batches makes it imperative to transform a new show into a smash hit as quickly as possible. *Variety* observed that "the numbers for *Survivor* all the more amazing given that *Survivor* had only 13 weeks to generate viewer interest and such a rabid following . . ." (Kissell and Schneider 19).

Survivor's relatively low cost and high ratings potential made the show imminently marketable worldwide, especially in the wake of CBS's purchase of television syndication giant, King World, in 1999. King World collaborates closely with international partners to produce shows carefully tailored to specific national markets, and creates customized promotional advertisements for international licensees (Compaine and Gomery 218). Overseas broadcasters that have licensed the American format of *Survivor* and created their own versions include China's CCTV, the Middle East satellite platform Gulf DTH, South Africa's SABC, Mexico's Televisa, and stations in Scandinavia, Eastern Europe, and throughout Asia (Guider 1).

The global popularity of *Survivor* is attributable, in part, to CBS's use of the economies of scale provided by the size of the U.S. television audience, to sell the program cheaply in developing countries. The proven commercial appeal of *Survivor's* format, and the relatively low cost of reality television production, also encourage foreign broadcasters to create their own versions of the program. . . .

The formation of advertising agencies with global reach provides evidence of the role of advertising in propagating the overseas proliferation of reality television. . . . Global consolidation is encouraged because the larger an advertising agency, the more leverage it has getting favorable terms for its clients with global commercial media (McChesney 86). "More and more, what (advertisers) want is to distribute their global dollars into fewer agency baskets," the *Wall Street Journal* observed in 1998 (Beatty 1).

The rise of transnational advertising agencies also enables sponsors such as Proctor & Gamble to penetrate developing countries with the offer of "free" programming, through which advertisers underwrite programming of general appeal, and provide it free of charge to financially struggling broadcasters (Schiller 330). The top 10 global advertisers alone accounted for some 75 percent of the $36 billion spent by the 100 largest global marketers in 1997 (McChesney 84). Advertising sponsorship thus plays a pivotal role in determining the type of programming made and broadcast by foreign television producers in their native markets.

The competition for audiences and advertisers created by the proliferation of broadcast, cable, and satellite television overseas has led broadcasters in other countries to seek low-cost programming with immediate ratings potential attractive to advertisers. . . .

The consequence of an increasing number of channels in formerly public television markets competing for funding and audiences is that broadcasters must spend greater and greater sums on marketing to get their shows noticed, intensifying pressures on program funding. The pressures on overseas networks to control production costs has in turn led to the concentration of television production in the hands of companies most able to supply low-cost, high volume programming. . . .

The adaptability of reality television shows to local cultures and the convertibility of the format into a virtual infomercial for sponsors' products raises a concern about the role of reality television in propagating the culture of consumption, in both the United States and other nations targeted by transnational capitalism. . . .

CONSUMPTION OF REALITY TELEVISION: TRANSFORMING CITIZENS INTO CONSUMERS

The global success of reality television is attributable to the practice of licensing the format of a show to overseas broadcasters for adaptation to specific markets. The strategy of formatting springs from the principal of product differentiation, through which network executives attempt to replicate a successful show by blatantly imitating it. Hits are so rare on network television that network executives think that a bald imitation stands a better chance of getting ratings than a show that stands alone. This results in the repackaging of old forms in slightly different permutations (Gitlin 77–85). In the wake of *Survivor*'s success, television executives aggressively pursued imitations of it, as the number of reality television hours on broadcast television skyrocketed from four-and-a-half to 19 hours a week between Fall, 2002 and Fall, 2004 (McNary 21).

Paralleling this proliferation of reality television programming was the repetition of what the *New York Times* called a "hamsters-in-a-box" narrative design. The strategy of casting individuals on the basis of type, and forcing them to work and live together, became cross-pollinated with various genres, including game shows, gross-out contests, makeovers, dating programs, situation comedies, and satires (Nussbaum 2). The minimal difference between these many shows stems from the pressure of the marketplace to duplicate a financially successful show.

Financed by advertisers interested in cultivating new consumers abroad, the development of reality television as a format that flexibly incorporates national ideologies on a nation-by-nation basis further suggests that reality TV is first and foremost a commodity. In licensing the *Survivor* format from a British production company, CBS found a program that can be tailored on a market-by-market basis around the world, by integrating the game show and the adventure drama into a hybrid formula. Rather than democratizing global television programming, this trend organizes citizens into consumers by reifying capitalism as an ideology and a way of life. The design of *Survivor* as a game show/adventure/drama hybrid facilitates the placement of products in competitive circumstances that blend adventure and consumption.

In this way, the premise of the show—game show competitors seeking adventure in exotic locations that render global politics invisible—fuels demand for a lifestyle of conspicuous consumption around the world. The director of marketing for Sony's AXN Action TV Network, on which *Survivor* airs in East Asia, exclaimed that "the focus on action and adventure is something that's really picking up—it's a new lifestyle for the young in Asia, a fact borne out by the rise in sales of four-by-four vehicles, for example" (Osborne 32).

The design of *Survivor* also affirms consumption as a way of life, both by attracting advertising and by enabling its producers to develop lucrative licensing deals that extend its shelf life. By organizing leisure time around the consumption of both these programs and pricey ancillary merchandise, *Survivor* encourages viewers to participate in a commodified system of exchange. While merchandising tie-ins have been around since the advent of television, they are now far more commonplace. There are now 150 *Survivor*-themed products available, ranging from CDs to bug spray, to board games, and bandanas (Madger 150). Reality television's organization of the audience into consumers socializes the public into behaving like a market, and as consumers rather than citizens.

CONCLUSION

This chapter argues that the worldwide proliferation of reality television is a product of the increasing concentration of ownership in the television industry, the globalization of commercial TV, and the fragmentation of the worldwide audience. The dependence of the U.S. and other governments on capital investment has led to the implementation of policies that enable the largest media corporations to curtail access to prime time television through in-house production and co-production, and by favoring programs that offer the lowest risk and the highest potential for ratings. The privatization of formerly public overseas broadcasters has also led television programmers in developing nations to seek out inexpensive programming capable of attracting advertisers and viewers.

The first casualty of this trend is educational programming. Television producers, advertisers, and networks know that programs that are too long, too difficult to comprehend, or simply too boring will lead viewers to switch channels. In this way, reality television turns attention away from issues such as poverty in developing countries. The victory of a contestant from the African country of Zambia over a competitor from Tanzania on *Big Brother Africa* provided, according to *Variety,* "a welcome distraction from nationwide strikes in the impoverished country, where most people earn less than $1 a day" (De Jager 19). While some celebrate reality television's global popularity as a sign of the democratization of television production and distribution, a political economic study of reality television compels us to consider that economic determinism limits the possibilities of reality television's potential for democratic communication.

NOTE

1. Prime time refers to a twenty-two hour weekly period spanning 8PM to 11PM Monday through Saturday, with an extra hour on Sunday.

REFERENCES

Beatty, Sally. "Survey Expects Pace of Mergers to Pick Up on Madison Avenue." *Wall Street Journal* 21 May 1998: 1.

————. "Who Owns Prime Time? Industrial and Institutional Conflict over Television Programming and Broadcast Rights." *Framing Friction: Media and Social Conflict.* Ed. Mary S. Mander. Urbana: University of Illinois Press, 1999. 125–160.

Bing, Jonathan and Justin Oppelaar. "'Rat' Race to Publish 1st Survivor Book Begins." *Variety* 28 August–3 September 2000: 4.

"Burnett Likes Mad Ave." *Advertising Age* 19 May 2003: 3.

Compaine, Benjamin and Douglas Gomery. *Who Owns the Media?: Competition and Concentration in the Mass Media.* Mahwah, N.J.: Lawrence Erlbaum Associates, 2000.

De Jager, Christelle "Big Bro' Gives Reality New Meaning." *Variety* 15–21 September 2003: 19.

Fiske, John. "Global, National, Local? Some Problems of Culture in a Postmodern World." *Velvet Light Trap* 40 (1997): 58–66.

Fry, Andy. "Europe Secure as Leader of Reality Programming." *Variety* 25 September–1 October 2000: M4.

Gitlin, Todd. *Inside Prime Time.* New York: Pantheon Books, 1983.

Guider, Elizabeth. "Eye Floats *Survivor* World-wide." *Variety* 18 January 2001: 1.

Harvey, David. *The Condition of Postmodernity.* Boston: Blackwell, 1989.

Jhally, Sut. "The Political Economy of Culture." *Cultural Politics in Contemporary America*, Eds. Ian Angus and Sut Jhally. New York: Routledge, 1989. 65–81.

Kissell, Rick. "*Survivor* Fittest in All Demos." *Variety* 31 July–6 August 2000: 20.

Kissell, Rick and Schneider, M., "Summer Serves as Eye-Opener." *Variety* 28 August–3 September 2000: 19.

Littleton, Cynthia. "Dialogue: Mark Burnett." *Hollywood Reporter.* 26 May 2004. 18 Aug. 2004 <www.hollywoodreporter.com/thr/crafts/feature/display.jsp? vnu_content_id=10011523184>

Madger, Ted. "The End of TV 101: Reality Programs, Formats, and the New Business of Television." *Reality TV: Remaking Television Culture.* Eds. Laurie Oullette and Susan Murray. New York: New York University Press, 2004: 137–156.

McCarthy, Michael. "Also Starring (Your Product Name Here); Brands Increasingly Make Presence Known in TV Shows." *USA Today* 12 August 2004: B1.

———. "Sponsors Line Up *Survivor* Sequel." *USA Today* 9 October 2004: B1.

McCartney, Neil. "Can You Hear It Now?" *Variety* 29 March–4 April 2004: C1.

McChesney, Robert W. *Rich Media, Poor Democracy: Communication Polities in Dubious Times.* New York: The New Press, 1999.

McNarv, Dave. "Coming to Terms with Reality." *Variety* 4–10 October 2004: 21.

Nussbaum, Emily. "The Woman Who Gave Birth to Reality TV." *Variety* 22 February 2004: 2.

Osborne, Magz. "AXN Packs Reality Fare, Hopes Viewers Will Follow." *Variety* 5–11 February 2001: 32.

Raphael, Chad. "The Political Economic Origins of Reality TV." *Reality TV: Remaking Television Culture.* Eds. Laurie Ouellette and Susan Murray. New York: New York University Press, 2004. 119–136.

Schiller, Herbert. "The Privatization of Culture." *Cultural Polities in Contemporary America.* Eds. Ian Angus and Sut Jhally. New York: Routledge, 1989. 317–332.

Schneider, Michael and Joseph Adalian. "Nets Get It Together." *Variety* 22–28 May 2000: 15.

"TV's Peeper Producers are Powerhouses." *Variety* 25 September–1 October 2000: 1.

54

A SHOT AT HALF-EXPOSURE
Asian Americans in Reality TV Shows
Grace Wang

From the start of the sixth season of *Dancing with the Stars,* it seemed almost inevitable that ice skater Kristi Yamaguchi would win the top prize. The graceful poise and athleticism that helped her capture gold in the 1992 Winter Olympics translated well into the realm of ballroom dancing. Throughout the season, Yamaguchi appeared to have little difficulty learning and mastering new dance moves. But having the winner be a foregone conclusion on a show structured around the drama of a competition hardly seemed an ideal way to generate viewer excitement or ratings. And thus, for the Olympian who "brought golden precision to the floor," a different narrative about obstacles faced and overcome needed to be constructed about her character during the season. It soon became clear to viewers that the primary narrative arc structuring Yamaguchi's character on the show would be her inability to express emotions through her ballroom dancing and the personal barriers she would face learning to feel and show passion.

Dancing with the Stars is a popular reality TV show where an assortment of "stars" ranging from B-list Hollywood actors to professional athletes are paired with professional dancers and taught to perform a variety of ballroom dances. Each week, the judges and television audience collectively vote off a celebrity until a winner is finally chosen. Like many other reality TV programs, the show follows a fairly predictable format. Before the contestants perform their dance numbers, they are introduced in brief, easily digestible clips that provide tantalizing glimpses into their inner thoughts and personal biography. Yamaguchi, the cheerful ice skating champ turned mother of two, reflected early in the season, "It is not in my nature to be so open with my emotions." And just in case viewers failed to intuit her lack of emotion while dancing such fiery ballroom styles as the tango and rumba—dances that even casual viewers know are supposed to embody intensity, passion, and lust—a panel of expert judges was on hand to assess her performance. After Yamaguchi's tango in the third week, judge Len Goodman exhorted, "Sharp! Clean! Clear! Always delivered with extreme precision . . . [but I need] more emotional engagement. Lust! I want you to be a dirty girl. Release that for us to see!" Always the model competitor, Yamaguchi does learn to "release" her emotions over the course of the season and eventually wins the coveted top prize.

I begin this essay with Yamaguchi's character construction on *Dancing with the Stars* as it offers an entry point for understanding one of the central narratives that influences Asian American representation in the reality TV format. In what follows, I argue that while reality TV programs open up a space for greater representation of racialized minorities, these shows also adhere to, and authenticate, racialized narratives and stereotypes by embodying them in the characters of "real" people.

. . . If reality TV has been credited with diversifying television culture, this diversification has also depended on fueling drama and conflict through the deliberate casting of disparate characters that will generate tension over the course of the season (Braxton 2009; Stanley 2007). Rather than represent a wide range of "real people" who reflect the diversity of the nation, reality TV repackages difference into comfortably familiar stock characters and stereotypes. Individuals are chosen to represent certain types and then slotted (self-consciously or not) into a limited array of available characters: the angry black woman, the

From Grace Wang (2010), "A Shot at Half-Exposure: Asian Americans in Reality TV Shows." *Television & New Media*, 11:404–427. Reprinted with permission of SAGE Publications.

conservative Christian, the fabulous gay (usually white) man, the nonwhite immigrant grateful for the opportunities afforded to him or her in the United States, and so forth (Collins 2008). To make "real" people, who are obviously complex and contradictory, understandable to viewers in thirty- or sixty-minute time slots, reality shows turn them into "characters." Individuals frequently become stand-ins for only a few of the most visible (and charged) aspects of their identity. Contestants seeking to win a reality TV competition quickly learn to perform their racial, gender, class, and sexual identities on demand or risk being sent home.

THE TECHNICAL BUT UNFEELING ASIAN: HISTORICIZING RACIALIZED NARRATIVES

. . . Since the mid-1960s, journalists and scholars have frequently depicted Asian Americans as model minority subjects whose hard work ethic, compliant temperament, and self-sufficient nature have led to their relative material success. Much has been written about the ideological function that model minority discourses serve in disciplining other racial minority groups for their purported cultural "inferiorities" while also continuing to buttress white superiority and celebrate U.S. meritocracy (Kim 2003; Palumbo-Liu 1999; Osajima 1988). Model minority myths also help perpetuate the racial and cultural difference of Asian Americans by depicting members of this group—regardless of their generational status—as embodying "Asian" rather than "American" cultural values. Such a construction contributes to the continued elision between Asians and Asian Americans and the perpetually "foreign" status that Asian Americans hold in the U.S. racial imaginary.

While virtues such as discipline and diligence are valorized in the U.S. context, these purportedly "model" traits can become deviant when pushed to excess. Political scientist Claire Jean Kim (2003, 46) notes that during the 1980s, U.S. popular media portrayed Korean merchants as so hard-working, driven, and self-sacrificing as to seem "barely human." Taken to its zealous extreme, the unrelenting work ethic of Asians appears to evacuate them of both creativity and feeling. As Kim further observes, such narratives have a long historical precedent: "The construction of Asians/Asian Americans as self-immolating robots dates

back to discussions of Chinese immigrant labor and Japanese kamikaze pilots during the 1800s and World War II respectively." Similar discourses about the North Vietnamese as "subhuman" enemies who lacked feeling and individuality and placed little value on human life also circulated in the United States during the Vietnam War.

While the construction of Asians and Asian Americans as "quasi-robots" performs a dehumanizing function, it has also been used to domesticate the success that Asians and Asian Americans achieve in the United States. During the 1980s, an era marked by U.S. anxieties over the escalating ascendancy of Japan in the global economy, the United States positioned Japan as its cultural inverse. The conformist, unfeeling, and mechanical nature of Japanese culture specifically, and Asian cultures generally, stood in implicit contrast to the United States, which promotes individuality, free thinking, and ingenuity. . . . Aligning Japan's high-tech advancements with a culture of robot-like efficiency, discipline, and control allowed for the threat of Japan's economic growth to be contained and managed through the framework of what David Morley and Kevin Robins have termed *technoorientalism*.[1] Within such a context of anxiety over techno-orientalism, Asians and Asian Americans become the implied foil for normative white Americans, whose balanced pursuit of work and innovation would, in the long run, prove more successful.

More recently, the specter of Asian and Asian American success has led literary critic Min Song (2008, 16) to suggest the emergence of a new construction of model minority success in U.S. popular media—the "super minority." As Song observes, in such a characterization, "Asian Americans become less of a model whose successes specifically berate blacks and other racial minorities and more a kind of, for lack of a better term, super minority whose successes berate *everyone* who fails somehow to succeed." Such a narrative can be detected in media descriptions of the "new white flight"—white families who leave high-achieving suburban school districts that have become "too Asian." In this instance, the descriptor "too Asian" becomes a referent for a broad range of racialized anxieties about the ways that having an "over-representation" of Asian Americans transforms schools into excessively competitive environments, where the drive for academic achievement comes at the expense of the "whole" child (Egan

2007; Jaschik 2006; Hwang 2005). . . . By coding expertise in fields such as math and classical music as the consequence of discipline and relentless practice—rather than creativity, passion, or even inventiveness—what counts as talent and skill is transformed to diminish the achievements of Asian Americans. Moreover, while the unremitting drive and work ethic of Asian Americans might lead to particular types of success, these same qualities also limit their ability to reach the highest echelons of their professions, where creativity—in addition to technical mastery—is required.

Contestants need a narrative to be interesting in a reality TV competition over the course of a season, and for racialized characters these narratives frequently fall into a longer history of racialized discourses and stereotypes. . . . As a site that recycles and reworks racialized narratives onto "real" individuals, reality TV represents a critical new laboratory for understanding the maintenance of racial hierarchies in the contemporary U.S. context.[2] . . .

FINDING "HEART" AND "SOUL" ON *TOP CHEF*

Hung Huynh, a Vietnamese immigrant, won the third season of *Top Chef* (original episodes aired June through October 2007, but, like other Bravo programs, the episodes constantly replay). Similar to the other contestants on the show, he arrived with an impressive resume, having worked his way through some of the nation's most celebrated restaurants. Yet few contestants matched Hung's arrogance. . . . Relentlessly self-centered, Hung's attitude was best summarized by his mantra: "I'm here for myself, I came here by myself, and hopefully I can win this by myself." Not just mere braggadocio, however, Hung backed his arrogant swagger with an extensive arsenal of culinary skill and knowledge. His deft use of classic French techniques—depicted on *Top Chef* as representing the backbone of all fine culinary cuisine—brought him praise throughout the season.

Hung shined in challenges that focused on technique. He butchered chickens in such record time that even the head judge, chef Tom Colicchio, was left chuckling and shaking his head in astonishment.[3] In another challenge, Hung outperformed his contestants by replicating a signature dish served at the fancy French eatery

Le Cirque that looked and tasted most close to the original. And in a challenge meant to showcase the competitors' knowledge of classical training, he garnered abundant praise for his beautifully presented and executed dish by a panel of culinary luminaries at the French Culinary Institute. At the same time, however, the adulation Hung received was tempered with reservation. For while he was arguably the best chef technically, his food seemed to lack a certain elusive quality we might term "soul." Throughout the season, a swirl of questions consistently trailed Hung: Where was his passion? Where was his heart? One of the three finalists, Dale—the self-anointed "big gay chef" of the season—commented, "Hung is the best technical cook. But in my world, the best food has heart and when you don't have one it doesn't taste good."[4] This sentiment seemed to be shared by the judges, who complimented Hung for his technique but praised other contestants for dishes that "sang" and had "soul."

. . . In the episode before the finale, head judge Colicchio deftly summarized Hung's limitations this way: "You [Hung] are technically the best chef up here. Technically. But we don't see you in the food at all [pause . . . drum sounds dramatically in the background]. You were born in Vietnam?" Already knowing the answer, Colicchio quickly continued, "We need to see you in the food. Somewhere, we need to see Hung." In this particular iteration, Hung became a proxy for his nation of birth. Finding Hung, and presumably his soul, would involve tasting Vietnamese flavors in his food and, in so doing, returning to his "roots," his ethnic heritage, and his place of birth.

Colicchio's suggestion that Hung look "homeward" to Vietnam invoked a straightforward and accessible narrative for successfully performing "ethnic soul." For Hung to cook food that showcased his skills and knowledge in the fundamentals of classic French cuisine somehow inferred that he was not being himself. Yet similar pressures were not placed on his fellow white competitors. In fact, one of Hung's fellow finalists, a white woman from Texas, described her signature style of cuisine as drawing on Asian flavors. Thus, while the whiteness of the other finalists insulated them from any implicit (or explicit) expectation to draw on certain influences and flavor profiles in their food, as a clearly marked "ethnic" contestant, Hung needed to authenticate himself through a narrowly defined conception of passion to win over the judges. The image of Hung facing a white judge advising him to reveal his "soul" by looking to Vietnam—a nation long colonized by France and subject to imperial blunders by the United States—visually symbolized the bind that Asian Americans face when navigating fields of culture that continue to be governed by white privilege.[5] French food, it seems, could never authenticate a Vietnamese chef's "soul," regardless of the historical relationship of colonialism that linked these two nations. Since *Top Chef* presents the techniques and standards of Europeans and white Americans as universal, racialized minorities are cast either as "soulless" when they better their white counterparts at those skills or as unsophisticated and lacking proper training when they do not.[6]

. . . In the complex interplay among character construction, perception, and expectation operating in *Top Chef,* Hung appeared to be a quick study. He knew that the primary customers he needed to please were the panel of judges.[7] And if the judges wanted Hung to authenticate his passion for cooking through a particular construction of himself and his food, then he would willingly oblige. And thus, whether or not he believed himself to have a special connection to Vietnamese cuisine, Hung seemed to realize just how much authority the trope of "returning to one's roots" and cooking from one's "own" ethnic and national culinary tradition held on *Top Chef.*

On screen, Hung's persona transformed completely following judge Colicchio's caution that despite having superior technical skills his food communicated neither passion nor a sense of his identity as an individual born in Vietnam. While the process of judging on *Top Chef* demands a performance of authenticity—a declaration of love and passion—the change in Hung's character was so abrupt as to feel forced, even for a reality TV competition clearly edited to reveal, over the course of a season, the personal motivations that drive each contestant's passion for cooking. Writing about the *Top Chef* finale, Frank Bruni (2007), a restaurant critic for the *New York Times* at the time, appeared unconvinced by what he described as Hung's "transparent groveling and obsequiousness to the judges' panel. . . . On the heels of a comment that he didn't seem to cook with enough heart or soul, Hung suddenly morphed—at least semantically—into one big, red beating heart that had been marinated for 24 hours in essence of soul."

. . . The redemption of Hung's character and "soul" took place on the level of discourse—the narratives he used to frame his life story—and in the flavors contained in the dishes he promised to deliver in the finale. Arguing for his spot in the final challenge, Hung linked cooking to the very soul of his being. For the first time on the show, he spoke of a childhood spent sleeping in the kitchen and learning to cook from his mother. He described his mother as "the greatest chef in the world" and cooking as inherent to his family bloodline: "I cook with so much love and I get that from my mother. I grew up in the kitchen, sleeping in the kitchen. Cooking all my life. And when I think about my mom's food, I get so emotional. I get tingly. Because it's all about soul." The details Hung revealed about his personal background were equally compelling. His father risked his life escaping postwar Vietnam on a fishing boat headed for the United States when Hung was an infant; he did not see his father again until he was nine years old. Through hard work, sacrifice, and determination, his family eventually got off welfare by opening a restaurant. Winning the title "top chef" would, as Hung put it, make his mom proud *and* show the viewing public that "through hard work every immigrant can achieve the American Dream." And thus, whether the result of careful editing, a self-conscious recrafting of his on-screen persona, or a blend of both, by the finale Hung was less the self-centered braggart talking up his superior technique and skills and more the earnest immigrant who wanted, in his own words, to "win it for all immigrants in America." Hung scripted his family inheritance as twofold: he gained the flavors of home and family from his mother (a narrative replete with the gendered slippage between mother, food, and "homeland") and inherited the classic American story of self-reliance and immigrant success from his father.

In the final challenge, Hung showcased Vietnamese flavors in his food—palm sugar, coconut, and "ocean-scented rice"—and was rewarded not only with the title of "top chef" but also with praise for finally marrying "passion with technique." Colicchio lauded, "You put together a fabulous meal, and we're really happy to see you in your food." When the judges announced his win, an elated Hung exclaimed, "I'm so excited! I worked so hard to get here and to prove myself. And I have so much support from America."

. . . In interviews conducted outside of *Top Chef* and the Bravo network, viewers gain a sense of how Hung negotiated his television persona, as many of these interviews reveal the deliberateness with which he constructed his reality TV persona. He was media conversant enough to realize that *Top Chef* was as much a cooking competition as it was a reality TV program that depended on conflict and drama from its contestants. As Hung observed, being an interesting and outspoken character on the program would garner the most media exposure and ensure a lengthier stay on the show: "I wouldn't say I was the bad boy, but the most controversial contestant. That's the character I wanted to create from the beginning. I'm the most talked-about contestant. Either you love me or you hate me. It gets you more exposure. . . . It's a way to stay on the show, and it made good TV" (Smith 2007). Hung was clearly aware that he was playing a character crafted in concert with specific professional goals.

Hung's savvy also extended to the narratives he performed to satisfy the judges. For while he repeatedly emphasized the importance of passion, love, and soul toward the end of the *Top Chef* season, in interviews outside the show Hung continued to maintain that "technique is more important than soul and love, and creativity" (Tieu 2008). In one interview, Hung noted that he would donate a portion of his winnings to Buddhist temples and use another portion to travel to Spain and "experience life, learn, cook, [and become] *more* technical!" As he scoffed later in that interview, "When was the last time you walked out of a restaurant and said, 'That steak was so soulful, I'm definitely going back?' No. You say it was cooked perfectly, it was seasoned perfectly. . . . Why am I being dissed for having some technical skills?" (Lalli 2007). Thus, while *Top Chef* created an aura around "soul" that erased the typically racialized and immigrant labor involved in running a restaurant, such a media-constructed fantasy held less currency outside the realm of television. As Hung noted, in the day-to-day work of running a business, dishes need to be replicated with technical precision, and "heart" will

not keep a restaurant afloat: "Just because you have passion and love for the food doesn't mean you can operate a restaurant. You do need the training and the skills and the techniques to produce food for a $30 million operation. Passion just doesn't do that for you" (Smith 2007). Such media reports suggest how consciously Hung went about trying to create a television character that would not only keep him on the show but also win over the judges who ultimately controlled his fate in the competition.

Hung willingly participated in the reality TV competition and accepted the specific parameters set forth by *Top Chef*. If the television program needed him to embody the role of the grateful Vietnamese immigrant who cooks food inspired by the flavors of his homeland, he did his part and hoped that the editing process would go his way. In an article that appeared a few days before the finale aired, Hung seemed hopeful that he had performed enough "soul" and gratitude to secure the win: "Everything is going to make sense in the end, if they edit it right" (Lalli 2007). At the same time, he seemed to brace against the limitations placed on him, including the one-dimensional and expected version of ethnicity offered to him within the context of the show. For such a simplistic performance of ethnicity revealed neither the complexity of his life experience nor his food. As Hung questioned in an interview, "What does that mean when [Colicchio] says, 'We don't see Hung'? What should I do, make sweet and sour chicken and wontons? I'm trained in French food. I love French food. That is me" (Lalli 2007).

. . . On *Top Chef*, the nuance of Hung's life story and his multilayered relationship to cuisine were compressed into an easily digestible story of immigrant success achieved through hard work, humility, gratitude, and maintaining one's ethnic heritage and "roots." Hung's narrative on *Top Chef* revealed not only how the trope of being technical but lacking "heart" and "soul" is placed on Asian Americans but also the conflicts that racialized minorities encounter competing in fields of culture that continue to be governed by white privilege. . . .

NOTES

1. See Morley and Robins (1995).

2. Space limitations prevent a fuller analysis of racial representation across a range of reality

TV shows. While the rapid proliferation of new reality TV programs produced each year makes it somewhat difficult for critical scholarship to keep pace, several scholars have insightfully analyzed how reality TV incorporates the tenets of multicultural discourse in the United States by celebrating racial and ethnic diversity through the mere fact of representation itself and by personalizing, decontextualizing, and containing racism to the realm of individual conflict. See, for instance, Kim and Blasini (2001) and Kraszewski (2009).

3. At the same time, Hung's impressively fast skills were also portrayed on the show as making him, quite literally, a menace in the kitchen. Contestants noted that Hung ran quickly and carelessly around the kitchen with his knives in hand, ready at any minute to accidentally slice off the limb of an unsuspecting competitor.

4. It is worth noting that while Hung reveals himself to be bisexual during the reunion show, his queerness never becomes part of his narrative arc. It might be that to foreground Hung's queerness *and* his identity as a racialized immigrant would have muddled his character construction too much for a

show that depends on the easy legibility of its characters.

5. It is worth noting that included in the panel of judges is Padma Lakshmi, who is of South Asian descent. However, as the host of the show, her capital seems primarily located in her attractiveness rather than in her culinary expertise.

6. See Priscilla Ferguson (2004, 4) for a fascinating account of how the French came to dominate Western concepts of sophisticated culinary cuisine. As Ferguson notes, from the nineteenth century to the present era, French culinary customs, restaurant practices, and discourses of gastronomy have retained their special place as an "ideal of culinary. . . . French cuisine supplies a point of reference and a standard."

7. Hung, like many other *Top Chef* contestants, frequently noted the importance of pleasing the judges first and foremost regardless of the particular demographic being targeted for the challenge (which ranged from "cowboys" and "cowgirls" at a rodeo to members of the Elks club).

REFERENCES

Betts, Kate. 2004. Visions from the East. *Time,* September 20. http://www.time.com/time/magazine/article/0,9171,699434,00.html.

Blasini, Gilberto Moíses and Kim, L.S. 2001. The Performance of Multicultural Identity in U.S. Network Television: Shiny, Happy, POPSTARS (Holding Hands) *Emergences: Journal for the Study of Media and Composite Cultures* 11 (2): 287-307.

Boncompagni, Tatiana. 2008. Korea opportunities. *FT.com,* January 5. http://www.ft.com/cms/s/2/3a1b5eb6-ba6b-11dc-abcb-0000779fd2ac.html.

Bourdain, Anthony. 2007. *The nasty bits: Collected varietal cuts, usable trim, scraps, and bones.* New York: Bloomsbury.

Braxton, Greg. 2009. The greater reality of minorities on TV. *Los Angeles Times,* February 17.

Bruni, Frank. 2007. The *Top Chef* finale: Of bad lobster and tame cake. *New York Times,* October 4.

Chung, Hye Seung. 2006. *Hollywood Asian: Philip Ahn and the politics of cross-ethnic performance.* Philadelphia: Temple University Press.

Cohen, Lara. 2006. In her own words: From refugee to *Project Runway. US Weekly,* March 20, 120–21.

Collins, Sue. 2008. Making the most out of 15 minutes: Reality TV's dispensable celebrity. *Television & New Media* 9:87–110.

Dominus, Susan. 2008. The affluencer. *New York Times,* November 2.

Egan, Timothy. 2007. Little Asia on the hill. *New York Times,* January 7.

Ellick, Adam. 2007. Boulud settling suit alleging bias at French restaurant. *New York Times,* July 31.

Elliot, Charles. 1995–1996. Race and gender as factors in judgments of musical performance. *Bulletin of the Council for Research in Music Education* 12 (7): 50–56.

Feldman, Jenny. 2006. Being a good Asian daughter, I thought I should become a buyer or work on the business side instead of trying to design. *Elle*, August.

Feng, Peter X. 2000. Recuperating Suzie Wong: A fan's Nancy Kwan-dary. In *Countervisions: Asian American film criticism*, ed. D. Hamamoto and S. Liu, 40–58. Philadelphia: Temple University Press.

Ferguson, Priscilla. 2004. *Accounting for taste: The triumph of French cuisine*. Chicago: University of Chicago Press.

Fisher, Ian. 2008. Is cuisine still Italian even if the chef isn't? *New York Times*, April 7.

Go, Kitty. 2005. Eastern exposure. *Financial Times*, January 8.

Hendershot, Heather. 2009. Belabored reality: Making it work on *The Simple Life* and *Project Runway*. In *Reality TV: Remaking television culture*, 2nd ed., ed. S. Murray and L. Ouellette, 243–59. New York: New York University Press.

Holmes, Su. 2004. "Reality goes pop!" Reality TV, popular music, and narratives of stardom. *Television & New Media* 5:147–72.

Hwang, Suein. 2005. The new white flight. *Wall Street Journal*, November 19.

Jaschik, Scott. 2006. Too Asian? *Inside Higher Ed*, October 10. http://www.insidehighered.com/news/2006/10/10/asian.

Kim, Claire Jean. 2003. *Bitter fruit: The politics of black-Korean conflict in New York City*. New Haven, CT: Yale University Press.

Kingsbury, Henry. 2001. *Music, talent, and performance: A conservatory cultural system*. Philadelphia: Temple University Press.

Kraszewski, Jon. 2009. Country hicks and urban cliques: Mediating race, reality, and liberalism on MTV's *The Real World*. In *Reality TV: Remaking television culture*, 2nd ed., ed. S. Murray and L. Ouellette, 205–22. New York: New York University Press.

Lalli, Nina. 2007. Hung speaks: "What should I do, make sweet and sour chicken?" *Village Voice*, October 1. http://blogs.villagevoice.com/food/archives/2007/10/hung_speaks_wha.php.

Manalansan, Martin. 2009. The empire of food: Place, memory, and Asian "ethnic" cuisines.

In *Gastro polis: Food and New York City*, ed. A. Hauck-Lawson and J. Deutsch, 93–107. New York: Columbia University Press.

Morley, David, and Kevin Robins. 1995. *Spaces of identity: Global media, electronic landscapes and cultural boundaries*. London: Routledge University Press.

Osajima, Keith. 1988. Asian Americans as the model minority: An analysis of the popular press image in the 1960s and 1980s. In *Reflections on shattered windows: Promises and prospects for Asian American studies*, ed. G. Okihiro, 165–174. Seattle: University of Washington Press.

Palumbo-Liu, David. 1999. *Asian/America: Historical crossings of a racial frontier*. Stanford, CA: Stanford University Press.

Parasecoli, Fabio. 2009. The chefs, the entrepreneurs, and their patrons: The avant-garde food scene in New York City. In *Gastropolis: Food and New York City*, ed. A. Hauck-Lawson and J. Deutsch, 116–31. New York: Columbia University Press.

Senior, Jennifer. 2007. The near fame experience. *New York Magazine*, August 6. http://nymag.com/news/features/35538/.

Severson, Kim, and Adam Ellick. 2007. A top chef's kitchen is far too hot, some workers say. *New York Times*, January 17.

Silverstein, Michael, and Neil Fiske. 2003. *Trading up: The new American luxury*. New York: Portfolio.

Smith, Nina. 2007. *Top Chef's* controversial Hung wins—and says he deserves it. *TV Guide*, October 5. http://www.tvguide.com/news/top-chef-hung-35797.aspx

Song, Min Hyoung. 2008. Communities of remembrance: Reflections on the Virginia Tech shootings and race. *Journal of Asian American Studies* 11 (1): 1–26.

Stanley, Alessandra. 2007. The classless utopia of reality TV. *New York Times*, December 2.

Stokes, Martin. 1994. *Ethnicity, identity and music: The musical construction of place*. New York: Berg.

Tieu, Hong Hoa. 2008. Hail to the chef: Cooking his way to the top. *BN Magazine*, March 28. http://news.newamericamedia.org/news/view_article.html?article_id=4b076d2bc03de735409ee094a90255f2

THE RACIAL LOGIC OF *GREY'S ANATOMY*

Shonda Rhimes and Her "Post-Civil Rights, Post-Feminist" Series

Kristen J. Warner

Episode 2 of *Grey's Anatomy* (2005–) Season 3 begins as Dr. Preston Burke (Isaiah Washington) lies in his hospital bed "recovering" from a gunshot wound to the hand with his resident girlfriend, Dr. Christina Yang (Sandra Oh), by his side, when his door suddenly bursts open to reveal his parents. Aesthetic markers signify that the elders are well-to-do . . . individuals who are understandably surprised to find their son and his significant other in a compromising position—in a hospital bed, no less. Donald and Jane Burke come to tend to their son and also make judgments on his personal entanglements. Dressed in an expensively regal navy St. John suit with her hair carefully coiffed and her makeup designed to look natural and fresh, Jane wanders through the corridors of Seattle Grace meeting Burke's friends and offering advice in an extremely sophisticated fashion. Meanwhile, Donald spends the majority of the episode sitting quietly and reading the paper in Burke's hospital room . . .

As a black viewer, what shocked me about the characters Donald and Jane Burke is that iconic African American actors Diahann Carroll and Richard Roundtree portrayed them. Carroll [was a] celebrated entertainer of the 1960s and one of the first African American leads of [a] prime-time television series, *Julia* (NBC 1968–1971), and Roundtree [was a] former model turned actor most famous for his role as John Shaft in *Shaft* (1971). . . . [M]y summation of how the viewing audience meets Donald and Jane Burke . . . is a wonderful example of one of the show's most vital yet unarticulated components: race. . . . [T]hough these two actors' histories are informed by them breaking racial barriers in Hollywood, *Grey's* insistence on not seeing their characters as racialized beings ultimately neutralizes Carroll and Roundtree's achievements.

Returning to the scene with Jane and Donald catching Burke and Christina in the act, Jane takes issue with Christina because she considers her a woman with "loose morals." Jane clearly disapproves of Christina but interestingly enough, the race of the woman her son is dating is never brought up. Given the generational gap between Burke and his parents, it would have made sense that the young woman's racial makeup be acknowledged. Even though Burke might not notice her Asian difference, Civil Rights era parents surely do. Instead, Jane articulates that regardless of how similar they are with regard to ambition and socioeconomic status, Christina is unilaterally not good for him. This lack of racial acknowledgment is not by accident.

To the contrary, the way that creator, executive producer, and head writer Shonda Rhimes imagines her characters illustrates the conscious effort she exerts to normalize and rehabilitate viewer attitudes regarding this interracial romance: "It's not about the fact that she's Asian and he's Black. It's about the fact that she's a slob and he's a neat freak. That's what the whole relationship is all about" (Barney 2006, 3). Rhimes's failure to acknowledge racial difference between these two characters of color in favor of framing it as a more simplistic "odd couple" trope is not an accident. In fact, her neutralization of race within her self-fashioning of this series is quite intentional. Fogel makes an astute observation connecting Rhimes's

Television & New Media 2015, Vol. 16(7) 631–647. © The Author(s) 2014. Reprints and permissions: sagepub.com/journalsPermissions.nav DOI: 10.1177/1527476414550529.

fashioning of her show to its depiction of race: "Shonda Rhimes has conceived Seattle Grace as a frenetic, multicultural hub where racial issues take a back seat to the more pressing problems of hospital life: surgery, competition, exhaustion and—no surprise—sex" (Fogel 2005). In other words, race has little value within this text in comparison with the sexy and seemingly racially neutral aspects of television's nighttime soap dynamics in the foreground.

HISTORICAL PRECEDENTS TO *GREY'S*

But *Grey's* is not the first prime-time dramatic series, or even more specifically, the first prime-time medical series to deploy race neutralization as a solution to racial inequity. . . . One response, the evacuation of cultural specificity for racialized characters, also known as racial colorblindness, has televisual antecedents preceding Rhimes's hit series. *Julia* was not a medical show per se (Turow 1989, 201), but her position as an African American nurse who worked with a white doctor set up the dynamics for the medical genre. . . . *Julia* was shaped around a black female lead and pursued a colorblind agenda by rarely addressing the cultural differences that marked the stratification lines that forced people of color into subordinate positions. Smith-Shomade argues that *Julia* presented a utopic and sanitized 1960s America incongruent from the systemic racism the Civil Rights movement fought to eradicate:

> Julia never alluded explicitly to this phenomenon or to the civil and social unrest raging on American streets. The show implied that . . . harmony could be achieved if we could all just get along. Look, watch Julia do it. Julia ran for three years, with Julia never having a steady companion, promotion, or confrontation. This blind-eye approach paved the way for 1990s "no color lines" programming. (Smith-Shomade 2002, 14–15)

The blind-eye approach also framed *Julia's* characterization. *Julia* was heavily criticized for constructing a "White Negro," for playing it safe not to scare away white viewers, for sugarcoating its messages. Although all of that may be true, the show's "whiteness" middle-classness, and inoffensiveness

did not defuse its threat to entrenched racist positions. The historical positioning of *Julia* as a forerunner in colorblind television compels us to not forget that part of the reason assimilation occurs is to connect a society together for consumption. The series analogized through the titular character's desire to become upwardly mobile through her nursing career, that the more common ground racial groups had with whites, the more likely she (and by extension, a black audience) would attain the material signs of upward mobility. In Julia's case, the more she "got along," the more successful/accepted she became—at least in theory. Bodroghkozy (1992, 156–57) points out that although *Julia* was designed to be so racially neutral as not to offend audiences, hostile viewers still felt there was too much black on their television screens.

In contrast to *Julia,* 1970s medical dramas attempted to mainstream U.S. counterculture as a way to brand their networks as edgy. *The Interns* (CBS 1970–1971) featured an integrated cast that reflected the commercially viable *Mod Squad*-esque formula for rebellion and relevance. The series was short lived, only lasting one season. If nothing more than serving as an ancestor to the contemporary medical genres such as *E.R.* and *Grey's Anatomy,* one of the achievements of *The Interns* was that it did feature women and African Americans in central roles. Yet, the series served what, according to Phillips (2000, 50–52), had become a staple of the medical genre in that era: support of the white male lead. This convention had the potential to render the bodies of color powerless to express their difference—which, given the cultural context of the time, may have proven a valuable goal. If the genre implicitly placed gender and race at the center of its structure only to make those identities unimportant, then it makes more sense how the evacuation of cultural specificity so easily became legitimized as a solution to television's racial disparity.

Ultimately, what these medical shows suggest is that the networks have not been responding to blacks' desire to be seen as much as they are responding to what and how much white viewers want to see of black life. Thus, the 1990s and present-day programming seem on the surface progressive because there are so many medical shows and other kinds of hour-long dramas that feature black casts. Gray (2004, 84) points to the real complexities of this programming especially concerning the prime-time drama:

Ironically, it seemed that the hour-long drama was finally about to deliver the goods, presenting programs with multiracial casts, devoting story lines to complex depictions of Black life, and locating such programs in integrated workplace settings.

Gray's quote brings into focus the networks' logic in greenlighting Rhimes's *Grey's Anatomy.* New York Times television critic Fogel subtly questions the intentions of the show: "*Grey's Anatomy* has differentiated itself [from other medical shows] by creating a diverse world of doctors—almost half the cast are men and women of color—and then never acknowledging it" (Fogel 2005). . . . A strategy of quantity over quality representation, *Grey's* illustrates how diversity is more gimmick than innovation.

RHIMES'S *GREY'S:* BLINDCASTING AS PUBLIC RELATIONS MIRACLE

Grey's Anatomy appeared on ABC's midseason lineup in March of 2005. Five surgical interns . . . compete and negotiate their work and love lives with each other and their supervisors. . . . Much like *Julia* and *The Interns, Grey's* is not about medicine. Rhimes asserts,

> *Grey's Anatomy* is more about, not necessarily being a medical drama as it is about people who are starting a job, and on a bad day you kill somebody. On a good day, you save a life. To me, it's surgery and it's competition, and that feels fresh. It's also very much about their personal lives (Rhimes 2005, *Tavis Smiley Show*).

Rhimes's differentiating how *Grey's* operates with different narrative interests than medical dramas aligned with more standard procedural conventions forwards a smart discursive tactic she will deploy throughout her career. Focusing on her show's generic difference allows her to divert attention from her position as a black female showrunner. What's more, Rhimes's tireless work ethic also becomes a deflection tool. Indeed, much of the discourse surrounding Rhimes is quite similar to the discourse surrounding her show—a proponent of diversity, yet a believer in universality. She is, on one hand, celebrated as one of the only black, female executive producers of

a prime-time network drama, and, she is, on the other hand, racially neutralized as a hardworking individual with a strong work ethic (Fogel 2005; Johnson 2005). In 2012, while participating in a public panel on her newest hit series *Scandal* (ABC 2012–) at the Paley Center's annual PaleyFest, a female fan asked Rhimes for advice on how women could break into the male-dominated television industry. Rhimes responds,

> Y'know Betsey [Beers co-executive producer of Scandal] and I have talked about this a bunch because we get asked this question a lot like "you're two women in Hollywood. How does that work?" And I remember saying that I'm too busy working to be worried about the fact that somebody else has a problem with my vagina. Really, the idea that being a woman is a problem in this town is something I just don't have time for. Like I don't have the time to worry that somebody has a problem that I'm a woman or that I'm a woman of color. That's like exhausting. So I don't have time to worry about your thing cause we're too busy doing our thing ourselves. (Scandal Cast and Creators 2012, Paleyfest)

Here Rhimes's way of circumventing the very clear structural impediments to accessing industrial employment for women and, with regard to this essay, women of color, is to displace the issue altogether. In other words, systemic issues can exist but if one is immersed in her work, she cannot feel the effects of her limitations. As a powerful showrunner at the time of this writing presiding over three prime-time dramatic series at ABC, Rhimes's position allows her the privilege to feel relatively immune to the disadvantages women of color in the television industry regularly face. Yet, Rhimes's reluctance to acknowledge her unique position does not mean she was unaware she was selling a safe version of race to audiences. To the contrary, I argue that the way she self-presents as a colorless female writer is a discursive strategy deployed to divest race from its cultural contexts for herself and her cast. That is to say, in the same manner that Rhimes disavows any racially specific politics, her cast of characters practices a similar strategy that results in difference that is only skin-deep.

For the television industry, Rhimes brought back public discussions of race on television in a positive way. The discourse surrounding the *Grey's* cast is both celebratory and self-congratulatory in tone. Newspaper articles implicitly acknowledge the lack of people of color on television and see *Grey's* as a corrective for years of neglect (Barney 2006; Fogel 2005). Her innovative blindcasting could, if properly deployed, change the visual representation of minorities on the small screen ultimately satisfying watchdog racial action groups that threaten potential advertising revenue. The tension between groups like the National Association for the Advancement of Colored People (NAACP), the National Association of Latino Independent Producers (NALIP), and the networks emerged around the Fall of 1999. Just a few years prior to *Grey's,* the NAACP and NALIP threatened to boycott the networks in response to the complete lack of diversity in their Fall premiere lineups. Quelling talk of boycotts with promises to be intentional about diversity, the networks tried to make use of every opportunity to prove they had changed. One of those opportunities came when the networks realized they could make casts more racially diverse without having to acknowledge difference. This innovation, called blindcasting, insisted that as opposed to the traditional method of network executives, casting directors, and talent managers generating casting breakdowns that explicitly listed the race and ethnicity of each character for auditioning purposes, the producer not specify the race of any of the roles. Ironically, blindcasting is not new or innovative. Traditionally considered a large part of U.S. theatrical history, blindcasting allowed Rhimes to audition a variety of actor types for each of the characters and ultimately hit pay dirt for both the showrunner and the network helping the show become a runaway success because it exemplified the notion of a multicultural, yet, paradoxically, post-racial society.

Rhimes's engagement with blindcasting as a progressive social practice is thus tethered to a double-minded ideology that informs how she approached *Grey's* and television in general. In nearly every interview (Fogel 2005; *Nightline* 2005), Rhimes makes the same point about her views of society:

> I don't think anybody is colorblind in this world, do you know what I mean? I think I'm a product of being a post-feminist, post-civil rights baby born in an era after that happened, where race isn't the only thing discussed. And I

just felt like there's something interesting about having a show in which your characters could just be your characters. (Robichaux 2006)

Although Rhimes's quote is rich, it is important to note the ambiguity of her position. It is necessary for her to at once acknowledge that although she (and all of us) has to "see" race, the post-racial moment we currently abide within allows us to not make it a meaningful aspect of identity. In fact, the way she self-fashions her own autobiography illustrates how her work ethic overshadowed any identity politic that may have helped her along the way. While in her mid-thirties, Rhimes tells the story of her foray into television as the former feature film screenwriter and graduate of University of Southern California's film program. After adopting her infant daughter, Rhimes took a sabbatical from film scripts, stayed at home, and watched television. Not impressed with the current stock of female-led shows, she wrote the pilot for *Grey's Anatomy* and when it became a hit surprised herself as well as the networks and trade press (Johnson 2005). Her biographical narrative not only gives credence to the (false) notion that anyone can write and transform a script into a network development deal, but similar to her quote at PaleyFest, it also normalizes Rhimes's position as a black female writer neglecting the data that suggest she holds a place few can manage. Indeed, according to the 2011 Writers Guild of America (WGA) Hollywood Writers Report, women writers remain underrepresented by factors of 2 to 1 for television writers whereas minority writers remain underrepresented by factors of 3 to 1.

Regardless of data, Rhimes deploys her normalizing narrative to carve out a so-called neutral space for her work. What's more, her investment in normalizing nonracialized characters exemplifies the liberal individualist discourse of a post-racial America. In this revisionist history, all the sins of the past are absolved in the heroic efforts of a few dissidents during the Civil Rights era. Critical race theorists, such as Peller (1990), argue this discourse emerged when America's "race problem" needed a solution that would not divest whites of their privilege. Proponents of liberal individualism believe that the irrationality of prejudice can only be overcome through logical behavioral modifications such as not just seeing people as individuals but as individuals like themselves: "The ideal [of colorblindness] was to transcend stereotypes in favor of treating people as individuals free from racial group identification" (Peller 1990, 769). Being "free" from racial group identification is the crux of postrace ideology because separating an individual from his or her group status also disconnects the person from a historical trajectory of disenfranchisement. The individual alone becomes responsible for her lot in life and cannot claim racism as an injustice or an issue. . . . For Rhimes, who successfully participates in this post-racial space, the greatest benefit of the era is *not* having to make race an issue.

Depicting racialized characters but not making race an issue becomes one of the creative challenges of *Grey's*. The common refrain among most reports on the show focuses on how the multiracial cast "just happened" organically without intention. In terms of racial construction in the first four seasons of the series, three of the eight doctors are African American and one of the interns is Asian American. All three African American cast members are all in positions of authority. . . .

Rhimes adds to the illusion of blindcasting with her reasoning:

It's not necessarily intentional. We have a really diverse cast, which was important to me that we bring in actors of every color for every role. I wanted a world that looked like the world I lived in. You said that they seem to a lot of times be the heroes. Well, one of them is the chief of surgery, one of them is the resident that trains the interns, and one of them is a surgeon. And like all of the other characters, they are at times petty, heroic, tired, angry, not interested in their jobs, interested in their jobs. I feel like they're three-dimensional characters, which, when you only have one character of color in a show, doesn't necessarily get to happen. So I don't necessarily think that they're intentionally heroic. (Robichaux 2006)

Rhimes is inconsistent in her rationale: if the casting was not necessarily intentionally diverse, then why does it benefit the dimensionality of the characters to have more than one person of color on the show? The paradox of diversity and colorblindness that Rhimes participated in does not allow for this type of dissonance. Instead, what Rhimes puts forth here is that regardless of their skin color—or how that color correlates to racialized identity—these characters are as normal

as the white characters in terms of their behaviors. They are no more or less heroes than the others.

Rhimes's logic is put to the test in the Season 2 episode "Into You Like a Train." The major storyline concerns a train accident in which two of the passengers, Bonnie and Tom, are impaled on a metal pole. Realizing that they will be only able to save one of the skewered patients, the Seattle Grace doctors must decide which person they will save: young, white, soon-to-be married Bonnie or Tom, an older, black man. Tom makes the decision for them offering to give his life for Bonnie's as she has more life to live. The optics of an older black man and a young white woman impaled together are notable for two reasons. In this storyline, discourses on the privileges of white femininity as innocent and protected are applied in the existential conversations the doctors have concerning which life is more valuable. In addition, the trope of an Aesop-like magical negro sacrificing himself for the betterment of a white woman is recirculated around the image of them bound together. As Okorafor-Mbachu (2004) posits, the magical negro is often deployed as a plot device "dropped into the story to help the [white] protagonist along." By focusing on their difference in age and not race, Rhimes can plausibly deny her choice to make the black man the hero who sacrifices his life for hers, by stressing that it is not his racial identity—or the cultural attitudes associated with that identity—that informs his decision but rather that he is old and content with the life he has lived. In a karmic twist, Tom's goodness is rewarded when Bonnie does not survive and he does. Again, even if one reads Tom as hero in this circumstance, the storyline neutralizes his cultural specificity in such a way that it becomes difficult to connect to a larger history of racialization and black men. Tom is an everyman who in this instance "happens" to be portrayed by an African American actor. On the surface, this sounds like an equitable statement; however, we must remember that representation does not exist in a vacuum but rather continues along a historical trajectory of naturalized stereotypes and racialized tropes, the magical negro notwithstanding (Bogle 2001). Thus, as much as Rhimes may desire all of her characters to be the same, historical representations prevent this from becoming a reality.

The desire to avoid conversations within the text about race mirrors the absence of those conversations in real life around the difficulty of black professionals to gain equal access to capital and resources. Take, for example, the special placement of Drs. Webber, Burke, and Bailey in high-ranking positions at Seattle Grace. Considering that the actual population of Seattle is 3.6 percent black (Balk 2013), and only a quarter of that demographic have professional careers, the probability of three African American doctors in powerful positions at the same hospital is unlikely. The blindcasting of those actors in the roles hence works to displace and neutralize conservative fears of minority takeovers by creating the aspirationally utopic space Rhimes envisioned. As long as the actors were hired raceblind for the parts and just "happen" to be African American, then it is not a conspiracy that they are in highly coveted positions. Cast member Isaiah Washington affirmed this utopia: "Right now, three of us (blacks) are in charge at Seattle Hospital and no one is questioning that because we're good at what we do" (*Jet* 2006). Washington seems to understand the improbability of his and the others' authoritative positions on the show. Post-race politics that deploys colorblindness as a strategy ultimately allows these cast members to be in these positions because whatever subversion their racial difference may have caused has been stripped away in favor of a feel good sentiment that diversity and corporate multiculturalism are effective societal tools. Further complicating this choice is that it is hard to persuade actors who want to work to fight for a reality where they do not "happen" to be characters of color. In interviews, James Pickens Jr. (Chief Webber) often expresses his delight with the representation without identification the blindcasting process allows: "The world is just a much bigger place than Black judges and Black cops" (Fogel 2005). Pickens is rightly addressing the one dimensionality of roles people of color frequently are placed in. However, his blindcast characterization is probably only a step-up in dimensionality.

GREY'S AS COLORBLIND PROTOTYPE FOR SOCIETY

In interviews, Rhimes describes her vision of a diverse American landscape as it related to casting *Grey's*: "I basically walked in saying I didn't write anybody's race into the script" (Duffy 2006, P1).

Shocked that television did not normally participate in her blindcasting process, Rhimes set out to make her diverse cast "normal." In a very telling *Nightline* segment called "America in black and white," Rhimes and the cast discuss the racial aspects of *Grey's*. Discussing how the race of the characters is less important than their experiences, Rhimes posits,

> It's not shocking if the guy running the hospital is Black. It's not shocking if the surgeon is Black. If you accept it as reality instead of making it a very special episode of *Grey's Anatomy* where people discuss race which would make me . . . uh . . . crazy, it seems like the show could be about something more and once you start seeing these people as people [rather than by] the color of their skin, you begin to maybe see the people in your grocery store as more than the color of their skin. (*Nightline* 2006)

This quote reveals many of the show's politics. First, Rhimes's discussion of a reality that transcends race is significant because it demonstrates a belief that television representation alone can change preconceived notions about racialized groups. The problem of course is that because these characters are divorced from their cultural specificities, they are reduced to stereotypically shallow characterizations devoid of context from their marginalized group of origin. In addition, the quote describes Rhimes's discomfort with television episodes that intentionally focus on race. I concede that when television programs make race an explicit theme, it is usually an appeal to some universal, effectively white, human experience that operates to ultimately reinforce the goals of liberal individualism. Rhimes's approach, balking at any utterance of race talk with regard to dialogue, plot points, or character development, works to make the discussion of racialization seem unnecessary and inauthentic.

One of the problems that arises from Rhimes's mode of disavowal is that the actors of color inadvertently step into racial tropes. Put simply, when characters of color are written normatively [read: white] and their history is not considered, the text becomes a breeding ground for unintentional stereotypes. *Grey's* Dr. Preston Burke and Dr. Miranda Bailey are useful examples because of no fault of their own, their characterizations are often ensnared by unintentional stereotypes. The lack of cultural specificity, for example, reduced Burke's highly ambitious perfectionism to that of a "superspade," an African American stereotype characterized by the ability to excel in talent and skill. Similarly, the unintentional pitfall Bailey (portrayed by Wilson) stumbles into is equally telling. While she received what Henderson coins a "mammy makeover," for the most part Bailey still finds herself as the caretaker of her (mostly) white residents. It is in later seasons that viewers learn she has a husband (although his only on-camera appearance on *Grey's* was as a patient who nearly dies from a brain hemorrhage after a car accident while she was in labor delivering their son). Doubling down on the pitfalls associated with blindcasting, in the *Nightline* segment mentioned earlier, Chandra Wilson recounts that Rhimes initially cast a tall, blonde haired, blue-eyed woman as the original Miranda Bailey—which may also explain the nickname given pre-casting, "the Nazi." . . .

However, it is important to realize that while Burke and Bailey were perhaps not racialized in Rhimes's imagination, once Isaiah Washington and Chandra Wilson were hired, their roles became imbued and loaded with a litany of racialized tropes that a writer would have to consciously circumvent. . . .

In the abovementioned *Nightline* segment, the interviewer asks [Patrick] Dempsey about the competition between him and Washington for the role of Dr. Derek Shepherd:

> At the time, Ellen [Pompeo, lead actress on *Grey's*] had been cast as the lead and Burke's part was cast with a different actor and so there was a screen test between Isaiah and me . . . it was wide open . . . it would have been interesting if he was McDreamy [Shepherd's nickname] and I was Dr. Burke. But that could work too . . . uh . . . y'know. (*Nightline* 2006)

Washington's comments conflict with Dempsey's more optimistic outlook. Washington asserts,

> ABC didn't want me to be Dr. Shepherd, they wanted Patrick Dempsey so there's your answer . . . it's not daring . . . it's not daring. That is off limits . . . [Interviewer cuts in: "So you're saying that's still . . ."] Oh [guffaws], it's not going anywhere . . . I'll be disappearing on you like Dave Chappelle if I said anything different. (*Nightline* 2006)

Perhaps a foreshadowing for Washington, these interview remarks demonstrate the fascinating (and frustrating) awareness on the part of Washington, and presumably others, of the unlikelihood of a black character being the leading man in *Grey's*. Still, according to the logic of blindcasting, if Washington had been cast as McDreamy, his character would have exhibited the same traits as Dempsey-as-McDreamy. Again, the politics of colorblindness insist that there be the illusion of equal opportunity. Both Washington and Dempsey concur that the screen test was "wide open" and that the results were simply a case of the "best" man winning. However, Washington's tepid acknowledgment of the network's implicit demands for a white lead[1] comes as close to a provocative statement about racial issues as the publicity around the show will allow. Put simply, casting a black male lead against a white female lead on a broadcast television series is industrially considered a difficult coupling to sell to a mainstream, white audience.

Washington's self-knowledge of his own industrial expendability forwards the realization that for all of its good intention, blindcasting ultimately alienates characters of color from the material realities of racism. Burke, Bailey, and Richard Webber (James Pickens), the Black Chief of Surgery, never acknowledge the predicament they are in as African American doctors in a predominately white hospital and how that placement contributes toward how others receive them. This is not to say that as racialized subjects they do not necessarily recognize themselves as black; rather, the point is that they do not see their blackness as a factor in how they have attained their success or are perceived by their white counterparts. Double consciousness, that is, "this sense of always looking at one's self through the eyes of others, of measuring one's soul by the tape of a world that looks on in amused contempt and pity" (Du Bois 2007, 5), is a component of black life in America. The disacknowledgment of that in the circumstances these three characters have found themselves in is disingenuous. As insincere as the dissonance Rhimes's characters find themselves in, the point is clear: the goal of post-race identity is denying this double consciousness because to possess it undermines their very deracialization. In an interview about her new ABC series *Scandal*, Rhimes affirms this point. When questioned as to whether she sees her blindcasting approach . . . as problematic, Rhimes responds,

> When people who aren't of color create a show and they have one character of color on their show, that character spends all their time talking about the world as "I'm a Black man blah, blah, blah," she says. That's not how the world works. I'm a Black woman every day, and I'm not confused about that. I'm not worried about that. I don't need to have a discussion with you about how I feel as a Black woman, because I don't feel disempowered as a Black woman. (Paskin 2013) . . .

"ARE THERE INTERRACIAL RELATIONSHIPS ON THE SHOW?" THE RACE-NEUTRALIZING POWER OF COUPLING

Burke and Bailey's characters are not the only examples of *Grey's* experiment with colorblindness within the text. Rhimes "unintentionally" places her characters in interracial relationships. When asked about it in interviews, she feigns surprise that her characters are (1) racialized and (2) in interracial relationships. Her explanation for those couplings is predictably downplayed: "It's what I had planned for the characters" (*Nightline* 2006). Returning to the Burke/Yang romance best illustrates Rhimes's disinterest in the cultural signifiers and expectations of her characters' racial backgrounds.

From the beginning of their relationship, Burke and Yang never talked about race. In fact, the only differences and struggles that they had involved their cleaning habits. Recalling this essay's introduction, Rhimes's provocative statement hoping that viewers would not get caught up on their racial differences but focus instead on their idiosyncrasies was part of why the relationship works. Chito Childs (2009, 48) reinforces *Grey's* strategy to neutralize the racial aspects of Burke/Yang's interracial union:

> On *Grey's Anatomy*, the top surgeon Preston Burke, who is involved with an Asian American medical intern Cristina Yang, is presented as having "transcended . . . racial origin and, in so doing, have become normal." The racialized message is still received yet in a

color-blind package like contemporary racism and promotes an assimilationist perspective that encourages the view that race does not matter.

Racial transcendence functions not only as a narrative structure for the characters, but also as a lens for audiences to look past the obvious cultural reasons that may make interracial romances difficult. Moreover, transcendence offers yet another reason to plausibly deny why these televisual romances generally always fail. With regard to Burke/Yang, this so-called racially transcendent relationship came to a bracing halt in Season 4 of *Grey's* thanks to an off-set scandal leading to ABC dismissing Isaiah Washington[2] in reaction to the publicity crisis he created for the network. Regardless, the lack of race discussion was cowardly. As one columnist wrote, "Face it, some writers are just afraid of going there. Taking on cultural differences isn't easy, so they simply make believe they don't exist" (Chito Childs 2009, 48).

In addition to the Burke/Yang romance . . . the show revealed a second interracial romance with a backstory that was harder to racially transcend. As a way of neutralizing the racial stakes of this illicit affair, Chito Childs (2009, 37) argues that placing the romance in the past generates a sort of racial displacement:

> Beyond not showing interracial couples, another strategy of invisibility is to have an interracial union that happened in the past. By placing the relationship in the past, the show can claim to be racially progressive while not having to deal with actually presenting an interracial relationship.

In the show, Meredith Grey discovers that decades before her arrival at Seattle Grace, Chief of Surgery Dr. Webber had a long-term affair with her mother Dr. Ellis Grey. In the show, Webber faithfully visited Meredith's mother in her nursing home until her death. Interestingly, Grey suffered from Alzheimer's, a disease that narratively allowed writers to not only make the past the present for melodramatic purposes but also to easily erase that history and detach it from its strong ties to U.S. racial tensions. Grey would frequently relive moments between Webber and herself but because her memory is eaten away, she can never name race as a factor in the ending of their affair. Although it may be understood that contemporarily individuals are raceblind, even thirty years ago, race did matter. Yet, there was not a single mention of race or racial tension in their relationship. . . .

IN THE END, DOES THE *GREY'S* EXPERIMENT WORK?

In a 2005 *New York Times* article, ABC President of Entertainment Stephen McPhereson said in response to *Grey's Anatomy* hit status, "The face of America is a diverse canvas . . . and the fact that this show represents a lot of those different aspects, you would be silly to think that doesn't have something to do with its success" (Fogel 2005). In many ways, *Grey's* does represent the American scene but only in superficial ways. Yes, the world is a diverse canvas, but there are many diverse cultural experiences that deserve space in the televisual world. Ignoring those cultural differences in the favor of . . . colorblindness and diversity is a dishonest maneuver designed to ensure comfort at the expense of resonance for people of color. This dishonesty only fuels fires of complacence and negligence when it comes to race relations. Cultural specificity does not mean that the show needs to have a racial problem . . . solved every week; however, there does need to be a nod to the world not just as Shonda Rhimes envisions it or experiences it as an individual but to the world as it *actually* is. . . .

Rhimes developed several other series with ABC after her success with *Grey's*. The spinoff, *Private Practice,* also boasted an integrated cast— yet was not explicitly defined as a blindcast program. . . . [I]n January 2012, Rhimes and ABC launched the premiere of *Scandal*. Based on the life of black public relations crisis manager Judy Smith, and portrayed by Kerry Washington, Rhimes did not blindcast the lead role of Olivia Pope. In an interview, she describes the casting process for Pope:

"We auditioned every actress of color in town, every one, and I wanted everyone to have a chance," Shonda explained. "So it was really difficult because we saw a ton of actresses." (Paskin 2013)

That Rhimes intentionally cast a woman of color for the lead role is wholly different from the way she cast *Grey's* or *Private Practice*. Yet, Rhimes's race politics remain in play on *Scandal*. Rhimes's self-fashioning as post-Civil Rights and post-feminist is smart because it guarantees the network that she has no secret revolutionary agendas and will serve their primary demographic. Thus, although the casting for Pope was about intentionally auditioning women of color, the actual part required the actress to transcend the fixed reality of her race so she could become the character Rhimes (and ABC) needed her to be.

What Rhimes's decision may suggest is the difficulty in configuring racial parity and acceptability. Quite literally Washington's leading status may be equivalent to the hiring of two or three more actors of color. Rhimes's negotiation of the value of that position for a woman of color tethered to the creation of a series based on a black woman's life for network television has been a worthy investment. . . . What's more, Rhimes's desire to build an interracial affair between Pope and the white lead, Republican President of the United States Fitzgerald Grant suffers the same fate as the other interracial romances she creates on her other shows. As expected, their doomed love affair was not at all about racial boundaries, but in the vein of Yang and Burke's "she's messy and he's neat" dynamism, in the case of Olivia and Fitz, it was that he was married and she felt guilty. . . .

Rhimes's blindcasting works to acknowledge difference in ways that will cause the least amount of discomfort to white audiences while providing an illusion that under liberal individualism, the marketplace will do right by historically marginalized individuals. This is a post-racial network world indeed.

NOTES

1. It is important to note that Washington never made Rhimes the executor of ideology; rather, she represents the equal opportunity employer. ABC's standards are in question.

2. According to E! Online writer Gina Serpe (2006), leading co-stars Washington and Patrick Dempsey succumbed to mounting tensions coming to blows after Dempsey

defended co-star T. R. Knight against Washington uttering a homophobic epithet at the actor. ABC rebuked Washington, sending him to a rehabilitation center for anger management. Once he completed treatment and produced a pro-tolerance public service announcement, the network terminated him.

REFERENCES

Balk, Gene. 2013. "Census: Washington Getting Less White, Older; Asians Growing Fastest in State." *The Seattle Times,* June 12. http://blogs.seattletimes.com/fyi-guy/2013/06/12/census-washington-getting-less-white-older-asians-growing-fastest-in-state/.

Barney, Chuck. 2006. "In Living Color; There Are Many Shades of Love When It Comes to TV's Interracial Couples." *The Augusta Chronicle,* February 15, P1.

Bodroghkozy, Anikio. 1992. "'Is This What You Mean by Color TV?': Race, Gender and Contested Meanings in NBC's *Julia.*" In *Private Screenings: Television and the Female Consumer,* edited by Lynn Spigel and Denise Mann, 156–157. Minneapolis: University of Minnesota.

Bogle, Donlad. 2001. *Toms, Coons, Mulattoes, Mammies, and Bucks: An Interpretive History of Blacks in American Films.* New York: Bloomsbury.

Chito Childs, Erica. 2009. *Fade to Black and White: Interracial Images in Popular Culture.* Lanham: Rowman & Littlefield.

Duffy, Mike. 2006. *Grey's Anatomy* Creator Says Diverse Cast Reflects the Real World. *Detroit Free Press,* March 22, P1.

Fogel, Matthew. 2005. "'*Grey's Anatomy*' Goes Colorblind." *The New York Times,* May 8. http://www.nytimes.com/2005/05/08/arts/television/08foge.html.

Gray, Herman S. 2004. *Watching Race: Television and the Struggle for Blackness.* Minneapolis: University of Minnesota Press.

Hoffman, Melody K. 2006 "*Grey's Anatomy* Stars: Pump Life into TV Medical Drama." *Jet,* April 24, 59.

Johnson, Pamela K. 2005. "The Cutting Edge: Shonda Rhimes Dissects *Grey's Anatomy.*" *Written By,* September. http://www.wga.org/writtenby/writtenbysub.aspx? id=883.

Okorafor-Mbachu, Nnedi. 2004. "Stephen King's Super-Duper Magical Negroes." *Strange Horizons,* October 25. http://www.strangehorizons.com/2004/20041025/kinga.shtml.

Paskin, Willa. 2013. "Network TV Is Broken. So How Does Shonda Rhimes Keep Making Hits?" *The New York Times,* May 9. http://www.nytimes.com/2013/05/12/magazine/shonda-rhimes.html?pagewanted=all

Peller, Gary. 1990. "Race Consciousness." *Duke Law Journal.* Vol 1990, no. 4, 769.

Phillips, Deborah. 2000. "Medicated Soap: The Woman Doctor in Television Medical Drama." In *Frames and Fictions on Television: The Politics of Identity within Drama,* edited by B. Carson and M. Llewellyn-Jones, 50–52. Portland: Intellect Books.

Robichaux, Mark. 2006. "Rhimes' Anatomy." *Broadcasting & Cable,* February 26. www.broadcastingcable.com/article/102990-Rhimes_Anatomy_.php.

Serpe, Gina. 2006. "Grey's Apology." *Eonline,* October 26. http://www.eonline.com/uberblog/b53612_greys_apology.html.

Smith-Shomade, Beretta E. 2002. *Shaded Lives: African-American and Television.* New Brunswick: Rutgers University Press.

Turow, Joseph. 1989. *Playing Doctor: Television, Storytelling, and Medical Power.* Ann Arbor: University of Michigan Press.

Writers Guild of America. 2011. "Recession and Regression: 2011 Hollywood Writers Report." Writers Guild of America. http://www.wga.org/uploadedFiles/who_we_are/hwr11exe-csum.pdf.

PERFORMING CLASS

56

Gilmore Girls *and a Classless Neoliberal "Middle Class"*

Daniela Mastrocola

Within its first episode, *Gilmore Girls* (2000–2007) foregrounds a class-based conflict, articulated as a generational tension between the show's two primary families, the senior Gilmores, Emily and Richard . . . and the "Gilmore girls," their daughter, Lorelai. . . . and granddaughter, Rory. . . . In many respects, this conflict serves as the series' primary narrative propellant: for example, Lorelai, the protagonist, must leave her chosen life in the quirky, colorful world of Stars Hollow and return to the symmetrical, monochromatic world of her parents' house in Hartford, Connecticut, to beg them to pay for her daughter's private school tuition.[1] During this episode, audiences learn that Lorelai left her parents' wealthy household at the age of seventeen with her then one-year-old daughter to escape the restrictions of an upper-class lifestyle ("Pilot"). Lorelai takes refuge in Stars Hollow, working for room-and-board as a maid at the Independence Inn, where she has become the manager fifteen years later, when the series begins. Despite the importance of class to the series' narrative arc, it is surprisingly difficult to definitively characterize Lorelai's class membership.

[This chapter attempts] to make sense of Lorelai's ambiguous class membership and . . . to understand how the characters' performances of class identities normalize hegemonic discourses that obfuscate the material consequences of wealth and income inequalities. . . . [The] two Gilmore matriarchs, Emily and Lorelai . . . are presented as near-total opposites in terms of their individual and relative relationships to the common indicators of class (wealth, occupation, and lifestyle); concentrating this analysis on Emily and Lorelai thus serves to explicate the narrative devices and internal logic according to which the program relationally articulates class categories. . . .

RE-CLASSIFYING NEOLIBERALISM

Neoliberalism, characterized broadly as the "ideological software" for global capitalism (Peck and Tickell 389), expounds the alleged death of class; according to this mode of social organization, professional success and material security are the responsibility of private individuals. This logic renders useless any notion of class consciousness—that is, awareness of one's place and degree of agency within broader socioeconomic and political structures, especially as it relates to those who hold a similar place. State resources are increasingly directed at facilitating trade and economic growth, while social services are diminished, if not eliminated, especially if they are perceived as a hindrance to free market privatization. In contrast with the so-called "golden age of capitalism," wherein the welfare state intervened in the market in order to redistribute wealth and protect the working class, albeit to a limited extent (McClintock and Stanfield), *neo*liberalism signals the commodification of all public and social goods. . . . It fosters a citizen-as-consumer subjectivity that encourages individuals to purchase displays of wealth as evidence of individual success and social membership, while denying structural sources of poverty and inequality. The individual is a self-produced entrepreneur, and the failure to achieve financial security or the life of her choosing is her fault (Walkerdine). . . .

Contemporary Marxists have taken up the challenge of resurrecting and redefining notions of class and class consciousness, such that the idea of a working or systemically exploited and underprivileged class may serve as a meaningful basis upon which to capture the pain and injustices caused by wealth inequality and mobilize resistance to the widespread violence of market fundamentalism. In the United States, the working class includes a majority of Americans who work for a living but have little control over their lives, are subject to routine exploitation in their working environments, and may experience periods of under- and unemployment (Zweig). In addition to income, class is also defined in relation to occupation (e.g., manual or service, management or ownership), education, and lifestyle or taste (including how one spends income) (Ehrenreich; Leistyna). In other words, the contours of class are sketched in relation to [both] economic and cultural dimensions. . . .

In order to understand how *Gilmore Girls* contributes to the broad public discourse about classlessness in contemporary America, the representation of the series' ambiguously-classed protagonist must be analyzed in relation to both these material and cultural markers of class. An overemphasis on the *signification* of class affiliation may encourage a distorted reading of class that is reduced to practices of consumption, particularly with regards to taste and lifestyle. For example, even in poor American communities, one finds cheap, knock-off displays of middle- and upper-class wealth, often purchased with credit (Ewen 24–73; Pascale 357). Purchasing such displays of wealth—for example, a home, car, entertainment, or clothing—may shield working class individuals from the continued stigmatization of poverty (Leistyna). This may, in turn, reinforce the individualist mantra of personal success, to the extent that one's ability to display wealth is used as a measure of personal achievement, regardless of working conditions or financial security. This perpetuates the notion that class is no longer a useful basis upon which to organize *resistance:* under these conditions, "It's much more commonsensical that we think of ourselves as individual members of an imaginary middle-class rather than collective members of a working class" (Gray). In other words, the symbolic articulation of class may bear little resemblance to one's economic position but may nonetheless be used to project an image of individual achievement that reinforces a supposed middle-class identity or, by virtue of middle-class ubiquity, classlessness.

This may explain why a majority of Americans define themselves as simultaneously classless or belonging to an elusive but much lauded middleclass, despite worsening economic and labor conditions (Asner). For example, conservative estimates indicate that at least sixty-one percent of Americans self-identified as middleclass between 2000 and 2008, during the time *Gilmore Girls* aired (Newport). However, forty-nine percent of the American population is poor or low income, based on current government poverty rates, and seventy-nine percent live in danger of poverty or unemployment ("Current US Poverty Statistics"). . . . Neoliberalism's female subjects, in particular, are encouraged "to look the part, sound the part and . . . make themselves and their homes over to conform to this middle-class aesthetic" (Walkerdine 242). This is coupled with the stigmatization of a working class identity: as Robin Kelley remarks, "Somehow, in this [American] culture, being working class is a failure." Taken together, these factors make a classless identity seem not only logical but desirable. It also perpetuates neoliberal notions of social mobility, to the extent that people can purchase displays of wealth that mask their poverty and distract from the value of class consciousness for the improvement of working conditions.

Pascale's study of the subjective measurements of class in America is a prime case in point. In her effort to understand how class has been made to appear irrelevant, she speaks to diverse individuals about how they self-classify. Many of her interviewees define themselves as middle-class or classless, despite huge variations in income and asset ownership (Pascale 350). For example, four of her five multimillionaire participants defend their middle-class status with reference to those elements of class commonly associated with notions of cultural and social capital: those with whom they maintain relationships, the type of leisure activities in which they participate, and their economic origins (for example, if they began poor and acquired assets later in life). They also distance themselves from an upper-class label, not on an economic basis, but because they do not feel themselves to exhibit the "pretentiousness" of upper-class lifestyles, while admitting that they enjoy leisure activities like "yachting and extensive world travel" (Pascale 350–351). For those with significantly less (or no) income or asset ownership, Pascale's study shows a middle-class or classless identity (or both) is asserted on the basis of being ordinary (like everyone, as in the majority "in the middle"), and the self-identification of class is positioned in non-economic terms (e.g., based on ethnic or cultural affiliations), avoiding the stigmatization of poverty (354–375). . . .

Pascale proposes that "Class must be understood as performative" and that "the everyday 'doing of class' and the hegemonic discursive formations upon which such doing relies, disorganizes the recognizable presence of wealth and poverty and effectively subvert[s] the capacity for collective identity based on class interests" (349). In other words, she argues that addressing *how* Americans perform and experience their class identities is a generative means by which to understand how economic measurements of class have receded so thoroughly to the far corners of common sense discourse in the U.S., so as to make class categories appear objectively meaningless. . . . Because opportunities for social mobility are allegedly equally available to all people, it makes little sense to speak of (semi)static social classes that categorize one's place in relation to external systems and structures—systems and structures which, in fact, constrain and/or enable individual and collective choices. Emptied of meaningful content, being middleclass comes to mean and be experienced as classlessness. It is with this conception of a middleclass that the remainder of the article proceeds to offer a critique of *Gilmore Girls*. . . .[2]

CONSTRUCTING A CLASSLESS MIDDLE-CLASS FANTASY

Throughout the series, class is constructed and expressed on the basis of interpersonal antagonisms between the two Gilmore family matriarchs, Emily and Lorelai. There is little doubt of Emily's economic and cultural membership in upper-class high society. She and her husband live in a historic mansion furnished by expensive antiques. She is financially sustained by inherited wealth and her husband's high-paying though ill-defined job in the insurance industry. In fact, during the episode "Help Wanted," Lorelai presses to understand exactly what her father does at his international insurance consulting firm—*how* he labors—to which Emily vaguely though confidently responds, "He consults on matters relating to international insurance." Clearly money is in large supply, and the details of its procurement are

trivial. In terms of vehicular mobility, throughout the series audiences see Emily driving both a Mercedes and Jaguar; she also considers purchasing shares in a plane. . . .

Culturally, Emily's behavior is governed by notions of proper etiquette reminiscent of British aristocracy. She is President of the Daughters of the American Revolution and regularly orchestrates charity fundraisers. She associates primarily with other upper-class, white housewives with whom, for example, during an afternoon tea party, she contemplates which Founding Father would have made the best lover. . . . Her behavior is also marked by an entitlement that she strives to pass onto future generations of upper-class wealth. When traveling with her granddaughter, she reminds her on multiple occasions to expect pampering from those in her employ: "Rory, I told you before, you do not move luggage." . . . Toward the end of the series, Emily leads a young girl through her initiation into high-society social etiquette, including which cutlery to use and the type of conversation to make around the dinner table, demonstrating her mastery of such skills: "Think of things in the middle three sections of the Sunday *New York Times*—travel, arts and leisure, Sunday styles—and forget the rest of the paper exists!" . . . This highlighted component of her class membership is, however, depicted unfavorably.

Functioning as a proxy for other upper-class women, Emily figures as an emotionally stifled character who is unable to forge intimate relationships (Rossi 89). For example, she is unable to express hurt when her daughter withholds news about her engagement; instead, when Lorelai finally confesses, she replies curtly, "Well, I think that's very nice. I certainly hope we'll be in town for it, but if not I promise we'll send a nice gift. Now excuse me, I'm going to check on the roast." . . . Her adherence to social customs is continuously presented as a hindrance to her expression of authentic emotions; for example, when her husband's business partner, Jason, dismisses her plans to organize a traditional launch party, she is obliged to hide her offense and hurt behind polite sarcasm. . . . While, as Matthew Nelson points out, many of the series' upper-class characters are depicted as "arrogant, unlikable, and unpleasant" (204), Emily's character also serves to invoke pity from the audience. Audiences are, therefore, shocked when, while drinking with her daughter, she momentarily displays an emotional vulnerability that stands in stark opposition to her usual highly composed demeanour. Viewers see a glimpse of resistance to the heteropatriarchy of her upper-class lifestyle as she laments the code of proper behaviour that required she leave the financial management of her household to her husband:

> Sure, I went to Smith, and I was a history major, but . . . I was always going to be a wife. I mean, the way I saw it, a woman's job was to run a home, organize the social life of a family, and bolster her husband while he earned a living. It was a good system, and it was working very well all these years. Only when your husband isn't there . . . you realize how dependent you are. . . .

This moment, however, passes quickly, suggesting that this display of vulnerability is owed entirely to her intoxication. In other words, the scene points to a systemic issue in the relationship between gender and financial dependence and then quickly retreats as Emily hastily dismisses the moment of exposure upon the sobriety of the next morning. While the moment may pass within the show, the broader economic realities to which it points do not—namely, how women of different economic classes are constrained by economic gender norms (granted, Emily's is not the most sympathetic of cases). The show leaves the issue unresolved without further investigation, much less any form of resolution.

In contrast to Emily's definitive display of upper-class membership, Lorelai's class membership is significantly harder to define as it is articulated primarily by comparison to that of Emily. In other words, it is suggested that Lorelai belongs to a lower or middle class largely because she does not exhibit the same indicators that are used to construct Emily's high-class membership. In some ways, this relational articulation of class is not surprising, given that "locating the middle class as a material and subjective experience requires [that] it be located both against others above and below it" (Walkowitz 122). However, within this series, this relational configuration projects an image of Lorelai as classless and thereby enables the series to dodge a sincere and direct engagement with the class inequalities to which it makes reference. Using relative terms and comparisons avoids dealing with the disparities in fixed wealth and working conditions and contributes to the misrecognition of self and others' class membership in a way that reinforces the ambiguous neoliberal notion of a middle class. Furthermore, Lorelai internalizes this relative logic in a way that allows her to claim a kind of impoverished credibility—as someone who "started with nothing" and overcame poverty by the show's conclusion, despite her wealthy roots. . . .

To begin with, in contrast with the Gilmore mansion, Lorelai and Rory live in a two-bedroom household that Emily routinely criticizes. . . . Although humble by comparison, it is hardly the picture of impoverishment. Inside it lacks no amenities, even if it is smaller, disorganized, and considerably more colorful. It is not a definitive picture of a working class home from, for example, *Married with Children* or *Roseanne*.[3] There are, nonetheless, a few subtle references to the challenges that Lorelai overcame while furnishing her house that remind viewers of her financial limitations, including brief mention of a second-hand bedroom set and a couch purchased on credit and paid for over many months. . . . These moments of flirtation with a working class identity are, however, quickly obscured by a neoliberal middle-class image of personal freedom. For example, when Lorelai and her on-and-off-again boyfriend contemplate purchasing a nearby mansion, she opts not to, not because she lacks the funds or credit, but because of her sentimental attachment to her home. . . . Lorelai also drives a Jeep Wrangler, which Emily disapprovingly describes as "an army vehicle" . . . but which was, nonetheless, purchased as a new car with none of the rust, obnoxious sounds, or damage that one might expect of a woman who figures as comparatively poor with limited disposable income. As with her home, when her car breaks down during the final season—at which point she has become the co-owner of an inn with seemingly greater income—she acknowledges that she can now afford a more luxurious car but stays true to her chosen roots and, instead, purchases a replacement engine so she can keep the original car. She performs a kind of allegiance to the show's distorted image of an impoverished identity *by choice*. . . .

The primary point of class distinction between Emily and her daughter is that Lorelai is a waged laborer, managing the Independence Inn for the first half of the series, whereas Emily manages her household on the backs of women hired as maids. Indeed, Emily's management of her household is one of the primary sites upon which audiences encounter her dispositional failings as an entitled and exploitive member of the upper class. Her behavior exemplifies the pretentiousness from which Pascale's multimillionaire research participants seek to distance themselves (350). To begin, Emily demands a dehumanizing perfection from her maids while also taking credit for the fruits of their labor. For example, she insists that she deserves recognition for the preparation of meals, not because she actually cooked or served the food but because she commanded her maid's preparation of it: "*I* told her [the maid] to make it! You're enjoying duck because *I* requested duck!" . . . Furthermore, she cycles through a new maid every episode because she holds unattainable expectations of her employees. During one episode, she is on the phone with her lawyer preparing to defend herself in court for firing a maid merely because the maid walked too loudly: "Every time she went to the pantry, I thought she was marching on Poland. Oh, I see, because I want things a certain way, I'm unreasonable?" . . . She displays the same expectation of total appeasement from her lawyer as she did the maid, insisting that the lawyer miss his daughter's dance recital to "turn [his] little near-luxury car around, go back to [his] office, and fax [her] that libelous scrap of paper" immediately. Beneath the comedic extremes of scenes like this are all the markings of class privilege that equate extreme wealth with increased value as a human being. However, because the scene is coated with humor and filtered through Emily's perspective, audiences never actually confront the pain and humiliation endured by her maids who are fired as quickly as they are hired, despite performing all of their expected duties. . . .

As noted previously, the series begins fifteen years after Lorelai leaves her parents' house; in apparent retaliation to her mother's mistreatment of maids, Lorelai becomes a maid at the . . . Independence Inn. When the series begins, audiences are to understand that she worked her way up the employee ladder to become the Inn's manager. In her words, "I worked my way up. I run the place now. I built a life on my own with no help from anyone" . . .[4] The narrative's lapse in time conceals the type of labor involved in this process. In fact, audiences never actually see Lorelai labor as a maid. They do not see the struggle, challenges, or humiliations that normally characterize service work. To be sure, one deleted scene included as a DVD extra depicts a young Lorelai in a maid's outfit and toddler Rory in the Inn, although it is hardly the picture of labor: the girls are seen twirling and dancing in the Inn's empty entranceway. . . . Instead, Lorelai epitomizes the neoliberal entrepreneur whose independent hard work and determination are rewarded by upward mobility. It is a narrative familiar from a series like the *Cosby Show* that perpetuates a fantasy of upward mobility by highlighting an exceptional case in which structural barriers were overcome by a deserving protagonist (Jhally and Lewis 72–73).

In many ways, Lorelai's cultural displays of class membership, including her lifestyle and tastes, are also rooted in her resistance to that of her parents. . . . Emily's behavior is constrained by upper-class customs, in her chosen world Lorelai is free spirited and prone to vulgar, witty, and emotional outbursts that, by comparison, confer an authenticity onto Lorelai's character.[5] Indeed, she defends her escape from her parents' house as a means to safeguard her eclectic and outspoken personality: "I had nothing in that house. I had no life. I had no air. You [Emily] strangled me." . . . It is worth remembering that her parents' house was marked by all the privileges of upper-class wealth, including rarified educational opportunities, world travel, and endless commodities. Yet, like Emily's character, this lifestyle figures as unpleasant and undesirable, a source of suffering from which Lorelai has no choice but to escape, and she takes refuge in the comparatively more ordinary (lower-class) world of Stars Hollow. In this world, she is free to be her true down-to-earth self. For example, when Emily tries to make her family engage in dinner table discussion about "current events, historical events and intellectual trivia" like the Kennedys, Lorelai's retort marks her connection to the world of popular culture trivia, rather than a socially removed, presidential family: "Did you know that a butt model makes $10,000 a day?" . . .

Lorelai's financial limitations also make her a likeable character, permitting her an authenticity that is denied to Emily. While Emily is always seen wearing stiff and symmetrical blazers and pant suits, Lorelai regularly displays her "thing for fringe," sporting jeans, tassels, and rhinestones that further convey her character's approachability. . . . Lorelai is also resourceful, designing and sewing numerous outfits throughout the series; on two occasions, she repairs Emily's clothing, who would presumably be dependent on her maids to complete such tasks. . . . Lorelai eats meals served in vending machines, makes fun of George W. Bush, Jr. because "he's stupid and his face is too tiny for his head," and opts for VHS cassettes of movies recorded off television rather than DVDs with special effects because the former include "the original commercials, which is half the fun." . . . She is fun and cool, and her poverty is a source of pleasure for her and the audience. Rather than experiencing her independence from her parents as a painful loss of resources, she and the audience can relish her decision to be part of the real world in which (a distorted version of) poverty is represented as fun.

Other moments that point to Lorelai's poverty are also performative in ways that undercut their seriousness, making them a source of comedic pleasure. A prime case in point is Lorelai and Rory's relationship to food. Throughout the series, audiences see Lorelai and Rory preparing to consume an absurd amount of junk food.[6] . . . This display of excessive eating habits is a familiar marker of television's "white trash" stereotypes, normally a "particularly consequential transgression for women" in terms of their respectability (Bettie 141). Because *Gilmore Girls* portrays these eating habits with a light-hearted comedy, some critics have read them, instead, as a refreshing countercultural critique of commonplace on-screen depictions of women eating salads or nothing at all (e.g., Valenti). However, Lorelai and Rory's idealistically thin bodies challenge the legitimacy of this performance. They may be read instead as eating habits intended to superficially rebel against a world of wealthy delicatessens that also normalize overconsumption. They are the working class eating habits familiar from a series like *Roseanne* without the accompanying body sizes of Roseanne and her husband, Dan. In this way, viewers can enjoy as the women plan to feast on copious amounts of fast food without engaging the politics of food insecurity and waste or mainstream fat phobia especially "in the U.S., where weight is inversely correlated with socioeconomic status [and] fat, itself, becomes associated with 'lowbrow' status" (Bettie 138). The women and their viewers can have their cake and eat it too, so to speak.

In a related scene of total absurdity, Rory points to the presence of healthy food in their fridge as indication that her mother might be financially struggling: Rory compares the presence of cheese, vegetables, and bread in her mother's fridge to the fridge from her childhood with left-over pizza and cold fries, reading the former as indication that her mother may be trying to reduce her spending. . . . This exchange is, of course, counter to the reality of working class families who rely on fast-food restaurants because they do not have access to the healthier options available in grocery stores. . . . It is a distorted performance of a real kind of poverty. There is an indication that Lorelai is, in fact, reducing her expenses, but the means by which she tries to save money is part of the show's inverted depiction of reality. Lorelai's use of coupons is similarly performative. She relied on coupons at some point in her and her daughter's life off screen, although they are treated on screen as though reliance on them is optional and not a matter of necessity for working class families. . . .

MOMENTS OF THE REAL: RUPTURES IN THE FANTASY

Throughout its 153 episodes, *Gilmore Girls* features a few moments of the real, that is, moments when working class poverty becomes a source of humiliation and hindrance on the quality of its characters' lives. In these moments, poverty is not displayed or chosen; it is imposed, although its systemic sources are concealed. The most obvious example is Lorelai's inability to pay for Rory's tuition to Chilton, a private secondary school, and Yale University. Although these moments are significant indicators of the benefits Rory reaps from her access to familial wealth (because her grandparents ultimately pay for her to have these opportunities), one moment is more to the point of poverty than high-priced educational opportunities.

The episode entitled "Secrets and Loans" begins with Lorelai rising pleasantly out of bed, putting on her robe, smiling as she sees her daughter, and retrieving her daily newspaper off the white front porch with a coffee mug in hand, all while Doris Day's "Que Sera Sera (Whatever Will Be, Will Be)" plays in the background. It is a moment of idyllic, picture-perfect American middle-class life. Suddenly, the music stops as Lorelai's foot sinks through the porch: Lorelai and Rory's home—the physical epicentre of their family unit—has been infested with termites, the damage from which will cost $15,000 to repair. In keeping with her generally fun disposition, Lorelai first approaches the repair cost with humor. However, this humor quickly fades, and Lorelai spends the rest of the episode trying desperately to find a bank that will lend her money for the repair. Despite flirtation, aggression, and begging, she is unable to secure the loan. Per the dominant neoliberal narrative of individualized success, Lorelai experiences her inability to get the loan as a personal failing, describing herself as "one of the biggest losers in Stars Hollow." Rory and Sookie, Lorelai's best friend, attempt to restore Lorelai's sense of personal value by reminding Lorelai of her contributions to their community. Lorelai, however, is forced to accept that her community involvement is irrelevant to banks. Like the lyrics of Day's song suggest, Lorelai is powerless over the structural forces that determine her credit-worthiness:

SOOKIE: You're an upstanding citizen, you're an active part of the community.

RORY: Yeah, you made all of the donkey outfits for the Christmas festival last year.

SOOKIE: You organized the Save the Historic Oak Tree campaign.

RORY: And you played Tevye in the, uh, Stars Hollow Community Theater production of *Fiddler on the Roof.*

LORELAI: Yes, well, five and a half stars from the *Stars Hollow Gazette,* unheard of 'til that time.

SOOKIE: They [the bankers] should take that into account.

RORY: Yes, they should.

LORELAI: Yes, they should, but they won't.

Here audiences see the economic limits of symbolic displays of class affiliation and neoliberal notions of personal achievement. If the show is accepted at face value, Lorelai performs as neoliberalism's model middle-class citizen who independently supports her family and contributes to her community. Yet these are insufficient to grant her access to the economic capital needed to repair her home. This is a prime opportunity for the show to level a social critique against the class disparities with which it otherwise engages light heartedly. Instead, the episode depoliticizes what is, in fact, a structural problem (McCullough 246): it falls back on an interpersonal resolution, when Emily co-signs her daughter's loan—an option not necessarily available to all women. In other words, this crisis points to a systemic flaw in the neoliberal narrative of individual achievement and gaps in the image of an autonomous, individualized middle class, yet the narrative retreats quickly to a familial resolution that refocuses the issue on the personal dynamics between Lorelai and her mother. . . . Indeed, when Lorelai and Emily leave the bank, their entire conversation centers around what Emily expects to receive in exchange for the co-signature, not the failure of a system that leaves Lorelai unable to repair her home without her parents' help or what might have happened to Lorelai if, like many women in her situation, she did not have access to her parents' wealth.

CONCLUSION

A "best of both worlds" strategy characterizes Lorelai's performance as a classless protagonist who simultaneously typifies an economic middle-class fantasy and advantageously performs a working class cultural identity. Against the failings and shortcomings of her definitively upper-class mother, Lorelai performs the image of an anti-class hero whose eccentricities are beyond *class*ification. In terms of cultural displays of class affiliation, Lorelai rejects her parents' lifestyle and codes of conduct and, in doing so, creates an impression of their class's undesirability. She is fun and authentic in contrast with her stiff and stifled mother. Economically, she performs the image of an independent, self-made neoliberal entrepreneur who can pick-and-choose from the market of symbolic identities available to her, as she autonomously constructs a life of her own choosing. She appears classless—beyond the restriction of any one class category and, as such, fulfils the empty image of the neoliberal middle class. When the harsh realities of economic inequalities momentarily interrupt this neoliberal fantasy—precisely the kinds of humiliation that a coherent working class could unite against—her recourse to her parents' wealth casts systemic issues through the lens of an interpersonal conflict, thereby "[disorganizing] the recognizable presence of wealth and poverty and effectively subvert[ing] the capacity for collective identity based on class interests" (Pascale 349).

If one accepts that television narratives articulate normative truths that enter into public discourse and reinforce or resist dominant ideologies (Stern 172), then *Gilmore Girls* is a prime indicator of and contributor to neoliberal notions of an autonomous individual made in the image of a classless middle-class American. . . . At best, the series points to a lack of political commitment on the part of its producers, and at worst, it perpetuates a neoliberal fantasy that glosses over the harsh realities of working class life in ways that distract from the value of class consciousness. This seemingly class-based show exploits economic disparities in the articulation of a classless neoliberal middle class.

NOTES

1. Erin Johns and Kristin Smith make a similar observation, citing class as one of the series' "major propellants" (30).

2. This is not to suggest that a middle-class cannot or does not exist; rather, that the majority of Americans who identify as middle-class would be more accurately characterized as working class people who have achieved limited improvements in their standard of living, as Zweig suggests.

3. In fact, one economist estimates that the real-life cost of Lorelai's home would be $2.8 million (Adamczyk).

4. Stern offers a similar reading of the show's emphasis on Lorelai's *decision* to leave her parents' home, attributing it to "the postfeminist politics of individual decision-making separated from institutional constraints" as well as a denial of the community network on which Lorelai heavily relied for support (175–176).

5. Justin Rawlins makes a related argument, suggesting that the intertexual banter that characterizes the dialogue throughout Stars Hollow serves to distinguish the town from the senior Gilmore residence, because the former allows its inhabitants to "play with culture" (52). For Rawlins this narrative strategy has a democratizing function by opening the possibility that "cultural capital may be available to all," including the characters and their audiences (49). Instead, this article sketches the material limits of this free play.

6. To be sure, audiences very rarely see Lorelai or Rory actually consume the food that has been ordered (Mintz and Mintz 236).

WORKS CITED

Adamczyk, Alicia. "How Can Lorelai Gilmore Afford a $2.8 Million Home?" *Time*. 20 Oct. 2015. Web. 20 Feb. 2017.

Asner, Ed, narrator. *Class Dismissed: How TV Frames the Working Class*. Dir. Loretta Alper. Media Education Foundation, 2005. Film.

Bettie, Julie. "Class Dismissed? *Roseanne* and the Changing Face of Working-Class Iconography." *Social Text* 45 14.4 (1995): 125–49. *JSTOR*. Web. 20 Feb. 2017.

"Current US Poverty Statistics." *Kairos: The Center for Religions, Rights, and Social Justice*. Kairos. 2015. Web. 19 Oct. 2016.

Ehrenreich, Barbara, interviewee. *Class Dismissed: How TV Frames the Working Class*. Dir. Loretta Alper. Media Education Foundation, 2005. Film.

Ewen, Stuart. *All Consuming Images: The Politics of Style in Contemporary Culture*. New York: Basic Books, 1999. Print.

Gray, Herman, interviewee. *Class Dismissed: How TV Frames the Working Class*. Dir. Loretta Alper. Media Education Foundation, 2005. Film.

Jhally, Sut, and Justin Lewis. *Enlightened Racism: The Cosby Show, Audiences and the Myth of the American Dream*. Boulder: Westview Press, 1992. Print.

Johns, Erin K, and Kristin L. Smith. "Welcome to Starts Hollow: *Gilmore Girls,* Utopia, and the Hyperreal." Gilmore Girls *and the Politics of Identity.* Ed. Ritch Calvin. Jefferson: McFarland, 2008. 23–34. Print.

Kelley, Robin D. G., interviewee. *Class Dismissed: How TV Frames the Working Class.* Dir. Loretta Alper. Media Education Foundation, 2005. Film.

Leistyna, Pepi, interviewee. *Class Dismissed: How TV Frames the Working Class.* Dir. Loretta Alper. Media Education Foundation, 2005. Film.

McClintock, Brent, and James Ronald Standfield. "Welfare State." *Encyclopedia of Political Economy.* Ed. Phillip Anthony O'Hara. Vol. 2. London: Routledge. 1999. 815–819. Print.

McCullough, John. "Rude and the Representation of Class Relations in Canadian film." *Working on Screen: Representations of the Working Class in Canadian Cinema.* Ed. Malek Khouri and Darrell Varga. Toronto: University of Toronto Press, 2006. 246–276. Print.

Mintz, Susannah B., and Leah E. Mintz. "Pass the Pop-Tarts: The *Gilmore Girls'* Perpetual Hunger." *Screwball Television: Critical Perspectives on* Gilmore Girls. Ed. David S. Diffrient and David Lavery. Syracuse: Syracuse University Press, 2010. 235–256. Print.

Nelson, Matthew, C. "Stars Hollow, Chilton, and the Politics of Education in *Gilmore Girls.*" *Screwball Television: Critical Perspectives on* Gilmore Girls. Ed. David S. Diffrient and David Lavery. Syracuse: Syracuse University Press, 2010. 202–213. Print.

Newport, Frank. "Fewer Americans Identify as Middle Class in Recent Years." *GALLUP.* 28 Apr. 2015. Web. 18 Oct. 2017.

Pascale, Celine-Marie. "Common Sense and the Collaborative Production of Class." *Cultural Sociology* 2.3 (2008): 345–367. *SAGE Journals.* Web. 20 Feb. 2017.

Peck, Jamie, and Adam Tickell. "Neoliberalizing Space." *Antipode* 34.3 (2002): 380–404. *Scholars Portal.* Web. 20 Feb. 2017.

Rawlins, Justin O. "Your Guide to the Girls: Gilmore-isms, Cultural Capital, and a Different Kind of Quality TV." *Screwball Television: Critical Perspectives on* Gilmore Girls. Ed. David S. Diffrient and David Lavery. Syracuse: Syracuse University Press, 2010. 36–56. Print.

Rossi, Leena-Maija. "Daughters of Privilege: Class, Sexuality, Affect and the *Gilmore Girls.*" *Working with Affect in Feminist Readings: Disturbing Differences.* Ed. Marianne Liljeström and Susanna Paasonen. New York: Routledge, 2010. 85–98. Print.

Stern, Danielle M. "It Takes a Classless, Heteronormative Utopian Village: *Gilmore Girls* and the Problem of Postfeminism." *The Communication Review* 15.3 (2012): 167–186. *Scholars Portal.* Web. 20 Feb. 2017.

Valenti, Lauren. "I Went on the 'Gilmore Girls Diet'—and I Lost Two Pounds." *Marie Claire.* 28 Jan. 2016. Web. 20 Feb. 2017.

Walkerdine, Valerie. "Reclassifying Upward Mobility: Femininity and the Neo-Liberal Subject." *Gender and Education* 15.3 (2003): 237–248. *Scholars Portal.* Web. 20 Feb. 2017.

Walkowitz, Daniel. "The Conundrum of the Middle-Class Worker in the Twentieth-Century United States." *The Making of the Middle Class: Toward a Transnational History.* Ed. Ricardo López and Barabara Weinstein. Durham: Duke University Press, 2012. 121–140. Print.

Zweig, Michael, interviewee. *Class Dismissed: How TV Frames the Working Class.* Dir. Loretta Alper. Media Education Foundation, 2005. Film.

57

DON'T DROP THE SOAP VS. THE SOAP OPERA

The Representation of Male and Female Prisoners on U.S. Television

Hannah Mueller

INTRODUCTION

When Piper Chapman (Taylor Schilling), the White upper-class protagonist on the Netflix prison series *Orange Is the New Black (OITNB,* Netflix 2013–present), first arrives at Litchfield Penitentiary to serve her sentence for money laundering in a drug cartel, her counselor Sam Healy (Michael Harney) welcomes her with the words: "This isn't *Oz*" (Friedman, Kohan, & Trim, 2013). Within the context of the show's narrative, his comment aims to reassure the intimidated woman that she has nothing to worry about. On a meta-reflexive level, however, the statement puts *OITNB* into an explicit intertextual correspondence with another television show: the prison drama *Oz* (HBO, 1997–2003), one of the most iconic representations of incarcerated people on U.S. television that became famous primarily for its excessive use of physical and sexual violence. By setting itself apart so explicitly from the provocatively violent *Oz* in its very first episode, *OITNB* seemed to make a purposeful programmatic statement about what it was, or rather wasn't, going to be.

The show's ambition to present a different perspective on prison life appeared to be validated by a chorus of television critics who were quick to praise *OITNB* for opening a new chapter in the representation of prisoners in American popular culture. Unlike previous shows set in correctional facilities, many suggested, *OITNB* did not buy into the sensationalist notions about prison that American audiences are so familiar with, offering instead a more nuanced and humanizing representation of incarcerated people. A common opinion among reviewers was the claim that *OITNB* was

unusually "realistic": Hank Stuever (2013) wrote in the *Washington Post,* for example, that the series created a "believable and unembellished realm" that worked "almost like a documentary report from within." Stuever explicitly used the label of realism to distinguish *OITNB* from other recent popular representations of prison, such as the hyperviolent *Oz.* However, when *Oz* first aired on television in the late 1990s, it had been precisely the show's obsession with violence and rape that had prompted critics to employ the label of realism as well, among them Stanley Crouch (1998) in the *New York Times,* who had gone as far as to say that *Oz* "set another standard for realism."

The confident and repeated assessments of both *Oz* and *OITNB* as realistic, unembellished, and honest are particularly noteworthy because, as Bill Yousman (2009) points out, they are often made by "critics, most of whom, presumably, have never been in prison" (p. 141). Lara Stemple (2007) sarcastically comments on this phenomenon: "To hear the critics tell it, OZ is *real.* . . . Either these critics learned everything they know about prison from fiction; or 'realism' is just a term which means life in OZ is really, really bad" (pp. 166–167). Bill Tush (2000) on *CNN* frankly admitted to his lack of personal experience in a commentary on *Oz:* "It's really true to life. I mean, I don't know what it's like in the big house, but. . . . This is such a real-looking set."

This readiness to judge representations of penal culture from a position of rather unapologetic ignorance is what Michelle Brown (2009) identifies as a central feature of what she calls the "penal spectator." Brown argues that the U.S. prison-industrial complex is stabilized and perpetuated by the fact

---

This piece is an original essay that was commissioned for this volume.

that the privileged—those in control of capital or power—experience prison from the perspective of the outsider, the penal spectator. The penal spectator gets to know prison culture exclusively through its cultural representations, for instance on television, and is "so disconnected from the practice of punishment as to simply be a voyeur." Yet this viewer still evaluates these images from a position of "profound privilege, authority, and moral justification" (p. 12) This means that televisual representations of prisoners are not merely fictional fantasies of spaces unfamiliar and inaccessible to the average HBO and Netflix customer. These images also directly generate, influence, and steer public discourses on crime and punishment: in short, they both result from and in return inform the ideological structures at the foundation of the prison-industrial complex.

Oz and *OITNB* portray prison life, in many regards, in diametrically opposite ways. While *Oz* became legendary for its shocking brutality, *OITNB* has been lauded for its both humorous and humanizing portrayal of prisoners. Yet, public media and television spectators praised both shows as "realistic" portrayals of prison life. In this chapter, I argue that the assessment of both *Oz* and *OITNB* as "realistic," despite their significant differences, is not an arbitrary contradiction. Rather, it is due to the way in which audiences' cultural fantasies about prisoners are influenced by assumptions relating to gender and sexuality. *OITNB*, I argue, is not so much (or at least, not *only*) symptomatic of a changing public perspective on incarcerated people in the early 21st century, but in fact makes visible a gender distinction in the public perception of prisoners in the United States. Counselor Healy tells Piper upon her arrival at Litchfield: "This isn't *Oz*," and immediately adds: "Women fight with gossip and rumors." On the narrative level of the series, this addendum exposes the seemingly friendly corrections officer as prejudiced and misogynist—his worldview allows him to neatly divide the (prison) population into violent men and scheming women. However, his statement can also serve as an apt description of the prison television genre as a whole, *OITNB* itself included. In fact, the heavily gendered tropes and stereotypes employed in the representation of male and female prisoners on scripted television significantly influence popular narratives about the cycle of crime, punishment, and recidivism in the United States.

NOT A HAPPY PLACE

The differences between televisual representations of men's and women's prisons often start with the choice of genre and setting. On U.S. television, male prisoners appear primarily on drama shows like *Oz, Prison Break* (FOX, 2005–2009, 2017), and *Sons of Anarchy* (FX, 2008–2014), or on procedurals like *Criminal Minds* (CBS, 2005–present) and *Hawaii Five-0* (CBS, 2010–present). These genres draw their suspense from their protagonists' frequent encounters with violence and danger, and prison provides a convenient background for this setup. Consequently, the representations of men's prisons in these programs show almost exclusively maximum-security facilities and prisoners who, in the vast majority, appear to be incarcerated for violent offenses. Recurrent images of heavy walls, fences, steel gates, or constant video surveillance create a claustrophobic atmosphere. Long shots of the iconic cellblock invoke memories of animal shelters or zoos, thus not so subtly drawing a comparison between prisoners and caged animals.

These images are noticeably absent from shows set in women's prisons, which in contrast to the dark dramas populated with male prisoners tend to lean toward the comedy and soap-opera genre; from the short-lived sitcom *Women in Prison* (Fox, 1987–1988) to Fiona Gallagher's (Emmy Rossum) stint in jail on the dark comedy *Shameless*, to the Netflix dramedy *OITNB*. The female prisoners on these shows are not housed in cellblocks—instead the camera shows cramped low-security dorms, where crowds of women mingle in confined spaces. This holds true even when the low-security setting seems to be at odds with the program's narrative. The written memoir *Orange Is the New Black: My Year in a Women's Prison* (Kerman, 2010) that provided the inspiration for the Netflix show *OITNB* makes it clear that the majority of women in the facility are incarcerated for low-level, nonviolent offenses. In a clear divergence from the nonfiction book, the TV show provides Piper's fellow prisoners with significantly more violent histories, from manslaughter to murder. These offenses certainly make for more dramatic story lines, but would in reality likely lead to confinement in a higher-security state facility, thus making the show's setting in a federal minimum-security facility fairly implausible. The same is true for *Shameless:* When Fiona is on the bus taking her to prison, the woman next to her mentions that they are headed to Decatur Correctional Center, a minimum-security facility, right before telling her that she was convicted of stabbing a pregnant woman (Pimental & Hemingway, 2014), an offense that seems to warrant incarceration at a higher security level. Yet the minimum-security setting of *OITNB* is diegetically necessary, because it provides the backdrop for the chaotic, unruly interactions between prisoners, staff, and visitors from which the show draws not only much of its dramatic, but more important, also its comedic effect.

This correlation between gender, genre, and carceral setting is important because it serves to justify the specifically gendered aspects of prison life different TV shows focus on in their representation of penal culture. The gendering of prison scenarios can be illustrated for example by a comparison of scenes set in the prison shower room, which serves as a focal point for many popular fantasies about prison. The prison shower is intriguing because it reveals prisoners' bodies fully to the eyes of the audience, thus inviting viewers to unabashedly revel in their voyeuristic role both as *television* spectators (in line with Laura Mulvey's [1975] seminal film-theoretical concept of the cinematic gaze as voyeuristic) and as *penal* spectators, who consume images of carceral culture from an outsider position and thus, according to Brown (2009), have to be ultimately thought of as voyeurs.

As a common trope circulating in pop culture, the men's prison shower room in particular has long been almost synonymous with the notion of violence, and more specifically, rape. In a 2014 segment on the American prison system, *Last Week Tonight* host John Oliver lamented the ubiquity of "dropping the soap" references in U.S. media, which callously reduce male prisoners to a rape joke, complaining that "we are really comfortable making jokes about one of the most horrifying things that could potentially happen to them."

Television shows set in men's correctional facilities similarly reiterate this stereotype of the prison shower as a place of unpleasant encounters and threats, of physical and sexual assault. In the *Criminal Minds* episode "Lockdown" (Davis, Williams, & Gibson, 2015) for example, a murder scene opens with the shot of a shower faucet, followed by the backside of a naked prisoner who appears to be alone in the shower room. Familiar

with the trope of the prison shower, the audience knows immediately that the man is in danger and can accurately predict his subsequent violent death.

In contrast, the shower rooms in the women's prisons depicted on *OITNB* and *Shameless* fulfill very different functions. On the one hand, the shower on *OITNB* permits for the reiteration of a trope as old and persistent as the popular joke about dropping the soap: the fantasy of circumstantial lesbian sex behind bars. In the pilot episode, the spectator gets to follow Piper's gaze when she witnesses fellow prisoners Nicky (Natasha Lyonne) and Morello (Yael Stone) perform oral sex in one of the shower stalls. Yvonne Swartz Hammond (2016) confirms "while cultural representations of rape in men's prison realize our worst fears about prison sex, *OITNB* plays off fantasies about lesbian sex . . ." (pp. 80–81).

More frequently, however, shower scenes in the depicted women's facilities highlight the lack of hygiene and privacy in prison, marking the shower as a place of humiliation and disgust. In fact, the opening scene of *OITNB*'s pilot episode establishes the protagonist's resentment toward the prison shower. In a flashback voice-over, Piper talks about her life-long love for baths and showers: "It's my happy place," she says, only to continue, as the camera cuts to a shot of her shivering miserably in the prison shower stall: "*Was* my happy place."

MALE PRISONERS: THE PENIS SYSTEM

These scenes set in different prison showers are indicative of the public perception of life in men's and women's correctional facilities. Scripted television continues to perpetuate the idea of the male prisoner as a caged animal whose violent potential is waiting to be set off by the smallest spark. The closed-off setting of the maximum-security prison is presented as an effective and deadly trap locking the protagonist, and by proxy the television spectator, in with the brutal killers. *Prison Break* (Scheuring & Ratner, 2005) and *Oz* (Fontana & Martin, 1997) set the stage for this constellation in their respective pilot episodes. Both shows introduce the television audience to the prison by having the protagonist, upon his arrival, witness one prisoner stabbing another without providing any explanation for the horrifying act—ominous beginnings establishing the prison as a place of ruthless violence without reason. The atmosphere of senseless violence that is so typical for shows set in men's prisons is further illustrated by the noticeably frequent representation of violent riots. On television, these riots tend to be caused by very minor incidents, like a broken A/C unit in the *Prison Break* episode "Riots, Drills and the Devil: Part 1" (Santora & Mandel, 2005) or a small cell block fire in the *Hawaii Five-0* episode "Olelo Ho'Opa'I Make/Death Sentence" (Cwik & Spicer, 2013). During these riots, the prisoners frequently perpetrate excessive violence against corrections officers: In the *Criminal Minds* episode "Lockdown," for example, the prisoners step out of their suddenly unlocked cells and immediately stab a CO in cold blood. In *Prison Break*'s "Riots, Drills and the Devil," the previously peaceful inhabitants of the infirmary suddenly turn aggressive when they discover that other prisoners are rioting: They jump out of their beds and threaten the female doctor with rape and death. To make the cliché complete, the doctor is a White woman and the man who threatens her most vehemently is a tall, muscular Black man.

This representation is rather at odds with the empirical data showing that actual prison riots are fairly rare, and usually the result of several coinciding influential factors. Commonly suspected causes for riots include "inhumane conditions, bad food, brutal staff, economic factors, racial tensions, incarceration rates, political disempowerment, the presence of young violent prisoners, external social upheavals, building-design problems and overcrowding" (Boin & Rattray, 2004, p. 47). In fact, Arjen Boin and William Rattray argue "that much must go wrong, for quite some time, before a prison explodes into collective violence" (p. 48).

In contrast, U.S. television paints a rather skewed picture of prisoners' readiness to revolt by presenting their riots as an ultimately senseless but basically natural occurrence, an inevitable consequence of the prisoners' inherently violent nature. This naturalization of violence is also used to explain the escalation of racial tensions: In the *Prison Break* episode "Allen" (Scheuring & Watkins, 2005), the newly incarcerated Michael Scofield (Wentworth Miller) asks about the reasons for an escalating feud between Black and White inmates, and is told by another prisoner: "Same reason you don't put cats and dogs in the same cage. They don't get along." *Oz,* too, presents violence in prison as a quasi-natural principle founded in competitive masculinity. In the first episode, narrator Augustus Hill (Harold Perrineau) explains this basic rule of prison life to the television spectator: "They call this the penal system. But it's really the penis system. It's about how big, it's about how long, it's about how hard. Life in Oz is all about the size of your dick, and anyone who tells you different ain't got one."

Men's prisons, in these televisual texts, are presented as hypermasculine microcosms structured by the Darwinist law of raw violence. Both *Oz* and *Prison Break* demonstrate how the initiation into prison life confronts their White[1] upper-class protagonists with this basic rule. Tobias Beecher (Lee Tergesen) on *Oz* is sexually enslaved, and unwillingly branded with a swastika by the leader of the Aryan Brotherhood; Michael Scofield on *Prison Break* is beaten up, threatened with rape, and mutilated as another prisoner cuts off his toe.

FEMALE PRISONERS: MAINTAINING YOUR EYEBROWS

The female protagonists of *OITNB* and *Shameless,* on the other hand, face challenges of a very different kind. When Fiona Gallagher first arrives in prison in the *Shameless* episode "Emily" (Pimental & Hemingway, 2014), a fellow prisoner in the dorm tries to trick her into consuming drugs right before she is called out for a urine test. When Piper Chapman, shortly after her arrival at Litchfield, makes the mistake of insulting the prison cook in *OITNB*'s "I Wasn't Ready," she is served a blood-soaked tampon by the kitchen crew: At the end of the episode, the audience watches her retching miserably behind the building. Both incidents seem to confirm Counselor Healy's statement that women fight with "gossip and rumor," relying on intrigue and scheming instead of brute violence. But Piper's encounter with the bloody tampon sandwich also foregrounds, just like her negative feelings toward the prison shower, the persistent sensation of revulsion and disgust. For her, the most difficult part about the adjustment to prison life is not the threat of physical or sexual violence, but instead an exclusion from what *OITNB* presents as basic feminine needs: privacy, cleanliness, healthy food, and access to makeup and fashion.

While male prisoners on TV mostly undergo strip searches with nonchalant resignation, both *OITNB* and *Shameless* highlight the women's shame and humiliation when faced with the forced lack of privacy in prison, from shared toilets and showers to the degrading strip searches. *Shameless,* for example, has certainly earned its reputation for hardly ever shying away from showing nudity and sex, but when Fiona has to strip naked at the county jail after her arrest in "Iron City" (Wells & Ponsoldt, 2014), the camera pans away from her body and remains focused on her pained face, highlighting the humiliating nature of the search.

OITNB's portrayal of women's attempts at beautification under the most dire circumstances takes a more light-hearted approach, but it similarly reaffirms stereotypes about female prisoners' priorities. Before Piper leaves to serve her sentence at the beginning of the series, her best friend Polly (Maria Dizzia) instructs her sternly: "You focus on how you are going to maintain your eyebrows behind bars. You may not come back with a unibrow." Her reprimand serves as a motto for the following episodes of the show, in which incarcerated women diligently shave their legs, dye their hair, apply nail polish and makeup, and find creative, often comical ways to make up for the lack of access to beauty products.

In fact, *OITNB* frequently stages women's struggles with the terrible conditions of prison life as a source of humor, in particular in regard to stereotypically feminine issues like hygiene, health care, and food. The prisoners' reactions of disgust in the face of dirty bathrooms, moldy food, vermin, and bodily fluids are often played up for laughs, which helps the series maintain its comedic tone, but also has the unfortunate effect of making the women's fully justified revulsion appear exaggerated, squeamish, even hysterical.

This creates the impression that the incarcerated women's behavior is silly, sometimes naïve and even childish, a characterization that is spelled out explicitly several times over the course of *OITNB*. When a group of prisoners get into a physical altercation over an ice cream cone in the episode "Tit Punch" (Ramirez & Briesewitz, 2013), a guard groans, like a long-suffering father talking to his daughters: "Please tell me you aren't fighting over ice cream!" During the election for the prisoner's council in "WAC Pack," (Morelli & Trim, 2013) Piper similarly compares her fellow inmates' antics

to a high school competition. Whereas fights between different groups of prisoners along lines of race, ethnicity, and class in men's prisons are presented as expressions of the merciless law of the fittest's survival, in *OITNB* these conflicts are likened to animosities between school girls. This comparison not only downplays racial and class-based social tensions, it also reiterates minority stereotypes as material for comedy. *OITNB*'s first season for instance casts as its "mean girl" Tiffany "Pennsatucky" Doggett (Taryn Manning), a fanatically religious redneck meth addict who represents an "openly ridiculed cultural archetype—white trash" (Sered, 2016, p. 128), and on whom the White prisoners with middle- and upper-class backgrounds look down in disgust.

Pennsatucky is not the only case in which other characters' reactions of distaste seem to be turned into a joke at the expense of underprivileged groups. The revulsion experienced by Piper on *OITNB* and Fiona on *Shameless* is caused not only by the abysmal conditions of incarceration, but frequently also by the personal habits of their fellow prisoners, who tend to be less White, less skinny, less young, and less conventionally beautiful than the protagonists. When Piper is sent to the detention center in Chicago in the episode "Thirsty Bird" (Herrmann, Kohan, & Foster, 2014), she visibly recoils when her cellmate, an older, overweight Black woman, uses the toilet in front of her. Both Piper and Fiona also act disturbed by the sexual advances of Black women, thus treating Black lesbianism as threatening. While their reaction could be interpreted as a commentary on Piper's and Fiona's racial prejudice, the shows implicitly reproduce this bias in their persistent reaffirmation of conventional ideals of beauty. Lauren DeCarvalho and Nicole Cox (2015), for example, point out that on *OITNB,* "onscreen sexual relations between two women are typically reserved for thin, white women" (p. 74), like those of Piper and her lover Alex (Laura Prepon).

THE CONSEQUENCES: WE AIN'T EVER GONNA CHANGE

These different representations of prison life have a direct effect on the respective shows' explanations of criminal acts, and their perspective on rehabilitation. The naturalization of violence in representations of men's prisons leaves spectators with the impression that rehabilitating male prisoners is pointless because they are born to be criminals. On *Oz,* new characters are regularly introduced with a flashback to their time before prison, but these scenes focus exclusively on the crimes they committed—reducing their characterization to their identity as cold-blooded criminals. In the episode "Visits, Conjugal and Otherwise," the narrator lectures the television audience on genetic predisposition, claiming that people's fates are determined by their parents' DNA: "Maybe they passed you some cell that makes you drink or do drugs, even if you don't wanna. Even if it's killing you. These gene things are like the shackles they put on us here" (Fontana & Gomez, 1997). *Criminal Minds* presents a similarly fatalistic view by citing theories of social conditioning: In "Damaged," a serial killer on death row is analyzed by a FBI profiler, who tells him that his family history destined him to be a murderer: "I think deep down you know, . . . you . . . never had a chance" (Davis & Bernero, 2008). But not only are the male prisoners on television predestined for a life of crime, they also don't seem to be interested in leaving it behind. Tim McManus (Terry Kinney), the administrator running the experimental prison block Emerald City on *Oz,* is portrayed as a naïve reformist who believes in rehabilitation and has to be told by the prisoners themselves that they are monsters, and that they like it that way: "Let me tell you something, coach," one prisoner says in "The Routine," "Even with all your good intentions, all your reforms and your overhaul policies, I ain't ever gonna change. We ain't ever gonna change. None of us." The show uses McManus's feeble, and ultimately doomed, attempts at rehabilitation for a critique of liberalism and ultimately for an argument in favor of even harsher punishment.

While male prisoners' identity is frequently reduced to their crime, representations of women in prison generally take their time to tell audiences how they ended up behind bars. Their crimes require explanation, because as Jodie M. Lawston (2001) argues, incarcerated women "perplex society because they do not fit the traditional mold of what a prisoner is 'supposed' to be: male, and in contemporary society, of color" (p. 1). *OITNB* uses a similar flashback structure as *Oz,* but instead of focusing on the women's crimes, the flashbacks

give the spectator insight into their lives. Unlike the male prisoners on *Oz* or *Criminal Minds,* the women on *OITNB* and *Shameless* are not predestined to become criminals, but for the most part are shown as falling victim to the wrong kind of romance. As the flashbacks on *OITNB* and Fiona's story on *Shameless* show, many of them are seduced, tricked, or forced into a criminal lifestyle by their lovers. And yet, more subtly, there is also a certain inevitability to the path that leads these women into prison. On *OITNB,* a considerable number of the women at Litchfield Penitentiary have in common complicated, broken family backgrounds. With predictable regularity, their problems can be traced back to absent or negligent mothers. In particular the mothers of Black, Hispanic, and lower-class inmates are presented as absent, careless, or promiscuous. Anna Marie Smith (2015) rightly criticizes "the series' promotion of the idea that our social problems can be traced back to the absolute failure of low-income black women and Latinas to meet a minimum standard where parenting is concerned" (p. 277). But even the mothers of White prisoners from wealthy families, like Piper or Nicky, are portrayed in a negative light: They are self-absorbed and emotionally distant. *OITNB*'s representation of female prisoners as often silly, immature high school girls further supports the impression that their criminal actions are a direct result of their mothers' failure at parenting. Even more so, the shows seem to suggest that their mothers' negligence predestines them to fail as mothers themselves. On *Shameless,* Fiona is the oldest of six children from a mother who is bipolar, emotionally abusive, and for the most part absent. Her parents' behavior is not only the source of the family's poverty, but also depicted as the reason for the children's emotional problems. In the Season 4 episode "There's the Rub" (Holmes & Nutter, 2014), Fiona's chaotic love life and her weakness for recreational drugs lead to her toddler-age baby brother accidentally overdosing on cocaine. Thus, the show suggests that her mother's negligence is not only what leads to her incarceration; it also causes her to become a negligent mother figure herself.

A similar discourse is invoked on *OITNB,* where many prisoners are failed by their mothers and failing as mothers at the same time. This constellation becomes particularly obvious in the relationship between Daya (Dascha Polanco) and her mother Aleida Diaz (Elizabeth Rodriguez), both imprisoned in Litchfield Penitentiary. Their relationship is so toxic that a heavily pregnant fellow inmate complains that the two could serve as a "cautionary tale" that makes her wonder whether perhaps having children is a mistake ("Moscow Mule," Ramirez & Abraham, 2013). When Daya herself is impregnated by a corrections officer, she tells her mother that she is afraid the cycle of bad parenting is going to continue with her own child: "Do you want me to end up like you?" she asks. "I'm already in prison. All I need is five different baby daddies and an ass tattoo of a dog" ("Fucksgiving," Heder & Trim, 2013). This argument is spelled out even more explicitly in the figure of Pennsatucky, who has had five abortions by the time she goes to prison. When she expresses the feeling that she failed her unborn children in the episode "Mother's Day" (Kohan & McCarthy, 2015), another prisoner comforts her by telling her that she did society a favor: "You were a methhead white trash piece of shit. And your children, had they been born, would have been methhead white trash pieces of shit. So by terminating those pregnancies you spared society the scourge of your offspring. I mean, if you think about it, it's . . . a blessing."

CONCLUSION

At first glance, representations of female prisoners on contemporary U.S. television may indeed appear as more sympathetic than those of their male counterparts. Male prisoners, in particular men of color, continue to be likened to animalistic predators, and most shows imply that they are incarcerated not as a consequence of systemic social and racial inequality, but because they are by nature violent and need to be caged. Consequently, efforts at rehabilitation, as they are shown in the work of Tim McManus on *Oz*, are presented as pointless, because the men in prison neither want to nor can be changed.

Incarcerated women, especially those from lower-class backgrounds, on the other hand, are presented as immature girls, who end up in prison primarily because their mothers failed at the task of adequate parenting, which makes them vulnerable to the seduction of romantic partners who drag them into a life of crime. Yet they, too, are ultimately presented as immune to rehabilitation. Both *OITNB* and *Shameless* suggest that the women's complicated family backgrounds, in particular their absent or negligent mothers, have emotionally affected them in a way that predestines them to fail at motherhood themselves, thus continuing the cycle of bad parenting, crime, and incarceration. While shows like *OITNB* and *Shameless* offer more insight into the systemic conditions of poverty, discrimination, and abuse that lead to incarceration, this has to be understood at least partly as an attempt to explain the reasons behind the incarceration of women as what society considers "atypical" criminals. Ultimately, these shows still present a relationship of cause and effect that blames female criminality on failed motherhood, thus once again foregrounding individual responsibility over social inequality and a flawed criminal justice system.

The assessment of *OITNB* as "realistic" is consequential, in this context, in the way it influences television spectators' assumptions about the causes of incarceration and the makeup of the prison population in the United States. Compared to shows like *Oz*, *OITNB* might easily succeed in making its characters appear more "human," that is, sympathetic, to the penal spectator. At the same time, however, its representation of female prisoners comes with its own problems. On the one hand, the way in which this portrayal is tied to specifically gendered elements of life in a women's prison means that the sympathetic view only extends to female prisoners, while leaving the image of the male prisoner as violent animal untouched. In fact, *OITNB* reiterates this image itself in "Thirsty Bird," when Piper encounters male prisoners at the detention center. On the other hand, the show's take on the conditions of incarceration derives humor from the women's deprivation of what is portrayed as stereotypically feminine needs, such as fashion and makeup, thus downplaying the horrendous living conditions in most American correctional facilities. And finally, *OITNB*'s portrayal of failed motherhood, in particular when it comes to lower-class women and women of color, ultimately lays the blame for increasing rates of incarcerated women firmly at the feet of these same women, and suggests that bad mothering leaves a mark on women that ultimately also makes them resistant to efforts at rehabilitation.

NOTE

1. Actor Wentworth Miller is actually mixed-race/White-passing, but his character Michael Scofield is White.

REFERENCES

Boin, A., & Rattray, W. A. R. (2004). Understanding prison riots: Towards a threshold theory. *Punishment & Society, 6*(1), pp. 47–65.

Brown, M. (2009). *The culture of punishment: Prison, society, and spectacle.* New York: New York University Press.

Crouch, S. (1998, September 20). My favorite show; Stanley Crouch on "Oz." *New York Times.* Retrieved from http://www.nytimes .com/1998/09/20/magazine/my-favorite-show-stanley-crouch-on-oz.html

Cwik, S., & Spicer, B. (2013, January 20). Olelo Ho'Opa'I make/death sentence. In B. Spicer, *Hawaii Five-0.* New York: CBS.

Davis, J., & Bernero, E. A. (2008, April 2). Damaged. In R. Dunkle, *Criminal minds.* New York: CBS.

Davis, J., Williams, V. & Gibson, T. (2015, March 4). Lockdown. In R. Dunkle, *Criminal minds.* New York: CBS.

De Carvalho, L., & Cox, N. (2015). Queerness (un)shackled. In A. Trier-Bieniek (Ed.), *Feminist theory and pop culture* (pp. 65–76). Rotterdam: Sense Publisher.

Fontana, T., & Gomez, N. (1997, July 14). Visits, conjugal and otherwise. In T. Fontana, *Oz.* New York: HBO.

Fontana, T., & Martin, D. (1997, July 12). The routine. In T. Fontana, *Oz.* New York: HBO.

Friedman, L., Kohan, J. & Trim, M. (2013, July 11). I wasn't ready. In N. K. Tannenbaum, *Orange is the new black.* New York: Netflix.

Heder, S., & Trim, M. (2013, July 11). Fucksgiving. In N. K. Tannenbaum, *Orange is the new black.* New York: Netflix.

Herrmann, T., Kohan, J. & Foster, J. (2014, June 6). Thirsty bird. In N. K. Tannenbaum, *Orange is the new black.* New York: Netflix.

Holmes, D., & Nutter, D. (2014, February 9). There's the rub. In M. Hissrich, *Shameless.* Chicago: Showtime.

Kerman, P. (2010). *Orange is the new black: My year in a women's prison.* New York: Spiegel & Grau.

Kohan, J., & McCarthy, A. (2015, June 11) Mother's Day. In N. K. Tannenbaum, *Orange is the new black.* New York: Netflix.

Lawston, J. M. (2011). From representations to resistance. How the razor wire binds us. In J. M. Lawston & A. Lucas (Eds.), *Razor wire women: Prisoners, activists, scholars, and artists* (pp. 1–17). Albany: State University of New York Press.

Morelli, L., & Trim, M. (2013, July 11). WAC pack. In N. K. Tannenbaum, *Orange is the new black.* New York: Netflix.

Mulvey, L. (1975) Visual pleasure and narrative cinema. *Screen, 16*(3), 6–18.

Oliver, J. (2014, July 20). Incarceration in the United States. In J. Oliver, *Last week tonight.* New York: HBO.

Pimental, N., & Hemingway, A. (2014, March 30). Emily. In M. Hissrich, *Shameless.* Chicago: Showtime.

Ramirez, M., & Abraham, P. (2013, July 11). Moscow mule. In N. K. Tannenbaum, *Orange is the new black.* New York: Netflix.

Ramirez, M., & Briesewitz, U. (2013, July 11). Tit punch. In N. K. Tannenbaum, *Orange is the new black.* New York: Netflix.

Santora, N., & Mandel, R. (2005, September 26). Riots, drills and the devil: Part 1. In P. Scheuring, *Prison break.* Los Angeles: FOX.

Scheuring, P., & Ratner, B. (2005, August 29). Pilot. In P. Scheuring, *Prison break.* Los Angeles: FOX.

Scheuring, P., & Watkins, M. (2005, August 29). Allen. In P. Scheuring, *Prison break*. Los Angeles: FOX.

Sered, S. (2016). Pennsatucky's teeth and the persistence of class. In A. K. Householder & A. Trier-Bieniek (Eds.), *Feminist perspectives on Orange is the new black: Thirteen critical essays* (pp. 128–139). Jefferson, NC: McFarland.

Smith, A. M. (2015). "*Orange* is the same White": *Orange is the new black,* Netflix, 2013, 2014. *New Political Science, 37*(2), 276–80.

Stemple, L. (2007). HBO's OZ and the fight against prisoner rape: Chronicles from the front line. In M. L. Johnson (Ed.), *Third wave feminism and television: Jane puts it in a box* (pp. 166–188). London/New York: I.B. Tauris.

Stuever, H. (2013, July 11). Netflix's "Orange is the new black": Brilliance behind bars. *The Washington Post.* Retrieved from https:// www.washingtonpost.com/entertainment/tv/ netflixs-orange-is-the-new-black-brilliance-behind- bars/2013/07/11/d52f911e-e9aa-11e2-8f22- de4bd2a2bd39_story.html.

Swartz, Hammond, Y. (2016). Cleaning up your act: Surveillance, queer sex and the imprisoned body. In A. K. Householder & A. Trier-Bieniek (Eds.), *Feminist perspectives on Orange Is the New Black: Thirteen critical essays* (pp. 77–94). Jefferson, NC: McFarland.

Tush, B. (August 26, 2000) *Showbiz this weekend.* New York: CNN.

Wells, J., & Ponsoldt, J. (2014, February 16). Iron city. In M. Hissrich, *Shameless*. Chicago: Showtime.

Yousman, B. (2009) *Prime time prisons on U.S. TV: Representation of incarceration*. New York: Peter Lang.

58 DONALD TRUMP AND THE POLITICS OF SPECTACLE

Douglas Kellner

I first came up with the concept of media spectacle[1] to describe the key phenomenon of US media and politics in the mid-1990s. This was the era of the O.J. Simpson murder case and trial, the Clinton sex scandals, and the rise of cable news networks like Fox, CNN, and MSNBC and the 24/7 news cycle that has dominated US politics and media since then.[2] The 1990s was also the period when the Internet and New Media took off so that anyone could be a political commentator, player, and participant in the spectacle, a phenomenon that accelerated as New Media morphed into Social Media and teenagers, celebrities, politicians, and others wanting to become part of the networked virtual world joined in.

The scope of the spectacle has thus increased in the past decades with the proliferation of new media and social networking like Facebook, YouTube, Twitter, Instagram, Skype, and the like that increases the breadth and participation of the spectacle. By "media spectacles" I am referring to media constructs that present events which disrupt ordinary and habitual flows of information, and which become popular stories which capture the attention of the media and the public, and circulate through broadcasting networks, the Internet, social networking, smart phones, and other new media and communication technologies. In a global networked society, media spectacles proliferate instantaneously, become virtual and viral, and in some cases becomes tools of sociopolitical transformation, while other media spectacles become mere moments of media hype and tabloidized sensationalism.

Dramatic news and events are presented as media spectacles and dominate certain news cycles. Stories like the 9/11 terror attacks, mass shooting, Hurricane Katrina, Barack Obama and the 2008 U.S. presidential election, and in 2011 the Arab Uprisings, the Libyan revolution, the UK Riots, the Occupy movements and other major media spectacles of the era, cascaded through broadcasting, print, and digital media, seizing people's attention and emotions, and generating complex and multiple effects that may make 2011 as memorable a year in the history of social upheaval as 1968.[3]

In today's highly competitive media environment, *"Breaking News!"* of various sorts play out as media spectacle, including mega-events like wars, other spectacular terrorist attacks, extreme weather disasters, or, political insurrections and upheavals. These spectacles assume a narrative form and become focuses of attention during a specific temporal and historical period, that may only last a few days, but may come to dominate news and information for extended periods of time. Examples include the O.J. Simpson Trial and the Clinton sex/impeachment scandal in the mid-1990s, the stolen election of 2000 in the Bush/Gore presidential campaign, and natural and other disasters that have significant destructive effects and political implications, such as Hurricane Katrina, the BP Deepwater Horizon Oil Spill, or the Fukushima-Daiichi nuclear catastrophe. Media spectacles can even become signature events of an entire epoch as were, arguably, the 9/11 terrorist attacks which inaugurated a historical period that I describe as Terror War (Kellner, 2003).

I've argued since 2008 that the key to Barack Obama's success in two presidential elections is because he became a master of media spectacle, blending politics and performance in carefully

From Kellner, D. (2016). American Nightmare: Donald Trump, Media Spectacle, and Authoritarian Populism. *Transgressions, 117.*

orchestrated media spectacles (Kellner, 2009, 2012). Previously, the model of the mastery of presidential spectacle was Ronald Reagan who everyday performed his presidency in a well-scripted and orchestrated daily spectacle. Reagan was trained as an actor and every night Ron and Nancy reportedly practiced his lines for the next day performance like they had done in their Hollywood days. Reagan breezed through the day scripted with a teleprompter and well-orchestrated media events, smiling frequently, and pausing to sound-bite the line of the day.

Now in the 2016 election, obviously Donald Trump has emerged as a major form of media spectacle and has long been a celebrity and master of the spectacle with promotion of his buildings and casinos from the 1980s to the present, his reality-TV shows, self-aggrandizing events, and now his presidential campaign. Hence, Trump is empowered and enabled to run for the presidency in part because media spectacle has become a major force in US politics, helping to determine elections, government, and, more broadly, the ethos and nature of our culture and political sphere, and Trump is a successful creator and manipulator of the spectacle.

I would also argue that in recent years U.S. wars have been orchestrated as media spectacle, recalling Bush Jr's 2003 Iraq shock and awe campaign for one example. Likewise, terrorism has been orchestrated as media spectacle since the 9/11 attack that was the most spectacular and deadly attack on the US heartland in history. As we know too well, school and mass shootings which can be seen as a form of domestic terrorism, have become media spectacles with one taking place in 2015 in Virginia on live TV, while the stock market, weather, and every other form of life can become part of a media spectacle. Hence, it is no surprise that political campaigns are being run as media spectacles and that Knights of the Spectacle like Donald Trump are playing the spectacle to win the presidency, although it is far from certain that the Donald will become King of the Spectacle.

Trump's biographies reveal that he was driven by a need to compete and win,[4] and entering the highly competitive real estate business in New York in the 1980s, Trump saw the need to use the media and publicity to promote his celebrity and image. It was a time of tabloid culture and media-driven celebrity and Trump even adopted a

pseudonym "John Baron" to give the media gossip items that touted Trump's successes in businesses, with women, and as a rising man about town.[5]

Trump derives his language and behavior from a highly competitive and ruthless New York business culture combined with an appreciation of the importance of media and celebrity to succeed in a media-centric hypercapitalism. Hence, to discover the nature of Trump's "temperament," personality, and use of language, we should recall his reality-TV show *The Apprentice* which popularized him into a supercelebrity and made the Donald a major public figure for a national audience. Indeed, Trump is the first reality-TV candidate who runs his campaign like a reality-TV series, boasting during the most chaotic episodes in his campaign that his rallies are the most entertaining, and sending outrageous Tweets into the Twitter-sphere which than dominate the news cycle on the ever-proliferating mainstream media and social networking sites. Hence, Trump is the first celebrity candidate whose use of the media and celebrity star power is his most potent weapon in his improbable and highly surreal campaign.[6]

THE APPRENTICE, TWITTER, AND THE SUMMER OF TRUMP

Since Trump's national celebrity derived in part from his role in the reality-TV series *The Apprentice*,[7] we need to interrogate this popular TV phenomenon to help explain the Trump phenomenon. The opening theme music "For the Love of Money," a 1973 R&B song by The O'Jays, established the capitalist ethos of the competition for the winning contestant to get a job with the Trump organization, and obviously money is the key to Trump's business and celebrity success, although there is much controversy over how rich Trump is, and, so far, he has not released his tax returns to quell rumors that he isn't as rich as he claims, that he does not contribute as much to charity as he has stated, and that many years he pays little or no taxes.

In the original format to *The Apprentice*, several contestants formed teams to carry out a task dictated by Trump, and each "contest" resulted with a winner and Trump barking "you're fired" to the loser. Ironically, some commentators believe that in the 2012 presidential election Barack

Obama beat Mitt Romney handily because he early on characterized Romney as a billionaire who liked to fire people, which is ironic since this is Trump's signature personality trait in his business, reality-TV, and now political career, which has seen him fire two campaign managers and more advisors by August 2016.

The Apprentice premiered in January 2004, and after six seasons, a new format was introduced: *The Celebrity Apprentice.* The celebrity apprentice series generally followed the same premise as the original, but with celebrities as contestants participating to win money for their chosen charities, rather than winning a job opportunity with the Trump organization. There have been seven seasons of *The Celebrity Apprentice* since 2008, although NBC announced on June 29, 2015 that it was severing all business ties with Trump due to the latter's comments about Mexican immigrants, but has said its relationship with the producer of the series Mark Burnett and the show will continue.

When NBC started negotiating with Trump concerning the reality TV-series in 2002, according to NBC producer Jeff Gaspin, the network was not sure that the New York-centric real estate mogul would have a national resonance and the initial concept envisaged different billionaires each season hiring an apprentice. The show immediately got good ratings and Trump became a popular TV figure as he brought the contestants into his board room in Trump Tower, appraised their performances, insulted and sometimes humiliated those who did not do well, and fired the loser.[8]

The Apprentice's TV Producer Mark Burnett broke into national consciousness with his hit reality-TV show *The Survivor,* which premiered in 1992 a neo-Darwinian epic of alliances, backstabbing, and nastiness. The series provides an allegory of how one succeeds in the dog-eat-dog business world in which Donald Trump has thrived, and spectacularly failed as many of the books about him document. Both Burnett and Trump share the same neo-Darwinian (a)social ethos of 19th century ultracompetitive capitalism with some of Donald Trump's famous witticisms proclaiming:

- When somebody challenges you unfairly, fight back—be brutal, be tough—don't take it. It is always important to WIN!

- I think everyone's a threat to me.

- Everyone that's hit me so far has gone down. They've gone down big league.

- I want my generals kicking ass.

- I would bomb the shit out of them.

- You bomb the hell out of the oil. Don't worry about the cities. The cities are terrible.[9]

In any case, *The Apprentice* made Trump a national celebrity who became well-known enough to run for president and throughout the campaign Trump has used his celebrity to gain media time. Further, *The Apprentice* provided a Trumpian pedagogy of how to succeed in the cut-throat corporate capitalist business world with the show illustrating what aggressive, highly competitive, and sometimes amoral tactics are needed to win and gain success, and provided for a generation the message that winning was everything and that losing was devastating.[10]

In addition to his campaign's ability to manipulate broadcast media, Trump is also a heavy user of Twitter and tweets obsessively throughout the day and night. Indeed, Trump may be the first major Twitter candidate, and certainly he is the one using it most aggressively and frequently. Twitter was launched in 2006, but I don't recall it being used in a major way in the 2008 election, although Obama used Facebook and his campaign bragged that he had over a million "Friends" and used Facebook as part of his daily campaign apparatus.

Twitter is a perfect vehicle for Trump as you can use its 140 character framework for attack, bragging, and getting out simple messages or posts that engage receivers who feel they are in the know and involved in TrumpWorld when they receive his tweets. When asked at an August 26, 2015, Iowa event as to why he uses Twitter so much, he replied that it was easy, it only took a couple of seconds, and that he could attack his media critics when he "wasn't treated fairly." Trump has also used Instagram—an online mobile photo-sharing, video-sharing and social networking services that enables its users to take pictures and short videos, and share them on a variety of social networking platforms, such as Facebook, Twitter, Tumblr and Flickr.

Twitter is perfect for General Trump who can blast out his opinions and order his followers what to think. It enables Businessman and Politician

Trump to define his brand and mobilize those who wish to consume or support it. Trump Twitter gratifies the need of Narcissist Trump to be noticed and recognized as a Master of Communication who can bind his warriors into an on-line community. Twitter enables the Pundit-in-Chief to opine, rant, attack, and proclaim on all and sundry subjects, and to subject TrumpWorld to the indoctrination of their Fearless Leader.

Hence, Trump is mastering new media as well as dominating television and old media through his orchestration of media events as spectacles and daily Twitter Feed. In Trump's presidential campaign kickoff speech on June 16, 2015, when he announced he was running for President, Trump and his wife Melania dramatically ascended down the escalator at Trump Towers, and the Donald strode up to a gaggle of microphones and dominated media attention with his drama. The opening speech of his campaign made a typically inflammatory remark that held in thrall news cycles for days when he stated: "The U.S. has become a dumping ground for everybody else's problems. [Applause] Thank you. It's true, and these are the best and the finest. When Mexico sends its people, they're not sending their best. They're not sending you. They're not sending you. They're sending people that have lots of problems, and they're bringing those problems with us. They're bringing drugs. They're bringing crime. They're rapists. And some, I assume, are good people."

This comment ignited a firestorm of controversy and provided a preview of Things to Come concerning vile racism, xenophobia, Islamophobia, and the other hallmarks of Trump's Cacophony of Hate. Debate over Trump's assault on undocumented immigrants would come to dominate daily news cycles of the Republican primaries and would continue to play out in the general election in Fall 2016. In the lead up to the first Republican primary debate in Fall 2015, Donald Trump got the majority of media time, and his daily campaign appearances and the Republican primary debates became media spectacles dominated by Trump. Every day that Trump had a campaign event, the cable news networks would hype the event with crawlers on the bottom of the TV screen proclaiming "Waiting for Trump," with air-time on cable TV dominated by speculation on what he would talk about. Trump's speeches were usually broadcast live, often in their entirety, a boon of free TV time that no candidate of either party was awarded. After the Trump event, for the rest of the day the pundits would dissect what he had said and his standing vis-à-vis the other Republican candidates. If Trump had no campaign event planned, he would fire off a round of Tweets against his opponents on his highly active Twitter account—which then would be featured on network cable news discussions as well as social media.

Hence, Trump's orchestration of media spectacle and a compliant mainstream media was a crucial factor in thrusting Trump ever further into the front runner status in the Republican primaries and winning for him the overwhelming amount of media attention and eventually the Republican nomination. The first major quantitative study released notes that from mid-June 2015 after Trump announced he was running through mid-July, Trump was in 46% of the news media coverage of the Republican field, based on Google news hits; he also got 60% of Google news searches, and I will bet that later academic studies will show how he dominated all media from newspapers to television to Twitter and new media to social networking during the Republican primaries and then during the general election.[11]

At a press conference on August 26, 2015, before his appearance at a rally in Dubuque, Iowa, Trump bragged how all three US cable news networks, as well as the other big three networks and even foreign news networks, were following him around all day, broadcasting all his live campaign appearances, and even his appearance for Jury duty in New York one day (he didn't have to serve and cable news anchors led off that night with ordinary people who had been waiting all day to see if they would be enrolled to serve on a jury who were asked what Trump had been doing all day, if he'd said anything, and so on, clearly a waste of news space and sign that Trump was dominating Republican primary coverage).

The August 26, 2015 Iowa event was the day that a Univision anchor Jorge Ramos tried to interrupt Trump's press conference to challenge Trump on immigration, in which Trump had his operatives throw Ramos out, but then let him back in to create another media spectacle of Trump vs Ramos as they battled it out debating immigration, letting Trump dominate yet another news cycle.

The same day, Trump bragged about how one major media insider told him that it was the "Summer of Trump" and that it was amazing how he was completely dominating news coverage. Trump also explained, correctly I think, why he was getting all the media attention: "RATINGS," he explained, "it's ratings, the people love me, they want to see me, so they watch TV when I'm on." And I do think it is ratings that leads the profit-oriented television networks to almost exclusively follow Trump's events and give him live TV control of the audience. In his 1989 book, *Fast Capitalism,* and *Speeding Up Fast Capitalism,* a sequel to his earlier book, Ben Agger presented a framework for analyzing mutations in society, culture, and politics that have made possible a Donald Trump.[12] Without a media-saturated "fast capitalism" and media-centric politics, new technologies like Twitter and social networking, and a celebrity culture that has morphed into politics, there could never be a Donald Trump. Trump's ability to dominate the mediascape of contemporary capitalism and now sectors of the political scene is facilitated by quasi-religious beliefs that the allegedly successful businessman (who may or may not be a billionaire) has the qualifications to lead, and there is no doubt but that his celebrity status attracts devoted followers.

NOTES

1. On my concept of media spectacle, see Douglas Kellner, *Grand Theft 2000. Media Spectacle and a Stolen Election.* Lanham, Md.: Rowman and Littlefield, 2001; *Media Spectacle.* London and New York: Routledge, 2003: *From September 11 to Terror War: The Dangers of the Bush Legacy.* Lanham, Md.: Rowman and Littlefield, 2003: *Media Spectacle and the Crisis of Democracy.* Boulder, Col.: Paradigm Press, 2005: and *Media Spectacle and Insurrection, 2011: From the Arab Uprisings to Occupy Everywhere.* London and New York: Continuum/Bloomsbury, 2012.

2. I provide accounts of the O.J. Simpson Trial and the Clinton sex/impeachment scandal in the mid-1990s in *Media Spectacle.* op. cit.: I engage the stolen election of 2000 in the Bush/Gore presidential campaign in *Grand Theft 2000.* op. cit. and describe the 9/11 terrorist attacks and their aftermath in *From 9/11 to Terror War,* op. cit.

3. See Kellner. *Media Spectacle and Insurrection,* 2011.

4. See Michael D'Antonio, *Never Enough: Donald Trump and the Pursuit of Success* (New York: Thomas Dunne Books, 2015); Gwenda Blair, *The Trumps* (New York: Simon and Schuster, 2000): and Michael Kranish and Marc Fisher, *Trump Revealed. An American Journey of Ambition, Ego, Money and Power.* New York: Scribner, 2016. Blair's chapter on "Born to Compete," op. cit., pp. 223ff., documents Trump's competitiveness and drive for success at an early age.

5. Marc Fisher, Will Hobson, "Donald Trump 'pretends to be his own spokesman to boast about himself.' Some reporters found the calls disturbing or even creepy; others thought they were just examples of Trump being playful." *The Independent,* May 13, 2016 at http://www.independent.co.uk/news/world/americas/us-elections/donald-trump-pretends-to-be-his-own-spokesman-to-boast-about-himself-a7027991.html (accessed August 9, 2016).

6. For my take on celebrity politics and the implosion of entertainment and politics in U.S. society, see Douglas Kellner, "Barack Obama, Media Spectacle, and Celebrity Politics" in *A Companion to Celebrity,* Edited by P. David Marshall and Sean Redmond. Malden, MA, and Oxford, UK. Wiley-Blackwell, 2015: 114–134. See also Mark Wheeler. *Celebrity Politics.* Cambridge, UK: Polity 2013. The best study of Trump, the media, and his long cultivation and exploitation of celebrity is found in Timothy L. O'Brien, *TrumpNation: The Art of Being the Donald.* New York: Grand Central Publishing, 2016 [2005].

7. Trump's book *The Art of the Deal,* co-written with Tony Schwartz (New York: Ballantine Books. 2005 [1987]), helped introduce him to a national audience and is a key source of the Trump mythology: see Blair, op. cit., 380ff. I discuss Trump's three books below.

8. Gaspin was quoted in CNN, *All Business. The Essential Donald Trump,* September 5, 2016.

9. *Quotations From Chairman Trump,* edited by Carol Pogash. New York: Rosetta Books, 2016, pp. 30, 152–153.

10. On *The Apprentice,* see Laurie Ouellette and James Hay, *Better Living Through Reality TV,* Malden, MA: Blackwell, 2008.

11. Ravi Somaiya. "Trump's Wealth and Early Poll Numbers Complicate News Media's Coverage Decisions," *The New York Times,* July 24, 2015 at http://www.nytimes.com/2015/07/25/business/media/donald-trumps-wealth-and-poll-numbers-complicate-news–medias-coverage.html (accessed July 22, 2016).

59 IS THIS TVIV? ON NETFLIX, TVIII AND BINGE-WATCHING

Mareike Jenner

In 2007, online DVD rental service Netflix announced the introduction of a video-on-demand (VOD) service. By 2014, Netflix not only offers a large online library of film and TV in North and South America, the Caribbean, Denmark, the United Kingdom, Ireland, Sweden, Norway, Finland and the Netherlands, but even offers original content in the form of serialized drama and comedy, featuring a number of stars ranging from Kevin Spacey to Will Arnett, directors like David Fincher or writers like Jenji Kohan. Netflix has moved into territory that sets it apart from familiar structures of production, broadcasting, or branding of television.

Netflix does signal a change within the digital television landscape. How permanent and significant this change actually is, only time will tell (though with companies and VOD platforms like Amazon and Hulu now offering original content, Netflix's impact seems both permanent and significant). As such, the title question of this [chapter], is this TVIV?, is clearly hyperbole. As Derek Kompare (2005) argues,

> . . . it is impossible to gauge exactly what "television" will be in another decade or so [. . .]. However, it is clear that the centralized, mass-disseminated, "one-way" century is largely ceding to a regime premised instead upon individual consumer choice, and marked by highly diversified content, atomized reception, and customizable interfaces. . . . These changes around television are also part of a larger conceptual shift across all media, as the aesthetic, technological, industrial and cultural boundaries between previously discrete forms (text, film, broadcasting, video, and sound recordings) are

increasingly blurred, challenging established practices and paradigms. (p. 198)

This [chapter] is concerned with issues of how to conceptualize Netflix in light of its relatively new role as producer and distributor of original content rather than "just" VOD and DVD rental service. It is argued here that Netflix (as representative of VOD as producer of original content) signals a significant shift in a new media landscape and problematizes known terminologies. The first part of this article will explore how Netflix relates to periodizations of television history and the concept of television itself. It will then move on to discuss what Netflix *is* and how it is positioned in its current media environment. In a third step, this [chapter] will consider how Netflix deliberately positions itself as similar, but also decidedly different from other media, by looking specifically at the case study of *Arrested Development* (Fox, 2003–2013, Netflix, 2013), Season 4, alongside looking specifically at the case study of *Arrested Development* (Fox, 2003–2013; Netflix, 2013), . . . the concept of independent scheduling and binge-watching. . . .

WHAT IS TVIV?

. . . [T]he division of television history into such eras is never unproblematic. Roberta Pearson (2011) summarizes the "periods" of U.S. television as follows:

> In the United States, TVI, dating from the mid-1950s to the early 1980s, is the era of channel scarcity, the mass audience, and three-network

From Jenner, M, (2016). Is this TVIV? On Netflix, TVIII and binge-watching, *New Media and Society*, 18 (2), 257–273.

hegemony. TVII, dating from roughly the early 1980s to the late 1990s, is the era of channel/network expansion, quality television, and network branding strategies. TVIII, dating from the late 1990s to the present, is the era of proliferating digital distribution platforms, further audience fragmentation, and, as Reeves et al. (2002) suggest, a shift from second-order to first-order commodity relations. (Location 1262–1266)

While TVIII is marked by certain technological advances and connected branding and programming strategies, what is signaled by Netflix and other VOD platforms exclusively available online is a move away from the television set. One significant marker of TVIII is its move towards multiplatform forms of distribution and storytelling, but it has always kept some (however tenuous) link with the technology, branding and programming strategies, and social connotations television traditionally carries. Constructions of "television" associated with TVI and TVII have frequently been subverted in the TVIII era by technological developments (ranging from DVD box sets to TiVo or illegal downloads), audience behavior (in accordance with the possibilities of new technology) and industry (particularly, Home Box Office [HBO]'s efforts to redefine serialized drama as "high culture"), but has still sought to align itself with the familiar medium. Yet, Netflix seems to signal a move away from the medium, its branding strategies, associated viewing patterns, technologies, industry structures, or programming.

As Pearson also points out, while the division of television history into certain periods is certainly helpful, they can only be understood as broad guideposts in a complex discursive formation of what we understand as television. . . .

Netflix does not change existing modes of broad- or narrowcasting. It does not even draw into question the role of DVDs and DVD culture, as Netflix does not offer any "extras," such as commentaries, photo galleries, gag or blooper reels, cast and crew interviews, making-ofs and so on, nor does it offer an alternative to the (possibly fetishized) object of a DVD and DVD box sets. However, it does draw into question previous notions of multiplatform as television, due to its independence from more traditional modes of a branding infrastructure that links online

streaming to existing television channels (as will be discussed in more detail later on).

Michael Curtin (2009) argues that the Hollywood writers' strike in 2007 and 2008, which was dominated by questions of writer's shares of the profits gained through distribution via DVD and Internet and through the sale of material based on their diegetic universes, such as video or online game tie-ins, signaled a significant shift in the contemporary media landscape:

> The 2007–2008 TV season therefore proved to be something of a tipping point for the industry, a moment of crisis when executives and creative talent were again forced to revisit the issues of synergy and intermedia strategy. In part, they needed to recalibrate daily practices, audience-measurement techniques and revenue-sharing formulas, but at a deeper structural level they needed to rethink the spatial logic of electronic media. . . . Yet during the 2007 season, prime-time audiences for each of the four leading networks averaged roughly 5 percent of television households, only a fraction of what they had attracted during the classical era. Interestingly, daily television viewing remained high—in fact, higher than in the 1960s, at 4 hours 35 minutes—but it was coming from more centres and flowing through more circuits than ever before: via DVD, cable, satellite and broadband; via Telemundo, Spike, Netflix and YouTube. (pp. 12–13)

In light of this proliferation of media outlets through which audiences consume television content, Curtin argues for an understanding of television, particularly post-2007 television, as matrix media. The advantage of this term is that it acknowledges the ever-increasing complexity of the medium. Furthermore, it moves beyond a periodization of television that proves to be quite limiting when discussing shifts in such a complex media landscape. Netflix actually is a perfect example of the disruption of distinctions between film, television, DVD, and online video platforms such as Vimeo or YouTube: "the matrix era is characterized by interactive exchanges, multiple sites of productivity and diverse modes of interpretation and use" (Curtin, 2009, p. 13). . . . Curtin's argument that a significant shift happened around 2007, further away from more "traditional" concepts of industry, audience behavior and the medium of TV, is not without its merits as it signals that there is a difference between the TVIII of the early 2000s when premium cable channels became more dominant and 2007, incidentally also the year Netflix moved its content online, National Broadcasting Company (NBC) extended its multiplatform presence, and in the United Kingdom, British Broadcasting Corporation (BBC) iPlayer was launched. However, trying to pinpoint a specific moment when a change or shift in the discursive formation of television happened seems to work against the advantage the term matrix media has in relation to a periodization like TVI, II, III and IV. Yet, possibly, TVIV can be understood as an era of matrix media where viewing patterns, branding strategies, industrial structures, the way different media forms interact with each other, or the various ways content is made available shift completely away from the television set. The term *matrix media* to describe what TVIV could be also emphasizes the fluidity of the term.

WHAT IS NETFLIX?

Netflix started out in 1997 as an online-based DVD rental service. The majority of its business is still to stream content that was previously shown in cinemas or on television. As such, Netflix has always been more associated with the medium of DVDs and the Internet (as the name already suggests) rather than broadcasting and original programming. It may not be too surprising that, along with television broadcasters offering multiplatform services, it was the struggling business of video rental services that now dominates the business of VOD services, thus reinventing itself for a new era in film and television distribution. As Cunningham and Silver (2012) point out,

> [In 2007] Netflix placed 10,000 titles from its 90,000 film library on-line in "Watch Instantly" mode as a free value-added service to its large base of existing Netflix customers who had to use their ID and password to watch those films. In 2010, it transformed its core business model from a monthly subscription for DVDs-delivered to the home, migrating its customers to a U.S. $7.99 monthly subscription service for

unlimited movie and TV downloads via Watch Instantly, plus an extra $2 monthly fee for unlimited DVDs delivered to the home. Netflix is clearly focused on preparing its customers for the digital transition and eventual demise of the bricks and mortar video store when VOD replaces DVD optical discs as the second window after cinema release. (Location 1581–1587)

Netflix's strategy to grab customer's attention involved a move away from its original business model as exhibitor of film content. Orienting itself more towards Hulu, "a joint venture between NBC-Universal, Fox Network and Disney through its ABC TV network subsidiary" (Cunningham & Silver, 2012, p. 1593), which streams mostly television content, Netflix has now moved into the business of being producer of serialized drama. Most other streaming services are linked to a television branding infrastructure and offer a chance to catch up with missed programs, but Netflix now offers the first—and for long periods of time only—chance to watch its original dramas. The streaming service thus moves away from its previous business model where it only provided film and TV dramas that had already been shown elsewhere and are often already available on DVD, to being the first in the chain of media exhibition. By turning the familiar chain of first, second, and third market distribution on its head, Netflix offers a distinctively different form of media distribution. Of course, this change does not come out of nowhere: online dramas are now a common occurrence on YouTube and many TV series offer webisodes to extend the diegetic universe, for example, critically acclaimed cable TV drama *Battlestar Galactica* (SciFi, 2004–2009). Yet, the individual instalments distributed online tend to be between 2 and 5 minutes long, thus constituting a format significantly different from most TV drama. While Netflix may not copy the format, it certainly takes a cue from a system of distribution where the online form is the first link in a chain.

Often hyped as a "new HBO," and comparing itself to HBO (Hastings & Wells, 2013), Netflix actually offers a different kind of TV revolution than previously associated with the premium cable channel: Netflix is simply not TV (p. 7). Where HBO revolutionized television aesthetics and narrative structures, the slogan "it's not TV. It's HBO" implied a promise of content that was somehow different from the familiar "mainstream" fare commonly associated with the medium rather than a rejection of the technological infrastructure. Netflix offers content in the form of serialized dramas, but it is hardly this aspect that serves to set it apart from cable channels such as HBO, American Movie Classics (AMC), Showtime, and Fox eXtended (FX), or even network channels like Columbia Broadcasting System (CBS), American Broadcasting Company (ABC), and NBC. The VOD service offers none of the more "traditional" television genres, such as news, game shows, sporting events, or other programs associated with TV's live aesthetics. Furthermore, it is largely disconnected from the technological or branding infrastructure associated with television—network or cable. Catherine Johnson (2012) describes a brand as an

> . . . interface/frame [that] manages the interactions between consumers, products and producers. . . . In relation to the television channel, the brand is communicated to the viewer through programme production and acquisition, scheduling, on-screen advertising and ancillary products related to the channel and/or its programming. (pp. 17–18)

While the BBC iPlayer, for example, also offers the streaming of content, and channels in most Western countries offer similar services, they tend to be linked with the brand identity of a specific channel which serves as frame or interface: in order to watch a program on iPlayer, cbs.com, or RTL, now, viewers have to familiarize themselves either with this particular channel's schedule or be familiar enough with the brand to know that they may find content they are interested in on their website. Alternatively, audiences may go directly to websites such as thedailyshow.com . . . in search of a specific program. Thus, these streaming services are inherently linked with the medium of TV and its cultural connotations, even though the technological infrastructure is different and the streaming of content implies a disconnect from TV schedules.

On the other hand, Netflix certainly draws on television's branding strategies. Johnson (2012) points out how branding in U.S. television became important as the market was deregulated in the 1970s and 1980s and new cable channels emerged:

> Even with the developments in satellite technology, these cable channels could not hope to compete with the reach of the free-to-air national networks. As a consequence, they focussed on offering differentiated programme services to specialized niche audiences. This was important, as cable was funded by a combination of advertising and subscription, and so cable operators and networks had to persuade audiences that it was worth paying the extra subscription for their services and advertisers that they could offer valuable audience segments to justify the lower ratings that they gained than network television. (p. 16)

Netflix does not have to justify itself to advertisers in a "traditional" sense, as the information on the company on the *New York Times Business* website states that "The Company obtains content from various studios and other content providers through fixed-fee licenses, revenue sharing agreements and direct purchases" ("Netflix, Inc.," 2013). Thus, while Netflix is accountable to shareholders and its partners in revenue sharing, it tends to be the company that advertises itself to subscribers rather than advertisers:

> The Company markets its service through various channels, including online advertising, broad-based media, such as television and radio, as well as various partnerships. In connection with marketing the service, the Company offers free-trial memberships to new and certain rejoining members. ("Netflix, Inc.," 2013)

However, by offering creative and budgetary freedom to television *auteurs* like Mitch Hurwitz and Jenji Kohan, hiring actors like Robin Wright or Jason Biggs or directors like Joel Schumacher or Jodie Foster, Netflix seems to follow HBO's example of creating a brand identity where "quality" content helps construct the brand:

> . . . over the second half of the 1990s HBO developed a brand identity as the home of quality television in the USA that drew on a wide range of its programming, but was centred on the shift towards producing adult, edgy, authored and high-budget original drama

series. While the brand identity was initially constructed through the promotional efforts of HBO itself, and then increasingly depended on these signature shows to stand in for the network, it also increasingly depended upon critical acclaim within the media more broadly to support its claim to be the home for creative talent. (Johnson, 2012, p. 32)

As more and more cable channels have adapted this strategy, HBO's brand faces increasingly harsh competition. Netflix only recently adapted the strategy by offering its own original drama, relying mostly on (social) media buzz with original programming shaping the brand identity. Thus, while drawing on familiar formats and marketing strategies from TVIII, Netflix is also clearly positioned as something other than television through forms of distribution, business model (assumed), viewing practices and marketing.

What will be considered in more detail here is Netflix's production and distribution of Season 4 of *Arrested Development*. Through this, Netflix managed to position itself in relation to the "cult" TV show, offered an original approach to the series through a slight change in format, a changing narrative perspective and a different narrative structure. In the run-up to the season's publication on Netflix, what seemed to be particularly highlighted in press statements and interviews was the text's suitability for the practice of binge-watching, which now seems to be an encouraged mode of viewing all Netflix series, as recent reviews of the second season of *House of Cards* (Netflix, 2013–present) seemed to confirm. Although the season brought in a disappointing number of new subscriptions, the textual strategies employed by Season 4 of *Arrested Development* are quite telling in terms of how Netflix positions itself within the broader television landscape.

ARRESTED DEVELOPMENT, BINGE-WATCHING, "CULT" TV, AND NOT TV

Season 4 of *Arrested Development* . . . premiered on May 26, 2013 on Netflix. This was significant in a number of ways: First, the series had previously run on network channel Fox, but had been cancelled after only three seasons in 2006 due to low ratings. Yet, the series has managed to attain a "cult" status (as disputed as the term is), and a follow-up film has been rumored for years. Second, all 15 episodes of the season were put online at once. Netflix argued at the time that this was a response to assumed viewer behavior of the so-called binge-watching, supposing that viewers would wish to watch more than one episode in one sitting or, at least, schedule their *Arrested Development* consumption as they pleased. Third, the text of Season 4 seems aware of this transition in viewer behavior: the narrative structure is different from the first three seasons, seemingly responding more to the needs of self-scheduled, rather than scheduled, television. *Arrested Development,* Season 4, functions well as a case study as it shows how Netflix positions itself in relation to TVIII, "cult" or "quality" TV and encourages specific modes of viewing. More so, by building on a familiar "cult" text and associated (assumed) practices of watching the series, Netflix seems to also "teach" its audiences how to watch Netflix.

Seasons 1–3 of *Arrested Development* were well received by critics, and the series was nominated for and won a number of prestige awards during its run.[1] With its indie film aesthetics, its often outrageous humor that sometimes made it seem like a parody of itself, and its witty commentary on contemporary politics, it seemed to function as a network counterweight to a still emerging cable "quality" TV market. Yet, due to low ratings, Fox cancelled the series in 2006, which possibly contributed to its "cult" status as a series whose worth had not been recognized by the network or "mainstream" audiences. . . . The cast has often re-enforced this "cult" narrative in interviews and repeated it in the run-up to Season 4 (see, for example, Kelly, 2013).

Yet, while this narrative has been used as marketing strategy for the DVDs of the series and its Netflix season, these complaints are not unwarranted. In 2005, a *Chicago Tribune* article by Maureen Ryan (2005) claimed,

> The conventional wisdom says Fox's Emmy-winning comedy "Arrested Development" is a cult success but a commercial failure. The conventional wisdom may well be wrong. The critically acclaimed show, which returns from Fox's baseball break with two episodes featuring guest star Charlize Theron on Nov. 7, is indeed ratings challenged, but it's surprisingly dominant

in another arena. Fox won't release sales totals, but executives at the company's home-video division say "Arrested," which chronicles the misadventures of the dysfunctional, formerly rich Bluth family, has sold very well on DVD. . . . Season 2 of the show has spent much of the past week at the top of Amazon.com's boxed-set best-sellers chart, where the Season 1 boxed set can usually be found among the chart's top 40 releases. And that commercial success, along with critical praise, a shelf-full of industry awards and a ferociously supportive Internet fan base, has helped keep the show alive, at least for a while.

Thus, *Arrested Development* can be viewed as part of a general movement in the early 2000s where DVD box sets of TV series became increasingly popular and, in some cases, even seemed to replace the scheduled television experience. While hardly a ratings-hit in its original run on Fox, the series seems to have an active afterlife (even before its resurrection on Netflix) on DVD, through online streaming and (often illegal) downloads and with an avid fan base. . . .

Netflix's choice of *Arrested Development* seems to consciously draw on the fandom and related viewing practices. The practice of binge-watching associated with the DVD culture becomes central. Debra Ramsay (2013), in a blog post on *CST online,* addresses one quite significant problem with the marketing of a TV series (or season) as material for binge-watching:

> Just what constitutes a televisual "binge"? Does it involve watching more than one episode of one series concurrently, and if so, how many constitute a "binge"? Or is it watching an entire season or more—sometimes described in somewhat more respectable terms as "marathon" viewing—in an uninterrupted session? Why would watching consecutive hours of television, but viewing different programmes during that time, not be considered a "binge"? Which raises the question of why an extended period of consuming television should be considered 'binging' in the first place.

In her blog post, Ramsay admits to watching a whole season of *Supernatural* (CW, 2005) in 1 day, but for those who do not watch TV professionally, anything above four episodes may seem excessive, though they may also describe themselves as binge-watchers. A recent survey by Harris Interactive conducted on behalf of Netflix seems to define a binge as watching two to three episodes in a row (see Spangler, 2013). At any rate, what exactly constitutes a binge is likely to be different for everybody and defined through highly individualized terms and practices. . . . A major factor of binge-watching is that it is disconnected from scheduled television. As Jason Jacobs (2011) argues, such viewing practices serve to remove any "pollution" of the text through advertising breaks:

> The difference between the VCR—the earliest domestic weapon against interruption and chronological authority of the broadcast schedule—and digital television technology seems to be that the various ways to own, time-shift or otherwise mine texts are promoted as the obvious and routinized ways to interact with the medium rather than viewing the schedule in real time. 'Who wants to watch adverts, promos and the rest of the connective tissue of the television flow?' seems to be the compelling appeal to common sense that digital television marketers deploy most frequently. (Location 3125)

The practice of binge-watching implies not only viewers' desire for autonomy in scheduling when they want to watch what, but also a wish for a "pure" text (as Jacobs terms it) that is distinctively not part of the television flow.

Another factor in binge-watching is the text itself. The kind of attention demanded by some series seems to make it necessary for viewers to consciously make a decision to focus entirely on the series, something only possible if viewers can schedule autonomously. Jason Mittell (2010) argues,

> Complex comedies like *Arrested Development* encourage the freeze-frame power of DVDs to catch split-second visual gags and pause the frantic pace to recover from laughter. These televisual strategies are all possible via scheduled flow, but greatly enhanced by viewing multiple times via published DVDs. Having control of when and how you watch also helps deepen one of the major pleasures afforded by complex narratives: the operational aesthetic. . . .

While Seasons 1–3 of *Arrested Development* already rejected the familiar sitcom formula, relying on complex jokes and story lines that easily extend beyond one episode or even season, Season 4 complicates the matter further by developing an even more complex narrative structure. . . . Each episode focuses on one character of the Bluth family who, after falling out in the last episode of Season 3, all went their separate ways. The individual story lines intersect at varying points, leaving "mini-cliffhangers" in the middle of episodes. In light of this, it is particularly the first episode, "Flight of the Phoenix" of Season 4 that seems confusing as it provides a number of scenes that are difficult to decode without the information provided later on. . . . As such, Season 4 of *Arrested Development* demands more attention from viewers through its narrative structure.

The case of *Arrested Development* shows quite clearly how Netflix positions itself in relation to DVD culture, fandom, and associated viewing practices. The season seems to mostly function as a way to "teach" audiences how to watch Netflix in the long term. It is hard to measure how successful this idea of "teaching" viewers using a familiar text as starting point has been. Furthermore, nothing akin to ratings has been published by Netflix (possibly because the figures could be disproportionate to media buzz). . . . Thus, its success was measured by the audiences it attracted instantly rather than over a long period of time. . . . The failure to attract numbers of new subscribers proportionate to the preceding media buzz immediately translated into a drop in share prices (see Brown, 2013). Quite possibly, it was this aspect (along with a mixed review in the influential *New York Times* by Mike Hale, 2013) that fed into an overall impression that critics remained unimpressed, though most reviews in the mainstream press seem to echo the title of Dan Zak's (2013) review in *The Washington Post* that it is "A Chore to Watch and a Delight to Decrypt."[2] This suggests that an immediate desire for viewing numbers akin to Nielsen ratings, in other words a "traditional" way to measure commercial success in a TVI, II, and III era, proved to be destructive to the Netflix brand and the text, possibly eliminating chances for a film revival or another season of *Arrested Development* and silencing long-term media buzz. Thus, the season's supposed failure also serves as an argument why "traditional" ways of measuring the "success" of

serialized drama and conceptualizing the audience and their viewing practices seem insufficient in an era of self-scheduled binge-watching. After all, a major aspect of viewer autonomy is that it should not matter if audiences watch the season on the day it is released or months, even years, later. Thus, *Arrested Development* seems to fall victim to changing concepts of how to measure audience reactions and commercial "success" once again. Yet, the series' resurrection positions Netflix as a corporation that panders to binge-watchers in general (even though they may not be attracted by this particular text). . . .[3]

Netflix, thus, builds on models of individualized viewing practices and self-scheduling of TV. . . .

The contemporary media landscape feeds into this current state where consumer behavior and individualized identity construction are intrinsically linked. Jacobs (2011) argues that

> it is true, however, that digital television threatens the universal experience of television's social function. Digital television's promises of control imply disconnection and separateness from the usually nationally socialized presence of television. (Location 3225)

Yet, these moments of socializing can happen online as one's viewing behavior is shared on Facebook or tweeted. Thus, viewing behavior (and consumer behavior) is projected as part of one's (online) identity and can be commented on by others. Furthermore, the "water-cooler" moment in other social interactions is hardly gone as viewers are still likely to discuss their viewing experiences, despite the fact that these are not synchronized. Thus, what you watch (or rather, what you publicly share about it) may take on a different meaning, in particular as middle-class tastes have strongly gravitated towards serialized drama with high production values and complex narrative structures, such as *House of Cards*.[4]

As such, the blurring of lines between production, distribution, and exhibition may only be a logical consequence of a marketplace that panders to consumers who link consumer habits and identity construction. In other words, Netflix's tailor-made product can only function in a system of distribution where this process is also individualized.

CONCLUSION

This [chapter] has explored how Netflix's move to producer, distributor, and exhibitor of its own content links in with a TVIII media landscape, consumer behavior, and viewing habits of serialized content and a contemporary capitalism and social sphere. In this, it analyzed the ways Netflix fits neatly into the way we use the terminology of TVIII, but also how it is decidedly different from existing formats (with other corporations like Amazon quickly following its example). As such, the shift Netflix signals may be significant enough to allow for a terminology of TVIV.

The company also ties in with a discourse in contemporary capitalism where media corporations never appear to be exclusively producer, exhibitor, and distributor of content, but additionally seem to be linked in with other markets, as with the ubiquitous Amazon. Recently, even the online version of the renowned *Spiegel* started offering the streaming of films in Germany, blurring lines between news magazine, news website, television, and cinema. As such, Netflix may be best understood as a signifier for shifts within the media industry where the understanding of clearly differentiated media forms becomes obsolete. After all, Netflix as a company may not survive in the long run against competitors like Amazon or in the face of battles surrounding "Net neutrality" in the United States (meaning that Internet providers need to provide the same bandwidth for all content, a rule under revision at the time of writing), but as a business model that introduced "independent" (disconnected from established television channels) VOD, it is likely to have a long-lasting legacy. . . .

Yet, if television is defined less through the technology used and more through formats (particularly, it seems, the format of serialized drama) and we can schedule it ourselves, then the way to ask for our attention changes significantly. In other words, increasingly complex narrative structures demand our attention in a way scheduled television rarely can. In this sense, Netflix may be viewed as part of a television matrix, but, apart from offering serialized content, it signals a further move away from what is still understood as television. A key aspect here is Netflix's independence from branding infrastructures that link television with online media. Instead, orienting itself more toward much more prolific online-based companies like Amazon or Google, Netflix builds its own brand, a premium online channel independent from more "traditional" forms of channel branding in network and cable television with even smaller "niche" audiences with the autonomy to build their own schedule. *Arrested Development,* Season 4, shows just how much Netflix ties in with an already existing discourse surrounding "cult" and "quality" TV and viewer autonomy.

The shift signaled by Netflix concerns issues of technology, but maybe more important, branding and programming strategies, viewing practices independent from scheduling that lead to a complication in how audience behavior needs to be understood and "success" of a program measured, as well as how familiar associations with the concept of television are not "merely" subverted, but changed completely. In a matrix media and (potentially) TVIV landscape, this does not eliminate existing and familiar concepts of what "television" is, but it extends them significantly and introduces a range of other media forms and discourses to this matrix.

NOTES

1. During its original run, *Arrested Development* was nominated for 22 prime-time Emmys and won 6, 3 Golden Globe awards and winning 1, nominated 3 times for a Screen Writers Guild award and was nominated and won a number of other awards.

2. metacritic.com, looking at 21 (U.S.) reviews, states that the critical reception of the season has been overwhelmingly positive, with no negative reviews and only six mediocre ones,

scoring 71 (not much below *House of Cards*'s score of 76). This still places Season 4 as the least popular of the series among critics and also in fan ratings, but the overall response seems to be positive, though not overly enthusiastic.

3. In this, *Arrested Development* would not be the first series to be resurrected to help introduce viewers to a different kind of television viewing. Other examples would be *Dragnet*

(National Broadcasting Company [NBC], 1951–1959 and 1967–1970) or *Battlestar Galactica* (American Broadcasting Company [ABC], 1978–1979 resurrected by SciFi, 2004–2009).

4. The first two episodes of the second season of *House of Cards* were even shown at the *Berlinale* film festival in 2014, securing its position as "high culture." Some aspects that play into contemporary notions of "quality" are a willingness to challenge the norms of television, often through a supposed transgression of social norms (see, for example, Ritzer, 2011, pp. 26–53 or Akass & McCabe,

2007, p. 66), an association of creative staff with cinema or other "quality TV" or "high art" (see, for example, Thompson, 1996, p. 59 and pp. 150–152 or Feuer, 2007, pp. 146–157), or a pandering to the so-called quality demographics, which Ellen Seiter and Wilson (2005) describe as " young, affluent viewers, with money to spend, and with the cultural capital that translates into recognition by industry tastemakers with Emmys and other prestige awards. The label 'quality' indicates audiences that would not otherwise want to be associated with the debased television form or the audiences that regularly watch it (p. 140)"

REFERENCES

Akass, K. & McCabe, J. (2007) Sex, swearing and respectability: Courting controversy, HBO's original programming and producing quality TV. In K. Akass & J. McCabe (Eds), *Quality TV: Contemporary American television and beyond* (pp. 62–76). London: I.B. Tauris.

Brown, A. (2013, May 29). Netflix shares take a hit from disappointing "Arrested Development" reviews. *Forbes Online.* Retrieved from http://www.forbes.com/sites/abrambrown/2013/05/29/netflix-shares-take-a-hit-from-disappointing-arrested-development-reviews/

Cunningham, S. & Silver, J. (2012). On-line film distribution: Its history and global complexion. In S. Cunningham & D. Iordanova (Eds), *Digital disruption: Cinema moves On-Line* (pp. 33–66). St Andrews, UK: St Andrews Film Studies.

Curtin, M. (2009). Matrix media. In J. Tay J & G. Turner (Eds), *Television studies after TV: Understanding television in the post-broadcast era* (pp. 9–19). London: Routledge.

Feuer, J. (2007). HBO and the concept of quality TV. In K. Akass & J. McCabe (Eds), *Quality TV. Contemporary American television and beyond* (pp. 145–157). London: I.B. Tauris.

Hale, M. (2013, May 26). A family streamed back to life. *New York Times.* Retrieved from http://www.nytimes.com/2013/05/27/arts/television/arrested-development-on-netflixcom.html?

action=click&;module=Search&region=searchResults&mabReward=relbias%3Aw&url=http%3A%2F%2Fquery.nytimes.com%2Fsearch%2Fsitesearch%2F%3Faction%3Dclick%26region%3DMasthead%26pgtype%3DHomepage%26module%3DSearchSubmit%26cont entCollecti on%3DHomepage%26t%3Dqry262%23%2Farr ested%2520development&_r=0

Hastings, R. & Wells, D. (2013). Q3 13 letter to shareholders. Retrieved from http://ir.netflix.com/ results.cfm

Jacobs, J. (2011). Television, interrupted: Pollution or aesthetic? In J. Bennett & N. Strange (Eds), *Television as digital media (console-ing passions)* (pp. 255–282). Durham, NC and London: Duke University Press.

Johnson, C. (2012). *Branding television.* New York: Routledge.

Kelly, S. (2013, May 24). A huge mistake: *Arrested Development* cast criticise Fox's 2006 cancellation. *RadioTimes.* Retrieved from http://www.radiotimes.com/news/2013-05-24/a-huge-mistake-arrested-development-cast-criticise-foxs-2006-cancellation

Kompare, D. (2005). Rerun nation: How repeats invented American television. New York: Routledge.

Kurosawa, A. (1950). *Rashomon.* Japan: Daiei Motion Picture Company.

Mittell, J. (2010). *Serial boxes. Just TV.* Retrieved from http://justtv.wordpress.com/2010/01/20/serial-boxes/

Netflix Inc., company information. (2014, April 28). *New York Times.* Retrieved from http://topics.nytimes.com/top/news/business/companies/netflix-inc/index.html

Pearson, R. (2011). Cult television as digital television's cutting edge. In J. Bennett & N. Strange, (Eds), *Television as digital media (console-ing passions)* pp. pp. 105–131). Durham, NC and London: Duke University Press.

Ramsay, D. (2013). Confessions of a binge watcher. *CST Online.* Retrieved from http://cstonline.tv/confessions-of-a-binge-watcher

Reeves, J. L., Rogers, M.C., & Epstein, M. (2002). *The Sopranos* as HBO brand equity: The art of commerce in the age of digital reproduction. In D. Lavery (Ed.), *This thing of ours: Investigating* the Sopranos (pp. 42–57). New York: Columbia University Press.

Reitman, J. (2007). *Juno.* USA: Fox Searchlight.

Ritzer, I. (2011). Fernsehen Wider Die Tabus. Sex, Gewalt, Zensur Und Die Neuen US-Serien. Berlin: Bertz + Fischer.

Ryan, M. (2005, October 21). There's always money in the banana stand: *'Arrested Development's'* stealth success. *Chicago Tribune.* Retrieved from http://featuresblogs.chicagotribune.com/entertainment_tv/2005/10/theres_always_m.html

Seiter, E., & Wilson, M. J. (2005). Soap opera survival tactics. In G. R. Edgerton & B.G. Rose (Eds.), *Thinking outside the box: A contemporary television genre reader* (pp. 136–155). Lexington, KY: The University Press of Kentucky.

Spangler, T. (2013, December 13) Netflix survey: Binge-watching is not weird or unusual. *Variety.* Retrieved from http://variety.com/2013/digital/news/netflix-survey-binge-watching-is-not-weird-or-unu-sual-1200952292/

Thompson, R. J. (1996). Television's second golden age: from *Hill Street Blues* to *ER*. New York: Continuum.

Zak, D. (2013, May 29). 'Arrested Development' Season 4 review: A chore to watch and a delight to decrypt. *The Washington Post,* 29 May. Retrieved from http://articles.washingtonpost.com/2013-05-29/entertainment/39595417_1_arrested-development-patriarch-chore

SOCIAL MEDIA, VIRTUAL COMMUNITY, AND FANDOM

As discussed elsewhere in this book, there is a robust debate within media studies regarding the degree to which consumers internalize mediated messages into the way they make sense of the world. Those scholars working within the more **Marxist**-based paradigm of political economy tend to focus on the powerful impact that **hegemonic ideology** has on the way consumers construct their notions of reality, identity, and even commonsense. More recently there has been a shift toward emphasizing not only **active audience** members, who read media texts against the grain, but also media fans, those consumers who are most highly engaged in making new meanings out of given cultural texts—sometimes producing not just variant interpretations but also new texts of their own. In this section, we focus on fan activity and audience activism—showing some of the many ways that people go beyond a passive relation to media culture. We also include chapters that are critical of the tendency in some of this work to diminish the power of the media industries in shaping the public consciousness or to overlook the ways that participatory media can be used to reinforce rather than challenge racism, misogyny, and other regressive ideologies.

We begin this section on audience activism and participation in media production with the optimistic approach of media scholar Henry Jenkins III (VIII.60), who has devoted much of his career to studying media fandom and audience activity. As a theorist of what is sometimes called **media convergence,** Jenkins argues:

> Media convergence . . . involves the introduction of a much broader array of new media technologies that enable consumers to archive, annotate, transform, and recirculate media content . . . it alters the relationship between existing technologies, industries, markets, genres, and audiences. (p. 513)

In Jenkins's view, we need to attend to the ways two different but related forms of media convergence interact if we are to understand the dizzyingly unstable contemporary world of media production and consumption:

> *Corporate convergence*—the concentration of media ownership in the hands of a diminishing number of multinational conglomerates that thus have a vested interest in ensuring the flow of media content across different platforms and national borders
>
> and
>
> *Grassroots convergence*—the increasingly central roles that digitally empowered consumers play in shaping the production, distribution, and reception of media content. (p. 514)

Jenkins questions the "media imperialism" argument of some media critics who claim that giant media corporations and cultural products based in the West completely dominate global media production and consumption. Focusing on how audience and fandom studies complicate our understanding of the power dynamics between consumers and texts, he urges us to look carefully, through ethnographic study, at the ways in which regional and local audiences may actually read imported cultural texts like Disney products "in radically different ways . . . against the backdrop of more familiar genres and through the grid of familiar values" (p. 514). And beyond simply looking in more nuanced ways at how U.S. cultural texts are received in other nations, Jenkins points to the importance of understanding the digitally assisted ways U.S. media consumers, particularly the sophisticated group he calls "pop cosmopolitans," now embrace, appropriate, and help to circulate imported Asian cultural goods, such as Japanese anime and manga or Bollywood films.

In recent years, media scholars with a critical political economy perspective have also been taking a closer look at how Internet-based fan activities operate within the context of corporate domination of the Internet. These critics address a range of individual and group activities, from enthusiastic consumption of online cultural products and the creation of communities based on that consumption; to the production and distribution of new narratives like fan fiction, remixed videos, or the creation of online identities through social media and gaming platforms.

Picking up on the term "prosumer" introduced by Alvin Toffler in the early 1980s—to indicate "the progressive blurring of the line that separates producer from consumer"—Christian Fuchs (VIII.61) looks at the political economy of Facebook, in particular its privacy policy, which enables the platform to gather, store, and own personal information and cultural products its users provide. In contrast to what some media scholars refer to as "celebratory" studies of participatory culture on the Internet, Fuchs emphasizes not the creativity or pleasure produced through social media, but the corporate profit derived from the user's labor. He writes uncompromisingly "prosumption is used for outsourcing work to users and consumers, who work without pay. In this model, corporations reduce their investment costs and labor costs, destroy jobs, and exploit consumers who work for free" (p. 519). He cites the example of a 13-year-old Facebook user bombarded by targeted advertisements (that are obviously based on personal data sold by Facebook), and calls this boy "the prototypical Facebook child worker."

Fuchs follows his incisive critique of Facebook's "use of targeted advertising and economic surveillance . . . legally guaranteed by Facebook's privacy policy" (p. 520) with an appeal to readers to consider a contrasting "socialist internet privacy politics." He offers several strategies for "advancing the decommodification of the internet," (p. 520) from the relatively modest policy of opt-in only online advertising, to the development and support of corporate-watch organizations and noncommercial, collectively organized alternative Internet platforms.

Continuing the focus on the commodification of the Internet and social media, Alice Marwick and danah boyd (VIII.62) examine how social media enables celebrities to market themselves to fans. They show how "networked media is changing celebrity culture, the ways that people relate to celebrity images, how celebrities are produced, and how celebrity is practiced" (p. 525). Because celebrities are now branded "products" that help generate enormous profit for both the companies that use their names and for themselves, they can be viewed both as commodities and as producers of media texts. According to Marwick and boyd, actors, musicians, reality TV stars and other "highly followed people" are adapting their self-presentation practices to the demands of the new social media world, expending "emotional labor maintaining a network of affective ties with their followers." As the authors point out, "even the famous must learn the techniques used by 'regular people' to gain status and attention online" (p. 533).

While online attention such as this is typically assumed to be positive, Andrea Braithwaite (VIII.63) provides a case study of malevolent online culture by examining #Gamergate—a controversy over misogynistic discourse that circulated across multiple social media platforms utilized by the online gaming community. Because the video game industry has historically designed and marketed its products to White heterosexual males, "geek masculinity" (such as valuing technical prowess over athletic ability) has been associated with "real" gamers. Because geek masculinity both adopts and rejects aspects of hegemonic masculinity, some men view the increasing diversity of the gaming community as a threat. In an attempt to retain their "gamer identity," these young men turned to social media to "discipline unruly female voices" that were challenging the sexism, racism, and homophobia that exists within game culture (p. 538). Braithwaite believes "#Gamergate has refocused popular discussions about gaming cultures into ones about gender, launched female game developers and critics into the public spotlight, and raised additional questions about social media as an avenue for gendered harassment and threats" (p. 536). Ultimately, Braithwaite's analysis of #Gamergate goes beyond game culture and speaks to important issues surrounding new media, gender, and power.

While Braithwaite turned a critical eye to the online gaming community's use of social media, Lisa Nakamura (VIII.64) investigates other types of content created by fans of *World of Warcraft,* the massive multiplayer online role-playing game (MMORPG). Nakamura examines how the hostility that many players feel about the game's unintended subsidiary practice of "gold farming, or selling in-game currency to players for real money," has taken a visual and specifically racialized (anti-Chinese) form. Fan-produced *machinima* (homemade music videos using visuals appropriated from within the online world and distributed on the Internet) stereotype the "gold farmers" as multitudes of faceless Chinese workers, who pose a threat to the more casual players who cannot hope to compete with their relentless labor. Nakamura argues that in this case participatory media, often seen by enthusiasts as extending the world of mainstream texts "in truly **liberatory** ways," can also be used by fans destructively and divisively:

> If indeed machinima extend the world of gameplay, how are players co-creating this world? . . . A closer look at user produced content from Warcraftmovies.com reveals a contraction and retrenchment of concepts of gender, race and nation rather than their enlargement. (p. 551)

Braithwaite and Nakamura both demonstrate that digital media is not free from regressive hegemonic ideologies. However, new platforms do have the potential to open up spaces for some marginalized groups. Through auto-ethnography and archival research, Jennifer Cole and colleagues (VIII. 65) explore how online platforms facilitated the formation and maintenance of an alternative community run by and developed for women with disabilities. The authors view digital technologies as an opportunity for the GimpGirl Community members "to move beyond externally imposed definitions of who they are, experiment with self-representation and forge their own sense of identity" (p. 558). These online platforms allow members to "develop a capacity to perform as agents of self- and social transformation" (p. 557). One member uses "an avatar with a wheelchair when speaking to non-disabled people about the GGC, and an able-bodied avatar when speaking to her peers." Another writes: "My avatar looks very much like me in real life, minus the signs of disability that I rarely display in *Second Life* because in my head I don't really picture myself as disabled" (p. 558).

In addition to creating a sense of community, as in the GimpGirl example, interactive media platforms can also increase the visibility of marginalized groups. In the next chapter, Christine Bacareza Balance (VIII.66) shows how YouTube has become "an alternative avenue of cultural production" for Asian American performers (p. 562). Beginning her chapter with the story of an undergraduate's satirical response video, mocking White racial stereotyping of Chinese immigrants in another student's video, Balance discusses the various ways Asian American YouTube performers have contributed to and benefited from "social media's democratic promise" (p. 564). First she notes the prominence of Asian Americans in viral video production:

> All but absent in the Hollywood star system and on the Billboard charts, Asian Americans . . . dominate YouTube's Most Subscribed lists. . . . Today's Asian American creative hopefuls do not merely accede to but actively exploit social media and information sharing platforms such as YouTube, Facebook, Twitter and blogs . . . as their new "calling card." (p. 562)

Beyond the boost that the viral capability of these platforms has given to independent artists, Balance explores how YouTube captures a large Asian American audience through speaking "to the simultaneously virtual and material aspects of Asian American identity" (p. 564). In the context of frustration with "the model minority myth's discursive containment," she argues Asian American youth audiences may be hungry to see and hear expressions of the "paradoxical feelings of Asian America: cultural alienation and, yet, the desire to belong" (p. 566).

While new media technologies can thus enable community development and cohesion, it is important to also remind ourselves of the potential damage individuals and groups can suffer when the Internet amplifies the politics of hate and fear. In the next chapter, by Nadia Yamel Flores-Yeffal, Guadalupe Vidales, and April Plemons (VIII.67), a description and analysis is offered of what is termed "the Latino cyber-moral panic process in the United States." Drawing on the work of sociologist Stanley Cohen, the authors define "moral panic" as "the reaction of a society against a specific social group based on beliefs that the subgroup represents a major threat to society" (p. 569). They focus on the case of anti-immigration sentiments directed against Latino/as to show how online technologies have enabled a rapid and widespread panic. The authors combined an online **ethnography** with a **content analysis** of anti-immigrant websites, and observed not only that the classic moral panic stages were effectively promoted online, but also that the Internet enabled a new stage which the authors call "a call for action"—through requests for donations and the promotion of particular political and civil activities. The chapter is an important reminder that online technologies potentially enable social activism of all kinds—not just that which would tend to spread democracy and decrease inequalities in society.

We end this anthology with a timely contribution by Yarimar Bonilla and Jonathan Rosa (VIII.68) that highlights the ways digital media can indeed be used to challenge social inequality and draw attention to injustice. As the authors note, "Social movements have long used media and technology to disseminate, escalate, and enlarge the scope of their struggles" (p. 581). In response to the brutal murders of Michael Brown and Trayvon Martin activists brought visibility to state-sanctioned police violence against young Black men through the creation and widespread adoption of hashtags such as #BlackLivesMatter, #Ferguson, #HandsUpDontShoot, #IfTheyGunnedMeDown, and #NoAngel. In addition, many social media users included "selfies" that reflect the hashtag in an effort to represent their solidarity with the victims and the movement. Within this context, social media facilitates a new form of digital activism that speaks "to the long history of inaccurate and unfair portrayal of African Americans within mainstream media and to the systematic profiling and victim blaming suffered by racialized bodies" (p. 582).

In this last section of our book, we have seen that despite increasing conglomeration and monopolization of media industries by giant corporations, there are still spaces left where individuals and communities can build affirmative identities, create and distribute cultural representations of themselves and others, and in general resist and challenge hegemonic representations. There are even opportunities to use Internet platforms for organizing media activism and social activism more generally. Nevertheless, we end with the caveat that no amount of participatory production, consumption, and distribution via the Internet can stand in for what our society still needs: fair and equal access for noncorporate entities, individuals and groups, to the whole range of cultural production.

Broader political efforts are still necessary to pressure mainstream media producers and owners to create and distribute more accurate and diverse representations. No doubt, achieving a more democratic system of media ownership and access in the current era will require a very high and sustained level of citizen activism—including working to challenge media policies favoring corporate control, such as the deregulation of broadcast media and the dismantling of Internet neutrality regulations. For those interested in the relationship of media to democracy, the efforts of active audiences and media activists should be encouraged and supported.

POP COSMOPOLITANISM

60

Mapping Cultural Flows in an Age of Media Convergence

Henry Jenkins III

If there is a global village, it speaks American. It wears jeans, drinks Coke, eats at the golden arches, walks on swooshed shoes, plays electric guitars, recognizes Mickey Mouse, James Dean, E.T., Bart Simpson, R2-D2, and Pamela Anderson.

Gitlin 2001

The twain of East and West have not only met—they've mingled, mated, and produced myriad offspring, inhabitants of one world, without borders or boundaries, but with plenty of style, hype, and attitude. In Beijing, they're wearing Levis and drinking Coke; in New York, they're sipping tea in Anna Sui. While Pizzicato Five is spinning heads in the U.S., Metallica is banging them in Japan.

Yang, Gan, Hong and the staff of A. Magazine, *1997*

I have spent my career studying American popular culture, adopting an approach based on older notions of national specificity. In recent years, however, it has become increasingly difficult to study what's happening to American popular culture without understanding its global context. I mean this not simply in the predictable sense that American pop culture dominates (and is being shaped for) worldwide markets but also in the sense that a growing proportion of the popular culture that Americans consume comes from elsewhere, especially Asia. This chapter represents a first stab at explaining how and why Asian popular culture is shaping American entertainment.

The analysis must start with the concept of media convergence. Most industry discourse about convergence begins and ends with what I call the black box fallacy: sooner or later all media are going to be flowing through a single black box in our living rooms, and all we have to do is figure out which black box it will be. Media convergence is not an end-point; rather, it is an ongoing process occurring at various intersections among media technologies, industries, content, and audiences. Thanks to the proliferation of channels and the increasingly ubiquitous nature of computing and telecommunications, we are entering an era when media will be everywhere and we will use all kinds of media in relation to each other. We will develop new skills for managing that information, new structures for transmitting information across channels, new creative genres that exploit the potentials of those emerging information structures, and new modes of education to help students understand their impact on their world. Media convergence is more than simply the digital revolution; it involves the introduction of a much broader array of new media technologies that enable consumers to archive, annotate, transform, and recirculate media content. Media convergence is more than simply a technological shift; it alters the relationship among existing technologies, industries, markets, genres, and audiences. This initial wave of media changes exerts a destabilizing influence, resulting in a series of lurches between exhilaration and panic. Yet media convergence is

From Jenkins, H., "Pop Cosmopolitanism: Mapping Cultural Flows in an Age of Convergence." In Marcelo M. Suarez-Orozco and Desiree Baolian Qin-Hilliard (eds) (2004), *Globalization: Culture & Education in the New Millennium.* Berkeley: University of California Press.

also sparking creative innovation in almost every sector of popular culture; our present media environment is marked by a proliferation of differences, by what Grant McCracken calls "plenitude" (see McCracken 2003). . . .

In this chapter I focus on the interplay between

Corporate convergence—the concentration of media ownership in the hands of a diminishing number of multinational conglomerates that thus have a vested interest in ensuring the flow of media content across different platforms and national borders

and

Grassroots convergence—the increasingly central roles that digitally empowered consumers play in shaping the production, distribution, and reception of media content.

These two forces—the top-down push of corporate convergence, the bottom-up pull of grassroots convergence—intersect to produce what might be called global convergence, the multidirectional flow of cultural goods around the world. Ulf Hannerz is describing global convergence when he writes: "[World culture] is marked by an organization of diversity rather than by a replication of uniformity. . . . The world has become one network of social relationships and between its different regions there is a flow of meanings as well as of people and goods" (Hannerz 1990, p. 237).

Global convergence is giving rise to a new pop cosmopolitanism.[1] Cosmopolitans embrace cultural difference, seeking to escape the gravitational pull of their local communities in order to enter a broader sphere of cultural experience. The first cosmopolitans thought beyond the borders of their village; the modern cosmopolitans think globally. We tend to apply the term to those who develop a taste for international food, dance, music, art, or literature—in short, those who have achieved distinction through their discriminating tastes for classical or high culture. Here, I will be using the term pop cosmopolitanism to refer to the ways that the transcultural flows of popular culture inspire new forms of global consciousness and cultural competency. Much as teens in the developing world use American popular culture to express generational differences or to articulate fantasies of social, political, and cultural transformation,

younger Americans are distinguishing themselves from their parents' culture through their consumption of Japanese anime and manga, Bollywood films and bhangra, and Hong Kong action movies. This pop cosmopolitanism may not yet constitute a political consciousness of America's place in the world (and in its worse forms, may simply amount to a reformation of orientalism), but it opens consumers to alternative cultural perspectives and the possibility of feeling what Matt Hills calls "semiotic solidarity" with others worldwide who share their tastes and interests (Hills 2002). . . .

Pop cosmopolitanism cannot be reduced to either the technological utopianism embodied by Marshall McLuhan's "global village" (with its promises of media transcending the nation-state and democratizing cultural access) or the ideological anxieties expressed in the concept of media imperialism (with its threat of cultural homogenization and of "the West suppressing the Rest," as Ramaswami Harindranath describes it [see Harindranath 2003, p. 156]).

The media imperialism argument blurs the distinction between at least four forms of power—economic (the ability to produce and distribute cultural goods), cultural (the ability to produce and circulate forms and meanings), political (the ability to impose ideologies), and psychological (the ability to shape desire, fantasy, and identity). Within this formulation, Western economic dominance of global entertainment both expresses and extends America's status as a superpower; the flow of cultural goods shapes the beliefs and the fantasies of worldwide consumers, reshaping local cultures in accordance with American economic and political interests. The classic media imperialism argument ascribed almost no agency to the receiving culture and saw little reason to investigate actual cultural effects; the flow of goods was sufficient to demonstrate the destruction of cultures.[2] Ethnographers have found that the same media content may be read in radically different ways in different regional or national contexts, with consumers reading it against the backdrop of more familiar genres and through the grid of familiar values. Even within the same context, specific populations (especially the young) may be particularly drawn toward foreign media content while others may express moral and political outrage. Most will negotiate with this imported culture in ways that reflect the local interests of media consumers rather than the global interests of media producers.

To be sure, there is probably no place on the planet where one can escape the shadow of Mickey Mouse. Entertainment is America's largest category of exports. The Global Disney Audiences Project, for example, deployed an international team of scholars to investigate the worldwide circulation of Disney goods. They found that in eleven of eighteen countries studied, 100 percent of all respondents had watched a Disney movie, and many of them had bought a broad range of other ancillary products (Wasko, Phillips, and Meehan 2001). But while still strong, the hold of American-produced television series on the global market has slipped in recent years (Foroohar 2002; Klein 2002). Local television production has rebounded, and domestic content dominates the prime evening viewing hours, with American content used as filler in the late-night or afternoon slots. Hollywood faces increased competition from other film-producing nations—including Japan, India, and China—that are playing ever more visible roles within regional, if not yet fully global, markets. Major media companies, such as Bertelsmann, Sony, and Universal Vivendi, contract talent worldwide, catering to the tastes of local markets rather than pursuing nationalistic interests; their economic structure encourages them not only to serve as intermediaries between different Asian markets but also to bring Asian content into Western countries. Many American children are more familiar with the characters of Pokemon than they are with those from the Brothers Grimm or Hans Christian Andersen, and a growing portion of American youth are dancing to Asian beats. With the rise of broadband communications, foreign media producers will distribute media content directly to American consumers without having to pass by U.S. gatekeepers or rely on multinational distributors. At the same time, grassroots intermediaries will play an increasingly central role in shaping the flow of cultural goods into local markets.

Adopting a position that if you can't beat them, merge with them, the American entertainment industry has become more aggressive in recruiting or collaborating with Asian talent. Sony, Disney, Fox, and Warner Brothers have all opened companies to produce films—aimed both at their domestic markets and at global export—in Chinese, German, Italian, Japanese, and other languages. American television and film increasingly remake successful products from other markets, ranging from *Survivor* and *Big Brother,* which are remakes of successful Dutch series, to *The Ring,* a remake of a Japanese cult horror movie, and *Vanilla Sky,* a remake of a Spanish science fiction film. Many of the cartoons shown on American television are actually made in Asia (increasingly in Korea), often with only limited supervision by Western companies.

Some have argued that Hollywood entertainment has always been global entertainment. Whereas many national cinemas respond to a relatively homogenous local market, Hollywood has had to factor in the tastes of a multicultural society. Richard Pells writes: "The United States has been a recipient as much as an exporter of global culture. . . . American culture has spread throughout the world because it has incorporated foreign styles and ideas. What Americans have done more brilliantly than their competitors overseas is repackage the cultural products we received from abroad and then retransmit them to the rest of the planet" (Pells 2002; also see Olson 1999). Pells sees this as an ongoing development that has shaped the evolution of American pop culture, not simply a cosmetic shift in response to recent economic trends or cultural developments.

These shifts complicate any simple mapping of the relationship among economic, political, and cultural power. We still must struggle with issues of domination and with the gap between media have and have-not nations, but we do so within a much more complicated landscape. . . . Arjun Appadurai writes, "Electronic mediation and mass migration . . . seem to impel (and sometimes compel) the work of the imagination. Together, they create specific irregularities because both viewers and images are in simultaneous circulation. Neither images nor viewers fit into circuits or audiences that are easily bound within local, national, or regional spaces" (Appadurai 1996, p. 4).

STRATEGIES OF CORPORATE CONVERGENCE

The flow of Asian goods into Western markets has been shaped through the interaction of three distinct kinds of economic interests: (1) national or regional media producers who see the global circulation of their products not simply as expanding their revenue stream but also as enhancing national pride; (2) multinational conglomerates that no longer define their production or distribution decisions in national terms but seek to identify potentially valuable content and push it into as many markets as possible; and (3) niche distributors who search for distinctive content as a means of attracting upscale consumers and differentiating themselves from stuff already on the market. For example, in the case of world music, international media companies, such as Sony, identify international artists and market them aggressively in their local or regional markets. As those artists are brought westward, the companies make a commercial decision whether they think the musicians will open mainstream, in which case the companies retain distribution rights within the United States, or niche, in which case they subcontract with a boutique label or third-party distributor (Levin 2002).

In a compelling analysis of the impact of Japanese transnationalism on popular culture, Koichi Iwabuchi draws a distinction between the circulation of cultural goods that are essentially "odorless," bearing few traces of their cultural origins, and those that are embraced for their culturally distinctive "fragrance" (Iwabuchi 2002). In some cases, mostly where these goods are targeting niche or cult audiences, these goods are strongly marked as coming from some exotic elsewhere; in other cases, especially where they are targeted to the mainstream, their national origins are masked and the content retrofitted to American tastes.

As Iwabuchi has documented, Japanese media industries sought ways to open Western markets to their "soft goods," or cultural imports, based on the overseas success of their hardware and consumer electronics. Seeking global distribution for locally produced content, Japanese corporations such as Sony, Sumitomo, Itochu, and Matsushita bought into the American entertainment industry. They saw children's media as sweet spots in Western societies. Much as Hollywood's ability to compete in international markets rests on its ability to recoup most of its production costs from domestic grosses, the success of Japanese-made comics and animation meant that these goods could enjoy competitive prices as they entered Western markets. In Japan, manga constituted 40 percent of all books and magazines published, and more than half of all movie tickets sold were to animated films (Ahn 2001). More than two hundred animation programs were aired each week on Japanese television, and about seventeen hundred animated films (short or feature length) were produced for theatrical distribution each year. Japanese media producers had created a complex set of tie-ins among comics, animated films and television series, and toys, which allowed them to capitalize quickly on successful content and bring it to the largest possible audience. They hoped to export this entire apparatus—the programs, the comics, and the toys—to the West. In the domestic market, anime and manga appealed to a broad cross-section of the public, but as they targeted the West, Japanese media companies targeted children as the primary consumers of their first imports. As this generation matured, the companies anticipated that they would embrace a broader range of Japanese-made media. . . .

TACTICS OF GRASSROOTS CONVERGENCE

. . . . Grassroots convergence serves the needs of both cosmopolitan and local. A global communication network allows members of diasporic communities to maintain strong ties with their motherlands, ensuring access to materials and information important to their cultural traditions and preserving social connections with those they left behind (Punathambekar 2003). Cosmopolitans use networked communication to scan the planet in search of diversity and communicate with others of their kind around the world. . . .

The pop cosmopolitan walks a thin line between dilettantism and connoisseurship, between orientalist fantasies and a desire to honestly connect and understand an alien culture, between assertion of mastery and surrender to cultural difference.

These same paradoxes and contradictions surface when we turn our attention to American fans of Japanese anime, the otaku. Otaku is a Japanese term used to make fun of fans who have become such obsessive consumers of pop culture that they have lost all touch with the people in their immediate vicinity. American fans have embraced the shameful term, asserting what Matt Hills calls a "semiotic solidarity" with their Japanese counterparts (Hills 2002); constructing their identity as "otaku" allows them to signal their distance from American taste cultures and their mastery over foreign content. While a minority of otaku are Asian or Asian American, the majority have no direct ties to Japan. . . .

Initially, anime, like Bollywood videos, entered the United States through small distributors who targeted Asian immigrants. Fans would venture into ethnic neighborhoods in search of content; in New York and San Francisco they turned to a handful of Japanese bookstores for manga that had not yet been translated or distributed in North America.[3] The Web enabled fans to start their own small-scale (and sometimes pirate) operations to help import, translate, and distribute manga and anime. . . .

Ethnographers who have studied this subculture disagree about the degree to which otaku seek any actual connection with real-world Japan or simply enter into an imaginary world constructed via anime genres. As Susan Napier writes, "the fact that anime is a Japanese . . . product is certainly important but largely because this signifies that anime is a form of media entertainment outside the mainstream, something 'different'" (Napier 2000, p. 242; see also Newitz 1994; Tobin 1998). Napier suggests that fans are attracted to the strange balance of familiar and alien elements in Japanese animation, which openly appropriates

and remakes Western genre conventions. Some anime fans do cultivate a more general knowledge of Japanese culture. They meet at sushi restaurants; clubs build partnerships via the Internet with sister organizations in Japan. Members often travel to Japan in search of new material or to experience the fan culture there more directly; some study the Japanese language in order to participate in various translation projects. As American fans go online and establish direct contact with their Japanese counterparts, they create an opening for other kinds of conversation. Discussion lists move fluidly from focus on anime- and manga-specific topics onto larger considerations of Japanese politics and culture. These different degrees of cultural engagement are consistent with what Hannerz has told us about cosmopolitanism more generally: "[In one kind of cosmopolitanism], the individual picks from other cultures only those pieces which suit himself. . . . In another mode, however, the cosmopolitan does not make invidious distinctions among the particular elements of the alien culture in order to admit some of them into his repertoire and refuse others; he does not negotiate with the other culture but accepts it as a package deal" (Hannerz 1990, p. 240). What cosmopolitanism at its best offers us is an escape from parochialism and isolationism, the beginnings of a global perspective, and the awareness of alternative vantage points. . . .

NOTES

1. For another take on what I am calling pop cosmopolitanism, see Roberts 2001.

2. For overviews of the debates on media imperialism, see Tomlinson 1991, Howe

1996, Liebes and Katz 1990, and Featherstone 1996.

3. On manga fandom, see Schodt 1996; Kinsella 2000; and Macias and Horn 1999.

REFERENCES

Ahn, J. (2001). Animated subjects: On the circulation of Japanese animation as global cultural products. Paper presented at the Globalization, Identity and the Arts Conference, University of Manitoba, Winnipeg.

Appadurai, A. (1996). *Modernity at large: The cultural dimensions of globalization.* Minneapolis: University of Minnesota Press.

Featherstone, M. (1996). Localism, globalism and cultural identity. In *Global local: Cultural production and the transnational imaginary.* Rob Wilson and Wimal Dissanayake, eds. Durham: Duke University Press.

Foroohar, R. (2002). Hurray for Globowood: As motion-picture funding, talent and audiences go global, Hollywood is no longer a place, but a state of mind. *Newsweek International,* May 27.

Gitlin, T. (2001). *Media unlimited: How the torrent of images and sounds overwhelms our lives.* New York: Metropolitan.

Hannerz, U. (1990). Cosmopolitans and locals in world culture. In *Global culture: Nationalism, globalization, and modernity.* M. Featherstone, ed. London: Sage.

Harindranath, R. (2003). Reviving "cultural imperialism": International audiences, global capitalism and the transnational elite. In *Planet TV.* L. Parks and S. Kumar, eds. New York: New York University Press.

Hills, M. (2002). Transcultural Otaku: Japanese representations of fandom and representations of Japan in Anime/Manga fan cultures. Paper presented at Media-in-Transition 2: Globalization and Convergence Conference, Massachusetts Institute of Technology, Cambridge, MA.

Howe, D. (1996). Commodities and cultural borders. In *Cross-Cultural Consumption: Global Markets, Local Realities.* London: Routledge.

Iwabuchi, K. (2002). *Recentering globalization: Popular culture and Japanese transnationalism.* Durham: Duke University Press.

Kinsella, S. (2002). *Adult Manga: Culture and power in contemporary Japanese society.* Honolulu: University of Hawaii Press.

Klein, C. (2002). The globalization of Hollywood. Paper presented at the Modern Language Association conference, New York, NY.

Levin, M. (2002). Independent distributors and specialty labels move product in the U.S. by such international artists as Shakira. Copyright 2002 BPI Communications, Inc. Used with permission from Billboard, November 2.

Liebes, T., and E. Katz (1990). *The export of meaning: Cross-cultural readings of Dallas.* Oxford, UK: Oxford University Press.

Macias P., and C. G. Horn, eds. (1999). *Japan edge: The insider's guide to Japanese pop subculture.* San Francisco: Cadence Books.

McCracken, G. (2003). Plenitude. http://www.cultureby.com/books/plenit/cxc_trilogy_plenitude.html.

Napier, S. (2000). *Anime from Akira to Princess Mononoke: Experiencing Japanese animation.* New York: Palgrave.

Newitz, A. (1994). Anime Otaku: Japanese animation fans outside Japan. *Bad Subjects* 13. http://eserver.org/bs/13/Newitz.html.

Olson, S. R. (1999). *Hollywood planet.* New York: Lawrence Erlbaum.

Pells, R. (2002). American culture goes global, or does it? *Chronicle of Higher Education,* April. http://chronicle.com/free/v48/i31/31 b00701.htm.

Punathambekar, A. (2003). *Bollywood bytes: A story of how I found an Online Adda.* New York: New York University Press.

Roberts, M. (2001). Notes on the Global Underground: Subcultural Elites, Conspicuous Cosmopolitanism. Paper presented at the Globalization, Identity and the Arts Conference, University of Manitoba, Winnipeg, http://www.umanitoba.ca/faculties/arts/english/media/workshop/papers/roberts/roberts_papcr.pdf.

Schodt, F. (1996). *Dreamland Japan: Writings on modern Manga.* Berkeley, CA: Stone Bridge.

Tobin, J. (1998). An American Otaku or, a boy's virtual life on the Net. In *Digital diversions: Youth culture in the age of multimedia.* J. Sefton-Green, ed. London: University College of London Press.

Tomlinson, J. (1991). *Cultural imperialism.* Baltimore: Johns Hopkins University Press.

Wasko, J., M. Phillips, and E. R. Meehan, eds. (2001). *Dazzled by Disney? The global Disney audiences project.* London: Leicester University Press.

Yang, J., and D. Gan, T. Hong, and the staff of A. Magazine, eds. (1997). *Eastern Standard Time: A guide to Asian influence on American culture from Astro Boy to Zen Buddhism.* Boston: Houghton Mifflin.

61

THE POLITICAL ECONOMY OF PRIVACY ON FACEBOOK

Christian Fuchs

THE POLITICAL ECONOMY OF FACEBOOK

Alvin Toffler (1980) introduced the notion of the prosumer in the early 1980s. It means the "progressive blurring of the line that separates producer from consumer" (Toffler 1980, 267). Toffler describes the age of prosumption as the arrival of a new form of economic and political democracy, self-determined work, labor autonomy, local production, and autonomous self-production. But he overlooks that prosumption is used for outsourcing work to users and consumers, who work without pay. In this model, corporations reduce their investment costs and labor costs, destroy jobs, and exploit consumers who work for free. Free labor produces surplus value that is appropriated and turned into corporate profit. Notwithstanding Toffler's uncritical optimism, his notion of the "prosumer" describes important changes in media structures and practices that can therefore be adopted through critical studies. . . .

. . . New media corporations do not (or hardly) pay users for the production of content. A widely-used accumulation strategy is to give the users free access to services and platforms, let them produce content, and to accumulate a mass of prosumers that are sold as a commodity to third-party advertisers. No product is sold to the users; the users are sold as a commodity to advertisers. The more users a platform claims, the higher the advertising rates. The productive labor time that is exploited by capital involves, on one hand, the labor time of paid employees, and, on the other hand, all of the time spent online by users. New media corporations pay salaries for the first type of information labor, but not for the second type. . . .

What does it mean that Facebook prosumers work for free and are exploited? Adam is a thirteen-year-old pupil and heavy Facebook user. He has two thousand Facebook friends, writes fifty wall postings a day, interacts with at least forty of his close contacts and colleagues over Facebook a day, updates his status at least ten times a day, and uploads annotated videos and weekend photos, often showing him with his girlfriend in the countryside. Yet there is one thing that puzzles him. The advertising at the right-hand side of his profile frequently relate to what he has done last weekend or what he intends to do next weekend. Adam wonders how this happens and feels uneasy about the fact that his personal data obviously serves inscrutable economic ends that he cannot control in terms of which personal data and usage behaviors are stored, assessed, or sold. The answer to Adam's dilemma is that Facebook closely monitors all of his contacts, communication, and data, selling this information to companies, which then send targeted advertisements to him. Facebook thus profits and could not exist without the unpaid labor that Adam and millions of his fellow Facebook workers conduct. Adam is the prototypical Facebook child worker.

. . . With the rise of user-generated content, open access social networking platforms, and other ad-based platforms, the web seems to approach TV or radio in their accumulation strategies. The users who upload photos and images, write wall posting and comments, send mail to their contacts, accumulate friends, or browse other profiles on Facebook constitute an audience commodity that is sold to advertisers. The difference between the audience commodity for traditional mass media and for the internet is that, in the latter case, the users are also content producers

From Christian Fuchs (2012), "The Political Economy of Privacy on Facebook," *Television & New Media,* 13 (2), 139–159. Reprinted with permission of SAGE Publications.

who engage in permanent creative activity, communication, community building, and content-production. In the case of Facebook, the audience commodity is an internet prosumer commodity.

Surveillance of Facebook prosumers occurs via corporate web platform operators and third-party advertising clients, which continuously monitor and record personal data and online activities. Facebook surveillance creates detailed user profiles so that advertising clients know and can target the personal interests and online behaviors of the users. Facebook sells its prosumers as a commodity to advertising clients; their exchange value is based on permanently produced use values, that is, personal data and interactions. . . .

Data surveillance is the means for Facebook's economic ends. Facebook permanently monitors users for economic ends, which means that no economic privacy is guaranteed to them. Since it remains unknown to users what specific information and data contributes to targeted advertising, they cannot control their data use or protect themselves from its commodification.

The use of targeted advertising and economic surveillance is legally guaranteed by Facebook's privacy policy (Facebook privacy policy, version from December 22, 2010, http://www.facebook.com/policy.php, accessed on May 29, 2011). Facebook's privacy policy is a typical expression of a self-regulatory privacy regime, in which businesses define their own personal user data processes. In general, U.S. data protection laws cover government databanks, leaving commercial surveillance untouched in order to maximize its profitability (Ess 2009, 56; Lyon 1994, 15; Rule 2007, 97; Zureik 2010, 351). Facebook's terms of use and its privacy policy are characteristic for this form of self-regulation. When privacy regulation is voluntary, the number of organizations protecting the privacy of consumers tends to be very small (Bennett and Raab 2006, 171).

SOCIALIST PRIVACY IDEALS AND SOCIAL NETWORKING

. . . What could socialist privacy protection policies on Facebook look like? One basic insight here is that the protection of consumers,' prosumers' and workers' privacy can only be achieved in an economy that is not ruled by profit interests, but is controlled and managed by prosumers, consumers,

and producers, thereby ending the need for privacy rules that protect us from domination. If there were no profit motive on internet platforms, then there would be no need to commodify the data and behaviors of internet users. Achieving such a situation is not primarily a technological task, but one that requires changes in society.

. . . The overall goal of socialist internet privacy politics is to drive back the commodification of user-data and the exploitation of prosumers by advancing the decommodification of the internet. Three strategies for achieving this goal are the advancement of opt-in online advertising, the civil society surveillance of internet companies, and the establishment and support of alternative platforms.

Opt-In Privacy Policies

Gandy (1993) argues that an alternative to opt-out solutions for targeted advertising are opt-in solutions that are based on the informed consent of consumers. . . .

Opt-in privacy policies are typically favoured by consumer and data protectionists, whereas companies and marketing associations prefer opt-out and self-regulation advertising policies in order to maximize profit (Bellman et al. 2004; Federal Trade Commission 2000; Gandy 1993; Quinn 2006; Ryker et al. 2002; Starke-Meyerring and Gurak 2007). Socialist privacy legislation could require all commercial internet platforms to use advertising only as an opt-in option, which would strengthen the users' possibility for self-determination. Within capitalism, forcing corporations by state laws to implement opt-in mechanisms is certainly desirable, but at the same time it is likely that corporations will not consent to such policies because they would likely reduce the actual amount of surveilled and commodified user data significantly, resulting in a drop of advertising profits. Organizing targeted advertising as opt-in instead of as opt-out (or no-option) does not establish economic user privacy, but is a step toward strengthening the economic privacy of users.

Corporate Watch-Platforms as Form of Struggle against Corporate Domination

To circumvent the large-scale surveillance of consumers, producers, and consumer-producers, movements and protests against economic surveillance are necessary. . . .

Critical citizens, critical citizens' initiatives, consumer groups, social movement groups, critical scholars, unions, data protection specialists/groups, consumer protection specialists/groups, critical politicians, and critical political parties should observe closely the surveillance operations of corporations and document these mechanisms and instances, in which corporations and politicians take measures that threaten privacy or increase the surveillance of citizens. Such documentation is most effective if it is easily accessible to the public. The internet provides means for documenting such behavior. It can help to watch the watchers and to raise public awareness.

In recent years, corporate-watch organizations that run online platforms have emerged.[1] Transnationale Ethical Rating aims at informing consumers and research about corporations. Its ratings include quantitative and qualitative data about violations of labor rights and human rights, employee layoffs, profits, sales, earnings of CEOs, boards, president and managers, financial off-shore operations, financial delinquency, environmental pollution, corporate corruption, and dubious communication practices. Dubious communication practices include an "arguable partnership, deceptive advertising, disinformation, commercial invasion, spying, mishandling of private data, biopiracy and appropriation of public knowledge" (http://www.transnationale.org/aide.php, accessed on March 21, 2011). The topics of economic privacy and surveillance are here part of a project that wants to document *corporate social irresponsibility*. Privacy is not the only issue addressed here, but corporate watch platforms can be situated in the larger political-economic context of corporate social irresponsibility (the counterpart of the CSR ideology).

Alternative Internet platforms

. . . It is not impossible to create successful non-profit internet platforms, as the example of Wikipedia, which is advertising-free, open access, and donor financed, shows. Diaspora is the best-known alternative social networking site that has developed an open-source alternative to Facebook. It is a project created by four New York University students, Dan Grippi, Maxwell Salzberg, Raphael Sofaer, and Ilya Zhitomirskiy. Diaspora defines itself as "privacy-aware, personally controlled, do-it-all, open source" (http://www.joindiaspora.com,

accessed on November 11, 2010). It is not funded by advertising, but by donations. Three design principles of Diaspora are choice, ownership, and simplicity: "Choice: Diaspora lets you sort your connections into groups called aspects. Unique to Diaspora, aspects ensure that your photos, stories, and jokes are shared only with the people you intend. Ownership: You own your pictures, and you shouldn't have to give that up just to share them. You maintain ownership of everything you share on Diaspora, giving you full control over how it's distributed. Simplicity: Diaspora makes sharing clean and easy—and this goes for privacy too. Inherently private, Diaspora doesn't make you wade through pages of settings and options just to keep your profile secure" (http://www.joindiaspora.com, accessed on March 21, 2011).

The Diaspora team is critical of the control of personal data by corporations. It describes Facebook as "spying for free" and the activities of Facebook and other corporate internet platforms in the following way. Salzberg opined, "When you give up that data, you're giving it up forever. . . . The value they give us is negligible in the scale of what they are doing, and what we are giving up is all of our privacy" (http://www.nytimes.com/2010/05/12/nyregion/12about.html). In an online video Zhitomirskiy added, "For the features that we get on blogs, social networks and social media sites, we sacrifice lots of privacy. . . . The features that we get are not anything special. . . . What will happen. . . . when one of these big large companies just goes bust, but has as one of its assets all of your personal data and all of our personal data, our communications, our photos, our comments? . . . They are in power to do what they please with it" (http://vimeo.com/11242604).

The basic idea of Diaspora is to circumvent the corporate mediation of sharing and communication by using decentralized nodes that store data that is shared with friends. Each user has his or her own data node that he or she fully controls.

Diaspora aims to enable users to share data with others, and, at the same time, to protect them from corporate domination by sacrificing their data to corporate purposes in order to communicate and share. Diaspora can therefore be considered as a socialist internet project that practically tries to realize a socialist conception of privacy.

. . . There are diffuse feelings of discontent with Facebook's privacy practices among many users. These have manifested into groups, such as those against the introduction of Facebook Beacon, news feed, mini-feed, as well as the emergence of the web 2.0 suicide machine (http://suicidemachine .org/), and the organization of a Quit Facebook Day (http://www.quitfacebookday.com/). These activities are mainly based on liberal and Luddite ideologies, but if they were connected to ongoing class struggles against neoliberalism (such as those of students in the aftermath of the new global capitalist crisis and the protests against austerity measures, unemployment and inequality in countries like Greece, Spain, Portugal, etc.) and the commodification of the commons, they could grow in importance. Existing struggles could be connected to the attempts to establish opt-in policies, corporate social media watchdogs, and alternative social media. . . .

NOTES

1. Examples of corporate watch organizations are: CorpWatch Reporting (http://www .corpwatch.org), Transnationale Ethical Reporting (http://www.transnationale.org), The Corporate Watch Project (http://www .corporatewatch.org), Multinational Monitor (http://wwww.multinationalmonitor .org), Crocodyl: Collaborative Research on Corporations (http://www.crocodyl.org), Endgame Database of Corporate Fines (http:///.endgame.org/corpfines.html), Corporate Crime Reporter (http://www .corporatecrimereporter.com), Corporate Europe Observatory (http://www.corporate europe.org), Corporate Critical Database (http://www.corporatecritic.org).

REFERENCES

Andrejevic, Mark. 2002. The work of being watched. *Critical Studies in Media Communication* 19 (2): 230–48.

Arendt, Hannah. 1958. *The human condition,* 2nd ed. Chicago: University of Chicago Press.

Bellman, Steven, Eric J. Johnson, Stephen J. Kobrin, and Gerald L. Lohse. 2004. International differences in information privacy concerns: a global survey of consumers. *Information Society* 20 (5): 313–24.

Bennett, Colin, and Charles Raab. 2006. *The governance of privacy.* Cambridge, MA: MIT Press.

Bolin, Göran. 2005. Notes from inside the factory. *Social Semiotics* 15 (3): 289–306.

Bolin, Göran. 2009. Symbolic production and value in media industries. *Journal of Cultural Economy* 2 (3): 345–61.

Bruns, Axel. 2008. *Blogs, Wikipedia, Second Life, and beyond. From production to produsage.* New York: Peter Lang.

Culnan, Mary J., and Robert J. Bies. 2003. Consumer privacy. Balancing economic and justice considerations. *Journal of Social Issues* 59 (2): 323–42.

Dussel, Enrique. 2008. The discovery of the category of surplus value. In *Karl Marx's Grundrisse: Foundations of the critique of the political economy 150 years later,* edited by Marcello Musto, 67–78. New York: Routledge.

Ess, Charles. 2009. *Digital media ethics.* Cambridge, UK: Polity.

Etzioni, Amitai. 1999. *The limits of privacy.* New York: Basic Books.

Federal Trade Commission. 2000. *Privacy online: fair information practices in the electronic marketplace.* http://www.ftc.gov/reports/privacy2000/privacy 2000.pdf.

Fuchs, Christian. 2009a. Information and communication technologies and society. A contribution to the critique of the political economy of the Internet. *European Journal of Communication* 24 (1): 69–87.

Fuchs, Christian. 2009b. *Social networking sites and the surveillance society. A critical case study of* the usage of studiVZ, Facebook, and MySpace by students in Salzburg in the context of electronic surveillance. Salzburg/Vienna: Research Group UTI.

Fuchs, Christian. 2010a. Labour in informational capitalism. *Information Society* 26 (3): 179–96.

Fuchs, Christian. 2010b. Social networking sites and complex technology assessment. *International Journal of E-Politics* 1 (3): 19–38.

Fuchs, Christian. 2010c. Some reflections on Manuel Castells' book "Communication Power." *tripleC* 7 (1): 94–108.

Fuchs, Christian. 2010d. studiVZ: social networking sites in the surveillance society. *Ethics and Information Technology* 12 (2): 171–185.

Fuchs, Christian. 2011a. A contribution to the critique of the political economy of Google. *Fast Capitalism* 8 (1).

Fuchs, Christian. 2011b. *Foundations of critical media and information studies.* New York: Routledge.

Fuchs, Christian. 2011c. The political economy of WikiLeaks: Power 2.0? Surveillance 2.0? Criticism 2.0? Alternative media 2.0? *Global Media Journal—Australian Edition* 5 (1).

Gandy, Oscar H. 1993. *The panoptic sort. A political economy of personal information.* Boulder, CO: Westview.

Habermas, Jürgen. 1989. *The structural transformation of the public sphere.* Cambridge, MA: MIT Press.

Hearn, Alison. 2010. Reality television, the Hills, and the limits of the immaterial labour thesis. *tripleC* 8 (1): 60–76.

Held, David. 1996. *Models of democracy.* Cambridge, UK: Polity.

Hesmondhalgh, David. 2010. User-generated content, free labour and the cultural industries. *Ephemera* 10 (3/4): 267–84.

Jenkins, Henry. 2008. *Convergence culture.* New York: New York University Press.

Jhally, Sut. 1987. *The codes of advertising.* New York: Routledge.

Jhally, Sut, and Bill Livant, Bill. 1986. Watching as working: The valorization of audience consciousness. *Journal of Communication* 36 (3): 124–43.

Johnson, Deborah G., and Kent A. Wayland. 2010. Surveillance and transparency as sociotechnical systems of accountability. In *Surveillance and democracy,* edited by Kevin D. Haggerty and Minas Samatas, 19-33. New York: Routledge.

Karatani, Kojin. 2005. *Transcritique: On Kant and Marx.* Cambridge, MA: MIT Press.

Kücklich, Julian. 2005. Precarious playbour. Fibreculture Journal 5, http://five.fibreculture journal.org/fcj-025-precarious-playbour-modders-and-the-digital-games-industry/.

Lee, Micky. 2011. 2011. Google ads and the blindspot debate. *Media, Culture & Society* 33 (3): 433–47.

Livant, Bill. 1979. The audience commodity. *Canadian Journal of Political and Social Theory* 3 (1): 91–106.

Lynd, Staughton. 1965. The new radicals and "participatory democracy." *Dissent* 12 (3): 324–33.

Lyon, David. 1994. *The electronic eye. The rise of surveillance society.* Cambridge, UK: Polity.

Macpherson, Crawford Brough. 1973. *Democratic theory: Essays in Retrieval.* Oxford, UK: Clarendon Press.

Manzerolle, Vincent. 2010. Mobilizing the audience commodity: Digital labour in a wireless world. *Ephemera* 10 (3/4): 455–69.

Marcuse, Herbert. 1955. *Eros and civilization.* Boston, MA: Beacon Press.

Marx, Karl. 1843a. Critique of Hegel's doctrine of the state. In *Early writings,* 57–198. London: Penguin.

Marx, Karl. 1843b. On the Jewish question. In *Writings of the young Marx on philosophy and society,* 216–48. Indianapolis, IN: Hackett.

Marx, Karl. 1867. *Capital. Volume 1.* London: Penguin.

Meehan, Eileen. 1993. Commodity audience, actual audience. The blindspot debate. In *Illuminating the blindspot,* edited by Janet Wasko, Vincent Mosco, and Manjunath Pendakur, 378–97. Norwood, NJ: Ablex.

Mill, John Stuart. 1965. *Principles of political economy.* 2 vols. London: University of Toronto Press.

Moglen, Eben. 2003. *The dotCommunist Manifesto.* http://emoglen.law.columbia.edu/publications/dcm.html

Murdock, Graham. 1978. Blindspots about Western Marxism. *Canadian Journal of Political and Social Theory* 2 (2): 109–19.

Negri, Antonio. 1991. *Marx beyond Marx.* London: Pluto.

Nissenbaum, Helen. 2010. *Privacy in context.* Stanford, CA: Stanford University Press.

Pateman, Carole. 1970. *Participation and democratic theory.* Cambridge: Cambridge University Press.

Quinn, Michael. 2006. *Ethics for the information age.* Boston: Pearson.

Rule, James B. 2007. *Privacy in peril.* Oxford: Oxford University Press.

Ryker, Randy, Elizabeth Lafleur, Chris Cox, and Bruce Mcmanis. 2002. Online privacy policies: an assessment of the fortune E-50. *Journal of Computer Information Systems* 42 (4): 15–20.

Smythe, Dallas. 1977. Communications: Blindspot of Western Marxism. *Canadian Journal of Political and Social Theory* 1 (3): 1–27.

Smythe, Dallas W. 1978. Rejoinder to Graham Murdock. *Canadian Journal of Political and Social Theory* 2 (2): 120–27.

Smythe, Dallas W. 1981/2006. On the audience commodity and its work. In *Media and cultural studies,* edited by Meenakshi G. Durham and Douglas M. Kellner, 230–56. Malden, MA: Blackwell.

Starke-Meyerring, Doreen and Laura Gurak. 2007. Internet. In *Encyclopedia of privacy,* edited by William G. Staples, 297–310. Westport, CT: Greenwood Press.

Tännsjö, Torbjörn. 2010. *Privatliv.* Lidingö: Fri Tanke.

Tavani, Herman T. 2008. Informational privacy: Concepts, theories, and controversies. In *The handbook of information and computer ethics,* edited by Kenneth Einar Himma and Herman T. Tavani, 131–64. Hoboken, NJ: Wiley.

Toffler, Alvin. 1980. *The third wave.* New York: Bantam Books.

Turow, Joseph. 2006. *Niche envy. Marketing discrimination in the digital age.* Cambridge, MA: MIT Press.

Zureik, Elia. 2010. Cross-cultural study of surveillance and privacy: Theoretical and empirical observations. In *Surveillance, privacy and the globalization of personal information,* edited by Elia Zureik, Lynda Harling Stalker, Emily Smith, David Lyon, and Yolane E. Chan, 348–59. Montreal: McGill-Queen's University Press.

TO SEE AND BE SEEN

62

Celebrity Practice on Twitter

Alice Marwick and danah boyd

INTRODUCTION

Networked media is changing celebrity culture, the ways that people relate to celebrity images, how celebrities are produced, and how celebrity is practiced. Gossip websites, fan sites, and blogs provide a plethora of new locations for the circulation and creation of celebrity, moving between user-generated content and the mainstream media. The fragmented media landscape has created a shift in traditional understanding of 'celebrity management' from a highly controlled and regulated institutional model to one in which performers and personalities actively address and interact with fans.

CELEBRITY THEORIES

. . . Although famous people represent an increasingly significant part of mass media, for many academics, they personify the trivial, dangerous decadence of American culture (Ewen, 1989; Lowenthal, 1961). In keeping with this viewpoint, people who enjoy consuming celebrity culture have been pathologized, portrayed as miserable or lonely, or seen as cultural dupes (Feasey, 2008; Jensen, 1992). However, celebrity images are culturally pervasive; they have become part of our day-to-day lives (Turner, 2004: 17) and part of the raw material through which we construct identities and engage in public discourse (Feasey, 2008; Gamson, 1994). More recently, fandom has become a subject of study in its own right (Baym, 2000; Jenkins, 1992, 2006b). In the tradition of active audience studies, theories of 'participatory culture' examine how people draw from media texts to create

and produce their own cultural products (Jenkins, 2006a; Lessig, 2004). Understanding not only how the celebrity construct functions as a product within media industries, but how and why people make meaning from celebrity culture in their daily lives, is essential as we see the process of celebrification trickling down to blog writers, social network site participants, YouTube stars, and other social media users (Senft, 2008). Celebrity can now be practiced by a greater number of people.

. . . Reality TV popularized a behind-the-scenes, self-conscious examination of celebrity construction; online, this goes one step further. Theresa Senft defines 'micro-celebrity' as a technique that 'involves people "amping up" their popularity over the Web using techniques like video, blogs, and social networking sites' (2008: 25). 'Micro-celebrity' describes a prevailing style of behavior both online and off, linked to the increase in popularity of 'self-branding' and strategic self-presentation (Hearn, 2008; Lair et al., 2005). This phenomenon was first noted in camgirls, young women who broadcast images of themselves 24/7 to interested audiences (Snyder, 2000). Their strategic micro-celebrity is distinct from the inadvertent fame resulting from internet memes, such as the 'Star Wars Kid' and 'Tron Guy'. Micro-celebrity involves viewing friends or followers as a fan base; acknowledging popularity as a goal; managing the fan base using a variety of affiliative techniques; and constructing an image of self that can be easily consumed by others. As we will see, these resemble techniques that extremely famous people use to manage audiences on Twitter, rather than relying on formal access brokers like managers and agents to maintain the distance between themselves and fans.

From Alice Marwick and danah boyd (2011), "To See and Be Seen: Celebrity Practice on Twitter," *Convergence*, 17: 139–158. Reprinted with permission of SAGE Publications, Ltd.

While the distinction between micro-celebrity and 'real' celebrity might once have been a question of popularity, approachability, or mainstream status, this article looks at how 'traditional' celebrities have adopted techniques formerly characterized as 'micro-celebrity'. We view celebrity practice as a *continuum* that can be practiced across the spectrum of fame rather than a schism. This essay examines how celebrity is practiced by the very famous, yet we are interested in the larger cultural shifts indicated by these celebrity performances and recognize the need for research on the daily practice of celebrity by non-famous individuals.

In this chapter, we define celebrity as a *practice*. Whenever possible, we refrain from referring to people as celebrities, preferring to use 'celebrity practitioners' or 'famous people' to avoid the binary implications of the noun. However, since celebrity-as-noun is the prevalent usage within both scholarly and public discourse, we use it in reference to other works and discourses.

TWITTER AND METHOD

The microblogging site Twitter lets people post quick 140-character updates, or 'tweets', to a network of followers. Twitter asks participants 'What's happening?' resulting in a constantly-updated stream of short messages ranging from the mundane to breaking news, shared links, and thoughts on life. In Twitter's directed model of friendship, users choose others to 'follow' in their stream, and each user has his or her own group of 'followers'. There is neither a technical requirement nor social expectation of reciprocity (particularly with famous people, although this differs by user group). Tweets can be posted and read from the web, SMS, or third-party clients for desktop computers, smartphones, and other devices. This integration allows for instant postings of photos, on-the-ground reports, and quick replies to other users. The site launched in 2006 and broke into the mainstream in 2008–2009, when user accounts and media attention exponentially increased. Twitter had approximately 18.2 million users in May 2009 (Nielsen Company, 2009), increasing to 27.2 million by January 2010 (Quantcast Corporation, 2010). As of 2010, the most-followed Twitter users are well-known organizations like CNN and Whole Foods, very famous people and public figures, from

President Barack Obama to actor Ashton Kutcher and pop star Britney Spears. While Twitter can be used as a broadcast medium, the dialogic nature of Twitter and its ability to facilitate conversation has contributed substantially to its popularity.

This popularity has contributed to media fascination with the site. Unlike individuals famous primarily for their affiliation with social media properties, such as Tila Tequila on MySpace or Tay Zonday on YouTube, Twitter attracts actors, pop stars, authors, politicians, and others with established fame, such as Oprah Winfrey, Senator John McCain, Shaquille O'Neal and Weird Al. Although people known primarily for their online presence, like marketer Pistachio and video blogger iJustine, are well-represented on Twitter, the most-followed Twitter users are, for the most part, the conventionally famous.

Given this, we used Twitter to understand how celebrity is practiced through interactions between famous people and fans, friends, and other practitioners on Twitter. Part of the appeal of Twitter, as we will discuss, is the perception of direct access to a famous person, particularly 'insider' information, first-person pictures, and opinionated statements. Those celebrities who use Twitter primarily to 'broadcast' publicity information are seen as less authentic than those using the tool for dialogue and engagement with fans. One of our first methodological tasks was to work out who authored accounts of famous people.

We collected data from all people in the 300 most-followed Twitter accounts (as measured by Twitterholic.com during May and June 2009), including actors, musicians, technologists, politicians, reality television stars, and so forth for a total of 237 individuals; the remaining 63 accounts were media, companies, and organizations. . . . All the accounts we looked at were public. The messages we analyzed are also public; we use the actual usernames of both fans and highly followed people in this article, since the tweets are publicly searchable and accessible (while tweets are only publicly searchable for 21 days, they can always be directly accessed from the user's page). Twitter allows for private, person-to-person tweets that do not appear on public pages, called direct messages (DMs). This chapter references several practices that Twitter users have developed to facilitate conversation on the site, namely @replies, retweets, and hashtags. @replies, or 'at-replies', are public tweets that use a '@+username' convention to refer to other Twitter users; these can be used to identify people, address tweets to particular users and attribute quotes (Honeycutt and Herring, 2009). @replies are common on Twitter and 42 per cent of tweets in our sample are @replies.

The second type of common user practice we tracked was the retweet (RT), a repost of another person's tweet (see boyd et al., 2010, for a comprehensive look at retweeting). This is less common, and only 5 per cent of tweets in our sample were retweets. Hash tags, or the # sign followed by a word, mark tweets with descriptive terms. On sites like Delicious, Amazon.com, and Flickr, tags are used for many purposes, only one of which is classifying the tweet's subject matter (Golder and Huberman, 2006). On Twitter, tags are typically used to group tweets together by subject, such as a conference or meme; 6 per cent of the tweets in our sample included hashtags.

PERFORMING CELEBRITY ON TWITTER

Like other public genres of social media, Twitter requires celebrity practitioners to negotiate a complicated social environment where fans, famous people, and intermediaries such as gossip columnists co-exist. These multiple audiences complicate self-presentation, since people present identity differently based on context. Erving Goffman's 1959 work *The Presentation of Self in Everyday Life* suggested that people, like actors, navigate 'frontstage' and 'backstage' areas in any given social situation. This can be understood in terms of place. For instance, a restaurant's floor is frontstage, since employees must interact in front of an audience of bosses and customers. More candid talk between servers can take place backstage, away from the watchful eye of the employer. These concepts can also be understood in terms of content. For instance, intimate details about one's life are understood as part of the 'backstage' while professional communications can be seen as a 'frontstage' performance. However, frontstage and backstage are always relative as they depend on audience, context, and interpretation.

Goffman's work is related to symbolic interactionism, a sociological perspective which maintains that meaning is constructed through language, interaction, and interpretation (Blumer, 1962; Strauss, 1993). Symbolic interactionists claim that identity and self are constituted through constant interactions with others—primarily, talk. Individuals work together to uphold preferred self-images of themselves and their conversation partners, through strategies like maintaining (or 'saving') face, collectively encouraging social norms, or negotiating power differentials and disagreements. What Goffman refers to as 'impression management' takes place through ongoing adjustment to perceptions of audience judgment (1959).

Very famous people constantly navigate complex identity performances. The ostensible disconnect between a famous person's public persona and 'authentic' self is fueled by tabloid magazines, paparazzi photos, and gossip columns that purport to reveal what a particular starlet is 'really' like. Celebrity scandals often involve the exposure of personal information to the public, such as outing someone as queer or the dissemination of photos, 'sex tapes', answering machine messages, emails, and other purportedly backstage documents. This tricky territory has traditionally been navigated with the help of assistants, agents, public relations personnel, bodyguards, and other mechanisms that broker access between famous person and fan. On Twitter, however, this infrastructure is not available. As we will see, celebrity practice involves the appearance and performance of backstage access to the famous, presuming that the typical celebrity persona involves artifice. . . . Determining whether readers are watching an 'authentic' individual or a performed 'celebrity' persona is not entirely the point; it is the uncertainty that creates pleasure for the celebrity-watcher on Twitter.

Simultaneously, celebrity practice reinforces unequal power differentials. While Twitter users who do not use the site instrumentally may think of their followers as friends or family (Marwick and boyd, 2010), celebrity practice necessitates viewing followers as fans. Performing celebrity requires that this asymmetrical status is recognized by others. Fans show deference, creating mutual recognition of the status imbalance between practitioner and fan. In return, fan–practitioner relationships move beyond parasocial interaction, the illusion of a 'real', face-to-face friendship with a performer created through watching television shows or listening to music (Horton and Wohl, 1956). In parasocial relationships, or what John Thompson calls 'mediated quasi-interaction' (J Thompson, 1995: 98), a fan responds to a media figure 'as if s/he was a personal acquaintance' (Giles, 2002: 289); in contrast, Twitter suggests the possibility of interaction. There is no singular formula for celebrity practice; it consists of a set of learned techniques that are leveraged differently by individuals.

Public Recognition and Fan Maintenance

Like much social media, Twitter creates a 'context collapse' (boyd, 2008) in which multiple audiences, usually thought of as separate, co-exist in a single social context. The practice of celebrity involves negotiating these multiple audiences to successfully maintain face and manage impressions. Celebrity practitioners use public acknowledgment, in the form of @replies, to connect with others. Fans @reply to famous people not only in the hope of receiving a reply, but to display a relationship, whether positive or negative. If fans receive @replies back, they function as a mark of status and are publicized within the fan community. Celebrity practitioners' public acknowledgment of friends, peers, and colleagues is rarely critical, primarily adhering to frontstage norms of public appearance. Famous people mention fans to perform connection and availability, give back to loyal followers, and manage their popularity.

Celebrity practice requires constant interaction with fans to preserve the power differentials intrinsic to the performed 'celebrity' and 'fan' personas. Celebrity practitioners approach this in different ways. . . . For example, when Mariah Carey tweets about her friend Jasmine Dotiwala, an MTV producer and gossip columnist, she chooses to identify her by her Twitter username:

> MariahCarey: @jasminedotiwala just sang the Vegas remix of "these are a few of my favorite things and did a little dance in a terry cloth robe" hilarious

This establishes intimacy between Carey and her followers by sharing personal details from her life while publicly identifying jasminedotiwala as a friend—a performance of backstage access—and inviting her followers to check out Jasmine's Twitter stream. This maintains the power differential

between an average fan and the singer's intimate friend, since Jasmine is marked as someone who spends time with Mariah in person. It also provides a public endorsement of Jasmine's Twitter stream.

While some highly followed users reference others without being prompted, others will acknowledge friends as a favor to direct attention their way. This is particularly visible through the practice of retweeting:

> KevinRose: RT: @garyvee announcing my 1st business book http://tinyurl.com/garyveebook – congrats to @garyvee, crush it!
> Greggrundberg: RT @WilfridDierkes "watch My Name is Earl tonite cause if it gets canceled my family is moving in w/you." Peeps please watch. Save us all!!

Both these tweets demonstrate publicly articulated relational ties: between Digg founder Kevin Rose and motivational speaker Gary Vaynerchuk, and between actor Gregg Grunberg and producer Greg Garcia. This practice suggests insiderness between the participants, but it also highlights the dynamics of attention on Twitter.

Public acknowledgment, of either friends or fans, is not always positive. Twitter user Leproff sends an angry tweet to Republican politician Newt Gingrich about Reagan, who responds tersely:

> Leproff: @newtgingrich I do not agree when you say that USSR collapsed because of Ronald Reagan. This is a historical lie!
> NewtGingrich: @Leproff do you really believe the soviet union would have disappeared without rea-gab. Read peter schweizers book reagans war

Gingrich's tweet reinforces his image as an ornery conservative, but the act of responding also shows that he takes time to talk directly with followers. The potential of such interactions implies that fans are faced with accountability to the actors and singers they gossip about. Some famous people directly address gossip, for instance:

> LilyRoseAllen: and no i didnt say that stuff, ive never met cheryl, or her husband, noe david beckham. please dont believe that rubbish.

NewtGingrich: A false story was planted this morning about my sueing twitter. This is totally false and we have repudiated it with the media

Hollymadison123: @PerezHilton Criss and i r not back together. lol!

Rumor-mongering, whether by follower or gossip columnist Perez Hilton, can theoretically be directly corrected. Of course, fans may choose to believe the rumor even if the famous person chooses to reject it and not all fans read all tweets written by a celebrity. As with any other medium, correcting a rumor on Twitter can be more challenging than starting one. . . .

Intimacy

Twitter allows celebrity practitioners to create a sense of closeness and familiarity between themselves and their followers. Highly followed accounts vary in performed intimacy; while some mostly broadcast information about an upcoming tour or book, others write about personal subjects, post exclusive content, or chat about their daily lives. This type of strategic revealing found on confessional talk show appearances, tell-all autobiographies, and magazine interviews has been criticized as 'second order intimacy' (Rojek, 2001: 52) or the 'illusion of intimacy' (Schickel, 1985: 4; Turner, 2004). This point of view maintains that performed intimacy is synonymous with parasocial interaction and a poor substitute for actual interaction.

While it is true that the practice of celebrity involves strategically managed self-disclosure, we should not be so quick to judge the closeness created by Twitter as false and second-best. First, Twitter does provide the possibility of actual interaction with the highly followed person, in the form of a direct message or @reply. Second, the 'lifestreaming' function of Twitter encourages 'digital intimacy' (C Thompson, 2008). The many seemingly insignificant messages serve as phatic communication (Miller, 2008); rather than sharing meaningful information, many tweets serve a social function, reinforcing connections and maintaining social bonds (Crawford, 2009). If we accept that Twitter creates a sense of ongoing connection with one's real-life acquaintances and friends, following a famous person's tweets over a period of time may create an equally valid feeling of 'knowing' them. Finally, as we will see in the following case studies, users can and do let things slip via Twitter that would never be revealed in an interview with *People* magazine.

On Twitter, performative intimacy is practiced by posting personal pictures and videos, addressing rumors, and sharing personal information. Picture-hosting services, such as YFrog and Twitpic, allow users directly to post cameraphone pictures to Twitter. Famous people frequently use these services, creating the illusion of first-person glimpses into their lives. . . . Similarly, streaming video services like uStream are used by musicians like Bow Wow and Snoop Dogg to broadcast studio recordings and live performances, while others post funny videos, take questions from fans, or host live events. Shaquille O'Neal, for instance, filmed himself lipsynching and tweeted the link to his followers. While these pictures and videos add a visual dimension, they are still strategically chosen by the practitioner, in contrast to the unauthorized candids found in tabloids and gossip blogs.

As we have seen, other famous people use Twitter to directly address rumors. The same technique is used to respond to fan criticism or comments. For instance, Shaq retorted to a follower who said his sneakers were ugly:

@Naimthestar yea dats why I sold 80 million pair since 1992 at 3 dollars per pair comn to me, do the math

In addition to publicly recognizing and responding to a fan concern, this information makes the fan feel that they possess insider, candid knowledge about the sports star. Contentious discussions are not uncommon:

Jake_Banks: @ddlovato the Jonas Brothers, are just a disney fabrication who did not earn their fame and thusly are undeserving of such a large spotlight

Ddlovato: @Jake_Banks It's funny that you call them a "disney fabrication" but they have fans of ALL ages and they do deserve the spotlight.

Ddlovato: They've been touring and working extremely hard for years and they still haven't stopped. They're the hardest working people I know of. . . .

These exchanges demonstrate how Twitter has contributed to changes in the parasocial dynamic. While parasocial interaction is largely imaginary and takes place primarily in the fan's mind, Twitter conversations between fans and famous people are public and visible, and involve direct engagement between the famous person and their follower. The fan's ability to engage in discussion with a famous person de-pathologizes the parasocial and recontextualizes it within a medium that the follower may use to talk to real-life acquaintances. As we have seen, Twitter makes fans accountable for rude comments, taking the subjects of gossip out of the realm of fantasy and repositioning them as 'real people'. Traditional settings for in-person celebrity–fan interactions, such as autograph signings and award ceremonies, are highly managed and limited in scope. In contrast, although Twitter conversations are mediated, they appear off-the-cuff, contributing to a sense that the reader is seeing the real, authentic person behind the 'celebrity'.

Authenticity and Sincerity

In *Sincerity and Authenticity*, Lionel Trilling (1972) distinguishes authenticity from sincerity. He conceptualizes authenticity as a display of the hidden inner life, complete with passions and anguish, while sincerity is the opposite of hypocrisy—honesty without pretense. Both these elements matter on Twitter. The intimacy engendered by celebrity tweets provide the glimpse into the inner life that fans want, while at the most basic level, fans want to ensure that the person tweeting is sincerely who they claim to be. Twitter is generally a site where personal disclosure and intimacy are normative (Marwick and boyd, 2010), so access, intimacy, and affiliation are valueless if an account is fake or written by an assistant. The process involved in vetting whether a person is really who they claim to be reveals the appeal of celebrity practice for fans: the potential for disclosing the 'truth', the uncensored person stripped of PR artifice and management.

Users frequently debate whether Twitter accounts are written by who they claim to be. The site truthtweet.com verifies or debunks accounts like Tina_Fey and The_Pitts. During our research, accounts for Seth Rogen, Michael Phelps, and Tina Fey were identified as impostors and subsequently shut down (Tina_Fey was renamed 'FakeTinaFey'

and the comedian Tina Fey took over Tina_Fey). Some of these demonstrably false accounts are valued for their satirical value or effective impersonation, such 'FakeSarahPalin' whose tweets include things like 'This "death panel" thing is really taking off! Suck it, Luntz, you got p0wned Palin style. Srsly!!!' In June 2009, Twitter introduced verified accounts that certify 'genuine' famous people. Not all 'celebrity' accounts are written by the purported individual. In our own efforts to account for authenticity of Twitter accounts, we focused on the signals of authenticity. Judith Donath discusses how subtle online signals function as identity cues, given the dearth of physical evidence (1998). Given the presence of typos in most participants' tweets, we expect that 'real' celebrity practitioners will make grammatical or spelling mistakes. Tweets that are personal, controversial, or negative—in other words, that contradict the stereotype of the overly managed 'celebrity' account—signal greater authenticity than safely vetted publicity messages. If the writer interacted with fans, used the first-person voice, and posted candid snapshots, they seemed more authentic, as did their use of mobile clients such as Tweetie or Twitterberry. Of course, our assessment is only based on the available signals; we have no way of validating our best guesses. Similarly, fans carefully evaluate the *sincerity* of celebrity accounts.

Trilling's alternative meaning of authenticity, as passion and interiority, is also crucial to Twitter's appeal. 'Authenticity' is a social construct that is ultimately always relative and context dependent (Bendix, 1997; Cheng, 2004); it seems that self-disclosure, and therefore what it means to be authentic, is expected more on Twitter compared to other venues. While we accept that a *Cosmopolitan* cover story on pop star Katy Perry will probably be a bit boring, we anticipate that Perry's Twitter feed will be in keeping with her glamorous, wacky image. Celebrity practice that sticks to the safe and publicly consumable risks being viewed as inauthentic, while successful celebrity practice suggests intimacy, disclosure, and connection. . . .

Mariah Carey: Fan Relationships with Celebrities

The pop singer Mariah Carey has been releasing successful albums for 20 years, and has a devoted, loyal fan following which she calls her 'lambs'. While Carey is the best-selling female artist in the

USA, her volatile career has included two highly publicized marriages, a divorce, the failed film *Glitter*, and a televised mental breakdown. Perhaps because of these personal tribulations, her fans send her intimate public messages that often resemble a quick text to a friend:

> OMJitsReva: @MariahCarey On my way to NYC be there in 21 hours, yep I'm catchin teh greyhound . . . hope ur in town and i c u
>
> halima12: @MariahCarey hey, been in the garden with sugapie dunking her in the pool & givin her a ride on the lilo. been playin E¼MC2:) watcha up 2?
>
> ShayneFly: @MariahCarey Had to put our family dog to sleep tonight. I know you know how it hurts. Im missing a piece and my stupid face is all wet:(

These messages both demonstrate the power of parasocial interaction and how Twitter changes it. Fan LaurenDayMakeUp responded to our question about her Twitter interaction with Mariah, 'I follow @MariahCarey becoz she has been with me through her music everyday of my life 4 the last 15 years! She inspires me!' But unlike listening to music, social media suggests the possibility of the media figure responding, which intensifies the interactive credibility.

> MariahCarey: Trying to DM as many nice folks as possible. Thanks for all the love as always. I love twitter cos I can really stay in touch w/you. (Cont)

Fans know that Mariah uses Twitter to communicate directly with friends and fans, meaning she may potentially respond to them. As a result, fans directly ask for responses:

> Rochyta: @Mariahcarey We miss you, Mariah! I had a terrible day today. It would be great to read a "hi" from you.Te quiero muchi´simo. Roci´o-Spain.
>
> OriginalJengsta: @MariahCarey Today is my birthday and my birthday wish is to get a Twitter shout-out from MC -can you swing it?? -Nancy Jeng

Receiving a message from a highly followed individual is a status symbol in itself. User OMJitsReva writes on her profile, 'Check my FAVs [favorite tweets] for celebs that have tweeted me back! I feel like a mini-celebrity.' This is also a public performance of access. Users tweet to Mariah not only to feel a sense of connection with her, but also to publicly acknowledge the lack of distance between themselves and the singer.

> AviHBF: @dieguitoLAMB Mariah DM'd me today!
>
> DieguitoLAMB: @AviHBF OM*G!!! YOU LUCKY GURL!
>
> LoyalLamb88: @AviHBF Wow! That's awesome. . . .

AviHBF brags about receiving a direct message; the responses show the value of this within the fan community. One fan, MiMiGreat, posted 'Mariah wrote me a DM!!!!!!!!!!!!!!!!!!' upon receiving her own message. Notably, Mariah uses private direct messages rather than public @replies. This could be a way to avoid public accountability, but it also means that fans can claim that Mariah wrote to them even if she did not. Mariah's tweet about 'loving Twitter' and the excited responses from fans comprise a performance of fan interaction. Mariah could claim to interact with fans privately without actually doing so, or could have an assistant write DMs. For Mariah Carey and her fans, Twitter seems to be about the perception of availability and fan access.

Miley Cyrus: Celebrity Relationships with Celebrities

Celebrity practitioners also interact with other famous people on Twitter, creating revealing performances of what appear to be intimate interactions. Truly private interactions between famous people, with no public audience, are invisible to fans. Highly publicized romantic relationships and friendships covered by gossip magazines create the illusion of insider access, but are still public. Twitter allows the public visibility of casual friendships between famous people, which both creates a sense of insiderness for fan observers and requires celebrities to navigate carefully. Celebrities must constantly shift between performing their stage persona, concealing or revealing personal information, and creating intimacy and authentic self-presentation for the benefit of their fans. At times, it becomes difficult to discern what is performance and what is 'real'; this is precisely the kind of juxtaposition that fans love.

Teen star Miley Cyrus began a public feud with fellow singer/actors Demi Lovato and Selena Gomez after posting a mocking parody of the girls' home-made video series on YouTube (Beer and Penfold-Mounce, 2009). Speculations on the origin of the feud include internal Disney rivalry; conflict over Gomez being labeled the 'Next Miley Cyrus' by the press; and tension after Lovato dated Cyrus' ex-boyfriend, teen idol Nick Jonas. The feud was heavily covered by the entertainment press, fueled by Nick's brother Kevin wearing a 'Team Demi and Selena' t-shirt in public. Cyrus, Lovato, and Gomez have publicly denied a feud and were photographed in late 2008 having dinner, presumably a staged event as damage control to counteract fallout from the rumors (Kidzworld, 2009). While Lovato and Gomez are publicly 'best friends' who continue to present themselves as such, Cyrus and Lovato engaged in a somewhat surprising ongoing series of public interactions on Twitter:

Ddlovato: Now I'm with my other two best friends in the entire world . . . @selenagomez and @mileycyrus. What an amazing day.: D

MileyCyrus: @ddlovato is one of the bestest friends in the world:)

Ddlovato: @mileycyrus I'm comin'! You better visit me on tour!!! Idk how long I can go without seeing you:)

MileyCyrus: @ddlovato I dont know if I've ever needed someone as badly as I need you right now. . . . I miss you sweet girl.

Ddlovato: @mileycyrus awww:(make me tear up why don't ya?! I love you so much. I've ALWAYS got your back.

These tweets can be viewed as strategic frontstage performances. It's irrelevant whether or not Miley, Demi and Selena actually are friends, since the frequency and emotional tone of the messages mark them as performative—Cyrus and Lovato want their fans to know that they are friends. . . .

While an agent or manager may have been the impetus for Lovato and Cyrus's public declarations of friendship, similar public declarations take place on social network sites among non-celebrities every day. Interactions between users create publicly visible relationship lines, marking friendship, romantic entanglements, breakups, flirtations, rivalries, and alliances. It is not surprising that celebrities—particularly teenage girls whose peer group conduct their social lives via social media—do the same thing. The scrutiny may become too much; in October 2009, Miley Cyrus left Twitter in a whirlwind of publicity, stating in a home-made rap video posted on YouTube 'Everything that I type and everything that I do, all those lame gossip types take it and they make it news' (MandyMiley 2009).

The Cyrus–Lovato 'feud' demonstrates that reading conversations as performative or real is neither neat nor easy. Celebrity is practiced through scripted attempts to give backstage access. But just as actually getting backstage at a rock show does not provide true access to the band, neither does reading tweets provide insider access. The performance of celebrities interacting with no thought of fans, press, or managers on Twitter is actually managed interaction that creates the perception of intimacy. That is not to say that celebrities do not let things slip on Twitter; this is precisely why studios such as Disney and Dreamworks see Twitter as a liability (Wallenstein and Belloni, 2009). There is indeed a tension between deliberate self-presentation—what Erving Goffman called impressions 'given'—and unintentional self-presentation, or information 'given off' (1959). It is the inability to tell what is strategic and what is accidental, as well as what is truthful and what is not, that makes Twitter so enjoyable for fans.

SIGNIFICANCE

. . . New media not only provides new outlets for the exploration of celebrity, but complicates the dynamics between celebrity practitioners, their audiences, and those who occupy spaces in-between. Interactions between famous people are typically brokered through entertainment media or kept from public view; Twitter allows famous people to make their conversations publicly visible. This requires celebrity practitioners to navigate skillfully the performative friendships, feuds, and negotiations with others, all in front of their fans and the mainstream media. Twitter also disrupts the expectation of parasociality between the famous person and the fan. The study of celebrity culture has primarily focused on fans as separate from celebrities, but the ability of famous people to read and reply to fans has given rise to new sets of practices and interactions. Celebrity practitioners must harness this ability to maintain ongoing affiliations and connections with their fans, rather than seem uncaring or unavailable. Thus, Twitter creates a new expectation of intimacy. Rather than handing off fan management to an agent or fan club, celebrity practitioners must expend emotional labor maintaining a network of affective ties with their followers. Thus, even the famous must learn the techniques used by 'regular people' to gain status and attention online. Twitter demonstrates the transformation of 'celebrity' from a personal quality linked to fame to a set of practices that circulate through modern social media.

REFERENCES

Baym N (2000) *Tune In, Log On: Soaps, Fandom, and Online Community*. Thousand Oaks, CA: SAGE.

Becque S (2007) Big Damn Fans: Fan Campaigns of Firefly and Veronica Mars. Senior thesis, Departments of Sociology and Anthropology, Mount Holyoke College, MA, USA.

Beer D and Penfold-Mounce R (2009) Celebrity gossip and the new melodramatic imagination. *Sociological Research Online* 14(2–3). URL (consulted July 2009): http://www.socresonline.org.uk/14/2/2.html

Bendix R (1997) *In Search of Authenticity: The Formation of Folklore Studies*. Madison: University of Wisconsin Press.

Blumer H (1962) Society as symbolic interaction. In: Rose AM (ed.) *Human Behavior and Social Processes*. Boston, MA: Houghton Mifflin, 179–192.

Boorstin D (1961) *The Image: A Guide to Pseudo-Events in America*. New York: Athenaeum.

boyd d (2008) Taken out of Context: American Teen Sociality in Networked Publics. PhD dissertation, University of California, Berkeley.

boyd d, Golder S and Lotan, G (2010) Tweet, tweet, retweet: Conversational aspects of retweeting on Twitter. HICSS–43. IEEE: Kauai HI, 6 January.

Braudy L (1986) *The Frenzy of Renown: Fame and Its History*. New York: Oxford University Press.

Cheng VJ (2004) *Inauthentic: The Anxiety over Culture and Identity*. New Brunswick, NJ: Rutgers University Press.

Cohen N (2009) When stars Twitter, a ghost may be lurking, *The New York Times*, 26 March. URL (consulted December 2009): http://www.nytimes.com/2009/03/27/technology/internet/27twitter.html

Crawford K (2009) These foolish things: On intimacy and insignificance in mobile media. In: Goggin G and Hjorth L (eds) *Mobile Technologies: From Telecommunications to Media*. New York: Routledge, 252–265.

Donath J (1998) Identity and deception in the virtual community. In: Kollock P and Smith M (eds) *Communities in Cyberspace*. London: Routledge, 29–59.

Donath J (2007) Signals in social supernets. *Journal of Computer-Mediated Communication* 13(1). URL (consulted July 2009): http://jcmc.indiana.edu/vol13/issue1/donath.html

Dunbar RIM (1996) *Grooming, Gossip, and the Evolution of Language*. Cambridge, MA: Harvard University Press.

Dyer R (1986) *Heavenly Bodies: Film Stars and Society*. London: BFI Macmillan.

Ewan S (1989) *All Consuming Images: The Politics of Style in Contemporary Culture*. New York: Basic Books.

Feasey R (2008) Reading Heat: The meanings and pleasures of star fashions and celebrity gossip. *Continuum: Journal of Media & Cultural Studies* 22(5): 687–699.

Gamson J (1994) *Claims to Fame: Celebrity in Contemporary America*. Berkeley: University of California Press.

Giles DC (2002) Parasocial interaction: A review of the literature and a model for future research. *Media Psychology* 4(3): 279–305.

Goffman E (1959) *The Presentation of Self in Everyday Life*. Garden City, NY: Doubleday Anchor Books.

Golder S and Huberman BA (2006) Usage patterns of collaborative tagging systems. *Journal of Information Science* 32(2): 198–208.

Hearn A (2008) 'Meat, mask, burden' Probing the contours of the branded 'self'. *Journal of Consumer Culture* 8(2): 197–217.

Honeycutt C and Herring SC (2009) Beyond microblogging: Conversation and collaboration via Twitter. Proceedings of the Forty-Second Hawaii International Conference on System Sciences (HICSS–42). Los Alamitos, CA: IEEE Press.

Horton D and Wohl RR (1956) Mass communication and para-social interaction: Observations on intimacy at a distance. *Psychiatry* 19(3): 215–229.

Jensen J (1992) Fandom as pathology. In: Lewis L (ed.) *The Adoring Audience: Fan Culture and Popular Media*. New York: Routledge, 9–29.

Jenkins (1992) *Textual Poachers*. New York: Routledge.

Jenkins (2006a) *Convergence Culture*. New York: New York University Press.

Jenkins (2006b) *Fans, Bloggers, and Gamers: Exploring Participatory Culture*. New York: New York University Press.

Kachka B (2008) Have we reached the end of book publishing as we know it? *New York Magazine*, 14 September. URL (consulted July 2009): http://nymag.com/news/media/50279/

Kidzworld (2009) *Miley timeline: Nick Jonas and Miley Cyrus relationship 2009*. Kidzworld. com. URL (consulted June 2009): http://www .kidzworld.com/article/18635-niley-timeline-nick-jonas-and-mileycyrus-relation ship–2009

Knoppner S (2009) *Appetite for Self Destruction: The Spectacular Crash of the Record Industry in the Digital Age*. New York: Simon & Schuster.

Lair D, Sullivan K and Cheney G (2005) Marketization and the recasting of the professional self. *Management Communication Quarterly* 18(3): 307–343.

Lessig L (2004) *Free Culture*. London: Penguin Books.

Lowenthal L (1961) *The triumph of mass idols. Literature, Popular Culture, and Society*. Englewood Cliffs, NJ: Prentice-Hall, 109–140.

MandyMiley (2009). *Goodbye Twitter*. YouTube. com 9 October. URL (consulted October 2009): http://www.youtube.com/watch?v=2tSOTQPUQoU

Marshall PD (1997) *Celebrity and Power: Fame in Contemporary Culture*. Minneapolis: University of Minnesota Press.

Marshall PD (2006) *The Celebrity Culture Reader*. New York: Routledge.

Marwick A and boyd d (2010) I tweet honestly, I tweet passionately: Twitter users, context collapse, and the imagined audience. *New Media and Society*. Published online before print, 7 July.

McLeod K (2002) *The private ownership of people*. In: McLeod K Owning Culture, New York: Peter Lang, ch. 6.

Miller V (2008) New media, networking, and phatic culture, *Convergence* 14(4): 387–400.

Murray S (2004) 'Celebrating the story the way it is': Cultural studies, corporate media and the contested utility of fandom. Continuum 18(1): 7–25.

Nielsen Company, the (2009) Nielsens Social Media QuickTake: May 2009. *Nielsen.com*. URL (consulted June 2009): http://blog.nielsen .com/nielsenwire/wp-content/uploads/2009/06/ nielsen_pr_090619.pdf

Quantcast Corporation (2010). Twitter.com. *Quantcast.com*. URL (consulted March 2010): http://www.quantcast.com/twitter.com

Rahman M (2006) Is straight the new queer? David Beckham and the dialectics of celebrity. In: Marshall PD (ed.) *The Celebrity Culture Reader*. New York: Routledge, 223–228.

Rojek C (2001) *Celebrity*. Chicago, IL: Reaktion Books.

Schickel R (1985) *Intimate Strangers: The Culture of Celebrity*. New York: Doubleday.

Senft T (2008) *Camgirls: Celebrity and Community in the Age of Social Networks*. New York: Peter Lang.

Snyder D (2000) Webcam women: Life on your screen. In: Gauntlett D (ed.) *Web. Studies:*

Rewiring Media Studies for the Digital Age. London: Arnold, 68–73.

Sternbergh A (2004) Cruise control: The publicist behind the movie star. *Slate*, 5 April. URL (consulted December 2009): http://www.slate.com/id/2098277/

Strauss AL (1993) *Continual Permutations of Action.* New York: Aldine De Gruyter.

Thompson C (2008) Brave new world of digital intimacy. *The New York Times* 7 September. URL (consulted February 2009): http://www.nytimes.com/2008/09/07/magazine/07awareness-t.html? r=1

Thompson JB (1995). *The Media and Modernity.* Stanford, CA: Stanford University Press.

Trilling L (1972) *Sincerity and Authenticity.* Cambridge, MA: Harvard University Press.

Turner G (2004) *Understanding Celebrity.* Thousand Oaks, CA: SAGE.

Wallenstein A and Belloni M (2009) Hey, showbiz folks: Check your contract before your next tweet. *The Hollywood Reporter: THR Esquire*, 15 October. URL (consulted December 2009): http://www.thresq.com/2009/10/check-your-contract-before-your-next-tweet.html

63

IT'S ABOUT ETHICS IN GAMES JOURNALISM?

Gamergaters and Geek Masculinity

Andrea Braithwaite

At the end of August 2014, many online gaming communities erupted into vicious arguments—ostensibly about ethics in video game journalism, but more pointedly about gender, privilege, and gaming. #Gamergate has refocused popular discussions about gaming cultures into ones about gender, launched female game developers and critics into the public spotlight, and raised additional questions about social media as an avenue for gendered harassment and threats. #Gamergate highlights aspects of dominant gaming cultures that many of its participants already know: they skew toward straight White males, and calls to recognize the full breadth of who plays games are met with hostility from "real" gamers. As games become an increasingly popular pastime across demographic categories, conversations about who counts as a gamer increase—in number, volume, and, often, negative tone. #Gamergate provides one perspective on the cultural fissures around this redefinition.

When tracking #Gamergate discussions across social media platforms, we see Gamergaters on a crusade to save an innocuous male pastime from killjoy critics. Pejoratively referred to as social justice warriors (SJWs), Gamergaters discipline and discredit these critics as the wrong kind of women, who need to be put back in their place. Gamergaters situate themselves as the "real" victims, oppressed by calls for diversity and at risk of losing "their" games to more inclusive ones. Thus, #Gamergate is about more than games: as a set of anxieties, rhetorical strategies, and targeted hate campaigns, #Gamergate is an articulation of technology, privilege, and power.

GAMING AND GENDER

Historically, game companies have imagined an audience filled with young, White, heterosexual males. Kline, Dyer-Witheford, and de Peuter (2003) describe how "the young male niche . . . was perceived as the key to dominance in the whole business," and game companies have tended to court this demographic (p. 250). This industry construction of "gamer" is often reflected in the content of games themselves. Many games center on powerful White male protagonists, with women as damsels in distress or sexualized background decorations (Cassell & Jenkins, 2000; Kennedy, 2002; Sarkeesian, 2013). Non-White characters are frequently villains or obstacles, if they exist at all (Brock, 2011, Higgin, 2009). These patterns contribute to the dominant image of "gamer" as a White male, for the "lack of portrayals of marginalized groups in video games is often tied to the fact that the industry rarely recognizes members of these groups as gamers" (Shaw, 2011, p. 28).

Yet recent research suggests that gaming is a widespread activity. The Entertainment Software Association (ESA) notes that 42% of Americans regularly play video games, their average age is 35, and 44% of them are female (ESA, 2015). Even with such popularity, "gaming publics remain

From Braithwaite, A., (2016). It's About Ethics in Games Journalism? Gamergaters and Geek Masculinity, *Social Media and Society*, 2 (4).

a contentious area where identity, as viewed from the outside, is continually negotiated and bounded by the many groups which participate within the technological space" (Salter & Blodgett, 2012, p. 413). On discussion boards like Reddit and in the comments sections for YouTube videos, participants haggle over what the label "gamer" really means and who can use it. . . . a gamer is not just someone who plays games, and someone who plays games is not automatically a gamer. Rather, "being a gamer is defined in relation to dominant discourses about who plays games, the deployment of subcultural capital, the context in which players find themselves, and who are the subjects of game texts" (Shaw, 2013, para 1; see also Shaw, 2014).

These are all shifting categories. The ESA report, for instance, illustrates the gap between the image and reality of who plays games, a reality that cannot be easily read off the games themselves. Fans, critics, and players engage in often-contentious debates about these texts. Calls for different kinds of content reveal the importance of representation and the reluctance of many players to critically confront their games:

> [P]osters who want to engage in sociopolitical discussions face an up-hill battle. The forum may overwhelmingly reject the idea that sociopolitical issues are valid concerns when it comes to entertainment and delegitimize posters who raise such concerns by launching ad-hominem attacks and characterizing them as not true video game fans. (McKernan, 2015, p. 245)

Attempts to intervene in privileged discourses of gamer identity, or to draw attention to games' often limited representations, regularly return sexist, racist, and homophobic slurs (Gray, 2014). This is not to suggest that everyone who plays games, participates in, or even lurks on gaming-oriented social media and websites is racist, sexist, or homophobic. Yet, as many have noted, such "toxic technocultures . . . are enabled and propagated through sociotechnical networks such as Reddit, 4chan, Twitter, and online gaming" (Massanari, 2015, p. 5; see also Braithwaite, 2014; Condis, 2014; McKernan, 2015; Nakamura, 2013a,

2013b; Salter & Blodgett, 2012). #Gamergate is another instance of social media's ability to make misogyny public.

Concretely measuring the size of a movement like #Gamergate is challenging, since it is easy for a single user to create multiple anonymous accounts on Twitter, Tumblr, Reddit, and 4chan. Some suggest #Gamergate comprised approximately 10,000 participants, based on the number of active subscriptions to key #Gamergate sites . . . (devomet, in FEMAcampcounselor, 2014), or the increased number of Twitter followers for vocal #Gamergate advocates ("So just how popular is #GamerGate?," 2014). The largest estimate, of 400,000, is based on the number of views for the most popular #Gamergate YouTube videos and is admittedly "super generous" (De La Cruz, 2015, sec. 4b) since it cannot account for potential multiple views by a single person. On social media, however, prominence is not only a matter of size but also a matter of being heard and of who hears you. . . . Increasingly, being heard means being hateful, as our "technologies and cultures of social media interpellate particular subject-positions, normalizing behaviours that would seem inappropriate in other contexts" (Shepherd et al., 2015, p. 3).

#Gamergate, notably, is heard not only by gamers but also by mainstream press. Recounted in high-profile outlets like *The New York Times* (Wingfield, 2014a), *Rolling Stone* (Collins, 2014), and *The Colbert Report* (Comedy Central, 2014), #Gamergate brings discussions about gaming cultures and gamer identity to the forefront of cultural commentary. Much of this attention zeroes in on #Gamergate's treatment of women, emphasizing how "gamer" is generally contingent upon gender. Such misogyny is a key component in understanding Gamergater as an iteration of geek masculinity. Geek masculinity is a gender identity characterized in part by "a strong interest in technology and playing computer games. . . . These performances of expertise, skill, and knowledge are not only sources of social connection and pleasure, but also work as important markers for inclusion and exclusion" (Taylor, 2012, p. 111; see also Dunbar-Hester, 2008; Kendall, 2011). Like other gender identities, geek masculinity is relational:

it is understood relative to forms of femininity as well as to hegemonic masculinity.

. . . Geek masculinity expresses a different configuration of masculinity, incorporating some elements of hegemonic masculinity (such as judgment and mastery) while often renouncing others (such as sporting or athletic cultures) (Taylor, 2012). Formed and re-formed, geek masculinity is a way of *doing* gender in a specific situation and for a specific end (Connell, 1995/2005; see also Butler, 1990).

In this situation, geek masculinity is conditioned by practices that have historically equated technological access and prowess with masculinity (Wacjman, 1991), as well as popular perceptions that gaming is a "guy thing" (Burrill, 2008; Cassell & Jenkins, 2000). At the same time, geek masculinity also disavows stereotypically masculine interests in favor of technology and gaming, meaning "those who identify with geek culture often feel marginal, as their interests are marked by the dominant culture as odd or weird" (Massanari, 2015, p. 4). For the gaming industry, however, this dedicated male audience has been lucrative and courted nearly exclusively during the industry's early years (Cassell & Jenkins, 2000; Kline et al., 2003). Gamergaters are working to maintain the dominance of this geek masculinity in gaming, as its position is challenged by SJWs' arguments for equality and inclusivity.

Such arguments illustrate how the gaming industry is growing and changing. This is due in part to the increasing popularity of "casual" games like *Candy Crush* and *Farmville,* which are "easy to learn to play, fit well with a large number of players and work in many different situations" (Juul, 2010, p. 5). Often associated with women and femininity (Anable, 2013; Juul, 2010; Taylor, 2012), these games are helping redefine what counts as gaming and impacts

> who is able to lay claim to titles like "fan" or "gamer" . . . what happens when new users lay claim to those titles, and how some fans are reacting to the loss of their privileged relationships with content producers. (Condis, 2014, p. 199)

We can see some of these reactions in #Gamergate's reliance on discourses of battle, exclusion, and victimization.

#GAMERGATE AND CRITICAL DISCOURSE ANALYSIS

. . . While #Gamergate discussions often contain vastly different stances, the consistent use of a single hashtag encourages us to treat these differences in concert with each other (Chess & Shaw, 2015). I offer one way of understanding #Gamergate: as a misogynist claim to games and gamer identity. . . .

To do so, I entered #Gamergate discourse by looking at sites like Reddit, 4chan, 8chan, Tumblr, Twitter, and YouTube, where #Gamergate discussions are most active. . . .

In particular, I focused on instances of aggressive, hateful discourse that are increasingly "natural" and "quite acceptable" online (see also Gray, 2014; Shepherd et al., 2015). I paid specific attention to how these discourses invoke gender since one of the primary ways #Gamergate has been characterized by participants and the popular press is as an attack on women (Collins, 2014; Dewey, 2014; Hathaway, 2014; Wingfield, 2014a). I discovered that #Gamergate discussions which focus on gender rely on three particular rhetorical figures and storytelling strategies (van Dijk, 1993, p. 264): crusader imagery, disciplining unruly female voices, and claims that "real"— that is, male—gamers are the actual victims of #Gamergate. . . .

THE #GAMERGATE CRUSADE

Accounts chronicling #Gamergate usually point to the 16 August 2014 release of "The Zoe Post" as its beginning (Hathaway, 2014; Kain, 2014). Written by Eron Gjoni (2014), this blog entry details the messy and convoluted end of his romantic relationship with independent game designer Zoe Quinn, who had recently released a free game called *Depression Quest.* Gjoni accuses Quinn of cheating on him with, among others, a journalist from the gaming site *Kotaku.* The implication that Quinn had traded sex for a favorable review circulated on well-trafficked forums like Reddit and 4chan, despite evidence to the contrary (Totilo, 2014). When it seemed like no prominent gaming news sites were going to report on Gjoni's intensely personal missive, these discussions turned into declarations of corruption in games journalism.

Actor Adam Baldwin tweeted his concern about the situation, tagged it #Gamergate, and the hashtag stuck.

#Gamergate's stated purpose—to advocate for more transparent and ethical games journalism—was overshadowed by a barrage of largely negative attention directed at Quinn, Brianna Wu (a game developer), and Anita Sarkeesian (a feminist pop culture vlogger who had already received rape and death threats for her Tropes vs Women in Video Games series; Sarkeesian, 2012). After following the #Gamergate hashtag from 1 September to 23 October 2014, *Newsweek* concluded that "GamerGaters cares less about ethics and more about harassing women," based on a significant discrepancy between the number and nature of tweets aimed at critics like Wu and Sarkeesian, and those directed toward game journalists (Wofford, 2014, para 13).

Twitter is one of many social media spaces Gamergaters use. On YouTube, for instance, the video "#GamerGate: For Those Who Stand and Fight" (PowerIndustry, 2014) captures the bombastic tone of much #Gamergate rhetoric. Nearly 9 min long, the video features black-and-white gameplay footage from a variety of first-person shooters and wartime games, intercut with website headlines and stills from Sarkeesian's Tropes vs Women series. A calm male voice-over establishes a moral trajectory for Gamergaters, scripting them as dauntless crusaders in a corrupt, uncaring world:

> The shield of deception and lies has never once stopped even the weakest parry from the sword of truth. For it is truth that has driven back the darkness of the primordial age. It has turned huts to nations and nations to civilizations. It has pumped electricity into your home and put the sun as the centre of the solar system. It has brought the world closer to becoming the sons of God we were meant to be. (PowerIndustry, 2014)

Here, Gamergaters have a manifest destiny. The video envisions #Gamergate as a battle between forces of darkness and light, in which Gamergaters fight to preserve the purity and goodness of games. Gamergaters' references to war create a "narrative framing to set themselves as 'the good guys'" on a quest for truth (Salter & Blodgett, 2012). This fervor recurs across social media networks. For example, a resource thread

for Gamergaters on 4chan's /v/ (video games) board is titled "World War /v/ Part 10" (2014). Similarly, when #Gamergate-supported group The Fine Young Capitalists (2014) resolved a dispute with frequent #Gamergate target Zoe Quinn, they titled the resolution "Peace Treaty." Such binary logic is a typical tactic on social media, and Gamergaters employ it here to script #Gamergate as a "zero-sum struggle—justified as a moral struggle—against (perceived) threats" (Srauy, in Shepherd et al., 2015, p. 4).

8chan posters draw upon this same imagery in a thread about Sarkeesian's 29 October 2014 appearance on *The Colbert Report.* Speaking as one soldier to many more, one commenter posts, "The war is still there for you in the mornin' soldier. Rest when you can, fight when you must, but always, always keep your head in the game" (cited in Futrelle, 2014c, para 20).

The reminder to "keep your head in the game" anchors Gamergaters' dominance in video games. Gamergaters see themselves at distinct advantage, their victory guaranteed by their gaming expertise. Redditor Piroko (2014) makes this explicit in "EVE Online as a model for the Culture War." Referencing the sandbox multiplayer game (MMO) *EVE Online,* Piroko (2014) says,

> Wars between rival alliances fighting in EVE Online, and the conflict between gamers and social justice warriors, are very similar. They are both culture wars, and are won or lost not by destroying your opponent's assets, but by driving your opponent to fail cascade.

Piroko positions #Gamergate as a war game and holds up the large-scale assaults in *EVE Online* as a strategic model for Gamergaters. As commenter zabchob says, "Great post, thanks for this. Eve PVP really does demonstrate just how formidable gamers can be as opponents, and how a common identity can really strengthen resolve" (in Piroko, 2014). In this way, Gamergater becomes a collective identity by invoking typical gaming experiences, as games are used as both a justification and a blueprint for behavior.

The idea of being at war colors much of #Gamergate rhetoric. "The projection of this heroic struggle into the subtext of the community's discourse is reflected in the rhetoric of villains and enmity, of outsiders and insiders," and of

Gamergaters themselves as mythic heroes (Salter & Blodgett, 2012, p. 402). The role of champion is also combined with that of consumer. Gamergater Oliver Campbell's tweets during 2015's E3 convention effectively illustrate this conflation. He sets up #Gamergate as a learning moment for game developers: "Developers, I want you to look at something: #gamergate is made of gamers; we are hype as FUCK for this E3. Anti-GG is . . . well, look." As he explains, Gamergaters are crusaders *because* they are consumers:

> Right now, in our industry, we have those who are trying to tear it apart for personal gain. And your customers are fighting to PROTECT YOU.
>
> Those same customers who gave you thunderous applause today
>
> . . . have spent almost a year of their lives fighting to protect you. (Campbell, 2015)

DISCIPLINING THE ENEMY

#Gamergate's status as a pitched battle between crusaders and SJWs relies on clearly defined boundaries: between Gamergaters and agitators, between customers and critics. In #Gamergate, gamers don't criticize games, and critics don't play them: "Who do you make games for? Do you make them for the perpetually and chronically offended? Or do you make games for gamers?" (Campbell, 2015). This exclusionary logic is central to social media, as a "toxic technoculture often relies [on] an Othering of those perceived as outside the culture" (Massanari, 2015, p. 5). A war game needs enemies to defeat, and #Gamergate has a range of strategies for discrediting its detractors.

Some of these directly invoke past wartime propaganda. Gamergaters have repurposed Nazi-era anti-Semitism, going after Sarkeesian on Twitter with slurs like "Jewkeesian" (McCormack, 2014). Gamergaters also create caricatures of Sarkeesian as the avaricious Jew, reproducing past forms of dehumanization to legitimize #Gamergate's attacks (Nyberg, 2014; Savannah, 2014). Other tactics work similarly. In a post on the KotakuInAction subreddit, Luzarius (2015) offers a method for dealing with Sarkeesian: "Let's praise her when she says something right and criticize her when she says something only a non-gamer

with an agenda would say." This rhetoric of obedience training frames critics as willful and stubborn, in need of "one man who is a real gamer to show her the ropes and she'll tone down her ways" (Luzarius, 2015).

Game developer Brianna Wu also receives dismissive attacks. Many on 8chan, for instance, target her appearance: "Stop calling that rotten faggot a she, you are insulting every real woman in existence comparing them to that creature" ("Fuck Her," 2015, no. 640646). Gendered pronouns and phrases are changed from her to him, from "woman-splain" to "freak-splain," because "you only get to be called She if you can pass, this one cannot, whats his real name again?" ("Fuck Her," 2015, no. 640982). Here, #Gamergaters attempt to discredit Wu based on her self-presentation. By not meeting their ideals of sexual attractiveness and availability, Wu must be lying about her gender; if Wu is lying about her gender, then anything else she says cannot be taken seriously. These comments are meant to discipline critics, not only because Sarkeesian and Wu are vocal proponents of improving games and gaming environments but also because they are women. As Salter and Blodgett (2012) note, "Women within the hardcore gaming public are given tightly bound roles to play and punished for stepping outside them" (p. 411). Women can only be one of three things: sex objects, invisible, or the enemy (Salter & Blodgett, 2012). Since Sarkeesian and Wu do not promote themselves as sex objects and refuse to remain silent or invisible, they *must* be the enemy.

For many Gamergaters, evaluating women's sexual behavior takes precedence over critiquing ethical transgressions in games journalism: "Understandably, the focus was kept on her [Zoe Quinn] for awhile because even though the target should have always been Kotaku/Grayson, she's a superhumanly awful whore and everyone was disgusted by her" ("#GamerGate—FLOOD #PAX," 2014, no. 260980887).

4chan Internet Relay Chat (IRC) logs dated shortly after the release of Gjoni's "The Zoe Post" illustrate Gamergaters' preoccupation with policing female sexuality:

> The 4channers express their hatred and disgust towards her; they express their glee at the thought of ruining her career; they fantasize about her being raped and killed. . . . And then

there is the ongoing discussion of her vagina, described variously as "wide," large enough to "fit 12 dicks at once" and "a festering cheese-filled vagina" that leaves "a trail of cunt slime" wherever she goes. (Futrelle, 2014d, paras 15 and 18)

In #Gamergate, women's primary value lies in service of a domineering, aggressive masculinity. For example, in 8chan's "Women of Gamergate thread!" (2015), commenters post pictures of women associated with #Gamergate "to brighten our spirits . . . SO show off those tits, asses, vagina's" (no. 213587). Some are panned based on appearance: "why are her breasts sagging, fucking disgusting" (no. 221844). . . . A woman's worth lies in her desirability, and not her interest in a shared pastime. Sex is a form of discipline, administered by a real man to maintain the appropriate pattern of gender relations:

I feel like I would probably fuck Zoe. But not out of a loving sense of sexual attraction. More of that "hate fuck" sense where you just want to assert your dominance as a male on her, a primal savagery. (EronLovesZoe, cited in Futrelle, 2014d, para 35)

The crowdsourced cartoon figure Vivian James also illustrates Gamergaters' perception of "right" and "wrong" women. Born from the video game subreddit (/v/) to support The Fine Young Capitalists' game development project, Vivian James is drawn as a pale redhead, clad in jeans and a striped hoodie, and 4chan's clover pinned in her hair (DrMobius, 2014). "Low-affect" and "loves video games," Vivian James is meant to somehow mitigate accusations that #Gamergate is misogynistic (DrMobius, 2014). As a fictional female gamer, however, her actions and opinions are determined entirely by her creators. In some instances, Vivian James represents broader #Gamergate themes: a depiction of her as the goddess of war greets visitors to The Fine Young Capitalist's website, and an image of her hollering "Get off your high horse, bitch!" appears frequently on Twitter and Tumblr.

In others, Vivian James is, like the other women of #Gamergate, considered solely as a sex object. 8chan posters swap images of Vivian James in sexually suggestive poses ("Mods Are Asleep," 2015): her pants half-down; taking off her hoodie to reveal her bra; posing like a pin-up model in underwear and knee-high socks; playing video games in nothing but lingerie. Many are more explicit: reclining naked with legs spread; having sex with another woman; masturbating with a console controller; being aggressively penetrated by the male cartoon figure used to represent 4chan—Vivian James is calling him Daddy, while he yells "DON'T CUM SO FAST YOU FUCKIN' CASUAL."

Spaces like 8chan offer Gamergaters the opportunity to participate in a discourse that reduces women, both real and fictional, to sex objects. When the shape of a woman's breasts is enough reason to ignore her, the possibilities for generating a thoughtful conversation are greatly diminished. These tactics turn "the seemingly social spaces of Web 2.0 into tools for the exclusion and perpetuation of a male-dominated gaming social public" (Salter & Blodgett, 2012, p. 402).

#GAMERGATE'S REAL VICTIMS

Designed to demonstrate that they have been unfairly labeled misogynists, Vivian James is part of Gamergaters' argument that they are the real victims. Gamergaters see themselves as besieged by SJWs whose critiques are personal and political, and part of an insidious plot to destroy gaming entirely. Gamergaters "refuse to standby idly while the emphasis in gaming is taken away from quality and focused on social politics" ("An Open Letter," 2014). As Condis (2014) incisively notes, "'ideology' or 'politics' is always the label given to what *someone else* cares about" (p. 207). SJWs are talking about ideology, while *real* gamers are talking about games.

Games are thus only the beginning, a culture war's early salvo from which Gamergaters have the most to lose. Chess and Shaw (2015) argue that such logic can be more fully grasped "if we look at it in term of a combination of *perceived* persecution and an examination of the anxieties that a conspiracy is articulating" (p. 217). Some Gamergaters are haunted, for instance, by the specter of a gaming press complicit in the SJW agenda. This sentiment is a response to the publication of a handful of opinion pieces about the current state of gaming cultures and communities, with titles like "We might be witnessing the 'death of an identity'" (Plunkett, 2014), "The end of gamers" (Golding, 2014), and "'Gamers' don't have to be your audience. 'Gamers' are over" (Alexander, 2014). These, and other similar articles, draw attention to the same kind of information contained in the ESA (2015) report: video games are increasingly popular and are being played by a diverse range of people. Ergo, the columnists contend, the label "gamer," and the cultures around it, should adapt in turn. Gamergaters point to the stereotype of "lonely basement kids" and "people who know so little about how human social interaction and professional life works" as evidence that gamers have been maligned and belittled for decades (Alexander, 2014, paras 3 and 12). At the same time, "gamer" is a point of shared history, solidarity, and often gender identity; predictions of its demise are taken personally: "By having male spaces where they can feel safe, they don't feel like their refuge is under attack. Gaming is one of those refuges. Instead you've got feminists storming the castle walls and poking these guys with sticks" (DaNiceGuy, cited in Futrelle, 2014b, para 1).

"Gamer" is thus a protective barrier. For Gamergaters, more diverse and inclusive games can only come at the expense of their own sense of identity. This feels less like an industry's evolution and more like an attack:

> yes i may be an evil cis gendered "white" male, however through out my earlier life i was the outsider, the person to, while not out right shun, just not to be interacted with. It wasnt until, for the most part, i was able to get a constant access to the internet was i able to feel like i belong anywhere. even to this day due to the earlier outcasting do i have trouble connecting to anyone. Gaming/In ernet has let me belong, not feel so alone and fuck these people for demonizing it and me over and over and over again. (CynicCorvus in gekkozorz, 2015)

In seeing themselves as the real victims, Gamergaters assume moral superiority. Their aggressive and misogynistic claims circulate on social media as an expression of this position, "disguis[ing] hate as a moral campaign against a perceived immoral threat" (Srauy, in Shepherd et al., 2015, p. 5). Gamergaters' feelings of victimization also highlight the close ties between gamer as a gendered

identity and gamer as a consumer category. As many comments suggest, "there is a genuine sense of loss, watching games become mainstream and accessible" (Juul, 2010, p. 151). This loss is bound up with geek masculinity so that arguments for inclusivity are understood as attacks on men:

> Have you not noticed? GAMER is a proxy word for MEN. They want to eradicate GAMER culture? Yeah, guess who that really means. The SJws won't be happy until male culture as we know it has vanished, consigned to the aether like a memory or a fleeting moment of "what could have been." (fingerjesus, cited in Futrelle, 2014a, para 7)

In some respects, Gamergaters are correct. Large video games companies have long benefitted from targeting young White males (Cassell & Jenkins, 2000; Kline et al., 2003).

Now, the

> rage we see expressed by threatened individuals and groups seems to be based on at least two factors—sexist (as well as racist, homophobic and ageist) beliefs about the abilities and proper place of female players, and fears about the changing nature of the game industry. (Consalvo, 2012, para 8; see also Gray, 2014)

Expanding the range of audible consumer voices means capturing more effectively the types of games being played and the kinds of people who play them. Gamergaters see this as betrayal. As one Voat commenter says,

> it feels like I'm running out of places to go . . . gaming is mine
>   . . . it is the single hobby that takes precedent above all my other hobbies, even reading. I would sooner die than lost this bastion of nerddom. (AustNerevar in mnemosyne-0000, 2015)

The historically privileged position "gamer" has in relation to the gaming industry been internalized as a right by Gamergaters who identify with the term, and efforts to broaden the category are an incursion into the proper order of things.

Yet identifying how men have been favored as a demographic is not victimization. Making the conceptual leap from one to the other means ignoring the power imbalances the gaming industry has grown up with: "It is difficult to understand those involved in the GamerGate movement as 'persecuted'—the movement is inhabited by people who, by and large, are representations of the power structures that have been built into gaming culture for decades" (Chess & Shaw, 2015, p. 216). The language of privilege, rights, and loss indicates that, at its core, #Gamergate is about power. Gamergaters' threats to boycott games and companies—dubbed Operation Disrespectful Nod (Dewey, 2014)—demonstrate that video games are most useful as a staging point in a social media struggle over whose voices should be heard.

THE FUTURES OF ONLINE HARASSMENT

At the end of September 2014, Intel pulled its ads from game development news site *Gamasutra*, in response to Gamergaters' campaign to have Leigh Alexander's (2014) "'Gamers' are over" opinion piece read as bullying (Wingfield, 2014b). Despite their anxieties, Gamergaters—as the self-proclaimed vanguard of typical gamers—remain a visible and powerful category of consumers. Their intimidation tactics also take the form of threats against some of the most vocal female critics in gaming. For example, Anita Sarkeesian canceled a talk at Utah State University in October 2014 after the school received an email claiming, "If you do not cancel her talk, a Montreal Massacre style attack will be carried out against the attendees, as well as students and staff at the nearby Women's Center" (Anon., quoted in Neugebauer, 2014). The invocation of the Montreal Massacre is telling, as it suggests these gendered anxieties persist beyond social media and gaming.

#Gamergate is a compelling and often frightening point on a continuum of male behavior Michael Kimmel (2013) calls an "aggrieved entitlement" to use violence to reclaim privileges seen as rightfully belonging to men. #Gamergate's

articulation across social media gives us a window into how Gamergaters' grievances take shape via the righteous rhetoric of a crusade, the objectification and exclusion of women, and the argument that gamer masculinity itself is under siege. Such sentiments stick to #Gamergate, as it relies on social media as spaces in which aggressive, sexualized attacks against women are seen as reasonable, even moral modes of argumentation.

The "discursive environments of sexism, racism, and homophobia deserve critical attention because they are central to games culture," and in #Gamergate these environments are leveraged to create an atmosphere of fear and paranoia among women who speak out (Nakamura, 2013b, p. 4; see also Gray, 2014). #Gamergate claims to be rooted in a desire for more ethical and transparent games journalism. . . . However, the repeated use of the #Gamergate hashtag in misogynistic performances of geek masculinity makes such a stance more difficult to see.

Instead, #Gamergate appears to be most adept at using social media to produce and reproduce reactionary narratives about gender, technology, privilege, and power. These sentiments move quickly across social media platforms, reinforcing the premise that women are not welcome—in gaming, or online. In many ways, #Gamergate is simply Internet business as usual; much of the vitriol chronicled here is routinely found in other virtual places. Yet, and importantly, #Gamergate made this kind of "ordinary" harassment newsworthy, calling our collective attention to the sustained abuse many people endure in order to participate in online spaces. By bringing "gamer" out of the basement and into the light, we can see more clearly the challenges we face as we work toward more inclusive communities.

REFERENCES

Alexander, L. (2014, August 28). "Gamers" don't have to be your audience: "Gamers" are over. Gamasutra. Retrieved from http://www.gamasutra.com/view/news/224400/Gamers_dont_have_to_be_your_audience_Gamers_are_over

Anable, A. (2013). Casual games, time management, and the work of affect. Ada 2. Retrieved from http://adanewmedia. org/2013/06/issue2-anable/

Braithwaite, A. (2014). "Seriously, get out": Feminists on the forums and the war(craft) on women. *New Media & Society* 16, 703–718.

Brock, A. (2011). "When keeping it real goes wrong": Resident Evil 5, racial representation, and gamers. *Games and Culture* 6, 429–452.

Burrill, D. A. (2008). *Die tryin': Videogames, masculinity, culture.* New York, NY: Peter Lang.

Butler, J. (1990). Gender trouble: Feminism and the subversion of identity. New York, NY: Routledge.

Campbell, O. (2015, June 16-18). [Tweets]. Retrieved from http://gamergate-news.tumblr.com/image/121736262135

Cassell, J., & Jenkins, H. (Eds.). (2000). *From Barbie to Mortal Kombat: Gender and computer games.* Cambridge, MA: MIT Press.

Chess, S., & Shaw, A. (2015). A conspiracy of fishes, or, how we learned to stop worrying about #GamerGate and embrace hegemonic masculinity. *Journal of Broadcasting and Electronic Media* 59, 208–220.

Collins, S. T. (2014, October 17). Anita Sarkeesian on GamerGate: "We have a problem and we're going to fix this." *Rolling Stone.* Retrieved from https://www.rollingstone.com/culture/features/anita-sarkeesian-gamergate-interview-20141017

Comedy Central. (2014, October 30). The Colbert report—Gamergate—Anita Sarkeesian. YouTube [Video]. Retrieved from https://www.youtube.com/watch? v=9L_Wmeg70TU

Condis, M. (2014). No homosexuals in Star Wars? Bioware, "gamer" identity, and the politics of privilege in a convergence culture. *Convergence* 21, 198–212.

Connell, R. W. (2005). *Masculinities* (2nd ed.). Berkeley: University of California Press. (Original work published 1995)

Consalvo, M. (2012). Confronting toxic gamer culture: A challenge for feminist game studies scholars. Ada 1. Retrieved from http://adanewmedia.org/2012/11/issue1-consalvo/

De La Cruz, L. (2015, August 17). Almost no one sided with #GamerGate. Superheroes in Racecars. Retrieved from http://superheroesinracecars.com/2015/08/17/almost-no-one-sided-with-gamergate/

Dewey, C. (2014, October 20). Inside Gamergate's (successful) attack on the media. *The Washington Post.* Retrieved from http://www.washingtonpost.com/news/the-intersect/wp/2014/10/20/inside-gamergates-successful-attack-on-the-media/

DrMobius. (2014). The birth of Vivian James [Image]. Retrieved from http://imgur.com/gallery/iGYhtyX

Dunbar-Hester, C. (2008). Geeks, meta-geeks, and gender trouble: Activism, identity, and low-power FM radio. *Social Studies of Science* 38, 201–232.

Entertainment Software Association. (2015). Essential facts about the computer and video game industry. Retrieved from http://www.theesa.com/wp-content/uploads/2015/04/ESA-Essential-Facts-2015.pdf

FEMAcampcounselor. (2014, October 12). How popular is gamergate, really? Reddit [Discussion]. Retrieved from https://www. reddit.com/r/GamerGhazi/comments/2j23qd/

The Fine Young Capitalists. (2014, September). Peace treaty [Archived webpage]. Retrieved from https://web.archive.org/web/20140903000841/http://www.thefineyoungcapitalists. com/PeaceTreaty

Fuck her—scum meme? (2015, March 28). 8chan [Discussion]. Archived at https://web.archive.org/web/20150330005726/ http://8ch.net/gg/res/640606.html

Futrelle, D. (2014a, September 21). Men's Rightsers take up arms against the video game destroyers. And Kroger supermarkets. Never give up! Never surrender! Wehuntedthemammoth. Retrieved from http://wehuntedthemammoth.com/2014/09/21/mens-rightsers-take-up-arms-against-the-vidya-game-destroyers-never-give-up-never-surrender-and-dont-shop-at-kroger/

Futrelle, D. (2014b, October 16). The top four Men's Rightsiest things said about the recent threats against Anita Sarkeesian. Wehuntedthemammoth. Retrieved from http://wehuntedthemammoth.com/2014/10/16/the-top-four-mens-rightsiest-things-said-about-the-recent-threats-against-anita-sarkeesian/

Futrelle, D. (2014c, October 30). The top 22 most ridiculous things said by 8channers about Anita Sarkeesian's appearance on the *Colbert Report*. Wehuntedthemammoth. Retrieved from http://wehuntedthemammoth.com/2014/10/30/the-top-22-most-ridiculous-things-said-by-8channers-about-anita-sarkeesians-appearance-on-the-colbert-report/

Futrelle, D. (2014d, September 8). Zoe Quinn's screenshots of 4chan'sdirtytrickswerejusttheapp etizer. Here'sthefirstcourse of the dinner, directly from the IRC log. Wehuntedthemammoth. Retrieved from http://wehuntedthemammoth.com/2014/09/08/zoe-quinns-screenshots-of-4chans-dirty-tricks-were-just-the-appetizer-heres-the-first-course-of-the-dinner-directly-from-the-irc-log/

#GamerGate—FLOOD#PAX#PAZ2014 #PAXPRIME #Gamergate. (2014, August 31). 4chan [Discussion]. Retrieved from https://archive.moe/v/thread/260976252/#q260980887

gekkozorz. (2015, June 29). DiGRA is back again, this time under hashtag #digraa. Let them know what you really think. Reddit [Discussion]. Retrieved from http://www.reddit.com/r/KotakuIn Action/comments/3b16tu/digra_is_back_again_this-time_under_hashtag/

Gjoni, E. (2014, September 12). The Zoe post. Retrieved from https://thezoepost.wordpress.com/

Golding, D. (2014, August 28). The end of gamers [Tumblr]. Retrieved from http://dangolding.tum-blr.com/post/95985875943/the-end-of-gamers

Gray, K. (2014). Race, gender, and deviance in Xbox Live: Theoretical perspectives from the virtual margins. New York, NY: Routledge.

Hathaway, J. (2014, October 10). What is Gamergate, and why? An explainer for non-geeks. Gawker. Retrieved from http://gawker.com/what-is-gamergate-and-why-an-explainer-for-non-geeks-1642909080

Higgin, T. (2009). Blackless fantasy: The disappearance of race in massively multiplayer online role-playing games. Games and Culture 4, 3–26.

Juul, J. (2010). A casual revolution: Reinventing video games and their players. Cambridge, MA: MIT Press.

Kain, E. (2014, September 4). GamerGate: A closer look at the controversy sweeping video games. Forbes. Retrieved from http://www.forbes.com/sites/erikkain/2014/09/04/gamergate-a-closer-look-at-the-controversy-sweeping-video-games/

Kendall, L. (2011). "White and nerdy": Computers, race, and the nerd stereotype. The Journal of Popular Culture 44, 505–524.

Kennedy, H. W. (2002). Lara Croft: Feminist icon or cyberbimbo? On the limits of textual analysis. Game Studies, 2(2). Retrieved from http://www.gamestudies.org/0202/kennedy/

Kimmel, M. (2013). Angry white men: American masculinity at the end of an era. New York, NY: Nation Books.

Kline, S., Dyer-Witheford, N., & de Peuter, G. (2003). Digital play: The interaction of technology, culture, and marketing. Montreal, Quebec, Canada: McGill-Queen's University Press.

Luzarius. (2015, June 17). Do feminists want immersion and equality OR censorship in gaming? Reddit [Discussion]. Retrieved from http://www.reddit.com/r/KotakuInAction/comments/3a9623/discussion_do_feminists_want_immersion_and/

Massanari, A. (2015). #Gamergate and the Fappening: How Reddit's algorithm, governance, and culture support toxic technocultures. New Media & Society. Advance online publication. doi:10.1177/1461444815608807

McCormack, N. [noahmccormack]. (2014, October 20). Someone is going to write a book with a chapter titled "Based Mom vs Jewkessian." The book will be very good or very bad [Tweet]. Retrieved from https://twitter.com/noahmccormack/sta-tus/524330936951787521

McKernan, B. (2015). The meaning of a game: Stereotypes, video game commentary and colour-blind racism. American Journal of Cultural Sociology 3, 224–253.

mnemosyne-0000. (2015, June 28). You are not sexist. You are not a monster. I think more people need telling this. Voat [Discussion]. Retrieved from https://voat.co/v/KotakuInAction/comments/178517

Mods are asleep, post Vivian! (2015, March 24). 8chan [Discussion]. Retrieved from https://web.archive.org/web/20151111072955/ http://8ch.net/gg/res/632377.html

Nakamura, L. (2013a, December 10). Glitch racism: Networks as actors within vernacular internet theory. Culture Digitally. Retrieved from http://culturedigitally.org/2013/12/glitch-racism-networks-as-actors-within-vernacular-internet-theory/

Nakamura, L. (2013b). "It's a nigger in here! Kill the nigger!": User-generated media campaigns against racism, sexism, and homophobia in digital games. In K. Gates (Ed.), *The international encyclopedia of media studies*. Retrieved from https://lnakamur.files.wordpress.com/2013/04/nakamura-encyclope-dia-of-media-studies-media-futures.pdf

Neugebauer, C. (2014, October 15). Terror threat against feminist Anita Sarkeesian at USU. *Standard Examiner*. Retrieved from http://www.standard.net/Police/2014/10/14/Utah-State-University-student-threatens-act-of-terror-if-feminist.html

Nyberg, S. [srhbutts]. (2014, October 31). "We're inclusive and accepting!" says #gamergate, before drawing racist caricatures of women they dislike [Tweet]. Retrieved from https://twitter.com/srhbutts/status/528425149393928192/photo/1

Piroko. (2014, November 25). EVE Online as a model for the culture war. Reddit [Discussion]. Retrieved from http://www.reddit.com/r/KotakuIn Action/comments/2nfxci/eve_online_as_a_model_for_the_culture_war/

Plunkett, L. (2014, August 28). We might be witnessing the "death of an identity." Kotaku. Retrieved from http://kotaku.com/we-might-be-witnessing-the-death-of-an-identity-1628203079

PowerIndustry. (2014, October 28). #GamerGate: For those who stand and fight [Video]. YouTube. Retrieved from https://www. youtube.com/watch? v=CavKAh40YCE

Salter, A., & Blodgett, B. (2012). Hypermasculinity & dickwolves: The contentious role of women in the new gaming public. *Journal of Broadcasting and Electronic Media, 56*, 401–416.

Sarkeesian, A. (2012, July 1). Image based harassment and visual misogyny. Feministfrequency. Retrieved from http://feministfrequency.com/2012/07/01/image-based-harassment-and-visual-misogyny/

Sarkeesian, A. (2013). Tropes vs women in video games. Feministfrequency. Retrieved from http://feministfrequency.com/tag/tropes-vs-women-in-video-games/

Savannah. [leftygirl]. (2014, October 26). #Gamer Gate supporters are using an anti-semitic caricature to defame Anita Sarkeesian . . . who is Armenian, not Jewish [Tweet]. Retrieved from https://twitter.com/leftytgirl/status/526543341014380544

Shaw, A. (2011). Do you identify as a gamer? Gender, race, sexuality, and gamer identity. *New Media & Society 14*, 28–44.

Shaw, A. (2013). On not becoming gamers: Moving beyond the constructed audience. Ada 2. Retrieved from http://adanewme-dia.org/2013/06/issue2-shaw/

Shaw, A. (2014). Gaming at the edge: Sexuality and gender at the margins of gamer culture. Minneapolis: University of Minnesota Press.

Shepherd, T., Harvey, A., Jordan, T., Srauy, S., & Miltner, K. (2015). Histories of hating. *Social Media + Society 1*, 1–10.

So just how popular is #GamerGate? (2014, October 10). Cathode debris [Tumblr]. Retrieved from http://cathodedebris.tumblr.com/post/99675407383/so-just-how-popular-is-gamergate-how-many-of

Taylor, T. L. (2012). Raising the stakes: E-sports and the professionalization of computer gaming. Cambridge, MA: MIT Press.

Totilo, S. (2014, August 20). In recent days. Kotaku. Retrieved from http://kotaku.com/in-recent-days-ive-been-asked-sev-eral-times-about-a-pos-1624707346

van Dijk, T. A. (1993). Principles of critical discourse analysis. *Discourse & Society 4*, 249–283.

Wacjman, J. (1991). *Feminism confronts technology*. University Park: Pennsylvania State University Press.

Wingfield, N. (2014a, October 15). Feminist critics of video games facing threats in "GamerGate" campaign. *The New York Times*. Retrieved from http://www.nytimes.com/2014/10/16/technol-ogy/gamergate-women-video-game-threats-anita-sarkeesian. html? smid=pl-share&_r=1

Wingfield, N. (2014b, October 2). Intel pulls ads from site after "Gamergate" boycott. *The New York Times*. Retrieved from http://bits.blogs.nytimes.com/2014/10/02/intel-pulls-ads-from-site-after-gamergate-boycott/

Wofford, T. (2014, October 25). Is GamerGate about media ethics or harassing women? Harassment, the data shows. *Newsweek.* Retrieved from http://www.newsweek.com/gamergate-about-media-ethics-or-harassing-women-harassment-data-show-279736

Women of Gamergate thread! (2015, June 29). 8chan [Discussion]. Retrieved from http://8ch.net/gamergatehq/res/213587.html

World war /v/ part 10. (2014, August 29). [Discussion]. Retrieved from https://archive.moe/v/thread/260450712/

"DON'T HATE THE PLAYER, HATE THE GAME"

The Racialization of Labor in World of Warcraft

Lisa Nakamura

Massively Multiplayer Online Role Playing Games (MMOs) such as *World of Warcraft* (*WoW*), *Lineage II,* and *Everquest* are immensely profitable, skillfully designed, immersive and beautifully detailed virtual worlds that enable both exciting gameplay and the creation of real time digitally embodied communities. This year, *World of Warcraft* surpassed 10 million users, confirming games economist Edward Castronova's (2005) predictions for exponential growth, and these players are intensely interested in and protective of their investments in the virtual world of Azeroth. This stands to reason: as Alexander Galloway (2006) writes, "virtual worlds are always in some basic way the expression of Utopian desire." One of their primary rallying points as a group has been to advocate strongly that Blizzard regulate cheating within the game more stringently; however, the definition of cheating is unclear, despite the game's End User License Agreement (EULA), since many players break these rules with impunity, a state of affairs which is actually the norm in MMO's.[1] As Mia Consalvo (2007) argues, it makes much less sense to see cheating within games as a weakness of game design or a problem with player behavior than to see it as an integral part of game culture, a feature that keeps players from getting "stuck" and quitting. "Cheating" thus benefits players and the game industry alike. However, cheating is as varied in its forms as is gameplay itself, and some varieties are viewed by players as socially undesirable, while others are not.

Though Consalvo (2007) stresses the extremely subjective ways that MMO players define cheating, asserting that "a debate exists around the definition of cheating and whether it actually hurts other players [and] players themselves see little common ground in what constitutes cheating" (p. 150), real-money trading (RMT), or buying and selling in-game property for real money, is widely considered the worst, more morally reprehensible form of cheating. In particular, the practice of gold farming, or selling in-game currency to players for real money, usually through resellers such as IGE or EBay, is especially disliked. Leisure players have been joined by worker players from poorer nations such as China and Korea who are often subject to oppression as both a racio-linguistic minority, and as undesirable underclassed social bodies in the context of game play and game culture.[2] These "farmers," as other players dismissively dub them, produce and sell virtual goods such as weapons, garments, animals, and even their own leveled-up avatars or "virtual bodies" to other players for "real world" money. As Consalvo (2007) writes, the "gill-buying practice is viscerally despised by some players" (p. 164). . . .

Though as T. L. Taylor (2006) notes, MMOs are distinguished by their "enormous potential in a fairly divisive world," the "fact that people play with each other across regions and often countries" as often as not results in ethnic and racial chauvinism: "as a tag the conflation of Chinese with gold farmer has seemed to come all too easy and now transcends any particular game" (p. 321). Robert Brookey (2007) expands upon this claim; in his analysis of gaming blogs, he discovered "overt racist attitudes" towards Chinese farmers; most importantly, that "some players, who harbor negative feelings toward Chinese farmers, do not

From Nakamura, L. (2009). "Don't hate the player, hate the game": The racialization of labor in *World of Warcraft. Critical Studies in Media Communication*, 26(2), 128–144. Copyright © National Communication Association, reprinted by permission of Taylor & Francis Ltd. (http://www.tandfonline.com) on behalf of The National Communication Association.

believe that these feelings denote racial discrimination." Thus, though it is the case that players cannot see each others' bodies while playing, specific forms of gamic labor, such as gold farming and selling, as well as specific styles of play have become racialized as Chinese, producing new forms of networked racism that are particularly easy for players to disavow.

Unlike the Internet itself, MMOs have *always* been a global medium, with many games originating in Asia.[3] Korea has been a major player in the industry from its beginning, but Asian players are numerous even in American-run MMOs such as Blizzard's *WoW;* in 2008, the number of simultaneous players on Chinese *WoW* servers exceeded 1 million, the most that have ever been recorded in Europe or the U.S. ("Blizzard," 2008). Thus, though gold farmers are typecast as Chinese, most Asian players are "leisure players," not player workers. . . .

Perhaps because most digital game scholars are players themselves, the economics of gold farming are usually discussed in the scholarly literature in terms of their negative impact upon the "world" of leisure players, who buy gold because they lack the time to earn virtual capital through "grinding" or performing the repetitive and tedious tasks that are the basis of most MMOs. However, as Toby Miller (2006) has advocated, digital games scholars need to attend to its medium's political economy, and to "follow the money" to its less glamorous, less "virtual" places, like games console and PC manufacturing plants, gold farmer sweatshops, and precious metals reclamation sites—in short, to China. Yet while many players are fairly unaware that their computer hardware is born and dies, or is *recycled,* in China, they are *exceptionally* aware of the national, racial, and linguistic identity of gold farmers. Gold farmers are reviled player-workers whose position in the gamic economy resembles that of other immigrant groups who cross national borders in order to work, but unlike other types of "migrant" workers, their labors are offshore, and thus invisible—they are "virtual migrants."[4] However, user generated content in and around MMOs actively visualizes this process. Machinima fan-produced video production racializes this reviled form of gameplay as "Oriental" in ways that hail earlier visual media such as music videos and minstrel shows. Gold farming, a burgeoning "grey market" labor practice in a disliked and semi-illegal industry that as Consalvo (2007) notes, may soon outstrip the primary games market as a source of revenue, has become racialized as Asian, specifically as Chinese. . . .

WoW and other virtual worlds have been touted for their democratic potential—as Castronova (2005) puts it:

> People entering a synthetic world can have, in principle, any body they desire. At a stroke, this feature of synthetic worlds removes from the social calculus all the unfortunate effects that derive from the body . . . all without bearing some of the burdens that adhere to the Earth bodies we were born with. (pp. 25–26)

The social calculus of race, nation, and class are burdens borne by Chinese gold farmers, Chinese leisure players, and ultimately, the gaming community as a whole. Hatred of Chinese gold farmers drives *WoW* users to produce visual and textual media that hews closely to earlier anti-Asian discourses, media that they broadcast to other users through forums, general chat in-game, and "homemade" videos.

World of Warcraft is a virtual world where significant numbers of people are conducting their psychic, financial, and social lives. This massively multiplayer online game continues to roll out content for its users in the form of expansion packs, frequent software updates, action figures and a feature film in development, and an extensive content-rich and frequently updated website for its community of users. Users are invited by Blizzard to get involved in some aspects of this world's production by contributing interesting screenshots, machinima, personal narratives, and advice on gameplay to their site, and even in cases when they are not, players actively produce in defiance of its wishes. Topics that the game industry may wish to avoid because they may seem divisive, or may reflect badly on the virtual world, are confronted frequently in participatory media created by its users.

MACHINIMA AS USER-GENERATED RACIAL NARRATIVE: THE MEDIA CAMPAIGN AGAINST CHINESE PLAYER-WORKERS IN *WOW*

Machinima is a crucial site of struggle over the meaning of race in shared digital space, and it is a central part of the culture of MMOs such as *World of Warcraft*. Machinima has recently become the object of much academic interest because it exemplifies the notion of participatory media, an influential and useful formulation that is the basis for Jenkins' (2006) book *Convergence Culture*. In it, Jenkins describes how machinima are prime examples of users' seizing the right to contribute to media universes in defiance of industry wishes, standards, and control; their value lies in the ability to produce counternarratives whose impact lies in their active subversion of the narrow messages available in many dominant media texts. Machinima literally extend the storyspace of the games upon which they are based, and the most interesting of these actively work to reconfigure their original meanings in progressive, socially productive ways. Jenkins explains that transmediated storyspaces which exist across media platforms permit increased opportunities for engaged users like fans to insert their own content into these "synthetic worlds," to use Castronova's (2005) phrase—while game developers like Blizzard provide limited, licensed, and fairly tightly controlled virtual space for players to navigate, users extend this space by writing fan fiction, creating original artwork, and making their own movies or machinima using images, narratives, and tropes from the game.

While part of the pleasure of *World of Warcraft* consists in navigating its richly imaged, beautifully rendered spaces, users must rely upon the company to provide more of this valuable commodity in the form of expansion packs such as "The Burning Crusade" and "The Wrath of the Lich King," eagerly anticipated and extremely profitable products for which users are willing to stand in line for days at a time. Machinima permits users to expand this space for free; while navigable space is still tightly controlled by the company—unlike in *Second Life,* users are unable to build their own structures or objects to insert in the world—machinima allows users to extend its representational or narrative space, creating scenarios that are genuinely new because they depict activities or behaviors impossible in the space of the game. This is a fascinating area of study, and one that is a thriving and integral part of *WoW* in particular. The struggle for resources integral to the structure of MMOs can also be re-envisioned as the struggle to own or claim virtual space and to police national boundaries as well.[5] Player-produced machinima accessed from Warcraftmovies.com make arguments about race, labor, and the racialization of space in *World of Warcraft*.[6] These highly polemical texts employ the visual language of the game, one of the most recognizable and distinctive ever created for shared virtual play, to bring into sharp relief the contrast between the privileges of media production available to empowered players with the time and inclination to create machinima, and those who are shut out of this aspect of *WoW* by their status as worker players. Participatory media is a privilege of the leisure class; active fandom is too expensive a proposition for many digital workers, who as Dibbell explains poignantly, can't afford to *enjoy* the game that they have mastered, much less produce media to add to it.[7]

Unsurprisingly, there are two tiers of this type of user production—Blizzard frequently solicits screenshots, holds art contests, and showcases user-produced machinima that become part of the "official" canon of the game. However, there is extensive traffic in content that is not endorsed by the developer, but which is nonetheless part of the continuing rollout of the world. Racial discourse is a key part of this rollout. If the official *World of Warcraft* game is a gated community, one that users pay to enter, its covenants consist in its EULA [End-User License Agreement]. However, part of Jenkins' (2006) argument is that media technologies such as the Internet have made it impossible to "gate" media in the same way. The "underground" machinima I will discuss in this chapter build and expand the world of *WoW* in regards to representations of race in just as constitutive a way as its official content. As Lowood (2006) notes, *WoW* players have been creating visual moving image records as long as, or perhaps even longer than, they have been playing the game. Thus, machinima is anything but a derivative or ancillary form in relation to *WoW,* for its history runs exactly parallel, and in some sense, slightly in advance of the game itself—as Lowood notes, users were employing the beta version of *WoW* to make machinima before the game was available to the public. Lowood claims, "*WoW* movies, from game film to dance videos, have become an integral part of the culture shared by a player community" (p. 374).

If indeed machinima extend the world of gameplay, how are players co-creating this world?

Anti-farmer machinima produces overtly racist narrative space to attach to a narrative that, while carefully avoiding overt references to racism or racial conflict in our world, is premised upon a racial war in an imaginary world—the World of Azeroth. While Jenkins (2006) celebrates the way that fans, particularly female fans, have extended the worlds of *Star Trek* in truly liberatory ways, inserting homosexual narratives between Captain Kirk and Spock that the franchise would never permit or endorse, a closer look at user produced content from Warcraftmovies.com reveals a contraction and retrenchment of concepts of gender, race, and nation rather than their enlargement.

Warcraftmovies.com, the most popular *World of Warcraft* machinima website, organizes its user generated content under several different categories. "Underground" machinima deals with topics such as "bug/exploit," "exploration," and "gold farming." "Ni Hao (A Gold Farmer's Story)" by "Nyhm" of "Madcow Studios" has earned a "4 x Platinum" rating, the highest available, from Warcraftmovies.com, and it is also available on *YouTube,* where it has been viewed 533,567 times, has been favorited 1,998 times, and has produced 981 comments from users ("Ni Hao"). This extremely popular, visually sophisticated machinima music video features new lyrics sung over the instrumental track of Akon's hit hip hop song "Smack That." This polemical anti-Asian machinima's chorus is:

> I see you farmin' primals in Shadow moon Valley, 10 cents an hour's good money when you are Chinese, I buy your auctions you sell my gold right back to me, feels like you're bendin' me over, you smile and say "ni hao" and farm some gold, "ni hao" it's getting old, ni hao, oh.

The claim that "10 cents an hour's good money when you are Chinese" displays awareness that the farmers' incentive for exploiting or "bending over" better-resourced players comes from economic need. Another part of the video shows a "farmer" shoveling gold into a vault, with the subtitled lyric "IGE's making bank now." The International Gaming Exchange is one of the largest re-sellers of gold, avatar level-ups, and other virtual property, and it is an American business, not an Asian one. Nonetheless, this commentary on the gold farming economic system resorts to the full gamut of racial stereotypes, including a Chinese flag as the background for a video scene of a sexy singing female Troll in a scanty outfit flanked by the human "farmers" wielding pickaxes and shovels.

Later in the video, a Chinese gold farmer is killed by another player, who comments as he kneels next to the corpse that "this China-man gets fired, that's one farmer they'll have to replace, not supposed to be here in the first place." . . . Clearly, Asian players, specifically those suspected of being "farmers" but as this image [suggests], all "China-men" have a diminished status on *WoW:* many American players fail to see them as "people." . . . The video depicts them as all owning exactly the same avatar, a male human wearing a red and gold outfit and wielding a pickaxe. This dehumanization of the Asian player—they "all look the same" because they all *are* the same—is evocative of earlier conceptions of Asian laborers as interchangeable and replaceable. . . .

CONCLUSION

The anti-Asian racial discourse in "Ni Hao," as well as that noted in Brookey's (2007), Steinkuehler's (2006), and Taylor's (2006) research are not necessarily representative of the *WoW* population as a whole (though it must be said that while *YouTube* and Warcraftmovies are full of machinima or trophy videos of farmer-killing replete with racist imagery, there are no pro-farmer user-produced machinima to be seen).[8] Machinima is a breakthrough medium because it differs from previous mass forms of media or performance; it is the product of individual users. However, like the minstrel shows that preceded it, it shapes the culture by disseminating arguments about the nature of race, labor, and assimilation. . . .

Similarly, it is certainly not the case that games must be entirely free of racist discourse in order to be culturally important or socially productive, in short, to be "good." No multiplayer social game could meet that criterion at all times. On the other hand, if we are to take games seriously as "synthetic worlds," we must be willing to take their racial discourses, media texts, and interpersonal conflicts seriously as well. As Dibbell (2006) claims, it is constraint and scarcity—the challenge of capital accumulation—that makes MMOs pleasurable, even addictive. Game economies based on cultures of scarcity engender Real Money Transfer, and as long as this form of player-work is socially debased and racialized, it will result in radically unequal social relations, labor types, and forms of representation along the axes of nation, language, and identity. Asian worker players are economically unable to accumulate avatarial capital and thus become "persons"; they are the dispossessed subjects of synthetic worlds. As long as Asian "farmers" are figured as unwanted guest workers within the culture of MMOs, user-produced extensions of MMO-space like machinima will most likely continue to depict Asian culture as threatening to the beauty and desirability of shared virtual space in the *World of Warcraft*.

NOTES

1. Players of *WoW* regularly use an arsenal of "mods" and "add-ons" that are circulated on player boards online; though these are technically in violation of the End User License Agreement (EULA), many players consider the game unplayable without them, especially at the terminal or "end game" levels. Blizzard turns a blind eye to this, and in fact tacitly condones it by posting technical updates referring to the impact of add-ons on game performance.

2. See T. L. Taylor (2006), on in-game language chauvinism and the informal enforcement of "English only" chat in *WoW* even by players of non-Anglophone nationalities.

3. See Chan (2006), as well as the January 2008 special issue of *Games and Culture* on Asia, volume 3, number 1, in particular Hjorth's (2008) introductory essay "Games@Neo-Regionalism: Locating Gaming in the Asia-Pacific."

4. See (Aneesh, 2006).

5. As Brookey (2007) argues, national boundaries have been reproduced in cyberspace, and the location of the servers that generate these virtual environments are used to demarcate the borders. These respondents claim that if Chinese players experience discrimination on U.S. servers, it is because they have crossed the border into territory where they do not belong and are not welcome.

6. The phrase "player-produced machinima" is in some sense a redundant one, since machinima is from its inception an amateur form; however it is becoming an increasingly necessary distinction as professional media producers appropriate it. *South Park*'s "Make Love Not Warfare" was co-produced with Blizzard Entertainment, and Toyota has aired a 2007 commercial made in the same way. See http://www.machinima.com/film/view&id= 23588. In an example of media synergy, *South Park* capitalized on the success and popularity of the episode by bundling a *World of Warcraft* trial game card along with the DVD box set of its most recent season.

7. See Dibbell (2007) for an eloquent account of "Min," a highly skilled worker player who took great pride in being his raiding party's "tank," a "heavily armed warrior character who . . . is the linchpin of any raid" (p. 41). His raiding team would take "any customer" into a dangerous dungeon where a lower level player could never survive alone and let them pick up the valuable items dropped there, thus acting like virtual African shikaris or Nepalese porters. Min greatly enjoyed these raids but was eventually forced to quit them and take up farming again when they proved insufficiently profitable.

8. UC San Diego doctoral candidate Ge Jin's distributive filmmaking project on the lives of Chinese worker players in MMOs can be viewed at http://www.chinesegoldfarmers .com.His films, which can also be viewed on *YouTube,* contain documentary footage of Chinese worker players laboring in "gaming workshops" in Shanghai. His interviews with them make it clear that these worker players are well aware of how despised they are by American and European players, and that they feel a sense of "inferiority" that is articulated to their racial and ethnic identity.

REFERENCES

Aneesh, A. (2006). *Virtual migration: The programming of globalization*. Durham, NC: Duke University Press.

Blizzard Entertainment's *World of Warcraft:* The Burning Crusade surpasses one million peak concurrent player milestone in mainland China. (2008). *PR Newswire: United Business Media*. Retrieved May 28, 2008, from http://ww.pmewswiie.com/news/indexmail.shtml? ACCT=104&STORY=/www/story/04–11–2008/000479086&EDATE=

Brookey, R. A. (2007, November). *Racism and nationalism in cyberspace: Comments on farming in MMORPGS*. Paper presented at the National Communication Association Annual Convention, Chicago.

Castronova, E. (2005). *Synthetic worlds: The business and culture of online games*. Chicago: University of Chicago Press.

Chan, D. (2006). Negotiating Intra-Asian games networks: On cultural proximity, East Asian games design, and Chinese farmers. *Fibreculture, 8*. Retrieved May 28, 2008, from http://journal fibreculture.org/issue8/issue8_chan.html

Consalvo, M. (2007). *Cheating: Gaining advantage in videogames*. Cambridge, MA: The MIT Press.

Dibbell, J. (2006). *Play Money*. New York: Basic Books.

Dibbell, J. (2007, June 17). The life of the Chinese gold farmer. *The New York Times Magazine*, 36–41.

Galloway, A. (2006). Warcraft and Utopia. *1000 days of theory*. Retrieved April 11, 2008, from ctheory.net/printer.aspx? id=507

Hjorth, L (2008). Games@Neo-regionalism: Locating gaming in the Asia-Pacific. *Games and Culture, 3*(1), 3–12.

Jenkins, H. (2006). *Convergence culture: Where old and new media collide*. New York: New York University Press.

Lowood, H. (2006). Storyline, dance/music, or PvP? Game movies and community players in *World of Warcraft. Games and Culture, 1*(4), 362–382.

Miller, T. (2006). Gaming for beginners. *Games and Culture, 1*(1), 5–12.

Ni Hao: A Gold Farmer's Story. Retrieved November 7, 2007, from http://youtube.com/watch? V=odllf5NEI00

Steinkuehler, C. (2006). The mangle of play. *Games and Culture, 1*(3), 199–213.

Taylor, T. L (2006). Does *WoW* change everything? How a PvP server, multinational player base, and surveillance mod scene cause me pause. *Games and Culture, 1*(4), 318–337.

GIMPGIRL GROWS UP

Women With Disabilities Rethinking, Redefining, and Reclaiming Community

65

Jennifer Cole, Jason Nolan, Yukari Seko,
Katherine Mancuso, and Alejandra Ospina

INTRODUCTION

. . . This study explored the key members, events, issues, and technologies of GimpGirl Community (GGC) (http://gimpgirl.com), which was founded in 1998 as a forum for women with disabilities, run by women with disabilities. We focused on the lived experiences of GGC members: how they actively shape and nurture this online community for like-minded individuals; how they maintain and moderate social interaction among members; and what path the community has taken in the past twelve years. The study could be considered a reflective narrative inquiry and learning exercise in which key members of the GGC took initiative in setting the research agenda, conducted their own inquiry, and organized and presented their analysis in collaboration with co-authors/academic mentors who wanted to help the group share their story with the academic community. By documenting the organizing efforts of GGC moderators and their learning experiences over the past decade, we were able to inquire into the connections between online technologies and the capabilities people need to develop and maintain communities.

INITIATING INQUIRY

We were particularly interested in what initially drove GGC members to develop an online community, how the community solved problems, and how various online technologies (from text-based to more recent mixed-media virtual environments) were adapted to meet the diverse needs of members. Our investigation was inspired by the method of narrative inquiry: qualitative research that examines narratives to understand the meanings people ascribe to their experiences (Trahar, 2009). Narrative inquiry takes diverse modes of filed texts—oral, written, visual—as data sources to look for deeper understanding of 'lived experience' (Clandinin and Connelly, 2000; van Manen, 1997). We saw the value of how, based on various narrative elements, narrative inquirers interrogate how the life experiences of individuals get woven into a story, for whom and for what purpose, and what cultural discourses it draws upon.

. . . For our inquiry, digital archives of the twelve years of GGC activity constituted archived texts that include postings to the community listservs, blog entries, minutes from staff meetings, and online dialogues among the members. Formulation of this article took place solely online with members in different parts of the world, and incorporated recent scholarly contributions from the group (Cole, 2009; Cole and Mancuso, 2009; Mancuso and Cole, 2009; Ospina et al., 2008).

Along with archival materials, we chose to focus on auto-ethnographic reflections of the founding member Jennifer Cole, as her experiences best portray the overall structure and development of the community. It is not unusual for an author of an auto-ethnography to consult with various other people and materials, but it is less common for multiple authors to agree on a single voice to represent a community. Lather (1995) used this approach and noted the challenges of telling stories on behalf of marginalized individuals, as well as the concomitant necessity to do so. Jennifer's

From Jennifer Cole, Jason Nolan, Yukari Seko, Katherine Mancuso, and Alejandra Ospina (2011), "GimpGirl Grows Up: Women with Disabilities Rethinking, Redefining and Reclaiming Community." *New Media & Society* 13:1161–1179. Reprinted with permission of SAGE Publications, Ltd.

auto-ethnographic writings were nurtured by online discussions and one-on-one dialogues between the co-authors, as they collaboratively reconstructed memories of the community. . . .

. . . By investigating Jennifer's narrative in the context of various episodes and incidents in the collective life of the GGC, we explored issues of inclusivity and exclusivity crucial for maintaining a safe and open space for participants, as well as the experiments in identity construction performed by some GGC members. These experimentations presented a counterpoint to conventional assumptions about women with disabilities that construct them as asexual service recipients without autonomy or agency.

GENESIS OF THE GGC

Inspired by her participation in the DO-IT program for teens with disabilities (http://www.washington.edu/doit/), Jennifer and her mentor Len Burns founded The Center for Breaking Away, a non-profit organization for disabled youth transitioning to adulthood. This organization originally housed the GGC project, but was dissolved after the GGC project outgrew the center. The GGC was founded in 1998 as a collaboration of young women with disabilities who shared a dissatisfaction with pre-existing services and communities, which appeared incapable of fulfilling the needs of these youth in transition to adulthood. For Jennifer, a chief motivation for creating the GGC was to fight back against abusive situations she had encountered, and to counterbalance her early heteronomous role of being a passive daughter/child with a disability. She noted in an online conversation with the co-authors:

> I started it [the GGC] when I was 18 or 19 I think. Just after I left an abusive home. It started as me battling back against that and forming community to help each other through those tough times. Many people with disabilities feel like when we are no longer cute kids, we get thrust out into the world without much support. This is what the GGC was made for, to offer direct peer-to-peer support. . . . Interestingly, we came across many women who were just out of abusive situations or actively in abusive situations and I was so glad that they found somewhere to go and didn't have to create it.

The GGC was intended as an online-based group connecting isolated members with shared interests. Most of the founding members were teens who had met each other through the DO-IT program or similar organizations, and so the GGC was initially founded by and for young women, who created a safe and informal space for sharing ideas and experiences, discussing issues involved in the transition to adulthood, and for offering information and peer-to-peer support unavailable in formal settings. The domain gimpgirl.com was registered in February 1998; this was initially Jennifer's personal website, but was almost immediately given over to GGC. Jennifer was the first leader, though governance changed over time. She thought of herself as running and growing a non-profit.[1] The GGC website was one of the first sites dedicated to women with disabilities based on self-diagnosed disability, without restrictions on age, sexual orientation, or types of disability. The website included links to news from the disability community and resources for women with disabilities. Other areas showcased art and writing of members, as well as fun activities such as quizzes and polls.

. . . The name 'GimpGirl' originated as a nickname Jennifer's friends called her when she was a teenager: '[The nickname] didn't have any particular meaning other than who I was, and a big part of who I am is getting beyond terminology, which still carries in what we do today.' By sharing her nickname with the group, Jennifer motivated herself and other GGC members to 'get each other through life' beyond any given terminology. Jennifer suggested that what underlies the active use of controversial language was a challenging spirit against conventional discourse surrounding women with disabilities. She noted:

> [The term 'GimpGirl' was] Not offhand. I know even before we started [the group in 1998], people in the disability community were calling themselves gimps (mostly on the West Coast) and crips (mostly on the East Coast). It was a source of 'cheeky' pride . . . . While the language we use has definitely sparked some controversy, it is who we are and so it has withstood the controversy. Within the disabilities community there always seems to be some set of politically acceptable language that we are supposed to use to make people feel better, and

part of our stand is that we can choose how we react to whatever language people use. Our goal is not to be popular or be politically acceptable, but to get each other through life.

Jennifer's subversive moniker also mirrored her expectation that the name and logo of the community would remind participants that they are the ones who give power to words, and would encourage them to distance themselves from the ever-changing 'politically correct' institutional language that defines and shapes much of the identity of women living with disabilities. . . .

. . . GGC members and their families became increasingly accepting; one mother of a GGC member sent an email to Jennifer, commenting: '[At first,] "GimpGirl" seems rude but when I think more on the term, it is upfront and confident and takes away any sense of pity.'

THE GROWTH OF THE GGC AND USE OF ONLINE TECHNOLOGY

One important characteristic of the GGC is its active search for, and implementation of, new technologies to facilitate member participation in community development and maintenance. The community has transcended any specific technology and has morphed through listservs, interactive virtual worlds, websites, blogs, and various social networks. Rather than abandoning old tools and moving onto new ones, the GGC has actively sought effective technologies to develop and deliver desirable content for its members. Before adopting a new form of communication, staff consults with board members and the community to see how many are already using a particular technology and how accessible they found it. The administrators then further research the technology with regard to usability and accessibility, to ensure that a benefit to some would not exclude others. . . .

. . . On 18 July 2003, the GGC created an account on the LiveJournal platform (http://gimpgirl.livejournal.com/) in an effort to rejuvenate and diversify access and to reduce duties for moderators. The GGC later transferred all existing lists to this social networking platform, making the LiveJournal group the main venue for communal activities. In this system, users were able to maintain their own accounts and benefited from a variety of available communities. LiveJournal also had community archives that were more immediate and engaging to new members. . . . Even after the GGC opened facilities in Second Life in 2008, the GimpGirl LiveJournal community remains the GGC's third largest community, with over 275 members worldwide who discuss wide-ranging subjects from bras and yeast infections to discrimination and victories.

The GGC's next major evolution came when Dr Mark Dubin of 3D Embodiment (http://3demb.com/) donated a quarter-sim parcel in *Second Life,* September 2007. The parcel was designed as a multi-use campus, with meeting rooms, a dance and pool area on the roof, an amphitheatre for presentations and events, a mall where members could sell items they had created, and a small apartment building where some members have homes. By February 2008, the parcel was fully developed and opened to the public, just in time for the GGC's tenth anniversary. This event was highly successful; members and supporters showed up to celebrate and hang out with their peers in this synchronous environment. After a decade of transitional homes, this incarnation marked a coming-of-age for the GGC, an all-volunteer group that had always worked on the fringe of the disability community without institutional support or formal funding. The launch was so successful that by March 2008 the parcel was redesigned by new volunteers to further increase accessibility and services. It also attracted support from Ryerson University's Experiential Design and Gaming Environment lab.[2]

. . . Expansion into *Second Life* sparked another wave of development in membership, activities, and staff. *Second Life* helped bring in outside resources by allowing a broader network of supporters from the large group of pre-existing disability and non-profit communities. As social networks become more popular to keep in touch with friends and family (Wellman et al., 2006), more people and organizations are willing to venture into virtual environments such as *Second Life*. The GGC was initially composed of a close-knit community of women who knew one another, but now it has extended to a larger community.

Since expanding to *Second Life* in 2008, the GGC has worked to expand and govern the community, and is using online community building tools to reach a wider range of women with disabilities and form a rich and nuanced web of people and resources. It has hosted a series of online public forums on *Second Life* in which the members join professionals or scholars outside the membership; this has raised the GGC's public profile, engaged a wider range of dialogue, and clarified the complex issues surrounding women with disabilities. The GGC also extended its presence to Facebook and MySpace (later deleted due to inactivity and usability issues) on 17 February 2008 and later opened a Twitter account 2 April 2008. Meanwhile, the GGC redesigned its main website, utilizing the open-source Moodle software to add forums, a wiki, and a membership system. The website re-release was announced on 12 April 2008....

BEYOND THE MYTH OF NORMATIVITY: COMMUNITY, IDENTITY, AND TECHNOLOGY

A consistent theme throughout this inquiry is the notion of being doubly marginalized: living as women and as individuals with disabilities. From a Foucauldian perspective, people with disabilities live immersed in a pathological discourse of disability, as an object of disciplinary power. They are forced to become the subject matter of professional groups, who constantly define the meaning of living with disabilities, resulting in the systematic closure of opportunities for agency.... The possibility of autonomy in day-to-day life is highly dependent on the willingness and ability of service providers and personal care assistants to see them as individuals with unique needs and goals. With potentially limited mobility and access to resources necessary to independently claim their own identity, they are often designated as the 'docile' population.... GGC members have strived to overcome the 'double silence' of women with disabilities by resisting the stereotypical view of living with disabilities, thereby claiming the status of subjects with agency (Ferri and Gregg, 1998: 433)....

. . . While the community has successfully maintained an openness to all forms of disability by intentionally educating themselves about the needs of members, staff members have had to work in uncharted territory without models to emulate or apply. The need to create a safe and nurturing space for members must be balanced by a concomitant act of social engagement with larger disability communities, academic and medical communities, and the public at large. Because the goal of the community was to be inclusive and to give voice to those under-represented or marginalized, its model could not be fixed, but had to remain fluid and open to continual re-assessment and reconfiguration to ensure that power remained with all members. As the community has grown, the GGC has needed not only to consider the safety of members but also to reach outside its walls to interface with the public and advocate for public support and communication.

By using a variety of online tools, the GGC has helped members develop a capacity to perform as agents of self- and social transformation. The system also helps empower participants to involve themselves in their own lives by providing information and broadening their experience with others in similar situations. Meanwhile, staff members are aware of the potential exclusivity of ICTs, due to financial requirements and other factors involved in getting online. To participate, members must purchase a computer and have access to the internet (financially difficult for many women with disabilities) and be technically savvy enough to interact with others via online-mediated platforms. This, according to Jennifer, may explain why many of the GGC members are 'computer geeks.' Despite these limitations, ICTs are the only way for many GGC members to shift discourse from an institutional/medical location to a community of their own. By doing so, Jennifer and other members have developed their own skills and strategies for using various forms of online technology, structuring community, negotiating participation, developing and maintaining community standards, and resolving conflict. Jennifer noted:

> While online technologies certainly exclude a huge population, at the same time they are also very inclusive to many people because they reach into where they are. Many of us who are bedbound (like myself most days) and don't always have the same opportunities to be involved in face-to-face groups. Also for people who have issues socializing in face-to-face situations, either because of shyness or

communication issues (for whatever reason), online environments are much easier.

Another challenge related to the use of online platforms is the issue of validity, stemming from the lack of face-to-face interaction among participants. While online forums are a good way to get a broad range of input from different people, participants accustomed to face-to-face interactions occasionally voiced concern about the GGC's fundamental reliance on online media. One former volunteer explained that some saw the GGC as 'not real enough,' because members rarely saw one another face-to-face. The concern is valid, because the GGC does not have an office, and members interact using text and avatars, sometimes supplemented by voice/video chat. However, the situation has been gradually changing, as the administrators have consistently encouraged other members to balance online and offline relationships. Drawing on her experience of gaining support from people she first met online, Jennifer explained how online technologies can help users overcome isolation in real life:

> I think a lot of us who have issues [with social-izing in face-to-face situations] eventually use [online platforms] to make friends face-to-face. Not all of us, obviously. But it's definitely a tool. In meetings we talk a lot about what people can do to meet friends face-to-face, how to find other support groups, how to socialize, etc. Not that I'm any great expert myself, but it's some-thing we try to encourage to help people bal-ance their lives.

Interactive platforms such as *Second Life* encourage members to work within a synchronous open-ended environment where they can directly interact with others via avatars. Having a visible representation of oneself on *Second Life* certainly allows members to explore their identity in a more 'realistic' environment. Members visualize their online identity in various ways; some members incorporate their real-life disabilities in their avatars, while others do not, and still others fluctuate from one choice to another. Alejandra changes her avatar's appearance depending on the representation she wants to portray, using an avatar with a wheelchair when speaking to non-disabled people about the GGC, and an able-bodied avatar

when speaking to her peers. Jennifer describes her avatar:

> My avatar looks very much like me in real life, minus the signs of disability that I rarely display in Second Life because in my head I don't really picture myself as disabled. It's not part of my personal image of myself, not because I think appearing with a disability is in any way less of an option. It's just what feels comfortable to me most of the time.

Jennifer's story invites a particular and resisting reading of ICT policy, with the goal of encouraging disabled people to live 'normal' and 'integrated' lives (Moser, 2006). For Jennifer and other members, visual representations of self in the form of a *Second Life* avatar can vividly reflect how they understand their disability and identity in a variety of ways, as well as how they teach others about the disability community. Alejandra's occasional use of different avatars and Jennifer's disinclination to picture herself 'as disabled' exemplify how the *Second Life* virtual platform allows GGC members to express a subjective understanding of disability, unbounded by the stigmas ascribed to their real-life bodies. In other words, the ability to choose how to present themselves allows the members to express their identity in ways that work for them, without relying on conventional narratives of medical intervention or rehabilitation. Given *Second Life's* role as identity playground, the members become capable of creating their own meanings, to open up rather than close down the meaning of living with disabilities. By working toward transcending the myths of 'normativity' and thus being perceived as something other than helpless, they reconstruct their way of being-in-the-world as one of the privileges of life. For GGC members, who are often defined by institutions and medical definitions of their disability with limited opportunities for autonomous social exploration, ICTs represent an opportunity to move beyond externally imposed definitions of who they are, experiment with self-representation and forge their own sense of identity.

LOOKING FORWARD

. . . The GGC has much to share on many levels: as a model of a self-sustaining online community;

a community that maintains itself across a myriad of intersecting ICTs simultaneously; an example of how to resist institutional appropriations of identity and definitions of self for women with disabilities; and as an inclusive women-centered space that tailors itself to the needs of its members wherever they are and however they define themselves. The GGC is a unique community that has had the opportunity to come into its own and grow alongside the proliferation of the Web 2.0 phenomenon. Members of the community have made choices regarding the technologies they use and how they integrate them in order to meet the needs of as many members as possible. Over the past decade,

the GGC and its members have changed their lives, and have been shaped by the choices they have made in how they engage in ICTs. With the wider adoption of ICTs by society at large, we will continue to look for new ways in which to challenge institutional/medical discourses, as well as public perceptions of women with disabilities. As well, we consider the further exploration of various ICT tools central to our goal of bringing women with disabilities together in order, not only to share our stories and coconstruct community, but to discover and create new opportunities for us to engage more fully with the world around us, both socially and economically. . . .

NOTES

1. After 12 years of activity, the GGC finally achieved this goal in January 2010. The GGC officially became a program of People Helping People (http://www.phpnw.org) to give the GGC 501(c)3 nonprofit status and the support of an organization with the same goals and passion to support the independence of people with disabilities.

2. Just before this article was published the GGC parcel in *Second Life* moved to the EDGE lab's sims at http://slurl.com/secondlife/Research%20Edge/50/58/282

REFERENCES

Barron K (1997) The bumpy road to womanhood. *Disability & Society* 12(2): 223–240.

Bowker N and Tuffin K (2002) Disability discourses for online identities. *Disability and Society* 17(3): 327–344.

Chen W and Wellman B (2005) Minding the cyber-gap. The Internet and social inequality. In Romero M and Margolis E (eds) *Blackwell Companion to Social Inequalities.* Oxford: Blackwell.

Clandinin DJ and Connelly FM (2000) *Narrative Inquiry.* San Francisco, CA: Jossey-Bass.

Cole J (2009) GimpGirl Community: Supporting the lives of women with disabilities. Paper presented at Sex::Tech Conference, San Francisco, CA, 22–23 March.

Cole J and Mancuso K (2009) GimpGirl Community: Women with disabilities. Paper presented at 2nd Virtual Praxis, Online, 21–22 November. Available at: http://people.cohums.ohio-state.edu/collingwood7/minerva/conference09_jennylin.html (consulted March 2010).

Dobransky K and Hargittai E (2006) The disability divide in Internet access and use. *Information, Communication and Society* 9(3): 313–334.

Ferri BA and Gregg N (1998) Women with disabilities: Missing voices. *Women's Studies International Forum* 21(4): 429–439.

Finn J (1999) An exploration of helping processes in an online self-help group focusing on issues of disability. *Health and Social Work* 24(3): 220–231.

Haythornthwaite C (2008) Learning relations and networks in web-based communities. *International Journal of Web Based Communities* 4(2): 140–158.

Hine C (2000) *Virtual Ethnography.* London: Sage.

Hughes B (2005) What can a Foucauldian analysis contribute to disability theory? In Tremain S (ed.) *Foucault and the Government of Disability.* Michigan: University of Michigan Press.

Katz J and Rice R (2002) *Social Consequences of Internet Use: Access, Involvement, and Interaction.* Boston, MA: MIT Press.

Kendall L (1996) MUDder? I hardly know 'Er! Adventures of a Feminist MUDder. In Cherny L and Weise E (eds) *wired_women*. Seattle, WA: Seal, 207–233.

Lambek M (2005) Our subjects/ourselves: A view from the back seat. In Meneley A and Young DJ (eds) *Auto-ethnographies*. Toronto: Broadview Press, 229–240.

Lather P (1995) The validity of angels: Interpretive and textual strategies in researching the lives of women with HIV/AIDS. *Qualitative Inquiry* 1(1): 41–68.

Mancuso K and Cole J (2009) GimpGirl community's best practices for facilitating an accessible community in a virtual world. Poster presented at IEEE Accessing the Future Conference, Boston, MA, 20–21 July. Available at: http://ewh.ieee.org/conf/accessingthefuture/documents/mancuso.pdf (consulted July 2009).

Mazar R and Nolan J (2009) Hacking say and reviving ELIZA: Lessons from virtual environments. *Innovate* 5(2). Available at: http://www.innovateonline.info/index.php? view=article&id=547 (consulted July 2009).

Morris M and Ogan C (1996) The internet as mass medium. *The Journal of Communication* 46(1): 39–50.

Moser I (2006) Disability and the promises of technology: Technology, subjectivity and embodiment within an order of the normal. *Information, Communication and Society* 9(3): 373–395.

Nolan J and Weiss J (2002) Learning cyberspace: An educational view of virtual community. In Renninger A and Shumar W (eds) *Building Virtual Communities*. Cambridge: Cambridge University Press.

Ospina A, Cole J and Nolan J (2008) GimpGirl grows up: Women with disabilities rethinking, redefining, and reclaiming community. Paper presented at Internet Research 9.0, Copenhagen, 15–18 October.

Pendergrass S, Nosek M and Holcomb J (2001) Design and evaluation of an internet site to educate women with disabilities on reproductive health care. *Sexuality and Disability* 19(1): 71–83.

Rheingold H (1994) *The Virtual Community: Homesteading on the Electronic Frontier*. Reading, MA: HarperPerennial.

Sponaas-Robins R and Nolan J (2005) MOOs: Polysynchronous collaborative virtual environments. In Zemliansky P and Amant K St (eds) *Workplace Internet-based Communication*. New York: Idea Group, 130–156.

Trahar S (2009) Beyond the story itself: Narrative inquiry and autoethnography in intercultural research in higher education. *Forum Qualitative Sozialforschung/Forum: Qualitative Social Research* 10(1): Art 30. Available at: http://www.qualitative-research.net/index.php/fqs/article/view/1218/2654 (consulted September 2010).

Valentine G and Skelton T (2009) An umbilical cord to the world. *Information, Communication and Society* 12(1): 44–65.

van Dijk J and Hacker K (2003) The digital divide as a complex and dynamic phenomenon. *The Information Society* 19: 315–326.

van Manen M (1997) *Researching Lived Experience*. London, Ontario: Althouse.

Wellman B, Hogan B, Berg K et al. (2006) Connected lives: The project. In: Purcell P (ed.) *Networked Neighbourhoods*. London: Springer, 161–216.

Young DJ and Meneley A (2005) Introduction: Auto-ethnographies of academic practices. In Meneley A and Young DJ (eds) *Auto-ethnographies*. Toronto: Broadview Press, 1–22.

HOW IT FEELS TO BE VIRAL ME

Affective Labor and Asian American YouTube Performance

Christine Bacareza Balance

On March 15, 2011, just days after University of California–Los Angeles undergraduate Alexandra Wallace posted (and subsequently took down) her incendiary "Asians in the Library" video log (vlog) on YouTube, another video set ablaze Facebook walls and Twitter accounts. Jimmy Wong's "Ching Chong! Asians in the Library Song"—a satirical love song addressed to Wallace—distinguished itself from the hundreds of other ranting and remix response videos. Opening with an excerpt from the offending party's original post—as she mockingly renders a scene of Asians answering their cell phones in the library with an "Ooooh, Ching Chong Ling Long Ting Tong," Wong's video quickly shifts into a style and staging commonly associated with online vlogs. Seated and directly addressing the camera, he is framed by his home studio's accoutrements: computer and electronic keyboard on his left side and a row of cables neatly hanging on the wall behind him. Stuttering in a thick Asian accent and, in turn, deriding Wallace's own orientalist rendition, a guitar-strapped Wong introduces his song into a boom microphone that hangs near his face: "Greetings, Miss Alexandra Wallace. I'm not most . . . how you say . . . politically correct person. So please . . ." (head bows quickly) "do not take offensive. Thank you."

Viewers familiar with the "Asians in the Library" video would recognize that this introduction riffs on Wallace's own preface: while she is not the most "politically correct person," she *does* have Asian friends, and hopes, in the end, that viewers do not take offense. Wong strums a single chord, signaling a magical transformation, as the video again cuts to Wong, now guitarless but seated in the same position. This new version of Wong purrs into the

microphone without an Asian accent or tone of deference. With his recording studio–style headphones on, his seductive vocal style recalls Asian American radio disc jockey Theo Mizuhara ("Theo" on Los Angeles R&B/hip-hop station 92.3 the Beat), often assumed to be African American by unsuspecting listeners because of his deep and soothing voice. This sexier Wong calls to Wallace—"Oooh girl"—before launching into his own rendition of her library scene: "Don't think I didn't see you watching me talking on my phone yesterday . . . all sexy . . . All Ching Chong Ling Long . . . Baby, it's just code . . . It's just the way that I tell the ladies that it's time for me to get funky."

For Wong, "getting funky" means launching into an acoustic ode to Wallace, a remix and reclamation of words and phrases lifted from her original video post. The song culminates in a repeating chorus, one that "wrings the musicality of the original Ching Chong" bit while satirizing its incommensurability: "Ching Chong . . . It means I love you . . . Ling Long . . . I really need you . . . Ching Chong . . . I still don't know what that means." The song's arrangement of vocal melody and harmony, acoustic guitar, and lo-fi percussion are simple and catchy. Yet the video's visual elements—the main frame of Wong is surrounded by small boxes or PiPs (picture in pictures) of him performing each portion of the music—requires a professional style of multichannel editing. Here, Wong's video evidences the unstable divisions between amateur and professional that is characteristic of the video-sharing website YouTube, ones that have helped redefine contemporary media production.

Since its initial posting, "Ching Chong! Asians in the Library Song" has garnered almost

Christine Bacareza Balance, "How It Feels to Be Viral Me: Affective Labor and Asian American YouTube Performance" from *WSQ: Women's Studies Quarterly* 40, Nos. 1 & 2, (Spring/Summer 2012): 138–152. Copyright © 2012 by the Feminist Press at the City University of New York. Used by permission of the publishers, www.feministpress.org. All rights reserved.

4 million hits worldwide, received coverage from both Asian American and mainstream U.S. press outlets, and landed the twenty-three-year-old actor/musician a role in an upcoming indie film. As a video that was able to spread quickly and across many screens, the "Ching Chong! Asians in the Library Song," in all respects, was a viral hit. While its popularity must be characterized as unexpected or accidental, in order for a YouTube video to "go viral," it must actually incorporate emotional hooks: key signifiers that catch the attention and sensibility of a particular audience. While sites like YouTube, by hosting such videos, enable the process of viral video making, these videos' successful transmission—from one user to the next—requires what media scholar Henry Jenkins has termed a larger participatory culture of related blogs, social networking sites, and mass media coverage (Jenkins 2006).

With these paradoxical and performative features, viral media has ushered in, according to journalists and industry insiders, a new generation of "Asian American YouTube stars." All but absent in the Hollywood star system and on the Billboard charts, Asian Americans—such as Ryan Higa (NigaHiga), Kevin Wu (KevJumba), and Wong Fu Productions—dominate YouTube's Most Subscribed lists.[1] Paying serious attention to this phenomenon of Asian American YouTube stars, either lauded for its democratizing potential (giving Asian American "unseen talents" a performance stage) or disparaged for its industry-driven tendencies (making visible an otherwise "unseen niche market"), I instead imagine other types of value that the stars hold for their youth audiences. It requires that we revisit this phenomenon, one branded as unforeseen, and locate it within a longer cultural history produced by the laborious acts of "feeling Asian American." As "production(s) defined by combination of cybernetics and affect" (Hardt 1999, 97), these YouTube performances— vlogs, webisodes, and musical covers—function as forms of affective labor for young Asian Americans today. While I respectfully engage the analytical language of media studies, my purpose falls more in line with a central theoretical concern of performance studies: to envision what these enactments might *mean* for their audiences. It is a perspective that falls out of reception studies' qualitative scope and one often concealed by the whitewash of fan studies.

I also want to think beyond a prevalent discourse that celebrates YouTube as a means for Asian Americans to infiltrate the mainstream and, therefore, "change da game."[2] With breakthrough celebrities such as Legaci (pop star Justin Bieber's touring backup vocalists) and Charice Pempengco (child star turned daytime television darling), many critics have heralded YouTube as a launching pad for Asian Americans, a group otherwise lacking representation in U.S. mainstream pop culture. Yet others maintain the opposite view: it is actually young Asian Americans whose "aesthetics and business sense have helped change the face of online video" (Kun 2010). As illustrated in discussions at the Conference for Creative Content (C3), which took place in June 2011 at Visual Communications' annual Los Angeles Asian American film festival, today's Asian American creative hopefuls do not merely accede to but actively exploit social media and information-sharing platforms such as YouTube, Facebook, Twitter, and blogs as what was described at C3 as their "new calling card." To further aid this generation in "negotiating and navigating between community and commerce," C3 panels focused on the entrepreneurial nuts and bolts necessary to succeed online: copyright and intellectual property rights; effective modes of branding, distribution, and news reporting; and crafting performances to capture audiences. And if their hands-on approach to "becoming a YouTube star" was not enough of a draw, the organizers also summoned Asian America's celebrity power as panelists—bloggers Phil Yu and Diana Nguyen, YouTube trendsetter Wong Fu Productions, and *Glee* star Harry Shum.

Along with its ability to infiltrate and infect, the viral has the power to replicate. So, while some journalists and media organizations view YouTube as an open stage for Asian American performers, artists themselves look to the website as an alternative avenue of cultural production. As twenty-four-year-old Korean American rapper Dumbfoundead (Jonathan Park) noted in a recent *Koream* magazine article, "Asians got tired of waiting to get into the mainstream. With YouTube, you don't have to wait for somebody to sign you, or give you a budget of millions of dollars to make a film; you can just do it. We're like, 'YouTube's here. We're going to smash it up with this YouTube thing'" (Eun and Ma 2010). With "no third party, no money-sucking managers, or closed-minded

Hollywood executives," Asian Americans do not simply leverage but actually dominate YouTube's topten-channel lists, designating them as celebrities on the video-sharing site. Encompassing "highly visible and successful 'homegrown' performers and producers," as defined by Joshua Green and Jean Burgess, the category of "YouTube celebrity" or "YouTube star" consists of entrepreneurial vloggers such as Jimmy Wong, cultural producers who collaborate with other artists and partake in the site's daily life as active consumers (2009, 91). As a communication genre, vlogs derive from such media antecedents as "webcam culture, personal blogging, and the more widespread 'confessional culture' that characterizes television talk shows and reality television—while also adhering to current social media mandates to 'invite critique, debate, and discussion'" (94). At the same time, while "digital visuality" online "can reinstate an understanding of race as always visible and available to the naked eye," according to media scholar Lisa Nakamura, on the Internet (unlike in cinema) "users have the option to perform their identities in ways that are not possible elsewhere" (2008, 205). No longer simply broadcasting media, YouTube's celebrity system also requires its stars to post responses to their viewers' comments, follow other users' videos, and maintain public profiles through other Web 2.0 channels (Facebook, Myspace, Twitter). Tapping into and taking part in the "affective economies" of these media and networking platforms, YouTube stars are often required to extend their performances beyond these virtual arenas.[3]

To succeed in today's participatory culture, with its own logic of affective economics, the larger U.S. entertainment industry has had to rethink how it does business. No longer able to merely distribute content in a top-down fashion, organizations and performers—whether amateur or professional, nonprofit or profit driven—are forced to devise new forms of audience outreach and engagement. In Asian America, the International Secret Agents (ISA) showcase and nonprofit organization Kollaboration are two grassroots examples of this new affective economics model as they both capitalize on a niche audience's emotional attachment to performers ("people like me") by presenting YouTube celebrities live in performance. Started in 2008 by Southern California's Wong Fu Productions and hip-hop group Far East

Movement, ISA has since showcased popular Asian American performers, from YouTube celebrities A. J. Rafael, Ryan Higa, and Jennifer Chung to reality TV contestants/hip-hop dance crews Quest Crew and Poreotics, in cities such as Seattle and New York as well as the Los Angeles ethnoburbs San Gabriel and Cerritos. With five sold-out concerts in the past three years, according to Wong Fu Productions' website, ISA "prov[es] that there is a voice, face, and desire for Asian Americans in the mainstream world" (see ISA [http://isatv.com/?page_id=66]). While both ISA and Kollaboration employ YouTube for the purposes of publicizing and programming their events, Kollaboration—with its tagline "Empowerment Through Entertainment"—actually auditions brand-new performers on YouTube for its seasonal acoustic as well as electric concert-competitions. Established eleven years ago in Los Angeles' Koreatown (where its headquarters are still based), Kollaboration has spread across the nation, with local chapters, or Kollaboration Cities, in Asian American centers: San Francisco, Seattle; New York; Washington, DC; Toronto; Chicago; Atlanta; Houston; and Tulsa. Extending the reach of YouTube stars—from home computer screens onto concert stages—ISA and Kollaboration's community-based efforts also map today's Asian America.

According to *Koream* writers Elizabeth Eun and Julie Ma (2010), before YouTube's advent in 2005, "it all seemed self-indulgent and borderline narcissistic . . . uploading videos of yourself belting out pop songs or talking to an invisible audience." Yet despite the ways online media has changed the aesthetics and business of entertainment, most YouTube video performances are still popularly perceived as being amateurish in their look and feel—"narcissistic" and "self-indulgent" musical or spoken solo performances addressed to a built-in computer camera, with little else in terms of lighting, backdrop, or editing. These are consumer-based productions. However, as critics have noted, the probability of a YouTube video's "going viral" hinges precisely on the qualities of authenticity and earnestness. "Not targeted nor read as necessarily containing material for general audiences," Patricia Lange notes, these viral hits often contain "stereotypical, spontaneous, and . . . numerous in-jokes and references that many general viewers would not understand in the way the creators intended" (2009, 73). In other words, to catch an already distracted viewer's attention, viral videos must exude an air of amateur production—versus the slick, professional, and therefore controlled aesthetics of mainstream Hollywood or television sources—and mobilize key signifiers that resonate with a particular community or subculture.

Once struggling in a constrictive media system that viewed its films and performances as unprofitable and the idea of an Asian American audience as moot, indie Asian American artists have reaped the most benefit from social media's democratic promise. Already engaged in analog forms of virality (such as DIY filmmaking, word-of-mouth advertising, and informal networks of production), Asian American artists and entrepreneurs have easily shifted into digital mode. In the nonprofit sector, Asian American theaters and arts organizations mobilize social media in order to publicize upcoming productions, assist in fund-raising campaigns, and archive highlights from past productions or major events. At the same time, some of the most successful Asian American artists on YouTube—Wong Fu, Legaci, Charice, and KevJumba, for example—had years of performance experience and training under their belt before uploading their first YouTube video. In the case of Wong Fu Productions, which started circulating its work via email in the late 1990s, the video-sharing website was merely a cheap and easy alternative for sharing film shorts and music videos, especially with friends who lacked high-speed Internet connections. In all these cases, YouTube was the means, not the ends, to producing and distributing their work.

Yet how do we account for the popularity of YouTube stars and their performances among today's Asian American youth? In other words, besides just continuing a tradition of DIY cultural production, what purpose do these Asian American YouTube performers—their videos and the ways in which they are shared—actually serve? These questions arise for me not only in the space of this essay or during my private moments of writing and researching but also, and more so, in the public spaces of teaching, when students share and retell their fandom for certain YouTube performers and performances—or when I notice swooning from thirty-and-under Asian Americans huddled around computer screens, see them standing in line for tickets to a YouTube college tour show, or hear them screaming from their seats at a recent Kollaboration Acoustic 5 showcase. Is there something about YouTube—a genre of new media dependent upon the viral, as a "politics of form and form of politics"—that speaks to the simultaneously virtual and material aspects of Asian American identity?[4]

At once an all-too-easy catchall term (among census takers, public health researchers, and marketers) for an endlessly diverse population—of various ethnicities, nations, and classes, fluent in a number of different languages/dialects and with divergent immigration histories—"Asian American" originated as a highly contested, simultaneously political and cultural term during the civil rights, anti–Vietnam War, and student movements of the 1960s and 1970s. Purposefully pan-ethnic, it signaled the interlocking, oft-forgotten histories of U.S. war and empire in Asia and earlier Asian immigration to the United States as well as the mutually material and representational effects of these historical events and conditions. According to early Yellow Power proponents, while early twentieth-century U.S. popular representation of Asians focused on "contagious divides"—the discursive lines between U.S. modernity and Orientalized otherness drawn across Asian bodies—since the end of World War II and the Cold War's onset, one particular myth of racialization has prevailed (Shah 2001). Published in 1966, in the aftermath of the Moynihan report and amid rising domestic racial tensions, the main themes of the *U.S. World and News Report* article "Success Story of One Minority Group in the U.S." continue on in the "model minority" myth. Painting a portrait of the Chinese and Japanese as hardworking, obedient, self-reliant individuals whose drive toward assimilation is matched only by their fervent adherence to "traditional Asian values"— filial piety, humility, and sacrifice—the model minority myth is a neoliberal form of racialization.[5] It at once promises U.S. citizenship and belonging to those Asian subjects ("obedient, self-reliant individuals) who must also perform a racialized script that marks them as forever foreign ("traditional Asian values"). In this frequent collapse between "Asian" and "Asian American," model minority discourse has prescribed the parameters of Asian American-ness, setting the terms for political debate within Asian America.[6]

Against this discursive containment, scholars such as Kandice Chuh, Laura Kang, Lisa Lowe, and Karen Shimawaka have helped us fine-tune a working definition of "Asian American," one that reminds us of its supple and performative nature, an identity constituted by multiple and competing epistemologies. . . . As Lowe eloquently outlined in her seminal *Immigrant Acts,* Asian American culture is a "countersite to U.S. national culture" where "contradictions are read, performed, and critiqued"; it functions as a "medium of the present" that "mediates the past," remembering fragmented histories while reimagining political futures (Lowe 1996, 65). Likewise, against community-based discursive containment—the kind that espouses notions of Asian Americans as culturally, socially, and politically homogeneous, attempts to expel radical Asian otherness through anti-immigrant sentiments, or even falls prey to the assimilationist lure of performing "model minority"-ness—I want to consider the political potential and critical possibilities offered by Asian American YouTube performances, as staged and everyday performances of affect and participation. . . . As mentioned above, the success of viral media depends upon (1) a niche or subculture's active participation through online networks (i.e., websites, blogs, and social networking directed at its particular needs/concerns) and (2) its knowledge of and ability to craft emotional hooks, key signifiers that touch upon a shared set of affective investments and affiliations. Asian America's particular use of viral media points to this virtual diaspora's simulated and representational elements and, in turn, to the performative and affective dimensions of the "symbolic ethnicity" of Asian Americans.

A 2001 Pew Internet and American Life Project reported that "fully 75% of English-speaking Asian-American adults have used the Internet," surpassing the numbers for all other English-speaking ethnic and even white American groups and making them "the most wired racial or ethnic group in America," "the young and the connected" (Spooner 2001, 2). Unlike their ethnic or even white counterparts, Asian American Internet users were "proportionally much more likely than others to get information about financial matters, travel, and political information" as well as "to use the Internet as a resource at school or at work" (2). In this comparative race-based research study, the report's author cites the challenges to surveying and collecting coherent data within this pan-ethnic community: heterogeneity of languages, high levels of language retention, and a lack of proper translation services. Thus, with its English-only survey,

the Pew report depends upon and, in turn, perpetuates a limited definition of "Asian American."

Alongside a critique of this domesticating discourse, the trope of Asian American "hyperconnectivity" requires a deeper inquiry into the causes and effects of this group's long-standing Internet use and early adoption of Web 2.0 technologies—social networking sites like Friendster, Myspace, Facebook; short message services; and Internet telephone providers such as Skype. For both U.S. and foreign-born Asian Americans who maintain connections to homeland politics and family networks, these digital technologies allow for quick, inexpensive communication across time zones and national borders. Therefore, as Linda Leung has noted, the Asian diaspora is an imagined community "experienced largely over the Internet" and best "characterized as 'virtual'" (2008, 10). While the virtuality of Asian America traffics in both the simulated and representational, it also gestures toward an extensive cluster of real-world implications and everyday situations. The explosion of Korean pop (K-pop) culture globally, in the past decade, exemplifies this interplay between the virtual and material. Although the Internet's role in disseminating state-sponsored and market-driven forms of K-Pop culture is vital, as cultural anthropologist Jung-Sun Park observes, Korean American youth (U.S.-born and 1.5 generations as well as *yuhaksaeng,* students who study abroad) and their "consumption, dissemination, and to some extent, creation, of trans-Pacific popular culture"—as they participate in K-Pop-oriented websites and forums and share with friends, family, and other fans the latest news and songs from abroad—plays an equally crucial role (2008, 161). Alienated from mainstream U.S. popular culture, the Korean American youth whom Park interviews find a sense of belonging, a "feeling at home," in K-Pop's style and culture.

In the registers of emotion and affect, Asian American youth also work through and against the specter of the model minority as a prescriptive racial fiction. Throughout its popular cultural history, Asian America has propagated the "grander passions" of anger, rage, and shame (Ngai 2005, 6). Like today's YouTube videos, 'zines of the 1990s yesteryears, with their espousal of punk and indie subcultures' DIY credo, also toed the lines "between commercial and D.I.Y., between mainstream and marginal" (Rubin 2003, 14). In the case of highly successful print publications that survived their digital transformation into online 'zines—Eric Nakamura and Martin Wong's *Giant Robot,* Mimi Thi Nguyen's *Exoticize This!,* and Sabrina Alcantara-Tan's *Bamboo Girl*—the tone of Asian America's talk-back to mainstream U.S. industries and representation took on the punk aesthetic of "gleeful opposition to decorum and propriety" by expressing itself in ways that "fl[y] directly in the face of the 'polite Asian' stereotype" (Rubin 2003, 15–16). If model minority status was maintained through deference, then these cultural forerunners instead chose to express anger and rage, emotions falling outside the boundaries of this racial fiction. Ironically, model minority rhetoric actually figures Asians as *unfeeling* or, as Wesley Yang vividly described in his recent *New York* magazine article "Asian Like Me," "a mass of stifled, repressed, abused, conformist quasi-robots" (2011, 22). Derived as they are from this 'zine publishing tradition, it is no wonder that some of today's most popular Asian American blogs still contain emotionally charged terms—the blogs *Angry Asian Man, Disgrasian,* and *You Offend Me You Offend My Family* (*YOMYOMF*). Through these particularly salient examples, we might hone our understanding of Asian American as a "symbolic ethnicity." According to Rachel Rubin, the categorical term of "Asian American" is "symbolic, because of its rhetorical and deliberative nature, but, nonetheless possessed of real-world implications" (2003, 5). As a mode of identification, it holds the possibility of being a "deliberative and motivated thing: experiential rather than biological, grounded in the present as much or more than in the past" (5). For Asian American 'zine writers, this "deliberative and motivated thing" registered as an "attitude," a particular way of expressing one's being-in-the-world. In the case of YouTube performances, such as Jimmy Wong's "Ching Chong! Asians in the Library" parody, the Asian American attitude today references a broader set of emotions than just anger and rage but still performs the affective labor of transforming alienating episodes into a common understanding. . . .

For Davis Jung, producer of the recent Conference for Creative Content, Wong Fu Productions' 2006 "Yellow Fever"—the group's first You-Tube video and response to the common narratives of Asian American masculinity—arrived at a critical point in his life. In his online essay "How New Media Gave Me a Voice," Jung narrates familiar tales for Asian Americans—the perpetual mispronunciation of one's name, the attempt to cultivate a love for genres of whiteness (country music, Classical Civilization major), and, of course, the lack of "role models" or "words" to articulate one's self—in order to capture the paradoxical feelings of Asian America: cultural alienation and, yet, the desire to belong. Bored and procrastinating, one fall evening in 2007, the then college-age Jung stumbled upon the University of California–San Diego collective's video link and clicked it. "I cannot tell you how many times I watched that video. It reached out and shook me. It made me laugh, and later on, it made me cry. It excited me, it incited me. It made me question everything that I had ever assumed about myself. It made me question what it meant to be 'normal.'"

Appearing at the end of his essay, this moment of cultural discovery serves as Jung's final word, his response to the question continually raised regarding the value of YouTube for Asian Americans. Pivoting between the dualities of culture and commerce, business and cultural resource, node and network, the rhetoric regarding the content-sharing website vacillates between characterizing it as "culturally generative" (for the several roles it plays as "high volume website, broadcast platform, media archive, social network") and seeing it as merely another "'top-down' platform for distributing popular culture" (Snickars and Vondereau 2009, 13). Yet, as Jung's anecdote so vividly reminds us, we need another set of protocols: an audience-centered analysis of the value of Asian American YouTube performances. By invoking a certain set of shared affects for these Asian American youth audiences, these YouTube stars' vlogs, song parodies, skits, and cover performances produce something "intangible: a feeling of ease, well-being, satisfaction, excitement, passion—even a sense of connectedness or community" (Hardt 1999, 96). Breaking out of the model minority myth's discursive containment, these emerging online personalities restage and respond to the banal and ridiculously racist moments of Asian America's everyday life, performing the affective labor of transforming alienation into humor, hate into love. Unexpectedly, a story or a song might catch us. Moved by these performances, we cannot help but share them, infecting others with the feeling.

NOTES

1. The most spectacular examples: comedic vlogger "KevJumba" (Kevin Wu): no. 9 Most Subscribed Comedian (All Time), 1.4 million subscribers, over 150 million views; character actor/comedian "NigaHiga" (Ryan Higa): You-Tube no. 1 Most Subscribed (All Time), 3.4 million subscribers, over 746 million views; directorial/writing collective Wong Fu Productions (Wesley Chan, Ted Fu, and Philip Wang): 785,394 subscribers, over 95 million views.

2. From the title of a panel at the 2010 San Francisco Asian American Film Festival: "Changing da Game: YouTube Legends and the Future of Online Media" (Center for Asian American Media 2010).

3. In this particular case, I am referencing Burgess and Green's use of "affective economies" to describe the participatory culture of emotional attachments and investments expressed on YouTube. Other scholars such as Sara Ahmed and Henry Jenkins have also written about the "affective economies" of political language and actions between racialized individuals within the nation-state (Ahmed 2004) and the logics of "affective economics" as propagated and perpetuated by reality television shows such as *American Idol* (Jenkins 2006).

4. I am borrowing this notion of "the politics of form and the form of politics" to discuss the critical and political work enacted by cultural productions from Jodi Kim's (2010) recently released *Ends of Empire: Asian American*

Critique and the Cold War. Thanks also to Joshua Chambers-Letson (2009) for his essay "Contracting Justice: the Viral Strategy of Felix Gonzalez-Torres," which models different ways that a term such as the "viral" can be mobilized as a conceptual meeting point for an interdisciplinary discussion of bodies, the law, and artistic form.

5. In some aspects, the political difficulties faced by a term such as "Asian American" find a kinship with the similarly vexed identity category of "Latino." As Jose Esteban Muñoz has questioned, "Latino does not subscribe to a common racial, class, gender, religious, or national category, and if a Latino can be from any country in Latin America, a member of any race, religion, class, or gender/sex orientation, who then is she? What, if any, nodes of commonality do Latinas/os share?" (Muñoz 2000, 67) Yet, in other ways, "Asian American" has historically served as an umbrella term that has unified seemingly disparate groups. For the purposes of this essay, I draw on the spirit of Muñoz's focus on affective performances, or ways of "feeling brown," as a site for mobilizing different forms of what Norma Alarcon (1996) has designated an "identity-in-difference."

6. It bears repeating here that, within this containment logic of the "model minority," "Asian" more often refers to East Asian Americans (i.e., Chinese, Japanese, and sometimes Korean) rather than Asian/Asian American ethnicities such as Filipinos, South Asians, and Southeast Asians.

WORKS CITED

Ahmed, Sara. 2004. "Affective Economies." *Social Text* 22(2):117–39.

Alarcon, Norma. 1996. "Conjugating Subjects in the Age of Multiculturalism." In *Mapping Multiculturalism,* ed. Avery F. Gordon and Christopher Newfield. Minneapolis: University of Minnesota Press.

Bryman, Alan. 2004. *The Disneyization of Society.* Thousand Oaks, CA: Sage.

Burgess, Jean, and Joshua Green. 2009. "The Entrepreneurial Vlogger: Participatory Culture Beyond the Professional-Amateur Divide." In *The YouTube Reader,* ed. Pelle Snickars and Patrick Vondereau. Stockholm: National Library of Sweden.

Center for Asian American Media. 2010. "Changing da Game: YouTube Legends and the Future of Online Media." http://www.youtube.com/watch? v=98ayDYf UMtk

Chambers-Letson, Joshua. 2009. "Contracting Justice: The Viral Strategy of Felix Gonzalez-Torres." *Criticism* 51(4):559–87.

Chuh, Kandice. 2003. *Imagine Otherwise: On Asian Americanist Critique.* Durham: Duke University Press.

Eun, Elizabeth, and Julie Ma. 2010. "How YouTube Transformed the Asian American Arts Scene." *Koream,* September. http://iamkoream.com/coverstory-youtube-stars/

Hardt, Michael. 1999. "Affective Labor." *boundary 2* 226(2): 89–100.

Hyon, Soyoung Sonjia. 2011. "Anxieties of the Fictive: The Immigrant and Asian American Politics of Visibility." PhD diss., University of Minnesota.

Jenkins, Henry. 2006. *Convergence Culture: Where Old and New Media Meet.* New York: New York University Press.

Jung, Davis. 2011. "How New Media Gave Me a Voice." http://asianfilmfestla.org/2011/films-events/c3-conference-for-creative-content/how-newmedia-gave-me-a-voice/

Kang, Laura. 2003. *Compositional Subjects: Enfiguring Asian/American Women.* Durham: Duke University Press.

Kim, Jodi. 2010. *Ends of Empire: Asian American Critique and the Cold War.* Minneapolis: University of Minnesota Press.

Kun, Josh. 2010. "Unexpected Harmony: YouTube Helps Legaci's Breakout." *New York Times,* June 18, AR1.

Lange, Patricia. 2009. "Videos of Affinity on YouTube." In *The YouTube Reader,* ed. Pelle Snickars and Patrick Vondereau. Stockholm: National Library of Sweden.

Leung, Linda. 2008. "From 'Victims of the Digital Divide' to 'Technoelites': Gender, Class, and Contested 'Asianness' in Online and Offline Geographies." In *South Asian Technospaces,* ed.

Radhika Gajjala and Venkataramana Gajjala. New York: Peter Lang.

Lowe, Lisa. 1996. *Immigrant Acts: On Asian American Politics.* Durham: Duke University Press.

Muñoz, Jose Esteban. 2000. "Feeling Brown: Ethnicity and Affect in Ricardo Bracho's *The Sweetest Hangover (and Other STDs).*" *Theatre Journal* 52(1): 67–79.

Nakamura, Lisa. 2008. *Digitizing Race: Visual Cultures of the Internet.* Minneapolis: University of Minnesota Press.

Ngai, Sianne. 2005. *Ugly Feelings.* Cambridge: Harvard University Press.

Park, Jung-Sun. 2008. "Korean American Youth and Transnational Flows of Popular Culture Across the Pacific." In *Transpop: Korea Vietnam Remix* (exhibition catalogue), ed. Viet Le and Yong Soon Min. Seoul: Arko Art Center, Arts Council Korea.

Rubin, Rachel. 2003. "Cyberspace Y2K: Giant Robots Asian Punks." Occasional Paper, Institute for Asian American Studies. Boston: Institute for Asian American Studies, University of Massachusetts Boston.

Shah, Nayan. 2001. *Contagious Divides: Epidemics and Race in San Francisco's Chinatown.* Berkeley: University of California Press.

Shimakawa, Karen. 2002. *National Abjection: The Asian American Body Onstage.* Durham: Duke University Press.

Snickars, Pelle, and Patrick Vondereau. 2009. "Introduction." In *The YouTube Reader,* ed. Pelle Snickars and Patrick Vondereau. Stockholm: National Library of Sweden.

Spooner, Tom. 2001. "Asian Americans and the Internet: the young and the connected." Pew Internet and American Life Project. Washington, DC: Tides Center.

Visual Communications. 2011. "C3 Conference" (schedule). http://asianfilmfestla.org/2011/films-events/c3-conference-for-creative-content/

Yang, Wesley. 2011. "Asian Like Me." *New York,* May 16, 22–29.

THE LATINO CYBER-MORAL PANIC PROCESS IN THE UNITED STATES

Nadia Yamel Flores-Yeffal, Guadalupe Vidales, and April Plemons

67

According to Cohen (1972), 'moral panic' is the reaction of a society against a specific social group based on beliefs that the subgroup represents a major threat to society. Usually, the information spread is exaggerated or fabricated by what Becker (1963) calls 'moral entrepreneurs' who create a threatening situation with inflated rhetoric and develop a sense of fear against the subgroup. Commonly, this rhetoric is spread with the use of popular and mass media (e.g. newspaper headlines, radio shows, television programs, web-sites, weblogs, and/or discussion forums). Such outlets divert society's attention from more pressing issues affecting American society and those who are in control utilize resources such as 'politics, social status, gender, wealth, religious beliefs, and mobilization of the masses' to dominate, both, 'materially and ideologically', the information targeting the subordinate group (Adler & Adler 2009, p. 152).

Today, an immigrant subgroup is being targeted and victimized by a moral panic—Latinos/as, particularly, Mexican immigrants (Massey 2007; Chavez 2008; Perez *et al.* 2008). Such demonization of a specific subgroup of immigrants is not new in the United States. Throughout history, US immigration policies have been described as unfair and capricious procedures in which the US government acts without any regard to the immigrant's rights and needs (Calavita 1992, 1996; Ngai 2004; Massey 2007). First, the United States enacted the Chinese Exclusion Act in 1882, which discriminated against Chinese immigrants. Then, European immigrants at the turn of the twentieth century, such as Russian Jews, German Catholics and Italians, faced a second wave of

discrimination where the same rhetoric previously used against the Chinese was also utilized to demonize and dehumanize these new immigrants (Brodkin 1999; Foner 2000; Ngai 2004; Portes & Rumbaut 2006).

Chavez (2008) states that the new 'Latino Threat Narrative is part of a grand tradition of alarmist discourse about immigrants and their perceived negative impact on society' (p. 3). He further argues that immigrant Latinos are labeled 'illegal aliens' to emphasize their criminal status, which presents them as a group of criminal outsiders unworthy of social services, educational support and legalization.

. . . Due to online technological advances, this negative perception has increased and become more pervasive; 'moral entrepreneurs' have facilitated the spread of information in ways never imagined against Latinos. The near instantaneous spread of cyberspace information directly affects the process in which contemporary moral panics take place. In this chapter, we use the case of the anti-immigrant sentiment against Latinos in the United States to explore the extent to which online technology influences the classic moral panic stages as previously presented by scholars before the use of internet technology. . . .

THE CLASSIC MORAL PANIC STAGES

According to the classic moral panic process framework, a full-blown moral panic is the final stage in the moral campaign process: awareness, moral conversion, and moral panic. Through

From Nadia Yamel Flores-Yeffal et al. (2012), "The Latino Cyber-Moral Panic Process in the United States." *Information, Communication and Society*, 14:4, 568–589. Reprinted by permission of the publisher (Taylor & Francis Ltd., http://www.tandf.co.uk/journals).

these stages, public morality can be constructed, manufactured, and spread. In the 'awareness' stage, a message is generated in relation to a problem by citing statistics, case examples, presenting 'experts' to justify their claims, and using intense rhetorical methods. The second stage, 'moral conversion' draws upon 'elements of drama, novelty, or cultural myths' in which entrepreneurs utilize wide media coverage and often seek celebrities or political leaders to convince the masses (p. 149). Through these surrogate sponsors, moral entrepreneurs legitimize their claims and convince the public to join the movement. In the final stage, 'moral panic', there is a temporary and widespread concern about a problematic issue promoted both by the media and legislative attention. Furthermore, formal and informal communication outlets draw attention to a specific targeted group, or 'folk devils', who become the scapegoats for larger social ills. . . .

THE CONSTRUCTION OF LATINOS AS A THREAT

Prior research demonstrates that people of color are commonly perceived as a possible threat to society (King & Wheelock 2007), and Latino immigrants are not an exception. Huntington (2004) published 'The Hispanic Challenge', in which he asserts that Latinos, especially Mexicans, represent an extremely dangerous threat to the United States and its culture because of their failure to assimilate, failure to learn English, and failure to adopt the Protestant values. Then, a 2005 report from the Pew Hispanic Center announced there were 12 million unauthorized immigrants living in the United States, and 75 percent were Hispanic (Passel 2005). More recently, the 2006 HR 4437 law, also called 'the Border Protection, Antiterrorism, and Illegal Immigration Control Act', was the catalyst for immigration marches where millions of people marched on the streets in protest of the proposed legislation and calling for immigration reform. These marches were broadcasted globally, and it has been claimed that an anti-immigrant backlash against Latino immigrants began as a result of the 2006 immigrant Marches (Perez et al. 2008). In 2006, the US Census Bureau announced in major newspapers that the US Hispanic population was 'projected to

nearly triple, from 46.7 million to 132.8 million, from 2008 through 2050. Its share of the total US population was expected to double from 15 to 30 percent by the year 2050; thus, one in three US residents would be Hispanic' (Broughton 2008). Given this, Latino immigrants would outnumber all the other racial and ethnic groups in the United States, including the non-Hispanic White population, therefore, representing a possible numeric threat to the nation (Chavez 2008; Feagin 2009).

American nativist rhetoric was strongly associated with issues related to the preservation of national sovereignty, such as the protection of US territory from an invasion (Chavez 2001). The immigrants' utilization of the Mexican flag as a symbol of their nation is perceived as a racial threat and the 'browning' of United States. Also, other problems are perceived as a threat such as the economic burden that immigrants represented and the multiculturalism agenda they embraced. . . .

In addition, immigrant groups have been described as 'contaminated communities', and 'popular rhetoric about immigration often operates by constructing metaphoric representations of immigrants that concretize the social "problem"' (Cisneros 2008, p. 569). Immigrants also have been identified in cyberspace as 'the immigrant problem' (Sohoni 2006). In this way, immigrants become degraded images and not human beings. Goode and Yehuda (1994) argue 'folk devils' are used as metaphors or symbolic representations of moral panics; they are shrouded in myths and empirical falsehoods. Therefore, in this paper, we introduce the term *Latino cyber-moral panic*, in which we claim that the use of cyber technology has provided a dangerous platform in which the already existent anti-immigrant movement has become more dangerous against Latinos. Here, false and manipulated information transforms Latino immigrants into the contemporary American 'folk devils', or those perceived as threatening the social order and blamed for much of society's problems (Cohen 1972).

MORAL ENTREPRENEURS AND THE USE OF INTERNET TECHNOLOGY

Media outlets tend to include such allegations against the subgroup, in this case against the Latino immigrants in the United States, into their media content and emotionally charging otherwise dispassionate subjects to maximize their audiences (McRobbie & Thornton 1995). Also Shoemaker and Reese (1996) note that 'the more deviant people or events are, the more likely they are to be included in media content and the more likely they are to be stereotyped' (p. 270). Alarmist websites, internet blogs, social networking sites such as Twitter and Facebook, internet forums, television programs, video hosting sites such as YouTube, radio talk shows and billboard propaganda, among other types of public free expression in the era of the reflexive and interactive Web 2.0, are utilized to spread the information, which generally includes hate content instantaneously at low cost, and to an even larger audience than newspaper and TV consumers. As Castells et al. (2008) state, the 'public sphere' is culturally and politically critical because it is the 'space where people come together as citizens and articulate their autonomous views to influence the political institutions of society' (p. 2). The public sphere refers to the ability to form social opinions as a result of rational public debate (Habermas 1991[1973]) which has been revived with the use of the internet technology (Papacharissi 2002). In addition, the internet allows for the access to tools which permit individuals to engage in new social and political action, have instant access to social network outlets and exchange of information at a distance (Bowen 1996; DiMaggio et al. 2001; Castells et al. 2007; Van Laer & Van Aelst 2010).

Actors at the top of the power structure who are active in the movement and who enjoy greater access to the internet utilize different features, such as derogatory images, exaggerated pictures and discriminatory cartoons to effectively spread the Latino cyber-moral panic to others, which is then reproduced and transmitted by individuals mainly also via cyberspace. Social power online is no longer simply at the hands of the few or elite. While moral entrepreneurs and politicians can exert 'considerable influence' over media and social thought, the audience is equally as active in creating, reproducing, and influencing content (Castells 2007). In either case, the internet allows a new form of cyberspace socialization containing a number of technological advances used as outlets for people to exchange information, enjoy relative anonymity and share their social views and values

to untapped mass audiences (DiMaggio et al. 2001; Bergh & McKenna 2004).

The moral entrepreneurs penetrate the mass media using alarmist reports often cited by major newspapers. Such alarmist news produced by those reports help sell more newspapers and reach a larger audience given that, at the time of writing this paper, most newspapers were published via cyberspace which is now playing a more 'decisive role' in shaping social movements (Castells et al. 2008). . . .

THE STUDY

We utilized a multi-method approach in cyber space consisting of online ethnographic research followed by content analysis of anti-immigrant websites. . . .

Our online ethnography consisted of online participant observation, field notes and data documentation from various cyber social networks including anti-immigrant and pro-immigrant websites, US government websites, documents and reports about immigration online, blogs and forums (both pro-and anti-immigration), online newspaper articles, forums, Facebook, *YouTube,* emails and online video hosting since May 2006. The authors have observed evidence of the moral panic through visiting these sources. For example, one of the authors has been an online participant-observer of an anti-immigration forum which began before the 2006 immigrant marches and spent an average of two hours per day discussing immigration issues and gathering information from other websites, blogs, forums, and news articles mostly available online and posted by other forum participants. She also obtained information concerning the main sources and how arguments that supported the anti-immigrant sentiment were originated. In addition, the three authors have been conducting content analyses of several talk radio programs and political news television shows, and collecting data from talk radio websites, Twitter posts, and Facebook updates also related to the same television and radio programs, where the discussion of anti-immigrant issues are the norm.

. . . During the preliminary stages of our research, while constructing our snowball sample of websites, we unintentionally discovered the anti-immigrant movement in cyberspace is led by the following three 'think tank' organizations via their websites:

1. The Center for Immigration Studies (CIS)

2. NumbersUSA

3. The Federation for American Immigration Reform (FAIR).

We realized most of the sites, if not all, had links to the three think tanks named above, which illustrates the degree of the trio's influence. Others identified the 'trio' as very influential in the anti-immigrant movement (Beirich 2009), and noted that their websites did not utilize nativist language (Sohoni 2006). These are what Daniels (2009) refers to as 'cloaked websites', because the anti-immigrant agenda is not apparent to online visitors. We argue the founders, board of directors, supporters and site creators or moderators are, in fact, the moral entrepreneurs leading the incrimination against Latino immigrants. Other moral entrepreneurs are from media outlets, such as political commentators, talk radio hosts, and politicians, but the data suggested the central moral entrepreneurs behind the cyberspace movement are FAIR, NumbersUSA and CIS, all three in particular.

The content analysis of the anti-immigrant website subsample revealed that one of the main strategic processes in attacking the subgroup was with the creation of metaphors and extensive use of images portraying Latino immigrants as 'folk devils'. This strategy increases the phobia by presenting the immigrants as inhumane and inferior to Americans. Another awareness-promoting strategy was the use and manipulation of images and words in order to portray an extremely negative image of the Latino immigrants to site visitors. For example, Latino immigrants were portrayed as dangerous, possible terrorists, killers, drug addicts and were accused of spreading diseases, such as the H1N1 virus, being dirty and living in crowded and unsanitary conditions. They were blamed for taking the jobs of Americans, reducing their wages, being a burden to society by not paying taxes, stealing identities, utilizing medical facilities, asking for welfare financial benefits, Medicaid, food stamps, or using fraudulent documents to vote among other claims.

Most sites posted claims together with other text disclosures stating that the sites and arguments had 'nothing to do with race' or being negative toward immigrants, but rather that their goals were only making people aware of the sudden increase in immigration statistics and the possible burdens this could represent to the American society. Most provided neither empirical evidence, nor empirical statistics to support their claims, but instead provided inflated statistics and pictures (which were altered and/or fabricated) that were posted next to each claim. For example, websites commonly juxtapose pictures of a young, smiling, blond haired child with one of a brown-skinned person's criminal mug shot, followed by a picture of a coffin to imply the child was murdered by an immigrant. However, there is no evidence of the picture's validity, or if the story's circumstances are even accurately associated with the people in the images.

User-created posts and comments and blogs linking to anti-immigrant sites revealed that, in general, site visitors rarely questioned the claims or content of the images. On the contrary, visitors began reproducing the links of exaggerated claims on additional blogs, forums, Facebook or Twitter pages and private sites to spread awareness to others, which exponentially spread the information in today's participatory, often user-created, Web 2.0. For example, a hoax about immigrant statistics (found by us in 2006) was circulating online that was said to have been published by *Los Angeles Times,* but the *Los Angeles Times* (2007) published a disclaimer (Internet Immigration Hoax 2007; http://latimesblogs.latimes.com/readers/2007/11/internet-immigr.html) stating this was false. The statistics stated that, '95% of warrants for murder in Los Angeles are for illegal aliens', and, that 'Over 300,000 illegal aliens in Los Angeles County are living in garages'. The hoax targeted Latinos, as it was supposed to have been published by *Los Angeles Times* and included statistics about Spanish speaking radio stations, etc. These false statistics spread online via anti-immigrant websites and newcomers believed the statistics enough to copy and paste them over and over in other forums, blogs, private websites, etc without questioning their validity or fact-checking. The claim appeared legitimate since it cited the *Los Angeles Times,* and, as of 13 September 2010, we found the phrase, 'Over 300,000 illegal aliens in Los

Angeles County are living in garages' resulted in 1,570,000 hits from the Yahoo search engine, and the phrase 'of warrants for murder in Los Angeles are for illegal aliens' yielded 9,690,000 results. Therefore, internet users spread the information and fear to others on the internet in order to make everyone else aware of the Latino threat (Chavez 2008). . . .

Given that their claims could not be supported by any academic empirical evidence or governmental reports, the moral entrepreneurs, led by the three organizations listed above (FAIR, CIS, and NumbersUSA) created a system of revolving information that we call the *Recycling Factory* in cyberspace. In this original process, each organization creates statistical reports and recycles them continuously to the other organizations. Each cites the other, and almost all of the sites used the reports to support their unsubstantiated statements. . . .

The content analysis of our sub-sample revealed a new stage that is absent in Adler and Adler's original three stages of the moral campaign process. We name this new stage the '*Call for civil action*' which includes various forms of calls for action, either civil or political. It is through this stage that individuals personally participate and directly contribute to the anti-immigrant movement. Prior moral panic research has never before identified at this stage, the direct participation by the individuals being converted. The internet is providing a new 'meta-medium' in which the public sphere can be utilized as a means to gather financial, political, social, and cultural support (DiMaggio et al. 2001).

. . . Some urge the boycott of American companies supporting immigration by offering detailed information about how and why to carry it out. Others invite citizens to become "minutemen"[1] and/or volunteer to protect the borders, as well as the reporting of undocumented immigrants. In fact, we found minuteman websites for almost every state in the nation, even those not in close proximity to the border. There were calls for donations which can be paid with a credit card or PayPal (a secure form of online payment). Some sites, such as FAIR also provide site visitors with information on how they can make recurrent donations to the organization. In fact, aside from making one-time donations, a person can contribute to FAIR's cause literally from the moment they

join the work force until after their death. From 401K plans (where donations will be matched dollar for dollar) to endowments, FAIR provides information on how one can include their organization and cause as a beneficiary of a life insurance policy or will. Site visitors are asked to directly participate in funding, supporting, and furthering the movement through this new stage, a call to action (found at: http://www.fairus.org/site/Page Navigator/support/other_ways_to_give.html).

Other forms of obtaining money from upset citizens was through the sale of minuteman videos, gold or silver coins, documentaries about immigration, hats, shirts, and bumper stickers with various patriotic anti-immigrant phrases, such as 'no amnesty' or 'no invasion'. A more extreme case sought donations to construct billboards all over the nation with the message, 'Stop the Invasion, Protect our Borders' (Melamed 2006). More importantly, revenue accumulated from these sites can be used to 'make campaign contributions and sway political candidates, to fund research favorable to their [movement] and to lobby against unfavorable legislation' (Adler & Adler 2009, p. 152).

. . . A successful tactic utilized by the cyberspace movement is the invitation to engage in political action by contacting politicians. This pervasive strategy includes elaborate information charts about how to contact legislators, current legislation for congressmen to vote on, petitions to sign, and where to rally in favor of or against a political proposition related to immigration, etc. They even include direct links to legislators and offer ready-to-send messages which can be sent asking for immediate action related to immigration issues. For example, visitors can browse their state's list of congressmen to find out their stance and voting records on anti-immigration legislation. At NumbersUSA, those congressmen with highest regard, or the 'best' anti-immigration voting records, win the title of 'True Reformers'— those who 'promise to support all or nearly all of NumbersUSA's top immigration priorities'. Of course, site visitors are provided a link to that congressman's personal website and encouraged to contribute to the 'True Reformer's' political campaign, in the hope of ensuring their re-election and support for the nativist movement (http://www.numbersusa.com/content/true-reform ers.html).

Finally, evidence from the sites' content analysis revealed that most sites posted evidence of the movement's successes. . . .

For example, FAIR's annual report claims that their number of site visitors in 2007 surpassed the 1 million mark and received over 6 million views, a significant increase from previous years (FAIR Annual report 2007). Evidence of the pro-immigrant movement's failures was commonly seen in reminders of the lack of immigration reform, successes of government intervention and new legislation, and the massive raids and deportations that have taken place in the past few years (Moreno 2007). Reports also show lower numbers of Mexican immigrants crossing the border to the United States, although Mexican immigrants in the United States are not returning to Mexico (Passel 2005; Passel & Cohn 2009). Unfortunately, the number of hate crimes which result from the Latino cyber-moral panic movement has yet to be measured. One example of a hate crime, which resulted as a consequence of this movement, is the case of a minuteman activist who was accused of killing a man and child in their own home:

> An outspoken anti-immigration activist who was at the center of a series of violent crimes in Everett earlier this year now stands accused of the home-invasion killings of an Arizona man and his 9-year-old daughter. Shawna Forde, 41, and two associates in her Minuteman American Defense group are charged with two counts of first-degree murder, one count of first-degree burglary and one count of aggravated assault, according to the Pima County Sheriff's Department in Arizona. (North et al. 2009)

Shawna Forde, the activist mentioned above, besides being a minuteman volunteer, was also found to be one of the executive directors of FAIR. Forde, who further jeopardized the organization's reputation for the murders of the immigrants, was ultimately found guilty and sentenced to death ('Jury decides on death penalty for woman who headed vigilante squad' 2011). . . .

CONCLUSION

. . . In this research, we used as an example, the Latino cyber-moral panic and found empirical evidence to support that Adler and Adler's three classic moral panic stages have taken place, but in a more effective manner with the use of new online technologies.

A new stage not previously identified was conceptualized called a 'call for action', where donations, political action, and civil action are promoted and enforced via cyberspace. Through calls for donations, moral entrepreneurs collect funds from the movement's panic victims to pay for other forms of propaganda and further spread the moral panic. Similar internet tools have already been identified as being key instruments for the direct participation of individuals in other political and social movements around the world (Bowen 1996; Van Laer & Van Aelst 2010).

. . . The results presented here indicate that the continually evolving online technologies, if used in a negative way, can be extremely dangerous against specific subgroups of people. Future moral panics could occur and progress even faster than today and more efficiently could aid in the creation of legislation, hate crimes, and social suppression against the 'folk devils' being targeted. Furthermore, if moral panics indeed provide an avenue for social reproduction of particular ideologies (Beisel 1997; Gatson 2007), then cyber-moral panics could then become a dangerous never-ending source of social reproduction of suppressing and discriminatory ideologies against specific subgroups of people. Future research should be conducted to examine the role of politicians as a type of secondary moral entrepreneurship with the goal of political benefit. . . . In addition, more research should explore the power of civil and political action with the help of cyberspace technology, and whether it can also be used for a more positive cyber movement in which the targeted groups, instead, could acquire some kind of benefit which could help them to succeed instead of placing them in a disadvantaged position in society.

NOTE

1. According to Chavez (2008), the Minutemen are a group of civilians whose final goal is 'to monitor the Arizona–Mexico border in the hopes of locating clandestine border crossers.

However, this surveillance operation also had a larger objective: to produce a spectacle that would garner public media attention and influence federal immigration polices' (p. 132). According to the Minuteman Project Command Center, their organization is 'a multiethnic, immigration law enforcement advocacy group.—Operating within the law to support enforcement of the law.—The power of change through the power of peace' http://www.minutemanproject.com/organization/about_us.asp.

REFERENCES

Adler, P. & Adler, P. (2009) 'Constructing deviance', in *Constructions of Deviance: Social Power, Context, and Interaction*, eds P. Adler & P. Adler, Wadsworth, Belmont, California, pp. 147–154.

Arsenault, A. & Castells, M. (2006) 'Conquering the minds, conquering Iraq: the social production of misinformation in the United States—a case study', *Information, Communication & Society*, vol. 9, no. 3, pp. 284–307.

Bakardjieva, M. & Feenberg, A. (2001) 'Involving the virtual subject: conceptual, methodological and ethical dimensions', *Journal of Ethics and Information Technology*, vol. 2, no. 4, pp. 233–240.

Baker, P. (2001) 'Moral panic and alternative identity construction in Usenet', *Journal of Computer-Mediated Communication*, vol. 7, no. 1.

Becker, H. S. (1963) *Outsiders: Studies in the Sociology of Deviance*, Free Press, New York.

Beirich, H. (2009) 'The Nativist lobby: three faces of intolerance' in *A Report from the Southern Poverty Law Center,* ed. Mark Potok, Montgomery, Alabama, pp. 1–21 [Online] Available at: http://www.splcenter.org/sites/default/files/downloads/splc_nativistlobby.pdf (10 January 2011)

Beisel, N. (1997) *Imperiled Innocents: Anthony Comstock and Family Reproduction in Victorian America,* Princeton University Press, Princeton, NJ.

Ben-Yehuda, N. (1986) 'The sociology of moral panics: toward a new synthesis', *The Sociological Quarterly*, vol. 27, no. 4, pp. 495–513.

Bergh, J. A. & McKenna, K. Y. (2004) 'The Internet and social life', *Annual Review of Psychology*, vol. 55, pp. 573–590.

Berry, D. M. (2004) 'Internet research: privacy, ethics and alienation—an open source approach', *The Journal of Internet Research*, vol. 14, no. 4, pp. 323–332.

Bowen, C. (1996) *Modem Nation: The Handbook of Grassroots American Activism Online*, Random House, New York.

Brodkin, K. (1999) *How Jews Became White Folks and What That Says About Race in America*, Rutgers University Press, New Brunswick, NJ.

Broughton, A. (2008) 'Minorities expected to be the majority in 2050', *CNN.com*, [Online] Available at: http://edition.cnn.com/2008/US/08/13/census.minorities/index.html (11 August 2009).

Calavita, K. C. (1992) *Inside the State: The Bracero Program, Immigration and the INS*, Routledge, Chapman and Hall, Inc, New York.

Calavita, K. (1996) 'The new politics of immigration: "balanced-budget conservatism" and the symbolism of proposition 187', *Social Problems*, vol. 43, pp. 284–305.

Castells, M. (2007) 'Communication, power and counter-power in the network society', *International Journal of Communication*, vol. 1, pp. 238–266.

Castells, M., Qui, J., Fernandez-Ardèvol, M. & Sey, A. (2007) *Mobile Communication and Society: A Global Perspective,* MIT, Cambridge, MA.

Castells, M., Qui, J., Fernandez-Ardèvol, M. & Sey, A. (2008) 'The new public sphere: global civil society, communication networks, global governance', *The ANNALS of the American Academy of Political and Social Science*, vol. 616, no. 1, pp. 78–93.

Chavez, L. (2001) *Covering Immigration Popular Images and the Politics of the Nation*, University of California Press, Los Angeles.

Chavez, L. (2008) The *Latino Threat: Constructing Immigrants, Citizens, and the Nation*, Stanford University Press, Palo Alto, California.

Chou, R. S. & Feagin, J. R. (2008) *The Myth of the Model Minority: Asian Americans Facing Racism*, Paradigm Publishers, Boulder, CO.

Cisneros, D. J. (2008) 'Contaminated communities: the metaphor of immigrant as pollutant in media representations of immigration', *Rhetoric & Public Affairs*, vol. 11, no. 4, pp. 569–602.

Cohen, S. (1972) *Folk Devils and Moral Panics*, Routledge Press, London.

Cornwell, B. & Linders, A. (2002) 'The myth of "Moral Panic": an alternative account of LSD prohibition', *Deviant Behavior*, vol. 23, pp. 307–330.

Daniels, J. (2008) 'Searching for Dr. King: teens, race & cloaked websites', in *Electronic Techtonics: Thinking at the Interface*, eds Erin Ennis Harry Halpin, Paolo Mangiafico, Jennifer Rhee et al., Lulu Press, Durham, NC, pp. 94–116.

Daniels, J. (2009) *Cyber Racism: White Supremacy Online and the New Attack on Civil Rights*, Rowman & Littlefield, Lanham, MD.

DiMaggio, P., Hargittai, E., Neuman, W. R. & Robinson, J. P. (2001) 'Social implications of the internet', *Annual Review of Sociology*, vol. 27, pp. 307–336.

Feagin, J. (2009) *The White Racial Frame*, Routledge Press, New York.

Federation for American Immigration Reform. (2007) 2007 *Annual Report, FAIRUS.org*, Washington DC, [Online] Available at: http://www.fairus.org/site/DocServer/2007_Annual_Report.pdf? docID=2402 (18 October 2009).

Federation for American Immigration Reform (2009) 'US Immigration Policy and Legislation', *FAIRUS.org*, [Online] Available at: http://www.fairus.org/site/PageNavigator/legislation (18 October 2009).

Federation for American Immigration Reform (2010) 'The fiscal burden of illegal immigration on United States taxpayers', *FAIRUS.org*, [Online] Available at: http://www.fairus.org/site/DocServer/USCostStudy_2010.pdf? docID=4921 (23 November 2010).

Fisher, D. R. & Boekkooi, M. (2010) 'Mobilizing friends and strangers: understanding the role of the internet in the step it up day of action', *Information, Communication & Society*, vol. 13, no. 2, pp. 193–208.

Foner, N. (2000) *From Ellis Island to JFK: New York's Two Great Waves of Immigration*, Russell Sage Foundation, New York.

Fox, N. & Roberts, C. (1999) 'GPs in cyberspace: the sociology of "virtual community"', *The Sociological Review*, vol. 47, no. 4, pp. 643–671.

Gajjala, R. (2000) 'Cyberethnography: reading each "Other"', [Online] Available at: http://personal.bgsu.edu/~radhik/Cyberethnography.pdf (10 September 2010).

Gajjala, R. (2002) 'An interrupted postcolonial/feminist cyberethnography: complicity and resistance in the "Cyberfield"', *Feminist Media Studies*, vol. 2, pp. 177–193.

Garcia, A. C., Standlee, A. I., Bechkoff, J. & Cui, Y. (2009) 'Ethnographic approaches to the internet and computer-mediated communication', *Journal of Contemporary Ethnography*, vol. 38, no. 1, pp. 52–84.

Gatson, S. (2007) 'The body or the body politic? Risk, harm, moral panic, and drug use discourse online', in *Real Drugs in a Virtual World: Drug Discourse and Community Online*, eds Edward Murguia, Melissa Tackett-Gibson & Ann Lessem, Lexington Books, Lanham, MD, pp. 23–44.

Gerstenfeld, P. B., Grant, D. R. & Chiang, C. P. (2003) 'Hate online: a content analysis of extremist internet sites', *Analyses of Social Issues and Public Policy*, vol. 3, no. 1, pp. 29–44.

Goode, E. & Yehuda, N. B. (1994) *Moral Panics: the Social Construction of Deviance*, Blackwell, Massachusetts.

Habermas, J. (1991 [1973]) 'The public sphere', in *Rethinking Popular Culture: Contemporary Perspectives in Cultural Studies*, eds C. Mukerji & M. Schudson, University of California Press, Berkeley, CA, pp. 398–404.

Hine, C. M. (2000) *Virtual Ethnography*, Sage Publications Ltd, Thousand Oaks, CA.

Huntington, S. (2004) 'The Hispanic challenge', *Foreign Policy*, vol. 141, pp. 30–45.

Internet Immigration Hoax (2007) 'A conversation on newsroom ethics and standards', *Los Angeles Times*, 28 November, [Online] Available at: http://latimesblogs. latimes.com/readers/2007/11/internet-immigr.html (12 November 2009).

Jury decides on death penalty for woman who headed vigilante squad (2011) CNN Justice News, February 22, 2011, [Online] Available at: http://articles.cnn.com/2011-02-22/justice/arizona.double.killing_1_shawna-forde-death-penalty-anti-illegal-immigration?_s=PM:CRIME (25 February 2011).

King, R. D. & Wheelock, D. (2007) 'Group threat and social control: race, perceptions of minorities and the desire to punish', *Social Forces*, vol. 85, pp. 1255–1280.

Los Angeles Times (2007) 'Internet immigration hoax', [Online] Available at: http://latimesblogs.latimes.com/readers/2007/11/internet-immigr.html (10 September 2010).

Marwick, A. E. (2008) 'To catch a predator: The Myspace moral panic', *First Monday*, vol. 13, no. 6, [Online] Available at: http://first monday.org/htbin/cgiwrap/bin/ojs/index.php/fm/article/viewArticle/2152/1966#author (12 November 2010).

Massey, D. S. (2007) *Categorically Unequal: The American Stratification System*, Russell Sage, New York.

McRobbie, A. & Thornton, S. (1995) 'Rethinking "Moral Panic" for multi-mediated social worlds', *British Journal of Sociology*, vol. 46, no. 4, pp. 559–574.

Melamed, S. (2006) 'Politics writ large: illegals go home', *MediaLifeMagazine.com*, [Online] Available at: http://www.medialifemagazine.com/artman2/publish/Alternative_media_43/Politics_writ_large_Illegals_go_home-5721_printer.asp (18 October 2009).

Moreno, S. (2007) 'Immigration raid leaves Texas town a skeleton', *Washington Post*, [Online] Available at: http://www.gorena.org/pdf/287g-Cactus.pdf (18 October 2009).

Ngai, M. M. (2004) *Impossible Subjects: Illegal Aliens and the Making of Modern America*, Princeton University Press, Princeton, NJ.

North, S., Holtz, J. & Writers, H. (2009) 'Activist Shawna Forde charged in double slaying: woman with troubled past in Evertt now accused in Arizona', *The Herald*, [Online] Available at: http://heraldnet.com/article/20090613/NEWS01/706139922/1054#Activist.Shawna.Forde.charged.in.double. slaying (13 August 2009).

Papacharissi, Z. (2002) 'The virtual sphere: the internet as a public sphere', *New Media & Society*, vol. 4, no. 1, pp. 9–21.

Passel, J. S. (2005) *Estimates of the Size and Characteristics of the Undocumented Population*, Pew Hispanic Center, Washington, DC.

Passel, J. S. & Cohn, D. (2009) *Mexican Immigrants: How Many Come? How Many Leave?* Pew Hispanic Center, Washington, DC, [Online] Available at: http://pewhispanic.org/reports/report.php? ReportID=112 (18 October 2009).

Perez, H. L., Benavides, C., Malagon, M., Velez, V. & Solorzano, D. (2008) 'Getting beyond the "symptom", acknowledging the "disease": theorizing racist nativism', *Contemporary Justice Review*, vol. 11, no. 1, pp. 39–51.

Portes, A. & Rumbaut, R. (2006) *Immigrant America: A Portrait*, 3rd ed, University of California Press, Los Angeles.

Rheingold, H. (1993) *The Virtual Community: Homesteading on the Electronic Frontier*, Addison-Wesley, Reading, MA.

Schafer, J. A. (2002) 'Spinning the web of hate: web-based hate propagation by extremist organizations', *Journal of Criminal Justice and Popular Culture*, vol. 9, no. 2, pp. 69–88.

Shoemaker, P. J. & Reese, S. D. (1996) *Mediating the Message: Theories of Influences on Mass Media Content*, Longman, New York.

Sohoni, D. (2006) 'The "Immigrant Problem": modern-day nativism on the web', *Current Sociology*, vol. 54, no. 6, pp. 827–850.

US Census Bureau. (2006) 'The Hispanic population in the United States: 2004 detailed tables', Census.gov. [Online] Available at: http://www.census.gov/population/www/socdemo/hispanic/cps2004.html (10 October 2009).

Van Laer, J. & Van Aelst, P. (2010) 'Internet and social movement action repertories: opportunities and limitations', *Information, Communication & Society*, vol. 13, no. 8, pp. 1146–1171.

Ward, K. (1999) 'The cyber-ethnographic (Re)construction of two feminist online communities', *Sociological Research Online*, vol. 4, no. 1, [Online] Available at: http://www.socresonline.org.uk/4/1/ward.html (21 December 2010).

#FERGUSON

68

Digital Protest, Hashtag Ethnography, and the Racial Politics of Social Media in the United States

Yarimar Bonilla and Jonathan Rosa

On Saturday, August 9, 2014, at 12:03 p.m., an unarmed black teenager named Michael Brown was fatally shot by a police officer in Ferguson, Missouri, a small town on the outskirts of St. Louis. Within the hour, a post appeared on the Twitter social media platform stating, "I just saw someone die," followed by a photograph taken from behind the beams of a small wooden balcony overlooking Canfield Drive, where Michael Brown's lifeless body lay uncovered, hands alongside his head, face down on the asphalt.[1] Immediately following the incident, community members assembled to demand an explanation for why this unarmed 18-year-old had been seemingly executed while reportedly holding his hands up in a gesture of surrender, pleading "don't shoot." The impromptu gathering soon turned into a sustained protest marked by daily demonstrations and violent confrontations with highly armed local police—all of which were documented in detail across social media platforms like Twitter, Instagram, YouTube, and Vine.

Occurring on the heels of other highly publicized killings of unarmed black men—such as Eric Garner (who died as a result of an illegal chokehold by New York City police just weeks before the events in Ferguson), Oscar Grant (whose death was emotionally portrayed in the award-winning film *Fruitvale Station* released just one year prior), and 17-year-old Trayvon Martin (whose 2012 killing sparked national outcry and spurred numerous forms of activism)—the death of Michael Brown quickly captured the imagination of thousands across and beyond the United States.[2] Protestors from around the nation flocked to Ferguson to participate in demonstrations calling for the arrest of the officer responsible for the fatal shooting. Television viewers tuned in across the country to watch live news coverage of the violent confrontations between the protestors and the highly armed local police. Images of these confrontations circulated widely in national and international news coverage, and news of these events quickly went "viral" across social media. During the initial week of protests, over 3.6 million posts appeared on Twitter documenting and reflecting on the emerging details surrounding Michael Brown's death; by the end of the month, "#Ferguson" had appeared more than eight million times on the Twitter platform. . . .

Much will be written about Michael Brown: about his portrayal in the media, his treatment by the police, and both the circumstances and consequences of his death. Much will also be written about the protestors who immediately gathered at the site of his killing and about those who remained, under intense police harassment, long after the media spotlight faded.[3] But what are we to make of the eight million tweets? What do they tell us about this event, its place in the social imagination, and about social media itself as a site of both political activism and social analysis?

In 1991, a homemade VHS tape of Los Angeles resident Rodney King being brutally beaten by four police officers sparked outrage across the country and galvanized thousands in what is widely recognized as one of the most influential examples of citizen journalism in the United States (Allan and Thorsen 2009).[4] Today, 56 percent of the U.S. population carries video-enabled smartphones, and the use of mobile technology is particularly high among African Americans.[5] The increased use and availability of these technologies has provided marginalized and racialized populations with new tools for documenting incidents of state-sanctioned violence and contesting media representations of racialized bodies and marginalized communities. In many cases—such as police officers' use of a chokehold in the murder of Eric Garner—the use of mobile technology to record and circulate footage of events has played a key role in prompting public outcry.[6] In the case of Ferguson, video footage of the fatal shooting of Michael Brown has yet to surface, but informal journalism was used to document the scene in the direct aftermath of his murder, to publicize the protests that ensued, and to bring attention to the militarized police confrontations that followed.[7] Through social media, users were able to disseminate these accounts to a broad audience and to forge new mediatized publics. . . . In this essay, we explore how and why platforms like Twitter have become important sites for activism around issues of racial inequality, state violence, and media representations. . . .

[I]t is necessary to begin by distinguishing the town of Ferguson, Missouri, from "hashtag Ferguson" and to recognize how each of these contributed to the formation of the larger "event" of Ferguson. As those familiar with Twitter know, the hashtag symbol (#) is often used as a way of marking a conversation within this platform. The hashtag serves as an indexing system in both the clerical sense and the semiotic sense. In the clerical sense, it allows the ordering and quick retrieval of information about a specific topic. For example, in the case of Ferguson, as details were emerging about the protests forming at the site of Michael Brown's death, users began tweeting out information with the hashtag #Ferguson. The hashtag in this case provided a quick retrieval system for someone looking for updated news on the unfolding events. But, in addition to providing a filing system, hashtags simultaneously function semiotically by marking the intended significance of an utterance . . . hashtags allow users to not simply "file" their comments but to performatively frame what these comments are "really about," thereby enabling users to indicate a meaning that might not be otherwise apparent. Hence, someone could write, "Decades of racial tension and increasing suburban poverty boiled to the surface last night" followed by the text "#Ferguson," as a way of creating a particular interpretive frame. Hashtags thus operate in ways similar to library call numbers:

They locate texts within a specific conversation, allowing for their quick retrieval, while also marking texts as being "about" a specific topic.[8]

In addition, hashtags have the intertextual potential to link a broad range of tweets on a given topic or disparate topics as part of an intertextual chain, regardless of whether, from a given perspective, these tweets have anything to do with one another. Thus, a tweet in support of Ferguson protestors and a tweet in support of Officer Darren Wilson could both be coded and filed under #Ferguson. Moreover, a tweet about racial disparity in Missouri, such as "racism lives here," and one about a night out on the town in St. Louis could both be marked #STL. . . .

In the case of #Ferguson, patterns emerged in which Twitter became a platform for providing emergent information about the killing of Michael Brown and for commenting on the treatment of the officer who shot him. For example, one user posted, "Prosecutors get real friendly when they have to adjudicate one of their own. But they'll move heaven and earth hunting POC down. #Ferguson."[9] In contrast, other tweets recontextualized the situation in Ferguson as part of global affairs (e.g., "#Egypt #Palestine #Ferguson #Turkey, U.S. made tear gas, sold on the almighty free market represses democracy"), while others critiqued the appropriation of this event (e.g., "seriously though, @FCKH8 never posted ANYTHING on their Facebook page in support of #Ferguson until it was time to sell some t-shirts"[10]). Meanwhile, some tweets combined these genres, such as those involving self-promotion of one's own broader commentary on Ferguson (e.g., "People are talking about #Ferguson all over the world. Here's a interview I did for a newspaper in Italy," along with a link to an Instagram photo of a newspaper story) and juxtapositions of #Ferguson with commentary on mundane aspects of one's everyday life (e.g., "It's 3:30 . . . I'm acting like I don't gotta be up at 7:30 #Ferguson #HandsUp #MichaelBrown"). . . .

In addition to these intertextual considerations, hashtags also have the interdiscursive capacity to lasso accompanying texts and their indexical meanings as part of a frame. Linkages across hashtags and their accompanying texts—which comprise both other hashtags (e.g., #Ferguson, #MichaelBrown, #HandsUp, etc.) and additional commentary—frame #Ferguson as a kind of mediatized place.[11] It is in this sense that much like one could go to the library, stand in front of a call number, and find texts on a particular subject, one could go onto Twitter, type #Ferguson, and find a large number of posts on the subject at hand. But what is the relationship between this mediatized place—as it is experienced from outside the boundaries of the geographical context with which it is associated—and everyday life in what might be understood as Ferguson proper? How does the mediatization of Ferguson, Missouri, through #Ferguson lead to the formation of new "ad hoc publics" (Bruns and Burgess 2011)?[12]

The types of publics created by Twitter emerge from the hashtag's capacity to serve not just as an indexing system but also as a filter that allows social media users to reduce the noise of Twitter by cutting into one small slice. However, this filtering process also has a distorting effect. Social media create a distorted view of events, such that we only get the perspective of the people who are already in our social network (Garret and Resnick 2011; Pariser 2012; Sunstein 2009). . . .

Part of the problem of engaging in hashtag ethnography, then, is that it is difficult to assess the context of social media utterances. Moreover, a simple statement of fact—for example, that there were eight million Ferguson tweets—tells us very little. How many were critical of the police? How many were critical of the protestors? How many were posted by journalists (both professional and amateur)? Beyond knowing that people tweeted, we know little about what those tweets meant to their authors and their imagined publics. We do not know, for example, how many of the eight million tweets were aimed at a national audience (and thus appropriately hashtagged for quick retrieval and retweet) versus how many were aimed at a smaller group of followers with the contextual information necessary to assess both the explicit and implicit uses of hashtags and other references. . . .

[S]ome have argued that in assessing the importance of Twitter in the Ferguson protests, we must take into account that, despite the enduring digital divide within the United States, the percentage of African Americans who use Twitter (22 percent) is much higher than that of white Americans (16 percent; Bryers 2014). While these simple figures tell us little about the ways and frequency with which these groups use the system and to what ends, the significance of what has been called "Black Twitter" (Florini 2014; Sharma 2013) should not be overlooked. As we discuss below, Twitter affords a unique platform for collectively identifying, articulating, and contesting racial injustices from the in-group perspectives of racialized populations. Whereas in most mainstream media contexts the experiences of racialized populations are overdetermined, stereotyped, or tokenized, social media platforms such as Twitter offer sites for collectively constructing counternarratives and reimagining group identities.[13]

In the case of Ferguson, it is worth noting that, at least initially, the most common use of the #Ferguson hashtag was to convey information about the unfolding events.

Before the mainstream media had caught up to what was happening, the mass of hashtagged tweets was a way of calling attention to an underreported incident of police brutality. Well aware of the algorithmic nature of Twitter, users were purposefully hashtagging to make Ferguson "trend."[14] However, once Ferguson had stabilized as an important news event, many began tweeting about the events without necessarily marking their posts with a hashtag. Some local residents, for example, marked their tweets #STL (i.e., the common hashtag for a post referencing St. Louis), and others did not mark their tweets at all. The only way to really know what these tweets were "about" was to view them in the context of the individual tweeters themselves: when they were posting, what they had previously posted, who they had begun following, and what they were retweeting.

By looking only at tweets marked #Ferguson, one would miss out on a large number of posts that were "about" Ferguson even though they were not marked as such.[15] . . .

However, recognizing that hashtags can only ever offer a limited, partial, and filtered view of a social world does not require abandoning them as sites of analysis. Rather, we must approach them as what they are: entry points into larger and more complex worlds. Hashtags offer a window to peep through, but it is only by stepping through that window and "following" (in both Twitter and non-Twitter terms) individual users that we can begin to place tweets within a broader context. This kind of analysis requires us to stay with those who tweet and follow them after hashtags have fallen out of "trend." Only then can we better understand what brings them to this virtual place and what they take away from their engagement.[16]

THE WHOLE WORLD IS TWEETING

Social movements have long used media and technology to disseminate, escalate, and enlarge the scope of their struggles: Transistor radios allowed Cuban guerrilla fighters to transmit from the Sierra Maestra; television coverage transformed the riots in Selma, Alabama, into a national event; and e-mail accounts allowed Zapatistas in Chiapas to launch global communique's. #Ferguson did what many of these other tools did: It allowed a message to get out, called global attention to a small corner of the world, and attempted to bring visibility and accountability to repressive forces.[17]

One of the differences between Twitter and these earlier forms of technology, however, is its multivocality and dialogicality (Bakhtin 1981). Twitter does not just allow you to peer through a window; it allows you to look through manifold windows at once. On #Ferguson, you could watch six simultaneous live streams. You could read what protestors were tweeting, what journalists were reporting, what the police was announcing, and how observers and analysts interpreted the unfolding events. You could also learn how thousands of users were reacting to the numerous posts. In the era of transistor radios and television sets, one did not necessarily know what listeners or viewers yelled back at their machines, but on Twitter one can get a sense of individual responses to mediatized events.

E-mail, television, radio, and print have long managed to open up windows into the experience of social movements, but the dialogicality and temporality of Twitter create a unique feeling of direct participation. Twitter allows users who are territorially displaced to feel like they are united across both space and time. . . .

#Ferguson and its attendant live streams created a . . . feeling of shared temporality—particularly during the protests and confrontations with police. As opposed to someone who might *post about* Ferguson on Facebook, users on Twitter felt like they were *participating in* #Ferguson, as they tweeted in real time about the unfolding events, rallied supporters to join various hashtag campaigns (discussed below), and monitored live

streams where they could bear witness to the tear gassing and arrests of journalists and protestors. Engaging in these activities is akin to participating in a protest in the sense that it offers an experience of "real time" engagement. . . .

It was partly because of this heightened temporality that, as others have noted, the news surrounding Michael Brown's death dominated Twitter much more than Facebook.[18] Facebook moved too slowly for the eventfulness of Ferguson. For the denizens of #Ferguson, the posts on Facebook were "yesterday's news"—always already superseded by the latest round of tweets.[19]

HASHTAG ACTIVISM VERSUS "REAL" ACTIVISM?

Many have disparaged hashtag activism as a poor substitute for "real" activism, and, indeed, some suggest that the virality and ephemerality of social media can only ever produce fleeting "nanostories" (Wasik 2009) with little lasting impact. However, it is important to examine how and why digital activism has become salient to particular populations. It is surely not coincidental that the groups most likely to experience police brutality, to have their protests disparaged as acts of "rioting" or "looting," and to be misrepresented in the media are precisely those turning to digital activism at the highest rates. Indeed, some of the most important hashtag campaigns emerging out of #Ferguson were targeted at calling attention to both police practices and media representations, suggesting that social media can serve as an important tool for challenging these various forms of racial profiling.

The first of these campaigns was inspired by eyewitness reports that Michael Brown had his hands up in the air as a sign of surrender and had uttered the words *don't shoot* just before he was shot and killed by Officer Darren Wilson. Initial activism around Michael Brown thus revolved around the hashtag #HandsUpDontShoot, often accompanied by photos of individuals or groups of people with their hands up.[20] . . .

Through this campaign, users sought to call attention to the arbitrary nature of racialized policing, the vulnerability of black bodies, and the problematic ways in which blackness is perceived as a constant threat.[21] Because Michael Brown was allegedly shot while holding his hands up, #HandsUpDontShoot also became a tool for contesting victim-blaming or respectability narratives rooted in the belief that one can control the perception of one's body and the violence inflicted on it. These efforts echoed a previous "meme" that emerged in response to the killing of another unarmed African American teenager, Trayvon Martin, two years earlier.[22] Shortly following Martin's killing, a recording of the 911 call made by George Zimmerman, the killer, describing Martin as someone "suspicious" wearing a "dark hoodie," circulated widely in the press. Fox News commentator Geraldo Rivera suggested that the hoodie was "as much responsible for Trayvon Martin's death as George Zimmerman" (Geraldo Rivera: "Leave the Hoodie at Home" 2012). Rivera argued that hoodies had become emblematic of criminal behavior, given their ubiquitous presence in crime-suspect drawings and surveillance footage of petty theft. This argument elides the role that race plays in structuring the hoodie's alternate status as an innocuous piece of clothing versus a sign of criminality or deviance. That is, hoodies are only signs of criminal behavior when they are contextualized in relation to particular racialized bodies.[23] Many commentators sought to draw attention to this point. In the wake of Trayvon Martin's death, the hoodie became a powerful symbol, with events like the "Million Hoodie March" drawing hundreds of supporters. Online activism at the time included the circulation of images of users wearing hoodies, marked with the hashtags #HoodiesUp and #WeAreTrayvonMartin in a sign of solidarity.

Immediately following Trayvon Martin's killing, many social media users changed their profile pictures to images of themselves wearing hooded sweatshirts with the hoods up. Similarly, in the wake of Michael Brown's death, many posted profile pictures of themselves with their hands up. These instances show how the seemingly vacuous practice of taking "selfies" (i.e., photos of oneself) can become politically meaningful in the context of racialized bodies. These images represent acts of solidarity that seek to humanize the victims of police brutality by suggesting that a similar fate could befall other similarly construed bodies.[24]

Two of the other popular memes that emerged in the wake of #Ferguson also focused on representations of black bodies and, specifically, on media portrayals of Michael Brown. The first of these emerged as a response to the photograph that mainstream media initially circulated in the wake of his death. The image sparked controversy because it showed Michael Brown making a hand gesture that, for some, represented a peace sign and, for others, a gang sign. Like Trayvon Martin's hoodie, the very same hand gesture could be alternately interpreted as a sign of peace or criminality depending on the racialized body with which it is associated. In response, Twitter users began using the hashtag #IfTheyGunnedMeDown to post contrasting pictures of themselves along with various versions of the question "which picture would they use?" For example, 18-year-old Houston native Tyler Atkins (featured in a *New York Times* article about the meme) posted a picture of himself after a jazz concert in his high school, wearing a black tuxedo with his saxophone suspended from a neck strap. This was juxtaposed with a photo taken while filming a rap video with a friend, in which he is wearing a black T-shirt and a blue bandanna tied around his head and his finger is pointed at the camera. . . .

Once again, these images represent an act of solidarity. They suggest that anyone could be represented as either respectable and innocent or violent and criminal—depending on the staging of the photograph. This campaign speaks to larger concerns over privacy in an era when private photos and surveillance footage are routinely leaked, hacked, and repurposed to nefarious ends. More importantly, it also speaks to an acute awareness among young African Americans of how black bodies are particularly vulnerable to misrepresentation by mainstream media (Vega 2014).

The final hashtag campaign we mention here speaks directly to this issue. It emerged in response to a *New York Times* profile of Michael Brown released on the day of his funeral, which described the 18-year-old as "no angel" (Elignon 2014). The piece suggested that Brown "dabbled in drugs and alcohol" and had been involved in "at least one scuffle with a neighbor." Many saw this as a tasteless, unfair portrayal and an extension of the attempted smear campaign carried out by the local police, who had released what they themselves admitted was "unrelated" surveillance video of a purported act of shoplifting at a convenience store. In response, Twitter users began using the hashtag #NoAngel to highlight the mainstream media's inability to acknowledge the possibility of black victimhood or innocence. For example, one person tweeted, "I am #NoAngel, so I guess I deserve to be murdered too. Yep, perfectly acceptable to gun down a person if they aren't a Saint."

The use of hashtags such as #HandsUpDont-Shoot, #IfTheyGunnedMeDown, and #NoAngel speak to the long history of inaccurate and unfair portrayal of African Americans within mainstream media and to the systematic profiling and victim blaming suffered by racializied bodies. Their use suggests that while social media might seem like a space of disembodied engagement, for many, social media can become an important site in which to foreground the particular ways in which racialized bodies are systematically stereotyped, stigmatized, surveilled, and positioned as targets of state-sanctioned violence.[25] These hashtag campaigns, which seek to identify the insidious nature of contemporary racism, can thus be understood as a powerful response to the "racial paranoia" (Jackson 2008) associated with African Americans' ongoing experiences of abject inequality in an age of alleged colorblindness.

The effort to bring attention to this inequality is powerfully captured by the hashtag #BlackLivesMatter, which emerged in July 2013, after George Zimmerman was acquitted of Trayvon Martin's murder. Many Twitter users also drew on this hashtag in response to the killing of Michael Brown. It is important to understand #BlackLivesMatter not simply as a general statement about the inherent value of black life in the face of state-sanctioned racial violence but also as a reflection of the ways that social media can become a site for the revaluation of black materiality. As illustrated in the memes described above, participants often used photos of themselves to contest the racialized devaluation of their persons. . . .

ALL THAT IS TWEETED MELTS INTO AIR?

It is clear that platforms like Twitter have become essential to contemporary social actors, but the long-lasting effects of digital modes of activism remain hotly debated. For some, these acts represent fleeting moments of awareness, quickly replaced by the customary innocuousness of social media pleasantries. For others, however, participation in forms of digital activism prove

transformative in unpredictable ways. For, although Twitter activism is said to be fleeting by nature, it is also inherently aggregative. It is thus important to recognize that the reactions to the death of Michael Brown did not spark in a vacuum; they were fueled by accumulated frustrations over previously mediatized moments of injustice and guided by previous digital campaigns. This aggregative effect powerfully positions different instances of racialized brutality not simply as isolated contemporary phenomena but as long-standing systematic forms of violence associated with what has been described as a "state of racial expendability" that is fundamental to the logics of U.S. sovereignty (Marquez 2012).[26]

As Johnetta Elzie, a 25-year-old protestor profiled in the magazine the *Nation,* explained, "We saw it with Trayvon Martin. We saw it with Jordan Davis—but I always felt away from everything. Then I saw Brown's body laying out there, and I said, 'Damn, they did it again!' But now that it happened in my home, I'm not just going to tweet about it from the comfort of my bed. So I went down there" (Hsieh and Rakia 2014). Elzie's words hint at how face-to-face and digital forms of activism work in interrelated and aggregative ways. Although she draws a distinction between tweeting from the comfort of her home and physical presence at an event, her narrative shows how these contexts are interrelated and build on each other—even beyond the confines of one particular historical event or hashtag campaign.

The article goes on to describe how Elzie encountered other activists involved in the protests through their shared use of social media, stating, "They quickly developed a tight-knit community, sustained by their addiction to social media. Together, they live-tweeted, Vined and Instagrammed every protest, through the sweltering days and tumultuous nights, as well as the direct actions taking place elsewhere in the St. Louis area." The group eventually took on the name Millennial Activists United and shifted their role from "documenting" their actions to "generating" new forms of social community, for instance, through the use of #FergusonFriday to create a space for reflection on the movement, the creation of a daily newsletter *This Is The Movement* to spread news and reflection pieces about unfolding events, and the organization of national "fireside" conference calls during which activists based in Ferguson could speak directly with those following the events from afar.[27] The ways these activists shift seamlessly across spaces and modes of engagement underscore the slippery boundary between analog and digital forms of activism. Indeed, it is unclear if #HandsUpDontShoot and #JusticeForMichael-Brown represent the use of political slogans as hashtags or if they represent the use of hashtags as slogans. This ambiguity reflects the dynamic, multimodal nature of these activist efforts.[28]

In the wake of Michael Brown's killing, new sites of struggle have appeared, fueled by both the events in Ferguson and by the events of #Ferguson, #HandsUp, and #JusticeForMichaelBrown. Some of these efforts are visible through digital windows like #BlackLivesMatter, #FergusonOctober, and #FergusonFriday, but others are not necessarily marked and codified for easy digital retrieval. [Those] interested in these social worlds should thus remain attentive to the possibilities of hashtag ethnography while still being prepared to read between and go beyond the digital lines.

POSTSCRIPT

On November 24, 2014, after a grand jury released its decision not to indict Darren Wilson, Ferguson went viral once again, with over 3.5 million tweets appearing in a matter of hours under the hashtag #FergusonDecision. That evening, and in the days that followed, protestors took to the streets across the nation and beyond to decry the decision, the overall handling of Michael Brown's case by the justice system, and racialized police brutality more broadly. Demonstrators staged "death-ins" at city intersections and shopping malls, they lined suburban sidewalks face down in memory of Michael Brown's lifeless body, and they brought traffic in several cities across the United States to a halt, shutting down multilane highways, bridges, tunnels, and modes of public transportation. Many wore T-shirts proclaiming "I am Mike Brown" and held signs calling for the need to "Indict America." These demonstrations led social media users to claim that "#Ferguson is everywhere," emphasizing the connection between online and offline forms of protest.

The release of the grand jury hearing transcripts also offered a new view of the events as narrated by Darren Wilson, who had until that moment remained silent. His testimony—particularly his description of Michael Brown as "a demon," as a larger-than-life figure, and his use of the pronoun *it* to refer to the 18-year-old—offered further insight into the distorted lens through which black bodies are read by representatives of the state. Michael Brown and Darren Wilson were both 6'4" tall and weighed 290 pounds and 210 pounds, respectively, yet, in his testimony and in television interviews, Wilson said he felt like "a 5-year-old holding on to Hulk Hogan." Wilson's characterization of himself as a child and of Brown as a superhuman monster became part of an exculpatory narrative in which the unarmed teenager was framed as the true threat, not the police officer who shot and killed him. In his testimony, Darren Wilson affirmed that he had done nothing wrong and expressed no remorse for his actions. Describing the moment of Michael Brown's death, he stated that, as the bullets entered the young man's body, "the demeanor on his face went blank, the aggression was gone, it was gone, . . . the threat was stopped." Wilson's reverse logic, sanctioned by the state, presents a narrative in which an unarmed teenager is a terrifying aggressor and an armed police officer is an innocent victim. This inversion underscores the significance of affirming that #BlackLivesMatter in a context where they are disproportionately viewed as threats by state forces and mainstream institutions.

The same week of the Ferguson grand jury decision, news broke of the fatal shooting of 12-year-old Tamir Rice by Cleveland police after a 911 caller reported a "guy" with a gun. The gun was probably fake, the caller had said, and "it" (referring to Rice) was "probably a juvenile," but, still, the mere sight of the boy with a toy gun "is scaring the shit out of me," the caller insisted. Police were dispatched, and they shot the boy dead within two seconds of encountering him. This event made clear once again state agents' distorted views of black Americans, especially teenagers— how their very bodies are perceived as looming, larger-than-life threats and how any objects in their possession (e.g., candies, sodas, toys, articles of clothing) are read as weapons.

Once again, the media focused not on state action but on the worthiness of black bodies. Local news immediately ran profiles of Rice's parents, noting that they both had "violent pasts" (his father had been charged with domestic violence and his mother with drug possession). This history, reporters argued, could help explain why Tamir Rice would be inclined to play with a toy gun in a public place. Under fire for its coverage, the Northeast Ohio Media Group claimed, "One way to stop police from killing any more 12-year-olds might be to understand the forces that lead children to undertake behavior that could put them in the sights of police guns." There was no discussion of a national "gun culture," as there often is in incidents involving youth and guns (though, in this case, the "gun" was a toy), nor was there any discussion of the structural violence that Rice and his family engaged with on a daily basis or of the distorted ways young black bodies are viewed when they end up "in the sights" of police guns.

Within this context, social media participation becomes a key site from which to contest mainstream media silences and the long history of state-sanctioned violence against racialized populations. Upon announcing the Ferguson grand jury decision, St. Louis prosecutor Robert McCulloch claimed that media coverage, and particularly social media, had posed "the most significant challenge" to his investigation. Social media cast a spotlight on this small Missouri township, but more importantly, by propelling Ferguson into a broader, mediatized, virtual space, social media users were able to show that "#Ferguson is everywhere"—not only in the sense of a broad public sphere but also in the sense of the underlying social and political relationships that haunt the nation as a whole.

NOTES

1. For a timeline of events in these early moments, see Laurie 2014. At present, it remains an open question to what extent Twitter posts should be treated like confidential "data" obtained from human subjects or like quotations from published texts. Throughout this article, we have thus thought carefully about when to quote, cite, or paraphrase from Twitter posts. We have used the real names of Twitter users when discussing tweets that went "viral" or were featured in mainstream media reports. However, when quoting or paraphrasing from unreported tweets, we have chosen not to reproduce the username of the author—erring on the site of privacy at the expense of offering proper attribution. Legally speaking, Twitter users have agreed to publish their posts by accepting the platform's "terms of service," and in this sense tweets operate similarly to YouTube videos, which are publicly available, archived, and citable. Indeed, the Library of Congress is currently in the process of archiving all public tweets dating back to 2006. However, it is unclear whether individual users of the service are fully aware of this archival possibility and its implications. For, although Twitter posts are public, they are not necessarily imagined to be permanent: At present, any post can be retroactively deleted, user-names can be easily changed, and entire accounts can be erased. (These actions are achieved much more easily on Twitter than on Facebook.) Among journalists, these questions have been hotly debated. Although one can easily cite Twitter users without their permission, some feel that "journalists should let people know when they're performing journalism," as one commentator suggests (Chittal 2012). Among scholars, there have been similar debates. Many argue that researchers should not depend on corporate user agreements and should instead obtain informed consent from individual users before harvesting posts as "data" (see boyd and Crawford 2012; Zimmer 2010; Zimmer and Proferes 2014). This issue becomes all the more complicated as we increasingly learn of how corporations like Facebook and Twitter are harvesting their own data for internal research, marketing, and development purposes.

   Although it is important to debate the ethical concerns surrounding "Twitter research," we would caution against viewing these as entirely new, or disconnected from previous methodological and ethical debates in social science research. The fact is, these issues speak to long-standing anthropological concerns regarding "misinformed consent" through either a user agreement or a signed institutional review board form (du Toit 1980; Sankar 2004; Wax 1980), the implications of using "naturally occurring" versus "elicited" communication (Dobrin 2008; Wolfson 1976), and the larger question of the general role and purpose of the "native voice" in anthropological texts (Bonilla n.d.; Trouillot 2003). Engagement with these questions in the context of digital platforms should thus not be set apart from discussions of "analog" methods and ethical concerns.

2.   Some commentators have noted the greater attention directed toward these events as compared to miscarriages of justice involving black women, such as Renisha McBride (who was murdered while seeking help following a car accident), Marissa Alexander (who was not afforded access to the same "Stand Your Ground" defense used to exonerate George Zimmerman in the killing of Trayvon Martin; she received, instead, a mandatory minimum sentence of 20 years for firing a warning shot in the air after she was attacked by her husband), and Mariene Pinnock (whose beating at the hands of California Highway Patrol officers was captured on video). For a discussion of the intersectional politics of race and gender that shape this disparate coverage, see Gebreyes 2014.

3.   The protests in Ferguson did not quickly fade. Indeed, as this article was being drafted, a new hashtag, #FergusonOctober, began trending as people from across and beyond the United States gathered in Ferguson from October 10 to October 13, 2014, "to build momentum for a nationwide movement against police violence." See Ferguson October 2014.

4.   One could go even further back historically and examine how the image of Emmett Till, released by his mother for publication in *Jet* magazine, served as an important catalyst for the Civil Rights movement. See Adams 2004 to listen to firsthand accounts of this decision and its impact.

5.   A recent study by the Pew Research Center (Smith 2013) indicates that 53 percent of white Americans, 64 percent of African

Americans, and 60 percent of U.S. Latinos/as own smartphones.

6.   While some audiences have interpreted increased mediatization of such events as a sign of increased rates of police brutality, many others have pointed out that police brutality has always been rampant in communities of color, particularly African American and Latina/o communities. These perspectives represent contrasting, racialized chronotopes (Agha 2007; Bakhtin 1981; Silverstein 2005), or space-time constructions. From the vantage point of predominantly white communities that have not faced it, police brutality is often viewed as a practice taking place "there" and "now" (i.e., a specifically contemporary phenomenon in communities of color); from the vantage point of people of color who have faced police brutality in their communities for generations, such brutality is often viewed as a practice that has "always" taken place "here" (i.e., it is a long-standing, ongoing phenomenon in predominantly minority communities). These contrasting racialized chronotopes shape perceptions of the scale of police brutality and responses to it.

7.   The importance of citizen journalism and journalistic uses of social media became even more evident once it was revealed that local police and the U.S. government collaborated to establish a no-fly zone over the Ferguson area in efforts to resist aerial media coverage of confrontations between protestors and the militarized police force (Gillum and Lowy 2014). For more on the tactics used during the Ferguson protests and their possible violation of civil rights, see the report released by Amnesty International (2014). It is worth noting that Ferguson marked the first time the organization deployed observers within the United States.

8.   While a full assessment of Twitter is beyond the scope of this article, a few demographic trends are worth noting. Despite early statistical dominance, the United States is no longer the per capita leader in Twitter activity; however, it remains the nation with the highest number of users (Lipman 2014). Within the

United States, urban dwellers are much more likely than suburban or rural residents to use Twitter, a fact that is certainly relevant to any comprehensive account of social movements (Duggan and Brenner 2013). There is also a seeming feedback loop between political unrest and language usage: For example, the use of Arabic surged in 2010 as Twitter became a clearinghouse for information about demonstrations in Turkey, Egypt, Tunisia, and beyond (Seshagiri 2014). And, within different languages, some studies suggest the hashtag itself functions differently (see Weerkamp et al. 2011). As anthropologists grapple with virtual field sites, it will be important to keep in mind how geographic differences contour the experience of online interaction.

9. POC is an acronym for people of color. "@FCKH8" is the Twitter handle of a company that sells T-shirts with activist themes. The author of this tweet is accusing the company of using the events in Ferguson as an opportunity to generate profit.

10. John Postill (2014) has noted the ways that the use of multiple, novel hashtags reflects savvy social media users' understanding that Twitter rewards novelty over raw numbers in its trending algorithms. The relationships between these hashtags and their accompanying texts can be conceptualized as comparatively "type-" and "token-" oriented interdiscursive links (Silverstein 2005). Whereas token oriented interdiscursivities highlight particular events (e.g., accounts of the shooting of Michael Brown and specific police responses to protests in a given moment), type-focused interdiscursivities address issues related to genres of communication and interaction (e.g., police brutality in general, patterns in media coverage surrounding the victimization of racialized peoples). Collectively, these interdiscursivities constitute the mediatized eventness of #Ferguson (Agha 2011) and the potential ways it can be recontextualized in relation to other such particular events and genres of events (Briggs and Bauman 1992).

11. Crucially, the leaky boundaries that correspond to publics more broadly certainly pertain to mediatized publics (Gal and Woolard 2001). That is, the publicness and counterpublicness (Warner 2002) of #Ferguson must be understood as a performative context with the potential to be mobilized as part of social projects across individual and collective scales.

12. In addition to "Black Twitter" we must also think about "Media Twitter" and how journalists negotiate professional norms in their Twitter use (Lasorsa et al. 2012). In the context of the Ferguson protests, several journalists used Twitter to document the challenges they were facing as they covered the events, including the possibility of arrest. Attention to these practices is essential to the project of "provincializing" digital media (Coleman 2010:489).

13. Trending is also achieved through "retweeting"—a crucial aspect of Twitter engagement. Any user's tweet can be "favorited," "retweeted," and "quoted" by another user. The number of favorites and retweets, which can be seen on the original tweet, is often interpreted as a sign of a given tweet's popularity. Abbreviations such as MT (i.e., modified tweet) and RT (i.e., retweet) can be used to manually quote or retweet. This range of quotation practices leads to debates about authorship and disputes over whether users are strategically quoting popular users to attract more followers. In the context of #Ferguson, particular users, such as Antonio French (alderman of St. Louis's 21st Ward) and Wesley Lowery (a reporter for the *Washington Post*), emerged as key informants whose on-the-ground accounts in Ferguson were retweeted by thousands of Twitter users. As an article in *USA Today* documents, over the course of the Ferguson events, Antonio French experienced a huge surge in popularity, going from around four thousand to 121 thousand followers in less than a month. See Mandaro 2014. This surge did not go unnoticed by local residents, some of whom have tweeted that politicians used the events to further their own careers.

14. This point is not exclusive to posts about Ferguson. Broadly speaking, in analyzing

Twitter usage, we must think carefully about when and why users feel the need to hashtag their posts. For example, users who post commentary about a specific TV show while that show is being broadcast often do not use a hashtag, presumably because they are tweeting to followers who are also watching the show at that moment in time. These tweets are not retrievable through hashtag searches, and, indeed, it is impossible to know what they are "about" unless one is viewing the tweets in real time or carefully reading a given user's timeline. Thus, the hashtag is just one possible way of creating eventness via Twitter.

15. Among those who write about "digital worlds" there is significant debate about the kinds of lines that should be drawn between "online" and "offline" realms (see Horst and Miller 2012). However, it is worth noting that many who tweeted about #Ferguson from outside Missouri eventually felt the need to visit the town of Ferguson and noted a sharp difference between these two sites. (See, e.g., Browne 2014; Cooper 2014.) Jalani Cobb (2014), who wrote about Ferguson for the *New Yorker,* argued that, during his reporting on the events, he developed a "between-the-world-and-Ferguson view of the events."

16. In considerations of the use of social media to articulate shared interests and mobilize political action, the recent history of its role in antiauthoritarian movements throughout the Middle East and Africa looms large. On the one hand, it is revealing to draw transnational connections between movements opposing closed regimes abroad and the struggles of subjugated populations within liberal democratic states. In the case of the Arab Spring, many studies point to the constitutive role of social media in not only information dissemination but also tactical maneuvers and strategic negotiations (see Howard et al. 2011; Lotan et al. 2011). On the other hand, it is methodologically dangerous to always jump to the scale of the "global rhetoric of 'spectacle,'" as Nishant Shah (2013:667) puts it, by rendering all such movements comparatively legible under broad monikers like "digital activism." Hence, the task of assessing the limits and promises

of #Ferguson as a field site requires sensitive attention to how technological changes run up against the persistent and embodied legacies of structural violence.

17. Several commentators at the time noted how the Ferguson events played out differently on Facebook versus Twitter. One researcher compared the "virality" of Ferguson on Twitter with that of the "Ice Bucket Challenge" on Facebook—a digital activism campaign that sought to raise awareness about amyotrophic lateral sclerosis (ALS). While there were, overall, many more news articles written about Ferguson than about the Ice Bucket Challenge in August of 2014, stories about Ferguson generated an average of 256 Facebook referrals compared with 2,106 referrals for stories about the Ice Bucket Challenge. Ice Bucket stories on Facebook also received a much larger number of "likes," "shares," and comments than Ferguson stories. One proposed reason for the pattern is Facebook's much more restrictive algorithms, but, more generally, Facebook is not regarded as a forum for hard news, tending more toward "friends and family and fun" (McDermott 2014). The fact that Ice Bucket Challenge posts often used the native video app within Facebook (rather than linking to an outside service) also explains why they dominated users' news feeds, as these types of posts are given priority within the Facebook algorithm. Notably, one user tried to "hack" the Facebook algorithm by faking a change in marital status and using the fake announcement to post commentary on Ferguson. See Warzel 2014. Others tried to "hack" the Ice Bucket Challenge itself; for more, see http://www.icebuckethack.com/, accessed October 15, 2014.

18. The "slowness" of Facebook vis-à-vis Twitter is generally attributed to the Facebook algorithms. Unlike Twitter, which shows all posts in reverse chronological order, Facebook orders posts using an algorithm that takes into account a user's behavior on the site and across the web. Some argue that Facebook's algorithm operates as a form of censorship, weeding out controversial topics and racially charged posts. See Tufekci 2014.

19. For more on the story behind the production of this image, see Lee 2014.

20. For a historical analysis of the production of "black criminality," see Muhammad 2010.

21. Memes might be best understood as mediatized tropes. That is, memes are citational representations that circulate in forms such as hashtags, photos, and videos. In some cases, such representations are explicitly recognized as memes. See Know Your Meme 2007–14.

22. Like Trayvon Martin's hoodie, whose sign value was construed in relation to race, the meaningfulness of the bag of candy and can of iced tea he was carrying with him at the time of his death were also racially construed and, in fact, rematerialized altogether as weapons and drug paraphernalia. George Zimmerman, Trayvon Martin's killer, allegedly thought that the candy and can of iced tea were potentially guns or other weapons; other commentators speculated that Martin was using these items to make recreational drugs. Here, ideas about race transform not just a sign's value (e.g., as a relatively unremarkable piece of clothing or a sartorial practice associated with criminality, as in the case of the hoodie) but the fundamental ontology of a given sign (e.g., as a bag of candy or a gun, a can of iced tea or drug paraphernalia), thus reflecting the semiotic power of race and racialization (Rosa 2010).

23. Perhaps the most recognizable of these images was a photo of the Miami Heat basketball team wearing hooded sweatshirts with the hoods up that famed NBA player Lebron James posted to Twitter with the hashtag #WeAreTrayvonMartin. See ESPN.com 2012.

24. Some commentators have pointed to the importance of the body not simply as a vehicle for marches or demonstrations but as a strategic choreographic tool deployed through practices such as the gestures associated with #HandsUpDontShoot. See Kedhar 2014.

25. Twitter also became a site in which to draw connections between what was taking place in Ferguson and state-sanctioned violence in other political contexts. Some Twitter users suggested that the killing of Michael Brown and militarized police response to protestors was analogous to the Israeli treatment of Palestinians. This was evident in posts such as "Where I come from, what some call 'rioting' we call an uprising #Ferguson #Gaza #Palestine #intifada" and "The Palestinian people know what it means to be shot while unarmed because of your ethnicity #Ferguson #Justice." Some Palestinians took to Twitter to offer those in Ferguson advice on how to avoid and respond to tear gas, including messages such as "#Ferguson solidarity," "To #Ferguson from #Palestine," and "#Palestine stands with #Ferguson." Meanwhile, other posts pointed to the U.S. involvement in both of these situations; one user, for instance, posted a picture of a teargas canister with the message, "Made in USA teargas canister was shot at us a few days ago in #Palestine by Israel, now they are used in #Ferguson." See Molloy and agencies 2014.

26. The phrase #Ferguson has been used not only on social media but also on other canvases such as posters and T-shirts. During October 2014, #Ferguson morphed into #FergusonOctober as a temporal rallying cry for demonstrations against police violence held in Ferguson throughout the month in preparation for the announcement of whether Officer Darren Wilson would be prosecuted for the killing of Michael Brown. In addition to this adaptation of #Ferguson, #HandsUpDontShoot has been invoked on posters and other organizing materials urging interested parties to text "HANDSUP" to a particular number for updates on what is going on in Ferguson and in the broader effort to eradicate police violence. Thus, there are powerful coordinating relationships between digital and offline contexts such as #Ferguson and Ferguson proper as well as relationships between digital modalities such as the circulation of information via Twitter and cellular text messages.

27. For more on these activities, see http://www.hashtag-ferguson.org/ and http://fergusonfireside.org/.

REFERENCES

Adams, Noah 2004 Emmett Till and the Impact of Images: Photos of Murdered Youth Spurred Civil Rights Activism. NPR Morning Edition. http://www.npr.org/templates/story/story.php?storyId 1969702, accessed November 15, 2014.

Agha, Asif 2007 Recombinant Selves in Mass Mediated Spacetime. *Language and Communication* 27(3):320–335.

Agha, Asif 2011 Meet Mediatization. *Language and Communication* 31(3):163–170.

Allan, Stuart, and Einar Thorsen, eds. 2009 *Citizen Journalism: Global Perspectives.* New York: Peter Lang.

Amnesty International 2014 On the Streets of America: Human Rights Abuses in Ferguson. http://www.amnestyusa.org/research/reports/on-the-streets-of-america-human-rights-abuses-in-ferguson, accessed November 15, 2014.

Bakhtin, Mikhail 1981 *The Dialogic Imagination: Four Essays.* Caryl Emerson and Michael Holquist, trans. Austin: University of Texas Press.

Bonilla, Yarimar In press *Non-Sovereign Futures: French Caribbean Politics in the Wake of Disenchantment.* Chicago: University of Chicago Press.

boyd, danah, and Kate Crawford 2012 *Critical Questions for Big Data. Information, Communication, and Society* 15(5):662–679.

Briggs, Charles L., and Richard Bauman 1992 Genre, Intertextuality, and Social Power. *Journal of Linguistic Anthropology* 2(2):131–172.

Browne, Rembert 2014 The Front Lines of Ferguson. Grantland.com, August 15. http://grantland.com/features/ferguson-missouri-protest-michael-brown-murder-police/, accessed October 15, 2014.

Bruns, Axel, and Jean Burgess 2011 The Use of Twitter Hashtags in the Formation of Ad Hoc Publics. Paper presented at the European Consortium for Political Research conference, Reykjavik, August 25–27.

Bryers, Alex 2014 #Ferguson: Social Media More Spark than Solution. Politico.com, August 20. http://www.politico.com/story/2014/08/ferguson-social-media-more-spark-than-solution-110202.html, accessed October 15, 2014.

Chittal, Nisha 2012 How to Decide What Can Be Published, What's Private of Twitter and Facebook. Poynter.com, March 29. http://www.poynter.org/latest-news/making-sense-of-news/167704/how-to-decide-what-can-be-published-whats-private-on-twitter-and-facebook/, accessed October 15, 2014.

Cobb, Jalani 2014 Between the World and Ferguson. New Yorker.com, August 26. http://www.newyorker.com/news/news-desk/world-ferguson, accessed October 15, 2014.

Coleman, Gabriella 2010 Ethnographic Approaches to Digital Media. *Annual Review of Anthropology* 39: 487–505

Cooper, Brittney 2014 "I Am Not Afraid to Die": Why America Will Never Be the Same Post-Ferguson. Salon.com, September 3. http://www.salon.com/2014/09/03/%E2%80%9Ciamnotafraidtodie%E2%80%9Dwhyamericawillneverbethesamepostferguson/, accessed October 15, 2014.

Dobrin, Lise 2008 From Linguistic Elicitation to Eliciting the Linguist: Lessons in Community Empowerment from Melanesia. *Language* 84(2):300–324.

Duggan, Maeve, and Joanna Brenner 2013 Social Networking Site Users. Pew Research Internet Project. February 14. http://www.pewinternet.org/2013/02/14/social-networking-site-users/, accessed October 15, 2014.

du Toit, Brian M. 1980 Ethics, Informed Consent, and Fieldwork. *Journal of Anthropological Research* 36(3):274–286.

Elignon, John 2014 Michael Brown Spent Last Weeks Grappling with Problems and Promise. *New York Times,* August 24, 2014.

ESPN.com 2012 Heat Don Hoodies after Teen's Death. ESPN.com, March 24. http://espn.go.com/nba/truehoop/miamiheat/story/_/id/7728618/miami-heat-don-hoodies-response-death-teen-trayvon-martin, accessed October 15, 2014.

Ferguson October 2014 About. http://ferguson october.com/about/, accessed October 15, 2014.

Florini, Sarah 2014 Tweets, Tweeps, and Signifyin': Communication and Cultural Performance on "Black Twitter." *Television and New Media* 15(3):223–237.

Gal, Susan, and Kathryn Woolard 2001[1995] Constructing Languages and Publics: Authority and Representation. In *Languages and Publics: The Making of Authority.* Susan Gal and Kathryn Woolard, eds. Pp. 1–12. Manchester, UK: St. Jerome's Press.

Garret, Kelly R., and Paul Resnick 2011 Resisting Political Fragmentation on the Internet. *Daedalus* 140(4):108–120.

Gebreyes, Rahel 2014 How Race, Gender and Fatigue Have Affected the Coverage of Renisha McBride's Death. http://www.huffingto-npost .com/2014/07/24/renisha-mcbride-trayvon-martin-gendern5615011.html, accessed October 15, 2014.

Geraldo Rivera: "Leave The Hoodie At Home" 2012 YouTube video, 3:02, from Fox New Broadcast on March 23. Posted by tpmtv. https://www .youtube.com/watch? v 2Yyqkcc-a8U, accessed October 15, 2014.

Gillum, Jack, and Joan Lowy 2014 Ferguson No-Fly Zone Aimed at Media. http://bigstory.ap.org/ article/674886091e344ffa95e92eb482e-02be1/ ap-exclusive-ferguson-no-fly-zone-aimed-media, accessed November 15, 2014.

Horst, Heather, and Daniel Miller 2012 *Digital Anthropology.* London: Berg Publishers.

Howard, Philip, Aiden Duffy, Deen Freelon, Muzammil Hussain, Will Mari, and Marwa Mazaid 2011 Opening Closed Regimes: What Was the Role of Social Media during the Arab Spring? Project on Information Technology and Political Islam. http://pitpi .org/wp-content/uploads/2013/02/2011˙Howard-Duffy-Freelon-Hussain-Mari-Mazaid˙pITPI.pdf, accessed October 15, 2014.

Hsieh, Steven, and Raven Rakia 2014 After #Ferguson. *Nation.* October 27, 2014.

Jackson, John L. 2008 *Racial Paranoia: The Unintended Consequences of Political Correctness: The New Reality of Race in America.* New York: Basic Civitas.

Kedhar, Anusha 2014 "Hands Up! Don't Shoot!": Gesture, Choreography, and Protest in Ferguson. Feministwire, October 6. http://thefeministwire .com/2014/10/protest-in-ferguson/, accessed October 15, 2014.

Know Your Meme 2007–14 Know Your Meme Home. http://knowyourmeme.com, accessed October 15, 2014.

Lasorsa, Dominic, Seth Lewis, and Avery Holton 2012 Normalizing Twitter: Journalism Practice in an Emerging Communication Space. *Journalism Studies* 13(1): 19–36.

Laurie, Julia 2014 10 Hours in Ferguson: A Visual Timeline of Michael Brown's Death and Its Aftermath. MotherJones.com, August 27. http:// www.motherjones.com/politics/2014/08/time-line-michael-brown-shooting-ferguson, accessed October 15, 2014.

Lee, Jolie 2014 Hands Up: Howard U. Photo of Students in Solidarity Goes Viral. *USA Today,* August 14. http://www.usatoday.com/story/news/ nation-now/2014/08/14/hands-up-ferguson-michael-brown-howard-brown/14044865/, accessed October 15, 2014.

Lipman, Victor 2014 Top Twitter Trends: What Countries Are Most Active? Who's Most Popular? Forbes.com, May 24. http://www.forbes .com/sites/victorlipman/2014/05/24/top-twitter-trends-what-countries-are-most-active-whos-most-popular/, accessed October 15, 2014.

Lotan, Gilad, Erhardt Graeff, Mike Ananny, Devin Gaffney, Ian Pearce, and danah boyd 2011 The Revolutions Were Tweeted: Information Flows during the 2011 Tunisian and Egyptian Revolutions. *International Journal of Communication* 5:1375–1405.

Mandaro, Laura 2014 300 Ferguson Tweets: A Day's Work for Antonio French. *USA Today,* August 26. http://www.usatoday.com/story/news/ nation-now/2014/08/25/antonio-french-twitter-ferguson/14457633/, accessed October 15, 2014.

Marquez, John 2012 Latinos as the "Living Dead": Raciality, Expendability, and Border Militarization. *Latino Studies* 10(4):473–498.

McDermott, John 2014 Why Facebook Is for Ice Buckets, Twitter Is for Ferguson. Digiday.com, August 20. http://digiday.com/platforms/facebook-twitter-ferguson/, accessed October 15, 2014.

Molloy, Mark, and agencies 2014 Palestinians Tweet Tear Gas Advice to Protesters in Ferguson. *Telegraph,* August 15. http://www.telegraph.co.uk/news/worldnews/northamerica/usa/11036190/Palestinians-tweet-tear-gas-advice-to-protesters-in-Ferguson.html, accessed October 15, 2014.

Muhammad, Khalil Gibran 2010 *The Condemnation of Blackness: Race, Crime, and the Making of Modern Urban America.* Cambridge, MA: Harvard University Press.

Pariser, Eli 2012 *The Filter Bubble: How the New Personalized Web Is Changing What We Read and How We Think.* New York: Penguin Press.

Postill, John 2014 Democracy in an Age of Viral Reality: A Media Epidemiography of Spain's Indignados Movement. *Ethnography* 15(1):51–69.

Rosa, Jonathan 2010 Looking like a Language, Sounding like a Race: Making Latina/o Panethnicity and Managing American Anxieties. Ph.D. dissertation, Department of Anthropology, University of Chicago.

Sankar, Pamela 2004 Communication and Miscommunication in Informed Consent to Research. *Medical Anthropology Quarterly* 18(4):429–446.

Seshagiri, Ashwin 2014 The Language of Twitter Users. NYTimes.com, March 9. http://bits.blogs.nytimes.com/2014/03/09/the-languages-of-twitter-users/, accessed October 15, 2014.

Shah, Nishant 2013 Citizen Action in the Time of the Network. *Development and Change* 44(3):665–681.

Sharma, Sanjay 2013 Black Twitter? Racial Hashtags, Networks, and Contagion. *New Formations: A Journal of Culture/Theory/Politics* 78(1):48–64.

Silverstein, Michael 2005 Axes of Evals: Token versus Type Interdiscursivity. *Journal of Linguistic Anthropology* 15(1):6–22.

Smith, Aaron 2013 Smartphone Ownership 2013. Pew Research Center, June 5. http://www.pewinternet.org/2013/06/05/smartphone-ownership-2013/, accessed October 15, 2014.

Sunstein, Cass 2009 Republic.com 2.0. Princeton: Princeton University Press.

Trouillot, Michel-Rolph 2003 *Global Transformations: Anthropology and the Modern World.* New York: Palgrave Macmillan.

Tufekci, Zeynep 2014 What Happens to #Ferguson Affects Ferguson: Net Neutrality, Algorithmic Filtering and Ferguson. Message, August 14. https://medium.com/message/ferguson-is-also-a-net-neutrality-issue-6d2f3db51eb0, accessed October 15, 2014.

Vega, Tanzina 2014 Shooting Spurs Hashtag Effort on Stereotypes. *New York Times,* August 12.

Warner, Michael 2002 *Publics and Counterpublics.* New York: Zone Books.

Warzel, Charlie 2014 How Ferguson Exposed Facebook's Breaking News Problem, BuzzFeed News, August 19, http://www.buzzfeed.com/charliewarzel/in-ferguson-facebook-cant-deliver-on-its-promise-to-deliver#2e4wmxb, accessed October 15, 2014.

Wasik, Bill 2009 *And Then There's This: How Stories Live and Die in Viral Culture.* New York: Penguin.

Wax, Murray 1980 Paradoxes of "Consent" to the Practice of Fieldwork. *Social Problems* 27(3):272–283.

Weerkamp, Wouter, Simon Carter, and Manos Tsagkias 2011 How People Use Twitter in Different Languages. Paper presented at ACM WebSci, 3rd International Conference on Web Science, Koblenz, June 14–17. http://www.websci11.org/fileadmin/websci/Posters/90˙pap-er.pdf, accessed October 15, 2014.

Wolfson, Nessa 1976 Speech Events and Natural Speech: Some Implications for Sociolinguistic Methodology. *Language in Society* 5(2):189–209.

ALTERNATIVE CONTENTS INDEX

MEDIA LITERACY AND MEDIA ACTIVISM ORGANIZATIONS

Many organizations address the issues in media culture explored throughout this book. In this section we provide a selective list of nonprofit and educational organizations that provide reliable critical media analysis and alternative media related to media literacy and race, class, gender, and sexuality. Organizations in this section provide a mix of educational materials for young adults and educators, opportunities to engage in media education, activism, and production, and critical media analysis and reporting. Drawing on information and language from the organizations' websites, this section highlights a number of organizations, along with their missions, a brief description of their available resources and activities, and information on how to connect with their content and initiatives.

About Face

About Face equips women and girls with tools to understand and resist harmful media messages that affect their self-esteem and body image. About Face offers real-world and online media literacy and media activism for teen girls. Its website provides educational resources, action guides, and a gallery of media complete with critical analysis and actionable information about media producers. About Face offers many ways to engage, from providing information for conducting letter-writing campaigns to educational resources for adult advocates and educators. This organization also offers workshops and speaking engagements in the San Francisco area.

www.about-face.org

Action Coalition for Media Education

The Action Coalition for Media Education (ACME) is a network of media educators and other stakeholders working to extend critical media literacy through education, media reform, and media activism. The organization is open to educators, students, activists, health professionals, media producers, and concerned members of the public. ACME offers a wide variety of media education resources and hosts occasional summits and trainings.

https://acmesmartmediaeducation.net

Adbusters

Adbusters is a global network of culture jammers and artists working to change the way information flows, the ways corporations wield power, and the way meaning is produced in our society. Adbusters publishes a magazine and maintains an active website.

https://adbusters.org

Adios Barbie

Adios Barbie's mission is to broaden the concepts of body image to include people of all ages, cultures, gender abilities, sexual orientations, races, and sizes. It creates articles, campaigns, lectures, and events that redefine perceptions of beauty.

www.adiosbarbie.com

Alliance for Community Media

The Alliance for Community Media promotes civic engagement through community media.

The alliance serves students, professionals, and institutions concerned with local-access media. The organization advocates for public policy supporting media access for all citizens. It supports local media producers with resources, events and conferences, the annual Hometown Film Festival, and a job board for students and media professionals. This organization also offers scholarship awards.

www.allcommunitymedia.org

Alliance for Media Arts and Culture

The Alliance for Media Arts and Culture fosters and fortifies the culture and business of independent media arts. Through dialogue, collaboration, research, and advocacy, it connects, organizes, and develops organizations. The alliance is a membership organization that supports artists and individuals creating digital media. For people interested in producing alternative media, it offers a host of supports, including leadership training and regular convening events.

www.thealliance.media

Alliance for Women in Media

The Alliance for Women in Media advances the influence and impact of women in all forms of media by facilitating collaboration, education, and innovation. The alliance is a professional organization for media professionals interested in gender equity behind the camera and quality representation in front it. Membership is open to women and men working in the media field or related professions. This organization is also open to students interested in pursuing a career in media. Annual Gracie Awards celebrate women in media, and travelling symposia address relevant industry topics. Student scholarships are available through this organization.

http://allwomeninmedia.org

Association for Media Literacy

The Association for Media Literacy is an organization based in Canada that is made up of teachers, librarians, consultants, parents, cultural workers, and media professionals concerned about the impact of the mass media on contemporary culture. The association seeks to help people develop a more informed and critical understanding of the nature of media. The association offers lesson plans for teachers and a resource section online, and workshops and speakers offline.

www.aml.ca

California Newsreel

California Newsreel is the oldest nonprofit social issue documentary film center in the country. California Newsreel has a large library of social justice documentaries, with a heavy emphasis on issues of race and justice. California Newsreel hosts outstanding documentaries on race, gender, and sexuality such as the collected works of Marlon Riggs, including *Black Is . . . Black Ain't, Color Adjustment, Ethnic Notions,* and *Tongues Untied.*

www.newsreel.org

Campaign for a Commercial-Free Childhood

Founded in 2000, Campaign for a Commercial-Free Childhood (CCFC) has built a powerful movement to end the exploitive practice of marketing to children and promote a modern childhood shaped by what's best for kids, not corporate profits. Its advocacy is grounded in the evidence that child-targeted marketing undermines healthy development and the belief that society bears responsibility for, and benefits immeasurably from, the wellbeing of children. Their website features a range of resource materials and information.

www.commercialfreechildhood.org

Center for Media Democracy

The Center for Media Democracy (CMD) is a nonpartisan media watchdog group focused on exposing corporate spin and government propaganda. CMD produces award-winning investigative journalism covering politics, corporations, environmentalism, the justice system, and other issues for its three publications: *PR Watch, SourceWatch,* and *Bankster.*

www.prwatch.org

Center for Media Literacy

The Center for Media Literacy (CML) is an educational organization that provides leadership, public education, professional development, and educational resources nationally and internationally. A great resource for students is CML's reading room, which catalogs hundreds of articles on media culture. CML also offers a large number of curriculum and educator resources.

www.medialit.org

Center for Public Integrity

The mission of the Center for Public Integrity is to enhance democracy by revealing abuses of power, corruption, and betrayal of trust by powerful public and private institutions. The organization provides nonpartisan, original reporting on a wide range of issues in the United States and abroad, with a special focus on politics, the environment, and social justice.

www.publicintegrity.org

Center on Media and Child Health

The Center on Media and Child Health educates parents and the public on media and their effects on the physical, mental, and social health of all children. The center provides a database of research on children and media. It hosts a searchable database, along with active social media sites with daily info for parents.

http://cmch.tv

Color of Film Collaborative

The Color of Film Collaborative is a nonprofit organization that works to support media makers of color and others who have an interest in developing and creating new, diverse images of people of color in film, video, and the performing arts. The collaborative supports independent filmmakers of color with production support, screening and distribution, and workshops.

www.coloroffilm.com

Common Sense Media

Common Sense Media is dedicated to improving the lives of kids and families by providing trustworthy information, education, and the independent voice they need to thrive in a world of media and technology. Common Sense Media provides age-based ratings and reviews of media, including videos, apps, and games for parents and families. It also offers educator programs and advocates on behalf of families to promote digital literacy and improve media rating systems to empower parents.

www.commonsensemedia.org

The Critical Media Project

The Critical Media Project is designed to serve high school instructors and other educators who seek to incorporate media literacy into the classroom. Its website offers a wide range of media artifacts that explore the politics of identity across issues of race and ethnicity, class, gender, and sexuality.

http://criticalmediaproject.org

Culture Reframed

Culture Reframed responds to the pornography crisis by providing education and support to promote healthy child and youth development, relationships, and sexuality. Its research-driven programs teach parents and those in the education and helping and health care professions how to recognize and respond to the role pornography can play in sexual violence, unhealthy relationships, Internet and sex addictions, negative self-image, sexual dysfunction, depression, sexually transmitted infections, injuries, and other health problems. Culture Reframed aims to empower participants to create positive and lasting change in families and communities harmed by the sexually abusive and hypersexualized media that marks the digital age.

www.culturereframed.org

FAAN Mail

FAAN Mail is a media literacy and activist project formed by and for women of color. The organization works to engage corporate media producers in critical dialogue and to engage communities through education, dialogue, and activism. FAAN Mail provides an active hub for those interested in addressing media representations and misrepresentations of women of color. It provides a vibrant online community both through its website and through social network engagement on Facebook and Twitter. It also provides workshops to colleges and community organizations interested in learning more about and addressing the representations of women of color in the media. FAAN Mail holds and posts talk-back sessions, in which members address media constructions in real time and share analysis with the wider community. FAAN Mail also offers workshops and speakers.

https://faanmail.wordpress.com

Fairness and Accuracy in Reporting

Fairness and Accuracy in Reporting (FAIR), the foremost national media watch group, has been offering well-documented criticism of media bias and censorship since 1986. It works to invigorate the First Amendment by advocating for greater diversity in the press and by scrutinizing media practices that marginalize public interest, minority, and dissenting viewpoints. FAIR offers excellent and extensive independent reporting and analyses of media across the whole spectrum of public interest issues affecting youth, minorities, the elderly, and the environment—online, on the radio, and via its YouTube channel. It also offers opportunities to take action through regular action alerts.

http://fair.org

Free Press

Free Press is a national, nonpartisan nonprofit advocating for universal and affordable Internet access, diverse media ownership, vibrant public media, and quality journalism. Free Press is an active organization fighting restrictive media ownership policies and advocating for wider dissemination of the tools for media production, including low-power FM stations. Free Press offers a multitude of ways readers can advocate for a better media environment, from online petitions to support for community media startup projects.

www.freepress.net

Geena Davis Institute on Gender and the Media

The mission of the Geena Davis Institute on Gender and the Media is to spotlight gender inequities in media and entertainment companies through cutting-edge research, education, training, strategic guidance, and advocacy programs in order to dramatically alter how girls and women are reflected in media. The organization advocates within the media industries for improved representation. It offers a variety of media education tools online, including research on media representation of women and girls, content for adults and young people, and curricula for educators.

https://seejane.org

Global Critical Media Literacy Project

In 2015, The Global Critical Media Literacy Project (GCMLP) was created under the Media Freedom Foundation's nonprofit umbrella by Project Censored, the Action Coalition for Media Education, and Sacred Heart University's Media Literacy and Digital Culture graduate program. The GCMLP provides pedagogy and curricular models for educators working in a variety of disciplines. The GCMLP empowers and engages students with meaningful learning and an educational pathway from junior college to graduate school and an opportunity for civic engagement in their communities. The GCMLP and its participants offer critical media literacy classroom activities and assignments, student- and faculty-generated content on the GCMLP website, and a service-learning component to participating faculty's curricula, in which students collaborate with one another and with faculty to produce works for publication, and more.

http://gcml.org

Mass Media Literacy

Mass Media Literacy is committed to ensuring that children have access to comprehensive media literacy education. They work with school systems, libraries, community groups, and legislators to deliver training, curriculum, research, and other resources that promote comprehensive media literacy education.

www.massmedialiteracy.org

Media Education Foundation

The Media Education Foundation (MEF) produces and distributes documentary films and other educational resources to inspire critical thinking about the social, political, and cultural impact of American mass media. From films about the commercialization of childhood and the subtle, yet widespread, effects of pop-cultural misogyny and racism, to titles that deal with the devastating effects of rapacious consumerism MEF offers resources designed to help spark discussion about some of the most pressing, and complicated, issues of our time. Their aim is to inspire students to think critically and in new ways about the hyper-mediated world around them.

www.mediaed.org

Media Literacy and Digital Culture Master's Program

The goal of Media Literacy and Digital Culture (MLDC) is to graduate master's students who have the media literacy skills necessary to critically analyze the intersections of media and culture while fostering their creativity and social awareness. MLDC brings together the theory and practice of communication within the contemporary media environment with a specific focus on vulnerable populations and social inequality.

http://sacredheart.edu/mldc

Media Watch

Media Watch's mission is to challenge, through education and action, abusive stereotypes and other biased information commonly found in the media. Media Watch is a nonprofit focusing on media depictions of gender and race. It creates educational media literacy videos focused on the harms of gendered representations and hosts a media literacy education blog and public lectures in addition to providing other resources.

www.mediawatch.com

National Association for Media Literacy Education

The National Association for Media Literacy Education's mission is to expand and improve the practice of media literacy education in the United States. The association is an active membership organization made up of educators, students, and media activists. It provides opportunities for networking and professional development among members through conferences, a resource hub, and publications.

https://namle.net

Paper Tiger Television

Paper Tiger Television is an open nonprofit volunteer video collective. The organization believes that increasing public awareness of the negative influence of mass media and involving people in the process of making media is mandatory for the long-term goal of information equity.

Paper Tiger Television produces short videos on critical media literacy and other social justice issues. It also offers community workshops and materials for those interested in hosting their own community screenings.

http://papertiger.org

Project Censored

Project Censored educates students and the public about the importance of a truly free press for democratic self-government. They expose and oppose news censorship and promote independent investigative journalism, media literacy, and critical thinking. Project Censored's work—including its annual book, weekly radio broadcasts, campus affiliates program, and additional community events—highlights the important links among a free press, media literacy, and democratic self-government.

http://projectcensored.org

Snopes

Snopes has been operating since 1995 and is the Internet's go-to source for urban legend information. This is an excellent source for debunking viral stories.

www.snopes.com

Spy Hop

Spy Hop's mission is to mentor young people in the digital arts to help them find their voices, tell their stories, and be empowered to effect positive change in their lives. Spy Hop works with youth to produce film, music, and design. The organization offers educational workshops for youth and educators and maintains a website rich with high-quality youth media.

http://spyhop.org

Understand Media

Understand Media's website provides media literacy information for students, teachers, and adults. The site features media literacy video lessons, a podcast, and a blog on media issues.

www.understandmedia.com

Vision Maker Media

Vision Maker Media shares with the world stories that represent the cultures, experiences, and values of Indigenous people. This organization offers training, support, and distribution to help Native media makers share stories. Its website also offers educational guides for Native-themed productions suitable for higher ed.

www.visionmakermedia.org

Weave News

Founded in 2007, Weave News is a global community of citizen journalists who are committed to weaving a better world. This organization is directed by a team of staffers who assist contributors in sharing their work via investigative blogs, Big Questions videography, multimedia projects, and other initiatives. They aim to investigate underreported stories, highlight alternative perspectives, and promote grassroots media-making and critical media literacy.

www.weavenews.org

Women Action and the Media

Women Action and the Media (WAM) is an independent nonprofit dedicated to building a robust, effective, inclusive movement for gender justice in media. WAM is a grass-roots organizing and advocacy group that encourages participants to take action to increase gender representation of women in front of and behind the camera, including increasing their ownership of and roles in media production. They offer multiple ways to engage, from joining an established local chapter to creating one's own.

www.facebook.com/WomenActionMedia/

Women Make Movies

Established in 1972 to address the underrepresentation of women in the media industry, Women Make Movies is a multicultural, multiracial, nonprofit media arts organization that facilitates the production, distribution, and exhibition of independent films and videos by and about women. The organization serves both established and emerging artists. Women Make Movies fosters feminist media by providing distribution services, funding and support, and workshops for women to produce independent feminist media.

http://wmm.com

GLOSSARY OF TERMS

Active audiences. See *Audience, active audience, audience reception.*

Activism, media activism, media activists. Media activists include those who organize, educate, and lobby to challenge the mass media stories and images they consider harmful to society or derogatory to particular groups. Some media activists also produce counterhegemonic media texts as a way to raise consciousness about the economic, social, and political inequalities inherent in capitalism. Others act as public interest advocates who urge policymakers to ensure public access to media for historically disenfranchised groups.

Address, subject address. See *Subject position.*

Agency. See *Resistance.*

American Dream ideology. This refers to the belief, particularly strong for immigrants in the 19th and 20th centuries, that the United States offers unlimited opportunities for freedom, economic success, and happiness for all who are willing to work hard. In the context of media studies, this ideology is often discussed along with individualism and neoliberalism.

Appropriation. This term can refer, in a neutral sense, to how we make sense of the meanings encoded into cultural texts and incorporate these into our daily lives. Cultural critics also use this term frequently to highlight power relations in an unequal society. Thus, appropriation can refer to the process whereby members of relatively privileged groups "raid" the culture of marginalized groups, abstracting cultural practices or artifacts from their historically specific contexts. Frequently this involves co-optation, by which a cultural item's resistant or counterhegemonic potential is lost through its translation into the dominant cultural context. Adding insult to injury, appropriation frequently means profit for the appropriator as in the example of White rock-and-roll musicians who benefitted from the creative labor of uncompensated Black artists.

Audience, active audience, audience reception. Developed partly in response to the classical Marxist notion that ideology is all-powerful and, hence, audience members are at the mercy of the ideas of the ruling class, the concept of the active audience stresses the ways audiences are involved in actively constructing meaning from the text. There is debate within media studies as to just how much

agency audience members have to construct their own meaning. Some scholars argue that given the polysemic nature of all texts, there are multiple ways to decode the ideological messages embedded in the texts. Others, most notably those within more critical cultural studies, follow Stuart Hall and argue that there are three main possible audience responses: dominant reading, preferred reading, and oppositional reading (see *Encoding/decoding* entry). Today, some media scholars apply the concept of the active audience to those who produce their own media across a range of media platforms as a way to disrupt or play with the hegemonic meanings embedded in corporate-controlled media.

Authoritarianism. Authoritarianism has been discussed by scholars as both a personality trait and a political ideology. Cultural theorist Theodor Adorno and his coauthors (1950) famously described the authoritarian personality as one that values obedience, conformity, and respect for power. As an ideology authoritarianism is considered hostile to political freedom and dissent and is closely related to Fascism in its belief in powerful forms of centralized leadership. Critical media studies scholars have explored the tendencies of cultural texts to either reinforce or challenge authoritarian values.

Binary. In critical race, gender, and sexuality studies, this refers to the "either/or" conceptualization of "race" as Black/White or "gender" as masculine/feminine, or sexuality as straight/gay in contrast to a system allowing for multiple racial, gender, and sexual identities.

Black feminist perspective. See *Feminism, Black feminism, feminist media studies.*

Capitalism, capitalist. An economic system based on private (rather than public or collective) ownership of the means of production, the market exchange of goods and services, and wage labor. This book tends to adopt a perspective critical of the ways capitalist ownership of the media shapes and limits content.

Class, social class. A much-debated term in both sociology and economics. It tends to be used by sociologists to refer to a social stratum whose members share certain social, economic, and cultural characteristics. However, critical sociologists use a modified version of the classic Marxist usage, which defined class as a group of people occupying a similar position within the social relations of economic production. Whereas Marx argued that there are only two major classes under capitalism, the bourgeoisie (owner class) and the proletariat (worker class), critical sociologists distinguish five: the ruling class, the professional/managerial class, small-business owners, the working class, and the poor.

Codes, semiotic codes, media codes. A term used in semiotics-influenced media studies to refer to rules and conventions that structure representations on a number of levels—some specific to certain media, such as narrative film or advertising photographs, and others shared with different modes of communication. Audiences learn to "read" the conventional verbal, visual, and auditory features that make up the "languages" or "sign systems" of media and other cultural forms in much the same way children learn the complex, often arbitrary systems of meaning in natural languages. Also see *Semiotics* and *Encoding/decoding*.

Commodity. Any object or service that can be bought and sold in the marketplace. Marxists argue that capitalism reduces all aspects of life, and even people themselves, to commodities.

Conglomeration, conglomerates. In the context of media studies, this refers to the merging of two or more large media corporations into mega-corporations with great economic, political, and cultural power.

Consumerism/consumerist. Consumerism is an economic system and set of cultural values that encourages the production of consumer products and services, and accords social status to their purchase, display, and consumption. Consumerism is often associated with the capitalist system that relies on rising production and sales, achieved through branding, promotion, and mass media advertising. The term *consumerism* is frequently used in a critical manner, especially in the context of media and cultural studies, to suggest the excesses of materialist culture and conspicuous consumption, as well as the negative environmental impacts of rising production and waste. Consumerism can also refer to a movement to use information and laws to protect consumers from false advertising and dangerous or defective products.

Content analysis. A social scientific method of describing and analyzing the "content" of a range of media texts, either in qualitative or quantitative terms. Quantitative content analysis (counting the number of times certain types of material appear) is especially useful for describing the broad contours of a large quantity of texts, but it tends to miss the more subtle and complex ways texts construct meaning.

Convergence, media convergence. This term has been used to refer to many different processes in the current fast-changing media business environment. Henry Jenkins (2006) has usefully clarified the term this way: "the flow of content across multiple media platforms, the cooperation between multiple media industries, and the migratory behavior of media audiences who will go almost anywhere in search of the kinds of entertainment experiences they want" (p. 2).

Co-opt, co-optation. See *Appropriation*.

Counterhegemonic, antihegemonic. See *Hegemony, hegemonic*.

Critical race theory. In contrast to older approaches to "race" that assumed "White" or Euro-American norms and focused on "non-White" identities as "the problem," critical race studies are based on the assumption that the proper object of study is the construction of hierarchical racial categories by which "White privilege" comes to seem "natural." Critical race theorists have argued that White supremacist ideologies are commonplace rather than exceptional. Critical race theorists are also concerned with challenging the Black/White *binary* that has dominated U.S. academic discourse on "race," rendering invisible anyone who cannot be made to exemplify one of these two artificially constructed categories. In general, critical race theorists view "race" as a purely historical construct in the service of political goals. See Omi and Winant (1993).

Critical, critical theory, critical media theory, critical media pedagogy. Also see *Marxism*. "Critical" in media studies does not necessarily mean negative or derogatory. Critical studies is an approach to the analysis of social and cultural phenomena that highlights the dominant role of White supremacy, patriarchy, and capitalism, and the social inequalities that result from these ideologies and practices.

Cultivation, media cultivation. Cultivation is a theory of media influence advanced by the late media scholar George Gerbner (1998) and his colleagues that challenges more traditional theories of media effects by suggesting that the consequences of growing up with television, in particular, are subtle, gradual, but ultimately powerful. Positing that television has become the primary storyteller throughout much of the contemporary world, cultivation scholars survey television viewers and find, over the course of repeated and ongoing studies, that the more television a person watches, the more likely they are to accept television's often distorted and misleading narratives and images, particularly when it comes to issues such as violence, race, gender, and so forth.

Cultural studies. An approach to the study of communication in society that is drawn from a number of sources, including Marxism, semiotics, sociology, literary and film analysis, psychoanalysis, feminism, and critical race and postcolonial theory. As used in this book, it locates the production, textual construction, and consumption of media texts in a society characterized by multiple systems of inequality. Of key importance is the study of the role of media in the production and reproduction of these systems of inequality. See Chapter 1 in this reader for an extended discussion of this approach.

Culture, popular culture. *Culture* is a term with many different meanings, depending on the school of thought in which it is employed. In anthropology, it refers to everything created by humans, including artifacts or objects, ideas, institutions, and expressive practices. In traditional humanities fields such as art history and literature, culture has tended to be conceptualized as the high-status arts of the wealthy and socially dominant, such as oil paintings, opera, ballet, or poetry. Cultural studies rejects this view of culture as elitist, replacing it with the more anthropological usage. In particular, cultural studies takes as its area of study all the expressive, meaningful, interactive aspects of everyday life, including forms of popular culture (like magazines, video games, popular music, social media, etc.) that traditional scholarship may dismiss as trivial or unworthy of serious analysis.

Decode. See *Encoding/decoding.*

Deconstruct. To deconstruct (or analyze, "take apart") a cultural text is to first understand that texts are constructed within a political, economic, and social context that to greater or lesser degrees shapes the encoded meaning of the text. Texts are seen as holders of meaning and, as such, need to be carefully deconstructed using an array of methods. Over the years, however, media scholars have recognized that audiences don't necessarily make the dominant reading and have explored, often using ethnographic methods, the ways audiences deconstruct or unpack the texts. While scholars may deconstruct the text using different methodologies, it is only by careful research of the audience that we can understand the connection, or lack of it, between the encoding and decoding ends of the communication chain.

Discourse(s), discourse analysis, discursive. Within cultural studies, discourse analysis examines how power relations in societies are sustained by and reflected in a variety of specialized ways of speaking and writing, such as those of elite institutions and groups—for example, medical professionals, religious institutions, and academics—as influentially articulated in French historian Michel Foucault's *The History of Sexuality.*

Discursive. See *Discourse(s), discourse analysis, discursive.*

Emergent media. This term is used to distinguish newer forms of media such as digital, mobile, Internet-based, and social media from what is sometimes called "old" or traditional media like newspapers, magazines, radio, film, and television.

Encoding/decoding. "Encoding/Decoding" is the title of an influential article by British cultural studies scholar Stuart Hall (1980). Hall proposes that meaning does not simply reside in a media text's codes but is the result of a complex negotiation between specific audiences and texts. In contrast to former critical media theorists who assumed that audiences had little control over meaning and were vulnerable to being "brainwashed" by the media, Hall proposed three possible audience responses to the dominant ideology contained in the media text's codes, or three distinct reading positions corresponding to audiences' different social situations: dominant reading (accepting the preferred meaning), negotiated reading (accepting aspects of the preferred meaning but rejecting others), and oppositional reading (rejecting the preferred meaning).

Ethnography. This is a social research method first used by anthropologists and now adopted by some cultural studies scholars for understanding the role of media audiences in the production of meaning. In ethnographic media studies research, audience members are typically interviewed about their understandings of the media text, or they participate in guided discussions in focus groups. The study can also involve participant observation, which requires that the researcher become a part of the group studied for a specified period to understand directly the context in which the media text reception takes place. For an example of an ethnographic media study, see Radway in this reader. Also see *Audience, active audience, audience reception.*

Fans, fandom studies. Ethnographic media audience studies sometimes focus on specialized groups of audiences—the enthusiasts or fans, who seem to exemplify the "active audience" phenomenon in a particularly intensive way. As Henry Jenkins showed in his original study of *Star Trek* fans, excerpted in this volume, a fan community can go beyond consumption of a media text to a more active relationship, in which new texts are created by fans who borrow ("poach") from and creatively rewrite aspects of commercial media texts, especially when the original texts are found lacking in some way. Fans can bond with one another over their strong relationships with selected media texts, using passionate and interactive revision of such texts as one basis for community. Fandom studies tend to emphasize the potential of grassroots media culture productivity to undermine or challenge the dominance that corporate producers exercise over media culture.

Feminism, Black feminism, radical feminism, feminist media studies. A multidisciplinary approach to social analysis, rooted in the contemporary women's movement(s) and the lesbian/gay/bisexual/transgender/queer (LGBTQ) liberation movement. Emphasizing gender as a major organizing feature of power relations in society, feminists argue that the role of media and popular culture is crucial in the construction and dissemination of gender ideology and, thus, in gender socialization. As Bob Jensen explains in his chapter in this book, "Radical feminism opposes patriarchy, the system of institutionalized male dominance, and understands gender as a category that established and reinforces inequality. The goal is the end of—not accommodation with—patriarchy's gender system and other domination/subordination dynamics" (p. 292). Feminists of color have critiqued the tendency in some feminist theory to privilege gender over other categories of experience; in particular, cultural analysts with a Black feminist (sometimes called "womanist") perspective have brought to the foreground the ways gender is "inflected" or modified by race and class factors. See Patricia Hill Collins (2000).

Feminist film theory. This strand of cultural studies, which was particularly influential in the 1980s, combines a feminist view of the centrality of gender in cultural analysis with a generally psychoanalytic orientation to the study of audience reception of film. Feminist film theorists working through textual analysis have explored such issues as gendered spectatorship, the ways the film text, through its formal codes, "addresses" or speaks directly to the hypothetical or ideal viewer as either male or female. An early formulation by Laura Mulvey (1975) asserted that any viewer of classic Hollywood narrative film was encouraged by plot, camera work, and editing to adopt a "masculine subject position" and share in the male gaze of both the film's protagonist and the camera while looking at a female object of desire.

Gay and lesbian studies, lesbian/gay/bisexual/transgender/queer (LGBTQ) studies. See *Queer theory, queer studies*.

Gaze, male gaze. See *Feminist film theory*.

Gender, gendering, gendered. Whereas sex differences (anatomical and hormonal) between genetic males and genetic females are biological in nature, gender is a social concept by which a society defines as "masculine" or "feminine" one particular set of characteristics and behaviors and then socializes children accordingly. These criteria can vary tremendously over time and between cultures, and even between different social groups within the same culture. Some contemporary scholars argue that both gender and sexuality (erotic desires and identities, sexual object choice, sexual practice) are more accurately understood as continuums, rather than in binary (only two, either/or) categories. Gender is now commonly understood to be constructed in "intersectional" relationships with other aspects of social identity, such as race and class. Media theorists and critics generally try to locate their gender analysis within specific social contexts, distinguishing, for example, representations of Black middle-class masculinity of a particular time and place from other masculinities.

Gendered subjectivity, sexual subjectivities. See *Gender, gendering, gendered and subject position*.

Genre. *Genre* comes from the French word meaning "type" or kind. In media studies, it refers to a collection of texts categorized according to their similar content and style. A specific text is part of a genre when it uses certain codes and conventions that are familiar to viewers. Examples of media genres discussed in this book include reality TV shows, advertisements, and hip-hop music. Genres are not always discrete entities, because the codes and conventions of one genre can leak into another—as in the case of pornography, where pornographic codes and conventions of representing women's bodies have seeped into pop culture, resulting in what some scholars call hypersexualization of the media environment.

Globalization, global media. In this age of giant multinational media conglomerates and new digital and Internet technologies that allow for wide distribution of corporate-produced cultural products from the richer nations across the globe, the term *globalization* means different things for different media critics. Some, such as Robert McChesney (2008), warn of the dangers of cultural imperialism, which they see as threatening the integrity and autonomy of local cultures around the world, particularly those in the Global South that lack the wealth and industrial technologies necessary to compete with the onslaught of Hollywood-produced imagery. Others, including Henry Jenkins (2006), argue that the process is more one of cross-cultural "flow" and see the imperialistic model as too deterministic. Also see *Convergence, media convergence*.

Hegemony, hegemonic, counterhegemonic. A term utilized by Italian Marxist theorist Antonio Gramsci to refer to the process by which those in power secure the consent of the socially subordinated to the system that oppresses or subordinates them. Rather than requiring overt force (as represented by the military or police), the elite, through their control of religious, educational, and media institutions, attempt to persuade the populace that the hierarchical social and economic system is fixed and "natural," and therefore unchangeable. According to Gramsci, however, such consent is never secured once and for all but must continually be sought, and there is always some room for resistance through subversive (counterhegemonic) cultural work.

Heterocentrism, heteronormativity. These terms refer to the placing of heterosexual experience at the center of attention, or the routine assumption that heterosexuality is "normal" and any other expression of sexuality is "deviant."

Heterosexism. A term coined by analogy with *sexism,* the basic definition of heterosexism is discrimination or prejudice against queer people by heterosexual people. As with *racism* and *sexism,* this book takes the view that structural or institutional forces underpin social inequalities, rather than individual prejudiced attitudes. Thus, heterosexism would refer to the heterosexual ideology that is encoded into and characteristic of the major social, cultural, political, and economic institutions of our society. Heterocentrism, similarly, refers to the centrality of the heterosexual perspective in a society. Also see *Race, racism, postracial* and *Sexism.*

Homophobia. A psychological concept, referring to deep-seated fear of homosexuality, in others or in oneself. Also see *Heterosexism* and *Heterocentrism, heteronormativity.*

Hypersexuality, hypersexualized. *Hypersexual* is a controversial term in media studies used to describe the increasingly sexualized imagery of young women found in pop culture. Some scholars argue that these images represent female sexual empowerment, while others see them as the outgrowth of a culture steeped in pornographic codes and conventions. Feminists have pointed out that this new hypersexual look is formulaic in that it requires strict adherence to a set of codes and conventions that are difficult for most women to conform to, especially women who are disabled, heavier, or older. In her chapter in this book, Rosalind Gill argues that the increasing hypersexuality of images results in a "self-policing narcissistic gaze," where "the objectifying male gaze is internalized to form a new disciplinary regime" (p. 253).

Ideology. This term was traditionally used by Marxists to refer to ideas imposed on the proletariat (working class) by the bourgeoisie (owners of the means of production) to get the subservient classes to consent to their own oppression. Today, critical theorists tend to use a broader concept of ideology that emphasizes the way ideas embedded in all our social institutions (legal, educational, political, cultural, economic, familial, military, etc.) create a dominant commonsense understanding of reality that supports the status quo. For a definition of ideology, see the essay by Stuart Hall in this reader.

Image, imagery, media image. This term refers to any representation of social reality in media culture, as in "images of women in advertising." However, the word *image* as commonly used—as in "mirror image"—tends to suggest a more direct, uncomplicated, and less artificial or constructed relationship with "reality" than most scholars now propose for media representations. Image also refers, of course, to a specifically visual representation. See Sut Jhally's chapter on "Image-Based Culture" in this volume.

Individualism. Individualism is a political philosophy, moral stance, or ideology that accords primacy to individual interests and desires. It is also a methodology that takes individual people, rather than social groups, classes, or nations, as the unit of analysis. Individualism is often contrasted with socialism or communitarianism, in which the society or community has systemic qualities with values and attributes that cannot be reduced to the level of individuals. Proponents of individualism generally presume that people are sovereign entities capable of making informed decisions in their own interests, that the pursuit of individual interests does not have a major negative impact on others, and that efforts to regulate individual behavior are intrusive, immoral, or counterproductive.

Intersectionality. An approach to describing and analyzing social identity that recognizes multiple strands that combine with one another in complex ways. In a world characterized by race, class, ability, age, gender, and sexual inequalities, among others, an intersectional analysis allows us to study how different forms of inequality work together to limit the life chances of oppressed groups. Adopting such an approach has implications for social activism because it demands building coalitions of groups to form social movements that can address multiple oppressions.

Intertextuality. John Fiske (1987) has explicated a theory of intertextuality to help explain the way audiences experience a wide variety of media texts as interrelated, allowing their knowledge of one to influence their reading of another. For example, if a primary media text is a specific book, film, or television show, then a secondary text might be "studio publicity, journalistic features, or criticism" about the primary text, and tertiary texts might include viewers' letters, gossip, and conversation about the primary text (Fiske, 1987, pp. 108–109). Commercial intertextuality refers to the practice of media text promoters' using a multiplicity of media platforms to make a particular text highly visible and attractive to the intended target audience. Also see *Text, media text.*

Lesbigay, LGBTQ. See *Queer theory, queer studies.*

Liberatory. Like *emancipatory* or *progressive*, this term is used in critical cultural studies to indicate what the critic sees as a positive political impact, in which a socially subordinate group gains greater power or freedom (liberation or emancipation from oppression).

Liminal, liminality. A term used by anthropologists and cultural studies scholars to mean an area or condition of ambiguity or mixture, at the border between two different conditions.

Marxism, Marxist, Marxian. A general theory of historical change originally developed by 19th-century German philosopher Karl Marx. Marx argued for the centrality of economics in social history and developed a critique of capitalism that has had a major influence on political theory and on social revolutions in the 19th and 20th centuries. In the realm of cultural studies, classic Marxism argued that the economic structure of society (the "base") shapes major cultural institutions (the "superstructure"), including the military, legal system, educational system, arts, and media. This is because, according to Marx, "the class which has the means of material production at its disposal has control over the means of mental production" (Marx & Engels, 1938). For a modification of classic Marxist ideas of this relationship, see *Hegemony.*

Masculinities, masculinist. See *Gender, gendering, gendered.*

Media, mass media, mass communications media, mediated, media culture. The term *media* is originally the plural of medium (such as television, film, radio, internet, etc.). It has become a shorthand way of referring to the whole range of technologically assisted means by which images and messages can be created and distributed by producers for later consumption by "the masses" (vast numbers of people). "The media" is sometimes a shorthand way of referring to news media in particular, but in the context of this book, we are referring primarily to entertainment media culture. To say that communication is "mediated" is to draw attention to its highly secondhand character (as opposed to real-time, face-to-face, traditional cultural forms, such as storytelling, live theater, acoustic musical performances for live audiences, etc.).

Media literacy/media literacy skills. The goal of media literacy is to educate people to think critically about the way media texts are produced, constructed, and consumed, and to provide skills that help deconstruct the ideological messages encoded in texts. Critical media literacy includes an analysis of political economy where the study of the production, consumption, and distribution of the text is located within the wider context of capitalist control of media institutions. Recently, many media literacy experts have argued that a major component of media literacy is to teach media production skills as a way to deepen an understanding of how mainstream media is constructed and to encourage people to create independent (noncorporate) media that challenge the hegemonic representations of corporate-owned media.

Media platforms. A media platform is a technical mechanism by which text, images, video, and sound are presented to media users. These can include traditional platforms such as television, newspapers, and radio, as well as relatively new social media platforms on the internet, such as Facebook, Twitter, YouTube, blogs, and online news sources. In media studies, the concept of media platforms is significant because the use of different platforms has implications for ownership, control, privacy, influence, and access.

Misogyny. Literally, this word means "hatred of women," and its use emphasizes the emotional or psychological basis for sexism. Feminist cultural critics analyze how misogyny and sexism are embedded in culture, often in ways that make social arrangements in which males are allocated supremacy over females seem natural or inevitable.

Multicultural, multiculturalism. As used in this book, *multiculturalism* refers to a movement affecting curricula, teaching methods, and scholarship in a variety of fields within universities and colleges in the United States. The broad objectives of activists in this movement include democratizing knowledge and education by bringing to the foreground and validating the experiences and perspectives of those groups unrepresented, misrepresented, marginalized, or culturally and socially dominated in our society.

Multidisciplinary, interdisciplinary. An approach that encourages students and educators to cross the boundaries between traditional academic disciplines or areas of knowledge (such as history, literature, sociology, philosophy, economics, or political science) to more effectively capture the complexity of the topics studied.

Negotiated reading. See *Encoding/decoding.*

Neoliberalism. This term refers to an ideology that has become dominant in the economic policies of the wealthier nations, and of international lender organizations such as the World Bank, in the past several decades. Unlike the economic theories of John Maynard Keynes, which emphasized the role of government intervention in the economy to promote the well-being of citizens, this view greatly emphasizes (and some would say exaggerates) the beneficial workings of the unregulated private sector, through the magic of the workings of the free market. Embedded in this ideology is the idea that every individual is equally able to protect herself or himself from economic disaster—an idea that easily leads to "blaming the victim" when individuals do not achieve economic stability. In the context of cultural studies, critics argue that certain types of media texts, such as makeover reality programs, Judge Judy, or talk radio, encode and promote neoliberal ideas, teaching that the individual can and must empower herself or himself without government support.

New media. This term generally refers to communication technologies that enable users or consumers to directly interact with one another and with media texts, in contrast to traditional, older mass media technologies such as newspapers, radio and television broadcasts, films, and recorded music. New media would include blogs, social networking sites, online games, interactive websites such as YouTube, and many other examples that will be current by the time you read this book.

Objectify, objectification, objectifying. Literally, "to make into an object"; more figuratively, to dehumanize a person. In the context of feminist theory, objectification of women is implied by excessive emphasis on body parts and external appearances, especially in media representations designed to sexualize female bodies.

Oppositional reading. See *Encoding/decoding*.

Orientalism. Perhaps most associated with the late Edward Said because of his book by the same name, *Orientalism* is a term critical scholars use to refer to the attitudes and practices of Westerners in regard to the nations and people of the so-called Orient, including Asia and the Middle East. Said (1979) discusses Orientalism as a form of discourse that aids in situating non-Western people as alluring and mysterious and simultaneously backward, even primitive, and dangerous and untrustworthy. As Said wrote, Orientalism is "a Western style for dominating, restructuring, and having authority over the Orient" (p. 3). The term is used frequently in cultural and postcolonial studies as a way to critically examine cultural discourses of inclusion and exclusion ("us" and "them"), and the "Othering" of members of outgroups. Also see *Postcolonialism*.

Patriarchal, patriarchy. Literally meaning "rule by the father" and referring to family (and clan) systems in which one older man had absolute power over all members of the group, including women, children, and younger male relatives and servants. As used by contemporary feminists, it is a concept developed to examine and critique continuing male domination of social institutions such as the family, the state, the educational system, and the media.

Political economy. In critical theory, a perspective that "sets out to show how different ways of financing and organizing cultural production have traceable consequences for the range of discourses and representations in the public domain, and for audiences' access to them" (Golding & Murdoch, 1991, p. 15). This often involves studying who owns the media industries, how ownership influences media content, and how media is funded.

Polysemic text. A polysemic text is one that is "open" to various readings or has multiple meanings. Cultural studies scholars currently disagree regarding how relatively "open" or "closed" most media texts are. Also see *Encoding/decoding*.

Pornification. Journalist Pamela Paul is often credited with introducing this term in her book *Pornified: How Pornography Is Damaging Our Lives* (2006). It refers to the way pornography, as both a discourse and an industry, has increasingly come to dominate our cultural landscape and shape sexual relationships. Within the feminist community, there is a long-standing debate regarding the degree to which pornification is an expression of misogyny, or an example of women's sexual agency. This book, working within the critical cultural studies paradigm, contains chapters that see pornification as inextricably linked to the increasing commodification of all aspects of our lives, and the attendant erosion of sexual agency and creativity.

Pornography. Most broadly, this refers to sexually explicit visual and/or written texts designed to produce sexual arousal in consumers. The definition has been politicized and was strenuously contested during the 1980s, when feminists proposed city ordinances by which the production and distribution of certain classes of pornography could be prosecuted as civil rights violations, rather than under traditional anti-vice criminal law. Anti-pornography feminists argued that pornography is a form of violence against women in its production and consumption. Against this position, there are some who argue that pornography provides a space for sexual creativity and power for women.

Postcolonialism. A critical approach to the legacy of colonialism and imperialism, primarily by European powers, in terms of the political, cultural, and economic impacts on formerly colonized countries, and the enduring inequalities in relations between them and Western countries. Postcolonialism draws from postmodernism to understand how colonialism was not just a military phenomenon but, rather, was structured and legitimated through media and cultural representations that portrayed the superiority of Western civilization, arts, and science, and the inferiority of colonized people and their cultures. Postcolonialism investigates how many of the traditional conceptions of superiority and inferiority are perpetuated in media images and texts, and how these contribute to ongoing economic inequalities, harsh immigration policies, military interventions, and other phenomena. Also see *Orientalism*.

Postfeminism. This term has been used to describe and critique a period of reaction against feminism that began in the 1980s, when some women sympathetic to the goals of feminism nevertheless refused to name themselves as feminists. As used by feminist media critics, however, it tends to refer to the idea embedded in some cultural texts that all the goals of the women's movement have already been achieved. In this way, it is parallel to postracial discourse. Also see *Race, racism, postracial*.

Post-Fordism. This refers to the strategies adopted by multinational corporations in seeking to maximize profits by diversifying products and marketing them in new ways in response to global flows of labor and consumption patterns. (It contrasts with "Fordism," which was the 20th-century mass production and distribution system developed by auto manufacturer Henry Ford, based on standardizing factory production of goods for mass consumption.) In the context of global media, post-Fordism refers to changes in the ways producers and distributors of media products must operate as they seek to capture both national mass audiences and diverse local and niche markets in other parts of the world.

Postmodernism. Literally meaning "after modernism," this term describes an influential philosophical movement of the latter 20th century that reacted to and challenged many dominant 19th- and earlier 20th-century Western ideas based on "modern" scientific certainty and authority, including faith in social progress driven by science and reason. The postmodern era (roughly corresponding to the years after World War II, though some theorists would point to earlier 20th-century roots) is characterized by fragmentation of states and other sources of authority and a general skepticism regarding scientific progress and large-scale social projects and ideologies, whether religious or political. In the postmodern era, it is claimed that there is a greater awareness of the intersectionality of identities—that people are constructed, for example, through categories such as nation, ethnicity, class, and gender, and that these categories might be unstable and fluid. Postmodernism also claims that media culture does not merely reflect a preexisting reality; rather, these texts construct our notions of common sense, our systems of meaning, our identities, and the larger social reality. From a postmodern perspective, however, this does not lead to large-scale ideological manipulation or brainwashing, because the use of fragmented media sources by people with complex and unstable identities cannot lead to predictable or determinate outcomes.

Postracial discourse. See *Race, racism, postracial*.

Preferred reading. A concept developed by Stuart Hall to circumscribe the degree of "openness" (polysemy) of media texts. According to Hall (1980), the structure of mainstream media texts always "prefers" or strongly suggests a "correct" meaning that tends to promote the dominant ideology. Within cultural studies, there continues to be a lively debate over whether a preferred meaning can be said to be a property of the text; some would argue that the making of meaning ultimately resides with audiences. Like Hall, most critical media scholars understand that meaning results from the interactions between texts and audiences. Also see *Encoding/decoding*.

Progressive. The term *progressive*, when applied to politics, has a long and varied history. For the purposes of this book, it is used to describe a particular approach to understanding both how society is structured and a way of thinking about how to bring about social change. Progressive thinkers tend to believe contemporary societies are based on unjust and unequal economic systems. Progressives argue for a fairer and more just distribution of economic, cultural, and political resources, and believe that only by organizing and movement building can we bring about macro social change.

Public sphere. This is a concept drawn from the work of Jurgen Habermas and other philosophers and political scientists to indicate those areas of social existence where individuals from diverse communities interact, debate, and create discourses that help to define the terms by which we live. Habermas often wrote about this in optimistic terms, referring to "ideal speech situations" where all stakeholders would be given an equal voice. Other scholars have been skeptical about the possibility of this ever coming to fruition in societies that are marked by inequality and conflict.

Queer theory, queer studies. An interdisciplinary and politically radical approach to cultural studies that emphasizes the instability and fluidity of gender and sexuality categories, in contrast to the view that sexual identity is a fixed, permanent "essence." The term *queer* is adopted to reclaim it in a positive sense from derogatory usage, as well as to create a more inclusive vision of the areas of study.

Race, racism, postracial. Also see *critical race theory*. Although the political importance of "race" as a social category is evident in today's world, most scholars agree that "race" is a convenient fiction with complex historical significance but no biological reality. In everyday usage, racism can be used to mean holding or displaying prejudiced or bigoted attitudes or indulging in discriminatory behavior toward someone else on the basis of that person's apparent race, ethnicity, or skin color. However, in critical theory, and in this book, we use the term to refer specifically to the White-supremacist ideology encoded into and characteristic of major social, cultural, political, and economic institutions. Postracial discourse is based on the belief that in the post–civil rights era, race is no longer a major factor in determining one's access to resources, respect, and equality. This view is linked with the ideology of meritocracy, which assumes that individuals inevitably succeed in life and are rewarded in society as a result of their individual hard work and motivation. Those who critique these concepts argue that such a view fails to see and acknowledge structural inequalities in our society, such as White privilege, male privilege, straight privilege, or class privilege, that provide hidden advantages to some people from birth.

Representation, cultural representation, media representation. *Representation* is a term used to include all kinds of media imagery (through words, pictures, sounds, or all of these) that, no matter how convincing their likeness to everyday social reality, are always to be recognized as illusions. Media representations such as situations in reality television shows or depictions of gangster life contained in hip-hop videos should be understood not as direct mirrorings of "real life." Rather, they are always the result of artistic and economic judgments by their producers, "constructions taken from a specific social and physical viewpoint, selecting one activity or instant out of vast choices to represent, and materially made out of and formed by the technical processes of the medium and its conventions" (King, 1992, p. 131).

Resistance, resisting. In critical cultural studies, this can refer to the refusal of the reader, viewer, or audience to take up or accept the preferred reading and/or the subject position encoded in the media text, therefore resisting its power to reinforce hegemonic ideas. There is still debate among cultural studies scholars on how much opportunity for resistance texts offer (how "open" or polysemic they are). Many scholars have criticized a tendency to "romanticize" the idea of the interpretive community's resistance. Others question the notion that audience resistance is in and of itself positive, citing the resistance of those with conservative social ideologies to texts whose preferred meaning is politically progressive. Finally, it has been asserted that resistive readings of specific texts do not necessarily translate into political resistance to cultural hegemony. (A related term, *agency,* refers to the degree to which a consumer of culture can be understood to be a free agent whose choices must be respected by the cultural critic, as opposed to merely being a passive victim of cultural brainwashing.)

Semiotics, semiology. Semiotics is a linguistics-based field of study that has had an important influence on the way cultural studies scholars discuss the codes in media texts. It is concerned with the study of signification, or the ways both languages and nonlinguistic symbolic systems operate to associate meanings with arbitrary elements, such as words, visual images, sounds, colors, or objects. According to semiotics, signs actually consist of two elements—that which is signified (the meaning) and that which signifies (the image, sound, word, etc.). Also see *Encoding/decoding.*

Sexism. Coined by the women's movement in an analogy with racism, sexism is used in several ways. In common usage, it can refer to prejudicial or disrespectful attitudes or discriminatory behavior on the part of individuals toward others on the basis of their perceived gender. In this book, we use it to refer specifically to male-supremacist or patriarchal ideology encoded into and characteristic of the major social, cultural, political, and economic institutions of a society.

Sexuality, sexualities, heterosexuality. Sexuality involves erotic identities, desires, and practices. Historians have established that heterosexuality emerged as a normative or hegemonic concept in response to the discovery by 19th-century medical discourses of variant or what were then called "perverse" sexualities. See D'Emilio and Freedman (1998). Also see *Gender, gendering.*

Signifier, signified. See *Semiotics, semiology.*

Social networking. Social networking on the Internet refers to the use of interactive websites that provide a forum for interaction among users who share interests or are otherwise connected. Social networking sites such as Facebook, Instagram, Snapchat, Pinterest, and LinkedIn invite users to provide information about themselves through a personal profile and then interact with others through chat and messaging, forming groups of "friends," sharing pictures and video, or posting about personal activities or current events. Social networking is widely acknowledged to be causing far-reaching changes in contemporary culture, social interaction, and the structure of communities, though there is considerable disagreement regarding the nature and overall benefits of these changes.

Spectacularize, spectacle. These terms are used in media studies to refer critically to the tendency of contemporary media culture to create ever more visually entrancing and emotionally exciting events (spectacles) to attract and retain audiences.

Generally, it is argued that media spectacles increasingly replace the kind of substantive and thoughtful discourse needed to ground an authentic democracy. See Kellner (2005).

Spectatorship. See *Feminist film theory*.

Stereotype. This popular term was often used in 1970s media criticism and activism to describe and critique reductive, much-repeated social imagery (as in "Uncle Tom and Aunt Jemima are racist stereotypes"; "June Cleaver and Playboy centerfolds are sexist stereotypes").

Subject position. A concept developed within literary and film criticism, which claims that narrative texts produce through their codes an ideal "viewing position" or subject position, from which the narrative is then experienced by any viewer/reader. A male viewer could be invited by a particular text to view it from a feminine subject position, for example, just as a heterosexual reader might temporarily occupy a queer subject position. A related term for this process is *interpellation*—which means that the text can be read as figuratively "hailing" or "calling out to" a particular ideal type of reader.

Text, media text. This term is used broadly and can refer to any communicative or expressive media product, from a song lyric or magazine ad to a dramatic TV show or online video game. Textual analysis, or a close examination of how particular media texts generate meaning, is one of the key methods of contemporary cultural studies.

Textual analysis. See *Text, media text*.

Transgender. This is an umbrella term for individuals whose gender identity does not match their assigned birth gender and whose gender identity, expression, or behavior is not consistent with that culturally associated with their assigned sex at birth. The existence of trans people is often seen as an example of the fluid nature of gender identity; at the same time, there is debate within the scholarly community regarding the degree to which conformity to any socially defined gender is either counterhegemonic or hegemonic. Also see *Gender, gendering, gendered*.

Transgressive. A term often used positively in cultural criticism to indicate the writer's approval of an act that challenges and/or flaunts traditional (oppressive) rules or social or cultural hierarchies.

Whiteness. Using critical race theory, many media scholars seek to highlight the economic, legal, and cultural construction of White people as a social and material category. It is argued that Whiteness has been developed as a social category to legitimize racism by arguing that people with "white skin" are naturally and biologically superior. In media studies, theorists examine how media images help normalize Whiteness through its overwhelming presence, which paradoxically renders it "invisible" and thus less likely to be critically examined.

Womanism. A term coined by novelist and essayist Alice Walker to refer to Black feminism. See *Feminism, Black feminism, Feminist media studies*.

GLOSSARY REFERENCES

Adorno, T. W., Frenkel-Brunswik, E., Levinson, D. J., & Sanford, R. N. (1950). *The authoritarian personality*. New York: Harper & Row.

Collins, P. H. (2000). *Black feminist thought: Knowledge, consciousness, and the politics of empowerment* (2nd ed.). New York: Routledge.

D'Emilio, J., & Freedman, E. (1998). *Intimate matters: The history of sexuality in America*.

Fiske, J. (1987). *Television culture*. London: Methuen.

Gerbner, G. (1998). Cultivation analysis: An overview. *Mass communication and society* 1(3/4), 175–194.

Golding, P., & Murdoch, G. (1991). Culture, communications and political economy. In J. Curran & M. Gurevitch (Eds.), *Mass media and society* (pp. 15–32). London: Edward Arnold.

Hall, S. (1980). Encoding/decoding. In S. Hall, D. Hobson, A. Lowe, & P. Willis (Eds.), *Culture, media and language* (pp. 128–138). London: Hutchinson.

Jenkins, H. (2006). *Convergence culture: Where old and new media collide*. New York: New York University Press.

Kellner, D. (2005). *Media spectacle and the crisis of democracy*. Boulder, CO: Paradigm.

King, C. (1992). On representation. In F. Bonner, L. Goodman, R. Allen, L. Janes, & C. King (Eds.), *Imagining women* (pp. 131–139). Cambridge, UK: Open University Press.

Marx, K., & Engels, F. (1938). *German ideology* (R. Pascal, Trans.). London: Lawrence & Wishart.

McChesney, R. W. (2008). *Communication revolution: Critical junctures and the future of media*. New York: New Press.

Mulvey, L. (1975). Visual pleasure and narrative cinema. *Screen, 16*(3), 6–18.

Omi, M., & Winant, H. (1993). On the theoretical concept of race. In C. McCarthy & W. Crichlow (Eds.), *Race, identity, and representation in education* (pp. 3–10). New York: Routledge.

Paul, P. (2006). *Pornified: How pornography is damaging our lives*. New York: Henry Holt.

Said, E. (1979). *Orientalism*. New York: Vintage Books.

AUTHOR INDEX

SUBJECT INDEX

ABOUT THE EDITORS

Gail Dines is professor emerita of sociology and women's studies at Wheelock College in Boston. She has been researching and writing about the pornography industry for well over 20 years. She has written numerous articles on pornography, media images of women, and representations of race in pop culture. Her latest book is *PORNLAND: How Pornography Has Hijacked Our Sexuality* (2011). She is a cofounder of the activist group Stop Porn Culture!

Jean M. Humez is professor emerita of women's and gender studies at the University of Massachusetts, Boston, where she taught courses in both women's studies and American studies and chaired the Women's and Gender Studies Department. She designed and taught an undergraduate "Women and the Media" course early in her career and, through her interest in media text analysis, came to collaborate with Gail Dines on this book. She has also published books and articles on African American women's spiritual and secular autobiographies and on women and gender in Shaker religion. Her most recent book is *Harriet Tubman: The Life and the Life Stories* (2004).

Bill Yousman is an assistant professor in the School of Communication and Media Arts at Sacred Heart University in Fairfield, Connecticut, where he directs the graduate program in Media Literacy and Digital Culture. He is the former managing director of the Media Education Foundation. His research focuses on both media literacy education and the construction of racial ideologies in media images and narratives. He has published numerous essays in peer-reviewed journals and anthologies. His first book, *Prime Time Prisons on U.S. Television: Representation of Incarceration,* was published in 2009. His most recent book is *The Spike Lee Enigma: Challenge and Incorporation in Media Culture* (2014).

Lori Bindig Yousman is an associate professor in the School of Communication and Media Arts at Sacred Heart University in Fairfield, Connecticut, where she teaches in the graduate program in Media Literacy and Digital Culture. Her research is grounded in critical television studies and media literacy with a focus on the construction and commodification of young femininity. She is the coauthor of *The O.C.: A Critical Understanding* (2013) and author of *Dawson's Creek: A Critical Understanding* (2008) and *Gossip Girl: A Critical Understanding* (2015).

ABOUT THE CONTRIBUTORS

Lee Artz is an associate professor in the Department of Communication and Creative Arts at Purdue University Northwest. He has written numerous articles on cultural diversity and democratic communication for leading journals. His most recent book is *Global Entertainment Media: A Critical Introduction* (2015).

Christine Bacareza Balance is an assistant professor of Asian American studies in the School of Humanities at the University of California, Irvine. Her research interests include Filipino American studies, performance studies, popular music studies, Asian American cultural studies, queer/feminist theory, and U.S. popular culture. In 2012 to 2013 she was a Ford Foundation Postdoctoral Fellow. Her newest publication, *Tropical Renditions: Making Musical Scenes in Filipino America,* was published in April 2016 by Duke University Press.

Elena Bertozzi is an associate professor in both the medical sciences and the game analysis, and design at Quinnipiac University. She is the director of the Engender Games Group lab, which has developed games to teach midwives in rural Mexico (*Atendiendo el Parto in Casa*) and the *Emergency Birth!* Game, which received a Silver Medal at the Serious Game Competition in 2011. Her latest book is *The Clitoris and the Joystick: Play, Pleasure, and Power in Cyberspace* (2012).

Ian Bogost is an author and game designer. He is the Ivan Allen College Distinguished Chair in media studies and professor of interactive computing at the Georgia Institute of Technology, founding partner at Persuasive Games LLC, and a contributing editor at *The Atlantic.*

Yarimar Bonilla is an associate professor at Rutgers University School of Arts and Sciences in the Department of Anthropology. Her research and teaching interests include social movements, colonial legacies, and questions of race, sovereignty, and citizenship across the Americas. She currently serves on several committees, including the board of the *Journal of Latin American and Caribbean Anthropology,* amongst others. Her most recent book, *Non-Sovereign Futures: French Caribbean Politics in the Wake of Disenchantment,* was published in 2015.

danah boyd is a senior researcher at Microsoft Research; a research assistant professor in media, culture, and communication at New York University; a visiting researcher at Harvard Law School; a fellow at Harvard's Berkman Center; and an adjunct associate professor at the University of New South Wales. Her research examines social media, youth practices, tensions between public and private, social network sites, and other intersections between technology and society. She is also a coeditor of *Hanging Out, Messing Around, Geeking Out: Living and Learning With New Media* (2009).

Andrea Braithwaite is senior lecturer of communication and digital media studies at the University of Ontario, Institute of Technology. Her research interests include gender and sociability in gaming communities, representations of sexualized violence, and digital media and feminist activism.

Richard Butsch is a professor of sociology, American studies, and film and media studies at Rider University, and he teaches in the areas of media, culture studies, and social psychology. He is author of *The Citizen Audience: Crowds, Publics, and Individuals* (2007) and editor of *Media and Public Spheres* (2009). He is currently writing a history of screen culture and a book on the representation of manual labor and laborers in 20th-century America.

Jane Caputi is a professor of women, gender, and sexuality studies, and communication and mass media at Florida Atlantic University. She is the author of several books, most recently *Goddesses and Monsters: Women, Myth, Power and Popular Culture* (2004). She also produced the educational documentary *The Pornography of Everyday Life,* distributed by Berkeley Media. Her recent published works include "Re-Creating Patriarcy: Connecting Religion and Pornography" in *Wake Forest Journal of Law & Policy* (2011).

Dianne C. Carmody is an associate professor of sociology and criminal justice at Old Dominion University. Her research interests include intimate partner violence, school violence, and rape victimization. She has published numerous articles on violence against women in journals such as *Justice Quarterly, American Journal of Criminal Justice,* and *Affilia: Journal of Women and Social Work.*

Jay Clarkson is an assistant professor of communication at Indiana State University. He studies media representations of gender and sexuality and the proliferation of addiction narratives to explain media consumption patterns. He is author of several articles, including "Contesting Masculinity's Makeover: *Queer Eye,* Consumer Masculinity, and 'Straight-Acting' Gays" (2005).

Jennifer Cole is a founding member and director of the GimpGirl community. She is also a research associate in the Experiential Design and Gaming Environments (EDGE) Lab at Ryerson University. She has worked with Oregon Public Health to create state policy recommendations around women with disabilities and sexual health.

Victoria E. Collins is an instructor in the Department of Sociology and Criminal Justice and a research and administrative assistant at the International State Crime Research Consortium at Old Dominion University. She is also an instructor at the Samaritan House/Virginia Beach Law Enforcement Training Academy. Her research interests include state crime, transnational crime, and violence against women. She has published numerous articles in journals such as the *International Criminal Justice Review* and *Contemporary Justice Review.*

David P. Croteau taught about the sociology of media as an associate professor (retired) in the Department of Sociology and Anthropology at Virginia Commonwealth University. He is the author of *Politics and the Class Divide: Working People and the Middle-Class Left* and coauthor, with William D. Hoynes, of *Experience Sociology.*

Sander De Ridder holds a master's degree in communication sciences, with focus on visual culture, and film and television studies. He earned a PhD in communication sciences from Ghent University in Belgium. Currently, he is working on a research project, funded by the Special Research Fund (BOF), Ghent University. The project aims to understand intimate storytelling as mediated practice in social networking sites, thereby specifically focusing on youth culture. The project starts from a democratic concern, inquiring how gender and sexuality are socially and culturally organized in current popular participatory media environments.

Frederik Dhaenens is a researcher at the Department of Communication Studies at Ghent University and a lecturer at the School of History, Culture and Communication at Erasmus University Rotterdam. He is also a member of Centre of Cinema and Media Studies (CIMS) (Ghent University). His former and current research starts from queer theoretical and/or cultural studies perspectives and focuses on gender and lesbian, gay, bisexual and transgender (LGBT) themes in media and popular culture. He has published in *European Journal of Cultural Studies, Sexualities, Popular Communication,* and *Television & New Media.*

Gail Dines is professor of sociology and women's studies at Wheelock College in Boston, where she is also chair of the American Studies Department. She has been researching and writing about the pornography industry for well over 20 years. She has written numerous articles on pornography, media images of women, and representations of race in pop culture. Her latest book is *PORNLAND: How Pornography Has Hijacked Our Sexuality* (2011). She is a cofounder of the activist group Stop Porn Culture!

Kirsty Fairclough-Isaacs is a lecturer in media and performance in the School of Arts and Media at The University of Salford, United Kingdom. Her research is focused on the analysis of contemporary media, in particular the phenomenon of celebrity and how it impacts everyday life. She is coeditor, alongside colleagues Ben Halligan and Rob Edgar, of *The Music Documentary* (2013), the first full-length study of music documentaries, from rockumentary to mockumentary. Her recent published work includes *Beyonce: Celebrity, Feminism and Pop Culture* (2017).

Nadia Yamel Flores-Yeffal is an assistant professor of sociology at Texas Tech University. She specializes in Latin American demography, Mexican–U.S. migration, and international migration from El Salvador. Her research focuses on the social networks of migrants from Latin America, the use of the Internet to spread the anti-immigrant sentiment in the United States, and human capital transferability among migrants from Latin America. Her recent published works include "Other South Africans after Apartheid: The Relationship Between Household Income and Race in Adults Over 50 in the Cape Area of South Africa" (coauthoried with C.C. Dunham, *Sociological Imagination,* 2015) amongst others.

John Bellamy Foster is a professor of sociology at the University of Oregon and also editor of *Monthly Review*. His writings focus on the political economy of capitalism and economic crisis, ecology and ecological crisis, and Marxist theory. He has published more than 100 articles, written and edited more than a dozen books, and received numerous awards and honors. His latest book (coauthored with Paul Burkett), *Marx and the Earth: An Anti-Critique,* was published in 2016.

Christian Fuchs is a professor of social media at the University of Westminster Communication and Media Research Institute. He is editor of the journal *tripleC: Communication, Capitalism & Critique.* His research interests include social theory, critical theory, and critique of the political economy of media.

Rosalind Gill is a professor of cultural and social analysis at City University of London. Her research interests include cultural and creative labor, gender and media, media and intimate life, the dynamics of discrimination and inequality, and discursive, visual, and psychosocial methods. She is the author of numerous articles on media and sexualization, and her most recent book is *Aesthetic Labor: Beauty in Politics in Neoliberalism* (2017). She is currently working on a 4-year Marsden (Royal Society) project exploring how "tween" (9- to 12-year-old) girls negotiate living in an increasingly sexualized culture.

Karen Goldman is assistant director for external relations, development, and assessment at the Center for Latin American Studies and research associate in the Department of Hispanic Languages at the University of Pittsburgh where her work promotes community outreach and exchange with primary and secondary schools. She has published several journal articles and book chapters on gender themes in Spanish and Latin American film. Her recent work includes "Saludos Amigos and The Three Caballeros: Representations of Latin America in Disney's 'Good Neighbor' Films" in *Diversity in Disney Films: Critical Essays on Race, Ethnicity, Gender, Sexuality and Disability* (2013).

Stuart Hall was one of the founders of British cultural studies and was director of the Centre for Contemporary Cultural Studies at Birmingham University for many years. He has written numerous articles and books on cultural studies, race, and representation, including *Encoding and Decoding in the Television Discourse* (1973), *Cultural Studies: Two Paradigms* (1980), and *Cultural Representations and Signifying Practices* (1997). Hall retired from the Open University in 1997 and is now a professor emeritus.

Jonathan Hardy is senior lecturer in media studies at the University of East London. He writes on media and advertising, communications regulation, and international and comparative media. His books include *Critical Political Economy of the Media* (2014), *Cross-Media Promotion* (2010), *Western Media Systems* (2008), and *The Advertising Handbook* (2009; coedited). He is secretary of a U.K. media reform group, the Campaign for Press and Broadcasting Freedom.

William D. Hoynes is professor of sociology and former director of both the American Studies Program and the Media Studies Program at Vassar College. He received his PhD in sociology from Boston College and joined Vassar's Sociology Department in 1992. Hoynes is a cultural sociologist whose research explores contemporary media and culture in the United States, with a special focus on the relationships among journalism, the structure of the media industry, and practices of democratic citizenship.

Sue Jackson is senior lecturer in the School of Psychology at Victoria University of Wellington, New Zealand. Much of her previous research and publication work has centered on young women's negotiation of sexuality and the ways sexuality is represented in girls' popular culture. Currently her research centers on a project examining preteen girls' engagement with popular culture in their everyday lives, supported by the NZ Royal Society Marsden Fund.

Henry Jenkins III is the Provost's Professor of communication, journalism, and cinematic arts at the University of Southern California and was previously the director of the MIT Comparative Media Studies Program and the Peter de Florez Professor of humanities. He is the author and/or editor of 12 books on various aspects of media and popular culture, including *Convergence Culture: Where Old and New Media Collide* (2006). His latest book (coauthored with Neta Kligler-Vilenchik) is *By Any Means Necessary: The New Youth Activism* (2016).

Mareike Jenner is a lecturer in media studies at Anglia Ruskin University. Her PhD was awarded from Aberystwyth University in 2013. Her research interests are video-on-demand, television genre, gender, and contemporary television. Her monograph *American TV Detective Drama* is about to be published in Palgrave Macmillan's Crime Files series.

Robert Jensen is a professor in the School of Journalism at the University of Texas, a founding board member of the Third Coast Activist Resource Center, and a member of the board of Culture Reframed. Jensen's latest book, *The End of Patriarchy: Radical Feminism for Men* (2017), offers a critique of the pathology of patriarchy that is at the core of today's crises.

Sut Jhally is a professor of communication at the University of Massachusetts at Amherst and founder and executive director of the Media Education Foundation. He is the author of numerous books and articles on media, including *The Codes of Advertising* (1990) and *Enlightened Racism* (1992). He is also the producer and director of a number of media literacy films and videos for classroom use, including *Dreamworlds: Desire/Sex/Power in Music Video; The Price of Pleasure: Pornography, Sexuality and Relationships;* and *Hip Hop: Beyond Beats and Rhymes.*

Helen Johnson is an honorary research fellow in the School of Social Science at the University of Queensland. Her articles have appeared in a range of national and international journals. She has contributed to significant publications, particularly those focusing on issues of gender and development, and she has written policy and reports for a number of governments and companies. Her research interests currently include globalization, social change, and mixed heritage; gender, development, and social impact assessment; and gender, labor, and knowledge work in Malaysia, among others.

Chris Jordan is an assistant professor of film studies in the Department of Theatre, Film Studies, and Dance at St. Cloud State University. He is the author of *Movies and the Reagan Presidency: Success and*

Ethics (2003), and essays and articles on film and television. He has also published chapters in *Devised and Directed by Mike Leigh; Gender, Race, and Class in Media* (3rd ed.); and *How Real is Reality TV?* His journal publications also include *Journal of Information Ethics, Velvet Light Trap, Television & New Media,* and *The Democratic Communique.*

Jackson Katz is an educator, author, independent scholar, and lecturer on issues of gender, race, and violence. He is cofounder of Mentors in Violence Prevention (MVP), one of the longest-running and most widely influential sexual assault and relationship abuse prevention programs in high schools, colleges, sports culture, and the military in North America and beyond. He is creator of the award-winning *Tough Guise* video series, and author of *The Macho Paradox: Why Some Men Hurt Women and How All Men Can Help,* and *Man Enough? Donald Trump, Hillary Clinton and the Politics of Presidential Masculinity.* He lectures and trains widely in the United States and around the world.

Douglas Kellner is a distinguished professor of education at UCLA and is author of many books on social theory, politics, history, and culture, including works in cultural studies such as *Media Culture and Media Spectacle* (2003). His book *Guys and Guns Amok: Domestic Terrorism and School Shootings From the Oklahoma City Bombings to the Virginia Tech Massacre* won the 2008 Association of Educational Service Agencies AESA award as the best book on education. He has also published *Cinema Wars: Hollywood Film and Politics in the Bush-Cheney Era* (2009) and *Media Spectacle and Insurrection, 2011: From the Arab Uprisings to Occupy Everywhere!* (2012).

C. Richard King is a professor of comparative ethnic studies at Washington State University. He is the author or editor of more than a dozen books, including *Team Spirits: The Native American Mascots Controversy* (Nebraska, 2001) and *Native Athletes in Sport and Society: A Reader* (Nebraska, 2006).

Michael J. Lee is an assistant professor of communication at the College of Charleston and has had several award-winning conference papers in his research area of political communication. His work has been published in such journals as the *Quarterly Journal of Speech* and the *Journal of Applied Communication Research.* His most recent book is *Creating Conservatism: Postwar Words That Made an American Movement* (2014), which earned four national book awards in the field.

Dafna Lemish currently serves as the associate dean for programs of the School of Communication and Information and professor of journalism and media studies at Rutgers State University. She is the founding and current editor of the *Journal of Children and Media* and combines her interests in children with gender representations and feminist theory in her investigation of the gendered nature of mediated childhoods. She has published seven books and more than 100 refereed journal articles and book chapters in several languages, and is the first recipient of the Teresa Award for the Advancement of Feminist Scholarship, the Feminist Scholarship Division of the International Communication Association (2009).

George Lipsitz is a professor of Black studies and of sociology at the University of California at Santa Barbara and studies social movements, urban culture, and inequality. He is the author of more than half a dozen books and numerous articles, and his latest book (coauthored with Daniel Fischlin and Ajay Heble) is *The Fierce Urgency of Now: Improvisation, Rights, and the Ethics of Cocreation* (2013). He is also the chair of the board of directors of the African American Policy Forum and is a member of the board of directors of the National Fair Housing Alliance.

Sean Lockwood is an assistant professor of ancient history and classics at Trent University in Canada. He specializes in funerary monuments in Anatolia dating from the Persian Empire to the early Roman Imperial period. He investigates the identities of those who created these monuments through analyses of ancient textual and archaeological evidence.

James Lull is professor emeritus of communication studies at San Jose State University, California, specializing in media and cultural studies. He has published 12 books, as well as dozens of journal articles, chapters, and essays, and has lectured throughout the world on the interplay between communication and culture. His latest book is *The Moon Will Not Be Eaten by the Clouds* (2014).

Katherine Mancuso is a social media consultant and instructor at Tech Liminal and a volunteer community liaison for the online community GimpGirl. Her interests include digital media, online education, community building, and accessibility.

Joanna Mansbridge is an assistant professor at Bilkent University in the Department of American Culture and Literature. Her research interests include modern and contemporary American theater, performance studies, film and visual culture, and gender studies. Centered on cultural materialist, feminist, and queer theory, her work focuses on history and material effects/affects of performance, attentive to all levels of cultural production. Her book *Paula Vogel* was published in 2014.

Alice Marwick is a 2016–17 fellow at the Data & Society Research Institute, the director of the McGannon Communication Research Center, and an assistant professor of communication and media studies at Fordham University. Her work examines the impact of the large audiences made possible by social media on individuals and communities from a social, cultural, and legal perspective. Current research interests include the impact of socioeconomic status on privacy practices, data-mining and social media, gendered online harassment, and Internet celebrity.

Daniela Mastrocola is currently a graduate student and lecturer at York University in the Communication and Culture department. Her selected works include "Another One Bites the Dust? The Transition from CHRY 105.5FM to VIBE105" and "The Canadian Seal Wars on CBC News."

Robert W. McChesney is the Gutgsell Endowed Professor in the Department of Communication at the University of Illinois at Urbana-Champaign. In 2002 he was the cofounder of Free Press, a national media reform organization. He served as its president until April 2008 and remains on its board of directors. He has written numerous books and articles, including *Rich Media, Poor Democracy: Communication Politics in Dubious Times* (2000), and his work has been translated into 30 languages. His latest book is *Blowing the Roof Off the Twenty-First Century* (2014).

James McKay is a professor and honorary research consultant at the Centre for Critical and Cultural Studies at the University of Queensland. He has published widely on topics such as gender, race, nationalism, globalization, and popular culture. He is a former editor of the *International Review for the Sociology of Sport* and is on the editorial board of *Men & Masculinities*. His most recent publication is "Assessing Sociologies of Sport: Revisiting the Sociological Imagination" in the *International Review for the Sociology of Sport* (2015).

Candace Moore is an assistant professor in the Department of Screen Arts and Culture at the University of Michigan. Her research and teaching interests include film history, cultures of consumption, and feminist and queer media studies. She has published a number of articles on Showtime's *The L Word*. Her newest book, *Marginal Production Cultures: Infrastructures of Sexual Minority and Transgender Media* (2017), concentrates on considerations of how race, sexuality, and gender nonconformity complicate media production and distribution practices.

Amanda Moras is an associate professor of sociology and the assistant dean of student success for the College of Arts and Sciences at Sacred Heart University in Fairfield, Connecticut. Her professional interests include racial and ethnic relations, sociology of violence, gender, sexualities, labor and immigration, feminist theory, and qualitative methodologies.

Michael Morgan is an emeritus faculty member in the Department of Communication at the University of Massachusetts, Amherst. His areas of interest include television, media effects, cultivation theory, and analysis; international and intercultural effects of media and mass communication; new media technologies; media and identity; media institutions and policy; and media and the family.

Wesley Morris is the critic at large for the *New York Times* and a contributing writer for the magazine. He received the 2012 Pulitzer Prize for Criticism for his work with *The Boston Globe*.

Leigh Moscowitz is a public relations sequence head and associate professor at the University of South Carolina in the College of Information and Communications. Her research focuses on the various ways gendered and sexual identities are represented in news and popular culture. Her current research projects include coverage of child abductions in the news as well as the televisual production of class and gender in popular shows. Her latest book is *Snatched: Child Abductions in U.S. News Media* (2015).

Hannah Mueller is an instructor of television and media studies in New York City. She holds a Ph.D. and an M.A. from Cornell University, and a Magister (M.A.) from Konstanz University (Germany).

Dara Persis Murray is an assistant professor in the Department of Communication and Media at Manhattanville College. She teaches courses on communication theory; advertising, public relations, and culture; gender and media; and public speaking. Her research interests include consumer culture, digital culture, visual culture, popular culture, celebrity culture, reality television, beauty/the body, and popular feminism. She has published articles in *Feminist Media Studies* and *Celebrity Studies*.

Lisa Nakamura is the Gwendolyn Calvert Baker Collegiate Professor in the Department of American Cultures at the University of Michigan, Ann Arbor, where she is also the coordinator of digital studies. She serves on the steering committee of the Fem Tech Net Project, which is a network of educators, activists, librarians, and researchers interested in digital feminist pedagogy. She is the author of *Digitizing Race: Visual Cultures of the Internet* (2007) and *Cybertypes: Race, Ethnicity, and Identity on the Internet* (2002), as well as many journal articles. She is also coeditor of *Race in Cyberspace (2000)* and *Race After the Internet (2011)*.

Jason Nolan is an assistant professor in the School of Early Childhood Studies at Ryerson University. He is founding coeditor of the journal *Learning Inquiry* and coeditor of the *International Handbook of Virtual Learning Environments*. His areas of research include concept development in science, social technologies for young children, identity construction online, critical thinking and reflective practice, teacher education, and children's information privacy online in social networks.

David Nylund has been a practicing therapist with more than 25 years of clinical experience in a broad array of settings, including community mental health, nonprofit agencies, managed care, and private practice. He is also an associate professor of social work at California State University, Sacramento. He is the author of several books, including *Beer, Babes, and Balls: Masculinity and Sports Talk Radio* (2007).

Alejandra Ospina is a liaison for GimpGirl Community. She has spoken about GimpGirl in a number of forums, including interviews and virtual and on-site presentations. She presented a version of "GimpGirl Grows Up" at the Ninth Association of Internet Researchers (AoIR) Conference, prior to its publication.

Shannon E. M. O'Sullivan is a doctoral candidate at University of Colorado Boulder in the College of Media, Communication and Information, where she is also a lecturer. Her research centers on representations of the U.S. working class on television through the theoretical framework of intersectionality. She has previously worked as a reporter and freelance contributor for a weekly business newspaper in Buffalo, New York.

Laurie Ouellette teaches media and cultural studies at the University of Minnesota. She is the author of *Viewers Like You? How Public TV Failed the People* (2002) and coauthor of *Better Living Through Reality TV: Television and Post-Welfare Citizenship* (2008). She is coeditor (with Susan Murray) of *Reality TV: Remaking Television Culture* (2008). She also edited *The Media Studies Reader* (2010), and her most recent book is *Lifestyle TV* (2016).

Gilad Padva teaches in the Department of Film and Television at Tel Aviv University. He publishes extensively about cinema and television studies, gender and queer theory, media aesthetics, visual communications, camp subculture, and popular music. His articles have appeared in many journals, including *Cinema Journal, Feminist Media Studies, Sexualities, Journal of Communication Inquiry,* and *Women and Languages.*

Rosemary Pennington is an assistant professor in Miami University's Department of Media, Journalism & Film. She received her PhD in mass communication from Indiana University's Department of Journalism. Pennington's research interests include global communication as well as Muslims and the media.

April Plemons is a lecturer of sociology at Sam Houston State University. Her research and teaching interests include sexuality studies, gender, deviance/crime, and media. She is author of the article "Commodifying Fido: Pets as Status Symbols" (2012). She is a director and branch cocreator of Long Way Home, a nonprofit dedicated to saving animals that traditional shelters and animal control facilities have deemed unadoptable, placing them into a thriving foster system and finding them forever homes.

Janice Radway is the Walter Dill Scott Professor of communication studies and a professor of American studies and gender studies within the Weinberg College of Arts and Sciences and is past president of the American Studies Association. Her current research interests are in the history of literacy and reading in the United States, particularly as they bear on the lives of women. Her book, *Reading the Romance: Women, Patriarchy and Popular Literature,* originally published in 1984, received the Fellows Book Award as a "classic" in the field from the International Communication Association.

Momin Rahman is an associate professor of sociology at Trent University in Ontario, Canada. His research interests include sexuality and citizenship, as well as celebrity culture, and he teaches courses on the relationship between Muslim cultures and gender/sexuality politics. He is coauthor of *Gender and Sexuality: Sociological Approaches* (2010).

Guillermo Rebollo-Gil attended the University of Florida as a graduate student and frequently is an online commentator on political issues and more. He is currently at Universidad del Este in Puerto Rico. His published works include "Black Women and Black Men in Hip Hop Music: Misogyny, Violence and the Negotiation of (White-Owned) Space" in *Popular Culture* (2012) and "A New Heroic Figure: Female Protestors and Precarity in Puerto Rico" in the *Journal of Feminist Scholarship* (2016).

Mary F. Rogers, a longtime professor of sociology and anthropology at the University of West Florida, and a pioneer in women's studies, died unexpectedly in 2009. She taught courses in feminist theory, social change and reform, social justice and inequality, and qualitative research. She was the author of *Barbie Culture* (1999, 2002) as well as *Contemporary Feminist Theory: A Text Reader* (1997). She was coauthor, with C. D. Garrett, of *Who's Afraid of Women's Studies: Feminisms in Everyday Life* (2002). With Susan E. Chase, she coedited *Mothers and Children: Feminist Analyses and Personal Narratives* (2001).

Jonathan Rosa is an assistant professor at the University of Massachusetts Amherst where he also works as a sociocultural and linguistic anthropologist. His work centers on the conaturalization of language and race as a way of understanding patterns of societal exclusion and inclusion. His recent published works include "Undoing Appropriateness: Raciolinguistic Ideologies and Language Diversity in Education" (*Harvard Educational Review,* 2015) amongst others.

Michael Salter is a senior lecturer in criminology and a member of the Sexualities and Genders Research Network at the Western Sydney University. His publications include studies on child abuse, violence against women, and the gendered implications of new technology. His book *Crime, Justice and Social Media* was published in 2016.

John Sanbonmatsu is an associate professor of philosophy at Worcester Polytechnic Institute in Massachusetts. He is author of *The Postmodern Prince: Critical Theory, Left Strategy, and the Making of a New Political Subject* (2003), and he is editor of the anthology *On the Animal Question: Essays in Critical Theory and Animal Liberation* (2011).

Juliet Schor is a professor of sociology at Boston College. Her research over the past 10 years has focused on issues pertaining to trends in work and leisure, consumerism, the relationship between work and family, and women's issues and economic justice. The author of numerous articles, her most recent book is *True Wealth: How and Why Millions of Americans Are Creating a Time-Rich, Ecologically-Light, Small-Scale, High Satisfaction Economy* (2011).

Yukari Seko obtained her PhD in the Communication and Culture Programme at York and Ryerson Universities, Ontario, Canada. Her research interests include user-generated content on social media, identity practice online, multimodal self-expression, digital surveillance, and aesthetics of pain. Her dissertation theorizes photographs of self-harm on Flickr as a form of aesthetic self-disclosure.

James Shanahan is the dean of the Media School at Indiana University and is a mass media effects researcher, which focuses on cultural indicators, cultivation theory, media effects, and public opinion. His most recent book (co-edited with Michael Morgan and Nancy Signorielli) is *Living With Television Now* (2012). His most recent publication is "Social Media Cultivating Perceptions of Privacy: A Five-Year Analysis of Privacy Attitudes and Self-Disclosure Behaviors Among Facebook Users," published in *New Media and Society* (2016).

Raka Shome recently (2011–2012) served as the Margaret E. and Paul F. Harron Endowed Chair in Communication at Villanova University, Pennsylvania. She is the author of numerous articles, and her current interests are exploring new relations of postcoloniality; Asian modernities; the rhetoric of "new India"; and Whiteness, particularly new formations of Whiteness and White femininity. She now is a visiting senior fellow at the National University of Singapore. Her recent book, *Diana and Beyond: White Femininity, National Identity, and Contemporary Media Culture,* was published in 2014.

Kay Siebler is a professor of English and the coordinator of the new gender and power studies minor at Missouri Western State University in St. Joseph, Missouri. She is currently working on a book titled *Queer Identity in the Digital Age.*

Gloria Steinem is a well-known feminist activist, organizer, writer, and lecturer. Steinem was a founder in 1972 of *Ms. Magazine,* the first national women's magazine run by women, and she continues to serve as a consulting editor. She has been published in many magazines and newspapers in the United States and other countries and is also a frequent guest commentator on radio and television. Her books include *The Revolution From Within: A Book of Self-Esteem* (1992), *Outrageous Acts and Everyday Rebellions* (1983), *Moving Beyond Words* (1993), *Marilyn: Norma Jean* (1986), and, most recently, *Doing Sixty and Seventy* (2006). She recently published her autobiography *My Life on the Road* (2015). She is also an editor of *The Reader's Companion to U.S. Women's History* (1998).

Tiina Vares is senior lecturer in sociology at the University of Canterbury, Christchurch, New Zealand. Her research interests lie in the areas of gender, sexualities, the body, and popular culture with a focus on the reception of popular cultural texts. She is currently working on the research project *Girls, 'Tween' Popular Culture and Everyday Life,* supported by the New Zealand Royal Society Marsden Fund.

Guadalupe Vidales is an assistant professor of criminal justice at the University of Wisconsin at Parkside. She is the author of "Arrested Justice: The Multifaceted Plight of Immigrant Latinas Faced With Domestic Violence," in *Journal of Family Violence* (2010).

Grace Wang is an assistant professor in American studies at the University of California at Davis. Her research and teaching focus broadly on race, immigration, transnationalism, multiethnic U.S. literature, music, and popular culture. She is currently working on a book, *Soundtracks of Asian America,* that critically interrogates the cultural role music plays in the production of Asian American identities.

Jamie Warner is a professor at Marshall University in West Virginia. Her research interests include the intersection of political theory and political communication—specifically, how irony, parody, and humor work within a democratic system. She has published articles in both political science and communications journals, including *Polity, Popular Communication,* and *Politics & Gender.* She is currently at work on a book on political culture jamming.

Kristen J. Warner is an assistant professor in the Department of Telecommunication and Film at the University of Alabama. Her research interests are centered at the juxtaposition of televisual racial representation and its place within the media industries, particularly within the practice of casting. She has contributed an essay on race and primetime television in *Watching While Black: Centering the Television on Black Audiences* and is completing her manuscript entitled *The Cultural Politics of Colorblind TV Casting* (2015).

Bill Yousman is an assistant professor in the School of Communication and Media Arts at Sacred Heart University in Fairfield, Connecticut, where he directs the graduate program in Media Literacy and Digital Culture. He is the former managing director of the Media Education Foundation. His research focuses on both media literacy education and the construction of racial ideologies in media images and narratives. He has published numerous essays in peer-reviewed journals and anthologies. His first book, *Prime Time Prisons on U.S. Television: Representation of Incarceration,* was published in 2009. His most recent book is *The Spike Lee Enigma: Challenge and Incorporation in Media Culture* (2014).